America

The Complete Story

America
The Complete Story

GLOBAL BOOK PUBLISHING

PUBLISHER	Gordon Cheers	**ILLUSTRATIONS**	Mike Gorman
ASSOCIATE PUBLISHER	Margaret Olds		Vicky Short
MANAGING EDITOR	Anna Cheifetz		Robert Taylor
SENIOR EDITOR	Dannielle Doggett		Spike Wademan
EDITORS	Loretta Barnard	**GRAPHS**	Mike Gorman
	Fiona Doig	**PICTURE RESEARCH**	Gordon Cheers
	Kate Etherington	**TYPESETTING**	Dee Rogers
	Vanessa Finney	**INDEX**	Glenda Browne
	Scott Forbes		Dee Rogers
	Sue Grose-Hodge	**PUBLISHING ASSISTANT**	Erin King
	Denise Imwold	**PRODUCTION**	Bernard Roberts
	Heather Jamieson		
	Ariana Klepac		
	Margaret McPhee		
	Susan Page		
	Merry Pearson		
	Bernard Roberts		
	Anne Savage		
	Sarah Shrubb		
	Marie-Louise Taylor		
	Margaret Whiskin		
ADDITIONAL TEXT	Scott Forbes		
ART DIRECTOR	Stan Lamond		
SENIOR DESIGNER	Mark Thacker		
COVER DESIGN	Bob Mitchell		
DESIGNERS	Louise Buchanan		
	Cathy Campbell		
	Joy Eckermann		
	Alex Frampton		
	Moyna Smeaton		
	Alex Stafford		
	Veronica Varetsa		
CARTOGRAPHER	John Frith		
ADDITIONAL CARTOGRAPHY	Ian Faulkner		
CONTOUR SHADING	John Gittoes		
MANAGING MAP EDITOR	Valerie Marlborough		
MAP EDITORS	Jan Watson		
	Jennifer Lake		
	Heather McNamara		
	Janet Parker		
	Joan Suter		
CARTOGRAPHIC CONSULTANTS	Ed Antczak		
	Michael L. Camarano		
	Tony A. Huegel		
	John King		
	Jill R. Sandvik		
	William C. Tucker		
	Lillian J. Wonders		
PHOTO LIBRARY	Alan Edwards		

First published in 2001 by
Global Book Publishing Pty Ltd
1/181 High Street
Willoughby, NSW 2068
Australia
tel 61 2 9967 3100 fax 61 2 9967 5891
email globalpub@ozemail.com.au

Reprinted 2002

ISBN 1 74048 102 X

Illustrations from the Global Illustration Archives
© Global Book Publishing Pty Ltd 2001
Photographs from the Global Photo Library (except
when credited otherwise on page 864)
© Global Book Publishing Pty Ltd 2001
Text © Global Book Publishing Pty Ltd 2001
Maps © Global Book Publishing Pty Ltd 2001

The publisher would be pleased to hear from photographers
interested in supplying international photographs.

Printed by Sing Cheong Printing Co. Ltd, Hong Kong
Film separation Pica Digital, Singapore

Cover images
Back cover from left to right: Steam train, Colo.; Statue of Joan of
Arc, New Orleans, La.; Brooklyn Bridge, New York City, N.Y.; Fall
foliage, Colo.; Buckman Tavern, Lexington, Mass.; Road near Aspen,
Colo.; Statue, Rockefeller Center, New York City, N.Y.; Big Sur, Calif.
Front cover from left to right: Route 66 sign, Calif.; Casino lights,
Las Vegas, Nev.; Wheat farmer, Lyons, S.C.; Times Square, New York
City, N.Y.; Railway line, Nev.; Rodeo, Springfield, Ill.; Manhattan sky-
line, New York City, N.Y.; Golden Gate Bridge, San Francisco, Calif.

Captions for images in the preliminary pages
Page 1: Native American totem pole, Montpelier, Indiana
Page 2: Native American Indian Chief, Washington, DC
Pages 4–5: Mountains in Denali National Park, Alaska
Pages 6–7: Denali National Park, featuring Mt McKinley, Alaska
Pages 8–9: Landscape near Moab, Utah
Pages 12–13: Bryce Canyon National Park, Utah

Captions for images on the chapter opening pages are listed
on page 848.

Photographers are acknowledged on page 864.

Contributors

Michael G. Barbour is a Professor of Plant Ecology at the University of California, Davis. His research has included studies on the distribution, dynamics, and ecology of vegetation and component species of coastal dune scrub, tidal salt marsh, grassland, desert scrub, and montane conifer forest in Alta and Baja California, along the Pacific and Gulf of Mexico coastlines, and in Argentina, Australia, Israel, and Spain. He is the co-author or co-editor of textbooks on introductory plant biology, plant ecology, the vegetation of California, and the vegetation of North America.

Jennifer Berry is a freelance journalist who has traveled the globe for the past 20 years—14 of which she has spent driving over 160,000 miles across America's backroads and freeways. She has written features for *GQ Australia* and travel articles for a number of publications, including *The Sunday Times, The Quorum, Vacations, World Travel Magazine, Breakaway,* and *Escape.* Jennifer has also been involved in several travel-related television productions on the American West. She currently lives in Sydney.

Dominic Buchanan is a freelance journalist, editor, and writer. For well over a decade he has contributed articles to national magazines, metropolitan daily newspapers and web sites. His writing covers art, film, theater, literature, and travel. He is currently writing on the arts in Canberra, Australia

Colin Burgess is the author of many adult and juvenile non-fiction books on subjects as varied as the Australian prisoner-of-war experience and humorous aviation tales. These days he is concentrating on writing about his favorite topic: human spaceflight. His most recent book is a biography of teacher, Christa McAuliffe, who was killed when the *Challenger* space shuttle exploded shortly after take-off. He is currently finalizing a manuscript on the lives of the eight NASA astronauts who lost their lives prior to the *Apollo* Moon landings.

George O. Carney is Regents Professor of Geography at Oklahoma State University, where he has taught the courses Introduction to Cultural Geography and Geography of Music for over 30 years. Other teaching and research interests include the cultural geography of Oklahoma and the preservation of historic properties in Oklahoma.

Dr Carney has authored or edited more than 80 publications, as well as six books—the most recent being *Baseball, Barns, and Bluegrass: A Geography of American Folklife.* Recent awards for teaching and research include the National Council for Geographic Education Geography Excellence in Media Award (2000), and the Association of American Geographers Distinguished Teaching Award (2000).

Anna Cheifetz is an editor and writer with over a decade of publishing experience. She holds an MA in History from York University, UK, and was awarded the 1990 Catherine Mackichan prize for history writing. She has managed a series of medical journals and contributed to a variety of publications on topics such as history, art and design, gardening, lifestyle, and entertaining in both the UK and Australia.

Jeffrey M. Chusid is an architect, and the director of the Historic Preservation Program at the University of Texas at Austin School of Architecture. He has worked with notable firms in California and consulted on preservation projects from California to Bosnia–Herzegovina. Jeffrey has written, lectured, and curated exhibitions about the California

architecture of Frank Lloyd Wright. He was also director of the Wright-designed Samuel Freeman House in Los Angeles for 12 years; founded the preservation program at the University of Southern California; and has taught at Sci-Arc, California Polytechnic University in Pomona, and at Harvard University.

Joan Clemons was born in Los Angeles and received her formal education at the University of California (UCLA), and the University of Minnesota. She taught geography, environmental science, and geology at Los Angeles Valley College where she chaired the Earth Science Department. She was a Visiting Professor at UCLA and directed the California History/Geography Project and the GLOBE Science Project. Joan was a founding member of the National Geographic Society's California Geographic Alliance. Recently, she has been involved in research in Australia, New Zealand, and Southern Africa.

Ivan Coates has a long-standing interest in American history, culture, and politics. He earned a degree with First Class Honours at the University of Sydney and won the University Medal for his thesis on contem-porary American history. He has traveled widely in the United States, and is currently attempting to master and enjoy the art of juggling, involving a PhD, freelance writing, university tutoring, and looking after a lively and engaging son.

Terry Coffey is a freelance writer living in New Castle, Indiana. He has written short works of fiction, poetry, and nonfiction, and has contributed to publications such as *The American Legion Magazine* and *Life*, among others, as well as on the Web. Terry is also an award-winning radio news reporter and producer with over a decade of experience.

Robin Doughty is a faculty member in the Department of Geography at the University of Texas. Robin has a long-standing interest in wild animals, notably birds. He has written seven books on topics such as the feather trade, recovery of the endangered whooping crane, and the impact of early a settlers on Texas wildlife. A recent book about the spread of eucalypts outside Australia, tackles environmental, and international issues connected with plantation forestry, and the diffusion of alien organisms. He has just completed a book about the purple martin.

Dr Paul D. Edson is Associate Professor of Humanities and Social Sciences at Embry-Riddle University in Daytona Beach, Florida, where he teaches courses in history, geography, and anthropology. Born and raised in northern California, Paul Edson earned his PhD in anthropology at Indiana University. He has been on the faculties of Loyola University in Chicago, Wayne State University in Detroit, and the University of South Florida in Tampa, on the staffs of the College of Art and Design in Detroit and of the Detroit Institute of Arts, and is a past president of the Florida Conference of Historians.

Catherine Fallis is the fifth woman in the world to earn the title of Master Sommelier. Introduced to wine while backpacking in Europe, her more formal education began with Kevin Zraly at Windows on the World in New York City, where she was the first person to work both as Assistant Cellar Master and Wine School Coordinator. She is currently proprietor of Planet Grape, a Wine Content Provider and Consultant Sommelier Service. She co-authored the *Global Encyclopedia of Wine*, and contributes to *Decanter*, *Epicurean*, *Wine Business Monthly*, *Wines and Vines*, WineToday.com (*New York Times*), and other publications.

Tony Huegel, a native of Wisconsin, earned a bachelor's degree in journalism from the University of California at Berkeley. He has worked as a reporter for newspapers in California, Wyoming, and Idaho, and is the author of *Backcountry Byways*, a guidebook series, dedicated to helping travelers explore the backcountry roads of the American West. His travel experience encompasses journeys around North America, Central America, North Africa, and Europe. Tony is a regular contributor of travel articles to a variety of different magazines.

Tom Hyland is currently a writer and educator in Chicago. He writes about wine and food for several publications including *The Underground Wine Journal*, *The Quarterly Review of Wines*, *Epicurean*, the *Chicago Tribune*, and the *San Francisco Examiner*. Tom is also an avid fan of architecture and has spent much of his time in and around Chicago, as well as in southern Wisconsin, exploring the works of Frank Lloyd Wright.

Denise Imwold is a freelance writer and editor who has also worked for many years as a bookseller. She is from Baltimore, Maryland and feels equally at home in the United States, Ireland, and Australia (where she currently lives). Denise holds a Bachelor of Arts Degree in English Literature and a Postgraduate Diploma in Editing and Publishing from Macquarie University in Sydney. She has contributed to a wide range of publications in such fields as literature, travel, sport, health, and spirituality.

Jean G. Kropper is an author, designer, teacher, and worldwide traveler. She was born near Boston, and graduated from the University of Vermont (USA) with a BA in fine art in 1982. Jean began working in graphic design first in Boston, then in Sydney, Australia, where she still lives. In 1991, she began exhibiting her artwork and teaching art workshops around Australia and the United States. She is the author of numerous magazine articles and three non-fiction books.

Timothy Long is a Wine Educator and student in the Master of Wine program in Wisconsin. He teaches wine classes, presents restaurant staff-training seminars, and assists clients in developing effective retail and restaurant wine programs. Relentless travel and tasting are, of course, vital to his business, or so he says.

Tom L. McKnight was born and raised in Dallas, Texas. His formal education includes an MA from the University of Colorado and a PhD in geography and meteorology from the University of Wisconsin. He has spent most of his professional life based at the University of California, Los Angeles (UCLA), where he served as Chair of the Geography Department from 1978 to 1983, and is now a Professor Emeritus. He has also taught temporarily at nine American, three Canadian, and three Australian universities.

Mary Annette Pember has worked in mainstream print journalism for 15 years. An enrolled member of the Red Cliff Band of Wisconsin Ojibwe, she is currently president of the Native American Journalists Association (NAJA) and a freelance photojournalist/writer in Cincinnati, focusing exclusively on Native topics. In the past, her photojournalism has dealt primarily with social issues in the United States, Nepal, and India. Her work has been widely published in newspapers and magazines including *Life*, *Time*, *Newsweek*, and the *New York Times*. She has won numerous awards including several from the National Press Photographers Association; this year she was named Best Photographer by NAJA.

Peter Rose graduated from the University of North Carolina in Chapel Hill and served with the 10th Special Forces Group (Green Berets) in the Bavarian Alps. He has been a reporter and editor at newspapers in five states, including *The Arizona Republic* in Phoenix, where he had assignments around the world. He has also been an editor at two US national magazines, is the co-author of the book *Boise & Sun Valley*, and has written film treatments and screenplays in Los Angeles.

Elizabeth Schweitzer is one of 10 Master Sommelier's in the world. She has written many articles on a variety of topics, such as travel, lifestyles, wine and spirits, and inspiration. She lives in southern California, enjoys the outdoors and listening to music. She is a prolific reader and loves to travel.

Barry Stone is a graduate of the Australian College of Journalism in Sydney and a compulsive traveler. He has long been a regular contributor of travel articles on countries from Indonesia to Monaco for newspapers as well as for the in-flight magazines of some of the world's largest airlines. His passion, however, is the United States. From exploring its back roads to hiking National Park trails in over 30 states, its astounding geographic diversity and varied communities have provided him with a limitless source of insight and inspiration for the written word.

Roger W. Stump is Professor of Geography and Planning, and Religious Studies, at the State University of New York, Albany. He began his work on the geography of American religion in graduate school at the University of Kansas in the late 1970s, and since then has published numerous articles and book chapters on this topic. Most recently he is the author of *Boundaries of Faith: Geographical Perspectives on Religious Fundamentalism*.

Luba Vangelova is a freelance journalist whose articles range from topics such as FBI forensic courses to South African walking safaris. Her work has appeared in dozens of print and online publications, including *National Geographic Traveler*, *The New York Times*, and *Wildlife Conservation* magazine. She has also contributed to a series on home renovation, appeared on a syndicated radio travel program, and consulted on a television script. She has lived and traveled extensively on five continents.

Dr Cynthia Waddell is an Adjunct Assistant Professor in the Geography Department at Florida State University. Recipient of FSU's Thomas Campbell Award and the PIE Award for Outstanding Teaching, she has taught a number of courses including Crime in the United States, Serial Killers, Organized Crime, Southern History of the United States, and Methods of Teaching. Her various publications include articles on Southern history and teaching the Holocaust. Dr Waddell is currently completing a history of crime in the United States.

Barney Warf is Professor and Chair of Geography at Florida State University. His research and teaching interests lie within the broad domain of regional development—straddling contemporary political economy and traditional quantitative, empirical approaches. In the first topic area he has written on social theory, postmodernism, and localities issues; in the second, his work centers on producer services, telecommunications, military spending, and international trade. He has co-authored or edited two books, 20 book chapters, and 60 refereed articles. His teaching interests include urban and economic geography, social theory, and East Asia.

CONT

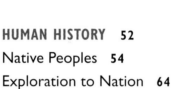

E N T S

PART I

THE STORY OF AMERICA

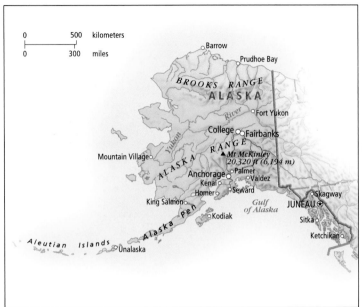

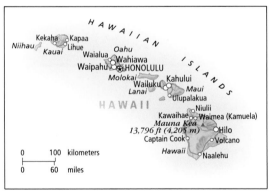

NORTH

| 0 | 200 | 400 | 600 | kilometers |
| 0 | | 200 | | 400 | miles |

America Fact File

Official name United States of America

Capital Washington, DC

Land area (50 states, excluding water) 3,536,278 square miles (9,158,960 sq km)

Highest point Mt McKinley, Alaska, 20,322 feet (6,194 m)

Lowest point Death Valley, California, 282 feet (86 m) below sea level

Longest river Missouri River, 2,500 miles (4,023 km)

Largest lake Lake Michigan, Michigan, 22,300 square miles (57,757 sq km)

Highest average annual rainfall Mt Waialeale, Hawaii, 460 inches (11,684 mm)

Lowest average annual rainfall Death Valley, California, 5 inches (27 mm)

Highest recorded temperature 134°F (57°C) at Death Valley, California, July 10, 1913

Lowest recorded temperature −81°F (−63°C) at Prospect Creek, Alaska, January 23, 1971

Population 281,421,906 (April 1, 2000)

Population density 70 per square mile (27 per sq km) (1993)

Urban v. rural population 75.2% urban, 24.8% rural (1997)

Population growth rate 0.91% (1999–2000 est.)

Projected population (2051) 405–407 million

Birth rate 14.5 per 1000 population (1999)

Death rate 8.8 per 1000 population (1999)

Life expectancy 74.2 for males, 79.9 for females (2000 est.)

Infant mortality 6.82 per 1000 births (2000 est.)

Country of birth of population USA 90.3%, Mexico 2.6%, Philippines 0.53%, China and Hong Kong 0.36%, Cuba 0.35%, Vietnam 0.35%, India 0.31%, El Salvador 0.28%, Dominican Republic 0.25%, Great Britain 0.24%, Korea 0.22%, other 4.21% (1999)

Country of birth of immigrants Mexico 19.9%, China 5.6%, India 5.5%, Philippines 5.2%, Dominican Republic 3.1%, Vietnam 2.7%, Cuba 2.6%, Jamaica 2.3%, other 53.1% (1998)

First language English 87.3%, Spanish 7.6%, French 0.75%, German 0.68%, Italian 0.58%, Mandarin (Chinese) 0.55%, Tagalog (Filipino) 0.37%, Polish 0.32%, Korean 0.28%, Vietnamese 0.22%, other 1.35% (1990)

Religious affiliation Protestant 56%, Catholic 28%, Jewish 2%, other 6%, no religion 8% (1989)

Employment by sector Services 80%, Industry 18%, Agriculture and mining 2% (1999)

GDP $9.255 trillion (1999 est.), $33,900 (per capita 1999 est.)

Major exports Computer and electronic products 25.2%, Transportation equipment 16.4%, Machinery (except electrical) 11.5%, Plastics and rubber products 10.3%, Electrical equipment, appliances, and components 3.5%, Food manufacturing 3.3% (2000)

Major imports Computer and electronic products 20.7%, Transportation equipment 17.5%, Oil and gas 8.6%, Machinery (except electrical) 6.6%, Chemicals 5.9%, Apparel and accessories 5.2% (2000)

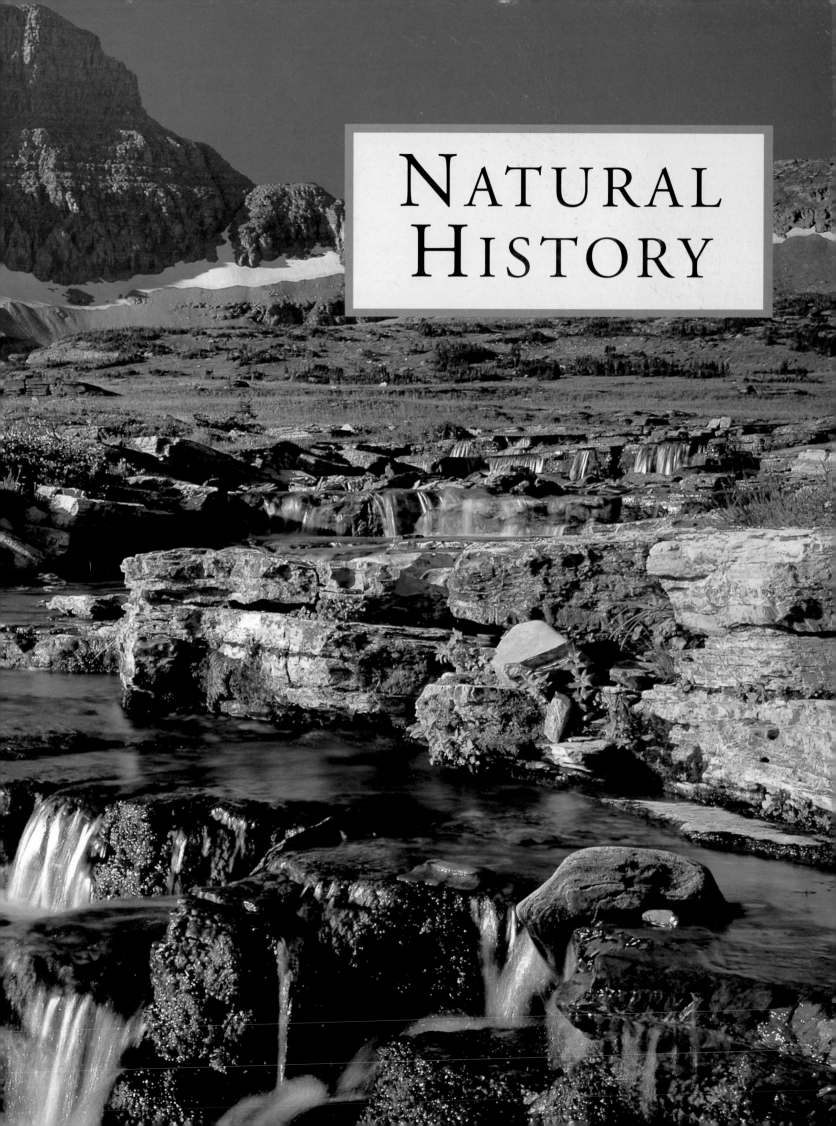

NATURAL HISTORY

One of many rivers that flow from the eastern uplands to the Atlantic Ocean, the Roanoke River stretches for 410 miles (660 km) through the southern Appalachians to Albemarle Sound in northeast North Carolina.

In western Texas, arid plains and salt flats surround the rugged Guadalupe Mountains, site of the state's highest peak, 8,749-foot (2,667-m) Guadalupe Peak.

PHYSICAL GEOGRAPHY

The Lay of the Land

For the most part, the United States of America occupies a mid-latitude location, lying entirely north of the Tropic of Cancer, except for the far-flung state of Hawaii, and with only Alaska extending north of the 50th parallel of north latitude. The country's physical features vary widely; indeed, it could be said that diversity is what best characterizes the geography of the United States.

Topographic regions

The mainland's major topographic features divide it into four regions: the western ranges, the central plains, the eastern uplands, and the Atlantic seaboard.

THE WESTERN RANGES

In the West, a series of mountain ranges and valleys is interspersed with numerous desert basins and plateaus. The western mountain complex has two major prongs. In the coastal states (Washington, Oregon, and California), a series of steep-sided ranges more or less parallels the coast between Mexico and Canada. It varies in height from only a few hundred feet in parts of the Coast Ranges of Oregon and Washington to more than 14,000 feet (4,270 m) in California's Sierra Nevada and Washington's Cascade Mountains. Between these ranges lie several major valleys including the Central Valley of California and the Oregon's Willamette Valley.

The second of these prongs is formed by the Rocky-Mountain Cordillera, which consists of a series of southeast–northwest-trending mountain ranges that rise abruptly from the central plains and stretch, with only one significant interruption, all the way from central-north New Mexico to Canada's Yukon Territory. These mountains are characterized by high elevations— more than 50 peaks in Colorado alone reach above 14,000 feet (4,270 m)—great variations in altitude, ruggedness, and spectacular scenery. Only in the Wyoming Basin is there any significant stretch of terrain that is not mountainous.

Between the coastal ranges and the Rocky Mountains lies an extensive area of arid land incorporating a wide variety of terrain. The southern and southwestern portions of this land are known as "basin and range" country, and consist of numerous discrete, short, rugged mountain ranges separated by flat, alluvial-filled valleys. In the "Four Corners" country to the east, where the states of Utah, Arizona, Colorado, and New Mexico meet, plateaus, mesas, cliffs, and buttes dominate the landscape. To the north, the Columbia and Snake rivers wind through lava plateaus and rolling hills.

THE CENTRAL PLAINS

A vast area of low-lying land—the Great Plains—occupies the central portion of the country, widening significantly in the north. Although some parts of this region, such as the High Plains of Texas, are remarkably flat, the landscape is generally characterized by undulating terrain or low, flat-topped hills. The surface is highest in the west, where parts of the plain are more than 6,000 feet (1,830 m) above sea level, dropping in height to the east at an average rate of 10 feet per mile (1.9 m per km); at the eastern margin of the plains, the average elevation is less than 1,500 feet (460 m). Great aprons of alluvial deposits line the Rocky-Mountain front and major river valleys, and glacial deposits thinly cover the surface north and east of the Missouri River.

THE EASTERN UPLANDS

Along the eastern edge of the Great Plains, the Appalachian uplands extend from Alabama to the Gulf of St Lawrence. Although the Appalachians are often referred to as mountains, much of the chain is made up of low, forested hills. From Pennsylvania southward, the terrain consists of a remarkable sequence of parallel valleys and long, steep-sided ridges. To the west lie the so-called Allegheny and Cumberland plateaus, which are in fact clusters of low hills separated by abrupt, narrow valleys.

North of Pennsylvania, the landscape of the Appalachians is much more varied, although hills and low mountains still dominate. The most conspicuous ranges here are the Adirondacks in New York, the Green Mountains in Vermont, and the White Mountains in New Hampshire.

To the west of the Appalachians, a number of similar but smaller and lower ranges rise from the inland plains. The Ozark uplands are the remains of an eroded plateau, which now form an amorphous cluster of low, rounded hills. Separated from the Ozarks by the Arkansas River valley, the Ouachita Mountains of western Arkansas and eastern Oklahoma form an area of east–west-trending linear ridges and valleys similar to the southern ridge-and-valley section of the Appalachians.

THE ATLANTIC SEABOARD

On the Atlantic coast, a coastal plain stretches south from New England, widening as it curves southwest through Georgia and Florida to link up with the southern margin of the central lowland. This is one of the flattest portions of North America, with most of the region sloping gently seaward at a rate of only a few feet or even a few inches per mile, and continuing underwater at the same angle for more than 100 miles (61 km) as a continental shelf. The uniformity of the southeastern landscape is broken only by low (10–50-feet [3–15-m]) riverine bluffs alongside broad river valleys or, particularly west of the Mississippi River, low linear ridges (called cuestas) that parallel the coast.

As a result of submergence in recent geologic time, the eastern coastal margin of the continent is exceedingly irregular, with many extensive drowned valleys (estuaries) and bays, swamps, lagoons, as well as low-lying sandbar islands.

Outside the Lower 48

Two states are entirely separate from the US mainland: Alaska and Hawaii. Alaska has the highest and most heavily glaciated mountains of the continent. Along the south coast is the long, remarkably rugged, and ice-draped Chugach Range. To the north lie the

The Snake River meanders through the valley of Jackson Hole, beneath the jagged Teton Range in Wyoming. Part of the Rocky-Mountain Cordillera, the Tetons include a dozen peaks higher than 12,000 feet (3,660 m).

A narrow, windblown strip of sand dunes, marshland, and beaches, Ocracoke Island is one of the barrier islands that make up the Outer Banks of North Carolina.

A popular snorkeling destination, Hanauma Bay Beach Park is located on the southern tip of Oahu, the third-largest island in the Hawaiian archipelago.

equally dramatic Kenai Mountains, which in turn give way to the Wrangell Mountains and the Alaska Range, the continent's mountain chain, topped by Mt McKinley at (20,320 feet [6,194 m]). A vast interior lowland separates the Alaska Range from the towering Brooks Range, beyond which lies an extensive northern coastal plain facing the Arctic Ocean.

Located in the northern Pacific Ocean, 2,088 miles (3,363 km) southwest of San Francisco, the state of Hawaii encompasses a 1,600-mile (2,560-km) string of eight major islands, several islets, and coral reefs. The islands are the summits of undersea volcanic peaks.

Islands

The Hawaiian Islands are not the only islands that form part of the United States; indeed, approximately 5,000 islands lie just off the mainland. Those located

off the East Coast are generally small and sparsely populated, with one major exception: Long Island, whose 1,400 square miles (3,600 sq km) support more than 7.5 million people. Most other East-Coast islands are long, narrow, low-lying sand ridges. The extensive chains of islands off the North Carolina and Texas coasts, for example, represent barrier sandbars at an extreme stage of development: long, narrow, and flat, they encompass lagoons and sounds that are in the process of being filled in as the coastline extends outward.

Other islands, such as those along the Georgia and Mississippi coasts, are more varied in origin, ranging from erosional remnants to old beach ridges. The Florida Keys are different again: the eastern keys are the exposed remains of an elongated, fossilized coral reef cut by tidal channels into a series of separate islands, whereas the western keys consist of limestone shoals upraised from an earlier seafloor.

The smooth, regular, and steep Pacific coast has few coastal indentations or islands, with only the six Channel Islands off the southern California coast encompassing much acreage. Alaska, on the other hand, is replete with islands. The greatest concentration can be found along the panhandle, where a bewildering array of bays, inlets, channels, and fjords indent the coastline, forming hundreds of forested peninsulas and islands. Collectively, these islands are known as the Alexander Archipelago, with Prince of Wales Island being the largest in the group.

Only a few islands lie off the south coast of Alaska, although Kodiak Island is the second-largest in the

nation. Off the west coast, the Aleutian Islands are a volcanic chain surmounting the crest of a submarine ridge that extends for 1,200 miles (1,900 km) west from the tip of the Alaska Peninsula. The chain includes some 60 volcanoes, about half of which are active. North of the Aleutians in the Bering Sea lies a scattering of a half-dozen medium-sized islands, of which St Lawrence is the largest.

Waterways

Two prominent drainage systems, the Great Lakes–St Lawrence and Mississippi–Missouri, dominate the hydrography of North America. The five Great Lakes (Superior, Huron, Erie, Ontario, and Michigan, the first four being shared by the United States and Canada) drain northeastward into the Atlantic Ocean via the relatively short St Lawrence River. Many rivers flow into the Great Lakes, but all are short and the watershed of the lakes is remarkably small: it is, for example, only one-sixth the size of the drainage area of the Mississippi–Missouri system.

The Mississippi River and its many tributaries drain an enormous area of the central United States. The Mississippi itself flows almost due south from central Minnesota to the Gulf of Mexico at New Orleans. Its principal left-bank tributary is the Ohio, which drains much of the northern Appalachians and the Midwest, and is in turn fed by the Tennessee River, which drains much of the southern Appalachians and adjacent areas. The far-reaching Missouri River, which emanates from the northern Rocky Mountains of Montana and gathers tributaries all across the central-north part of the country, is the major right-bank tributary of the Mississippi.

The well-watered east shore of the United States is drained by a host of rivers, most of which are of moderate length but carry large quantities of water. West of the Mississippi, the rivers that enter the Gulf of Mexico are longer but have a lower volume of flow.

In the West, the rivers that flow into the Pacific Ocean vary greatly in form, length, and volume. The Colorado River is a lengthy desert stream that drains much of the arid Southwest and eventually debouches into the Gulf of California in northern Mexico. The complex Sacramento–San Joaquin system drains much of California. The Columbia, the principal river of the Pacific Northwest, originates in Canada and traverses some 465 miles (745 km) before crossing into the United States; it is then joined by its main tributary, the Snake, before flowing for another 300 miles (480 km) to the coast, this part of its course forming the state boundary between Oregon and Washington. Alaska's hydrography includes two extensive river systems, the Yukon and the Kuskokwim, as well as several dozen smaller rivers, most of which carry considerable quantities of water.

It is noteworthy that thousands of square miles in the western United States are not served by external drainage. Particularly in Nevada, Utah, and California, interior drainage basins abound. Most hold either shallow or dry lakes (Utah's Great Salt Lake is the most conspicuous example) and are fed by streams that usually flow only intermittently.

Outside of the glaciated regions of the North (primarily New England, New York, and the Upper Lakes states), the interior basins of the arid West, and the flat limestone country of central and southern Florida, the United States has relatively few natural lakes for its size. However, numerous artificial lakes or reservoirs have been constructed, especially in the southeastern, central-south, and southwestern states. In most cases, this has involved the damming of rivers, resulting in fingerlike bodies of water that extend for long distances along former stream valleys. Such waterways are now prominent features on large-scale maps of almost any area from Carolina to California.

The steep cliffs on the Oregon side of the Columbia River Gorge have given rise to an abundance of dramatic waterfalls, including 176-feet (54-m) Horsetail Falls.

The Geologic Inheritance

Zion National Park in Utah includes striated sheets of sandstone that formed from ancient desert sands and were then fashioned by water and wind.

PLATE MOVEMENTS

This cross-section shows how the westward movement of the North American Plate forces the Pacific Plate to subduct, depositing sediments on, and thereby expanding, the western side of the continent. In contrast, the East and especially the shield formation beneath the central plains are relatively stable.

The United States encompasses a remarkable variety of geologic formations, ranging from some of the world's oldest mountains to vast sedimentary deposits laid down by ancient oceans, and entire landscapes fashioned by glaciers. Furthermore, most parts of the country are still very much under construction, meaning that numerous geologic processes can be viewed as they occur.

A continent takes shape

The oldest rock formations in the United States have been dated to more than 3 billion years ago. Around that time, a large area of crust began to form in the region, which grew significantly during the next 400 million years or so. Some time after 2.5 billion years ago, tectonic activity split this crust into fragments. Several of the fragments then merged, about 1.8 billion years ago, to form a block of land, or craton, which now underpins the Canadian Shield and the Great Plains. This was the core around which the continent began to take shape.

Substantial evidence exists to suggest that approximately 500 million years ago a total of five continents existed on Earth. About 450 million years ago, these continents drifted together and merged to form the supercontinent of Pangaea. For the next 200 million years or so, Earth had but one landmass and a single ocean. Subsequently, Pangaea began to rift and break up, initially into two enormous sections—the continents of Laurasia in the Northern Hemisphere and Gondwanaland in the Southern Hemisphere.

Phases of mountain building, or orogenies, associated with the formation and break-up of Pangaea thrust the Appalachian Mountains upward to the height of today's Himalayas and also gave rise to crustal deformation that commenced the construction of the ancestral Rocky Mountains.

Westward expansion

Following the break-up of Pangaea, a new phase of geologic development began—one that continues today. Rifting off the eastern side of the continent formed an ocean, and lava from the mantle rose through a fracture in the seafloor, solidifying as it cooled to form an undersea mountain range called the Mid-Atlantic Ridge. The buildup of lava along the ridge slowly pushed the tectonic plates on either side of the fracture outward, widening the sea and eventually creating the Atlantic Ocean.

Seafloor spreading, as this phenomenon is known, has since carried the United States, which is located on the North American Plate, westward at a rate of about 1 inch (2.5 cm) a year or $15\frac{1}{2}$ miles (25 km) every million years. Along its western edge, the North American Plate collides with the Pacific Plate, which is moving generally northwestward. The collision forces the thinner Pacific Plate beneath the thicker continental plate—a process known as subduction.

During subduction, seafloor sediments, island chains, and even small pieces of continental crust are deposited or "emplaced" along the edge of the thicker plate, which also buckles and rises, forming mountains. In North America, the earliest emplacements occurred around 200 million years ago near the present-day Nevada–Utah border; subsequent dockings have gradually extended the western side of the landmass and thrown up several mountain ranges. The Sierra Nevada, for example, began to take shape about 10 million years ago and is still in the early stages of growth. Although easily eroded, the 10,000-foot (330-m) San Gabriel Mountains continue to rise because they are being pushed up faster than rain and snow tear them down.

Subduction also generates intense heat, melting rock deep within the crust. This molten rock may rise to the surface through fractures in the plate edge,

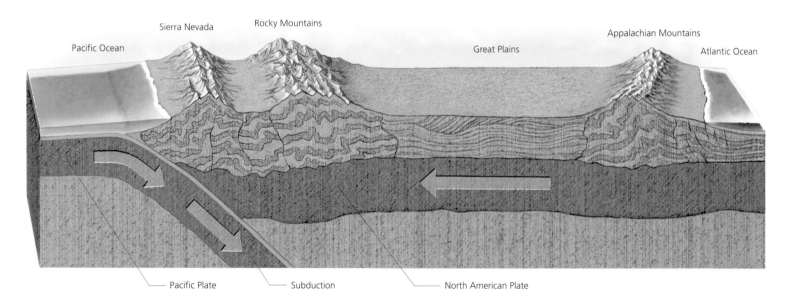

Pacific Ocean   Sierra Nevada   Rocky Mountains   Great Plains   Appalachian Mountains   Atlantic Ocean

Pacific Plate   Subduction   North American Plate

forming volcanoes and hot springs. Volcanic activity has occurred all along the margin of the North American Plate, and today two major chains of active volcanoes still line the West Coast. One stretches along the entire south coast of Alaska; the other, the result of subduction of the small Juan de Fuca and Gorda plates that lie between the Pacific and North American plates, runs from British Columbia down through Washington, Oregon, and California. This was the site of the most recent major eruption in the United States, when Mt St Helens blew its top in May 1980. The explosion claimed 60 lives, flattened 230 square miles (600 sq km) of forest, set off enormous mudflows that choked hundreds of miles of waterways, and created a huge ash cloud that spread 930 miles (1,500 km) to the east. Fortunately, the blast was directed away from the nearby city of Portland.

Far offshore, a different kind of volcanic activity gave rise to the Hawaii Islands. They began to form about 70 million years ago as the Pacific Plate moved slowly over a newly formed hot spot—a column of especially hot magma that rises persistently to the surface from deep within the Earth's mantle, creating volcanoes. The volcanoes that rose above sea level formed islands. The hot spot is now located under the Big Island of Hawaii and fuels its active volcanoes.

Fault lines

Along the western edge of California, the North American and Pacific plates move past each other in opposite directions; here, the boundary between the plates is known as the San Andreas Fault. Movement along this boundary is not smooth and regular: the plates may not shift at all for decades, then suddenly jump a few feet in seconds. Such movements create shock waves that reverberate throughout the region and are more commonly known as earthquakes.

Plate movements are also responsible for some of the West's most dramatic topographic features. East of the Sierra Nevada and the Coast Ranges lies a series of valleys and mountain chains that stretches across eastern California, Nevada, parts of Utah, Arizona, New Mexico, and western Texas. The valleys here are flat-floored basins—hence the use of the term "basin and range" to describe this region. The basins were formed by a process called block faulting, whereby

The highest mountain chain in North America, the Alaska Range is crowned by 20,320-foot (6,200-m) Mt McKinley.

Top: At Zabriskie Point in Death Valley National Park, California, fine-grained mudstone deposits have been eroded by water to form multihued, parallel ridges.

blocks of land bounded by faults are pushed upward or drop downward as a result of plate movements. Occurring repeatedly over the last 25 million years or so, block faulting has created row after row of north–south-trending, parallel basins and ranges. The mountains average 4,000 feet (1,300 m) in height, though the difference between basin floor and summit may be as much as 10,000 feet (3,300 m). Outstanding examples of these basins include Death Valley and Lake Tahoe in eastern California.

Along the Continental Divide

During the Precambrian era—the name for the earliest period of geologic history, extending from the formation of Earth to 570 million years ago—the ancestral Rocky Mountains were thrust up and leveled off several times in succession. However, the most significant period of mountain building in the Rockies was the Laramide Orogeny. The result of the ongoing subduction along the western side of the continent, it occurred between 70 and 40 million years ago and resulted in enormous folds and slabs of crust being thrust upward in an easterly direction, especially in Wyoming and Idaho.

Southwest of the Rockies lies a more stable part of the continent, the Colorado Plateau. Between 570 and 286 million years ago, this area was repeatedly flooded by seas which deposited layer after layer of sediment. These deposits eventually turned into an enormous block of sedimentary rock, which has since been little affected by deformation of any kind.

About 20 million years ago, as a result of tectonic activity, the block was significantly uplifted. Rivers have since cut deep into the plateau, allowing scientists to examine layers of geologic history. In the Grand Canyon, the Colorado River has exposed deposits that date back to the earliest days of the continent, including sandstone formed from an ancient desert, shale deposited by a river system about 280 million years ago, limestone formed from the remains of marine creatures, and Vishnu Schist, a metamorphic rock created 2 billion years ago when two large landmasses collided.

Under ancient seas

Beneath the Great Plains to the east of the Rocky Mountains lies the original shield formation around which North America coalesced. Its remoteness from the continental margins protected it from most of the mountain-building collisions and fractures that occurred in peripheral areas, and, as a result, this inland region has remained geologically stable for most of the last 500 million years or so.

During the Jurassic Period (208–144 million years ago), the plains were inundated by a shallow sea. As it retreated, the mud, sand, and silt beneath it turned to stone, encasing the remains of many dinosaurs that had inhabited the area. The region is now one of the world's most significant sources of dinosaur fossils.

Further layers of sediments were deposited by another sea during the Cretaceous Period (144–98 million years ago) and subsequently by rivers flowing east from the Rockies and west from the Appalachians.

Since they were thrust upward by a series of processes occurring between 500 and 250 million years ago, the Appalachians have been slowly rounded and worn down by water and wind to a fraction of their former height. They were also modified by volcanic activity that followed the break-up of Pangaea, evidence for which includes 200-million-year-old granite intrusions found in New Hampshire.

As the rifting of the Atlantic Ocean pushed the Appalachians westward, faults formed along the eastern edge of the continent, which then dropped downward. Layers of sediments carried eastward from the Appalachians by rivers then covered this margin, forming the Atlantic Coastal Plain.

Fashioned by ice and water

Successive ice ages, beginning about 2 million years ago and occurring repeatedly until 10,000 years ago, saw great glaciers cover hundreds and sometimes thousands of square miles of northern North America. During the most recent glacial period, which occurred 10–15,000 years ago, ice sheets 2–3 miles (3–5 km) thick blanketed much of the northern United States. As they moved south, as far as the Missouri and Ohio rivers, they scoured much of the land, eventually dumping enormous quantities of glacial debris where they halted. Long Island is perhaps America's most prominent example of a rock pile bulldozed into position by a massive river of ice.

The glaciers produced different results, depending on the underlying terrain and the thickness of the ice. In the West, isolated channels of ice ground along mountain valleys, deepening and steepening them to create dramatic features such as Yosemite Valley. In the Northeast during the last ice age, the ice was five times as thick and the land much lower. Glaciers consequently spread over large areas, smoothing the terrain and reshaping existing river valleys to create features such as the Finger Lakes of upstate New York.

The melting of the glaciers at the end of the last ice age flooded enormous areas of the continent. In the northern United States this created the Great Lakes, the largest accumulation of fresh water on Earth. In the Columbia River Basin of the Northwest, the floodwaters rushed seaward, forming the series of east–west ridges that now characterizes the basin, and stripped topsoil from low-lying land.

Nowhere is the role of water in the continual refashioning of the landscape more apparent in the United States than along the shore of the Gulf of Mexico. The Mississippi River has been depositing bits and pieces of middle America here for eons. Recently, the accumulation of sediments below and alongside the river has raised the waterway so that it now sits some 20 feet (6 m) above the nearby city of New Orleans, which consequently has to be protected by levees. Moreover, the river has begun to change course and, if left to its own devices, would soon bypass New Orleans and reach the Gulf of Mexico via a shorter (and lower) route through the Atchafalaya Bayou. For decades, the US Army Corps of Engineers has struggled to keep this vital waterway close to the city by building ever-higher levees and a huge concrete diversion channel 100 miles (160 km) north of the city. Some day, they will probably lose that battle.

Alaska's glaciers include several "surging" glaciers, which, in short bursts, may advance as much as 100 feet (330 m) in a single day.

OPPOSITE: The Grand Canyon of the Yellowstone in Yellowstone National Park, Wyoming, was gouged out by massive flash floods triggered by the melting of glaciers at the end of the last ice age.

At the height of the last ice age, about 18,000 years ago, glaciers stretched across Canada and into the northern United States.

GLACIATION DURING THE LAST ICE AGE

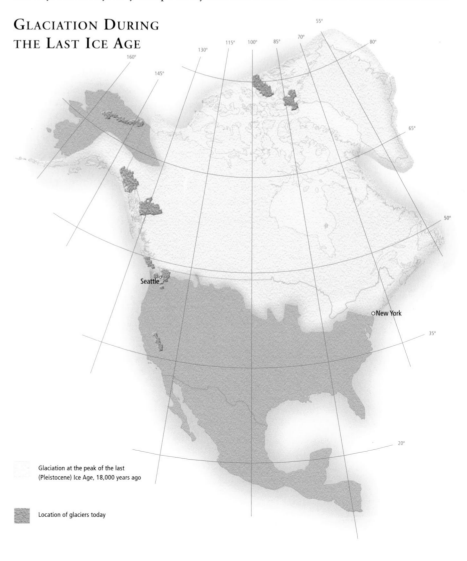

Glaciation at the peak of the last (Pleistocene) Ice Age, 18,000 years ago

Location of glaciers today

Weather and Climate

New Hampshire receives more than 60 inches (150 cm) of snow each year. Many of the state's heaviest snowfalls are brought by storm systems that originate over the Atlantic Ocean.

As is typical of mid- and high-latitude parts of the world, most of the United States has a climate marked by distinct seasonal changes. Generally, summer is hot and is the season of maximum precipitation; winter is cold and somewhat drier; and spring and fall are stimulating seasons of transition. There are, however, some major exceptions to these generalizations, particularly on the Pacific coast, where winter is the wet season and summer is quite dry. Furthermore, the nation's latitudinal location means that it often experiences extremes of weather. Hurricanes affect the East Coast, especially Florida, between June and November. Tornadoes can happen anywhere and at any time, but the largest and most destructive ones occur in a belt known as Tornado Alley, which stretches from Texas north to Iowa, through Oklahoma, Kansas, Missouri, and Nebraska.

National patterns

Over most of the conterminous states, warm, moist air from the south meets cold, dry air from the north in continually varying patterns. The resulting weather systems are continually pushed toward the East Coast by the general westerly flow of air that predominates in most midlatitude regions of the world. Some of the systems form around low-pressure cells (midlatitude cyclones), which attract air masses of different temperatures, producing frontal disturbances, stormy or unsettled weather, and sometimes abundant precipitation. Others are dominated by high-pressure cells (anticyclones), which bring clear skies and extreme temperatures (usually low, but sometimes high).

These broad patterns of air circulation combine with major topographic features (most notably north–

CLIMATE ZONES

- Tundra
- Subarctic
- Highland
- Marine West Coast
- Humid continental with cool summers
- Humid continental with warm summers
- Steppe
- Desert
- Mediterranean
- Humid subtropical
- Tropical

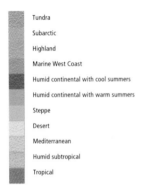

Alaska

Hawaii

south trending mountain ranges) and supplies of moisture (especially from oceans to the west, east, and south) to produce plentiful precipitation along the northern portion of the West Coast, on the windward sides of western mountain ranges, and across the southeastern part of the continent. Drier conditions prevail in the Alaskan Arctic, over much of the Great Plains area, and particularly in the interior West due to the remoteness of these regions from sources of oceanic moisture. This general pattern is modified by a variety of factors, particularly cold-air invasions from the north in winter and onshore flows of warm, moist air from the Gulf of Mexico in summer.

Climate zones

The combination of air-circulation and precipitation patterns creates the following broad climatic zones.

In the southeastern quarter of the country, the climate is classified as *humid subtropical*. Summer here is characterized by high humidity, which often combines with high temperatures to create uncomfortable conditions for the region's inhabitants. Winter is short and relatively mild, although significant cold spells occur several times each year. Precipitation is spread throughout the year, with a tendency toward a maximum in summer, except in Florida, where rains associated with hurricanes result in a fall maximum.

A large area of the central-east United States has a *humid continental with warm summer* climate. This is a result of interaction between warm tropical air masses from the south and cold polar air masses from the north (with the former tending to dominate in summer, the latter in winter), which results in frequent weather changes throughout the year. Summers are warm to hot and are the time of highest rainfall; winters are cold with considerable snowfall.

In the Northeast, a broad east–west band of the country experiences a *humid continental with cool*

Pacific Ocean, bringing alternating periods of rain and sunshine. Summer is virtually rainless because stable, subtropical high-pressure conditions dominate the region at this time of year. In coastal areas, sea breezes moderate temperatures year-round, but inland zones experience hot summers and cool winters.

The *marine west coast* climate of the Pacific Northwest is characterized by long, relatively mild, extremely wet winters and short, relatively dry summers. The extended, wet winter is the result of the frequent movement across the region of maritime polar air and associated fronts. Exposed, elevated slopes on the mountains of the northwest coast receive some of the highest levels of precipitation (both rain and snow) in the world.

The climate of central and southern Alaska is classified as *subarctic*. Winter, the dominant season, is long, dark, relatively dry, and bitterly cold. Summer lasts only a short time, but the long hours of daylight result in several weeks of warm-to-hot weather. Rainfall is scanty in summer, but evaporation rates are generally low. Winter snowfall is meager, too, but little melting takes place between October and May.

Arctic Alaska has a *tundra* climate. The region is virtually a cold desert and there is little precipitation during any season; however, evaporation rates are also low. Winter is very long and dark, although not as cold as in the subarctic area. Summer is short and cool.

The principal mountain ranges of the United States have a *highland* climate. However, generalizations about this climatic category can be made only with reference to particular elevations or exposures. Usually, temperature and pressure decrease with altitude, whereas precipitation and windiness increase.

The climate of the Hawaiian Islands is truly *tropical,* which means that the weather is warm and wet year-round. Northeasterly trade winds blow almost continuously across the islands, and the height and orientation of the mountain ranges are the major determinants of temperature and rainfall variations. Hurricanes occur in the region, but only rarely.

summer climate. It is distinguished from the previous climatic type by its shorter, milder summer and its longer, more rigorous winter.

The Great Plains and intermontane areas of the West have a *steppe* climate, which is essentially a semi-arid climate with marked seasonal temperature extremes. Summers are hot, dry, and windy, and punctuated by occasional, abrupt thunderstorms; winters are cold, dry, and windy, with intermittent blizzards. Cold continental air masses and warm air masses from the Gulf of Mexico often meet in this region, giving rise to bouts of intense and dramatic weather such as hail, heat waves, tornadoes, and windstorms.

The *desert* climate of the Southwest is characterized by clear skies, brilliant sunshine, and long periods without rain. Only at higher elevations does significant precipitation occur. Summer is long and can be scorchingly hot, with temperatures rising well over 100°F (38°C) for extended periods in the interior; winter is brief and mild.

Central and coastal California have a *Mediterranean* climate. Regular frontal systems move in from the

LEFT: A cold front moves in over the western edge of the Great Plains. Low-pressure systems originating in the Pacific Ocean often weaken over the Rockies, but may then regain strength as they move eastward across the plains.

BELOW LEFT: The hot, humid conditions that prevail in the Southeast during summer encourage many of the region's residents to vacation at coastal resorts such as Virginia Beach, Virginia.

Extreme Weather

The combination of the United States' location and topographical and climatic factors make many parts of the country susceptible to extremes of weather. Among the most notable instances of wild weather are the following:

Highest recorded temperature: 134°F (57°F); Death Valley, California; July 10, 1914

Lowest recorded temperature: −81°F (−63°C); Prospect Creek, Alaska; January 23, 1971

Highest rainfall (in 24 hours): 43 inches (109 cm); Alvin, Texas; July 25–26, 1979

Highest rainfall (in one year): 739 inches (1,878 cm); Kukui, Maui, Hawaii; December 1981 to December 1982

Highest snowfall (24 hours): 76 inches (195.6 cm); Silver Lake, Colorado; April 14–15, 1921

Highest snowfall (one season): 1,140 inches (2,895.6 cm); Mt Baker, Washington; 1998–99

Deadliest hurricane: Galveston, Texas; September 8, 1900; 6,000 people killed

Deadliest tornado: Tri-State Tornado; March 18, 1825; 695 people killed

Deadliest flood: Johnstown, Pennsylvania; June 1, 1889; 2,209 people killed

Most destructive flood: Mississippi River; summer 1993; $15–20 billion worth of damage

Most destructive drought: Dust Bowl drought, Midwest; 1934–41; 50 million acres (20 million ha) affected

Most destructive blizzard: East Coast; March 11–14, 1888; 5 feet (1.5 m) of snow, 400 deaths, $20 million worth of damage

Most destructive natural disaster: Hurricane Andrew, Florida; August 24, 1992; $26 billion worth of damage

FLORA

America's Diverse Vegetation

The fall foliage of the quaking aspen (Populus tremuloides) gilds hillsides at Mt Sneffels, Colorado.

Arctic tundra
Boreal forest
Eastern deciduous forest
Southeastern pine savanna
Tallgrass prairie
Mid-grass prairie
Shortgrass prairie
Central California bunchgrass prairie
Intermountain shrub steppe
Chihuahuan desert
Sonoran desert
Mojave desert
Intermountain desert
Mediterranean woodland & scrubland
Lowland temperate conifer forest
Montane conifer forest
Mixed grass, scrub, Madrean woodland
Subtropical forest & wetlands
Tropical rainforest

Alaska

The contiguous states encompass most of the world's major vegetation types, including alpine tundra, conifer forests, deciduous forests, subtropical forests, semiarid woodland and scrubland, deserts, and freshwater wetlands, while the far-flung states of Alaska and Hawaii add, respectively, arctic tundra and tropical lowland and montane rainforests to this already extensive list. Indeed, only a small number of vegetation types are not found in the United States, among them tropical grassland, tropical floodplain, evergreen rainforest, extremely arid desert, subtropical grassland, and subtropical thornscrub.

Viewed from a high-flying aircraft, the American landscape appears green, continuous, and healthy. But this is a false impression. The nation's plant cover has been altered dramatically by humans—subtly but pervasively by Native Americans for tens of thousands of years, and much more drastically by European and then American settlers in the past 400 years. Large areas of forest and grassland have been replaced by agricultural fields, pastures, homes, and cities; riparian vegetation along waterways has been cut for timber or degraded by artificial levees; even remote arctic tundra, boreal forest, and arid desert have been modified by livestock, invasive plants, and new fire regimes, and are now crisscrossed with roads and dotted with oil rigs and pipelines. The following survey, which divides the country's vegetation types into seven broad categories, describes both what once existed and what remains.

DOMINANT NATURAL VEGETATION

Washington
Montana
North Dakota
Minnesota
Maine
Oregon
Idaho
South Dakota
Wisconsin
Michigan
Vermont
New Hampshire
Massachusetts
Rhode Island
New York
Wyoming
Nebraska
Iowa
Pennsylvania
Connecticut
New Jersey
Nevada
Utah
Colorado
Kansas
Illinois
Indiana
Ohio
West Virginia
Virginia
Delaware
Maryland
California
Arizona
New Mexico
Oklahoma
Arkansas
Missouri
Kentucky
Tennessee
North Carolina
South Carolina
Mississippi
Alabama
Georgia
Texas
Louisiana
Florida

Hawaii

Tundra

Tundra is a Lapp word meaning "treeless hill." Ecologically, the term refers to short herbaceous vegetation growing at low elevations above the Arctic Circle, but it also applies to meadow-like vegetation on high mountains farther south as well as taller, shrubby vegetation growing on well-drained soils. Common plant growth forms include perennial broad-leaved herbs, sedges, grasses, mosses, and lichens. In the most severe arctic or alpine habitats, plants grow only in patches; in slightly more temperate areas, ground cover may be continuous.

ARCTIC TUNDRA

The growing season in the Arctic is measured in weeks rather than months, maximum summer temperatures and solar intensity are low because of the low angle of the sun (even though there may be 24 hours of daylight in summer), and soil remains permanently frozen (as "permafrost") below a relatively shallow rooting zone within 3 feet (1 m) of the surface. Despite this shallow soil, three times as much plant biomass lies below ground as above ground, probably because the tundra environment is so harsh and the warmest, best-protected part of it is located just under the soil surface.

Plants that grow on the tundra of mainland Alaska are either identical to, or very similar to, those found in Canada, Finland, Russia, and the Aleutian Islands. There is, in fact, a common circumboreal arctic flora that numbers just over 1,000 species, and two-thirds of these plants occur in Alaska. Most are thought to have evolved in, and spread from, the mountains of central Asia during the past 3 to 6 million years. Relative to other plant communities, arctic tundra is very young.

Arctic tundra can be divided into four main subcategories. Tall-shrub tundra grows on well-drained, coarse soils on wide river floodplains. Its dominant shrubs are alder (*Alnus crispa*), willow (*Salix* species), and birch (*Betula* species), which may reach 15 feet (5 m) tall. A shorter shrub tundra, standing about 1.5 feet (0.5 m) tall, covers rolling uplands; it includes additional woody species such as cloudberry (*Rubus chamaemorus*), huckleberry (*Vaccinium* species) and turpentine-smelling Labrador tea (*Ledum* species). Meadow tundra is found on poorly drained soils and in depressions, becoming especially abundant at higher latitudes. Near the northern limit of vegetation, the polar desert has less than five percent cover; the plants are either very compact, low-growing perennial herbs called cushion plants, or mosses and lichens.

Apart from areas around oil fields, pipeline routes, and roads, relatively little of the Alaskan tundra has been disturbed. Human populations have always been low here, and the sea rather than the land has provided them with their main food supplies. However, tundra is one of the most fragile ecosystems: even a single pass by a heavy vehicle can kill plant cover and open up the soil surface to the sun, resulting in melting of the permafrost and consequent soil erosion.

ALPINE TUNDRA

A similar range of treeless vegetation types, known generally as alpine tundra, occurs near the peaks of mountains far to the south, primarily the Rockies, the northern Coast Range of Washington State, and the central Cascades and Sierra Nevada. The elevation of the alpine tundra zone increases to the south, being less than 5,000 feet (1,650 m) in British Columbia but more than 11,000 feet (3,650 m) in California. Although the growing season is short, sunlight is stronger and daytime temperatures higher than in the Arctic. Consequently, permafrost is less continuous and species richness significantly higher.

Conifer forests

A range of conifer-forest types occurs in America, varying with climate and elevation. The low-elevation forest that grows in cold climates of the far north is known as boreal forest. A similar vegetation type called subalpine forest grows at high elevations in mountains to the south. At lower elevations in the warmer climate zones of the south, a third type made up of much larger trees is known as montane conifer forest. Along the west coast, this type blends with a fourth category, lowland temperate conifer forest.

BOREAL FOREST

North America's boreal forest lies mainly within Canada but extends west into Alaska and south into the northeastern United States. Like tundra, this vegetation has been changed little by indigenous peoples; however, European and American settlers have clearcut large areas amounting to 20 percent of the original forest.

Boreal forest is made up of relatively small, short-lived trees that form a dense cover, creating a shaded habitat low in plant and animal diversity. The forest is two-layered, consisting of an overstory of spruce (*Picea* species), fir (*Abies* species), larch (*Larix* species), and pine (*Pinus* species), and an understory of mosses, lichens, and perennial herbs. Wet meadows, floating bogs, and small lakes dot the forest.

Wildfires play an important role in the maintenance of this ecosystem. They are usually started by lightning strikes during dry spells, but only rarely— every 200 years or so—are the air and vegetation dry enough to catch fire and the wind strong enough to spread the fire over a large area. Given these conditions, a crown fire may spread over thousands of acres until stopped by a change in the weather, open water, or topographic features. Most boreal plants are adapted to survive wildfire and some even require fire to complete their life cycles or to grow at maximum rates.

SUBALPINE FOREST

A similar type of forest can be found in the subalpine zone of mountains to the south, just below the alpine tundra. In the transition zone between forest and alpine tundra, the conifers become more widely spaced and stunted and develop multiple trunks, before being eliminated altogether by the lack of sufficient warmth during the growing season. The transition zone, which

Abundant throughout the boreal forest, Norway spruce (Picea abies) has needle-like leaves and tough, 5–7-inch (12.5–17.5-cm) cones. The species is widely used for ornamental Christmas trees.

TOP: Many alpine flowers, such as mountain larkspur (Delphinium barbeyi), bloom near the transition zone between alpine tundra and subalpine forest.

OPPOSITE: In Denali National Park, Alaska, sparse stands of conifers bloom along waterways amid wider expanses of arctic tundra.

LEFT: The Colorado blue spruce (Picea pungens) is one of the most attractive of subalpine forest species, though its leaf-cover tends to become more sparse as it reaches old age.

Typical of montane conifer forests and lowland temperate conifer forests, the Douglas fir (Pseudotsuga menziesii) is one of the most widespread conifers. It can grow to a height of 200 feet (61 m) and measure up to 6 feet (2 m) in diameter. On mature trees, the bark may be as much as 10 inches (25 cm) thick.

RIGHT: Olympic National Park in Washington State is the site of the largest undisturbed stands of old-growth lowland temperate conifer forest in the United States. The forests are watered by up to 167 inches (4,175 mm) of rain each year.

may be 1,000 feet (300 m) wide, is called the timberline. Its elevation varies with latitude by about 300 feet (100 m) per degree and also increases with distance from the coast. In the White Mountains of New England, for example, it is located at only 5,700 feet (1,900 m), whereas on the San Francisco Peaks of Arizona it is found at almost twice that height, 11,100 feet (3,700 m).

The same genera of trees typically grow in both subalpine and boreal forests, but the species are different: subalpine fir (*Abies lasiocarpa*) and Engelman spruce (*Picea engelmannii*) instead of boreal balsam fir (*Abies balsamifera*) and white spruce (*Picea glauca*); lodgepole pine (*Pinus contorta*) and bristlecone pine (*Pinus aristata* and *Pinus longaeva*) instead of jack pine (*Pinus banksiana*); alpine larch (*Larix lyallii*) instead of northern larch (*Larix laricina*); mountain hemlock (*Tsuga mertensiana*) instead of western hemlock (*Tsuga heterophylla*). Subalpine species are also longer-lived, typically enduring for close to 1,000 years and, in the case of the record-breaking bristlecone pine, up to 5,000 years. Because the growing season is so short, even ancient bristlecones are not large; in fact, they are mostly dead, with only a small part of the tree remaining alive after other parts have died over the centuries.

MONTANE CONIFER FOREST

In the Rocky Mountains, Cascades, Sierra Nevada, and Coast Ranges of the west—and to a lesser degree in the Appalachian Mountains of the east—a species-rich and somewhat open conifer forest grows just below the subalpine zone. This is the picturesque forest made famous by photographs of national parks such as Sequoia, Yellowstone, and Yosemite. Here, tall trees in open colonnades tower above scattered oak and dogwood, clusters of evergreen shrubs, and a seasonal scattering of perennial forbs and grasses. Ponderosa pine (*Pinus ponderosa*) and Douglas fir (*Pseudotsuga menziesii*) are the most widespread (and most heavily cut) species, but others are found depending on the region: grand fir (*Abies grandis*), white fir (*Abies concolor*), Pacific silver fir (*Abies nobilis*), and red fir (*Abies magnifica*); sugar pine (*Pinus lambertiana*) and western white pine (*Pinus monticola*); western

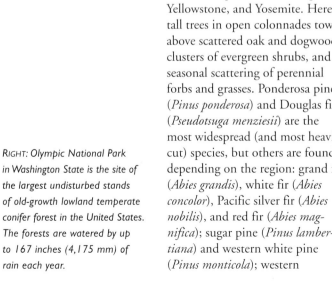

hemlock; incense cedar (*Calocedrus decurrens*); and, in 75 localized stands through the central Sierra Nevada, Sierra big tree (*Sequoiadendron giganteum*), a relative of the coast redwood (*Sequoia sempervirens*).

Montane conifer forests are fire-dependent. Slow-moving, cool-burning surface fires, usually started by lightning in late summer or fall, revisit a given acre every 15–50 years. The surface fires consume litter, herbs, shrubs, saplings, and pole-size trees, but merely scar mature trees. Native Americans were aware of the natural role of fire and purposely set fires more frequently to keep meadows and forests near villages open. European and American settlers, however, have tended to put fires out as soon as possible; a century of fire-suppression management has changed the forests from open and pine-dominated to dense and fir-dominated. The stands are now so thick that if a surface fire were to start it would quickly ladder up into the overstory, killing all the trees; a full recovery might then require 200 or more years to complete. In addition, the intensified competition among plants has led to large numbers of trees being wiped out during episodic droughts, such as the 1987–92 drought in the Cascade–Sierra Nevada chain which killed 20 percent of the local forest.

LOWLAND TEMPERATE CONIFER FOREST

A famous, but relatively small, forest hugs the western coast of the United States and has been identified as the most luxuriant and productive forest in the world, with a greater biomass and level of annual growth than even tropical rainforest. Known as the Pacific Northwest temperate rainforest, it is dominated by massive, long-lived conifer species which rise above a rich understory of broad-leaved trees, shrubs, herbs, and mosses. This forest extends from Cook Inlet, Alaska, southward in a continuous belt to northern California and then in increasingly isolated patches to the Big Sur Coast of central California.

The overstory conifers include western hemlock, Sitka spruce (*Picea sitchensis*), Douglas fir, and several cedar species (*Chamycyparis* and *Thuja*). South of the

Oregon–California border, one other species joins the mix and soon begins to dominate: coast redwood, perhaps the tallest tree in the world. It thrives in the local climate, which is characterized by abundant rainfall, moderate temperature changes across all seasons, summer fog, and little hard frost. Redwoods can grow as high as 300 feet (100 m), wider than 9 feet (3 m), and live for more than 2,000 years.

The value of Douglas-fir and cedar timber is high, but that of redwood even higher because it contains natural substances that inhibit fungal and bacterial decay. One old-growth coast redwood tree may be worth $50,000. Consequently, much of the coastal forest was logged intensively in the late 1800s and early 1900s, with the result that more than 50 percent of the stands are second-growth forest. These are not only much less impressive than the old-growth stands, but less suited ecologically to supporting certain rare birds and mammals. Remaining old-growth stands are largely restricted to Olympic National Park in Washington State and several other national and state parks in Washington, Oregon, and California.

Scattered along the rest of the California coast are patches of several other lowland conifer forest types, made up mainly of closed-cone pines and cypresses. Among the best-known species are Monterey pine (*Pinus radiata*) and Monterey cypress (*Cupressus macrocarpa*). These trees are relatively short-lived and modest in stature compared to the species found in the temperate rainforests, and they grow on soils that are drought-prone and low in nutrients. However, when transplanted and grown without competition they thrive in a variety of environments and on many soil types. As a result, they have been planted throughout the world as sources of lumber and ornamentals; indeed, Monterey pine (also called radiata pine) is the widest-planted timber tree in the world. Ironically, it is an endangered species in its natural habitat because natural populations have been degraded and fragmented by urban development and are threatened by a recent outbreak of pine canker disease.

Another lowland pine-dominated vegetation type grows on the Atlantic coast, from New Jersey to Florida and eastward to Louisiana. Its trees are scattered, creating only a savanna or woodland over a grassland of perennial grasses and forbs. Several pines are common here, including shortleaf (*Pinus echinata*), slash (*Pinus elliottii*), longleaf (*Pinus palustris*), and loblolly (*Pinus taeda*). All not only tolerate frequent surface fires, but require fire in order to maintain dominance. Fires are usually started by lightning strikes and, if the grass is dry enough and the wind strong enough, spread quickly across the savanna. Pines ten years old or more have tall enough canopies and thick enough bark to survive, whereas hardwood saplings and trees do not. As long as fires sweep a given acre every three to six years, the vegetation remains pine savanna. But if fires are suppressed for half a century, the pine savanna is replaced by a hardwood deciduous forest. Because of this, fires are now purposely set and managed in many areas to maintain pine's dominance.

The southeastern pine forest was logged intensively during the first third of the twentieth century and is still being logged today. The pines are also "bled" for their sap, which is collected in pails, then heated and treated to yield resin, pitch, turpentine, and other commercial products.

Deciduous forests

The eastern third of the United States was once covered by a vast forest of winter-deciduous trees. European and then American settlers thought of this forest as a wilderness, though they noted a park-like mosaic of open-understory forest and meadow-like clearings. They were unaware that these features had been created by indigenous peoples through their use of fire, which was deployed to clear land for crops and villages, to attract or drive away animals, and as a tool of war. In their turn, the settlers modified the landscape much more dramatically, replacing forest with cropland and inadvertently introducing exotic species (such as tree-of-heaven [*Ailanthus altissima*], and kudzu vine [*Pueraria lobata*]) that became naturalized, spread aggressively, and altered the remaining forest.

The original deciduous forest had a complex, four-layered architecture. The overstory, up to 200 feet (61 m) tall, and was a mix of oak (*Quercus* species), hickory (*Carya* species), maple (*Acer* species), beech (*Fagus* species), basswood (*Tilia* species), tulip tree (*Liriodendron tulipifera*), buckeye (*Aesculus* species), ash (*Fraxinus* species), elm (*Ulmus* species), and walnut (*Juglans* species). Below was a discontinuous layer of understory species such as dogwood (*Cornus* species) and hop hornbeam (*Ostrya virginiana*). The third level consisted of shrubs such as evergreen rhododendron (*Rhododendron* species) and soft-leaved viburnum (*Viburnum* species), and the fourth layer, the forest floor, was made up of seasonally present perennial

The pale, elegant paper birch (Betula papyrifera) can grow to a height of 60 feet (18 m). Its name derives from the fact that its bark peels off in long, paper-like strips. Native Americans used the paper birch to build canoes and make items such as baskets.

In Yellowstone National Park, Wyoming, many of the lodgepole pines (Pinus contorta) that make up 80 percent of the park's forests require fire to release the seeds inside their hard cones.

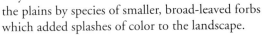

herbs, ferns, and mosses. In addition, Virginia creeper (*Parthenocissus quinquefolia*) and briar lianas (*Smilax* species) made their way up trunks and into the tallest canopies. Only a few hundred acres of such forest remain today, in isolated groves in state parks.

WESTERN RIPARIAN FOREST

Another kind of deciduous forest exists in the more arid West as a riparian belt along streams and rivers. Although the climate here is hotter and drier, the trees' roots are in contact with a water table, so they do not experience drought. The presence of these narrow strips of deciduous forest in the West, far from the closely related eastern forest, suggests that a single deciduous forest—which probably began to fragment about 20 million years ago as a result of climate change—was once continuous throughout the Northern Hemisphere of both Old and New Worlds.

Grasslands

Grassland generally replaces forest where one or more of the following occurs: the climate becomes more arid; the incidence of wildfire rises above once every decade; the possibility of drought occurring for one or more years in succession becomes as likely as every few decades; and the soil becomes more finely textured and deeper. At about 95 degrees west longitude, along a line running north through Arkansas, Missouri, Iowa, and Minnesota, most of these conditions are met. Here, the eastern forests once gave way to vast prairies that spread west to the edge of the Rocky Mountains, where they changed to other kinds of grassland including intermountain shrub steppe and warm desert steppe. Today, except for a few small protected areas that have never been plowed, the prairies have been replaced with farms.

THE CENTRAL PRAIRIES

Early travelers likened the central prairies to an enormous sea, the wind-whipped grasses resembling oceanic waves. On the eastern fringe of the plains, the grasses grew head-high and were a mixture of tufted forms (bunchgrasses) and rhizomatous forms (sodgrasses). With increasing aridity to the west, the grasses shortened to waist and ankle height and were primarily bunchgrasses. Although the grasses were the tallest plants, they were outnumbered across the plains by species of smaller, broad-leaved forbs which added splashes of color to the landscape.

Sadly, almost nothing remains of these vast natural grasslands. Settlers found the black soil ideal for farming and soon cleared huge swaths. Today, more than 90 percent of the tallgrass and mid-grass prairies, and more than 80 percent of the shortgrass prairie has disappeared. Efforts to restore small areas with plantings and through the use of prescribed fire have been variously successful, and a few parks and preserves contain pieces of the original, unplowed prairie. But these parks are like zoos: small, fenced-in relics where curious tourists and ecologists gather to stare.

INTERMOUNTAIN SHRUB STEPPE

A band of grassland mixed with shrubs once extended from the western flanks of the Rocky Mountains through southern Idaho and into eastern Washington and Oregon and the foothills of the Cascade Range. The dominant grasses were wheatgrass (*Pascopyrum smithii*), fescue (*Festuca* species), and wild rye (*Elymus* species) bunchgrasses, accompanied by short shrubs of sagebrush (*Artemisia tridentata*), an element from the cold desert to the south.

This shrub steppe has been severely degraded by purposely set fires, overgrazing, and the accidental introduction of aggressive annual grasses and forbs, in particular cheatgrass (*Bromus tectorum*, downy brome) from Eurasia. Relatively small areas of this grassland at one time extended south into the Willamette Valley of Oregon and to the north coast and Central Valley of California. These areas have also been enormously changed by introduced species, overgrazing, and conversion to agriculture. Today, less than one percent of these peripheral grasslands remain in their original condition.

WARM DESERT STEPPE

Warm desert steppe occurs in parts of Texas, New Mexico, and Arizona, at elevations just above the desert zone. Another bunchgrasss type, its grasses—tobosa (*Hilaria mutica*), galeta (*Hilaria jamesii*), and black grama (*Boutelou eriopoda*)—differ from those already described in that their maximum growth occurs in the warm or hot summer rather than the cooler early spring. They are, for this reason, called "warm season" grasses, in contrast to "cool season" grasses.

Characteristic of northeastern deciduous forests, maple trees (Acer species) produce dazzling displays of color in fall.

The rain shadow on the eastern side of the Sierra Nevada Mountains creates an abrupt transition from well-watered montane conifer forest to relatively arid intermountain desert. Consequently, the foothills are characterized by a mix of semiarid scrub and conifers.

This grassland has also been much modified by humans in the past 150 years. In this case, the most significant change has been caused by the suppression of fire, a management strategy that inadvertently allows desert shrubs to spread. Originally, the fires regularly destroyed the shrubs, allowing the grasses to dominate all except for more rocky areas.

Deserts

According to climatologists and vegetation scientists, most American deserts are not true deserts but semi-arid lands because their climate is too humid and they receive more than 5 inches (120 mm) of rain a year—the defined maximum for real desert. Only in one or two areas, notably in Death Valley National Park and at the head of the Gulf of California, where mean annual rainfall is around 1 inch (25 mm), does the precipitation fall far below this level.

Four distinctive kinds of what is commonly called desert exist in the United States: intermountain (also called Great Basin, basin-and-range, cold, or high desert), Mojave, Sonoran, and Chihuahuan.

INTERMOUNTAIN DESERT

The intermountain desert, which stretches across western Utah, Nevada, northeastern California, northwestern Arizona, and into New Mexico, is the most northerly desert type. Land elevation in this environment ranges from approximately 3,600 feet (1,200 m) to 4,800 feet (1,600 m); winters can therefore be severe, with hard frosts and snow. The landscape is generally characterized by row upon row of forested mountain ranges rising above gently sloping bajadas that lead to internally drained playas

or sinks. The rocky bajadas support desert scrub, but the playas have only a low cover of specialized salt-tolerant shrubs and grasses. The dominance of sagebrush shrubs gives the scrub vegetation a monotonous blue-green appearance. Native cacti, which include two *Opuntia* species, are uncommon because most cacti species are frost-sensitive and incapable of surviving this environment's cold winters. Modest numbers of annual plant species add color in spring, then disappear until the next year.

MOJAVE DESERT

To the south is the smallest of the four deserts, the Mojave. As in the intermountain zone, most of the precipitation falls in winter, which limits the amount of plant cover. Elevations are generally lower than those of the cold desert, and winter conditions not so extreme. Cacti are strikingly more abundant, but the dominant shrub is a brown-green plant known as creosote bush (*Larrea tridentata*) for the odor of its resinous leaves. Few animals can eat this plant, which helps explain its abundance. Other prominent species include Joshua trees (*Yucca brevifolia*), desert wash smoke trees (*Psorothamnus spinosus*), cactus-like desert coachwhip (*Fouquieria splendens*), and an array of annual forbs and grasses. Wet years in the Mojave produce strikingly colorful shows of annual plants—so dense in places that they appear to form a solid carpet. Outstanding examples of protected Mojave vegetation can be found in Death Valley and Joshua Tree National Parks.

SONORAN DESERT

The hottest and lowest desert, occupying southeastern California and southern Arizona, is the Sonoran, which extends south into Mexico. Plant life here is diverse and even bizarre, plant cover is extensive, and biodiversity is high. A typical Arizona landscape includes small paloverde and iron-wood trees, tall creosote-bush and acacia (*Acacia* species) shrubs, shorter burrowbush (*Ambrosia dumosa*) and brittlebush (*Encelia farinosa*) subshrubs, cacti ranging from 12-foot (4-m) saguaros (*Carnegiea gigantea*) and chollas (*Opuntia echinocarpa*) as tall as humans, to barrel (*Ferocactus* species) and pincushion (*Mammillaria* species) cacti that hug the ground, and two crops of annuals (one that flowers in spring and another that flowers in summer). Precipitation falls in both winter and summer. Elevations are mainly below 1,800 feet (600 m), so hard frost is almost unknown, and summer temperatures can be very high.

LEFT: The wide, flat, scrub-covered plains by Highway 389 in northwestern Arizona are typical of the intermountain desert zone.

BELOW LEFT: Death Valley National Park, California, is one of the few places in the United States where true desert can be found. At Stovepipe Wells, prevailing northwest winds have piled up sand grains deposited by rivers into enormous sand dunes.

Synonymous with Sonoran desert, the saguaro cactus (Carnegiea gigantea) grows extremely slowly, taking 10 years to reach a height of 1 inch (2.5 cm), and up to 150 years to attain its maximum height of 50 feet (15 m) and weight of 10 tons (10 t). A single saguaro can store as much as 200 gallons (757 l) of water.

Siuslaw National Forest protects a strip of temperate conifer forest measuring 135 miles (217 km) by 27 miles (44 km) on the coast of Oregon. Heavy rainfall fuels the growth of large tree species including western hemlock (Tsuga heterophylla), Douglas fir (Pseudotsuga menziesii), and Sitka spruce (Picea sitchensis), which are often cloaked with mosses such as the rare pohlia mosses (Pohlia species).

CHIHUAHUAN DESERT

The most easterly desert, the Chihuahuan, is also principally a Mexican desert and extends only a short distance into western Texas and southern New Mexico. The soils are often rich in limestone or gypsum and as a result harbor rare and endemic plants. Creosote bush is the dominant species, but it is joined by a diversity of of yuccas (*Yucca* species) and agaves (*Agave* species)—plants with basal rosettes of large, stiff, thorny leaves and tall flowering stems. Only summer annuals grow here because there is little winter rain. The best protected example of this desert is in Big Bend National Park, Texas.

Mediterranean and Madrean woodlands and scrublands

The terms "Mediterranean" and "Madrean" are used to refer to two environment types that have different kinds of semiarid climate but share a similar flora. Traditionally, "Mediterranean" describes the winter-wet climate and evergreen vegetation of countries bordering the Mediterranean Sea. In the United States, this combination occurs in the foothills and coastal basins of California. Common vegetation types here include mixed evergreen forest, oak woodland, chaparral, and coastal scrub. "Madrean" refers to the summer-wet climate and scrubby vegetation types of the Sierra Madre Occidental foothills in Mexico. A similar climate and range of vegetation can be found along the western foothills of the Rocky Mountains in Colorado and New Mexico. The main vegetation types are chaparral and oak woodland.

MIXED EVERGREEN FOREST

Mixed evergreen forest grows between 1,800 feet (600 m) and 4,500 feet (1,500 m) in the Coast Ranges of southern Oregon and northern California and in the Transverse and Peninsular Ranges of southern California. It can be thought of as a transition zone between montane conifer forest above and oak woodland below.

Mixed evergreen forest has a dense canopy but because the leaf litter is so thick, almost nothing grows in the understory; however, mosses usually cover tree trunks and boulders. The trees are a rich combination of conifer, broad-leaved evergreen, and winter-deciduous species. The conifers include Douglas fir, ponderosa pine, and Coulter pine (*Pinus coulteri*); the broad-leaved evergreens consist of coast and canyon live oaks (*Quercus agrifolia* and *Quercus chrysolepis*), chinquapin (*Chrysolepis chrysophylla*), madrone (*Arbutus menziesii*), and California bay (*Umbellularia californica*); and the deciduous trees are mainly black oak (*Quercus kelloggii*), big-leaf maple (*Acer macrophyllum*), hazelnut (*Corylus cornuta*), and dogwood (*Cornus nuttallii*). Few old-growth stands of this forest remain. When it is logged for Douglas fir, the hardwoods stump-sprout and create dense thickets in which the conifers have difficulty reestablishing themselves.

OAK WOODLANDS

Californian oak woodland occurs in a warmer, drier, lower-elevation habitat than mixed evergreen forest. It has a two-layered structure: an open canopy of evergreen and deciduous oaks over a continuous understory of grasses and forbs. These grasses used to be an upland extension of the bunchgrass prairie that dominated lowland California. The bunchgrasses have been better maintained in this forest than at lower elevations where introduced annuals dominate. Among the species still commonly found here are melic grass (*Melica* species), California fescue (*Festuca californica*), needlegrass (*Nasella* species), bluegrass (*Poa scabrella*), and wild rye (*Elymus glaucus*). Oak species include blue oak (*Quercus douglasii*), interior live oak (*Quercus wislizenii*), and coast live oak, Oregon white oak (*Quercus garryana*), black oak (*Quercus velutina*), valley oak (*Quercus lobata*), and Engelman oak (*Quercus engelmannii*); associated trees include California buckeye (*Aesculus californica*), California black walnut (*Juglans californica*), and foothill pine (*Pinus sabiniana*). Madrean oak woodland has an even richer array of oak species and many species of short pines.

Oak woodlands once supported the highest population densities of native Californian peoples, partly because acorns played a central role in their diet. These forests were also traversed by European settlers coming into California, and many California cities were given names that relate to this vegetation type, such as Oakland, Woodland, Encino, and Hollywood—an ironic practice given that the trees were soon cleared for agriculture and urban expansion, and exploited for timber and fuel. In more recent times, introduced diseases such as sudden oak death (SOD) have been spreading along the coast.

Several deciduous oak species appear to have had minimal regeneration success during the twentieth century; many acorns are produced each year and germinate, but few seedlings survive to become saplings. Possible causes may be overgrazing by livestock and deer, high populations of gophers (which eat the acorns), or competition from introduced grasses and forbs. Evergreen oaks seem to be unaffected.

CHAPARRAL

Chaparral is a dense, one-layered, scrubby vegetation type composed of rigidly branched shrubs with small leaves. It typically grows on steep slopes with shallow or coarse-textured soil, in the same elevation zone that supports oak woodland. However, chaparral tends to occupy the hottest and driest sites and those most often affected by wildfire.

Californian and Madrean chaparral are dominated by different species of manzanita (*Arctostaphylos*), ceanothus (*Ceanothus*), silk tassel (*Garrya*), scrub oak (*Quercus*), and coffee berry (*Rhamnus*). Uniquely Californian shrubs are chamise (*Adenostoma* species) and Christmas berry (*Heteromeles arbutifolia*). In contrast to the evergreen Californian chaparral, Madrean chaparral is winter-deciduous.

Understory herbs are only scattered, except immediately after a wildfire. Hot, intense fires occur every 25–75 years. Most shrub species eventually resprout, and within a half-dozen years the shrub layer has closed over again, although at a shorter height than before the fire. Within 20–30 years, the prefire structure of the scrub is reestablished.

COASTAL SCRUB

A lower-elevation, coast-facing version of chaparral, called coastal scrub, dominates steep slopes all along the California coast. In the north, the vegetation consists of soft-leaved bush lupines (*Lupinus arboreus*), coffee berry (*Rhamnus californica*), and coyote brush (*Baccharis pilularis*) above a dense understory of reedgrasses (*Calamagrostis* species) and perennial herbs from the nearby coastal prairie. In the south, the vegetation has an even more open overstory of very odorous, drought-deciduous subshrubs, including California sagebrush (*Artemisia californica*) and several sage (*Salvia*) species, and an understory of annual grasses and forbs. The southern coastal scrub is considered to be endangered because much of it has been displaced by urban development and the remainder is degenerating to grassland because of the competitive nature of exotic herbs and a changed fire cycle.

Hawaiian rainforests

The isolation of the Hawaiian Islands had major consequences for its flora and vegetation. There is a high level of endemism; a small number of species, most of which evolved from a small number of colonizing species; and poor competitive abilities against exotic species brought to Hawaii by humans.

More than 80 percent of Hawaii's vegetation has been destroyed. Originally, the two most important vegetation types were lowland tropical forest and montane tropical forest. Lowland tropical forest dominated areas below 2,000 feet (660 m), but most was cleared by native Hawaiians for agriculture 700 years ago. It is likely that its overstory comprised tree palms, leguminous trees, and the eucalyptus relative ohia (*Metrosideros polymorpha*).

Montane tropical rainforest is still common on most of the islands. Growing at elevations between 1,800 feet (600 m) and 6,000 feet (2,000 m), it is overwhelmingly dominated by ohia trees, often accompanied by koa (*Acacia koa*), and has an understory of diverse shrubs and ferns. Many perennial herbs grow epiphytically on the upper trunks and branches of emergent trees, alongside several species of lianas. The wettest areas also incorporate large expanses of tree ferns interspersed with bogs rich in mosses, sedges, and grasses.

Unfortunately, the ecological integrity of montane forests and wetlands is gravely threatened by the presence of feral pigs and the large number of invasive plants that have been introduced to Hawaii.

Tropical hibiscus (Hibiscus rosa-sinensis) is found throughout Hawaii. In addition to seven native species, hundreds of imported varieties and hybrids grow on the islands, ranging in color from shades of red and pink to yellow, lavender, white, and gold.

LEFT: Though closely associated with the Hawaiian Archipelago in the popular imagination, the coconut palm (Cocos nucifera) is not native. It either floated to the islands from the South Pacific or was introduced by Polynesian settlers, who used it as a source of food, drink, and building materials.

FAUNA

The Evolution of American Fauna

Known as Eubrontes, these dinosaur tracks in Dinosaur State Park, Connecticut, were probably made by a small carnivorous dinosaur such as Dilophosaurus, about 200 million years ago.

RIGHT: The beautiful armadillo (Dasypus bellus) was one of a number of giant armadillos that roamed the continent when humans first arrived 20,000 years ago. Its bony scutes offered effective protection from predators, but it nevertheless became extinct about 11,000 years ago.

About two-thirds of all the animal species that have ever lived no longer exist. Furthermore, since the emergence of mammals in the geological record a little more than 200 million years ago, more mammal species have become extinct than are alive today. The principal reason for this is that some groups of animals were able to adjust to the changes brought about by continental drift, mountain building, climate change, and even catastrophic events such as asteroid impacts, whereas others were not.

Influences on evolution

Approximately 200 million years ago, tectonic plate movements began to break up Pangaea, the single supercontinent that had existed for 200 million years or so, forming a northern continent called Laurasia, which included modern-day North America, Europe, and Asia, and a southern continent known as Gondwanaland, which incorporated present-day South America, Africa, India, Australasia, and Antarctica. Both landmasses supported major groups of vertebrate or backboned animals, the oldest of which were the reptiles, which had first appeared about 335 million years ago, giving rise to the dinosaurs about 100 million years later. Mammals emerged around 215 million years ago, and birds, which seem to have evolved from flying reptiles, appeared approximately 160 million years ago.

Around the time when Pangaea broke up, the region that would become North America

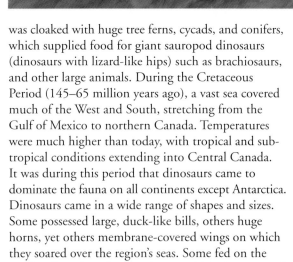

was cloaked with huge tree ferns, cycads, and conifers, which supplied food for giant sauropod dinosaurs (dinosaurs with lizard-like hips) such as brachiosaurs, and other large animals. During the Cretaceous Period (145–65 million years ago), a vast sea covered much of the West and South, stretching from the Gulf of Mexico to northern Canada. Temperatures were much higher than today, with tropical and subtropical conditions extending into Central Canada. It was during this period that dinosaurs came to dominate the fauna on all continents except Antarctica. Dinosaurs came in a wide range of shapes and sizes. Some possessed large, duck-like bills, others huge horns, yet others membrane-covered wings on which they soared over the region's seas. Some fed on the first flowering plants and trees, which also appeared at this time; others were meat-eaters, such as the famous Tyrannosaurus Rex, with its 6-inch (15-cm) teeth capable of ripping huge chunks of flesh.

At the end of the Cretaceous Period, a range of lizard, snake, and bird families were also present, together with fur-bearing cat- and rat-like placental mammals and older marsupials, the ancestors of Australia's koala and kangaroos. Newer placental mammals were generally smaller than the more abundant dinosaurs.

Beginning about 70 million years ago and persisting for tens of millions of years, earth movements, including volcanic eruptions, lava flows, faulting, and mountain building, resulted in the formation of the Rocky Mountains and the Sierra Madre Oriental in Mexico. At the same time, sea levels began to fall, exposing vast expanses of marine sediments. Land dinosaurs, pterosaurs, and huge sea reptiles like the mososaurs vanished, together with ammonites and

The Smilodon, a saber-toothed cat, inhabited North America until about 12,000 years ago. The size of a lion, it had massive jaws with 7-inch (17.5-cm) incisors.

groups of marine invertebrates. Mammals became more abundant, gained in body size, and gave rise to species that began to feed off newly evolved grasses. Bees, butterflies, and wasps emerged to feast on the abundant nectar supplied by the greatly increased range of flowers, plants, and shrubs.

It now seems that the demise of the dinosaurs was the result of a single catastrophic event rather than these and other gradual environmental changes. The most likely explanation is that an asteroid impact some 65 million years ago, possibly off the Yucatan Peninsula, created tidal waves, forest fires, and clouds of ash and dust, all of which drastically altered the climate, in turn killing off the plants on which the dinosaurs depended. The harsh conditions lasted for many years, affecting the movements and migrations, feeding strategies, competition, reproduction, and survival of other animal groups, too.

The demise of the megafauna

There have been major ice advances and retreats of continental ice sheets and mountain glaciers in the northern hemisphere during the past 2 million years or so. In North America, the most recent, so-called Wisconsin Ice Age, which may have begun about 100,000 years ago, involved the spread and retreat of glacial and tundra conditions over what is now the northern tier of the Midwestern states. When the ice withdrew, conditions would have been similar to those in Alaska or Siberia today; as conditions once again grew colder, the tundra would become an icy desert where life was highly precarious. In the lower-latitude tropics and subtropics, changes in forest, grassland, and desert vegetation depended upon moisture regimes, including the rise and fall of lake levels in western America. Desert-adapted flora and fauna prospered in dry spells, and retreated during the wetter times. Among the most successful at coping with the vagaries of the climate were deer, javelina, bison, collared peccary, pronghorn, moose, and bear.

When the first humans reached North America around 20,000 years ago, the continent's fauna also included bison, horses, and camels, as well as a range of giant mammals, or megafauna. Among their number were mammoths standing 10 feet (3 m) tall with 16-foot (4.8-m) curved tusks, huge woodland musk oxen, beavers the size of modern-day bears, ground sloths as large as today's oxen, and giant armadillos, one Texan species of which was as big as a present-day rhinoceros. Giant herbivorous mammals like these were found also in Eurasia and Australia.

Controversy surrounds the reasons for the subsequent disappearance of the megafauna in North America and elsewhere. Some authorities argue that climate changes associated with the close of the last ice age gradually reduced the habitats upon which the animals depended, eventually leading to their extinction. Others attribute the disappearance of the megafauna to diseases carried by the first humans to reach the continent. Another hypothesis, developed more than 40 years ago by Paul S. Martin, a geosciences professor, suggests that it was the appearance of specialized human hunting communities in North America around 15,000 years ago that caused the extinction of more than 20 mammal species, including horses and camels. According to this "Pleistocene Overkill" theory, the hunters, wielding finely wrought, flaked blades and projectile points, entered North America by crossing from Asia to Alaska, then spread rapidly southward through an ice-free corridor at a rate of about 100 miles (160 km) a decade, reaching the southern edge of South America in 1,000 years or so. Large herbivores in the tundra zone and others in the tropics failed to cope with the sudden arrival of these new, mobile predators, and gradually succumbed to hunting pressures.

Following the demise of the megafauna, some North American peoples continued to hunt large mammals such as deer, bison, moose, and bear for their flesh, sinews, and skins; others switched to plant collecting and hunting smaller animals. About 6,500 years ago, agriculture began in the central valley of Mexico and spread north, reaching the Southwest about 2,500 years later. Farther north, peoples of the western deserts managed to adjust to the vagaries of climate and the varying abundance of prey and continue to hunt. Their key food was the American bison, which was widely distributed across the central plains. However, fluctuations in moisture over several millennia made the plains hotter and drier, limiting the bison's range, so that some 8,000 years ago these hunters settled in lowland riparian areas where they depended on migratory bison and local game.

In the late seventeenth century, Native Americans gained access to horses and weaponry imported by early European colonists. This led to a gradual decline in populations of large mammals such as the American bison, a decline that would become increasingly rapid as European settlers advanced westward.

The mountain goat (Oreamnos americanus) is thought to have originated in Eurasia and reached North America via a land bridge that formed in the Bering Strait during the early Pleistocene age.

Descended from a small fox-sized animal called Hyracotherium, the modern horse (Equus caballus) first appeared about 2 million years ago. Hunted to extinction in America soon after the arrival of humans, it was reintroduced by Spanish explorers in the 1600s.

Wildlife in Peril

Communities of the black-tailed prairie dog (Cynomys ludovicianus) once covered 100 million acres (40 million ha) from Mexico to Canada. Today, they occupy just 1 million acres (400,000 ha), mainly on the Great Plains.

European explorers and settlers arriving in North America in the late eighteenth and early nineteenth centuries were astonished by the abundance and diversity of the continent's wildlife. Waterfowl literally clouded the skies, blocking out the sun; fish choked rivers and creeks; and huge herds of pronghorn antelope crowded short-grass plains amid enormous colonies or "towns" of prairie dogs that stretched from horizon to horizon. For settlers, coming from a continent where animal populations had been depleted by centuries of hunting and habitat destruction, this plenitude was a godsend.

Working collectively and utilizing modern technologies, such as guns, axes and plows, the new Americans soon began to alter the landscape and impact on its animal inhabitants to a far greater extent than indigenous peoples had done. Few European immigrants expressed qualms about this. For a start, the superabundance of wildlife suggested that these resources were virtually unlimited. Even large mammals, such as bison and deer, appeared so plentiful that shooting a few seemed to barely make a dent in their incredible numbers.

Moreover, according to then-widespread beliefs, human activities, such as land clearance, farming, and the construction of settlements, improved and "civilized" nature rather than degraded it. Important sources of food and barter, such as waterfowl, quails, prairie chickens, and wild turkeys, were therefore harvested for the greater good. Any animal that impeded the "march of progress" deserved eradication. Eliminating "savage" creatures that threatened humans or livestock, such as alligators, wolves, cougars, bobcats, and jaguars—even crop-thieving parrots and doves—was an act of civic virtue.

Over a period of decades, and especially toward the close of the 1800s, unregulated shooting and trapping of native mammals and birds resulted in catastrophic declines in the numbers of many species. The slaughter was facilitated by the expansion of railroads, significant improvements in the efficiency of firearms, and the contemporary development of refrigeration. Bison numbers may have once reached 50 million, but by the end of the nineteenth century only small remnant populations remained. Between 1872 and 1874 alone, market hunters killed 4.3 million bison on the southern plains. In the South and Midwest, entire communities would stop work to take pot shots at immense flocks of passenger pigeons. It has been estimated that there were around 9 billion passenger pigeons in America in 1800; by 1914, the species was extinct.

Preserving wildlife

In the 1880s, articles began to appear in sporting magazines and scientific journals descrying the rapid diminution of native mammal and bird populations. Authors called for restraints on exploitation and for enforceable laws that would prevent the extinction of key species. The Audubon Society, founded in February 1886 by George Bird Grinnell, editor of *Forest and Stream*, appealed for a halt to the slaughter of wild birds for their ornamental feathers. Grinnell pointed out that declines in bird populations affected farmers and horticulturists, who depended on swallows, kingbirds, bluebirds, and other insectivorous species to rid their crops of bugs. Within three years, the Audubon Society had more than 50,000 members including many children and teachers who responded enthusiastically to the society's suggestion that

The North American bison (Bison bison) was hunted almost to extinction in the late-nineteenth century, when bison hides were much in demand for making leather machine belts. The killing was highly inefficient, with most of the carcasses being left to rot where the animals died.

Americans take pleasure in observing animals rather than shooting them. Within a decade or two, other conservation organizations and wildlife groups began to lobby for laws and restrictions on hunting for the table or hat, and to work to change popular assumptions about killing animals.

At the beginning of the twentieth century, both federal and state authorities became increasingly involved in animal protection. In 1900, the *Lacey Act* prohibited the interstate shipment of illegally taken game birds, and the importation of nonnative species (typified by the European starling). In 1913, the *Federal Migratory Bird Law* gave federal authorities the right to establish closed seasons and regulate bag limits and weapons used in hunting migratory birds. Three years later, the passing of the *Migratory Bird Treaty Act*, signed by the United States and Britain (on behalf of Canada), made it unlawful to sell or barter migratory bird species or their eggs.

In 1903, President Theodore Roosevelt set aside Pelican Island in Indian River, Florida, as a bird refuge. The island was an important nesting site for brown pelicans, which were then shot regularly by millinery agents for their wing feathers. This executive order was the precedent for more than 100 migratory waterfowl refuges spanning 1 million acres (400,000 ha) that now exist across the nation. Linked to this effort to protect habitat for native wildlife was the decision to capture and transplant certain mammals and birds into areas where overhunting had exterminated them. For example, in the early 1940s, white-tailed deer from the Aransas National Wildlife Refuge in Texas

were transplanted several hundred miles to ranches on the Edwards Plateau in north-central Texas. Landowners agreed to protect introduced deer so that populations would rise high enough to sustain some hunting. Other transplants in Texas have included beaver, quail, antelope, and wild turkeys. Federal taxes levied on arms and ammunition under a 1937 statute assisted in funding such reintroductions.

A major breakthrough in animal conservation came with the inclusion of nongame species in wildlife laws, most notably the *Endangered Species Preservation Act* of 1966 and its subsequent reformulation in 1973. The act is implemented by the Fish and Wildlife Service within the Department of the Interior, which establishes regulations for identifying and listing threatened species, and sets up programs to assist in their recovery.

One famous animal that has benefited from this program is the whooping crane, North America's tallest wild bird. Fifty years ago, its numbers had fallen so low that scientists began to transplant eggs from wild nests in Canada and hatch them in a Wild Bird Research Center in Patuxent, Maryland. Birds raised in captivity were then reintroduced to the wild. Similar captive breeding programs have helped reestablish peregrine falcons, which were decimated by pesticide-residue build-up, red wolves in northeastern North Carolina, and California condors in the Grand Canyon.

Fortunately, the public is interested and concerned about the fate of indigenous species, and prepared to support programs that assist in their recovery, whether they involve polar bears and caribou on the Arctic tundra, red-cockaded woodpeckers in the pinelands of Louisiana and Texas, or Mexican gray wolves in Arizona. Right across the nation, there is an overwhelming desire to protect the nation's natural heritage, preserving it for future generations, so that they too might be inspired by the variety and abundance of the United States' wild creatures.

After being pursued by hunters for its feathers in the late-nineteenth century, the brown pelican (Pelecanus occidentalis) was further threatened in the 1960s and 1970s by the widespread use of DDT in pesticides. Pelican populations plummeted, but recovered to some extent following the banning of DDT.

The white-tailed deer (Odocoileus virginianus) made a remarkable recovery in the second half of the 1900s after being nearly wiped out by hunters. Taking advantage of forest clearance, which encourages the growth of the shrubs on which the species feeds, it has extended its range and raised its population to an all-time high.

America's Animal Communities

*In spring, when snows melt, the white-tailed ptarmigan (*Lagopus leucurus*) sheds its white winter plumage. This bird is usually found near willow trees, its principal source of nourishment year-round.*

*The Columbian ground squirrel (*Spermophilus columbianus*) inhabits the Rocky Mountains of western Montana, Idaho, Oregon, Washington, and Canada's British Columbia.*

The United States supports an astonishing array of wildlife, including 346 species of mammals, 836 kinds of birds, 277 species of reptiles, and 230 types of amphibians. Some of these creatures are distributed widely across the nation. This is the case, for example, with many wetland animals such as beaver, muskrat, otter, and turtles, and many highly mobile bird species. Other animals are widespread because they have adapted successfully to a range of habitats. White-tailed deer have gradually extended their range across much of the Lower 48 states; coyotes hunt in deserts, mountains, and woodlands. However, as a result of adaptation to specific climate and vegetation types, the majority of animals belong to distinctive ecological communities associated with each of the United States' major environments.

Tundra

Winter on the Alaskan tundra is a time of extreme cold, fierce blizzards, and almost total darkness. Plants are concealed by snow, and moisture in liquid form is in short supply. To escape these privations, many summer residents migrate south to warmer climes. They include huge herds of caribou (*Rangifer tarandus*), the region's major herbivore, as well as a wide range of birds, notably ducks, geese, and plovers. Many winter residents cope by hibernating. Small mammals such as voles and lemmings bury themselves under the snow, feeding sporadically on stored plants and seeds. Most of the animals that remain above ground have developed adaptations to the extreme conditions. Several species, including the arctic fox (*Alopex lagopus*) and snowy owl (*Nyctea scandiaca*), swap their summer colors for a white winter coat. Larger mammals such as the gray wolf (*Canis lupus*), polar bear (*Ursus maritimus*), and lynx (*Lynx lynx*) are protected by dense fur, and, in the case of the polar bear, a specially adapted circulatory system that constantly transfers warm blood from the heart to vulnerable extremities.

With the return of spring, the snow melts, hardy plants poke through the frozen soil, clouds of insects emerge from hollows, and the days lengthen. Waterfowl and shorebirds fly back to the tundra to feast on this bounty and to breed, small mammals emerge from their burrows, and the caribou herds sweep north across the plains to tundra calving grounds, pursued by their enemies, the gray wolf and grizzly bear (*Ursus arctos*).

A similar cycle occurs in alpine tundra, which covers the highest peaks of mainland mountain ranges including the Rockies, Cascades, and Sierra Nevada. Here, several species descend to lower elevations or, in the case of birds, fly to warmer regions in winter. Year-round residents include medium-sized mammals such as the yellow-bellied marmot (*Marmota flaviventris*), which survives on its body fat during hibernation, and smaller creatures such as pikas, which have insufficient body fat to hibernate and therefore have to tunnel beneath the snow to reach buried plants and supplies set aside in summer. Larger alpine creatures able to weather the big freeze by virtue of body mass and efficient insulation include mountain goats, mountain lions, and bighorn sheep.

Boreal and subalpine forests

As well as providing a winter refuge for many tundra species, conifer forests host their own animal communities. South of the arctic tundra lies the immense swath of the great northern conifer, or boreal, forest, which in the United States covers much of Alaska and parts of the far Northeast. Conditions here are still sufficiently severe to pose major challenges to animal life. Large size is one protection against the cold and, as a result, many of this environment's mammals, including the grizzly bear, moose, and elk, dwarf their relatives elsewhere. The herbivores of the boreal forest, which include moose, elk, deer, and caribou, have limited supplies of grasses available to them; as a result, some, such as the moose, have adapted to

feeding on aquatic plants, which are found in abundance in bogs and riparian valleys. The gray wolf and grizzly bear are the major predators of these large animals; smaller herbivores, which include the snowshoe hare, marmots, squirrels, and pikas, keep a wary eye out for lynx, wolverine, pine marten, and red fox.

Undoubtedly, the most renowned resident of the boreal forest is the brown or grizzly bear. Growing to 7 feet (2.1 m) in length and reaching a height of 3.5 feet (1.2 m) or more at the shoulder, grizzlies are omnivorous and therefore able to cope with wide variations in food supplies. In turn, their large food intake allows them to build up sizable reserves of fat that see them safely through their winter hibernation. Although relatively common in the boreal forest and on the edge of the arctic tundra, grizzlies have been virtually eliminated from the Lower 48 states, where fewer than 1,000 individuals remain.

Wetlands in the boreal zone, known as muskeg, serve as summer breeding grounds for an abundance of waterfowl, including swans, cranes, geese, and ducks, which migrate south to the Gulf states during the non-nesting season. Migratory songbirds also nest among northern conifers in summer, returning south in fall. Among the species that reside in boreal forests year-round are the common raven (*Corvus corax*), black-capped chickadee (*Parus atricapillus*), boreal chickadee (*Parus hudsonica*), and pine grosbeak (*Pinicola enucleator*) which, as its name suggests, has a large bill that is specially adapted for extracting seeds from pine cones.

The subalpine community, which occurs below alpine tundra, is made up of a similar range of animals,

The elk (Cervus elaphus) is found in most western states (where it is especially common in the Rockies), and in some parts of the east, notably Pennsylvania. Adult male elk grow antlers bearing six tines and measuring up to 5 feet (1.5 m) in length. Despite its weight, a bull elk can run at up to 35 miles per hour (55 kph).

The Alaskan brown bear (Ursus arctos middendorfi) is the largest subspecies of the brown or grizzly bear, weighing up to 1,700 pounds (770 kg).

Found throughout the Lower 48 states and Alaska, but common in the Northwest, the bald eagle (Haliaeetus leucocephalus) was selected as the national bird of the United States in 1782.

including grizzly bear, wolf, deer, and large cats such as the mountain lion and bobcat, but often includes other species from adjacent lower-level habitats.

Montane and lowland temperate conifer forests

Animals occupy similar niches within the cool, moist environments of the montane conifer forests, which cover many western mountain slopes and parts of the Appalachians, and the lowland conifer forests of the Pacific coast. Elk, antelope, and deer are the major herbivores; gray wolves, mountain lions, and grizzly bears are their main predators. Grizzlies are rare and generally confined to high, remote areas; black bears far outnumber them at lower elevations. Small mammals include a range of squirrels, martens, chipmunks, weasels, and voles. The abundant moisture in coastal forests supports significant numbers of amphibians, notably salamanders. Especially common in coastal redwood forests, they include the Pacific giant salamander (*Dicamptodon tenebrosus*), North America's largest at 6 inches (15 cm) in length.

Among the most notable birds in montane and lowland temperate conifer forests are the bald eagle (*Haliaeetus leucocephalus*), which gathers in forests surrounding salmon-rich rivers, especially in Alaska, and the northern spotted owl (*Strix occidentalis*), symbol of the successful 1980s conservation campaign to save the old-growth forests of the Pacific Northwest. One unusual inhabitant of the lowland temperate conifer forest is a seabird, the marbled murrelet (*Brachyramphus marmoratus*). It has been known to science for 200 years, but its nesting habits remained a mystery until 1990, when researchers discovered a colony in British Columbia, Canada, that was home to as many as 50,000 birds. This revealed that the murrelet nests in the high, mossy boughs of large conifers like Douglas firs. Other nesting sites have since been located in the western United States.

Deciduous forests

In eastern forests, where few old-growth stands remain, animal habitats have been greatly disrupted. Only in protected zones, including major national parks such as Shenandoah and Great Smoky Mountains, do the original communities survive intact. The major herbivore is the widespread white-tailed deer (*Odocoileus virginianus*) which has taken advantage of the eradication of its major predator, the gray wolf, to expand its range. Another predator, formerly widespread in the Southeast, the red wolf (*Canis rufus*), was almost wiped out by settlers and has only recently been reintroduced to certain areas. Other carnivores include the red fox, coyote, and bobcat.

The deciduous forest's temperate climate and abundance of seeds and plants also support the nation's largest populations of black bears and a plethora of small, often arboreal mammals including opossums, skunks, raccoons, squirrels, woodchucks, and chipmunks. Deciduous forests also harbor a surprisingly large number of amphibians: the Great Smoky Mountains, for example, are home to the world's biggest assemblage of salamanders.

Birdlife is prolific, too, with a range of families occupying different niches. Towhees, wrens, grouse, and nightjars favor the forest floor; woodpeckers, chickadees, nuthatches, and thrushes occupy the middle layers, and tanagers and vireos generally confine themselves to the canopy. Birds of prey, such as hawks and owls, tend to patrol clearings or forest edges where they have a clear view of passing prey. Many of the bird species in deciduous forests, including vireos, warblers, and thrushes, are migratory, flying long distances to wintering grounds in South America before returning in spring.

Grasslands

Now vastly diminished, the grasslands of the Great Plains were once home to immense populations of hoofed grazers, including perhaps as many as 50 million bison, 40 million pronghorns, and large

numbers of elk, bighorn sheep, and deer, as well as predators such as wolves, grizzlies, and coyotes.

Following the rapid clearance of the prairies and introduction of domestic livestock, bison numbers fell to about 300 individuals at beginning of the twentieth century. Breeding programs and the expansion of the national park and wildlife refuge systems saved the species from extinction. Today, up to 200,000 bison (*Bison bison*) inhabit a range of parks and preserves across the nation, including Yellowstone National Park and Wichita Mountains National Wildlife Refuge. Most live in an environment that at least approximates the original prairie ecosystem, though wolves, elk, and grizzlies are seldom present. Pronghorns have also made a comeback, with 1 million now distributed across the country.

The lack of cover on the plains meant that small mammals such as prairie dogs, badgers, jack rabbits, and pocket gophers had to live in burrows. Prairie dogs (*Cynomys ludovicianus*) dig extensive networks of

Characteristic of deciduous woodlands, tree squirrels feed principally on plants, nuts, and seeds. Their long tail, strong claws, and powerful hind legs make them highly agile climbers.

The bison (Bison bison) is America's largest land animal. Males can measure up to 6 feet (1.8 m) in height and weigh as much as 2,000 pounds (900 kg).

tunnels and chambers known as "towns," which include "listening rooms" near the surface, from where these buff-colored rodents can listen and sniff for predators.

Abandoned prairie-dog towns often become nesting sites for snakes and birds including the burrowing owl. Such strategies are critical where trees are in short supply and the skies are dotted with the silhouettes of hawks, kestrels, and vultures. Other birds take their chances in the open, relying on the cover provided by dense thickets of grass or by camouflaged plumage, as sported by the common nighthawk (*Chordeiles minor*). The eradication of native prairie habitats has drastically limited the distribution of many grassland birds; others, such as the great-tailed grackle (*Quiscalus mexicanus*) and brown-headed cowbird (*Molothrus ater*), have adapted successfully to human habitats and expanded their ranges significantly.

Arid and semiarid regions

As a result of variations in climate and vegetation, each of the four main kinds of desert (intermountain, Mojave, Sonoran, and Chihuahuan) of the Southwest and the Mediterranean and Madrean regions of the West has a subtly distinctive animal community. However, some species range across these habitats, though they may be confined to particular zones within them, and all have to cope with this environment's major challenge: a lack of water.

Large mammals are generally absent from Mediterranean zones; from the arid region usually confined to the cooler, wetter intermountain desert of the Great Basin; and from the highest ranges of other deserts. Species found in these areas include bears, mountain lions, bobcats, mule deer, and desert bighorn sheep. These animals may enter warmer zones when water is available but will quickly retreat during dry spells.

Birds are able to travel long distances to find water and even migrate to more productive lands during prolonged droughts. As a result, they are distributed more widely across arid zones. Among the most characteristic species are the rock wren (*Salpinctes obsoletus*), Gambel's quail (*Callipepla gambelii*), and the highly distinctive greater roadrunner (*Geococcyx californianus*), noted for its bizarre appearance and its habit of running at high speed along the ground. Hummingbirds are also common locally, particularly in the Sonoran Desert; many species migrate north from Mexico and South America in spring to feed on desert blooms. Several desert birds, such as the scrub jay (*Aphelocoma coerulescens*) and California quail (*Callipepla californica*), are also native to chaparral and other Mediterranean zones in California.

Many desert creatures conserve energy and moisture by being active only at dawn or dusk, or even, as is the case with species such as the kit fox (*Vulpes macrotis*) and the desert kangaroo rat (*Dipodomys deserti*), only at night. Some lie low during the dry season: certain ground squirrels and gophers, for example, retreat to their burrows and enter a state of dormancy—a form of hibernation known as estivation. Reptiles are particularly well adapted to arid

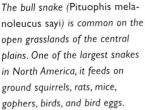

*The bull snake (*Pituophis melanoleucus sayi*) is common on the open grasslands of the central plains. One of the largest snakes in North America, it feeds on ground squirrels, rats, mice, gophers, birds, and bird eggs.*

conditions, having a high tolerance of heat and an ability to lower their metabolism which allows them to survive on much lower quantities of food than warm-blooded animals. Desert kangaroo rats extract all the moisture they require from seeds, and can live an entire lifetime without drinking a single drop of water.

Desert communities are often centered on plants, particularly certain kinds of cactus. A large saguaro cactus, for example, may provide a nesting site for gila woodpeckers and red-tailed hawks, as well as a breeding ground for honeybees. Similarly, a single cholla may host cactus wrens and white-winged doves, and supply food and water for wood rats in the form of discarded branches.

Hawaiian tropical forests

Since they began rising from the sea more than 70 million years ago, the islands of Hawaii have remained isolated from other landmasses. Animals could colonize this archipelago only by flying or floating across thousands of miles of open ocean. Just one flying mammal, the hoary bat (*Lasiurus cinerius*), and one marine mammal, the Hawaiian monk seal (*Monachus shauinslandi*), made the trip. Not a single reptile or amphibian arrived.

Even among birds, only a handful of species reached the islands, more than likely blown off course during migration. But as a result of gradual adaptation to the various niches available, those few birds evolved into 70 different species. The most remarkable process of adaptation occurred among finches, which evolved from a few birds into 54 species, now known collectively as the Hawaiian honeycreepers. Two of these birds, the scarlet-plumaged iiwi (*Vestiaria coccinea*) and apapane (*Himatione sanguinea*), are the most prominent creatures in Hawaiian tropical forests.

In all, an extraordinary 96 percent of Hawaiian wildlife is endemic; unfortunately, since the arrival of humans and their domestic animals, a large number of species has been wiped out, including 23 kinds of honeycreeper.

Beyond the land

In addition to these vegetation zones, the United States has a wide variety of wetland, seashore, and ocean habitats. There are an estimated 105.5 million acres (4.25 million ha) of wetlands in the Lower 48 states, although that is less than half of what existed during the colonial period. These waterways support aquatic mammals such as beavers, muskrats, and otters, reptiles and amphibians including frogs, toads, and turtles, countless fish and insect species, and enormous numbers of waterbirds, the most conspicuous of which are ducks, herons, rails, coots, loons, and grebes. Distinctive wetland habitats include the Great Lakes and the swamps of the Southeast, home of the American alligator (*Alligator mississippiensis*).

Along seashores, too, birds are the most prominent animals, among them vast numbers of seabirds, such as cormorants, shearwaters, scoters, and albatrosses; and shorebirds, including plovers, sanderling, whimbrel, and dunlin. Many species, from crabs to cormorants, are ubiquitous year-round; others are associated with particular regions and seasons. In fall, huge colonies of elephant seals gather to breed at Año Nuevo on the California coast, while, just offshore, gray whales migrate south to wintering grounds in Baja California. In April, on the barrier islands of the Texas coast, loggerhead sea turtles haul themselves ashore to lay their eggs in the sand. In late spring, at Cape May in the Northeast, thousands of horseshoe crabs come ashore to spawn, their eggs in turn attracting more than 1 million seabirds belonging to more than 20 species.

Once common in the Southeast, the gopher tortoise (Gopherus polyphemus) has come under threat from habitat destruction, hunting, the prevention of fires (which create a suitable habitat), and the gassing of burrows to kill rattlesnakes. As a result, numbers have declined by about 80 percent during the last 100 years.

An immature turkey vulture (Cathartes aura) watches for prey from a prominent perch in Everglades National Park, Florida. Turkey vultures are carnivorous, feeding on live prey such as small mammals and birds as well as carrion and garbage.

Protecting the Environment

Almost two centuries of technological development have taken a heavy toll on the natural environment of the United States. As the country's industries and population have grown, so have the demands placed on natural resources such as air, water, soil, and forests. Emissions from factories and machines have filled the atmosphere with harmful gases, and residues from manufacturing processes, agriculture, and settlements have polluted waterways. Fortunately, however, Americans are becoming increasingly mindful of the widespread and often irreparable damage being done to the environment and a concerted effort is now being made by legislators, conservation groups, and individuals to prevent the permanent loss of many important resources.

The conservation movement

Americans first became aware of the harm they were doing to their environment in the mid-nineteenth century. Among the first to warn of the dangers of overexploitation and suggest that public lands should be preserved as wilderness were journalist George Bird Grinnell, founder of the Audubon Society; Transcendentalist writers Ralph Waldo Emerson and Henry David Thoreau; and George Perkins Marsh, author of *Man and Nature* (1864), which was later republished with the more descriptive title *The Earth As Modified by Human Action: Man and Nature*. In 1872, the federal government finally responded to such concerns by setting aside 2 million acres (810,000 ha) of forest in the Yellowstone region as the world's first national park; in 1891, it passed the

Forest Preserve Act creating Yellowstone Timberland Reserve, the nation's first federal forest reserve.

The late nineteenth century also saw the birth of the Sierra Club, which was founded in 1892 by a group of nature-lovers including writer and prominent conservationist John Muir. The organization initially focused its campaigns on the preservation of Yosemite National Park, which had been created in 1890, but subsequently addressed a much wider range of issues, in turn helping to raise public awareness of the need for conservation. The presidency of Theodore Roosevelt (1901–09) also resulted in a number of important initiatives, including the formation of the US Forest Service and the setting aside of more than 16 million acres (6.5 million ha) of national forests. Perhaps surprisingly, conservation also received a boost from World War II. President Franklin Roosevelt used unemployed men to staff the Civil Conservation Corps (CCC), which planted trees, restored silted waterways, provided flood control and soil-erosion protection, and carried out many other preservation projects.

In the 1960s, a number of key events prompted widespread concern regarding the environmental impact of activities such as agriculture, mining, manufacturing, and energy production. In 1961, Rachel Carson published *Silent Spring*, a devastating study of the impact of pesticides on natural food chains. In 1969, the oil-polluted Cuyahoga River caught fire and burned; later the same year, oil leaking from an offshore well coated California beaches and wildlife. Increasing public anger forced the government's hand: between 1962 and 1970, 16 major conservation and environmental legislation acts were passed. The *Wilderness Act* of 1964 established the National Wilderness Preservation System, designed to leave lands "unimpaired for future use and enjoyment as wilderness." The *National Environmental Protection Act* of 1969 led to the foundation in 1970 of the Environmental Protection Agency (EPA), a federal body charged with implementing and enforcing environmental legislation. Its role has brought it into conflict with industries seeking to develop natural resources, and its requirement that all federal agencies file an environmental impact statement (EIS) or an environmental assessment (EA) before any major legislation or project can proceed has resulted in claims that it simply creates a layer of unnecessary bureaucracy,

In attempting to minimize waste, Americans have become ever-more adept at recycling a wide variety of materials. These discarded tires are being used to limit soil erosion in Nebraska.

North Carolina State University's Solar House at Raleigh aims to demonstrate the efficient use of solar energy to homebuilders and homeowners. Increased use of solar power could help reduce levels of damaging emissions created by fossil-fuel combustion.

This wind-power plant at Foot Creek Rim, Wyoming, produces sufficient energy to power between 15,000 and 25,000 homes. In total, the United States' wind-power systems could meet the energy needs of 600,000 to 800,000 average households.

LEFT: The Northeast's high concentration of factories, such as this petroleum plant in New Jersey, makes the region a major contributor to air pollution. Ozone output regularly exceeds safety standards, while levels of acid deposition, toxic contaminants, and carbon monoxide are also high.

but most conservationists regard the agency as an essential safeguard against rampant development.

Following the creation of the EPA, other, more specific legislation was also passed, including the *Clean Water Act* (1972), *Safe Drinking Act* (1974), *Water Quality Act* (1987), and *Clean Air Act* (1990).

Air pollution

The burning of fossil fuels, particularly in factories and in the combustion engines of vehicles, produces gases and particulate material which, if present in sufficient quantities, can combine to create an atmospheric haze known as smog (a term originally coined from the words "smoke" and "fog"). Smog can be highly detrimental to human health, especially that of children and older citizens, exacerbating asthma, respiratory problems, and eye infections. All major cities produce smog, but in many places, such as Chicago, New Orleans, and Honolulu, the haze is dispersed by frequent strong winds or rain. Severe air-pollution problems most often arise when local to-

pography and weather patterns combine to trap stagnant air in pockets or basins, as occurs regularly in metropolitan areas such as Los Angeles, Albuquerque, Denver, and Portland.

Some of the gases emitted by factories and automobile engines, including carbon dioxide, chlorofluorocarbons, nitrous oxides, and ozone are also thought to be contributing to global warming. All are already present in the atmosphere and play an important role in trapping heat reflected from Earth's surface. But the enormous increase in the levels of these gases as a result of such emissions is intensifying this effect and gradually raising atmospheric temperatures.

Under the *Clean Air Act*, the EPA established the National Ambient Air Quality Standards for specific pollutants considered harmful to human health and the environment. Daily measurements are taken in most major cities and warnings are issued if levels of these pollutants exceed the set standards. Many newspaper and television weather bulletins include graphs of daily pollution indices, and all states are now required by law to produce such information and monitor changes in emission levels. At the same time, conservation groups are campaigning to limit global warming by persuading individuals to reduce energy and automobile use and upgrade to more fuel-efficient vehicles, and by persuading politicians to introduce legislation limiting emissions from factories and vehicles, such as the proposed *Clean Power Act* and *Clean Smokestacks Act* of 2001.

Urban runoff via storm sewers is one of the leading causes of river pollution. In 1998, the EPA assessed 23 percent of the nation's rivers and found that 35 percent of those waterways were polluted.

Protecting waterways

Throughout America, rivers, streams, lakes, wetlands, and oceans have been affected by waste from industries, farms, and homes, and, as a result, most of the country's drainage systems, including the Mississippi–Missouri, Hudson, Ohio, and Colorado rivers, now suffer significant levels of pollution. The most common pollutants include nitrates, phosphates, and pesticides.

Toxicity and acidity levels in waterways have also been raised dramatically by acid rain, especially in the Northeast. Acid rain forms when water vapor in the atmosphere combines with sulfur and nitrogen oxides emitted by cars and factories to produce dilute forms of sulfuric and nitric acids. These acids also kill plants.

The damming of major rivers has resulted in further environmental problems. Blocking the flow of water often disrupts natural ecosystems, and dams frequently collect silt and debris, which in turn reduces oxygen levels in the water.

Ocean pollution is particularly severe in shallow coastal areas, where urban waste tends to accumulate; this is a major problem on the northeastern seaboard and in the Gulf of Mexico between Brownsville and Florida. The Pacific coast has fewer pollution problems because its steep continental shelf allows currents to disperse contaminated water; but this in turn threatens deep-sea environments.

Overall, it has been estimated that 218 million Americans live within 10 miles (16 km) of a polluted lake, river, or ocean, and that 40 percent of the nation's waterways are unsuitable for fishing or swim-

ming. That is at least an improvement on 1970, before the introduction of the Clean Water Act, when 65 percent of waterways were considered unsuitable for fishing or swimming. Sources of pollution are gradually being eliminated and water and industrial-waste treatment facilities have improved greatly in recent years. However, stronger enforcement of environmental laws and continued preservation of wetlands are required if further progress is to be achieved.

Deforestation

Although forests cover about 35 percent of the conterminous states, only a tiny proportion of this consists of virgin forest. Indeed, since the early seventeenth century, between 95 and 97 percent of native virgin forests have been cleared. Most of the remaining old-growth forests are in the western United States and Alaska, and these areas have become the focus of conservation efforts in recent years. One of the most significant campaigns took place in the 1980s when the government proposed the harvesting of old-growth trees in the Pacific Northwest. Conservationists successfully used the *Endangered Species Act* of 1966 to block this development, arguing that the logging could result in the disappearance of the endemic and endangered northern spotted owl.

Forests are still threatened by commercial development, however—even some of those on public lands. National forests, for example, are managed under the principle of sustainable and multiple use, meaning that some logging and mining is permitted; it is estimated that 52 percent of national forests have been detrimentally affected by such activities. The Worldwide Fund for Nature has calculated that, in total, one-third of American forests have little or no protection and are therefore vulnerable to exploitation.

The creation of national parks and wilderness areas has, however, helped protect some old-growth

A woodchipping plant in Alabama. The ongoing clearance of native forests and the damming of rivers have contributed to this state having the highest rate of species extinctions in the Lower 48.

areas, and the implementation of selective cutting rather than clear cutting has limited habitat loss and erosion in certain areas. Other initiatives, such as the foundation of private reserves by conservation groups such as the Nature Conservancy and the adoption of recycling to minimize demand for wood products, are also contributing to the preservation of the nation's forests. Conservationists claimed a major victory on this front in January 2001 when President Clinton introduced the Wild Forest Protection Plan, banning development in the remaining 58.5 million acres (23.7 million ha) of untouched land within national forests.

Preserving the land

Soil erosion and land degradation have long had a detrimental effect on the nation's agricultural productivity. As early as the 1930s, soil depletion resulting from overuse, poor cultivation practices, and drought created enormous dust bowls across the central United States. More recently, the increased use of pesticides, fungicides, and rodenticides has raised toxicity levels in soils, and, in turn, exacerbated water pollution.

Some progress in dealing with these problems has been made. Improved irrigation systems, crop-rotation programs, and organic pesticides have been widely introduced. Waste and toxic materials are now regularly recycled, and technological innovations are gradually limiting the effects of land degradation. In many areas, these strategies have significantly reduced or even arrested soil erosion.

Solid waste

The ultimate consumer society, with a population of more than 280 million, the United States produces immense quantities of solid waste. At one time, such waste material was simply deposited in open dumps or oceans, or even burned. Fortunately, most of these practices are now prohibited. Today, waste from many urban areas is accommodated in sanitary landfills, which are lined to prevent seepage into surrounding groundwater. Once at capacity, landfills are often covered over, reclaimed, and used as recreational areas. Honolulu, Los Angeles, New Orleans, Chicago, and Atlanta are among many cities that include parks or similar recreational areas created in this way. In some cases, treated sewage water is even used to create ornamental lakes and fountains.

Recycling is undoubtedly one of the keys to reducing solid waste, and recycling programs are now widespread. Furthermore, increasing numbers of products are being made from recycled materials such as paper, newsprint, and certain types of plastic and glass. Many large urban areas have mandated the sorting of waste products in order to facilitate recycling. In Los Angeles, the effective sorting of trash has created a sustainable industry based on recycling glass and plastics for use in road beds and buildings.

In total, approximately 25 percent of the United States' solid waste is now recycled, while more than 55 percent is deposited in landfills, with most of the remainder being incinerated. However, the cost of recycling remains prohibitive, and in some areas where the population is small or widely scattered, and financial support from government unavailable, such programs are not yet viable.

America's industries released 7.7 billion pounds (3.5 billion kg) of toxic chemicals into the atmosphere during 1999, according to a survey by the EPA.

Automobile recycling programs are helping to reduce levels of solid waste. It has been estimated that 75 percent of a vehicle's components by weight can be reused or recycled.

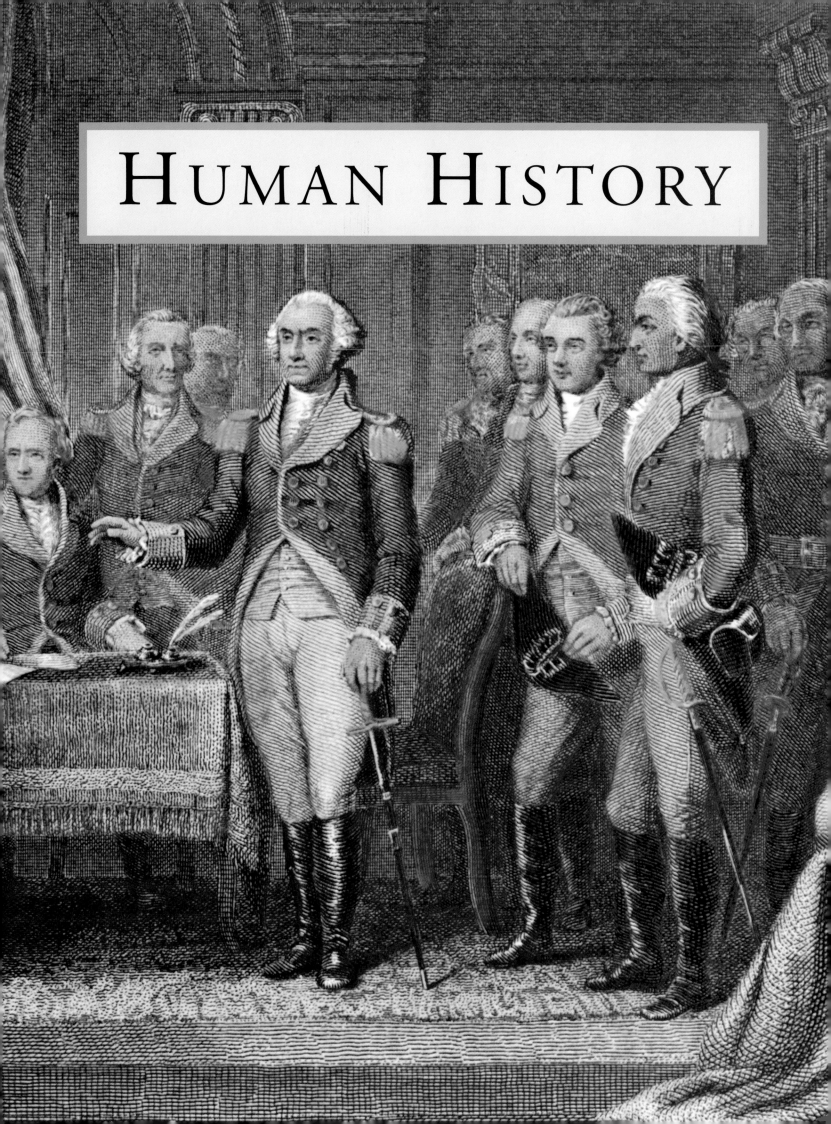

HUMAN HISTORY

NATIVE PEOPLES

Prehistory

During the Eastern Archaic period, southern deciduous forests, such as these, expanded northwards. This led to a change in subsistence practices as hunting was gradually replaced by the gathering of plants, nuts, and seeds, and basic agriculture.

When the Age of Discovery brought European explorers to the New World, the newcomers found an enormous, uncharted land filled with strange plants and animals, and populated by remarkably varied native cultures. Where these "Indians" had come from was not an immediate concern during the contact period, but today the question is the starting point for any understanding of American prehistory.

The first Americans

The most widely accepted explanation for the first peopling of America points to the north. The first Americans seem to have been of Asian origin, and geographical and climatic evidence makes a land migration from Asia possible around the dates of earliest human evidence in the New World (around 9500 BC). During peak periods of glaciation, Siberia and Alaska were connected. During a key inter-glacial period, about 14,000 BC, bands of big-game hunters, it is argued, moved from northeast Asia across the Bering land bridge, then through an ice-free corridor into a new land. They discovered a place that teemed with herds of large herbivorous mammals vulnerable to the hunting techniques and technologies of a sophisticated new predator. The hunters thrived, reproduced, and spread throughout the continents.

For decades the land bridge hypothesis has dominated discussion of the first Americans. Recent evidence, however, suggests

Three species of mammoth lived in North America during the Ice Age, from 2 million to 8,000 years ago, and were hunted by early peoples. These were the Columbian mammoth (Mammuthus columbi), Jefferson's mammoth (M. jeffersonii), and the woolly mammoth (M. primigenius). As the glacial ice-sheets retreated north, climatic changes radically altered plant and animal habitats, resulting in the extinction of the megafauna.

plausible alternatives, such as the idea of multi-point peopling of the New World. Very early sites in far southern Chile don't fit comfortably into the established model. Perhaps coastal populations of northeast Asia entered the Americas along the Pacific before the land bridge formed and followed the coast rapidly south. Unfortunately, evidence of coastal movement is scanty, for as the Ice Age ended, sea levels rose and inundated the coastal shelves where evidence of such movements would be expected.

Other evidence and hypotheses abound. Skeletal remains suggest different migrating populations contributing to the Paleo-Indian mix. Kennewick man, found in Washington State in 1996 and thought to date from around 6400 BC, displays cranial characteristics significantly different from modern Native Americans. Was he from a different ancestral population?

Artifactual evidence

Some researchers assert significant correlation between artifacts of the early European Solutrean culture and the American Paleo-Indians. Migration from Europe across the Atlantic Ocean could explain the similarities. Opponents counter that the similarities are more sensibly understood as examples of parallel or convergent cultural development.

Clovis

The earliest generally accepted cultural identity in America is based on unique fluted projectile points (arrowheads and spearheads), that date to the Paleo-Indian period around 13,500 BC. They were first found in Clovis, New Mexico, and are called simply "Clovis." Without Asian correlates, these indigenous tools are found throughout the Americas. Following Clovis, around 9000 BC, was a new type of fluted projectile point. Named Folsom after the New

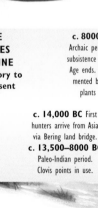

NATIVE PEOPLES TIMELINE Prehistory to the Present	c. 8000–1700 BC Archaic period. Changes in subsistence strategies as Ice Age ends. Hunting supplemented by gathering of plants and fishing.	c. 300 BC–AD 500 Hokoham people develop irrigation agriculture. c. AD 600 First cliff dwellings are built at Mesa Verde, Colorado.	1541 Francisco Vasquez Coronado arrives in the Southwest seeking gold; the Zuni people first encounter the horse.
	c. 14,000 BC First hunters arrive from Asia via Bering land bridge. c. 13,500–8000 BC Paleo-Indian period. Clovis points in use.	c. 1700 BC Woodland period. Pottery and basic agriculture appear. c. 1200 BC First mound buildings built in the Midwest and Southeast.	1000 Peak of Mogollon and Anasazi cultures; pueblo centers are built in New Mexico. 1492 Christopher Columbus arrives on San Salvador Island, home of the Arawak.

Mexico site of the first find, these points were found with the bones of an extinct Ice Age species of bison.

A number of archeological sites have yielded artifacts suggesting a pre-Clovis culture. The significance of crude stone choppers has met with skepticism, and concerns about the accuracy of dating continues to fuel the debate. The most persuasive find thus far has probably been that of the Meadowcroft Rockshelter in Pennsylvania. The meticulous excavation at this site yielded dates earlier than Clovis—to around 17,000 BC. However, the dates have been challenged by other scholars.

Following the Paleo-Indian period was the Archaic period, a dynamic period of change and adaptation beginning at the end of the Pleistocene epoch, or Ice Age, around 8000 BC.

Adapting to local conditions

Responding to a changing landscape, the Native Americans had to develop new strategies to exploit local resources. Throughout America during the Archaic period, hunting was increasingly supplemented by the gathering of plants, seeds, and nuts. This resulted in a vast knowledge of local food plants, and ultimately led to gardening and agriculture.

In the Eastern Archaic period, the southern deciduous forests expanded north. More extensive tool kits were developed including atlatls (spearthrowers) and ground stone tools. Wild dogs were domesticated, and some of America's first dwellings appeared.

Parallel developments occurred in the west, with regional Archaic adaptations in the Plains, the Plateau, Great Basin, and Southwest. Some Plains groups maintained semi-nomadic big-game hunting. In riverine areas fishing became important. In areas like the Pacific Northwest and parts of California, abundant resources were able to support dense populations living in large villages.

The development of pottery and agriculture

The Woodland period followed the Archaic in the east after 1700 BC. It was marked by the first appearance of pottery and the beginning of basic agriculture with local plants as well as Mexican cultivars of pumpkin and gourds. Gardening was a logical extension of gathering as people familiar with useful local plants protected those of particular value, thus providing a more dependable food supply.

In the Southwest, maize and squash appeared in New Mexico. Hohokam culture established an irrigation agriculture between 300 BC and AD 500. The Mogollon and Anasazi people peaked around AD 1000, establishing pueblo centers including Chaco Canyon in northwestern New Mexico. Chaco's Pueblo Bonito had as many as 800 rooms and was the center of a thriving occupation zone thought to have been on a trade route to Mexico. By AD 1150 the astonishing cliff dwellings of Mesa Verde had also been established. These sites were all abandoned by the late 1200s.

In the Midwest and Southeast, mound buildings appeared round 1200 BC, first in the south as at the Poverty Point complex in Louisiana, then in the Ohio River valley in the 500s BC. Earthen mounds varied in size and shape and some, but not all, were used for burials. Later mound builders included the Hopewell, based in southern Illinois between 100 BC and AD 400, and the Mississippian, who built platform mounds that recall Mexican sites.

The people who inhabited the mound buildings at Cahokia in Illinois developed a sophisticated culture which included ceremonies and festivals. Archeological evidence from copper plates found there show that status in the form of decoration was important. Cahokia was the center of a cultural zone that may have had a population of 30,000. It included the great Monks Mound covering 16 acres (6 ha). The Cahokia culture peaked between AD 1050 and 1250, and was abandoned by 1500 before European contact. The reason for this, as for the decline of many early American centers, continues to be debated.

TOP LEFT: Arrow- and spearheads, ("Clovis points") were first found in New Mexico. Dating back to around 13,500 BC, the extremely sharp points were used to kill Ice Age megafauna.

ABOVE: Petroglyphs (rock carvings) in the White Mountains, north of Rock Springs, Wyoming, testify to ancient occupation of the site.

BELOW: Cliff dwellings several stories high perch in a shelf in the Superstition Mountains near Phoenix, Arizona.

1607 British colonists settle Jamestown, Virginia, on Powhatan land. **1620** Puritans arrive at Plymouth Rock, on Wampanoag land.	**1675** "Prince Philip's War," the first combined tribal effort to drive out the British. **1763** Ottowa Chief Pontiac leads rebellion against British in the Great Lakes area.	**1790–91** Chief Little Turtle leads Algonquian victory against the Americans. **1803** The Louisiana Purchase results in the loss of more Indian land.	**1838–39** "Trail of Tears"—4,000 out of 18,000 Cherokee die while being moved from their land in winter.	**1864** "The Long Walk." The US Army enlists Kit Carson to remove the Navajo to a camp in Bosque Redondo, New Mexico. This involves a 300-mile (483-km) trek.	**1878** Chief Joseph is defeated in Nez Perce war and surrenders to life on a reservation. **1886** Geronimo surrenders to American troops.	**1934** Indian Reorganization Act attempts to improve conditions on reservations. **1944** National Congress of American Indians formed to press for self-determination.	**1973** Protest at Wounded Knee, South Dakota. **1992** Navajo and Hopi tribes are given back nearly 2 million acres (809,380 ha) of their land in Arizona.
1550 The Seneca, Cayuyga, Mohawk, Oneida, and Onondaga tribes of the northeast form the League of Five Nations.	**1621** Chief of Wampanoags, Massasoit, makes treaty with John Carver, the Governor of Plymouth, which the new settlers fail to honor.	**1769** Father Junipero Serra arrives on Chumash land in California. He subsequently sets up 20 missions to convert the "neophytes."	**1810** Rebellion led by Shawnee Chief Tecumseh. **1830** Indian Removal Act—over 100,000 people are moved to land west of the Mississippi River.	**1840s** Westward expansion by pioneers and gold miners intensifies disputes over land. **1860** Start of the Indian Wars as the government attempts to remove tribes.	**1876** General Custer is defeated by Lakota chiefs Sitting Bull and Crazy Horse at the Battle of Little Bighorn, Montana. **1877** Crazy Horse killed.	**1890** Massacre of Wounded Knee ends the Sioux struggle to save their lands. Many turn to the Ghost Dance religion. **1924** Native Americans are granted US citizenship.	**1968** American Indian Movement (AIM) formed in Minneapolis. **1969** AIM members begin a 19-month siege on Alcatraz as a civil rights protest.

Native Alaskans dip-netting for hooligan fish in Turnagain Arm, south of Anchorage. Sustainable management of the environment and its resources continues to be practiced by indigenous peoples.

Native Peoples before European Contact

In the fifteenth century there may have been 1,000 or more distinct Native societies inhabiting the land which would become the continental United States and Alaska. Some are known only by brief references in the records of European explorers, and others may have disappeared before European contact.

Cultural development everywhere begins at the most basic level of subsistence and survival. In America, the diversity of natural environments—Arctic conditions in Alaska, arid deserts in the southwest and Great Basin, dense forests in the northwest and northeast, and the prairies and plains of the geographical center—shaped the material culture, social and political organization, art, and religion of the Native peoples living in these areas. Although considerable movement and intermixing of peoples and cultural artifacts has occurred throughout Native American history, these areas provide a framework for discussing their history and culture before European contact.

The Arctic

Standing apart both geographically and culturally from "the lower 48" states, Alaska's Native peoples represent two distinct culture patterns, the Arctic and the Subarctic. The peoples of the Arctic tradition in Alaska are now known as "Inuit" or "Aluet." They represent one distinct language family, Eskimo–Aleut. Living in a land of ice and snow, of long cold winters, and permanently frozen soil (permafrost) and tundra, the Inuit were primarily hunters and foragers, an effective subsistence pattern in such an inhospitable region. Prey animals included large sea mammals and caribou, and all parts of the animals were used for food, fuel, and

tools. Kayaks and umiaks were used in transportation and hunting, and igloos were the preferred house structure although wooden dwellings covered with sod were also built. Artwork consisted of baskets made from spruce root, elaborate carvings from wood, bone, and horns, and finely tanned clothing. Storytelling was considered a high art among the Inuit who were also skilled in singing and social drumming and dancing.

The Subarctic

South of the Arctic tundra is the subarctic area located in the boreal forest north of the Great Lakes. Since this area is north of the limits of Native agrarian activity, the peoples here existed in nomadic hunter-gatherer bands. Animals, including caribou and moose, were hunted or trapped, and fishing provided an important supplement to the subsistence base. Skins were used to cover tipi-like dwellings in the summer, earth-covered lodges were used in the winter. These peoples had strong oral traditions, and storytelling and singing abilities were greatly prized. The two largest language groups were the Algonquians in the east and Athapaskans in the west, and tribes included the Beaver, Cree, Chipewyan, Slavey or Slave, Gwich'in, Naskapi, and Montagnais.

The Northwest Coast

The temperate climate, rivers, and forests of the coastal zones of Oregon and Washington State ensured substantial food supply and allowed the establishment of dense settled populations. Salmon was the most important food source among these peoples and is still revered in their mythology. Northwest Coast society was complex, with a ranking system based on both personal wealth and heredity.

The affluence of the coastal society of the northwest is illustrated by the "potlatch," a feast and public gift-giving that usually took place to commemorate life-cycle changes or the initiation of a new chief. It was an ostentatious show of wealth and rank and is still practiced today—to a more modest degree—for births, marriages, deaths, and other important events.

Northwest Coast artworks were usually stylized animal figures representing the owner's lineage, painted or carved on housefronts or onto wooden poles. The

DISTRIBUTION OF NATIVE AMERICAN TRIBES

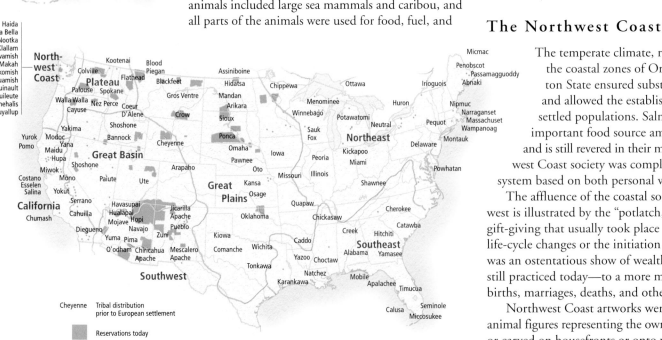

Cheyenne   Tribal distribution prior to European settlement

Reservations today

famous "totem poles" were primarily funerary objects. These carvings were intimately linked to religion and social hierarchy and were dramatic public symbols of ancestry, wealth, and social status.

These groups were also skilled canoe builders, using mostly red cedar which was also used to build their rectangular plank houses. Some tribes from this area are the Chinook, Kwakiutl, Makah, Tsimshian, and Haida. Most were primarily Salish speakers.

California

The "Mediterranean" climate of the California culture area, which includes the west and central area of modern California, provided plentiful natural resources, including wild game, fish, and edible plants. Acorns were among the dietary staples.

This area is separated from eastern traditions by the mountains of the Sierra Nevada range. The topography is diverse, from hot inland valleys to the extensive Pacific coastline, and the people belonged to many different cultural traditions organized around an extended family village structure. Of the 300,000 or more Natives, few were organized in tribes in the truest sense of the word. Groups such as the Chumash, Hupa, Shasta, Maidu, Cahuilla, Miwak, Pomo, Wailaki, and Yoruk formed as many as 500 "tribelets" or small villages clustered around larger satellite groupings. As many as 300 different language dialects of more than 100 separate languages were spoken throughout the area. Though the availability of wild food made agriculture mostly unnecessary, the area still managed to support population densities as high as any in eighteenth-century America.

These people were known for their fine basketry and rock art which often depicted ceremonial rites. Dwellings were mostly open-air structures with pole frameworks and mat coverings. In winter, people sometimes made their homes partially underground and covered their houses with earth, grass, and mats.

The Plateau

In the interior of the American Northwest, east of the coastal mountain ranges, lies the Plateau cultural area. It includes eastern Washington State, northern Idaho, western Montana, northeast and central Oregon, and extends north into Canada south of the boreal forest. Winters in the north of the region are near-Arctic; whereas summers in the southern, semiarid Colombian plateau are desert-like.

The people of the plateau were fishers, hunters, and gatherers, with salmon an important food source. The distinct tribal groupings included the Cayuse, Coeur d'Alene, Kootenai, Salish, Nez Perce, Colville, Kalispel, Umatilla, and Yakima. Most spoke dialects of Salish although the Kootenai spoke an entirely separate, isolated language. Dwellings were frequently semi-subterranean pit houses covered with earth, or above-ground long houses covered with mats, depending on the season. These tribes integrated the use of horses into their lifestyle during the eighteenth century. Able to move quickly with buffalo and other animal herds, they began to abandon their semi-sedentary ways during the eighteenth century and moved with the availability of their food source, using hide-covered tipis for shelter. These peoples were known for their exquisite tanning skills and their finely made baskets.

LEFT: The mountains of the Alaska Range, an area that has sustained indigenous groups for centuries. The region's long, cold winters, frozen soils, and tundra have shaped the subsistence patterns and lives of the Native population.

BELOW: The Alaska moose (Alces alces gigas), a member of the deer family, is still hunted by indigenous people.

BOTTOM: The Zuni people first encountered the horse around 1540, when Francisco Vasquez de Coronado arrived in the Southwest. By the early 1700s, horses were more widely available. The animal allowed native peoples to migrate to new territories and hunt more widely, but its use also facilitated the spread of disease.

The Great Basin

South of the Plateau is the Great Basin, a high desert region covering today's eastern Oregon, southern Idaho, western Wyoming, most of Utah and Nevada, parts of California, and extreme Northern parts of Arizona and New Mexico. Tribes such as the Shoshone, Bannock or Paiute, Ute, and Washoe developed a distinct cultural identity in response to the challenging environment. Surrounded by mountains, the basin sees little rainfall; in the infamous Death Valley, daytime temperatures peak around 140°F (60°C). Mostly gatherers and small game hunters, the people of this inhospitable land needed to exploit all available food sources to survive, including roots, seeds, nuts, reptiles, and insects. Pinon seeds were a dietary staple.

Most people lived in small, nomadic family groups and had only loose tribal affiliations. These people lived in wickiups in the summer, constructed from brush and reeds over willow poles. Like other groups, they took advantage of the availability of horses in the eighteenth century and adopted elements of the Plains lifestyle. The Great Basin peoples were known for their singing and drumming abilities, basketry and use of rock art on their surrounding landscape. All spoke Shoshonean dialects.

A riverbed in Canyon de Chelly National Monument, Arizona, shows evidence of agricultural activity. The area has been home to different groups of Native Americans including Pueblo, Hopi, and Navajo tribes. The Navajo people who settled here after AD 1000 were farmers.

RIGHT: Animals, people, and symbols are carved into the rock face at Newspaper Rock in Utah, representing 2,000 years of Archaic, Basketmaker, Fremont, and Pueblo cultures.

A necklace, featuring brass beads, grizzly bear fur and fierce-looking claws, made for a man of the Great Plains.

The Southwest

From southern Colorado and Utah, the Southwest culture area encompasses most of Arizona and New Mexico and continues south deep into modern Mexico. An arid zone, it is characterized by cactus, mesquite bushes, juniper, and other evergreens. This area is environmentally diverse with buttes, canyons, mesas, deserts, and forests.

Tribes such as the Apache, Havasupai, Hopi, Pima, Navajo, Tohono O'odham, Yagui, and Zuni were culturally and linguistically diverse and included farmers such as the Pueblo, descendants of the Anasazi cultural tradition, as well as hunters and gatherers descended from the Hohokam, Mogollon, and Hakataya.

On the continent, this is the site of the longest continuously human inhabited area outside of Mesoamerica. It is estimated that the first inhabitants of the Southwest arrived roughly between 23,000 BC to 10,000 BC. At that time farmers used irrigation canals for their crops of corn, beans, and squash. Dwellings included apartment-like adobe pueblos as well as hogans—log-framed houses of six to eight sides, covered with adobe and wood. Southwestern art had a strong, rich tradition in pottery, weaving, turquoise and silver jewelry, and basket-making. Elaborate sand paintings, used as ceremonial objects, were destroyed after use. Southwestern tribes were well known for their ceremonial chanting.

The Great Plains

The Great Plains encompass an enormous swath of land in the center of the continent, stretching from the Mississippi River to the Rocky Mountains and from the Canadian border to central Texas. Though the region includes some mountain ranges and plateaus, it is largely a vast country of grassland plains which has limited rainfall.

Inhabitants of this area were either sedentary or semi-nomadic prairie farmers. The Great Horse Culture, for which the people of the Plains are best known today was, in fact, the result of European contact. Originally introduced by late fifteenth-century Spanish settlers in California, horses reached the Plains around AD 1700. Horses offered easy mobility and spurred many agriculturists to turn almost exclusively to hunting, following the great buffalo herds as they migrated. Before the horse, hunters on foot would drive the great herds over cliffs. Dogs were used as pack animals to move with the hunters over the prairie.

This labor-intensive hunting method meant that buffalo were not a dominant food source for the Plains peoples. After 1750 and the introduction of the horse, however, the buffalo became a staple food. All parts of the animal were used: bone for implements and skin for coverings of pole tipis.

The term "Sioux" refers to a large language group spoken by at least 13 separate tribes. They were the Lakota, Nakota, Dakota, and several subdivisions of these. Other tribes included the Osage, Assiniboine, Ponca, Cheyenne, and Comanche. Artwork carried out by Plains peoples included tanning, beadwork, quillwork, and "winter counts"—pictorial tribal histories painted on buffalo hides.

The Southeast

The southeast was a largely forested zone of mostly warm-temperate climate, including mountain ranges, coastal plains, river valleys, salt marshes, and even subtropical environments (Florida's Everglades). Most Natives here lived in villages in the many river valleys, developing large-scale farming supplemented by hunting and gathering. Crops included corn, beans, squash, tobacco, and sunflowers. The peoples of the Southeast formed centralized towns that were socially and politically complex. Dwellings were constructed of pole frames covered with walls of grass matting and clay plaster. The Seminoles, however, lived in chickees —pole structures covered with mats, well suited to their subtropical environment.

The peoples of the Southeast were a mix of many different language families, including Muskogean, Siouan, Algonquian, and Iroquoian. Some of the best-known tribes were the Cherokee, Choctaw, Chickasaw, Creek, and Seminole, the so-called Civilized Tribes. White people dubbed them "Civilized" during the early nineteenth century because the tribes' customs and lifestyles seemed to be similar to their own in that their farming, governance, and dress resembled

that of European settlers. It is believed that many of these tribes descended from the mound-building cultures of the Ohio Valley. These groups were best known for their baskets and pottery.

The Northeast

A wide range of distinct native cultures developed in this enormous area stretching from the Atlantic coast to the Mississippi River and from the Great Lakes to the area of modern Virginia, North Carolina, and Tennessee. For all its environmental variability, the Northeast was extensively forested, and the forests of conifer and deciduous trees provided the foundation for local cultural adaptations. The region is characterized by severe winters and mild, short summers. Wood was used for fuel, shelter, transportation, and tools. Foods included wild rice, bracken ferns, maple sugar, fish, shellfish, deer, elk, moose, bear, and other game.

Two main language divisions define this region, Algonquian and Iroquoian. The Algonquian tribes (Anishinabe, Ho-Chunk, Menominee, Potowatami) lived in bark-covered long houses or wigwams—hunting, fishing, and foraging in small family bands. The Iroquois (Cayuga, Mohawk, Oneida, Onandaga, Seneca) who made up the famous Iroquois League, lived in large, extensive villages and had highly structured governments linking more than 17,000 people and comprised of 50 hereditary chiefs, each with specific responsibilities. The creators of the United States system of government used the League as a model of democracy.

The Anishinabe were known for their intricate "Spirit Writing"—pictographic recordings of ceremonial life on birch bark. Other tribes used wampum or shell bead, woven into intricate designs and used for tribal recordings and ceremonial purposes. The Northeast tribes were also known for their intricate birch bark baskets and canoes as well as baskets which were made from ash trees. They were expert tanners and decorated hides with quillwork. The Mahican, Abnaki, and Miami were just some of the many tribes that lived in this area.

TOP: A brushwood frame covered with grass or reed mats made a temporary shelter, or wickiup, for nomadic travelers of the arid West and Southwest.

MIDDLE: Arikara Indians were sedentary farmers and seasonal hunter–gatherers who lived in earth lodges like this one, in villages. They inhabited Dakota territory from AD 1150 to 1832.

BOTTOM: A small band of Native Americans—people of the Mogollon culture—lived in cliff dwellings in the thirteenth century. About a dozen families occupied 40 rooms in natural cavities 175 feet (53 m) above the canyon floor in Gila, Arizona.

Native Peoples Since European Contact

The loss of land and autonomy is expressed in this weeping wooden sculpture at the Museum of the Cherokee Indian in North Carolina. Cherokees are people of Iroquoian lineage who lived in Georgia, East Tennessee, and western North and South Carolina. Resistance to the encroachment of white settlers on their territory met with military force.

A Native American family pose for the camera. The Indian Removal Act of 1830 evicted them from their territories and confined them to reservations.

The arrival of Europeans in America signaled the beginning of a full-blown genocide for Native peoples. It is estimated that there were 7 to 10 million indigenous people inhabiting the country at the time of European contact in the early fifteenth century. By 1900, however, there were fewer than 230,000.

Since the Native people had no resistance to Old World diseases such as smallpox, measles, and typhus, entire villages and tribes were wiped out within the first 100 years following European contact. This paved the way for European settlers, since large areas of the land were conveniently "uninhabited." More insidious and long-term destruction, however, quickly followed.

Early struggles for land

Settlers, missionaries, explorers, and even entrepreneurs believed they carried the power of divine providence when they arrived in the New World. The notion of European racial, religious, and cultural supremacy justified decades of theft, murder, warfare, forced removal, and deception, and government programs were designed to deprive Native people of their land.

Christopher Columbus, who landed in San Salvador in 1492, described the indigenous people (who were mistakenly dubbed "Indians") as "gentle, sweet, mannerly, and decorous." However, their generosity, tolerance for other religions, group ownership of land, and differing social customs were seen as weaknesses and proof that their ways were "blasphemous to God."

British settlers in Jamestown, Virginia in 1607, and Puritans who called themselves "pilgrims" in Massachusetts in 1620, were initially welcomed and tolerated by the tribes they encountered. The Native peoples were shocked and confused, however, by their guests' insatiable lust to own the land as the concept of individual land ownership did not exist in Native culture. Worse still, the Jamestown colonists grew large crops of tobacco which quickly depleted the soil and fed their need to acquire more territory. Chief Powhatan and his people, disgusted by the colonists' use of their lands, retaliated by kidnapping several of the settlers. Among those hostages was John Smith, leader of the colony. Legend has it that Pocahontas, daughter of Chief Powhatan and a Christian convert, successfully pleaded with her father to spare Smith's life.

Years of bitter fighting continued between the settlers and the Powhatans. After several colonists were killed during a Powhatan revolt, the corpses' mouths were stuffed with dirt to remind the white men to stop devouring the land. Their warnings went unheeded, however, and most of the Powhatans were eventually killed or driven out by 1675.

The first Thanksgiving took place in Massachusetts after the Wampanoag tribe helped the pilgrims survive their first winter in 1620. Massasoit, chief of the Wampanoag, humored the newcomers by signing a friendly treaty (the first treaty signed between settlers and Native people) with the British Puritans in 1621, allowing them use of lands for settlement and farming. The Puritans, however, failed to honor the treaty. In retaliation, Metacomet, son of Massasoit (crowned "Prince Philip" by the British in an effort to control him) organized the first multi-tribal effort in 1675 to drive out the British. Joined by the Narragansett and other tribes, Prince Philip's War lasted one year, and hundreds of settlers were killed. In the end, however, the tribes were no match for the superior weapons and sheer numbers of the British.

As Europeans continued to thrive in America, Native people grew more dependent on their trade goods, often trapping animals for pelts rather than hunting and gathering. They were further demoralized by European insistence that they accept alcohol in trade.

For the settlers, their success in dominating the Native population reinforced their belief that they were preordained by God to rule the new land.

The Native peoples' nature-based religions were dismissed by Christian missionaries and Puritans as "ungodly." The Puritans set about saving the souls of their savage and primitive neighbors, convinced that evangelism was their "errand in the wilderness." Indeed, this notion of saving the Native soul continued to justify the brutality that characterized the European colonization and settlement of the United States.

Towards the nineteenth century

In their efforts to drive out the whites during the late eighteenth and early nineteenth centuries, northern and southeastern tribes formed pan-tribal confederacies of warriors. These alliances were sometimes supported by the British or French in their fight to gain control of the New World from the encroaching American settlers. Dynamic and visionary leaders called on their people to renounce the white man's tools, technologies, and alcohol. Prophets from among the Shawnee, Delaware, Ottawa, Cherokee, and others called for spiritual rebirth. Above all, they sought the return of their lands and way of life.

Ottawa war leader Chief Pontiac led tribes from the Great Lakes area, attacking garrisons there and throughout the Ohio Valley in 1763. The Pontiac Rebellion dwindled to an unsuccessful halt largely due to the distribution of smallpox-infected blankets by British General Amherst during the siege of Fort Pitt along the Ohio River. This early use of "germ warfare" was a common practice among the Europeans in their efforts to rid America of its indigenous people.

Miami leader Little Turtle led Algonquian tribes on two of the most successful revolts against the American army in 1790 and 1791. The goal was to establish the Ohio River as a boundary for white expansion. When the British withdrew their support of Little Turtle and his army, however, they were forced to cede much of their land to the Americans in the Treaty of Greenville in 1793.

Other unified rebellions ensued including the campaign led by the great Shawnee chief Tecumseh in 1810 in the Ohio Valley and Indiana territory. The rebellion failed and he was killed in 1813. Short-lived, unsuccessful Native revolts continued but, by the 1820s, tribes were resigned to ceding their territory east of the Mississippi.

Finally, under the leadership of President Andrew Jackson, Congress developed a solution to the "Indian problem." Jackson convinced Congress to pass the *Indian Removal Act* of 1830, which forcibly removed over 100,000 Native people to a "permanent" Indian frontier west of the Mississippi. Thousands of Native people perished during these cruel removal marches including over 4,000 Cherokees who died on the "Trail of Tears" in the winter of 1838–39. Jackson also established the Bureau of Indian Affairs under the control of the War Department.

This permanent frontier, later known as Oklahoma, was "given" to more than 100 tribes in exchange for title to their lands west of the Mississippi. Many tribes

resisted, with a few members remaining in hiding on their lands during Removal. In the end, however, the tribes yielded to the overwhelming coercion by US authorities and signed away their homelands. A notable exception, in 1832, was Osceola, Chief of the Seminoles, who was said to have stabbed his knife into the treaty document. He and his tribe fled into the Florida Everglades with over 200 US troops unsuccessfully pursuing them. The Seminoles never signed a treaty with the US government.

By the 1840s, thousands of pioneers and settlers began streaming west. The discovery of gold in Sacramento, California in 1848 added to this mass emigration through Native land west of the Mississippi. Pioneers began stripping the land of its resources and quickly clashed with tribes along the trails. White hunters killed millions of buffalo on the plains, reducing their numbers from an estimated 40 million in 1800 to fewer than 1,000 by 1895. They killed the buffalo simply for sport or for buffalo robes, prized in the east. The Plains tribes, on the other hand, viewed the buffalo as a sacred gift from the Creator and used this gift sparingly, utilizing every part of the buffalo for clothing, housing, and implements as well as food. The clash between the world view of the new arrivals and that of the Native peoples was the basis of many of their conflicts. Non-indigenous people saw the earth's resources as something to be controlled and

The bravery and war-like demeanor of Native Americans were much admired by European settlers. This did not prevent the newcomers from using any means available to drive indigenous people from their lands.

The American bison, also known as the buffalo, formed a central part of the economy and culture of Native peoples. Its large-scale destruction by European settlers for meat and hides, and then for sport, provoked wars. The bison is now protected and can only be hunted under licence.

The gravestone of George Armstrong Custer (1839–76), who led the 7th US Cavalry to a devastating defeat by a combined force of eastern Sioux and northern Cheyenne warriors in 1876. All his men, numbering over 200, died in the Battle of Little Bighorn, which lasted only an hour.

exploited. Native people viewed the earth and its resources as gifts to be acknowledged and nurtured.

Further west in California, the Gold Rush provided open season on killing Native people. In the 1850s, miners and ranchers murdered men, women, and children with impunity, a government bounty on Native scalps fueling the frenzy of murder that characterized the "settling" of California.

During western expansion, the new Department of the Interior was assigned to oversee the Bureau of Indian Affairs in 1849, a relationship that continues today. Although the Fort Laramie treaty was signed by several Plains tribes in 1851, allowing safe passage for settlers, these settlers did not honor their side of the treaty. During Red Cloud's War, Red Cloud, chief of the Oglala Dakota people, and his followers forced a closure of the Bozeman Trail until US forces agreed to sign a second treaty in 1868 guaranteeing closure of forts along the trail as well as preservation of the sacred Black Hills.

The Indian Wars

The great Indian Wars between 1860 and 1890 were a concerted effort by the US government to eradicate indigenous peoples and their cultures through bloodshed and forced assimilation. At Sand Creek in southeastern Colorado in 1864, US forces led by Colonel John Chivington massacred an encampment of peaceful Cheyenne and Arapaho people led by Chief Black Kettle. Over 100 women and children and several dozen men were killed and their bodies horribly mutilated. Black Kettle and his people were again attacked, this time by General George Custer under orders from the famous Indian fighter General Philip Sheridan who is credited with the phrase, "The only good Indians I ever saw were dead." Once again, mostly women and children as well as Black Kettle were slaughtered during the attack at Washita River.

After gold was discovered in the Black Hills in 1874, miners swarmed into this

area which by treaty was off-limits to whites. Angered by this intrusion onto land that they viewed as holy, and by the many army massacres and broken treaties, Indians retaliated. When General Custer was sent to remove the remaining tribes to reservations, he and his army were destroyed at the Battle of Little Bighorn in Montana, led by Lakota chiefs Crazy Horse and Sitting Bull. Retribution by the US army was unrelenting. Hold-outs to the reservation system were hunted down mercilessly. Crazy Horse was executed in 1877. Chief Joseph of the Nez Perce and his people tried to flee army forces but surrendered to life on an Idaho reservation in 1877. In 1881 Sitting Bull and his people also surrendered.

The surrender of land and freedom

Primarily using trickery and force, the US government convinced tribes to sign over 300 treaties from 1778 until 1871. Most of the treaties required Native peoples to surrender their traditional lands. The reservation land assigned to tribes was usually the least desirable. Available game and resources were quickly depleted on these small sites and the Native people were forced to depend on meager government rations for survival. Cut off from their traditional subsistence lifestyle, the reservation system became a recipe for despair for Native people. Predictably, the ills of poverty, including substance abuse, disease, hunger, and unemployment quickly developed.

The 1887 *General Allotment Act* or *Dawes Act* further reduced Native territory by assigning individual ownership of small tracts of land to the heads of Native households. "Unassigned" lands in the former Native territory were then opened for settlement by whites in 1889.

Desperate over wretched conditions on the Lakota reservations, many people turned to the Ghost Dance, a religion founded by Paiute prophet Wovoka that promised a return of the Indian way of life. Unnerved and fearful of a possible uprising, soldiers overreacted, arresting and killing Sitting Bull and finally massacring his people who had sought refuge with Chief Big Foot at Wounded Knee in South Dakota. Over 300 unarmed men, women, and children were butchered by US forces during the winter of 1890 at Wounded Knee. Thus was the end of armed Native resistance. For most Americans, Native Americans quickly became denizens of a bygone era and were forgotten.

In the late nineteenth century, Native identity came under further attack by the US government and missionaries. Children were taken, sometimes forcibly, from their families and moved to boarding schools off the reservations where they were taught vocational skills and forbidden to speak their Native languages or maintain their culture in any way. The motto of these schools was "Kill the Indian, Save the Man." As part of an organized effort to assimilate Native people into white culture, indigenous dances and religious ceremonies were banned on reservations, and practitioners were often jailed.

In 1973 an armed group of Native Americans occupied the Pine Ridge Indian Reservation at Wounded Knee, southwestern South Dakota, for 71 days. At the end of 1890 the last major armed conflict between whites and indigenous people took place here when Big Foot led his band of Miniconjou Sioux against the 7th US Cavalry.

In 1934, however, shamed by the terrible conditions they had seen on the reservations, reformers convinced Congress to pass the *Indian Reorganization Act* (IRA). The act repealed allotment, allowed self-governance, and introduced programs to support agriculture, education, and economic development.

Despite the fact that Indians were not granted US citizenship until 1924, many fought in both World Wars. A group of over 400 Navajo men participated in the Marines "Code Talker" program during World War II, transmitting military communiqués in Navajo, a "code" the Japanese were never able to break.

The year 1944 saw the formation of the National Congress of American Indians, an intertribal group of Native people dedicated to self-determination.

The move toward assimilation, however, reared its head again in the 1950s in the form of the Termination and Relocation programs. Termination sought to remove tribes from their trust relationship with the United States. Some reservation land was allotted to tribal members and the remainder was sold to non-Indians. Between 1954 and 1964, over 100 tribes were terminated. Some are still working to regain federal recognition today. The Relocation Program offered moving expenses and a 30-day living allowance to Indians who agreed to move to cities such as Minneapolis, Chicago, Cleveland, San Francisco, and others. However, this meant that they were then cut off from Bureau of Indian Affairs (BIA) services.

The fight for rights

Influenced by the civil rights movement in the 1960s, Native people began pushing for equal rights, self-determination, and sovereignty. Young militants formed the American Indian Movement (AIM) in Minneapolis in 1968 in response to police brutality against Indians. To call attention to their cause, a group of AIM members and other Indians in 1969 began a 19-month siege on Alcatraz Island, an abandoned federal prison in San Francisco Bay. They cited a government agreement that unused federal property could be returned to reservation status. The activists maintained that Alcatraz was remarkably like most reservations: there were no modern facilities, water, or arable land, and no employment opportunities. Later, in 1972, a group of Native Americans staged a protest called the "Trail of Broken Treaties." Demonstrators occupied the BIA building in Washington DC and called for a return to original treaty promises.

Responding to traditional tribal members' claims in 1973 about corruption within the Pine Ridge reservation government, AIM and other protesters took over the tiny community of Wounded Knee in South Dakota. The protest focused international attention on the conditions faced by Native people in the United States. Seventy-one days of gun battles and negotiations later, the protest ended peacefully. The Federal Bureau of Investigation, however, relentlessly pursued and harassed protest participants. In 1975, two FBI agents were killed during a gunfight with AIM members. One of the members, Leonard Peltier, was arrested and convicted of the murders. He is currently incarcerated at the Leavenworth federal penitentiary in Kansas. Supporters continue to call for his release, maintaining that he is innocent, a victim of retribution by a repressive, racist government.

Today, Native people are a vital part of modern America, yet they continue to maintain their identity and traditions as tribal peoples. Of the 2.4 million Native Americans living in the United States, about half live on approximately 550 reservations and the others live in cities and rural areas. The pursuit of self-determination and sovereignty has contributed to the ability of many tribes to begin to regain their lands and treaty rights through the courts, revitalize their communities' governments and economies, and revive and strengthen their traditions.

A statue commemorates Wampanoag Indian chief Massasoit, chief of Massachusetts (1590–1661). He and his people achieved peaceful relations with the Puritans in Plymouth Colony during his lifetime. The advantages of trade and cooperation palled after his death, however, as the settlers continued to take over more land. His son subsequently led a revolt against the colonists.

Early Exploration and Discovery

Columbus' ships, the Niña, Pinta and Santa María, reached the New World in October 1492. The Santa María never made it back to Spain; it was accidentally run aground on Hispaniola (modern-day Haiti and the Dominican Republic) and broken up to provide building materials for a fort.

Europeans, separated from the Americas by a wide ocean instead of a narrow strait, did not discover the North American continent until thousands of years after the first Asians crossed into present-day Alaska. By then, the Asian migrants' descendants had spread throughout North and South America.

The accidental discovery

Europeans first glimpsed the New World in about the year 1000. By then, Vikings had discovered and colonized the previously uninhabited islands of Iceland and Greenland. Around this time, a Viking ship was caught in a storm, drifted off course and came within sight of an unknown landmass before finding its way

As European explorers fanned out across the Americas, the familiar forms of the continents began to take shape on charts. This 1553 map reflects information gathered by contemporary Spanish expeditions into the interior of North America.

back to Greenland. A man named Leif Ericsson heard this tale, gathered a crew, and set off to explore.

Ericsson reached what is now Newfoundland, and established a settlement in an area he named Vinland. But the Vikings' colonization efforts were frustrated by conflict with the local indigenous people. The Vikings abandoned their settlement after a few years, and their exploits were gradually forgotten.

Columbus heads west

The continent was not rediscovered for another five centuries, and once again it was by accident. In the fifteenth century, many European countries were eager to find an efficient trade route to eastern Asia. A sea route, if one could be found, seemed the most promising option. While Portugal concentrated on exploring a southern route around Africa, a Genoese navigator named Christopher Columbus sought to convince Spain to sponsor an expedition in another, much riskier direction: west.

Educated Europeans had already accepted that the earth was spherical. It therefore made sense that someone sailing west from Europe would eventually reach Asia. The question was how long such a journey might take. No one knew if any islands existed beyond the Azores, 800 miles (1,300 km) due west of Portugal. An unbroken ocean voyage of more than 15,000 miles (24,000 km)—one contemporary estimate of the distance from Europe to Asia—would be impossible for a ship of those times.

Six years after first hearing Columbus' proposal, Spain's Queen Isabella and King Ferdinand finally agreed to fund his venture, although they were not very optimistic. On August 3, 1492, Columbus set off with three small ships and 90 crewmen, mostly former prisoners granted freedom in exchange for their service. They sailed first to the Spanish-owned Canary Islands off Africa's northwest coast. Then on September 6, they headed west with the trade winds, toward the unknown horizon.

The sailing was smooth, but the crew grew increasingly restless and worried as the weeks passed with no sign of land. Finally, on October 12, a crew member sighted an island, part of the present-day Bahamas. Columbus was convinced they had reached Asia, and called the inhabitants they encountered "Indians." The party explored several more islands and built a fort on the one they named Hispaniola (now Haiti and the Dominican Republic). Thirty-nine crewmen remained at the fort; Columbus and the rest sailed back to Spain, to a hero's welcome.

Columbus made three more voyages back to the region. Finding the fort destroyed on his first return, the crewmen all presumably having been killed by Indians, he ordered a second, stronger fort built and manned. Hispaniola thus became Europe's first permanent base in the region. Columbus then discovered several more Caribbean islands, and set foot on the mainland in South and Central America. But he went to his grave still believing it all to be Asia.

A whole new world

That belief was shared by another Italian navigator, John Cabot, who explored Newfoundland's coast on England's behalf in 1497. On his second voyage in 1498, Cabot may have ventured as far south as New England. With no sign of Asia's expected riches, the English rulers lost interest in further exploration for the time being. But in Cabot's wake, fishermen from many European nations arrived to harvest the bountiful waters from Newfoundland to Maine.

It was to be yet another Italian-born navigator, Amerigo Vespucci, exploring South America on Portugal's behalf, who in 1504 declared it to be a different continent entirely, a "new world." He realized that two oceans, not one, must separate Europe from Asia. It is for Vespucci that the Americas are named.

Over the next three decades, various Spanish travelers explored the Americas south of the Rio Grande River, finding gold and the great Aztec and Inca civilizations. Vasco Núñez de Balboa was the first among them to see the Pacific Ocean, while venturing west across the Isthmus of Panama in 1513.

The Spaniards paid less attention to what is now the United States, aside from a few incursions into its southern regions in failed quests for wealth and immortality. In 1513, Juan Ponce de León sailed north from the Caribbean in search of a rumored fountain of youth and more slaves. He discovered Florida instead. In 1528, Pánfilo de Narváez explored Florida's Gulf Coast. He then traveled inland seeking gold and civilizations to match what his compatriots had found in Mexico and Peru, but eventually gave up.

On the return journey, some of de Narváez's men were shipwrecked on what is now the Texas shore and imprisoned by Indians. During their incarceration, they heard rumors of great wealth somewhere farther north. One of them escaped and repeated the tales upon his return to Mexico. Hernando de Soto followed up these rumors in 1539, leading 500 men and 200 horses through the southeastern United States. Another expedition led by Francisco Vásquez de Coronado explored Texas and the southwestern United States, discovering the Grand Canyon in the process.

The Northwest Passage

Spain was not the only nation exploring the New World in the early 1500s. Although Spain's Ferdinand Magellan had demonstrated, in 1520, that one could indeed reach the Indies by sailing west and rounding South America, there was speculation that perhaps a faster route existed via North America. A race to find the "Northwest Passage" began. Giovanni da Verrazano's French-sponsored 1524 expedition failed in its quest, but in the process explored a large portion of North America's east coast, from North Carolina to Newfoundland. A decade later, France's Jacques Cartier found the Gulf of St Lawrence and the St Lawrence River in the area he named Canada.

Vast tracts of inland North America, as well as much of its western coast, were still unexplored by Europeans. But already, some were beginning to see the area in a different light—as a place to begin anew, far from the religious turmoil gripping Europe.

Throughout the Americas, statues of Columbus, such as this one in Stanford, Connecticut, have been erected to honor the Italian navigator's role in opening up the Americas to European settlement.

This nineteenth-century etching by W. H. Powell shows Spanish explorer Hernando de Soto on the banks of the Mississippi River. De Soto became the first European to cross the river, near present-day Memphis, Tennessee, during his expedition of 1539.

Early Settlement

This carving of the Archangel Michael is typical of the religious sculptures produced by Spanish missionaries in the Southwest during the eighteenth century.

Of the 102 pilgrims aboard the Mayflower, 35 had been living in the Netherlands, from where this painting shows them departing.

For more than half a century after Columbus' discovery of the New World, Europeans regarded the land north of Mexico as an area whose resources could be exploited by way of short forays rather than permanent settlements. But religious troubles arising from the Reformation inspired different ideas. In the mid-1500s, some persecuted Protestants began to think of the distant, mostly empty land as a refuge where they could live and worship as they pleased.

Religious exiles and opportunists

The first such group to turn thought into action were the French Huguenots. One of their leaders asked for and received royal permission to settle in North America. Thirty Huguenot would-be settlers arrived in what is now South Carolina in 1562. But they soon grew homesick and returned to Europe. Two years later, a larger group of Huguenots sailed to Florida. That attempt at colonization also proved short-lived: the Spanish, staunchly Catholic and believing themselves the rightful owners of all of North America, destroyed the settlement. To ward off further incursions, the Spanish built their own fort at St Augustine in 1565. St Augustine therefore became the first permanent European settlement in what is now the continental United States.

This failed to deter England, whose seafarers regularly plundered ships along North America's Atlantic coast. Hoping that a land base would boost the

nation's profits from either trade or plunder, Walter Raleigh obtained Queen Elizabeth I's blessing to found a colony on Roanoke Island (in modern-day North Carolina) in 1585. The settlers did not take to their new home and left the following year. A second colonization attempt on Roanoke Island in 1587 met a worse end: a supply ship returned four years later to find no trace of the 125 settlers.

Two decades later, growing economic hardship prompted the English to disregard these first aborted attempts and try again. Two private companies settled the coast between present-day North Carolina and Maine. Their promoters easily recruited gentlemen and working class people eager for profits or simply for a chance to farm their own land. The companies' first 100 colonists arrived in 1607, establishing Jamestown, near the mouth of Virginia's James River.

Expecting a paradise, the settlers instead found hunger and disease. Half perished within the first six months. But with the help of local tribes and fresh influxes of people and supplies, the settlement survived. By 1612, the settlers had even found a profitable economic venture: tobacco.

Settlement in Plymouth

While Jamestown was beginning to thrive, a group of Protestant sect members known as Puritans also received royal permission to settle in Virginia. They departed England in 1620, but instead of sailing to Virginia, they headed farther north, in order to avoid living among non-Puritans. They anchored their ship, the *Mayflower*, at Plymouth in modern-day Massachusetts. Because the site fell outside the Virginia Company's jurisdiction, the 101 settlers had to govern themselves. They formalized their committment to this undertaking in a document known as the "Mayflower Compact."

The Plymouth settlement also struggled to survive its first winter, and quickly lost half its inhabitants to hunger and disease. The following spring, local tribes taught the new arrivals about local agriculture, and, as a result, the settlement soon celebrated its first successful harvest. It also welcomed new arrivals from England. King Charles I, happy to rid the country of Puritans, gave permission to the newly formed Massachusetts Bay Company to settle New England. About 1,000 Puritans arrived in 1630; another 20,000 followed over the next dozen years.

The settled area expanded quickly. Among the Puritans were many educated people who did not want their geographic isolation to limit their horizons. They founded the colony's first college, Harvard, in 1636. But their own experience with religious persecution did not prevent them from persecuting others in turn. The new colonies of Rhode Island and Pennsylvania were eventually established by religious discontents seeking refuge from the Puritans.

While the English settlements in New England, Virginia, and Maryland were expanding, other European nations were establishing their own colonies along North America's eastern seaboard. The French had settled Acadia, in southeastern Canada, and were expanding along the St Lawrence River. However, their main priority was trade rather than permanent settlement. Farther south, the Netherlands had built settlements in Manhattan, along the Hudson River, and along the the present-day Connecticut and New Jersey coasts. There was even a New Sweden, which stretched along the Delaware River to just south of Philadelphia. Spain, which had initially claimed all of North America, protested against these incursions but was too weak to prevent them. It did, however, maintain its interests in the south and west, which consisted of a few scattered settlements in present-day Florida and New Mexico, as well as Mexico itself.

Territorial disputes

Friction among the countries inevitably grew as their colonies spread. For some, this meant the end of their North American presence. The Dutch took over New Sweden in 1655. The English, in turn, forced the Dutch to surrender New Netherland. This was precipitated by Charles II's desire to reward loyalists in the aftermath of England's civil war. He decided to offer them property in North America, unconcerned that some of the land in question already belonged to another country. By 1670, the English colonies thus stretched from Maine to the Carolinas.

As they spread out, the settlers bought some of their land cheaply from Native Americans, who frequently misinterpreted the purchases as mere land-use agreements and resented their subsequent evictions. This led to ambushes and reprisals, and, ultimately, war. The first Native American war erupted in 1675 in Rhode Island; a year later, native peoples had forever lost their hold on New England.

France was also intent on expanding its North American interests. In the second half of the 1600s, French explorers and missionaries ventured into the vast interior from their bases around the Great Lakes. In 1682, Robert Cavelier, Sieur de la Salle, traveled down to the Gulf of Mexico and claimed for France all the land in the Mississippi River basin. This huge tract of territory, stretching from the Appalachian Mountains in the east to the Rocky Mountains in the west, was given the name Louisiana. Spain, meanwhile, had spread farther into what is now the southwestern United States.

The boundaries separating these countries' claims were ill-defined, and the series of wars fought between England and France in Europe, which began in 1689, soon spilled over into North America. As the English colonies spread westward, France strengthened its grip on the interior, establishing a chain of forts linking its settlements around the Great Lakes to those along the Gulf of Mexico.

The pivotal conflict proved to be the French and Indian War, which took place between 1754 and 1763. With the aid of British troops, the more numerous British colonists won several decisive battles against French colonists and their Native American allies. On the brink of defeat, France secretly ceded all its territories west of the Mississippi to Spain. The following year, in 1763, France was forced to surrender the rest of its North American holdings—the Louisiana territory east of the Mississippi, and everything north of the Great Lakes—to Great Britain, which also obtained Florida from Spain (in exchange for colonies elsewhere in the world). The British Empire now dominated the continent.

Early relations between the Plymouth colony and local native peoples were cordial. Massasoit, chief of the Wampanoag, signed a treaty with the pilgrims in 1621 and remained their ally until his death around 1656.

BELOW: In the seventeenth and eighteenth centuries, young European women would demonstrate their mastery of needlework and literacy by making decorated panels of linen called "samplers." This example was made by Hannah Taylor of Rhode Island and is dated August 18, 1774.

BOTTOM: Early colonial furniture tended to be functional, though decorative features, such as the geometric panels on this early eighteenth-century blanket chest, gradually became more common.

Revolutionary War

History enthusiasts reenact an engagement from the Revolutionary War. At any one time, the American Continental Army consisted of just 20,000 men, most of whom were farmers. In contrast, the British force was made up of around 42,000 professional soldiers as well as 30,000 German mercenaries.

Having wrested a vast part of North America from France and Spain, Great Britain had become the world's greatest imperial power by 1763. Yet it was largely because of the costly war through which Britain gained its empire that it would go on to lose a significant portion of it just two decades later.

Britain's war debts

Cultural, economic, and social differences between the mother country and its American colonies were growing year by year, so the political ties would probably have loosened, if not broken, regardless of developments. But Britain hastened the process by trying to force the colonists to help pay off the empire's war debts.

The British, who thought of colonies as profit generators for the mother country, saw nothing unreasonable in this. From the beginning, the colonies had supplied Britain with crops, and in turn, British manufacturers had enjoyed a monopoly in American markets. The empire had also ensured the colonies' military protection. This arrangement had run relatively smoothly for the first 150 years, during which time the colonists had become accustomed to a significant degree of self-government.

But now Britain had to pay off its war debts and fund the additional forces needed to protect its large

empire. Unwilling to further tax themselves, British Parliamentarians decided to shift part of the burden onto the American colonists. From now on, Britain would enforce its Navigation Acts, which imposed tariffs on certain goods entering or leaving the empire's ports, unless they were carried in British ships. Americans, unwilling to enrich British merchants at their own expense, had long flouted these laws. Britain dispatched its navy to end the smuggling, and also expanded the list of goods covered by the Navigation Acts. Thus the *Sugar Act* was passed in 1764.

This law proved highly unpopular with the colonists, especially the affected merchants (New England's thriving rum trade relied on sugar). They argued that they could not be taxed without the consent of either themselves or their representatives, and that therefore Parliament, which contained no colonial representatives, could not tax the colonists.

The *Stamp Act*

Britain brushed aside the protests and sought ways to raise even more revenue. In late 1764, Parliament considered a resolution that would impose a stamp tax on the colonies. It would require legal and commercial documents and transactions, as well as printed materials, to bear special stamps bought from Britain. While considering this legislation, Parliament explicitly asserted its right to directly tax colonists, hoping to thereby stifle any dissent.

Instead, protests poured in. But they were ignored, and the *Stamp Act* became law in 1765. British–colonial relations, already testy because of Britain's failure to consider colonists' views on various local regulations, were now seriously damaged.

The dissent united the colonies, which had long resisted cooperation because of their many economic, religious, political, and cultural differences. Printers, fearing the stamp tax would be detrimental to their businesses, fanned the flames of opposition by publishing numerous critical pamphlets and newspapers. Some protests escalated into riots. Reasoning that a coordinated strategy would help their cause, the colonies convened a Stamp Act Congress, a forum for colonial delegates to discuss and perfect their plans. Only nine colonies were represented, and their delegates issued relatively moderate proposals. But the Stamp Act Congress marked an important milestone: it was the first American body whose authority was accepted by all of the colonies.

Meanwhile, the tumult over the *Stamp Act* was spawning a radical new party, whose members called themselves "patriots." They opposed using, or even allowing distribution of, the required stamps. They called for the colonies to sever their trade links with Britain. They rallied supporters with the slogan, "no taxation without representation." But their protest went deeper than taxes—it spoke of a fundamental refusal to be governed in any way by a remote body in which colonists were not represented.

In the face of such strong opposition, the British Parliament backed down and repealed the *Stamp Act* in 1766. But to save face, it also passed a *Declaratory Act* reiterating its right to do as it wished with regard to the colonies. It underscored this the following year by passing a sweeping set of acts that imposed new duties on tea and other goods; removed the colonial assemblies' control of payment of colonial officials; and set up new colonial districts that functioned without juries.

These acts affected an even greater number of colonists, many of whom greatly resented this new assault on their rights. Resistance to British rule gradually became stronger and better organized. Massachusetts towns led the way by passing import restriction agreements. Passions intensified, until a 1768 riot in Boston prompted Britain to send in two regiments of soldiers to restore and maintain order.

Military occupation of Boston

Although Britain dissolved colonial assemblies that resisted the new legislation, the military occupation of Boston strengthened the colonies' resolve. Britain had long insisted that it maintained a standing army in North America for defense purposes. It was now clear that its soldiers would also enforce obedience to Parliament, if necessary. The nonimportation protest movement spread.

Both sides then proceeded to raise the stakes. In Massachusetts, leading patriot Samuel Adams tried but failed to mount an armed resistance to the British soldiers. So he persuaded the colony's House of Representatives to meet unofficially instead. Britain denounced this and called for prosecutions for treason. The nonimportation movement spread futher still, until it was taken up by all the core colonies, except New Hampshire, by early 1770.

Britain finally relented. All the new duties it had imposed were repealed, except for the one on tea. On the day the measure was proposed in Parliament, however, Boston erupted once more as a result of tensions between locals and British soldiers. A mob had attacked a Customs House, forcing the guards to fire in self-defense. Five Bostonians were killed, and the incident was branded the "Boston Massacre." The British subsequently withdrew their army.

Once the duties were officially repealed, calm was restored and trade resumed. But relations between colonists and the mother country remained strained. Parliament passed another contentious law in May, 1773. The *Tea Act* was designed to help Britain's nearly bankrupt East India Company by lifting export burdens to allow it to compete better in the American market. The act also allowed the company to sell its tea directly. American colonists would receive lower-priced tea, but at the expense of American tea smugglers and honest middlemen. Moreover, the duty tax on tea would remain in place. Benjamin Franklin, then Pennsylvania's agent in London, denounced this strategy as a subversive plot to entice Americans to surrender their principles of no taxation without representation in return for cheaper tea.

The son of a Huguenot immigrant, Paul Revere was a highly successful silversmith before he took up the cause of independence. His famous ride wasn't his only contribution: he was one of the ringleaders of the Boston Tea Party and later produced arms for the colonial militias.

The colonies' bountiful farms were a rich source of supplies for Britain. But it was the imposition of taxes on colonial produce that would drive the dependencies away from the mother country.

A pipe band performs at the July 4 celebrations in Washington. The capital's colorful Independence Day parades attract crowds of up to 400,000 spectators.

On June 17, 1775, the American forces made a heroic stand at Bunker Hill, Boston. Although eventually overwhelmed, they inflicted such heavy casualties that George Washington was able to easily displace the British army early in the following year.

Resistance spread, and when the first tea ships arrived in Boston in November, 1773, colonists refused to let them unload their cargo. Discussions led nowhere. Finally, a mob led by patriots dressed as Native Americans ran to the harbor and dumped the contents of more than 300 tea chests into the water. The "Boston Tea Party," as this event came to be known, inspired the inhabitants of other colonial ports to undertake similar revolts.

As the opposition movement grew, its principles evolved. Parliamentary authority, not just the power to levy colonial taxes, was more widely questioned. Economic complaints were turning into political ones.

By now Britain had lost its patience with the colonies, and passed what became known as the Intolerable Acts. Among other things, they gave colonial governors more powers, and ordered Boston's port closed until the colonists paid for the ruined tea. The colonies responded by convening the First Continental Congress in Philadelphia on September 5, 1774. Only Georgia did not send a representative. All agreed not to import British goods or obey the new laws.

Confronting British forces

The restless colonies had also begun to train and arm militias. On April 18, 1775, the British dispatched a secret expedition to either seize or destroy a colonial militia armory in Concord, Massachusetts. The

Boston radicals learned of the plan that night. Patriots Paul Revere and William Dawes rode through the countryside, alerting their fellow colonists. The next morning, a group of militia volunteers (known as Minutemen) confronted the British expedition at Lexington. The first shots of the Revolutionary War were fired during the ensuing battle.

It did not take long for war to break out elsewhere in the colonies. In May, a Second Continental Congress met and appointed George Washington, a Virginia planter and soldier, as overall commander of the growing American army.

Throughout the conflict, the colonists benefited from the British forces' many blunders. The colonists were also more motivated than their opponents, battling as they were for their fundamental interests. But the Continental Army had its share of problems, including inexperience and the civilian authorities' failure to keep up with soldier payments, supplies, and reinforcements. Fortunately, Washington's inspired leadership made up for many problems.

The British made a major error early in the war, when they failed to take Boston while its high points were undefended. They finally secured one of them, Bunker Hill, but incurred such devastating losses that the remaining British soldiers proved no match for Washington's forces once they arrived. In March, 1776, the British withdrew to Halifax and the patriots jubilantly claimed Boston.

French were eager for revenge on Britain after their defeat in the Seven Years' War and had already been covertly helping the American rebels.

Franklin's case was strengthened when the Continental Army won another victory, this time in Saratoga, New York. Because of their poor planning and communication, the British forces led by General John Burgoyne were forced to surrender to General Horatio Gates on October 17, 1777. This victory was somewhat offset by Britain's capture of Philadelphia—that loss precipitated the worst months of the war for Washington's army, which had to pass the bitter winter without blankets or other provisions in Valley Forge, Pennsylvania.

Nevertheless, the Saratoga victory convinced France that the rebels' war was winnable. With France's official entry into the conflict in 1778, the previously see-sawing balance of fortunes now favored the rebels. Spain also sided with the rebelling colonies, as did the Netherlands. And more and more Americans joined the patriot party.

A symbol of American freedom, the Liberty Bell was rung on July 8, 1776, to celebrate the first public reading of the Declaration of Independence. It is engraved with the words "Proclaim liberty throughout all the land unto all the inhabitants thereof." This replica stands outside the Treasury Department in Washington.

ABOVE LEFT: At the Battle of Trenton, Washington's forces defeated a British battalion of 1,400 men under the command of the Hessian Colonel Johann Rall. After the battle, the injured Rall was brought before Washington then taken to his quarters, where he died of his wounds.

Fighting for liberty

As the war progressed, calls for independence grew louder. Thomas Paine's influential pamphlet, "Common Sense," urged people to fight for liberty. These sentiments were shared by Congress, where a committee led by Virginia's Thomas Jefferson drafted a declaration of independence promoting every man's right to "life, liberty, and the pursuit of happiness." The delegates approved the document on July 4, 1776. Congress then drew up the Articles of Confederation to serve as a governing blueprint for the new nation.

On the battlefield, however, Britain regained the upper hand, driving Washington's troops out of New York and New Jersey later that year. Washington halted the retreat in Pennsylvania and, on Christmas Day, turned his troops around and mounted two quick strikes across the Delaware River. The two victories, at Trenton and Princeton in New Jersey, were strategically important and also boosted the patriots' morale.

Assistance from France

Meanwhile, Benjamin Franklin, then America's best-known and most urbane scientist and statesman, was in Paris, wooing the French to the patriots' side. The

British surrender

The decisive moment came in Yorktown, Virginia, not far from the site of the first English settlement at Jamestown. General Charles Cornwallis was caught there, waiting to be rescued by the British Navy. Washington saw an opportunity for a decisive victory and marched his troops south from New Jersey. With French help, they blocked sea and land escape routes and mounted a siege. Cornwallis surrendered on October 19, 1781, and the war effectively ended. Some 80,000 British sympathizers from the American colonies fled to what became English-speaking Canada.

The Treaty of Paris settled the peace terms on September 3, 1783. The spoils went to the United States. Not only was American independence recognized, but the new country's boundaries were defined to be the Great Lakes in the north and the Mississippi River in the west, encompassing a large, nearly empty territory in addition to the settled seaboard states (apart from Florida, which reverted to Spain).

A new nation had been born, its existence based on principles of individual liberty that flew in the face of the long-established political order. Now it was left to the United States to wrestle with the implications of its founders' ideals, a struggle that continues today.

REVOLUTIONARY WAR TIMELINE	MAY–JUNE 1775 15,000 rebels converge on Boston. British, led by General William Howe, capture Bunker Hill on June 17, but sustain heavy losses.	FEBRUARY 27, 1776 Rebel troops inflict a heavy defeat on British forces at Moore's Creek Bridge, North Carolina.	AUGUST 1776 General William Howe leads assault on New York from sea, landing on Long Island, routing American forces, and driving them into New Jersey.	JULY 1777 British army under General John Burgoyne marches south from Canada, seizing rebel stronghold at Fort Ticonderoga, New York.	OCTOBER 1777 After his forces are blocked at Freeman's Farm, New York, Burgoyne's army is defeated then forced to surrender at Saratoga on October 17.	1781 Led by General Charles Cornwallis, British attempt to expand control in South, with only limited success. Cornwallis establishes base at Yorktown, Virginia.	1782–83 Loyalists flee as peace treaties are drawn up, the last British soldiers leaving New York on November 25, 1783. Washington returns to city in triumph.
	APRIL 19, 1775 British commander Thomas Gage's dispatch of troops to destroy militia armory at Concord results in first battles at Concord and Lexington.	NOVEMBER 1775 American forces invade Canada, capturing Montreal but failing to take Quebec despite a lengthy siege.	MARCH 1776 Washington's men seize Dorchester Heights near Boston and begin bombardment that forces British to leave city on March 17.	DECEMBER 1776–JANUARY 1777 On the brink of defeat, Washington seizes Trenton and Princeton, thus reviving rebel fortunes.	SEPTEMBER 1777 Howe lands at Chesapeake Bay and defeats Washington at Brandywine Creek. On September 25, he enters Philadelphia.	1778 France's entry into war provides Americans with much-needed support. 1779–80 British establish strongholds at Savannah and Charleston, Georgia.	SEPTEMBER–OCTOBER 1781 Bolstered by a large French force, rebel armies lay siege to Yorktown. British surrender entire army on October 19.

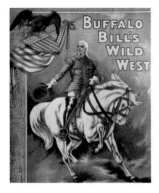

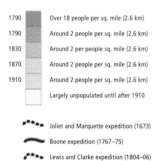

Few played a greater role in establishing the iconography of the West than Buffalo Bill Cody. From 1883 until his death in 1917, this former army scout toured his Wild West shows, featuring "genuine" Indians and cowboys and reenactments of historical events, all over the world, to immense acclaim.

EXPANSION WEST

This map charts the westward movement of the frontier over time, as expeditions, rail lines, and settlers progressed across the interior of America.

1790	Over 18 people per sq. mile (2.6 km)
1790	Around 2 people per sq. mile (2.6 km)
1830	Around 2 per people sq. mile (2.6 km)
1870	Around 2 people per sq. mile (2.6 km)
1910	Around 2 people per sq. mile (2.6 km)
	Largely unpopulated until after 1910

- Joliet and Marquette expedition (1673)
- Boone expedition (1767–75)
- Lewis and Clarke expedition (1804–06)
- First transcontinental railway (1869)

Expansion Westward

From the time of the first permanent English settlement in Jamestown until the end of the nineteenth century, the American frontier remained a moving target. Progress was perpetually linked with expansion; after all, the land and its resources appeared infinite. So when the newly independent United States found itself in possession of a vast, mostly uninhabited territory stretching from the Appalachian Mountains to the Mississippi River, its policy was never in doubt—settle the land.

The *Land Ordinance*

Congress quickly devised a blueprint for how to transfer this government land into private hands. The *Land Ordinance*, drafted by Thomas Jefferson and passed in 1785, decreed that the federal territory would be surveyed and divided up into townships. These would then be subdivided into 1 square mile (2.6 sq km), rectangular plots, which would be sold for not less than $1 per acre. This opened the way for land speculators to buy sections, subdivide them, and sell them at a profit.

The newly acquired land was not completely empty. There were Native Americans, of course, but also some white settlers. Adventurous backwoodsmen such as Daniel Boone had blazed trails into Kentucky and Tennessee before the Revolutionary War. Settlers had followed in their wake. Slave-owning planters later moved in and displaced many of these small farmers, who, in turn, headed north to settle Ohio, Indiana, Illinois, Michigan and Wisconsin. Here they were joined by New England farmers who had headed west in search of more fertile land. Some displaced settlers, including Boone himself, continued westward across the Mississippi, where they obtained land grants from the Spanish.

In 1803 came the first of several land acquisitions that, by the close of the century, would see the United States expand to the Pacific Ocean and beyond. Napoleon Bonaparte, eager for war funds and sensing that France would have difficulty holding on to the vast Louisiana Territory it had recently re-acquired from Spain, sold it to the United States for about $15 million. This extended the boundaries of the United States to the crest of the Rocky Mountains.

The Lewis and Clark expedition

At the time, this territory was still largely unexplored. President Jefferson therefore commissioned two army officers, Meriwether Lewis and William Clark, to survey the land, recommend good trading sites, and look for a water route to the Pacific. Lewis and Clark set off from Camp Wood, near St Louis, in May, 1804, and followed the Missouri River to North Dakota. There, they enlisted a Frenchman and his Native American wife, Sacagawea. Thanks in part to Sacagawea's presence, Lewis and Clark received help from Native Americans along most of their route. The party eventually crossed the Continental Divide and floated down the Columbia River to the Pacific Ocean. By the time they returned to St Louis, their journey had lasted 28 months and covered 7,689 miles (12,145 km). Lewis and Clark's journals included valuable, detailed descriptions of the area's geography, plants, and animals.

The government sponsored several more expeditions into other parts of the newly acquired land. Reports of large beaver populations lured trappers and traders eager to cash in on the European demand for pelts for making hats. These trappers and traders crisscrossed, further opening up the new territory until the felt-hat fashion (and most of the beavers) died out by the mid-1830s.

New technologies also facilitated westward migration. The first steamboats began operating west of Appalachia in 1811; they soon replaced rafts on the Mississippi, decreasing both the time and cost of water travel. The Erie Canal opened in 1825, connecting the East Coast to the Ohio and Mississippi River valleys. Most significantly of all, the first American steam locomotive was built in 1825 (trains finally penetrated the West almost two decades later).

The promise of a better life (if not outright riches) was the frontier's perennial drawcard. A major depres-

sion hit the country in 1837 and convinced many easterners to pull up stakes and try their luck elsewhere; the 1840s therefore marked the beginning of the country's major westward migration. Over the next three decades, more than 300,000 pioneers in "prairie schooners" (cloth-covered wagons) wound their way along the four major westward trails. The most popular of these was the Oregon Trail, which stretched 2,000 miles (3,200 km) from Independence, Missouri to Oregon City near the Pacific coast. The pioneers' oxen-pulled wagons were loaded with household possessions and enough nonperishable foods to last the long, arduous journey across the seemingly endless plains and high-mountain passes. Traveling in large groups for safety, the pioneers endured rough terrain, extreme weather, and attacks by Native Americans. Disease and accidents claimed many lives.

A manifest destiny

At the beginning of this great migration, the land to which many were heading, in California and in Oregon, belonged to Spain and Great Britain, respectively. Soon, Americans began agitating for the United States to take over the Oregon Territory, which extended to the north into modern-day Canada, and the British decided to negotiate a compromise. In 1846, they agreed to extend the existing border with Canada, along the 49° north latitude line, all the way

to the Pacific Ocean. The United States thus gained about three-fifths of the Oregon Territory, and the nation, for the first time, spanned the length of the entire continent. America's "manifest destiny," its seemingly inevitable expansion over the continent, was coming to pass.

This was true not just in the west. In the South, the newly independent Mexico and the United States were clashing over Texas. It officially belonged to Mexico, but many Americans had long considered it theirs by virtue of the Louisiana Purchase, and settlers poured into the area during the mid-1830s. In 1836,

This contemporary image of the bar of a gambling saloon in Sacramento, California, highlights the diverse ethnic origins of those drawn west by the gold rush.

Top: In the 1840s, a steady stream of settlers flowed across the prairies of the interior to the West. By 1845, about 6,000 Americans had already settled in Oregon.

Beartooth Pass, Montana, which reaches a height of 10,974 feet (3,347 m) and is blocked by snow in winter, is typical of the daunting terrain faced by pioneers as they journeyed westward.

the settlers declared their independence from both countries. The Mexicans then tried to reclaim the land by force. They won several battles, including the siege of the Alamo, a San Antonio fort that Davy Crockett and 186 other men died protecting. But the Americans overpowered the Mexican army in another key battle, and in 1836, the captured Mexican leader, Antonio López de Santa Anna, was forced to sign a treaty recognizing Texas' independence.

The trouble did not end there. Texans claimed an area about three times the size of the province they had originally settled, and also indicated they would be willing to give up their independence and join the United States. In response, the United States sent a force to the area, and in 1846, the Mexican War began. To further antagonize Mexico, the United States encouraged a settlers' revolt in California, also still in Mexico's possession (though American pioneers had settled there as well). The Mexicans were no match for the United States army, and the war ended a year later. Under the 1848 Treaty of Guadelupe Hidalgo, the United States gained all Mexican

The fringed buckskin shirt, coonskin cap, and long rifle have strong associations with Davy Crockett (1786–1836). This Tennessee politician's adventurous image, pioneering background, and tragic death at the Alamo made him an American folk hero.

territory from Texas to California. This land made the United States almost as large as Europe.

The first American mass-migration into this area began even while the Mexican War still raged. Like some of the earliest immigration to America, it was prompted by a desire to escape religious persecution. Joseph Smith had founded the Church of Jesus Christ of Latter-Day Saints (whose members came to be called Mormons) in upstate New York in 1830, and Smith and his follower Brigham Young had recruited many people to the sect. Some Americans, however, objected to the Mormons' beliefs and practices, which included polygamy. Young therefore led the Mormons west to Illinois and Missouri, but they were persecuted there, too, so he took them farther west. The first Mormon party arrived in Utah's then-uninhabited Great Salt Lake basin in 1847; by 1848, some 5,000 Mormons had arrived, and their numbers continued to grow.

Gold rushes

Another mass-migration into the former Mexican territory occurred soon afterward. A sawmill builder found gold in a creek near Sacramento, California, in January, 1848. During the following year, speculators poured into California from the United States and overseas. Only a small percentage of them became rich.

This was the first of many mineral strikes that would open up the western mountain regions in the coming decades. By the late 1870s, gold or silver had been found in every territory of the Far West. Colorful mining camps sprang up throughout the region, although rough topography and harsh climate kept the mountain populations relatively small. Busts often followed hard on the heels of the booms. Some of the mining camps became ghost towns; others developed into agricultural centers, especially after the last remaining swath of empty land, the Great Plains, finally began to fill up in the 1860s.

The Wild West

The plains west of the Missouri River had been called the Great American Desert since the first explorers had claimed that the region's seemingly poor soil and inadequate water would make them unsuitable for agriculture. However, Texas cattlemen, eager to find new pastures, reasoned that if the plains could support vast buffalo herds, they should also support cattle. They began moving huge herds north in the 1860s, hiring cowboys to drive the cattle from Texas to Kansas and Missouri; from railroads there, they could be sent to slaughterhouses in Chicago and elsewhere. The "Wild West" of popular imagination—cowboys riding into dusty frontier towns marked by saloons, painted women, sheriffs, and vigilante justice—developed in this era.

Farmers were also drawn to the Great Plains by the *Homestead Act* of 1862, which promised 160 acres (64 ha) of public land to the head of every household, provided he or she was (or was planning to become) a citizen and was at least 21 years old. In return, the family had to pay a small fee and settle on the land for at least five years. Migration increased after the Civil War, encouraged by the expanding railroads (the first transcontinental railroad link was established in 1869).

Pioneering families overcame many challenges, including a scarcity of trees for lumber, limited water sources, isolation, and severe winters. They also clashed with the Native Americans of the plains, formidable warriors with nowhere left to retreat. A series of conflicts rocked the region—Native Americans fought (and generally lost) at least 200 battles between 1869 and 1876. The last major native–settler altercation ended with the capture of Chiricahua Apache leader Geronimo in Arizona in 1886. By then, Native Americans had already been made wards of the government, and almost all were living on reservations. Whites had destroyed their livelihoods by decimating the vast buffalo herds that had roamed the prairies (their hides were sought after for making industrial machinery belts). Almost 4 million buffalo were killed in 1871 alone.

Farmers also clashed at this time with cattlemen, who resented the settlers erecting fences that prevented their stock from reaching previously open pastures and water sources. Shortly afterward, however, expanding railroads in the South rendered long cattle drives obsolete, and by 1886, the cowboy era had ended, a mere 20 years after it had begun. Many farmers' livelihoods were destroyed a few years later by a series of droughts, and some returned to the East to start all over again.

After the 1890 census, the frontier was declared closed. By this time, settlers had even spread beyond the mainland. An 1880 gold strike had lured a few to Alaska, which the United States had bought from Russia in 1867 for $7,200,000. (Many more settlers followed in their wake when gold was found on the Klondike River in 1897.) And American missionaries and traders had been settling in Hawaii, a key port of call en route to Asia, since the early 1800s (the islands eventually became a territory in 1898).

However, it was only the contiguous frontier—"the meeting point between savagery and civilization," in the words of one contemporary historian—that no longer existed. Many pockets of free land remained. Land-hungry settlers also had their eye on Oklahoma, which had been deemed a Native American Territory in the mid-1800s. After a few white incursions were driven out, expansionists pressured the government into opening up the land. Congress finally acquiesced, and from 1890 onward settlers swarmed into the area to establish themselves under the *Homestead Act*.

From that time on, the frontier existed primarily in certain forms of popular entertainment. "Buffalo Bill's Wild West," a show staged by William Cody and fellow frontier veterans, played to great acclaim in the United States and Europe from 1883 until the early 1900s. By then, frontier life had firmly established itself in the national folklore.

This Baltimore bridal quilt was made in 1847. The American tradition of quilt-making dates from the late eighteenth century; styles became increasingly elaborate throughout the 1800s.

Contemporary artists did much to create the enduring myth of General Custer's "Last Stand" at the Battle of Little Bighorn in 1876. Reluctant to depict the reality of this calamitous defeat, they portrayed Custer and his men as heroes, fighting to the end for America and "civilization."

Slavery

Abraham Lincoln was implacably opposed to the division of the country along pro- and anti-slavery lines, arguing that it must be "all one thing, or all the other."

Right: Stereotypical depictions of black people continued to be used to sell Southern products long after slavery was abolished, as this late-nineteenth-century trade card demonstrates.

Despite emancipation, African Americans continued to face prejudice, limited opportunities, and poverty. This photograph shows a black neighborhood in Thomasville, Georgia, in 1895.

The social practice that has arguably had the greatest impact on America's history—and continues to shape its present—is the one eventually came to be known as "that peculiar institution," slavery. The idea was neither new, nor unique to North America—slavery had been practiced on other continents since antiquity. But it had never before been practiced in a nation founded on the principle of equality.

The Atlantic slave trade was effectively launched in the 1400s, when Portuguese explorers tracing the west African coast were offered war captives in exchange for material goods. They accepted the offer, reasoning that these people were little different from animals. The Africans would in fact benefit from the arrangement, the Portuguese rationalized, if they converted to Christianity as a result.

Soon after the discovery of the New World, Europeans realized that slaves could help them exploit its riches. Native Americans were captured and enslaved, but tended to run away or die too quickly to satisfy the owners. In 1501, Spain's rulers consented to let African slaves be brought to Hispaniola (now Haiti and the Dominican Republic), thus introducing black slavery to the Americas.

Black slaves were no more content with enslavement than Native Americans; their first revolt took place in 1522, but was quickly put down. Native enslavement continued for many years, but the level of black slavery soon surpassed it throughout Central and South America. The practice subsequently spread to the North American mainland when Spaniards brought black slaves to Florida in 1581.

FOOLED DIS TIME CULLY DIS COTTON AINT GWINE TO BREAK

Importing slaves to the colonies

A few decades later, English settlers in Virginia were struggling to grow enough tobacco to satisfy the market. There were too few Englishmen in Virginia to meet the labor demand, and fewer still who were willing to toil on big tobacco farms. So the colonists decided to import slaves. In 1619, a Dutch ship arrived with about 20 African captives; others followed. Profits grew, and slave labor soon underpinned the economy.

The practice developed more slowly in the Northern colonies—the first slaves were imported into what was then New Netherland in 1655—and was never taken up as eagerly or as widely as in the South, partly because large-scale farming was uncommon and white immigrants were happy to carry out other work.

Some Northerners even voiced their disapproval. In 1652, Rhode Island became the first colony to outlaw the practice, and in 1688 the Quakers of Germantown, Pennsylvania, who had experienced persecution themselves, issued North America's first antislavery petition.

Such protests remained on the fringes, however, and the Atlantic slave trade reached its height in the 1700s. It was a triangular trade. English merchants traded iron, cloth, and other goods for slaves in western Africa. They shipped the slaves to the Caribbean, where they sold them to plantation owners and purchased sugar with the proceeds. Finally, they returned to England, where they sold the sugar. The trans-Atlantic segment became known as the "Middle Passage." Slaves were manacled in the holds of ships, and many perished en route. Survivors were either put to work on Caribbean plantations or re-sold on the North American mainland.

Antislavery legislation

During the Revolutionary War period in the 1770s and 1780s, the ideals of freedom and equality began to circulate in the American colonies. Some pondered whether slavery could coexist with the new nation's principles. Many influential people thought it could not, and New England, Pennsylvania, and Delaware soon passed antislavery laws. Not all opposition to slavery was highminded; some Northerners simply didn't want their region overrun by blacks.

In April, 1776, Congress passed a war measure forbidding additional slaves to be imported into the 13 rebelling colonies (the slave importation ban finally became a federal law in 1808). Later that year, the Declaration of Independence proudly announced that "all men are created equal." But an explicit denunciation of the slave trade was deleted from the final draft, in deference to South Carolina and Georgia.

Indeed, the belief in black inferiority was so widely entrenched that the general public, even in the North, could hardly be described as being opposed to slavery. The Constitution, significantly, did not forbid the practice; the Bill of Rights contained no right not to be enslaved. It was therefore left to each state to decide if slavery was acceptable.

The cotton industry

In 1793, Eli Whitney invented the cotton gin, a machine that revolutionized cotton production and boosted the demand for field hands. Soon the supply of cotton picked by slaves was vital to the Southern economy. Thus, at the same time that the antislavery movement was gaining support and spreading (all states north of Maryland had outlawed it by 1819, and Britain freed all its slaves in 1833), Southerners were increasingly coming to depend on it.

A few Southern antislavery groups surfaced; in 1822, one paid for freed slaves to be recolonized in Africa, helping establish the country of Liberia specifically for this purpose. But in general, Southern whites closed ranks. Plantation owners enjoyed their power and prosperity. Besides, they had invested heavily in their slaves, and believed the Southern economy could not survive without them. Poorer whites, meanwhile, felt threatened by the idea of having to compete against millions of freed blacks. And their poverty seemed slightly more bearable while there was another, even more disadvantaged group to look down on.

More than 4 million slaves lived in the South by the mid-1800s. Their situations varied, but their lives contained little joy or comfort. Plantation overseers whipped them and forced them to work from daybreak to sundown. They were often dirty, barefoot, and dressed in rags. In the cause of white solidarity,

the few laws that existed to protect slaves were frequently not enforced. Many slaves ran away, sometimes in an effort to trace and rejoin their spouses or children, who were often sold separately.

Slavery splits the country

Northern antislavery—and Southern resistance to it—gathered strength as the 1800s progressed. Over the years, sympathetic Northerners helped thousands of slaves escape northward along the "Underground Railroad." The more radical abolition movement grew out of the antislavery movement in 1831, when Boston's William Lloyd Garrison founded a journal called the *Liberator*. In 1852, the injustices arising from the harsh new *Fugitive Slave Law* prompted Harriet Beecher Stowe to dramatize the slaves' plight in the popular and influential novel *Uncle Tom's Cabin*.

Abolitionist John Brown's failed attempt to capture an armory and incite a slave rebellion in Harpers Ferry, Virginia, and Lincoln's election on the antislavery Republican ticket, prompted 11 Southern states to secede from the Union in the winter and spring of 1861. The remaining states refused to recognize the Confederate States of America, and the Civil War began in April, 1861 (see page 78–81).

"Juneteenth"

The war's subtext, slavery, was finally brought to the fore when Lincoln signed the Emancipation Proclamation on January 1, 1863, freeing all Confederate slaves. In practical terms, this war-time declaration was unenforceable. But it had a significant moral impact and served notice of the country's future policy in this area. Eventually, in January, 1865, Congress approved the Thirteenth Amendment to the Constitution, outlawing slavery. The war ended later that year. The last American slaves to learn that they were free heard the news on June 19, 1865, a day celebrated ever since as "Juneteenth."

On cotton plantations, slaves not only gathered the crop but operated the cotton gins that transformed the industry. Proprietors, meanwhile, enjoyed an increase in quality and profits.

Drying tobacco. A strong demand for tobacco in Europe during the early seventeenth century brought about the transportation of the first slaves from Africa to America.

Civil War

The seeds of the Civil War, which erupted in 1861, were sown at the time of the founding of the American republic, almost a century earlier. The United States Constitution proved to be a document subject to interpretation, and one lingering point of contention was how the rights of the individual states' were to be balanced against the powers of the federal government. Two trains of thought developed, with one side supporting a strong union and the other favoring greater independence for the states. The two issues that drove many people to favor one side or the other were economics and slavery.

The effect of a protectionist tariff

In 1816, the federal government passed the United States' first protectionist tariff, in order to discourage dependence on foreign manufactured goods and, in turn, boost domestic manufacturing industries. These fledgling industries were concentrated in the North-east; the South, in contrast, remained heavily agri-cultural. Consequently, the tariff created ill-feeling among Southerners, who resented having to buy more expensive goods in order to help the North.

The industrial states, on the other hand, felt that they did not receive sufficient assistance from the first tariff, nor even from two subsequent increases. They lobbied for further controls, which were contested by the South. But following political maneuvering, in 1828 the party that opposed the increases ended up approving an exceptionally strong measure known as the "Tariff of Abominations." South Carolina passed a resolution denouncing it; some within the state went even further, arguing that states had the right to nullify federal laws within their borders.

The issue of slavery

But it was slavery that drove the biggest wedge between North and South and pushed the question of states' rights to the fore. The Constitution left it to individual states to decide whether or not to allow slavery. After the invention of the cotton gin in 1793, slaves became an integral part of cotton production, and thus crucial to Southern economies. Northerners, whose econo-mies were never tied to slavery, began to disapprove of the practice (or at least of having it in their midst). The states north of the Maryland–Pennsylvania bor-der had abolished slavery by 1819; those south of the so-called Mason–Dixon Line retained it.

This troubled the South, which felt threatened by the country's changing demographics and expanding borders. The industrializing, prosperous North was far more populous than the agrarian South, and the population gap was widening. Under proportional representation, Northerners would wield more and more political power in the House of Representatives. The last political line of defense for Southern interests (particularly the continuation of slavery) seemed to lie in the Senate, where each state was allotted two seats, regardless of population. It was thus essential that the South maintain a balance between the num-ber of slave states and free states in the growing na-tion. The Missouri Compromise of 1820 appeared to reinforce this idea by allowing slavery to exist in any new territories that fell below the 36°30' north latitude line (marking Missouri's southern border), as long as residents approved of it.

But by 1831, the growing Northern antislavery movement had spawned a radical fringe element, the abolitionists. They wanted slavery to end everywhere, immediately, by whatever means necessary. They were

Colonel Jesse Alexander is one of 17,000 soldiers buried at Vicksburg National Cemtery, Mississippi, the largest Civil War cemetery in the United States.

not popular, even in the North. But an 1831 slave rebellion in Virginia, though an isolated incident, alarmed Southerners, who saw it as evidence that Northern abolitionists were fomenting violent uprisings.

Settling the tariff issue

The lingering tarrif issue reinforced Southerners' sense of grievance. In 1832, rates were finally lowered, but not sufficiently to please South Carolina, which passed an ordinance declaring the recent tariff acts unconstitutional. A state convention also nullified them within South Carolina's borders, and threatened secession if the federal government tried to collect payments by force. President Andrew Jackson denounced these actions, prompting South Carolina to raise troops in defiance. But calmer heads prevailed, and a compromise that included a lower tariff was soon accepted. South Carolina suspended its nullification ordinance. The tariff issue, at least, was settled. But the underlying problem of defining the limits of states' rights endured.

The problem resurfaced in the 1840s, when it became clear that the Missouri Compromise would not work out in the slave states' favor. Several new southwestern territories had been settled by people opposed to slavery. Balance in the Senate appeared on the verge of slipping away. Southern talk of secession rose.

Congress struck a compromise in 1850; the concession to the slave states was a more strident *Fugitive Slave Act.* Yet its injustices also increased the abolitionists' ranks. Guerrilla warfare broke out in the new territory of Kansas, whose stance on slavery the North and South were both trying to influence. Meanwhile, more free states joined the Union, tipping the balance in the Senate.

The Confederate States of America

The spark that helped ignite a full-blown crisis came in October, 1859, when a militant abolitionist called John Brown attempted to capture an armory in Harpers Ferry, Virginia, intending to incite an armed slave rebellion. Although he was quickly captured and hanged, Southerners viewed the incident as a portent of what Northerners might attempt in the future. A year later, Abraham Lincoln, a member of the anti-slavery Republican party, was elected president. At this point, the Southern states realized there was no future for slavery if they remained in the Union.

As a result, on December 20, 1860, South Carolina seceded. It was followed by Mississippi, Florida, Alabama, Georgia, Louisiana, and Texas. In February, delegates from those states met in Montgomery, Alabama, and framed a constitution for the "Confederate States of America." This was to be a voluntary merger of equals. Jefferson Davis of Mississippi, a former planter and Secretary of War under Franklin Pierce, was appointed its president.

The Civil War was one of the first conflicts to be recorded by photographers. Some traveled with soldiers, setting up studio tents, recording battles, and providing combatants with portraits of themselves and their comrades.

At the Battle of Arkansas Post, or Fort Hindman, Union soldiers eventually overwhelmed the Confederate defenders after a two-day siege in January, 1863.

The Confederate battle flag is the best-known of three flags adopted by the South during the war. The 11 stars of the "Southern Cross" represent the 11 Confederate states.

Fighting begins

The Union tried to entice the rebel states back by passing constitutional amendments promising not to interfere with slavery. But the time for discourse had passed. The first shots of the war were fired at 4:30 am on April 12, 1861, when the Confederates began to bombard Fort Sumter, South Carolina, the only Union fort within their borders that had refused to surrender. The fort soon fell, but this aggression provoked indignation throughout the North and volunteers flocked to join the Union army.

The Northern public's primary concern was to keep the Union intact. They believed the country's wealth, strength, and continued progress depended on it. Secession would weaken the Union, lead to further fragmentation, and nullify the country's experiment in self-government.

The Confederacy gained an important new member when Virginia seceded from the Union on April 17. Arkansas, Tennessee, and North Carolina followed. There were now 11 Confederate states. Twenty-three states remained in the Union, four of them (Missouri, Kentucky, Maryland, and Delaware) slave-owning.

The Confederacy was greatly outnumbered in terms of population. The Union also had a stronger economy, more industries, a vast railroad network, and a navy. But the Confederacy felt it had more at stake and could therefore battle on until the Union lost its enthusiasm for the fight. It also hoped that Great Britain would support its cause because of that country's dependence on cotton.

The Massachusetts Militia encounters opposition from pro-Confederate locals as it passes through Baltimore, Maryland. Although it remained part of the Union, Maryland was a slave-owning state and the loyalties of its citizens were thus divided.

The Confederate capital was moved to Richmond, Virginia, 105 miles (168 km) south of Washington. One early Virginia conflict, known later as the First Battle of Bull Run, ended in Union defeat in June, 1861. This made the North realize that it would have to better train its recruits and expect considerable sacrifices. The following April, on the western front, the Battle of Shiloh, Tennessee, ended in a draw, although it resulted in 13,700 Union and 10,700 Confederate casualties. The bloodiness that would mark this war was driven home to both sides.

An important Union strategy was the use of its navy to block Southern ports and prevent supplies reaching the Confederacy. The Union also targeted the Mississippi River, hoping to cut the Confederacy in two and sever a major supply route. Union forces captured the northern Mississippi region and then New Orleans. By the summer of 1862, only a small stretch of river remained in Confederate hands.

In Virginia, several Union attempts to capture Richmond were aborted due to poor military decisions. The generals who commanded the Army of the Potomac, as the Union's eastern forces were called, also faced a formidable foe in General Robert E. Lee. Lee secured many victories for the Confederates, including the Second Battle of Bull Run in August, 1862.

To court British public opinion, which was fiercely antislavery, and forestall any attempt by the British to side with the Confederacy, Lincoln prepared a document proclaiming all slaves in the seceded states would be freed. But he wanted to announce it after a significant Union victory. That came in September, 1862, at Antietam, Maryland, when General George B. McClellan drove Lee's invading forces back to Virginia. Lincoln issued his Emancipation Proclamation a few days later. It achieved nothing from a legal standpoint, but it did influence the British and also gave the Unionists another, higher reason to continue the fight.

None of this could make up for poor military decisions, however, and two months later the Union suffered a disastrous loss at Fredericksburg, after Ambrose E. Burnside ordered a suicidal attack against a well-fortified position held by Lee's troops. Another heavy loss followed in May, 1863.

That same month, the Union's Ulysses S. Grant laid siege to Vicksburg, Tennessee, the primary remaining Confederate stronghold along the Mississippi River. Rather than send his troops to Vicksburg's aid, Lee decided to remain in Virginia. He hoped that just one

more decisive victory was needed to turn some of the existing Union sentiment against the war into a resounding chorus. Congress had passed a compulsory draft that spring, prompting riots. The worst of these were in New York, where soldiers had to restore order.

In June, Lee marched his troops northward to Pennsylvania, a free state. The Army of the Potomac, under George G. Meade, followed. This led to the bloodiest battle of the Civil War, the Battle of Gettysburg. After three days of fighting, 28,000 Confederate soldiers and 23,000 Union soldiers lay dead or wounded. Lee, having lost more than a third of his army, retreated to Virginia.

A day after that battle had ended came news that Vicksburg had surrendered. A few days later, the entire Mississippi River was controlled by the Union. The following spring, the separate Union armies were placed under Grant's command. They began to concentrate on conquering the Confederate armies rather than on capturing their cities.

In May, 1864, Grant led one Union army across the Potomac into Virginia, while General William T. Sherman moved another Union army south from Tennessee into Georgia. By July, both had launched sieges, Grant on Petersburg (near Richmond), and Sherman on Atlanta. Neither assault brought fast results, and both Union armies suffered heavy casualties. In the North, public calls for peace increased.

Finally, at the beginning of September, the Confederate forces pulled out of Atlanta, and Sherman quickly occupied it. Meanwhile, Grant sent cavalry officer Philip Sheridan to Virginia's Shenandoah Valley. He drove out the Confederate forces and scorched the fertile farmland. Lincoln's popularity surged and he was reelected for a second term.

Confederate surrender

In Georgia, Sherman's 60,000 men torched Atlanta and then marched to the sea, leaving in their wake a blazing swath of land, 270 miles (440 km) long by 60 miles (97 km) wide. They then moved north, pinning down the Confederate forces in the Carolinas and Virginia. A few months later, Lee finally retreated from Petersburg and Richmond. Pursued by Grant, Lee surrendered his army on April 9, 1865. Other Confederate armies gave up over the next two months, and the last surrender took place in Galveston, Texas on June 2. The war that had torn apart a nation and claimed almost 1 million lives was over. To this day, it

remains the bloodiest American conflict in terms of the number of lives lost in proportion to the population.

Lincoln favored a conciliatory policy toward the renegade states. But he would not live to pursue that policy, for on April 14, 1865, he was assassinated by a Confederate sympathizer named John Wilkes Booth. The more radical elements of Lincoln's party assumed control. Their mood for revenge was exacerbated by the Southern states' intransigence—even before the Thirteenth Amendment to the Constitution had taken effect in December, 1865, outlawing slavery, the Southern states began passing "Black Codes," a system of laws designed to perpetuate the newly freed African-Americans' social and economic inferiority.

In March, 1867, Congress passed the *Reconstruction Act*. The former Confederate states (except for Tennessee, the only one to vote in favor of the Fourteenth Amendment, which extended citizenship to blacks) were to be treated as conquered provinces and ruled by military governors. Liberal laws and constitutions were forced through. Unfortunately, the official ranks contained more than a few Northern opportunists interested only in increasing the Southern states' debts for personal gain.

Eventually, the Southern states were readmitted into the Union and the Northern "carpetbaggers" driven out. By 1876, conservative state governments were in place throughout the former Confederacy, and Reconstruction was over. However, the bitter memories of the war and its aftermath would linger well into the next century.

The fall of the town of Vicksburg on July 4, 1863, was a breakthrough for the Union as it brought almost the entire Mississippi River under Northern control. The town is now the site of the Vicksburg National Military Park and Cemetery, one of the best-preserved Civil War battlefields.

CIVIL WAR TIMELINE	JULY 1861 Union army marches on Southern capital, Richmond, Virginia. Routed by Confederate forces at Bull Run, it is forced to retreat to Washington.	APRIL 1862 Confederate army counter-attacks Grant at Shiloh, but he holds his ground and Southern forces retreat to Mississippi. Union navy seizes New Orleans.	AUGUST 1862 Lee defeats Union army at Second Battle of Bull Run, drives Northern force out of Virginia, and proceeds to invade Maryland.	APRIL–MAY 1863 Union forces attack Lee in Virginia but are defeated at Chancellorville and obliged to retreat. Lee invades the North once more.	JULY 4, 1863 After a two-month siege, Grant finally takes Vicksburg, Mississippi, bringing most of the region under Northern control.	JUNE 1864 After a costly southward advance, Grant traps Lee's forces at Petersburg, outside Richmond, Virginia. The ensuing siege lasts for ten months.	APRIL 1865 Grant takes Richmond on April 3 and Lee surrenders six days later. Remnant Confederate forces continue fighting, but by June war is over.
	FEBRUARY 1861 War begins after Southern forces bombard Union outpost at Fort Sumter in Charleston, South Carolina, forcing Northern army to depart.	FEBRUARY 1862 Union forces under Brigadier-General Ulysses S. Grant capture key Southern strongholds of Forts Henry and Donelson in Tennessee.	JULY 1862 General George McClellan leads Union advance on Richmond, but is blocked by Confederate forces under General Robert E. Lee during Seven Days' Battles.	SEPTEMBER 1862 McClellan blocks Lee's advance at Battle of Antietam Creek, Maryland, where 24,000 men die. Lee retreats to Virginia.	JULY 1-3, 1863 Lee's force runs into Union army at Gettysburg, Pennsylvania. The ensuing battle results in over 50,000 casualties. Lee's army retreats south.	NOVEMBER 1863 Following Battle of Chattanooga, Grant drives Lee out of Tennessee. Union army led by General William T. Sherman seizes Knoxville.	SEPTEMBER–DECEMBER 1864 Sherman captures Atlanta, cuts a swath of destruction through Georgia, and then captures Savannah.

Immigration

A Vietnamese settler tends Asian vegetables in a Florida garden. Immigrant importation of traditional foods has greatly enriched American cuisine.

Immigrants disembark from the SS Prince Frederick Wilhelm at Ellis Island in 1915. Once they had been "processed," immigrants would normally travel to their final destination by rail.

Benjamin Franklin once complained that there were so many Germans moving to the English colonies that they would soon take over and that eventually everyone would speak German. Franklin's view of the situation was, however, somewhat skewed. Germans were clustered in the region around his hometown of Philadelphia, but in fact made up only 10 percent of the total colonial population of the United States. Franklin's ill-feeling toward the immigrants, however, resonates to the present. Native Americans constitute less than 2 percent of the population of the United States, making the other 98 percent immigrants or their descendants, yet resentment toward newcomers is a recurring characteristic of the immigrant experience in America.

In the seventeenth and eighteenth centuries, two-thirds of immigrants lived in economic bondage, either as indentured servants or slaves, and a few thousand were convicts. Yet despite this, the United States has come to represent freedom and opportunity for millions of people. A push-pull combination of forces brings the foreign-born to America, whether legally or otherwise. Pushed out of their homeland by financial stagnation, starvation, war, religious persecution, or other hardship, they are also drawn by the promise of stability, freedom, and financial success.

Fitting in

Each wave of newcomers, regardless of their place of origin, follows a distinctive social and economic pattern of adjustment and assimilation. Historically, immigrants tended to move in groups made up of extended family or former neighborhoods or villages. Many arrived without the necessary funds to move inland, resulting in congregations of newcomers in coastal cities, where they settled in the same areas as previous immigrants from their region. To this day, the proximity of their homes is often identified by the addition of the prefix "Little" or suffix "town" to their nation of origin, as in "Little Italy" and "Chinatown."

As a group, immigrants usually experience economic and social discrimination. Gradually they assimilate, and the children learn to speak English better than their parents, who lament the loss of the old culture. They become politically active, finan-

cially successful, and move on, no longer needing the support network provided by the old neighborhood. Within three or four generations, the neighborhood begins to change, as a new group with a different culture moves into the area.

In the process of assimilating, newcomers introduce words, place names, foods, celebrations, and spirit into the western European, Protestant culture that originally gave rise to the nation.

The arrival

Immigrants have been arriving since the 1630s, with peaks in the early 1850s, 1901–1910, and the 1980s. Since records began to be kept in 1820, over 56 million people have moved to American shores. Some 80,000 people left the British Isles for the New World in the first "Great Migration" of the 1630s, and the Irish dominated the flood of 2 million newcomers that arrived between 1845 and 1855. The mid-nineteenth century influx was the greatest proportionate migration in history, made possible by improvements in transportation. The third wave of nearly 9 million people arrived from southern and eastern Europe in the first decade of the twentieth century. If illegal-immigrant estimates were added to the numbers of legitimate arrivals in the 1980s, that decade would surpass all earlier totals. This last great wave of immigrants came from the Philippines, Korea, and other Asian nations, as well as Mexico and Latin America.

The classic arrival on American shores took place at Ellis Island in New York City's harbor, where the Statue of Liberty was often the first glimpse immigrants had of their new homeland. For 62 years, from 1892 to 1954, some 12 million immigrants were processed there. Ellis Island was only for the masses who arrived in steerage, as those who could afford first or second class were checked aboard the ship. Nearly half of America's population today is descended from ancestors who passed through Ellis Island.

A land of opportunity

Immigrants would have poured into the United States even if conditions in their homelands had not compelled them to leave. The economic pull of an expanding capitalist system was very powerful in the nineteenth and twentieth centuries, and increased settlement was essential to meet the demand for labor. By 1860, the textile industry was burgeoning, and the labor force in the mills of a place like Lowell, Massachusetts, was 50 percent Irish. The Irish built the canals in the 1820s, moved into mining and constructing railroads, and operated the steel mills following the Civil War. Immigrants became associated with certain

regions and trades: Poles, Slavs, and Italians with the mines of Pennsylvania; Greeks with New England textiles; and Polish Jews with the needle trades in New York City. When iron workers arrived from Sweden in the 1880s, most knew just three words of English: "Charlie," "Deere," and "Moline," referring to Charlie, the president of the John Deere Plow Company, of Moline, Illinois, where they knew a job was waiting. Women and children generally worked in the mills and provided domestic service.

The federal government itself encouraged migration during the Civil War by establishing a "contract labor" system reminiscent of the traditional indentured servant arrangements. The government paid the passage of potential workers and provided their wages for a period of time afterward. However, when businesses made a similar offer to attract workers for the railroads and other heavy tasks, abuses of the system led the government to outlaw the practice in 1885. The workers responded to poor wages, long hours, and unsafe conditions in the railroads and other industries with strikes and efforts at unionizing, but unity was often difficult to achieve because of ethnic divisions in the workforce.

Poor wages resulted in desperate living conditions for the majority of new arrivals in the nineteenth and early twentieth centuries, but successful mastery of the language and customs of America usually developed within a generation. Immigrants looked to those who preceded them to help find housing and jobs, and learn the rules of the system. Immigrant aid societies efficiently tended to the newcomers' needs, and after the Civil War young women of middle- and upper-class backgrounds, such as Jane Addams, established Settlement Houses in major northern and eastern cities, to provide language and culture classes, medical

By the 1870s, more than 40,000 Chinese immigrants lived in San Francisco, mainly in the city's Chinatown. Their numbers subsequently fell as a result of more restrictive immigration policies, then rose again from the 1960s onward. San Franciscans of Chinese origin now number over 100,000.

Many of America's immigrant communities have succeeded in preserving culinary traditions while adapting them to local tastes. In this 1960 photograph, two Jewish men savor a Chinese meal prepared by Chinese chefs according to kosher guidelines.

treatment, legal advice, and other assistance to immigrants living in crowded slums. Churches instituted Sunday School classes to assist in language acquisition, and the need to teach immigrant children about American ways encouraged the adoption of compulsory education and funding for public schools.

The politics of immigration

The politics of immigration reflect deep American prejudices that manifest themselves in restrictive legislation, lack of governmental protection, and discrimination. The nation's first immigration law, in 1790, aimed at restricting citizenship rather than movement, and allowed naturalized citizenship for "free white people" only. Later in the 1970s, the *Alien and Sedition Act* extended the length of residency required for naturalization in an effort to curb the growing popularity of the opposition Democratic–Republican Party, the first political home for most newcomers to the country for more than 200 years.

No laws attempted to curb the flow of the Irish in the middle of the nineteenth century, but they found abundant discriminatory signs in shops and boarding houses, such as "No Irish need apply." In the 1830s, when Catholicism became the nation's largest denomination, an acrimonious debate over whether to adopt the Catholic Bible or the Protestant Bible in Philadelphia schools spilled into the streets, and during New York City's Civil War draft riots, which dwarfed the antiwar protests of the 1960s, thousands of Irish joined in the melee.

IMMIGRATION TO AMERICA 1821–1989

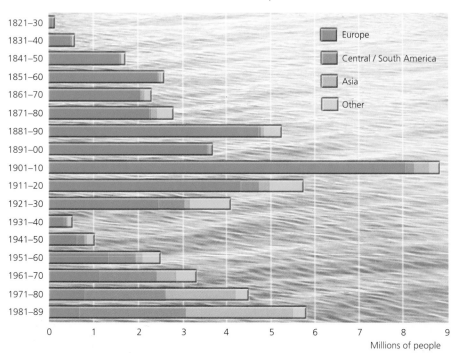

IMMIGRATION TO AMERICA 1821–1989

Legend:
- Europe
- Central / South America
- Asia
- Other

Y-axis (decades): 1821–30, 1831–40, 1841–50, 1851–60, 1861–70, 1871–80, 1881–90, 1891–00, 1901–10, 1911–20, 1921–30, 1931–40, 1941–50, 1951–60, 1961–70, 1971–80, 1981–89

X-axis: 0 1 2 3 4 5 6 7 8 9
Millions of people

Throughout the nineteenth century, immigration inspired the foundation of political organizations purporting to defend the native-born against the onslaught of foreigners. One of these organizations was nicknamed the "Know Nothings" for their rule of responding "I know nothing" when asked about their secret organization; it later became the American Party of the 1850s. Their platform was nativist and discriminatory. While the native-born were able to unite, immigrants were rarely able to bridge the ethnic gap in favor of coalition. Often the competition between ethnic groups for employment became violent, as when 10,000 Irish railroad workers clashed with a similar number of Chinese in the Utah desert upon the completion of the transcontinental line at Promontory Point in 1869. Clashes between the two groups also occurred in California throughout 1870s.

The Irish, experienced at organizing themselves against English rent-collectors and absentee landlords, enthusiastically entered the political arena and became the foundation of political machines in every major city in the North and Northeast. The Chinese and Japanese were less successful politically, and failed to prevent a series of acts, beginning in 1882, that stopped immigration from China. A "Gentlemen's Agreement" with Japan in 1905 had a similar aim.

Many people of Eastern European origin found a political home in the American Socialist Party, which elected 33 mayors and one Congressman in 1912, and consistently outvoted Republicans in the state of Florida for much of the twentieth century. The Socialists had little national power, however, and could not block passage of the most restrictive immigrant legislation in the nation's history, the *Immigration Act* of 1924. This act established quotas biased in favor of Western Europe. The result was a growth in the number of illegal immigrants from Mexico, Cuba, and other Latin American countries. Periodic legislation also prohibited the immigration of prostitutes, the insane, and anyone likely to need welfare.

The incarceration of immigrant Americans

During the first "Red Scare" immediately following World War I, immigrants of Eastern European descent were particularly targeted for arrest and incarceration in violation of the writ of habeas corpus and due process. Over 200 were summarily deported aboard a ship nicknamed the "Red Ark" for having communist, anarchist, or socialist beliefs, or simply for not being able to speak English. A protracted trial and appeal in the mid-1920s failed to save the lives of Nicola Sacco and Bartolomeo Vanzetti, accused of murder but convicted more for their immigrant status and anarchistic philosophy than by the evidence.

The most heinous action by the government occurred during World War II, when both Japanese immigrants and their American-born children were forced to give up their property and move to internment camps on the West Coast for security reasons. Some German Americans were publicly harassed, but the government took no action against them or Italian Americans. The Supreme Court sanctioned the treatment of the Japanese Americans at the time, but subsequent decisions condemned their treatment and ordered reparations for the property losses. Mexican workers allowed entry into California during the war, to make up for the labor shortage when the Japanese Americans were incarcerated, fought local nativists and military personnel stationed in Los Angeles in the "Zoot Suit" riot of 1943.

New quotas

The legal climate did not alter until the *Immigration Act* of 1965, which established quotas favoring the Western Hemisphere. The end of the Vietnam War led to an increase in the Asian population and a subsequent rise in tension, which erupted in violence in Texas.

Anticommunist sentiment opened the door to a flow of refugees from Central America and Cuba in the 1980s, and several riots followed in Miami, Florida. In 1987, the Immigration Service offered 10,000 special visas to citizens of nations historically prevented by law from moving to the United States; a staggering 1.4 million people applied.

Koreans and Hispanics clashed in Los Angeles at the end of the twentieth century, and criminals continued to prey on their own kind, most notably in the "sweatshops"

discovered in the computer industry in the 1990s. Entrepreneurs from various Asian countries had set up houses inhabited by a dozen or more of their compatriots, who were employed as computer operators and programmers and worked extraordinarily long hours in appalling conditions.

Nativist thinking later inspired the California legislature to attempt to deny welfare access to naturalized citizens. Today, legislatures debate bilingual education, and English-only amendments are repeatedly proposed in Congress.

Enriching America's culture

The government's rhetoric of opportunity and equality appears hypocritical when considered in the light of the litany of intolerance and injustice, but conditions in the United States have almost always been better than those the immigrants left behind, and economic, political, and social success are at least attainable. The contributions of individual immigrants to the arts, science, business, and industry have been enormous, and the strength and size of the nation's middle and upper classes, and the ever-increasing numbers who continue to arrive, help validate the rhetoric. In 1990, the United States welcomed more than twice as many immigrants as all other countries in the world combined. For the first time, the majority came not from Europe, but from Mexico and the Philippines. The Hispanic community now extends up the East Coast and north to Chicago, as well as into the Pacific Northwest, and, with Asian-Americans, is the fastest-growing segment of the nation's population.

Cigar roller Roberto Ramirez demonstrates his craft in his shop in Tampa, Florida. Almost 17 percent of Florida's population is of Hispanic or Latino origin.

The Gilded Age

Advances in glass manufacturing led to a boom in art glass in the late nineteenth century. Louis Comfort Tiffany, the maker of this window (1890), became the leading producer of this type of high-quality, iridescent glassware.

Remarkable social and economic changes swept through the nation after the Civil War. Some states, most notably in the Northeast, had already developed manufacturing bases. But the pace of industrialization now accelerated, thanks in part to transportation and communication breakthroughs and the establishment of rail networks. Trains had only penetrated half the continent in 1865; just four years later, the first transcontinental line was opened. By 1890, there were five such lines.

American inventors such as Thomas Edison were equally prolific—he patented the phonograph and electric light bulb in the late 1870s. In 1876, the telephone, invented by Alexander Graham Bell, caused a sensation at the Centennial Exposition in Philadelphia. The first long-distance telephone service connected Boston with New York in 1884, the same year that the world's first skyscraper, a 10-story marvel, was built in Chicago. By the end of the century, the United States had become the world's technological and industrial leader.

Changes on the social front

The industrial boom, dwindling frontier lands (the frontier was officially deemed closed in 1890), and agricultural innovations that enabled fewer farmers to produce more crops, prompted many Americans to permanently abandon their family farms. The proportion of Americans living in cities doubled between 1860 and 1900, by which time 40 percent of the population was based in urban centers.

A train travels over the newly completed bridge at Promontory, Utah in 1869. The bridge marked the creation of the first trans-continental rail link in America, as it joined the Union Pacific to the Central Pacific railroad.

The country's overall population also swelled, almost doubling from 1870 to 1900. Much of the increase came from overseas. Many of the new arrivals came from southern and eastern Europe. Their customs, languages, and religions differed from those of the vast majority of Americans, who traced their roots to northern and western Europe. A nativist backlash developed. Its supporters successfully pushed for a law to exclude Chinese immigrants, but otherwise failed to stem the tide.

The lot of southern African-Americans worsened after Reconstruction, once conservative state governments had regained power throughout the South. Tennessee passed the first so-called "Jim Crow" segregation law in 1881. Similar legislation was soon passed through-out the region, legally sanctioning the separation of the races. An 1896 Supreme Court decision ruled that segregation was constitutional if it provided for "separate but equal" facilities. In reality, this was rarely the case.

Corruption spreads

Rising wages elevated many families to the middle class. But the country's economic progress was marred by endemic corruption. Land speculators hyped worthless properties in the frontier regions. Brash opportunists flocked to the booming railroad industry, hawking counterfeit stocks, manipulating accounts, and enriching themselves at the expense of naive investors. "Robber barons" such as Jason "Jay" Gould and Cornelius Vanderbilt grew spectacularly

rich. Author Samuel Clemens (aka Mark Twain) captured the titans' shallow acquisitiveness (and gave the era its name) in his 1873 novel, *The Gilded Age.*

The government's laissez-faire policies facilitated corruption. Moreover, many lawmakers actively encouraged it, as long as they could pocket their share of the spoils. Corruption infiltrated all government ranks; even Congressional seats could be bought. A system of patronage perpetuated the abuses by allowing officials to give public-payroll jobs to people they could manipulate. The most notorious crooked politician was New York City's William Marcy "Boss" Tweed. He headed Tammany Hall, a party committee that effectively controlled city politics. During his tenure, Tweed and his appointees skimmed up to $20 million from government coffers.

Corruption even changed the outcome of the 1876 presidential election. Democrat Samuel J. Tilden won the majority of the popular vote. He would have also prevailed in the decisive electoral college vote (in which electors are supposed to vote according to their states' results), but Republican operatives tried to tamper with several key states' returns. Congress set up a commission to judge the corruption charges. But its members simply voted along party lines, effectively giving the presidency to Republican Rutherford B. Hayes.

Business influence expands

Many emerging business leaders soon realized they could gain more by cooperation than competition. A wave of consolidations swept through many industries. Some went so far as to form trusts, which effectively gave the member businesses a monopoly over an industry, allowing them to set whatever prices they wished. The first and best known of these was the Standard Oil Trust, which John D. Rockefeller and his associates formed in 1882.

Although some of the best known business titans were self-made men, most came from privileged backgrounds. With immense wealth came immense power; they were not reticent to wield it, usually in the service of increasing their bounty. Yet many among them were equally interested in giving money away, endowing libraries and other public institutions.

Agitation for reform

The tycoons' largesse didn't extend to their customers or employees. Workers enjoyed no social safety net; they were at their employers' mercy, particularly during the depressions of the mid-1870s and mid-1890s. Like the business owners, laborers saw the advantage of banding together. The first effective, national union was the Knights of Labor, formed in 1869. The group first tried to improve workers' lives through politics and education. Then it began to apply economic pressure, usually in the form of strikes. In 1886 alone, some 600,000 workers were involved in nearly 1,600 strikes. They were opposed by both

business owners and the government, which sometimes, in the interests of keeping order, sent troops to break the strikes. Violence often ensued, and some strikers paid for their activism with their lives.

The labor unions met with limited success: their strikes prevented railroad wage cuts in 1885, for example. But their hard-won public sympathy dissipated as a result of the 1886 Haymarket riot, when anarchists exploded a bomb at a strike protest meeting, killing seven police officers.

Nevertheless, widespread public outrage finally forced some feeble economic and political reforms. Patronage, though it didn't disappear, lost some of its power after Congress passed an Act in 1883 to curtail the practice. Under pressure, the federal government also intervened on behalf of consumers. The 1887 *Interstate Commerce Act* ordered railroads to, among other things, charge reasonable and consistent rates. The Interstate Commerce Commission, established to oversee the Act, became the first regulatory commission in the nation's history, establishing a precedent that in economic standoffs, the government's role was to protect the powerless.

The vaguely written 1890 *Sherman Antitrust Act* also proved an important step in curbing businesses' power. These early measures, though largely ineffective, established the principle that businesses were subject to human laws, and in so doing, set the stage for the more meaningful reforms of the twentieth century.

Cable cars pass through Market Street, San Francisco in 1895, providing public transportation for the rapidly increasing numbers of metropolitan residents.

Patented by Thomas Edison in 1877, the phonograph allowed the recording and reproduction of sound. Uncle Sam doffs his hat to the new invention in this advert for the Triumph model.

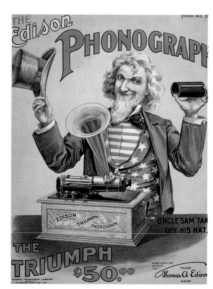

THE AMERICAN CENTURY

1900–1909

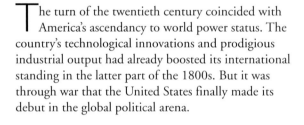

The Wright brothers demonstrate their airplane to observers. The use of a four-cylinder gasoline engine allowed the Wrights to make the world's first powered flight on December 13, 1903.

As the mass production of cars initiated a new era of personal transportation, companies targeted new motorists with advertisements such as this for tires (c. 1909).

The turn of the twentieth century coincided with America's ascendancy to world power status. The country's technological innovations and prodigious industrial output had already boosted its international standing in the latter part of the 1800s. But it was through war that the United States finally made its debut in the global political arena.

An imperial legacy

The Spanish–American War—fanned by unscrupulous newspaper publishers who ran inflammatory stories with little regard for truth—had lasted just four months in 1898. Spain was by then a mere shadow of its former self; its navy easily fell to the superior American fleets it faced in Cuba and the Philippines. At the end of the conflict, the United States acquired several former Spanish colonies in the Caribbean (Puerto Rico) and the Pacific (Guam and the Philippines). (Also in 1898, but unrelated to the war, the United States annexed Hawaii and, a couple of years later, acquired the South Pacific islands now known as American Samoa.)

The United States suddenly had a far-flung empire. Some Americans considered this natural and inevitable. America's domestic frontier had finally been settled; growth seemed to demand overseas expansion. Besides, the other world powers of the time all had empires. Current social Darwinist theories also legitimized colonialism by deeming it natural that strong nations conquer weak ones, leaving the fittest to survive.

Unrest in the Philippines

But not all Americans liked the implications of empire. Some argued that it violated the nation's founding principle of self-determination, most notably in the case of the Philippines. Unlike the other colonies, the Philippines had millions of native inhabitants who yearned for independence, and were willing to fight for it, in a guerrilla war that began in 1899. America ruthlessly retaliated and finally quelled the rebellion in 1902. But they also granted the Filipinos partial self-rule (which turned into almost complete home rule in 1916). At the cost of more than 4,000 American soldiers' lives and the lives of some 20,000 Filipinos, the Philippine Insurrection proved longer-lived and far bloodier than the Spanish–American War that had set the stage for it.

Caribbean interests

Closer to home, the United States dominated the Caribbean in a less brutal fashion. It had promised Cuba independence as a result of the Spanish–American War, and reluctantly lived up to its promise. But the United States kept a hand in Cuban affairs by agreeing to withdraw its soldiers only if Cuba, in turn, would agree to allow the United States to interfere in the country's affairs whenever Cuba's independence or financial stability were threatened. The United States also wanted to use Guantánamo Bay as a naval base. Cuba had little choice but to accept the terms.

The United States also found other ways to carve out a regional sphere of influence. To minimize the risk of violent international conflicts erupting in Latin America, President Theodore Roosevelt announced that the United States would henceforth step in to collect defaulted foreign national debts in the region. The United States had become the self-appointed police officer of the Western Hemisphere.

The Panama Canal

The time was now ripe for the United States to act on a long-standing ambition—to build a canal across Central America, to give American merchants easier access to Pacific markets. The Spanish–American War, fought in the Pacific and the Caribbean, helped convince the government that such a project was also a military necessity.

First, some long-standing obstacles had to be overcome. The most pressing of these was the threat of tropical diseases such as yellow fever. This problem was all but eliminated when US military surgeon Walter Reed, working in Cuba after the Spanish–American War, determined that yellow fever was spread by mosquitoes rather than poor sanitation. Controlling mosquito populations, it was reasoned, should keep the disease in check. The next problem was diplomatic. An 1850 agreement with Britain stipulated that neither nation would monopolize such a canal, if one were built; yet there seemed little point in building a canal that would benefit other countries. So in 1901, the Americans managed to convince the British (then preoccupied with the Boer War) to sign a new treaty giving the United States full control over any canal it built.

The question now became where to build it. The Central American isthmus was at its narrowest (41 miles [65 km]) in Panama. But the terrain there was hilly. Further north, a longer passage through Nicaragua could be dug at sea level. However, worries about volcano activity eventually scuttled that option, and Panama prevailed.

The final stumbling block involved getting permission from Colombia, whose borders encompassed Panama. The Colombian senate rejected a proposed treaty. Some Panamanians hinted to the United States that, if they could be assured of American assistance, they may revolt and press for independence. The United States gladly obliged and, as soon as American warships arrived to block Colombia from retaliating, the Panamanians declared their independence. The new nation of Panama then signed a canal treaty with the United States, leasing it an 11-mile (18-km) wide strip of land in perpetuity. In return, the United States promised to guarantee Panama's independence.

Construction began in May, 1904; the first ships passed through the finished canal a decade later, in August, 1914.

Prosperity and problems

While Americans asserted themselves on foreign soils, great numbers of foreigners were landing on American shores. Immigration reached historic heights (not surpassed since) from 1905–07, when 3,400,000 people were admitted into the country.

Technological innovations were also transforming society and shrinking the world. The first trans-Atlantic radio telegraphic transmission was made in 1901. Henry Ford introduced the assembly line (which made cheap automobiles possible) in 1903; the first Model T, costing just $850, was produced in 1908. Also in 1903, Orville and Wilbur Wright flew the world's first plane in Kitty Hawk, North Carolina.

But the nation's prosperity masked a plethora of social problems and general disaffection. Commercial and local government power had become concentrated in the hands of big corporations and political bosses. Laissez-faire policies gave businesses free rein to exploit workers and overlook safety and other considerations. A variety of groups (together known as the Progressive movement) agitated for reform on many fronts. They worked to relieve suffering in urban slums, and campaigned for women's suffrage, alcohol prohibition, natural conservation, and consumer safety legislation, among other things. Roosevelt, himself a Progressive, pushed through a moderate reform agenda. His legacies include the *Pure Food and Drug Act* of 1906 and the setting aside of millions of acres of land as national parks.

Factory workers at the Ford Motor Company plant in Detroit, Michigan, assemble a Model T automobile. Launched in 1908, the car was so popular that Ford opened a second large factory in 1910 to increase production.

Chamber cranes in the Pedro Miguel locks, Panama, during the construction of the Panama canal c. 1908. The canal, completed in 1914, provided shipping with a passage from the Atlantic to the Pacific, without the need to pass around the tip of South America.

1910–1919

America's premier wildlife artist, Charles Livingston Bull (1874–1932), was commissioned by the army to produce this World War I recruitment poster.

RIGHT: Suffragettes march through the streets of New York in 1916 to support President Woodrow Wilson's campaign for women's votes.

Economic and political reforms

The reform movement continued well into the century's second decade. Its popular appeal was reflected in the election of Woodrow Wilson, an idealist and a Progressive, in 1912. A number of important economic and political reforms were passed during Wilson's two terms. The sixteenth amendment to the Constitution legalized a federal personal income tax. The seventeenth amendment allowed for the direct election of senators, stripping some power away from party bosses. The *Clayton Antitrust Act* strengthened and extended the existing *Sherman Antitrust Act*, and gave employees the right to strike in certain situations. The Federal Reserve System, granting the government some control over the nation's financial institutions, was also established during this period to help stabilize the economy.

Although American expansionism had run its course, the United States continued to throw its weight around the region. It interfered in several minor Caribbean issues. More significantly, in 1913, it refused to recognize Mexico's self-appointed new president on moral grounds (he had ordered a rival killed). The United States helped Mexican rebels to oust him, going as far as to occupy the coastal town of Vera Cruz. Other Latin American countries denounced the American response as arrogant imperialism.

War in Europe

During World War I, crystal radios such as this were used to convey messages in the field. Containing crystalline minerals that could detect radio signals, they did not need electrical power or batteries.

But more pressing international problems soon drew America into European affairs. Conflicting territorial ambitions had prompted the European powers to align themselves into two factions: the Central Powers (Germany and Austria-Hungary) and the Allies (Great Britain, France, and Russia). The stage was set for war; all that was needed was a crisis to spark it. That came in June 1914, when the heir to the Austro-Hungarian throne was assassinated in Sarajevo, an outpost of the Austro-Hungarian empire. Austria-Hungary accused neighboring Serbia of complicity and declared war. Russia promptly backed Serbia, and the other countries fell in line on one side or the other. By August, the Great War (as World War I was then called) had begun.

Wilson hoped to keep the United States out of the conflict, and urged Americans to act and think neutrally. Nevertheless, many Americans sympathized with the Allies, especially following reports of German brutality in Belgium. American banks also lent money to Great Britain and France.

In Europe, Germany was trying win the war by capitalizing on the Allies' weak points. Aware of Britain's dependence on imported food, Germany decided to try and starve the nation by blockading its ports, using a formidable new German invention, the submarine. Germany declared a blockade zone around Britain and warned all ships, including neutral ones, to stay away. The United States, mindful of its commercial interests, refused to sever its sea links with Britain. On May 7, 1915, a German submarine torpedoed the liner *Lusitania* off the Irish coast. Almost 1,200 people, including 128 Americans, went down with the ship. In the face of vigorous American protests, Germany promised to end its blockade.

The United States then learned of German plans to sabotage American factories making materials for the Allies. Alarmed, Wilson directed the country to begin military preparations. Meanwhile, the war in Europe dragged on. British ships severed Germany's sea links, hurting Germany enough to convince it, in early 1917, that it could not win the war without relaunching its submarine blockade on Britain. The United States again refused to sacrifice its commercial interests, and ignored the warnings. One of its vessels, the *Housatonic*, was promptly sunk by a blockading German submarine.

America enters the war

Britain then intercepted a telegram revealing German plans to encourage Mexico to reconquer its one-time territories in the United States, should the United States enter the war on the side of the Allies. Britain forwarded this message to the Americans, who were indignant. Then, in March, the Russian revolution ended the czars' reign. The Great War now pitted democracies (the Allies) against autocracies (the Central Powers). After a German submarine sank yet another American ship, the United States declared war on Germany in April, 1917. Wilson justified it as a drastic but necessary step to "make the world safe for democracy."

Wilson wasted little time in establishing a military draft and preparing to send troops to Europe for the first time in the country's history. The first contingents, led by General John J. Pershing, landed in France in June. More soldiers arrived and trained throughout the winter while the Germans hung back, preparing what they hoped would be their final push. They had already broken the Eastern Front and, in March 1918, forced the Russians to sign a peace treaty relinquishing a great deal of territory. They could now afford to focus all their attention on the Western Front, along France's northeast border.

In late March, the Germans broke through the front and advanced toward Paris. The Allies were losing hope when the Americans finally joined the battle in force. Fighting as independent units, as Pershing had demanded, the Americans stopped the German advance at Château-Thierry, then took the offensive at nearby Belleau Wood. The Americans won the battle, though at a high cost (half the soldiers were either killed or wounded). The Germans recovered and prepared another advance. They were again met by American soldiers, who were reinforced by Allied troops. Together they forced the Germans back.

Finally an American army half a million strong attacked the German line in September, forcing it to retreat almost to the German border. Austria-Hungary realized the war was lost and surrendered in early November. Germany followed suit a week later, and the armistice was announced on November 11, 1918.

The war had cost 8,400,000 lives, 53,400 of them American. Another 63,000 Americans had died outside of battle (mostly of influenza), and 204,000 had been wounded. Yet America's losses paled in comparison with Europe's devastation. Of the world's great powers, only the United States and Japan emerged from the Great War undiminished. And of the two, one stood higher—the United States had become the world's most powerful nation.

After the war

Wilson hoped the country could use its new-found status to ensure a lasting world peace. He championed the idea of a League of Nations (written into the Treaty of Versailles) that would peacably resolve future conflicts. But Congressional Republicans opposed him, fearing it would make the United States subordinate in times of war. Wilson tried to rally public support for the treaty, but Congress rejected it.

Meanwhile, the war had encouraged intolerance and xenophobia to flourish domestically. The Anti-Radical Division (later the Federal Bureau of Investigation) was established in 1919 to ferret out subversives. Also that year, the prohibitionists—who had played on anti-German sentiments to turn the public against beer brewers (many of whom were of German descent)—celebrated the passing of the eighteenth Amendment to the US Constitution. It outlawed the alcohol trade and launched the Prohibition era.

Barrels of beer are emptied into the sewer by authorities as prohibition begins. In January 1919, Congress outlawed the manufacture, sale, and transport of "intoxicating beverages."

A new era of postwar fun and travel is captured by this seaside postcard from the 1920s. An airship, hot air balloon, and airplanes show the new transport options available.

1920–1929

Lingering post-war xenophobia, together with the anti-radical sentiments that swept through the United States in the wake of Russia's 1917 Bolshevik revolution, culminated in a national "Red Scare" at the turn of the decade. The newly established precursor to the FBI, having declared war on socialists, communists, and other radicals, arrested thousands of suspects in the first half of 1920. Many were innocent people tarred by association or circumstance. In the name of national security, government officials violated civil liberties with impunity, until the scare died down later that year.

The dawn of the 1920s also coincided with what would prove to be the Progressive movement's last hurrah: the ratification of the nineteenth amendment to the US Constitution, giving women the right to vote. Two decades of reform agitation and a world war had wearied the public. People yearned for a return to "normalcy," as 1920 Republican presidential candidate Warren G. Harding called it. After winning office, Harding and a like-minded Congress steered a pro-business course. His administration also negotiated history's first effective arms-reduction agreement with the world's other great naval powers.

Growing intolerance

There was considerably less political will to combat intolerance. Responding to anti-immigrant sentiments, Congress sharply curbed immigration in 1921. The *Emergency Quota Act* limited the annual intake from each country to three percent of the existing US residents from that country. Thus ended America's greatest immigrant influx, which had seen almost 25 million people enter the country over the previous four decades. In 1924, President Calvin Coolidge (who had succeeded Harding upon his death the previous year) signed the *National Origins Act*, which made the quota system permanent (it was finally dismantled in 1965). The Act also lowered the acceptable annual intake to two percent of existing US residents from each country, and introduced a formula to guarantee that the majority of future immigrants would come from northwest Europe. The Act completely excluded Asians.

The Ku Klux Klan also seized on the national mood. The group's hate campaign against African-Americans, Jews, and Catholics spread from the South to other regions, particularly the Midwest and North, where many African-Americans had migrated in search of better opportunities. The group's membership rose to more than 3 million in the mid-1920s, before corruption and other scandals caused the numbers to diminish.

Urbanization

Much of the intolerance was fundamentally a reaction against the rapid pace of change across American society. The population base had permanently shifted from rural to urban areas: the 1920 census showed that, for the first time, more than half of all Americans lived in urban centers with more than 2,500 inhabitants. The migration continued throughout the decade—by 1930, about 45 percent

A doorman stands outside the famous Cotton Club, opened in 1923 in Harlem, New York City. Cashing in on demand for alcohol and entertainment, many gangsters opened clubs during the prohibition years which produced a booming jazz music scene.

Prohibition also left its mark on the decade (it was not repealed until 1933). Alcohol consumption actually increased as people either made their own "moonshine," ordered supplies from "bootleggers," or flocked to the countless illegal bars known as "speakeasies." Lucrative profits from the illegal alcohol trade, combined with inadequate government enforcement, led to a rise in organized crime. Larger-than-life gangsters such as Chicago's Al Capone gained international notoriety during their brief and violent careers.

Economic collapse

The period's prosperity also spawned greed. By the mid-1920s, the booming economy had encouraged many people to speculate on the stock market. The "greater fool" principle—promising an endless chain of speculators—convinced people to continue buying shares even as their prices skyrocketed. After exhausting their cash reserves, people borrowed money to buy more stocks. By 1928, the stock market valuation was swinging up and down erratically. New President Herbert Hoover sensed that a sharp downturn might follow, but was reluctant to allow the federal government to interfere.

The stock market was not the only danger sign; various other economic factors were portents of trouble. The agriculture sector had been struggling for a decade. Many poorly managed and little super-vised banks had overextended themselves. Consumer spending was stagnating. By spring 1929, factory production began to decrease. The stock market continued to perform erratically until early October. Then on October 18, the value of many blue-chip company stocks dropped sharply. Other stocks followed suit. By October 24, people were talking about a "panic." The New York banking community bought large quantities of stocks to try to stabilize prices, and the market responded with a brief and partial recovery.

But then on October 29, 1929, "Black Tuesday," the market crashed. More than 16 million shares were traded that day. The 50 leading stocks lost half of their value, on average, in just two months. People's life savings evaporated. The nation realized that its economy was profoundly sick.

Increased prosperity, the building of new highways, and cheaper cars led to a motoring boom and the popularity of automobiles such as this 1920s Lanchester.

LEFT: Panicked stock traders crowd the sidewalks outside the New York Stock Exchange on October 29, 1929 ("Black Tuesday"), the day the American stockmarket crashed.

of Americans lived in just 96 urban areas that each had more than 100,000 inhabitants.

Manufacturing now surpassed farming as an occupation. Rising productivity translated to higher wages and mass prosperity. Thanks to expanded consumer credit schemes, more and more people could afford to buy recently invented products such as washing machines. Cheap automobiles and new highways facilitated movement and enabled suburbs to grow up around cities. Radios and movies expanded the horizons of people's daily lives.

The Roaring Twenties

Women, emboldened by their voting rights victory, wanted to retain the independence they'd enjoyed during the Great War while the men were fighting overseas. The emancipated "flappers" rebelled by discarding their corsets, and by smoking and drinking in public. Young people in general rebelled against attempts to restore pre-war social conventions.

But affluence and carefree attitudes also masked a hollow materialism and an erosion of shared values, as articulated by authors like F. Scott Fitzgerald. The men and women who came of age in the 1920s were called "the Lost Generation." They were portrayed as struggling (unsuccessfully) to find meaningful values in an unstable society. They embraced a new type of music, jazz, whose loosely structured style grew out of the songs of dispossessed Southern slaves.

The mass production of radios, such as this five-valve battery wireless (1925) with amplifier on top, created a new national audience for popular entertainment. By 1928, over 75,000 radios per week were being produced.

1930–1939

Built in just 14 months in the depths of the Depression, the Empire State building was winner of a contest to design the tallest building in the world. This plaque, inside the building, celebrates its official opening by President Hoover on on May 1, 1931.

RIGHT: President Roosevelt delivers one of his weekly radio "fireside chats" to the nation.

The wives of unemployed workers line up to receive hand-outs of food from the New Hope Mission, New York City, during the Depression.

The Great Depression

The 1930s were a time of domestic and international upheaval. The stock market crash in October 1929 had plunged the country into the Great Depression. Bewilderment turned to despair as industrial production stagnated and unemployment soared. In the spring of 1930, almost four million American workers were unemployed. The number doubled within a year and continued to grow, until by 1933, almost a third of the workforce (between 13 and 16 million people) was without work. Those who kept their jobs didn't necessarily fare much better, as wages plummeted. Farmers, already struggling, found it even more difficult to make a profit; many lost their farms.

Although other industrialized nations had well-established, centralized social safety nets, the United States left such tasks to private charities and local governments. The scope of the Great Depression soon overwhelmed these institutions, leaving many people on their own to face malnutrition and the threat of starvation. President Herbert Hoover, a self-made man who championed the virtues of rugged individualism and unbridled capitalism, steadfastly refused to give direct federal relief to individuals. Instead, his administration tried (with little success) to stimulate business and private charity.

The economic crisis spread to Europe and the rest of the world in 1931. The global money pinch, in turn, caused foreigners to withdraw their money from American stocks and banks, further harming the US economy. More than 500 American banks failed that

October. Hoover persuaded the nation's insurance companies to halt foreclosures. He also convinced remaining banks to pool their money to save troubled financial institutions.

These initiatives failed to reverse the economic slide. But Hoover persevered. In January, 1932, the government established a Reconstruction Finance Corporation to lend money to businesses. That summer, Hoover signed an *Emergency Relief Act* authorizing the government to loan money to states for welfare programs. But he continued to oppose direct federal welfare proposals.

Social unrest had grown as the situation worsened. "Hunger riots" broke out in some areas as desperate

people looted grocery stores. In the spring of 1932, about 30,000 war veterans arrived in Washington to pressure Congress into passing a proposal that would allow veterans' bonuses (due for payment in 1925) to be paid immediately. The House of Representatives passed the bill, but the Senate rejected it. The veterans, who had camped on the city's Anacostia River flats, resisted police eviction efforts. Hoover ordered federal troops to drive the "bonus army" out. In the ensuing struggle, two veterans and a baby were killed, and more than 1,000 people were injured. The government's heavy-handedness outraged the public.

A new deal

Americans showed their desire for new leadership by voting overwhelmingly for Democrat Franklin Delano Roosevelt in the 1932 presidential election. Calling for a "new deal for the American people," Roosevelt had signalled plans to experiment with ways to solve the nation's economic woes. His optimistic inaugural address urged Americans to maintain hope for the future.

Working with a largely Democratic Congress, Roosevelt quickly set to work. He ordered all banks to close for a "bank holiday," then allowed only the better-managed ones to re-open. The federal government granted itself powers over the remaining banks and all gold transactions. (This was the first of many expansions of federal powers during Roosevelt's tenure.) Roosevelt also launched his weekly radio "fireside chats," to both reassure and inform the public about how his plans were progressing.

Roosevelt's overall plan involved cutting federal costs where possible, then redirecting that money (supplemented by borrowed funds) toward massive spending programs to relieve want and revive the economy. Congress went into a legislative frenzy to pass the so-called New Deal. Among its first initiatives was the Civilian Conservation Corps, which employed 500,000 youths in a variety of conservation projects. The government also committed federal funds to state welfare programs; subsidized farms and regulated farm prices; helped farmers stave off foreclosures; and paid workers to develop the impoverished Tennessee Valley.

Reform for recovery

The most ambitious of Roosevelt's early initiatives was the *National Industrial Recovery Act*, giving the government broad powers to regulate many aspects of the economy. It was roundly criticized, and a government report later found that it actually exacerbated economic problems. The Supreme Court eventually deemed the Act unconstitutional. Nevertheless, it helped set the stage for a landmark piece of labor legislation—the 1935 *Wagner Labor Relations Act*— which forbade employers to use unfair labor practices.

The unions seized on this to launch a massive labor organization drive.

More reforms followed, in line with Roosevelt's dictum that the government should lead society and resolve conflicts. In 1935, the Works Progress Administration was established to provide work for unemployed people. Over the next six years, the WPA spent about $11 billion employing 3.5 million people to work on some 250,000 projects. These ran the gamut from writing books to constructing public buildings. Through other initiatives, the government supported young people who wanted to continue their education, and introduced electricity to previously unserved rural areas. As the economy began showing signs of recovery, the spending was rolled back. But the economy foundered again, and the programs were resurrected.

Roosevelt also signed various consumer protection laws, including the *Securities and Exchange Act* to police stock and bond sales. He also established the Federal Deposit Insurance Corporation which insured bank deposits up to $5,000 against loss. One of the most significant pieces of legislation, however, was the *Social Security Act*. In 1935, this Act brought the United States in line with other industrialized nations by guaranteeing basic security against unemployment, disability, and old age. Also that year, a system of graduated taxes was introduced to place the biggest financial burden on the wealthy.

Unrest in Europe

Late in the decade, international developments grew more ominous and began to distract Americans from their domestic woes. A series of aggressive moves by Japan (which seized the Chinese province of Manchuria in 1931), Italy (which invaded Ethiopia in 1935, and Albania in 1939), and finally Germany (which, after annexing Austria in 1938, seized Czechoslovakia in 1939) prompted the European powers to form alliances. Matters came to a head in September 1939, when Germany (allied with Russia) invaded Poland. Great Britain and France honored a pledge to Poland, and declared war on Germany. Europe once again plunged into battle.

Built at Black Canyon on the Colorado River between 1931 and 1935, the Hoover Dam provided much needed employment as well as electricity and water for the Southwest.

LEFT: Growth in advertising and mass market production in the 1930s led to the appearance of identifiably American products. In 1938, journalist William Allen White described Coca-Cola as "the sublimated esssence of all that America stands for."

Champagne celebrations mark the end of prohibition in this contemporary print. Bowing to public pressure, Roosevelt finally repealed the ban on alcohol in February 1933.

1940–1949

B25 bombers are assembled at the North American Aviation factory, Kansas City, in 1942.

During World War II, many American companies produced patriotic, war-related advertisements, such as this Coca-Cola score pad from 1943.

Escalating world conflict

The 1940s began with Europe embroiled in its second large-scale war in less than 25 years. Having already appropriated Austria, Czechoslovakia and Poland, Germany turned its sights westward. By July, 1940, Germany's Adolf Hitler had conquered Denmark, Norway, Luxembourg, the Netherlands, Belgium and France. His rapid advance through Europe troubled the still neutral United States, which began to worry that it too would be unable to withstand a direct German attack. Still maintaining its neutrality, it began to build planes and naval vessels. In September, 1940, America's first peace-time draft began enlisting all men between the ages of 21 and 35 for a year's military service.

An overwhelming majority of Americans sympathized with the Allies (Great Britain and France), rather than the Axis powers (Germany and Italy). America's claims to neutrality eroded later that year, when it sent planes, destroyers and munitions to England, to help it fend off a prolonged German air attack. Then Congress passed the *Lend-Lease Act*, allowing the United States to supply war materials to any country whose defense it deemed vital to its own interests; by 1942, some three dozen countries were receiving such goods.

Tensions between the United States and Germany grew in 1941, as Germany continued expanding its borders. It conquered Greece and Yugoslavia, then turned against its former ally, Russia. The United States seized Axis ships and froze Axis assets.

Germany retaliated, sinking American merchant ships and firing at American destroyers.

The United States had also been keeping a close eye on Japan, which had imperial ambitions of its own. To serve notice that it would not stand by and give Japan control of the Pacific Rim, the United States moved its Pacific fleet from San Diego to Pearl Harbor, Hawaii. It also restricted trade with Japan and gave aid to China, whose Manchurian province the Japanese had conquered. Japan raised the stakes in September, 1940, when it signed a mutual defense treaty with Germany and Italy. When US–Japan talks stalled, war seemed inevitable.

The United States enters the War

On December 7, 1941, Japanese planes attacked Pearl Harbor. Within an hour, much of America's Pacific Fleet was destroyed or badly damaged, and more than 2,000 American military personnel were killed. An outraged United States immediately declared war on Japan. Four days later, Germany and Italy honored their treaty with Japan and declared war on the United States, which reciprocated. The European conflict had turned into a second global war.

The United States launched a massive mobilization effort. Within a year, it had manufactured almost 50,000 war planes. Its war goods production soon equalled that of all three Axis powers combined, and eventually surpassed it. About 15 million American men joined the armed forces, while women took up the slack within industry. The war finally accomplished what the New Deal had attempted: to achieve full employment. Corporations and individuals also contributed to the war effort by buying war bonds and paying high taxes. The government applied price controls and rationed food, clothing, gas, and other items.

Americans of Japanese descent had never been popular on America's West Coast, where most of them had settled. Now they were also suspected of being spies and traitors. So President Franklin Delano Roosevelt (re-elected for an unprecedented third term in 1940) ordered them removed from their homes and detained. More than 100,000 Japanese-Americans waited out the war in special internment camps, until the Supreme Court struck down the executive order several years later.

War in the Pacific

The real enemy, meanwhile, wasted no time in extending its reach: by mid-1942, Japan controlled the Philippines, Hong Kong, Guam, Burma, all of Southeast Asia south of Thailand, and a number of Pacific islands. It also threatened Australia, Hawaii, and even India. American troops, working with local scouts, had tried to defend the Philippines. But they had been greatly overmatched in battles on the Bataan Peninsula and Corregidor. The Japanese forced prisoners of war from those campaigns on what became known as the "Bataan Death March," a long trek on which thousands of captives died of disease and hunger.

But the tide soon turned, as the United States made good use of its aircraft carriers to win a series of Pacific battles, including ones on Midway Island, and on Guadalcanal in the Solomon Islands. After the Battle of the Bismarck Sea in March 1943, the Japanese would remain on the retreat for the duration of the war.

Germany pushed back

Roosevelt wanted to first defeat Nazi Germany (which he considered a greater threat to world democracy and US interests), and then Japan. Just as the Americans were finally gaining the upper hand in the Pacific, Germany suffered massive defeats in Europe and North Africa. Although the Germans had advanced more than 1,000 miles (1,600 km) into Russia by the summer of 1942, its soldiers were not prepared for the bitter Russian winter to follow. The Russians trapped several hundred thousand Germans in Stalingrad until they surrendered in January 1943.

Meanwhile, a German sweep through Northern Africa toward the Suez Canal was finally repelled in Egypt in late 1942 by British forces led by Lieutenant General Bernard L. Montgomery. Then in May 1943, American and British troops under US Lieutenant General Dwight D. Eisenhower battled Marshal Erwin Rommel's remaining German Afrika Korps in Tunisia, forcing Rommel to surrender 300,000 troops.

The Allies could now turn their attention to liberating Europe. Allied troops entered southern Italy in June 1943. The Italian dictator, Benito Mussolini, was forced to resign the following month, and the Allies eventually captured much of southern Italy. But German troops stubbornly resisted further Allied advances on that front.

In the North Atlantic, the German submarine threat had finally been subdued. So the United States sent a flood of men and equipment

Cadets Rosemary Krier of Stokie, Illinois (a former schoolteacher), Mary H. Bolin of Washington DC, and Helen A. Wick of Pittsburgh, Pennsylvania (a pharmacist), outside the US Midshipmen's School at Northampton, Massachusetts, May 28, 1943. The women were part of the first contingent of cadets picked from the ranks to attend a seven-week course in the Marine Corps Women's Reserve Officers Candidate Class.

New York's 69th battalion wade toward the beach at Butaritari Island in the Pacific on December 13, 1943. Heavy fire, shell holes, and treacherous coral on the sea floor hampered the advance. A strategic base for the Japanese since 1941, the Americans successfully took the island after three days of fighting.

The medals of a World War II veteran commemorate the action and bravery of American troops during wartime.

The "Big Three"—Roosevelt, Churchill, and Stalin—meet at Yalta on the Black Sea, February 4–11, 1945. The Yalta conference decided tactics for the closing stages of the war and postwar policies for the division of power and land in Europe

to Britain. In a highly secret operation, Eisenhower led almost 3 million American, British and Canadian troops across the English Channel and onto the beaches of Normandy, in northern France, on "D-Day," June 6, 1944. Six weeks later, the American forces finally broke through the German front.

The liberation of Europe

Over the next two months, the Allies swept through France, liberating town after town. (They had also finally succeeded in driving the Germans back in Italy, and had liberated Rome in early June.) Then they drove the Germans out of Belgium, Luxembourg, and the southern Netherlands. By October, American forces had penetrated Germany's western border. Hitler ordered one last offensive against the American line, in the Ardennes mountains of Luxembourg and Belgium. The "Battle of the Bulge," another Allied victory, ended in January 1945.

By this time, the Russians, who had advanced across Germany's eastern border, were within 30 miles (50 km) of Hitler's headquarters in Berlin. The Americans continued pushing from the west, and by April, the two Allied armies met. On April 30, Hitler committed suicide in his bunker, Berlin lying in ruins around him. Within a week, Germany, Austria, and Italy had surrendered. The war in Europe was over.

The final struggle against Japan

Fighting in the Pacific, however, continued. The previous October, the United States, which had by then captured all major Japanese bases in the Pacific Ocean, reached the Philippines. Led by General Douglas MacArthur, American troops regained the capital, Manila, in February 1945. They then moved on to capture two outer Japanese islands, Iwo Jima and Okinawa.

Yet the Japanese appeared unlikely to surrender quickly or easily. As it happened, by the summer of 1945, the United States had developed a powerful new weapon, far more destructive than anything that had been used in war up to that time. Scientists assigned to the top-secret "Manhattan Project" had successfully harnessed the power of atomic energy. The first atomic bomb was tested in the desert of Alamogordo, New Mexico that July.

President Harry Truman (who, as Roosevelt's vice-president, succeeded him when he died shortly after winning his fourth term in 1944) decided to use this new weapon to force Japan's hand. On August 6, the American plane *Enola Gay* dropped an atomic bomb on the city of Hiroshima, killing more than 78,000 of its 344,000 residents. Another 37,425 people were injured, and 13,500 were reported missing. Three days later, the United States dropped a second atomic bomb, this time on Nagasaki, killing 38,500 people. Japan finally surrendered on September 3, 1945, ending World War II.

The war had claimed some 50 million lives around the world. Cities and countries lay in ruins. The United States emerged as the sole world power to have retained its wealth and not suffered great physical damage. It had also benefited from the immigration of European artists and intellectuals who had fled totalitarian regimes before and during the war.

Europe's future is decided

By the time Japan surrendered, the Allied leaders had already discussed postwar policies for Europe, making decisions that would influence the course of world events for the remainder of the century. Roosevelt, the Soviet Union's Joseph Stalin, and Great Britain's Winston Churchill had conferred for the last time in Yalta, on the Black Sea coast, in February, 1945. They had agreed to let European countries solve their postwar problems democratically. They had also decided which Allied power would liberate each occupied country, a decision that ultimately determined where communism and capitalism would hold sway. Great Britain and the United States had also secured Stalin's promise to help in the war against Japan; in return, they had granted the Soviets concessions in China and Korea.

The Pearl Harbor attack had taught the United States the importance of maintaining defense forces and actively working for world peace. Isolationism was abandoned in favor of a program of international cooperation and security. To try to guarantee that, this time, the postwar peace would hold, 50 countries signed the Charter of the United Nations in mid-1945. (The World Bank and the International Monetary Fund had been created the previous year, to promote international economic cooperation.)

A member of the US navy is welcomed home by his family in New York City. Despite the loss of nearly 36,500 navy personnel, the United States had amassed the largest and most powerful naval force in the world by the end of the war in 1945.

Truman, Churchill (replaced partway through by Clement Attlee), and Stalin then met in Potsdam, Germany, in July and August 1945. This conference proved largely inconclusive, apart from the decision on how to partition Germany. One section of the country would be given to Poland; the rest would be divided into four administrative zones, governed separately by Russia, Britain, the United States, and France. The capital, Berlin, which fell in the Russian zone, was also to be divided. The Western powers later combined their zones for economic reasons, creating the Federal Republic of Germany (West Germany). The Soviet Union established a communist government in its zone, which then became the autonomous German Democratic Republic (East Germany).

The Cold War begins

Before long, Stalin had propped up sympathetic communist regimes throughout much of Eastern Europe, and was supporting communist uprisings elsewhere in the world. The United States saw the spread of communism as a threat to its capitalist, democratic way of life. So when Great Britain stopped helping Greece and Turkey quash their communist insurgencies in 1947, Truman called on the United States to step in with financial assistance. The Truman Doctrine, in which the president stated that the United States should help all free peoples resist "subjugation," marked the start of America's policy to contain the spread of communism.

Truman was also convinced that the United States should help rebuild Europe. A healthy Europe would make a better trading partner. And unless Europeans could be rescued from starvation and helped on the road to economic stability, they might again succumb

to totalitarianism. It also seemed a good way to curb the westward expansion of communism. In 1948, the *European Recovery Act*, better known as the Marshall Plan, began giving American funds and technical assistance to any European country that could present a viable recovery plan. About $13 billion was doled out over the next five years.

Stalin forbid Eastern European countries from applying for these funds, thereby solidifying the division of Europe and the enmity between America and the USSR. The Cold War, an indirect struggle for supremacy between the capitalist United States and the communist Soviet Union, had begun.

For its part, the Soviet Union tried to solidify its control over East Germany. It blocked overland access routes to West Berlin in April, 1948. Over the next year, American and British planes dropped almost two and a half tons of food and fuel to the city. The "Berlin airlift" finally ended when the Soviets lifted their blockade.

In 1949, the United States, Canada, and 10 Western European nations created the North Atlantic Treaty Organization, pledging to integrate their defenses and to treat an attack on one as an attack on all. (Four more European nations joined later.) That same year, the Soviet Union tested its first atomic weapon. Two ideologically opposed super-powers now had the power, not only to drive world events, but to destroy humanity.

The Marine Corps War Memorial in Washington DC records the raising of the American flag at Mount Suribachi on the island of Iwo Jima on February 23, 1943. One of the last territories to be recaptured from the Japanese, the success at Iwo Jima signified the conclusion of the American Pacific campaign.

1950–1959

A new prosperity

A decade and a half of deprivation and sacrifice gave way to prosperity and complacency after World War II. War-time industries and technological developments were adapted to peace-time uses. New labor-saving devices and leisure goods (including televisions) poured onto the market. Americans, flush with war-time savings, snapped them up, eager for the trappings of the good life they had been denied for so long. By giving millions of war veterans money for housing, college educations, and even business ventures, the 1944 "G.I. Bill" helped swell the ranks of the middle class. The expanding economy caused personal disposable incomes to rise by about 17 percent between 1947 and 1960.

Economic security and the war's end prompted the younger generation to settle down en masse to raise families, producing a demographic "baby boom." In an era of relatively low immigration, the population rose from 140 million in 1945 to 179 million in 1960. Suburbs sprang up and appealed to many young families searching for tranquil domesticity.

Yet the complacent mood was tempered by the knowledge that the world's two enemy superpowers, the United States and the Soviet Union, both possessed weapons of mass destruction. The fate of humanity now rested partly in American hands; the country could no longer afford to remain aloof from the rest of the world.

Rosa Parks, December 21, 1956 in Montgomery, Alabama after the Supreme Court ruling that banned segregaton on the city's public transportation.

RIGHT: Postwar prosperity fuelled a motoring boom as Americans took to the roads in new cars such as this Cadillac Fleetwood.

Senator Joseph McCarthy waves to delegates at the Republican National Convention, July 9, 1952. Exploiting "Red" fears, McCarthy conducted a series of communist witch hunts from 1950, targeting leading members of the armed forces and government.

The Korean War

Cold War tensions soon led to armed conflict. At the end of World War II, the Allies had decided to temporarily divide Korea at the 38th parallel. The division hardened when a Soviet-backed communist government was installed in the Democratic People's Republic of Korea (North Korea). In June, 1950, North Korea invaded South Korea (formally known as the Republic of Korea). President Harry Truman, mindful of how a policy of early appeasement had allowed Hitler to conquer much of Europe, urged prompt resistance to the communist invasion.

The United Nations Security Council voted unanimously to order North Korea to withdraw from the South (conveniently, the Soviet Union was boycotting the Security Council at the time of the vote). UN troops were dispatched to the peninsula to force North Korea's compliance. Commanded by American General Douglas MacArthur, and heavily reliant on American men and materials, the UN forces quickly met their objective.

But after driving the North Koreans out of the South, MacArthur attempted to unify the entire peninsula by force. He pressed on and invaded North Korea, pinning the communists near the Chinese border. China, itself firmly in communist hands, saw this as an act of Western aggression. It intervened and pushed the UN forces back to the 38th parallel by mid-December. It became clear the war would drag on indefinitely unless the United States could accept a compromise. Protracted negotiations finally resulted with an armistice on July 27, 1953. It re-established a national border at the 38th parallel; over 54,000 Americans had died in a war that had ended in a draw.

The "Red Scare"

The seemingly interminable Korean War had irritated many Americans. Anti-communist sentiments were nothing new; they had only briefly been suspended during World War II, while the United States and the Soviet Union had fought a common enemy. Many Americans blamed the "loss" of China (a communist regime had gained control in 1949) and the Soviets' atomic bomb prowess on spies and traitors in their midst. A few sensational espionage cases (most notably Ethel and Julius Rosenberg, and former State Department official Alger Hiss) helped confirm such fears.

The House Un-American Activities Committee launched a series of investigations and hearings to root out communists from a variety of professions. The committee members particularly targeted Holly-

wood personalities because of the ensuing publicity. Many former communists or communist sympathizers lost their jobs; those who refused to discuss colleagues were jailed for contempt of Congress. Suspects were blacklisted by their industries.

A senator from Wisconsin, Joseph R. McCarthy, decided to exploit the issue for his own personal gain. Truth was no barrier for McCarthy. He grabbed the national spotlight in 1950 when he claimed to have a list of State Department employees that the Secretary of State himself knew to be communists. The country, now linked by national media and transportation, proved eager to enlist in the witch hunt.

McCarthy targeted the very pinnacles of power, including the president's administration. He was finally exposed as a mendacious bully in 1954, when a Senate subcommittee launched televised hearings to examine his charges against the Army. The Senate later censured him. His influence evaporated, helped by a thawing in relations with the Soviet Union.

A redirection of energies

President Dwight D. Eisenhower, who in 1953 became the first Republican to occupy the White House in two decades, was committed to a policy of détente. Peaceful coexistence was backed up by nuclear arsenals on both sides. But the Soviet launch of the first man-made satellite, *Sputnik I*, in 1957, convinced Americans they had fallen behind in the technology race. Eisenhower's answer was to launch an ambitious space exploration program and boost spending on science education.

Another government program with wide-reaching repercussions was the 1956 *Interstate Highway Act*, the most ambitious public works project ever undertaken. The federal government committed more than $33 billion to build a network of highways across the country. American lifestyles—where people lived, worked, shopped, and vacationed—began to revolve around automobiles.

Moves for civil rights

Further change was also brewing behind the veneer of 1950s social stagnation. The two world wars had given American blacks new opportunities and encouraged them to question their status as second-class citizens. The National Association for the Advancement of Colored People filed a series of lawsuits to challenge the South's Jim Crow (segregation) laws. Thousands of blacks also forced changes more directly. Inspired by Rosa Parks, a black woman who refused to give up her seat at the front of a bus (the area reserved for whites), they began boycotting segregated services.

In 1954, the Supreme Court ruled in *Brown v Board of Education of Topeka, Kansas*, that separate educational facilities were inherently unequal and therefore unconstitutional. But Southerners often resisted the required integration efforts. One such incident prompted Eisenhower to send federal troops

to protect black students enrolling in Central High School in Little Rock, Arkansas in 1957. That same year, Congress passed the first civil rights act since 1875, to protect black voting rights.

Teenagers and other rebels

Meanwhile, changing social patterns increasingly separated adolescents from the world at large and encouraged them to develop a distinct subculture. Marketers reinforced this notion as they sought to capitalize on the teenagers' new affluence. Rock 'n' roll, a fusion of urbanized rhythm and blues and country music that first hit the national scene in the mid-1950s, reflected teenage rebellion. Its sexually explicit lyrics and inter-racial aspects outraged adults, even as it made stars out of performers such as Elvis Presley.

Rebelliousness was taken further by the "beats," young adults who expressed their alienation from society through experimental literary forms and roving lifestyles. Their heroes included the poet Allen Ginsberg and the writer Jack Kerouac, whose stream-of-consciousness novel *On the Road* became a sensation in the late 1950s.

Elvis Presley brings rock 'n' roll to a Hollywood stage, California, June 22, 1956.

A lapel button from the 1956 presidential campaign promotes the re-election of Republican Dwight Eisenhower. Eisenhower won a landslide victory (457 votes to 73), on the basis of his earlier successes in tackling "Korea, Communism, and Corruption."

1960–1969

A half-dollar coin from 1966 commemorates John F. Kennedy, assassinated on November 22, 1963, as his motorcade wound through Dallas, Texas.

A new generation

As the 43-year-old President John F. Kennedy announced in his 1961 inaugural address, the torch had passed to "a new generation." After more than a decade of conformity, the nation was ready for action and new ideas. America's youngest elected president appeared set to deliver.

Foreign affairs demanded much of Kennedy's attention. Eager to stay ahead of the Soviet Union in the Cold War arms and technology race, Kennedy urged the United States to send a man to the moon before the end of the decade. He also launched the Peace Corps, a program that enlisted American volunteers to work on practical projects in developing nations. Youthful idealism could thus be harnessed to win foreign friends for the United States.

Communism had already taken hold virtually in America's backyard, in Cuba. A US-backed coup failed at Cuba's Bay of Pigs in April 1961. Then a full-blown crisis erupted the following year, when the CIA discovered the Soviets were building missile bases in Cuba. Kennedy launched a naval blockade

but, hoping to defuse the situation, also hinted at a willingness to compromise. The Soviets relented and withdrew their missiles; in turn, the United States promised never to invade Cuba. Tensions subsequently thawed enough for the two superpowers to agree on a nuclear weapons Test Ban Treaty in 1963.

The Vietnam War

That same year, the United States deepened its involvement in an ongoing conflict in Vietnam. The United States had long feared that communism could spread from North Vietnam to South Vietnam, and from there to the rest of Asia. Now, worries that an unpopular regime in South Vietnam would boost support for Viet Cong communist rebels, moved the United States to meddle in a leadership overthrow. Kennedy also authorized the US military to assist South Vietnam in a clandestine war against North Vietnam, which actively supported the Viet Cong.

The pretext for open warfare came in August, 1964, when American ships approached the North Vietnamese mainland too closely and were allegedly fired upon. Kennedy's successor, Lyndon Johnson, decried what he called "unprovoked aggression" and convinced Congress to approve the Gulf of Tonkin Resolution, a de facto declaration of war.

However the United States had grossly underestimated its enemies, and was repeatedly stymied by the Viet Cong's guerrilla tactics. As the US presence in Vietnam grew to more than half a million troops, many Americans began to question the war on both practical and moral terms. In October 1967, an anti-war rally in Washington drew 200,000 protesters. Peace talks began in 1968, but there was no settlement on the horizon.

Student protesters and "hippies"

The Vietnam War quagmire (and Kennedy's assassination in 1963) marked a certain loss of innocence for America. The war also helped galvanize a student protest movement that had developed as an offshoot of the black civil rights cause. The increasingly independent teenagers of the 1950s were now university students. Civil rights introduced them to protest techniques; the "beats" had given them a model for countercultural experimentation. They developed their own "hippie" subculture, emphasizing peace, love, drugs, music, and a general disregard for social norms and entrenched authority. To the many idealists among them, all things seemed possible.

The University of California at Berkeley introduced civil disobedience to the academic world in 1964, when students demanded political free speech on campus. Soon students there and elsewhere began to protest against the Vietnam War, and in

John F. Kennedy at his desk on his first day in office, January 21, 1961. The youngest man ever elected president, he pledged to revitalize society through social, economic, and civil rights reform.

Dr Martin Luther King, Jr delivers his "I have a dream" speech in front of the Lincoln Memorial, Washington DC, August 28, 1953, during the March for Jobs and Freedom. The final speaker at the rally, drawing over 200,000 civil rights protesters, King outlined his vision of a racially integrated, peaceful America, where all could live freely and equally.

favor of participatory democracy and social justice. They staged mass demonstrations, strikes, and teach-ins, and sometimes occupied buildings to dramatize their demands. Violence occasionally erupted, as when police battled student protesters at the 1968 Democratic Convention in Chicago.

However, discrimination was so deeply entrenched, even in the North, that many blacks despaired that legislation could improve their daily lives quickly, if at all. Frustration mounted. In 1964, race riots convulsed many Northeastern cities. The following year, Los Angeles' Watts neighborhood erupted in violence, leaving 34 people dead and more than 1,000 injured. Black radicals called for racial unity and an independent black existence. But most blacks continued to support King's vision of integration, and felt a terrible sense of grief when he was assassinated in Memphis, Tennessee on April 4, 1968.

Civil rights victories and setbacks

Meanwhile, the black civil rights struggle continued. The direct, nonviolent protest movement grew in the 1960s when black college students (and white sympathizers) began disobeying Southern segregation ordinances. The first "sit-in" protest to gain national attention took place in February, 1960, when four black students refused to leave a Woolworth lunch counter where they had been denied service.

The following year, black and white "Freedom Riders" from the North poured into the South to challenge discrimination on buses and trains. They were greeted by mobs and arrests, prompting the nation's Attorney-General to order federal marshall protection. The Student Nonviolent Coordinating Committee also provoked many arrests by encouraging local community action on many fronts. Television news programs beamed scenes of Southern intransigence (including police attacking peaceful marchers with dogs and high-pressure fire hoses) around the nation, galvanizing Northern support for civil rights. Major churches joined with labor unions and black organizations to give the movement a broad support base.

Martin Luther King, Jr, an eloquent Baptist minister from Montgomery, Alabama, emerged as the movement's most prominent leader. He led various protest marches and boycotts in the South. Then in August 1963, he organized the March on Washington for Jobs and Freedom. About 200,000 demonstrators turned up to hear him deliver the rousing "I have a dream" speech, which conjured up his vision of an integrated, peaceful America. The following year, President Johnson signed the nation's most significant piece of civil rights legislation. Among other things, the *Civil Rights Act* outlawed discrimination in public places and granted the government supervisory authority over employment practices.

A decade of upheaval

Women had also begun to agitate for across-the-board equal rights in the 1960s. Betty Friedan's 1963 book, *The Feminine Mystique*, exposed the limitations and corrosive effects of the idealized suburban homemaker role. The 1963 *Equal Pay Act* and the 1964 *Civil Rights Act* (which also prohibited discrimination on the basis of sex) helped advance the concept of sexual equality. But in practice such laws had only limited effects, at least in the beginning. Groups such as the National Organization for Women staged protests, organized women's "consciousness-raising" sessions, and filed lawsuits to try to end sexual discrimination.

Pressure groups championed causes such as environmentalism and consumer protection legislation. President Johnson himself had tried to push through an ambitious "Great Society" program, which included "War on Poverty" legislation. But insufficient funds and the distraction of the Vietnam War stunted its effectiveness.

By the end of the decade, the country was reeling from the many changes and fissures in society. The assassination of both King and presidential candidate Robert Kennedy in 1968 reinforced a widespread sense that the country had lost its way. One of the decade's few remaining bright spots came in July, 1969, when US astronaut Neil Armstrong became the first man to walk on the moon, fulfilling Kennedy's grand vision.

Buzz Aldrin, photographed by Neil Amstrong, stands by the American flag at Tranquility Base, on the Moon, July 20, 1969. The successful Apollo 11 mission made Armstrong and Aldrin the first men to set foot on the Moon. They spent a total of 21.6 hours on the Moon's surface collecting samples, installing equipment, and taking photographs.

1970–1979

Leaving Vietnam

Despite ongoing peace talks and a gradual pull-out of American troops begun in the late 1960s, the Vietnam war was still raging at the start of the new decade. In April, 1970, the United States invaded a section of neutral Cambodia, in order to attack South Vietnamese communist rebel (Viet Cong) bases. This sparked a new wave of anti-war demonstrations back home, followed by outrage when National Guardsmen shot dead four student protesters at Ohio's Kent State University.

A peace agreement was finally signed in January 1973. This allowed the South Vietnamese leader to remain in office, while the Viet Cong were permitted to keep their recent gains. The United States withdrew its last troops two months later. But fighting between North and South Vietnam continued. The communists completed their takeover of South Vietnam in 1975, forcing American civilians to flee Saigon. Some 58,000 Americans had died in an unpopular war the United States had failed to win.

Even as the United States was learning to accept defeat in that conflict, it was enjoying an easing of tensions in the wider Cold War. President Richard Nixon made an unprecedented visit to China in 1972, setting the stage for "a normalization of relations" after more than two decades of hostility between the two countries. Nixon then travelled to Moscow to meet with the Soviet leader. Their tête-à-tête smoothed the way for the Strategic Arms Limitation Talks (SALT) treaty and a grain sale agreement.

The Watergate scandal

Nixon was re-elected in a landslide in 1972. But his popularity soon plummeted as a series of scandals engulfed his Republican administration. The most damaging of these was the Watergate affair. Five men had been caught breaking into the Democratic National Committee's headquarters in Washington's Watergate complex a few months before the election. Rumors soon began to circulate that the burglars, who had been trying to install bugging devices, had White House connections. One of them confessed to taking hush money, and implicated three high-ranking Republicans.

A chain of accusations prompted several high-level resignations. Nixon maintained his innocence, but withheld tapes of key White House conversations requested by a Senate committee that had opened hearings on the matter in May 1973. In the face of mounting indictments, accusations, and resignations, Congress launched impeachment hearings in July 1974. The following month, the Supreme Court ordered Nixon to surrender the requested tape transcripts, which proved his complicity in the cover-up. With impeachment a foregone conclusion, on August 9, 1974, Nixon became the first American president to resign. His vice-president, Gerald Ford, replaced Nixon, and pardoned him for any crimes he may have committed. But he couldn't erase the public's cynicism toward government in the wake of Nixon's many abuses of power.

The energy crisis

The economic picture was also bleak during this period. The 1960s economic boom had given way to an unprecedented combination of inflation and recession, labeled "stagflation." The United States recorded its first trade deficit that century in 1971. Then an energy crisis hit home in 1973, further aggravating the situation. Incensed by America's support of Israel in the Yom Kippur War, Arab nations embargoed oil shipments to the United States. They soon resumed exports, but at inflated prices. As the effects of quadrupled oil prices rippled through the economy, the inflation rate rose to 12 percent.

Coming hard on the heels of the Vietnam defeat, Watergate, and a decade of violent social conflict, the economic problems reinforced a national sense of disillusionment and diminished hopes for the future. It seemed an ironic time to celebrate 200 years of nationhood. Yet the 1976 Bicentennial celebrations proved wildly popular, and helped restore some faith in the country.

Reforms continue

Activism continued on some fronts, albeit more quietly than in the 1960s. The women's liberation movement hit its stride in terms of raising awareness and challenging sex roles. It also secured more

President Richard Nixon, April 29, 1974, in the midst of the Watergate scandal. In this address, Nixon agreed to hand over edited transcripts of taped White House conversations, which he said would clear him of any involvement and "tell it all."

Anti-Vietnam War protesters in Washington DC, May 24, 1970. Holding a sign that reads "sociologists for peace," the students demonstrate their support for the four student protestors killed by National Guardsmen in April at Ohio's Kent State University.

Congress, environmentalists blocked dams and other ecologically destructive projects.

Yet the country also suffered two of its worst environmental disasters in the late 1970s. An abandoned canal filled with chemical waste had been filled in and developed as a housing estate in Love Canal, a neighborhood of Niagara Falls, New York. In 1978, state officials detected toxic chemical leaks in area residents' homes. Then in 1979, a nuclear reactor on Pennsylvania's Three Mile Island malfunctioned. Although the accident resulted in minimal health risks, it greatly increased public fears about the safety of nuclear energy.

Egyptian President Anwar Al Sadat, Jimmy Carter, and Israeli Prime Minister Menachim Begin sign the Camp David Accord in the East Room of the White House, Septermber 17, 1978. The agreement set out a framework for peace in the ongoing Arab–Israeli conflict.

LEFT: Marchers carry a tree along Fifth Avenue, New York City at the first annual Earth Day gathering, April 22, 1970. The nationwide marches, in which millions participated, protested against environmental pollution.

legislative victories, including laws giving girls and women equal access to all federally funded school programs. Feminists celebrated the Supreme Court's 1973 *Roe v Wade* decision, which found most state restrictions on abortion unconstitutional. But the Equal Rights Amendment, finally passed by Congress in 1972, failed to get the required number of state ratifications (though in the end, various individual laws more or less achieved the same aims).

The gay liberation movement also matured in the 1970s. It had effectively begun on June 28, 1969, when police raided the Stonewall Inn, a homosexual bar in New York's Greenwich Village. The patrons had decided to fight back. The ensuing "Stonewall Riots" gave birth to gay activism. Organizations sprang up to encourage gay pride and to fight discrimination based on sexual preference.

The environmental movement reached critical mass at the first annual Earth Day gatherings in 1970. Environmental groups multiplied and lobbied Washington for legislative solutions to the country's pollution problems. Nixon created the federal Environmental Protection Agency, and signed the *National Environmental Policy Act*, which required environmental impact assessments for major federal actions. The *Clean Air Act* was passed in 1970, and the *Clean Water Act* followed two years later. Outside

The "me decade"

Activists encountered plenty of resistance. The environmental and consumer protection movements, in particular, were denounced by some for challenging the nation's material well-being. But many liberals had also lost their enthusiasm after a decade of protest. When Native Americans occupied Wounded Knee, South Dakota in 1973 to protest government Indian policies, few outsiders lent their support.

A magazine captured the prevailing mood when it referred to the 1970s as the "me decade." Self-actualization and good times trumped working for social change. Disco music and the party culture it promoted swept the nation. Over-the-top clothing styles ruled the day.

Yet the hedonism only glossed over people's nagging doubts about America's prospects. President Jimmy Carter, elected in 1976, couldn't tame the high inflation rate that he inherited from his predecessors. His most significant achievements came in the foreign affairs arena, which he imbued with a humanitarian focus. His most hard-won victory came when Israel and Egypt pledged to end their 30-year-old state of war after lengthy negotiations at the presidential retreat in Camp David, Maryland in September, 1978.

1980–1989

Held hostage

The 1980 presidential campaign was overshadowed by a hostage crisis on the other side of the world. An Islamic revolutionary movement led by the Ayatollah Ruhollah Khomeini had overthrown the regime of the US-supported Shah of Iran in early 1979. After the United States admitted the Shah for medical treatment, Iranian militants seized the American embassy in Teheran in November 1979 and held 66 of its occupants hostage. President Jimmy Carter tried desperately to resolve the crisis before the November 1980 election. However an attempted rescue mission in April failed, and eight would-be rescuers were killed.

Republican Ronald Reagan handily won the election. Shortly afterward, with Iran by this time pre-occupied with other issues, negotiations for the hostages' release got underway. They were finally freed on Inauguration Day, January 20, 1981, in return for the American release of some $8 billion worth of Iranian assets.

"Morning in America"

Reagan, a former Hollywood actor and California governor, had also promised voters that his conservative stewardship would revive the long-stagnated economy. Congress passed his main proposals, which involved cutting income taxes by 25 percent over a period of three years, and slashing federal spending on social programs. His supply-side economics theory hinged on the assumption that money that otherwise would have gone to pay taxes would now be invested in new economic activities, and that the taxes levied on the resulting income would ultimately lead to a net revenue gain.

The economy continued its slide until 1983, when unemployment reached almost 11 percent, a level not seen since the Great Depression. But then oil prices began to drop, inflation slowed, and the economy began to recover, just in time for Reagan to win re-election. (He won in a landslide against a Democratic ticket that included Geraldine Ferraro, the first major-party female vice-presidential candidate in the nation's history.)

Reagan's economic prescription also involved deregulating numerous industries, including banking and airlines. A short-term result was financial volatility. Some financiers sensed an opportunity for extraordinary profits in the new economic climate. One of them, Michael Milken, promoted the use of high-risk, high-yield "junk bonds" to finance corporate takeovers. The wave of mergers and acquisitions grew from 94 deals worth $18 billion in 1980, to 11,346 deals worth $452 billion in 1990.

Wall Street greed seemingly knew no bounds, and numerous financial scandals were uncovered and prosecuted. Glitz and ostentatious spending were the fashion of the day. Even many former hippies embraced bourgeois values and became "yuppies," a term coined in the 1980s to describe the new breed of affluent, consumerist young urban professionals.

But the domestic picture was by no means uniformly rosy. The rising economic tide lifted yachts higher than dinghies—the disparity between rich and poor grew, and average individual incomes in real terms were lower during the late 1980s than in the early 1970s. The unraveling of the government social safety net also exacerbated a wide range of social problems. The ranks of the homeless multiplied. Drug use increased.

It also became clear that the economic recovery was built on shaky ground. Government tax revenues did not rise as predicted. At the same time, the federal budget grew, because Reagan's attack on "big government" had not applied to the military; on the contrary, defense spending rose significantly. The budget deficit ballooned. Toward the end of the decade, the United States, long a creditor nation, had become the world's largest debtor nation. And then the stock market crashed on October 19, 1987, dropping more than 22 percent in one day.

The information age

Just as manufacturing had outpaced agriculture early in the century, now "knowledge workers" outnumbered producers of tangible goods. Many routine jobs had already been eliminated by large mainframe computers and other machines. Now jobs—and lifestyles—were being further transformed by personal computers. Once only the province of hobbyists, these desktop machines reached the mass market in the late 1970s, then took off in the 1980s. The IBM PC, introduced in 1981, soon became the world's most popular personal computer. As such

Entrance to Financial Ratings House, 25 Broadway, New York, home of financiers Standard & Poor. Personal and corporate investors exploited the favorable economic climate during the mid-1980s to take risks on the buoyant stock market.

RIGHT: The New York Post *reports the crash of the American stock market, October 19, 1987. The Dow Jones Industrial Average fell by almost a third, with stocks losing $1 trillion of their value.*

Dan Fylstra of VisiCorp uses an IBM PC XT and an Apple II, February 15, 1984, to demonstrate the earliest spreadsheet programs marketed. Increased availability of desktop computers and software transformed work and home life during the 1980s.

machines became cheaper, more powerful and easier to use, they were applied to an increasing array of tasks in homes, schools and offices.

The end of the Cold War

Another old paradigm was ending, though this was hardly apparent at the start of the decade. Relations with the Soviet Union had been strained since the Soviet invasion of Afghanistan in December 1979. The following year, Carter embargoed the sale of grain and high technology products to the Soviet Union, and convinced the United States Olympic Committee to boycott that summer's Olympic Games in Moscow. The Soviet Union (and other Eastern Bloc nations) later boycotted the Los Angeles Olympics in 1984.

Reagan's strong anti-communist view was reflected in his description of the Soviet Union as the "evil empire." But his view softened when reform-minded Mikhail Gorbachev became the new Soviet premier in 1985. The two leaders met that year, at the first United States–Soviet summit in six years. Two years later, they negotiated an intermediate-range nuclear forces (INF) treaty, the first such agreement requiring the parties to destroy existing weapons.

Gorbachev's "perestroika" and other reforms gathered a momentum of their own. The Soviet Union's days were numbered. In 1989, communism foundered in some half dozen Eastern European countries. The Berlin Wall was demolished that

November, marking the end of an "Iron Curtain" across Europe. After more than four decades, the Cold War had finally ended.

American interventions overseas

Reagan, whose tough stance was credited with speeding communism's demise, acted decisively in foreign affairs. He sent aid to Contra rebels trying to overthrow Nicaragua's leftist regime. He also ordered a bombing on Libya in 1986, in retaliation for a Libyan-sponsored terrorist attack in Germany that killed two Americans. In 1989, the new president, George Bush supported a coup attempt against Panama's Manuel Noriega, who had been implicated in drug trafficking. When the overthrow effort failed, Bush ordered an invasion of Panama. Noriega was eventually brought to the United States to stand trial.

America's prominence and aggressiveness made it a target in the growing number of international terrorist incidents. The worst incident came in 1983, when terrorists blew up US marine barracks in Lebanon, killing 241 American personnel who had been sent to the country on a peace-keeping mission.

Reagan had publicly insisted that he would never negotiate with terrorists. But in 1987, members of his administration were found guilty of illegally selling arms to Iran in exchange for the release of hostages, then using the profits to fund the Nicaraguan Contra rebels. Reagan's high popularity briefly dipped, but he emerged from the scandal virtually untainted, living up to his moniker as the "Teflon president."

US President Ronald Reagan and Soviet leader Mikhail Gorbachev at a welcoming ceremony for the Washington Summit at the White House, December 9, 1987. The summit culminated in the signing of the INF treaty—the first US–Soviet treaty to agree the destruction of nuclear weapons.

From 1990 onwards

At the Oklahoma City National Memorial, Oklahoma City, 168 chairs mark the lives lost in the bombing of a federal office building on April 19, 1995—the worst terrorist attack in US history up to that time.

RIGHT: American servicemen salute as the flag is raised again at the US embassy in Kuwait, February 27, 1991, following the retreat of Iraqi forces as a result of Operation Desert Storm.

BELOW: President Bill Clinton on April 8, 1998—the day a second government steward was called to testify before the federal grand jury investigating the President's alleged relationship with ex-White House intern Monica Lewinsky. On December 19, the case concluded with Clinton's impeachment for obstructing justice and for perjury in connection with his relationship to Lewinsky. The senate acquitted him of these charges.

War with Iraq

War and terrorism have been sobering book-ends to a dizzying period of technology-driven change in the United States.

Iraq's invasion of Kuwait in August 1990 was viewed as a harbinger of Iraqi domination of the Middle East, and a threat to America's oil supply. After Iraqi President Saddam Hussein ignored United Nations-imposed troop withdrawal deadlines in early 1991, the United States launched a devastating air assault followed by a ground war. A multinational force (including troops from other NATO countries and Arab allies) liberated Kuwait City after only four days of combat. An immediate cease-fire led to an official peace agreement two months later. Thanks to their high-tech weapons systems, victory had cost fewer than 150 American combat deaths.

The Soviet Union's disintegration that same year left the United States the world's sole remaining superpower. As the decade wore on, America's drastically reduced military force began to redefine its role, becoming more involved in humanitarian and peacekeeping missions in such hot spots as Haiti, Somalia, and the Balkans.

Economic ups and downs

A brief recession hit the country at the start of the decade. It was marked by a wave of corporate retrenchments that gutted the ranks of middle management, as businesses sought to become more streamlined and competitive for the global market. More than one million payroll jobs were eliminated in the last half of 1990 alone. Democrat Bill Clinton seized on people's economic insecurities to defeat George Bush in the 1992 presidential election.

The economy had already begun its recovery by the time Clinton assumed office. But he reversed the growing federal deficit trend, so that by the end of the decade, the United States was enjoying its largest budget surpluses in three decades, as well as its longest peace-time economic expansion ever.

Investors cheered the corporate restructurings, pushing the stock market to unheard-of levels even while the recession was still on. Yet those early gains proved minuscule when compared to the stock market's rise over the second half of the decade, when the Dow Jones index tripled in

value. Investing turned into a national obsession. Everyone wanted to get rich quickly, and many did—the number of millionaires quadrupled over the course of the decade.

The Internet

The driving force behind the longest bull market in United States history was a technology revolution involving personal computers and the Internet. Originally developed as a networking tool for American defense researchers in the late 1960s, the Internet gained mass appeal in the mid-1990s, thanks to the invention of the user-friendly World Wide Web. Millions of Americans began to communicate by e-mail and to form virtual communities based on shared interests rather than geography.

A gold rush mentality developed when people began looking for ways to commercially exploit the new medium. Online companies proliferated, with the help of plentiful venture capital. Speculators bid up the shares of "dot-coms," and spoke of a "new economy" that transcended established profit and loss rules. The stock market bubble finally burst in early 2000, and the American economy slid into a brief recession the following year.

Many people became self-employed free agents out of choice or necessity. The number of corporate mergers also increased, creating huge multinational concerns across a number of industries. And the Microsoft Corporation benefited from the booming

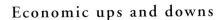

personal computer and software markets to became one of the most profitable and powerful companies in the country's history.

Globalization

The communications revolution (and government policies) also enabled greater international movement of capital in the "global village." For its part, the United States reaffirmed its commitment to globalization in 1993, when Congress passed the North American Free Trade Agreement (NAFTA).

American culture and brands, popular exports since mid-century, became ubiquitous around the world. But not everyone shared in the bounty. Many low-skilled American industrial jobs had already been exported to cheaper overseas labor markets, starting in the 1980s. A fragmented backlash against globalization reached critical mass when protesters disrupted the World Trade Organization conference in Seattle in November 1999.

Tabloid culture and impeachment

Ironically, the communications revolution also broke down the concept of the mass audience, as media outlets multiplied and targeted increasingly niche audiences. But some stories still held mass appeal, particularly sensational real-life dramas such as the investigation of President Clinton for perjury in a sexual harrassment case.

Clinton—whose two terms in office were dogged by a succession of financial, sexual and assorted other scandals—in 1998 became only the second United States president to be impeached. However, the Senate acquitted him of the charges, allowing him to serve out his term. Nevertheless, the Democrats lost the presidency in the 2000 election, when George W. Bush was eventually awarded the presidency after a drawn-out and hotly contested counting process.

Terrorism hits home

America was feeling generally secure, despite new threats that had emerged within the country's own borders. A couple of American military veterans bombed a federal office building in Oklahoma City, Oklahoma in April 1995, killing 168 people, to protest against a government they considered illegitimate. Other disaffected citizens around the country rallied around militia movements that together claimed about 100,000 members. Their main gripes concerned gun control legislation and the government's handling of a 1993 standoff in Waco, Texas, which cost the lives of 76 militant religious sect members. Violence also reached the country's playgrounds, as a spate of school shootings rocked the nation.

But nothing—not even the foreign terrorist bombing of New York's World Trade Center in February 1993, which killed six people—prepared the nation or the world for the horrific events of September 11, 2001.

Flight-trained terrorists working for exiled Saudi Arabian warlord Osama bin Laden hijacked four American planes almost simultaneously. They crashed one into the Pentagon and two into the World Trade Center towers, which caught fire and collapsed. Passengers on the fourth plane struggled with the hijackers, causing the plane to crash in a Pennsylvania field. The total death toll exceeded 3,200, including passengers, people in the Pentagon and World Trade Center buildings, and rescue workers including police and firemen.

A stunned nation responded with a flurry of flag-waving patriotism. President Bush launched a retaliatory "war on terrorism" against the shadowy bin Laden and his global al Qaeda terrorist network, which opposed America's support of Israel and what bin Laden saw as general interference in Middle Eastern affairs. With the help of other western and Arab allies, the United States bombed Afghanistan, where bin Laden was based. The coalition succeeded in toppling Afghanistan's fundamentalist Islamic regime, but bin Laden remained at large.

Meanwhile Americans had to learn to live with new security measures, curtailed civil liberties, and the ever-present threat of new terrorist attacks, especially after a spate of anthrax-tainted letters claimed several lives and caused widespread panic about handling mail.

An online stock trader checks the financial markets over the Internet. The development of browser software and the Web in the last decade of the century revolutionized business and personal communications, creating a global marketplace.

The twin towers of the New York's World Trade Center burning after terrorists flew hijacked passsenger planes into first the north tower (right) and then the south tower on September 11, 2001.
REUTERS/SEAN ADAIR

GOVERNMENT
AND THE
ECONOMY

Campaign signs in Syracuse, New York. During the 2000 election, campaign costs for all parties and candidates are thought to have surpassed $3 billion.

Government and Politics

The political institutions of the United States derive from a combination of the English heritage of restricted representative government, the Enlightenment philosophy that located power in the governed, and a colonial experience of isolation and distance which demanded self-rule. The system is intended to distribute power in order to prevent any one person or group from accumulating a dangerous degree of control, and to protect the numeric minority from the majority. Over the years, however, the application of egalitarian principles has been limited by gender, race, and ethnicity, and by class biases.

Democracy and the Constitution

The principles of governance are outlined in the Constitution of 1788, the oldest written plan of government in the world. The Constitution replaced the Articles of Confederation, the plan adopted in 1781 after the colonies declared independence from Great Britain. The fledgling Americans were accustomed to powerful state governments and feared a strong central government such as they had experienced under British rule. As a result, they denied the Confederation adequate authority to carry out its responsibilities. The Confederation Congress, for example, requested taxes from each state government, but had no means to compel payment. And, indeed, the states rarely paid. The Articles also failed to create a national military force, relying on the will of the states to provide a militia, which they failed to do when an anti-tax rebellion erupted against state collections in Massachusetts in 1786.

Frightened by such sentiments, the political and financial leaders of the young nation gathered in Philadelphia in the heat of the summer of 1787 to discuss a new plan of government. Instead of revising the Articles of Confederation, they replaced them with

a new plan, the Constitution, which divided power more evenly between central, or federal, government and the state governments. The new document aimed to establish principles rather than anticipate specifics, and promised a republican or representative form of government.

The Constitution's longevity is the result of its flexibility, which derives partly from the amendment process. Amendments to the document can be made through a two-step process of proposal and ratification. They can be proposed at the national level through Congress, with the approval of two-thirds of each house, or at the state level, with the approval of two-thirds of the legislatures. Ratification is usually handled by the state legislatures, but Congress also has the power to authorize special conventions for ratification. In either case, three-fourths of the states must approve the amendment.

The Constitution established that national elections would be held every two years and presidential elections every four years, but it left other election issues to state control, thus preserving local prejudices instead of creating national standards. It further limited democracy by allowing voters direct control over only the House of Representatives, and not the Senate, presidency, or judiciary.

The right to vote is essential to republican democracy, but English traditions imposed class and gender constraints on political involvement, a situation only partially rectified by the Enlightenment, which dismissed women as unworthy of citizenship. In America, racial restrictions developed gradually throughout the colonial period, legalizing and institutionalizing discrimination against all nonwhites in spite of the Enlightenment exaltation of the individual.

The two centuries following the adoption of the Constitution were an erratic progression toward near-universal suffrage as women and African-Americans gained then lost and regained the franchise. Slaves of either sex never voted, but propertied women in New Jersey and free, propertied blacks in several states voted temporarily in the early years of the new Republic. Both lost the franchise, women by 1800 and free blacks by 1840, ironically at the same time that unpropertied white males gained the vote. Black participation did not resume until after the Civil War, when the Reconstruction Amendments—the Thirteenth (1865), Fourteenth (1868), and Fifteenth (1870) additions to the Constitution—abolished slavery and prohibited

The president is chosen not by the voters, but by the electors of the Electoral College. The number of electors in each state equals the number of senators in the state (always two) plus the number of representatives (which depends on the state's population). The totals are shown below.

Alaska   3

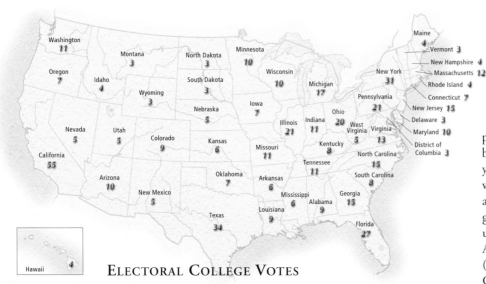

Washington 11
Montana 3
North Dakota 3
Minnesota 10
Maine 4
Vermont 3
New Hampshire 4
Oregon 7
Idaho 4
South Dakota 3
Wisconsin 10
New York 31
Massachusetts 12
Rhode Island 4
Wyoming 3
Michigan 17
Pennsylvania 21
Connecticut 7
Iowa 7
Ohio 20
New Jersey 15
Nevada 5
Nebraska 5
Illinois 21
Indiana 11
West Virginia 5
Virginia 13
Delaware 3
Maryland 10
California 55
Utah 5
Colorado 9
Kansas 6
Missouri 11
Kentucky 8
North Carolina 13
District of Columbia 3
Arizona 10
Oklahoma 7
Arkansas 6
Tennessee 11
South Carolina 8
New Mexico 5
Mississippi 6
Alabama 9
Georgia 13
Texas 34
Louisiana 9
Florida 27

Hawaii 4

ELECTORAL COLLEGE VOTES

The inauguration of George Washington as the first president of the United States took place in New York on April 30, 1789, after Washington had won the unanimous approval of the Electoral College. His selection was also popular with the city's citizens, who turned out in large numbers to congratulate him.

A group of suffragettes gathers outside the Woman Suffrage headquarters in Cleveland, Ohio, in 1912. Suffragettes won voting rights for women in nine states between 1910 and 1914, forcing other states to soon follow suit. Full suffrage was finally granted in 1920 with the passing of the Anthony Amendment, which says that the right to vote "shall not be denied … on account of sex."

disfranchisement on racial grounds. As soon as federal troops left the South in 1876, however, southern states began to impose literacy, financial, and other restrictions on suffrage with the aim of excluding both former slaves and poor white men, whose Populist Movement threatened elitist rule by the 1890s. It was not until 1965 that the *Voting Rights Act*, subtitled "An Act to Enforce the Fifteenth Amendment," abolished the poll tax and literacy requirements; even then, enforcement was achieved only after loss of life and property.

Other racial and ethnic minorities were excluded from the political system by the Constitution, which named Indians as an ineligible group, and by the first *Immigration and Naturalization Act* of 1790, which extended naturalized citizenship to "free whites" only. Native Americans gained citizenship gradually, a process completed in 1924, but naturalized citizenship continued to elude Asian settlers well into the twentieth century, and Americans of Asian descent were also denied due process and other rights until the end of World War II. Age discrimination was addressed in the Twenty-Sixth Amendment (1971), which extended the franchise to eighteen-year-olds.

In addition to an expanded franchise, voters increasingly sought greater influence over elected officials and legislation. In the twentieth century, they demanded and won the right of initiative and referendum, the power to suggest and comment on proposed and existing legislation at state and local levels, and the power of recall, which allows voters to remove an unpopular official from office before the end of the term. The United States Senate, state judiciaries, and many local offices, though not the presidency, also gradually came under direct control of the ballot.

Campaigners supporting the legalization of soft drugs gather at a rally in Washington DC. Since being chosen as the site of the national capital in 1790, the city has been a focal point for a wide variety of interest groups eager to attract popular and political support for particular issues. The rights to free speech and assembly were established by the Bill of Rights (1791).

The single most serious limitation on democracy in the opening years of the twenty-first century is the continued existence of the Electoral College system, which creates a barrier between voters and direct selection of the president. Under the system, voters choose electors, who in turn choose the president. The number of electors, 538, is determined by totaling the number of senators and representatives and adding three for the residents of the nation's capital. The creation of the system was a reflection of the Constitution writers' distrust of the masses. In the modern era, its impact is not to preserve elitist control, but to give undue weight to presidential votes cast in the states with the smallest populations. Three times it has resulted in presidents who did not receive the majority of the electoral votes. It may be, however, that the system's extremely inconsistent standards, which were exposed during the 2000 presidential election, and the rapid developments in Internet possibilities will soon combine to revolutionize the selection process for the Chief Executive.

The Bill of Rights

Ratification of the Constitution, which was carried out by state legislatures in the fall of 1787, was accomplished amid much public debate. The most searing criticism was directed at the lack of a Bill of Rights, a feature of most state constitutions of the time. The writers pledged to rectify the omission if the document otherwise met with public approval, and subsequently one of the first orders of business when Congress first opened was to craft a series of amendments to protect the rights of the people.

Collectively called the Bill of Rights, the first 10 amendments were approved by the states in 1791. The Constitution itself had provided some safeguards, such as forbidding ex post facto laws that would punish an act that was legitimate when committed, and Bills of Attainder, which punish without due process. The original document also guaranteed the writ of habeas corpus, the right to appear in court, and the right to know charges. The Bill of Rights added specific protections for property, freedom of speech, press, and assembly, and increased the rights of persons accused of a crime to include protection from unreasonable searches and seizures, the right to an attorney and a fair and speedy trial, and the right to remain silent. The Bill of Rights applied only to the federal government until after the Civil War when the Fourteenth Amendment and subsequent court rulings extended coverage to the actions of state governments.

Political parties

The Constitution contains no provisions for regulating political parties because when the document was written they had yet to evolve. Within a generation, however, nascent parties coalesced around the opposing interpretations of the Constitution presented by Thomas Jefferson and Alexander Hamilton. They divided over the size and role of the national government, elitism, and democracy, and economic interests. Jefferson's followers, who tended to be commoners fearful of a powerful central government, called themselves Democratic Republicans, and evolved into the modern Democratic Party. Hamilton, on the other hand, attracted men of business and commerce who looked to the government to provide institutions, such as banks, that would further their economic development. By 1856, Hamilton's political descendants were calling themselves Republicans.

Party development paralleled the evolution of white male suffrage, as common men gained control of the political process in the 1820s and 1830s by organizing voters locally and linking them nationally. At the same time, they imposed democracy within political parties through the adoption of the convention system, whereby candidates are chosen by the entire membership of a party instead of by a party elite under the old caucus rules.

A binary split characterized the political landscape from the beginning, with each party defining itself broadly enough to absorb third parties as they appeared. Consensus, rather than coalition, resulted. To enable the wide variety of views within each party to be heard, primaries were instituted— elections held within the party to choose the representative who would stand for president at the next general election. The South abused the primary system following the Civil War, using it as a tool to evade the mandate of the Fifteenth Amendment, but the worst of the abuses have been curtailed and the system is still used by both parties. Recent efforts to reform the political process have focused on the excessive influence of money, a situation that is difficult to change

because restrictions run counter to freedom-of-expression guarantees in the First Amendment.

Division of power

The powers of national, or federal, government are noted principally in the first three articles of the Constitution. The primacy of the federal or national government is established in Article VI, which proclaims the laws of the United States as the "supreme law of the land … the laws of any state notwithstanding." The federal government is expressly forbidden to pass certain laws violating individual rights, and the states are similarly prohibited from similar types of legislation. Furthermore, the states are not allowed to conduct foreign affairs such as entering into treaties or imposing tariffs. The Tenth Amendment (1791), known as the "states' rights" amendment, gives the states broad control over any matters not assigned to the federal government. For most of the nineteenth century, defining the boundaries between federal and state power dominated the discourse on constitutional interpretation, and the limit of state power was the question underlying the Civil War.

Responsibility and authority are further divided between three branches within the federal government, which were modeled on those of existing state governments: the legislature, the executive, and the judiciary. Each has the power to "check" the actions of the other two. Of the three branches, the legislature and executive work together most closely. Congress has a noticeable tendency to temporarily surrender power to the executive, especially during war, and occasionally has expanded the power of

the presidency permanently, such as in the area of settling labor disputes.

THE LEGISLATIVE BRANCH: CONGRESS

The authors of the Constitution intended that the branches of government would be equal in influence and prestige, but they betrayed a bias in favor of the legislature in the structure of the Constitution itself and in the level of detail included in the Articles. Article I, the longest segment of the Constitution, established a bicameral body, reflecting the simultaneous desire for and fear of democracy, and recognizing the recent autonomy enjoyed by state units under the Articles of Confederation. The makeup of each of the two houses, the Senate and the House of Representatives, reflects a compromise reached at the convention in 1787, between states with large populations and those that were more sparsely settled. The structure of the Senate appeased the small states by mandating two senators from each state regardless of size or population. As of 2001, that number totaled 100.

Membership of the House of Representatives depends on the population of the state, with each state guaranteed at least one representative. The current total number of members is 435.

The necessary qualifications for membership of either the House of Representatives or the Senate are

Designed by Maya Lin, the Civil Rights Memorial at Birmingham, Alabama, records the names and deeds of 40 people who gave their lives in the struggle for civil rights.

LEFT: A lapel button used during an election in the late nineteenth century. Such badges came into use in the 1880s and are still a feature of political campaigns.

Seat of the US legislature, the Capitol was designed in 1792 by William Thornton, a British-born doctor with no architectural training. Congress first assembled here in November 1800.

minimal and the number of terms that can be served unlimited. Members of the House of Representatives are, however, subject to regular voter scrutiny through short, two-year terms. Members of the Senate, where the states rather than the citizens are paramount, hold office for six years. Originally, senators were even more aloof from the people, being elected by state legislatures instead of popular vote until the Seventeenth Amendment in 1913.

Congressional responsibilities are noted both broadly and specifically in the Constitution. Broadly, Congress is obliged to "provide for … the general Welfare of the United States" and "make all Laws which shall be necessary and proper" for carrying out their duties. It is given specific responsibility for financial matters such as coinage, taxes, and credit; defense issues, including the declaration of war, and funding and regulating all military and militia; and the administration of the seat of national government, the District of Columbia. Specifically, the House of Representatives controls the introduction of taxation and other financial bills, while the Senate has sole confirmation power over treaties and presidential appointments; other bills can originate in either house.

Legislation must be passed by both houses, usually after scrutiny by various committees. The president's signature is necessary before the bill becomes law, but even if the president vetoes a bill, it can be enacted if two-thirds of both houses pass it again. Vetoes are rare, as are overrides. Free debate is assured by immunity from prosecution in all cases except treason, felonies, and breach of the peace, while members attend to their duties.

Each house determines its own operating rules. The Representatives choose their own Speaker, but the Constitution imposes the executive vice president on the Senate as its president, though the document limits his or her voting rights to breaking tie votes. Power is constrained by the rules of parliamentary procedure, the structure and composition of committees (where bills often die from inaction), and the authority of the Speaker and the Senate President, who influence the flow of legislation and committee assignments. The Senate has a unique weapon in the filibuster, the right of a member to speak uninterrupted for any length of time and thereby prevent discussion or vote on a controversial matter, unless two-thirds of the members vote otherwise. Power in both houses is also tempered by the imposition of the requirement for a super-majority of two-thirds to pass or prevent a bill, a tool established in the Constitution.

Congressional history is replete with sterling moments, ranging from the passage of amendments expanding the doctrine of equality to impassioned speeches supporting the concept of Union. However, it is also littered with financial scandals, ranging from irregular railroad financing in 1879 to ABSCAM, a bribery sting operation by the Federal Bureau of Investigation that resulted in the indictments of seven congressmen in 1979. More controversial are actions deriving from Congress's power to investigate, a function not specifically identified but implicitly "necessary and proper" for the legislature to carry out its duties. Prior to World War II, most investigations were a liberal response to the inertia of conservatives, and resulted in banking reform and the exposure of corruption. The irrational fear of communism prevalent after World War II changed the politics of Congressional investigations, resulting in the House of Representatives Un-American Activities Committee's harassment of suspected communists, uncooperative journalists, and finally of the Army itself, which in turn tarnished the reputation of the House. The same tactics were revived when the office of the Independent Counsel was created in response to President Richard Nixon's (1969–74) abuse of appointive power during the Watergate investigation. The office was allowed to expire after a multibillion-dollar impeachment failed to remove President Bill Clinton (1993–2001)

THE EXECUTIVE BRANCH: THE PRESIDENCY

Every four years, the president is expected to bridge the gap between partisanship and national unity in the three months separating the election in November from the inauguration in January. The presidency is the only office that represents the nation as a whole. Authorized to execute laws, the president also exercises limited legislative power and judicial power, suggesting an agenda for Congress through a State of the Union address and holding the power of veto over Congressional acts, and appointing federal judges and Supreme Court Justices, subject to Senate approval. Foreign policy is largely controlled by the president, through the role of commander-in-chief of the armed

The Presidents

1789–97	George Washington
1797–1801	John Adams
1801–09	Thomas Jefferson
1809–17	James Madison
1817–25	James Monroe
1825–29	John Quincy Adams
1829–37	Andrew Jackson
1837–41	Martin Van Buren
1841	William Henry Harrison
1841–45	John Tyler
1845–49	James Polk
1849–50	Zachary Taylor
1850–53	Millard Fillmore
1853–57	Franklin Pierce
1857–61	James Buchanan
1861–65	Abraham Lincoln
1865–69	Andrew Johnson
1869–77	Ulysses Simpson Grant
1877–81	Rutherford Birchard Hayes
1881	James Abram Garfield
1881–85	Chester Alan Arthur
1885–89	Stephen Grover Cleveland
1889–93	Benjamin Harrison
1893–97	Stephen Grover Cleveland
1897–01	William McKinley
1901–09	Theodore (Teddy) Roosevelt
1909–13	William Howard Taft
1913–21	Thomas Woodrow Wilson
1921–23	Warren Gamaliel Harding
1923–29	John Calvin Coolidge
1929–33	Herbert Clark Hoover
1933–45	Franklin Delano Roosevelt
1945–53	Harry S. Truman
1953–61	Dwight David Eisenhower
1961–63	John (Jack) Fitzgerald Kennedy
1963–69	Lyndon Baines Johnson
1969–74	Richard Milhous Nixon
1974–77	Gerald Rudolph Ford
1977–81	James (Jimmy) Earl Carter
1981–89	Ronald Wilson Reagan
1989–93	George Herbert Walker Bush
1993–2001	William (Bill) Jefferson Clinton
2001–	George W. Bush

...UNTIL JUSTICE ROLLS DOWN LIKE WATERS AND RIGHTEOUSNESS LIKE A MIGHTY STREAM.
DR. MARTIN LUTHER KING, JR.
AUGUST 28, 1963

forces and the power to propose treaties of alliance and trade (although treaties, like appointments, depend on Senate approval).

Created by Article II of the Constitution, the office of president was a new entity, neither monarchy nor ministry in function and power, but with a precedent in the governorships that were a feature of the Revolutionary period. In theory, the office is open to any natural-born citizen aged 35 or older with 14 years' residency. Four Constitutional amendments addressed the election, inauguration, and succession of the president, but only one, the Twenty-Second (1951), made a change in the power of the office by limiting the incumbent to two four-year terms.

Other Constitutional restrictions on presidential actions prohibit treason, bribery, and undefined "high crimes and misdemeanors," for which a president may be removed from office. The removal process begins when the House of Representatives prepares Articles of Impeachment; this is followed by a hearing to determine whether the Senate should hold a trial. Conviction in the Senate results in loss of office. Congress threatened two presidents with impeachment, John Tyler (1841–45) and Richard Nixon, and impeached but failed to convict two others, Andrew Johnson (1865–69) and Bill Clinton. Nixon, who resigned rather than face removal, had

previously lost his vice president, Spiro Agnew, as a result of financial improprieties. The double abdication resulted in a new president, Gerald Ford (1974–77), and vice president, Nelson Rockefeller, who were chosen by Congress and had no popular or electoral mandate. No fewer than six presidents died while in office, either as a result of illness or of an assassin's bullet.

Personality, personal philosophy, circumstances, and available resources have all shaped the tenure of successive presidents. Success or failure depends on how well the incumbents meet national needs and accomplish their own agenda, and on what changes they impose on the office and government. The most successful presidents often directly follow the worst, and offer a clear, alternative interpretation of the Constitution. George Washington (1789–97), Abraham Lincoln (1861–65), and Franklin D. Roosevelt (1933–45) have been chosen in varying arrangements as the three "greatest" presidents in every significant survey since 1948. All came to power with the support of the majority of both houses of Congress and successfully shepherded the nation through the gravest periods in its history: respectively, the founding of the nation, the Civil War, and the Depression and World War II. Unquestionably honest, they made aggressive use of available resources and presided over fundamental changes in public policy during periods of critical change. They also conveyed comfort and provided commanding leadership during crises.

America's sixteenth president (1860–65) and undoubtedly one of its most distinguished leaders, Abraham Lincoln displayed courage, compassion, and eloquence. His two most significant achievements were the preservation of the Union during the Civil War and the abolition of slavery.

ABOVE LEFT: Commander-in-chief of the colonial forces during the Revolutionary War and president between 1788 and 1797, George Washington began his career as a surveyor and farmer before being appointed military adjutant of southern Virginia in 1752.

OPPOSITE: The Martin Luther King Jr Memorial Garden in Raleigh, North Carolina, commemorates the country's most charismatic civil rights campaigner.

The presidency of Theodore Roosevelt (1901–09) was marked by stricter government regulation of large corporations, a strategy that won the incumbent wide-spread popular support. At the same time, Roosevelt pursued a vigorous foreign policy, which raised America's profile overseas and even earned him the 1906 Nobel Peace Prize for helping to end the Russo-Japanese conflict.

The presidents at the other end of the spectrum influenced hardly anyone, failed to repudiate discredited policies, failed to present alternatives, or were simply corruptible. Two of the three most often designated as least successful, Franklin Pierce (1853–57) and his successor James Buchanan (1857–61), offered uninspired leadership in the decade before the Civil War. Warren G. Harding (1921–23), most often chosen as the worst president, had a record of philandering to rival John F. Kennedy (1961–63) and Bill Clinton. Harding also appointed some of the most corrupt officials to hold executive office.

The national penchant for rewarding warriors with civilian office elevated seven men to the presidency, with mixed results. Washington and Theodore Roosevelt, for example, made excellent presidents; others, such as Jackson, Taylor, and Grant were less successful appointments. Revisionist emphasis on personal failings such as Woodrow Wilson's racism and Thomas Jefferson's (1800–08) long liaison with a slave resulted in downward adjustments in their ratings. Between the best and the worst, most presidents conduct themselves with a sense of their place in history, responding to both an established order and pressures for change.

Broad chronological developments in the characteristics of each presidency reflect the changing geographic, economic, and social order of the nation. A patrician air befitting the nation's founders characterized the political culture of the first six men to hold the office. Andrew Jackson (1829–37), the first "common man" to serve, benefited from expanding the franchise to all free white males. A frontiersman, he came to power as leader of the first national constituency organized locally and broadly into the Democratic Party. Presidential power during this partisan period lay in control over appointments. Theodore

Created by sculptor Gutzon Borglum between 1927 and 1941, the Mount Rushmore memorial incorporates portraits of presidents Washington, Jefferson, Theodore Roosevelt, and Lincoln, who symbolize, respectively, the founding, political philosophy, expansion and conservation, and preservation of the nation.

Roosevelt (1901–09) combined a boisterous personality with a philosophical devotion to progressive reforms, and curtailed the patronage system in favor of a civil service bureaucracy. Power in the first half of the twentieth century lay in the support of interests outside of the party, such as labor groups and farmers, and in the control of expanding executive agencies, such as the Department of the Interior. Richard Nixon's victory in 1968 represented a fourth cultural shift in the office, based on a new coalition of corporate heads and Southerners, centered outside of the beltway of traditional political power in Washington, DC. Nixon and subsequent presidents made extensive use of mass communication to appeal directly to the public. They created fiefdoms that were burdened by both partisan politics and bargains with special interest groups.

THE JUDICIARY

The watchdog on the activities of presidents, Congress, and the states is the judiciary, which was established by Article III of the Constitution. The third branch of government was given the least attention by the writers, and when the new national government took up residence in the new Capitol Building in Washington, DC, in 1800, the Supreme Court was, significantly, confined to the basement.

Although the creation of the Supreme Court was another innovative American contribution to government, the founders had little previous experience with a successful judicial structure and left much of the creation of the judiciary to Congress. The Constitution addresses only the creation of the Supreme Court. It defines the court's "original jurisdiction," which is the power of the court to be the first to hear a case, but limits that jurisdiction to disputes among states or involving diplomats and foreign affairs. The most important task assigned to the Supreme Court is to serve as the final arbiter in appeals coming from other courts. To complete the system, Congress passed a series of acts, most notably the Judiciary Act of 1789, which were the source of the three-tiered hierarchy of, from bottom to top, the Federal District Courts, Federal Appeals Courts, and the US Supreme Court.

The most fundamental power of the Supreme Court, judicial review—the authority to declare unconstitutional the actions of the president, Congress, or states—was not identified specifically in the Constitution, although the writers were familiar with the concept from their state courts and from the courts of England. Chief Justice John Marshall (1801–35), considered the greatest chief justice, rectified the matter in *Marbury v. Madison*, a case involving executive appointments which came before him in 1803. Marshall crafted the Court's intent to legitimize the power of the national government over the states, to impose discipline on the legislative and executive branches, and to safeguard a stable, free-flowing market.

More often than not, the Supreme Court's decisions over the past two centuries have followed Marshall in augmenting the power of the national government at the expense of the states, a tendency that has been the topic of intense legal debate. Notable exceptions have occurred mainly during the most turbulent periods of history, such as the buildup to the Civil War, the second Industrial Revolution, and the Depression, when institutions were reshaped. Although technically correct, the Dred Scott ruling of 1857, which denied legal recourse to slaves, is considered the worst decision the Supreme Court ever made. The Court's dedicated attempt to undermine the New Deal in the 1930s by denying the federal government the power to intervene in the economy resulted in a serious threat by Franklin Roosevelt to destroy the integrity of the Court. Roosevelt suggested that he might ask Congress to create more seats on the Supreme Court, thereby permitting him to appoint justices more likely to approve his programs. The court then backed down.

Supreme Court decisions often generate controversy, but only four have been overridden by amendment in over 200 years. Despite repeated threats of impeachment and even occasionally threats of death, for the last half of the twentieth century the Court championed civil and individual rights against the states, striking down institutionalized racism and sexism and upholding Congressional and executive efforts to create a more egalitarian society.

The writers intended to create an "independent judiciary," removed from political corruption, and thus specified that all federal judges and Supreme Court justices would hold appointment for "good behavior," but no other qualifications were stipulated. As a result, politics permeates the appointment, confirmation, and functions of the judiciary and in turn, the judges and justices influence politics.

This state of affairs was highlighted during the presidential election in December 2000, when the Supreme Court halted the recount of the Florida ballot and, in a partisan five-to-four vote, decided to allow a partial tally to become official, thus giving the election to George W. Bush, despite the fact that his rival Al Gore had won a larger proportion of the popular vote. That involvement was an aberration in that justices traditionally attempt to remain aloof from purely political issues and avoid ruling on relations between the other branches of government. It damaged a glowing reputation for integrity, just as failure to reform the election process has cost the other branches and the political parties dearly in trust and prestige.

Yet the harm is not irreparable. The power of money and the tendency toward reform are both part of the American tradition. The changes that have been wrought to the Constitution and the social order derive from the same basic principles upon which the plan of government was based: that a democratically elected republican form of government would protect the general welfare of the people, who were free to express their approval and disapproval in a variety of peaceful, legal ways, regardless of their gender, ethnicity, or class.

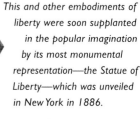

US
Supreme Court

13 US Circuit
Courts of Appeal

94 US District Courts

BELOW LEFT: The United States' district courts constitute the trial courts of the federal system. The 94 judicial districts are divided into 13 regional circuits, each of which has a federal court of appeal. The Courts of Appeal may, in turn, refer certain cases, most notably those regarding federal law or the Constitution, to the nation's ultimate arbiter, the US Supreme Court.

This wrought-iron weather vane, made in 1880, depicts Liberty carrying the Stars and Stripes. This and other embodiments of liberty were soon supplanted in the popular imagination by its most monumental representation—the Statue of Liberty—which was unveiled in New York in 1886.

Resources

The United States is blessed with a remarkably wide range of natural resources that has long been the linchpin of its steady economic growth. These resources can be divided into the categories of agriculture, minerals, and timber.

Agriculture

The American agricultural industry has been predicated upon the fortuitous combination of a benevolent climate and an enormous supply of arable land. The utilization of these resources has been accentuated by long-term developments such as capital intensification, the use of fertilizers, and the selective genetic breeding of crops. Over the years, these trends have combined to create exponential increases in efficiency that have resulted in the most productive agricultural industry in the world. At the same time, however, they have also led to the agricultural share of the labor force dwindling dramatically and to agriculture becoming agribusiness.

The national agricultural industry arose out of a patchwork of diverse crops and local practices that developed in different ways. In the early nineteenth century, steamships opened up the agricultural regions along the Mississippi River, making cities such as St Louis and New Orleans important points of transshipment. Settlers arriving in this area discovered an enormous region with tens of millions of square miles of flat, relatively stone-free agricultural land; a lengthy growing season; reasonably high, relatively predictable amounts of annual rainfall; and rich,

fecund soils. The subsequent unfolding of the Euro-American "frontier" in the nineteenth century laid the basis for the wholesale commercialization of the Midwest and Great Plains. The region has since been dedicated primarily to the production of spring and winter wheat as well as corn and hogs in the eastern Midwest (Indiana through Iowa) and cattle in the "beef belt" stretching from Texas to North Dakota. Much of the corn and wheat sorghum is used for animal feed. The upper Midwest is mainly given over to the production of dairy products.

In California, the Central Valley is similarly fertile and has become the world's leading producer of fruits and vegetables. National citrus production is concentrated in southern California and Florida. Sugar production relies on sugar cane grown in southern Florida and Louisiana, and sugar beets in Hawaii. The Pacific Northwest is the United States' leading producer of apples. Cotton and tobacco cultivation have long been confined to the South, to a large degree west and east of the Appalachian Mountains, respectively. From the eighteenth century onward, cotton production formed a major link between the Southern economy and the textile mills in the Northeast and in Britain.

The size and productivity of American agriculture are mirrored by its exports. The United States sells one-half of all traded agricultural products in the world, and is by far the world's leading exporter of grain (although it is a net importer of meat). Such exports are a major source of foreign revenues, rivaling those of manufacturing.

Despite its abundance, agricultural land has been threatened by an increasing number of social and environmental problems, including soil erosion and the loss of topsoil, groundwater extraction and pollution, saltwater intrusion in coastal areas, and rural-to-urban land conversion, as a result of which agricultural areas on the periphery of cities are swallowed up by urban sprawl.

A maintenance crew carries out repairs on an oil well at Burbank, Oklahoma. Oil reserves are scattered across the United States, but the major sources are Alaska, Texas, California, and Louisiana.

ABOVE RIGHT: Wheat fields in Montana. The United States is the world's third-largest wheat producer after China and India.

Bingham Canyon Copper Mine, near Salt Lake City, Utah, is one of the world's most productive open-pit copper mines. Measuring 2 1/2 miles (4 km) wide and 1/2 mile (0.8 km) deep, it is the largest excavation on Earth.

Minerals

The United States is fortunate to possess enormous, if unevenly distributed, coal deposits. Indeed, so large are the deposits that they could theoretically satisfy national energy demands for the next 300 years.

Throughout the nineteenth century, rising demand for coal—particularly as a consequence of the rapidly expanding manufacturing base of the Northeast and Midwest—resulted, predictably enough, in the exploitation of the rich seams of anthracite in the Appalachian Mountains, particularly in western Pennsylvania, Kentucky, and West Virginia. Employment in coal production reached its peak during the 1920s, when it generated approximately 750,000 jobs, but has declined steadily ever since. During the 1970s, rising energy prices and environmental concerns regarding the high sulfur content of Appalachian coal fostered the creation of mining communities in the Rocky Mountains (particularly Colorado and Utah) centered on the exploitation of low-sulfur bituminous coal and oil shale.

The American petroleum industry, which began in 1859 in Pennsylvania, hinged initially upon the exploitation of modest Midwest reserves. However, the industry subsequently shifted to Texas, Oklahoma, and Louisiana, where much larger reserves were found including sizable fields of oil and natural gas. Twenty-five thousand wells are now located offshore on the shallow continental shelf of the Gulf of Mexico.

Because crude oil is generally transported by pipeline, cities in this region have become termini for a vast network of pipes linked to metropolitan regions throughout the nation. Oil refining and storage services here also form the basis of the American petrochemicals industry. The 1970s energy crisis and resulting high oil prices induced petroleum companies to begin extraction in northern Alaska's Prudhoe Bay, from where crude oil is now transported to the state's southern coast via the Trans-Alaska pipeline. Despite this sizable domestic supply, however, the voracious American appetite for energy has generated a demand for imported petroleum, which today comprises more than one-half of the nation's total usage.

Although its population represents only four percent of the world's people, the United States consumes about one-third of its energy. In addition to coal, petroleum, oil shale, and natural gas, the American energy supply includes substantial quantities of hydroelectric power, which are generated by the 75,000 or so dams scattered around the country. In addition, nuclear power stations produce about 20 percent of the national energy supply.

The extraction of America's mineral wealth has been primarily a western phenomenon, creating a broad swath of communities whose fortunes rose and fell in a series of dramatic boom-and-bust cycles. The California Gold Rush of the 1850s attracted miners from all over the world to the Rocky Mountains and Pacific Northwest. Copper extraction has long been concentrated in Arizona and western Montana,

although declining world prices have recently led to numerous mines being shut down. In Idaho, Nevada, Utah, Colorado, and, to a lesser extent, Wyoming and New Mexico, open-pit mining of lead, zinc, nickel, tin, uranium, gold, molybdenum, tungsten, and silver continues, although employment levels have declined in the face of enormous capital intensification. In the South, mining of phosphate and sulfur occurs; however, as the highest-grade ores have gradually been exhausted and low prices have discouraged new supplies, many smaller mining communities have become ghost towns.

An oil well in Texas. In 2001, the United States' oil reserves were estimated at 21.8 million barrels, making it the twelfth largest producer in the world. Despite this, the nation imports more than 50 percent of its oil needs, mainly from Canada, Saudi Arabia, Venezuela, and Mexico.

Timber

The immense forests that once stretched across the North American continent were cleared rapidly by European settlers as they spread westward. The completion of the transcontinental railroads in the late nineteenth century opened a new chapter in American forestry, integrating the enormous stands of large coniferous trees in the Pacific Northwest into the national economy. The complex of timber, lumber, pulp, and paper production companies located in Washington, Idaho, Oregon, and northern California soon became the largest source of wood products in the world. The use of clear-cutting techniques dramatically altered the forest landscapes and stimulated environmental concerns regarding habitat destruction. Today, relatively few virgin forests remain intact, and those that do lie almost entirely in the national parks erected during the early twentieth century. As a result, American timber production has increasingly come to rely on scientific forestry and monocultural tree farms for perpetual forest production.

A high proportion of the nation's timber is used to make paper, and the United States is by far the world's largest manufacturer of paper and paper products.

Working the Land

The Amish communities of Ohio and Pennsylvania generally buck the historical trend toward mega-farming. Amish farms typically cover just 50 acres (20 ha) or so and include a range of crops such as corn, tobacco, and peanuts.

AGRICULTURAL REGIONS

Agriculture's share of the labor force may have declined dramatically, but it still dominates the physical landscape. The sector's broad regional characteristics were established by the beginning of the twentieth century.

- Dairy belt
- Spring wheat belt
- Winter wheat belt
- Atlantic fruit and vegetable belt
- General farming
- Corn belt
- Columbia Basin wheat region
- Grazing and irrigated crops region
- Gulf subtropical crop belt
- Old cotton belt
- Mediterranean agriculture
- Pacific dairy and fruit crops

During the colonial era, nearly all of the residents of the English and Spanish colonies in what would become the United States were farmers. Spatial patterns of land use formed two distinct configurations: small family farms in the Northeast, and a mix of family farms and large, commercial operations in the central and southern colonies. At the end of the eighteenth century, Thomas Jefferson spoke glowingly of farmers as the nation's future, describing them as the embodiment of liberty and advocating that the government give 50 acres (20 ha) of land to every white male. His political nemesis, Alexander Hamilton, who advocated using the land to support manufacture and commerce, was more prescient. However, Jefferson's campaign created an enduring American myth: the farmer as a sacred symbol of moral purity, rugged individualism, and the Puritan work ethic.

The agricultural revolution

The history of American farming is dominated by three themes: increasing efficiency, dwindling economic and political influence, and greater federal involvement in the agricultural sector. Jefferson pioneered new methods of tilling and fertilizing, and initiated newsletters to educate farmers and create a sense of community. But his advice on scientific farming was largely ignored at a time when it was more economical for farmers to wear out the land and move on than to engage in prudent management. In the first quarter of the nineteenth century, thousands of acres, especially in the South, were left barren as farmers moved westward.

Steady reform resulted in the first agricultural revolution of the 1840s, and by 1850 the changes taking place were as profound as those that had occurred in the textile trades during the first Industrial Revolution. The evolution was uneven, however, and interrupted by a dramatic increase in a form of tenant farming called sharecropping following the Civil War and the droughts of the late 1870s. Under this system, farmers provided labor in exchange for a plot of land, equipment, and a small share of the yield. The practice was common in up to one-third of the farms in the West, and characterized 50 to 60 percent of farms in the South. There, it was brutally enforced and resulted in widespread poverty until the 1930s, when it began to be alleviated by President Roosevelt's New Deal policies.

As southern farmers sank into indigence, western farmers struggled to bring the Great Plains under cultivation in the face of drought, blizzards, fires, and grasshopper plagues. In the last quarter of the nineteenth century, especially in Minnesota and the Dakotas, mechanized megafarms transformed western farming, bringing up to 30,000 acres (12,000 ha) at a time under cultivation. These "bonanza farms" then overpowered smaller spreads economically and politically.

As the 1900s progressed, technological developments, including new machines, tools, fertilizers, hybrid and selectively bred seeds, and new labor configurations, increasingly enhanced the efficiency and wealth of the farming sector nationwide.

Farmers as a political force

Farmers, whether consciously organized or not, shaped political, military, and economic policies throughout the nineteenth century. They established a powerful tradition of political leadership by providing four of the first generation of presidents, and were prominent among the secession movements in the South.

The farmers' political influence reached its peak near the end of the century, when southern and western farmers formed the Populist Party, the third-largest political party in American history, in 1892. It grew out of government-sponsored social clubs that were established after the Civil War to address the social isolation endemic in farm communities. The Populists failed to topple the two-party system, but nearly all of their platform was eventually adopted: direct election of senators, graduated income tax, depositors' insurance, an eight-hour workday, and restrictions on immigration. Unsophisticated and racist, the Populists nonetheless were the vanguard of a worldwide trend toward liberalism that accelerated in the twentieth century.

Government intervention

In a context philosophically dedicated to a free-market system, government intervention evolved in the nineteenth and twentieth centuries from indirect support for education and communication to direct subsidies and price supports. In the nineteenth century, the federal government built roads and canals to enable

FRUIT
TIMBER
WHEAT
BARLEY
SPRING WHEAT
TIMBER
CATTLE
HOGS
DAIRY CATTLE
DAIRY CATTLE
SHEEP
CORN
SOYBEANS
POTATOES
CATTLE
CATTLE
CORN
CORN HOGS CORN
FRUIT
CORN HOGS SOYBEANS
GRAPES
CATTLE
CATTLE
VEGETABLES
TOBACCO
CITRUS
WINTER WHEAT
SOYBEANS
TOBACCO
COTTON
CATTLE
CHICKENS
DAIRY CATTLE
COTTON
CATTLE
CHICKENS
SOYBEANS
PEANUTS
COTTON
CHICKENS
SHEEP
CATTLE
SUGAR
SUGAR
COTTON
CITRUS

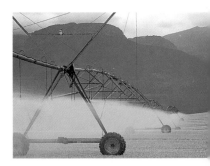

Western farmers have long been dependent on irrigation. The lack of water was addressed by the federal government in 1902 when it set up the Bureau of Reclamation and a series of dams and irrigation systems.

ABOVE LEFT: A Tennessee farmer at a local market. The worldwide trend toward trade liberalization has forced American farmers to compete more directly with overseas producers.

farmers to ship their produce to the urbanized East, and Congress funded military operations to protect farmers from angry Native Americans. During the Civil War, Congress passed a trio of acts that increased federal involvement in farming by setting up the Department of Agriculture, creating a new land policy (the *Homestead Act*), and establishing land-grant (agricultural) colleges (the *Morrill Act*).

The *Homestead Act* made huge tracts of free and low-cost acreage available in the West, tripling the number of farms by 1920. The colleges continued Jefferson's attempts to promote the scientific study of farming. Initially, they specialized in the study of animal husbandry, chemistries for fertilizers, herbicides, and insecticides, and the genetics of seeds. They also became administrators for county agents, providing funding and research data to men and women who demonstrated products and techniques and assisted farmers through meetings and regular newsletters.

In the early twentieth century, government activism became steadily more direct. Congressmen from the farming states sponsored legislation outlawing price collusion perpetrated by the corporations that purchased farm goods, the railroads that shipped them, and the manufacturers of farming supplies. They also exempted farmers' cooperatives from antitrust laws, and refined the rules governing rural credit, making it easier for farmers to obtain loans between harvests.

Capital-intensive farming

The first two decades of the twentieth century were agriculture's golden era, when farm wealth increased faster than manufacturing. Farmers began to adopt the culture of business and formed associations similar to those of their urban counterparts, as well as regional marketing organizations. The drive toward business efficiency culminated in the formation of the American Farm Bureau Federation in 1920, a national organization created to put farmers in contact with manufacturers and assist with financial needs.

By World War I, regional production patterns had emerged, the Northeast and upper Midwest specializing in dairying, poultry, and truck farming; the Mid-

west in corn, grain, and hogs and cattle; and the Great Plains in "wavin' wheat," as immortalized in the musical *Oklahoma*. The South relinquished its exclusive hold on cotton to begin truck farming and soybean cultivation, and California emerged as the most diverse region. In the 1920s, the number of farms peaked at 6.4 million.

Increased global competition and decreased regulation of the market at home then tipped farming into an economic depression ahead of the rest of the nation. In response, Roosevelt's New Deal of the 1930s established federally funded price supports, curbed overproduction through compensation, and improved the lives of millions of families through the provision of electricity, flood control, and recreational facilities.

New methods continued to transform the profile of farming, making it increasingly capital intensive rather than labor intensive. In the second half of the twentieth century, the number of farms in the United States declined from 5.5 million in 1950 to 1.5 million in 1995, while the average size rose from 200 to 500 acres (81 to 203 ha). Urban development encroached on 300 million acres (120 million ha). Advancements in agricultural science once more produced improvements in efficiency. Chemicals became more effective and seeds began to be genetically engineered.

Genetically modified produce was a common topic of debate as the twenty-first century began. The discussion took place in a context of falling trade barriers, a trend embraced by the United States (see page 133). Government subsidies continue to be paid to farmers—reaching $25 billion in 2000—and national protectiveness is ending only slowly. The trend toward free trade is often presented as a threat to the traditional farm, but 90 percent of farms are still family-owned. At the same time, however, the percentage of Americans engaged in agriculture has declined to just two percent, and farmers no longer command the political power they wielded in the nineteenth century.

Agricultural land near Batesville, Arkansas. Hard, labor-intensive effort was required to plow the thick turf of the central prairies, earning farmers the sobriquet "sodbusters" as well as a chapter in the book of farmer mythology.

The Rise of Manufacturing

US industry enjoyed a decade of expansion in the 1990s, although signs of a downturn appeared at the dawn of the new millennium.

The changing profile of the workforce reflects the declining significance of agriculture, the steady growth of manufacturing, and a rapid shift in the economy toward services in the postwar period.

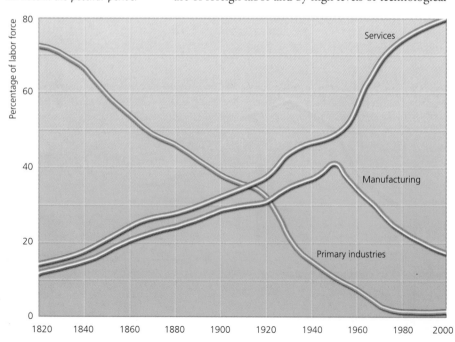

The emergence of manufacturing industries in North America marked the gradual formation of the largest single economy in the history of the world. Capitalizing on vast mineral resources and abundant agricultural land, the United States witnessed the rise of industry after industry, a process that generated enormous job opportunities, increased social mobility, and pushed up wages, and attracted tens of millions of immigrants from abroad. From the beginning, American industrialization was characterized by the use of foreign labor and by high levels of technological innovation, although such developments were uneven both temporally and geographically, reflecting various waves of change that transformed specific markets, products, technologies, and labor forces. In general, however, the growth of industries resulted in exponentially rising rates of productivity, and enormous social and spatial transformation.

For most of its early history—that is, prior to the 1830s—the United States was essentially a preindustrial nation, in which most economic activity centered around the utilization of raw materials, particularly through agriculture. The census of 1790, the first in the nation's history, recorded that 95 percent of the population lived in rural areas. Handicraft production was clustered primarily in the seaboard cities of the East Coast (including Boston, New York, Philadelphia, and Baltimore), which served as centers of trade with Europe.

By the 1830s, the emerging textile industry, which was then concentrated in southern New England, was pioneering the formation of the nation's industrial base. Linked to the garment industry in New York, textile production formed the basis of primary industry in Massachusetts, Rhode Island, Connecticut, and southern New Hampshire for more than a century, drawing large numbers of Irish immigrants into the labor force. In the 1920s and 1930s, the industry, drawn by lower wages and unionization rates, made a sudden shift to the South, primarily to the Piedmont states of North and South Carolina and Georgia, which remain the largest producers of American textiles to this day.

The emergence of an industrial superpower

Following the Civil War of 1861–65, the industrialization of the United States accelerated markedly. By 1890, manufacturing output surpassed that of agriculture and the United States overtook Great Britain as the world's leading industrial power. Along the East Coast, Connecticut and Philadelphia became notable centers of shipbuilding. In New York City, the garment industry flourished, drawing tens of thousands of German and eastern European Jews into the labor market. Light manufacturing flourished in many places, including activities such as sugar refining and the production of rope, pencils, caskets, and household goods. On the global stage, the United States was becoming an economic superpower: by 1913, it generated one-third of the world's industrial output; following World War II, this share would rise in some industries to 50 percent.

Much of the growth of manufacturing was concentrated in the "Manufacturing Belt," a broad swath of communities that extended from western New York State (and southern Ontario) across the southern shores of the Great Lakes, including cities such as Buffalo, Pittsburgh, Youngstown, Cleveland, Gary (Indiana), Chicago, and Milwaukee. Later, with the emergence of the automobile industry, Detroit became an important addition to this list. In contrast, manufacturing did not begin in earnest in the South until the 1920s, with the exception of the steel industry in Birmingham, Alabama. The Manufacturing Belt remained the primary locus of American industry for well over a century, until it was besieged by waves of deindustrialization in the 1970s.

The railroads were a key factor in the growth of the nineteenth-century economy, linking the expanding areas of the frontier West with the growing cities of the East and Midwest. Financed largely by British capital, the railroads extended progressively westward, opening up Midwestern agricultural and mining regions. Federal land grants expedited this process considerably. By the 1850s, railroads had reduced the pull of the Mississippi and Ohio River system, to the detriment of the South, and allowed western resources to flow eastward, just as many easterners were moving west. Construction of railroads provided a steady source of demand for the growing iron and steel industry and employed large numbers of immigrants (especially Irish in the East and Chinese in the West). In the 1870s, the size of the American railroad network surpassed that of all the European networks combined. By the 1880s, three lines—the Northern Pacific, Central Pacific, and Southern Pacific—completed the economic integration of the continent, facilitating regional specialization and a decline in the cost of many goods.

The late nineteenth century saw an unprecedented period of corporate growth and consolidation. Technological innovations, such as electricity and the telephone, raised productivity to new heights; national markets gradually displaced local ones, and large corporations with multiple offices and branch plants steadily swallowed smaller ones in a rapid round of oligopolization. This process was reflected in the rise of so-called "robber barons" who made fortunes in different industries, including Andrew Carnegie in steel, John D. Rockefeller in petroleum, Jay Gould and Cornelius Vanderbilt in railroads, the Dupont family in chemicals, and J.P. Morgan in banking. Yet others assumed control of the sugar, burlap, and barbed wire sectors.

Industrialization also saw the rise of labor unions and mounting class conflict, including violent strikes. Early organizations, from the Knights of Labor to the Industrial Workers of the World, disappeared in the heat of class warfare. The cautious, pragmatic American

LEFT: The rapid growth of large manufacturing companies gave rise to a wide range of smaller businesses engaged in producing services and materials, such as Sweet-Orr, a producer of heavy-duty clothes for factory workers.

A shipyard in Wisconsin. The national shipbuilding industry, which first took shape at the end of the nineteenth century, is centered on the Great Lakes and the eastern seaboard, especially Philadelphia and Connecticut.

The expansion of iron and steel production in the late nineteenth century coincided with greatly increased demand, especially from burgeoning railroad companies. Southern Pacific was founded in 1865 and established much of California's rail network.

Federation of Labor flourished, merging in the 1930s with the Congress of Industrial Organizations to become the largest working-class umbrella group.

Iron and steel

The iron and steel industry assumed pride of place in American industry during the late nineteenth century. Prior to this period, iron production tended to be organized around small-scale factories, many of which were dispersed in rural locations throughout the Northeast. Such operations relied upon wood and charcoal fuel and served local markets. In the 1880s and over the next four decades, however, several changes decisively reshaped the sector. The Bessemer process of open hearth furnaces made the production of steel relatively cheap, and led to the appearance of large, vertically integrated mills. The rise of the US Steel Corporation increased the domination of the industry by just a few companies; by 1901 it had become the world's largest corporation, producing 60 percent of the nation's steel output. The restructuring of the industry was geographically uneven, being centered on the cities of the Manufacturing Belt, which enjoyed certain advantages, such as easy access to Appalachian coal, Lake Superior iron ores, and Great Lakes water transport. Consequently, the major steel-producing cities were Hamilton (Ontario), Buffalo (New York), Youngstown and Cleveland (Ohio), Gary (Indiana), Chicago (Illinois), and above all, Pittsburgh (Pennsylvania), the epicenter of US Steel and the Carnegie empire.

Coal miners maintain a picket line during an industrial dispute at Window Rock, Arizona. Union membership declined significantly during the latter part of the twentieth century, falling from 20.1 percent in 1983 to 13.5 percent in 2000. Membership in manufacturing is, however, higher than average, at 14.8 percent.

Age of the automobile

Steel's triumphant ascendancy was soon matched by American dominance in another, albeit newer, industry: automobiles. Although car manufacturing originated in Europe, where producers catered to an upper-class clientele, the automobile and its production soon assumed distinctively American characteristics under the aegis of Henry Ford.

Ford's first automobile-production plant, in Dearborn, Michigan in 1902, became the nucleus for an expanding web of firms clustered within the general vicinity of Detroit, and added a new layer to the already robust industrial landscape of the Manufacturing Belt. Ford revolutionized the process of mass-production, introducing the moving assembly line and employing management methods developed by Frederick Taylor, such as time-and-motion studies. Early automobile production was strongly vertically integrated: coal and iron ore entered the plant, and finished cars came out. The new methods broke the industry into distinct sectors, each producing and assembling different parts. So profound was the impact of Ford's approach that the adoption of similar mass-production methods in other industries came to be known as "Fordism."

Unlike the Europeans, Ford also made the automobile affordable to the middle class and paid his own workers above-minimum wages. As a result, the swelling, urbanized middle class generated an enormous growth in the demand for automobiles during the 1920s. This in turn boosted the fortunes of suppliers of components, such as the tire manufacturers of Akron, Ohio, the capital of the nation's rubber industry. However, as automobile production expanded, the industry became increasingly oligopolized, so that today just three firms—General Motors, Chrysler, and Ford—generate 95 percent of national automobile output.

The postwar years

The apex of American manufacturing was unquestionably the decades immediately following World War II. With their rivals in economic and political disarray, American firms, many of which metamorphosed into multinational corporations, disproportionately dominated the world's industrial markets, particularly in capital-intensive sectors such as steel, aerospace, and automobiles. Throughout the 1950s and

most of the 1960s, Manufacturing-Belt cities enjoyed standards of living that were the envy of much of the world. Meanwhile, Los Angeles began to rival Midwestern cities as a major manufacturer of aircraft, petrochemicals, rubber, plastics, and automobiles.

This era of expansion and affluence did not last indefinitely, however. Beginning as early as the late 1960s, and accelerating markedly after the "petroshocks" of the 1970s, American manufacturing firms suffered a growing crisis of profitability as their competitive edge declined in the face of mounting foreign competition. Western European and Japanese firms led this onslaught, and were soon joined by others from the newly industrialized countries of East Asia (Taiwan, South Korea, Hong Kong, and Singapore in the 1960s and 1970s, followed by Thailand, Malaysia, and the Philippines). Wave upon wave of plant closures decimated many communities in the Manufacturing Belt, leaving depressed local economies in their wake. Manufacturing's share of the labor force declined from a post-World War II high of over 40 percent to the current level of 18 percent. Membership of unions suffered accordingly. Some firms responded by evacuating their industries altogether; others even relocated to other countries, particularly to Mexico; yet others engaged in a process of "downsizing" and technological change to re-establish their competitive viability (as occurred in the steel industry with the introduction of minimills).

The electronics revolution

The brightest spot in the otherwise bleak American manufacturing landscape remained the electronics industry, part of a broader constellation of "high technology" firms through which the United States still enjoys considerable success. Although the industry's roots extend back to the first radio and tele-

The completion of a transcontinental railroad in 1869 provided a major boost to the development of American industry. The West's abundant raw materials could be readily shipped to manufacturing centers in the East, and consequent population growth in the West soon resulted in the creation of local industrial bases.

LEFT: Cleveland, Ohio, is the largest in a chain of industrial centers that stretches along the southern shore of Lake Erie.

vision producers of the 1920s, it was the microelectronics revolution of the 1970s that brought the most radical change and financial gain. World War II provided much of the impetus for this revolution, and the defense forces have since developed close associations with major electronic firms.

By the 1990s, the process of miniaturization, the digitization of information, rapid declines in the production and retail costs of computers, and exponential increases in memory and processing power had had an enormous impact on every sector of the economy, in turn raising productivity and reshaping the skills and occupations of the workforce. Although low-end consumer electronics manufacturing has largely left the nation for low-cost production centers overseas, the United States retains a distinct competitive advantage in high-end computer hardware and software.

Services and Finance

A telecommunications tower in Wisconsin. The use of telephone networks for the transfer of digital data has resulted in a vastly increased demand for telecommunications services.

Each day, about 6,500 traders and staff throng the floors of the trading rooms at the Chicago Mercantile Exchange, one of the nation's leading futures trading centers. Originally founded in 1874 as a farm-products market, it is now linked to a number of overseas exchanges by means of a global electronic trading system.

Since World War II, the American economy has become progressively dominated by services. Approximately 80 percent of the nation's employment and gross national product (GNP) is now supplied by services, and more than 90 percent of all new jobs are generated in this sector.

Services can be broadly defined as the production of intangibles. The sector comprises a heterogeneous collection of industries, including finance and real estate, business services (such as legal services, advertising, accounting, engineering and architecture, and public relations), wholesale and retail trade, transportation, communications and the media, health care, education, public services, entertainment (including tourism), and nonprofit organizations. The growth of the services sector has brought about enormous changes in American society, refashioning labor markets, particularly for women, and affecting patterns of settlement, incomes, occupations, skill levels, education, and rates of unionization.

Finance services

Financial services form possibly the most influential part of the sector. They comprise a variety of businesses, including commercial, investment, and savings banks, and insurance companies. Essentially, the central function of these industries is to link borrowers and savers, greasing the wheels of commerce and consumer demand through loans, the stock and bond markets, and a variety of newer instruments.

Because of the central importance of this sector to the national money supply, and hence interest, inflation, and exchange rates, financial markets in the United States have been closely regulated by the state. In 1913, the Federal Reserve—the American national bank—was established, with broad authority to shape the national money supply and, as a result, inflation, interest, and exchange rates. Throughout the Depression of the 1930s, various regulations were implemented, including the *Glass-Steagall Act*, to separate commercial and investment banking (thereby preventing banks from buying or selling stocks) and to prohibit interstate banking. This was motivated primarily by the smaller, regional banks' fear of their New York rivals' growing power. The result of this legislation was a highly fragmented, decentralized banking system, with over 10,000 banks. Most financial institutions are therefore small and serve local clients; however, it is the large "money-center"

The New York Stock Exchange dates back to 1792, when a group of 24 traders met under a buttonwood tree at 68 Wall St and signed an agreement to trade with each other exclusively. Today, more than 200 million shares are traded here every day.

banks (particularly those based in Manhattan) that continue to dominate the industry.

In 1947, the American domestic regulatory structure was complemented by an international one in the form of the Bretton-Woods Agreement. It established the International Monetary Fund and the World Bank, and also fixed international currency exchange rates to the US dollar, which, in turn, was pegged to gold at $35 per ounce.

The relatively stable banking system set in place in the 1930s worked well for half a century; for example, bank failures were relatively uncommon until the 1980s. However, starting in the 1970s, a series of changes transformed the industry. One of the most important was the rapid rise in the price of petroleum as the result of reduced OPEC quotas. This led to widespread inflation, high interest rates, recession, and unemployment, and accelerated the process of deindustrialization.

The collapse of the Bretton-Woods Agreement in 1971 also had far-reaching implications for the American economy and was followed in 1973 by the shift to floating exchange rates. The technological changes unleashed by the microelectronics revolution saw the advent of automatic teller machines and telecommunications networks, including electronic funds transfer systems. The deregulation of finance brought about the end of interstate banking restrictions, prohibitions on foreign membership in stock exchanges, and the relaxation of controls over pension and mutual funds, generating new sources of investment. Among the results of these changes were a steady round of mergers in banking and the growth of new centers to rival the traditional capital of finance, New York, such as Charlotte, North Carolina.

Additionally, the expansion of American multinational corporations overseas, the steady growth of the European market, declines in trade barriers, and large federal government budget deficits in the 1980s all contributed to a steady globalization of finance as foreign sources of capital were attracted to higher real interest rates in the United States. Today, American finance has become firmly internationalized, and integrated into a seamless web of digital money that crosses national borders with ease.

After a slow but steady climb in the first half of the century, inflation has soared since the 1970s. Goods worth a dollar in 1910 would have cost around $4 in 1970, but would fetch $18 today.

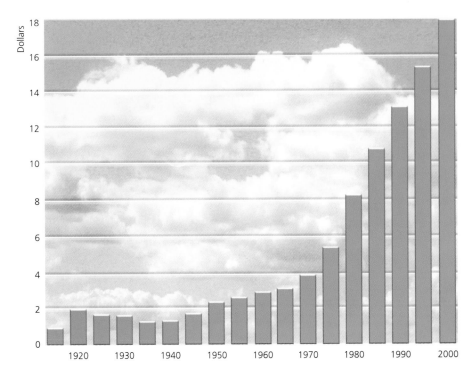

International trade is not only influenced by the performance of domestic economies, but also by fluctuations in global markets. Changes in currency exchange rates, in particular, alter the values of exports and imports, and can make the difference between a deficit and a surplus.

Trade

America's trade relations have long played a major role in the development of its relationships with other nations. The levels and type of trade, and the preferred trading partners, have all varied over time in response to changing international geopolitical circumstances, the value of currencies, and protectionist legislation. The largest bilateral trading partner has long been Canada, although Japan recently became the largest source of imports; Mexico is the third-largest trade partner, in part due to the numerous assembly plants that dot the United States–Mexico border. Trade since World War II has risen more rapidly than the gross national product; in 2000, exports comprised about 11 percent of US GNP, and imports about 13 percent. Thus, roughly one-quarter of the American economy is directly affected by trade. Some argue that the relatively small share of American GNP devoted to trade indicates its minor importance compared to the domestic economy, but it is essential to note that this estimate does not reflect the financial impact of trade on firms that compete with imports, or financial flows that are not measured in the merchandise trade balance.

Agricultural and manufactured goods

The United States enjoyed healthy trade surpluses in the halcyon years after World War II, and continues to be a major exporter of agricultural commodities—indeed, the United States still exports one-half of all foodstuffs traded internationally. By the 1970s, however, the recovery of foreign producers in many sectors, particularly in critical industries such as steel, automobiles, shipping, and machinery, flooded the United States with imports, leading to a sustained series of mounting trade deficits. Large federal gov-

Rising imports have seen the balance of payments in the goods trade drop ever deeper into the red. This is partly the result of increased competition from overseas producers.

ernment deficits in the 1980s, which drove up the American dollar relative to its trading partners, accentuated this problem. This transformation was accompanied by a shift in the geographic locus of trade: whereas historically the bulk of the nation's trade was with its European partners, the rising importance of East Asia, particularly Japan and the newly industrialized countries of Southeast Asia, has made trans-Pacific flows larger than trans-Atlantic ones. The shift has been mirrored by the changing status of trading centers on the East and West coasts: in terms of the volume of goods exported, the ports of Los Angeles and Seattle now surpass their counterparts in New York, Boston, Baltimore, and Philadelphia.

Sale of services

Although most public attention focuses on the merchandise trade (agricultural and manufactured goods), American trade also includes international trade in services, which is included in the current account. American exports of services (which comprise one-third of total foreign revenues) include flows of repatriated profits, government revenues, and income from tourism, but are most pronounced in sales of film and television shows and legal, advertising, accounting, computer software, construction, and engineering services. Unlike merchandise trade, in which the country suffers a trade deficit, the United States enjoys a modest surplus in trade in services. Employment related to foreign exports of services is concentrated in a handful of large metropolitan regions, primarily New York, Chicago, Los Angeles, San Francisco, and Seattle. The main markets for such trade are concentrated in western Europe.

Legislative controls

American trade has long been shaped by legislation designed to hamper or restrict imports through tariffs, quotas, and nontariff barriers—measures

Although the gap has narrowed in recent years, agricultural exports still outstrip agricultural imports. Wheat is by far the largest export commodity, followed by horticultural products (fruit, vegetables, and nuts).

FAR LEFT: The growing importance of Asian markets has increased trading activity in the West. Japan, China, Korea, and Taiwan are now among the United States' top ten trading partners.

BELOW LEFT: The United States still leads the world in the production of coarse grains such as corn, barley, and rye, but a number of other producers, most notably Argentina, China, and the European Union, have recently increased their share of the market at America's expense.

typically advocated by economic sectors whose competitiveness is threatened by imports.

The *Smoot-Hawley Act* of the 1930s, for example, unleashed a protectionist war over virtually all agricultural and manufactured goods, exacerbating the effects of the Great Depression. Downturns in the business cycle have been frequently accompanied by calls for trade restrictions. The automobile, steel, and textile industries, for example, became leading advocates of limited imports during the decline of American manufacturing in the 1970s. However, compared to many other nations, protectionism in the United States has been minimal. With highly competitive industries in many sectors, America has long been the world's leading proponent of "free trade," and has pioneered many developments in this area, including the various rounds of negotiations held to debate and develop the General Agreement for Trade and Tariffs (GATT) and the World Trade Organization. The abolition of trade restrictions with Canada included the 1965 Auto Pact, recently expired, the United States–Canada Free Trade Agreement of 1988, and, as of 1994, the North American Free Trade Agreement (NAFTA), which includes Mexico. NAFTA will lead to a progressive incorporation of the three North American economies but falls short of the far more comprehensive economic integration currently in operation in the European Union, which expedites the free flow of inputs, including labor, as well as outputs.

BELOW: In recent years, the balance of trade in services has moved in almost precisely the opposite direction to that in goods, registering a surplus.

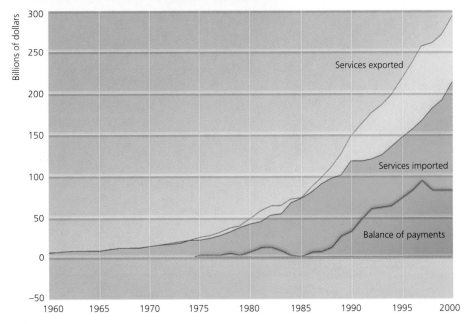

Billions of dollars

Services exported

Services imported

Balance of payments

300
250
200
150
100
50
0
−50

1960　1965　1970　1975　1980　1985　1990　1995　2000

CULTURE, ARTS, SCIENCES

CULTURE AND SOCIETY

Native American Culture

A Native American participates in an Independence Day parade in Washington DC. While Native people today are a vital part of modern America, they also maintain their tribal identity and traditions.

Spirituality

Spirituality is the focus of Native American life. Native religions endure today despite past attempts to prohibit and crush them. Often under the guise of celebrating the white men's holidays, Native people would conduct ceremonies, thus keeping their cultures alive.

Not surprisingly, the religions of Native Americans are diverse; however, they do share certain qualities and beliefs. Life is viewed as a continuing cyclical unity between people and the earth which is envisioned as a living being, often called "mother." Other living things are seen as relatives with whom kinship must be nurtured and honored. For instance, The Plains people value the circle as a sacred shape, a symbol of the interconnectedness of all life. The purpose of most Native religious ceremonies is to restore or ensure harmony between humans and the earth.

Typically, tribal religions are closely tied to sacred places where certain cer-

The totem pole is a carved record of a clan's traditional knowledge, preserving legends from one generation to another.

emonies may be practiced, often in conjunction with an equinox or change of season. The sacred place may be a river, mountain, or valley—a center from which wisdom and understanding flow. So rooted are tribal people to their sacred places that they continue to return to their ancestral homelands to participate in ceremonial life.

In an apparent recognition of Native peoples' deep religious ties, the US government passed the *American Indian Religious Freedom Act* in 1978 which reads, "Henceforth it shall be the policy of the United States to protect and preserve for American Indians their inherent right of freedom to believe, express, and exercise traditional religions, including but not limited to access to sites, use and possession of sacred objects, and the freedom to worship through ceremonials and traditional rites."

Later, however, as wealthy developers challenged the establishment of sacred places on valuable land, the courts reinterpreted the Act and ruled that the Bill of Rights did not apply to specific areas, even if their destruction prevented the religious ceremony from being practiced. Tribes continue to fight this decision both via organized protests and in the courts.

Other important legislation affecting Native culture and religion includes the *1990 Native American Grave Protection and Repatriation Act*. Under this Act, tribes have power to reclaim ancestral remains and sacred objects from museums and universities and repatriate them to sacred land. This has helped to revitalize the practices of certain ceremonies in some tribes.

Among other positive results of the 1960s and 1970s has been a renewed pride and interest in indigenous religions and cultures, especially among the younger Native generation. The Peyote Religion or Native American Church, a pan-tribal religion that emerged during the late nineteenth century, has grown in popularity among some tribes. The Church integrates many Christian beliefs and practices in its ceremonies, which involves the ritual eating of peyote, a hallucinogenic cactus. This is also part of the Traditional Unity Movement of the 1970s that incorporates elements of the Sweat Lodge, Sun Dance, and Sacred Pipe Ceremonies.

Generally speaking, practitioners of Native religions do not proselytize or recruit, despite recent

Quillwork and beadwork are often used by the Northeastern tribes to adorn tanned articles of clothing. Nature-based patterns demonstrate the links between art, life, and the earth.

Powwows are festivals of Native life and culture. Dancing is an important part of the celebrations, and is performed in traditional ceremonial dress.

The burial tipi of the wife of a Crow chief in Montana, circa 1895. For Native Americans, the cycle of life—birth, coming of age, marriage, procreation, and death—is a profoundly spiritual journey linked to the land.

The Hopi people of the Southwest are deeply religious. The kachina dolls (tihu), are a highly developed Hopi art form, and represent divine ancestral and nature spirits that act as a channel between the Hopi and the spirit world.

claims by certain New Age shamans who claim to have been instructed by their ancestors to teach non-Indians (usually for a large fee). These people often have clearly spurious ties to their tribes. Religious experience among traditional Native people is a highly personal, intimate matter, not to be shared lightly. It should be noted, however, that legitimate religious leaders may accept financial support for underwriting the costs of ceremonies.

Clearly, although the Native American may not own the land in the political sense, they are the spiritual owners of the earth.

Arts

In many ways, life and art are inseparable for Native peoples. Their holistic world view regarding the interconnectedness of life permeates art, crafts, literature, the performing arts, and all things "creative."

Special objects are often used in religious ceremonies, therefore much of Native art has strong spiritual connections. Even the design of everyday objects may depict celebrations of a sacred life force. Articles of clothing or other items might be decorated with images drawn from dreams, which are seen as powerful insights into one's relationship with the earth. Examples include the quillwork and beadwork used to embellish tanned goods of the Northeastern tribes, which are also influenced by fauna and other nature-based patterns.

The pottery of the Pueblo tribes and weaving by the Navajo are exquisite examples of function and art. Rugs and pottery of the Southwestern tribes are prized by art collectors all over the world.

Art in the form of superior craftsmanship is also evident in the creations of Native artisans. Nearly all tribes have a tradition of basketry made from available natural materials. Some examples are the fine cedar root vessels woven by the Plateau tribes.

Navajo turquoise and silver jewelry. Navajo people started working with silver in the late nineteenth century, and their work is in great demand all over the world.

Native art is also based on family position and clan affiliation. Traditionally, the Northwestern tribes honored their kin groups and mythology in the form of massive totem poles and house posts carved from wood, depicting stylized animal forms. Successful contemporary sculptors such as Haida artist Bill Reid are influenced by their tribes' ancient art forms.

The tradition of "Spirit Writing" among the Anishinabe of the Northeast has also inspired today's Native painters. Ancient accounts of ceremonies from the Midewiwiin Society or Grand Medicine Society (an Algonquian religion) in the form of pictographs were recorded on birch bark scrolls. These scrolls have influenced contemporary Anishnabe painters such as Miishibinijima and Zoe Wood-Salomon. Their work and others form the Manitoulin school of art.

Ho-Chunk artist Truman Lowe's towering sculptures of tree saplings, branches, and other natural items are clearly influenced by his relationship to the earth. He is involved with the newly formed Museum of the American Indian—an endeavor by the Smithsonian Institution of Washington DC to showcase the culture and art of Native Americans. The Smithsonian recently acquired the Heye Foundation Collection of Native Art from New York and decided to construct a new building to house this and other collections. The plan is to create a museum that will celebrate the vibrancy of contemporary Native art and present historical data and materials in a way that celebrates the culture as a living entity.

Native peoples have relied primarily on oral traditions to communicate history, religion, and other important events. Generally, Native Americans did not traditionally have a history of written languages, although Sequoyah, the son of a Cherokee woman and a British trader, did develop an 86-character syllabary of his mother's Cherokee language in 1821. Storytelling is considered a high art among Native Americans. Stories and songs are used to educate and entertain as well as worship. This very much underscores Native peoples' belief that their cultures, as well as the earth, are living entities that must be constantly reaffirmed.

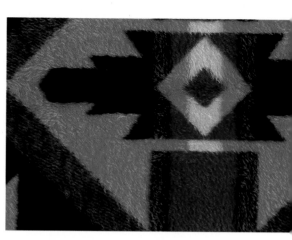

An intricately designed Native American blanket from Tennessee. In recent years, there has been an artistic renaissance among many of the Southeastern Native peoples.

Several forms of pictographs have been used among tribes to record important historical and religious events: the Oglala's winter counts, elaborate paintings on buffalo skins; Iroquois weavings of wampum beads which recorded historical events; and ancient picture writing on rock formations from the Great Basin, Plateau, and Southwest regions.

Today, many Native writers draw on their storytelling heritage to create fiction and other forms of literature. An early influence on today's Native journalists was the crusading journal of Yavapai Carlos Montezuma entitled, "Wassaja: Freedom's Signal for the Indians," which included his speech "Let my People Go." He helped found the Society of American Indians (a precursor to the National Congress of American Indians) in the early twentieth century. Currently, the Native American Journalists Association presents its annual Wassaja award to a Native journalist who has demonstrated exceptional journalistic integrity.

Many talented contemporary Native writers use their unique heritage to produce a distinct form of modern American literature. Internationally known Native writers include Louise Erdrich, Leslie Marmon Silko, Vine Deloria Jr, Scott Momaday, Sherman Alexie, and many others.

Another exciting art form is the development of modern Native music. Musicians like Keith Secola and his Wild Band of Indians and Joy Harjo and her band Poetic Justice integrate traditional drumming, chanting, and rock 'n' roll into their songs. Ulali, an intertribal group of Native women, creates a cappella music influenced by song and chant styles from the Southeast. There are also popular Native rap groups such as Without Reservations and Litefoot, as well as the newly popular rhythm and blues band, Indigenous.

The fabric of contemporary Native American art and culture is rich and diverse, its base of tradition and spirituality highlighted and enriched by modern perspective. Clearly, despite a history of near annihilation, Native peoples and cultures continue to grow and flourish in today's America.

A member of the Catawba tribe in South Carolina threads beads. Native American artists and artisans work within a framework of tradition and ancient motifs— individuality is of less importance.

The American Identity

America's multicultural history is represented by children dancing at Penn's Landing, Philadelphia, the site where Dutch colonist William Penn landed in 1682.

Inspiring the national anthem— the Star-spangled Banner—*the American flag is the most potent symbol of national identity and patriotism.*

America's identity is based on a vision of the country as a land of immigrants with a limitless frontier, an ethnic melting pot of the world's people where economic opportunities are abundant, and individual freedom is guaranteed. Initially, the essence of American identity was based upon Judeo-Christian laws and beliefs developed in Western Europe and transported to the North American continent with the first colonists in the seventeenth century. Formed by the influences of Western civilization, the character of the country and its people centered around Western European religions, languages, and ideologies. Urban and agricultural patterns were also consistent with methods developed in the European environment. The indigenous Native American population was rapidly overwhelmed, dismissed, and relegated to marginal lands, only barely surviving to become minor contributors to the American identity.

Rights for all citizens

With independence from Great Britain and the amalgamation of the colonies into a republic in 1776, the American Constitution began to foster a new sense of identity as it began the process of establishing individual rights, freedom of expression, democratic principles of law, and guaranteed rights for all citizens. Close inspection of the early documents, however, indicate that women, Native Americans, African-Americans, minorities, and children were not guaranteed such rights.

Uniquely different versions of the American experience began to emerge during the twentieth century as vast numbers of immigrants arrived from both European and non-European countries. This forced reform of the country's legislation as new interpretations of what it meant to be American and confidence in an American identity evolved. The different multicultural strands began to be reflected in civil rights legislation and affirmative action options which provided opportunities for women, Native Americans, African-Americans, Hispanic, and other disenfranchised populations—a process that continues today.

Diverse dreams

Cultural pluralism created by the contributions of a wide spectrum of immigrant groups over the past two centuries have shaped a rich and varied cultural mosaic of values and beliefs that collectively make up the American identity. From a basically small town rural community, America's culture and its identity have come to be associated with: an aggressive pursuit of goals and economic success; a belief in the importance of nature; a belief in individualism and individual freedoms; and a love of things new (ideas, music, landscapes, houses,).

The notion that any newcomer to the United States could seek, through hard work and dedication, the "American dream" of affluence, ownership of land, freedom from oppression, and cultural satisfaction is a profoundly American belief.

However, the reality of the American identity did not offer opportunities for everyone to accomplish this "American dream." Throughout the early 1900s, discrepancies in opportunities and options for many Americans prohibited economic and social mobility. Ethnic and racial groups in America were relegated to racially segregated neighborhoods, forced to attend segregated schools, and were denied access to medical assistance and affordable housing. Employed predominantly in low-paying jobs, most were unable to take advantage of economic and educational opportunities.

In 1942, the internment of over 110,000 Americans of Japanese ancestry from communities on the West Coast not only reflected the inherent racism still present in America, but also the willingness of government leaders to violate the federal Constitution.

World War II marked the transition to the "civil rights revolution." Defending democracy abroad stirred demands for racial justice at home, and with peace came new challenges against inequality and discrimination. Racial discrimination became un-American in the post-World War II years. Rosa Park's refusal to sit in the back of the bus in Montgomery, Alabama, and Martin Luther King's boycott of buses led to a victory for African-Americans and affirmed their power to transform the conditions of their lives through a grass-roots movement.

All languages, all faiths

As civil liberties and reforms began to occur nationwide in the mid-twentieth century, America's cultural identity continued to evolve. Variation in English usage led to regional differences or local dialects; the use of non-English languages in the home and the complex issue of bilingualism produced distinctive patterns within the United States. Signs in Spanish, Portuguese, Vietnamese, Hebrew, Chinese, Korean, and Tagalog are among the many indices of cultural pluralism that can now be seen across the national landscape. Naming of places reflects the variation in cultural identity, origins, and the country's history.

Although the dominant religion in America is Christian-based, there are a great many variations in the denominations and systems of practice and beliefs. In addition, recent immigrants have preserved their religions and these faiths have become part and parcel of the American culture. Islam, Buddhism, Hinduism, and Judaism are found imposed on the landscape through holy buildings, cemeteries, and other edifices.

America does not belong to one ethnic or racial group, and Americans have been constantly redefining their national identity from the moment of first contact with Native Americans on the shores of Virginia. America's diversity can be seen across the continent in Ellis Island, Angel Island, Chinatown, Harlem, South Boston, the Lower East Side, places with Spanish names like Los Angeles and San Antonio, or Native American names such as Iowa, Delaware or Massachusetts. The origin of the Bing cherry is Ah Bing, a Chinese immigrant who developed the fruit. Corn, tomatoes, and tobacco were Native American staples grown in the eastern portion of North America. The term "okay" is taken from a Choctaw word. Jazz, blues, and rock 'n' roll developed from the musical traditions of West African slaves transported to America's shores. The skills of the American cowboy were learned from the vaqueros of Central America. When Americans sing "God Bless America," "Easter Parade," and "White Christmas" they owe the words to Israel Baline, a Jewish immigrant who changed his name to Irving Berlin.

America's colonial society originally drew its identity and cultural heritage from the shores of Europe. As the nation developed, however, the history and promises of this society became intimately and unforgettably intertwined with the exploitation of minority labor from other countries and with land taken from Native Americans. America has become a country of immigrants who have held to their customs and traditions, and blended them with those of the first colonists. Today, the American identity reflects diverse cultures from indigenous Native Americans to the most recent immigrant, as well as a continued desire for freedom and equality.

TOP: At the Annual Delta Jubilee, the flags that have flown over Mississippi show the political and cultural forces—French, Spanish, English, and Confederate—that have shaped the history and identity of the state today.

ABOVE: Symbolizing freedom, the iconic Statue of Liberty in New York has welcomed new arrivals to American shores since 1886.

LEFT: Annual July 4 parades to mark the colonies' achievement of independence from Great Britain in 1776 (America's birthday), provide the opportunity to celebrate being American.

Religion

Religion plays a prominent role in American society and culture. In striking contrast to other countries at a similar level of socioeconomic development, the United States continues to display very high rates of religious participation and commitment. Surveys consistently reveal that over 90 percent of Americans claim some form of religious affiliation, that 70 percent belong to a local religious congregation, and that over 40 percent attend religious services in a typical week. The religiosity of the American people has been attributed in part to the nation's constitutional guarantee of religious freedom. This guarantee makes religion a matter of private choice, but it has also fostered a strong tradition of religious voluntarism since religious institutions do not receive support from the state. Participation in religious organizations thus represents a major focus of communal activity among Americans and serves as a source of social identity.

Freedom of religious choice has also contributed to the characteristic diversity of religious affiliation in America. Over 80 percent of the population identify themselves as Christian, but that label encompasses a great variety of different groups. Protestants comprise a majority of the Christian population, outnumbering Roman Catholics by a margin of more than two to one. Adherents of the Eastern Orthodox churches represent a smaller minority. The Protestant majority itself contains further diversity. Baptists, Methodists, and Lutherans represent the most prominent categories of Protestant religious affiliation, but American Protestantism includes hundreds of other denominations and independent churches as well. Although American Catholics are unified organizationally, they too display considerable diversity in terms of their ethnic origins. Beyond the Christian majority, Judaism has traditionally comprised the next most prominent religious tradition in America. Although American Jews account for only about 3 percent of the population, the United States contains more Jews than any other country, including Israel. Like Christianity, Judaism in America encompasses a variety of distinct groups, from the more liberal Reform movement to very traditional Orthodox Jews. Finally, the diversity of religious affiliation in America has been significantly affected in recent decades by the immigration of increasing numbers of Muslims, Hindus, and Buddhists.

The distinctive religious composition of the American population reflects the influence of several factors. Immigration ranks as perhaps the most important of these factors. Early settlement patterns established various Protestant churches as the dominant feature of the religious landscape of colonial America, although many areas along the settlement frontier remained largely unchurched at that time. Mass immigration from northern and western Europe during the first half of the nineteenth century reinforced the Protestant character of American religion, but also brought a growing number of Roman Catholics from Ireland and Germany. Between the 1860s and the 1920s, as the sources of American immigration shifted toward southern and eastern Europe, the number of Roman Catholics entering the country rose sharply, as did the number of Jews. Since the 1960s, global demographic and economic trends and changes in American immigration law have resulted in increasing immigration

TOP: The traditional façade of the Triple I Temple in Milwaukee, Wisconsin, a city with over 900 churches of many denominations.

ABOVE: A patriotic Hare Krishna devotee participates in the annual Independence Day celebrations in Washington DC. The Hare Krishna movement was founded in the United States in 1965.

RIGHT: An old Russian church and cemetery at Ninilchik on the Kenai Peninsula in Alaska. Russian Orthodoxy was the official religion here before the territory was bought by the United States in 1867.

from Latin America and Asia. New migrants from Latin America have reinforced the nation's Christian majority, while immigration from East Asia, South Asia, and the Middle East has steadily increased the number of Muslims, Hindus, Buddhists, and adherents of other Asian religions.

The religious make-up of the American population has also been shaped by internal patterns of denominational growth. American history has seen several periods of widespread religious revival, during which a heightening of religious interest within the population has led to significant increases in church membership. These processes of revival have contributed in particular to the growth of various evangelical Protestant denominations. Periods of revival during the early and middle 1700s and, especially, the early 1800s led to substantial increases in membership for Baptist, Methodist, and Presbyterian churches, which still rank among the leading Protestant groups. Another period of revival during the late 1800s and early 1900s fostered the growth of newly established churches in the Holiness and Pentecostalist movements. Continuing these earlier trends, conservative Protestant denominations have consistently grown more rapidly than have more liberal groups since the 1950s.

A third important factor in the evolution of the religious composition of the American population has been the development of new religious movements. The combined influences of religious freedom and religious voluntarism have contributed to continuing processes of religious innovation since the early 1800s. Many new churches and denominations founded over the years have eventually disappeared, but others have been quite successful, both in the United States and abroad. The Mormons (or Latter Day Saints), Jehovah's Witnesses, Christian Scientists, and Seventh-Day Adventists are some of the more prominent groups that originated during the nineteenth century. During the 1900s, religious innovation brought about the appearance of various Pentecostal churches, the Black Muslim movement, and many forms of non-traditional religions.

These factors have produced a diverse religious landscape in America, but one that contains significant regional variations. Numerous regions are dominated by particular religious groups, for example. Protestant denominations dominate three large regions: the southern states, where the religious revivals of the 1800s gave Baptists and Methodists preeminence; the Upper Midwest, where German and Scandinavian immigration

created a strong Lutheran presence; and Utah and portions of surrounding states, where Mormons attempted to establish an isolated homeland. These three regions have also traditionally displayed the highest levels of religious participation in the United States. Major Roman Catholic concentrations have developed through the immigration of various European groups to the Northeast, of colonial French settlers to southern Louisiana, and of Hispanics to the Southwest. The states along the West Coast, on the other hand, tend to be more diverse religiously, and are generally characterized by lower rates of religious participation than other regions of the country. On a more local scale, urban areas which have traditionally attracted migrants also tend to contain a high degree of religious diversity. The Jewish population of New York City and the surrounding areas represents one of the world's major concentrations of Judaism. Similarly, urban centers in the Northeast and the "Sunbelt" states are developing major concentrations of Hindus and Muslims.

Finally, as in the case of many other areas of culture, American religion has had a significant impact globally over the years. American churches have generally been strongly committed to missionary activity, a trait that has its roots in the recurrent revivalism that characterizes America's religious history. As a result, the United States is the world's leading supplier of missionaries to foreign lands. One consequence of this trend is that within many religious groups that originated in the United States, including the Mormons, Seventh-Day Adventists, and Jehovah's Witnesses, a majority of members now live in other regions of the world. American religious groups have also led the way in the use of religious broadcasting to promote global evangelism. The emphases on innovation and commitment in American religion have thus had implications for areas far beyond the borders of the United States.

TOP: *Marchers celebrate the Friday before Easter in downtown Milwaukee, Wisconsin. Good Friday is not a public holiday in the United States, reflecting the official separation between the Church and state enshrined in the Constitution.*

ABOVE: *The main altar of the historic Mission San Carlos Borremeo del Rio Carmelo in Carmel, California. The mission was established by Padre Junipero Serra in 1769, the same year he founded California's first Catholic mission in San Diego.*

Sport

Spectators enjoy a game of baseball, known as the national pastime of America. In total, the baseball leagues now draw more than 100 million spectators each year, in addition to radio listeners and television viewers.

A model of an American football player at the Packer Hall of Fame, Green Bay, Wisconsin. The game has been played in the United States for over 140 years. An early version of the modern rules was developed in the 1880s and published in 1891 by Walter Camp, the "Father of American Football."

You could be forgiven for thinking that the United States is populated almost entirely by sports fans. Entire media networks are devoted to sport, and the average American household watches more than 180 hours of television sports programming a week. The education system invests heavily in providing time, resources, and training so that almost every child can participate in sports at school, university scholarships underwrite promising sports talents, companies invest billions of dollars in sports sponsorship, and Americans fork over similar amounts each year for tickets, team memorabilia, and sports-related collectibles.

Sports even feature prominently in the arts. One only has to think of Roy Hobbs in Bernard Malamud's novel *The Natural*, Casey in Ernest Thayer's poem "Casey at the Bat," movies such as *Pride of the Yankees*, *Hoosiers*, and *The Longest Yard*, and even musical compositions ranging from "Joltin' Joe DiMaggio" (swing), to "Centerfield" (rock), and "The Mighty Casey" (opera).

Successful athletes are widely regarded as heroes. They confirm that, in America at least, you can succeed using only your own wits and physical resources, and that sport can be a way out of poverty. A great equalizer, sport allows for the American ideal of rugged individual accomplishment and conforms with the capitalistic, laissez-faire philosophy on which the country was founded. In turn, a "work hard, play hard" attitude and a strong sense of national pride make Americans some of the world's strongest sports competitors and most ardent fans.

Early fixtures

The first European settlers found Native Americans already engaged in sports, including a stick and ball game the French called lacrosse. Despite opposition from church leaders, early settlers soon began taking up sporting pastimes. The first organized spectator sport was horse racing, which began in 1665 when the governor of New York, Richard Nicholls, established a racecourse at New Market on Long Island. Rowing regattas, foot races, cricket, and gouging (a form of no-holds-barred fighting) also became popular.

Although some of these activities no longer feature in the American sporting calendar, the range of sports enjoyed by Americans has widened ever since. Ice hockey, golf, and tennis have a wide following, and in recent years soccer has become one of the country's major growth sports, with nearly three million Americans attending professional matches, and about 20 million participating at some level. But the sports scene is still dominated by three home-grown games: baseball, American football, and basketball.

Baseball

Prior to the American Civil War, cricket and various forms of baseball, known as "rounders" or "town ball," were equally popular. However, the faster game of baseball gradually captured the American imagination. The rules that came to form the basis of the modern sport were drawn up in 1845 by

Alexander Cartwright for the New York Knickerbockers. The Knickerbockers played in the first official baseball game in 1846 on New Jersey's Elysian Fields, near New York. At that time, the game was played by amateur clubs and by colleges; the first professional team—the Cincinnati Red Stockings—was formed in 1869 and others soon followed suit. In 1871, delegates from ten clubs around New York met to form the National Association of Baseball Players, which became the National League of Professional Baseball Clubs (NL) in 1876. In 1900, the rival American League (AL) was formed.

With two established professional leagues, there was a clear need for another competition that would establish overall superiority. Thus was born the World Series, a play-off between the league champions which first took place in 1903. To date, the New York Yankees have won more World Series than any other team—26 of 96 played.

American football

Baseball may be recognized as the great American pastime, but football has been played here for just as long. Organized football matches began in Boston high schools around 1860, and the first intercollegiate game took place in 1869, when Rutgers and Princeton faced off in a contest that more closely resembled soccer. In 1902, the first major competition, the intercollegiate Rose Bowl, took place as part of the Tournament of Roses festival in Pasadena, California. College football has remained wildly popular ever since, with well over 36 million fans attending games annually.

The professional National Football League (NFL) was founded in an auto showroom in Canton, Ohio, in September 1920. Although early teams were based in small towns like Canton, the professional game became so popular that, in 1959, Dallas businessman Lamar Hunt decided to start another championship, the American Football League (AFL). In 1966, the two leagues merged, and, from 1967, a series of play-offs culminating in a final called the Super Bowl—

now America's biggest one-day sporting event—was used to decide the NFL championship. The NFL is now more popular than ever, but still falls short of the college game in attendances, attracting 14.2 million spectators in 2000.

Basketball

Unlike baseball and football, which have their roots in British sports, basketball is a truly American invention. It was devised in 1891 by Dr James Naismith, a physical education teacher in Springfield, Massachusetts, to keep football players active during winter. The game caught on quickly, especially in the midwestern state of Indiana, where metal hoops and open-ended nets were introduced. Another Indiana innovation was the backboard, designed to prevent home fans in the balconies acting as shot-blockers. In 1925, Naismith acknowledged that "basketball really had its origin in Indiana, which remains the center of the sport."

The professional game didn't catch on until the formation of the National Basketball Association (NBA) in 1949. The NBA's roots were in barnstorming teams that began touring in the 1920s, such as the Celtics from New York, who were so good that they were split up and divided among competing teams, and Abe Saaperstein's Harlem Globetrotters, who once went more than two decades without losing a game. In 1967, the American Basketball Association (ABA) was created to compete with the NBA, and soon boasted many of the sport's most electrifying players. In 1976, the ABA joined the NBA. Twenty million people now attend NBA games every year but, as with football, it's the college game that fulfils the American urge to support the "hometown team"— 29 million fans turn out for men's college basketball games annually, with nearly 9 million attending women's college games.

Baseball being played at Oriole Park Stadium at Camden Yards, Baltimore, Maryland. Abner Doubleday, a West Point cadet, has been credited with baseball's invention in 1839.

Arena football at the Gaylord Entertainment Center, Nashville, Tennessee. The modern sport has its origins in a game called "balldown," devised at Princeton University in the 1820s, in which players used their fists and, later, feet to move the ball.

The Media

The mass media plays such a pervasive role in American society that the cultural landscape would be significantly different without its influence. Newspapers, magazines, radio, television, and the Internet are all major players in everyday American life, shaping politics, social mores, and history itself.

The Saturday Evening Post has a venerable history. Founded in 1728 and edited in the eighteenth century by Benjamin Franklin, it was once a forum for colonial and revolutionary politics. It went on to promote original literature, publishing, among others, Edgar Allan Poe, James Fenimore Cooper, F. Scott Fitzgerald, Jack London, and Kurt Vonnegut Jr. Now in its third century of publication, the Post continues to promote new fiction, but focuses editorially on health issues.

A newsstand on Wall Street, New York, seems to offer readers a wide choice of publications. In reality, the media is dominated by a few large players.

Power of the press

Even before the Colonies declared independence from Great Britain, the media was used to help shape public opinion. In the 1760s, Sam Adams started a newspaper, the *Boston Gazette*, using it to oppose taxation and advocate colonial home rule. Adams also developed America's first newsgathering and distribution service, the *Journal of Occurrences*. The *Journal* presented news and political commentary to 35 newspapers, spreading Adams' views throughout the colonies. In particular, editorials in response to the "Boston Massacre" in March 1770 (when five Bostonians were shot by British troops during riots against taxation) were instrumental in turning public opinion against the British. Throughout the American Revolution, newspapers and pamphlets were used to affect opinion and morale.

By the 1820s, another freedom-based issue— slavery—was a hot topic in the media. Abolitionist publications such as the *Providence, Rhode Island Instigator* and the *New Orleans Liberalist* used the power of the printed word to convince Americans slavery was a sin. However, many mainstream newspapers promoted the opposite stance, and feelings ran high. The Reverend Elijah Lovejoy, who in 1834 founded the *St Louis Journal*, had three presses destroyed by people upset by his anti-slavery editorials in 1836–37, and was himself killed when a mob tried to destroy a fourth press on November 7, 1837.

There were other issues that helped develop advocacy journalism. One early example was the fight against corruption in New York politics, led at first in September 1869 by *Harper's Weekly*, and later joined by other publications. Cartoonist Thomas Nast (1840–1902), whose unrelenting visual attacks could reach even the illiterate, instigated the crusade against corruption. Nast was the first to prove how important visuals can be in determining how people react to a story or an issue.

Joseph Pulitzer, for whom America's most prestigious journalistic prize is named, started the *St Louis Dispatch* in the 1870s, forever changing the American media landscape. Pulitzer thought papers should be cheap and simply presented so working people could —and would want to—read them. He also believed they should fight in the public's interest—or what he thought was the public's interest. In 1883, Pulitzer started the *New York World*. By combining dramatic headlines and larger illustrations with news-style sports reporting as well as articles designed to lure female readers, Pulitzer made the *World* America's top newspaper. San Francisco publisher William Randolph Hearst went a step further. On "slow" news days, Hearst actually made news for the *Examiner* by creating outlandish events. Competition between Hearst and Pulitzer came to a head when Hearst began supporting rebels in Cuba trying to gain independence from Spain, and called for American involvement. Pulitzer at first was opposed to American involvement, but eventually supported it, later admitting he did so to increase circulation. Both fanned the flames of public opinion, painting the rebels as courageous and noble and the Spanish government as bad and corrupt. Then, in early 1898, the USS *Maine* blew up in Havana Harbor. More recent investigations have shown that the *Maine* explosion was an accident, but Hearst and Pulitzer screamed murder. Their editorial attacks eventually brought public and Congressional opinion so heavily in favor of reprisals that President McKinley was forced to declare war, despite Spain's attempts to solve the problem peacefully.

Radio waves

In December 1901, Guglielmo Marconi sent the first trans-Atlantic radio signal, forever making the world a smaller place. But it was in 1916, when a Westinghouse engineer began broadcasting programs from his garage in Wilkinsburg, Pennsylvania, that the age of American radio really began. These broadcasts were so popular with amateur radio operators that Westinghouse decided to build a new station, with the sole purpose of broadcasting. KDKA went to air in 1920.

As more receivers were sold to the public, more stations took to the airwaves. Baseball and football play-by-play, concerts, live coverage of news events

showed that entertainment could be designed for and targeted to specific groups of viewers. The 1947–48 season heralded another important first to television: NBC and CBS networks both started national news-casts,15 minutes long.

During the 1950s the sitcom, game shows, and westerns were introduced. There was also the first attempt to link juvenile crime and television violence. In 1958 Senator Estes Kefauver held Congressional hearings on the subject and wrote an article for *Reader's Digest* entitled "Let's Get Rid of Tele-Violence." By 1960 about 90 percent of American households had television sets and by 1963 Americans were getting more of their news from television than newspapers. The political possibilities also became evident in the 1960s. For example, during the 1960 presidential election, John Kennedy's performance in televised debates sealed his win. As the decade progressed, more Americans turned against their country's involvement in Vietnam after seeing images of the devastation of war and wounded American soldiers on television news broadcasts.

The 2001 US presidential election highlighted a new problem—that of anticipating events. The strong desire to "be first" with the news led rival media organizations to report that first George W. Bush, and then Al Gore, had won the state of Florida, and the presidency, long before the votes were all tallied. The networks had to recant and apologize to the public. Eventually, after weeks of court battle, Bush was declared the winner. Critics say the debacle shows how an increasing number of media outlets created a mega-competition that leads to errors.

and entertainment programs such as "Fibber McGee and Molly" and "The Shadow" were staples of radio programming. Even newspapers were taken with radio—for years many papers, not recognizing a competitor, freely printed broadcast schedules. Radio became part of the American family's daily life. During its golden age in the 1930s and 1940s, radio personalities were superstars. With the advent of television, however, radio's popularity declined. Advertisers and big money moved to the new medium, as did the stars. Although today nearly every American car has a radio and listenership is still high, especially during commutes to work, programming is mostly made up of low-budget talk shows and recorded music.

The age of television

January 7, 1927 is considered the official date of the invention of television. That's when Philo Farnsworth applied for the first patent on a television camera tube. Television's first drama, "The Queen's Messenger," was broadcast from Schenectady, New York, in 1928, but it wasn't until 1929 that RCA's Vladimir Zworykin demonstrated the first practical electronic system for TV transmission and reception. The RCA-owned National Broadcasting Company was soon broadcasting from New York City, and in 1939 the network broadcast the opening of the World's Fair and the first televised baseball game. In 1941 America's entry into World War II put television development on hold, but after the war America's revived industrial economy gave people the spending power to purchase the new television sets. In 1947 NBC created "Howdy Doody," a popular program which drew kids to television and

Controlling the media

Despite such concerns, electronic media, including the Internet, are more prevalent than ever, although all forms of media continue to have a powerful influence on American culture. A major concern in today's media marketplace is the concentration of ownership and control. Although there are more media outlets than ever before, the major networks, publishing houses, magazines, and newspapers are controlled by a handful of major corporations. While it is true that corporate ownership and the power to control public opinion have been there since the media began, it is now a bigger issue than ever for Americans, many of whom fear that control is in the hands of too few.

Cable News Network's logo identifies the company's head-quarters in Atlanta, Georgia. Started in 1980 by Ted Turner, it successfully exported its formula of responsible 24-hour news reporting around the world. In 1995 it merged with the cable company Time Warner. In 2001 falling ratings prompted the company's takeover by the Internet company America Online, her-alding changes in CNN's philo-sophy and public image.

LEFT: The Giardina family in New York watches daughter Susanna with President Eisenhower on a television fundraiser for the American Red Cross in March 1953. Politicians were quick to see the potential of the new medium for reaching potential voters in middle America.

The Lone Ranger and his faithful horse Silver feature in a game of the 1950s. The character started life on radio and went on to star in a popular television series which was enjoyed by children around the world.

The Place d'Armes Hotel in the French Quarter of New Orleans, Louisiana, is an example of the French colonial style of architecture, prevalent in the South and brought over by French settlers in the seventeenth century.

RIGHT: The adobe-style church of San Geronimo, Taos Pueblo, New Mexico, part of an earlier pueblo complex built around 1450 by descendents of the Anasazi tribe. Adobe, a mixture of clay, sand, and silt, dries to a hard mass in the sun and can be formed into bricks or poured into forms.

Architecture

The history of architecture in America shows the impact of several forces: repeated waves of immigration, abundant natural resources spread over a vast and varied landscape, a long-term affection for technological and industrial innovation, and a belief in the right of home ownership as a measure of freedom and democracy. For at least 500 years, a continuing influx of new inhabitants has brought the varying architectural styles, construction methods, craft traditions, and intellectual cultures of Europe, Africa, and Asia to the United States. The vast forests provided the most common of American building materials, wood, while quarries and ore deposits have supplied sand, stones, and metals. The country's topography, from seaside tidal lands to deserts, mountains, and fertile river valleys, has led to a varied set of architectural responses appropriate to the different climates and terrains. And, from independence onward, the ability of each American family to own land and a home has been seen as an indicator of the social and economic success of the United States.

The earliest inhabitants of North America, who arrived either over a land bridge from Asia or traveled northward from South America, established communities across the continent, some of which date back 10,000 years. By the time Europeans, especially the Spanish (who created the first permanent settlements in what is now the United States), British, French, and Dutch, began establishing their American colonies in the sixteenth century, Native American peoples were constructing their homes in many different forms. These included the tepees of nomadic tribes of the Great Plains, the log long-houses of the Pacific Northwest, sod houses in California and the upper Midwest, pole and bark houses in the southeast, and the dramatic cliff-dwelling pueblos of the Southwest. As much as these dwelling types have entered the American mythos, reappearing in twentieth-century roadside motels and ethnographic museums, their impact on the Europeans was relatively small, with the possible exception of the adobe architecture of the Southwest.

The Europeans instead brought their own architectural prototypes to the New World, many derived from medieval models. Even today, they form the basis of much of the residential architecture found across the country. Areas settled by the French, such as the Mississippi River valley, still have houses recognizably different from the areas settled by the English along the Atlantic seaboard. The English farmhouse model, in turn, was altered in

The house of Jonathan Harrington, near Boston, Massachusetts is typical of the New England style of architecture, built predominantly from wood, with oak frames, clapboard sidings, and central chimneys.

distinctive ways to respond to climatic conditions and material availability. Houses in New England tended to have central chimneys, and to be made of wood, while houses in the South pushed the chimneys to the outside, and were often made of brick.

By the late eighteenth century, at least in the major cities along the East Coast of America, architecture was beginning to develop a particular character while responding to the prevalent Georgian style of English building. The new Republic turned to classical Greek and Roman architecture to find stylistic precedents that represented the democracies of ancient times. The principal intellectual force behind these developments was America's third president, Thomas Jefferson, who was the architect for the University of Virginia and his own home at Monticello.

By the middle of the nineteenth century, several important developments made affordable housing more accessible to Americans. These included the invention of the balloon frame construction system and machine-made nails. The balloon frame used manufactured, identically sized, wood members, and allowed for the swift construction of homes by a growing construction industry. Machine-made nails were inexpensive, which meant that skilled carpentry was no longer required to connect the wooden pieces. These two developments during the 1830s set up what is essentially still the method for constructing millions of homes across the country each year. A few years later, the building of large-scale urban structures was similarly aided by the invention of the elevator and the steel frame. Both sets of innovations, domestic and commercial, essentially came out of Chicago. Stylistically, the buildings of America were influenced by the architecture of the Italian Renaissance, or by the freer styles of the Gothic and Romanesque. At the end of the century, H.H. Richardson's heavy stone version

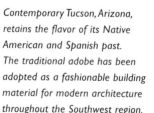

LEFT: Lower Manhattan skyline, New York. Skyscrapers, made possible by innovations such as steel-frame construction and elevators, came to prominence in the early twentieth century, due to a concentration of commercial activity in confined areas, the desire to make the most of commercial land purchases, as well as the demand for distinctive buildings to help publicize big businesses.

of the latter style could be found imitated from Texas to Boston to California, while domestically, similar stylistic moves could be found in the popular Queen Anne form of "Victorian" architecture. A few years later, Louis Sullivan combined Renaissance forms with Arts and Crafts ornamentation to help develop a formal language for the adolescent skyscraper.

Also by the end of the nineteenth century, large-scale engineering projects such as dams, canals, and bridges introduced the widespread use of concrete and helped to create the need for large factories that produced construction materials. Indeed, the first concrete grain silos of 1899–1900 would be cited as a model of strong, pure building by a later generation of European architects. While the United Kingdom-born Arts and Crafts movement would come to America (as would fascination with the architecture of Japan due to the opening of trade with that once-invisible nation), architects in the United States did not feel the need to view those traditions as a remedy for the ills of the Industrial Revolution the way Europeans did. America's most famous architect, Frank Lloyd Wright, even wrote a lecture in 1902 called the "Art and Craft of the Machine," to underscore the New-World view that good design in combination with industrial technology would be the appropriate direction to go. Frank Lloyd Wright's domestic architecture of the turn of the century, labeled the "Prairie Style," combined Japanese planning devices, Arts and Crafts furnishings and finishes, and products of the American construction industry. Another British import that was widely adopted was the bungalow, a house type originally created for the foothills of the Himalayas in India.

The period between the two world wars was marked by eclectic architecture which used multiple architectural styles and precedents (from Egyptian to Chinese, Mediterranean to English Tudor), by the lingering dominance of the Beaux-Arts (and its use of classical models, from Greek to Renaissance) for public buildings, and by the rise of Modern Architecture. Many architects tried new materials and forms in their architecture, such as the 1928 Lovell Hill house by Richard Neutra featuring an all-steel frame, and the concrete and redwood Double-House by Rudolph Schindler (both in Los Angeles). Others, such as

the inventor Thomas Edison, had also been trying to invent new and affordable ways to house America. The large Sears Roebuck department store chain developed a process for shipping the pieces of a home by rail— box by box according to the required construction sequence. Hundreds of thousands of these Sears homes were built, and many still exist today. Manufactured housing, often called mobile homes, remains an important source for inexpensive homes in the United States, especially in the South and West.

The advent of World War II brought a large number of European architects to the United States, as they escaped from the Nazis. Walter Gropius, Mies van der Rohe, Marcel Breuer, and others made their way to America, greatly influencing Modern Architecture. These architects, who themselves had been influenced by the work of Frank Lloyd Wright, took up important positions in American architectural schools and helped end the Beaux-Arts tradition in architectural education. After the war, the popularity of the shopping mall (first developed in the 1930s) along with the rise of the automobile and the interstate highways of the 1950s and 1960s led to an explosion of building across America in the form of the suburb and exurb, and new forms of planning such as "office parks."

Today, architects such as Frank Gehry have introduced new forms to architecture that combine ideas from contemporary art with the technology of the computer. Others, such as Peter Eisenman, have brought post-structuralist theories of language to their work. At the same time, vernacular architectural precedents, from sources as diverse as the Las Vegas strip and the architecture of the Pueblos, combined with issues of sustainability and the health of the environment, have led to a "critical regionalism" movement that supports the development of architectural styles appropriate to the many different conditions found across America. The centers of many older American cities, which suffered from the postwar rise of the suburbs, have become the focus of current design and planning efforts. However, America's belief in the technological, the phenomenon of continuing changes wrought by migrations from elsewhere around the world, and the importance of the home as the core element of the "American Dream" remain unchanged.

Contemporary Tucson, Arizona, retains the flavor of its Native American and Spanish past. The traditional adobe has been adopted as a fashionable building material for modern architecture throughout the Southwest region.

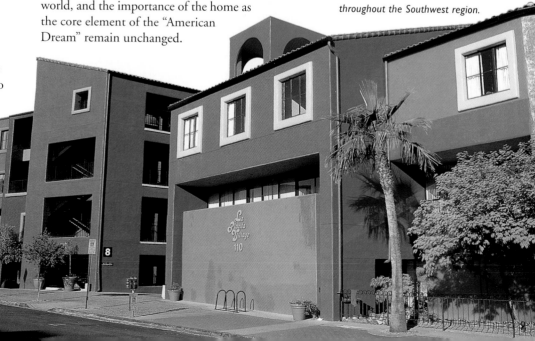

THE ARTS

Literature

Up from Slavery, the autobiography of writer and educator Booker T. Washington (1856–1915), was an eloquent account of the lives lived by many African-Americans before the Civil War brought emancipation to slaves. The author was born into slavery on a southern plantation, and went on to found the Tuskegee Institute in Alabama, a vocational school for African-Americans.

Ever since the first printing press began operation in Cambridge, Massachusetts in 1638, Americans have been producing literary works as diverse and as fascinating as the country itself. In the colonial period, these works for the most part consisted of Puritanical religious tracts (Cotton Mather), exploration accounts (Captain John Smith), and the political writings of a colony moving towards independence (Benjamin Franklin, Thomas Paine, and Thomas Jefferson). However, what we know as a distinctively national literature did not truly come into being until well into the nineteenth century. By this time, Independence had been achieved, Puritanism was dying, and people began to read increasingly for pleasure.

The nineteenth century

The first American writer to be recognized in Europe was Washington Irving, who entertained his readers with graceful, polished sketches and is best known for the stories "The Legend of Sleepy Hollow" and "Rip Van Winkle" (1820). James Fenimore Cooper's *The Last of the Mohicans* (1826) was one of a series of popular adventures known as "the Leatherstocking tales" that romanticized frontier life. The Gothic poems and tales of Edgar Allan Poe such as "The Raven" and "The Pit and the Pendulum" were poorly received in his lifetime (1809–49) but have endured, strongly influencing modern detective and horror genres.

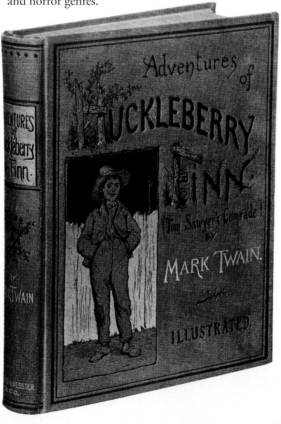

An enduring American classic, The Adventures of Huckleberry Finn *(1885) continues to delight generations of children. Despite author Mark Twain's mock-stern injunction to readers that, "persons attempting to find a moral in it will be banished," the book nevertheless makes a powerful case against the institution of slavery through its satirical humor.*

The poetic voices of the century were Emily Dickinson and Walt Whitman. Writing in the middle of the century, Dickinson, whose reclusiveness and rich interior life informed her verse, pondered the mysteries of nature and death in a refreshingly modern way. Whitman also broke with the conventions of form and content: the poems in *Leaves of Grass* (1855) are ebullient, sensual, and expansive, reflecting the boldness and energy of his young country.

Both at home and abroad, the novel was then flourishing as a major literary form, and the American masters were Nathaniel Hawthorn (*The Scarlet Letter*, 1850) and Herman Melville (*Moby Dick*, 1851), both of whom dared to explore deep moral and psychological themes in their writings.

This period is best known, however, for the influential group of writers known as the "Transcendentalists." Ralph Waldo Emerson, whose most famous essay, "Self Reliance," was written in 1841, left the Unitarian ministry, believing that "nothing is at last sacred but the integrity of your own mind." Henry David Thoreau retreated from mainstream society and recorded his contemplative years in essays such as "Civil Disobedience" (1849) and "Walden, or Life in the Woods" (1854). Thoreau went to jail for refusing to pay taxes to a government that condoned slavery. The debate over slavery and the resulting "War Between the States" produced *Uncle Tom's Cabin* (1852) by Harriet Beecher Stowe, and Stephen Crane's *The Red Badge of Courage* (1895) which remains the quintessential Civil War novel.

Two disparate writers dominated late nineteenth-century fiction: Henry James and Samuel Langhorne Clemens, known as Mark Twain. James wrote serious, sophisticated novels, such as *The Portrait of a Lady* (1881), dealing with complex human relationships. Twain was a humorist and spokesman for the common people. In his masterpiece, *The Adventures of Huckleberry Finn* (1885), Huck, a young boy, and Jim, a runaway slave, flee the demands of law and society to travel down the Mississippi River.

The early twentieth century

The turn of the century appropriately saw the emergence of several literary landmarks. Booker T. Washington became one of the first African-American writers to be published and is best remembered for *Up from Slavery* (1901). Kate Chopin's *The Awakening* (1900) was ahead of its time in its treatment of a woman's personal and sexual development, and became a classic feminist text. In *The Wonderful Wizard of Oz*, also published in 1900, L. Frank Baum created the first full-length original American fantasy.

The Imagist movement (1909–17), marked by free verse, colloquial language, and sharp, precise imagery, spawned such poets such as Carl Sandburg, Amy Lowell, William Carlos Williams, and Ezra Pound. An outspoken critic of American capitalism, Pound belonged to "the lost generation," a group of writers who lived and worked in Europe and included T.S. Eliot, Gertrude Stein, Djuna Barnes, Ernest Hemingway, and F. Scott Fitzgerald. Fitzgerald coined the term "the Jazz Age" to describe the heady, hedonistic 1920s. *The Great Gatsby* (1926) epitomizes the period and remains his best-loved work.

The novel most closely associated with the 1930s' Depression is John Steinbeck's *The Grapes of Wrath* (1939) which traces the journey of the impoverished Joad family as they leave the Dust Bowl of Oklahoma in search of a better life in California. According to eminent critic Harold Bloom, the character Tom Joad is the "perpetual icon of American social revolution."

The South experienced a literary revival between the World Wars, with such authors as William Faulkner (*The Sound and the Fury*, 1929) a virtuoso in his own unique brand of stream of consciousness; Thomas Wolfe (*Look Homeward,*

Angel, 1929); and Carson McCullers (*The Heart is a Lonely Hunter*, 1940). World War II was fictionalized in two major works: *The Naked and the Dead* by Norman Mailer (the 1948 novel which was to launch his long and controversial career) and James Jones' *From Here to Eternity* (1951).

Postwar literature

Despite, or perhaps because of, the political and social conservatism of the early postwar years, the 1950s produced a wealth of innovative writing. J.D. Salinger's *The Catcher in the Rye* (1951) expressed the insecurities and anxieties of troubled teenagers through its protagonist Holden Caulfield. Considered shocking in its day for its obscenities, the poem "Howl" (1956) established Allen Ginsberg as the bard of the Beat Generation. Jack Kerouac's *On the Road* (1957) is its prose counterpart. The author described his style as "spontaneous prose."

Harper Lee won the Pulitzer Prize in 1960 for *To Kill a Mocking-bird*, a compassionate novel about the themes of racism and tolerance in a small southern town. At the beginning

Gregory Peck as attorney Atticus Finch defends Brock Peters as Tom Robinson in the film of Harper Lee's bestselling book, To Kill a Mockingbird. Set in the deep South, where the author was brought up, the focus of the book is the accusation of rape made by a white woman against a black man. Written at a time when America was on the brink of enormous social change, its conclusion was a call to optimism, reflecting the belief that love could overcome hatred.

A stamp commemorates the short but productive life of writer Thomas Wolfe (1900–38). Look Homeward, Angel (1929) and Of Time and the River (1935) are autobiographical novels about the experience of growing up in a small mountain city in the South.

Novelist and short-story writer F. Scott Fitzgerald with his wife, Zelda, and child. He wrote about the world of the idle wealthy in the age of extravagance before the Depression in books like The Beautiful and the Damned *(1922) and* The Great Gatsby *(1925). He and Zelda moved to the French Riviera in 1924 where they lived a glamorous expatriate life, though* Tender is the Night *(1934) draws on the darker side of their troubled relationship.*

Pranksters" journeyed in a bus around America, a tour that was documented by Tom Wolfe in *The Electric Kool-Aid Acid Test* (1968). Norman Mailer's book *Why are We in Vietnam?* (1967) was another important work from this tumultuous revolutionary era.

John Updike said that "sex is the emergent religion." His novel *Couples* (1968), as well as Gore Vidal's *Myra Breckinridge* (1968), Philip Roth's *Portnoy's Complaint* (1969), and Erica Jong's *Fear of Flying* (1973) are examples of the literary works that came out of the "sexual revolution" of the late sixties and early seventies. *The Women's Room* (1977) by Marilyn French remains the definitive novel of the feminist movement. Postmodernism reached its peak during this period. *Gravity's Rainbow* (1973) is one of the novels that established Thomas Pynchon as an important figure in postmodernist fiction. Saul Bellow (*Humboldt's Gift*, 1975) was awarded the Nobel Prize in 1976 for his impressive body of work that would span five decades.

The 1970s and 1980s saw the flowering of a number of sensitive, imaginative writers such as Larry McMurtry (*Terms of Endearment*, 1975), John Irving (*The World According to Garp*, 1978), Anne Tyler (*Dinner at the Homesick Restaurant*, 1982), Armistead Maupin (*Tales of the City*, 1978), and the "cosmic/comic" Tom Robbins (*Even Cowgirls Get the Blues*, 1976). Several talented African-American women writers also came to prominence, most notably Alice Walker (*The Color Purple*, 1982), Toni Morrison (*Beloved*, 1987), and Maya Angelou (*The Heart of a Woman*, 1981).

Raymond Carver is described as the "minimalist" master of the short story, writing of "the daily responsibilities of life weighing on shoulders when nothing is certain." Carver's style, which reached a wider audience in 1976, with the publication of *Will You Please be Quiet, Please?* was to have a strong influence on the young writers Jay McInerney, author of *Bright Lights, Big City* (1984) and Bret Easton Ellis (*Less Than Zero*, 1985) whose early works dealt with the excesses of the 1980s and were known as "novels of cocaine culture" or "yuppie fiction." Tom Wolfe, who so accurately chronicled the hippie years, also examined greed in eighties' Manhattan in his best-selling *Bonfire of the Vanities* (1987), which first appeared in *Rolling Stone* magazine.

of the 1960s, the "confessional" school dominated the poetry scene in America and included such luminaries as Robert Lowell, Anne Sexton, John Berryman, and Sylvia Plath. Plath, who has become something of a cult heroine, is best known for *Ariel* (1965) and her autobiographical novel *The Bell Jar* (1961).

The title of Joseph Heller's 1962 novel *Catch 22* refers to a double-bind situation in which World War II airmen trying to escape from the horror of the conflict on grounds of insanity prove themselves sane in the attempt and thus ineligible. The phrase has become part of the popular lexicon and the novel itself became the bible of the anti-Vietnam War protest movement. Released in the same year, Ken Kesey's highly successful *One Flew over the Cuckoo's Nest* was set in a psychiatric institution—a metaphor for the society Kesey tried in various ways to escape from. Using his royalties, Kesey and his band of counterculturist "Merry

Recent developments

In the last two decades, readers have enjoyed a wealth of well-crafted, mass-market novels in specific genres. Popular authors include James Ellroy, James Lee Burke, and Patricia Cornwell (crime); Stephen King and Anne Rice (the supernatural); John Grisham (the law); Marion Zimmer Bradley (fantasy); and Tom Clancy (the techno-thriller).

Some thought-provoking novelists who were to have a major impact in the last decade of the century were Donna Tartt (*A Secret History*, 1992), E. Annie Proulx (*The Shipping News*, 1993), David Guterson (*Snow Falling on Cedars*, 1994), Barbara Kingsolver (*The Poisonwood Bible*, 1998), Paul Auster (*Timbuktu*, 1999), and Cormac McCarthy, whose 1994 novel *The Crossing* has been compared to *Moby Dick*.

At the close of the twentieth century, people were looking to the past to make sense of an uncertain future. Respected poet Robert Bly (*Iron John*, 1990), Clarissa Pinkola Estes (*Women Who Run with the Wolves*, 1992), and Thomas Moore (*Care of the Soul*, 1993) turned to ancient myths and folk tales, urging

their readers to live more simply. Charles Frazier chose the Civil War as the backdrop for his lyrical love story *Cold Mountain* (1997). Native American novelists Louise Erdrich and Michael Dorris went in search of the legendary lost diary of Christopher Columbus in *The Crown of Columbus* (1991).

Many writers searched their own cultural heritage and family history, both in fiction and auto-biography. Amy Tan's *The Joy Luck Club* (1988) bridges the gap between several generations of Chinese-American women. *Unto the Sons* (1992) is Gay Talese's account of his Italian immigrant forebears. In *Angela's Ashes* (1996), New York-born Frank McCourt tells of his childhood experiences in Limerick, Ireland, crossing the Atlantic again to pursue the American dream in his second book, *'Tis* (1999).

The Internet has emerged as an exciting new medium for literature, with notable works including Mark Amerika's on-line narrative *gammatron.com*. However, in whatever way the American tale continues to be told, as Flannery O'Connor once noted, "… in the long run, a people is known, not by its statements or statistics, but by the stories it tells."

Saul Bellow (1915–) autographs his Pulitzer Prize-winning novel Humboldt's Gift in 1975. He was born in Canada of Russian-Jewish parents, and moved to Chicago when he was nine.

A scene from Amy Tan's auto-biographical novel, The Joy Luck Club, which was made into a film in 1993. Born in Oakland, California, in 1952 to Chinese immigrant parents, she transformed her experience of a bicultural upbringing into the stories of four mother-daughter relationships.

American Art

Gilbert Charles Stuart, George Washington (Vaughan Portrait), *1795. Stuart was the creator of a distinctively American style of portrait. He was most famous for his images of George Washington in three main styles—the Lansdowne, the Athanaeum, and the Vaughan, or half-length type.*

The first Puritan settlers, arriving from northern Europe in the seventeenth century, rejected iconography and the graven image on religious grounds. Instead they brought a strong craft tradition, producing practical items such as chests and quilts decorated with plants, animals, and geometric designs which reflected the motifs and concerns of their daily rural life. By the early eighteenth century, the planter families of Virginia and North and South Carolina, growing rich on the flourishing tobacco trade, had begun to commission portraits as a way of displaying their new wealth and status. John Smibert (1688–1751), arriving from London in 1729, catered to this new audience, encouraging and directing a new market for art. The detail, light, and modeling of Smibert's society portraits established Classical Realism as the strongest influence on American art for the next century and inspired a new group of colonial artists, such as John Singleton Copley (1738–1815) and Benjamin West (1738–1820), to travel to Europe for training.

West never came back to America—he established a successful studio in London, became president of the Royal Academy, and court painter to George III. However, other American "neoclassical" artists who had traveled to Europe, such as Charles Willson Peale

(1741–1827), Gilbert Stuart (1755–1828), and John Trumbull (1756–1843) returned. They used the visual language of ancient Rome in their works to portray the spiritual, political, religious, and social ideals of the newly independent American Republic after the Revolutionary War in 1776.

While Classical Realism remained the governing style in painting, expansion west into new frontier lands in the mid-nineteenth century, the motivating spirit of Manifest Destiny (the idea that colonization was a necessary, God-sanctioned duty), and the growth of new settlements and cities began to produce landscapes of a distinctly American flavor. The romantic, atmospheric works of artists such as Asher B. Durand (1796–1886), Thomas Cole (1801–48) and, later, Cole's student Frederick Edwin Church (1826–1900), evoked the new spirit of discovery as railway lines began to open up the country. This group of artists based in the eastern states became known as the Hudson River school. Frederick Church's delicate, glowing use of tone and light—which was later to be termed Luminism— fitted the revelatory mood and influenced many American artists including John F. Kensett (1816–72), who used the technique to produce his renowned atmospheric seascapes.

Albert Bierstadt, The Rocky Mountains, Lander's Peak, *1863. Bierstadt, who was among the last exponents of the Hudson River School, is best known for his panoramic and grandiose interpretations of the American west, which were painted on an immense scale.*

As the process of industrialization quickened, depictions of the landscape as an untouched wilderness moved increasingly from realism to nostalgia and to moral and allegorical commentary. Artists of the Western school, in particular, reflected the sense of loss of a uniquely American landscape. Albert Bierstadt (1830–1902) and, then later, Frederick Remington (1861–1909), initially traveling west to the frontier lands to document the new territories, soon idealized and mythologized the landscape and battles between the new (pioneer) and former (Native American) occupants—establishing the still prevalent and popular perception of the Wild West.

The Civil War, the subsequent urban and industrial boom, and the slowing of westward expansion created new subjects and audiences for American art in the second half of the nineteenth century. The Civil War initiated a new interest in documentary realism (fueled in part by advances in photography) and the lives and concerns of everyday Americans. Artists Winslow Homer (1836–1910) and Thomas Eakins (1844–1916) depicted the lives of soldiers, African-Americans, children, and the thousands of urban dwellers crowding into America's new industrial centers.

With the closure of the frontier in 1890, American life increasingly meant urban life and the city became a new subject for art. Artists of the Ashcan School, such as Robert Henri (1865–1929) and George Bellows (1882–1925), living in New York at the turn of the century, showed the gritty realities of the industrial landscape and answered a new need for Americans to see their lives reflected in art.

Despite interest in this new "American experience," American artists and collectors continued the flow to Europe, confirming Paris, London, and Rome as

centers of the art world. The rising class of industrialist collectors, such as Rockefeller, Carnegie, Lockwood, and Morgan, commemorated achievements at home with epic landscapes by Bierstadt and Church, but spent most of their fortunes abroad, advertising their wealth and "taste" by investing in European masters. The society portraits and domestic interiors painted by expatriate artists such as John Singer Sargent (1834–1903), Mary Cassatt (1844–1926), and James McNeill Whistler (1844–1926) show the lives and concerns of wealthy Americans in Europe as well as American artists absorbing the influences of Impressionism.

In the early years of the twentieth century, America's growing power and confidence began to redirect the focus of world art. While Impressionism, Post-Impressionism, Fauvism, Cubism, and Futurism had lured American artists to Europe, Alfred Stieglitz (1864–1946) played a key role in bringing these movements to America. In 1913 the ground-breaking Armory Show at his Gallery 291 introduced the energy, colors, and abstract elements of avant-garde Modernism to the American public and promoted the emergence of New York as a new world center for art. Modernism provided American artists such as Joseph Stella (1877–1946), Charles Sheeler (1883–1965), and Charles Demuth (1883–1935) with a new visual language to interpret America's post-war industrial growth and optimism. Strong color, line, structure, and abstracted forms communicated the vibrancy of urban growth, mechanization, and mass production. The landscape was also reinterpreted by artists such as Georgia O'Keeffe (1887–1986). Drawn to New Mexico and the Southwest as an alternative to the thrust of the new cities, O'Keeffe used Modernist techniques to communicate the spiritual, primitive essence of nature found expressed in natural forms and the land.

A contemporary print (circa 1870) shows the appeal of the Hudson River and Catskill Mountain areas for eastern artists journeying from New York. The Hudson River School, active from 1825 to 1870, was an offshoot of the Romantic movement in art. Inspired by European artists such as Turner, and the writings of Washington Irving and James Fenimore Cooper, the Hudson River artists emphasized the scale and beauty of the American landscape.

Georgia O'Keeffe pictured with her husband, photographer Alfred Stieglitz. Married in 1924, the couple pioneered Modernism in America. Stieglitz promoted a number of Modernist artists through his New York Gallery 291 including O'Keeffe, whose semi-abstract style crystallized in the 1920s. She is best known for her closeup, large-scale depictions of flowers, animal bones, rocks, shells, and other natural forms.

Grant Wood, American Gothic, *1930. A major exponent of Midwestern Regionalism, a movement which flourished during the 1930s, Wood is best known for his satirical images of American provincialism, painted in a highly realistic style.* American Gothic *caused a sensation when it was first exhibited in 1930, at the Art Institute of Chicago, and propelled Wood's career from local to national recognition.*

Edward Hopper's (1882–1967) introspective, brooding city scenes reflect the change in mood as America moved from the energy of the 1920s into the Depression years. Experiments with abstraction were traded for realism and the comfort of the ordinary and recognizable, as artists re-examined the harsh realities of the people and landscape around them. While Hopper tackled isolation and dislocation in the urban landscape, "regional" artists such as Thomas Hart Benton (1889–1975) and Grant Wood (1892–1942) produced images of suburban and rural middle America that catered to the taste for escapist nostalgia. Rising to popularity in the 1930s and becoming a household name during the insecure years of the 1940s and late 1950s, Norman Rockwell (1894–1978) produced

illustrations that popularized a fictive "American Dream" of perfect family gatherings and "old fashioned" values in small-town America.

During and following World War II, European artists (including many Surrealists) seeking refuge in America rekindled interest in abstraction, in the spiritual role of art, and in the artistic process. Inspired by these new influences, Abstract Expressionists such as Willem de Kooning (1904–97) and Jackson Pollock (1912–56) began to explore the idea that the act of making art was as important as the end product, and that the surface of a work—its shape, texture, or color—could better communicate the artist's intention than imagery. Color field painters such as Mark Rothko (1903–70), Robert Motherwell (1915–91), and Barnett Newman (1905–70) also rejected representation, using planes of glowing color to express spiritual and emotional energy. Building on these ideas in the 1960s, artists of the Post Painterly Abstraction movement, such as Morris Louis (1912–62) and Helen Frankenthaler (1928–), concentrated on the communicative and expressive properties of color, staining large canvases with swirls and blocks of pigment.

While the Abstract Expressionists avoided recognizable imagery in their work as a means of visual communication, artists such as Jasper Johns (1930–) and Robert Rauschenberg (1925–) began to explore the power of mass-market iconography in the post-war boom years of America. During the 1950s television, film, advertising, and a wealth of new consumables provided America with a new collective cultural conscience, and provided artists with a new source of images. Known symbols and items, such as the American flag, numbers, or found objects, had an immediacy and power that could be appropriated by artists. Andy Warhol (1928–1987), Roy Lichtenstein (1923–97) and other Pop artists in the 1960s continued to break down the barriers between art and everyday life, using media-based, mass-produced images with a broad appeal.

In the late 1960s and 1970s, debate about what constitutes art and how it can best convey meaning promoted Minimalism among American artists looking for an alternative visual language to mainstream culture. Frank Stella's (1936–) all-black canvases, Robert Ryman's (1930–) all-white paintings, and Dan Flavin's (1933–96) neon tubes attempted to communicate directly with the viewer by focusing on the power of the object, its location, and choice by the artist. Earth artists such as Robert Smithson (1938–73) and James Turrell (1943–) also rejected commercialized imagery and the idea of a "product" by manipulating the natural environment, making temporary sculptures or installations using light, stone, and soil. Conceptual artists such as Bruce Nauman (1941–) channeled attention even more keenly on the power of the artist by incorporating videos, performances, and words rather than objects to present ideas.

The concept of marketing the artist rather than the artwork reached a new high point with the art market boom in 1980s America. Neo-expressionist artists such as Jean-Michel Basquiat (1960–88), Julian Schnabel (1951–), and Eric Fischl (1948–) rekindled interest in painting and exploited a new market of people who were desperate to invest in contemporary art. Questions of taste and what constitutes art were explored by Jeff Koons (1955–), whose kitsch reproductions of everyday objects parodied the art market and further broke down the barriers between high and low culture, art, and life.

While the demand for American art slowed down in the recession of the 1990s, American artists and buyers continued to be a major force in the world.

International institutions such as the Guggenheim, television, the Internet, and advertising now ensure the universal availability of American art and confirm the diversity of the current scene. Artists such as Cindy Sherman (1954–), John Currin (1962–), and Tom Friedman (1965–) continue to explore America's psychological, physical, and cultural landscape and identity, but the globalization of visual culture and frames of reference mean that American art is now a worldwide, not just a national, lexicon.

The Solomon R. Guggenheim Museum, New York. Mining heir Solomon R. Guggenheim (1861–1949) began collecting abstract art in the 1920s. In 1939 he founded the Museum of Non-Objective Painting to display his collection. The museum was renamed the Solomon R. Guggenheim Museum in 1952.

Music

A neon sign advertises BB King's blues club in Memphis, Tennessee. An African-American who grew up on a plantation and whose first ambition was to be a gospel singer, King (and his succession of guitars, always called Lucille) is regarded as one of the greats in the world of the blues.

RIGHT: By the 1930s, many families would have owned a bakelite radio like this one. Music was given generous air time and included the performances of dedicated studio orchestras.

American music developed from a myriad of origins and a number of different directions. Native American tribes provided the first in a series of many musical traditions, but the Old World forms and peoples of Europe were the main sources of the motley mixture that is the music of America. Some broad trends and patterns may be delineated in order to better understand the musical mosaic.

Music from the colonial era is divided into sacred and secular forms. New England worship music, specifically the psalmody, had a big effect on later southern music, including early country music, white and black spirituals, and modern gospel.

Increasing secularization

Secular music of the colonial period greatly influenced American music. British, Irish, and French ballads were popular. Most colonial ballads were transmitted orally from one generation to the next and became a major building block of American folk music. Other secular music centered around traditional fiddle tunes for formal dances such as the minuet and gavotte, and other dances like hornpipes, reels, and jigs.

The fiddle

The fiddle was the main instrument at colonial and frontier dances, and fiddle dance tunes are among the most genuine folk melodies preserved in America. The music of early string bands eventually evolved into bluegrass, a subgenre of country music. Fiddles were played across the country, from the fais dodos (all-night dances) of Cajun Louisiana, to the "house parties" and "kitchen sweats" in the Great Plains. The latter was the foundation for western swing, another substyle of country music.

Opera and other formal music

The increasing diversity and dispersion of the population, and growing commerce and prosperity furthered the secularization of eighteenth-century American society, and when the English ballad opera migrated across the Atlantic in the early 1700s it was enthusiastically received. The focal point of formal music was probably Charles Town (later Charleston) where, in 1762, the Saint Cecilia Society was founded, the first organization of its kind to achieve some permanence in America. The first foreign-language opera was staged in New York in 1825. The most lively operatic center was New Orleans, where a cosmopolitan French contingent had supported French opera since the late 1700s.

From the nineteenth century to the present, American music has been categorized into three major traditions: classical, popular, and folk. Classical orchestral music dominated the field of classical music during the nineteenth century when the first independent symphony orchestras were established.

Religion and the American musical tradition

Religious music became prominent in the 1900s. Spiritual folk songs and gospel hymns had their roots in evangelical songs of the revivalist movement in the American South and West in the late nineteenth century. Evolving from the gospel hymn in the 1920s and 1930s was the Southern gospel quartet music which used repeated refrain choruses sung in four-part harmony. Gospel quartet music remains a strong force in evangelical Christian music today.

Emergence of folk music

Two types of folk music emerged in America in the nineteenth century: hillbilly, the Anglo-influenced music of poor white southerners, and blues, the African-influenced music of poor African-American southerners. This music remained mostly unnoticed by the outside world until the 1920s, when the first field recordings were made, primarily by the Library of Congress. Musicologists generally agree that the country blues originated in the Mississippi Delta region. Over time, rural white southerners developed a body of songs celebrating landscapes and events of the American experience. As the music of the rural South diffused, several subgenres of country music emerged, defined by certain vocal and instrumental characteristics, including the singing cowboy, western swing, honky tonk, and bluegrass substyles.

Jazz was born in New Orleans, where this mural from the city's theater district is located. Often improvisational in nature, it first evolved from a combination of black and creole music.

and general morale, the 1930s saw expanding radio coverage for hillbilly and blues music, perhaps because their lyrics, which spoke of the hard times of the era, struck a chord in many people.

The advent of rock 'n' roll

After World War II, American popular music underwent a dramatic transformation. As had happened with jazz and blues, the main source of change was the music of African-Americans. In 1946 a new term, "rhythm and blues," replaced the outmoded label "race" music. Affluent white adolescents of the 1950s now turned to rhythm and blues because it was new to them and had danceable rhythms. In the early 1950s, an old blues term, "rock 'n' roll," was introduced to popularize rhythm and blues. Principal agents in the diffusion of rock 'n' roll included the transistor radio, 45 rpm records, the rise of the disc jockey, and "Top 40" radio. The major recording companies viewed the new music with skepticism, thus allowing small independent companies to capitalize on its growing popularity. The rock 'n' roll revolution of the 1950s effected a decentralization of the geographic centers for performance, recording, and publishing of popular music. Memphis, Philadelphia, Detroit, and Los Angeles now became as important as New York City.

During the 1960s, new forms of American rock 'n' roll emerged including the "surf sound" of southern California and the Detroit "Motown Sound." During the remainder of the twentieth century, more variants multiplied rapidly, including folk rock, heavy metal rock, punk rock, fusion, and alternative rock.

One of the few new developments in American music during the latter part of the twentieth century was rap. Some musicologists theorize that its roots are in the "talking blues" of an earlier era. Rap has since become an integral part of the "hip hop" culture that also includes vocabulary, clothes, and dance in its repertoire.

The future

As America begins a new century, new and recycled sounds are heard, such as Latin pop and "teeny bopper" music, which re-emerged in the late 1990s. American musical tastes and creativity resist any deterministic theory, and predicting future trends is virtually impossible. American people continue to experiment with musical forms and instrumentations, a trend that looks set to continue in our increasingly multicultural society.

A sign commemorates the beginnings of Motown, the record company that brought "Detroit Sound" to the world. Its many stars included the Supremes, Stevie Wonder, the Jackson Five, Marvin Gaye, and the Temptations.

LEFT: Memphis, Tennessee, was home to the king of rock'n'roll. Elvis began his recording career here in 1955 at Sun Studio.

Record players succeeded gramophones in the 1920s following the use of electricity in the recording process. This is the last Wurlitzer model to play only long-playing (78 rpm) records.

Jazz jazz jazz

Another significant development of the 1920s was jazz, an indigenous and unprecedented form of American music, which quickly achieved national popularity. New Orleans dominated the jazz scene from its inception although Kansas City, Chicago, New York City, and the West Coast eventually became important centers for later substyles such as swing, bebop, cool, avant-garde, and fusion. Some musicologists suggest that much American popular music evolved from the growing jazz movement.

Influence of technological changes

The prosperity which affected much of the American population following World War I changed popular and folk traditions. As well, significant technological developments which occurred in the 1920s—the establishment of commercial radio stations, the development of electrical recording, public address systems, and sound track for film—broadened the demographic for popular music, and composers, arrangers, and performers were expected to be more professional to cater to a more diverse and demanding audience. The commercialization of radio transmissions resulted in the birth of the popular music industry.

Then the Great Depression hit America, forcing many phonograph companies to curtail much of their operations. Yet despite the slump in business output

The potential value of a "brand" name like Hopalong Cassidy was recognized in the 1950s, when this publicity material was produced. Adapted from the novels by Clarence E. Mulford, Hopalong was the hero of 66 motion pictures. The star of the films, William Boyd, was astute enough to buy the television rights, licensing 52 episodes which were shown in America and around the world.

ABOVE RIGHT: A lobby card for Casablanca (1942), a classic from Hollywood's "Golden Age."

Elizabeth Taylor, Richard Burton, and George Segal fight it out in the emotionally harrowing film Who's Afraid of Virginia Woolf? (1966), adapted from Edward Albee's 1962 play.

Film

While it was the French Lumiere brothers, Auguste and Louis, who in 1896 first played a projected film to a paying public, it has been American artistry, technological advancement, and marketing that has established cinema as the fundamental and influential cultural force existing today. More than merely creating the most profitable mass entertainment industry in the country's history, cinema has become the main vehicle for promoting the American way to the world.

American cinema really began with the Nickelodeon—a peepshow device based upon Thomas Edison's Kinetoscope, where patrons could drop a nickel in a slot and view projections of moving pictures. The films only lasted a minute and often involved no more than street scenes or glimpses of celebrities like Buffalo Bill Cody, yet Nickelodeons became an immensely popular form of cheap entertainment.

But film manufacturers—precursors to the studios of the 1920s and 1930s—knew that to make more money they needed a higher class of patron (in terms of income). By 1910 they were targeting the emerging American middle class, creating theater screens big enough to project films before large crowds. Producers like David Wark (D.W.) Griffith (1875–1948) used new cinematic techniques (close-ups, changing points of view) and explored the medium's latent artistic and literary possibilities by adapting works by Shakespeare and Tennyson, and making movies that lasted over two hours. Along with Mack Sennet (1880–1960), Griffith also introduced a fresh art form—silent comedy, an amalgam of commedia dell'arte, vaudeville, and clowning—whose champion, Charlie Chaplin, became the defining image of the silent movie era.

The most fundamental shift in American film history came with the advent of sound. A parlous financial situation prompted Warner Brothers to take a chance on the new technology for a film adaptation of a Broadway play, *The Jazz Singer* (1927). This first "talkie" made over $2 million at the box office and in a single moment consigned silent film and most of its stars to history. Within two years 9,000 American theaters were wired for sound.

By the 1930s, the studios controlling film production—MGM, Paramount, 20th Century Fox, Warner Bros—had a reputation for harsh practice, technological proficiency, keen artistry, and dubious extravagance. Yet the system established a golden era, as can be seen by a partial list of 1939 releases: *The Wizard of Oz, Stagecoach, Gone with the Wind, Mr Smith Goes to Washington, Dark Victory*, and *Wuthering Heights*. The studios had created a product that was to become universally recognizable: the Hollywood feature film.

With World War II came perhaps Hollywood's finest hour as social institution and cultural force. Although American film registered its distaste for Nazism in films such as Chaplin's *The Great Dictator* (1940), its movement to "war production" ignited an economic and artistic boom that lasted until the 1950s. It also educed several masterpieces: Frank Capra's *The Philadelphia Story* (1941), Orson Welles' *Citizen Kane* (1941), Michael Curtiz's *Casablanca* (1942) among them. And though film noir classics like *The Maltese Falcon* (1941) had already introduced audiences to the criminality behind the picket fence of Middle America, post-war Hollywood emerged with a sequence of excellent "new realism" pictures that examined controversial social issues—adultery (*The Postman Always Rings Twice*, 1946), racism (*Gentlemen's Agreement*, 1947), and political corruption (*All the King's Men*, 1949).

Paranoia over communism saw the motion picture industry investigated by the House of Representatives Un-American Activities Committee (1947–52) run by Senator Joe McCarthy. Federal government Antitrust Laws broke up the studio monopolies by forcing the separation of controls over film production, distribution, and exhibition. At the same time, the sub-

urban migration of returning servicemen and the subsequent baby boom returned a generation of filmgoers from the theater to their homes, laying the groundwork for the rapid rise of television.

The failure of "widescreen" spectaculars—*Spartacus* (1960), *Ben-Hur* (1959), *Singin' in the Rain* (1952)—to arrest falling audience numbers also underlined how American tastes were becoming more sophisticated and varied. Society had changed and so must its entertainment. Films became more explicit in their depictions of drugs, violence, and sex. Simultaneously, a vivid new style of acting—Method—took off with a generation of actors including Lee Remick, Marlon Brando, Paul Newman, Montgomery Clift, and James Dean producing performances predicated upon a realist ideal of rawness and emotion. These developments polarized audiences, with the line drawn more by taste than age. But producers had begun to recognize the appearance of a new target market: teenagers.

The years 1965–75 could be considered America's period of auteur cinema, where the vision of the director rather than the studio was paramount. Younger talents like Stanley Kubrick (*2001: A Space Odyssey*, 1968), Sam Peckinpah (*The Wild Bunch*, 1969), and Mike Nichols (*Who's Afraid of Virginia Woolf?* 1966, *The Graduate*, 1967) forged a new identity for American cinema: intellectual, politically aware, philosophical, and individual. Artists such as Robert Altman (*MASH*, 1970), Martin Scorcese (*Mean Streets*, 1972, *Taxi Driver*, 1976), Francis Ford Coppola (*The Godfather*, 1972, *Apocalypse Now*, 1976), and to a lesser extent satirist Woody Allen (*Annie Hall*, 1977), extended the themes, structures, and visual composition of cinema and introduced realistic dialogue which vividly captured America's erratic response to the social and cultural emergencies of Watergate and the Vietnam War.

A nationwide economic downturn in the late 1970s soon had the studios reclaiming the keys to the cinematic kingdom. The success of two summer blockbusters in the mid-1970s—*The Exorcist* (1975) by William Friedkin and *Jaws* (1976) by Steven Spielberg—changed the way Hollywood did business, emphasizing the importance of saturation advertising and cross-promotion. Over the next 10 years Spielberg, often in collaboration with producer George Lucas, released lightweight family entertainment such as *ET: The Extra-Terrestrial* (1982) and the *Star Wars* trilogy (1977–83) supported by marketing campaigns equaling the film's production budget. They enjoyed spectacular billion-dollar aggregate grosses and producers such as James Cameron (*The Terminator*, 1984, *Titanic*, 1997) and Jerry Bruckheimer and Don Simpson (*Top Gun*, 1986) achieved similar success imitating the Spielberg/Lucas filmmaking and marketing model. Critics claimed that these glossy releases exchanged dialogue for state-of-the-art special effects,

had moved mainstream too far down-market, and were reducing an entire cinema culture to childishness. But there were many excellent offerings by artists who would shape American film for the next 20 years: Barry Levinson's *Diner* (1982), Phillip Kaufman's *The Right Stuff* (1983), John Sayles' *Matewan* (1987), Steven Soderbergh's *sex, lies, and videotape* (1989) and Spike Lee's masterpiece *Do the Right Thing* (1989).

The main legacy of the 1980s, however, was away from the silver screen. The restructuring that saw every major studio change its corporate owner meant Hollywood had been absorbed into the global communications industry. It no longer simply made films, it supplied and distributed filmed entertainment for a variety of markets and media outlets.

The introduction of new technologies such as cable television, pay-per-view, PC video games, compact discs, and then digital videodiscs (DVD) meant that in the 1990s Hollywood was able to attract consumers to buy and enjoy the associated products of films they hadn't actually seen. Movies such as *The Blair Witch Project* (1999) used the Internet to secure word-of-mouth promotion, allowing it to gross over $500 million while costing less than $2 million to make.

American film is now dominated as much by technology and marketing as by celebrity performers. This is consistent with its history—along with the periodic shifts of power and constantly advancing expertise, Hollywood's only constant has been its stars. American cinema has also remained consistent with its beginnings—it remains the dominant creative production force in world cinema, the innovator, and the standard bearer in this art form.

Gossip about film stars continues to provide fodder for what has become a vast mass entertainment industry. This somewhat tongue-in-cheek scandal sheet of the 1950s, featuring one of Hollywood's favorite stars, is now a collector's item.

LEFT: *Universal Studios was founded in Chicago in 1912 by Carl Laemmle, a pioneer filmmaker from Bavaria. The company moved to Los Angeles in 1915.*

A scene from *ET: The Extra-Terrestrial, about a group of children who befriend a gentle creature from another planet. The film, directed and produced by Steven Spielberg in 1982, was the most profitable movie ever made until Spielberg's dinosaur epic,* Jurassic Park, *overtook it at the box office in 1994.*

Theater

Chicago's theater district is in healthy shape. As well as new and experimental productions, classical theater is popular and drawing large audiences. The Chicago Shakespeare Theater, opened as part of a new entertainment complex in 1999.

Actors James Daly and Barbara Baxley read through the script of the comedy/drama Period of Adjustment with the playwright, Tennessee Williams (right) in New York in 1960. The play explored the dynamics of two relationships under stress and was later made into a film starring Jane Fonda.

Throughout its history American theater has reflected the nation's contradictory pursuit of an elusive panacea—the American Dream. Shaped by individuals as much as by cultural forces, such as war or civil rights, its story reflects shifts in ascendancy and innovation between Broadway and a network of regional and more alternative companies. But at its core, theater has been concerned most with the tension between America's asserted global identity and the individual's struggle for self-determination.

The first play performed on American soil was a comedy by Spanish explorers in 1598 and it was not until the late nineteenth century that America had formed a theatrical identity separate to its colonial ancestors. The Puritan settlers of the seventeenth century found little time after securing territory for cultural innovation and their stern condemnation of painted parlour games even extended to the arrest of three men in 1665 Virginia merely for the offence of "enacting a play." They were found innocent but theater evidently was not.

The late seventeenth century to the late 1890s was a period of modest evolution for theater as regional centers slowly began to develop. In 1714 *Androboros* by Robert Hunter was the first play to be published by an American. The first known theater was built in Williamsburg in 1716 and Walter Murray and Thomas Kean founded the first "professional" theater company in Philadelphia in 1749. But until the intercontinental railroad was completed in 1869, the small and scattered population was unable to sustain a professional theatrical community—offerings ranged from ebullient Buffalo Bill-type western shows by

travelling professional companies to re-enactments of popular localized tales, most often drawn from the Civil War by amateur local troupes.

Commercial American theater really began in 1898 with a consortium of six New York-based businessmen known as the Syndicate. This group combined celebrity casting and an efficient centralized bookings system with a network of contracted regional theater companies to tour productions. Although their monopolistic control soon led to accusations of bias and intimidation by the rest of theatrical community (from competing New York theater owners to actors who refused to sign Syndicate-only contracts), by the time their power had been effectively challenged the Syndicate had established the Broadway power base that remains to this day.

Their success marginalized more artistic endeavor until the arrival of the Little Theater movement between 1910 and 1917. Based in university campuses and small fringe companies, the movement popularized the works of European naturalists such as Ibsen and Zola. These playwrights' bleak renderings of tortured relationships inspired America's first world-class dramatist, Eugene O'Neill (1888–1953) to produce a series of seminal works including *Anna Christie* (1921), *The Hairy Ape* (1922), and *Long Day's Journey into Night* (1939–41), which eventually led to the winning of a Nobel Prize in 1936.

The interwar years were characterized by an intense period of activity in both commercial and experimental theater. The Theater Guild, established in 1918, played a seminal role. It raised the artistic level of commercial theater by expanding the choice of plays to include European avant-garde works by Sartre and Beckett while eschewing the "star system" of casting on Broadway. The Guild also founded season subscriptions for audiences and supported the US tour of the influential Moscow Arts Theater in 1923. The Guild had two important legacies: the creation of the Group Theater company in 1931, whose nascent belief in a difference between "true" acting and "theatrical" acting eventually spawned the Method style of the Actors Studio (1951), and the simultaneous discovery of social realist Clifford Odets (1906–63). Odets' compassionate dramas, including *Waiting for Lefty* (1935), exhibited a strong social conscience that grew out of the conditions caused by the Depression.

World War II saw the birth of a Broadway phenomenon—the musical spectacular. Based on a glossy fusion of catchy songs, comedy, dance, and expensive set design, teams such as

Oscar Hammerstein and Richard Rodgers (*Oklahoma!* 1943, *Carousel*, 1945, *South Pacific*, 1949, *The King and I*, 1951) and Alan Jay Lerner and Frederick Loewe (*Brigadoon*, 1947, *My Fair Lady*, 1956, *Camelot*, 1961) distracted a world-weary American audience with productions offering romantic whimsy and sure-to-please happy endings.

Combined with the rise in popularity of television and a resurgent Hollywood film industry, the success of musicals ironically underlined the need for, and then inspired, alternative theater. The term "off-Broadway" came to describe active theaters in Manhattan outside the Broadway strip and also a strand of idealism and political awareness that shunned the commercial imperatives of mainstream theater. Off-Broadway was to produce two native talents who would dominate the next half century in American theater: Arthur Miller (b. 1915) and Edward Albee (b. 1928).

Between 1940 and 1960 American theater began to articulate the social and moral consequences of the Depression, World War II, and the communist paranoia that accompanied the Cold War years. Authority and its servants were no longer blindly trusted and adversarial sentiment toward the Establishment was crystallized in Miller's two modern classics, *Death of a Salesman* (1949), in which a man's belief in the American Dream eventually kills him, and *The Crucible* (1953), an attack on the political and moral bankruptcy of the McCarthy era.

Edward Albee's pioneering absurdist short piece *The Zoo Story* (1959) heralded the experimentalism that was to dominate the 1960s, but his seminal works *Who's Afraid of Virginia Woolf?* (1962) and *A Delicate Balance* (1966) took America further down the road signposted by Miller. Albee and poetic realist Tennessee Williams (1911–83) both presented America from behind the 1950s' picket fence—a place of abrasive, internecine relationships, moral weakness, matriarchal dominance, and the desire for sexual and material gratification in the pursuit of happiness and success.

In the 1960s, theater's Anglo/American hegemony was breached and an expanding multicultural community began to establish its voice. Grants supplied by the Ford Foundation (1959) and the National Endowment of the Arts project encouraged the greatest expansion in theater production since the middle of the nineteenth century. This was accompanied by changes in production styles and values as companies replaced traditional scripts with performances that relied on lighting, set design, and sound and vision for impact.

The concept of theater as a vehicle for the detached contemplation of high-minded beauty or as the home of middle-class entertainment was increasingly anachronistic. Although musicals such as

Hair (1976) achieved spectacular Broadway success, writers during the 1970s and 1980s, such as Sam Shephard (b. 1943) and David Mamet (b.1947), produced confrontational works seemingly designed to undermine mainstream values and systems. They combined a literary use of language with visceral, unstable characters and settings. "Kinetic realism," as it was termed, showed how violence rather than reason or communication had seduced to become the resolution of choice in a materialistic, technology-dependent society.

Over the last 15–20 years strong regional companies, such as Steppenwolf in Chicago, and niche groups have set theater's agenda. By the mid-1980s there were over 100 women's theater groups nationwide and the formation of the Gay Theater Alliance (1978) had given homosexuality power as both a political and theatrical movement. Harvey Fierstein's (b.1954) *Torch Song Trilogy* (1982) and John Guare's (b. 1936) *Six Degrees of Separation* (1990) used their protagonists' homosexuality to explore issues such as social superficiality and artifice in modern America. However, it was the playwright Tony Kushener (b. 1956) who made gay issues accessible to national audiences in his Pulitzer and Tony Award-winning two-part work, *Angels in America* (1993–94).

Though film, television, and popular music may now eclipse it in terms of mass appeal, American theater in the twenty-first century remains integral to the expression and exploration of the national psyche and the perennial pursuit of its Dream. While Broadway still undeniably reflects its early Syndicate roots—supporting high-cost, mainstream productions such as the musicals of Andrew Lloyd Webber—politically active and substantially independent theater groups now increasingly represent America's cultural, social, economic, and political diversity.

The cast rehearses for a show by Rodgers & Hammerstein to be broadcast on television in 1954. The musical spectaculars created by two of Broadway's most successful librettists continue to attract large audiences.

LEFT: Tennessee Williams won his second Pulitzer Prize in 1955 for Cat on a Hot Tin Roof, *a play about emotional hypocrisy in a family of wealthy Southerners.*

A banner advertises one of the many theaters in Chicago. Respected regional theater companies such as Steppenwolf and the Goodman Theater are based here.

SCIENCE AND TECHNOLOGY

Invention and Innovation

Printer, diplomat, and scientist Benjamin Franklin (1706–90) performed some of the earliest experiments with electricity, and set up the first public library and fire service. The lightning rod, bifocals, and a revolutionary furnace stove number among his many innovations.

Throughout the short history of the United States, Americans have demonstrated that they have a flair for innovation. Their inventions have not only helped make their nation the world's leading technological power, but have also radically improved the lives of millions of people around the globe.

Early innovations

One of the country's earliest innovators was Benjamin Franklin. A highly influential ambassador and statesman, Franklin was also responsible for numerous inventions, including bifocal glasses (1783); the lightning rod (1752), which protects buildings and ships from lightning damage; the Franklin Stove (1740), a cast-iron stove that can be situated away from a wall; and watertight bulkheads in ships. He was also responsible for coining many of the terms that we use today in relation to electricity, including "positive," "negative," "conductor," and "battery."

Following the mechanization of the spinning process in England in 1764, demand for cotton from the United States increased greatly. This led Eli Whitney to develop the Cotton Gin in 1793, a machine that separated the cotton seeds from the fiber, a procedure that had previously been carried out by hand. Cotton production subsequently expanded dramatically, boosting the nation's economic prosperity.

One innovation strongly tied to the early history of the United States, and particularly the American West as portrayed in countless western movies, is the revolver—the first weapon that could be fired repeatedly without reloading. Samuel Colt patented his revolver in 1836. Although his first attempt at manufacturing the "six-shooter" bankrupted him, Colt then secured an order from the US government for 1,000 pistols during the Mexican War. The manufacture of interchangeable parts for his guns and the widespread use of the pistol during the American Civil War went on to make him a very wealthy man.

A contemporaneous development in a different field resulted in the invention of vulcanized rubber. Rubber had been widely used for waterproofing for some time, but had the disadvantage of freezing solid in cold weather and melting in hot weather. In 1839, Charles Goodyear discovered that mixing rubber with sulfur and then heating it—a process that became known as vulcanization—would create a material that was soft, pliable, and resistant to temperature variations. Vulcanization allowed the development of many modern rubber products, most notably car tires.

Communications and media

As America's population swelled in the mid-nineteenth century, the demand for improved communications and information services grew rapidly. Ever since Benjamin Franklin's experiments with electricity, scientists had dreamed of using this energy source to communicate over long distances. The dream became reality in 1838, when Samuel F.B. Morse introduced the telegraph and Morse Code, beginning a communications revolution that continues today.

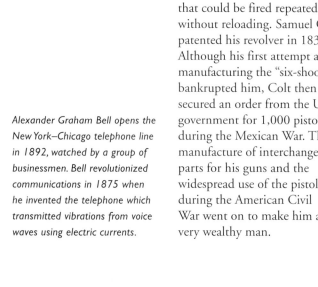

Alexander Graham Bell opens the New York–Chicago telephone line in 1892, watched by a group of businessmen. Bell revolutionized communications in 1875 when he invented the telephone which transmitted vibrations from voice waves using electric currents.

Traditional printing processes, involving unwieldy flatbed presses, made production of the first newspapers time-consuming and expensive. A major step forward occurred with Richard M. Hoe's idea of placing the type on a revolving cylinder. This innovation, called the Hoe Rotary "Lightning" Press and patented in 1847, increased print rates to 8,000 sheets (printing on one side) per hour, a huge rise in throughput. Further improvements led to a new and faster design, named the Hoe Web Perfecting Press, which was able to handle 18,000 sheets per hour and printed on both sides of the paper.

Throughout the 1800s, various attempts were made to make a machine that could produce standardized type on demand, but the results were generally less efficient than writing by hand. Finally, in 1867, Christopher Latham Sholes invented a practical and efficient machine, subsequently named a typewriter. In 1873, he signed a contract with the gunsmiths Remington and Sons of Ilion, New York, to manufacture it, and the first model, the Sholes and Glidden Type Writer, appeared in 1874. Mark Twain bought an early "Remington," as the machine was then known, and became the first author in history to submit a typewritten manuscript (*The Adventures of Tom Sawyer*) for publication in 1876.

Arguably the most significant invention of the nineteenth century was the telephone. On March 10, 1876, in Boston, Massachusetts, Alexander Graham Bell first transmitted speech via an electrical cable, addressing his assistant Watson with the now famous phrase "Mr Watson, come here. I want you." Later that year, he conducted a successful test over a 2-mile (3-km) distance. The first telephone exchange was set up at New Haven, Connecticut, in 1878.

Amateur photography received a huge boost in 1888 with the appearance of the first Kodak Camera, invented by George Eastman. It was a portable, hand-held machine with 100 exposures preloaded; when all the exposures were used up, the camera was returned to the manufacturer for processing and reloading.

Thomas Alva Edison, perhaps the most prolific inventor in American history, transformed everyday life in the nineteenth century with his hundreds of innovations relating to electric light and power, storage batteries, the telegraph, and the telephone. He invented the incandescent light bulb (1879), the phonograph (1877), and the mimeograph (1875), and helped develop early motion-picture machines.

Developments in transportation

Although the concept of lifting objects by mechanical means had been around for at least 2,000 years, by the mid-nineteenth century there was still no machine that could reliably and safely lift people. In 1853, however, Elisha Graves Otis perfected a safety device that made modern elevators possible. It consisted of a braking system that gripped the guide rails of an elevator only when tension was released from the hoist cable; that meant that if the cable broke, the elevator

would not fall. The first passenger elevators based on this system went into service in New York City in 1857 and were powered by steam; it was not until 1889 that the first electric elevators appeared. In turn, the refinement of elevator technology led to the proliferation of skyscrapers throughout the United States.

One notable early contribution to the development of transportation technology was the invention of the oil well. Before 1859, oil could only be found where it naturally seeped out of the ground. In that year, Edwin Drake combined a drill with a pumping mechanism to create an oil well. Implementing it for the first time at Titusville, Pennsylvania, he discovered oil about 70 feet (21 m) below the surface, a discovery that led to the first "black gold" rush.

The last major American invention of the 1800s was the submarine, which was developed in 1898. A prototype submarine had been invented in 1776 by American scientist David Bushnell, but it wasn't a practical form of transportation because it required that its pilot propel it by turning a hand-crank. Several craft made during the Civil War had similar limitations. A breakthrough occurred in 1894 when Simon Lake built a research craft called the Argonaut I, which was powered by a

Thomas Edison (1847–1931) pioneered the everyday use of electricity when he invented the incandescent light bulb in 1879. The bulb used a carbonized cotton thread as a filament.

The first hand-held Kodak camera, developed in 1888, cost $25 and popularized amateur photography. This Baby Brownie was Kodak's 1930s model.

The Wright brothers' first motor-propelled flight took place on December 17, 1903 in North Carolina. In this image, Orville Wright controls the plane, while Wilbur stands at the right.

Henry Ford's innovations in assembly line production allowed him to market this Model T Ford in 1908. It was the first mass-produced, affordable automobile.

gasoline engine and electric motor, and sailed it from Norfolk, Virginia, to New York City. In 1895, the intrigued US Navy awarded a contract to the John P. Holland Torpedo Boat Company to build a similar, craft, and in 1898 the company launched the first fully fledged submarine. It was over 50 feet (15 m) long, powered by electric and gasoline motors, and carried a torpedo tube and dynamite guns.

Another invention with obvious military applications was the airplane, whose development is credited to the brothers Orville and Wilbur Wright. They started by experimenting with a small biplane kite in 1899, then moved on to bigger gliders that could accommodate a pilot. The first of these was flown at Dayton, Ohio in the summer of 1899, but wasn't a great success because it failed to generate sufficient lift. However, once the Wrights had increased the wing area to 290 square feet (28 sq m), the glider worked more efficiently and by the end of the year had completed over 50 separate flights. Further experiments and adjustments resulted in a glider that completed more than 700 flights and was able to stay in the air for as long as 26 seconds. The next step was a powered machine. On December 17, 1903, at Kill Devil Hills, North Carolina, the Wrights managed to stay in the air for 59 seconds using an internal combustion engine mounted on a new frame. This finally demonstrated that heavier-than-air powered flight was possible. Over the next two years, the Wrights continued to refine their design and by 1905 they were able to stay in the air for 39 minutes at a time.

By this time, the first automobiles had appeared in the United States, built by entrepreneurs such as Ramson Eli Olds and James Packard. No fewer than 50 different companies were already manufacturing cars by 1898; but it was Henry Ford who made cars accessible to the general public, establishing a new age of personal transportation. In 1908, he introduced the first mass-market car, the "Model T," eventually selling more than 15 million of these vehicles. Cheap, efficient production was made possible by Ford's pioneering concept of the assembly line, which enabled his company to produce one complete car chassis every 93 minutes. His advances in assembly line technology were subsequently emulated by manufacturing industries around the world.

Toward the Space Age

As society became more complex, demand for greater calculating power grew; this fuelled the development of computers. Mechanical calculating machines had been used since the seventeenth century, but a major step forward in the United States occurred when Herman Hollerith devised a mechanical "statistical tabulator" to tabulate the results of the 1890 US Census. Hollerith subsequently founded the company that would become IBM and build the first general-purpose programmable computer.

One of the most significant contributions to the advancement of electronics and computing was the invention, in 1947, of the transistor by three physicists at Bell Labs, Walter H. Brattain, William B. Shockley, and John Bardeen. The transistor replaced much larger and less efficient vacuum tubes, allowing improvements in the design of products such as radios, telephones, and computers. Transistors also led directly to the development of integrated circuits—tiny, complete transistor and wiring circuits that form the basis of modern technology.

World War II provided the impetus for one of the major technological developments of the century—the atomic bomb. The United States began developing the bomb toward the end of the war, as part of a research program known as Manhattan Project. The first test was carried out on July 16, 1945, in the state of New Mexico. Later the same year the bomb was used to devastating effect against the Japanese cities of Hiroshima and Nagasaki, forcing the Japanese to surrender and marking the beginning of the "Atomic Age."

Military and more peaceful uses have been found for another notable invention of the postwar period, the laser. Created in 1960 by Theodore H. Maiman, a physicist at Hughes Research Laboratories, Miami, laser technology is now used in a wide range of applications, ranging from surgical instruments to compact disc players.

Perhaps the greatest achievement in human history took place on July 20, 1969, when astronauts Neil A. Armstrong and Edwin E. Aldrin landed on the Moon. The successful mission was the culmination of numerous innovations and thousands of hours of research by America's space program. One of the most significant subsequent developments in this field was the space shuttle, the first reusable spacecraft. Known originally as the Space Transportation System (STS), it was built by NASA and launched on April 12, 1981. It has now flown over 100 successful missions, with only one mishap in 1986.

The past 200 years have seen more technological developments than the previous 2000, and a high proportion of those innovations have originated in the United States. Having prospered in the Industrial Age, pioneered the Atomic and Space ages, and established itself as a leader in the Information Age, the United States is poised to play a major role in the next technological era—whatever that might be.

The installation of fiber optic cable across America since the 1980s has transformed the telecommunications industry. Providing fast, cheap access to data via phone or the Internet, it has made the nation a leader of the Information Age.

As part of America's nuclear testing program, Operation Crossroads, an atomic bomb was tested at Bikini Atoll in the Pacific Ocean on July 25, 1946. The underwater detonation projected a vast dome of water above the test ships on the lagoon.

Space Exploration

There are many defining moments in American history. One of these occurred on May 25, 1961, when President John Kennedy committed the nation to the goal of landing a man on the Moon by the end of the 1960s. Stung into action by rival Soviet space-flight achievements, President Kennedy had set the United States on a resolute course, not only to the Moon, but beyond. Today, that dream of space exploration and discovery continues.

On October 4, 1957, the history of the world changed forever when the then Soviet Union launched *Sputnik 1* into orbit. America responded on January 31, 1958, when *Explorer-1* soared into Earth's orbit atop a Jupiter-C research rocket.

Astronauts and cosmonauts

By the time the National Aeronautics and Space Administration (NASA) came into being in 1958 as the nation's civilian space agency, America had an impressive list of satellite launches. Despite this, the Soviet Union launched the first human into space in April 1961, when cosmonaut Yuri Gagarin's *Vostok* spacecraft carried him on a single orbit of the Earth.

Barely three weeks later, astronaut Alan Shepard became America's first man in space, with a 16-minute suborbital flight aboard his *Freedom 7* spacecraft. Soon after, NASA was committed to a manned lunar landing, and an enthralled nation gave itself over to a patriotic fervor that became known as "space fever."

THE RACE FOR THE MOON

John Glenn became America's first astronaut to orbit the Earth on February 20, 1962, by which time NASA had already established a timetable to beat the Soviet Union in an undeclared race for the Moon. Following

The Apollo 17 spacecraft sits atop its Saturn rocket before the last manned mission to the Moon in 1972. The crew landed for 75 hours and traveled 21 miles (34 km) over the Moon's surface in their lunar rover.

America's commitment to the space program has not been without human cost. The first manned Apollo flight, scheduled for January 27, 1967, ended in tragedy when astronauts Edward H. White, Virgil Grissom, and Roger B. Chaffee died in a launch pad fire.

the Mercury program was a series of two-man flights, during which astronauts practiced essential rendezvous techniques during protracted Earth-orbiting missions. The first of these *Gemini* missions was carried out in March 1965.

By now there were concerns that the Soviet Union was also aiming for a manned lunar flight. It had already accumulated an impressive list of space "firsts:" the first man and woman in space, the first person to walk in space, and the first multicrewed flight in a single spacecraft. However Project *Gemini* proved to be a monumental success, and in just 20 months, 10 manned flights took place.

PROBING DEEP SPACE

It was not just in the field of manned spaceflight that NASA performed magnificently. Robotic spacecraft were sent to our planetary neighbors, and out into the far reaches of the universe. Unmanned probes were landed on, or flew by, the Moon and planets in our solar system, and we began seeing captivating photographs taken on the surface of Mars. Launched in 1977, two unmanned spacecraft—called *Voyager 1* and *2*—achieved one of the most spectacular odysseys in spaceflight history, when they took us on a grand tour of our Solar System. Over several years the two spacecraft swept by Earth's outer planets, and sent back breathtaking photographs of worlds almost beyond our comprehension. These celestial encounters have instigated decades of study and evaluation, and further robotic probes will gradually add to our knowledge of what lies beyond our blue planet.

Even as robotic spacecraft explored our Solar System, and with space exploration now part of human destiny, NASA received a severe setback. On January 27, 1967, a launch countdown test of the first *Apollo* spacecraft was taking place at Cape Canaveral, when fire erupted in or near one of the wire bundles to the front left of Virgil ("Gus")Grissom's seat. The three astronauts died as a result. Following redesign work, the first three-man *Apollo* spacecraft was finally launched. In a bold move the next flight, *Apollo 8*, was sent into lunar orbit. Two more *Apollo* flights followed, then NASA was ready to make history.

A GIANT LEAP FOR MANKIND

Apollo 11 carried three men to the Moon, where astronauts Neil Armstrong and Edwin (Buzz) Aldrin landed their lunar module *Eagle* on the lunar soil. On July 20, 1969, Neil Armstrong became the first human being ever to walk upon another world. The mission planted an American flag and left a plaque to commemorate their achievement which said: "Here men from the planet Earth first set foot upon the Moon. July 1969 AD. We came in peace for all mankind."

As the *Apollo* program continued into the 1970s, more and more astronauts left enduring footprints on

This plaque in Arlington National Cemetery, Virginia, honors the crew of the Challenger space shuttle, which exploded seconds after its launch at the Kennedy Space Center in Florida on January 28, 1986. It is believed that the accident was caused by a critical combination of adverse weather conditions and mechanical failure.

Twenty years to the day after Gagarin's pioneering flight, space shuttle *Columbia* carried two astronauts into orbit, ushering in a new era of human space exploration. The four shuttles in NASA's fleet never achieved the agency's goal of up to 20 flights per year, but some remarkable feats of space science and satellite repair and retrieval were carried out, while massive robotic probes such as the Jovian probe *Galileo* began their long interplanetary journeys nestled in a shuttle's cargo bay. Meanwhile, space exploration was no longer the exclusive habitat of male test pilots, and women began to join NASA's astronaut training corps.

The considerable risks involved in spaceflight were realized on January 28, 1986, when shuttle *Challenger* and her crew of seven astronauts were destroyed in an explosion only 73 seconds after liftoff. Included in that ill-fated crew was a teacher named Christa McAuliffe, who would have been America's first civilian spacefarer. Once again NASA was faced with a re-evaluation of its procedures, hardware, and timetable, and when the shuttle program resumed some 20 months later many safeguards had been initiated.

A RETURN TO THE MOON?

Today, space shuttles continue to be launched from Florida's Kennedy Space Center, and scores of astronauts and cosmonauts are currently working on the construction of a massive space station to be known as Alpha. In cooperation with controllers at the Johnson Space Center in Houston, Texas, scientific and medical research will be carried out aboard this orbiting laboratory. Earth observation and oceanographic studies will continue to bring us a greater understanding of our planet, and the effects of global issues such as pollution and deforestation.

In years to come, it is expected that Alpha will provide a suitable space platform from which men and women will one day return to the Moon and even begin missions to Mars. Meanwhile, the exploration of the solar system continues under the administration of NASA's Jet Propulsion Laboratory in Pasadena, California. Under its supervision robotic probes are now mapping planets and asteroids, and landing to conduct geological evaluations of our celestial neighbors. The first steps have been taken, and America's outward urge will continue for the benefit of all humankind.

the Moon. By this time NASA had set its future sights on orbital science, and launched a series of manned flights to a vast space station known as Skylab. In 1975, America and the Soviet Union conducted a joint *Apollo/Soyuz* flight, during which astronauts and cosmonauts linked their spacecraft in orbit and tested compatible docking systems. It became known as the "handshake in space" mission, and was a precursor to the cooperative flights of today.

The space shuttle

Expendable space hardware had become a costly business for governments to justify, and a new space vehicle was now on the drawing boards. Known as the Space Shuttle, and designed to land on a conventional runway, this winged vehicle was intended to carry NASA's astronauts on increasingly routine flights into space.

TOP LEFT: *The first launch of space shuttle* Columbia *on April 12, 1981. Astronauts Robert Crippen and John Young's mission was to orbit the Earth.*

BOTTOM LEFT: *Nearly 20 years after the launch of* Columbia, *astronauts were able to install new equipment and perform complicated repairs outside their spacecraft. Here, Carlos I. Noriega waves for the camera, held by his space buddy, Joseph R. Tanner, on December 5, 2000. They were deploying a new solar array structure (seen at top of picture), an activity that involved three sessions of EVA (extravehicular activity).*

Computer Technology

Aerial view of the Santa Clara Valley in California. Now known as "Silicon Valley," this area 50 miles (80 km) from San Francisco is recognized as the technology center of the United States, specializing in the development and manufacture of computers and software.

Few inventions have had such an impact on modern society as the computer. In various guises, it now plays a vital role in many aspects of our daily lives, ranging from education and accounting to shopping and entertainment. The United States has long played a central role in the development of computer technology and has contributed many of the innovations that have made its increasing sophistication and ever-widening range of applications possible.

From tabulation to computation

The first major development in this field in the United States occurred in 1890 when Herman Hollerith built a mechanical "statistical tabulator" to collate that year's census results. His machine worked so well that he formed the Tabulating Machine Company, which eventually became International Business Machines (IBM). In 1938, IBM agreed to fund the construction, supervised by Howard H. Aiken at Harvard University, of the first programmable scientific calculator. Known initially as the Automatic Sequence-Controlled Calculator, and later as Mark I, it weighed 35 tons and consisted of 750,000 electromechanical parts. Instructions were fed into the machine using switches and punched tape. Mark I was able to cope with numbers up to 23 digits long, and handle in minutes calculations that had previously taken weeks. Soon, the military leased the machine to calculate ballistics problems.

Fifth-grade students in Arlington, Virginia use a computer in a science experiment. Computer technology has changed the face of education—even pre-school students are able to perform hi-tech tasks that help make learning fun.

The following year, an Iowa physics professor, John Atanasoff, and his assistant, Clifford Berry, constructed what has since been officially recognized as the first electronic digital computer. Built to carry out mathematical calculations, the Atanasoff-Berry Computer (ABC) incorporated many elements found in modern computers, such as regenerative memory.

The next milestone was the ENIAC (Electronic Numerical Integrator And Computer), a 30-ton (27 t) digital electronic computer built in 1945 by J. Presper Eckert and John W. Mauchly with the backing of the US government and the University of Pennsylvania. Instead of mechanical components, ENIAC used thousands of electronic vacuum tubes, which resulted in a major increase in processing speed—ENIAC

could complete calculations 1,000 times faster than any other contemporary machine.

Vacuum tubes were an improvement on the mechanical telephone relay switches used in the earliest computers, but still took up a lot of space and were prone to burn out. The introduction of the transistor in 1947—a much smaller and more reliable device—greatly increased efficiency and helped increase commercial sales. By the early 1960s, most large organizations had installed large "mainframes."

But the breakthrough that led to computers becoming ubiquitous was the creation, in 1958, of the integrated circuit, which was first patented by Jack Kilby at Texas Instruments. Kilby discovered that by using different chemicals it was possible to build thousands of electronic components onto one tiny slice of silicon. This in turn led to the development of microprocessors—programmable integrated circuits—which were first marketed by Intel in 1971. The increasing availability of microprocessors resulted in the computerization of a wide range of devices, from airplane and car instruments to automatic teller machines, microwave ovens, and video recorders. More significantly, it heralded the advent of the personal computer.

Personal computers

The first mass-marketed personal computer was the Apple II, which was built by Steve Wozniak and Steve Jobs and released by their company, Apple Computer, in 1977. By 1980, sales of Apple computers had reached $117 million. Inspired by this success, IBM introduced the IBM PC (Personal Computer) in 1981, which quickly became a popular business tool.

In the same year, Bill Gates and Paul Allen founded the software company Microsoft, whose early success was due mainly to the popularity of their program MS-DOS, which became the standard operating system for all IBM PCs. With the introduction of the Lisa in 1983 and the Macintosh in 1984, Apple revealed an alternative operating system. Known as a graphical user interface (GUI), it allowed the operator to accomplish computing tasks by moving pictures, or icons, around the screen by means of a mouse. This became so popular that Microsoft introduced its own Windows in 1990.

The refinement of microprocessors increased processing speeds rapidly: the Apple Macintosh 128K, released in 1984, had a clock speed of 8 Megahertz; the same company's G4, which appeared in 1999, offered a speed of 733 Megahertz. Sales expanded at a similar rate: by 1997, it was estimated that 40 percent of all American households owned a computer.

Computer networks

Over the past few years, increasing numbers of people have been using their computers to access the Internet. This network began as a computer network called ARPANET (Advance Research Projects Agency Network), which was set up in 1969 by the US Defense Department and designed to function even if other government systems were damaged. One of its first uses was the transmission of text messages known as electronic mail, or e-mail. The network was opened to non-military users in the late 1970s and then developed further by the National Science Foundation, becoming known as the Internet in 1983.

It was the development of the World Wide Web (WWW), however, that made the Internet accessible to the general public. This created a standard addressing system, known as "http" (Hyper Text Transfer Protocol), for all pages linked by the Internet, and allowed users to move directly from one page to another, anywhere in the world, using "hyperlinks"— electronic connections embedded within the pages. The system was devised in 1989 by an American scientist based in Switzerland, Tim Berners-Lee, but it wasn't until the appearance of the first web browsers— programs that facilitate navigation through the use of graphical interfaces—that net usage took off. The first widely used browser was Mosaic, which was developed at the University of Illinois by Marc Andreessen and released in 1993.

Greater interaction or convergence between the Internet, PCs, telephones, and even televisions is likely soon, and already the World Wide Web can be accessed on hand-held computers and mobile telephones. Increases in computer processing speed and storage capacity are also certain.

The Microsoft Corporation, founded by Bill Gates in 1981, and based in Washington State, is the worldwide leader in business and personal-computing software. Microsoft's user-friendly systems have helped to make computer technology accessible to the general public.

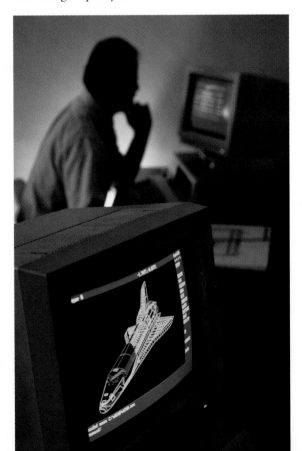

A graphics program is used to design a space shuttle on computer. Advances in computer-graphics technology have revolutionized fields such as art, architecture, advertising, animation, games, and special effects in film and television.

PART 2

PLACES IN AMERICA

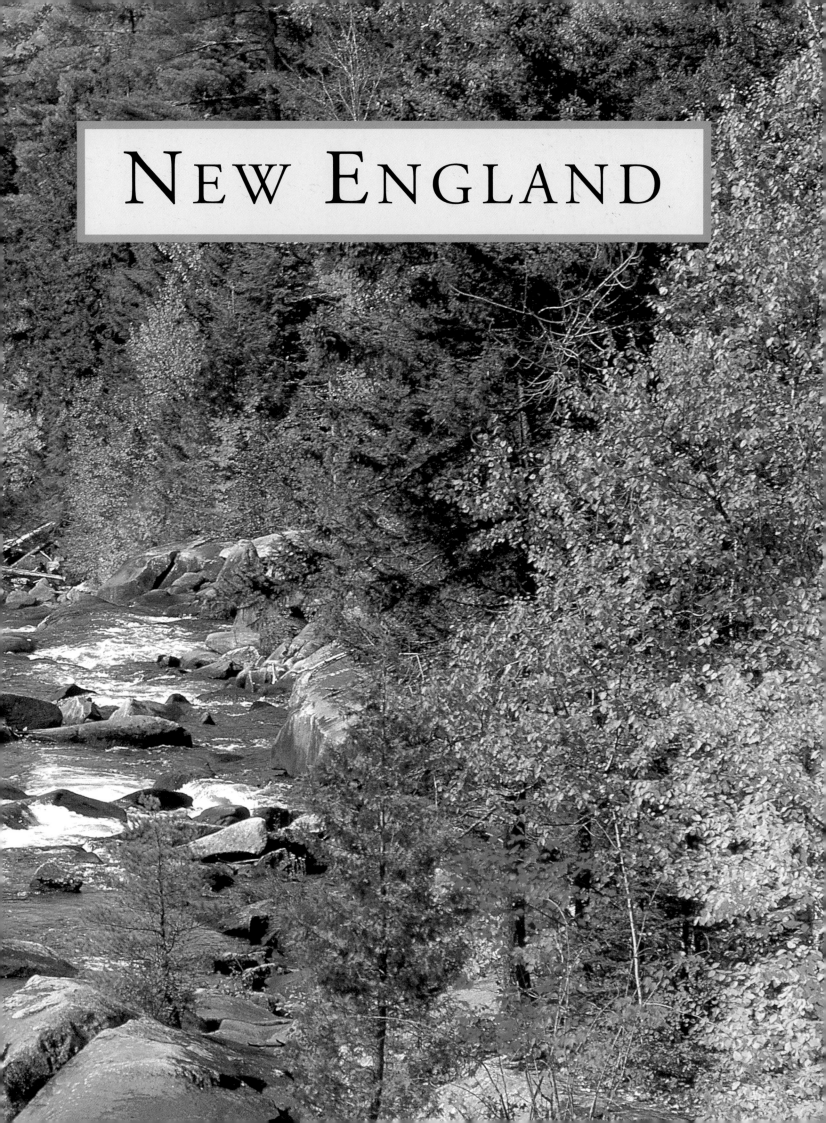

NEW ENGLAND

Fort Kent
Van Buren

Square
Lake

Presque Isle

St John River

Eagle
Lake

Chamberlain
Lake

Houlton

Chesuncook
Lake

Mt Katahdin
5,267 ft (1,605 m) ▲

Moosehead
Lake

MAINE

West Grand
Lake

Lincoln

Big
Lake

MOUNTAINS

Flagstaff
Lake

Dover-Foxcroft

Graham
Lake

Rangeley
Lake

Skowhegan

Bangor

Lower Richardson
Lake

Newport

Lake
Champlain

St Albans

Johnson

Mt Mansfield
4,393 ft (1,339 m) ▲

Errol

Rumford

Waterville

Ellsworth

Belfast

Bar Harbor

Burlington

South
Burlington

Winooski River

MONTPELIER ⚹

Barre

Berlin

St Johnsbury

Littleton

White Mts

Mt Washington
6,288 ft (1,917 m) ▲

AUGUSTA ⚹

Lewiston
Auburn

APPALACHIAN

Vergennes

Woodsville

NEW
HAMPSHIRE

Conway

Brunswick

Middlebury

Sebago
Lake

Westbrook

Portland

South Portland

Green Mountains

VERMONT

White River

Squam
Lake

Lake
Winnipesaukee

Lebanon

Biddeford

Rutland

Lake
Sunapee

Laconia

Winnisquam
Lake

Sanford

West River

Ludlow

Claremont

Rochester

Somersworth

Dover

Connecticut River

CONCORD ⚹

Bennington

Hillsborough

Manchester

Portsmouth

Harriman
Reservoir

Brattleboro

Keene

Derry

Newburyport

Mt Greylock
3,491 ft (1,064 m) ▲

North Adams

Nashua

Haverhill

Lawrence

Gloucester

Greenfield

Gardner

Fitchburg

Reading

Beverly
Salem

MASSACHUSETTS

Lowell

Burlington

Lynn

Pittsfield

Amherst

Quabbin
Reservoir

Hudson

Cambridge

Waltham

BOSTON ⚹

Massachusetts Bay

Northampton

Worcester

Needham

Holyoke

Norwood

Quincy

Mt Frissell
2,453 ft (748 m) ▲

Westfield

Springfield
Longmeadow

Webster

Woonsocket

Brocton

Provincetown

Windsor Locks

Jerimoth Hill
812 ft (248 m) ▲

Attleboro

Cape Cod
Bay

Cape Cod

CONNECTICUT

HARTFORD ⚹

Storrs

PROVIDENCE ⚹

Pawtucket

Taunton

Orleans

Torrington

New Britain

Willimantic

Cranston

Warwick

Somerset

Bristol

Waterbury

Meriden

Norwich

West
Warwick

Fall River

Tiverton

New Bedford

Hyannis

Monomoy I

Bristol

Danbury

Wallingford

RHODE
ISLAND

Newport

Nantucket
Sound

Lake
Candlewood

Shelton

New London

Westerly

Vineyard Haven

Rhode Island
Sound

New Haven

Martha's
Vineyard

Nantucket I

Bridgeport

West Haven

Long Island Sound

Norwalk

Fairfield

Stamford

Greenwich

NORTH

0   100   200   kilometers
0   60   120   miles

NEW ENGLAND

New England forms the northeast corner of the United States, and is made up of six states: Maine, New Hampshire, Vermont, Massachusetts, Connecticut, and Rhode Island. The pilgrims first arrived in New England at Plymouth, Massachusetts, in 1620. From then on, there were many fights over this territory with the French, the local Native Americans, and later with the British. Having to fight for their new land gave them a fierce pride that turned into patriotism after the Revolutionary War.

Education has always been valued highly here. Universities were often founded shortly after towns were established. Some of the early universities were Harvard in Cambridge, Massachusetts; Brown University in Providence, Rhode Island; Yale in New Haven, Connecticut; Dartmouth College in New Hampshire; and the University of Vermont. New England has been a center for education, research, and intellectual thought since the late 1700s. There are approximately 150 colleges and universities in Boston alone, including excellent schools in medicine and architecture. Consequently, the impact the area has on the USA is large, despite its small size of 66,608 square miles (172,515 sq km).

New Englanders have always taken themselves and their politics very seriously. The people are an unusual mix of puritan values, idealism, and progressive political ideas, often with a delightfully dry sense of humor. Local abolitionists fought slavery in the Civil War and supported votes for women. More recently, Vermont's Civil Union Law has validated gay and lesbian relationships. New England's largely democratic politicians have been very active nationally.

Geographically, the region has many mountains and sandy, rocky soils that are not suited to large-scale agriculture. The farmers became inventive, pragmatic, and philosophical. Long winters left time for intellectual thought; many artists, writers, and inventors have lived here. Waves of immigrants have come to build new lives and set up their own neighborhoods in the cities. Many religions live side by side, separate but tolerant of each other.

New England has a strong sense of place. The architecture is rich and varied because of the area's long history of European settlement and the mix of migrants, while the culture is both simple and sophisticated. There is much to see and do.

In Maine, drive along the seacoast in June, sampling lobsters, clams, and fresh fish, and watch the fishing boats. Go whitewater rafting on the Penobscot River, wander in the Acadia National Park, or tour the beautiful old sea captains' houses of Kennebunkport.

Skiers will be drawn to resorts in New Hampshire, Maine, and Vermont. Many places have extensive networks of trails for cross-country skiing.

Drive through New Hampshire over rivers that are spanned by red, covered bridges, or climb Mt Washington in the summer. Wander through an old graveyard and learn some local history. Take a canoe out on Lake Winnipesaukee and look for fish.

Vermont has dramatic changes of seasons, especially in the fall when the maple trees glow red and gold. Drive through Smuggler's Notch or the Appalachian Gap, crossing over the Green Mountains. Take a ferry across Lake Champlain at sunset.

In Massachusetts, there are many Revolutionary War sites to visit, such as the Boston Massacre, Old North Church, and the Boston Tea Party Ship. Nearby is Lexington and Concord, where the war started; Salem, where the witch trials were held; and coastal towns like Rockport, Gloucester, and Cape Cod.

In Old Lyme, Connecticut, visit some of the 60 nineteenth-century sea captains' houses. In Groton, see the world's first nuclear-powered submarine, the USS *Nautilus*, or climb aboard a whaling ship or square-rigger at the Mystic Seaport Museum.

Tour the Rhode Island mansions on Newport's Bellevue Avenue or Millionaires' Row. Sail along Narragansett Bay or surf on Narragansett Town Beach for some of the best surf on the east coast. Visit the state Capitol building in Providence, or rent a bicycle on Block Island and head for Mohegan Bluffs.

New England is sure to please anyone looking for culture, history, atmosphere, and natural beauty.

Stowe, in Vermont, has over 40 ski trails which are ideal for hikers and cross-country skiers.

Townshend Common in Vermont is reminiscent of an old village green in England.

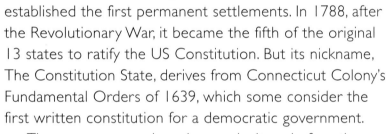

CONNECTICUT

New England's second-smallest and southernmost state (with a population of over 3 million) has a diverse natural beauty and rich history. Within its 5,544 square miles (14,359 sq km) are forested hills and coastal plains, colonial homes and urban skylines, corporate headquarters and ports that have seen both whaling ships and nuclear submarines. Its highest point is 2,380-foot (726-m) Mt Frissell. "Connecticut" comes from a Mohegan Native American word, *quinnehtukqut*, which means "place beside a long river" or "beside the long tidal river." The name is shared with the river that bisects the state.

A rowing crew from the Stonington School in Mystic, southeastern Connecticut, training on Mystic River.

The Dutch explored the area first. In 1633, English Puritans from Massachusetts established the first permanent settlements. In 1788, after the Revolutionary War, it became the fifth of the original 13 states to ratify the US Constitution. But its nickname, The Constitution State, derives from Connecticut Colony's Fundamental Orders of 1639, which some consider the first written constitution for a democratic government.

The economy was based on agriculture before the Revolutionary War; then the state became a manufacturing region. Insurance, banking, and production of jet aircraft engines, helicopters, firearms and nuclear submarines are mainstays today. In 1954 the first nuclear-powered submarine, the *Nautilus*, was launched at Groton, where it is now on display.

The 250-mile (402-km) Long Island Sound shoreline is popular with locals and tourists. Hammonasset Beach State Park, for example, at Madison, offers swimming, camping, birdwatching, hiking, and fishing. Visitors can sample nineteenth-century maritime life at Mystic Seaport, or visit Norwich's Mohegan Indian Burial Ground.

Connecticut can be reached by flying into New York City or Hartford. Rail lines connect many communities with New York City. Among its highways are two scenic byways, Hwy 169, in the state's northeastern corner, and the 38-mile (61-km) Merritt Parkway (Hwy 15), which goes through the panhandle. Bus service is available to most points in the state.

State motto *Qui Transtulit Sustinet* (He who transplanted still sustains)
State flag Adopted 1931
Capital Hartford
Population 3,405,565
Total area (land and water) 5,544 square miles (14,359 sq km)
Land area 4,845 square miles (12,549 sq km)
Connecticut is the 48th-largest state in size
Origin of name From the Mohegan and Algonquian word *quinnehtukqut*, meaning "beside the long tidal river" or a "place beside a long river"
Nicknames The Constitution State, The Nutmeg State
Abbreviations CT (postal), Conn.
State bird American robin
State flower Mountain laurel
State tree White oak
Entered the Union January 9, 1788 as the fifth state

Places in
CONNECTICUT

BRIDGEPORT

With 141,700 residents, this Fairfield County city is Connecticut's largest. Located in the southwest of the state, it was settled in 1639 at the site of a Pequonnock Indian village, where the river by the same name flows into Long Island Sound. It was first called Newtown, then Stratfield. In 1821, the whaling port and growing commercial center incorporated as a town and the name was changed to Bridgeport, after a drawbridge that once stood near the port. It officially became a city in 1836.

Showman and entrepreneur P.T. Barnum, who was born in nearby Bethel in 1810 and is buried in Bridgeport, helped turn the city into a manufacturing center. Charles Thurwood Stratton, who was only 25 inches (62.5 cm) tall when Barnum discovered him in 1842 and made him famous as "General Tom Thumb," was born here in 1838.

The arrival of railroads in the 1840s helped turn the city into an industrial center. During the American Civil War (1861–65), Bridgeport was an important source of military supplies for the Union army. Defense industries remained important until the late 1980s and early 1990s. The city is

Bridgeport's railway line was crucial to its previous manufacturing base.

home to the University of Bridgeport and a community college, and the Bridgeport Engineering Institute and Sacred Heart University are in neighboring Fairfield.

The city has a deep-water port, and is situated on major transportation routes between New York City, New Haven, and Hartford. Although it remains an important banking center, in 1991 financial difficulties, caused in part by Bridgeport's industrial decline, made it the first American city to file for bankruptcy.

Places of interest include the Barnum Museum; the Discovery Museum, with its interactive art and science exhibits; the Housatonic Museum of Art; and a zoo. From New York, it can be reached via I-95 and the Merritt Parkway. Ferries connect it to Port Jefferson on Long Island. Igor I. Sikorsky Memorial Airport provides air service. Railway connections include a direct route to New York City's Grand Central Terminal.
Map ref: page 222 B9

DANBURY

Like many New England locales, this city of about 65,600 shares its name with a city in England. Settled by eight families in 1684, it is located in an agricultural area of southwestern Connecticut. It was a military supply center during the Revolutionary War, and in 1777 British troops burned much of the town. It was incorporated as a city in 1889 and expanded west to the New York state line and north to manmade Candlewood Lake. From 1780 to 1956 it was a major hat manufacturing center, but it is now a diversified business and manufacturing hub. Today its economy includes manufacturers of machinery, textiles, chemicals, electronics, and plastics, as well as publishers and developers of energy and aerospace products. Union Carbide Corporation and First Brands Corporation are two prominent Danbury companies.

The city is the site of Western Connecticut State University. The 39-acre (16-ha) Charles Ives Center For The Arts, named for the

Eubrontes (fossilized dinosaur footprints) at the Dinosaur State Park.

Pulitzer Prize-winning composer born here in 1874, offers live performances in summer. The Danbury Museum and Historical Society operates the restored John and Mary Rider House (1785), a one-room schoolhouse, and the Dodd Hat Shop (1790).

Danbury can be reached by car via I-84 in Connecticut, and via I-684 from New York City. There are rail connections to New York City's Grand Central Terminal.
Map ref: page 222 B8

DINOSAUR STATE PARK

Some 200 million years ago dinosaurs roamed the region around Rocky Hill, in the Connecticut River Valley south of Hartford. Some left footprints in the mud and sediment. Over time the footprints became fossils, called eubrontes, Connecticut's official state fossil.

Two thousand eubrontes were accidentally uncovered here in 1966 during excavation for a new state building. Two years later the dinosaur trackway was made a state park. Five hundred of the fossil prints are now enclosed and visible beneath the Exhibit Center's large geodesic dome; the rest remain buried for preservation. The tracks range from 10 to 16 inches (4 to 6.4 cm) in length, and are $3\frac{1}{2}$ to $4\frac{1}{2}$ feet (1.1 to 1.4 m) apart.

The park is one of the largest dinosaur track sites in North America. Surrounding the Exhibit Center are more than 2 miles (3 km) of nature trails, plus a picnic area and an arboretum, with more than 250 species and cultivars of conifers as well as katsuras,

ginkgoes, magnolias, and other living representatives of some of the plant families that appeared during dinosaur times.

From May 1 to October 31, visitors can make plaster castings of tracks, if they bring a quarter-cup (63 ml) of cooking oil, cloth rags and paper towels, a 5-gallon (19-l) bucket, and 10 pounds (4.5 kg) of plaster of Paris.

Park grounds are open daily except on Thanksgiving, Christmas, and New Year's Day, but the Exhibit Center is only open Tuesday through Sunday.

GREENWICH

This New York City suburb has stately country homes, highly rated public schools, nine yacht clubs, a 522-acre (211-ha) Audubon nature preserve, an 18-hole golf course, 1,500 acres (608 ha) of parkland, and 32 miles (52 km) of beautiful Long Island Sound shoreline, complete with beaches, sailing facilities, and two islands.

With about 58,400 residents, Greenwich's 50 square miles (130 sq km) contain only small villages and neighborhoods. It is Connecticut's 10th oldest community. In 1614 Dutch explorer Adrian Block established a trading post here. Permanent settlement came in 1640.

British troops sacked the town several times during the Revolutionary War. Its evolution into a prestigious residential area began in 1848, when the arrival of the railroad prompted many wealthy New Yorkers to build their summer homes here. By 1928 the town, along the Merritt Parkway, topped the nation in per capita wealth.

HARTFORD

Connecticut's capital city is located at the northern end of the navigable portion of the Connecticut River, in the north-central part of the state. Since 1794, scores of insurance companies have made Hartford their base. Along with finance, insurance companies provide a multibillion-dollar service industry to augment the city's manufacture of firearms, machinery and aerospace products.

Hartford has grown to more than 133,100 people since 1614, when Dutch explorer Adrian Block sailed up the river into a region long occupied by Sicaog Native Americans. The Dutch established a trading post and fort, House of Hope, here in 1623. In 1635, English settlers from Massachusetts, led by the Reverend Thomas Hooker and Samuel Stone, established the first settlement. The settlement was named after Stone's birthplace—Hertfordshire in England.

In 1639 the settlement became part of Connecticut Colony, which was governed under the Fundamental Orders, considered by some the first written constitution for a democratic government.

Connecticut Colony encouraged the 13 British colonies on the road to rebellion almost a century before the Revolutionary War. In 1687, New England's new British governor, Sir Edmund Andos, ordered the colony to surrender the charter King Charles II had granted it 25 years earlier. The colonists refused, and hid the document in a large oak tree. Wind felled the

Boats from the state's last active fishing fleet moored at Stonington, near Mystic.

Charter Oak in 1856, but the site is marked by a plaque.

From 1701 to 1875, Hartford shared the seat of Connecticut government with New Haven. The dangers of shipping led groups of merchants to share the risks, and in 1810 the practice was formalized as the Hartford Fire Insurance Group. Now, the city is "the insurance capital of the world," a fact reflected in a skyline that includes The Travelers Tower, at 527 feet (161 m) one of the region's tallest, and Phoenix Home Life Mutual Insurance Company's glass-and-steel "boat building."

Inventive manufacturers helped turn Hartford into an industrial center. Gunmaker Samuel Colt, for example, pioneered the use of interchangeable parts, laying the foundation for mass production. The city is home to the nation's oldest continuously published newspaper, *The Hartford Courant* (begun in 1764), and the oldest public art museum, the Wadsworth Atheneum (1844). Authors Samuel Clemens (Mark Twain) and Harriett Beecher Stowe lived in the Nook Farm area.

The city boasts a symphony orchestra, ballet company, opera, and theater. Trinity College

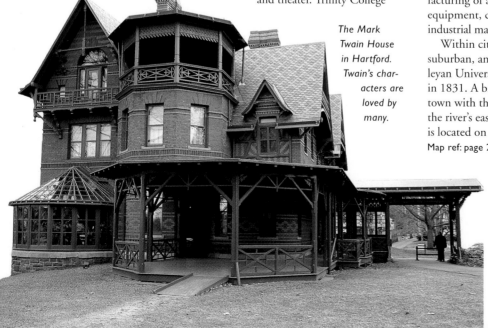

The Mark Twain House in Hartford. Twain's characters are loved by many.

was founded in 1823. The city is also home to Hartford Seminary, Hartford College for Women, Hartford Graduate Center, and the University of Connecticut School of Law. The University of Hartford (1877) is in West Hartford.

Visitors will find roving ambassadors—the Hartford Guides—stationed downtown, in red hats and khaki-and-white uniforms. They provide a range of services, from historical insights to help in emergencies.

Bradley International Airport, north of the city, provides air service. By car, access is via I-91 and I-84, and a number of US and state highways. A train service is also available.
Map ref: page 222 C7

MIDDLETOWN

This city of about 42,800, founded in 1650, occupies the west bank of the Connecticut River south of Hartford—it became a shipbuilding center and trading port. Middletown was once the state's largest and wealthiest city. Handgun manufacturer Simeon North built a factory here in 1799. Today, the city's economy hinges on the manufacturing of aircraft parts and equipment, computer equipment, industrial machinery and insurance.

Within city limits are rural, suburban, and urban areas. Wesleyan University was founded here in 1831. A bridge links Middletown with the city of Portland, on the river's east bank. Middletown is located on Hwy 9.
Map ref: page 222 C8

MYSTIC

This historic southeastern Connecticut seaport—part of the borough of nearby Stonington—was

settled in 1654 on the Mystic River, just north of Fishers Island Sound, an arm of Long Island Sound. It was a small but important fishing and whaling port before 1840; then it grew into a major shipbuilding center. At least 600 vessels were built and launched here between 1784 and 1919, including the Union Navy's ironclad *Galena*, built during the Civil War.

Today Mystic (population 2,600) has a major tourist attraction—Mystic Seaport, a private, not-for-profit educational institution dedicated to preserving and conveying New England maritime history. For an admission fee, visitors can stroll through a re-created nineteenth-century waterfront village that includes homes, shops, exhibits, the last surviving American wooden sailing ship—the *Charles W. Morgan*—and other historic ships and boats. There is a children's museum full of the toys, games, and clothing known to their nineteenth-century counterparts.

The nearby Mystic Marinelife Aquarium has more than 3,500 living sea creatures in 40 exhibits. Among them are Seal Island, an outdoor exhibit with seals and sea lions, and the Penguin Pavilion, an outdoor exhibit of African black-footed penguins. There are daily dolphin and whale demonstrations in the Marine Theater.

May through October, visitors can board the 1908 steamboat *Sabino* for daytime and evening excursions on the Mystic River. Also nearby are the Foxwoods Resort Casino and the Mohegan Sun Casino. Captain Nate Palmer, who discovered Antarctica in 1821, sailed from the town of Stonington—visitors can tour his 1852 mansion. Also in Stonington is the Old Lighthouse Museum, located inside an 1823 stone lighthouse.

Mystic and Mystic Seaport are located 10 miles (16 km) east of New London, just south of I-95. Trains serve Mystic daily from both New York City and Boston. There is also a ferry service to and from nearby points.
Map ref: page 222 D8

NEW BRITAIN

This central Connecticut city grew from a religious–agricultural community that was established by English Protestants amid a

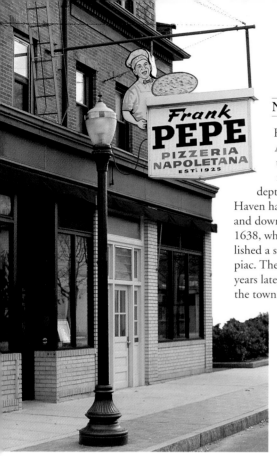

Little Italy, New Haven, has many excellent restaurants.

NEW HAVEN

From the pinnacle of American higher education and Yankee manufacturing prowess to the depths of urban decline, New Haven has seen its share of ups and downs. It traces its roots to 1638, when English Puritans established a settlement called Quinnipiac. The name was changed two years later, perhaps to highlight the town as a "new harbor," or to recall Newhaven, England. In 1665 the independent colony was combined with Connecticut Colony. In 1779, British military forces partially burned the town.

The city's harbor, on Long Island Sound, supported modest trade, but the harbor wasn't very deep, and its location (north of Long Island) was outside the main lanes of maritime commerce. In addition, New England farms could not generate the quantities of produce needed to support large shipments to Europe, so most of the city's foreign commerce was with the West Indies. By the mid-1800s, the railroads had begun to draw business away from maritime shipping; New Haven shipbuilding had peaked by the 1880s. The US Coast Guard, however, still has its Long Island Sound headquarters here.

In the following century, immigrants helped turn New Haven into a manufacturing center that either attracted or itself spawned such inventive minds as cotton gin inventor Eli Whitney, who attended Yale University, and native son Charles Goodyear, who developed vulcanized rubber.

The Old Lighthouse Museum at Stonington, near Mystic.

New Haven, with about 130,500 people, has struggled in recent decades with economic decline. It was among the first American cities to undertake urban renewal projects in the 1950s, and the first of the 1960s' anti-poverty programs was launched here in 1962.

Yale University, founded in 1701, continues to attract top quality students and faculty. The city's largest employer, the university has been central in the city's transition from a manufacturing center to a home for knowledge-based businesses such as biotechnology, health care, arts, and entertainment.

New Haven is also home to Southern Connecticut State University, Albertus Magnus College and a community college. The University of New Haven is in West Haven. Quinnipiac College is in nearby Hamden.

Visitors can tour Yale's Peabody Museum of Natural History and Yale University Art Gallery, the oldest university art museum in the western hemisphere. Three churches from about 1815 still preside over the city center's 16-acre (6.5-ha) green, which dates back to the 1600s.

New Haven can be reached on I-91 and many other highways. Tweed–New Haven Airport provides air connections to major airports in the region. The Metro-North Railroad connects New Haven with New York City's Grand Central Terminal.
Map ref: page 222 C8

swampland in 1686. Its name, chosen in 1754, reflects the origins and ancestry of many of its residents. Farming gave way to small industries here in the late 1700s, and many immigrants arrived from the mid-nineteenth century to about 1920. With so much hardware manufacturing, including tools, machine parts and bearings, it earned the nickname "Hardware City." But many industries closed or moved out in the second half of the twentieth century. The loss of high-paying industrial jobs in the 1960s and 1970s played a large part in New Britain's economic decline.

Today it is home to about 72,400 people. The New Britain Normal School, founded in 1849, is now Central Connecticut State College. The city is also home to the New Britain Museum of American Art, which has more than 5,000 paintings, graphics and sculptures from 1740 to the present, and the New Britain Youth Museum. Stanley Quarter Park includes a 27-hole golf course. Baseball fans head to Beehive Field from April through September to cheer the New Britain Rock Cats, the Class AA affiliate of the Minnesota Twins. New Britain is east of I-84, southeast of Hartford, which has rail lines and an international airport.
Map ref: page 222 C7

Gothic-style buildings of Yale University, New Haven. The university includes art galleries and a natural history museum.

NEW LONDON

From whaling boats to nuclear submarines, this southeastern Connecticut city of 28,500 residents, at the confluence of the Thames River and Block Island Sound, has had a long relationship with seafaring. English Puritans led by John Winthrop founded the settlement in 1646. In the nineteenth century it was one of many coastal Connecticut towns dependent on whaling and shipbuilding. During the Revolutionary War it was a base for privateers. British forces led by the American traitor Benedict Arnold attacked and burned the town in 1781.

Now an industrial city and summer resort, New London is heavily dependent on defense spending. Naval submarines are built across the Thames at Groton, home of the Naval Submarine Base New London. The US Coast Guard Academy is in New London, as is the Naval Underwater Systems Center, a Navy research center. The city is home to Connecticut College and a community college.

Places to visit include New London's historic downtown; the boyhood home of playwright Eugene O'Neill; Nathan Hale's Schoolhouse; the Lyman Allyn Art Museum; the Garde Arts Center; Ye Olde Town Mill, a gristmill built in 1650; and the restored Hempsted Houses, built in 1678 and 1758. The Harvard–Yale Regatta, a rowing (crew) competition, is held on the river each June.

New London can be reached by car on

The US Coast Guard Academy in New London. Around 275 cadets—over 5,000 apply—begin their four-year training each year.

I-95. Groton–New London Airport provides air service, and ferries travel to Block Island, Rhode Island, and Fishers Island and Long Island, New York. A rail service is also available.
Map ref: page 222 D8

NORWALK

A harbor on Long Island Sound and easy access to New York City, just 40 miles (64 km) to the southwest, have helped this city of 78,300 develop from an agricultural hamlet, founded in 1651, to a diversified industrial research center that is home to more than 200 manufacturers.

It was also within easy striking distance for British troops, who burned the town in 1779 during the Revolutionary War.

Once known for stoneware pottery, it became a bustling port in the nineteenth century. Today it produces scientific instruments, electronic systems, electrical devices, clothing, and marine equipment. Its attractions include many historic homes; the Maritime Aquarium, which features interactive exhibits about Long Island Sound's maritime history and marine life; and Depression-era WPA murals at City Hall.

A daily summertime ferry shuttles visitors between Hope Dock, next to the Maritime Aquarium, and Sheffield Island, the outermost of the Norwalk Islands in Long Island Sound.

I-95 and the scenic Merritt Parkway (Hwy 15) connect Norwalk to New York. The

The Lockwood-Matthews Mansion, in Norwalk.

Metro-North Railroad provides a train service. International and regional airports are less than an hour away.
Map ref: page 222 B9

NORWICH

In 1659, Major John Mason and the Reverend James Fitch led 69 families from Old Saybrook to land they purchased from the Mohegan people, where the Yantic and Shetucket rivers join to form the Thames River. Their community grew into an eighteenth-century shipping and shipbuilding center for southeastern Connecticut.

Norwich was forced to become more self-sufficient after the British government imposed the Stamp Act of 1764. Soon large mills were built along the Yantic, Shetucket, and

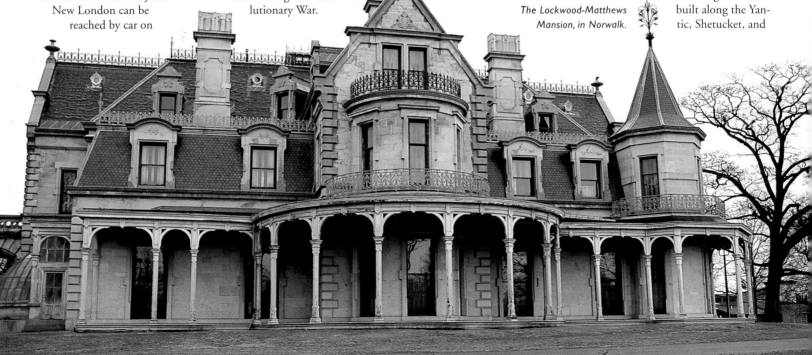

The Stamford Police badge.

Thames rivers. During the Revolutionary War, Norwich supplied ships and munitions as well as soldiers to the cause of independence. However, Norwich also contributed the brilliant military leader Benedict Arnold, who was born here in 1741—he later became America's most infamous traitor.

Steamship service between New York and Boston helped Norwich prosper early in the twentieth century. Today the city has a population of 37,400 people, and manufactures textiles, furniture, metal and paper goods, medical supplies, copper tubing, and electronic equipment.

Attractions include the Mohegan Indian Burial Grounds, the historic Norwichtown Green, and the Slater Memorial Museum and Converse Art Gallery.

The city can be reached by car on I-395.

Map ref: page 222 D8

PUTNAM MEMORIAL STATE PARK

This 183-acre (74-ha) park preserves the site of the Continental Army's 1779 winter encampment, under the command of General Israel Putnam. The Park consists of the remains of the encampment, plus reconstructed log structures, an interpretive trail, a museum, and enough space for hiking, fishing, and picnicking.

Admission is free, and the park is open every day. Putnam Memorial State Park is located in southwestern Connecticut's Fairfield County, on Hwy 58, 3 miles (5 km) south of Bethel.

STAMFORD

Just 40 minutes by train from New York City's Grand Central Terminal, this panhandle city has changed greatly from its origins as a Puritan village—it is now a bustling center of finance, and one of the nation's largest communities of corporate headquarters.

In 1640 Nathaniel Turner, agent for New Haven Colony, purchased 128 square miles (332 sq km) along the Rippowam River from the Siwanoy Native Americans. The price for the land is said to have been a dozen coats, hoes, hatchets, glasses, and knives, four kettles and four fathoms of white wampum.

The next year, 28 families left Wethersfield, south of Hartford, to establish a village, which was to be named for the river. The name of the village was later changed to Stamford (an old English word for "stony ford"), for the English town where many New England settlers had originated.

For 200 years Stamford's residents mostly farmed, fished, and gathered oysters. New York was their primary market. Stamford's transition to an industrial city began in the 1840s, when the New York, New Haven, and Hartford Railroad began regular services, and hundreds of immigrants arrived, fleeing the devastating potato famine in Ireland. In the 1860s the economy was bolstered by the success of the Yale & Towne Manufacturing Company's patented cylinder lock.

St John the Evangelist parish, Stamford. The town's buildings reflect its history.

Today the city is home to 108,100 people, and encompasses almost 40 square miles (104 sq km), from the New York state line to Long Island Sound in the south. Attractions include the 118-acre (48-ha) Stamford Museum and Nature Center, and the Whitney Museum of American Art at Champion, a branch of the museum in New York City. The city center, Stamford Downtown, offers a wide range of entertainment, restaurants and retail stores.

The city is divided by I-95 and the Merritt Parkway (Hwy 15). Metro-North Railroad provides an express train service from the Stamford Transportation Center to New York's Grand Central Station.

Map ref: page 222 A9

WETHERSFIELD

Founded in 1634, Wethersfield grew into a commercial center on the Connecticut River. Today it is a residential suburb of 25,700, just south of Hartford. Its past— it is one of the state's oldest communities—is reflected in its outstanding historic district, where visitors can see many pre-1800 structures, some still bearing their date of construction and the names of their original owners. Of particular interest is the Webb-Deane-Stevens Museum, which is made up of three eighteenth-century houses restored and furnished to depict colonial homes.

In 1781 General George Washington met with French General Comte de Rochambeau in the Joseph Webb House (1752) to plan the battle of Yorktown, where the American and French victory secured independence. Also of interest are the Cove Warehouse—one of several built in the 1600s, but the only one to survive the 1692 flood—and the Wethersfield Museum at Keeney Cultural Center (1893), which houses the Wethersfield Historical Society's collection.

Wethersfield can be reached via Hwy 99 south from Hartford.

Map ref: page 222 C7

The city of Stamford is ranked as the United States' eighth-largest business center.

MAINE

Maine has a population of over 1.2 million. It is known for its windswept rocky beaches, tidy seacoast villages of white wooden houses, picturesque lighthouses, and succulent lobster dinners. Its craggy mountains are covered with forests, ski resorts, and trails for hikers, hunters, and mountain bikers—its nickname, "Vacationland," is well deserved.

Eighty-nine percent of the state is covered in forest (over 17 million acres/7 million ha), made up of fir, spruce, and mixed hardwoods. The forests are home to many birds and animals, including moose, the state animal. These mountains and valleys are dotted with over 2,500 lakes. Moosehead Lake in the center of the state and Sebago Lake in the southwest are the biggest.

Maine has an extensive network of lakes and rivers, and fishing was vital to the early settlers; it remains important today. Fur trapping, lumbering, and ship building were successful industries for the new settlers. Textile mills and shoe-making factories built in the 1800s still

Maine's beautiful fall colors and winter snow make its mountain and lake country a beacon for tourists.

operate, but manufacturing has declined since the 1950s, and tourism has grown. Maine also produces potatoes, apples, oats, milk, eggs, beans, peas, broccoli, and hay—and 99 percent of the country's blueberries.

Abenaki Native Americans (Algonquian-speaking peoples) lived throughout the state when Europeans first arrived, but were decimated by smallpox soon after. The Penobscot and Passamaquoddy tribes lived in the central area of the state.

In the seventeenth century Maine was annexed to Massachusetts, but in 1819 Maine voted to separate. From the start, Maine's territory and resources were fought over by the British, French, Canadians, and the Americans. This kept settlers and investment away until Maine gained statehood. But the lack of industry had a good side—there were large areas of unpolluted wilderness, an ideal basis for tourism.

State motto Dirigo (I direct)
State flag Adopted 1909
Capital Augusta
Population 1,274,923
Total area (land and water)
33,741 square miles (87,389 sq km)
Total land area 30,865 square miles
(79,940 sq km)
Maine is the 39th-largest state in size
Origin of name Originally used to distinguish the mainland from the islands. It may also be a compliment to Henrietta Maria, consort of Charles I of England, said to have owned the province of Mayne in France
Nickname The Pine Tree State
Abbreviations ME (postal), Me.
State bird Chickadee
State flower White pine cone and tassel
State tree White pine
Entered the Union March 15, 1820 as the 23rd state

Places in
MAINE

AUGUSTA

Augusta (population 19,544) is inland from the coast on the Kennebec River, 55 miles (88 km) northeast of Portland on the I-95/495. It was originally settled in 1628 but was abandoned and then resettled in 1724. There was continuing violence during the French and Indian Wars and the War of 1812. Though Portland was the early capital, Augusta has been the capital since 1827—Augusta, being inland, was less vulnerable to attacks by sea from the French, British, or Native Americans.

In 1844, Augusta was already a center for lumber and had the raw materials for making paper. Paper mills quickly sprang up, using the local rivers as a water source, and the town grew as the paper industry blossomed.

Another industry also sprang up in Augusta in the mid-1800s. Each year the fresh, clean waters of the Kennebec River froze, and this provided the raw material for a huge industry—

Maine's State Capitol building, in Augusta.

ice. Refrigeration had not yet been invented, and ice was needed to preserve food. The river ice was cut into blocks, and hundreds of tons were shipped to cities and towns all over the United States, and even to the Caribbean. The ice men would take blocks of ice and sell them, door-to-door, from a horse-drawn cart. The invention of refrigeration completely destroyed this industry, and many people had to then leave Augusta to find other work.

Whitewater rafting and kayaking are popular on the Kennebec and the Dead River, and on the west branch of the Penobscot, timed with dam releases. It is a great way to see the wilderness.

The Maine State Museum in Augusta has wonderfully varied exhibits on quarrying, agriculture, shipbuilding, tools, Maine's gems, furniture making, glass making, and Maine's natural heritage. A feature is the "12,000 Years in Maine" exhibit on the Ice Age, which illustrates how the people lived and hunted then, and what they ate. One of the oldest remaining steam locomotives is here. There are many hands-on exhibits and children are very welcome.

Augusta has its own airport, and Portland International Jetport is not far away. Buses also service the area.
Map ref: page 221 H9

BANGOR

Bangor is on the Penobscot River, 129 miles (208 km) northeast of Portland on the I-95. The city is in what is called "Down East Maine," in the north woods. The term "Down East" is rather confusing when you look on a map, because it refers to the part of Maine that is actually further north and up the coast. The term comes from sailors; they were referring to ocean currents.

Bangor is the main center for businesses and shops in eastern

Ben and Bill's Chocolate Emporium in Bar Harbor—a great reason to visit!

and central Maine, and it is a good base for trips in the area. It has a population of 35,000, yet it feels like a small town.

The Cole Land Transportation Museum has over 200 vehicles to look at—there are full-size train engines, old cars, and shiny trucks. The museum displays cover the history of transportation in the early years of Maine's development. Bangor also has two golf courses, a symphony orchestra, and a ballet company. It is home to the Maine Shakespeare Festival.

Bangor has its own international airport, and buses service the area.
Map ref: page 221 K8

BAR HARBOR

Bar Harbor is on Mt Desert Island off the Atlantic coast (see feature on Acadia National Park, pages 190–191) and has a population of 4,589. In 1947, a huge fire burned down many of the elegant mansions across the island. Luckily, some of the impressive houses remained; many of them have been transformed into up-market guesthouses, inns, and restaurants since the fire.

Quite a number of hotels, motels, and shops have also sprung up in Bar Harbor in the last fifty years. Luckily, this doesn't detract from the beauty of the site, which is located on Frenchman's Bay.

The racing fleet is based in Northeast Harbor. Arcady Music Festival presents concerts on different sites on and near the island throughout the year. The Bar Harbor Festival runs from mid-July to mid-August.

Dr Robert Abbe founded Abbe Museum in 1928 to preserve and celebrate Maine's Native American Heritage. Visitors learn about several groups—the Micmac, Maliseet, Passamaquoddy, and Penobscot Indians. There are hands-on programs, workshops, and rotating exhibits covering 10,000 years of history. It is an award-winning museum, open May to October.

There is an airport in Bar Harbor, and Bangor International Airport is situated just 40 miles (64 km) to the northwest. Buses also service the area, and there is a car ferry that travels to Yarmouth, Nova Scotia.
Map ref: page 221 L9

BATH

Bath (population 9,950) is 38 miles (61 km) northeast of Portland on the I-95 and US-1. It began life as a shipbuilding center in 1607. The state's first sawmill was started in 1623, and many more came later. Lumber became Maine's most saleable resource. Shipbuilding grew after American independence and became a major industry in both Bath and Wiscasset (10 miles/16 km northeast).

Maine Maritime Museum and Shipyard documents the area's shipbuilding past. Visitors learn about the challenges these early adventurers faced. The wooden ships built then are a far cry from the guided missile frigates and merchant container ships built at the Bath Iron Works today.

Portland International Jetport is the nearest major airport.

Map ref: page 221 H10

BAXTER STATE PARK

Baxter State Park, in the center of the northern part of the state, north of Millinocket and about 100 miles (161 km) north of Bangor is the largest of Maine's 33 state parks. It has 202,064 acres (81,836 ha) of wilderness.

It is the fourth largest state-owned preserve in the United States and the largest public parkland in New England. It has moose, raccoon, deer, beaver, and caribou. Many birds live here, and more pass through on their annual migration. There are rare orchids,

Make sure you get to Baxter State Park early in the day—numbers are restricted.

ferns, alpine plants, and wildflowers, plus various kinds of fossils and interesting geology. Photographers, hikers, birdwatchers, mountain climbers, and nature lovers all find something here.

There are 46 mountain peaks, 18 of which are over 3,000 feet (915 m). Baxter Peak, at 5,267 feet (1,606 m), is the highest. There are 75 miles (121 km) of trails, some with delightful names, such as Pogy Notch Trail, Wassataquoik Lake Trail, Freezeout Trail, and

Knife Edge Trail. The most famous is the Appalachian Trail, which ends within the park.

Weather is changeable here, so visitors should always bring drinking water, extra warm clothing, a raincoat, and waterproof boots. There are campgrounds, bunkhouses, fireplaces, restrooms, and places to rent canoes.

Percival P. Baxter was a mayor of Portland, and later a two-term governor of the state. He admired the beauty of the area but was troubled by its being decimated by logging companies. He could not get the state to buy the land so he gradually bought land from logging companies himself, year by year. He donated the land to the state in two parcels, one in 1931 and one in 1962—and finally achieved his goal of having the land preserved as parkland.

The Baxter State Park Scenic drive is a good way to see the park. It is a 94-mile (151-km) rough dirt road (Tote Park Road) around Mount Kathadin, on the west and north end of the park. The road is very rough and there is a 20-mile (32-km) per hour speed limit, so the tour takes over two hours—but the rewards are tremendous. There are spectacular waterfalls, babbling brooks, delightful panoramic views,

whispering trees, and huge boulders left by the glaciers that formed these mountains.

Access to the park is from I-95 between May and October. No motorcycles, motorboats, or pets are allowed. Bangor International is the nearest major airport.

BRUNSWICK

Brunswick (population 20,778) is 20 miles (32 km) northeast of Portland on the I-95. It is the home of Bowdoin College, which was established in 1794. Bowdoin was built in an era when colleges and universities had beautifully landscaped campuses, impressive well-proportioned buildings, and grassy squares laced with wide paths. Henry Wadsworth Longfellow, the popular poet and linguist, was a senior here and became a professor of modern languages at the age of twenty-two.

The 110-acre (45-ha) campus is worth a wander, particularly the Bowdoin College Museum of Art. Here you can see paintings from Wyeth and Homer (both lived in Maine), Cassatt, and Raushenberg, as well as French, Italian, and Flemish masters, and portraits of Jefferson and Madison by Gilbert Stuart. The Peary–Macmillian Arctic Museum documents the first expedition to the North Pole, in 1909, by Admiral Robert Peary and Donald B. MacMillian. There are photographs, instruments, and other memorabilia.

Brunswick was also the home of Harriet Beecher Stowe (1811–96), the author of *Uncle Tom's Cabin*. Her novel, published in 1852, helped to change public opinion about slavery.

Portland International Jetport is the nearest major airport and buses service the area.

Map ref: page 223 H2

CAMDEN

Camden (population about 5,060) is a busy resort town 100 miles (161 km) northeast of Portland on the Atlantic coast. There is good shopping here and the restaurants are known for their tasty chowder and seafood pies. Many yachts, schooners, and a fleet of windjammers (originals and replicas) are based here on Penobscot Bay. Visitors are likely to see at least one

Maine has around 29,000 moose. They are the largest member of the deer family.

Surfing at Kennebunk Beach. It can be a year-round sport—for the determined.

of these elegant boats on the harbor at any time during summer.

Many cruises on these stately boats, to offshore islands, run from here. Five miles (8 km) north of Camden, in Lincolnville, reasonably priced ferries run to Isleboro Island across the Bay. The trip makes a good day out in fine weather, providing an impressive view of Camden from the water.

Just north of town is the Camden Hills State Park. It has 25 miles (40 km) of trails for hiking and mountain biking. You can hike or drive up Mount Battie and look down over the harbor.

Camden is almost midway between Bangor and Portland international airports.
Map ref: page 221 J9

Map ref: page 221 J9

KENNEBUNK

Kennebunk (population 9,101), Kennebunkport (population 3,495), and Kennebunk Beach are three adjacent towns in southern Maine, 27 miles (44 km) southwest of Portland. In the 1800s the area became busy with trade—the inland rivers and streams were perfect sites for sawmills and gristmills. Lumber was needed for shipbuilding on the Kennebunk River, and for houses, and repairs. As more people came there to work, farms grew to feed them. The town center of Kennebunk moved to the north side of the river. Up to 100 ships were built in a year in the early 1800s. The towns became the second richest in the state, with shipbuilders, owners, and captains building elegant houses in town.

However, after 1861, more and more steel ships were being built and the lumber and boatbuilding industries shrank dramatically. Shipping embargoes during the Civil War further reduced the industries. The boom ended and many people left. Luckily, the 1870s brought a growth in the popularity of summer houses and resorts along the coast. The 1880s brought growth to the Kennebunks as tourism gradually took the place of shipbuilding.

Kennebunk is full of white clapboard houses with shutters, and sea captains' mansions. Many wealthy artists and writers own houses here now, in place of the sea captains, and, as a consequence, there are a few stores in the area selling rare and used books. There are walking tours of the old houses to give visitors a good taste of the area's history. The Brick Store Museum has changing exhibits on the history and art of southern Maine, and one semi-permanent exhibit on Kennebunk in the Federal Period. The Taylor–Barry House Museum, built in 1803, is a good picnic spot in summer. Gooch's Beach and Middle Beach are meeting grounds for teenagers; the quieter Mother's Beach is ideal for families.

Kennebunkport is a scenic town with old captain's houses, boutiques, and restaurants. Dock Square, the town center, is a good place to begin a tour. Captain Lord Mansion, built in 1821, is now a guesthouse. Nott House, in the center of the village, has white Doric columns—it was built in 1853 in the Greek Revival style. All the carpets, wallpaper, and furniture are original.

The Wedding Cake House, built in 1821, is covered with ornate fretwork. All-white, it does, indeed, look as much like a wedding cake as any house could. The story behind it is that a sea captain had to leave in the middle of his own wedding and the house was a gift to his new bride to make up for the lack of a wedding cake. The house is a private residence, but the adjacent carriage house is a studio and gallery open to the public.

Both Kennebunk and Kennebunkport are perfect for taking a leisurely walk or drive around town. Guided walking tours run from Nott House from June to October, and there are also plenty of opportunities for self-guided tours. There are many beautifully maintained buildings of Colonial, Federal, Greek Revival, and Victorian styles. The town-house school is a white, one-room schoolhouse with a pretty peaked roof. It was used from about 1900 to 1951. The old Jail is to the left of the school, and is now open by appointment only.

The Seashore Trolley Museum exhibits an enchanting array of a century's worth of streetcars—from 1872 to 1972—from many cities around the world, such as Nagasaki, New York, Budapest, Boston, and Sydney, Australia. The highlight of the museum is a 4-mile (7.5-km) trolley ride with a stop at the restoration workshop.

South of Kennebunk is the Rachael Carson National Wildlife Refuge. It is a great place for retreating from the crowds in summertime on a relaxed self-guided tour. Visitors can wander the trails through salt marsh and spot shorebirds and waterfowl—there are over 200 species to see. Rachael Carson was a naturalist and author of *Silent Spring* and other books that helped begin the environmental movement.

Portland International Jetport is the nearest major airport.
Map ref: page 222 G3

Kennebunk's Wedding Cake House, built by George Bourne. The ornamentation is reminiscent of that on Milan's cathedral.

LEWISTON

Lewiston is on the Androscoggin River, on the ooposite bank from its twin city, Auburn. It is 35 miles (56 km) north of Portland, on I-95/495, and has a population of 39,390. It is the home to the renowned and respected Bates College, founded in 1855.

Bates College's Museum of Art displays new exhibitions—four to five times per year—from its collection of nineteenth- and twentieth-century prints and drawings.

Bates College's Special Collections, in the Ladd Library, are for lovers of rare books and handwritten manuscripts. Visitors can view hand-bound leather volumes made with handmade paper pages to understand the work involved in making books before binding became mechanized. The collections are strong in the areas of religion and natural history, and in photography and oral history.

The Edmund Muskie Archives preserve the personal papers and files of this former Democratic senator. There are also papers of the former governor of Maine, James B. Longley.

Portland International Jetport is the nearest major airport, and there is also the Lewiston–Auburn Municipal Airport, which is about 4 miles (6 km) southwest of the town. Buses also service Lewiston.
Map ref: page 220 G9

LUBEC

Lubec (population 2,099) is 239 miles (385 km) northeast of Portland and about 150 miles

Mulholland Lighthouse, built in 1885, is on the east side of Lubec Channel, near the F.D. Roosevelt Memorial International Bridge.

(241 km) east of Bangor. Just past Lubec, off Route 189, is Quoddy Head State Park. Next to the park is West Quoddy Head, the most easterly point of land in the United States, where visitors can watch the sunrise over the lighthouse. There are a number of walking trails that lead you along the top of the 80-foot (24-m) rocky cliffs and through thick evergreen forest. A wooden boardwalk leads you over a fragile peat bog.

Close to Lubec is Campobello Island, home to the Roosevelt Campobello International Park, the only International Park in the world. It is actually in New Brunswick, Canada, but the United States and Canada manage it jointly. The park covers 2,600 acres (1,053 ha) on the southeast end of the island.

It was established in 1964 in honor of Franklin D. Roosevelt, who was President of the United States from 1933 to 1945. There is the family's 35-room "Cottage," the grounds, bogs, forest, and beaches. The cheerful red house is welcoming, full of wicker furniture and family belongings. The upstairs bedrooms overlook the rugged coast of the bay and islands. There are walking trails, meadows, a lighthouse nicknamed "Sparky," coves for sailboats to land, and many fish to catch. It is open from May to October. Roosevelt came here for summers with his family as a child, and when he was newly married, and later as President.

It was here that Roosevelt contracted polio, when he was 39 years old with a wife and five children. Many areas are accessible for the handicapped.

Campobello Island is reached from Route 189 to Lubec, then over the FDR International Bridge to the Island. Bangor has the nearest major airport.
Map ref: page 221 N7

PORTLAND

Portland was so named because it was the closest US port to Europe. The city now has a population of 64,249 residents. Portland is a good place to begin a trip to Maine. There are many interesting historic sites, cultural attractions, shops, restaurants, lighthouses, and forts, plus the beauty of Casco Bay.

The British fleet destroyed most of the city of Portland—the capital of Maine then—during the Revolutionary War. In the War of 1812 it was severely damaged again. Maine had few defenses, and because it was a province of Massachusetts, building forts in Maine was not a priority. The capital was moved inland from Portland to Augusta in 1827.

Portland is on scenic Casco Bay, a beautiful place to watch the changeable weather. It is a deepwater port, as are Searsport and Eastport. The oldest ferry service in the nation runs here, from the state pier in Portland. There are trips to the outlying islands year-round, which are relaxing day trips in the summer months. The Portland Head is the oldest US lighthouse in continuous use, still guiding ships into the harbor.

The Portland Museum of Art, established in 1882, is today housed in a modern building designed by I.M. Pei and Partners. There are exhibitions of fine and decorative arts from the 1700s to the present. It houses Winslow Homer's *Pulling the Dory* and *Weatherbeaten*, as well as works of art by Andrew Wyeth, John Marin, Marsden Hartley, Monet, Renoir, and Picasso. Homer's and Wyeth's works give a good feel for Maine's coast and countryside. The museum also runs educational programs, art classes, videos, jazz breakfasts on Sundays, and talks on art and architecture.

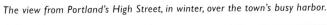

The view from Portland's High Street, in winter, over the town's busy harbor.

The Children's Museum of Maine has many hands-on exhibits that support learning and curiosity in both children and adults. It is a great place for children to burn off some extra energy.

Henry Wadsworth Longfellow, the popular poet, educator, and linguist was born in Portland in 1807. His childhood home, built in 1798, was the first brick house in Portland. It is an impressive three-story late Colonial-style house and most of the furnishings are original. Longfellow was the first American poet to write about American life and themes—previously, writers had looked to Europe for inspiration and culture.

Maine Historical Society and the Maine History Gallery are housed in the same building. The research library here is good for genealogy research.

The Neil Dow Memorial is a National Historic Landmark site. This was the home of General Neil Dow, who was an advocate of women's rights, the father of prohibition, and an abolitionist. The first floor is open for tours.

Tate House Museum was the home of Captain George Tate, a mast agent. This wooden house looks quite plain from the outside, but has some unique architectural details. It was built in 1755 and still has furnishings from the period. There is a huge fireplace and historically accurate gardens. It is open from June to September.

Victoria Mansion, built in 1858, is built in the style of an Italian villa, rather a surprise on the coast of Maine.

Portland is lucky to have the Museum of African Tribal Art, the only such museum in New England. It has rotating exhibits from its collection of 500 pieces. The displays are from 1,000 years of sub-Saharan African art. The collection has sculptures in bronze from the Benin and Yorba Kingdoms, including a leopard, made using the lost wax technique. This free museum is in the Portland Arts district.

Portland International Jetport is the busiest airport in the state. The city is also serviced by buses.
Map ref: page 222 G2

Portland lobster—fresh, cooked, and packaged—is famous all over the United States.

PRESQUE ISLE

Presque Isle (population 8,872) is in the far northeastern side of the state, near the Canadian border. Route 1 passes through here between Houlton on I-95 and the Canadian border. It is in the fertile plateau of Aroostook County ("Aroostook" is a Native American word meaning "beautiful river").

Potato production, centered in Presque Isle, is Maine's primary crop, earning one-quarter of the state's farm income.

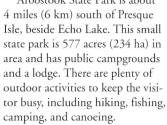

Portland's new Public Market, opened in 1997, showcases Maine's fresh produce.

Aroostook State Park is about 4 miles (6 km) south of Presque Isle, beside Echo Lake. This small state park is 577 acres (234 ha) in area and has public campgrounds and a lodge. There are plenty of outdoor activities to keep the visitor busy, including hiking, fishing, camping, and canoeing.

The Northern Maine Regional Airport is in Presque Isle.
Map ref: page 221 L3

WISCASSET

Wiscasset (population 3,700), a lovely old village, is on the Sheepscot River, 10 miles (16 km) northeast of Bath on US-1. It was settled in 1663, and was home to many sea captains and shipping magnates, and the hub for all shipping north of Boston. Today there are few boats built here, and most of the boat traffic is small pleasure craft. Fort Edgecomb (1808), an octagonal blockhouse, was built nearby to protect American ships from British and French raids.

Today, the bustle is gone but old cemeteries and churches preserve the area's history. Many of the old mansions have been converted to antique shops, art galleries, and guesthouses. It is now a center for artists and writers. The Maine Art Gallery exhibits local work.

Castle Tucker House was built in 1807 on a hill overlooking the Sheepscot River. This Federal-style house showcases the history of the town and of the families that lived there. There are ship portraits, furnishings from Victorian family life, keepsakes from foreign travel, and natural history exhibits about the area. The house is named for Captain Richard Tucker, who moved here with his young bride and managed the wharves and the iron foundry. The couple raised five children here. His business collapsed in 1871, so he took in boarders and began farming to feed his family. Years later, his daughter took over the house and preserved it as it had been in the late 1800s.

Nickels-Sortwell House has an imposing façade that is the centerpiece of Main Street. It is a three-story Colonial Revival-style house—white with black shutters, columns, and a central arched window. Captain William Nickels, a ship owner and trader, built it when business was booming. There was little time to enjoy the house because the Embargo Act of 1807 and the War of 1812 decimated the shipping industry. Many families involved in shipping went broke. It was changed to a hotel in 1830. The tide turned again as the house became a summer resort in the late 1800s. The house is open from June to October.

Portland International Jetport is the nearest major airport, 48 miles (77 km) southwest of Wiscasset.
Map ref: page 221 H10

Acadia National Park

Fall colors from birch, maple, and oak are often mixed with evergreens—spruce, pine, fir, and hemlock. Construction of the carriage roads that weave through Acadia National Park included much planting, to frame scenic vistas and to heal the scars of the roadbuilding work.

Acadia National Park, near Bar Harbor, was first established in 1916 as Sieur de Monts National Monument with 6,000 acres (2,430 ha) of land. Campaigner for the park, George B. Dorr, spent 43 years and much of his family money working to preserve the land, which had been donated by many individual owners, as a park. His work, and that of others, such as John D. Rockefeller Jr, made the park a reality. They understood how special the area was and worked hard to preserve it. On February 26, 1919, this land became Lafayette National Park, the first national park east of the Mississippi River. On January 19, 1929, the name was changed to Acadia National Park, as it is today.

Acadia National Park is known for its unusual combinations of mountain and ocean scenery. There are 17 mountains, huge pink granite boulders, wind-stunted trees, meandering woodland trails, and rocky beaches. Fall foliage, in late September and early October, is spectacular here, with the woods becoming a vibrant mix of red, orange, golden yellow, and many shades of brown. The park's paths become a carpet of color as the leaves fall. Snow closes many roads in the park between December and April.

Acadia is the fifth-smallest national park in the United States, but it is one of the country's 10 most visited. Over 3 million people visit the park every year, with the warmer summer months of July and August being the busiest.

Twenty thousand years ago this area was covered with glaciers up to 1 mile (2 km) thick. This rounded the tops of the mountains and scraped out valleys as it moved. It gave the area its feeling of wild, rather desolate beauty. A glacier created a spectacular natural fjord. It is called Somes Sound and is on Mt Desert Island near Somesville. It is the only true fjord on the east coast. More recently, evidence of the Wabanaki people from 6,000 years ago has been found in the area—it is unclear if they spent summers or winters here.

The majority of the park is on Mt Desert Island, originally named "L'Isle des Monts Deserts" by Samuel de Champlain. He came here on September 5, 1604, and saw barren mountains right on the ocean. The island does indeed have some barren mountains, but most of the mountains, back from the windy coast, are forested.

John D. Rockefeller Jr began coming to Mt Desert Island as a summer resident in 1917. He had big ideas, and the money and foresight to carry them out. He feared there would be nowhere to ride in horse-drawn carriages in peace without the newly invented automobiles roaring nearby.

Consequently, he initiated the building of 57 miles (92 km) of 16-foot (5-m) wide gravel paths designed for pleasant rides in his carriages. Though the age of carriages is long past, the paths are a wonderful legacy; they are perfect for walking, and feature many beautiful vistas. Forty-five miles (72 km) of Rockefeller paths are now part of the park. Sometimes visitors can pick blueberries along the way or hear the call of a loon. Other birds spotted within the park are owls, hawks, falcons, gannets, waxwings, finches, sandpipers, grouse, herons, cormorants, shearwaters, swallows, and golden eagles. Gilley Museum, in Southwest Harbor, is a must for birdwatchers.

Rockefeller also had 16 unique bridges built, from steel-reinforced concrete with facings of local granite, as part of these trails. They fit in well with their surroundings and have a rustic character. One bridge spans a 40-foot (12-m) waterfall. Most of the bridges and paths were donated to the park, along with 11,000 acres (4,455 ha) of Rockefeller's own land. The park grew gradually, as more and more locals donated their land, to its current size of 47,633 acres (19,291 ha), or over 40 square miles (104 sq km). This history of local owners donating land year by year explains the irregular shape of the park and why sections of it are on Mt Desert Island, adjacent islands, and the nearby Schoonic Peninsula.

As well as the Rockefellers, other very wealthy families, such as the Fords, Morgans, Vanderbilts, Carnegies, and the Astors came here during the summers from the gay 1890s to the Depression. They dominated the area for 40 years, with each family building opulent mansions, diminutively called "cottages," on the island. The Depression and World War II put a brake on their opulent lifestyles. The final chapter came in 1947, when a huge fire on the

Acadia National Park's broken-stone carriage roads and bridges were built between 1913 and 1940. They were carefully planned and constructed—they follow the contours of the land, and are built to survive local weather conditions. They are now being gradually rehabilitated as part of a long-term maintenance scheme.

island destroyed 67 estates. Few of the families ever returned to the island or rebuilt. Since then, a strip of reasonably priced hotels and motels has appeared along Frenchman's Bay, allowing for a different sort of summer visitor.

The park is entered via Routes 3 and 102 through Ellsworth. The visitor center in Hull's Cove is worth a visit to get an overview of the park and plan the time one wishes to spend there. It is open May 1 to October 31, seven days a week. There are maps, books, listings of tours and boat trips, and a short film about the park.

The Park Loop road is often crowded in summer months, but its 27 miles (44 km) of spectacular scenery gives a good idea of what the park has to offer. Rockefeller staked out much of the route himself, determined to make best possible use of the landscape for picturesque views. A landscape designer planted flowers and trees when the roads were built, to frame the views. The Park Loop road goes past Sand Beach, Thunder Hole, Otter Cliffs, and the Jordan Pond House, where you can snack on hot popovers and tea. On the western end of Mt Desert Island is Echo Lakes sandy beach. A lifeguard watches over everyone, so it's ideal for families. Seals, sea eagles, and osprey can often be seen from Indian Point in Blagden Reserve.

There are two large campgrounds in the park, and they book up quickly in busy months. There are other private campgrounds nearby—these are often quieter. Camping outside the campgrounds is not allowed. There is also a nature center, a museum, a bathhouse, and a place to rent horses. These are all closed in winter.

Finback, humpback, and minke whales can be seen 20 miles (32 km) off the coast on half-day boat trips out of Bar Harbor. The whales pass along the coast from mid-June to early October on their way south. It is difficult to appreciate just how big these animals are until they are seen on the open ocean.

Puffins, or sea parrots, are whimsical-looking sea birds with bright triangular beaks. They have re-established colonies on five offshore islands over the last 25 years, after having been hunted ruthlessly for many years. They nest in spring in rock crevices or in soft sandy soil. After that, they are mostly at sea until around the first week of August, when the young fledge. Though you cannot land on the islands, several of the whale-watching boats pass close by one of them (Petit Manan Island) in early summer.

Visitors arriving on a cold day when walking is less than attractive can still enjoy the park's magnificent views by driving up to the top of Cadillac Mountain (1,530 feet/467 m) on Schoodic Point. Snow closes many roads in the park between December and April.

There is an airport in Bar Harbor, and Bangor International Airport is only 40 miles (64 km) northwest of Bar Harbor. Buses also service the area.

This beautiful view is typical of the inland areas of Acadia National Park in early spring, as the snows begin to melt and the streams run faster. Soon the deciduous trees lining these banks will be budding into leaf.

Sand Beach, the only swimming beach in Acadia National Park, is not for the faint-hearted—water temperatures rarely rise above 55°F (12°C). In summer the beach has a lifeguard, but in winter the sand can be swept away by the storm waves—it is returned the following spring.

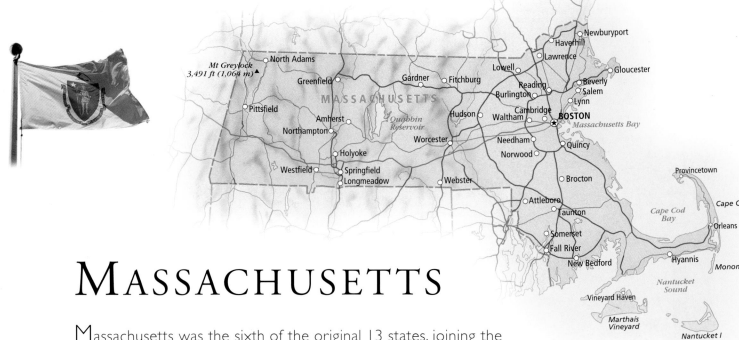

MASSACHUSETTS

Massachusetts was the sixth of the original 13 states, joining the Union in 1788 and including Maine until 1820. Its 9,241 square miles (23,934 sq km) sustain 6.3 million residents, making Massachusetts one of the most densely populated states. Boston is its capital, and New England's largest city. Summers in Massachusetts are hot and humid, and winters cold and snowy, but the Atlantic Ocean tends to moderate coastal temperatures.

The coastline measures almost 2,450 miles (3,924 km), counting inlets, bays, and coves. Its diverse landscape includes the rivers, lakes, and woods of the Berkshire Hills in the west (topped by 3,481-foot [1,062-m] Mt Greylock, the state's highest point), hardwood forests, farmlands, and beaches.

English Pilgrims established New England's first permanent European settlement at Plymouth in 1620. The Massachusetts Bay Colony and Boston were established in 1630, at the mouth of the Charles River. European diseases decimated the Massachuset peoples; immigration and domestic migration have since made Massachusetts an ethnic and racial melting pot.

This charming residential area in Lexington typifies Massachusetts and indeed the whole of New England.

More than 100 colleges and universities have been established in Massachusetts since Harvard College, the country's oldest, was founded in Cambridge in 1636. In the eighteenth century Boston spearheaded the Revolutionary War. In the nineteenth century Massachusetts led the nation into the Industrial Revolution with water-powered textile mills and shoe factories. The economy is now driven by service-oriented, defense, and high-technology fields.

Boston's Logan International Airport is the commercial air travel center for New England. There is a rail service from New York to Boston and the state has many major highways. Ferries link the mainland to coastal communities and resorts.

State motto *Ense Petit Placidam sub Libertate Quietem* (By the sword we seek peace, but peace only under liberty)
State flag Adopted 1908
Capital Boston
Population 6,349,097
Total area (land and water) 9,241 square miles (23,934 sq km)
Land area 7,838 square miles (20,300 sq km)
Massachusetts is the 45th-largest state in size
Origin of name From two Native American words meaning "great mountain place"
Nicknames The Old Colony State, The Bay State
Abbreviations MA. (postal), Mass.
State bird Chickadee
State flower Mayflower
State tree American elm
Entered the Union February 6, 1788 as the sixth state

Places in
MASSACHUSETTS

BROCKTON

Brockton, a suburb south of Boston with 92,800 residents, was settled in 1700, but it didn't incorporate as a city until 1881. A shoe manufacturing center in the nineteenth century, its economy is now diversified among 200 manufacturing, health-care, and distribution businesses. The city has a community college, a symphony orchestra and The Fuller Museum of Art. The city is just east of Hwy 24.

Map ref: page 222 F6

CAMBRIDGE

As the home of some of America's greatest universities—Harvard University and the Massachusetts Institute Of Technology—Boston's neighbor has educated some of the most important movers and shakers in the nation's history and is now home to 95,800 residents. It was founded in 1630 as Newtowne, on the Charles River opposite Boston, as a farming village, and was the capital of the Puritan Massachusetts Bay Colony until 1634. The colony established North America's first college here two years later,

with nine students and one master. In 1639 the college was named for its first major benefactor, English clergyman John Harvard. At the same time, the town's name was changed to recall the town in England where many of the Puritans had been educated.

In 1639 Stephen Daye brought America's first printing press here, and founded Cambridge Press. During the Revolutionary War, George Washington took command of the Continental Army on Cambridge Common on July 3, 1775. He then directed the siege of Boston from a house on Brattle Street that would later become the home of poet Henry Wadsworth Longfellow, now preserved as Longfellow National Historic Site. By 1846, when the town incorporated, it was becoming increasingly industrial, and remained so until after World War II. Major publishing houses located here as well. A subway line to Boston was completed in 1912. Today, besides higher education,

Harvard University was named for Englishman, John Harvard, its first major benefactor.

Cambridge is a center for academic research, business consulting, and high-technology ventures. Attractions include Harvard Square and adjacent Old Cambridge, the Harvard University Museum of Cultural and Natural History, and the MIT Museum. In summer and fall, Memorial Drive is closed to traffic between the start of the Alewife/Fresh Pond Parkway and Western Avenue, leaving it to joggers, walkers, and inline skaters. Bikers, walkers, and inline skaters can try the popular $10\frac{1}{2}$-mile (17-km) Minuteman Rail Trail. This follows an old railroad grade along the approximate route of Paul Revere's ride in April 1775 (which warned the American rebels of the approaching British troops, starting the Revolutionary War) and links Cambridge, Arlington, Lexington, and Bedford.

Map ref: page 222 F6

CAPE COD

Shaped like an arm flexing its biceps, the arc of Cape Cod is one of the East Coast's most recognizable landforms, and, with

its miles of beaches, one of its most popular summertime getaways. English Captain Bartholomew Gosnold named it in 1602 for the abundant codfish in the cape's waters. US-6 runs northeast along its 65-mile (105-km) length, from the Massachusetts mainland to Provincetown at its tip. In 1620 the Pilgrims first set foot in North America at Provincetown, today an artists' colony and tourist haven nicknamed "P'town."

The cape's width varies from about 20 miles (32 km), between Sandwich and Woods Hole, to a few hundred yards at the tip. Vacationers are drawn to its resort facilities as well as to its beaches, campgrounds, lakes and ponds, hills, sand dunes, and forests of scrub oak and pitch pine. Walkers, hikers, and bicyclists can explore the area's extensive trails. For walkers, bicyclists, and inline skaters, the 25-mile (40-km) Cape Cod Rail Trail, an old railroad grade, links Dennis, Brewster, Eastham, and Wellfleet for a more intimate look at the land. Sightseers can also take in the cape's lighthouses, including Chatham Light, at Chatham, and Cape Cod Light, at Truro. But for the mainland to the west, the cape is bounded by salt water: Cape Cod Bay to the north, the Atlantic Ocean to the east, Nantucket Sound to the south and Buzzards Bay to the southwest.

Besides Provincetown, Cape Cod has a number of cities and towns, including Barnstable, Hyannis, Orleans, and Wellfleet. The cape has long been known for fishing and, earlier, whaling. The prosperity it derived from the sea is reflected in the elaborate homes that wealthy sea captains built during the 1800s. Provincetown still makes some of its living from the sea, from a harbor that is one of the northeast's largest and safest.

About 44,000 acres (17,820 ha) of coastal marshland, glacial cliffs, and dense forests are protected from development as the Cape Cod National Seashore, with its headquarters in South Wellfleet. Plenty of lodging is available, from beach cottages to B&Bs, inns, and motels. A number of campgrounds serve campers and those driving recreational vehicles. Most beach parking areas require either a

The oldest institution of higher learning in America—Harvard University, Cambridge.

STATE FEATURE

Boston

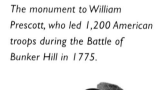

In Boston, colonial buildings stand amid the modern skyscrapers.

The monument to William Prescott, who led 1,200 American troops during the Battle of Bunker Hill in 1775.

COLONEL
WILLIAM PRESCOTT
JUNE 17, 1775

When an American strolls along the historic and hectic streets of Massachusetts' capital city for the first time, a sense of déjà vu may well arise. Boston Harbor, the Boston Massacre, the Boston Tea Party, the Battle of Bunker Hill, and the revelry of Irish-Americans on St Patrick's Day are so ingrained in the national identity that New England's largest and most influential city may well feel familiar.

There is evidence of Native American habitation as far back as 8,000 years. When the first Europeans, led by former Church of England cleric William Blackstone, settled the narrow Shawmut Peninsula at the mouth of the Charles River in 1625, the dominant native group was the Massachuset people. After the British Crown granted the Massachusetts Bay Company a charter to colonize the area in 1629, the company dispatched about 800 Puritans, led by John Winthrop, to establish the Massachusetts Bay Colony.

In 1630 the group settled in today's Charlestown, between the Mystic and Charles Rivers, but soon joined Blackstone across the river. The settlement was first named Trimountaine, after the three large hills that later residents excavated away for landfill. The theocratic Pilgrims later named their new home Boston.

Boston's early economy was based on providing English immigrants with food and supplies. In the 1640s, they turned to fishing, shipbuilding, and maritime trade, and the autonomous Massachusetts Bay Colony was on its way to becoming the most important city in British America. Boston was the third-busiest British port by 1700, and the largest city in the colonies until it was surpassed by Philadelphia in 1760.

When the Crown re-established control over the colony, its charter was annulled, and the colony's first royal governor, Sir Edmund Andros, arrived in 1686 replacing the intolerant Puritan clergy. He abolished the colony's representative assembly, and imposed taxes without the colonials' consent. After King James II was deposed and Andros was sent back to England, a new royal charter took effect in 1691 that extended the colony's authority to Plymouth and Maine. Importantly, it established an elected popular assembly and extended voting rights to property-owning non-Puritans.

Bostonians' opposition to taxation without representation reached fever pitch when Britain imposed a series of taxes to help pay the cost of the French and Indian War (1754–63). After opposition to the *Stamp Act* erupted into riots in 1765, the British government ordered the military occupation of Boston in 1768. Two years later British soldiers fired on a mob and killed five protestors.

In 1773 a group of Bostonians protested against a tax on tea by tossing almost 45 tons (41 t) of it into Boston Harbor.

(Visitors can reenact the moment at the Boston Tea Party Ship & Museum, at the Congress Street Bridge.) In 1775 British troops marched to Concord, launching the Revolutionary War. The Redcoats suffered terrible losses at the Battle of Bunker Hill, but won the fight. They later evacuated the city by sea on March 17, 1776, after General Washington positioned captured British cannon on Dorchester Heights, overlooking the city and harbor.

Boston Harbor, the center of maritime commerce after the Revolutionary War, saw its fortunes decline during the wars, embargoes, and blockades of the early nineteenth century. Boston's businessmen then turned to textile manufacturing, launching the Industrial Revolution in America with huge water-powered mills. As immigrants, particularly Irish fleeing the potato famine of the 1840s and 1850s, poured into Boston, cheap labor became readily available. As the city became dominant in banking, insurance, and the manufacture of inexpensive clothing, the grip of the upper-class Yankee (English-descendant) Republicans on city government began to give way to Irish Democrats, who saw control of government as a road to advancement. The city elected the first of many Irish-American mayors, Hugh O'Brien, in 1885.

Boston's economy peaked in 1920, but as the Great Depression deepened in the 1930s, it began a long and steep decline. Revival began in 1960, but the 1970s were marred by interracial strife over forced busing to desegregate public schools. Still, Boston's resurrection continued. Boston Harbor, once among the country's most polluted, has been cleaned up. The city is the largest center for banking and insurance in the northeast, and about 700 high-technology and electronics companies are in the Boston area. The US$10.8 billion Central Artery/Tunnel Project—The Big Dig, as its called—is being touted as the largest and most complex highway construction project in American history. Scheduled to be completed in 2004, it is expected to dramatically reduce the city's notorious traffic congestion.

It's easy to wander through the centuries in Boston, where history and modernity stand juxtaposed. High above buildings that were the foundry of the American nation—such as Faneuil Hall, where many rousing revolutionary meetings were held—stand modern edifices like the 60-story John Hancock Tower, New England's tallest structure.

The Boston National Historical Park links a variety of sites (including the 16 sites of the Freedom Trail) that help visitors gain a coherent view of the city's role in American history. The park visitor center is located at 15 State Street. The park includes South Boston's Dorchester Heights, where the colonial army, led by newly appointed General George Washington, installed a battery of cannon during the siege of Boston, thereby forcing the British to evacuate on March 17, 1776.

In the three-mile (4.8-km) Freedom Trail Walking Tour, visitors can stroll to 16 of Boston's—and the nation's—most important historic sites. Boston Common is a large green originally set aside in 1634 as a military training ground and public pasture. It also served for public hangings. From there the Freedom Trail zigzags past sites such as the Granary Burying Ground (1660), where lie the bones of three signatories of the Declaration of Independence, patriot Paul Revere, Boston Massacre victims, and Benjamin Franklin's parents. It passes the Old South Meeting House (1729); the Old State House, Boston's oldest public building (1713) and the site of the Boston Massacre (1770); Faneuil Hall (1740) and Quincy Market; the Paul Revere House (circa 1680); and the Old North Church (1723), from which a sexton signaled with two lanterns that British troops were leaving Boston to seize the militia's arms cache at Concord. From there, it crosses the Charles River to the Charlestown Navy Yard, where the oldest commissioned Navy ship, the USS *Constitution*, is anchored; then, finally, to the Bunker Hill Monument.

Located in the heart of Boston's historically upscale Beacon Hill neighborhood is the Boston African-American National Historic Site, which includes 15 pre-Civil War structures related to the history of the city's nineteenth-century African-American community and Boston's ardent opposition to slavery. It includes the African Meeting House, built in 1806, the oldest standing African-American church in the country.

Highlighting the contribution of women is the Boston Women's Heritage Trail, comprising four interesting walks that each require about one to one-and-a-half hours to complete.

For the aquatically inclined there is the New England Aquarium, which features more than 12,000 fish and aquatic animals. The Charles River and Boston Harbor both offer sailing, canoeing, and kayaking. The Boston Harbor Islands National Recreation Area provides a range of outdoor recreation opportunities, from hiking and camping to picnicking. Sweeping views of the region can also be gained from the John Hancock Observatory, atop the Hancock Tower, where elevators take visitors 740 feet (226 m) above Boston's streets.

Art lovers can take in Boston's Museum of Fine Arts, while technophobes and technophiles alike will enjoy the Computer Museum or the Museum of Science. Sports fans may want to see a Boston Red Sox baseball game at Fenway Park (built in 1912), a Celtics basketball game, or Bruins ice hockey match at the FleetCenter. The annual Boston Marathon is held on the same day as the Patriots Day celebration, the third Monday in April. St Patrick's Day (March 17) is one of the largest annual celebrations. The week preceding July 4 is marked by the waterfront Harborfest. On the Fourth itself, Bostonians bring picnic lunches to the banks of the Charles River to hear the Boston Pops Orchestra.

Logan International Airport provides commercial air service to Boston. The easiest and most affordable way to get around is the "T," the system of subways, buses, trolleys, boats, and commuter trains.

The USS Constitution, *the oldest commissioned Navy ship, is anchored at the Charlestown Navy Yard in Boston.*

The largest city in Massachusetts, Boston is the state's center of banking and insurance.

The Cape Cod area, once known for whaling, is now a favorite tourist destination.

resident sticker or a fee; access is free for walkers and bicyclists. The National Seashore beach charges per vehicle, pedestrian or bicyclist.
Map ref: page 222 H7

CHICOPEE

Chicopee was settled in 1641 at the confluence of the Connecticut and Chicopee rivers and adjacent to Springfield, just south of today's I-90. Its name is an Native American word for "birch bark place." In the 1800s it became known for the manufacture of textiles, firearms, bicycles, bronze statuary, and farm implements. Today the city of 54,500 produces sporting goods and electrical machinery. Westover Air Force Base and the College of Our Lady of the Elms are located here. The Polish Kielbasa Festival is held here in September.
Map ref: page 222 C6

CONCORD

This stately eastern Massachusetts town, settled in 1635, has a central place in the annals of early US history as the battleground where "the shot heard 'round the world" was fired. In 1774, it hosted the colony's first county convention and the first Massachusetts Provincial Congress which protested aspects of British rule.

On April 19, 1775, the Battle of Concord between British troops and colonial Minutemen, civilian volunteers who'd vowed to fight the British on a minute's notice, launched the military phase of the Revolutionary War. (An earlier skirmish that morning at Lexington, about 5 miles [8 km] east of Concord, was the first military

clash of the Revolution.) Some 800 British troops headed to Concord to capture or destroy the large cache of military supplies the colonists had stored there. Patriots Paul Revere, William Dawes, and Samuel Prescott had warned the militia of the impending attack. About 300 to 400 militia resisted the British advance at the North Bridge over the Concord River, with several losses on both sides. Finally, pursued by growing numbers of militia, the British retreated under steady gunfire to Boston. Despite the arrival of reinforcements at Lexington, the British suffered more than 270 casualties in the retreat, the colonists fewer

than 100. The latter's real victory lay in showing they could and would fight. The events are recalled at Concord-based Minute Man National Historic Park, 900 acres (365 ha) along original segments of what came to be known as Battle Road.

In the 1800s Concord was a literary and cultural center. It was home to Amos Bronson Alcott, who ran a school of philosophy, and his novelist daughter, Louisa May Alcott. Orchard House, where Louisa May Alcott wrote *Little Women* is now open to the public. Sleepy Hollow Cemetery is the final resting place of the Alcotts, Emerson, French, Hawthorne and Thoreau. Visitors can also take guided tours through The Old Manse, built in 1770 by the grandfather of writer and philosopher Ralph Waldo Emerson and named by another literary figure, Nathaniel Hawthorne, who lived in the house from 1842 to 1845. Just south of Concord is Walden Pond, immortalized by essayist

Henry David Thoreau, who lived there from 1845 to 1847. Walden Pond Reservation is on Hwy 126. Concord was also home to renowned sculptor Daniel Chester French, who created The Minute Man of Concord and the statue of a seated Abraham Lincoln in the Lincoln Memorial in Washington DC. About 1850, Ephraim W. Bull developed the popular Concord grape here.

The city of about 17,100 residents maintains its New England charm with many historic homes and sites. Visitors can take a walking tour, or even take to the Concord River in a canoe; this is an especially popular activity when the forests by the river are displaying their colorful fall foliage. Other points of interest include the Concord Museum and Emerson House, where Ralph Waldo Emerson lived from 1835 until his death in 1882.

Concord, which is now largely a residential suburb northwest of Boston, can be reached via scenic Hwys 119 and 2A (Lexington Road), which passes through Minute Man National Historic Site and links Concord with Lexington. Commuter train services to Concord are available from Boston's North Station.
Map ref: page 222 E5

Pretty Provincetown, Cape Cod, has one of the country's safest harbors, and is famous for its Bohemian atmosphere.

Shoppers at Fall River's many outlet stores can stop at this unusual McDonald's outlet for lunch.

FALL RIVER

In the decades following construction of Fall River's first cotton mill in 1811, its access to abundant water power and the port of Mt Hope Bay, an arm of Narragansett Bay, enabled "Spindle City" to grow into one of the country's most important cotton thread and cloth manufacturing centers. At least some residents got rich from the 120 mills that eventually sprang up—evident today in the Victorian mansions on the heights above the city. But serious labor unrest, including a textile workers' strike in 1904–05, demonstrated that not everyone felt they were sharing adequately in the city's good fortune, which declined along with the textile industry here in the 1920s.

Plymouth Colony settlers founded Fall River in 1656. Its name derives from the Native American word for the area, *Quequechan*, or "falling water." Today the city at the mouth of the Taunton River numbers almost 91,000 residents, and clothing manufacturers offer discount prices in many outlet stores. Fall River entered the annals of crime in 1892 with the trial of Lizzie Borden, who was acquitted of murdering her father and step-mother with an axe in a house that is now a B&B offering daily tours.

In addition to textiles and clothing, Fall River produces medical products, electrical equipment, and chemicals. Besides its many historic buildings, the city is the site of Battleship Cove, the final resting place of the 680-foot (207-m) USS *Massachusetts*, which survived 35 battles in the Atlantic and Pacific theaters in World War II. Two operational PT boats, the destroyer USS *Joseph P. Kennedy Jr*, and the World War II attack submarine USS *Lionfish* are also moored here. It is open to visitors daily except New Year's Day, Thanksgiving, and Christmas.

Displays of steam-powered transport can be found at the Marine Museum. Other attractions are Fall River Heritage State Park, which has exhibits depicting the city's textile and nautical history; and

The entrance to the John F. Kennedy Hyannis Museum, in Hyannis.

the Old Colony and Fall River Railroad Museum. Fall River is north of I-195, south of Boston, and south-east of Providence in Rhode Island, both of which are served by international airports.
Map ref: page 222 F7

FITCHBURG

Settled in 1720 on the North Branch of the Nashua River, this industrial city northwest of Boston is named for inventor John Fitch. It became a paper manufacturing center early in the 1800s, and now also produces fabricated metal, machinery, engines, electrical instruments, and plastic goods. It has about 39,800 residents, and is the site of Fitchburg State College and the Fitchburg Art Museum. The city is just north of Hwy 2, and a commuter train service to Fitchburg is available from Boston's North Station.
Map ref: page 222 E5

GLOUCESTER

Sebastian Junger's book *The Perfect Storm: A True Story of Men Against the Sea*, and the subsequent movie told of the dangerous and sometimes tragic business of fishing the North Atlantic from this picturesque Cape Ann port, northeast of Boston. A bronze statue of a fisherman is dedicated to the many Gloucester fishermen lost at sea. Founded by English fishermen in 1623, 17 years after French explorer Samuel de Champlain mapped the harbor, the settlement was named for Gloucester, England. It has been a fishing port ever since.

Like many coastal New England towns in the 1700s and 1800s, Gloucester also supported a ship-building industry. Today its historic buildings, narrow streets, old wharves, and artists' colony make it the center of a popular summertime resort area, with the region's rocky shore noted for whale-watching. Several firms offer whale-watching trips and coastal sightseeing excursions.

The city of 28,700 residents can be reached via Hwy 128 east. Paintings and drawings by Fitz Hugh Lane and other Cape Ann artists are displayed at Gloucester's Cape Ann Historical Museum. Other attractions include Beau-port, a 40-room house built between 1907 and 1934 by interior decorator Henry Davis Sleeper and Hammond Castle Museum, a medieval-style structure built by inventor Dr John Hay Hammond between 1926 and 1929. The two-day Gloucester Waterfront Festival is held in August.
Map ref: page 222 F5

HOLYOKE

Founded in 1745 as a farming community on the Connecticut River in the Pioneer Valley, Holyoke used water power and a system of canals built between 1847 and 1849 to become a textile and paper manufacturing center for south-western Massachusetts. It also became the country's first planned industrial center. It was named for Captain Elizur Holyoke, who explored the area in 1633. Just north of Springfield, on I-91, the city now numbers 43,700.

Holyoke celebrates its Irish heritage with one of the largest St Patrick's Day parades in the country. As the city where William G. Morgan invented volleyball at the local YMCA in 1895, it is home to the Volleyball Hall of Fame. Holyoke Heritage State Park has cultural and recreational programs, and includes the Children's Museum , with interactive exhibits, performances,

Hyannis has much to offer tourists, from historic homes and museums, to the waterfront; the area is also associated with the famous Kennedy family.

workshops, and a science discovery area. Mt Tom State Reservation, located north of Holyoke, offers visitors 1,800 acres (729 ha) on the western slope of Mt Tom, which stands 1,214 feet (370 m) above the valley floor. Its precipitous ridge is forested with pine, hemlock, hardwoods, and spruce. It is open daily, dawn to dusk, and a vehicle fee is charged.
Map ref: page 222 C6

HYANNIS

Cape Cod's Hyannis is a summer resort with the largest beaches on the cape and 14,120 permanent residents. It was settled in 1666 and named for a local Native American leader. It became a center of business after the railroad arrived in 1854.

Today Hyannis is one of the city of Barnstable's seven unincorporated villages, all with historic homes, beautiful beaches, and other vacation amenities. It is also a distribution point for fish and cranberries. America's best substitute for royalty, the Kennedy clan, made Hyannis and nearby Hyannis Port, site of the Kennedy family home on Nantucket Sound . A wonderful memorial to President

John F. Kennedy stands on Ocean Street. The John F. Kennedy Hyannis Museum, in the old downtown Town Hall Building on Main Street, has exhibits depicting the Kennedy family's time on Cape Cod during the years 1934 to 1963. In addition, the museum has opened an exhibit about the slain president's son, the late John Kennedy Jr. who died in a tragic plane crash.

The Cape Cod Central Railroad's first-class parlor cars, elegant dinner cars, and restored coaches make regular scenic excursions from Hyannis to Cape Cod Canal, via Sandwich. Hyannis Harbor Tours, from Pier 1 at the Ocean Street dock, offers a one-hour tour of Hyannis Harbor, a view of the Kennedy family's summer homes, and round-trip daily cruises to nearby Nantucket Island and Martha's Vineyard.

Hyannis is south of Barnstable, about 3 miles (5 km) south of US 6 on the southern side of Cape Cod. Air service is available at the Hyannis, Barnstable Municipal Airport. Ferries run between Hyannis, Nantucket Island, and Martha's Vineyard (schedules change seasonally).
Map ref: page 222 G7

LAWRENCE

In 1845, the need for waterpower to run huge textile mills drew Boston industrialists, led by American businessman and Congressman Abbott Lawrence, to the banks of the Merrimack River, 25 miles (40 km) northwest of Boston. The subsequent need for jobs drew thousands of poorly paid immigrant laborers to the planned industrial city of mills and canals that was built here.

At its peak the mills were producing 800 miles (1,287 km) of cloth a day, and the Washington Mills, built in 1886, were once the largest woolen mills in the country. But conditions were considerably harsh and unsafe for the workers, and in 1860 a factory collapsed, killing 88 people.

In 1912 Lawrence's workers launched the Bread and Roses Strike, one of the largest labor actions in American history. The massive strike of 23,000 workers, many of them women and children, followed decisions by the mill owners to increase the speed of factory looms and lower wages. Many deaths and mass arrests occurred when the state's National Guard and private and city police

were sent in against the strikers, resulting in a public outcry. Even though the mill owners backed down after two months and mill workers throughout New England won wage increases, the textile industry declined during the rest of the century. Today, the more diversified city of 70,200 residents manufactures electronic equipment, textiles, paper products, computers, and foodstuffs.

The Bread and Roses Strike is commemorated in the annual Bread and Roses Labor Day Heritage Festival in early September. The 23-acre (9.3-ha) Lawrence Heritage State Park, Boarding House Site records the story of Lawrence, whose immigrant heritage earned it the nickname "Immigrant City." A visitor center is located in a restored 1840s mill boarding house. Visitors can also tour the North Canal Historic District, composed of 70 properties featuring mills, factory boarding houses, locks, bridges, the North Canal, the 900-foot (275-m) Great Stone Dam and the Immigrant City Archives.

Lawrence is situated on I-495, and can be reached via I-93, traveling north from Boston.
Map ref: page 222 F5

LEXINGTON

This residential suburb northwest of Boston echoed with gunfire on April 19, 1775, when a skirmish between local militia, dubbed Minutemen, clashed with about 800 British troops in the first military action of the Revolutionary War. The troops were on their way to seize military supplies that were stored in nearby Concord. They were met on Lexington Common (Lexington Battle Green) by about 70 Minutemen, who had been alerted to the approach of the British by Paul Revere. When shooting broke out, eight Minutemen were killed, including their commander, Captain John Parker. However, the British were forced to retreat after confronting a larger force of Minutemen at the North Bridge in Concord. Nine hundred acres (365 ha), including segments of what came to be called Battle Road, are preserved at the Minuteman National Historic Site in nearby Concord.

Lexington, which was settled about 1640, now has about 29,000 residents. It was named for Lexington, England. Visitors can see the battle site and the Revolutionary Monument, dedicated in 1799 and believed to be the first monument commemorating the Revolutionary War. The town includes many historic buildings, some dating from the 1690s. Buckman Tavern, headquarters of the Minutemen, was built in 1709 and has furnishings from the Revolutionary War period. The changing exhibits of the Museum of Our National Heritage depict American history and culture. Much of the route used by the eighteenth-century American and British forces is now covered by Hwy 2A. However, bikers, walkers, and inline skaters can enjoy the popular 10½-mile (17-km) Minuteman Rail Trail (see entry on Cambridge, page 193).
Map ref: page 222 E6

LOWELL

Looking for a source of abundant water power to run cotton and woolen mills, a group of Boston investors dubbed the "Boston Associates" found what they needed just south of the New Hampshire state line, at the confluence of the Merrimack and Concord Rivers northwest of Boston. Originally settled by the English in the 1650s, Lowell was transformed from a farm village to an industrial hub during the Industrial Revolution by the construction of riverside mills and power canals in 1822. Named for early American cotton-textile manufacturer Francis Cabot Lowell, in the decades to come the city became a major textile manufacturing center that employed thousands of immigrants under poor conditions for low pay.

Eventually massive five- and six-story brick mills lined the river for nearly 1 mile (1.6 km), a sight so imposing that it became an almost obligatory stop for Europeans touring the United States. By 1850 almost 6 miles (10 km) of canals coursed through the city, powering 40 mill buildings, 320,000 spindles, and nearly 10,000 looms operated by more than 10,000 workers. The textile industry here declined steadily in the twentieth century, and many operations were moved to the South.

The fascinating story of Lowell and the Industrial Revolution is told at Lowell National Historic Park, which includes mills, workers' housing, the canal system, and industrial exhibits. Visitors can take one of the daily guided tours. The Boot Cotton Mills Museum is housed within the brick walls of a cotton mill built in 1873. It includes an operating weave room with 88 power looms and "mill girl" boardinghouses.

Today Lowell is home to about 103,400 residents, and it is the site of the University of Massachusetts at Lowell. High-tech businesses are beginning to revitalize the economy. Its cultural heritage also includes the Whistler House Museum of Art, the birthplace (1834) of painter James A. M. Whistler. Beat Generation writer Jack Kerouac (1922–69) was also born and raised in Lowell, and wrote five books set in the town. The New England Quilt Museum and the Sports Museum of New England are also here.

By car, the Lowell National Historical Park is accessible via the Lowell Connector from either I-495 or US-3. A commuter rail service is available from Boston's North Station to Lowell's Gallagher Terminal, where convenient shuttles to downtown Lowell can then be boarded.
Map ref: page 222 E5

LYNN

One of Massachusetts' oldest communities, this industrial city of 81,200 on Massachusetts Bay, a few miles northeast of Boston, was named Saugus when it was settled in 1629. In 1637 it was renamed for the English town of King's Lynn. Shoemaking began here in 1635, and eventually grew in importance to make Lynn the leading shoe manufacturing center in the country early in the twentieth century. That industry declined, and now Lynn's economy includes the manufacture of turbines, generators, jet engines, electrical lamps, and processed foods.

Places of interest include the Grand Army of the Republic Museum, and the Mary Baker Eddy Historical House, once the home of the founder of the Christian Science Church (tours are available). Lynn Woods Reservation, a 2,200-acre (891-ha) city park, offers hiking, rock climbing, picnicking, and cross-country skiing. The Lynn Heritage State Park Visitor Center at 590 Washington Street provides information about the city's history, as well as the histories of the towns of Nahant and Swampscott.

Historic Buckman Tavern, located in Lexington, was the headquarters of the Minutemen, who were led by Captain John Parker.

The lighthouse at Gay Head on Martha's Vineyard. The magnificent cliffs at Gay Head were carved out of the land by glaciers more than 100 million years ago.

Nearby is the landscaped 4½-acre (1.8 ha) Waterfront Park, with a long boardwalk and views across Lynn Harbor and Massachusetts Bay. Lynn can be reached via highways 1A and 107, and air service is available at Boston's Logan International Airport. Map ref: page 222 F5

MARTHA'S VINEYARD

A picturesque island between Vineyard Sound and Nantucket Sound, "the Vineyard," as it's often called, is one of "the islands." Seven miles (11 km) south of Cape Cod, it has beaches, lighthouses, colonial history, quaint cottages, proximity to Nantucket Island and about 11,700 residents. It is a longstanding, and pricey, resort destination for tourists and all types of vacationers, from celebrities and summertime renters to daytrippers.

It is thought that the first islanders came here before it was an island—before melting glaciers at the end of the last ice age raised the sea level enough to separate it from the mainland. It's had various names, but the one that has lasted was given by English Captain Bartholomew Gosnold, who is said to have named it for its native wild grapes and a female relative, perhaps a daughter or his mother-in-law. Some contend that the island's name was originally Martin's Vineyard.

The island was inhabited by Native Americans long before English farmers and shepherds arrived from the Boston area in 1642. The island provided safe harbor and supplies to sailing ships rounding Cape Cod through the nineteenth century. The largest of its six towns, Edgartown, is the site of the original settlement and

Repairing lobster traps, Menemsha, Martha's Vineyard.

a former whaling center. Commercial fishing continues at the village of Menemsha, and recreational fishing, including charter fishing, is popular from the island as well. Four large harbors make the Vineyard popular for sailing. Vineyard Haven is the only year-round ferry port. The island has two privately owned campgrounds, in Vineyard Haven and Oak Bluffs.

In addition to its popular, free public beaches there are some that are private. Other attractions include windsurfing, yachting, shopping at Oak Bluffs, viewing the colorful clay cliffs of Gay Head, The Vineyard Museum in Edgartown, and West Tisbury's Mayhew Chapel and Native American Burial Ground. In summer, many visitors leave their cars on the mainland and ride shuttle buses, bicycles, or mopeds around the picturesque island, which measures 20 miles (32 km) west to east and 10 miles (16 km) north to south. (Bicycles, mopeds and cars can be rented.) Particularly popular for pedaling is the narrow Edgartown-Oak Bluffs State Beach Park.

The island has an air service at Dukes County/Martha's Vineyard Airport. Car and passenger ferries operate daily from Woods Hole and Vineyard Haven year-round. In summer they also operate between Oak Bluffs and Woods Hole, Falmouth, Nantucket and Hyannis, and between Vineyard Haven and New Bedford. A ferry also shuttles between Martha's Vineyard and neighboring Chappaquiddick Island. Map ref: page 222 F8

NANTUCKET ISLAND

Another of "the islands" in Nantucket Sound south of Cape Cod, affluent and expensive Nantucket Island lies about 30 miles (48 km) from the mainland and 15 miles (24 km) southeast of Martha's Vineyard. It is smaller, less populous and more exclusive than its neighbor, but its Old New England maritime charm, particularly the quaint town of Nantucket, also makes it the destination of throngs of summertime visitors who come by plane, ferry, or yacht.

The crescent-shaped, sandy, and undulating island is about 14 miles (23 km) long, and ranges from 3 to 6 miles (5 to 10 km) wide. About 6,000 people live on this old seafaring isle. The town of Nantucket, with its cobblestone main street, narrow lanes, Quaker-style homes and period storefronts, is listed on the National Register of Historic Places. The entire 57-square-mile (148-sq-km) island is a National Historic Landmark, and comprehensive building restrictions ensure that even new properties will look old and quaint.

The island, along with three smaller privately owned adjacent islands, comprises all of Nantucket County. Its small size lends itself to exploration by foot, bike, moped, or shuttle bus. Lodgings abound, all of them expensive. Camping

is not only unavailable, it's strictly illegal.

As with Martha's Vineyard, Nantucket Island was home to Native Americans long before European settlers arrived in 1659. The settlers initially made their livings by raising sheep and farming, which stripped much of the once-wooded island of its natural coverings, and left the land exposed to the elements. Having depleted the land, the settlers turned to whaling, and after that tourism, now the mainstay of its economy.

With its numerous weathered cottages, historic homes, rose gardens, cozy inns, backroads, bike paths and beaches, there's no doubt why summertime visitors spill from ferries by the thousands for a day, weekend, or longer. Attractions and amenities abound for walkers, shoppers, bird watchers, anglers, sailors, or New England history buffs, though most of them come with a hefty price tag.

The town of Nantucket has four bicycle paths, ranging from hilly to flat to winding and varying in length from 2½ miles to 6 miles (4 to 10 km). Bike and moped rentals are readily available.

Seamen's Bethel, New Bedford, features in Herman Melville's sprawling whaling epic Moby Dick.

Sculpture outside the New Bedford Whaling Museum.

Handicapped-accessible shuttle buses, equipped to carry bicycles, transport visitors and residents around the island and to the public beaches in summer. Cars can be rented, but are considered unnecessary and are discouraged.

Popular places to visit include the Nantucket Whaling Museum, located inside a former candle-works and whale oil refinery; the Oldest House, a saltbox-style home built on Sunset Hill in 1686; the Peter Foulger Museum and Research Center, which depicts local history through exhibits of various artifacts; and the Brant Point, Sankaty Head, and Great Point lighthouses.

Access to the island is either by air or by boat. A daily ferry service is available year-round from Hyannis, and from Martha's Vineyard from early May to late October. Nantucket Memorial Airport has a range of commercial flights that connect to major mainland airports.
Map ref: page 222 G8

NEW BEDFORD

Settled about 1640 as part of Dartmouth, New Bedford expanded considerably after 1760 as its location—at the mouth of the Acushnet River, on Buzzards Bay across from Cape Cod—enabled it to grow into the country's dominant whaling port by 1820s. But prosperity based on whaling ended

when petroleum replaced whale oil for lighting and lubrication in the second half of the nineteenth century. The textile industry increased and continued to support the town into the 1920s, along with cod fishing. The latter became dominant after the textile industry collapsed, but now fishing boats have been dry-docked by the federal government's closure of severely depleted fisheries, leaving the city with a struggling economy.

Today, the city of almost 100,000 memorializes its seafaring heritage at the New Bedford Whaling Museum, one of the largest of its kind. Visitors can board a fully-rigged 89-foot (27-m) half-scale replica of the whaling bark *Lagoda* daily. Its history is also preserved in the New Bedford National Historical Park, a 13-square-block area of cobblestone streets and buildings dating as far back as the early 1800s.

Seamen's Bethel was dedicated in 1832 as a non-denominational whaler's chapel, with a ship's bow for a pulpit. Herman Melville, who himself sailed from New Bedford for the Pacific aboard a whaler in 1847, referred to it in his novel *Moby Dick*. Still a working church, it is open to visitors, who are asked to make donations.

New Bedford can be reached via Hwy 140 or I-195, or by air through New Bedford Regional Airport. A passenger ferry shuttles to Martha's Vineyard.
Map ref: page 222 F8

Plymouth Rock, landing place of the Pilgrims in 1620.

American currency, depicts the history of American paper-making. Pittsfield is also credited with holding the first country fair, on the village green in 1810.

Camping, hiking, and many other outdoor recreation opportunities can be found at Pittsfield State Forest, and at Onota and Pontoo-suc Lakes, between Pittsfield and the New York state line. South of Pittsfield, in the town of Len-ox, is Tanglewood, summer home of the Boston Symphony Orchestra.

Pittsfield is just east of New York, and north of I-90 via US-20/7.

Map ref: page 222 B5

PITTSFIELD

A relatively high city at 1,026 feet (313 m) above sea level, Pittsfield, in the Berkshire Hills of western Massachusetts, sits at the head-waters of the Housatonic River. Settled in 1761, it was named for the British statesman William Pitt. Pittsfield grew from an agricultural community to an industrial center that attracted immigrant workers from many countries early in the twentieth century and now num-bers about 46,300 people. It has long been a center of plastics research and manufacturing, particularly for General Electric.

Between 1850 and 1863, writer Herman Melville and his family occupied the nearby home called Arrowhead, where he completed his classic novel *Moby Dick*. The home is open for tours daily from Memorial Day through October 31. Also nearby is the Hancock Shaker Village, for 170 years (until 1960) a 1,200-acre (486-ha) religious community of the United Society of Believers in Christ's Second Appearing. Tours of the village are available.

In nearby Dalton, the Crane Museum of Papermaking, owned by Crane & Co., the sole sup-plier of the paper used to make

PLYMOUTH

After exploring the shore of Cape Cod from the site of today's Pro-vincetown, the Pilgrims anchored the *Mayflower* at Plymouth Bay, an offshoot of Cape Cod Bay, and came ashore in December 1620. It was the first permanent Euro-pean settlement in New England. Almost half of the original 102 Pilgrims who'd sailed from Ply-mouth, England, died during their first winter. Today's traditional Thanksgiving Day feast recalls the celebration the survivors held in 1621. Plymouth Colony prospered afterwards, and was merged with Massachusetts Bay Colony in 1691. The Pilgrims' landing is commemo-rated each December 21 during Forefathers' Day.

Southeast of Boston, Plymouth is a popular tourist destination and a city of 45,600 residents. A major attraction is Plimoth Plantation, a reproduction of the Pilgrims' village as it appeared in 1627. The Plantation is open April through November. Visitors can also tour the *Mayflower II*, a replica of a seventeenth-century sailing ship. Burial Hill, the site of a fort built in 1622–23, holds the remains of William Bradford, a Pilgrim leader and Plymouth Colony governor,

who died in 1657. Interestingly, Plymouth is also the site of the Cranberry World Visitor Center, which includes working bogs (where the cranberries are grown) and information on the cultivation and use of cranberries.

By car, Plymouth can be reached via Hwy 3 from Boston or Cape Cod. Train and bus services are available from Boston, although the train station in Plymouth is located about 2 miles (3 km) north of downtown.

Map ref: page 222 F7

PROVINCETOWN

The Pilgrims first set foot on North American soil at Provincetown, on the isolated northern tip of Cape Cod, in 1620 before exploring Cape Cod Bay and establishing New England's first permanent European settlement across the bay at Plymouth. Visitors can see a tall granite monument on High Pole Hill that commemorates both the landing and the signing of the Mayflower Compact, which empowered the Pilgrims to enact laws for the general good of their settlement—the colonies' first agree-ment to govern by the consent of the governed.

P'town, as it is nicknamed, has long been an artistic community, drawing painters, writers, and other creative sorts from all over the country to its oceanside Bohemian lifestyle. It still remains a fishing port with a permanent population of about 3,400 residents, but in summer it becomes a busy tourist mecca. Among its attractions are miles of nearby beaches (including Cape Cod National Seashore), shops, boutiques, and art galleries. Stelwagen Bank is a prime whale-watching site from mid-April through October.

Lodging options range from up-scale resort hotels, condominiums, and romantic inns to two commer-cial campgrounds. Provincetown marks the northern terminus of US-6. Ferries shuttle passengers between Boston and Provincetown in summer, and a year-round bus service is also available from Bos-ton. Cape Air provides a regional air service from Provincetown Municipal Airport.

Map ref: page 222 G6

Visitors can tour the **Mayflower II** at Plimoth Plantation, Plymouth.

QUINCY

Settled in 1625 just a few miles southeast of Boston, on Quincy (pronounced QUINN-zee) Bay, this suburb of 85,000 people is immersed in the early political history of the United States. It was part of Braintree until it became a separate entity in 1792 and was named for John Quincy, a colonial legislator and resident. It was home to four generations of the Adams family, and was the birthplace of two presidents—the second, John Adams; and the sixth, his son John Quincy Adams. John Hancock, president of the Continental Congress and the first to sign the Declaration of Independence, was born here in 1737.

The 14-acre (5.7-ha) Adams National Historic Site encompasses 11 structures, including the house where John Adams was born in 1735 and where he wrote his first letters to his future wife, Abigail Smith; the couple's nearby house, where John Quincy Adams was born in 1767 and where the Massachusetts Constitution was drafted; the Old House (1731), home to four generations of Adamses. At the United First Parish Church, the remains of both presidents and their wives are entombed in the family crypt.

Passes for the Adams National Historic Site can be purchased at the National Park service visitor center in town. A free trolley bus provides transportation to the site.

Quincy, a financial and industrial center, is known for shipbuilding, and was a major granite quarrying center in the eighteenth and nineteenth centuries. In 1826 the first commercial railroad in the country was built here to transport granite for the Bunker Hill Monument in Boston.

Boston's Logan International Airport is the nearest airport with a commercial airline service. By car, access is via I-93 and Hwy 128, or Hwy 3. Commuter train service is available from Boston.
Map ref: page 222 F6

SALEM

Although the town of Danvers (then Salem Village), just to the north of today's Salem, was the primary site of the witchcraft hysteria of 1692, Salem has strong ties

The Basketball Hall of Fame in Springfield is a must for sports lovers.

to the dark affair that was sparked by the bizarre behavior of two young girls. The "Witch House," home of Jonathan Corwin, one of the infamous trial judges, still stands at the corner of North and Essex streets. Built in 1642, it was the site of the preliminary witchcraft examinations. By the time the panic over alleged witches had spent itself, 19 people had been hanged on Salem's Gallows Hill, and one man had been crushed with stone weights.

Salem is a coastal city of about 38,100 residents, situated 16 miles (26 km) northeast of Boston on Salem Bay. By the end of the eighteenth century it had become an important port, and by the mid-nineteenth century it had become a manufacturing center. Its modern economy is based on tourism and professional services.

Writer Nathaniel Hawthorne was born here in 1804. His birthplace is part of The House of the Seven Gables Historic Site, which includes the house (built in 1688) that he featured in his famous tale. The Peabody Essex Museum is one of New England's largest, and is the oldest continuously operating museum in the country. Its extensive collections include 552 original documents

pertaining to the witchcraft trials, as well as 30 galleries, a research library and 11 historic houses. Additional attractions at Salem include a Pioneer Village—Salem 1630, and the Salem Witch Museum, while Salem Whale Watch offers whale-watching tours. The city's maritime history can be explored at the New England Pirate Museum and Salem Maritime National Historic Site.

Salem can be reached by car on a number of highways north from Boston. Ferry, bus, and commuter rail services from Boston to Salem are available as well.
Map ref: page 222 F5

SPRINGFIELD

With 157,000 residents, Springfield is Massachusetts' third-largest city. Located in western Massachusetts on the east bank of the Connecticut River in the Pioneer Valley, it has emerged from a long and diverse manufacturing history to become an insurance, banking, telecommunications, higher education, and transportation hub. Puritans arrived here in 1636, establishing a settlement called Agawam. First located on the west bank of the river, the settlement was soon relocated to the east bank and was renamed Springfield in 1640. As it evolved into a manufacturing center, plants turned out a wide range of products, from guns to board games, bicycles and motorcycles to airplanes. The first successful gasoline-powered automobile to be produced in the United States, the Duryea, was built here in 1893.

In 1787, Daniel Shays led an abortive attack on a federal arsenal here during an anti-tax uprising known as Shays Rebellion. The city's long history as a center of firearms research and manufacturing is depicted at the Springfield Armory National Historic Site. Established in 1794, the armory had produced more than nine million guns by the time it closed in 1968. Among them were the famous Springfield rifle and the Garand semiautomatic (M1) rifle.

Teacher James Naismith's development of basketball at Springfield in 1891 is remembered at the Basketball Hall of Fame. Children's author Theodor Seuss Geisel, also known as Dr Seuss, also grew up here, and is the subject of the Dr Seuss Museum. The Indian Motorcycle Museum recalls the period

Springfield is a thriving business and higher education city in western Massachusetts.

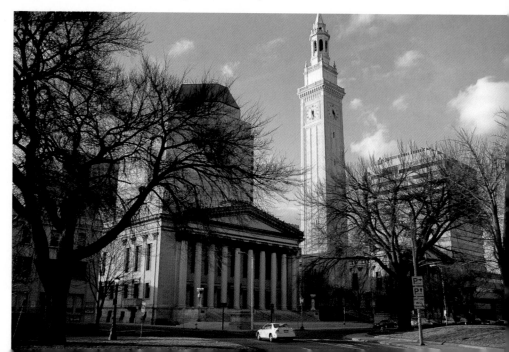

from 1901 to 1953 when the famous bikes were built here. Another attraction is the Springfield Library and Museums, with facilities devoted to history, science, and art. The city is also home to Western New England College, Springfield College, American International College and a community college. Springfield can be reached by car via I-90 and I-91.
Map ref: page 222 C6

STOCKBRIDGE

This western Massachusetts town of 2,400 is located in the Berkshire Hills, on the Housatonic River just south of the Massachusetts Turnpike (I-90). If it seems to evoke familiar views of a simpler, bygone time in America, that could be because the illustrator Norman Rockwell lived here and used it as a model. He died in 1978. The Norman Rockwell Museum at Stockbridge is home to more than 500 of his paintings and drawings. Chesterwood, the studio and summer home of early twentieth-century sculptor Daniel Chester French, maintained by the National Trust For Historic Preservations is open from late May to October. Tanglewood, the summer home of the Boston Symphony Orchestra and the site of the annual Berkshire Music Festival, is nearby.

Other attractions are the Berkshire Botanical Garden; Merwin House (1825), with its collection of European and American furniture; Mission House (1739), the home of John Sergeant, the first missionary to the Stockbridge Native Americans; and the Indian Burial Ground on Main Street.
Map ref: page 222 B6

STURBRIDGE

The modern city of almost 8,000 residents isn't the reason for coming to this south-central Massachusetts locale. The real attraction is Old Sturbridge Village, a re-created 1830s New England village. Spread over 200 acres (81 ha) of rolling fields and farmlands, Old Sturbridge Village is a living history museum comprised of more than 40 restored buildings relocated from around New England. The faithfully reproduced exhibits and activities are typical of an early nineteenth-century New England

hamlet—homes, a tin shop, a bank, printing office, meeting house, schoolhouse, even a law office. There are water-powered mills, craft shops, a blacksmith and cooper shop, even a functioning farm. The village also holds special events, including a Thanksgiving Day celebration.

Old Sturbridge Village is open daily April to December and weekends only in January to mid-February. The village is located on Hwy 20 in Sturbridge, at the junction of I-84 and the Massachusetts Turnpike (I-90). Parking is free, but there is an entrance fee for all but children age 6 and under. Tickets are good for two consecutive days. By car, the village is about an hour from Boston, 45 minutes from Hartford and 3 hours from New York City. The village can be reached by bus from Worcester, Boston, New York and Hartford.
Map ref: page 222 D6

WEYMOUTH

Established in 1635, this residential suburb on Hingham Bay, southeast of Boston, was the birthplace (1744) of Abigail Smith Adams, wife of President John Adams, the second president of the United States, and the mother of John Quincy Adams, the sixth president. The restored house, built in 1685, is at North and Norton streets. Guided tours are available Tuesday to Sunday, July 1 to Labor Day. Weymouth, a city of 54,100, can be reached by car via Route 3A.

The delightful farm at Old Sturbridge Village is always popular with children.

At Old Sturbridge Village, costumed "villagers" re-create a bygone lifestyle.

The Adams National Historic Site is located in nearby Quincy.
Map ref: page 222 F6

WORCESTER

With almost 170,000 residents, the so-called "Heart of the Commonwealth" is the state's second-largest city, located 45 miles (72 km) west of Boston on hills overlooking the Blackstone Valley. English settlers arrived here in the 1670s, naming the settlement Quinsigamond Plantation. The name was changed to Worcester in 1684. It has a long industrial history going back to the 1828 opening of the Blackstone Canal, which linked the city to Providence, Rhode Island. From 1906 to 1961, the city was home

to the Worcester Lunch Car Company, which produced more than 650 diners. Worcester is still known for its selection of vintage diners.

The city now is a financial, commercial, industrial, cultural, and educational hub for central Massachusetts. Its centers of higher education include Worcester Polytechnic Institute, Worcester State College, Assumption College, the College of the Holy Cross, the University of Massachusetts Medical Center, and Clark University, where rocket pioneer Robert H. Goddard was a professor. Goddard fired his first rocket at nearby Auburn in 1926. Worcester is also home to many biotechnology firms.

Places of interest include the Worcester Art Museum, which has more than 35,000 objects representing 5,000 years of art and culture; the Higgins Armory Museum, which has exhibits of weapons and armor from medieval and Renaissance Europe, feudal Japan, and ancient Greece and Rome; the Ecotarium, a 60-acre (23-ha) environmental museum and wildlife center; and the Worcester Historical Museum.

A rail service is available between Boston and Worcester and an air service is available at Worcester Municipal Airport. Several interstate highways and many state highways access Worcester as well.
Map ref: page 222 D6

NEW HAMPSHIRE

The state that would "live free or die," as its motto proclaims, was the first of the 13 colonies to adopt a provisional state constitution and government, thus breaking with Great Britain. It later cast the decisive vote to ratify the US Constitution. Today, although home to about 1.2 million people, it ranks 40th in population, yet it wields enormous political influence nationally every four years as the first state to hold a presidential primary election.

New Hampshire covers only 9,283 square miles (24,043 sq km) but has the highest and most rugged mountains in the Northeast. It also has one of the country's largest freshwater lakes. Its rounded mountains, boulders, and numerous lakes are reminders of the region's glacial history.

The Androscoggin River in northern New Hampshire is particularly lovely during the colorful fall months.

The land was inhabited by Algonquian-speaking native groups when Europeans first arrived in the seventeenth century, but their populations were decimated when European diseases, to which the Native Americans had no resistance, spread rapidly through New England. English Captain Martin Pring made the first recorded visit in 1603; the first settlements followed 20 years later.

The state has short, humid summers and long, cold winters. It is bordered on the north by Quebec, on the east by Maine and the Atlantic Ocean, on the south by Massachusetts, and on the west by the Connecticut River, which flows south from its headwaters in northern New Hampshire to form the 250-mile (402-km) boundary with Vermont. Its 13-mile (21-km) coastline includes the estuary of the Piscataqua River, at Portsmouth, ensuring that seafaring, trade, and shipbuilding have all played important roles in the state's development.

Lumber, shipbuilding, fishing, agriculture, and maritime trade were mainstays during the eighteenth century. Now technology and light industries—and the absence of state sales and income taxes—bolster its economy, while tourists are drawn to its outdoor recreation opportunities, attractive covered bridges, and appealing fall colors.

State New Hampshire
State motto Live Free or Die
State flag Adopted 1909 (modified 1931)
Capital Concord
Population 1,235,786
Total area (land and water) 9,283 square miles (24,043 sq km)
Land area 8,969 square miles (23,230 sq km)
New Hampshire is the 44th-largest state in size
Origin of name Named for the English county of Hampshire
Nickname The Granite State
Abbreviations NH (postal), N.H.
State bird Purple finch
State flower Purple lilac
State tree White birch
Entered the Union June 21, 1788 as the ninth state

Places in
NEW HAMPSHIRE

CONCORD

New Hampshire's capital has grown from a trading post established in 1659 on the Merrimack River to a city of 37,850. It is the seat of Merrimack County, and the state's center for politics, finance, technology industries, commerce and transportation.

Located in the south-central part of New Hampshire, the settlement began as a land grant made in 1725 by the Massachusetts Bay Colony with the original name of Rumford. Commerce increased due to its riverside setting, and in 1741 a dispute began between Massachusetts and New Hampshire over which region had jurisdiction over Rumford. New Hampshire won, and in 1765 the town was renamed Concord to commemorate the unity of its people during the dispute. It was made the state capital in 1808.

In 1827 wheelwright Lewis Downing and coachbuilder J. Stephens Abbot launched a stagecoach factory. The Concord stagecoaches built here became a key means of travel in the American West through much of the nineteenth century. The town was also home to NASA's first civilian astronaut, Concord High School social studies teacher Christa McAuliffe, who died in the 1986 explosion of the space shuttle

Challenger. A planetarium in Concord is named in her memory, and is open to the public.

Visitors can also take in the Museum of New Hampshire History, which includes an early Native American canoe and an original Concord coach. Pierce Manse was the home and law office of former President Franklin Pierce from 1842 to 1848. Concord's historic State House, on Main Street, is said to be the oldest (1819) in the country in which a legislature still meets in its original chambers.

Near Concord are quarries where the state's famous white granite was mined for construction of the Library of Congress in Washington DC. A few miles north of Concord is Canterbury Shaker Village, which was established in 1792 and is now a museum and historic site.

Recreational opportunities include boating on the Merrimack River and upstream lakes, which also offer fishing and swimming. Concord can be reached by car on I-89/93/393 and bus services are available. Air links are provided by Concord Municipal Airport.
Map ref: page 222 E4

DOVER

Founded in 1623 on the falls of southeastern New Hampshire's Cocheco River, Dover, the seat

The impressive State Capitol building in Concord was built in 1819.

New Hampshire's lakes and rivers provide ample opportunity for fishing.

of Strafford County, is said to be New Hampshire's oldest permanent settlement, and the seventh oldest in the nation. It was settled by fishermen and traders who worked their way from the coastal site of Portsmouth, around Great Bay and up the Piscataqua River.

Its early economy was centered on fishing, farming, and shipbuilding. In the nineteenth century those ventures gave way to mills and factories. Now home to about 26,500 residents, it's still an industrial city, but it also has a high-technology component.

Dover can be reached by car via Hwy 16 northwest of Portsmouth. It is also serviced by rail on the Boston, Massachusetts, to Portland, Maine, route.
Map ref: page 222 F4

EXETER

Like New England itself, this quaint town of just 9,560 residents was founded in 1638 due to religious dissent. The Reverend John Wheelwright and his followers settled here, on the Squamscott River just 10 miles (16 km) from the

Atlantic, after they were expelled from the Puritan Massachusetts Bay Colony situated in Boston for supporting religious reformer Anne Hutchinson.

Its riverside location proved well suited for the construction of a mill. The river also provided access to Great Bay, the Piscataqua River and the seaport at Portsmouth. When the Revolutionary War broke out, the capital of New Hampshire was moved from Portsmouth to Exeter (the capital was later moved to Concord in 1808).

In 1781 Phillips Exeter Academy, now one of the nation's most prestigious preparatory schools, was founded in Exeter. Another place of interest is the American Independence Museum in the restored 1700s Ladd-Gilman House on Governor Lane. Early New Hampshire Governor John Taylor Gilman lived here during his 14 terms as chief executive. The museum also includes Folsom Tavern, built in 1775.

Exeter can be reached by car via Hwy 101 (also known as the Exeter-Hampton Expressway).
Map ref: page 222 F4

Local store, Jackson—with all this snow, it looks too cold for ice cream.

HANOVER

This western New Hampshire town of 9,530 residents, east of the Connecticut River in the hilly region between New Hampshire and Vermont, is dominated by the Ivy League Dartmouth College. This was founded in 1769 by the Reverend Eleazar Wheelock under a charter from King George III to establish a school "for the education and instruction of Youth of the Indian Tribes in this Land ... and also of English Youth and any others." The town itself was granted a charter in 1761, and the first permanent settlers arrived from Connecticut four years later.

Prominent among the campus sights is Dartmouth Row, which consists of four white Georgian buildings including a structure dating back to 1784. Other attractions include the 1928 red-brick Baker Memorial Library (which contains nearly one million volumes, and murals painted by the early twentieth-century Mexican artist Jose Clemente Orozco), the Hood Museum of Art, and the Hopkins Center for the Performing Arts.

Hanover is located at the junction of Hwy 120 and 10, about 6 miles (10 km) north of Lebanon. The city of Lebanon is serviced by a municipal airport. A bus service is also available.

Map ref: page 222 D2

JACKSON

Tucked into the White Mountains of eastern New Hampshire, this 200-year-old village of 700 residents has been drawing visitors to its wooded hills, rolling farmlands, steepled churches, and waterfalls since artists discovered it in the mid-1800s. First called Madbury, the village's name was changed in 1800 to Adams, after President John Adams. In 1829 the name was changed again to honor President Andrew Jackson.

Local farmers housed the early-day tourists until hotels were built to accommodate visitors arriving by train. In 1876 Charles Austin Broughton and his son Frank built a covered bridge over the Ellis River, one of only 55 of its type still in existence. Nicknamed "Honeymoon Bridge," newlyweds have made a tradition of being photographed there.

Visitors today come for Jackson's gabled inns, horse-drawn sleighs in winter, and New England charm. Jackson is the site of New England's oldest ski area, Black Mountain, opened in 1936. Other seasonal activities include hiking and biking in the White Mountains, cross-country skiing, snowshoeing, and fly-fishing.

The Conway Scenic Railroad, based in nearby North Conway, offers trips through the area from the end of June to mid-October.

Jackson lies west of the New Hampshire–Maine state line in Mt Washington Valley, just north of Hwy 302. It can be reached from North Woodstock via the scenic Kancamagus Hwy (Route 112), or Route 16 north from Portsmouth. A bus service is available.

Map ref: page 220 F9

KEENE

An old textile mill town on the Ashuelot River in southwestern New Hampshire, Keene is a city of 22,800 people located amid rolling wooded hills and river valleys. It is the seat of Cheshire County and the site of Keene State College.

The town was incorporated in 1753, and was named for British diplomat Sir Benjamin Keene. In 1770, the first meeting of the trustees of Hanover's Dartmouth College was held in Keene's Wyman Tavern, which was built in 1762. In 1775, the tavern served as the staging point for Minutemen traveling to fight the British after the Revolutionary War was sparked at Lexington and Concord in Massachusetts. The town center is marked by a gazebo and the steeple of the United Church of Christ, erected in 1787.

Keene entered the Industrial Revolution with the construction of the river-powered Faulkner and Colony Woolen Mill in 1838. Production ceased in 1953, and many of the former mill buildings are now shops and restaurants. Various light industries and insurance companies now bring diversity to the local economy.

Keene's Halloween Pumpkin Festival in late October is particularly popular. Other attractions include the Horatio Colony House Museum (1806) and the Monadnock Children's Museum. Visitors are also drawn to four nineteenth-century covered bridges in the vicinity of Swanzey, south of Keene. The annual Cheshire Fair, a traditional country fair, is held in Swanzey in early August.

The city of Keene lies east of the Vermont state line and north of the Massachusetts state line, at the junction of Hwys 9, 10, and 12. Air services are provided at Dillant-Hopkins Airport. A bus service is also available.

Map ref: page 222 D4

The town of Jackson boasts this quaint covered bridge, which was built over the Ellis River in 1876.

LACONIA

Home to about 17,000 residents, this central New Hampshire city, the seat of Belknap county, is in New Hampshire's Lakes Region. Nicknamed "City on the Lakes," the city limits reach into Paugus Bay and lakes Winnisquam and Opechee. However, these bodies of water are humbled by nearby Lake Winnipesaukee, at 72 square miles (186 sq km) the state's largest lake and a major resort area.

Since Laconia was settled in 1761, it has taken advantage of its proximity to water. A slow-growing community into the nineteenth century, its economy and population expanded after 1848 when railroad lines reached the town, then called Meredith Bridge. Water power helped Laconia become a major producer of textiles and clothing. It is now a popular winter and summer outdoor recreation area, although it still has some light industries.

Every June, Laconia and the surrounding area become a mecca for thousands of motorcyclists from all over the country, particularly Harley-Davidson riders. Enthusiasts arrive for Motorcycle Week, also known as The Nationals, centered on contests at the New Hampshire International Speedway, south of Laconia on Hwy 106.

The Amoskeag Mills in Manchester.

Laconia Municipal Airport provides a regional air service, and a bus service is also available.
Map ref: page 222 E3

LAKE WINNIPESAUKEE

New Hampshire's largest lake, a relic of the last ice age, attracts thousands of freshwater recreation enthusiasts each year. Lying just south of the White Mountains, it is surrounded by wooded hills. It covers 72 square miles (186 sq km), includes 235 islands and is as deep as 300 feet (92 m).

From boating to bass fishing, basking on a beach, swimming, water skiing or the 182-mile (293-km) scenic drive around its perimeter, "Winni" has a great deal to offer visitors—except solitude during its busy Memorial Day to Labor Day (end of May to early September) season. Particularly popular is Weirs Beach.

The lake can be reached by many highways, including I-93 from Boston. Laconia Municipal Airport provides regional air services, and a bus service is available.
Map ref: page 222 E3

MANCHESTER

With over 102,000 residents, this southern New Hampshire city astride the Merrimack River is the state's largest. During presidential election season, when New Hampshire holds the nation's first primary election, the city seems like the center of US politics as presidential hopefuls "press the flesh."

Manchester evolved from an eighteenth-century fishing and lumbering town to a nineteenth-century center for water-powered textile manufacturing. Incorporated as Derryfield in 1751, it was renamed after Manchester, England, in 1810, when cotton mills began churning out cloth. The factories eventually covered more than 8 million square feet (743,200 sq m), stretched for 1 mile (1.6 km), and shipped nearly 5 million yards (4,572,000 m) of cloth a week. The Amoskeag Mills, chartered in 1831, were once the largest in the world. The last of the mills shut down in 1935, the victim of cheaper labor in the South, and aging equipment.

The city is now New Hampshire's industrial, financial, and commercial hub, and home to four colleges, a campus of the University of New Hampshire, the New Hampshire Institute of Art, and a junior college. The Currier Gallery of Art houses European and American pieces from the thirteenth century to the present.

Manchester can be reached on a number of highways, including I-93. The city has its own airport and is served by several bus lines.
Map ref: page 222 E4

MT WASHINGTON

Rising 6,288 feet (1,918 m) above sea level, the granite summit of Mt

Lake Winnipesaukee, situated in the state's center, is popular with tourists.

Washington is the highest point in the northeastern United States. It dominates the Presidential Range of the White Mountains in northeastern New Hampshire. The summit can be reached by a hiking trail (the Appalachian National Scenic Trail crosses its upper slopes), by the historic (1869), coal-fired, first-of-its-kind Mt Washington Cog Railway. It is a 3-hour round-trip from Bretton Wood, or by car on the mostly paved Mt Washington Auto Road, which branches west from Hwy 16 south of Gorham. It takes at least two hours to drive to the summit because of the steep grades and sharp curves. Some hardy folks even bike to the top. Guided tours are available.

At the windy peak, first reached in 1642, the weather can change quickly from warm and sunny to stormy and Arctic cold. The world's highest wind speed— 231 mph (372 kph)—was recorded here on April 12, 1934. A 59-acre (24-ha) state park, weather station, and information center are located at the top. If conditions allow, visitors have a panoramic vista across the White Mountains and four states to the Atlantic Ocean and Canada.

Depending on the weather, the road is usually open from May until October, when it closes for winter. The annual Mt Washington Road Race, a footrace to the top of the mountain, is held in mid-June. Late June brings the Mt Washington Hillclimb, the country's oldest sports car hill climb.
Map ref: page 220 E9

NASHUA

With its jumble of malls and absence of a state sales tax, New Hampshire's second-largest city (population 82,285), the seat of Hillsborough County, has something of a bordertown shopper's feel to it. In addition to commuters who travel the highways northwest of Boston each day, Bay State bargain hunters stream up Hwy 3 to Nashua's malls and shops.

Sited where the Nashua River flows into the Merrimack, Nashua entered the Industrial Revolution in the nineteenth century by building water-powered cotton textile mills. Mill production ended after World War II, but the city has since diversified its economy. Now the textiles most visitors focus on are in the retail stores. *Money* magazine has twice selected southern New Hampshire's "gate city," one of the fastest-growing in New England, as the best place to live in America

The city is a medical center, and its light industries produce computer and paper products, electronics, chemicals, and beer. It is also the location of two educational institutions: Rivier College and Daniel Webster College. Access to Nashua is easy by car (Hwy 3) or bus.
Map ref: page 222 E5

PORTSMOUTH

Hip and urbane Portsmouth has transformed itself since the 1980s from a bygone maritime trading

High-quality, full-flavored beer is produced at the Portsmouth Brewery.

hub and Pentagon dependent, to a cosmopolitan port city of nearly 28,000 residents that competes culturally with Boston, which is just an hour to the south.

Long a struggling Atlantic port city at the mouth of the Piscataqua River, Portland was hit in the 1970s by the declining importance of the Portland Naval Shipyard (across the harbor in Maine), and again in the early 1990s when the federal government closed nearby Pease Air Force Base. Revitalization efforts since the 1980s, however, have reversed the city's decline, and it is now a cultural center noted for its restaurants, cafés, import shops, and harbor views.

The first settlers arrived at the estuary of the Piscataqua River early in the 1600s. In 1630 a group of settlers landed on the river bank, found it covered with wild strawberries and christened the spot Strawbery Banke. A 10-acre (4-ha) museum of the same name

preserves a historic waterfront neighborhood with more than 45 buildings constructed between 1695 and 1955.

Strawbery Banke grew from a fishing and farming village to a shipbuilding and trading center that took advantage of inland forests for masts and lumber, and an excellent harbor for far-flung trade. In 1653 the town was renamed Portsmouth.

Portsmouth was New Hampshire's colonial capital, both politically and commercially. By 1700 it had become one of the most important cities in the colonies. At the outbreak of the Revolutionary War, however, the capital was moved to Exeter. In the nineteenth century, Portsmouth harbor's trade and commerce was undermined by inland railroads and ports at larger cities. The city continued to decline during the twentieth century but the slide has now been notably reversed.

Besides its shopping, culinary, and cultural attractions, visitors can take in the Richard Jackson House (1664), the state's oldest structure, the Children's Museum of Portsmouth, harbor cruises, the Portsmouth Harbor Trail, (a walking tour through Portsmouth history) and the John Paul Jones House (1758), where the Continental Navy captain stayed in 1777 and 1781.

Portsmouth can be reached on I-95 north from Boston and is served by several bus lines.
Map ref: page 222 F4

WHITE MOUNTAIN NATIONAL FOREST

With more than 750,000 acres (303,750 ha), White Mountain National Forest is the largest alpine region east of the Rocky Mountains and south of Canada. It is located primarily in northern New Hampshire, although a portion extends into Maine. It encompasses the White Mountains and the northern reach of the Appalachian chain, and is the most rugged and heavily forested region of the state. Forty-eight peaks in the White Mountain National Forest exceed 4,000 feet (1,220 m), and in the mountains' Presidential Range, nine peaks rise above 5,000 feet (1,525 m).

Being within easy driving range of the Northeast's population centers, the forest attracts more visitors each year than Yellowstone and Yosemite national parks combined, making overuse an environmental concern. A parking permit is required to park in the national forest.

Attractions include back-country and alpine skiing, camping, trout fishing, fall foliage tours, snowmobiling, mountain biking, hunting, and canoeing. Hikers are drawn to 1,200 miles (1931 km) of trails, including the Appalachian National Scenic Trail. The 34-mile (55-km) east–west Kancamagus Scenic Byway (Hwy 112) winds between Conway and Lincoln, through some of New Hampshire's most unspoiled scenery.

Information centers are in Lincoln and Campton, and at the Saco Ranger Station at the east end of Hwy 112. The national forest can be reached on I-93 or Hwy 16, and a bus service is available to the village of Jackson.
Map ref: page 222 E2

New Hampshire's cool climate is ideal for maple trees. During fall, forests blaze with orange, red, and gold maple foliage.

RHODE ISLAND

The "State of Rhode Island and Providence Plantations" is the smallest state in America, but it has the longest official name. Between Connecticut, Massachusetts, and the Atlantic Ocean, it is about 48 miles (77 km) long and 42 miles (68 km) wide, and covers just 1,231 square miles (3,188 sq km). It includes many islands, one of which is in fact Rhode Island, but most of the state is in mainland New England.

Its population, about 988,000, ranks 43rd, but Rhode Island is the second most densely populated state, after

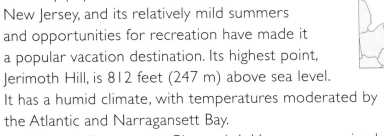

New Jersey, and its relatively mild summers and opportunities for recreation have made it a popular vacation destination. Its highest point, Jerimoth Hill, is 812 feet (247 m) above sea level. It has a humid climate, with temperatures moderated by the Atlantic and Narragansett Bay.

When Italian seaman Giovanni da Verrazzano arrived at Narragansett Bay in 1524, five Algonquian-speaking native groups occupied Rhode Island. They were decimated by European diseases. Puritan minister Roger Williams established the first permanent European settlement, Providence, in 1636. From the outset, Rhode Island was

Fishing boats at rest in Narragansett Bay at Bristol. The town has a long and distinguished maritime history, especially in shipbuilding.

a haven for people who advocated religious and political freedom.

Beginning as a farming, fishing, and shipbuilding area, Rhode Island was later part of the trade in slaves, rum, and molasses. The state industrialized in the 1800s, with textile mills. After World War II, jewelry, silverware, and machinery were its primary manufactured products. The state was hit hard in the 1970s when two US Navy bases were closed. Recovery began in 1993, focusing on service industries and higher education.

The main auto routes are I-95/295, US-1, 6, and 44, and State Routes 146 and 114. Theodore Francis Green State Airport provides service to and from Providence. There is a rail service to Rhode Island on the Washington DC–New York–Boston line. Ferries link the mainland to the islands, and bus services are widely available.

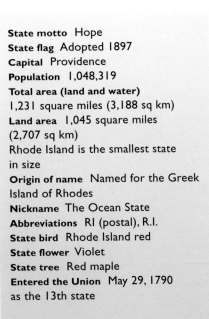

State motto Hope
State flag Adopted 1897
Capital Providence
Population 1,048,319
Total area (land and water)
1,231 square miles (3,188 sq km)
Land area 1,045 square miles
(2,707 sq km)
Rhode Island is the smallest state in size
Origin of name Named for the Greek Island of Rhodes
Nickname The Ocean State
Abbreviations RI (postal), R.I.
State bird Rhode Island red
State flower Violet
State tree Red maple
Entered the Union May 29, 1790 as the 13th state

Places in
RHODE ISLAND

BLOCK ISLAND

Block Island is a popular family vacation destination, with beaches, views from 200-foot-high (61-m) Mohegan Bluffs, two historic lighthouses, walking, biking, and nature trails, resorts, fishing, and children's activities. Particularly popular is 18-acre (7.3-ha) Block Island Beach Recreation Area. New Shoreham is the Island's only town.

The Island is 12 miles (19 km) south of the mainland, between Block Island Sound and Rhode Island Sound. Seven miles (11 km) long and 3½ miles (5.6 km) wide, it covers 11 square miles (29 sq km). It is named for Adrian Block, a Dutch explorer who visited in 1614. Settled in 1661, it now has about 850 year-round residents, and an estimated 10,000 in summer.

A ferry service is available from mainland Rhode Island at Newport, Providence, and Galilee, and at Montauk, Long Island, New York. Schedules vary seasonally. New England Airlines provides commercial air services between Block Island State Airport and Westerly.
Map ref: page 222 E9

BRISTOL

With its upscale eighteenth- and nineteenth-century waterfront houses, this city of about 21,900 residents between Mt Hope and Narragansett Bays recalls its prosperity as a seaport, and its role in the "triangular trade" among New England, Africa, and the West Indies in slaves, rum, and molasses.

Bristol was incorporated in 1680 as part of Plymouth Colony, and was annexed to Rhode Island in 1746. It has been a sailing and shipbuilding center since the seventeenth century, and is known for construction of America's Cup contenders and winners. Its downtown is noted for examples of colonial and Federal-style architecture. The city holds the oldest continuous Fourth of July celebration in the country.

Along its 15-mile (24-km) coastline are facilities for boating, swimming, and fishing. The western side of Colt State Park overlooks Narragansett Bay. The park has playing fields, picnic areas, walking and jogging trails, boating, and fishing. Nearby is Coggeshall Farm, a replica of an eighteenth-century working farm.

The 125-acre (51-ha) campus of Roger Williams University overlooks Mt Hope Bay. Other places of interest are Blithewold Mansion and Gardens, a 45-room summer home built on 33 acres (13 ha) in 1908 (picnicking is allowed); the Haffenreffer Museum of Anthropology, Brown University, which exhibits Native American arts and cultural items; and the Herreshoff Marine Museum and America's Cup Hall of Fame, which exhibits 35 classic yachts built between 1859 and 1947.

The city is on Hwy 114 southeast of Providence, and can be reached from Boston via Hwy 24. A ferry service operates year-round to Hog and Prudence islands.
Map ref: page 222 E7

Bristol's main street. The town takes special pride in its history and patriotism.

Newport's Chateau-sur-Mer displays design trends of the mid-nineteenth century.

NEWPORT

Since the late 1800s, this resort city of 28,200 residents on the island of Rhode Island (also known as Aquidneck) in Narragansett Bay has been a summer haven for the ultra-rich. Now less exclusive, the area's history is reflected in its summer "cottages," which are actually great estates and mansions.

There are a number of these mansions on Bellevue Avenue. Among those that are open for tours are The Astors' Beechwood Mansion and Victorian Living History Museum (1857); Belcourt Castle (designed in 1891); The Breakers (1895); and Chateausur-Mer (1852).

Also open to the public is Hammersmith Farm (1887), the childhood home of Jacqueline Bouvier and the site of the wedding reception for her and her new husband, John F. Kennedy, who used it as a summer White House during his presidency.

Religious refugees from the Puritan Massachusetts Bay Colony established the town of Newport in 1639. A safe harbor for many different faiths, the town saw Quakers arriving in 1657 (the Friends Meeting House built in 1699 still stands), followed by Sephardic Jews in 1658. Newport's Jewish heritage is preserved at Touro Synagogue National Historic Site, the oldest (1763) Jewish house of worship in the nation.

Narragansett Bay hosted the America's Cup Race from 1930 to 1983, and boatbuilding remains an active industry here. Newport also has a large fishing industry. The Bay was the principal port for the US Navy's Atlantic Fleet in the early 1900s.

Fort Adams State Park, a military installation from 1799 to 1945, is the venue for the annual Newport Jazz Festival, held in July, and for Ben & Jerry's Newport Folk Festival, in August. Other places of interest are the Museum of Yachting and the International Tennis Hall of Fame and Museum.

Newport's Naval heritage continues at the Naval War College, the Naval Education and Training Center and the Naval Undersea Warfare Center.

During the Revolutionary War, General George Washington met with the French General Comte de Rochambeau at the Old Colony House (1739) on Washington Square. The Declaration of Independence was read from its balcony in 1776. The US Constitution was ratified in the building in 1790. Newport shared the role of state capital with Providence until 1900.

The city's attractions include the public Gooseberry and Easton's Beaches, and nearby Sachuest and Third Beaches, which are located in Middletown. Walkers enjoy the 3-mile (5-km) Cliff Walk path between Easton and Bailey's Beaches (the latter is private). Harbor tours are also available.

Newport can be reached by car on Hwy 24 and Hwy 138. Ferries shuttle from Providence to Newport and Block Island.
Map ref: page 222 E8

PAWTUCKET

Situated next to Providence in northern Rhode Island at the Blackstone River falls, Pawtucket became the birthplace of the Industrial Revolution in the United States in 1793 when Samuel Slater built the country's first successful water-powered cotton mill. His success in duplicating British water-powered textile machinery launched the industrialization of the Blackstone River Valley and New England. The yellow clapboard mill building still stands at the 5½-acre (2.2-ha) Slater Mill Historic Site.

In 1986, Congress recognized the historic importance of the river valley between Worcester, Massachusetts, and Providence, and designated the 250,000-acre (101,250-ha) Blackstone River National Heritage Corridor. President Bill Clinton designated the Blackstone a National Heritage River. There are visitor centers related to the corridor in Pawtucket, Providence and Woonsocket.

The area was settled in 1671. It was named for the Wampanoag chief who led a Native American revolt sparked by land disputes with the Massachusetts colonies that largely destroyed the town in 1676. The town is now an industrial center on I-95 producing wire, electronic equipment, and glassware, and has about 72,600 residents.
Map ref: page 222 E7

PROVIDENCE

Rhode Island's capital and largest city has been revitalizing itself with a transition from a manufacturing economy to one that is service based. The city has removed concrete covers from rivers, built a modern convention center downtown, and emphasized the restoration and reuse of its historic structures. The city today is a center for finance, commerce, education, medicine, and the arts, and is one of the East Coast's most important seaports. It is particularly noted for jewelry, and claims to be the "costume jewelry capital of the nation."

Providence is on the Providence River at the head of Narragansett Bay; Puritan religious outcast Roger Williams founded the town as a haven for those who shared

Downtown Providence—new and old.

his belief in religious and political freedom. Williams named the city "for God's merciful providence unto me." By the early 1700s Providence, 27 miles (44 km) from the Atlantic Ocean, was a prospering seaport, profiting from shipbuilding and the "triangle trade" in rum, molasses, and African slaves with the West Indies and Africa.

In 1772, as tensions built between Great Britain and its American colonies, Providence residents burned the ship *Gaspée*, which Britain had dispatched to enforce its protective Navigation Acts. Rhode Island declared independence from Great Britain on May 4, 1776, in Providence—the city was a base for American and French troops during the Revolutionary War. Providence joined the Industrial Revolution in the nineteenth century, supported by an influx of immigrant labor. In 1900 the state capital, shared with Newport, was consolidated here.

The city is a center for higher education, being home to Ivy League Brown University, the Museum of Art–Rhode Island School of Design, Providence College, Rhode Island College, and Johnson and Wales University.

Among its historic buildings is the restored first Baptist church in America, built in 1775. Benefit Street's "Mile of History" has many original colonial homes as well as examples of early Federal and nineteenth-century architecture.

The Museum of Art–Rhode Island School of Design has a collection of more than 65,000 works of art. The city's 435-acre (176-ha) Roger Williams Park includes 10 lakes, flower gardens, and 9 miles (15 km) of roads. In the State House reposes Rhode

Island's original 1663 charter, granted by King Charles II.

Providence is reached by a large network of highways, including I-95 and I-195. It is 185 miles (298 km) from New York City, and 45 miles (72 km) from Boston. It has commercial air services (at Theodore Francis Green State Airport), rail services (at the Capitol Center Project), ferries that link the city to the islands, and a bus service.
Map ref: page 222 E7

WARWICK

With 85,400 residents, this city just 12 miles (19 km) south of Providence is Rhode Island's second largest. Samuel Gorton, who was expelled from the Puritan Massachusetts Bay Colony as well as from Roger Williams' more tolerant Providence, purchased the site, originally called Shawomet, from the Narrangansett people in 1643. After his imprisonment for blasphemy, he sailed to England and obtained the protection of Robert Rich, the second Earl of Warwick. Gorton returned to his settlement, and in 1648 named it for the Earl.

A textile manufacturing center in the nineteenth century, Warwick today is a suburban community known for its malls and outlet stores, and insurance and healthcare companies. Many of Providence's downtown retailers have moved to Warwick.

The city has 39 miles (63 km) of undeveloped coastline. Warwick City Park provides a public beach and recreational facilities. Swimming is available at Oakland Beach.

Warwick is reached on Hwy 117.
Map ref: page 222 E7

WESTERLY

Tucked into the western corner of Rhode Island, across the Pawcatuck River from Connecticut and north of Block Island Sound, this city of 16,500, settled in 1648, encompasses several villages: Westerly, Watch Hill, Bradford, and Avondale. Beach lovers come for the many public expanses of sand between Watch Hill and Weekapaug. The Flying Horse Carousel at Watch Hill was built in 1870.

Westerly is south of I-95 on US-1. Air services are available at Westerly State Airport. A bus service to Westerly is also available.
Map ref: page 222 D8

WOONSOCKET

This northern Rhode Island city of 43,900 was a major textile manufacturing center on the Blackstone River between 1840 and the 1950s. The mills employed thousands of French Canadians, whose story is told through exhibits in the Museum of Work and Culture.

Richard Arnold, Sr, an associate of Providence founder Roger Williams, established claims here in the 1660s, after which his family built a sawmill on the Blackstone River. The first textile mill was built in 1810—by 1842 there were 20 mills, producing primarily cotton cloth. But the industry collapsed in the 1920s and 1930s. Manufacturing, particularly of electronics and jewelry, remains important. High-technology firms, as well as finance and retail businesses, have also become prominent in the city's economy.

Woonsocket is on Hwy 126, near the Massachusetts state line.
Map ref: page 222 E7

Park and church in Westerly, a town that used to be a granite and textiles producer.

VERMONT

Vermont (population 608,827) is in the northeast of the United States, bordered by New York State to the west, Canada to the north, New Hampshire to the east, and Massachusetts to the south. It is known for its rugged mountains, clear rivers and lakes, and dairy farms.

The state has been modernized dramatically over the last 25 years. Cities and towns have grown and become more cosmopolitan, although Vermont remains the most rural state in the United States. The Native Americans in Vermont were mainly Abenaki, part of the Algonquian Nation, known as "People of the Dawn."

The state was first named when French explorer Samuel de Champlain explored the area in 1609—the name "Vermont" comes from the French words *vert mont,* referring to the green mountains he saw. British settlers came up from Massachusetts and Connecticut after the French and Indian Wars were resolved in 1760. Both Massachusetts and New Hampshire claimed the land. The Green Mountain Boys, a local militia, grew from settlers fighting these land claims in 1775. In 1777, Vermont was declared a republic and it kept its independence until March 4, 1791, when it was the first to join the Union after the original 13 states.

Pretty village churches like this one are dotted throughout Vermont.

The Green Mountains run vertically up the center of the state. Mount Mansfield is the tallest at 4,393 feet (1,340 m), and there are many peaks over 3,600 feet (1,098 m). The Connecticut River runs along the border with New Hampshire. The Long Trail (also called the Appalachian Trail) runs the full length of the state from Massachusetts in the south to Canada in the north.

Ferry travel is a relaxing way to cross over to New York State. Boat cruises leave from Burlington, giving spectacular views—particularly at sunset.

Vermont's interstate highways are always kept well ploughed and in good repair, so travel is interrupted as little as possible through the long, snowy winter. Vermont Transit buses have regular routes, and Burlington, Montpelier, and Bennington all have airports.

State motto Vermont, Freedom, and Unity
State flag Adopted 1923
Capital Montpelier
Population 608,827
Total area (land and water) 9,615 square miles (24,903 sq km)
Land area 9,249 square miles (23,955 sq km)
Vermont is the 43rd-largest state in size
Origin of name From the French *vert mont* meaning "green mountain"
Nickname The Green Mountain State
Abbreviations VT (postal), Vt.
State bird Hermit thrush
State flower Red clover
State tree Sugar maple
Entered the Union March 4, 1791 as the 14th state

Places in
VERMONT

BENNINGTON

Bennington is in the southeast corner of the state, at the junction of Route 9 and US-7. It is the third-largest city in Vermont, with a population of 16,132 residents. It was a manufacturing center in the 1800s, with famous Bennington Pottery, paper mills, and gristmills. The area is rich in history. The Vermont patriot and Revolutionary War hero, Ethan Allen, met with the Green Mountain Boys in the Catamount Tavern. In 1775 they recaptured Fort Ticonderoga from the British during the Revolutionary War.

Visitors can enjoy panoramic views of Bennington by taking the elevator up the 306-foot (93-m) Battle of Bennington Monument. It is a stone obelisk that commemorates the victory of General Stark over the British when they tried to take the town's stockpile of supplies. This victory contributed to the British Commander "Gentleman Johnny" Bourgoyne surrendering two months later. The monument is open from April to October.

The Bennington Area Chamber of Commerce provides a walking tour brochure that tells the stories behind many of the buildings in Old Bennington, the area just west of downtown. Here there are several brick Federal houses and white-columned Greek Revival houses circling the village green. Pulitzer Prize-winning poet Robert Frost is buried at the Old First Church at the corner of Monument Avenue and Church Street.

A charming cottage situated in the historic city of Bennington, in southeast Vermont.

The Bennington Museum has household items from life in the country as well as collections of art and craft from the area. There is the biggest public collection of the folk art of Grandma Moses, who lived and painted nearby. There are exhibits on the history of glassmaking in the United States, including some works by Tiffany, as well as a room devoted to Bennington Pottery.

Bennington College is a small co-ed college, well respected for its arts program. It is a lively place, despite the peaceful surroundings

of green meadows, dairy farms, and cornfields. The Vermont Symphony orchestra is in town all winter, and the Old Castle Theatre Company is housed in the Bennington Center for the Arts from April to October.

The William H. Morse State Airport is in Bennington. Trains and buses service the area.
Map ref: page 222 B4

BRATTLEBORO

Brattleboro (population 12,396) is in southeast Vermont at the intersection of the Connecticut and West Rivers, on US-5. It began as a frontier outpost in the 1700s, as did many other towns in the area. These outposts were used as trading centers and then gradually became towns. It became a resort town in the 1800s and, simultaneously,

manufacturing industries began to grow. It is still the main business center for southeastern Vermont, but manufacturing has declined since the 1950s.

This has become an area for people living alternative lifestyles and those taking part in political activism. More recently, the state approved recognition of gay and lesbian relationships through a ceremony of civil union.

The Brattleboro Museum and Art Center is housed in an old railway station. Visitors can view exhibits of local historical and artistic interest. One curious item is an Estey organ, from the time when Brattleboro was the headquarters of what was then the world's largest organ company.

Ice sculptures are now a part of winter carnivals, but that was not always so. Larkin G. Mead, a local resident in the 1800s, created an 8-foot (2.5-m) high snow angel at the junction of Routes 30 and 5. Using such a transient material as ice for sculpture was new. You can see a replica of the snow angel in the Brooks Memorial Library along with other artworks by Vermonters.

Near Brattleboro is Naulakha, meaning "jewel beyond price," a house built by Rudyard Kipling. He moved here in 1892 and bought 11 acres (4.5 ha) of meadow in a long strip and built his house so that there were views from each room. It was here that he finished writing *The Jungle Book*. He sold the house in 1902 and, today, it is restored and can be rented out from Britain's Landmark Trust. Eight people can sleep here in comfort.

Just outside Brattleboro, in the Connecticut River Valley at the foothills of the Green Mountains, is the Fort Dummer State Park. It is 217 acres (88 ha) of forest. There are camping sites available.

Trains and buses service the Brattleboro area.
Map ref: page 222 C4

BURLINGTON

Burlington is 38 miles (61 km) northwest of Montpelier on I-89, in the northwest of the state. It was founded in 1763. Burlington is the largest city in Vermont, with a population of 54,339, plus well over 20,000 students during the school year—Burlington is home

Picture-perfect farm near Arlington, north of Bennington.

Burlington has a variety of cafés and restaurants to tempt every palate.

to the University of Vermont. It is also the birthplace of the American philosopher John Dewey and was home to the Revolutionary War hero, Ethan Allen.

In the last 25 years, Burlington has become a much more cosmopolitan city. This is reflected in the variety of restaurants and shops available. Church Street Marketplace downtown is a good place to enjoy a cappuccino in a sidewalk café, to watch the passing parade, or to have a look in a boutique window or craft gallery. There are 165 shops, cafés, and restaurants in the Marketplace.

Today there are many new high-tech firms within commuting distance of Burlington, and university graduates have the possibility of

Robert Frost's grave at Bennington.

finding a challenging job locally and staying permanently in the area. Since more people are moving here from around the country, the population is becoming much more diverse.

The shoreline of Lake Champlain has recently been cleaned up and transformed. The 11 acres (4.5 ha) of Waterfront Park have picnic areas, and a 9-mile (14-km) cycle way. The park is used for weekend festivals and firework displays. Concerts are held here on Thursday evenings in summer, a perfect time to see the stunning sunsets over the lake.

Lake Champlain Aquarium (open May to September) and the Lake Champlain Basin Science Center are ideal for families. The Community Boathouse is a floating barge complete with a restaurant. Visitors can rent rowboats, sailboats, and rowing shells. There is scuba diving too, with three fascinating wrecks nearby to explore. Ice fishing is popular on the lake once winter has settled in and the ice is thick.

The Burlington music scene is vital and dynamic with jazz, rhythm-and-blues, rock, and folk music in bars and clubs around town. Locals have had the chance to see many more performers than are seen in other cities of similar size. Burlington is between Boston and Montreal and it was often a stop-off point for large bands on tour. This exposure fuels the local music industry.

Not so far from Burlington—a 45 to 60 minute drive—is Smuggler's Notch ski resort. It has trails for skiers of all levels, and is particularly known for its programs for families. The first triple black diamond run (the most difficult) in the east was named in 1996. There is also the Family Snowmaking Learning Center. Here there are snowmaking demonstrations and exhibits that explain snow crystals and the weather.

Shelburne Museum, a short drive south of Burlington, has 35 buildings of historic significance, which have been moved here and scattered over 100 acres (40 ha). There is a blacksmiths, lighthouse and private homes, from stately to small. Visitors can see candles made and quilts sewn. There is also a steam-powered side-wheeler boat and a collection of 200 carriages.

Burlington has an international airport, and trains and buses service the area.
Map ref: page 220 B8

CHELSEA

Chelsea is a picturesque village in central Vermont, just 20 miles (32 km) southeast of Montpelier. A good old-fashioned fiddling contest is held here each year. It is a good area for hunting and outdoor sports. Chelsea also has a covered bridge, one of many left in the state. These wooden bridges were covered to protect the road surface and the structure of the bridge from the weather.

Edward F. Knapp in Montpelier is the closest airport; Chelsea is also serviced by trains and buses.
Map ref: page 222 C2

EAST DORSET

East Dorset is located 20 miles (32 km) south of Rutland on US-7. During the late 1800s, East Dorset grew with the development of marble quarries and the lumber industry in the area. The town grew to 1,800 people, four or five times larger than today. The city of Washington DC was being built at that time, and many of Washington's public buildings were constructed from East Dorset marble. The marble was also used for the dramatic and elegant New York Public Library.

Today East Dorset is a sleepy town with some lovely old wooden homes and the Emerald Lake State Park nearby for picnicking, swimming and boating.

Rutland State Airport is the closest to East Dorset. Buses and trains service the area.
Map ref: page 222 C4

The University of Vermont in Burlington.

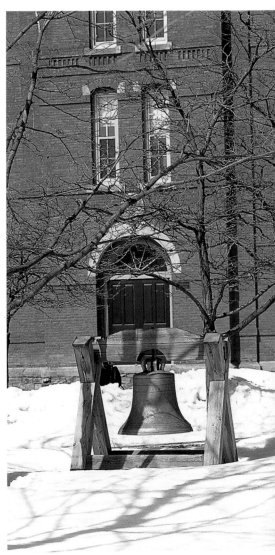

MIDDLEBURY

Middlebury (population 8,548) is located 30 miles (48 km) south of Burlington on the US-7, in the Champlain Valley. In the 1800s, the town was a center for wool and grain mills, and the marble industry. The town is still the economic and cultural hub of this peaceful farming region. Middlebury College is closely and cooperatively connected to the town. It is situated in a scenic lakeside valley.

Middlebury College has three libraries, each of which has exhibits and activities for both visitors and locals. Many cultural events are held at the university and it is a good idea for visitors to check what is on during their visit.

Downhill skiers can ski at the Middlebury College Snow Bowl. The Rickert Center for bicycle and ski touring is on Middlebury's Breadloaf campus. In winter cross-country skiing on snowy trails nearby is very popular.

When the snow is gone and the ground turns green again, mountain bikes travel these same trails. In summer you can take a picnic lunch and hike up the trails to enjoy the view. July brings the "Festival on the Green" to Middlebury. There are dance performances, music, and storytellers.

Somerset Reservoir and Lake Dunmore are nearby and are popular for bird watching, camping, and fishing in summer, and cross-country skiing in winter. Branbury State Park is also on a lake and has camping facilities.

There are many and varied high-quality restaurants or, for something low-key, visitors can try one of the many inexpensive places catering to students.

Around Middlebury is a rural area of rich farmland with dairy cattle, apple orchards, and hardwood timber forests. The University of Vermont Morgan Horse Farm is west of town and offers an interesting tour with information of the history of this durable Vermont breed.

There are distinctive red timber covered bridges dotted around this area on the east side of the Green Mountains.

The poet laureate, Robert Frost, spent 23 summers on a farm here, just east of Ripton. He began a well-respected writer's conference

Kayaking on the waterways around Middlebury is not for the faint-hearted.

at Middlebury College's Breadloaf campus. Visitors can see the landscapes and the kinds of people that inspired his work.

Middlebury has its own airport and Burlington International Airport is not far. Trains and buses also service the area.
Map ref: page 222 B2

MONTPELIER

Montpelier is on the shores of the Winooski River in the Green Mountains, in central-north Vermont.

Montpelier is surprisingly alternative and surprisingly small for a state capital. There is a mix of old tradition and a conservative outlook combined with progressive political ideas. It is 38 miles (61 km) southeast of Burlington. It is the smallest state capital in the United States, with a population of less than 10,000. It is the only state capital without a McDonalds restaurant. It was named as the state capital in 1805. Pick-up trucks with gun racks in the back window are frequently seen parked next to the latest Saabs and Volvos.

The current State Capitol was built in 1859, after two previous versions in wood. It is built from Barre Granite in the Greek revival style, with a shiny gold dome that gives a dramatic shape to the skyline. Its towering columns are 6 feet (2 m) in diameter. The dome is topped with a sculpture of Ceres, the Roman goddess of agriculture. A second sculpture, of Ethan Allen, is on the steps. There are regular tours of the interior.

Visitors can take a walk along State Street to the offices of the Vermont Historical Society. On the ground floor is the Vermont Museum, with historical exhibits on everything from covered bridges, panthers, costumes, and rural life. Nearby is the famous Vermont Culinary Institute and their two teaching restaurants. The tourist Information Center offers walking tours of the city.

Not far from Montpelier is the Rock of Ages Granite Quarry in Barre. This is the largest quarrier of granite in North America as well as the largest manufacturer of granite memorials. (The rock walls were used as a backdrop to the latest *Batman* film.) This massive quarry is an interesting find in this small town. It covers 50 acres (20 ha) with a seam of granite that is 500 feet (152 m) deep. The

logistics of cutting, drilling and lifting the rock up to the surface are impressive. Curbstones for cities all over New England, gravestones, monuments, columns, and cornerstones are cut and carved out of this enduring material. George Barron Milne, from Aberdeen, Scotland, founded the quarry. He came to the United States when he was 26 years old, and started the business in 1885. It now has over 1,000 employees.

The quarry is open to visitors between June and October and there is a shuttle tour around the quarry. There is also a gift shop. During the tour visitors get a real sense of the vastness of the quarry and get to watch master stone sculptors at work in the manufacturing facility (May to October).

The Edward F. Knapp Airport is in Montpelier and trains and buses service the area.
Map ref: page 222 C1

RUTLAND

Rutland (population 18,083) is 69 miles (111 km) south of Burlington in central Vermont. Rutland was built on railroading and marble quarry industries and still has an industrial character. Shopping malls and traffic lights are much more visible than the mansions of the people who made money here. A short drive, 4 miles (6 km) north, takes visitors to Proctor to see the Vermont Marble Exhibit. Here visitors can watch sculptors-in-residence and hear the screech of their cutters shaping the milky stone. The gallery shows both the industrial and decorative uses of marble and has exhibits on the quarrying process and a video on the industry's past. It is open from Memorial Day to October.

Rutland's Crossroads Arts Council produces events in theater, opera, music, and dance. The Vermont Symphony Orchestra performs here in winter and in Woodstock in the summer months, and Rutland hosts the Vermont State Fair.

Just east of Rutland, at the intersection of Routes 100 and 4, is the center of Vermont's ski country. The ski resorts Killington, Okemo, and Pico are here. Killington has impressive views from the summit, worth a trip, even for non-skiers. The ski resort is nicknamed the

"Beast of the East" or "Megamountain." The access road is heavily developed and the resort itself is well serviced with many facilities. It has the longest ski season in the East.

Rutland has its own airport and is serviced by trains and buses.
Map ref: page 222 C3

STOWE

Stowe (population 3,953) is the name of the town, the ski resort is "Stowe Mountain Resort", and the mountain is Mount Mansfield, but to many they are one and the same. Stowe is 22 miles (35 km) northwest of Montpelier on I-89 then Hwy 100. The town is dominated by 4,393 foot (1,340 m) Mount Mansfield, which is the tallest mountain in Vermont. The views from the top are awe-inspiring on a clear day. Visitors can either climb to the summit, drive up the toll road (summer only), or ride the gondola.

Skiers have been coming here since the 1930s when the industry was beginning. Free shuttle buses that pass all the lodgings along Mountain Road make it easy to get to the mountain. The January Stowe Winter Carnival and April's Sugar Slalom are enduring traditions. There are two restaurants

on the mountain and three base lodges providing a variety of services. Smuggler's Notch and Bolton are two other ski resorts located nearby.

The Von Trapp family, known from the movie *The Sound of Music*, moved here after escaping from Nazi-occupied Austria. Their Trapp Family Lodge has spectacular views over meadows and mountains. There is a series of summer concerts here and trails for walking or cross-country skiing depending on the season.

Stowe has a 5-mile (8-km) "recreational path" which begins behind the town's Community Church—or you can join it at many points along the way. It wanders through the beautiful river valley.

The Morrison-Stowe State Airport and the Edward F. Knapp Airport in Montpelier service the area. There are also bus and train services to Montpelier.
Map ref: page 222 C8

Skiing is a way of life on Mount Mansfield in Stowe. A ski patrol watches for people in trouble.

A Rutland store with a display of wood carvings.

WINDSOR

Windsor is a small town, with a population of 3,956, on the eastern border of the state 50 miles (80 km) north of Brattleboro on I-91. Land grant holders announced Vermont was to be an independent republic here in the Old Constitution House in 1777. The house has information on the Vermont Constitution, which was the first state constitution to found a public school system or prohibit slavery.

The longest covered bridge in the state (460 feet/140 m) is here, not far from Route 5. It crosses the Connecticut River that forms the border with the state of New Hampshire.

Windsor House, which was originally built in 1846 and later restored, is now home to the Vermont State Craft Center. It displays selected work from over 200 talented craftspeople.

Trains and buses service the Windsor area.
Map ref: page 222 D3

WOODSTOCK

Woodstock (population 3,398) is a very pretty town in central Vermont, just 20 miles (32 km) east of Rutland on the US-4. Well-maintained Federal-style houses circle the village green. There are boutiques, art galleries, and restaurants. It is a pleasant place to take a stroll year-round. The Rockefeller family, and George Perkins Marsh (the primary initiator of the Smithsonian Institution in Washington, DC) were deeply involved in the planning, historic preservation, and conservation in the area.

There is an annual winter carnival with cross-country skiing and snowshoeing demonstrations, guided tours, and games for children. The Raptor Center of the Vermont Institute of Natural Science is a non-profit center for education and research. There are 26 different species of birds of prey on show, including the magnificent bald eagle and peregrine falcon.

Many of the birds were brought here for care after an injury. There are 77 acres (31 ha) of nature preserve here with self-guided walking trails throughout.

Dana House, built around 1807, is home to the Woodstock Historical Society. Exhibits include an elegant sleigh, furniture, the town's charter, maps, paintings, and some silver.

Billings Farm, in Woodstock, is a living museum. It was first established in 1871 with cows imported from the Jersey Islands. It is an operational dairy farm, which also has a museum with photographs and a film on the history of the farm. Self-guided tours are also available on which visitors can see the restored farmhouse, built in 1890.

The ski area, Suicide Six, is the first ski tow in the United States; it was opened in 1934. There are several runs here for the adventurous skier, though the vertical drop is only 650 feet (198 m). There are 22 trails and two double chair lifts. There is an area for snowboarders with a half pipe. The Ski Touring Center has 37 miles (60 km) of trails, as well as rental equipment and lessons for cross-country skiers.

Rutland is the nearest center and has an airport. Woodstock is serviced by trains and buses.
Map ref: page 220 C3

STATE FEATURE

Mountains and Maple Trees

Driving the Mountains

Fall in New England is justly famous for the spectacular pageant of the changing colors of the leaves. The brightest glowing reds and golds are in the maple trees, the rust, greens, and browns are in the oaks, the darker greens are in the spruce and the soft yellows are in the fluttering birch leaves. In late September and early October many tree-lined roads are covered with vivid color. Vermont, with many tree-covered mountains and hills, is a perfect place to watch the foliage. The colors appear first up north and move south between the last week of September and the first two weeks of October—but the weather changes the timing every year, so exact dates are impossible to predict. Listed here are some of the special places to see this warm rainbow of color.

The glorious fall colors of the black maple (Acer nigrum) cover this mountain trail.

Northeast Kingdom

This a special area, in the northeast corner of Vermont, which is largely undeveloped. An especially pretty spot is Lake Willoughby, 28 miles (45 km) north of St Johnsbury. The dramatic scenery would not be out of place in the Scottish highlands. Glaciers carved out this 500-foot (152-m) deep lake. The cliffs on the lower reaches of Mt Pisgah and Mt Hor form the northern edge of Lake Willoughby. The scenery is fabulous for a visit any time of year. Hikers can climb the mountains for dramatic views.

Also in the Northeast Kingdom, is Peacham, an unspoiled, traditional village, northeast of Montpelier. There is the Bayley Hazen Country Store 1 mile (2 km) south of the village, a small archeological site to explore, and escorted ghost walks in the evening to learn some history of people who once lived here. The last week in September is the Northeast Kingdom Fall Foliage Fest, which runs for more than a week. There are church suppers, craft sales, and organ concerts, by talented local musicians, at the local church. Besides Peacham, several surrounding towns are involved, such as Barnet, Cabot, Plainfield, Gro-

ton, and Marshfield. The area is very good for cyclists too, with great scenery and less traffic than in many other parts of the state.

Smuggler's Notch

Visitors beginning at Stowe can drive northwest along Route 108 through Smuggler's Notch—a dramatic pass winding past massive boulders. Madonna Peak is on one side and Mount Mansfield is on the other. Small parking areas along the way are perfect for picnics and viewing the magnificent scenery. Snow closes the road in winter.

Visit Little River State Park, also near Stowe. It is 3½ miles (6 km) north of Route 2, 2 miles (3 km) east of Route 100. Visitors can see the changing colors from above by climbing Mount Mansfield or Camel's Hump on hiking trails. Another way to see the wonderful colors is to rent a boat and view them from the river.

Waitsfield to Bristol

In central Vermont, just southwest of Montpelier, is Waitsfield. Drive west through the Appalachian Gap, crossing the Long Trail. The road weaves through the mountaintops and comes down into Bristol for some of the best views in the state. The driving is tricky, but worth it. Just south of Waitsfield is Warren and the ski resorts Sugarbush and the wildly popular Mad River (no snowboards allowed).

At Stowe is the beginning of a 21-mile (34-km) road with stunning views of towering Mount Mansfield. Take Route 100 north, then Stagecoach Road, to Morristown, over to Morrisville and finally, turn south on Randolph Road. Try the Mountain Bike Shop on Mountain Road for organized cycling tours.

Southern Vermont

In early October the maple trees are still changing color further south. Visitors can wander from Arlington on Kelley Stand Road East to Green Mountain National Forest and any of the roads from there. They can continue over the mountains past Stratton Mountain Ski Resort then turn south on Route 100 to see Harriman and Somerset reservoirs. The reservoirs are halfway between Bennington and Brattleboro.

Peacham, in Vermont's Northeast Kingdom, was established in the year of American independence.

Many visitors to the United States think of visiting the big cities like New York, Los Angeles, or Las Vegas and forget about the large tracts of wilderness still here. Even along the well-developed east coast, there are unspoiled places. The Long Trail in the Green Mountains National Park is one. The Long Trail is a perfect place to watch the seasons change. You can still hike for days, weeks, or even months in the wilderness. The Long Trail runs north to south through the Green Mountains.

Maple Trees

Maple syrup is made from the sugar maple (*Acer saccharum*) and the black maple (*Acer nigrum*). Vermont is the largest producer of maple syrup in the United States. Thirty to 50 gallons of sap (115 to 190 l) are boiled down to make 1 gallon (4 l) of syrup. The season is only four to six weeks long, and the dates vary every year according to the weather. It starts in mid-January in the south of Vermont and in March further north. The sap stops running when the freezing nights end in mid-April. Native Americans made maple syrup in the Great Lakes region and in the St Lawrence River Valley, long before the arrival of European settlement.

Collecting sap begins with a walk in the woods with a bag of spouts and a hammer. The spouts are hammered into the trees and metal buckets are hung on a hook to collect the sap as it drips out. Most people now put plastic tubing onto the spile (or little spout that goes into the tree) and leave the tubes up all year. It saves time for serious producers. The tubes feed into a collection vat.

People who do still travel around to collect sap from buckets use an all terrain vehicle—a bit like a

skimobile with small tracks like a tank has—so it can travel easily on snowy or muddy ground. The sap only runs when the nights are still freezing—so it is a cold job to collect the sap.

The buckets are covered to keep out debris. Each hole can yield about 10 gallons (38 l) of sap. Genetics, the local weather conditions, and the soil all change the yield. A tree may produce sap for 100 years if cared for properly. Tapping the tree for sap does not damage the tree.

The buckets are taken off the trees and emptied into the gathering tank one by one, and then replaced on the tree. When the tank is full, it is pulled back to the sugarhouse to begin cooking. Once it is collected, the sap must be evaporated as soon as possible.

The sugarhouse is in a small clearing in the woods with a big woodpile against one wall. There is a vent in the roof to let out steam. The gathering tank is dragged inside and the sap is poured into a large flat evaporating pan, a bit like an over-sized baking pan. The pan sits on an "arch," a kind of firebox. A large slow-burning fire is built underneath to boil down the sap. Oil, gas, or coal can also be used as a heat source. The fire is tended through the day and checked hour by hour until only sweet sap is left. It is then strained and bottled while still hot. In spring visitors can see demonstrations of making maple syrup all over the state.

Baird Farm, Chittenden. Native Americans made maple syrup long before Europeans arrived in North America. Now, maple syrup production is a lucrative business.

When enough sap is collected, it goes back to the sugarhouse for processing.

Central and Northern Maine
Northern New Hampshire • Northern Vermont

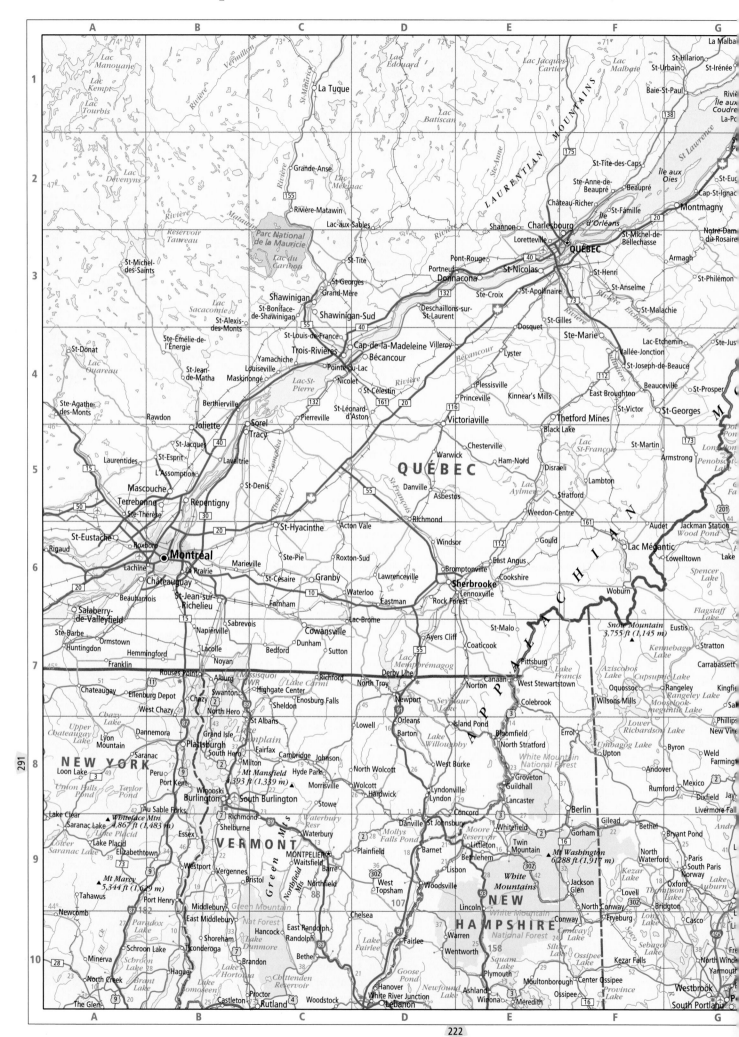

0   20   40   60   80   100 kilometers
0   20   40   60 miles

H   J   K   L   M   N   P

CANADA
UNITED STATES OF AMERICA

St-Pascal
St-Éleuthère
Pohénégamook
Pied-du-Lac
Lac Ste-Anne
St-Eusèbe
Dégelis
Lac-Baker
Edmundston
Madawaska
St David
Frenchville
Lille
Fort Kent
St-Jacques
St-Quentin

Beau Lake
Glazier Lake
Long Lake
Mt Carleton
2,680 ft (817 m)

St Francis
Soldier Pond
Dickey
Eagle Lake
Winterville
Square Lake
St-Léonard
Van Buren
Grand Falls
Drummond
Big Bald Mtn
2,500 ft (762 m)

Stockholm
Limestone
Four Falls
Aroostook
Plaster Rock
Three Brooks

Caribou
Washburn
Fort Fairfield

NEW BRUNSWICK

Portage
Presque Isle
Perth-Andover
Upper Blackville

Ashland
Westfield
Upper Kent
Bath
Juniper
Doaktown

Masardis
Mars Hill
Bristol
Florenceville
Boiestown
Astle

Bridgewater
Hartland
Stanley
Nashwaak Bridge
Gaspereau Forks

Oxbow
Monticello
Upper Woodstock
Woodstock
Millville
Taymouth
Chipman

Littleton
Burtts Corner
Minto

Smyrna Mills
Houlton
Meductic
Nackawic
Douglas
FREDERICTON
Youngs Cove

Island Falls
Linneus
Pokiok
Kings Landing
Lincoln

Patten
North Amity
Marysville

MAINE
Sherman Station
Haynesville
Orient
New Maryland
Oromocto
Geary
Jemseg
Gagetown

Mt Katahdin
5,267 ft (1,605 m)
Grand Lake
Harvey
Tracy
Springfield

Millinocket
Danforth
York Mills
Blissville
Hampstead
Hampton

East Millinocket
Macwahoc
Vanceboro
McAdam
Brockway
Hoyt
Oak Point

Norcross
Wytopitlock
Brookton
Welsford
Gondola Point
Quispamsis

West Seboeis
Mattawamkeag
Topsfield
Grand Bay
Westfield
Fairvale

Lincoln
Springfield
Waite
Saint John

Brownville Junction
Lee
Waite
Moores Mills

Greenville
Shirley Mills
Milo
Passamaquoddy
Indian Resn
Prince of Wales

Guilford
Howland
Princeton
Calais
St Stephen

Dover-Foxcroft
Passadumkeag
Woodland
St George
Maces Bay

Monson
Olamon
Big Lake
Alexander
St Andrews
Blacks Harbour

South Lagrange
Crawford Lake
Meddybemps
Perry
Eastport

Dexter
Milford
Old Town
Marion
Welshpool
Lubec

Harmony
Orono
Wesley
Whiting
North Head
Grand Manan I

Corinna
Amherst
Machias
Grand Harbour

Newport
Bangor
Brewer
Columbia Falls
Cutler
White Head I

Pittsfield
Hampden
Highlands
East Holden
Cherryfield
Harrington

Hinckley
Burnham
Dixmont
Green Lake
Waltham

Clinton
Unity
Frankfort
Franklin

Waterville
Winslow
Albion
Bucksport
Ellsworth
Milbridge
Jonesport
Weymouth

Waldo
Searsport
Trenton
Ashville

South China
Belfast
Bar Harbor
Gulf of Maine
NOVA SCOTIA

AUGUSTA
Liberty
Somesville
Acadia National Park
Bear Cove

Randolph
Gardiner
Camden
Sedgwick
Southwest Harbor
Salmon River

Union
Jefferson
Deer Isle
Bass Harbor
Port Maitland

Richmond
Newcastle
Rockland
North Haven
Acadia National Park
Yarmouth
Arcadia

Wiscasset
Owls Head
Isle au Haut
Wedgeport

Boothbay Harbor
Jansen I
Port Clyde
Matinicus I
NORTH

Southern New England • Eastern New York

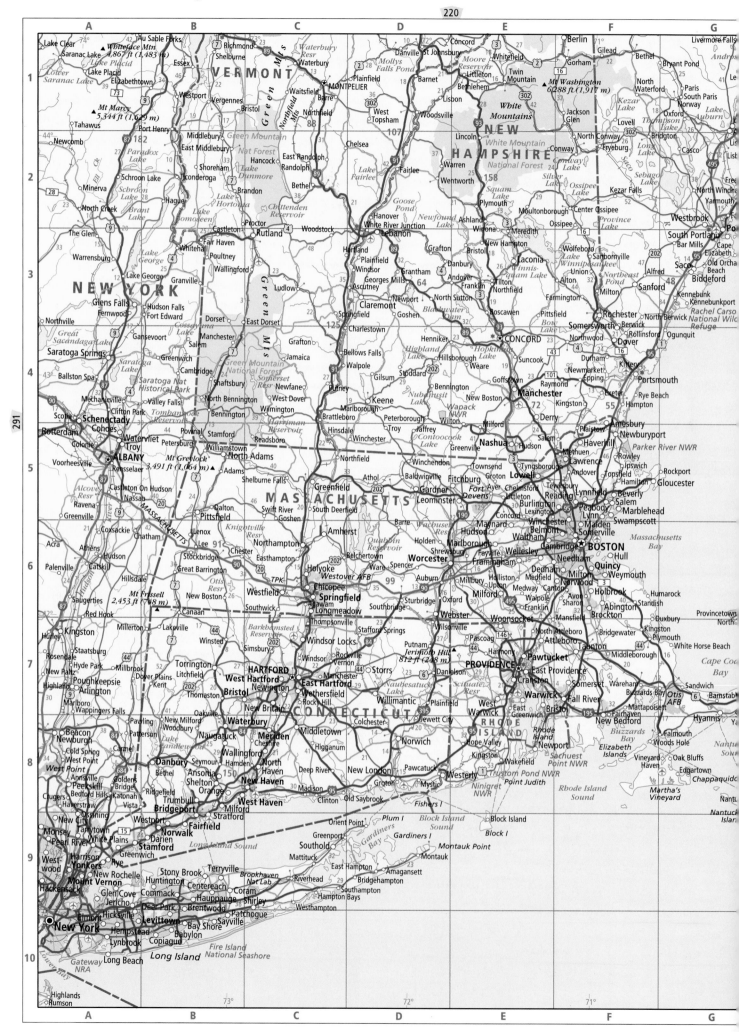

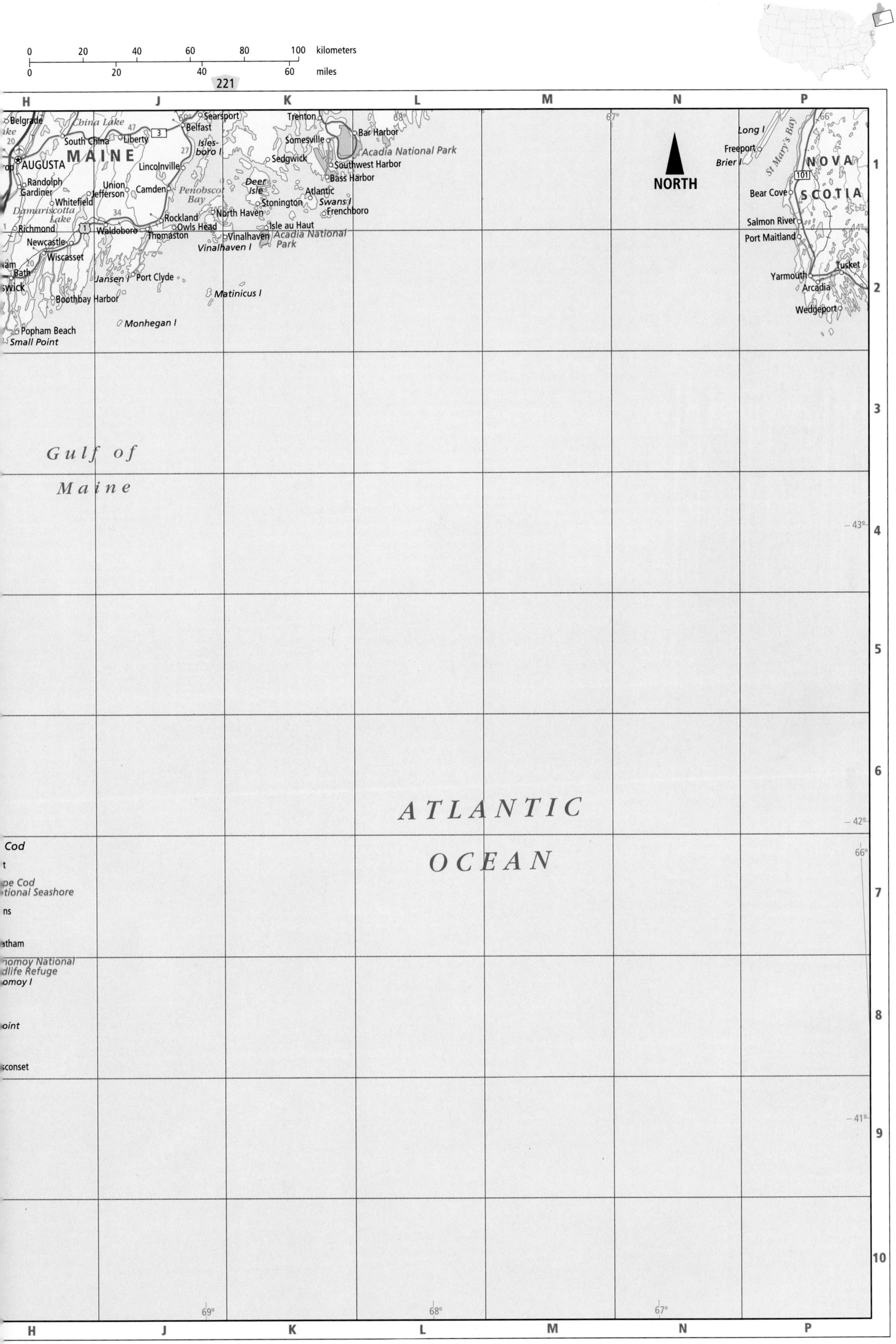

0 20 40 60 80 100 kilometers
0 20 40 60 miles

221

| H | J | K | L | M | N | P |

Belgrade China Lake **Searsport** Trenton 68° **Long I** 66°
Belfast Somesville **Freeport**
South China Liberty Isles- **Sedgwick** **Acadia National Park** **Brier I** **NOVA**
47 3 boro I **Southwest Harbor** **Bear Cove** **SCOTIA**
AUGUSTA **MAINE** Lincolnville Deer **Bass Harbor** **Salmon River**
Randolph 20 Union Camden Penobscot Isle Atlantic **Port Maitland**
Gardiner Jefferson Bay Stonington Swans I **NORTH**
Whitefield 34 Rockland **North Haven** Frenchboro **Yarmouth** **Tusket**
Damariscotta Lake Owls Head Isle au Haut **Arcadia**
Richmond 1 Waldoboro Thomaston Vinalhaven Acadia National **Wedgeport**
Newcastle Vinalhaven I Park
Wiscasset Jansen I Port Clyde
Bath Matinicus I
Boothbay Harbor
Popham Beach Monhegan I
Small Point

Gulf of

Maine

— 43°

ATLANTIC

OCEAN

— 42°
66°

Cod

e Cod
tional Seashore

ns

tham

homoy National
dlife Refuge
omoy I

oint

sconset

— 41°

| H | J | K | L | M | N | P |

69° 68° 67°

THE MID-ATLANTIC

0   100   200   kilometers

0   60   120   miles

Massena
Plattsburgh

St Lawrence River

Ogdensburg   Potsdam

Lake Champlain

Saranac Lake

▲ *Mt Marcy*
5,344 ft (1,629 m)

Adirondack Mountains

Watertown

NEW YORK

Glens Falls

LAKE ONTARIO

Oswego

Fulton   *Oneida Lake*

Rome   Utica

Saratoga Springs

Amsterdam

Greece Irondequoit
Rochester   Brighton
Niagara Falls
Tonawanda
Kenmore   Batavia
Depew
Buffalo
West Seneca
Mount Vernon
Hamburg

Great Sacandaga Lake

Schenectady
Rotterdam
ALBANY

Canandaigua
Geneva
Seneca Lake
Cayuga Lake
Auburn
Syracuse
Oneida

LAKE ERIE

Cortland

Keuka Lake

Dunkirk
Fredonia

Ithaca

Cobocton River

Hudson River

Kingston

Erie
Chautauqua Lake
Jamestown   Olean
Bradford

Corning
Elmira
Sayre

Susquehanna River

Binghampton
Endicott

Catskill Mountains

Poughkeepsie
Arlington

Warren

Mansfield

Towanda

Oneonta

Delaware River

Middletown
Newburgh
West Point
Peekskill

Pymatuning Reservoir

Meadville

PENNSYLVANIA

Carbondale
Scranton   Dunmore

Oil City

Clarion River

St Marys

Williamsport

Nanticoke   Wilkes-Barre

Tarrytown
White Plains
Southold

Sharon   Hermitage

DuBois

Susquehanna River

Berwick
Hazleton

Hopatcong   Oakland
Paterson
Yonkers

Hauppauge

New Castle

Bloomsburg
Sunbury

Parsippany
Morristown

Jersey City
Elizabeth
Perth Amboy

Patchogue
Bay Shore

Long Island

Butler

State College

Allegheny Mountains

APPALACHIAN MOUNTAINS

Pottsville

Phillipsburg
Allentown
Bethlehem
Emmaus

Newark
New York
Levittown
Long Beach

Aliquippa
Franklin Park
New Kensington
Murrysville

Indiana

Altoona

Hershey
Lebanon
Reading

New Brunswick
Somerville

Old Bridge
Freehold

Pittsburgh
Mount Lebanon
McKeesport
Greensburg
Johnstown

HARRISBURG

Pottstown

Princeton

Long Branch
Asbury Park

Washington

Carlisle

Columbia
Lancaster

Norristown
Bristol
Willingboro

Point Pleasant

TRENTON

Chambersburg
York

Broomall
Woodlyn

Philadelphia
Bellmawr

NEW JERSEY

Uniontown

▲ *Mt Davis*
3,213 ft (979 m)

Gettysburg

Hanover

▲ 448 ft (137 m)

Wilmington
Newark

Pennsville

Hammonton

Frostburg
Cumberland

Hagerstown
Westminster

Reisterstown
Frederick

Towson
Parkville

Aberdeen
Edgewood

Bridgeton

Vineland
Millville

Pleasantville
Atlantic City
Ocean City

▲ *Backbone Mtn*
3,360 ft (1,024 m)

Gaithersburg
Columbia
Elkridge
Baltimore

Pasadena
Crofton

DOVER

Delaware Bay

Wheaton
Bethesda
WASHINGTON
DISTRICT OF COLUMBIA

Beltsville
Suitland

Milford

DELAWARE

Clinton

ANNAPOLIS

Easton

Georgetown

Waldorf

Chesapeake Bay

Cambridge

La Plata

MARYLAND

Salisbury

Ocean City

Lexington Park

Potomac R

Scotland

Pocomoke City

THE MID-ATLANTIC

The Mid-Atlantic states—New York, New Jersey, Pennsylvania, Delaware, and Maryland, plus the District of Columbia—lie along the eastern seaboard, between New England and the South. Most have some Atlantic coastline, but the region is geographically diverse, extending west to the Appalachian Mountains, and north to the Great Lakes. Consequently, low-lying coastal areas may have warm-temperate climates and hot, humid summers, while the west and north endure cold winters and considerable snowfall.

Some of the continent's earliest settlements were established in the fertile Mid-Atlantic region. Settlers in these parts were not all from the British Isles, so this was North America's first melting pot. In the 1620s, the Dutch built settlements in Manhattan, up the Hudson River, and along the Connecticut and New Jersey coasts; New Sweden stretched along the Delaware River to just south of Philadelphia. The English settled Maryland in 1634. The Dutch eventually forced Sweden to relinquish its claims, and the English soon did the same to the Dutch; by 1670, the entire region was ruled by England. But the area's Dutch legacy is still evident in many place names.

After the handover, Pennsylvania's first English settlers were Quakers. Led by William Penn, they established a colony that was to be a model of tolerance. Pennsylvania soon became a haven for persecuted religious sects; even today, visitors to the state can see Amish, Mennonite, and other community groups leading traditional lifestyles.

Over a century later, the Mid-Atlantic colonies joined their northern and southern neighbors and declared independence from Britain. Philadelphia—by then a distinguished center for learning and progressive thinking—hosted the First and Second Continental Congresses. Some of the Revolutionary War's key battles were fought in Pennsylvania, New Jersey, and New York. Philadelphia was also the temporary national capital in the 1780s; the national seat of government later moved to the new District of Columbia, essentially a 68-square-mile (176-sq-km) segment of Maryland on the Potomac River.

Maryland and Delaware were border states during the Civil War. They remained part of the Union, despite having slave-owning residents. But the situation was considered volatile enough in Maryland for martial law to be imposed throughout the state. Some of the bloodiest Civil War campaigns were fought there and in Pennsylvania. Gettysburg's National Cemetery in southern Pennsylvania is still a somber reminder of the war that almost tore the nation apart.

The Mid-Atlantic states are the nation's most urbanized—the New York–Washington corridor is becoming one huge megalopolis. Traditionally a prime manufacturing center, the dual port of New York and New Jersey has become the country's largest shipping center. New York is the world's largest financial center and home to major stock exchanges. Delaware, known for chemical manufacture, is also a major banking center.

The Mid-Atlantic's economic base relies primarily on service industries. Once dependent on tobacco farming, Maryland now relies on government service jobs in the Washington, DC region, while its capital, Annapolis, is home to the US Naval Academy.

Chesapeake Bay, known for its crabs, is dotted with islands whose residents still have the Elizabethan accents of their forebears. Mountainous areas offer outdoor activities, including hiking, rafting, and even skiing. Fall is delightful, with mountains a riot of color.

Washington's Smithsonian Institution is a cultural storehouse fondly called the "nation's attic." There are also historic sites, museums for inventors such as Thomas Edison, Victorian seaside towns, wild barrier islands, preserved colonial towns, and honeymoon spots such as Niagara Falls and Pennsylvania's Poconos.

The breadth of its history, politics, and geography combined with its natural beauty all ensure the Mid-Atlantic caters to a rich tapestry of ideas and interests.

A snow-covered dummy with a traditional pumpkin head waits patiently for Halloween to arrive in New York State.

The Adirondacks region in upstate New York offers a wealth of outdoor activities, from hiking to fishing.

DELAWARE

The nation's second-smallest state—only Rhode Island is smaller—Delaware is one of the most densely populated states, even though about half the state is farmland. It has benefited from its waterways, ports, and proximity to Philadelphia, Baltimore, and Washington DC. Delaware's corporate tax and incorporation laws, less stringent than in other states, have induced many companies to locate their headquarters here. Northern Delaware has also become an important center for finance, insurance, and real estate.

Delaware shares the Delmarva Peninsula, between Delaware Bay and Chesapeake Bay, with eastern Maryland and Virginia. To the north is Pennsylvania, and to the northeast, across Delaware Bay and the Delaware River, is New Jersey.

The state is divided into two sections by the east–west Chesapeake and Delaware Canal. The small northern section is a somewhat hilly, industrialized, and heavily populated region dominated by the Wilmington metropolitan area.

Most of Delaware lies south of the canal. This is the more rural and agricultural coastal plain, with many beach-oriented resorts; the capital

Delaware has many historic homes, including this attractive house in Dover.

city, Dover, is here as well. Most of this area is less than 60 feet (18 m) above sea level, making Delaware the lowest state.

One of the original 13 states, Delaware is named for Virginia's first colonial governor, Thomas West, Lord De La Warr. Lenni Lenape Native Americans occupied the land when English navigator, Henry Hudson, sailing for the Dutch East India Company, discovered Delaware Bay in 1609. Sweden established the first permanent European settlement in 1638, at the site of today's Wilmington. The region came under English rule after several wars in the 1600s between the Dutch, Swedes, and British. After the Revolutionary War, Delaware was the first state to ratify the US Constitution, earning it "The First State" nickname.

State motto Liberty and Independence
State flag Adopted 1913
Capital Dover
Population 783,600
Total area (land and water)
2,396 square miles (6,206 sq km)
Land area 1,955 square miles
(5,063 sq km)
Delaware is the 49th-largest state
in size
Origin of name From the Delaware
River and Bay, which were named for
early Virginian governor Sir Thomas
West, Lord De La Warr
Nicknames The Diamond State,
The First State
Abbreviations DE (postal), Del.
State bird Blue hen chicken
State flower Peach blossom
State tree American holly
Entered the Union December 7, 1787
as the first state

Places in DELAWARE

BRANDYWINE VALLEY

The rural valley of Brandywine Creek, in the rolling wooded countryside north of Wilmington, spreads across northern Delaware and southeastern Pennsylvania, from Wilmington to West Chester. It is a landscape of covered bridges, great estates, gardens that bloom in spring, and woods that become a palette of hues in fall—perfect for the slices of America portrayed by the famous Wyeth family of artists.

Long dominated by the du Pont family, oligarchs of the American chemicals industry, the Brandywine Valley is rich in colonial history and pastoral scenery.

Fighting in the 1600s among the Dutch, Swedes, and English ended with the English gaining control over the region. During the Revolutionary War, in September 1777, the British defeated General George Washington and the Continental Army at the Battle of Brandywine Creek, in Pennsylvania, a few miles from the Delaware border. The fight is commemorated at Brandywine Battlefield Park at Chadds Ford, Pennsylvania.

In the 1790s, mills along Brandywine Creek near Wilmington made the area the country's largest source of flour. In 1802, French immigrant E.I. du Pont de Nemours built a gunpowder mill on Brandywine Creek, launching one of the world's largest chemical manufacturing companies and a family dynasty that has dominated the Brandywine Valley and, to a great degree, Delaware.

The valley's du Pont-built mansion-museums are prime tourist attractions. Winterthur Museum and Gardens, on Route 52 in Winterthur, is centered on Henry Francis du Pont's palatial nine-story chateau, famous for its collection of American decorative arts and antiques. Hagley Museum, on Route 141, 3 miles (4.8 km) north of Wilmington, is the site of the original du Pont mills and powder works. Longwood Gardens is a horticultural showcase, with 1,000 acres (405 ha) of conservatories, gardens, fountains, and woodlands.

The Brandywine River Museum and Conservancy, in Chadds Ford, Pennsylvania, on Route 1, is located in a Civil War-era mill on Brandywine Creek. It is known for its extensive collection of art by the Wyeth family.

Brandywine Creek State Park, just west of US-202 and north of Wilmington, was once a dairy farm owned by the du Pont family. It offers 14 miles (23 km) of hiking trails, wildlife viewing, and picnicking areas, as well as sledding and cross-country skiing in winter. A Civil War reenactment is held there in May.

Another annual event is the Winterthur Point-to-Point Races. Held in early May, it is an old-fashioned race featuring horses, antique carriages, and elegant tailgate picnicking.

Pennsylvania's Route 1 is the primary highway through the heart of the Brandywine Valley, but smaller roads north of Wilmington also take travelers through the valley.

The graveyards of Brandywine Valley reveal much about the history of the region.

DELAWARE SEASHORE STATE PARK

Delaware Seashore State Park was added to the state park system in 1965. With beaches, boating, surfing, windsurfing, sailboarding, camping, and a range of other activities, it's easy to see why this narrow, 2,018-acre (817-ha) strip of shore is Delaware's most popular state park.

The barrier island in southern Delaware has the Atlantic Ocean as its eastern boundary, while Rehoboth Bay and Indian Bay lie to the west. Until the late 1930s, natural alterations to the inlet channel between the bays and the ocean made the island inaccessible. In 1939, the federal government remedied the situation by constructing a pair of steel and stone jetties that made the Indian River Inlet more stable.

The beach located just north of the inlet is one of the few designated areas in the state for surfing. Dune crossings have been marked to indicate where 4WD drive vehicles have access to the beach. A permit is required to drive on the beach, which can be picked up from the park office.

Fishing is popular year-round on the beaches and banks of the Indian River Inlet. The New Road region provides easy access to the water for boats and sailboards via a manual boat launch. Visitors are also allowed to gather clams and crabs in some parts of the bays.

Burton Island has a nature trail that provides views of the salt marshes and bay islands. The park also hosts a sandcastle-building contest in July. The Indian River Marina has many services for anglers, including charter boats for ocean fishing. The campground is open mid-March to mid-November and can accommodate a variety of units from tents to large recreational vehicles.

There is a small daily entrance fee for Delaware-registered vehicles, and a slightly higher fee for out-of-state vehicles. Entrance fees are in effect May through October and some activities require additional fees. The park is south of Rehoboth Beach, on State Route 1.

Reenactments of war-time battles occur in parks throughout Brandywine Valley.

DOVER

Settled by Swedes in 1631, Dover replaced New Castle as the state capital in 1777. Today it has about 30,400 residents. In addition to its role as the seat of state and county government, this central Delaware city is a marketing center for agricultural southern Delaware. Nearby is Dover Air Force Base, the military's largest air-cargo terminal. The base has a public museum that exhibits vintage aircraft dating back to 1941.

The old State House, built in 1792, served as the seat of state government until 1933. In its Hall of Records is displayed the original deed to Delaware given to William Penn by England's Duke of York (later King James II) in 1682, and William Penn's order for the mapping of Dover, named for Dover, England.

Dover's Hollywood Diner opened in 1954

The city is noted for the preservation and restoration of numerous historic homes, particularly those built in the Georgian colonial style. Many restored eighteenth- and nineteenth-century homes can be seen around the Green, North and South State Street, and South Bradford Street. Brochures for self-guided tours of the city's most interesting buildings and attractions are available at the Delaware Visitor Center and the Sewell C. Biggs Museum, at 406 Federal Street.

Other local points of interest are the Delaware Agricultural Museum and Village, and the John Dickinson Plantation. The latter is the home of the man dubbed "Penman of the American Revolution" for his writings, including the Articles of Confederation that preceded the US Constitution. The site is on Kitts Hummock Road, 6 miles (9.7 km) south of Dover, on US-113.

Dover is reached by US-13/State Route 1. Air, rail, and bus services are available at Wilmington.

Map ref: page 293 K7

New Castle is renowned for its architecture, which includes buildings in the Federal and Colonial styles.

LEWES

Situated at the mouth of the Delaware Bay in southern Delaware, this maritime community traces its roots to the Dutch settlers who founded it in 1631 as an agricultural and whaling village. It has survived much since then, including destruction by Indians and attack by British forces during the War of 1812.

Today, its 2,300 residents host hordes of tourists and vacationers heading for its nearby bay and ocean beaches, which include Cape Henlopen State Park, Rehoboth Beach, Dewey Beach, and Delaware Seashore State Park. The beaches provide a range of aquatic activities, from sunbathing to swimming, fishing, boating, and hiking on nature trails. The 8,818-acre (3,571-ha) Prime Hook National Wildlife Refuge, 8 miles (13 km) north of Lewes off Route 1, provides marsh habitat for migratory waterfowl and native mammals, and more than 7 miles (11 km) of canoe trails.

The Seaside Nature Center has a variety of interesting exhibits, including large fish tanks, displays of stuffed birds, and whale and dolphin skulls; a self-guided interpretive trail that explains the human and natural history of Cape Henlopen; and a World War II observation tower that is open for tours.

Map ref: page 293 K8

NEWARK

The University of Delaware has made its home here—just east of the Maryland state line in northern Delaware—since it was founded in 1765. Not far away, at Cooch's Bridge, is the site of the only battle of the Revolutionary War fought in Delaware, on September 3, 1777. Although the Americans lost, it is said that the battle was the first in which Betsy Ross' newly designed flag of stars and stripes was flown. The battleground can be seen from a 90-foot (27-m) observation tower at Iron Hill Park, which is a popular mountain-biking, hiking, and picnicking venue.

The Newark area was settled in the 1690s. It became an iron-making center in the 1700s, and paper and textile mills were later built. It now has about 27,870 residents. It is located at the junction of Routes 2 and 273, north of I-95 and southwest of Wilmington.

Map ref: page 293 J6

NEW CASTLE

In 1682, Quaker leader William Penn landed here after English King Charles II granted him the region that had previously been controlled by Sweden and then Holland.

Located in northern Delaware on the Delaware River, 7 miles (11 km) south of Wilmington, New Castle served briefly as the capital of Delaware. During the Revolutionary War two signers of the Declaration of Independence—George Read and Thomas McKean—hailed from New Castle.

The town prospered through trade until a fire destroyed its business district in 1824. The arrival of the railroad in 1832 revitalized the town, but in the mid-1800s the lines were re-routed through Wilmington.

New Castle is noted for its Colonial and Federal architecture. Among its attractions is the 1730s Amstel House, which is now a museum. The Dutch House, built in the late seventeenth century, is thought to be the oldest brick house in the state, and is also now a museum. The Green, on Delaware Street between Third and Market streets, was laid out in 1655. The New Castle Court House, built in 1732, was occupied by the Colonial Assembly until 1776—it was here that Delaware adopted its constitution in September 1776.

New Castle can be reached on Route 9 from Wilmington.

Statue of William Penn, located in New Castle

Map ref: page 293 J6

ODESSA

Originally known as Cantwell's Bridge, this crossroads town south of the Chesapeake and Delaware Canal became an important grain-shipping port in the early 1800s, with access to Delaware Bay. Grain from the region's farms was shipped to the Delaware River, but when the railroad bypassed Odessa, and the American Midwest became the breadbasket of the world, its port days were numbered.

Among the places of interest are the Historic Houses of Odessa, a cluster of eighteenth- and nineteenth-century houses. The Collins-Sharp House—dating from the early 1700s—is one of Delaware's oldest houses.

Located on busy Route 1, Odessa has about 300 residents.
Map ref: page 293 J6

REHOBOTH BEACH

Rehoboth Beach is the closest beach to the District of Columbia. It is very popular and it may seem that this is where all Washington-ians come to escape the oppressive summer heat and humidity.

Refugees from inland summers find an array of maritime recreational activities at this popular beach resort town of 1,300 residents, on the Atlantic in southeastern Delaware. Just north of Rehoboth Beach is Cape Henlopen State Park, and to the south is Delaware Seashore State Park, where campsites are available. The four-day Rehoboth Beach Jazz Festival is held the weekend before Halloween, and the community hosts the Sea Witch Halloween Festival on the last weekend of October.

Rehoboth Beach was originally settled in the late 1600s. By 1873, when the first hotels were built near the beach, it was becoming a summer resort community—a change accelerated by the arrival of the railroad in 1878 and Route 1 in the 1920s.

Besides Route 1, visitors can take the year-round ferry between Lewes and Cape May, New Jersey.
Map ref: page 293 L8

WILMINGTON

Wilmington, with a population of 71,500, is the state's only large city and a metropolitan area where two-thirds of Delaware's population resides. As well as being an important port on the Delaware River, Wilmington is a national banking and finance center, and

Two-thirds of Delaware's residents live in Wilmington, the only large city in the state.

one of the world's largest centers for the chemical and pharmaceutical industries.

In the early 1800s, French immigrant E.I. du Pont and his two sons came here intending to establish a Utopian colony—instead they began gunpowder manufacturing. In 1803 their mill on Brandywine Creek, in Brandywine Valley, began producing gunpowder. Today, Wilmington is the headquarters of the chemical manufacturing and marketing giant E.I. du Pont de Nemours and Company—known simply as "DuPont"—which has to a great degree shaped the fortunes of Wilmington and Delaware. Many other corporations have also established headquarters here to take advantage of Delaware's lenient tax and incorporation laws.

Wilmington grew from a Swedish colony founded in 1638. By 1664 the settlement had passed from Swedish to Dutch and then English control. William Penn and the Society of Friends (Quakers) were granted a deed to the region in 1682. In 1739 it was named Wilmington for Spencer Compton, the Earl of Wilmington.

In addition to nearby Brandywine Valley, Wilmington has the Delaware Art Museum, which includes a collection of English pre-Raphaelite paintings, as well as paintings by various American artists. The Delaware Museum of Natural History has a variety of exhibits in natural settings. Holy Trinity (Old Swedes) Church, built in 1698, is thought to be the oldest active Protestant church in North America. Visitors can also tour the tall ship Kalmar Nyckel, a full-size replica of the 1638 ship that carried the first permanent settlers from Sweden to Delaware Bay. The ship features a 105-foot (32-m) main mast, cannon, 7,600 square feet (722 sq m) of sails, solid timbers, and elaborate wood carvings.
Map ref: page 293 K6

The sumptuous interior of Hotel du Pont in Wilmington is a lavish tribute to Delaware's "First Family."

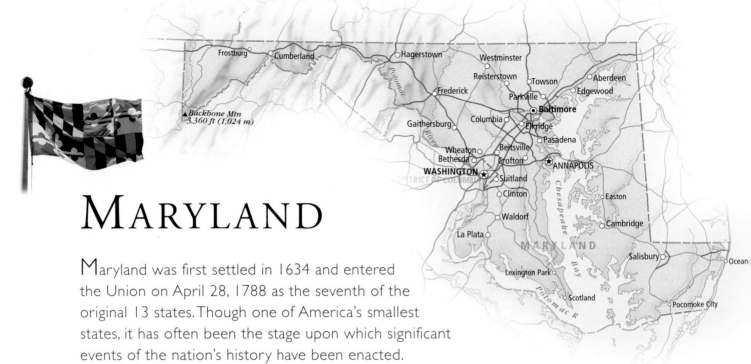

MARYLAND

Maryland was first settled in 1634 and entered the Union on April 28, 1788 as the seventh of the original 13 states. Though one of America's smallest states, it has often been the stage upon which significant events of the nation's history have been enacted.

The Treaty of Paris, which brought an end to the Revolutionary War and acknowledged the independence of the colonies, was ratified on January 14, 1784, by the Continental Congress sitting at Annapolis, the state's capital.

The port city of Havre de Grace only narrowly lost out to Washington DC as the site for the nation's capital. Maryland ceded land for the establishment of the District of Columbia in 1791. Because Maryland surrounds Washington DC, much of its economy is dependent upon government services, such as Department of Defense installations and the National Institutes of Health.

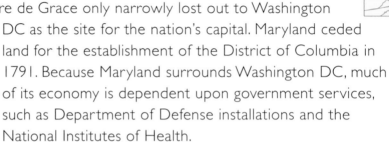

During the Civil War, perhaps the most pivotal battle of the entire conflict was fought in the farmlands west of Frederick around a trickling stream called Antietam Creek. That one day of confrontation saw the greatest loss of American lives ever to occur during a single day of war in the country's history, and Robert E. Lee's shattered Southern army retreated south back across the Potomac River.

This view of Annapolis from the Maryland State House shows many of the city's historic buildings.

Maryland's border with the Atlantic Ocean is a flat and often swampy expanse and includes two of the state's premier natural attractions, Assateague Island National Seashore, and the Blackwater National Wildlife Refuge. Chesapeake Bay cuts through the heart of the state, providing Maryland with a proud maritime heritage stretching back some 300 years.

Western Maryland includes Garrett County, with parklands and lakes that are ideal for hiking, camping, and fishing for trout. Forests cover two-fifths of the state.

With the exception of its urban areas, much of the state to the west of Chesapeake Bay is made up of farmlands and tiny rural communities. They are all connected to Maryland's proud history through landmarks, festivals, or monuments.

State motto *Fatti Maschii, Parole Femine* (Manly deeds, womanly words)
State flag Adopted 1904
Capital Annapolis
Population 5,296,486
Total area (land and water) 12,297 square miles (31,849 sq km)
Land area 9,775 square miles (25,317 sq km)
Maryland is the 42nd-largest state in size
Origin of name Named for Queen Henrietta Maria, consort of Charles I of England
Nicknames The Free State, The Old Line State
Abbreviations MD (postal), Md.
State bird Baltimore oriole
State flower Black-eyed susan
State tree White oak
Entered the Union April 28, 1788 as the seventh state

Places in
MARYLAND

ANNAPOLIS

Annapolis is the capital city of Maryland and the seat of Anne Arundel County. Settled in 1649, this historic city of 33,000 people is situated on the banks of the Severn River at its mouth on Chesapeake Bay.

Annapolis is a perfectly preserved blend of Colonial, Federal, and Victorian architecture; its buildings were spared the ravages of the Revolutionary War, the War of 1812, and the Civil War. The city boasts some 60 pre-Revolutionary houses, and the historic City Dock has been in use for more than three centuries.

The Maryland State House boasts America's largest wooden dome constructed without nails, and is the nation's oldest state capitol still in legislative use. The Treaty of Paris ending the Revolutionary War was signed there. The homes of three people who signed the Declaration of Independence can also be visited: William Paca, Charles Carroll, and Samuel Chase.

The William Paca House is one of the most impressive eighteenth-century Georgian mansions in Annapolis. This elegant landmark was constructed between 1763 and 1765 and has been meticulously restored to its original appearance. Well known for its 2 acre (0.8 ha), five-terraced pleasure garden, the house is furnished with period antiques, silver, and decorative arts.

Annapolis is home to two celebrated institutions of higher learning: the US Naval Academy and St John's College. The Naval Academy was formed in 1845 and occupies the site of old Fort Severn on a 338-acre (137-ha) campus built on the river. John Paul Jones is buried in its chapel crypt. St John's College is a liberal arts college founded in 1696 as King William's School, and is the third-oldest college in the nation.

Architectural historians offer weekend walking tours of the Historic District and US Naval Academy from April through to October, leaving from the visitor center in Cherry Grove Avenue.

Annapolis is 27 miles (43 km) south of Baltimore and is serviced by the Baltimore–Washington International Airport.
Map ref: page 293 H8

ASSATEAGUE ISLAND NATIONAL SEASHORE

Assateague Island is Maryland's premier natural attraction. A barrier island constantly reshaped by persistent waves, which raise sands from the gently sloping ocean floor, it totals 18,000 acres (7,290 ha), including its southern portion which lies within Virginia. It parallels Maryland's coastline for 24 miles (39 km), separated from the mainland by Chincoteague Bay.

The noon formation outside Bancroft Hall, at the US Naval Academy in Annapolis.

Main Street, Annapolis, is lined with historic buildings that exude old-world charm.

Visitor centers are operated by the National Park Service on both the Maryland and Virginian ends of the island. The Maryland center features beachcombing exhibits and a museum store.

In fall the poison ivy—vital to the island's ecosystem because its roots knit the dunes together—turns a brilliant red and sets this Atlantic island aflame. Fall also sees an end to summer crowds, and the island's infamous mosquitoes make way for the stunning monarch butterflies that make the island one of the stops on their annual migratory route.

Assateague's famous wild horses roam the marshlands. Descendants of domestic horses, they have reverted to a wild state and are actually the size of ponies, most likely due to their harsh environment and poor diet—almost 80 percent of their feed is a coarse salt marsh cord grass mixed with American beach grass. Their distinctive, bloated appearance is the result of a high concentration of salt in their diet that causes them to drink twice as much fresh water as domestic horses.

Assateague Island is home to nearly 300 species of bird. A bird checklist can be obtained from the visitor centers. Through spring and late summer, sandpipers, and other shorebirds probe the wet sand for food; Assateague's shallow bays are home to egrets and herons. Waterfowl, snow geese, black ducks, and mallards all escape harsher winters to the north on Assateague Island.

Camping on the beach is permissible, and nothing can beat an Assateague Island sunrise. But come prepared—mosquitoes can be horrendous from mid-May to October and high winds can send even the best-pegged tent soaring. An abundance of lodgings can be found north of Assateague Island at Ocean City.

Away from the beaches, half-mile (about 1-km) trails wind through lesser-known marshes, forests, and dune environments. The natural beauty of these areas prompted the *National Geographic* in 1996 to list Assateague State Park as one of the 10 best in the United States.
Map ref: page 293 L10

Baltimore's city skyline is an attractive backdrop for the marina at Inner Harbor.

BALTIMORE

Maryland's largest city, Baltimore (population 650,000) is situated at the head of the Patapsco River estuary, 15 miles (24 km) above Chesapeake Bay.

Baltimore is the birthplace of two of America's national treasures: its anthem, "The Star-Spangled Banner," written by Francis Scott Key; and George Herman Ruth Jr, known to all Americans as Babe Ruth, or just The Babe.

Babe Ruth was born on February 6, 1895, at 216 Emory Street near the Baltimore waterfront. The old family home was opened as a museum in 1974 and has been expanded since then to become the Archives of the Baltimore Orioles baseball team.

This statue in Bethesda commemorates the spirit and tenacity of pioneer mothers.

Baltimore was established in 1729. The US Navy's first ship, the *Constellation,* was launched in Baltimore in 1797, and its namesake, the last all-sail warship built (1854), has been moored in the city's harbor since 1968.

Baltimore was also the first Roman Catholic diocese in the United States and is home to the nation's first Catholic cathedral, the Basilica of the National Shrine of the Assumption of the Blessed Virgin Mary, constructed from 1806 to 1820.

Baltimore's endless charms range from a celebrated waterfront to fascinating neighborhoods and intriguing museums. The Baltimore Museum of Art's permanent collections include pieces by Picasso, van Gogh, and Matisse, and the Walters Art Gallery is famous for its Greek and Asian collections, boasting art and artifacts covering almost 5,000 years of history.

For a breathtaking view of the city, go to the Top Of The World Observation Level on the 27th floor of the World Trade Center, then end your day with a sunset trip on a water taxi to Fells Point, a working waterfront community that captures the spirit of a seaside port in the 1800s. Its cobblestone streets are lined with shops and restaurants with water views. The Lyric Opera House is home to the Baltimore Opera Company; the Baltimore Symphony Orchestra is found in the Joseph Myerhoff Symphony Hall.

Baltimore has long had an intellectual aura. Many colleges and places of higher learning call the city home, including the renowned John Hopkins University (1866), the Peabody Conservatory of Music (1857), and the University of Maryland, Baltimore (1807).

Baltimore has many examples of Victorian architecture, and one of the best is The Inn at Government House at 1125 North Calvert Street in the center of town. The meticulous restoration of this nineteenth-century mansion was completed in 1985, and it has served as the Official Guesthouse of the City of Baltimore since that time.

Baltimoreans, including artisans and craftspeople, volunteered their time to restore the mansion, and plaques commemorating their dedication are placed over the doors of some of the 18 guest rooms in appreciation. The woodwork and stained glass throughout the mansion are original to this 1889 masterpiece; some of the wood was covered in as many as 20 coats of paint prior to its restoration. Toothbrushes were used to strip paint from the spires of the Grand Staircase, and the green marble of the Library fireplace was quarried in Baltimore.

Baltimore is located just 35 miles (56 km) northeast of Washington DC on I-95. It is served by several airports, including the Baltimore–Washington International Airport and Washington's Dulles International Airport.
Map ref: page 293 H7

BETHESDA

Bethesda (population 63,000) is located in Montgomery County, a suburban area of Washington DC. The name is a corruption of the Hebrew "Bethsaida," meaning "house of healing". Some of Bethesda's best-known institutions are medical in nature: the Naval Medical Hospital and the National Institutes of Health.

Founded in 1887, the National Institutes of Health is today one of the world's foremost medical research centers and a focal point for research within the United States. The Naval Medical Center was established in 1942, and much of Bethesda's growth after World War II can be attributed to the establishment of various government facilities, which began in 1937 with the National Cancer Institute.
Map ref: page 292 G8

CAMBRIDGE

Cambridge is the largest city in Dorchester County on the eastern shores of Chesapeake Bay, a county almost surrounded by the waters of Chesapeake Bay and the Choptank and Nanticote Rivers. Founded as a plantation port in 1684 and named for Cambridge in England, this city of 11,000 people is entered via a drawbridge over Cambridge Creek, whose stores have been serving the community since the 1860s.

Featured in James A. Michener's epic *Chesapeake,* Cambridge has a long maritime history, which is depicted in the Brannock Maritime Museum.

The Oriole Baseball Stadium, Baltimore.

Step back in time with a visit to the historic community of Cumberland.

What brings most travelers to Cambridge, however, is the Blackwater National Wildlife Refuge: over 20,000 acres (8,100 ha) of marshes covering much of southern Dorchester County and providing a prime habitat for nesting and migrating birds. Over 250 bird species are found here including the northern loon, cormorants, and thousands of Canadian geese and ducks. It is also home to the endangered Delmarva fox squirrel.

Wildlife viewing is sensational along Wildlife Drive, drawing an estimated 75,000 visitors annually. The Marsh Edge Trail affords close-up looks at brackish marsh life, while the Woods Trail is a $^1/_2$-mile (about 1-km) loop through pines and mixed hardwoods.

In 1996, 129 bald eagles were counted in or near the refuge. Even when Chesapeake Bay freezes over in winter, eagles like the refuge because of the waterfowl prey that forage in its fields.

Blackwater National Wildlife Refuge is a short drive south of Cambridge and should not be missed when visiting the "Queen City on the Eastern Shore."
Map ref: page 293 J9

CRISFIELD

If ever a town owed its prosperity to the humble oyster it is Crisfield in southern Maryland, on the shores of Chesapeake Bay. In the 1800s, John Woodland Crisfield, attorney, congressman, and friend of Abraham Lincoln, saw the then tiny seaside hamlet of Somers Cove's potential for growth because of its seafood industry, particularly oysters, and was responsible for bringing the railroad to town in 1867. Grateful property owners dutifully renamed the town Crisfield in 1872, and the town's 200 years of relative isolation was to come to an abrupt end.

Oysters literally proved the town's foundation, with billions of shells used as road base, in buildings, and even on railroad tracks. Its harbor filled with sailing vessels, and in 1910 the Crisfield Customs House boasted the largest registry of sailing vessels anywhere in the nation.

In the 1920s the oyster supply became exhausted, but along came the Chesapeake Bay blue crab to restore the town's fortunes. Still found in huge quantities, they are a mainstay of Crisfield's economy today, as well as oysters, which are once again readily available.

Crisfield is the southernmost town in Maryland, located on the tip of a long, low-lying peninsula jutting southwards into Chesapeake Bay. The hundreds of coves and inlets along the 600-mile (965-km) shoreline of Somerset County make a perfect home for the finest clams, fish, oysters, and the Chesapeake Bay blue crab, said to be the most delicious in the world.

Crisfield's harbor also has the Somers Cove Marina, the largest state-owned marina in Maryland and one of the largest on the East Coast, with over 450 boat slips designed for all types of boats.

A few miles north of Crisfield is Janes Island State Park, 3,100 acres (1,256 ha) all but surrounded by Chesapeake Bay and ranking third among the state's parks in its variety of activities and amenities. There are 8 miles (13 km) of sandy beaches, hiking trails such as the White Tail and Blue Heron, nine waterfront log cabins, and numerous camping options.

Crisfield also provides easy access to Maryland's only inhabited offshore island, Smith Island. Legend has it that Ernest Hemingway once docked the *Pilar* at the island's only shop, the Driftwood General Store. Evidence of this is hard to come by.

The island has a special charm, with the streets of the island's three villages, Ewell, Rhodes Point, and Tylerton having no official names, nor the houses any numbers until recently. The people of Ewell refer to everything below the church as "down the field," and everything above the church as "over the hill." The island has no police. A distinctive Cornwall dialect is still retained, a remnant of the island's first inhabitants who arrived from Cornwall in the early 1700s.

Passenger ferries to Smith Island leave from Crisfield.
Map ref: page 293 J10

CUMBERLAND

Cumberland is the largest town in western Maryland, with a population of nearly 24,000. It is set amid the Allegheny Mountains, two and a half hours' drive from Baltimore and Washington DC. It occupies a spot on the Potomac River where it makes a large northward loop reaching to within 6 miles (9.7 km) of the border with Pennsylvania.

Cumberland's architectural gems include the 1820 Cowden House, a Georgian-style B&B. The Dent House (1890), a Queen Anne-style B&B, is named for George Dent, the surveyor of Cumberland. Together the houses are known as the Inn at Walnut Bottom, and are located on historic Greene Street.

Cumberland was Maryland's first Heritage Area and one of the state's first "Main Street" communities. History House has a museum with antiques. The Emmanuel Episcopal Church is located on the site of the former Fort Cumberland, established as a western outpost by British General Edward Braddock in 1755. By prior arrangement it is possible to tour the catacombs beneath this Gothic Revival church.

Cumberland's must-see attraction is the 184-mile (296-km) long Chesapeake and Ohio Canal, opened in 1850 and operated until 1924 as a transportation route hauling coal from western Maryland to Georgetown in the District of Columbia. Original structures include locks, lockhouses, and aqueducts, as well as the impressive 3,118-ft (951-m), brick-lined Paw Paw Tunnel. The canal's towpath provides a near-level trail through spectacular natural scenery and is perfect for hiking and biking. The National Park Service has a visitor center at the Chesapeake and Ohio Canal Terminus in Canal Street.

Cumberland is located on I-68 and is also served by the Cumberland Municipal Airport.
Map ref: page 292 D6

EASTON

Easton is a small town of just 10,000 people located along the tributaries of Chesapeake Bay in eastern Maryland. Talbot County's first courthouse was established there in 1711, and the town has been a center of trade and government ever since.

The town has retained its unique charm despite suffering three disastrous fires over the years (in 1810, 1855, and 1878), and has worked hard to preserve its architecture and landmarks.

The Historical Society of Talbot County offers tours through three restored homes: the James Neall House (1810), the Joseph Neall House (1795), and a seventeenth-century reconstruction named "Ending of Controversie." The Society's beautifully maintained gardens have won both state and national acclaim. Self-guided walking maps of historic downtown Easton are available.

The Academy Art Museum is the result of a merger between two historic buildings, creating five galleries, art and dance studios, conference rooms, and a light-filled atrium. The Academy is now the Eastern Shore's premier art museum and is nationally recognized for its exhibitions and performing arts programs. The historic 400-seat Avalon Theater was built in 1921 and has been restored to its original Art Deco splendor, offering a year-round schedule of performing arts and community events.

The Third Haven Friends Meeting House, built in 1682 on a Native American trail, is the oldest

Baltimore Harbor, a major trading center, was protected during the eighteenth century by Fort McHenry.

religious building still in use in the United States and the earliest dated building in Maryland.

Every year on the second weekend of November, up to 20,000 people from across the country come to Easton for the Waterfowl Festival, a three-day celebration of the arts, to view and buy some of the best wildlife art in the world. Up to 450 artists and artisans exhibit paintings, sculpture, carvings, decoys, and photographs in 18 sites across the colonial town.

The Bishop's House is a landmark of Talbot County and one of the finest B&Bs on Maryland's eastern shore. Located in Goldsborough Street, this 1880 Victorian mansion was the home of Philip Thomas, Governor of Maryland from 1848 to 1851.
Map ref: page 293 J8

Corn is grown in agricultural areas between Frederick and Gaithersburg.

ELLICOTT CITY

The main reason to travel to Ellicott City, located a few miles to the southwest of Baltimore in the Patapsco Valley, is to gain a glimpse into the way America used to be.

Ellicott City was founded as a Quaker community in 1772 by three brothers, John, Joseph, and Andrew Ellicott, who were looking to build a grist. They built the Jonathan Ellicott house and store and traded as Ellicott & Company.

In July 1827 the Army Corps of Engineers left Baltimore to examine a route west from Baltimore to Ohio, determining the best course through the Patapsco Valley. Charles Carroll, 91 years old and the only surviving signer of the Declaration of Independence, was there on July 4, 1828, to turn the first sod.

In 1830 the Baltimore and Ohio Railway constructed the "Old Main Line" to the town from Baltimore, thus challenging the existing form of transport, horse-drawn carriages. The famous race involving the steam-driven engine on wheels, *Tom Thumb*, and a horse-drawn car saw the *Tom Thumb* lose after a band blew off its boiler, but it was a hint of things to come. The horse may have won, but steam power was here to stay.

Today, Ellicott City's Historical Society is located in a pre-1790 building. Also in Ellicott City are the Firehouse Museum and the

County Courthouse at the summit of Mt Misery. The story of those who built the railroad can be found at the Baltimore and Ohio Railroad Station Museum.

In July 1868 a flood swept down the Patapsco Valley and wiped out much of the town. Among what can be seen today is one span of what was once a three-span bridge called the Oliver Viaduct, built to carry the railroad across Main Street and spanning the Tiber branch of the Patapsco River. The outline of the original turntable can still be seen on the south side of the station. Passenger services were discontinued in 1949.

Lodging options are limited in town, making Ellicott City preferable as a day trip from Baltimore.
Map ref: page 292 G7

FORT McHENRY NATIONAL MONUMENT AND HISTORIC SHRINE

This late eighteenth-century fort, once the guardian of Baltimore Harbor, became the inspiration for lawyer and poet Francis Scott Key to write the poem that became America's national anthem, "The Star-Spangled Banner," after it was defended bravely by American forces during the British attack on Baltimore on September 13, 1814. During the next century, Fort McHenry was still used occasionally as a military post, although it never again came under fire from enemy forces.

The beautiful gardens of Frederick's City Hall are a must-see for visitors.

Designated a national park on March 3, 1925, it became the only park in the National Park System to be designated a National Monument and Historic Shrine, on August 11, 1939.

Located 3 miles (4.8 km) southeast of the Baltimore Inner Harbor just off I-95, Fort McHenry began life as an earthen, star-shaped fort in 1776 during the Revolutionary War. It was called Fort Whetstone due to its location on Whetstone Point. Surrounded on three sides by water, enemy ships sailing into Baltimore would have no choice but to bypass the fort. The Revolutionary War passed without a shot being fired from the fort. In 1798 a new fort was built on the site and renamed Fort McHenry for James McHenry, Secretary of War under George Washington.

The fort became famous during the War of 1812, when British forces bombarded it constantly for 25 hours from ships moored outside Baltimore Harbor in the Patapsco River. Its valiant defenders held firm, though, and Baltimore was saved.

Union troops were stationed in Fort McHenry during the Civil War to help keep Baltimore from joining the southern cause, and the fort's guns were turned towards the city. After the Battle of Gettysburg, approximately 7,000 Confederate troops were detained within its walls.

The final garrison left the fort in 1912, and from 1915 to 1917 the city of Baltimore used the site as a city park and beach. Used as a hospital for returned soldiers in World War I, it was transferred to the care of the National Park Service in 1933.

Fort McHenry holds a vast store of archeological artifacts, many of which are in storage and have never been seen by the public.
Map ref: page 293 H7

The Memorial Bridge in Frederick features murals by William M. Cochran.

FREDERICK

Although the first settlers arrived in the area surrounding present-day Frederick as early as 1725, the town's formal beginnings can be traced to the laying out of Frederick Town in 1745.

A historic community, the very first act of rebellion against the English occurred in Frederick—the hated *British Stamp Act* was first repudiated from jurists in Frederick County in November, 1765. Frederick was also the launching spot for an expedition westward led by General Edward Braddock, along with a young Colonel George Washington and Benjamin Franklin, who met in Frederick to plan the march to capture Fort Duquesne from the French in 1755.

In 1778, during the Revolutionary War, the town of Frederick sent 1,700 men to support General George Washington at Valley Forge.

Frederick lies 51 miles (82 km) northwest of Washington DC at the junction of I-70 and Hwy 270 and contains examples of almost every major architectural influence found in nineteenth- and twentieth-century America: Federal, Greek Revival, Italianate, Queen Anne, Colonial Revival, and Second Empire. Its clustered church steeples grew from an early mix of Lutheran, Anglican, and Reformed traditions that were present in the town from its inception.

A walking tour of the Frederick Historic District, covering 33 city blocks, takes you past streetscapes of adjoining buildings, two to five bays in width and two to four stories in height, with gables or shed roofs. A few frame and log houses can also be found.

Frederick is Maryland's third-largest city with soil so rich it is said you can grow corn "as high as an elephant's eye." Today it has a population of approximately 50,000 and is a vibrant agricultural center. Fort Detrick, site of the US Army Medical Research Institute of Infectious Diseases, sees Frederick host to many firms specializing in biotechnology.
Map ref: page 292 F6

GAITHERSBURG

When the National Bureau of Standards moved into Gaithersburg in 1961, this community of 50,000 became known as the "Science Capital of the United States." Gaithersburg, with its 23 parks and 522 acres (211 ha) of parkland, has managed to retain many of its small-town qualities despite the influx of science-related industries since the agency now known as the National Institute of Standards and Technology came to town.

Gaithersburg is located in the heart of Montgomery County, with its southeastern border just 13 miles (21 km) away from the northwestern border of the nation's capital, Washington DC. Named after Benjamin Gaither who built a house there in 1802, its humble beginnings can be traced back to 1765 when it was a tiny agricultural settlement called Log Town.

Gaithersburg's famous Forest Oak tree grew on the site of Gaither's house, and was found to be 275 years old in 1975 when a boring was taken to determine its age. Sadly, this city landmark was blown over during a severe storm in 1997.

In 1899 the Gaithersburg Latitude Observatory was built as part of an international project to measure the earth's wobble on its polar axis. It closed in 1982, with computerization rendering manual observations obsolete.

Gaithersburg is now a hub for high-technology industries, with commercial agriculture almost non-existent.
Map ref: page 292 G7

One of the best times to visit Green Ridge State Forest is fall, when the foliage becomes a blaze of orange and gold.

GREEN RIDGE STATE FOREST

Green Ridge State Forest lies 14 miles (23 km) east of Cumberland in Allegany County, western Maryland. A 44,000-acre (17,820-ha) oak-hickory forest, it is Maryland's second-largest state forest. Located in the Ridge and Valley Province of the Allegheny Mountain chain, it enjoys the state's lowest rainfall of 36 inches (900 mm) and is known for its population of white-tailed deer, wild turkey, squirrel, ruffled grouse, quail, and fox.

Rich in history, Green Ridge State Forest was once the site for the Carroll Furnace, originally built as part of a steam-powered saw mill back in the 1830s. There are magnificent views from several lookouts such as Banners, Logroll, and Point Lookout, and elevation throughout the forest varies from 475 ft (145 m) at the Potomac River to 2,039 ft (622 m) on Town Hill.

Green Ridge State Forest has a permanent 12-mile (19-km) mountain bike trail with steady climbs and fast downhills. Exits are located along the trail to provide weary riders with a more moderate ride back to the trailhead. Bike trail maps can be obtained from forest headquarters. The Forest's streams are stocked with trout each spring.

Over 100 designated primitive campsites can be found throughout the Forest and at sites along the Potomac River. Nearby Flintstone has lodgings on the shores of the pristine Lake Habeeb, surrounded by the Allegheny Mountains and a Jack Nicklaus-designed golf course. A wider range of lodgings can be found 12 miles (19 km) further west along I-68 in Cumberland.

HAVRE DE GRACE

Havre de Grace could be found on nautical charts and in short histories about the upper Chesapeake Bay and Susquehanna River as early as the 1620s. The town with the lovely name "Harbor of Grace" was incorporated in 1785. Its streets reflect the fact that it narrowly lost out to Washington DC as the site for the nation's capital, with names such as Union, Adams, Washington, and Lafayette. General Lafayette often visited Havre de Grace and remarked how it reminded him of Le Havre in France.

With a population of 12,000, Havre de Grace is 39 miles (63 km) northeast of Baltimore along I-95. Its remarkable Historic District of some 800 buildings was shelled by the British in the War of 1812. After laying siege to Washington and burning the White House, they sailed to Havre de Grace where Lt John O'Neill manned a lone cannon at Concord Point and fired back.

White-tailed deer (Odocoileus virginianus seminolus), Green Ridge State Forest.

Havre de Grace was sacked and burned, with only two houses and St John's Episcopal Church spared. After the war, Lt O'Neill was released, and sixteen years later was made the keeper of Havre de Grace's famous lighthouse at Concord Point. Today it remains the most photographed and painted structure in this charming seaside town, as well as being the oldest lighthouse in continuous use on the East Coast.

Havre de Grace houses a Maritime Museum, the Steppingstone Museum on the site of a working farm, and the Decoy Museum. The latter features a history of duck and geese decoys, rough-hewn from wood, used to lure waterfowl to within range of the hunter's shotgun. Today they have become valuable collector's items, more likely to be found adorning a collector's mantlepiece than floating in a hunter's rig. With over 1,200 decoys, the museum represents a unique glimpse into this centuries-old piece of Chesapeake Bay culture, celebrating the art of decoy making which has made Havre de Grace the "Decoy Capital of the World."

Map ref: page 293 J6

OCEAN CITY

When the Atlantic Hotel opened its doors to the public in the tiny seaside village of Ocean City in 1875, no one could have envisioned what the next hundred years would bring. Today, Ocean City is Maryland's Miami Beach. Ten thousand hotel rooms, over 25,000 condominium units, plus apartments, beach houses, and 17 championship golf courses are spread along 10 miles (16 km) of the finest white-sand beach anywhere on the East Coast.

Despite the growth of shopping malls, water sports, and golf courses, its primary attraction is still the beach and its flashing boardwalk. Eco-cruises provide the opportunity to see porpoises and whales off Ocean City's coast, or take a trip to famous Assateague Island where wild ponies wander its beaches, roads, and trails.

Ocean City's 160 restaurants serve everything from eastern shore seafood fresh from the docks to a variety of ethnic cuisines. Seafood favorites include crab, lobster,

Winter activities in the Savage River State Forest include snowmobiling and skiing.

oysters, clams, and a bountiful selection of fish. After dining, you can stroll out onto the decking and look west across Sinepuxent Bay and another unforgettable sunset.

Ocean City is also known as the "White Marlin Capital of the World," attracting anglers from all over the United States. Members of the Ocean City Marlin Club have caught over 40,000 marlin, most of which have been released.
Map ref: page 293 K9

OLDTOWN

Southeast of Cumberland, along Hwy 51 on the border with West Virginia and on the banks of the Potomac River, can be found the near-forgotten community of Oldtown. It was the first settlement in what is now Allegany County in western Maryland. Early Indian settlements were established at a ford in the river, and the famous "Warrior Path" from the Indian nations of the north to the southern tribes crossed the Potomac here.

This out-of-the-way community failed to benefit from the construction of the western Maryland Railroad in 1905–10, and Maryland's highways have all bypassed it. When the Chesapeake and Ohio Canal Company went bankrupt in 1924, it declined even further.

Yet Oldtown remains a fascinating detour for lovers of history. The old stone house on Main Street was the home of Michael Cresap, who moved in with his wife in 1764. There was a jail in the basement, and the basement windows still have the original bars. It is the oldest house in Allegany County and is open on only two weekends each year: the first Friday to Sunday in June and the first Friday to Sunday in September. Special tours are available by appointment.

Downstream from Oldtown is the Paw Paw Tunnel, the most outstanding engineering feat of the Chesapeake and Ohio Canal, built to transport coal from western Maryland to Georgetown. Cut through over 3,000 ft (915 m) of solid rock, it eliminated 6 miles (9.7 km) of tortuous Potomac River bends, and took 14 years to build, surviving riots by the workers for non-payment of wages, a general strike in 1838, and the financial collapse of the Canal Company.

Finally completed in 1850, the tunnel today is in a remarkable state of preservation, but bring a flashlight because there is no lighting in the tunnel. Picnic facilities are nearby, and the drive from Oldtown to Paw Paw Tunnel through Green Ridge State Forest is a particularly scenic one.

Nearby Cumberland provides lodging options, and Green Ridge State Forest has over 100 primitive campsites throughout its vast area.
Map ref: page 292 D6

ST MARY'S CITY

St Mary's City in southern Maryland was established in 1634 when Governor Leonard Calvert sailed up a tributary of the Potomac River and into the world of the native Woodland Indians.

The 10,000-year Indian occupation of the Tidewater ended as the 200 settlers moved onto the site of the Yaocomaco Indian village and renamed it St Mary's City, at the same time celebrating the United States' first Catholic mass. Named after the Virgin Mary, it was to be the first European settlement in Maryland as well as the state's first capital from 1676 to 1694 when the capital was moved to Annapolis.

St Mary's sits at the end of a tidewater peninsula with the Patuxent River to the northeast,

Chesapeake Bay to the east, the Potomac River to the south, and the Wicomico River to the west. It is an hour and a half southeast of Washington DC along Route 5.

Historic St Mary's City is an 800-acre (324-ha) living history museum with interpreters in authentic seventeenth-century dress. It contains the reconstructed state house, a working tobacco plantation, a Woodland Indian hamlet, and a replica of the *Maryland Dove,* one of the two square-rigged ships that brought Maryland's first settlers from England.

The visitor center is located on Rosecroft Road just off Route 5, and exhibits 30 years of archeological research, including one of three lead coffins excavated in St Mary's City in 1992.

A charming B&B is The Brome-Howard Inn in Rosecroft Rd, a three-story Greek Revival farmhouse (circa 1840) offering three rooms and set on 30 acres (12 ha) of farmland with a frontage onto the St Mary's River.

A short drive south to the tip of the peninsula brings you to Point Lookout State Park, once the site of the largest Union prison for Confederate POWs. Built after the Battle of Gettysburg, it housed 52,000 Confederates, nearly 4,000 of whom died from disease and starvation. A huge obelisk stands over their mass grave, the only monument in the United States dedicated to an enemy. This picturesque peninsula offers swimming, fishing, boating, and hiking and has 143 wooded campsites. A visitor center is open seasonally.
Map ref: page 293 H10

SAVAGE RIVER STATE FOREST

Savage River State Forest, at 52,812 acres (21,389 ha), is the largest state forest in Maryland. It is set amid the Appalachian Plateau Region of Garrett County, about 150 miles (241 km) west of Baltimore.

Classified as a northern hardwood forest, it offers a year-round wealth of outdoor activities including snowmobiling, horseback trail riding, mountain biking, and flat-water canoeing on the Savage and Casselman Rivers, both of which have their origin around Big Savage Mountain. The rivers flow in opposite directions and are separated by the Continental Divide.

Trail maps, which include 10 miles (16 km) of cross-country ski trails, are available at the park office. Approximately 2,700 acres (1,094 ha) of Savage River State Forest has been designated as Big Savage Wildland.

New Germany State Park is a popular picnicking and camping site within the Forest and surrounds a 13-acre (5-ha) lake, formed by the damming of nearby Poplar Lick Run for milling operations.

Snow can arrive as early as November and may remain into late April. Wildlife ranges from black bears to brook trout, bobcats, racoons, and beavers, and over 100 species of bird call Savage River State Forest home.

The area comprises over 70 primitive campsites. Nearby Grantsville and the larger town of Cumberland offer plenty of lodging options.

Life is peaceful in small communities such as Oldtown.

Antietam National Battlefield Park

Monuments in Antietam National Battlefield Park commemorate the 23,000 casualties of the bloodiest battle in US history.

General Robert E. Lee's first invasion of the North during the American Civil War (1861–65) was a huge gamble with the potential of great rewards.

Maryland was with the Union during the Civil War, though considered a "border state" with sympathies divided between North and South. Slavery was legal, and Marylanders fought for both causes.

Lee led his 40,000 soldiers across the Potomac at White's Ford into Maryland in September 1862. Union General George McClellan pulled together a disorganized Union force and pursued, assuming Lee would march on either Washington or Baltimore.

Worrying that Union garrisons were threatening his supply lines behind him at Harpers Ferry and Martinsburg, Lee split his army in two. McClellan became aware of this when that famous order to separate—Special Order 191—was found on September 13, wrapped around three cigars in an abandoned Confederate camp by a Union corporal.

Moving quickly before Lee could reunite his army, McClellan engaged the Confederates at South Mountain on September 14, though failing to win a decisive victory. With both armies maneuvering and shadowing one another, they collided on the morning of September 17 on the ridges above the town of Sharpsburg and along Antietam Creek.

The ensuing battle produced the bloodiest day in American history, with over 23,000 casualties on both sides. Twice as many Americans were killed or wounded on that single day than in the War of 1812, the Mexican War, and the Spanish–American war combined.

During the Battle of Antietam, 500 Union and Confederate cannons boomed from dawn to dusk. Today, cannons have been placed on the battlefield to indicate the artillery sites used throughout the battle.

Antietam's rolling terrain was perfect for the artillery of both armies. With a combined total of 500 cannons on high ground, Blue and Gray enemy positions could be struck at will and from great distances. The cannon fire was so intense, Confederate Colonel Stephen Lee, commander of a key artillery position located where the visitor center is today, referred to Antietam as "Artillery Hell."

The battle centered around the Dunker church, the target of the Union attack. The fierce slaughter lasted five hours, and when it was over some 12,000 men lay either dead or wounded within a half-mile (about 1-km) radius of the church.

To the south of the Dunker church, Confederates entrenched in what was known as the Sunken Road (later as Bloody Lane) repulsed wave after wave of northern assaults, with massive losses for both sides. Eventually, Union troops found a vantage point from where they were able to fire down upon the road's defenders. Soon bodies were lying two and three deep.

Additional fighting at the Piper Farm saw 3,000 Union and 2,500 Confederate soldiers either dead or wounded. However, the sheer advantage in Union numbers allowed them to break the Southern brigades.

With the center of the Confederate army now wide open, McClellan overestimated Lee's reserve troop numbers, and a fresh Union division was not sent in. With Lee's army ruined and the end of the Confederacy in sight, a great opportunity to end the War Between the States was lost.

Lee and his Confederates lost 10,318 men (dead and wounded)—a quarter of his army. The Union lost 2,108 dead and a further 10,293 wounded. It was a turning point in the war. Lee's invasion had been halted, and it was enough of a "win" for the North for Lincoln to announce the Emancipation Proclamation, threatening to crush the South by destroying slavery, the basis of its economy and society. Any hope of support for the Confederacy from England and France was dashed, and the battle sealed the fate of the South.

Antietam National Battlefield is one of the nation's best preserved Civil War sites, with the Park boundaries encompassing the vast majority of the ground where action took place. Virtually no modern development has intruded there, and even the town of Sharpsburg remains relatively untouched.

The landscape has, however, undergone change, with the West and North Woods having been removed and the East Woods severely cut back. None of the wartime orchards exist today, and of the great cornfields, only the Miller Cornfield is still planted with corn. The battlefield looks very different to 1862, despite reforestation of the West and North Woods, which is still in progress.

The farmhouse of Philip Pry still stands on a hilltop on the east side of Antietam Creek. General McClellan selected this building as his headquarters, which offered only a marginal view of the ground held by Confederate forces. Two wounded Union generals were brought to the Pry farmhouse in the course of the battle.

The Prys returned after the battle to find their crops and livestock completely decimated. Despite being within the boundaries of the Park, the house is not open to the public.

The Dunker church was built in 1852. The Dunkers are now known as the German Baptist Brethren, the term "dunker" describing their baptismal ceremony. Striving for simplicity in their lives and their faith, the small church is plain and lacks a steeple; it was initially mistaken by Union officers as a schoolhouse.

After the battle the damage was repaired and services resumed. Destroyed by a severe windstorm in 1921, the property was acquired by the Government in 1951 and a new church was constructed in 1961 using materials from the original structure.

Today, the Sunken Road only partly resembles its 1862 appearance. The road east of where it bends near Roulette's Lane has eroded since the battle, while the western portion is no longer sunken at all.

Antietam National Cemetery was established on March 23, 1865, for the burial of those who died in the Maryland Campaign of 1862. Originally intended for the dead of both sides, such was the bitterness over the recent conflict, combined with the devastated South's inability to raise funds, that only Union dead are buried there. Two men—Aaron Good and Joseph Gill—spent their time after the war locating grave sites and identifying the occupants through letters, diaries, photos, marks on belts or cartridge boxes, and by interviewing relatives and survivors.

Antietam National Battlefield Park is located 1 mile (1.6 km) north of Sharpsburg on Route 65. The visitor center is open every day except Thanksgiving, Christmas and New Year's Day. A self-guided driving tour is 8 1/2 miles (14 km) long with 11 stops; walking and biking are also encouraged.

Sharpsburg is a small farming community of about 900 residents. There are no hotels in town but several delightful B&Bs, including Piper House, an 1840 restored farmhouse, which served as Confederate James Longstreet's headquarters directly south of "Bloody Lane."

Antietam National Battlefield Park is located 20 miles (32 km) west of Frederick in central Maryland, on the east bank of the Potomac River near the border with West Virginia.

The present-day Antietam National Battlefield Park is a solemn place to visit. One of the most evocative sites in the park contains the remnants of the Sunken Road (also known as Bloody Lane), where many soldiers fought and died.

NEW JERSEY

New Jersey is the most densely populated state in the United States, with nearly two out of three of its eight million citizens living within 30 miles (48 km) of New York City in the urban sprawl that begins south in Elizabeth and travels north through Jersey City, Newark, and Paterson. All of its 21 counties are classified officially as "metropolitan."

It may surprise some to learn there are wilderness areas throughout the state, such as the Great Swamp, a 7,400 acre (2,977 ha) refuge of marshes and wetlands not far west of New York City.

The Appalachian Mountains cut through the state's northwestern corner. The Appalachian Trail, the nation's premier wilderness pathway, follows the Appalachian Mountains' ridge line for 2,160 unbroken miles (3,475 km) from Georgia to Maine, and parallels the Delaware River and the Delaware Water Gap National Recreation Area. The Pine Barrens region of southern New Jersey offers a range of savannas, swamps, and hardwood forests in a wilderness that is largely pristine.

Pumpkins for sale in the lead up to Halloween.

New Jersey's urban centers may be the butt of jokes in New York comedy clubs, but there are some delightful places. The Atlantic seashore here, with its summer cottages, boardwalks, and seaside communities, offers year-round recreation, while Atlantic City receives over 37 million visitors a year who try their luck in the casinos that line its Boardwalk.

New Jersey's rolling hills and lakes in the northwest, down through the state's center with its wealth of well-preserved Revolutionary War monuments (much of the War was fought on New Jersey soil) and further south to the wilderness of Pine Barrens and the delights of the Atlantic seashore, all combine to ensure the fifth-smallest state in the Union can be proud of its heritage and can stand on its own, and not simply be regarded as a cultural adjunct of New York City.

State motto Liberty and Prosperity
State flag Adopted 1896
Capital Trenton
Population 8,414,350
Total area (land and water)
8,215 square miles (21,277 sq km)
Land area 7,419 square miles
(19,215 sq km)
New Jersey is the 46th-largest state in size
Origin of name Named for the English Channel Island of Jersey
Nickname The Garden State
Abbreviations NJ (postal), N.J.
State bird Eastern goldfinch
State flower Purple violet
State tree Red oak
Entered the Union December 18, 1787 as the third state

CARLISLE

Located in the rolling, rural hills of Cumberland County, 23 miles (37 km) west of Harrisburg in south-central Pennsylvania, this city of 18,400 has seen its share of historic events since its founding in 1751. Two local residents, James Wilson and George Ross, signed the Declaration of Independence. They were chosen to represent Carlisle at the Continental Congress in the First Presbyterian Church (1757), which still stands. It served as President George Washington's headquarters during the 1794 Whiskey Rebellion, a crucial test of the new federal government's authority in which grain farmers and whiskey producers rebelled against an excise tax on whiskey. Mary Ludwig, better known as Molly Pitcher, the heroine who provided water to and then fought beside American troops during the Battle of Monmouth (June 28, 1778) in New Jersey, lived here as well. A monument marks her grave in a cemetery on East South Street.

Carlisle Indian School, the first non-reservation school for Native Americans, was established in 1879 at Carlisle Barracks. Over 39 years it educated 6,000 Native American children, including 1912 Olympic champion Jim Thorpe. It is now site of the US Army War College and its Military History Institute.

At Carlisle Barracks, 1 mile (1.6 km) north of town on US-11, visitors can tour the Hessian Powder Magazine Museum, in a building that Hessian troops— German mercenaries hired by the British to fight against American forces during the Revolutionary War—constructed in 1777.

Carlisle can be reached via the I-76 and I-71.
Map ref: page 292 G5

CHADDS FORD

Located 28 miles (45 km) southwest of Philadelphia and just north of the Delaware state line, on US-1, Chadds Ford lies amid the picturesque Brandywine Valley, home to both the du Pont family of the industrial-chemical fame and the Wyeth family of artists.

During the Revolutionary War, on September 11, 1777, British forces led by General Sir William Howe defeated General George Washington and the Continental Army at the Battle of Brandywine Creek. The Battle is commemorated at the 50-acre (20.3-ha) Brandywine Battlefield Park. A visitor center houses exhibits about the Battle, which opened the way for the British occupation of Philadelphia. There is also the reconstructed farmhouse of Benjamin Ring and the preserved house in which George Washington's French ally, the Marquis de Lafayette, stayed.

The Brandywine River Museum and Conservancy is located in a Civil War-era mill on Brandywine Creek. It houses an extensive collection of work by three generations of Wyeth family artists.

Chadds Ford was settled in 1684 and it has about 2,000 residents today. It is named for ferryman, farmer, and tavern-owner John Chads. The restored John Chads House, built in 1725, stands in the Chadds Ford Village Historic District. The restored Barns-Brinton House was built in 1714 and used as a tavern. It still stands near Chaddsford Winery.
Map ref: page 293 K6

CHESTER

Swedes and Finns first settled here, on the banks of the Delaware River just a few miles southeast of today's Philadelphia, in 1644, making this industrial suburb one of Pennsylvania's oldest communities. Originally named Upland, it was the most important settlement in the region for a time. As the first capital of Pennsylvania Colony, it was the site of the Pennsylvania Assembly's first meeting, in 1682, the year that Quaker leader and colony founder William Penn first visited. Today, the city of almost 42,000 residents is a port of entry and shipbuilding center, with oil refineries and auto assembly plants as well as paper, chemical, and electrical equipment factories.

In Governor Printz Park visitors can see foundations remaining from the original settlement. Other historic attractions in the area include the old Chester courthouse. Built in 1724, it is said to be the oldest public building still in use in the United States. The Caleb Pusey House at Landingford Plantation in nearby Upland was built in 1683. It is the only remaining building William Penn is known to have visited.

Chester can be reached via I-95 from Philadelphia.
Map ref: page 293 K6

EASTON

Located at the confluence of the Delaware and Lehigh rivers, 58 miles (93 km), north of Philadelphia, this city of 26,300 residents played an important role in the settlement of the region. Thomas Penn, son of the Pennsylvania Colony founder William Penn, founded Easton in 1752 as the administrative center for the new Northampton County. The town was laid out with the same concept used in Philadelphia: a grid around a "great square." In this square, on July 8, 1776, residents heard a public reading of the Declaration of Independence.

In the nineteenth century, Easton's location at two rivers, the Morris Canal, and five railroads gave it easy access to the region's major cities and coal mines, enabling it to become one of the country's first industrial centers. During these boom times, Lafayette College was founded (1832), and the many distinctive homes and other buildings that now comprise Easton's historic districts were constructed.

Door decoration near Chester.

Visitors can take a walking tour through the historic downtown, to see the 1753 Bachman Tavern, and "Millionaires Row" lined with Victorian homes. Mule-drawn boat rides along Easton's canals are available at Hugh Moore Park, and paddleboats and canoes can be rented.

Two Rivers Landing, in downtown Easton, houses the Delaware and Lehigh National Heritage Corridor Visitor Center, the Crayola Factory, and the National Canal Museum. The Delaware and Lehigh National Heritage Corridor Visitor Center has exhibits depicting the region's history, cultures, canal system and industries. The Crayola Factory isn't where the famous colored crayons and markers are made. Instead, it lets visitors see how they are manufactured. It includes projects and activities for children. The National Canal Museum has exhibits depicting the history and technology of nineteenth-century canals and inland waterways. Hands-on exhibits include operating a lock model, and a model boat that can be piloted through the lock.

Easton can be reached by car via US-22, or by bus.
Map ref: page 293 K4

Chaddsford Winery, Chadds Ford, in the scenic Brandywine Valley.

ERIE

Erie, 126 miles (203 km) north of Pittsburgh in Pennsylvania's north-western corner, is the state's only port on the Great Lakes. Its name derives from the Eriez Native Americans who inhabited the area when the French explored it in the early 1600s.

With 102,640 residents, Erie is Pennsylvania's third-largest city. It is a major manufacturing and commercial city spawned by access to Lake Erie, the Erie Canal (1825), and railroads, which arrived in the 1850s. Its factories manufacture plastics, locomotives, boilers, engines, turbines, and paper.

In 1753 a French expedition built Fort de la Presque Isle on the peninsula that juts into Lake Erie. They later abandoned the site, which was then occupied by the British. Ottawa Native American Chief Pontiac organized a confederacy of Great Lakes and Ohio Valley tribes in 1763, who attacked and defeated the British. Still, a permanent settlement was established at Erie by 1795.

On September 10, 1813, during the War of 1812, American Commodore Oliver Hazard Perry used ships built at Erie to defeat the British Navy in the Battle of Lake Erie. The Erie Maritime Museum is the home port of the reconstructed US Brig *Niagara*, to which Perry transferred his command after his first brig, *Lawrence*, was severely damaged. The sunken remains of the *Niagara* were raised from the bottom of Misery Bay in 1913. In addition to exhibits depicting the region's maritime past, the museum features a replica of the mid-ship section of the *Lawrence*, and a section that was blasted with live ammunition fired from the current *Niagara*'s cannon.

Nearby Presque Isle State Park, a day-use-only area, occupies the sandy spit that extends into Lake Erie. It offers beaches, hiking, biking, swimming, scuba diving, waterskiing, boating, fishing, bird-watching, and picnicking. In winter, cross-country skiing, ice-skating, and iceboating are popular.

The Experience Children's Museum houses interactive science and humanities exhibits, and programs designed to teach children about energy, light, force and motion, weather safety, fossils, recycling, and much more.

The Erie Summer Arts Festival is held each June in Liberty Street Park, and features local, regional and national artists and performers. The four-day Harborfest is held in mid-summer, with musicians, hot-air balloons, and even a US Navy SEAL sky-diving demonstration.

Erie can be reached by train, bus or by car via I-90, I-86 and I-79; it has an international airport.
Map ref: page 290 B8

GETTYSBURG

Were it not for three hellish days in the summer of 1863, this cross-roads town founded in the 1780s north of the Maryland state line might still be as obscure as it was before the clash of Union and Confederate forces left 51,000 Americans dead, wounded or captured. Confederate General Robert E. Lee had marched his army into southern Pennsylvania, seeking a major victory in Union territory. On July 1, in the picturesque farmlands and woods just south of Gettysburg, Lee's 75,000-man Army of Northern Virginia collided with the 90,000-strong Army of the Potomac, led by General George Meade.

On July 3, when the Civil War's bloodiest battle was finally over, Lee was defeated, although he did escape with his army. The battle is often called the "high-water mark" of the Confederacy, a turning point from which the South never recovered. Three months later, Abraham Lincoln delivered his famous Gettysburg Address at the dedication of Soldiers' National Cemetery.

To today's 7,000 residents, the battle bequeathed a thriving tourist economy, centered on the nearly 6,000 acres (2,430 ha) of Gettysburg National Military Park. Visitors can drive 26 miles (42 km) of roads through the battlefield. Popular sites include the stone house where Lee had his headquarters, the Union lines on Cemetery Ridge, the scene of the costly last-ditch Confederate assault known as Pickett's Charge, and the Lincoln Room Museum in the Wills House, where Lincoln stayed and finished writing the Gettysburg Address.

There is no charge for touring the Park. There are fees to view the large electric map of the battlefield, and the Cyclorama, a large 360-degree painting completed in 1884 that depicts Pickett's Charge accompanied by a dramatic sound and light program. It is possible to tour the Park in a few hours, but a full day at least is recommended. Guided tours are available, as well as audio tapes for auto tours.

Gettysburg is also the location of the Eisenhower National Historic Site, the 231-acre (94-ha) farm that was the only home the former general and two-term Republican president and his wife, Mamie, ever owned. Access is via shuttle buses from the Gettysburg Military Park Visitor Center.

Silent guns at Gettysburg National Military Park, where 51,000 Americans were killled, wounded, or captured in one of the bloodiest battles of the Civil War.

The fine handiwork of an Amish quilt.

There is no public transportation into Gettysburg, which is 37 miles (60 km) southwest of Harrisburg, and is reached via US-15 and US-30. The closest airport is Harrisburg International.
Map ref: page 292 G5

HARRISBURG

Pennsylvania's capital city is located in the southern part of the state along the Susquehanna River. While the city itself counts only 52,400 residents, it is part of a metropolitan area of almost 588,000 people. The State Capitol, on Capitol Hill, is in a 13-acre (5.3-ha) park. The 600-room edifice has a 272-foot (83-m) high dome, bronze doors, murals, statuary, and stained-glass windows.

Across from the Capitol is the State Museum of Pennsylvania, which has free exhibits depicting Pennsylvania's pre-history and history. Among its permanent features is a gallery dedicated to Quaker leader and Pennsylvania Colony founder, William Penn. The nineteenth-century Brockerhoff House includes interior scenes depicting American home life in the early and late-nineteenth century. The exhibits include a full-scale replica of a Delaware Native American village, Peter Frederick Rothermel's huge mural of the Battle of Gettysburg, paleontology and geology exhibits, and a planetarium.

Look for the riverfront John Harris/Simon Cameron Mansion, the home of John Harris, Sr (a ferry operator and William Penn's ambassador to the colony's Native Americans), and John Harris, Jr, who laid out the city of Harrisburg in 1785 and donated land for the Capitol grounds. In 1863 the house became the home of Simon Cameron, a former US senator and President Abraham Lincoln's first Secretary of War.

The 40-acre (16-ha) Fort Hunter Mansion and Park occupies a bluff overlooking the Susquehanna River and the Blue Mountain Range. Fort Hunter is a restored nineteenth-century plantation with nine structures listed on the National Register of Historic Places. Benjamin Chambers, the founder of Chambersburg, originally settled the property in 1725. Faced with the increasing threats posed during the French and Indian War—also known as the Seven Years War (1754–63)—the British built a number of small forts in the area, among them Fort Hunter. The fort was later abandoned and former Continental Army Captain Archibald McAllister purchased the site, turning the property into a self-sufficient frontier village.

The authentic paddlewheeler *Pride of the Susquehanna* provides cruises on its namesake river from May through October. It is docked at City Island, across the river from the State Capitol.

The world's attention turned to the Harrisburg area in 1979 when loss of coolant threatened a catastrophic meltdown of the reactor core and release of radiation at the nuclear power plant on nearby Three Mile Island, on the Susquehanna River. It is the United States' worst nuclear accident.

Gifford Pinchot State Park is 17 miles (27 km) south of Harrisburg, between US-15 and I-83. It offers camping, swimming, boating, fishing, hiking, cycling, horseback riding, ice skating, and cross-country skiing.

Numerous highways, including interstates, intersect at Harrisburg, which is 106 miles (171 km) west of Philadelphia. Harrisburg has an international airport, and also railway and bus services.
Map ref: page 292 G4

HERSHEY

The home of Hershey Foods Corporation, this company town of 7,400 residents has proclaimed itself "The Sweetest Place on Earth." Located 14 miles (23 km) east of Harrisburg in the picturesque Lebanon Valley, Hershey proudly touts its chocolate heritage, with streets named Chocolate and Cocoa avenues.

Company founder Milton Hershey started out as an apprentice candymaker in Lancaster in 1872. After failed attempts to launch candy companies in various cities, he returned to Lancaster and founded Lancaster Caramel Company in 1886. In 1894 he established the Hershey Chocolate Company as a subsidiary, but in 1900 he decided to concentrate solely on chocolate and relocated to Derry Church, the rural Pennsylvania village where he was born. The town was renamed Hershey in 1906 and a community grew up around it. Hershey and his

Amish farms near the village of Intercourse, in Pennsylvania Dutch Country.

wife, Catherine, gave generously to the town; he died in 1945.

Hershey Park and Hershey Park Arena offer a wide range of family activities, including amusement rides, live entertainment, marine mammal presentations, and sporting events. Next to the Arena is the Hershey Museum. Hershey's Chocolate World is the visitor center for the company and the area. An automated tour ride explains chocolate production. Nearby is ZooAmerica North American Wildlife Park. Indian Echo Caverns, 3 miles (4.8 km) west of Hershey off US-322, offers guided tours through an underground world of stalagmites, stalactites, columns, and lakes.

Hershey is 14 miles (22.5 km) east of Harrisburg on US-322. Rail and bus services go to Harrisburg and its international airport.
Map ref: page 293 H4

INTERCOURSE

The village of Intercourse, a social and commercial hub for Amish and Mennonite farm families and other local residents, was founded in the Pennsylvania Dutch Country in 1754. Originally named Cross Keys, its name was changed to Intercourse in 1814.

Many visitors are drawn to Intercourse by the presence of the "Plain People," Protestant Amish and Mennonites descended primarily from seventeenth- and eighteenth-century German immigrants, who maintain a conservative, agricultural way of life. Many still reject such modern amenities as electricity, telephones, and automobiles. Their horsedrawn carriages are commonly seen on Lancaster County's roadways.

The village offers art galleries, museums, lodgings, camping, and Pennsylvania Dutch restaurants and specialty shops featuring local handcrafts. Buggy rides, tours, and B&Bs are also popular.

The People's Place is the center for Amish and Mennonite arts and crafts. It provides information about the Amish, Mennonite, and Hutterite people with a film and a museum with hands-on exhibits. The People's Place Quilt Museum, located across the street in the Old Country Store, houses a collection of antique Amish quilts.

Intercourse is located on state Route 340, 11 miles (17.7 km) east of Lancaster.
Map ref: page 293 J5

JOHNSTOWN

This southwestern Pennsylvanian city of 28,100 residents, once an iron- and steel-producing center, occupies a deep valley in the Allegheny Mountains where Stony Creek, the Little Conemaugh, and the Connemaugh rivers meet.

Since Swiss immigrant Joseph Johns settled here in 1793, the town has been both blessed and cursed by its waterways. They provided important transportation links for commerce and industry. But four times the city has suffered

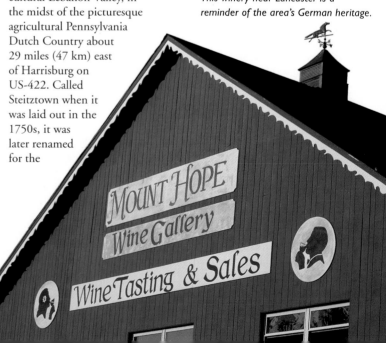

An Amish horse and buggy, commonly seen in the streets of Lancaster.

devastating floods. The South Fork Dam, east of the city on the Conemaugh River, failed in 1862 and 1889. The latter, infamous as the Johnstown Flood, sent a wall of water a half-mile (0.8 km) wide and about 75 feet (23 m) high through the town, killing 2,209 people and causing millions of dollars worth of damage. Another flood swept through the town in 1936, killing 25 and causing around US$40 million in damage. In 1977 yet another flood killed 85, and cost the city more than US$300 million dollars.

The Johnstown Flood Museum, at 304 Washington Street, has exhibits recalling the disaster of May 31, 1889. The 26-minute documentary film *The Johnstown Flood,* which won an Academy Award in 1989, plays hourly. A large 3-D relief map with sound effects and fiber-optic animation shows the path of the wall of water. The visitor center at the Johnstown Flood National Memorial, at the

site of the former South Fork Dam, has exhibits explaining the flood.

Johnstown is about 70 miles (113 km) east of Pittsburgh on state Route 56, between US-22 and US-219. It has a rail service plus regular commercial flights to and from Pittsburgh.

Map ref: page 292 D4

LANCASTER

Lancaster, with 55,550 residents, is the center of the Pennsylvania Dutch Country, a rich farming and popular tourist region settled by conservative Amish and Mennonite Germans, and other religious groups in the early 1700s.

Today, the horses and buggies that many of the "Plain People" use instead of automobiles, as well as their simple attire and picturesque farms, are reminders of a simpler time and lifestyle. The area's family-style Pennsylvania Dutch restaurants are famous for serving up platters of meat, home-baked breads, potatoes, fresh vegetables and other farm-country foods.

Lancaster served as the capital of the fledgling United States for a day during the Revolutionary War. Congress fled Philadelphia as British troops approached, stopping in Lancaster on September 27, 1777, on its way to York. From the 1760s through the early 1800s, Lancaster was the largest inland town in the American colonies and the country.

A block west of the city's hub, Penn Square, one of the country's oldest enclosed markets, is the

Fulton Opera House, built in 1852 and named for inventor Robert Fulton. The central market, located off Penn Square, dates back to the mid-1700s. Each Tuesday and Friday it comes alive with farmers, bakers, and butchers selling their products. Trinity Lutheran Church, also off Penn Square, is Lancaster's oldest congregation, dating back to 1729.

The Amish Farm and House, a working farm 5 miles (8 km) east of Lancaster, has exhibits depicting the Amish way of life.

The Landis Valley Museum, just north of Lancaster, has a "living history complex" interpreting rural Pennsylvania–German life from 1750 to 1940. Its historic buildings include farmsteads, a tavern and a country store.

The Historic Rock Ford Plantation, in Lancaster County Park, is the preserved eighteenth-century plantation of Edward Hand, adjutant general during the Revolutionary War.

Wheatland is the 1828 Federal style mansion of James Buchanan, the only Pennsylvanian to become president of the United States (1857–61). Costumed guides conduct one-hour tours, including tours by candlelight during the first two weeks of December.

Lancaster is located in south-eastern Pennsylvania between Philadelphia and Harrisburg via US-222 and US-30. Rail and bus services are available.

Map ref: page 293 H5

LEBANON

Lebanon is located in the agricultural Lebanon Valley, in the midst of the picturesque agricultural Pennsylvania Dutch Country about 29 miles (47 km) east of Harrisburg on US-422. Called Steitztown when it was laid out in the 1750s, it was later renamed for the

Lebanon of the Bible. With 24,800 residents, it is a center for the manufacture of chemicals, processed food, and textiles, as well as a commercial center for the surrounding area.

Among its historic churches are the 1760 Tabor United Church of Christ and the Salem Lutheran Church, also built in 1760 (tours by appointment).

The Stoy Museum and Hauck Memorial Library houses a variety of reconstructed rooms depicting bygone times, including a drugstore, doctor's office, one-room schoolhouse, toy shop and general store. Guided tours are available.

Map ref: page 293 H4

NEW HOPE

The charming village of New Hope, with just 1,400 residents and four streets, is a favorite destination for romantic weekends, art and antique shopping, visits to historic sites, ferry rides on the Delaware River and strolling on cobblestone walkways through alleys and side streets.

New Hope was founded in 1681 on the west bank of the Delaware River across from Lambertville, New Jersey, 42 miles (68 km) north of Philadelphia. An artists' and writers' colony, it has many guesthouses, fine restaurants, and shops. The village is just a few miles from Washington Crossing Historic Park, where General George Washington and his troops made their successful Christmas Night, 1776, crossing of the Delaware River during the Revolutionary

This winery near Lancaster is a reminder of the area's German heritage.

A panoramic view of the Pittsburgh city skyline and the Monongahela River just on nightfall, from Mount Washington.

War to attack German (Hessian) and British troops at Trenton and Princeton in New Jersey.

The Bucks County Playhouse is located in a mill building dating from the 1780s. Productions are offered May through December. In April-November, visitors can join one-hour mule-drawn barge trips on the Delaware Canal, narrated by a folk singer and historian.

The New Hope and Ivyland Railroad offers rail excursions on restored 1920s-vintage passenger cars, pulled by steam- or vintage diesel-powered locomotives, through the picturesque hills of Bucks County.

New Hope can be reached by car via US-202.

Map ref: page 293 L4

PHILADELPHIA

See Philadelphia, State Feature, pages 282–83

PITTSBURGH

Iron City. Steel City. Smoky City. Pennsylvania's second-largest city, once notorious for its heavy air pollution, has borne those dubious nicknames since the Industrial Revolution made it the world's leading steel producer by the late 1800s. Today, with the heyday of its smoke-belching blast furnaces a sooty memory and efforts to forge a post-industrial future for itself well underway, the new nickname for the home of nearly 370,000 residents is Renaissance City.

Although Pittsburgh still produces the metal that once gave it a booming economy, most of its big, aging steel mills, once the most productive in the world, have closed since a downturn began in the 1970s. Remaining production is focused now on specialty steels, and the city's economy has diversified into more service-oriented enterprises such as medical and industrial research.

About 90 hospitals service the area. The University of Pittsburgh is the region's largest employer. The University Health Center treats patients needing heart, lung, liver, and kidney transplants. More than 170 academic, industrial and governmental research laboratories, including nuclear research facilities, operate in the area as well. Manufacturing still employs more than 130,000 people in factories operated by such industrial giants as steelmaker USX Corp.; aluminum producer Alcoa; glass, paint, and chemical manufacturer PPG Industries; and the food products firm H.J. Heinz. Nonetheless, the economic downturn the city. has experienced since the 1980s has caused the population to decline from almost 424,000 in 1980 to less than 370,000.

Located in the western part of Pennsylvania, Pittsburgh is the nation's largest inland port. It sits amid hilly topography, where the confluence of the Allegheny and Monongahela rivers form the Ohio River. France and Britain traded control over the economically and militarily strategic area, originally inhabited by the Delaware and Shawnee Native Americans, during the French and Indian War or Seven Years War (1754–63) between France and England. In 1753, George Washington, then a young officer in the Virginia militia, surveyed the area for the Ohio Land Company of Virginia.

In 1758, General John Forbes re-established British control, named the site for British Prime

A heavy metal sculpture by Alexandr Brodsky, in Pittsburgh's city center.

Minister, William Pitt the Elder, and built Fort Pitt. European settlement was delayed until the 1770s by Native American uprisings, but by 1783 there were about a hundred families living here. Today, its blend of modern and historic architecture, its new parks and transportation systems, and numerous cultural sites show that the Pittsburgh of the twenty-

first century is unlikely to resemble the grimy Pittsburgh of the past.

The city has many places of interest to visitors, some of the best of which are named for the steel tycoon and philanthropist Andrew Carnegie (1835–1919). Fans of professional sports can follow football's Steelers, baseball's Pirates and hockey's Penguins.

Devotees of the performing arts can take in the programs at the Carnegie Music Hall while the Carnegie Museum of Art displays many Impressionist and post-Impressionist paintings, nineteenth- and twentieth-century American and European paintings, sculpture, films and architectural displays. Dinosaur Hall at the Carnegie Museum of Natural History displays a hundred full skeletons, including one of the famous *Tyrannosaurus rex*.

The Carnegie Science Center provides more than 250 hands-on exhibits focused on advances in science and technology. The Fort Pitt Museum, at Point State Park, provides insights into the early history of western Pennsylvania and the French and Indian War, with models, dioramas, a reconstructed trader's cabin, and artifacts.

Car-borne travelers can get to Pittsburgh via I-76 and I-79. The city is also accessible via its international airport, passenger trains, and bus services.

Map ref: page 292 B4

READING

Since two sons of Pennsylvania founder William Penn founded this city in 1748, Reading (pronounced RED-ing) has grown into an industrial center and commercial hub in the agricultural Pennsylvania Dutch region. Located on the Schuykill River in southeastern Pennsylvania, 63 miles (101 km) northwest of Philadelphia, the city is noted for

which presents the story of the pre-railroad canal transportation era, and the Heritage Center, an information center where special events are held throughout the year. In the Deppen Cemetery are 67 marked and unmarked graves dating from 1808 to 1915 that were relocated here to save them from inundation after the construction of Blue Marsh Lake. Also here is Wertz's Bridge, a covered bridge built in 1867,

Erie. From that point Scranton was chiefly a coal-mining city, but demand declined in the 1940s and many mines closed. Since the 1950s the city has implemented a series of plans to diversify its economy, which has a broad manufacturing base, a college, and a university.

The Pennsylvania Anthracite Heritage Museum, in McDade Park, tells the story of the people who came to this region to work in the mines, mills, and factories.

Amish people living in Lancaster County. It has an authentically furnished Old Order Amish farmhouse, a blacksmith shop, a one-room schoolhouse, a barn with animals, an operating smokehouse stocked with traditional Pennsylvania Dutch foods available for purchase, Amish buggies and wagons, and a picnic area.

The Mill Bridge Village in nearby Paradise dates from 1728. It is a restored colonial village with an operating 1738 water-driven corn mill. There are various working craftspeople, including a blacksmith, broom-maker, and quilter, as well as displays of Amish and Mennonite crafts. Buggy rides and a streamside picnic area are also available.

Next to the museum is the Lackawanna Coal Mine, where underground tours take visitors down 300 feet (92 m) on a walking tour through the mine's three veins.

Steamtown National Historic Site is downtown on 40 acres (16 ha) that were previously occupied by the former Delaware, Lackawanna, and Western Railroad. It preserves the history of steam railroading with one of the country's

The Railroad Museum of Pennsylvania is known for its collection of more than a hundred historic locomotives and train cars from the mid-nineteenth century through the twentieth century. Its huge indoor display area houses the museum's extensive Railway Education Program, which helps visitors understand the importance of railroading, from the era of wood-burning locomotives to modern diesel and electric locomotives. The National Toy Train Museum exhibits antique and modern toy trains.
Map ref: page 293 H5

Amish farms near Strasburg, a quaint town of interest to anyone who is keen on Amish heritage.

numerous eighteenth- and nineteenth-century buildings, many of which are located in three historic districts. These are: Callowhill, centered on the city's commercial area; Prince, which preserves nineteenth-century worker housing, factories, and commercial buildings; and Center Park, with some of the city's most impressive Victorian buildings.

During the Revolutionary War, Reading was a supply depot for the Continental Army, a hospital center, and prisoner-of-war camp. Today it produces electronic components, specialty steels, truck and car frames, textiles, and other products while also serving as a regional center for banking, insurance, and engineering services.

The Berks County Heritage Center in nearby Wyomissing is a complex of exhibits interpreting the region's history. It includes the Gruber Wagon Works, one of the nation's finest remaining examples of rural manufacturing, dating from 1882. There is also the C. Howard Heister Canal Center,

and the 5-mile (8-km) Union Canal Bicycle and Walking Trail, which follows the path once used for towing barges along the canal.

About 17 miles (27 km) southeast of Reading is French Creek State Park, set amid forested hills and farmlands. It offers camping and rental cabins year-round, fishing, boating, hiking, and picnicking. It can be reached via US-422 and Hwy 345.

Reading, which has 78,400 residents, can be reached by I-176 or US-222, or by plane.
Map ref: page 293 J4

SCRANTON

Like many post-industrial cities, this city of 81,100 residents in northeastern Pennsylvania has worked hard to remake itself in the wake of changing times. George W. Scranton and his associates developed it in 1840, building coal-fired iron furnaces here that used locally mined anthracite. By 1902, however, the iron and steel works were moved closer to Lake

largest collections of locomotives and rail cars. Train excursions are offered from Memorial Day weekend through the first weekend in November.

The Houdini Tour and Magic Show honors the memory of Ehrich Weiss (1874–1926), the Hungarian-born escape artist and magician better known as Harry Houdini. Visitors can see Houdini memorabilia, including props that he used, and a live magic show.

Scranton has an international airport and is 130 miles (209 km) from Philadelphia via I-380.
Map ref: page 293 J2

STRASBURG

Travelers keen on old-fashioned railroading and Amish heritage will find plenty of interest in this quaint town of 2,600 residents, 11 miles (17.7 km) southeast of Lancaster. The Amish Village, 1 mile (1.6 km) south of Strasburg on state Route 30, helps visitors learn about the history and customs of the 18,000

An actor wearing a costume from the time of Independence; Strasburg has plenty to offer the history buff.

TITUSVILLE

As the supply of whale oil for lighting declined and the Industrial Revolution increased demand for lubricants, entrepreneurs began to reconsider the slick film, often bottled and sold as medicine, that oozed up from the ground in Oil Creek Valley. The new Seneca Oil Company sent former railroad conductor Edwin L. Drake to Titusville, where oil had long been seen seeping to the surface, to see if large quantities of the burnable lubricant could be extracted. On August 27, 1859, Drake's derrick, located about a half-mile (0.8 km) south of Titusville, became the world's first successful oil well and launched Pennsylvania—and the world—into the era of oil.

Located in northwestern Pennsylvania, 106 miles (171 km) north of Pittsburgh, Titusville was founded in 1796 by surveyor Jonathan Titus. After Drake's discovery, the town quickly became the center of an oil-producing and refining area, with natural gas being produced on a large scale in the 1870s. By 1875 the oil wells began to dry up, and the boom towns they sprouted died. Pennsylvania remained the nation's top oil producer until production peaked in 1891, and the industry turned to richer reserves in the West. Today Titusville has about 6,400 residents. It is an industrial center producing textiles, lumber, steel and electronic equipment in the midst of an agricultural area.

The Drake Well Museum occupies the site of Drake's well. Visitors will find a replica of the derrick as well as exhibits depicting the early days of the oil industry, including still-functioning oil-field equipment. The adjacent 7,000-acre (2,855-ha) Oil Creek State Park has a 9.5-mile (15.3-km) paved bicycle trail through scenic Oil Creek Gorge, more than 52 miles (84 km) of hiking and interpretive trails through the historic and scenic area, and fishing and canoeing in Oil Creek. The Gerard Hiking Trail encompasses the entire Park. Scenic vistas, waterfalls, and historic sites are found along the trail, as well as two hike-in camping areas.

The Oil Creek and Titusville Railroad operates an excursion train on weekends and other days from May through October, using restored 1930s passenger cars.

Titusville can be reached via state Route 27 east from Meadville, state Route 8 north from Oil City and US-62, and state Route 27 southwest of Warren.

Map ref: page 290 B9

WILKES-BARRE

This northeastern city of 47,500 residents is a gateway to the Pocono Mountains, a 2,400-square-mile (6,216-sq.-km) region of woodlands, lakes, ponds, rivers, water-falls, ski areas and resorts that make it a mecca for outdoor recreation.

Colonists from Connecticut arrived in the Wyoming Valley in 1769, establishing a community on the Susquehanna River that they named for British Members of Parliament John Wilkes and Issac Barré, who defended the increasingly restive colonies in Parliament. Wilkes-Barre was burned twice in its history: in 1778, by British troops and Native Americans during the Revolutionary War; and in 1784, during the 16-year conflict over land claims in the Wyoming Valley known as the Yankee–Pennamite Wars. Many of the Yankee–Pennamite skirmishes occurred in Wilkes-Barre's River Common, now a 35-acre (14-ha) park dating from 1770. In 1972, Hurricane Agnes caused about $1 billion worth of damage.

From the early 1800s through to the 1940s it was a major center for mining the region's vast deposits of anthracite coal. Today, it has a somewhat more diverse economy that includes manufacturing, clothing, textiles, rubber and plastic products, aircraft parts, and processed foods.

The Sordoni Art Gallery, on the Wilkes University campus, houses paintings, sculpture, watercolors, photographs, and other works by late nineteenth- and twentieth-century American artists.

The F.M. Kirby Center for the Performing Arts is located in a restored Art Deco-style movie palace on Public Square. Home of the Northeastern Philharmonic Orchestra, it offers a variety of cultural events through the year.

Wilkes-Barre is 25 miles (40 km) southwest of Scranton on the I-81.

Map ref: page 293 J2

YORK

York, founded in 1735 in southeastern Pennsylvania, is a commercial, industrial and distribution center for the rich agricultural region known as Pennsylvania Dutch Country. During the Revolutionary War, it served as the temporary capital of the fledgling United States from September 30, 1777 to June 27, 1778, while British troops occupied Philadelphia.

It was here that the Continental Congress adopted the Articles of Confederation, an outline for a weak central government that was replaced by the current Constitution in 1788. Here, too, Congress received the news that British General John Burgoyne's 5,000-man army had surrendered to American forces following the Battles of Saratoga (New York), and that France would ally itself with the United States.

Downtown are the restored Golden Plough Tavern (1741) and General Horatio Gates House (circa 1751); both have direct links to America's history. Also downtown, the Bobb Log House (circa 1812) is a good example of a frontier Pennsylvania home, furnished to depict life in the 1830s.

Nearby is the York County Colonial Courthouse, a reproduction of the original courthouse where the Continental Congress met. Among the artifacts on display is an original copy of the Declaration of Independence.

Motorcycle enthusiasts can tour the Harley-Davidson Motorcycle Museum and final assembly plant for free. Engines are manufactured in Milwaukee, Wisconsin, then shipped to York, where the balance of each big bike is manufactured and assembled. The motorcycles on display in the museum range from the original 1906 model to contemporary motorcycles. The assembly plant can be seen by a 90-minute guided tour only.

York has about 42,200 residents. It is located 102 miles (164 km) west of Philadelphia, at the junction of I-83 and US-40. Bus services are available.

Map ref: page 293 H5

The world's era of oil began near Titusville; today we rely heavily on oil for gas to drive our cars.

A road sign near York warns of Amish buggies on the road.

STATE FEATURE

Philadelphia

Selling fruit and vegetables at the Italian Markets.

Philadelphia was founded in 1682 as a Quaker settlement that William Penn made the capital of his experiment in religious freedom and citizen participation in lawmaking. A century later it became the birthplace of a nation founded on the same ideals. Today, Philadelphia (a name taken from the Greek for "city of brotherly love") is not only the caretaker of national shrines that date from the country's founding, but also one of America's most important cultural, business, medical, and educational centers.

Penn laid out America's first planned city in a grid of rectangles, with large lots and wide streets that would leave space for gardens and orchards, and allow buffers between buildings to avoid the devastating fires and plagues that swept through crowded London in the seventeenth century.

It would be, Penn hoped, a "greene countrie towne." Instead, his city between the Delaware and Schuylkill rivers grew into Pennsylvania's largest city, a metropolis of 1.6 million complete with top-notch cultural amenities and persistent urban ills.

Philadelphia grew rapidly during its first century because immigrants and settlers were attracted to its tolerance of diversity and dissent. It eventually became the second-largest city in the British Empire, a major port city with commercial ties extending from China to the Mediterranean. It was the financial capital of the colonies and a center for the sciences.

During the Revolutionary War, Philadelphia became the political center of the 13 colonies' rebellion against Britain. The First Continental Congress met at Carpenters' Hall in 1774. From 1775 to 1783, the Second Continental Congress met in the Pennsylvania State House (now Independence Hall),

where delegates signed the Declaration of Independence on July 4, 1776, formally breaking with Britain. Here, too, they drafted the fledgling nation's constitution, the Articles of Confederation.

General George Washington's dwindling, poorly clad, sick and half-starved army spent the winter and spring of 1777–78 at nearby Valley Forge while British troops occupied Philadelphia. In 1787, with the war and independence won, Independence Hall was the scene of the Constitutional Convention, which produced the blueprint for federal government that still guides the country.

As the city grew more crowded, Penn's open spaces disappeared, bringing many of the urban problems he'd hoped to avoid, including yellow-fever epidemics that killed thousands between 1793 and 1820. Yet it saw the establishment of America's first bank, stock exchange, hospital, zoo, and free library.

Philadelphia was transformed in the nineteenth century into a gritty industrial center of almost two million people. Tensions between ethnic and racial groups flared as competition intensified for jobs in the textile and metals factories.

The twentieth century brought a decline in the city's fortunes despite a short-lived period of prosperity during World War II. Its manufacturing centers disappeared, its population declined, and much of the inner city became blighted by poverty, decaying buildings, and overcrowding. After World War II, African-American migrants from the South arrived seeking jobs in the city's declining industries. Unemployment and crime soared, and white residents migrated to the suburbs. Race riots broke out in the 1960s. Through the 1970s, the city government's tough-on-crime policies heightened racial tensions, which began to abate after Philadelphia's first black mayor, W. Wilson Goode, was elected in 1983 and efforts to revitalize the city were accelerated. A city-wide cleanup and restoration campaign continues today.

While Philadelphia still faces serious urban problems, it is showing up on lists of good places to live, work, dine, recreate, and do business. While large areas still suffer from poverty, poor schools, and high unemployment, the city and its environs boast historic sites, restored neighborhoods, world-class museums, and an enviable roster of colleges and universities. Philadelphia has also become a major center for the health-care industry in the United States.

History-minded visitors can begin a walking tour of the city at Penn's Landing, on the Delaware River between Market and Lombard streets. The site marks the spot where Penn landed in 1682. Independence National Historical Park (or Center City), located downtown, is a "must-see". At the visitor center, park

Chestnut Street, Philadelphia, as it was in the 1890s. The Drexel Building, which housed the Stock Exchange, and Independence Hall are on the right.

rangers can help plan a rewarding day taking in many important sites in the city and the nation. Among them are Independence Hall, Carpenter's Hall, the Liberty Bell Pavilion, and Congress Hall.

The Park includes Franklin Court, where Benjamin Franklin's brick house once stood. The Second Bank of the United States building (1824) now houses the Park's National Portrait Gallery. It has about 185 portraits from the late eighteenth and early nineteenth centuries, many of them by Charles Willson Peale (1741–1827).

Valley Forge National Historical Park, 20 miles (32 km) northwest of Philadelphia, preserves the site of the Continental Army's winter encampment. Visitors can see Washington's Headquarters, reconstructed huts, and the original entrenchment lines and fortifications.

In the Episcopal Christ Church (1727), plaques mark the pews used by Washington, Franklin, and Betsy Ross, the seamstress that legend says made the first United States flag.

Walkers will enjoy the area of early Philadelphia (Old City) immediately west of the Delaware River. Here, narrow cobblestone streets link points of historical interest amid numerous restored Georgian and Colonial-style buildings. Those seeking more natural settings can lose themselves in Fairmount Park to enjoy a hundred miles (161 km) of jogging and cycling paths or rowing on the Schuylkill River.

The city's original residential area is Society Hill. Named for the Free Society of Traders, a land company chartered by Penn, it mixes modern structures with restored eighteenth-century homes.

Philadelphia offers fans of professional sports football's Eagles, baseball's Phillies, hockey's Flyers and basketball's 76ers. The Penn Relays, held in April at the University of Pennsylvania, is one of the world's oldest and largest amateur track and field events.

The Academy of Natural Sciences (1812), has many permanent exhibits, including the Live Animal Center; Discovering Dinosaurs, with interactive

exhibits and touchable fossils; African Hall, with exhibits depicting that continent's environments.

Benjamin Franklin's contributions to science are memorialized at the Franklin Institute Science Museum. It includes hands-on exhibits related to science, industry, computers, physics, astronomy, history, and other disciplines. The University of Pennsylvania Museum of Archaeology and Anthropology, at 33rd and Spruce, is famous for its artifacts collected from around the world.

Visitors interested in the contributions of black Americans should take in the African American Museum. It has changing exhibits interpreting the history and culture of African-Americans.

Independence is celebrated every first week of July with the Philadelphia Freedom Festival. The New Year's Day Mummers Parade, said to date from the area's pre-Penn settlers from northern Europe, features thousands of flamboyantly costumed revelers.

Philadelphia has a nearby international airport as well as passenger train and bus service. By car, it can be reached via I-76 and I-95.

ABOVE: The Philadelphia Museum of Art (1876) is one of the world's top art museums, with a range of fine and decorative arts from Asia, Europe, and the United States spanning 2,000 years. Its collection includes masterpiece paintings, sculptures, prints, drawings, furniture, silverware, glassware, and architectural elements.

TOP: Philadelphia's city skyline and the Delaware River.

FEATURE

WASHINGTON, DISTRICT OF COLUMBIA

The reading of the Declaration of Independence is part of the Fourth of July celebrations each year in Washington DC.

Washington DC's National Independence Day parade moving down Constitution Avenue. The parade is made up of over 60 units and includes personalities, floats, marching bands, balloons, and costumed characters. It is a great flag-waving opportunity.

Washington DC, the capital of the United States, is a city of power and intrigue that is also full of fine restaurants and impressive museums. It is accessible by train, car, or plane—three major airports service the area. Above all, the city packs an enormous amount of diversity into a few neighborhoods: Georgetown, Adams-Morgan, Foggy Bottom, and Downtown.

Nestled on the Potomac River, the capital occupies only 61 square miles (158 sq km) of land in the District of Columbia, and is bordered by Maryland and Virginia. The cityscape is a striking blend of Roman and Greek architecture and tree-lined boulevards peppered with monuments and public galleries. The I-495 freeway, which circumnavigates downtown—"The Beltway"—barricades the city from the urban sprawl of its neighbors.

Washington remains a protectorate of the government. Approximately two-thirds of its 610,000 citizens work for the government or operate as lawyers and lobbyists representing billion-dollar corporations. The term "lobbyist" is thought to have originated in the lobby of the Willard hotel, which is near Capitol Hill and the White House.

While politics remains the undercurrent of the city's infrastructure, its wealth of attractions bring 20 million visitors each year. Few cities can boast as many museums in such a small area. However, as well as this vibrant culture, the city knows economic hardship. Beyond the fringe of downtown lie the predominately African-American and Hispanic communities, and the city's poorest residents. Riddled with street gangs and drugs, Washington's ghettos are invariably a shock for the uninitiated.

Washington is laid out as a grid, with alphabetical roads running east–west and numbered streets running north–south, and divided into four quadrants from the Capitol Building. It can be confusing, as there are identically named streets in each district. Mercifully, it has the Metrorail system and a good taxi service, and all the major tourist attractions are accessible on foot.

History

Washington DC became the nation's capital in 1800. Named for explorer Christopher Columbus, the District of Columbia was eventually named "Washington" in honor of the nation's first President. Washington's original "10 mile square," selected by Congress because it was midway between the New England and the Southern settlements, was procured from land ceded by its neighbors.

Washington was first settled in 1751 as a tobacco port. It evolved into a city after the Revolutionary War; the President commissioned French military architect, Pierre Charles L'Enfant, to prepare its blueprint. L'Enfant's vision was of a city of diagonal avenues and elegant roundabouts. He was dismissed, and Benjamin Banneker, an African-American engineer, brought his plan to fruition. L'Enfant's edict that the Capitol Building remain unblemished by towering buildings survived—the only vertical structure that deviates from Washington's horizontal skyline is the Washington Monument.

Washington became a center of discord during the years leading to the Civil War of 1861–65. It was just 100 miles (160 km) from the Confederate capital of Richmond, Virginia, and became a Union military base. The city's renaissance in the 1870s brought a beautification plan of esplanades and monuments. In the late 1990s, Washington DC began to clean up street crime—it is becoming an urbane city.

Adams-Morgan

The Adams-Morgan region is a colorful hybrid of Caribbean, African, and Hispanic nationalities. With streets pulsating to salsa, reggae, and rap, the neighborhood also overflows with ear-splitting record shops, funky cafés, and bars—it is an offbeat part of Washington's counterculture. The area was a beacon of community tolerance during the Civil Rights era.

Capitol Hill

The region around Capitol Hill is the center of Washington's attractions. The most well-known landmark is the Capitol Building. Home to America's legislative

branch since 1800, its magnificent dome, the Rotunda, is a symbol of democracy. Every deceased President since Abraham Lincoln lies in state beneath the *The Apotheosis of Washington* mural. The Capitol is linked to the Senate and House offices by a labyrinth of corridors and a subway system. Visitors can view Congress in full debate from public galleries. Free admission passes are available at the East entrance.

Directly behind the Capitol is the Supreme Court (1935), the judicial branch of the US government. Many historic rulings have been made under its marble walls—Brown vs the Board of Education, which abolished racial segregation in schools and sparked the Civil Rights Movement and, more recently, the Bush vs Gore contest for the presidency.

Next to the Supreme Court is the Renaissance-style Library of Congress, housing 100 million books in 460 languages. Crowned by a 160-foot (49-m)

The Capitol and the Reflecting Pool. The Capitol has housed the US legislature—the Senate and the House of Representatives—for nearly two hundred years, during which time it has been burnt, rebuilt, extended, and restored. It is the centerpiece of the Capitol complex, which consists of six Congressional plus three Library of Congress buildings, as well as the United States Botanical Gardens.

The Rotunda in the Capitol. This dome-shaped space is the Capitol's main circulation space, and is used for ceremonial occasions. It houses paintings and sculptures depicting the nation's important historical figures and events. It was conceived by Dr William Thornton, who won the design competition for the Capitol in 1793, but construction did not begin until 1818. It was completed in 1824, under the direction of Charles Bulfinch.

This massive African bull elephant stands in the entrance to Washington's National Museum of Natural History. The museum is a huge attraction, so be prepared for crowds. Among the most popular exhibits are the Dinosaur Room; the Discovery Room, where visitors can touch a range of objects, from petrified wood to elephant tusks; the O. Orkin Insect Room, an interactive exhibit where visitors can touch up to 60 species of insects; and the Janet Annenberg Hooker Hall of Geology, Gems, and Minerals, with its display of precious stones.

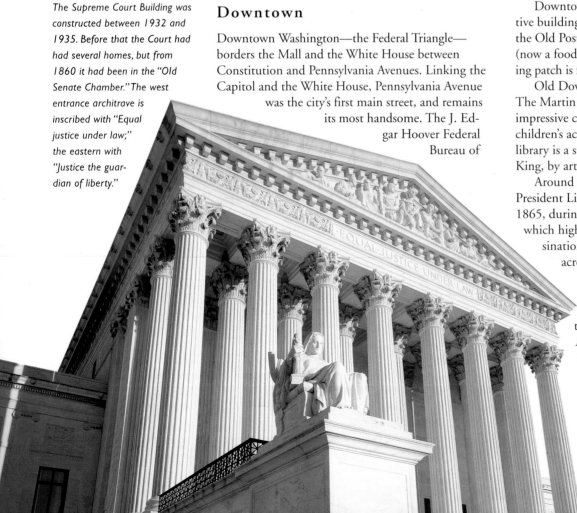

dome ceiling, the library's octagonal Main Reading Room in the Thomas Jefferson Building has mosaics and statues of academics. At the rear is the Folger Shakespeare Library, which houses the world's largest collection of Shakespeare's works. Though not open to the public, there are regular performances in the library's theater.

Two blocks north on Massachusetts Avenue is Union Station, a magnet for Capitol Hill's cadre during the Congressional lunch hour. Constructed in 1908, the marble structure recently underwent a US$165-million beautification. Along with servicing the East Coast network, the station's main hall, inspired by the Roman baths of Diocletian, also accommodates over 100 shops, numerous restaurants, and a massive food court.

A trail of colorful mosaics leads northeast from Union Station to the Capital Children's Museum, at 3rd Street. More of a mystical tour than a museum, it has three floors of animation, crafts, science, and two play areas. At 1st and Massachusetts is the National Postal Museum, which tells the story of the Pony Express and exhibits a fascinating collection of stamps.

Downtown

Downtown Washington—the Federal Triangle—borders the Mall and the White House between Constitution and Pennsylvania Avenues. Linking the Capitol and the White House, Pennsylvania Avenue was the city's first main street, and remains its most handsome. The J. Edgar Hoover Federal Bureau of Investigation (FBI) Building, at 935 Pennsylvania Avenue, holds a smorgasbord of criminal artifacts—pipe bombs, assault rifles, and the famous Tommy guns used in shoot-outs with Depression-era gangsters. Visitors can delve into the Bureau's 90-year history, and a modern-day "G-man" demonstrates the latest weapons in the underground firing range.

Directly opposite the FBI building is the National Archives. Showcasing the Declaration of Independence, the Constitution of the United States, and the Bill of Rights, the Archives recently acquired the personal papers of President Richard Nixon.

Downtown has many historic and commemorative buildings, including the US Navy Memorial and the Old Post Office, Washington's first skyscraper (now a food court). The Federal Triangle's last remaining patch is filled by the new Ronald Reagan Building.

Old Downtown boasts other famous landmarks. The Martin Luther King Memorial Library is an impressive cultural center that sponsors concerts, children's activities, films, and readings. Inside the library is a stunning mural portraying the life of Dr King, by artist Don Miller.

Around the corner is the Ford Theater, where President Lincoln was mortally shot on April 14, 1865, during a performance. The Lincoln Museum, which highlights the events surrounding the assassination, is in the theater's basement. Directly across the road is Peterson House, preserved as a museum, where visitors can view the room where the President died.

In 1968, the Smithsonian Institution opened the National Museum of American Art and the National Portrait Gallery. Housed in the former US Patent Office, the twin museums unveil America's history in a series of folk-art collections, photographs, sculptures, and biographic exhibits. The portraits in the Hall of Presidents and the adjoining Notable Americans Gallery are considered the Museum's highlights.

The Supreme Court Building was constructed between 1932 and 1935. Before that the Court had had several homes, but from 1860 it had been in the "Old Senate Chamber." The west entrance architrave is inscribed with "Equal justice under law;" the eastern with "Justice the guardian of liberty."

Dupont Circle

Dupont Circle is the heart of Washington's vibrant gay community. Once inhabited by the city's wealthiest, the area is now an eclectic mix of art galleries, outdoor cafés, and radical bookstores. For a more sedate experience, Dupont Circle mellows into an architectural showcase of international embassies along Massachusetts Avenue.

Foggy Bottom

The west-end neighborhood of Foggy Bottom is a mix of nineteenth-century town houses, trendy hotels, and second-hand bookstores. The district also flaunts the Corcoran Gallery of Art, the Renwick Gallery, and the Old Executive Office Building, now serving the Vice President and the National Security Council. The building's restored rooms and stained-glass rotundas are open to visitors. Another attraction is the Daughters of the American Revolution Museum on D Street, dedicated to preserving the legacy of the Revolutionary War.

Next to the Potomac River is The John F. Kennedy Center for the Performing Arts, which opened in 1971. With a concert hall, opera house, and a cinema complex, the center is largely responsible for maintaining Washington's reputation as a leading arts city. Next door is the Watergate complex, where the Nixon Watergate scandal unfolded.

Georgetown

Georgetown is Washington's oldest area and home to the city's powerful elite. Elegant Federal homes sit comfortably on cobblestone streets; the first American Catholic college, Georgetown University, was founded here in 1787. Its epicenter is on the corner of M and Wisconsin Streets, two of the area's busiest thoroughfares, full of restaurants, university pubs, and upscale boutiques. With its streets in constant gridlock, visitors should leave the car behind and soak up Georgetown's atmosphere on foot.

The Mall

L'Enfant's dream of re-creating the elegance of Paris' Champs-Elysées is a reality along the Mall. Linking the Potomac River to the Capitol, with the Washington Memorial center stage, the Mall has been the forum for countless political demonstrations, most vividly during the Civil Rights Movement in the 1960s. The Mall's tree-lined expanse hosts the Smithsonian Institution Museums and the National Zoo to the west. Just a 10-minute walk from the White House, the Smithsonian offers a glimpse into the worlds of aviation, science, and natural history, along with American history, the arts, and the country's archives. Even though each of the nine Smithsonian galleries is quite large, only one percent of their entire collection is ever on display—visitors should allow a couple of days to explore the museums. The most popular is the National Air and Space Museum. An IMAX theater features four films on aviation.

Visitors will find much memorabilia at the Museum of American History—from a demonstration lunch-counter used during the American Civil Rights Movement, to Dorothy's slippers from *The Wizard of Oz*.

Exploring the various art galleries takes considerable time and energy—start with the National Gallery of Art, one of the world's leading art museums. Linked by a subterranean walkway, the museum is divided into two galleries: the East Building houses twentieth-century art and the West Building exhibits medieval, Renaissance, and Impressionist paintings.

The Renaissance-inspired Freer Gallery of Art features an extensive collection of Asian and American art, including thirteenth-century Chinese silk paintings and James McNeill Whistler paintings.

One of the more recent additions to the Mall is the underground gallery of the National Museum of African Art, which has an impressive collection of ancient and modern African art.

The Washington Monument, a tribute to the "Father of His Country," George Washington. After leading the fight for American independence, Washington became his country's first President, shaping both the presidency and the relationships among the branches of government.

The Lincoln Memorial, built as a tribute to the man who fought to preserve the nation during the Civil War. It is designed to resemble a Greek temple, and has 36 columns, representing the states of the Union at the time of Lincoln's death. On the South wall the Gettysburg Address is inscribed; on the North wall is the President's inaugural address.

The Franklin D. Roosevelt Memorial, on the famous Cherry Tree Walk near the Mall, was dedicated in 1997. The monument traces 12 years of the nation's history through four open-air galleries, each representing one of Roosevelt's terms of office. It was designed by Lawrence Halpin, with walls—quotations from FDR carved in them—made from Cold Spring granite from South Dakota. The memorial has quiet pools and cascades, alcoves, and ornamental plantings, and is a place of peace in which to remember the achievements and dreams of this great President.

six years. A surge of public interest 37 years later allowed the monument to be completed. Surrounded by 50 American flags, the memorial is visible from nearly every city angle. Washington's skyline can be viewed from the observation deck.

Mirroring the Washington Memorial's colossal frame is the Reflecting Pool, modeled for the garden pools of the Taj Mahal and Versailles. It was captured in unforgettable images during Martin Luther King's Freedom March; film buffs will recall Forrest Gump wading through it at an anti-Vietnam demonstration.

Along with George Washington, Abraham Lincoln endures as the city's hero. The Lincoln Memorial, carved from marble, is illuminated by lights which also cast a glow over the Reflecting Pool. Likewise, numerous spotlights enhance Lincoln's gaze toward the Capitol Building—the very symbol of the Union he sanctified. Along with paying homage to the slain President, the memorial commemorates racial emancipation. Inscribed on a bronze plaque is Lincoln's historic Gettysburg Address of 1863. A century later Martin Luther King gave his "I Have A Dream" speech from its steps.

The most recent addition to the Mall is the Franklin D. Roosevelt Memorial. Opened in 1997, the plaza comprises four open-air granite chambers with dramatic sculptures and a cascading waterfall reflecting the peace that the President sought before his untimely death near the end of the World War II.

As well as galleries and presidential shrines, the Mall has military memorials. The most sobering is the Vietnam Veterans Memorial, a sweeping v-shaped wall. Inscribed in its black marble are the names of the 58,156 soldiers who died in combat. The Korean War Memorial, in contrast, depicts larger-than-life bronze soldiers trudging across a grassy embankment.

Along the Potomac's shoreline, the serene parkland of the Tidal Basin was originally constructed to protect the city from floods. Today it comes alive in spring with billowing cherry blossoms and hordes of tourists. At the park's apex lies the Jefferson Memorial, which pays homage to the nation's third President. Emulating the design of his Virginian estate, "Monticello," the memorial features a 19-foot (6-m) bronze statue of Thomas Jefferson as well as his contribution to the Declaration of Independence.

Children will enjoy the National Museum of Natural History (1910). The museum houses a collection of ice-age mammals, arthropods, and dinosaur fossils, along with the flawless 45-carat Hope Diamond. An insect zoo has hissing cockroaches and spine-tingling spiders in its live exhibits.

Near the end of the Smithsonian row is the Mall's original museum, built in 1855. The Smithsonian Castle's medieval structure contains the crypt of benefactor James Smithson, and serves as the Institute's main information center.

The Holocaust Museum, which opened in 1993, presents a haunting display. The exhibits include over 2,500 photographs, dimly lit chambers, barracks, and a kaleidoscope of haunting images and visual presentations. The museum is solemn and thought provoking—be cautious about taking young children there.

The Mall's verdant oasis also nurtures Washington's most famous monuments. Towering over it is the Washington Memorial, the largest freestanding obelisk in the nation. Construction began in 1848 but work stopped when private funding ran dry after

The White House

The most famous address in the nation is 1600 Pennsylvania Avenue. The office and residence of the nation's leader remains Washington's most popular attraction. Constructed in 1792 and first occupied eight years later by John Adams, the White House's neoclassical design has frequently been updated and painstakingly restored—most notably by former first lady Jacqueline Kennedy, in the early 1960s. During Bill Clinton's incumbency, security considerations saw Pennsylvania Avenue between 15th and 17th Streets closed to traffic. Now a pedestrian walkway, visitors can stroll parallel to the plain fencing that separates the South Lawn from the world. There are free tours which allow visitors a glimpse of the various state rooms. During the summer months there are lines for tickets at the White House Visitor Center.

Virginia Day Trips

Fifteen minutes from downtown Washington lie the historic attractions of neighboring Virginia.

Arlington National Cemetery was once the estate of Confederate war hero, Robert E. Lee. Now, simple headstones mark a sea of veteran graves dating to the Revolutionary War. The cemetery is also the final resting place of J.F.K. and his first lady, with an eternal flame honoring their graves. The Tomb of the Unknown Soldier is especially poignant—it cradles the graves of three servicemen, one each from World War II, the Korean War, and the Vietnam War.

From I-395, it is impossible to miss the Pentagon, headquarters of the Department of Defense. Pentagon tours were cancelled after the terrorist attack on the building on September 11, 2001. Close by is the Iwo Jima Memorial, dedicated to the marines who fought on this tiny Pacific island in 1943. Its graphic bronze sculpture depicting six soldiers struggling to raise the American flag in combat has come to symbolize the sacrifice of war.

The seaport of Old Town Alexandria incorporates many attractions, while retaining its historic sites. Most museums and galleries are around Market Square—there are antiquities and taverns dating back to the Revolutionary War. On Oronoco Street is the Boyhood Home of Robert E. Lee, and several buildings constructed during Washington's presidency.

Sixteen miles (26 km) from Washington DC is the Mount Vernon estate of George Washington, on the Potomac. Visitors can view the mansion (with many of its original furnishings), the slave quarters, and the tombs of George and Martha Washington.

Tips

Most Washington exhibits are open year-round, though the summer months see the longest lines. The city has hot, muggy summers (hottest in July and August), and bitterly cold winters (January and February). One of the best ways to view Washington is by Metrorail or Metrobus, which serve Downtown, Georgetown, and the fringe districts.

The Vietnam Veterans Memorial. This war was America's least popular, and the memorial was not constructed until some years after the war's conclusion—it was dedicated in 1982. It is by far the most visited memorial in Washington DC, and recognizes the sacrifice of those who served, while not reigniting the conflict that surrounded the war. It says goodbye, finally, properly.

The White House was built between 1792 and 1800. It was the work of James Hoban. During the War of 1812 it was burnt down, and so was reconstructed in 1815. It has been the home of every President since John Adams. The exterior remains much as it was in 1800, and the interior has been renovated according to the original floor plan. Presidents have, of course, made their own mark on the building, but it remains an iconic symbol of the presidency.

Western and Central New York • Northern Pennsylvania

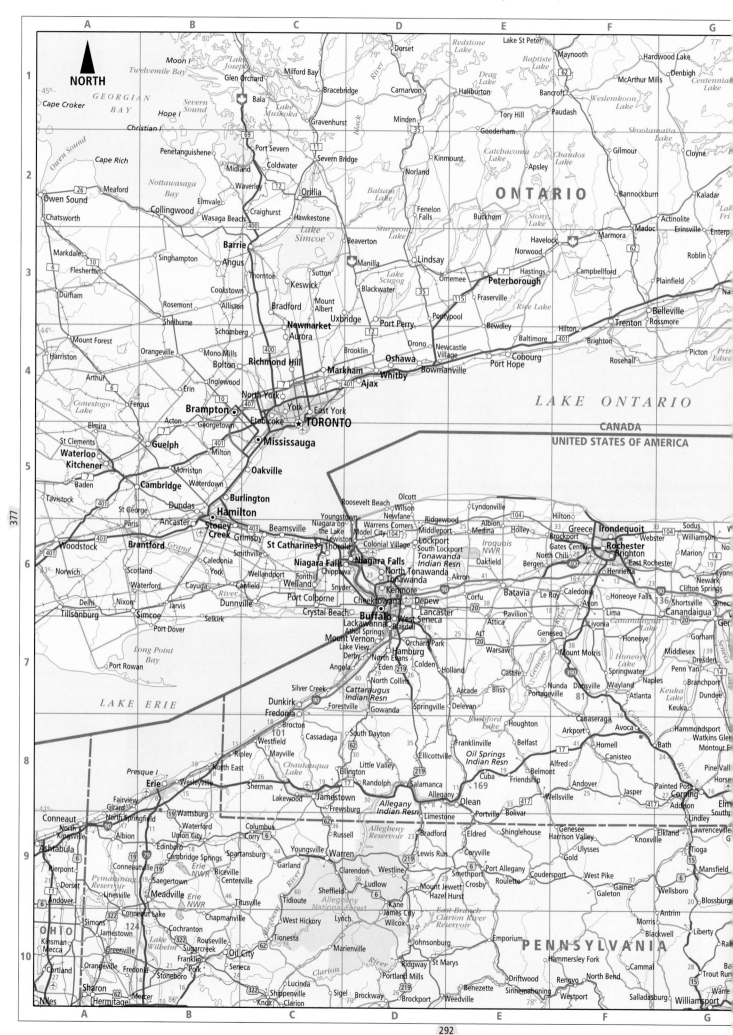

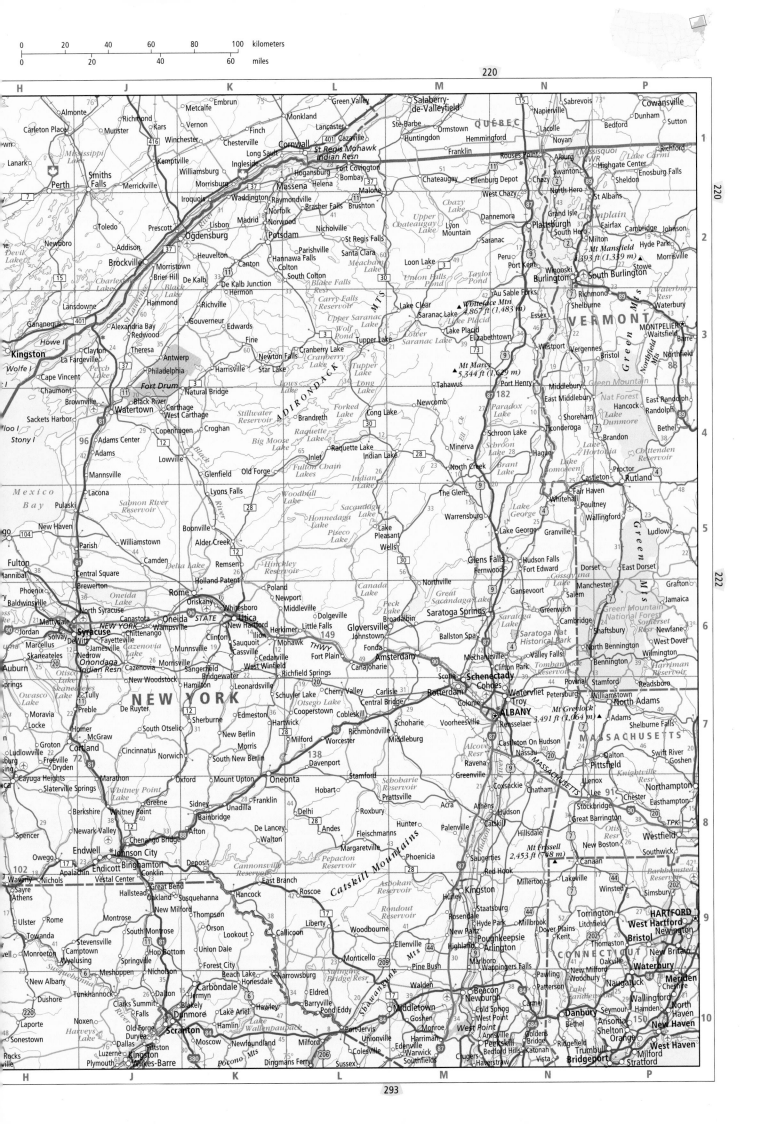

Southern Pennsylvania • New Jersey
Maryland • Delaware • District of Columbia

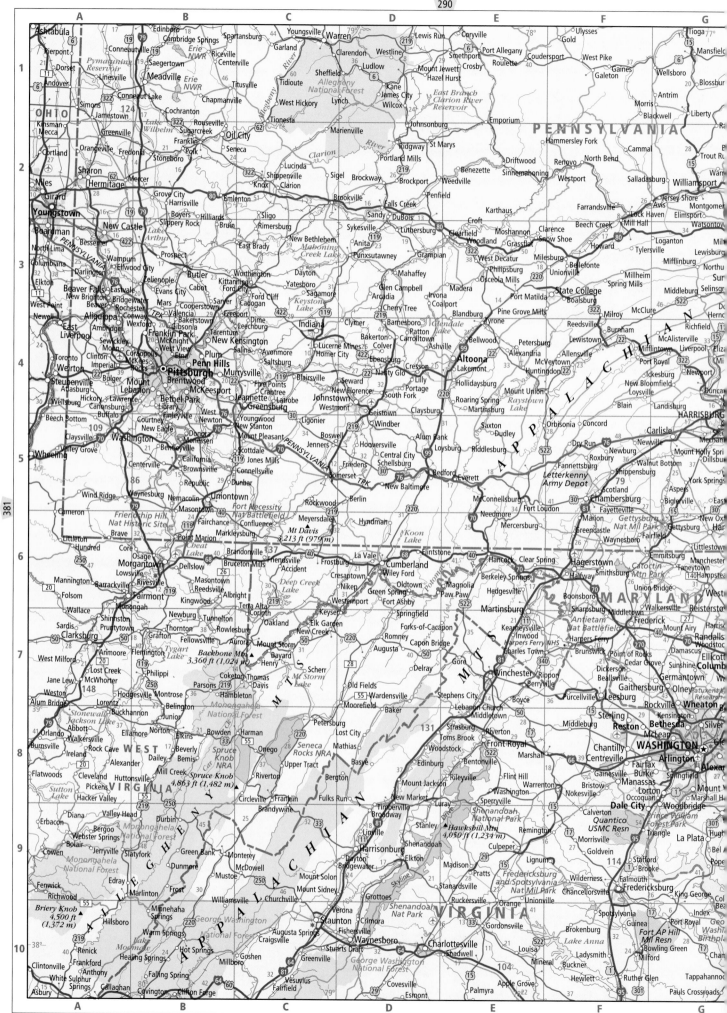

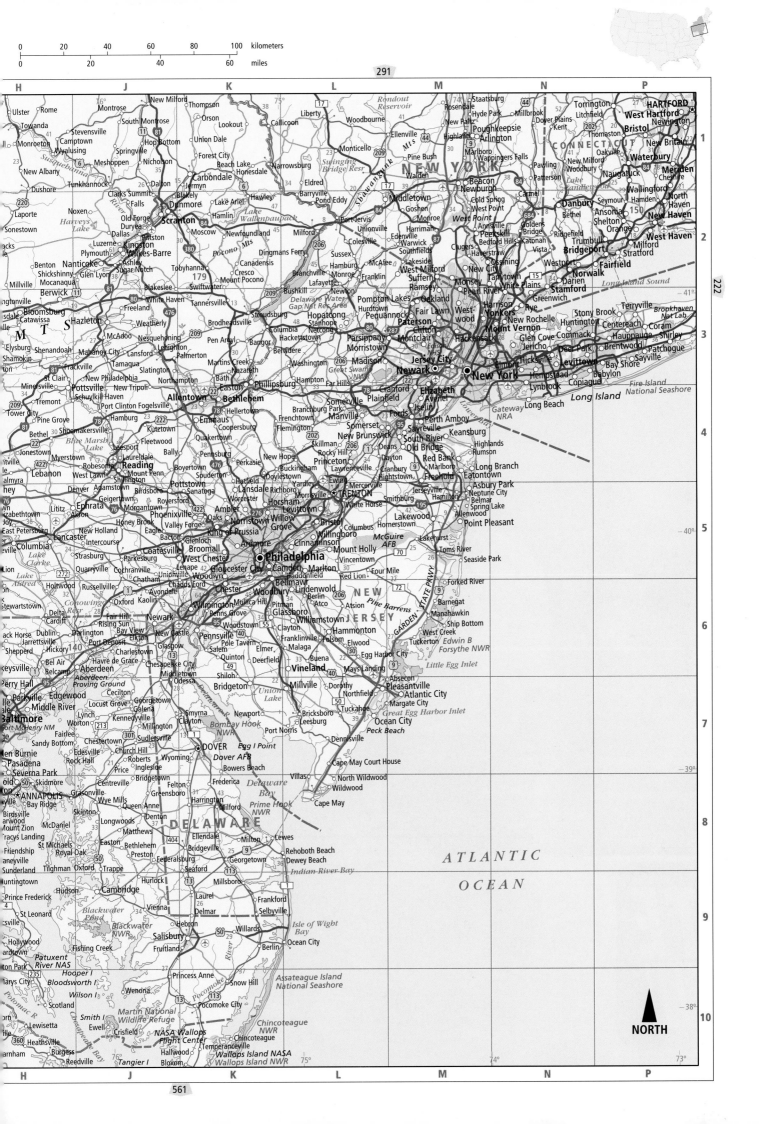

0 20 40 60 80 100 kilometers
0 20 40 60 miles

NORTH

The Midwest

▲ NORTH

0   100   200   300   kilometers
0   60   120   180   miles

Lake of the Woods

Thief River Falls

East Grand Forks

Upper Red Lake

International Falls

Bemidji

Lower Red Lake

Moorhead

Red River

Mesabi Range

Eagle Mtn ▲
2,301 ft (701 m)

Isle Royale

Lake Superior

Houghton

Mt Arvon ▲
1,979 ft (603 m)

Marquette

Sault Ste Marie

Leech Lake

Brainerd

Cloquet

Duluth
Superior

Ashland

Ironwood

St Ignace

Fergus Falls

Mille Lacs Lake

Morris

St Cloud

MINNESOTA

Lake Chippewa

Rhinelander

Iron Mountain

Escanaba

Beaver I

Alpena

Willmar

Rice Lake

Timms Hill ▲
1,951 ft (595 m)

WISCONSIN

Marinette

Whitefish Bay

Traverse City

Torch Lake

Lake Huron

Coon Rapids

Minneapolis
ST PAUL
Stillwater

Menomonie

Chippewa Falls

Wausau

Marshfield

Stevens Point

Green Bay
De Pere

Appleton

Lake Michigan

Cadillac

Houghton Lake

Big Rapids

Midland

Bay City

Chaska
Burnsville

Lakeville

Red Wing

Eau Claire

Wisconsin Rapids

Manitowoc

Ludington

Mount Pleasant

Saginaw

Marshall

New Ulm

Northfield

Faribault
Owatonna

Rochester

Winona

Onalaska

Oshkosh

Fond du Lac

Lake Winnebago

Sheboygan

MICHIGAN

Muskegon

Muskegon River

Grand Rapids

Wyoming

Owosso

Flint

Burton

Por

Mankato

Tomah

La Crosse

Beaver Dam

West Bend

Grand Haven

Holland

LANSING

Pontiac

Sterli

Det

Worthington

▲ 1,670 ft
(509 m)

Fairmont

Albert Lea

Austin

Sun Prairie

MADISON
Whitewater

Milwaukee
Waukesha

Racine

Battle Creek

Kalamazoo

Benton Harbor

Jackson

Ann Arbor

Rivervi

Spencer

Mason City

IOWA

Monroe

Janesville

Kenosha

Waukegan

Niles

Sturgis

Monroe

Sioux City

Fort Dodge

Cedar Falls

Waterloo

Dubuque

Charles Mound ▲
1,235 ft (376 m)

Beloit

Rockford

Arlington Heights

Evanston

Elgin

Chicago
Cicero

South Bend

Gary
La Porte

Crown Point

Warsaw

Bowling Green

Toledo

Defiance

Sandusky

Fostoria

Findlay

Bucy

Boone

Carroll

Ames

Marshalltown

Marion

Cedar Rapids

Clinton

Dixon

Sterling

Wheaton
Aurora
Bolingbrook

Markham

Joliet

Kankakee

Valparaiso

Fort Wayne

Lima

Mari

DES MOINES

Council Bluffs

Glenwood

Creston

Newton

Oskaloosa

Ottumwa

Indianola

Iowa City

Coralville

Davenport

Muscatine

Moline

Kewanee

Streator

Ottawa

Huntington

Logansport

Wabash

Van Wert

INDIANA

Warsaw

Maryville

Fort Madison

Burlington

Galesburg

Peoria

Pontiac

Lafayette

Kokomo

Frankfort

Marion

Anderson

Bellefontaine

▲1,257 ft
(383 m)

Campbell Hill ▲
1,550 ft (472 m)

Piqua

Urbana

Springfield

CO

Kirksville

Macomb

Keokuk

Pekin

Bloomington

Champaign

Urbana

Crawfordsville

Lebanon

Muncie

Richmond

Dayton

St Joseph

Quincy

Lincoln

Decatur

SPRINGFIELD

Taylorville

Plainfield

INDIANAPOLIS

Franklin

Shelbyville

Middletown

Hamilton

Wilmington

Hannibal

Jacksonville

Charleston

Mattoon

Terre Haute

Columbus

Northbrook
Bridgetown

Cincinnati

Portsmouth

Kansas City

Independence

Lees Summit

Moberly

Marshall

Mexico

Mark Twain Lake

ILLINOIS

Effingham

Bloomington

Bedford

Seymour

Madison

Belton

Columbia

Fulton

Alton

Vincennes

New
Albany

Clarksville
Jeffersonville

Warrensburg

Sedalia

Missouri River

St Charles

Granite City
St Louis

Carlyle Lake

Centralia

Washington

Jasper

Ohio River

JEFFERSON CITY

Harry S Truman Resr

Osage River

MISSOURI

Mehlville

Belleville

Mount Vernon

Evansville

Nevada

Lebanon

Rolla

Farmington

Herrin

Marion

Joplin

Carthage

Springfield

Taum Sauk Mtn ▲
1,772 ft (540 m)

Carbondale

Ohio River

Table Rock Lake

OZARK   PLATEAU

Cape Girardeau

West Plains

Poplar Bluff

Sikeston

Kennett

THE MIDWEST

The Midwestern states include those situated on the Great Lakes—Ohio, Michigan, Indiana, Illinois, Wisconsin, and Minnesota—as well as Iowa, reaching toward the west, and Missouri located to the south. This region is a formidable gathering of industrial might and fertile vastness, of pretty river valleys and far-flung prairies, of venerable trees and broad skies. The Midwest is also blessed with a plentiful supply of fresh water as well as a wealth of superb mineral resources.

With the exception of certain Great Lakes ridges and the hilly Ozarks in southern Missouri, much of the land is flat and rumpled, typically presenting a wide, low horizon covered in snow and ice during winter. Spring is brief and verdant, stirred by wind, and fall is a gorgeous melody of yellow hickories, wine-red oaks, flaming maples, purple ashes, and bright orange sassafras. Much of the land has been smoothed by glaciers, which melted about 10,000 years ago after extending as far south as Illinois and Ohio.

As elsewhere in the country, the Native Americans were the first inhabitants, leaving a unique legacy of immense burial mounds. Rapid development took place in the second half of the nineteenth century due to transportation breakthroughs: the railroads and the steamboat. Good soil and links with growing eastern cities encouraged the development of agriculture and food processing. Migrants from Europe and other parts of the United States poured in, and the economy boomed.

The Midwest is the center of the US car industry. Elwood Hayes built the first clutch-driven, gasoline-powered automobile and drove it in Kokomo, Indiana in 1894. Henry Ford introduced the assembly line to Detroit automobile production, an idea that spread to other industries. Since the early part of the twentieth century, the prosperity of the Midwest has been closely tied to manufacturing. Along the Great Lakes, from Superior to Cleveland, stretches a 1,000-mile (1,609-km) belt of factories, mills, refineries, breweries, blast furnaces, and machine-tool plants. Recessions have come and gone, and new industries have emerged, notably electronics, service, and finance.

Of the United States' 30 largest metropolitan areas, eight are in the Midwest. Chicago is the commerce capital of the Midwest; its spectacular museums, sculptures, architecture, shopping areas, restaurants, and night life make it an exciting and enjoyable place to visit. Indianapolis stages the most famous automobile race in the world, the Indianapolis 500. St Louis is home to the world's largest brewery, Anheuser-Busch. Cincinnati, "The Queen City," has a pleasing texture and layout. Detroit, the "Motor City," is known for cars and "the Motown sound." Minneapolis–St Paul is considered to be one of America's most liveable cities. Milwaukee has a rich multicultural heritage and a desirable lakeside position.

European-style town squares and plazas, beautiful fountains, majestic cathedrals, and towering war memorials are found in many towns and cities. Town halls and mansions proudly display a rainbow of historic styles from Victorian, Beaux-Arts, and Greek Revival to Romanesque, Queen Anne, and Italianate. Renowned architect Frank Lloyd Wright was born in Wisconsin, and many of his "organic" designs are found in the Chicago area.

The Midwest embraces its past through its festivals, museums, theaters, and music organizations. There are many excellent institutions of higher learning, including Notre Dame in South Bend, Indiana, Ohio State, and the University of Indiana.

A large number of top professional baseball, football, and basketball teams are located in the Midwest. Hiking, camping, boating, hunting, fishing, cross-country skiing, and snowmobiling are other popular pursuits in a region endowed with streams, lakes, beaches, and woodland refuges.

This eye-catching road sign is located on the I-29 between St Joseph and Kansas City in Missouri.

Farms in Michigan grow a range of produce, from peaches, cherries, and apples to corn, beans, and pumpkins.

ILLINOIS

Illinois, "The Prairie State," covers 57,918 square miles (150,008 sq km), making it the 24th-largest state in America. It has a population of over 12.4 million, which ranks fifth. It shares its borders with Wisconsin to the north, Indiana to the east, Kentucky to the southeast, and Iowa and Missouri to the west (separated by the Mississippi River). As befits its nickname, much of Illinois is rather flat. Most elevations are below 400 feet (122 m), with only a few spots in the northwestern and southern parts of the state rising above 1,000 feet (305 m).

Agriculture has always been an important staple of the state's economy, and today Illinois is one of the leading producers of corn and soybeans in the world. Wheat, beans, and dairy products are also important. Manufacturing is critical to the state's economy, with machinery, electronic equipment, and chemical products among the major entities.

The Chicago River, Illinois, has a river-walk that winds through the very heart of Chicago. The city's river playground can be explored by water taxi, tour boat or gondola.

Springfield is the state capital, while Chicago is the largest city. Located on the shores of Lake Michigan, Chicago is one of the world's most beautiful and resourceful cities. Because of its location along the lake's shores and right in the center of the country, Chicago is one of the transportation leaders in the United States—more railroad tracks are located here than anywhere else in America. Chicago's O'Hare International Airport is one of the busiest airports in the world.

Leading educational institutions in Chicago include the University of Illinois in Champaign-Urbana, the Northwestern University in Evanston, and the University of Chicago. Founded by John D. Rockefeller of Standard Oil fame (the Rockefeller Chapel is an awe-inspiring Gothic work), the University has produced more Nobel Prize winners in several fields (Literature, Economics, and Chemistry) than any other institution. The nuclear age was born here with the first chain reaction taking place in 1942.

State motto State Sovereignty, National Union
State flag Adopted 1915 (modified 1970)
Capital Springfield
Population 12,419,293
Total area (land and water) 57,918 square miles (150,008 sq km)
Land area 55,593 square miles (143,986 sq km)
Illinois is the 24th-largest state in size
Origin of name From a Native American word meaning "tribe of superior men," with a French suffix
Nicknames The Prairie State, The Land of Lincoln
Abbreviations IL (postal), Ill.
State bird Cardinal
State flower Violet
State tree White oak
Entered the Union December 13, 1818 as the 21st state

Places in ILLINOIS

AURORA

Aurora (population 142,900) is 50 miles (80 km) southwest of downtown Chicago in the Fox River Valley, and was settled in 1834. The fertile farm lands and water power attracted settlers as early as 1834. The railroad made its way here in the late 1840s and Aurora soon became a thriving community. The town is named for the Latin word "aurora," meaning "dawn," because Aurora was the first town in the state to install electric lights.

Aurora is located along a high-tech corridor with other cities such as Naperville, Joliet, and St Charles. The Fermi National Accelerator Laboratory, the world's largest energy particle accelerator, is located here. Self-guided tours are available and films are shown in the auditorium.

Local history is well preserved in Aurora. The Aurora Historical Museum specializes in nineteenth-century life, and the Blackberry Historical Farm Village is modeled on an 1840s farm. Children in particular will love the lambs and pygmy goats in the children's farm and enjoy going for the horse-drawn carriage and pony rides.

A treasured piece of history in Aurora is the Paramount Arts Center. Built in 1931 by the firm of Rapp and Rapp (they designed some of the country's most glorious movie palaces), the theater has now been restored to its original glory. With a seating capacity of over 1,800, the theater is booked for plays and musical performances throughout the year. Backstage tours are available for a small fee.

Michael Jordan, who loves the game of golf almost as much as basketball, opened his Golf Center here a few years ago. There are multiple levels of tees (heated whenever necessary) along with a short game area and putting greens.

Aurora can be reached by bus or train out of downtown Chicago. If coming by car, take the I-88 out of west suburban Chicago.
Map ref: page 376 A9

BLOOMINGTON-NORMAL

The twin cities of Bloomington-Normal (population 110,194) are located in the middle of Illinois, halfway between Chicago and St Louis. Founded in 1843, the Republican Party of Illinois had its origins here in 1856, when Abraham Lincoln made a speech that spelled out the political beliefs that would ultimately catapult him to the White House.

Today the city is known as a manufacturing center with a Mitsubishi auto manufacturing plant. There is also the Kathryn Beich Candy Company, maker of Bit O' Honey and the world-famous Beer Nuts, a popular snack.

Bloomington-Normal has two colleges, Illinois State and Illinois Wesleyan University. Attractions here include the American Passion Play, which is performed March–May and the Illinois Shakespeare Festival, which runs throughout summer. This event features three different plays that are performed on a rotating basis. For outdoor enthusiasts, Constitution Trail, a 9-mile (14.5-km) park is a popular venue for cyclists, joggers, and rollerbladers. Bloomington-Normal can be reached by bus, train, or the I-55/75 and the I-39.
Map ref: page 379 N6

CAHOKIA

Cahokia, a small town (population 16,391) in southwestern Illinois, is located between St Louis in Missouri and Columbia in Illinois. Settled in 1699, it is one of the oldest towns in the state. The first church was built here during that same year as part of a French mission.

While there are a few historic sites in town, such as the Cahokia Courthouse and the Holy Family Mission Log Church, the most significant attraction in this area is the historic site known as the Cahokia Mounds.

When the French arrived in Cahokia in the early 1700s, they discovered one of the world's most remarkable archeological sites. Preserved today, Cahokia Mounds is the only prehistoric city north of Mexico City. Archeologists have dated the original settlement to around AD 700, and their ruins are fascinating. It is believed that tens of thousands lived here, in this city that covered 6 square miles (16 sq km). These earthen mounds were built primarily for ceremony and 68 of the original mounds have been preserved.

One of the mounds is named Monks Mound, for the Trappist Monks who lived nearby in the early 1800s. This is the largest earthen mound in the Americas, its base covers 14 acres (6 ha) and its elevation is 100 feet (30 m).

There is no admission fee to come and visit this fascinating 2,000-acre (810-ha) site. There is also a museum here that further explains the lives of the primitive people that once lived here.
Map ref: page 383 K3

Aurora's Paramount theater opened in 1931, amid 2,000 roses thrown from a plane.

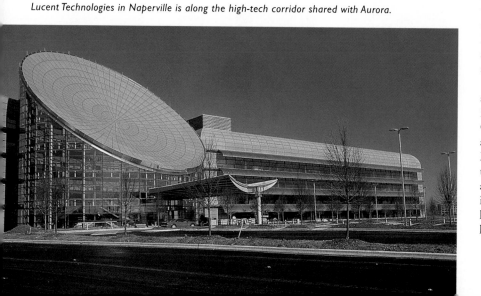

Lucent Technologies in Naperville is along the high-tech corridor shared with Aurora.

CARBONDALE

Surrounded by a number of lakes and rivers, Carbondale (population 20,681) sits at the far southern end of the state, about 40 miles (64 km) north of the border with Kentucky. Here locals speak with a noticeable Southern drawl, unlike the citizens who reside in the northern and central portions of the state.

The driving force of this city is Southern Illinois University (24,000 students). Visitors, however, are drawn here by the nearby Shawnee National Forest. Comprising 266,000 acres (707,730 ha), the forest is bordered on the east by the Ohio River and on the west by the Mississippi River. Unusual rock formations are one of the major attractions here and the forest offers a number of outdoor activities from swimming and boating to hiking and fishing.

Buses serve Carbondale as do trains, with a daily train to and from Chicago and as a stop on the famous "City of New Orleans" run. The I-57 and US-51 both run right through town.
Map ref: page 383 M5

CHAMPAIGN-URBANA

These two cities, separated only by a single street (Wright Street), are commonly referred to as one entity, although it did not start out that way. Champaign, with a population of 67,518, is the larger of the two cities. Urbana, which has a smaller population, at 36,395, is somewhat more of a commercial and industrial center. Urbana houses most of the campus of the University of Illinois.

Established in 1867, the University of Illinois (36,000 students) is one of the largest in the nation, and has one of the country's leading schools of architecture along with an influential computer department. Most historians credit the invention of the internet to a few computer experts at the University of Illinois.

On campus grounds, you will find the John Philip Sousa Library and Museum, which houses a music library along with authentic band costumes and instruments dating from Sousa's day. The Krannert Art Museum has sculpture and other art dating back to 4,000 BC.

Champaign-Urbana can easily be reached in several ways. Trains and buses serve the area, which can also be reached by taking the I-57 south from Chicago.
Map ref: page 380 A5

CHICAGO

Home to 2.9 million residents and located right on the shores of Lake Michigan, Chicago has one of the country's most beautiful shorelines, with the many giant skyscrapers of downtown dominating the view. The first skyscraper was built here in the late 1890s and, today, the 110-story Sears Tower is the tallest building to be found in the entire Western Hemisphere.

Chicago boasts of many cultural attractions, most notably being its Museum Campus, located on the shores of the lake, just a few minutes from downtown. Three museums are all within walking distance of each other—the Adler Planetarium with its laser

Joggers enjoy the miles of lakeside tracks along North Avenue Beach in Chicago.

star shows, the Shedd Aquarium with an oceanarium populated by dolphins and beluga whales, and the Field Museum, whose biggest attraction is Sue, the world's largest dinosaur. Another great attraction a few miles south, on the lakefront, is the Museum of Science and Industry, which houses a World War II U-Boat, along with state-of-the-art, hands-on science exhibits.

Major-league football, hockey, basketball, and baseball are great sources of pride for the city as are the dozens of blues clubs, many of which are open to the small hours of the morning. The restaurant scene here is among the best in the country, with many neighborhood eateries comparing well with the upmarket downtown sites. Outside of Los Angeles, there is no other city in the entire United States that has the wealth of Latin-cuisine restaurants as does Chicago.

Chicago was first incorporated as a city in 1834 and it suffered through its worst catastrophe in 1871 when much of the city was destroyed by fire. One of the few structures in the downtown area that survived the fire was the Water Tower, which still stands today on North Michigan Avenue, the heart of the city's shopping district.

The city was quickly rebuilt and became home to the finest in commercial architecture. Louis Sullivan was one of the early pioneers; his Auditorium Theatre and also the Carson, Pirie and Scott Department Store still stand today, both of which are lovingly restored.

There are several ways to see downtown Chicago—known as the Loop because the elevated public transit trains loop downtown—including river-boat tours. These tours in spring and summer last one or two hours and travel up and down the Chicago River, which runs through the heart of downtown. A walking tour is easy, and

Chicago's city skyline dominates the shoreline of Lake Michigan, as seen from North Avenue Beach.

highlights on one can include the Art Institute, home of the finest collection of French Impressionist paintings outside of France, the Rookery, with its sumptuous Frank Lloyd Wright-designed grand staircase, or any number of deep-dish pizza parlors, which are a well-known Chicago specialty.

One of Chicago's glories is its beautiful lakefront, covering some 30 miles (48 km) from north to south. Much of the credit for its uncluttered look goes to Daniel Burnham, who devised a master plan in the early twentieth century to enable Chicagoans to enjoy the lakefront amid parks and natural beaches. Lake Shore Drive, a reminder of roads that were built before the massive interstate highways, offers a lovely view of the lake and the surrounding environment. Thousands of Chicagoans jog or cycle along these trails during the warmer months, while others play golf or tennis, or merely relax in one of the parks and admire the natural beauty. Traveling along Lake Shore Drive is the best way to surround yourself with this city's charm—and it is free.

One of the city's biggest tourist attractions is the Taste of Chicago, held in Grant Park, located just west of the Lakefront and east of downtown. Here, people of all ages can feast on all types of delicacies, from pub foods to some rather delectable gourmet delights. This event is held for nine days and leads up to a memorable climax of a stunning Fourth-of-July fireworks show over the lake.

Known as the "Windy City," Chicago is easily reachable by plane at either Midway on the city's south side, or O'Hare Field, one of the world's busiest airports. Trains and buses also have many routes that arrive here. Brutally hot in the summer and equally cold and snowy in the winter, the weather is generally more moderate by the lakeshore.
Map ref: page 376 B9

DECATUR

Decatur (population 81,860) is located in central Illinois, east of Springfield and southwest of Champaign-Urbana. The city was founded in 1829 and, one year later, a young Abraham Lincoln settled less than 1 mile (1.6 km)

from here to begin studying law. Today, tourists can visit the Mt Pulaski Courthouse Site, built in 1848, where Lincoln argued cases.

Decatur has some 80 acres (32 ha) of Historic Districts within its limits, and several walking tours are available. Millikin Place, a housing development from 1909, was laid out by architect Walter Burley Griffin, the man who designed the master plan for the city of Canberra, Australia's capital. Griffin's wife, Marion Mahony, herself an architect, designed two of the houses here, while Frank Lloyd Wright designed another.

Millikin University is the leading school in Decatur. On campus, visitors can find the Birks Museum, with its collection of 1,000 pieces of china, crystal, pottery, some dating back to the fifteenth century. The Macon County Historical Complex showcases the city's past, including an 1850s school and log cabin.

The I-72 coming out of Springfield runs right through Decatur and later connects with I-57, which leads to Chicago. US-51, US-36, and Hwy 121 also lead into town.
Map ref: page 379 N7

EVANSTON

Located directly to the north of Chicago and on the attractive shores of Lake Michigan, Evanston is Chicago's largest suburb with a population of approximately 74,300. Right up until the mid-1970s, Evanston was a dry city, because no liquor was allowed to be sold within the city's limits. Today, that has changed and the cozy downtown area is now home to dozens of small restaurants that serve wine and spirits.

Looking north along Lake Michigan's shores toward Evanston, from Oak Street Beach in Chicago.

Evanston is the beginning of Chicago's North Shore, a collection of suburbs along Lake Michigan built by old money and populated by very large, expensive homes. While not as luxurious as towns like Winnetka, Kenilworth, or Lake Forest to the north, there is a lot of wealth in north Evanston. There are homes here designed by such architects as Walter Burley Griffin and Frank Lloyd Wright.

The tree-lined city is perhaps best-known as the home of Northwestern University. Many of the country's business leaders and leading journalists attended the school's graduate programs. Kendall College, which offers a full culinary degree program, is only a few blocks away.

Just north of the University on the lakefront is the Grosse Pointe Lighthouse, which is one of the most beautiful of all the remaining lighthouses on Lake Michigan. Visitors can climb to the top for a look down the lakeshore to downtown Chicago.

The Mitchell Indian Museum, open every day, offers a look into the lives of the Native American people. Another museum here, the Evanston Historical Society, is located in the former home of Charles Gates Dawes, Vice President to Calvin Coolidge.

Evanston can be reached via public transit out of downtown Chicago or by a drive north out of Chicago on Lake Shore Drive.
Map ref: page 376 B8

GALENA

Located in the far northwestern portion of the state, not far from Iowa, Galena has a population of 3,460 residents. In a state known for its flat prairies, Galena is a delight. There are many steep hills in this town, making walking a bit of a challenge, but worth the effort. For those with less stamina, bike rentals are available.

The number one tourist attraction is the home of Ulysses Grant, Civil War General and 18th US President. Galena locals gave the house to Grant, who lived here after the Civil War. Many original furnishings are still on display.

On Saturday mornings from May to October, the local historical society offers walking tours of the downtown area. For a small fee you are able to discover the wealth of the many luxury homes that were built here in the boom of the mid-nineteenth century. Many architectural styles, from Queen Anne to Federal, are represented.

Galena can be reached by bus or by car via US-20, west out of Rockford. Take Hwy 84 south out of town for a beautiful drive that overlooks the Mississippi River.
Map ref: page 379 L1

GALESBURG

Galesburg (population 33,706) is located in western Illinois, not far from the Iowa border. Founded in 1837, the town was named for George Washington Gale, a Presbyterian minister who wanted to establish a community to train other ministers. During the Civil War, Galesburg was a stop on the Underground Railroad.

Knox College, a small school of only 1,000 students is here. This is the site of the famous Lincoln-

Jefferson Street Bridge (1932) takes eastbound traffic over the Des Plaines River in Joliet.

Douglas Debates of 1858, where Stephen Douglas and Abraham Lincoln set out their differences in quest of a US Senate seat.

Galesburg was also the home of Carl Sandburg. As well as his poetry, Sandburg wrote a six-volume biography of Abraham Lincoln. The Carl Sandburg Historic Site showcases his birth cottage, now restored to its original condition.

Galesburg can be reached by train or by driving down the I-74 south from the Quad Cities on the Illinois–Iowa border.
Map ref: page 379 L5

JOLIET

Located 40 miles (64 km) southwest of Chicago, on the I-55, Joliet (population 106,221) was named for French explorer Louis Jolliet, who first saw the town in 1673. Much of the city's income over the past 100 years has revolved around the shipping industry. The Chicago Sanitary and Ship Canal is the passageway for a huge amount of barge traffic, while the Brandon Road Locks, just south of the city, is one of the busiest in the nation.

Today, income is brought in through riverboat gambling. Illinois legalized this form of gambling in the 1990s and Joliet was one of the first cities to take advantage. Two riverboats are docked on the Des Plaines River to allow easy access for those who want to try their hand at blackjack or roulette.

Visitors interested in the city's history should visit the Rialto Square Theater. Built in 1926, this vaudeville/movie theater is a reminder of the days when going to an evening's entertainment was a special event. Residents refer to it as a palace—the original design was patterned for the Hall of Mirrors at Versailles, France. Beautifully restored and refurbished, the theater seats almost 2,000 and is used for concerts, plays, and ballet.

Joliet is served by trains and buses as well as commuter trains that run out of Chicago. The I-55 or I-80 out of Chicago are the city's major thoroughfares.
Map ref: page 379 B9

MOLINE

Moline (population 43,768) is one of the Quad Cities. These four cities—two in Illinois and two in Iowa—sit in the shadow of the Mississippi River. Moline derived its name from the French word "moulin," meaning windmill, because many of these structures were built in this area to harness the power of the river.

Mention Moline to most people and their first thought is "John Deere." Moline is the world headquarters for the company, a leading manufacturer of farm, lawn, and gardening equipment. The John

Deere Pavilion is an architectural marvel, a glass and steel building designed by Eero Saarinen, who designed the Gateway Arch in St Louis. Free tours are available. The product building contains some current model plus more historic John Deere tractors. Nearby Rock Island, another of the Quad Cities, was once quite an important site for the military because Confederate prisoners of the Civil War were held here. These days, gambling boats are the most popular local attractions.

The I-74 and I-280 are the major roads here. Buses serve the Quad Cities and the nearest flights are via the Quad Cities Airport.
Map ref: page 379 L3

OAK PARK

Less than 10 miles (16 km) west of downtown Chicago, Oak Park (population 52,524) is celebrated for the architecture of Frank Lloyd Wright, who lived here between 1898 and1908. Wright's Home and Studio are open daily for tours and dozens of his famous "prairie-style" houses are located here and in Riverside, a wealthy suburb to the west. The houses are known for their long, horizontal features, which Wright claimed he designed to emulate the expanses of prairies that typify the Midwest.

One of Wright's most famous churches, Unity Temple, is located in Oak Park. This concrete structure is deceptively simple, without the usual religious ornamentation on the exterior. Inside, the beautiful light fixtures cast an elegant light on the sanctuary. Tours are available for a small fee.

Oak Park's other famous resident was Ernest Hemingway, who was born here in 1899. Visitors can tour his birthplace and also the museum devoted to the famous author, which is located just a few blocks further away.

Oak Park can be reached on the I-290, heading west out of downtown Chicago. Public transit trains out of downtown and the western suburbs also serve the town.
Map ref: page 376 B9

Farming country near the Iowa border in the vicinity of Galesburg.

The Saddle Bronc event at the National High School Finals Rodeo in Springfield—the world's largest outdoor rodeo, in which over 1,500 high-school students participate.

PEORIA

Peoria (population 112,936) is on the Illinois River in the state's north-central area. It is the oldest settlement in Illinois—explorers Louis Jolliet and Pere Marquette discovered the area in 1693.

Two famous educational institutions are in Peoria—Bradley University and Carthage College. Carthage was one of the first co-ed schools in the country. Its most famous student was former US President, Ronald Reagan. The school houses quite a collection of memorabilia from his movie and political careers.

Historic districts such as Glen Oak Avenue and High Street–Moss Avenue are lined with houses in many different styles, including Italianate and Queen Anne.

Famous Peorians include actor/comedian Richard Pryor, singer/songwriter Dan Fogelberg, and actor David Ogden Stiers. The phrase, "Will it play in Peoria?" referred to vaudeville acts in the early twentieth century, which would take their routine to Peoria for the locals' reaction before trying it in Chicago or other big cities.

Peoria is served by buses and can be reached by car by taking the I-55 north from Springfield.
Map ref: page 379 M5

SPRINGFIELD

The capital of Illinois, Springfield is located in the center of the state, some 200 miles (322 km) south of Chicago. Home to 111,454 residents, Springfield is best known as the adult home of Abraham Lincoln. Before being elected President in 1860, Lincoln spent a quarter of a century here as a lawyer and later as US Senator.

Many sites have been maintained as they were during Lincoln's life. These include his law office; the depot museum, where he bid farewell to Illinois as he left to take the Presidency; and his tomb. Almost every visitor here rubs the Lincoln statue's nose, which has since worn down to its original finish after 140 years.

Two other must-sees in Springfield include the State Capitol and the Dana-Thomas House. This is one of Frank Lloyd Wright's most famous Prairie-style houses, which contains some of the architect's most intricate art window panels.

For 10 days in August, the Illinois State Fair is held at the state fairgrounds in nearby DuQuoin. There is every type of entertainment from country music stars and 1960s rock bands to championship livestock—the fair aims to satisfy all tastes. Springfield is reached on the I-55, by bus or train out of Chicago and St Louis.
Map ref: page 379 M7

STARVED ROCK STATE PARK

Situated southwest of Chicago is the city of Utica, near the I-80 and I-39. Just 1 mile (1.6 km) south of this city lies Starved Rock State Park.

This is the most visited park in the state with over 1 million tourists per year. Over 2,400 acres (972 ha) in size, the park has been designed with everyone in mind, and campsites can accommodate everything from small cars to motor homes and big rigs.

Its name comes from the legend of the Illini tribe when surrounded by an enemy Potowatomi tribe atop the local bluffs. Without sufficient food, the Illini starved to death.

Situated on the Illinois River, fishing is a popular activity—walleye and white bass are the leading catches. Boaters have several lanes of direct access to the river.

Nature-lovers will have a field day in the park, with the 15 miles (24 km) of trails that wind their way around the bluffs and canyons. The St Louis Canyon has a 60-foot (18-m) waterfall that is an impressive icefall in the winter.

More than 200 species of birds have been identified in the park along with 175 different wildflowers. Lists describing these flowers and birds are available. The park's lodge, built in the 1930s by the Civilian Conservation Corps, has been recently refurbished. A huge rock fireplace adds to the warmth of the lodge, which has 72 deluxe rooms as well as a few cabins.

A few miles further east of the park is the Illinois Waterway Visitor Center, where visitors can see the operation of the locks and dam as well as viewing the 125-foot (37-m) majestic sandstone bluff for which the park is named.

John Deere, in Moline, manufactures quality tractors.

INDIANA

Indiana, in the Midwest, ranks among the top 10 states in both agricultural and industrial output. Because Indiana's railways, waterways, and ports provide access to the world, "The Crossroads of America" was selected as the state motto in 1937. The state has a population of over 6 million, which is 14th highest in the US, and its 36,420 square miles (94,328 sq km) make it the 38th largest.

The state's name, which means "land of Indians," recalls the many Native Americans who once lived here. Indiana people are known as "Hoosiers." One explanation is that it was the early pioneers' version of "Who's there?" Another is that in 1826 a canal contractor named Samuel Hoosier gave employment preference to men living on the Indiana side of the Ohio River. The men in his work gang were known collectively as Hoosier's men, which then shortened to Hoosiers.

The top two-thirds of Indiana is level or gently rolling; the southern part is somewhat hilly. The highest point, in the east near the Ohio state line, is 1,257 feet (383 m); the lowest, at 320 feet (98 m), is found in the southwestern corner.

Strolling musicians play at a festival to celebrate the year's harvest of sweet-corn in Middle-town, Indiana.

Indiana has more than 8,600 manufacturing plants, and manufacturing accounts for more than 25 percent of all Hoosier jobs. Top industries are auto parts, electronics, pharmaceuticals, agriculture, steel, chemicals, medical equipment, machinery, hardwood, manufactured housing, and recreational vehicles. The state is also a major agricultural exporter, with 16.4 million acres (6.6 million ha) of farmland and 65,000 farms. Principal products are corn and soybeans, pork, hay, dairy products, and chickens. Other major crops include tomatoes, melons, peaches, apples, and mint.

The two largest public seats of learning, Purdue University and Indiana University, are of national distinction, and the University of Notre Dame is one of the most prestigious Catholic universities in the world.

The state has more than 500 lakes, dozens of state parks, a national lakeshore, and a national forest.

State motto The Crossroads of America
State flag Adopted 1917
Capital Indianapolis
Population 6,080,485
Total area (land and water)
36,420 square miles (94,328 sq km)
Land area 35,870 square miles (92,900 sq km)
Indiana is the 38th-largest state in size
Origin of name Means "land of Indians"
Nickname The Hoosier State
Abbreviations IN (postal), Ind.
State bird Cardinal
State flower Peony
State tree Tulip tree
Entered the Union December 11, 1816 as the 19th state

Places in
INDIANA

BLOOMINGTON

Bloomington (population 60,600) is a tree-shrouded quarrying and university town with an old-time ambience and a modern tempo. Founded in 1818, it lies among rugged outcrops of limestone and is near some of the state's best outdoor recreational areas.

The University of Indiana, established in 1820, has a number of attractions for visitors. Of particular interest on the beautiful 1,850-acre (749-ha) campus are the Thomas Hart Benton murals on the University Theatre, Woodburn Hall, and the auditorium, painted for the 1933 Century of Progress Exhibition in Chicago.

The Indiana University Art Museum, designed by I.M. Pei, has an interesting permanent collection which includes works by Monet, Matisse, Picasso, Rodin, and Andy Warhol. There is also an Asian art gallery and African, Oceanic, and Art of Americas collections.

Mathers Museum, also on the campus, has changing exhibits on anthropology, history, and folklore from countries around the world. The Glenn A. Black Laboratory of Archeology displays artifacts relating to Indiana's history, going back to its first inhabitants and Native American cultures.

The Elizabeth Sage Historic Costume Collection and Gallery, affiliated with the university, pre-serves more than 6,000 items of clothing. The Monroe County Historical Society Museum displays Native American artifacts, quarrying tools, and nineteenth-century household items.

Bloomington is reached by car on Hwy 37, and by bus and plane.
Map ref: page 380 D7

COLUMBUS

Columbus (population 31,800) is known for its outstanding modern buildings, designed by acclaimed architects such as Edward Larrabee Barnes, Richard Meier, I.M. Pei, and Henry Weese.

First settled in 1820 on the banks of the White River, the city's economy is now largely based on farming and industry. The Columbus Area Chamber of Commerce provides visitors with tour information and printed material on the town's interesting architecture. Also worth seeing here is the Indianapolis Museum of Art Columbus Gallery which has changing exhibits of local and regional art.

The city lies just east of I-65, and US-31 runs through the city. Plane and bus services to Columbus are also available.
Map ref: page 380 E7

EVANSVILLE

Evansville is on the southwestern tip of the state, beside the Ohio River and across from Kentucky. With a population of 126,300, it is the largest industrial and trade center in southern Indiana, and combines the easy-going nature of the South with the get-up-and-go attitude of the more industrious North.

Evansville began as a ferry crossing on the Ohio River in the early 1800s and continued to grow as trade increased and the railroads were established. It has retained some of the atmosphere of its nineteenth-century prosperity, evident in its many fine public structures including the 1885 High Victorian Willard Library, designed by James and Merritt Reid; Henry Wolter's 1890 Old Vanderburgh County Courthouse; the 1890 Old Vanderburgh County Jail and Sheriff's Residence; and Old US Post Office and Custom House.

The Evansville Museum of Arts and Science exhibits Rivertown, a recreation of late nineteenth and early twentieth-century Evansville. It has a chest made by Abraham Lincoln and the engine, lounge car, and caboose of a train that evoke Evansville's railroad era. Artworks ranging from second-century Roman sculpture to contemporary American paintings feature in this hall of art, history, and science.

The Ohio River offers many opportunities for boating, swimming, waterskiing, and fishing. Wesselman Park has a number of sports fields, tennis and handball courts, baseball batting cages, and a fitness trail. There are hiking trails in the 200-acre (80-ha) park and

Bloomington has museums with Native American artifacts.

adjacent 200-acre Wesselman Woods Nature Preserve, which contains a virgin hardwood forest.

Mesker Park Zoo and Botanical Gardens cover 70 acres (28 ha) and house more than 700 animals in natural habitats surrounded by exotic plants, wildflowers, and trees. The Discovery Center focuses on the world's vanishing rainforests and animals. Also on the grounds are a butterfly house, children's zoo, paddle boats, and a train.

Reitz Home Museum showcases the restored 1871 mansion of John Augustus Reitz, once known as the "Lumber Baron." This French Second-Empire house has many original period furnishings.

The Angel Mounds State Historic Site is a large Native American settlement on a broad expanse of the Ohio River that was occupied between AD 1200 and 1450 by an estimated 3,000 members of the Mississippi Culture. They built 11 large earthen structures, including one 40 feet (12 m) high and others occupying as much as 4 acres (1.5 ha). They look like truncated pyramids, but were used as dwellings, not as burial chambers. An interpretive center displays exhibits and artifacts from an archeological dig. Replicas of their dwellings, their meeting house and temple are also exhibited. The village site of 103 acres (42 ha) is surrounded by about 300 acres (122 ha) of woodland.

Evansville is on I-64 and Hwys 62 and 66. It can also be reached by plane and bus.
Map ref: page 380 B10

A farm in northern Indiana, where the flat glaciated plains are ideal for growing crops. Landscape in the south is more hilly and varied.

A corn crop growing in Middletown, between the capital, Indianapolis, and Fort Wayne. Agricultural output still accounts for a significant part of Indiana's revenues.

FORT WAYNE

Fort Wayne (population 173,000) is the second largest city in Indiana. It lies at the confluence of three rivers in the northeast of the state. Now a manufacturing center surrounded by dairy and farming land, Fort Wayne was first settled by the Miami Native Americans. Their presence attracted French fur traders, who established a fortified trading post in the early 1700s. Fort Miami, as it was called, was rebuilt by the French in 1750 to stave off the British, who prevailed in 1760 due to the French and Indian War. During the American Revolution the site was a lawless settlement known as Miami Town, with a portage used by British and Americans.

For the next 30 years it was one of the most important fur-trading centers in the West. Two American armies were sent out by President Washington to establish a fort at the river junction, but they were defeated by the Miami under the leadership of their famous chief, Little Turtle. A third American army, under General "Mad Anthony" Wayne, overcame Little Turtle and set up a post across the river from Miami Town. Today's city of Fort Wayne is known by the name of the settlement that grew here, named for the general.

Now known as the "City of Attractions," Fort Wayne has 11 museums and historic sites within walking distance of downtown. The 1928 Embassy Theater houses a rare Grand Page organ, is home to a philharmonic orchestra, and stages touring Broadway shows, opera and ballet companies, and a venue for guest artists.

Garden-lovers will enjoy Fort Wayne's many botanical attractions. Lakeside Rose Garden is one of the largest in the nation with displays of 2,500 labeled plants. Foellinger-Freimann Botanical Conservatory consists of three gardens under glass. The Floral Showcase displays six distinct and colorful seasonal gardens each year. Many exotic plant species surround a waterfall in the Tropical House, while cacti feature in the Desert House.

The Fort Wayne Children's Zoo houses more than 1,200 animals and birds from around the world on 42 landscaped acres (17 ha).

The Lincoln Museum displays a wide collection of the personal possessions of President Abraham Lincoln and his family. These include the last portrait made of the president during his lifetime and the inkwell he used to sign the Emancipation Proclamation. Exhibits and audiovisual presentations focus on Lincoln's life from his boyhood

years to his law career and presidency. Touchscreen computers allow visitors to redecorate the White House as Mary Todd Lincoln did, fight a Civil War battle, and read Lincoln's mail. A library and archives are part of the museum.

Fort Wayne has an international airport. It is reached by I-69 and by US-27, US-24, and US-30. A bus service is also available.
Map ref: page 380 G2

GARY

The town of Gary (population 116,600) is tucked into the northwest corner of Indiana, 28 miles (45 km) from Chicago. It is located in what is known as the Calumet area, for the Grand and Little Calumet Rivers, and stretches for a distance of 30 miles (48 km) along the Lake Michigan shore. This now heavily industrialized region was formerly an expanse of high sand dunes and wild rice swamps which made it inhospitable to early development. In the late nineteenth century it became an industrial outpost of Chicago when financiers began looking for cheaper sites for their steel mills and oil refineries away from the crowded Illinois portion of Lake Michigan.

The town of Gary came into existence when US Steel purchased

9,000 acres (3,645 ha) of lake dune lands in 1905. It was named for company chairman Elbert H. Gary, and immigrant laborers poured in. Today, the Gary Land Company Building houses a small museum devoted to local history.

The town has some interesting twentieth-century industrial architecture. A good example can be seen at the 1909 headquarters of the American Bridge Company.

The Hobart Historical Society in the suburb of Hobart houses the 1915 brick Carnegie Library, an English Renaissance structure. The museum contains nineteenth-century household and farm items, a gallery of woodworking and wheel-making tools, and replicas of blacksmith and print shops.

Gary may be reached by car on I-90, and also by plane and bus.
Map ref: page 380 C1

LAFAYETTE

This city of 43,800 is surrounded by a broad ring of dairy farms and cattle operations. One of Indiana's best-known universities, Purdue, especially noted for its agricultural and engineering programs, is next door in West Lafayette. Its 140 buildings are clustered within a 1,579-acre (639-ha) campus that caters for 36,000 students.

Lafayette was founded on a plateau above the Wabash River in the year 1825 by riverboat captain William Digby. Digby named it for the Marquis of Lafayette, who served as a general under George Washington in the Revolutionary War. The Wabash and Erie Canal, which opened in 1843, extended the economic reach of Lafayette. Purdue, an early land grant college, was established in 1869.

The nineteenth century is preserved in the Downtown Lafayette Historic District, which includes the Tippecanoe County Courthouse, an enthusiastic blend of Gothic, Classical, Romanesque, and Renaissance styles which was built in the 1880s. The Tippecanoe County Historical Museum is located in the 1851 Gothic Revival house built by wealthy businessman Moses Fowler. It contains period furnishings, relics from Fort Quiatenon and the Battle of Tippecanoe, Native American artifacts, and nineteenth-century glassware, tools, clothing, and toys.

Tippecanoe is a big name in American history. The Battle of Tippecanoe was fought in 1811 between forces representing the two most influential men in the old Northwest, William Henry Harrison leading US troops and Shawnee Indian Chief Tecumseh. A group of warriors estimated at 600 to 700 attacked the camp of 1,000 US soldiers. The Native Americans withdrew, but there were many losses on both sides. The battle failed to break Native American resistance, and Tecumseh allied himself with the British in the War of 1812. In 1840 Harrison won the presidential election with the slogan "Tippecanoe and Tyler too," which referred to his victory against Tecumseh, and his vice-presidential running mate, John Tyler.

The Tippecanoe Battlefield Museum and Park marks Harrison's camp with a large obelisk. The 100-acre (40-ha) park is rugged and scenic woodland and marsh. The museum exhibits artifacts from the battle and literature from Harrison's 1840 presidential campaign. The Wabash Heritage Trail runs from this site to the golf course at Columbia Park, the largest park in Lafayette, which has plenty to entertain children and adults including a zoo, an amusement park, tennis courts, a swimming pool, and an outdoor theater.

The Greater Lafayette Museum of Art displays paintings by Indiana and other American artists, American pottery, contemporary art, and Latin American paintings.

Temporary exhibits feature historical themes in art, regional cultures, and local artists.

Access is via airport in adjacent West Lafayette and by car on I-90, Hwy 26, and Hwy 43, and bus.
Map ref: page 380 D4

MADISON

This handsome and historic Ohio Valley river town of 12,000, southeast of Columbus, has the special atmosphere of an attractive getaway spot which has managed to remain unspoilt by commerce. The shady streets are bordered by nineteenth-century Federal, Classical Revival, and Italianate buildings. Visitors can take a pleasant walk through town and along the river, and on summer mornings, local farmers sell their produce in town.

In the nineteenth century Madison was important as a port for settlers streaming into the Northwest Territory and for its major pork-packing industry, which competed with Cincinnati. The first railroad built in Indiana, the Madison and Indianapolis, was completed in 1847. Instead of benefiting the town, however, it siphoned off business from Madison and other towns along the Ohio River, relegating Madison to a small manufacturing center.

Indiana's leading nineteenth-century architect, Francis Castigan, came to Madison from Baltimore in 1837 and designed many of the buildings here, including two of the outstanding mansions in the Ohio Valley. One was commissioned by J.F.D. Lanier, a railroad promoter and wealthy financier who lent the state over US$1 million during a difficult period of the Civil War. His 1844 Greek Revival mansion overlooking the Ohio River has a cupola, a grand portico, and is decorated with delicate wrought iron. The interior contains period furnishings, opulent ornamentation, and a splendid spiral staircase.

The other Castigan-designed gem is Shrewsbury House, now a museum. It's an elegant Greek Revival building with intricate plasterwork, high ceilings, temple-like rooms furnished with period pieces, and a gorgeous three-story standing staircase. It was built for Charles Lee Shrewsbury, a shipping tycoon who made his fortune through investing in Virginia's salt mines.

A copy of New York's Statue of Liberty carries the flame in Madison.

The Dr William D. Hutchings Office and Hospital is another example of a restored Greek Revival building. It was the first and, until 1889, only hospital in the Ohio Valley between Louisville, Kentucky, and Cincinnati. It is open to the public and displays Dr Hutchings' medical instruments, books, and furnishings, all dating back to 1903 or earlier.

The Madison Railroad Station and Historical Society Museum is a restored 1895 railroad depot that houses the Jefferson County Historical Society Museum. The octagonal wooden depot displays railroad relics and other historical items. An antique railroad caboose can be seen in the grounds.

Nearby, 1,360-acre (551-ha) Clifty Falls State Park provides an excellent view of the Ohio River and the Kentucky hills. Walkers can explore trails leading to waterfalls, fossil beds, and a boulder-strewn canyon. The park has an inn, a swimming pool, and those interested in birds can observe the winter vulture roost.

Madison may be reached by car on Hwy 56 and Hwy 7, and US-421 and by plane.
Map ref: page 558 G2

Gary lies on the shores of Lake Michigan, a popular spot for canoeing and sailing.

MICHIGAN CITY

Michigan City (population 33,822) is a summer playground on the shore of Lake Michigan, popular for its fishing, sandy beaches and dunes, and theater.

Charter boats can be hired to fish from the lake. There are abundant coho and chinook salmon and brown, lake, and steelhead trout.

The Canterbury Theater stages summer shows, and the Dunes Summer Theater presents plays in summer and a workshop in winter.

The John G. Blank Center for the Arts exhibits art of regional, national, and international origin.

The 38-room Barker Mansion is the former estate of John H. Barker, founder of the Haskell & Barker Railroad Car Co. Built in 1857, it was modeled after an English Victorian manor house and includes baroque ceilings, a ballroom, and a sunken garden, as well as original furnishings and works of art.

At the Great Lakes Museum of Military History, military items from the Revolutionary War to the present are exhibited.

Washington Park, on the lakeshore, has a beach, marina, lighthouse museum, Coast Guard station, observation tower, and the Washington Park Zoo.

The nearby Indiana Dunes National Seashore emerged from the most recent Ice Age with an unusual ecosystem of plants, animals, and shifting dunes. Mt Baldy, the largest dune, is 120 feet (37 m) and it moves about 4–5 feet (1.2– 1.5 m) each year.

The lakeshore environment also includes swamps, bogs, and marshes. Plant life includes species that are not otherwise found in the area and a wide diversity of bird species land here for a rest on their north and south migration routes.

The Old Saulk Trail was once used by Native Americans, and may be hiked today. The homestead of French fur trader Joseph Bailly and the nineteenth-century Chelberg Farm may also be visited via hiking trails. Beaches, camping, fishing, and cross-country skiing are other park activities.

Michigan City is accessible by car on I-94, US-12, and US-421 and by plane and bus.
Map ref: page 380 D1

MUNCIE

This is an industrial city with a population of 71,000 62 miles (100 km) northeast of Indianapolis. The land was first occupied by the Munsee tribe of the Delaware Native Americans, which gave the city its name. The arrival of railroads and discovery of natural gas in the second half of the nineteenth century stimulated Muncie commerce. By far the best-known entrepreneurs are the Ball family, whose company, Ball Corporation,

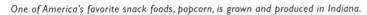

One of America's favorite snack foods, popcorn, is grown and produced in Indiana.

Summer visitors enjoy the variety of fish to be caught in Lake Michigan.

made widely used glass storage jars, and for whom the local university, Ball State, is named.

Ball State University, founded in 1918, is known for its state-of-the-art telecommunications production facility, and its planetarium and observatory. Part of the university is an area called Christy Woods which features arboretums, gardens, and greenhouses. Art-lovers will enjoy the university's Museum of Art which has a collection of seventeenth and eighteenth-century paintings, prints, and drawings, as well as contemporary works.

Minnetrista Cultural Center and Oakhurst Gardens has four galleries displaying local, national, and international exhibits on history, art, and science. Outdoor concerts and festivals are held in a pavilion.

Muncie's Children's Museum exhibits Garfield, the popular cartoon cat created by local artist Jim Davis. Hands-on exhibits allow kids an insight into the diverse lives of truck drivers, paleontologists, geologists, grocers, engineers, farmers, and even ants and birds.

At the National Model Aviation Museum, there is a range of models from simple balsa constructions to elaborate radio-controlled planes on display. Aeromodeling history is shown through flying models, engines, radio equipment, and model kits.

Muncie may be reached by car on US-35, Hwys 3, 32, and 67 and by plane and bus.
Map ref: page 380 F4

SOUTH BEND

This industrial city of 105,500 people, in the north central part of the state near the Michigan border, is best known for its Notre Dame University and remembered as the home of the famous Studebaker automobile last century.

South Bend takes its name from its position on the St Joseph River. In the seventeenth century a portage to the nearby Kankakee River provided explorers with a new water route between the St Lawrence and the Mississippi Rivers. In 1820 fur trader Pierre Navarre established a trading post here. Other traders settled in the area and the spot became known as Southhold and later South Bend.

In 1852, Henry and Clement Studebaker opened a blacksmith and wagon-building company in South Bend. Within 20 years, Studebaker was one of the world's largest manufacturers of wagons and buggies, and produced popular automobiles from 1902 until 1963.

Plow manufacturing became another big South Bend industry. In 1864 James Oliver discovered a process involving chilling which allowed iron in plows to be replaced with steel. The steel was harder and resisted the build-up of moist earth that clogged plow blades. Today, in addition to automobiles and plows, South Bend manufacturers produce goods ranging from automobile parts to guided missiles.

The University of Notre Dame was established in 1842 and has 10,126 students on a 1,250-acre (506-ha) campus. It is a Roman Catholic school noted for its bio-technology and vector biology research, and studies focusing on radiation, aerodynamics, and social ministry. It's also a major center for constitutional law studies. However, more than anything else Notre Dame is celebrated for its college football team, recognized as one of the best in the country.

The campus of Notre Dame is crowned by the magnificent golden dome of its administration building, the Basilica of Sacred Heart and Grotto of Our Lady of Lourdes. These are open to the public and may also be seen on guided tour. Restoration of the lighting fixtures, woodwork, and walls of the Victorian administration building has been undertaken recently at a cost of US$58 million. Murals painted by Luigi Gregori, a nineteenth-century Vatican artist who spent 17 years at Notre Dame, depict the life of explorer Christopher Columbus. The ornate basilica, built in the late 1800s, is adorned with gold and brass, and its ceiling and walls are decorated by Gregori's murals. The basilica is built in the shape of a Latin cross, and its chapels contain relics and works of art. The grotto is a reproduction of the famous Grotto of Lourdes in France.

Followers of football will enjoy the College Football Hall of Fame, which has a large display area of 58,000 square feet (5,500 sq m) for historic artifacts, mementos, photographs, and interactive installations as well as archives and a library.

Copshaholm, the Oliver Mansion, was built by the founder of the Oliver Chilled Plow Works, Joseph Doty Oliver, in 1895. He named his grand residence for the Scottish village in which he was born. Its 38 rooms feature leaded-glass windows, parquet floors, 11 fireplaces and nine bathrooms. Original contents include porcelains, glass, silver, prints, and bronzes. The extensive gardens have roses, a tea house, pergola, fountain, and carriage house.

At the Studebaker National Museum, horse-drawn and motorized vehicles manufactured in South Bend are on display. The Northern Indiana Center for History uses audiotapes, artifacts, and photographs to recreate the history of the St Joseph Valley.

The East Race Waterway is one of the few man-made whitewater kayaking and rafting courses in the world and is capable of matching the Colorado River in power. It is part of a 5-mile (8-km) system of

The Ohio River is a scenic waterway through some of Indiana's historic towns and marks the state's southern border.

parks that runs through downtown along the St Joseph River. National and international contests are held on the waterway.

South Bend is reached by car on I-72, US-31, and Hwy 2 and by plane and bus.
Map ref: page 376 D9

VINCENNES

This town of 19,900 residents is located on the banks of the Wabash River between Evansville and Terre Haute on the western edge of the state. During the eighteenth century it was almost entirely populated by descendants of its founders, the French troops who built Fort Vincennes in 1732. It was turned over to the British in 1763, then taken from them by George Rogers Clark for the state of Virginia. This act opened up the whole Northwest Territory, which became public domain in 1784 after Virginia ceded it to the United States. Vincennes

became the first town in Indiana and developed into a farming, business, and industrial center. It is now a shipping and trading center and the seat of Knox County. The area is noted for growing melons and raising livestock, and for its fishing and boating on the Wabash River.

Attractions include George Rogers Historical Park, which has a visitor center and museum, and Indiana Military Museum, which has an extensive collection of military memorabilia, past and present.

The Indiana Territorial Site, a two-story capitol building, was in 1811 the seat of government of a territory which included five of the present-day Midwestern states. A replica of the first newspaper shop in Indiana, where Elihu Stout published the *Indiana Gazette* in 1804, is preserved in the building.

Vincennes may be reached by car on US-41, US-50, and Hwy 67. It can also be reached by bus.
Map ref: page 380 C8

WARSAW

This town of 11,000 residents, 40 miles (64 km) west of Fort Wayne, is surrounded by the scenic lakes of Kosciusko County where excellent swimming, boating, and fishing are available.

One of the largest rotogravure printing plants in the United States is found here. Kosciusko County is also home to the world's largest duck farm, Maple Leaf Farms.

The Kosciusko County Old Jail Museum and Library goes back to 1871. It has a catwalk, two floors of jails, and an eight-room sheriff's residence. On show here are items relating to local history, including medical equipment, military artifacts and antique tools. There is also an exhibit that features gangster John Dillenger, who robbed the city police in 1934.

Warsaw can be reached by car on I-75, and also by plane.
Map ref: page 380 E2

STATE FEATURE

Indianapolis

The Soldiers and Sailors Monument is the hub of Monument Circle downtown.

Buildings along the distinctive city skyline of Indianapolis glint in the afternoon sun.

Indianapolis is the state capital and, with a metropolitan population of 1.3 million, by far the largest city in Indiana. It is best known for the Indianapolis 500 motor race, held every Memorial Day (May 30) when, in a loud and colorful blur of motion around a 2-mile (3-km) oval, high-tech, low-slung Indy cars reach speeds of more than 200 mph (320 kph) before boisterous packed crowds of half a million people.

Indianapolis and wheels go together. The city, in the middle of the state, was built in the early nineteenth century on the banks of the White River in the hope that the transportation opportunities the waterway offered would lead to growth and development. As it turned out, the river was too shallow most of the year for anything other than small boats. However, the city's central geographic position was an advantage as Indianapolis became a hub for east–west and north–south traffic. It boasts the title of "Crossroads of America" by virtue of the seven interstate and nine US highways that move through and around it.

Designed in a wheel pattern after Washington DC, the city grew out from Monument Circle, where a 285-foot (87-m) high monument to Indiana soldiers and sailors pays tribute to the more than 210,000 Hoosiers killed during the Civil War and more than 4,000 killed in the War with Mexico. Monument Circle and its surroundings—cobblestone streets, the Capitol, and the restaurants and night spots fanning out from the circle—present a spectacle reminiscent of Europe. Adding to the appeal are the Canal Walk and the five-block Veterans Memorial Plaza, which features the immense limestone and granite War Memorial Building, lovely gardens, woodland, bright grassy stretches, and a bewitching and playful water sculpture. It's hard to believe that not long ago central Indy was a bleak and dangerous eyesore. Since then a

progressive city government has spruced it up and made it safe. The new Circle Center mall is now *the* place to go to party, relax, and shop.

Before its centennial renovation in 1988, the interior of the Indiana Statehouse had been painted a drab green by prisoners. The $10 million makeover renewed original hand-painted details, brass chandeliers, and marble floors. The governor's office features a desk made of teak decking from the USS *Indiana*, the Supreme Court gleams with original brass spittoons, and just a few blocks west of Monument Circle the limestone shoulders and copper dome of the Capitol is bathed in light at night.

Downtown Indy abounds in historical edifices, most within walking distance of Monument Circle. The Madame Walker Urban Life Center at 617 Indiana Avenue features Egyptian and African design. The restored structure was built to house the business of C.J. Walker, America's first African-American self-made millionaire. The Indiana Theater at 134 W. Washington St is home to the Indiana Repertory Theater, the state's only professional resident theater company. The Spanish Baroque building, originally a 1920s' movie palace, offers three stages and a variety of performances. The elaborate Indiana Roof Ballroom on the sixth floor displays a starry domed "sky" and the decor of a Spanish village. Concerts, dances, and big New Year's Eve parties are held there. Union Station at 39 Jackson Place was built in 1888 as the nation's first grand railway station with the Union name. It saw 200 trains a day during the busy times of World War II. Now it's a marketplace loaded with specialty shops, restaurants, and an arcade for kids. The James Whitcomb Riley Home at 528 Lockerbie St in Lockerbie Square was home to the poet who penned such famous rhymes as "Little Orphan Annie" and "When the Frost is on the Punkin." The 1872 house, which is open to the public, is furnished with period pieces and the author's personal effects. The Middle East visits downtown Indy with the Murat Shrine Temple, a massive building right out of the Sahara with an exquisite Egyptian Room, where big-name concerts and holiday celebrations are held. Among many fine religious structures, the Scottish Rite Cathedral on N. Meridian St stands out. Its Tudor/Gothic wrap resembles a castle. The Masonic temple building has been lauded as one of the world's most beautiful buildings. Its ballroom has a magnificent black and white walnut parquet floor, and rare Russian white oak in the auditorium.

One of the keys to Indy's downtown redevelopment is Circle Centre. With other components in place—sports and performing-arts venues, hotels, a convention center, a zoo, museums, and housing—the one essential, missing ingredient was shopping. As in other cities, most of Indianapolis' major retailers had abandoned the downtown area for suburban malls. In 1995 the US$310 million, four-level shopping and entertainment complex was opened, and it has been a big hit. Circle Center not only keeps people in the city, but draws visitors from surrounding areas and far away. Its architecture combines the façades of eight venerable buildings with new construction that is both comfortable and contemporary. Arched skylights run the length of the mall and storefronts run the gamut from elegant to funky. The 100 tenants include Nordstrom, the Seattle-based department store famous for its customer service and quality merchandise, and the Parisian, a Georgia-based department-store chain that has an in-store jungle gym for restless kids.

Many of the best restaurants are downtown or in the affluent suburb of Broad Ripple, just to the north. Traditional American, Italian, and Chinese have been popular in the past, but in the last decade a wider variety of ethnic cuisines has come into the picture, including Indian, Korean, Ethiopian, and Russian.

When it comes to the performing arts, the outstanding Indianapolis Symphony Orchestra is one of America's few 52-week orchestras. It offers some 200 concerts a year for all tastes—classical, pop, a Yuletide celebration, and a Symphony on the Prairie series. For visual arts, the Indianapolis Museum of Art, founded in 1883, is one of the oldest art museums in the United States. Set in the beautifully landscaped riverside splendor of the former estate of Josiah K. Lilly Jr (the grandson of pharmaceutical company founder Eli Lilly), the museum is home to a superb collection of J.M.W. Turner watercolors and drawings, old master paintings, contemporary art, and remarkable collections of Chinese and African art.

Indianapolis was rolling woodland back in 1820, occupied by scattered Native American villages and two white settler families. It became the capital in 1824 because it was located near the center of the state and was thought to have such great potential for transport. By the Civil War (1861–65), the city had more than 100 manufacturing concerns. Today, Indianapolis is primarily a trade and manufacturing center, although government employment is significant, providing work for nearly a fifth of the labor force. There are more than 1,500 firms in the eight-county metropolitan area. Local products include pharmaceuticals, automobile parts, truck engines and bodies, jet engines, communication and electronic equipment, and rubber and paper goods. The city is among the leading US corn and grain producers, and is headquarters for many insurance companies.

The two largest educational institutions here are Butler University and Indiana-Purdue University at Indianapolis. Also in the city are Indiana University's Indianapolis Law School, the Graduate School of Social Services, the John Herron School of Arts, Marian College, the University of Indianapolis, and the Christian Theological Seminary.

But the city is best-known for its sports. Not only the Indianapolis 500, but two more of racing's notable events—the Brickyard 400 stock-car race and the International Hot Rod Association's US nationals—are held here. The presence of high-quality venues and high-quality events has led to the creation or relocation of some 250 racing-related businesses in Indianapolis ranging from engineering and design firms to racing organizations and equipment manufacturers.

Indianapolis also has two well-known professional sports teams, the Indianapolis Colts in the National Football League and the Indiana Pacers of the National Basketball Association. The minor league Indianapolis Indian baseball team and Indianapolis ice hockey team also have avid followings. As well, the Indianapolis Tennis Center showcases top international players. Many sports organizations have their headquarter here. The city has built or renovated more than US$168 million worth of sports facilities and Indy has hosted hundreds of events, including the Pan American Games and NCAA Final Four basketball games, earning it the title of "Amateur Sports Capitol of the World." The economic contribution to the city has been more than a billion dollars.

Indianapolis can be reached on I-70, I-74, I-65, and I-69. Its international airport is the largest in the state. It can also be reached by bus.

The State Capitol Building presides over the city's rejuvenated downtown area.

Players enjoy a game of roller hockey, a warm-season version of ice hockey, in Indianapolis, a city keen on amateur sports.

IOWA

Iowa's vast tallgrass prairies, born of ancient glacial forces and covered with the luxuriant growth of densely rooted prairie grasses, give this state a quarter of all the Grade A land in the United States, making it the breadbasket of the Midwest. The state's agricultural statistics are as big as they come: 90 percent of its land area is farmed, and the Iowa State Fair is the largest in the nation. Iowa ranks first in the United States in the production of pork, corn, and soybeans.

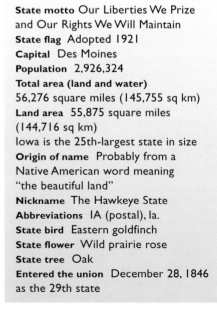

The state was settled largely by immigration from the eastern states and northwestern Europe. A significant proportion of the population is Caucasian, with German, Irish, or English heritage; German Protestants—the Amana Colonists—migrated to Iowa from Buffalo, New York, in 1855. The Amana Colonies are Iowa's main tourist attraction. Des Moines (population 191,000) has been the state capital since 1857, when the capital was moved there from Iowa City.

Winter temperatures can fall to 14°F (−10°C) in the north and to below −25°F (−32°C) in the extreme

The vast plains that are typical of Iowa stretch out along this lonely road near the state line. Much of this state is devoted to farming. In 1999 Iowa's 96,000 farms covered a staggering total of 33,000,000 acres (13,365,00 ha).

southeast. Although total snowfall is relatively small, the severity of the winter is often heightened by high winds that produce blizzard conditions and by prolonged periods of very low temperatures. Spring and fall are mild, but summers can be very hot and humid.

In the heartland of North America, Iowa is the only state to be bordered by two navigable rivers, the Missouri to the west and the Mississippi to the east. Its quaint "Main Street USA" towns (those that have taken part in a program of historic preservation) and politically conservative communities certainly reinforce the popular image of the state that is exemplified by the Grant Wood painting *American Gothic*.

In recent years, it seems the now-famous question asked by "Shoeless" Joe Jackson in the movie *Field of Dreams* has become the question most proud Iowans love to answer: "Is this Heaven?" "No, it's Iowa."

State motto Our Liberties We Prize and Our Rights We Will Maintain
State flag Adopted 1921
Capital Des Moines
Population 2,926,324
Total area (land and water) 56,276 square miles (145,755 sq km)
Land area 55,875 square miles (144,716 sq km)
Iowa is the 25th-largest state in size
Origin of name Probably from a Native American word meaning "the beautiful land"
Nickname The Hawkeye State
Abbreviations IA (postal), Ia.
State bird Eastern goldfinch
State flower Wild prairie rose
State tree Oak
Entered the union December 28, 1846 as the 29th state

Places in
IOWA

THE AMANA COLONIES

The Amana Colonies are a collection of seven communities spread over 26,000 acres (10,522 ha) along the Iowa River Valley in eastern Iowa, 15 miles (24 km) west of Iowa City. Their 1,700 residents are, for the most part, descendants of an early German religious movement known as the Colonies of True Inspiration who fled to the United States in 1842 to escape persecution in Germany. Initially settling in Buffalo, New York, they moved to the new state of Iowa in 1855 to escape increasing urbanization, building each village by hand.

These seven villages—Amana, Middle Amana, South Amana, East Amana, West Amana, High Amana, and Homestead—are laid

A blacksmith in Amana at his trade.

out in classic old-world style, and the entire settlement comprising some 475 historical sites and buildings is a national historic landmark, and also the state of Iowa's number-one tourist attraction.

The original colonists made all their own farm implements, formed their bricks from the local clay deposits, wove the fabric for their garments, printed and bound their own books, and pressed their own grapes for the village wines.

All goods were held in common, and this simple communal lifestyle continued for nearly 100 years until the people voted in 1932 to adopt a free-enterprise system. The

Amana Colonies have welcomed visitors ever since and are a popular place to visit.

Their churches are plain, with no stained glass or artwork to distinguish them. Anyone may attend, with men sitting on one side and women on the other. There are no ministers; lay elders from the community preside over services.

Each town has its own cemetery. Surrounded by a grove of pine trees, their residents are buried with plain stone markers, symbolizing equality in the eyes of God.

More than 1 million people visit the Amana villages every year. The community products, such as hardwood furniture, clocks, woolens, meats, cheeses, and wine, are available in a variety of shops throughout the villages. Restaurants serve thousands of visitors a day. Local specialties can be found at the Ox Yoke Inn in Amana while the Chocolate Haus makes its hand-dipped fudges and chocolates from 100-year-old recipes.

There are more than 500 hotel, motel, and B&B rooms available, as well as camping facilities. Special events and festivals are held year-round, and so life goes on for these descendants of the original settlers.
Map ref: page 379 J3

AMES

Situated in the geographical center of Iowa, Ames is a half-hour drive north of Des Moines near the junction of I-35 and I-80. This town is noted for its healthy and flourishing cultural environment, and the home of Iowa State University.

Ames was voted number two out of 189 small cities across America recently in terms of livability by *New Rating Guide to Life in America's Small Cities*. The rating is based on factors such as climate/environment, economics, health care, and public safety.

Historically a small town it was incorporated in 1870 with a population of just 844 and the town itself covered 12 city blocks. Today its population is approaching the 50,000 mark. It has 30 parks covering over 1,300 acres (526 ha), golf courses, and cross-country skiing is also available, thanks to Ames' average annual snowfall of 31 inches (79 cm). Cyclists are blessed with 42 miles (68 km) of bicycle paths.

Buildings in Amana are very plain and simple, reflecting the colonists' ideals.

The Campustown District is adjacent to Iowa State University and offers a plethora of shops and sights, and there's plenty to eat and drink on a student budget.
Map ref: page 378 E2

ANAMOSA AND STONE CITY

Anamosa lies 23 miles (37 km) northeast of Cedar Rapids in Jones County, eastern Iowa and has a population of 5,400. Known as the "Pumpkin Capital of Iowa," it is one of 15 US sites for the Great Pumpkin Commonwealth Weigh-off. Via international conference calls to other sites throughout the United States and Canada, the world's heaviest pumpkin is selected annually. The world record is for a 923 lb (419 kg) beauty, in 1994. However it is for the paintings of Iowa's greatest artist, Grant Wood, that Anamosa and the nearby town of Stone City owe their fame. Born on a farm near Anamosa in 1891, Wood painted some of America's most imaginative and original paintings of the 1930s, idealizing rural life in Iowa with iconic images of plain, small-town folk and conservative Midwestern values.

At the Grant Wood Tourism Center in Anamosa you can view a continuing exhibit of Grant Wood prints and photos from the original artists' colony he founded in Stone City during the summers of 1932 and 1933.

Some original murals painted by Wood from the old Chieftan Hotel in Council Bluffs are on permanent loan. Guided bus tours of Stone City are by appointment.

The annual Grant Wood Art Festival on the second Sunday of each June honors the artist and the legacy of the early Irish immigrants who settled in Stone City. Artists and entertainers from throughout the Midwest gather to exhibit their work amid replicas of the colorful wagons used as housing by some of the original 1930s students. Wood died in 1942 and he is buried at Riverside Cemetery, Anamosa.

Nearby Wapsipinicon Park was dedicated in 1923 and is one of Iowa's oldest parks. Spectacular views can be had from its limestone bluffs that hide rocky staircases, crevices, and caves. Deer, beaver, and wild turkeys frequent the Wapsi and Dutch creeks and surrounding forests and the Park has 30 campsites.
Map ref: page 379 J2

Anamosa is famous for its pumpkins.

BLAIRSBURG

Blairsburg is a tiny community that is 60 miles (97 km) north of the capital Des Moines near I-35 in Hamilton County. A rather sleepy district with a somewhat quaint history, it was founded in 1869 by John I. Blair, chief engineer of the Dubuque and Sioux City Railroad. Hoping to gain a concession of land, he approached a group of local investors who had laid out the town of Hawley about 12 years earlier. When they refused, he laid out his own town anyway, just a mile north of Hawley, and then named it after himself.

The town grew very slowly, and by 1880 only 44 people lived there. Peaking in 1980 at 288, the town has since been in gradual decline and today Blairsburg's population is listed at 269 people.

Prior to Blairsburg receiving electricity in the 1920s, the first state road that passed along the southern edge of town had lanterns strung in the trees to light the way for travelers. In recent years the Opera House has been restored and has become a focal point for the community with plays and other activities taking place there.

Highway traffic has diminished with the creation of I-35. Gone are the days when US-20 and US-69 brought travelers to the intersection known locally as "Blairsburg Corners," stopping at restaurants and gas stations. It's hard to imagine that Blairsburg's business district once stretched for several blocks. Nevertheless, it's only a small diversion from I-35, and it is well worth a stop.
Map ref: page 378 E1

The manufacture of farm equipment is a major industry in Burlington.

BOONE

The seat of Boone County, Boone (population 12,000) was named as a tribute to both frontiersman Daniel Boone and his son, Colonel Nathan Boone of the US Dragoons. Colonel Boone was one of the first to explore this region and give an account of its natural resources. It became the county seat in 1887.

Agriculture, railroads, and light manufacturing sustain the city's economy today. Boone has a host of city parks, including the 1,200-acre (486-ha) Ledges State Park, one of Iowa's oldest.

The wife of the US President Dwight Eisenhower, Mamie Doud Eisenhower, was born here. The home has been completely restored with original family furniture, and there is a museum plus a library featuring exhibits from the Eisenhower era. It is only one of two US First Lady birthplaces open to visitors. The home is open daily from June to October.

A beautiful trip along the Des Moines River Valley can be had on *The Iowan,* a steam locomotive that runs on weekends and holidays. The two-hour ride takes visitors across a 156-foot (48-m) high bridge offering superb views.
Map ref: page 378 E2

BURLINGTON

Burlington is a 167-year-old railroad town along on the banks of the Mississippi River. Once known as Catfish Bend, its 27,000 inhabitants live in a city that features extraordinary nineteenth-century charm. Settled in 1833 and named after Burlington in Vermont, it

Vegetables grown in Iowa include onions, cucumbers, potatoes, and sweet corn.

served briefly as the Wisconsin territorial capital (1837) and the Iowa territorial capital (1838–42). A bustling railroad hub since 1856, it is now a manufacturing center for tractors, electronic instruments, chemicals, and furniture.

Both the Sac and Fox Native Americans called the area "Shoquoquon," meaning "Flint Hills," for the abundance of flint-gathering sites in the area.

Located on scenic bluffs overlooking the Mississippi River, Burlington possesses the "crookedest street in the world," Snake Alley. Its residential showpiece is the Heritage Hill National Historic District. Almost 160 structures reflect a myriad of architectural styles including Greek and Gothic Revival, Queen Anne and Georgian, among others.

The town's convenience to commercial and cultural activities made the area socially desirable during the rather status-conscious period of 1870 to 1900.

Heritage Hill has an abundance of very impressive churches with high steeples, leading to Burlington sometimes being called the "City of Steeples."

Annual events include the Friday Festivals. There are six each year from late spring to early fall, and they involve afterhours live music, food, and fun at the Port of Burlington on the Mississippi riverfront. Visitors can view the giant steamboats

American Queen and *Delta Queen* that regularly dock next to the Port of Burlington Welcome Center.

The Schramm House B&B is at the top of Heritage Hill in the heart of the Historic District. This 1860s architectural masterpiece is a rather fine example of the Queen Anne style, with a brick first floor and clapboard siding on the second floor distinguishing it from other homes in the area. Its beautiful oak and walnut parquet floors, antique furnishings, and the two exterior porches make it an ideal place to lay one's head after a fascinating day exploring all this charming town has to offer.
Map ref: page 379 K5

CEDAR RAPIDS

Cedar Rapids is Iowa's second-largest city and it has a population of 115,000 residents. Incorporated in 1856, it was named after the swiftly flowing Red Cedar River. The town is centrally located in Iowa's eastern heartland on I-380.

Cedar Rapids' symbol is a very dramatic 60-foot (18-m) landmark, the Tree of Five Seasons, which is located at the corner of First Avenue and First Street SE. It marks the spot where the original settler, Osgood Shepherd, constructed Cedar Rapids' very first residence. By the 1870s the town had grown and became known as a grain-milling center.

Today the town is a principal industrial and business center with rich ethnic traditions and a love of the performing and visual arts. Approximately a quarter of the population is of Czech heritage, and the National Czech and Slovak

This truckwash in Council Bluffs sees a steady flow of business from Iowa's vast transportation industry, which takes the state's farming communities' produce to market.

Museum and Library is worth a visit to explore their cultural, political, and religious traditions. Included is an interesting variety of ethnic, gift, and specialty shops, plus a bakery and restaurants.

Historic Brucemore is listed on the National Register of Historic Places. This Queen Anne-style mansion is set in the midst of a 26-acre (11-ha) park and hosts a number of special events throughout the year, including outdoor theatre, which is on during July.

One of Cedar Rapids' true hidden treasures is the Belmont Hill Victorian B&B, which was built in 1882. Both the main dwelling and accompanying carriage house are on the National Register of Historic Places. The perennial gardens with centuries-old hardwood trees, and rooms with luxury appointments, ensure a pleasant stay.

Map ref: page 379 J2

COUNCIL BLUFFS

Council Bluffs has always found itself to be the focus of history in the Midwest. Explorers Lewis and Clark passed through in 1804 on their historic expedition to locate a northwest passage linking the Atlantic and Pacific Oceans. Their historic "council in the bluffs" with representatives of the Missouri and Oto Native Americans at White Catfish Camp (known today as Long's Landing) provided a model for future meetings, and eventually gave the town its name.

The town was called Miller's Hollow by the Mormons who originally settled the area in 1846, but the name was later changed to Council Bluffs at its incorporation in 1853. In 1859 Abraham Lincoln visited the city, and when he was elected President he declared it to become the eastern terminus of the Union Pacific Railroad, thus cementing its role as a key corridor in westward migration.

Council Bluffs today is a city of nearly 60,000 residents. It is located along the pleasant banks of the Missouri River and is ideally situated on I-80. This city offers a rich blend of history, natural beauty, and many cultural pursuits such as chamber music, jazz, opera, and also live theatre. Omaha, Nebraska, lies just across the river with attractions such as the Henry Doorly Zoo and Boys Town.

The Loess Hills Scenic Byway, Iowa's first designated scenic byway, runs through the city. Extending some 200 miles (322 km) from Sioux City to St Joseph, Missouri, down Iowa's western border, it was named among America's top 10 byways by *Scenic America*. "Loess" is windblown soil, and despite there being loess deposits found all over the world, nowhere—except in China—do they reach the heights found here—some hills of loess are 200 feet (60 m) above the adjacent valley floors.

Plants and animals that are found nowhere else in Iowa can sometimes be seen here, such as the prairie rattlesnake and the plains pocket mouse. The push is on to have the Loess Hills declared Iowa's first national park.

Council Bluffs has also carefully preserved its grand architectural heritage. The Historic Pottawattamie County Jail, or the "Squirrel Cage Jail," is a unique rotary designed oddity built in 1885. It is open during the months of April, May, and September.

General Dodge House is a 14-room Victorian home that was built in 1869 by Grenville Dodge, "the greatest railroad builder of all time." Five US Presidents have stayed there, and its exquisite parquet floors, cherry and butternut woodwork, and splendid location on a high terrace overlooking the Missouri Valley make it an ideal site to visit. It is also a great vantage point to appreciate the colorful history of this rather vibrant Midwestern city.

Map ref: page 378 B4

DAVENPORT

Davenport is Iowa's third-largest city (population 95,000) and the largest of what are known as the "Quad Cities" urban complex, which also includes Moline, East Moline, and Rock Island, all across the Mississippi River in Illinois.

Incorporated in 1838, eight years before Iowa became a state, its riverfront location was the site for the first railroad bridge to span the Mississippi River, in 1856. The development of both river and rail transportation assured the city's growth as a trading center. Main industries today are food processing, clothing, and farm machinery.

Of interest is the Village of East Davenport, a 120-acre (49-ha) historic district including homes dating to the 1830s and six blocks of specialty shops. Next-door is Lindsey Park, offering stunning riverfront views and was the site of Camp McClellan, a major Civil War training post for Union soldiers from Iowa and Illinois.

Davenport has two recreational trails—the Great River Trail runs 6½ miles (10.5 km) along the Davenport Riverfront, and the Duck Creek Parkway is a 13-mile (21-km) trail along Duck Creek through Bettendorf.

Map ref: page 379 K3

DES MOINES

With a population of 192,000, Des Moines is the capital city of the state of Iowa and the seat of Polk County. Located close to the geographical center of the state, it is situated at the confluence of the Des Moines and Raccoon Rivers.

Fort Des Moines was built in 1843, and when the Native Americans surrendered their land rights two years later the area was opened to European settlers. The towns of East Des Moines and Fort Des Moines were merged and incorporated as Des Moines in 1851. The state capital was moved to Des Moines from Iowa City in 1857, and the magnificent Capitol building stands today in the midst of a delightful 80-acre (32-ha) park.

A principal insurance center with several insurance companies having their headquarters here, Des Moines is also the commercial, manufacturing, and transportation center of the state. It is the site of Drake University (1881), Grand View College (1896), and the KRNT theater, one of the largest theaters in the nation. The city's

Reflection of the Capitol building in Des Moines.

Sherman Hill Historic District has many turn-of-the-century homes. The Iowa State fair, first held in 1878, is an annual Des Moines event that is worth seeing.
Map ref: page 378 E3

DUBUQUE

Dubuque is blessed with one of the most spectacular settings of any Iowan town. Sometimes called the "Masterpiece on the Mississippi," it meanders along huge limestone bluffs overlooking the Mississippi River, its hills dotted with gingerbread-style Victorian mansions that sit peacefully amid rocky outcroppings, tall trees, wildflowers, and soaring bald eagles.

Officially opened for settlement in 1833 and incorporated as a city in 1841, Dubuque has a population of 60,000 and is on Great River Road in northeastern Iowa at the confluence of three states: Iowa, Illinois and Wisconsin. It is named for Julien Dubuque, a French-Canadian fur trader who settled in the area in the 1780s.

Spared the glaciation that had scraped smooth the remainder of Iowa giving it its flat, seemingly endless tall-grass prairies, northeastern Iowa is the hilliest, most eroded part of the state—an area tourist brochures like to

The rich, flat plains of Iowa are dotted with weathered farmhouses and barns.

compare with the pastoral hills of Switzerland. Dubuque sits in a land of picturesque river valleys amid hardwood forests of hickory, elm, and oak. Surrounding well-kept farms and quiet rural communities complete the defining image of Iowan life.

Dubuque is the processing and transportation center of an agricultural area that produces grains and dairy products. Tourism has vastly increased since the introduction of legalized riverboat gambling, and river cruises are available on *The Celebration Belle*, an 800-passenger four-deck riverboat offering 100-mile (160-km) long day cruises from Dubuque to Moline, Illinois.

Historic sights abound and include the Ryan House, which was built in 1873. Boasting a solid walnut staircase, it houses the Dubuque County Historical Society. Iowa's oldest building is an early settlers' log cabin (1833) found within the grounds of the Mathias Ham House Historic Site on Lincoln Avenue. Both of these properties are listed on the National Register of Historic Places.

The Fenelon Place elevator is the world's steepest scenic railroad. Rising 189 feet (58 m) up from Fourth Street to Fenelon Place, it offers superb views of the historic Dubuque business district, the Mississippi River, and three states.

Half-an-hour's drive west of Dubuque on Hwy 20 takes you to Dyersville and the *Field*

Of Dreams movie site. Open from April through to November, the farm retains the famous baseball diamond set amid fields of corn where Kevin Costner pitched his curve ball to the legendary "Shoeless" Joe Jackson. Bring along your favorite bat and ball and relive the dream—the entry is free.
Map ref: page 375 L9

EFFIGY MOUNDS NATIONAL MONUMENT

Effigy Mounds National Monument extends along the high bluffs and lowlands of northeastern Iowa. It is located 3 miles (4.8 km) north of Marquette on Hwy 76. It was established in 1949 by presidential proclamation, and its 1,481 acres (599 ha) contain prehistoric Native American burial mounds that are unique in North America.

Prehistoric mounds are commonly found from the Midwest through to the Atlantic seaboard, but only in this region were they constructed as effigies of mammals, birds, and reptiles. One hundred and ninety-one mounds have been located, of which 29 are effigies. They were constructed from 500 BC through to AD 1300 by Eastern Woodland Native Americans, to receive the bodies of their departed. Some of these are quite monumental in scale, with the Great Bear Mound measuring 70 feet (21 m) across the shoulders and forelegs, 137 feet (42 m) in length, and 3½ feet (1 m) high.

Archeological finds within the Monument include some bone and copper awls used for sewing, and crude, heavily tempered pottery made with coarse pieces of crushed rock. The animals they hunted included deer, bear, and bison, plus the discovery of many weapons and tools such as the axe and the adz suggest a large population and a relatively prosperous lifestyle.

With the advent of the fur trade and the opening up of the West, Native American occupation of the land now within the boundaries of the Monument came to a close.

Located across the Mississippi River from historic Prairie du Chien, Wisconsin, Effigy Mounds National Monument contains a number of points of historical and scenic value. The military road from Prairie du Chien in Wisconsin to Fort Atkinson, Iowa, passes

Extinct forms of these modern-day bison once grazed around Effigy Mounds, where they were hunted with stones and spears.

through the Monument. For over a century the Monument's eastern boundary has provided sightseers with spectacular panoramas of the mighty Mississippi, and the many wildflowers, ferns, bird life, and animal populations provide the visitor with an area of biological diversity not found elsewhere in the entire National Park System.

The visitor center is open daily and contains not only museum exhibits but it also has an audio-visual presentation explaining the prehistory and natural history of Effigy Mounds.

A one-hour, self-guided walk along Fire Point Trail takes you past significant features such as the Little Bear Mound. A total of 11 miles (18 km) of hiking trails will have you viewing representations of falcons, eagles, bison, reptiles, turtles, and bears, all the while winding through natural features such as tall-grass prairies, wetlands, forests, and rivers.

No lodging or camping facilities are found within the Monument, but some campsites can be found at nearby Pikes Peak State Park and Yellow River State Forest in Iowa, and also at Wyalusing State Park, which is in Wisconsin.

Restaurants and lodging options can be found in some of the local communities, or in Prairie du Chien in neighbouring Illinois.
Map ref: page 375 K8

FORT DODGE

The seat of Webster County in north-central Iowa, Fort Dodge is situated at the juncture of the Des Moines River and Lizard Creek, 90 miles (145 km) northwest of Des Moines. With a population of 26,000, the city's economy centers on the production of gypsum, farm machinery, and chemical fertilizers.

The area was first settled by soldiers of the Sixth US Infantry in 1850 who foresaw the growth of a city and laid out the principal fort buildings in a line that would some day form a city street. A bronze plaque in downtown Fort Dodge marks the site of the original fort.
Map ref: page 378 D1

FORT MADISON

Situated on America's Great River Road, US-61, Fort Madison has a population of 11,620. It is located on a bend in the Mississippi River deep in the southeastern corner of Iowa where the River widens to almost 1 mile (1.6 km).

First settled in 1833, it contains seven beautiful city parks including the 250-acre (100-ha) Rodeo Park and the city's crown jewel, Riverview Park, which provides access to the Mississippi River. Spend a pleasant afternoon on an audio-guided driving tour of some of Fort Madison's most outstanding

examples of Victorian architecture, or visit nearby Shimek State Forest, which is Iowa's largest.

The town's foremost attraction is the reconstructed Old Fort Madison. The original, built in 1808 and named after US President James Madison, was America's first fort west of the Mississippi and was intended to secure the American frontier in the region.

The Fort was abandoned in 1813 after frequent attacks by the native Winnebago and Sauk. The soldiers of the 1st Regiment US Infantry set the Fort ablaze and escaped downriver in boats under cover of darkness. The original site of the Fort was rediscovered in 1965, and a stunning replica of Old Fort Madison now stands in Riverview Park just a few blocks from its original site.

Across the river in Illinois is the town of Nauvoo. A disease-infested swamp when it was first settled by Mormons in 1839, by 1844 it was the size of Chicago and considered by many to be the most beautiful city on the frontier. In 1846 most of the town's inhabitants went west to the Great Salt Lake Valley.

Today, after spending millions of dollars and over 20 years on its restoration, Nauvoo has finally been returned to its former glory and is worth seeing when in Iowa's beautiful "Riverbend" region.
Map ref: page 379 J6

IOWA CITY

Iowa City, population 60,000, is ideally located at the crossroads of I-80 and I-380 in east-central Iowa. It lost the title of state capital to Des Moines in 1857, although it retained the University of Iowa, established in 1847. The city's old capitol building is still standing on the University campus.

Its economy is centered around the University and its medical center. The University's art museum houses one of the world's largest collections of African sculpture, as well as twentieth-century works by Marc Chagall and Max Beckmann.

Self-guided walking tours of the four historic neighborhoods here include more than 80 buildings dating between 1840 and 1920. The 1851 Greek Revival Bostick Guest House, which was once used as a town hall, offers lodging in four spacious suites that come furnished with period antiques.

Ten miles (16 km) to the east of Iowa City lies the town of West Branch, with its 76 acres (31 ha) of native tall-grass prairie. It is adjacent to the Herbert Hoover National Historic Site.

While here you can also visit the small cottage where the 31st US President was born in 1874. There is also the first West Branch schoolhouse, and the Quaker Meetinghouse where the Hoover family worshipped. Also in the cottage grounds are the Hoover Presidential Library–Museum and the grave sites of President and Mrs Hoover.
Map ref: page 379 J3

Iowa as it once was: volunteers at the Neal Smith National Wildlife Refuge are re-creating the original Iowa prairie grasslands.

JEWELL (FORMERLY JEWELL JUNCTION)

The town of Jewell Junction was laid out at the junction of the north– south Des Moines and Minnesota Railroad, and the east– west Toledo and Northwestern Railroad in 1880. The name was eventually shortened to Jewell because the residents grew to dislike the "Junction" reference as the town began to prosper. Other towns in the vicinity that failed to attract the railroad, such as Lakin's Grove and Callanan, had many of their buildings put on skids in winter and pulled to Jewell over the frozen ground. Jewell had the first college in Hamilton County, established in 1893 by the Jewell Lutheran College Association.

The population of Jewell is now approximately 1,000, making it the second-largest town in what is a rather sparsely populated Iowa county. The town slogan is: "A Gem in a Friendly Setting."
Map ref: page 378 E1

NEAL SMITH NATIONAL WILDLIFE REFUGE

Twenty miles (32 km) east of Des Moines near Prairie City on Hwy 163, an ambitious attempt to re-create the state of Iowa as it was 150 years ago is underway. The Neal Smith National Wildlife Refuge is dedicated to the reconstruction of the tall-grass prairie that once covered 85 percent of Iowa and part or all of 12 other states. Volunteers collect seeds of some of the 200 species of prairie grasses still to be found in tiny remnants in cemeteries, roadsides, and railroad tracks throughout south-central Iowa.

The early pioneers saw the seemingly endless prairies and reasoned that if trees can't grow there then the soil must be poor, and so passed it by. Later, Iowa was found to have some of the richest

Boys playing ball in front of their Iowa home. The Iowa Cubs baseball team is an affiliate of the famous Chicago Cubs team.

soils in the world, helped by the winds coming down off the Rocky Mountains and mixing with moisture-rich winds coming up from the Gulf of Mexico. This led to the tall-grass prairies of Iowa, as distinct from the shorter, mixed-grass prairies of Nebraska, which received less rainfall.

At Neal Smith National Wildlife Refuge you can drive through this developing window-to-the-past and wander through the myriad prairie blooms. Or you can search for the bison herd that was introduced to help people better understand the bison's role in the shaping of the prairie. You can also participate in the planting of prairie seeds in the spring, and take a walk through the open-grown oaks of the "oak savanna"—scattered oases of groves whose spreading branches provided shade for the bison and elk.

The tall-grass prairies here once held a diversity of life: hundreds of plant species; nearly 100 species of mammals; 350 bird species; scores of amphibians, reptiles, and fish; and thousands of insect species. Neal Smith aims to increase the Refuge's biodiversity by restoring and restructuring the tall-grass prairie and savanna habitats so that one day elk, short-eared owls, glass

lizards, speckled snakes, and spotted skunks will once again become a part of the Iowan landscape.
Map ref: page 378 F3

SIOUX CITY

Sioux City is located in western Iowa on the banks of the Missouri River at its junction with the Big Sioux and Floyd Rivers. Settled in 1849 and named for the Sioux people, Sioux City has a population of 83,000 and is a processing, transporting, and commercial center for grain and livestock.

Some very fine examples of late nineteenth-century commercial buildings can be found along historic Fourth Street, where 15 of the buildings date from 1889 to around 1915. On the western edge of the city is a 135-acre (55-ha) area of native prairie ridges that make up Riverside Bluffs.

Stone State Park is 1,000 acres (405 ha) of wooded loess hills located at the northwestern edge of the city. It has over 70 types of wildflowers. Many of the old Park trails are believed to have been made by buffalo. It is also thought that the last wild buffalo in Iowa may have died within the boundaries of Stone Park.
Map ref: page 378 A1

WALNUT

In 1848 few settlers wanted to live in Pottawattamie County, Iowa. A land of rolling prairies but with no railroad and being quite far from the nearest

markets, the area that surrounds present-day Walnut was the last portion of the County to attract the land agent. Without a railroad, even paying $5 an acre seemed to be a rather steep price.

When in 1868 the Rock Island Railroad came and built Walnut Creek Station, later shortened to Walnut, settlers were far more easily drawn to the region's rich, fertile soil. Prosperity followed.

The present-day population of 850 is a little down on the 1,000 residents of 1878. It only has four gas stations and five restaurants. Yet Americans now flock to this tiny town in west-central Iowa to buy and browse for antiques—and there are lots of antiques here.

Walnut was officially named "Iowa's Antique City" in 1987, and is ideally situated on I-80, 85 miles (137 km) west of the capital Des Moines. Its 20 antique shops and malls housing over 250 dealers have fine antique furniture, primitives, glassware, linens, quilts, fishing lures, and toy-collectibles, and various precious gems from bygone ages on an almost infinite scale. Every year on the

Fathers' Day Weekend, the Walnut Antique Show and Walk attracts as many as 60,000 people from 25 states who come here in search of that something special. This annual event covers 17 city blocks, attracting dealers from across the country, and is heralded as one of the premier antique shows in the Midwest. Hot cider is consumed on Walnut's brick streets, and the town's "Fireman's Breakfasts" are a real treat.

Walnut's antique dealers are open seven days a week throughout the year, and at Christmas time, thousands of lights illuminate the turn-of-the-century storefronts that line Walnut's downtown area. Strolling carolers serenade passing shoppers and the romantic atmosphere can be enjoyed further by taking a horse-drawn carriage tour.
Map ref: page 378 C3

Antiques like this mid-nineteenth century love seat are plentiful in Walnut; the town is famous for its antique shops.

WATERLOO

On a July day in 1845 the covered wagons of George and Mary Hanna stopped on the east bank of the Cedar River. Their 18 × 24 feet (5.5 × 7 m) log cabin was destined to become Waterloo's first structure. They didn't receive their first neighbors for another year.

Today, Waterloo is a small city of 64,000 people, stretching along the banks of the Cedar River, 108 miles (174 km) northeast of Des Moines. It is one of Iowa's chief industrial centers for the manufacture of tractors and farm equipment. It also hosts the annual National Dairy Cattle Congress.

Waterloo is the home of the Waterloo/Cedar Falls Symphony Orchestra, one of northern Iowa's greatest cultural assets. The town also boasts four theaters including the Waterloo Community Playhouse, which has an international reputation for new plays.

The Cedar Valley Nature Trail is one of Iowa's premier "Rails to Trails" conversions, following the Cedar River south from Waterloo to Evansdale. Once a branch of the Illinois Central Gulf Railroad, it was abandoned in 1977 and was opened in 1984 as a recreational trail. The recycled crushed limestone surface is level and provides easy biking. Two restored rail stations located outside Gilbertville and Center Point are historical

Hogback Bridge, built in 1884, is one of six covered bridges found in Madison County, all near the small town of Winterset.

reminders of the days when the trail corridor was an important passenger link. The Trail takes in a great deal of variety of eastern Iowa's scenic diversity.
Map ref: page 379 H1

WINTERSET

Winterset, established in 1849, was very nearly called Independence but for the confusion many felt may occur with the several other towns in Iowa which bore that name. Named after the fourth US President, James Madison, it has a population of 4,300 and is the seat of Madison County.

Located 30 just minutes' drive southwest of the state capital Des Moines, pretty Madison County features densely wooded river valleys, majestic limestone bluffs, and gently rolling grasslands. It is also home to six famous covered bridges, and one very famous American movie actor.

When Robert James Waller first penned his great romantic novel *The Bridges of Madison County* he couldn't have known it would go on to sell 50 million copies around the world and even topple *Gone with the Wind* as the best-selling work of fiction of all time, turning the sleepy little town of Winterset,

Iowa, into a symbol of lost love for romantics the world over.

Despite it also being the birthplace of screen legend John Wayne, Winterset has not been the same since Clint Eastwood came to town to begin the filming of Waller's classic tale in 1994.

The most popular bridge and the one most heavily featured in the film is Roseman Bridge. Built in 1883 by Benton Jones, it measures 107 feet (33 m) in length and still sits in its original location. Holliwell Bridge, the longest of the six bridges at 122 feet (37 m), lies southeast of Winterset spanning over the Middle River.

Francesca's house, which had been abandoned for 35 years but was fully restored for the movie, lies in the northeastern portion of the County. It is open to visitors from May to October. The tour takes you through each room, including the kitchen where many of the scenes were filmed.

Winterset's Covered Bridge Festival is in its 30th year and is held on the second full weekend that occurs in October.

Winterset's other claim to fame began on May 26, 1907, when screen legend John Wayne was born in a tiny four-room timber home at 216 South Second Street, Winterset. Restored to reflect its 1907 appearance, an impressive collection of Wayne memorabilia includes the eye patch worn in the movie *True Grit*, a prop suitcase from the 1939 classic *Stagecoach*, and the hat worn in *Rio Lobo*.
Map ref: page 378 E4

Iowa's farm-equipment industry supports the state's agricultural base, with Waterloo boasting the country's largest tractor plant.

MICHIGAN

With no point farther than 6 miles (10 km) from water, vast tracts of forest, and a state park system with more than 14,000 camp sites, the "Great Lakes State" of Michigan is known as much for its outdoor attractions as it is for its pioneering role in the motor vehicle industry. Its two water-separated peninsulas border four of the five Great Lakes with 3,300 miles (5,300 km) of shoreline, much of it made up of sandy beaches which are popular in the summer. The landscape is dotted with more than 11,000 smaller lakes and is crossed by 36,000 miles (58,000 km) of rivers and trout streams.

Michigan covers 96,705 square miles (250,466 sq km), nearly half of which is water. The Lower Peninsula takes the form of a mitten-covered hand, a distinctive shape distinguishable from space. Agriculture, industry, and population are concentrated in the south; in the north are hardwood forests known for their blazing October colors, and the state's largest inland lake, 31-square-mile (80-sq-km) Houghton Lake. Moose, wolves, and black bears roam the pine-covered slopes of the smaller and more rugged Upper

Colorful South Pier lighthouse at Grand Haven on Lake Michigan.

Peninsula. The two are linked by a 5-mile (8-km) bridge across the Straits of Makinac.

Michigan's population of nearly ten million people makes it the nation's eighth most populous state. Detroit is its largest city, and Lansing is the capital. In 1837 Michigan became the 26th state to enter the Union. The name has Native American origins, as "Michigana" is widely recognized as the Algonquian term for "big water" or "great lake."

As the motor vehicle capital of the world, it should come as no surprise that the car rules in Michigan. Public transportation options are minimal and, with the exception of waterfronts and parks, walking or bicycling paths are non-existent. The economy is based on agriculture, fishing, forestry, mining, manufacturing, electronics, and trade. Michigan is also home to an emerging wine industry.

State motto *Si quaeris Peninsulam Amoenam Circumspice* (If you seek a pleasant peninsula, look around you)
State flag Adopted 1911
Capital Lansing
Population 9,938,444
Total area (land and water) 96,705 square miles (250,466 sq km)
Land area 56,809 square miles (147,135 sq km)
Michigan is the 23rd-largest state in size
Origin of name From the Native American word "Michigana" meaning "great lake" or "big water"
Nickname The Wolverine State
Abbreviations MI (postal), Mich.
State bird Robin
State flower Apple blossom
State tree White pine
Entered the Union January 26, 1837 as the 26th state

STATE FEATURE

Detroit

At Eastern Farmers Market, flowers are but one of the huge range of fresh produce available.

Detroit, in southeastern Michigan, is the state's largest city and largest port, and the seventh largest city in the nation. It is a leading industrial center and, as the world's foremost motor vehicle manufacturing center, has earned the nickname "The Motor City." Detroit faces Windsor, in Ontario, Canada, across the Detroit River, which is part of a vitally important waterway linking the lower and upper Great Lakes regions—Lake Erie to Lake St Clair. The waterway continues via the St Clair River to Lake Huron and the upper Great Lakes. The Detroit River is the narrowest point in this waterway. The city's strategic position on the left bank facilitated its early growth as a major port.

Detroit covers 139 square miles (360 sq km), spreading west from the river across a vast plain; lakes and rolling hills fringe the northwest. Summers are temperate, while winters are fairly cold. The greater metropolitan area includes Lapeer, Macomb, Monroe, Oakland, St Clair, and Wayne counties for a total area of 4,326 square miles (11,204 sq km). Detroit's population reached a peak of 1,850,000 in 1950; today the number hovers around 1,000,000. The population over the greater metropolitan area is about 4,700,000. Detroit has a large African-American community and the nation's largest Arab, Belgian, and Bulgarian communities.

As the motor vehicle industry grew, industrial suburbs formed a ring around the inner city, while residential suburbs formed an outer ring. The soaring buildings that make up the downtown skyline, most notably the landmark Renaissance Center and the Civic Center, are clustered around the shoreline across from Windsor. From here a network of highways and expressways spreads out like the spokes of a wheel. The city plan was modeled on the L'Enfant plan of Washington DC, which has major streets radiating out from a series of circles. However, in

Detroit's case, the major streets are up to nine lanes wide. Cars were at the heart of this and most other planning decisions in twentieth-century Detroit.

The city has its origins in the Fort Pontchartrain trading post, built on a bluff overlooking the strait here in 1701 by Antoine de la Mothe Cadillac and his soldiers to protect the waterways for French commercial interests. In 1760 Detroit surrendered to the British, and in the following years many of its French settlers relocated to St Louis, Missouri. In 1763, Chief Pontiac led his Ottawa tribe into battle against the European invasions, but lost out to the British, who retained control of Detroit—and the waterway it commanded—for the next 32 years. By 1805 Detroit was under American rule, although it was briefly reheld by the British in 1812–13.

The opening of the Erie Canal in 1825 transformed the Great Lakes into the world's largest inland waterway and enhanced Detroit's role as a trade center. By the 1840s it had grown to a city of 10,000. Abundant raw materials encouraged the building of ships, carriages, and furniture; mining in the Upper Peninsula initiated copper and iron smelting. A rail link with Chicago opened in 1852. Cheap and easy transportation led to another dramatic growth spurt. By 1900, Detroit was a major metal manufacturing center, the heart of the expanding motor vehicle industry, and the transportation hub for the Midwest. The city attracted inventors, engineers, and innovators such as Henry Ford and Ransom E. Olds.

The motor vehicle was the dominant influence on the city's economy until the recession of the 1980s. Detroit's other great claim to fame, the "Motown Sound," was created in the 1960s by Berry Gordy Jr in a basement studio. Soon the nation's airwaves were filled with hits from Motown artists Marvin Gaye, Smokey Robinson and the Miracles, the Supremes, The Temptations, and Stevie Wonder. Detroit has also seen some of the worst racial disturbances in the nation. In 1967 a week-long riot that took 43 lives marked the beginning of the inner city's downturn.

In the last decades of the twentieth century Detroit's decaying core became notorious for its crime, poverty, and widespread unemployment. The city center was a ghost town after business hours. Arson sprees on Devil's Night (the night before Halloween) made the headlines in the 1980s and early 1990s. During the recession, heavy industrial businesses such as motor vehicle manufacturing and metal production moved out of the city center.

The 1990s have seen a steady turnaround. Following the election of Mayor Dennis Archer in 1993, much has been accomplished in the fight against urban decay. New industries such as medical research, pharmaceuticals, chemicals, robotics, software, computer components, and high-tech research labs now support one-third of the economy. Ford Motor

Musicians at a recording session in one of the city's studios.

Company and General Motors (GM) still have their world headquarters here. A new theater district is emerging on the north side and construction has begun on countless new office buildings, hotels, and residences, and two new major-league sports stadiums. Citizen volunteers and city officials have teamed up to quell Devil's Night activities.

Any visit should include a tour of the Civic Center and Cobo Arena on the waterfront. The city center has one of the largest collections of early twentieth-century skyscrapers in the nation, most notably the Guardian, Penobscot, Book, and David Stott buildings. Lively Greektown, nearby, is known for its bakeries and restaurants. Just to the north is Trinity Lutheran Church, a small neo-Gothic cathedral dating from 1850, and the Eastern Farmers Market, built originally for hay and wood, and now housing a wholesale produce market, meatpacking center, flower market, fish market, and gourmet food center.

North of downtown in the New Center area is the Fisher Tower, an Art Deco skyscraper built in the 1920s, and the Motown Museum. The Cultural Center, near Wayne State University, includes the Detroit Science Center (with interactive displays for children), the prestigious Detroit Institute of Arts, the Detroit Symphony Orchestra Hall, and the Museum of African-American History (with its chilling full-scale model of chained slaves on a transport ship). The influential 1920s ceramics of Mary Chase Perry Stratton are on display at the historic Pewabic Pottery (on East Jefferson). In the outer areas Fisher Mansion, Edsel and Eleanor Ford House, Fair Lane, and Meadow Brook Hall are palatial reminders of the wealth of the auto barons. Fort Wayne, in the city's southwest, houses a museum of Detroit military history; the Great Lakes Indian Museum, Indian burial mound, and Tuskegee Airmen Museum are on the same grounds. Each Labor Day weekend Detroit hosts the Montreux Detroit Jazz Festival.

Belle Isle, the city's largest park, was designed by Frederick Olmsted, also responsible for New York's Central Park. Its 1,000 acres (400 ha) house a zoo, an aquarium, a conservatory, riding stables, the Detroit Yacht Club, and a marine museum. Each year the park hosts the Detroit Grand Prix, and it is also a popular spectator spot for the Gold Cup speedboat races. Other popular places include Rouge, Palmer, and Chandler parks, and the large freshwater beach on Lake St Clair.

From Detroit, I-94 runs east to Chicago. Detroit Metropolitan Airport, buses, and trains service the area. As in the rest of the state, cars are essential, though bus tours are available, and a monorail, the People Mover, circles the city center. A wealth of dining and lodging options are available in every price range. Detroit is a much safer place today than it was late in the twentieth century. However, as in any big city, the element of crime exists, so take precautions, especially after dark.

A driver waits beside his gleaming stretch limousine in downtown Detroit.

Aftermath of the civil disturbances of the 1970s and 1980s, an abandoned house near downtown Detroit.

Places in
MICHIGAN

ANN ARBOR

Ann Arbor (population 110,300), on the banks of the Huron River, is a major educational, medical, and research center, and a manufacturer of software and electronic equipment. Although the university defines Ann Arbor's character, it is much more than a college town. Rolling hills, forests, and farms surround the community, and the locals are friendly Midwesterners. Yet at the same time there is sophisticated urban culture. Many inhabitants commute to Detroit. The first settlers were land speculators who in 1823 began selling lots along the thickly forested riverbanks. It was soon a thriving milling center, and in 1837 lured the University of Michigan from Detroit; the area has seen steady growth ever since.

Ann Arbor has two central areas: the university's main campus, and the downtown shopping district. Public buses connect the two districts and also cover outlying areas, so a car is not necessary. Dining and lodging choices are plentiful in all categories.

Any itinerary should begin with a visit to the campus, where popular attractions include the Michigan Union, the Law Quadrangle, the Exhibit Museum, the Museum of Art, the Museum of Natural History, the Kelsey Museum of Archeology, the Gerald R. Ford Library, the Matthei Botanical Gardens, Nichols Arboretum, and

the Power Center for Performing Arts. Other attractions in the city include the Kempf House (an 1853 white-frame, Greek Revival structure with antique Victorian furnishings), the Ann Arbor Hands-On Museum, the National Center for the Study of Frank Lloyd Wright, the Waterloo Recreation Area, and Rolling Hills County Park.

The I-94, which runs through Ann Arbor's south side, links it to Detroit, 40 miles (64 km) to the east, and to Chicago, all the way across the state to the west. From the north or south, take US-23. Detroit Metropolitan Airport is the nearest major air hub.
Map ref: page 377 J7

BATTLE CREEK

Battle Creek (population 55,400) is an industrial center and grain-growing area at the junction of the Kalamazoo and Battle Creek Rivers in southern Michigan.

Known as "Cereal City," Battle Creek is home to Kellogg's cereals, and also manufactures pumps, motor vehicle parts, plastics, and paper. An 1825 fight between two land surveyors and two Native Americans here gave the river (and therefore the city) its name.

Kellogg's cereals are produced in Battle Creek.

In the 1850s, the area was a center of intense abolitionist activity and an important stop on the "Underground Railroad," the escape route for African-American slaves. Sojourner Truth, ex-slave, abolitionist, and women's rights activist, lived here near the end of her life and is buried in Battle Creek's Oak Hill Cemetery. Battle Creek also became headquarters for the Seventh Day Adventist religious group, which opened sanitariums here to promote temperance and health.

In 1876, physician John Harvey Kellogg joined the Western Health Reform Institute (founded on health principles advocated by Seventh Day Adventists) and spent the next 25 years developing this into a cutting-edge institution; known today as the Battle Creek Federal Center, it is open for visits and is on the National Register of Historic Places.

Along with hydrotherapy and exercise, Dr Kellogg's patients were given a vegetarian diet. By 1894, Kellogg had developed grain and nut products including a cereal-based flaked breakfast. Battle Creek became the location of cereal food manufacture when the doctor's brother W.K. Kellogg, and sanitarium patient C.W. Post both formed companies to market cereal products. The World's Longest Cereal Table is set up here every year in June during the Cereal City Festival.

Battle Creek Linear Park is an 11-mile (18-km) series of waterways and parks connected by a paved pathway; in the Park are the Leila Arboretum and the Kingman Museum of Natural History. Other Battle Creek attractions include the Kimball House Museum (a Queen Anne-style residence with exhibits relating to local health and medical history), Kellogg Bird Sanctuary, Binder Park Zoo with its Michigan Wetlands Encounter Trail, Willard Beach on Goguac Lake, and Fort Custer Recreation Area.

Battle Creek is on I-94 between Kalamazoo and Jackson, in Michi-

gan's heartland region, and is serviced by the Kalamazoo/Battle Creek International Airport. Lodging and dining options in the area are somewhat limited.
Map ref: page 376 F7

BAY CITY

Bay City (population 39,700) lies at the mouth of the Saginaw River on the Saginaw Bay in eastern Michigan. It is an industrial, trade, and tourist center, and a busy port on the St Lawrence Seaway, which services Great Lakes freighters as well as sea-going vessels. The surrounding agricultural area produces sugar beets, melons, and potatoes.

Two French Canadian fur traders settled here in 1831 and by 1836 had built a trading post and residence. The area grew into a thriving lumber center with 36 mills in operation by 1872. Along with the mills came lumber barons (the elegant mansions they built can be seen on Center Avenue), as well as the rowdy lumberjacks who patronized the Water Street saloons and contributed to a bawdy, colorful mill town atmosphere.

By the late 1800s, however, local lumber was depleted, the industry slumped, and Bay City shifted its focus to soft coal mining, commercial fishing, and growing sugar beets. The Material Girl, Madonna, is the city's claim to fame in the twentieth century. However, since she openly called her birthplace "the armpit of America" she has not been too popular with the locals.

Attractions in Bay City include historic Trombley House, waterfront Veterans Park, and the Riverwalk (all on the western side of the river), the Romanesque-style City Hall (listed on the National Historic Register), Center Avenue Historical District, the Historical Museum of Bay County, and the storybook theme park at Deer Acres. Water Street and Midland Streets are renowned for their antique shops.

Bay City Recreation Area, on the western shore of Saginaw Bay, features a Nature Center with displays on local history and wildlife, a beach, and a paved nature trail leading to Tobico Marsh (which is known for its wetland birds). The state's only Native American rock carvings can be seen in Sanilac Petroglyphs State Historic Park,

The "Barn Doctor" and his dog on their way to work, Ann Arbor.

near Cass City, 40 miles (65 km) east of Bay City. To the northeast, Hwy 25 follows the eastern shore of Saginaw Bay through fishing villages and coastal towns.

From the north or the south, take I-75. The MBS International Airport services nearby Saginaw, Midland, and Bay City. Cars are essential. Motels, fast food, and diners are the standard in these parts of the state.
Map ref: page 377 J4

DEARBORN

Dearborn is just west of Detroit in southeastern Michigan on the River Rouge. Industrialist Henry Ford was born here in 1863 and the city is now the international headquarters of the Ford Motor Company, and is also a major convention and tourist center. Its population of 96,400 includes the largest community of Arabic-speaking people in the country.

European settlement here dates from the late eighteenth century, when the banks of the river were subdivided into ribbon farms running back from the water in the rural French tradition. Dearborn was one of several townships established by American settlers who arrived after the War of 1812. It became a stop on the Chicago Road (today's Michigan Avenue)

and the Michigan Central Railroad and between the 1830s and 1875 was the site of a US military arsenal. In 1915 Henry Ford began construction of the famous Ford Motor Company Rouge Assembly Plant, where the assembly line method of mass production was perfected. Millions of tractors and Model T automobiles were assembled here during the 1920s.

The best known attractions in Dearborn are the Henry Ford Museum and the adjacent Greenfield Village; allow most of a day to visit both. The Museum is the Ford Motor Company's tribute to America's industrial awakening and is the largest indoor–outdoor museum in the country. It charts changing technology of the twentieth century, and in particular the impact of the motor vehicle.

The separate attraction of Greenfield Village features more than 80 historic buildings from the eighteenth and nineteenth centuries that were relocated to the site by Henry Ford. Lining several city streets, they include homes, shops, mills, schools, and stores, and the laboratories of such American luminaries as Lincoln, Edison, Carver, and Firestone.

The Henry Ford Estate, Fair Lane, was the automobile baron's home from 1915 until his death in 1947. This imposing mansion,

This 1950 Lincoln at the Henry Ford Museum in Dearborn carried US presidents.

surrounded by 72 acres (29 ha) of the original 3,000-acre (1,215-ha) estate, is listed as a National Historic Landmark and is open for public tours. Also worth a visit are the 1833 Commandant's Quarters, featuring military displays from the Civil War era, and McFadden-Ross House, with its nineteenth-century period rooms and extensive photographic archives. Both are housed in former arsenal structures and are operated by the City of Dearborn Historical Museum. Suwanee Park,

a late nineteenth-century family arcade, offers rides on steamboats, steam railroads, in a Model T, or in a horse-drawn carriage.

To reach the city of Dearborn, take Hwy 12 west from Detroit. Detroit Metropolitan Airport services the area, and both trains and buses stop here. Cars are essential. Lodging and dining options are very limited in Dearborn, apart from an extensive selection of Arabic restaurants.
Map ref: page 377 K7

A cluster of farm buildings on Route 37, typical of the larger farms of the Midwest. Agriculture is concentrated in the south of the state.

Keen fishermen trying their luck at a favorite spot on the Grand River, at Grand Rapids.

FLINT

Flint (population 136,000), on the river of the same name, is in southeastern Michigan's Saginaw Valley. It was the birthplace of General Motors (GM) and, despite plant relocations and closings in the 1980s and 1990s, Flint maintains its close links with the motor vehicle industry.

In pre-European times this was an important river crossing on the Pontiac Trail, part of a network of Native American wilderness routes, and the area itself was called "Pawanunling," meaning "river of flint." In 1819, prominent Detroit fur trader Jacob Smith persuaded the Ojibwa and Potawatomi tribes to withdraw, and founded a settlement here. Local sawmills provided the raw materials for road carts and katydids (two-wheeled vehicles used to haul logs), and by the 1890s Flint had become one of the largest carriage manufacturers in the nation and was known as "Vehicle City." When the Buick Motor Company came to Flint it hired successful local carriage-maker William C. Durant to promote its product. Durant masterminded the formation of General Motors; Buick, Cadillac, and Oldsmobile were the initial companies under the General Motors umbrella. European immigrants and African-Americans from the southern states supplemented the local workforce.

Flint is also known for its role in labor history, primarily a strike and other organized labor acts in 1936 and 1937 at the GM plant that garnered nationwide recognition for the United Auto Workers.

Flint Cultural Center consists of seven separate institutions on the campus of Flint College. Notable attractions include the Flint Institute of Arts (with a permanent collection ranging from Renaissance to contemporary works), the Robert T. Longway Planetarium, and the Alfred P. Sloan Museum. At Crossroads Village, which recreates nineteenth-century life, visitors can ride the steam-powered Huckleberry Railroad or cruise Lake Mott on a paddlewheel riverboat. Nearby is the carefully tended For-Mar Nature Preserve and Arboretum. The Genesee Recreation Area offers more than 4,000 acres (1,620 ha) of hiking and bicycling paths, a boat launch,

beaches, and fishing sites. There is camping at Timber Wolf and Wolverine, as well as picnicking at Stepping Stone Falls, Mott Lake.

Flint lies between Bay City and Detroit on I-75, and is serviced by buses and by its airport. Cars are essential. Chain hotels and restaurants make up the bulk of the hospitality market.
Map ref: page 377 J6

FRANKFORT

The harbor and resort area of the town of Frankfort curves around the picturesque shores of Betsie Lake in the upper western reaches of the Lower Peninsula. The sheltered waters here are fed by the Betsie River and open onto Lake Michigan. Route 22 runs along the lakeshore from Manistee to Frankfort, continuing north to the Point Betsie Lighthouse, Point Betsie Dunes Preserve, and into Sleeping Bear Dunes National Lakeshore in the Leelanau Peninsula. The population is less than 2,000, with the Coast Guard the largest employer.

The Father Marquette Historical Marker, at the mouth of the river next to the Coast Guard Station,

stands on the site where French explorer Father Jacques Marquette died in 1677. Researchers believe his "Rivière du Père Marquette" was actually the Betsie.

Facilities on Betsie Lake include a 40-slip marina, gas, electricity, and showers. The Lake's coho and chinook salmon draw fishing enthusiasts in season (spring and summer). Crystal Lake, not far north of Frankfort, is popular with windsurfers in summer, as is the Crystal Mountain Ski Area for snow sports in winter. A scenic drive about 20 miles (32 km) east on Hwy 31 reaches Interlochen State Park (with one of the few remaining stands of virgin white pine in the state) and the National Music Camp.

Manistee-Blacker Airport to the south, and Cherry City Airport in Traverse City to the northeast, are

the nearest flight facilities. Cars are essential. Lodging and dining options are limited in this area.
Map ref: page 376 E2

GRAND HAVEN

This lakeshore city and port situated at the mouth of the Grand River in southwest Michigan was first settled in 1834. Today it has an estimated population of 12,200. Its economy relies largely on port activities such as produce shipping, charter fishing, sport fishing, and recreational boating; it is also the location of a Coast Guard base.

A 2½-mile (4 km) boardwalk with shops and restaurants follows Grand River's south bank from downtown to Grand Haven State Park, on the sandy lakefront. Along the way is the Tri-Cities Historical Museum, featuring a "puffer belly"

Point Betsie Lighthouse near Frankfort on Lake Michigan's eastern shore; visibility is poor when violent storms are raging.

steam locomotive and three rail cars. Great Lakes fishing boats dock nearby at Chinook Pier, and for a bird's-eye view, the Michigan Balloon Corporation offers hot air balloon flights.

Grand Haven is located 10 miles (16 km) south of Muskegon on Hwy 31 and 30 miles (48 km) west of Grand Rapids on I-96. Muskegon County Airport services the area. Cars are essential. Accommodation is limited to camp sites in Grand Haven State Park (these need to be reserved) and basic motels. Dining options are limited.

Map ref: page 376 E6

GRAND RAPIDS

Grand Rapids, with a population of 200,000, is the state's second-largest city and the economic and political hub of western Michigan. It lies 30 miles (48 km) east of Lake Michigan's famed beaches.

Early inhabitants here were the Hopewell culture and the Ottawa people. Baptist missionaries arrived in 1825, and in 1826 fur trader Louis Campau established a trading post on the banks of the Grand River. Plentiful power (water from the rapids powered one of the Midwest's first hydroelectric plants), abundant raw materials, and easy transportation by water led to the city's specialty of furniture manufacture. This was the mainstay of the economy throughout most of the twentieth century, earning

Grand Rapids the nickname of "Furniture Capital of America." Information technology and tourism are now replacing furniture manufacturing, and the city is also headquarters of the Amway marketing organization.

Throughout his political career, Grand Rapids was the home of President Ford. The Gerald R. Ford Museum is a tribute to his life and career. For exhibitions on local history and nature, one can visit the Public Museum of Grand Rapids. Other attractions include the many impressive buildings of the Heritage Hill Historic District, the Norton Indian Mounds (the largest site of Hopewell culture in the state), the Grand Rapids Art Museum, the Frederik Meijer Gardens, the John Ball Park Zoo, and "La Grande Vitesse," a 43-foot (13-m)-high, 42-ton bright red metal sculpture by Alexander Calder in the Vandenberg Center, downtown. There are regular performances of opera, symphony, ballet, and professional theatre throughout the year, and the Grand Rapids Festival of the Arts is held each June. The Grand Rogue Campground, Canoe, and Tube Livery and Higher Ground Rock Climbing Center offer activities for outdoors enthusiasts. Cannonsburg Ski Area is a full-service ski resort.

Kent County International Airport, trains, and buses service the area. From Chicago, drive northeast on I-94 to I-196; from

Breaking ice on frozen Lake Michigan. Ski resorts in the area are popular.

Detroit, drive northwest on I-96. Cars are essential. Lodging and dining options are plentiful.

Map ref: page 376 F6

ISLE ROYALE NATIONAL PARK

Isle Royale, in Michigan's northwestern corner, is the largest island in Lake Superior. It lies 40 miles (64 km) off the Keweenaw Peninsula and, along with some 400 surrounding islets, makes up the 571,790-acre (231,395-ha) wilderness preserve of Isle Royale National Park. The nearest mainland (Ontario, Canada) is about 15 miles (24 km) away and the Park is about 18 miles (29 km) from Minnesota. Isle Royale itself is 44 miles (71 km) long and 8 miles (13 km) wide; there are no roads on the island.

Prehistoric Native Americans mined copper and fashioned tools here. Later the Ojibwa people inhabited the area and the Hudson's Bay Company operated a fur-trading post. The island came under US control in 1842; copper mining continued until 1883. Open from April to October, this remote Park receives fewer visitors per year than Yellowstone receives in a day. Ferries are available in peak season from Grand Portage, Minnesota, and Copper Harbor and Houghton, Michigan (the crossing takes up to six hours and can be rough). Seaplanes connect Houghton with Windigo and Rock Harbor on the island. A park entrance fee applies; 36 camp sites

are scattered throughout the Park. Ship-to-shore radio is the only form of available communication with the mainland.

Glaciers moving through the area eons ago created the region's long, narrow, deep inlets. The forests and wildflower-covered slopes provide sanctuary for beaver, mink, red fox, timber wolf, moose, and snowshoe hare populations. More than 200 bird species live here, including the osprey, herring gull, and bald eagle,. The 42 inland lakes are home to perch, walleye, and northern pike; trout are found in the streams.

Windigo, on the island's southwest end, has a National Park Service Information Center, marina, and camp store. Rock Harbor, in the northeast, has the same facilities plus a basic lodge and restaurant overlooking Tobin Harbor and a few cabins (both lodge and cabins fill up quickly). There are 165 miles (265 km) of rocky, rugged hiking trails including the popular Mt Ojibway Trail leading up 1,136 feet (346 m) for spectacular views. Take insect repellent because blackflies and mosquitoes abound. Boating, canoeing, and fishing are popular activities; swimming is less so because the water is icy cold. This is one of the most heavily regulated parks in the system. Dogs are prohibited, and the Park asks that you refrain from loud conversation and singing, and that you bring clothing and gear in camouflage rather than bright colors.

Map ref: page 372 B2

KALAMAZOO

Kalamazoo (population 81,100) is in southwestern Michigan halfway between Battle Creek and Lake Michigan, and due south of Grand Rapids. The city, river, and county share the Native American name meaning "where the water boils in the pot," a reference to the area's many bubbling springs. Kalamazoo is home to Western Michigan University and is a manufacturing center, most notably of paper and paper products.

Attractions in Kalamazoo include Bronson Park (where Abraham Lincoln made his only public speech in Michigan), Crane Park, the Kalamazoo Aviation History Museum, Gilmore-CCCA Car Museum, and the Kalamazoo Institute of Arts. Plays, musical comedies, opera, and other types of performances are on offer at the University, while those with an interest in the local brew can take the Kalamazoo Brewing Company's "Beer 101" tour. Visitors to the 1,000-acre (400-ha) Kalamazoo Nature Center, just 5 miles (8 km) north of the city, can choose from 11 varied nature trails.

Close by, to the northwest, are Bittersweet and Timber Ridge ski areas; Echo Valley Winter Sports Park, to the east, is open December to March for tobogganing and ice skating. Berrien County, to the southwest, is one of Michigan's two viticultural areas and location of the award-winning St Julian Winery (in Paw Paw). This, and five other wineries in the area, are popular for day trips from Kalamazoo.

Kalamazoo is on the Chicago–Detroit interchange, I-94. From Grand Rapids, take US-131 south. The Kalamazoo/Battle Creek International Airport serves the area. Cars are essential. Motels outnumber hotels, and dining options are equally limited.
Map ref: page 376 F8

KEWEENAW PENINSULA

Keweenaw Peninsula juts into Lake Superior from the remote northern reaches of Michigan's Upper Peninsula. Curving across its lower end is the Keweenaw Waterway (an arm of Portage Lake and a major shipping lane) which makes an island of the Peninsula's eastern part. The entire area is known as "Copper Country." Native Americans left behind evidence of mining dating from 5000–500 BC. In modern times the presence of pure, native copper led in 1843 to a copper rush, the nation's first major mining rush, which continued until the end of World War I and generated an estimated 10 times more revenue than the California gold rush.

When the copper ran out, the region went into a deep recession, but since the 1970s its rich heritage has gradually been restored, and in 1992 its abandoned mines, copper baron mansions, and ghost towns became the 1700-acre (690-ha) Keweenaw National Historic Park. Lumbering and tourism are now the main industries.

The largest communities, Hancock with a population of 4,600, and Houghton with a population of 1,900, face each other across the narrowest point of the Keweenaw Waterway. The Finns are the largest ethnic group; Finnish settlers founded Suomi College in 1896 and today Hancock is location of the Finnish American Center. Descendants of the skilled Cornish miners who came to work the copper mines represent the second-largest group.

Attractions include the A.E. Seaman Mineral Museum at Michigan Technological University in Houghton, the Quincy Mine No. 2 Shaft House and Norbert Steam Hoist, Maasto Hill Cross-Country Ski Trail, and Mont Ripley Ski Area. Whitewater paddling, hiking, camping, and mountain biking are popular activities.

The nearest airport is Houghton County Airport. By car, US-41 and M-26 are the main thoroughfares. Houghton is the best option for lodging and dining.
Map ref: page 372 C3

LANSING

Lansing (population 126,100) is the capital city of Michigan. Situated in the state's heartland at the junction of the Grand and Red Cedar Rivers, it covers an area of around 34 square miles (88 sq km) and overlaps three counties: Ingham, Eaton, and Clinton. It is an industrial center—the manufacture of motor vehicles, motor vehicle parts, and metal goods dominate (for more than a century it was home of the Oldsmobile). However, agriculture is also an important activity.

Settlers came here from Lansing, New York, in the 1840s, hence the name. They had purchased, at least on paper, plots in an existing community. When they arrived, they found they had been swindled. Many remained and the community formed around a sawmill. In 1847 Lansing was chosen to replace Detroit as state capital. By 1896, motor vehicle pioneer Ransom E.

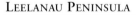

Maple syrup—popular throughout the region.

Olds had produced his first internal combustion vehicle here and within a decade Lansing's Oldsmobile Factory was the largest car producer in the nation.

The free tour of the State Capitol Building is one of the most popular tourist activities. Other attractions include the Michigan Historical Museum (which features a walk-through replica copper mine), the R.E. Olds Transportation Museum (where the first Oldsmobile is on display), the Turner-Dodge House and Park, the North Lansing Historic Commercial District, Potter Park Zoo, Fenner Nature Center, and the Impression 5 Science Center. Tours of the city by paddlewheel riverboat are available.

The Capital City Airport, trains, and buses service the area, and a public bus service covers the city and outlying areas. Cars are the best way of getting around. Lansing is halfway between Grand Rapids and Detroit on I-96. Lodging and dining options are plentiful in the capital city.
Map ref: page 377 H6

LEELANAU PENINSULA

The 28-mile (45-km) length of the Leelanau Peninsula projects north between Grand Traverse Bay and Lake Michigan. The rugged wilderness of the isolated Peninsula includes 98 miles (158 km) of Great Lakes shoreline, 142 inland lakes and ponds, and 58 miles (93 km) of streams. Ottawa Native Americans were the original inhabitants. Explorer and ethnologist Henry Schoolcraft came here in the 1820s and most likely created its name. Fishing and lumber settlements followed; today tourism and fishing support the economy.

Exhibits in the riverfront Leelanau Historical Museum, in Leland's Fishtown district, pay tribute to the diverse cultures that have shaped the history of the Peninsula. The well-restored Grand Traverse Lighthouse, at the tip of the Peninsula, now houses a

A group of students enjoy a Saturday afternoon break, Lansing.

A group of barns on a well-maintained farm, near Leelanau Peninsula. The Peninsula is an isolated area of wilderness between Lake Michigan and Grand Traverse Bay.

museum. Between Traverse City and Leland are eight wineries that offer public tours and tastings.

Sleeping Bear Dunes National Lakeshore was established in 1970 and is one of two protected shorelines in the state. Covering a vast 72,000 acres (29,000 ha), it encompasses the Manitou Islands and 35 miles (56 km) of the dune-covered western shoreline of Lake Michigan. The park is named after its landmark, the Sleeping Bear, an isolated dune far taller than its surroundings. According to Ojibwa legend, a forest fire in what is now

Wisconsin forced a mother bear and her two cubs to flee across the lake. Sleeping Bear is the mother who, after reaching the shore, climbed a bluff to watch for her young. The cubs never reached the mainland—North and South Manitou islands mark where they disappeared beneath the waves. There are two kinds of dune here— the low-lying hills of sand lining the southern shores, and the more dramatic "perched" dunes (mountains of sand that sit high above the beach on a rocky plateau). At 460 feet (140 m), Sleeping Bear

perched dune is by far the highest. The park provides a sanctuary for 200 bird species, porcupine, deer, coyote, and bass, bluegill, perch, and pike. Park highlights include the Dune Climb, the Maritime Museum, hiking, camping, and visiting the Manitou Islands. Entrance passes are available at the Philip A. Hart Visitor Center in Empire, the Platte River Ranger Station, the Pierce Stocking Scenic Drive, the Dune Climb, and the dock at Leland.

Traverse City is the nearest hub, and is serviced by Cherry Capital

Airport, which was named for the Peninsula's many cherry orchards. From there, drive west on Hwy 72 to the lakeshore, or north on Hwy 22 along the bay to Leland and Northport. Traverse City offers a wide range of dining and lodging options.

Map ref: page 376 F1

MARQUETTE

Marquette (population 23,000), on Lake Superior's south shore, is the largest city in the Upper Peninsula. Iron ore shipping, tourism, and dairy farming contribute to the economy. The Ojibwa people were the earliest inhabitants. Iron-ore mining here dates from 1846, with the establishment of the Jackson Mining Company, and the first iron forge was erected in 1849. The city is named for seventeeth-century explorer and missionary Father Jacques Marquette, who made canoe trips here in 1669–71.

Marquette is 50 miles (80 km) west of Munsing on Hwy 28, and 12 miles (19 km) west of Ishpeming on US-41. Marquette County Airport services the area. Cars are essential. Lodging and dining options are plentiful in the mid to low price range.

The southern edge of Sleeping Bear Dunes National Lakeshore, on Leelanau Peninsula, in winter. The area is a protected shoreline.

Popular attractions include the Marquette County Historical Society Museum, John Burt House, the Marquette Maritime Museum, the Michigan Iron Industry Museum, and the statue of Father Marquette. Great Lakes freighters are loaded at the city's historic Upper Harbor ore docks at Presque Isle Park. The Park is a popular spot for walking, jogging, skating, and bike riding. Northern Michigan University has the world's largest wooden dome, the Superior Dome, which spans 5 acres (2 ha). The school has been designated an Olympic Education Center, and is also home to the 5-acre (2-ha) Lee Hall Gallery, a technology and applied sciences center. Marquette's rugged beauty attracts outdoors enthusiasts, with hiking, camping, mountain biking, sea kayaking, rock-climbing, and snowshoeing popular activities. For the nature enthusiast, Seney National Wildlife Refuge, Hiawatha National Forest and Pictured Rocks National Lakeshore are all located nearby.

Map ref: page 372 D6

An elegant house on the shore of Lake Michigan at Petoskey. This summer resort town offers a range of activities.

MUSKEGON

Muskegon (population 42,000) is the largest city on the eastern shore of Lake Michigan and a major port on the southwestern coast of the Lower Peninsula. It extends about 5 miles (8 km) from the banks of the Muskegon River along the southern shore of Muskegon Lake and out to Lake Michigan and the Muskegon Channel. The name comes from the Ottawa people's "Muskego" or "river with marshes." French fur traders attracted by the easy access to the interior established a trading post here in 1810. European settlement dates from the 1830s, and from 1850 to 1890 this was a booming mill town with workers from Norway, Sweden, Ireland, Scotland, Germany, and Canada. During this time the city earned the nicknames "Lumber Queen" and "Red Light Queen" in reference to the numerous saloons, dance halls, and gambling halls. The pinelands were soon depleted, and by 1910 the last of the city's 47 mills had closed. Today, paper and metal products contribute to Muskegon's economy.

With 3,000 acres (1,215 ha) of parks, around 80 miles (130 km) of waterfront, and year-round fishing for coho, chinook salmon, lake trout, perch, and walleye, tourism is on the rise. Muskegon State Park covers 1,357 acres (550 ha) of swimming, fishing, and hiking areas. In winter, the Park's Muskegon Winter Sports Complex offers one of only two luge runs in the nation. Muskegon is also the location of the state's largest water park, the Adventure and Wildwater Amusement Park. The Gillette Nature Center at P.J. Hoffmaster State Park offers exhibits on dune history and ecology. The USS *Silversides* Maritime Museum, the Muskegon Historic District, Hackley and Hume Houses, Fire Barn Museum, John Torrent House, Hackley Public Library, Muskegon County Museum, and the Muskegon Museum of Art are other attractions well worth visiting.

Grand Rapids is to the southeast on I-96. Muskegon County Airport services the area. Cars are essential. Lodging and dining options are limited. Camping is a good alternative in season.

Map ref: page 376 E5

NORTHPORT

Northport is the last community on the northern tip of the Leelanau Peninsula. It is surrounded by water—Grand Traverse Bay to the east and Lake Michigan to the west. The horseshoe-shaped harbor here was one of the first areas on the Peninsula to be settled when Catholic missionaries arrived in 1849. By 1870 the population had grown to 2,500 and commercial fishing supported the economy.

One-person sailing boats rounding a mark in a race on Muskegon Lake, Muskegon. The city also offers year-round fishing.

A 250-room resort hotel built in the early 1900s burnt to the ground within five years. Today pleasure boaters visit the harbor. Leelanau State Park and Cat Head Point cover the remaining stretch of land to the north. Leland, Lake Leelanau, and the Sleeping Bear Dunes National Lakeshore are to the south. Cherry Capital Airport at Traverse City is the nearest facility. Cars are essential. From Traverse City, take Hwy 22 north.
Map ref: page 376 F1

PETOSKEY

This popular resort, with a population of 2,100, sits on picturesque Little Traverse Bay in the northern reaches of the Lower Peninsula, just south of the Straits of Makinac. The Ottawa and Ojibwa people settled here in the 1700s, and named the area after one of their tribe members, Petosega. Europeans arrived in the 1850s and established sawmills and a lime quarry along the waterfront. With the coming of the railroad in 1873, city-dwellers from Chicago and Detroit, attracted to the area's natural resources including the bubbling artesian springs, changed the face of Petoskey from an industrial center to an elegant summer resort. Resort hotels and shops opened; all but

one of these hotels have since burned down (the survivor was made out of brick), although a significant number of other historic buildings remain. In 1996, Petoskey was designated one of the 10 national treasures most worthy of fighting for by the National Trust for Historic Preservation.

The Gaslight District in downtown Petoskey covers eight blocks of historic Victorian structures housing shops and restaurants. The Little Traverse Historical Museum has exhibitions of Native American, pioneer, and Victorian life, as well as a display of Ernest Hemingway memorabilia. (Hemingway spent time here as a boy, and later, after World War I, came here to recuperate.) The 305-acre (123-ha) Petoskey State Park offers beaches, swimming, fishing, hiking, and cross-country skiing. Magnus Park is an optimal spot to hunt for Petoskey stones (fossilized coral), Michigan's official state stone.

Nearby Bay Harbor has a Yacht Club and an equestrian club. The Links, The Preserve, and The Quarry public golf courses have been ranked in the nation's top ten. Nearby ski areas include Boynte Highlands, Mt McSauba, Petoskey, Nubs Nob, and Boynte Mountain.

Emmet County Airport is the closest hub, but more services are offered in Traverse City at Cherry Capital Airport. From Traverse City, drive north along the bay on US-31. Cars are essential in these parts. Lodging and dining options are plentiful, especially at the upper end of the market.
Map ref: page 373 H8

PICTURED ROCKS NATIONAL LAKESHORE

One of two national lakeshore preserves, Pictured Rocks is in the center of the Upper Peninsula on the southern shores of Lake Superior. Only 5 miles (8 km) wide, the preserve hugs the coastline for 40 miles (64 km) from Munising to Grand Marais; inland, it adjoins Hiawatha National Forest and Lake Superior State Forest. The park is named for its dramatic, mineral-stained sandstone cliffs which have been eroded by glacial, wind, and water action into fantastic shapes. Soaring to 200 feet (61 m), they range in color from pink, red, yellow, and green to

brown and even blue, and fringe 15 miles (24 km) of the lakeshore. At Grand Marais the cliffs are replaced by the towering 200-feet (61-m)-high sand dunes and at Grand Sable Banks by a 12-mile (19-km) stretch of beach. The park entrance and visitor center is at Hwy 28 and H58 in Munising. Grand Sable's visitor center is open in summer only.

Munising Falls, located just inside the western boundaries, marks the beginning of the Lakeshore Trail, a 43-mile (70-km) segment of the North Country Trail that runs from New York to North Dakota. Miners Castle, Chapel Falls, Beaver Lake, Au Sable Lighthouse at Au Sable Point, and the Grand Sable Dunes are other popular attractions. Hikers, backpackers, and cross-country skiers have 21 miles (34 km) of trails to choose from.

The best way to see the cliffs is by boat—tour boats depart from Munising City, and Northern Waters in Munising offers kayak rentals and guided paddling trips. Three camp sites are accessible by car and offer pit toilets and water. Back-country camping is by permit only at one of 13 designated sites (most have no facilities). Even in the peak summer season, evenings are chilly, and waters are icy year-round. Just outside the park's eastern boundaries is Grand Marais, a quaint fishing village with a snug harbor much favored by kayakers. It offers affordable dining and lodging options with plenty of character.

Marquette County Airport is the closest facility. From Marquette, drive east along the lakeshore on Hwy 28. The Altan Shuttle, a county bus, runs along H58 in the park and is most convenient for backpackers and hikers. Otherwise, cars are essential. Roads are rough and sometimes unpaved.
Map ref: page 372 F5

Miners Castle, a spectacular formation in Pictured Rocks National Lakeshore.

Jack Locks Flea Market, Wyoming, a popular place to hunt for bargains.

PONTIAC

Pontiac (population 73,400) lies on the Clinton River in southeastern Michigan near Detroit. It is the seat of Oakland County and is named for Chief Pontiac of the Ottawa tribe who spent his summers here. Today it is an industrial, residential, and summer resort area. Eleven state parks and 400 lakes surround the city, which lies between Detroit and Flint on I-75.

The village established here by a group of Detroit businessmen in 1818 became a way station on the wagon trail to the West. By the late 1880s, its Pontiac Springs Wagon Works was one of the largest producers of wagons and carriages in the United States. Pontiac is still a major vehicle manufacturer, though for the last hundred years or so they have come with motors. The Pontiac Silverdome is an enclosed football stadium and home of the Detroit Lions, a professional team. Oakland University attractions include the Meadow Brook Art Gallery, Meadow Brook Hall, and Meadow Brook Theatre. In summer, outdoor enthusiasts are drawn to the lakes and state parks. In winter, they flock to the Alpine Valley Ski Resort near Milford.

Detroit Metropolitan Airport is the nearest major airport facility. Cars are essential.
Map ref: page 377 J7

SAGINAW

Saginaw (population 70,400) is in eastern Michigan on the Lower Peninsula just south of Saginaw Bay, an arm of Lake Huron. It sits on Saginaw River near its mouth on the Bay. The Chippewa people named this area "Land of the Sac (Sauk) People," or Saginaw. During the time of the Sauks, the swampy riverbanks were so thick with trees it was difficult for daylight to penetrate. Loggers arrived in 1816, and, until the forests were depleted in the 1890s, Saginaw was the lumber capital of the world. Today it is a commercial center for the surrounding sugar beet and bean farming areas as well as a manufacturing hub.

Attractions include the Japanese Cultural Center and Tea House, Saginaw Art Museum, Castle Museum of Saginaw County History, Marshall M. Fredericks Sculpture Gallery, Children's Zoo, and Anderson Water Park. Just to the south is the popular Bronner's Christmas Wonderland at Frankenmuth.

Saginaw is located between Flint and Bay City on I-75. MBS International Airport services the area. Cars are essential. Lodging and dining options are very basic.
Map ref: page 377 J5

SAULT STE MARIE

The oldest city in Michigan, Sault Ste Marie (population 1,800) is at the northeastern tip of the Upper Peninsula across from Sault Ste Marie, Ontario. It is on the south bank of the St Marys River, which connects Lake Superior with Lake Huron. Between the lakes elevation drops as much as 21 feet (6.4 m) and there is a hazardous stretch of rapids. The Sault Ste Marie Canals, also known as Soo Locks (there are three—two in Michigan and one in Ontario), allow ships to navigate this section of the River. The US Waterways, also known as St Marys Falls Canals, are four toll-free, parallel locks, each about 1 mile (1.6 km) long. From April to December about 100 vessels a day pass through; the locks are closed in winter as the river turns to ice. Eastbound freighters carry iron ore and grain. Westbound freighters carry coal and petroleum.

French fur traders began moving into the upper Great Lakes region. In 1668 Father Jacques Marquette founded Mission Ste Marie at an Ojibwa village overlooking the rapids. French forces arrived in 1671 and battled fiercely with some fourteen Native American tribes. Sault is the French word for "cascades," referring to the falls, hence the city's name.

The Soo Locks are the main attraction here, and the recommended first stop is the St Marys Falls Canal Visitor Center. Other attractions include the Federal Building, Lake Superior State University, the Museum Ship Valley Camp and Great Lakes Maritime Museum, the Tower of History, Haunted Depot, Schoolcraft House and Indian Agency, and John Johnston House.

The city lies at the end of I-75. Chippewa County International Airport services the area. Cars are essential. Lodging and dining options are somewhat limited.
Map ref: page 373 J6

WYOMING

The city of Wyoming, with a population of 71,000, is on the Grand River near Grand Rapids in southwestern Michigan. It was settled in 1832 as a farming and dairy center. From the 1930s on, Wyoming grew as a manufacturing center, most notably for aircraft and motor-vehicle parts. Grand Rapids is the nearest major hub.

Kent County International Airport, trains, and buses service Grand Rapids. Cars are essential. Indian Mounds Park is a Native American burial ground. Muskegon and Grand Haven are both popular day excursions.
Map ref: page 376 F6

A large barn complex. Although dubbed the motor vehicle capital of the world, agriculture is still vital to Michigan's economy.

MINNESOTA

Located in the north-central part of the country bordering Canada, Minnesota is well known for its cold, snowy winters and hot, humid summers. The Land of 10,000 Lakes, it is also famous for its sublime waterways. Ice hockey and iron-ore mining are part of the state character.

The Great Plains and prairies of the west meet the eastern woodlands and the coniferous forests of the north in Minnesota. The rumpled land left by glaciers forms basins for thousands of lakes. The highest point, Eagle Mountain, is 2,301 feet (702 m) above sea level, and Lake Superior, at 602 feet (184 m), is the lowest.

In 1850, the area that would become Minnesota had a population of about 5,000. By 1858, steamboat traffic and European immigration raised that number to 150,000, and statehood was attained. Waves of Scandinavians, Slavs, and other Europeans poured in until 1920. Although Southeast Asians are the most recent arrivals, 94 percent of the population is white.

Lake Itasca is one of 100 lakes at the headwaters of the mighty Mississippi River and one of many thousand in the entire state of Minnesota.

In the 1700s French explorers discovered the plant and animal resources that became the basis of the area's first industries: logging, fishing, and fur trading. Nowadays, the state of Minnesota leads the nation in the mining of iron ore. It is a big agricultural state, ranking high in livestock and crop production. Meat-packing, sugar-refining, and flour-milling are among its top industries. Although not considered a major manufacturing state, it has internationally known companies such as Minnesota Mining and Manufacturing (3M), Honeywell (missile controls, defense contracting), and agribusiness giant Cargill, one of the largest privately held companies in existence.

Minnesota is known for its excellent school systems, outdoor recreation, healthy residents, public services, and liberal attitudes to contemporary issues.

State motto *L'Etoile du Nord* (The North Star)
State flag Adopted 1893
Capital St Paul (see Minneapolis–St Paul, page 338)
Population 4,919,479
Total area (land and water) 86,943 square miles (225,182 sq km)
Land area 79,617 square miles (206,208 sq km)
Minnesota is the 12th-largest state in size
Origin of name From a Dakota Native American word meaning "sky-tinted water"
Nicknames The North Star State, The Gopher State, Land of 10,000 Lakes
Abbreviations MN (postal), Minn.
State bird Common loon
State flower Showy lady's slipper
State tree Norway pine
Entered the Union May 11, 1858 as the 32nd state

Places in
MINNESOTA

Attractive red pines dot the Chippewa National Forest's landscape and walking trails.

AUSTIN

Austin lies 80 miles (129 km) to the south of Minneapolis-St Paul near the Iowa border. The town is dominated by the Hormel Foods Corporation, which employs more than a third of all its 21,900 residents. Hormel is ranked the 24th largest food producing company in the Fortune 500, with latest sales figures of $3 billion a year. Its founder, George A. Hormel, was known as the "King of Spam." He started his meat-packing business in 1891 in an oak grove on the Cedar River, where his workers cut blocks of ice in winter to refrigerate their meat. Hormel used to urge his employees: "Originate, don't imitate."

The Hormel Museum tells the story of the company's success, and Hormel's downtown home is open for tours. The J.C. Hormel Nature Center, right on the former family estate, offers 8 miles (13 km) of nature trails through woods and wetlands, and in winter is used for cross-country skiing. Canoeing is possible there in summer.

The Mower County Historical Center exhibits contain a variety of historic structures, including the original Hormel building, a working blacksmith shop, an 1867 church, and a schoolhouse. Also in the center's three museums are Native American artifacts, antique fire engines, a hand-carved wooden circus set, and replicas of a pioneer home and train depot, which has

Statue of the famous lumberjack Paul Bunyan and his blue ox, Babe, in Bemidji.

a caboose and three railway cars.

Austin is reached by car on I-90, and on Hwys 16 and 218, and by bus. The nearest airport is in Rochester.
Map ref: page 374 G7

BEMIDJI

Bemidji is known far and wide for its original statue of the legendary logger Paul Bunyan and Babe the blue ox. The town of 11,200 is located 120 miles (193 km) west of Duluth in the north-central part of the state. The lake it surrounds, Lake Bemidji, is fed by the Mississippi River, which originates 31 miles (50 km) north in Itasca State Park. Within about a 50-mile (80-km) radius of Bemidji is some of the best fishing in the state. Large lakes in the area include Bemidji—"lake with crossing waters" in the Chippewa Native American tongue—Leech Lake, Cass Lake, the Cass Lake Chain of Lakes, and Lake Winnibigoshish. Panfish such as perch and crappie are abundant, as are northern pike, muskie, and walleye. Supplies of largemouth bass and trout are also plentiful.

During winter, ice fishing, cross-country skiing and downhill skiing at Buena Vista Ski Area, which offers 15 groomed downhill runs

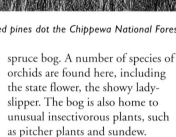

as well as a network of groomed cross-country trails, are popular.

The Paul Bunyan Trail, a 100-mile (160-km) paved multi-purpose route between Bemidji and Brainerd, is the longest snowmobiling course in the state. It is located in Lake Bemidji State Park, around 5 miles (8 km) north of town. Bog Walk, at 2 miles (3.2 km), is a self-guided interpretive nature trail that leads into a tamarack-black

spruce bog. A number of species of orchids are found here, including the state flower, the showy ladyslipper. The bog is also home to unusual insectivorous plants, such as pitcher plants and sundew.

Bemidji began as a trading post, later flourishing as a logging town. Dairy cows and farming replaced the lumber industry when timber supplies were depleted. New growth and controlled harvesting have rejuvenated the lumber industry, which is again a major livelihood.

The famous Paul Bunyan statue reaches a height of 18 feet (6 m). Constructed in 1937 beside Lake Bemidji, it shows Paul in a red-checkered shirt with a broad black moustache, blue billed cap, and red socks, standing beside the wide horns, wide eyes, and pale-blue cast of his faithful ox, Babe. It's a whimsical, playful depiction of simple lines and texture that long remains in the memory. The logging hero also gives his name to Bemidji's Paul Bunyan Playhouse, Minnesota's oldest summer theater, located in the Chief Theater.

The Bemidji Tourist Center offers a collection of Paul Bunyan memorabilia. Its Fireplace of the States was built with stones from each of the 50 states as well as from several Minnesota counties and the provinces of Canada.

Nearby Liberty Park has a statue of "Chief Bemidji," whose proper

name is Shay Now Ish Kung. The Carnegie Library Building, which is listed on the National Historic Register, houses the Bemidji Community Art Center.

Bemidji may be reached by car on US-2 and US-71, and by bus. The closest airports are in nearby Hibbing and Moorhead.
Map ref: page 370 D9

CHIPPEWA NATIONAL FOREST

The 1.6 million-acre (600,000-ha) Chippewa National Forest contains some of the largest lakes in the state—Winnibigoshish, Leech, and Cass—and more than 700 smaller bodies of water. It is located west of Grand Rapids in the north-central part of the state, about 80 miles (129 km) west of Duluth.

The forest contained some of Minnesota's grandest big pine country. Much of that timber was logged, but some of the magnificent woodland remains. Minnesota 46, a National Forest Scenic Byway, is called Avenue of the Pines because it travels through old-growth red-pine forest. Hwy 38, north of Grand Rapids, winds through rolling forest lake country.

Fishing, canoeing, waterskiing, bird-watching, and swimming are all quite popular in summer, while snowmobiling, cross-country skiing, and ice fishing take over in the winter. The forest is home to 200

pairs of nesting bald eagles, making it one of the country's greatest concentrations of these magnificent raptors. The eagle frequently builds nests on the top of giant white pines near the water.

Camp Rabideau is a Civilian Conservation Corps Camp from the 1930s, one of only three left from the original 2,650. About half its original 25 buildings still stand.

This is excellent hiking country. The 22-mile (35-km) Cut Foot Sioux Trail leads to Turtle Mound, a Native American effigy mound, and to Farley Tower, an old fire lookout. Along the 13-mile (21-km) Simpson Creek Trail, many bird species, such as eagles and osprey, can be seen. The 21-mile (34-km) Suomi Hills Trail near Marcell has trout and bass fishing. Lost Forty is a stand of virgin pine mistakenly missed by lumber companies. Trout Lake, with its several log buildings, is reached on a 5-mile (8-km) trail. The 68-mile (109-km) North Country Scenic Trail runs from west of Walker on Leech Lake to east of Remer. A 28-mile (45-km) Heartland Trail, passing woods and farms, offers a paved surface for bicycle riders. The Heartland Trail ends in Park Rapids, a town west of the lower part of the reserve. Three miles (5 km) north of Park Rapids is a recreated logging camp with a nature trail. Visitors may enjoy a lumberjack meal and watch the logging demonstrations.

US Forest Service naturalists conduct a variety of programs.

The Forest may be reached by car on Hwy 6, or by bus to nearby Grand Rapids. The nearest airport is located in Hibbing.
Map ref: page 370 F6

DULUTH

Duluth is a colorful and feisty port city located 156 miles (251 km) north and slightly east of Minneapolis-St Paul, which, because of its busy shipping life, industry and many things to do, seems much larger than its 85,000 population.

It is located on the western tip of Lake Superior beneath the cold and rocky North Shore cliffs, and extends along the lake for 24 miles (39 km). With the close of the last Ice Age around 10,000 years ago, lava formed the cliffs that run the length of the North Shore in the United States and Canada, towering above the largest freshwater lake (by area) in the world. Covering 31,500 square miles (81,585 sq km), Superior is the second only to deeper Russia's Lake Baikal in volume. Superior is a massive 350 miles (563 km) long and 160 miles (257 km) across, and is like an inland sea connected to distant ports and providing a passage to the entire world.

Superior's gentle majesty can be awakened by a strong nor'easter wind that hurls huge 20-foot (6-m) waves onto the shore. Hundreds of vessels have been sunk in its many storms, from small fishing boats to the 729-foot (222-m) ore boat, the *Edmund Fitzgerald*.

Flinty and lacking in nutrients, the lake has been a gigantic mystery of a fishing hole. Originally lake trout were plentiful in the in-shore areas and stream estuaries. The habitat of lake sturgeon, which once weighed as much as 300 pounds (136 kg), was wiped out by logging drives and sawmills a century ago. During the twentieth century, smelt and vampire-like sea lampreys entered the lake through the newly built Welland Canal and devoured the lake trout, brook trout, and lake herring. Recently steelhead, chinook, coho, and pink salmon have been introduced, and zebra mussels and river ruff have been carried in by the ballast tanks of foreign vessels. Today chartered deep-sea fishing boats, which range

in size from under 20 feet (6 m) to 100 feet (30 m) long, take anglers out on half-day and full-day trips as well as providing all the necessary equipment.

In addition to its active port, Duluth is an important grain center. Its harbor is protected by the long spit of Minnesota Point and has 49 miles (79 km) of dock line. Grain elevators, ore docks, and shipyards line the waterfront. Railroads thunder along the hillside, their sound mixing with the deep foghorns of freighters and ore boats outside the harbor.

The city was named for French explorer Daniel Greysolon, Sieur Duluth, who arrived in 1679. The Native American village that existed there was known as Fond du Lac and served as a gateway to what is now Minnesota and Canada.

Voyageurs in birch-bark canoes portaged a long stretch of rapids at the present site of Cooke State Park and traveled up the St Louis River to Canada or west to the Mississippi

River. Nowadays it is possible to hike along this historic passage, but a very good supply of insect repellent is necessary to fight the many swarming mosquitoes.

With the construction of locks at Sault St Marie on Lake Superior in 1855, shipping reached the large eastern cities on the lower Great Lakes and made Duluth a boom town. When the railroad arrived in 1870, Duluth rivaled Chicago as a grain-shipping port.

Downtown Duluth features a number of distinguished old buildings that point to its vigorous history, including the brownstone, chateau-like Depot, the Lake Superior Railroad Museum, the City Hall, Federal Building, St Louis Courthouse, the Karpeles Manuscript Museum, and Fitger's on the Lake, a renovated brewery housing more than two dozen shops and restaurants. Northeast of town on Superior Street lie the mansions of the late-nineteenth-century millionaires who built

Each year over 1,000 ships sail under Duluth's aerial lift bridge and into the port.

The picturesque streets of Duluth were once described as "a Lilliputian village in a mammoth rock garden."

Duluth and the lumber and iron-mining industries. One of the most luxurious estates, the Glensheen mansion, is open for public tours. The Jacobean mansion offers Georgian, Mission, and Art Nouveau furnishings and is set in 22 acres (9 ha) of landscaped grounds.

The Tweed Museum of Art, Sax Sculpture Library, and Marshall W. Alworth Planetarium are found at the Duluth campus of the University of Minnesota.

The Skyline Parkway follows a towering ridge along the lake and where the parkway intersects with 18th Avenue West stands the Enger Tower. It provides a fantastic lake overview. Also found on the parkway is the Hawk Ridge Nature Reserve, where each fall thousands of hawks, eagles, and falcons stop during their southern migration.

Duluth is home to Lake Superior Zoological Gardens, containing more than 80 exhibits with 500 species on 12 acres (5 ha); the Lake Superior and Mississippi Railroad, which offers a 12-mile (19-km) summer trip through dramatic hills along the St Louis River; the 8,800-acre (3,564-ha) Jay Cooke State Park, where the St Louis River is popular with kayakers. The recently opened Great Lakes Aquarium, America's first and only all-freshwater aquarium, presents active displays in tanks that exceed 120,000 gallons (454,200 l).

Duluth may be reached by car or bus along US-61 and Hwy 23. It has an international airport.
Map ref: page 371 J7

ELY

Ely bills itself as "the Canoe Capital of the World." The village has 4,000 residents and is located above Lake Superior near the Canadian border, 112 miles (180 km) from Duluth and 255 miles (410 km) from the twin cities of Minneapolis-St Paul.

This small town offers excellent access to Boundary Waters Canoe Area Wilderness and Quantico Provincial Park. It is encompassed by Superior National Forest, which has 2,021 lakes over 10 acres (4 ha) in size, with a total of 314,545 acres (127,390 ha) of water; it also contains 1,975 miles (3,178 km) of streams. Within Boundary Wilderness, 1,000 lakes of 10 acres (4 ha) or more can be reached by water.

Cross-country skiing and snow-mobiling are popular in winter, taking place on hundreds of miles of groomed trails in the area. Many resorts offer cabins for skiers and snowmobilers. Ely is at the end of the Taconite Trail, which runs through three state and one national forest, countless historical landmarks and numerous communities. Downhill skiing is offered at nearby Giants Ridge.

Berry picking is a very popular summer activity. Strawberries (in late June to mid-July), blueberries (from mid-July to mid-August), and raspberries (from July into August) are abundant. Waterskiing, fishing, boating, hiking, and golfing can also be enjoyed in the warm months. Walleye, lake trout, small-mouth bass, northern pike, black crappie, rainbow trout, largemouth bass, and bluegill all keep anglers busy. Beginners as well as experienced canoeists can enjoy boating the 1,500-plus miles (2,414 km) of the Boundary Wilderness' water trails. Canoe outfitters will often assist on choosing routes, selecting campsites, and supplying food or equipment. Motors are not allowed in designated areas so that canoe trips can be peaceful getaways and reach into areas that are not often visited.

Ely is home of the International Wolf Center, a multi-million dollar complex that examines one of the most elusive and misunderstood animals in the world.

Ely is the home or part-time residence of a number of known artists, writers, photographers, and adventurers. Former "On the Road" TV great Charles Kuralt bought the local Ely radio station in 1995 before dying in 1997. Jim Bradenburg is best known for his book on wolves and his work for *National Geographic*. Will Steger and Paul Schurke wrote the best-selling book *North to the Pole!* and they were once featured on a cover of *National Geographic*. Dorothy Molter, best known for her nursing skills and as "the Root Beer Lady of Knife Lake," was the last Boundary Wilderness resident. Then there is Dr Lynn Rogers, considered by many as "the Jane Goodall of black bears"—he is known for his innovative research and award-winning wildlife photography. And another is Bob Cary, who once ran for the Presidency on the independent Fishing Party ticket.

The Chippewa people have lived in Ely for centuries. In the eighteenth century, French traders known as "voyageurs" explored the area in search of fur, and most usually, beaver pelts. In the early nineteenth century, prospectors moved in. They searched for gold, which was never found. However, there were some rich and abundant iron ore deposits that were found along the Laurentian Divide.

Ely was incorporated as a village in 1888, just near the east end of Shagawa Lake. When the ore was discovered further west, the town moved in that direction to its present location south of Miners and Shagawa Lakes. At one time, Ely had 11 ore mines, the last of which closed in 1967.

Ely may be reached by car by following Hwy 169 and Hwy 1. The nearest airport in the area is in the town of Hibbing.
Map ref: page 371 J4

GRAND PORTAGE NATIONAL MONUMENT

Grand Portage National Monument is located on the western shore of Lake Superior just south of the US–Canada border. The portage bisects the reservation of the Grand Portage Band of Chippewa Native Americans, who in 1958 donated the land that became the national monument.

Mt Rose, which features several good overlooks, is probably the most accessible spot to view the

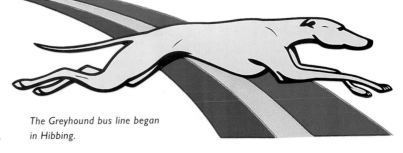

The Greyhound bus line began in Hibbing.

stockade at the national monument as well as to observe Lake Superior. The Mt Rose Trail begins across the road from the parking lot and it ascends to the summit of this 300-foot (92-m) hill.

Sometime after 1722 Grand Portage, the "Great Carrying Place," became an important hub in Canada's fur trade. Furs were transported by the legendary "voyageurs," hardy French-Canadian travelers who paddled their birch-bark canoes through the water network linking Montreal, capital of the Great Lakes fur trade, with northwestern Canada, the main source of the "soft gold" pelts. Separate waterways in the system were joined by trails or portages where the travelers carried their canoes and cargo overland. The routes that converged on Grand Portage totaled some 3,000 miles (4,827 km), and it became a regular meeting place for voyageurs coming from the west and Montreal men from the east.

These voyageurs, who are now credited with fueling the young nation's economy and opening new territory, lived romantic if somewhat arduous lives. Reputed to have sung French songs as they paddled, they apparently worked energetically and without complaint, exchanging comfort, health, and permanent homes for a life of adventure and camaraderie.

Voyageurs were hired to transport furs by the North West Company, a group of Highland Scots with an eye for a good location. They had set up their operation in Grand Portage in 1784. The company headquarters, which they located at the mouth of the Pigeon River, became the site of an annual mid-July gathering. At this regular gathering, the Montreal traders, voyageurs, and the Chippewa met to exchange goods and supplies.

The Grand Portage trading cycle continued until 1803, when the company moved upshore to Fort William. Grand Portage was indeed the largest post found anywhere within hundreds of miles. It included 16 wooden buildings all housed within a palisade. In the 1950s Grand Portage was designated as a national monument.

Visitors may explore the great hall, the kitchen, the fur press, the stockade, the lookout tower, and the warehouse.

The entrance to Grand Portage National Monument is from US-61, and is 36 miles (60 km) north of Grand Marais.
Map ref: page 371 N4

GRAND RAPIDS

Grand Rapids (population 7,976) is an old logging town of tall trees and stories, built on the Mississippi River 145 miles (233 km) north of Minneapolis-St Paul.

The story of the lumberjack era is well presented at the Forest History Center, operated by the Minnesota Historical Society. Visitors may walk through a logging camp modeled on the 300 camps that existed in Minnesota in 1900. Exhibits show lumberjacks sawing giant white pine by hand and moving the logs by sled or rail to the river. A movie shows a log drive down the Littlefork River in 1937, the last in Minnesota history. Also featured here is the tale of Paul Bunyan and Babe the Blue Ox, a 1914 story by copywriter William B. Laughead to advertise the Red River Lumber Company.

On Grand Rapids town square is the Central School History Center, a Romanesque building going back to 1895 where the past of the town and region are presented. The five period rooms at the Itasca County Museum depict Native American life, upper Mississippi exploration, pioneer days, and early commerce in town. Movie star Judy Garland was born in Grand Rapids. The museum's third floor is devoted to her: movie stills, posters, recordings, and interviews pay tribute to the little girl who became famous in *The Wizard of Oz*.

Other attractions include the Blandin Paper Company, which provides tours of its mill; the *Mississippi Melodie Showboat*, which presents summer musical-comedy shows; and the White Oak Society's recreation of a 1798 fur post just northwest of Deer River, where an annual fur trade rendezvous is staged on the first weekend of August.

Grand Rapids may be reached on US-169 and US-2, and by bus. The nearest airport is in Hibbing.
Map ref: page 370 G6

HIBBING

This town, 196 miles (315 km) north of Minneapolis-St Paul in the Mesabi Iron Range, is named for Frank Hibbing, who discovered here the largest deposit of naturally enriched iron that the world has ever known in 1892. A century later, huge production trucks were still hauling iron from the Hull-Rust-Mahoning, a combination of 50 mines that merged to form an open pit more than 3 miles (4.8 km) long, and 535 feet (163 m) deep.

Now a town of 18,046, Hibbing was moved 2 miles (3 km) south by log haulers to make way for the expanding mine. The Hibbing Historical Society and Museum in the Memorial Building portrays life in the early mining era.

The Palacci Space Theatre features a wrap-around screen and planetarium which puts on multimedia presentations on natural history, from dinosaurs to astronomy. Twenty miles (32 km) north of Hibbing is McCarthy Beach State Park, where a clutch of lakes dimples glacial hills. A beach flanks Sturgeon Lake beneath pure stands of birch and red pine.

Hibbing may be reached by car on US-169 and Hwy 73, by bus, and by plane.
Map ref: page 370 G6

Hibbing iron-ore mine, a massive iron-ore source with ore that is so soft and so close to the surface it can be obtained by open-cut mining.

Minnesota is a state of many lakes—there are thousands. This is Lake Itasca, the source of the Mississippi River, located in Lake Itasca State Park.

LAKE CITY

Located 65 miles (105 km) southeast of Minneapolis-St Paul, Lake City offers a commanding prospect of the Mississippi River. Softrock cones and thicket slopes launch themselves hundreds of feet above the water. High-angle ravines plummet down the palisades. In summer, cows graze on alpine slopes, and their bells can be heard below.

Lake City is home to 4,500 residents and has grown from its nineteenth-century beginnings—it now has the largest small-craft marina on the Mississippi River, seven recreational parks, and it hosts three annual festivals.

But what put the town on the map was the adventurous curiosity of an 18-year-old with $2 worth of pine boards. In 1922 Ralph Samuelson invented waterskiing here on Lake Pepin by skimming on his 8-foot (2.5-m) boards behind a motorboat.

This picturesque location produces one-quarter of the 700,000 bushels of apples harvested in Minnesota each year.

Wildlife includes tundra swans, turkeys, bald eagles, water fowl, foxes, and pheasants. The area has 500 miles (805 km) of marked snowmobile trails and more than 40 cross-country ski trails. There are also three very good downhill ski runs nearby.

Lake City may be reached by car on US-61 and US-63, and by bus. The nearest airport is in nearby Rochester.

Map ref: page 375 H5

Main street of Lake City, which has one of the finest marinas on the Mississippi River.

LAKE ITASCA

The slender thread of water gliding from the sandy shore of Lake Itasca and trickling through boulders is the headwaters of the mightiest river on the continent, the Mississippi. Lake Itasca is located in Lake Itasca State Park, about 85 miles (137 km) east of Moorhead. Established in 1891, the park is the oldest in the state and, at 32,000 acres (12,960 ha), it is second largest and one of the grandest. It contains towering stands of red and white pine scattered around more than 100 lakes.

Four other state forests circle around the villages of Park Rapids, Dorset, and Nevis. The ecosystem of grass, forests, and prairie provide habitat for over 200 bird species, including loons, eagles, osprey, swans, hawks, piliated woodpeckers, and American redstarts. Golf, fishing, horseback riding, hiking, hunting, snowmobiling, and cross-country skiing are some of the local outdoor activities available.

Lake Itasca may be reached by car on US-71. The nearest airport is located in Moorhead.

Map ref: page 370 D6

MINNEAPOLIS-ST PAUL (THE TWIN CITIES)

Half the people who live in Minnesota, or about 2.3 million people, live in the metropolitan area of Minneapolis-St Paul. The cities are located beneath the center of the state and east, and are near the Wisconsin border.

Minneapolis is perhaps best described as a small city, and it lies on the west of the country's most famous river, the Mississippi; St Paul, east of the river, is more like a big town. The two downtowns are joined by highways, city streets, commercial districts, and residential neighborhoods. St Paul is older, quieter, more cultured. Minneapolis is brighter, bigger, more vigorous. Minneapolis is a place of chrome, steel, and glass skyscrapers, while St Paul stands for stately brick and stone mansions of days gone by.

The skyline tells of the great dissimilarity of these "Twin Cities," a moniker that indicates their shared space despite their opposite appearance and character. The 57-story IDS skyscraper, the sandstone Art Deco Norwest tower, and the modern glass and stone of the First Bank Building, symbolizing industrial and corporate strength, dominate the Minneapolis skyline. In contrast, the copper dome and solid granite of St Paul's Cathedral and the state's Capitol dome, a copy of Michelangelo's cap for St Peter's Basilica in Rome, give St Paul a traditional, artistic air. However, both cities share an ethnic diversity with large numbers of Germans, Irish, Poles, Italians, Scandinavians, and Native Americans, along with newer communities of Southeast Asians and Hispanics.

Despite the existence of nearly 1,000 lakes in the Twin Cities area, Minneapolis and St Paul grew up as river towns. Native Americans had been settled in the area for thousands of years before Europeans arrived, who were attracted by the water, transportation, and food provided by the river.

After white settlement St Paul, with its ease of water navigation, became a transportation center for the Upper Midwest. In the case of Minneapolis, the water power that was harnessed from the 50-foot (15-m) St Anthony Falls helped this town to become a top flour-milling and lumber center.

In pioneer days, St Paul was the last bastion of the East; Minneapolis the gateway to the West. St Paul was flour mills and wheat traders; St Paul was steamboats and trains. Today these two cities share the same large Minneapolis-St Paul International Airport.

The Twin Cities have the same quality of water sparkle as does Scandinavia and together they are known as "the City of Lakes." These are not only located on the city outskirts: Loring Park and Lake, with its Canadian geese, mallards, and weeping willows, is only six blocks from the center of downtown Minneapolis. And four of the most beautiful lakes in the area are within 2 miles (3.2 km) of downtown, where the

The Frederick R. Weisman Art Museum in Minneapolis has a collection of over 13,000 objects.

headquarters of Cargill, General Mills, and Pillsbury recall the city's prominent wheat-milling past.

General Mills is the place of "Betty Crocker," the wholesome homemaker who whips up a plentiful mix of General Mills products. Agribusiness giant Cargill began in 1865 as a small Iowa wheat-trading business before spreading to a network of grain elevators across the upper Midwest. Today Cargill is one of the largest privately held companies in the world, employing 76,000 people at 1,000 locations in 66 countries. Another business mainstay, Honeywell, began as Minneapolis Heat Regulator Co., making thermostats for coal furnaces and boilers. When the company merged with Honeywell Heating Specialties Co. of Wabash, Indiana, it broadened its mission from thermostats to a variety of regulatory systems, including missile controls. With diversification it has become a corporate giant of the region and a major defense contractor.

What is perhaps the city's best-known company is the Minnesota Mining and Manufacturing, better known as 3M. Originally the company set up on the north shore of Lake Superior to make sandpaper. The deposit was inadequate, so it imported garnet abrasive. When

A hot-dog stand at the Landmark Center, Minneapolis.

a tramp steamer shipment of garnet turned out to be contaminated with olive oil, 3M then started a testing facility that was to become its world-renowned laboratory and research system. Today the company is known for manufacturing products as diverse as floppy disks and Post-It Notes.

Minneapolis is business, St Paul is history and government. The Capitol dominates the old river terrace overlooking downtown St Paul. The gold-leaf charioteer on its roof represents prosperity, its horse representing nature, and the woman representing civilization. The building is a masterpiece of the monumental Beaux-Arts Classical structures typical of late nineteenth-century statehouses. The Landmark Center, built of Minnesota pink granite, was once the Federal Court Building where gangsters of the Prohibition era went to trial. It is located north of Rice Park, established as a public square in 1849, and the cornerstone of one of St Paul's most attractive locations. The Landmark Center houses the Minnesota Museum

of American Art, the Ramsey County Historical Society, and it is also home to the Schubert Club Musical Instrument Museum.

To the west of Rice Park sits the Ordway Center for the Performing Arts, home of the St Paul Chamber Orchestra and also the Minnesota Opera. Completed in 1985, Ordway is a warm and elegant building replete with hardwood, copper, and brick. On West Seventh Street near downtown lies Irvine Park, one of the oldest residential areas of the city, where many of the original houses have been kept in good condition or restored.

As all this information indicates, the Twin Cities are best known for their rich culture. Together they have four major art museums, two big orchestras, the nation's foremost regional theater, scores of bookstores, terrific talent in jazz, pop, and gospel music, two of the finest science and history museums in the country, and a strong public radio and TV presence.

Just southwest of Loring Park in Minneapolis, the Guthrie Theater and Walker Art Center share space in an excellent arts complex that is right beside the 10-acre (4-ha) Minneapolis Sculpture Garden. The Guthrie was opened in 1963 by the British impresario Sir Tyrone Guthrie, who wanted to plant a high-quality repertory theater in America's heartland. Hundreds of performances later, his vision has borne impressive fruit. Some of the world's best directors, stage designers, costumers, and actors work there, and the shows are invariably high-quality and thought-provoking.

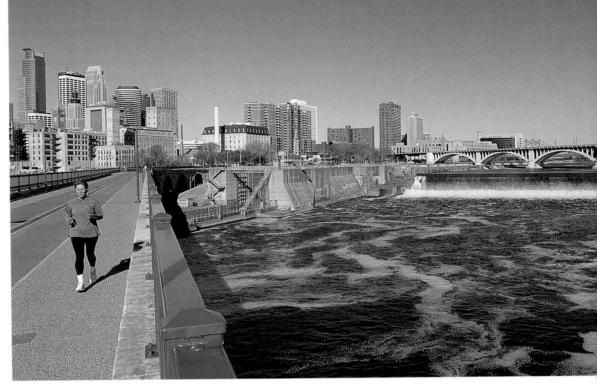

St Anthony Falls locks at St Paul. The water once powered wheat mills; three locks enable upstream navigation of the river.

The Walker Art Center's permanent collection of twentieth-century paintings, photographs, sculpture, and changing exhibits is considered one of the foremost contemporary collections in the country. The Walker also sponsors lectures, classes, and films. The Minneapolis Sculpture Garden, the largest of its kind in the country, is filled with more than 40 sculptures by internationally recognized artists from around the world. *Spoonbridge and Cherry*, created by Claes Oldenburg and Coosje van Bruggen, has become a trademark of Minneapolis.

The city's most unusual museum, the Museum of Questionable Medical Devices, on Main St SE, presents more than 200 exhibits relating to medical quackery. Displays include the MacGregor Re-

juvenator, which promised to reverse the aging process; three phrenology machines, claimed to indicate personality traits by measuring head bumps; the Solorama Bedboard, which vowed to cure brain tumors; and a foot-operated breast enlarger pump.

Minneapolis-St Paul is also known for its good schools, its friendliness, and its cold weather. The only cities in the continental US with colder climates are Duluth, Minnesota; Bismarck, North Dakota; and Great Falls, Montana. But the Twin Cities have done something about their icy disposition by building an extensive glass walkway system called the Skyway that connects shops, restaurants, and offices one story above the ground. And, as an example of caring for its freezing customers, Nicollet Mall in downtown Minneapolis offers heated sidewalks and piped-in classical music in its bus shelters.

St Paul makes the most of its wintry elements with its well-known St Paul Winter Carnival in late January and early February. The city crowns a king and queen, builds fabulous sculptures out of 300-pound (136-kg) ice blocks, runs a treasure hunt

and parades with Vulcans, devil's helpers who dress in red and imprint a black mark of charcoal on the women they kiss. Minneapolis answers with its summer Aquatennial, a 10-day event in late July of contests, entertainment, parades, and water sports—one boat race holds competition among vessels that are constructed entirely out of milk cartons.

Just south of the Twin Cities in Bloomington stands the most popular tourist draw in the state. The Mall of America attracts 40 million visitors annually, more than Disney World, the Grand Canyon and Graceland combined. The mall's 4.2 million square feet (399,000 sq m) include the 7-acre (3-ha) Knott's Camp Snoopy, the largest US indoor theme park with 23 rides; more than 400 specialty and department stores including Nordstrom, Macy's, Bloomingdale's, and Sears; and bars, restaurants and nightclubs, some of them themed, such as Planet Hollywood and Rainforest Cafe. Underwater Adventures is an inside-out mega aquarium in which visitors, tunneled by an acrylic wall, are surrounded by millions of gallons of water. The aquarium depicts habitats with appropriate species; a trout stream; a Minnesota lake; the Mississippi River; the Gulf Stream; and a reef off the coast of Belize with colorful fish, sharks, and stingrays. Do the shopping, then ride a roller coaster.

With 45,000 students and 250 fields of study, the University of

The Mall of America, the largest enclosed retail complex in the country, just south of the Twin Cities.

Minnesota in Minneapolis is one of the largest in the United States.

The Twin Cities boast of their sports teams. The Minnesota Twins of the American Baseball League play in the Hubert H. Humphrey Metrodome in downtown Minneapolis, as do the Minnesota Vikings of the National Football League.

The Minnesota Timberwolves of the National Basketball Association play in the Target Center of downtown Minneapolis. The University of Minnesota Gophers, members of the prestigious Big Ten Conference, play football in the Metrodome, basketball in Williams Arena, and ice hockey in Mariucci Arena.

Minneapolis-St Paul may be reached by car on I-94 and I-35, and by US-52, US-10 and US-61, and by Hwy 54. It can also be reached by bus and plane. Minneapolis-St Paul International Airport is the state gateway for domestic and foreign flights.
Map ref: page 374 F3

MOORHEAD

Moorhead has a population of 32,300 residents and lies 173 miles (278 km) to the northwest of Minneapolis-St Paul. It is adjacent to Fargo, North Dakota. This is quite a scenic spot on the Red River, and a center for farming, manufacturing, and dairying. Moorhead has many attractive old houses, including Comstock House, which was built in 1883. It is also home to Concordia College, well known for its music studies.

However, the town is perhaps best known for the *Hjemkomst*, the 77-foot (23-m) replica of an ancient Viking ship. Housed in the Heritage Hjemkomst Interpretive Center, it was built by Robert Asp when he was a junior-high school teacher. His idea was to sail it to Norway. Modeling it after a 1,000-year-old Jokstad Viking warship that might have journeyed across the ocean, Asp built the ship from native white oak in an old potato warehouse, but was then diagnosed with leukemia. He was able to sail the ship on

Lake Superior before he died. In 1982 a crew that included Asp's children sailed the ship from Lake Superior to Bergen, Norway, surviving a ferocious North Atlantic storm that cracked its hull.

Moorhead may be reached by car on US-10 and US-75, on I-94, and also by plane.
Map ref: page 370 A7

PIPESTONE

Located in the southwestern corner of Minnesota, 200 miles (321 km) from Minneapolis-St Paul, Pipestone, population 4,560, appears to be constructed of the same red stone that Native Americans used for pipes. However, the deep red building stone that is used for the many historic buildings is actually the harder Sioux quartzite that lies beneath much of the area.

The Pipestone National Monument preserves the sacred red stone quarries where Native Americans still quarry the red pipestone. Visitors may observe pipes and crafts being carved. A historic circle trail with a view of Winnewissa Falls leads through the coteau prairie.

Hunting, fishing and boating are recreational activities. Among summer events are the reenactment of a Civil War battle, a rendezvous festival, and Longfellow's legendary "Song of Hiawatha" pageant with a cast of 200. The Pipestone Center for the Performing Arts is home to several local performing groups and regional and national revues.

Pipestone may be reached by car on US-75 and Hwy 23. The nearest airport is in Minneapolis-St Paul.
Map ref: page 375 P6

RED WING

Red Wing is located about 61 miles (98 km) southeast of Minneapolis-St Paul and is beneath the limestone bluffs of one of the sharpest bends in the navigable Mississippi River.

This town is best known for the Red Wing Shoe Company, which employs 1,400 of the town's 15,135 residents and is particularly famous for its hiking, hunting, and work boots.

The centerpiece of the historic downtown area is the St James Hotel, which was originally built in 1874 to accommodate rail and river visitors. The Goodhue County Historical Museum is the oldest country museum in the state, dating back to 1869. A $2.4 million expansion in 1993 enlarged the facility, which provides quite a broad view of the

town and also the Mississippi Valley. Here there are exhibits of Red Wing pottery, a Dakota teepee, and it also presents the history of immigrants who arrived from Scandinavia, Germany, and the eastern United States during the mid-nineteenth century.

The T.B. Sheldon Memorial Auditorium, built in 1904 and

Boot production at Red Wing Shoe Company.

quite recently renovated, has a neo-Renaissance exterior with small faces popping out of it. Red Wing also has quite a few elegant historic houses that date from the mid-nineteenth century.

Red Wing may be reached by car or bus on US-61. The closest airport is in Minneapolis-St Paul.
Map ref: page 375 H5

Red Wing contains many graceful old homes, some of them dating back to the middle of the nineteenth century.

ROCHESTER

Rochester, home to the famous Mayo Clinic, is located 90 miles south of Minneapolis-St Paul. It has a population of 70,700.

William A. Mayo opened his medical practice here in 1863. The Mayo practice became a family affair when he was joined by his sons, William J. and Charles H., and was to prove incredibly innovative and experimental. The practice grew to today's 16,000 people, including about 2,000 doctors and residents-in-training. At the clinic and two affiliated hospitals, which comprise more than 30 buildings including the 19-story clinic, nearly 300,000 people are treated every year. The clinic established the world's first blood bank in 1930. In 1950 its doctors were awarded the Nobel Prize for discovering cortisone. The clinic also designed a mask and anti-blackout suit for test pilots, developed technology for open-heart surgery, advanced the use of lasers to destroy brain tumors, and used chemicals to dissolve gallstones without surgery. The Mayo Clinic tour visits several floors of the Mayo building, includes a film, and explores the historical displays in the Plummer Building. A Mayowood Mansion Tour visits the former residence of Dr Charles H. Mayo.

The Rochester Art Center features exhibitions of regional and national artists. The Olmstead County History Center features interpretive displays of the area's history, going back to a one-room schoolhouse and log cabin.

Rochester may be reached by car on US-52, US-14 and US-63, by bus, and by plane.
Map ref: page 375 H6

ST CLOUD

This town of 48,000, 72 miles (116 km) northwest of Minneapolis-St Paul, is known for its granite quarries. The fine-grain granite found in the region, ranging in color from coal-black to pink, has been used in some of the nation's finest buildings. The city's granite structures are from the first quarry at the present site of the Minnesota State Reformatory just after the Civil War (1861–1865). Reformatory grounds are secured by a wall of massive dark granite.

Entrance to the Mayo Clinic, Rochester's much-revered medical institution.

A Norwegian named John L. Wilson paid only $250 for the 325 acres (132 ha) where the St Cloud business district now exists, and lived in St Cloud until his death in 1910. Wilson named the city after Napoleon Bonaparte's hometown of St Cloud, France. The city's location on the Mississippi River helped it grow into a prominent industrial, business, and educational center.

St Cloud State University overlooks the west bank of the Mississippi. It has a planetarium.

On the east bank, in Riverside Park, are the Munsinger Botanical Gardens, which feature 80,000 annual plants as well as woodlands, fountains, ponds, and paths. Adjacent Clemens Gardens contain six formal gardens, one presenting more than 1,100 rose bushes, and another an all-white garden devoted to white flowers and flowering shrubs. Clemens also has a cast-iron and steel arbor embellished with red, yellow, purple, and blue flowering plants.

Saint John's Abbey and University, situated on the banks of Lake Sagatagan, has one of the world's largest collections of medieval documents and books. The Benedictine Monastery and university campus include a church, library, and science center designed by Marcel Breuer, the Hungarian-born American architect and furniture designer who was associated with the Bauhaus in the 1920s, and who is known for chairs with tubular steel frames.

The Stearns County Heritage Center houses the county historical museum, an archives and research center, and 8 miles (13 km) of interpretive nature trails. Museum exhibits include outdoor scenes, a log barn with antique farm equipment, Native American artifacts and lodges, a mock stone quarry, and changing displays.

Little Falls, 30 miles (48 km) northwest of St Cloud, was the childhood summer home of Charles A. Lindbergh, who in 1927 became the first airplane pilot to fly solo across the Atlantic Ocean. The house where Lindbergh lived, just south of Little Falls, is preserved with original furnishings and family possessions. It lies within the 600 wooded and grassy acres (243 ha) of Charles A. Lindbergh State Park, named for Lindbergh's father, who was a well-known Republican congressman. Just southwest of the park is the Charles A. Weyerhaeuser Museum which depicts early life in the area.

Twenty-six miles (42 km) southeast of St Cloud is the 1,500-acre (608-ha) Lake Maria State Park, which has 14 miles (23 km) of hiking trails and 17 remote camp sites spotted around Slough, Bjorkland, and Putnam Lakes.

St Cloud may be reached by car on I-94, Hwys 95 and 23, US-52, and by bus. The nearest airport is in Minneapolis-St Paul.
Map ref: page 374 E2

WINONA

Winona, 44 miles (71 km) east of Rochester, juts out into the Mississippi River and has the atmosphere of an island. Small lakes lie to the west, and the river curves around the long town shoulder to the east. Mark Twain called this part of the river "the Thousand Islands."

The town (population 25,399) was once a depot to restock steamboats with firewood and became a lumber center with 10 sawmills. Three museums look back at life along on the Mississippi. Latch Island moors nearly 100 boathouses and floating homes, the largest floating community in Minnesota.

Garvin Heights Park, 575 feet (175 m) above the Mississippi, has a 20–30-mile (32–48-km) vista of the river. Two National Register Historic Districts in downtown Winona comprise over 100 sites, forming one of the largest collections of Victorian commercial architecture in the region.

Winona may be reached by Hwy 66, and by bus. The nearest airport is in Minneapolis-St Paul.
Map ref: page 375 J6

The logging industry was once a major contributor to Winona's economy.

MISSOURI

Missouri, America's "Gateway to the West," lies at the geographical center of the continental United States. Its two major cities, St Louis and Kansas City, lie at opposite ends of the state and symbolize Missouri's bi-regional character. St Louis predates the nation; French traders built the settlement on the banks of the Mississippi River in 1764. Missouri was then part of the vast, unexplored Louisiana Territory, which belonged first to France and then Spain. Yet by the time the United States purchased it in 1803, American adventurers such as Daniel Boone had already pushed back the frontier and settled in the Missouri hinterlands.

The Mississippi River, memorialized by native son Mark Twain, brought in settlers from the East. Some of them remained in Missouri; others used it as a launching pad for the frontier lands of the Far West. President Thomas Jefferson commissioned Meriwether Lewis and William Clark to explore the newly acquired Louisiana Territory in 1804. They left from the vicinity of St Louis and returned 28 months later. Fur trappers followed in their wake, blazing trails that were later traveled by pioneers seeking better lives in Oregon, California, and Utah. The legendary Pony Express, which briefly serviced these far-flung settlers, also originated in Missouri.

The state's railheads were the end of the line for some of the great Texas cattle drives. Kansas City thus evolved into a major cattle-trading center. When horses eventually gave way to automobiles, the nation's first paved transcontinental highway, Route 66, passed through Missouri.

Today, visitors can relive some of this early history in Missouri's museums and historic towns. They can also experience Missouri's more recent contributions to the nation's culture in Kansas City's jazz clubs and barbeque joints, or Branson's country music halls, for instance. The state also boasts many caves, lakes, and forests for outdoor recreation.

The caretaker of the Pony Express Museum in St Joseph brings the thrilling history of that famous mail service to life.

State motto Salus Populi Suprema Lex Esto (The welfare of the people shall be the supreme law)
State flag Adopted 1913
Capital Jefferson City
Population 5,595,211
Total area (land and water) 69,709 square miles (180,546 sq km)
Land area 68,898 square miles (178,446 sq km)
Missouri is the 19th-largest state in size
Origin of name Named for the Missouri Native Americans, whose name means "town of the large canoes"
Nickname The Show-me State
Abbreviations MO (postal), Mo.
State bird Bluebird
State flower Hawthorn
State tree Flowering dogwood
Entered the Union August 10, 1821 as the 24th state

Places in
MISSOURI

ARROW ROCK STATE HISTORIC SITE

The small mid-Missouri town of Arrow Rock (population 100), about 40 miles (64 km) northwest of Columbia, preserves its frontier past at the Arrow Rock State Historic Site. The once-thriving town was established as a trading center in 1829, at the point where the Santa Fe Trail met the Missouri River. As river traffic dwindled, so did the town's population.

Guided walking tours (available from April through October) take visitors around the preserved town's dozen or so buildings, which include a pioneer home, a tavern, a jail, and a store. The Arrow Rock State Historic Site is open year-round and has a visitor center.

Columbia Regional Airport services the area.
Map ref: page 378 F9

BOONVILLE

Located on the Missouri River, about 20 miles (32 km) west of Columbia, Boonville (population 7,100) began as a distribution center for westward migrants.

Farms along the fertile Missouri River, like those near Boonville, grow a range of crops from soybeans to corn and other vegetables.

The town has buildings from the early and mid-1800s, including one of the oldest surviving theaters west of the Mississippi, and the Kemper Military School. Thespian Hall (built in 1855) hosts spring and fall concerts. The Boonville Area Chamber of Commerce can arrange tours of the historic districts, while the Friends of Historic Boonville office can supply maps for self-guided tours.

Ten miles (16 km) north of town on State Route 87 is Boone's Lick State Historic Site. Daniel Boone's sons produced salt from its two salt springs ("licks") in the early 1800s. Its picnic facilities are now open daily, year-round.

Columbia Regional Airport services the area. Boonville can also be reached by bus.
Map ref: page 382 E2

BRANSON

Once-remote Branson (population 3,700), just miles from the Arkansas border in southwestern Missouri, has grown into one of the nation's prime tourist attractions in the past decade. It first gained national attention in the early 1900s, thanks to Harold Bell Wright's best-selling novel, *The Shepherd of the Hills*. The book's homespun characters and Ozark-hill setting intrigued many Americans at a time when the country's population was growing increasingly urban and separated from its rural roots.

Branson's main drawcard today is its music scene. The section of two-lane State Route 76W that traverses Branson is known as 76 Country Boulevard or "The Strip." More than a dozen music theaters host top regional and national artists from May through October. While the emphasis is on country music, other styles are also on offer, including jazz, rock, gospel, and pop.

When not attending concerts, visitors to Branson can browse its many craft and antique shops and markets. There is also an old-fashioned dry goods store and a modern factory outlet mall. Among the half-dozen or so annual festivals is the National Festival of Craftsmen, from early September to late October. From spring through fall, visitors can see sound and light shows, take cruises and bus tours, and visit amusement parks. The Stone Hill Winery in Branson is open year-round.

Visitors interested in learning about old-fashioned Ozark lifestyles would want to visit the Shepherd of the Hills Homestead, 2 miles (3 km) west of Branson on State Route 76W. The working homestead has a preserved cabin, as well as a sawmill, smithy, and other shops. Guided tours are supplemented by shows, games, crafts, and scenic lookouts. There is also an outdoor amphitheater, where the novel's characters are brought to life nightly from late April through October. The homestead complex itself is open from April to December.

Visitors to Branson's Shepherd of the Hills Homestead can view a working sawmill and a blacksmith's workshop.

Three miles (5 km) further west is Silver Dollar City, a historical pioneer village crossed with a modern theme park. Roller coaster and water rides amuse thrill seekers, while those with a penchant for history or craftsmanship can watch artisans demonstrate traditional skills such as woodcarving and blacksmithing. The park fee includes admission to Marvel Cave, whose 3 miles (5 km) of passageways lie beneath the complex. Silver Dollar City is open almost continuously from April through December.

Popular activities at the three closest lakes include boating, swimming, fishing, and scuba diving. The visitor center has exhibits about area ecology and is a good place to see bald eagles from November through December. Houseboat rentals are also available at Table Rock Lake. An old-fashioned river showboat takes visitors on breakfast, lunch, and dinner cruises from the end of March to mid-December. An equally relaxing way to see the countryside is on the Branson Scenic Railway, which takes visitors on a 40-mile (64-km) round trip through the Ozark foothills, from mid-March to mid-December.

The city of Springfield, 45 miles (72 km) north on Hwy 65, has the closest airport. Branson is also serviced by buses.
Map ref: page 382 D8

CAPE GIRARDEAU

This Mississippi River town, in the state's far southeast, was founded as a French trading post in 1733. It was then settled by Spaniards lured to the area by cheap, tax-exempt land. After river trade diminished in the late 1800s, Cape Girardeau benefited from its position on the new railroad lines.

The town, which now has 34,400 residents, is dotted with parks, some of which overlook the river. Some of the best views can be had from Cape Rock, the site of the original trading post. The 57-mile (92-km) stretch of I-55 that connects Cape Girardeau with the town of St Mary in the north is also very scenic.

The Cape River Heritage Museum (open Wednesdays, Fridays, and Saturdays from March to December) interprets the area's

Conserving natural areas of Missouri is a priority.

history and culture. The Southeast Missouri State University Museum (open year-round, except during school vacations) has artworks and historical artifacts from the region and elsewhere. The Cape Girardeau Convention and Visitors Bureau has self-guided walking tour pamphlets of the historic downtown.

Ten miles (16 km) north of Cape Girardeau on State Route 177 is the Trail of Tears State Park. It contains part of the route covered by the Cherokees on their forced march from the East Coast to Oklahoma. Deer, turkeys, and foxes live in the Park's wooded hills and valleys; bald eagles can be seen there in the winter. Visitors can also venture out on the bluffs overlooking the Mississippi River.

The town is serviced by a municipal airport.
Map ref: page 383 L6

CARTHAGE

The local marble that was used in the Missouri State Capitol in Jefferson City can also be seen in several Victorian buildings in Carthage's historic square. The most unusual structure is the castle-like Jasper County Courthouse. Notable former Carthage residents include Myra Belle Shirley (also known as Confederate spy and outlaw Belle Star), as well as zoologist and nature television show host Marlin Perkins.

The town, located an hour's drive west of Springfield in southwestern Missouri, was also the site of a Civil War battle. An interpretive shelter commemorates the event at the Battle of Carthage State Historic Site. Elsewhere in and around town are markers explaining the various battle stages. Other periods of Carthage's history are commemorated in the Powers Museum.

What draws most visitors to this town of 10,700 is the Precious Moments Chapel. Artist Samuel J. Butcher made his name and fortune with his distinctive drawings of wide-eyed children. His creations usually appear alongside inspirational messages on greeting cards and porcelain collectibles. Butcher opened the Chapel in 1989. Its stained-glass windows and murals depict his Precious Moments children in biblical scenes. There is also a musical water and light show within a bronze sculpture garden.

Carthage and the surrounding area are serviced by buses and by Springfield Regional Airport.
Map ref: page 382 B7

COLUMBIA

Another of the many Missouri towns that prospered as an outfitting post for westward migrants (in this case thanks to its proximity to the Boone's Lick Trail),

Columbia has also distinguished itself through other enterprises. Area residents raised the funds to establish the first public university west of the Mississippi, in 1839. The University of Missouri is now one of three institutions of higher learning in this town of 69,100; the other two are Columbia College and Stephens College.

Six stately Ionic columns, all that remain of the university's first administrative building, now stand sentinel in Francis Quadrangle. Thomas Jefferson's original tombstone also lies nearby. The State Historical Society of Missouri, in the University's Ellis Library, has changing exhibits about the region. Also of interest is the Walters-Boone County Historical Museum.

As a vibrant college town and the hub of mid-Missouri, Columbia has a good assortment of cafés, restaurants, and shopping areas in its historic downtown area.

Columbia lies midway between St Louis and Kansas City on I-70, and is serviced by buses. It also has its own airport.
Map ref: page 382 F2

Parts of the Mississippi River near Cape Girardeau are reminiscent of days gone by.

Bald eagles (Haliaetus leucocephalus) are often seen near Hannibal in winter.

FULTON

This small mid-Missouri college town (population 10,000) is the site where Winston Churchill gave his famous "Iron Curtain" speech about the implications of a divided, Cold War Europe, on March 5, 1946. Fittingly, a section of the toppled Berlin Wall now stands on the campus of Fulton's Westminster College. It is part of the Winston Churchill Memorial and Library, whose focal point is the Church of St Mary, Aldermanbury. The 800-year-old original church was destroyed by the Great Fire of London in 1666. The architect Christopher Wren rebuilt the church, but this second building was damaged during the 1940 London Blitz. The remaining walls and columns were shipped to Fulton, then reassembled as a tribute to Churchill. In its basement there is a library, gallery, and museum with World War II memorabilia.

Columbia Regional Airport is 20 miles (32 km) from Fulton.
Map ref: page 382 G3

HANNIBAL

Mark Twain fans will recognize parts of Hannibal (population 18,000) from scenes in *The Adventures of*

Tom Sawyer and *The Adventures of Huckleberry Finn*. Samuel Langhorne Clemens (Twain's real name) spent his boyhood in this Mississippi River town, midway between St Louis and the Missouri–Iowa border, in the mid-1800s. The town's residents celebrate their famous son's fictional creations with dioramas, summertime outdoor dramas, and a life-size monument of his two young protagonists.

The must-see attraction is the Mark Twain Boyhood Home and Museum, which dates from 1843. The young Twain lived here for 11 years, until the age of eighteen. The house has been restored and furnished with period pieces. The museum next door has original manuscripts, photos, and Twain's writing desk, among other displays. Another highlight is the collection of Norman Rockwell oil paintings that were used to illustrate special editions of Twain's famous works.

Two miles (3 km) southeast of town on State Route 79 is the Mark Twain Cave. The nearby Cameron Cave can be explored by lantern-light on 90-minute tours that start at the Mark Twain Cave visitor center (appointments must be made between Labor Day and Memorial Day).

Those who want to steep themselves in Twain lore would do well to visit Hannibal during the week of July 4, when the town stages the National Tom Sawyer Days. One of the week's highlights is the fence-painting contest among Tom Sawyer look-alikes.

Hannibal was also the home of Margaret Tobin, better known as the Unsinkable Molly Brown after helping save passengers of the ill-fated *Titanic*. From April to December, the Molly Brown Dinner Theatre offers music revues recalling the 1920s to the 1950s.

Other attractions include a well-restored 1898 Art Nouveau river mansion, and a Dixieland riverboat dinner cruise.

Visitors in winter might see bald eagles on the high bluffs overlooking the Mississippi River. A good place to look for them is at the Saverton Dam, 9 miles (15 km) south of Hannibal on State Route 79. The next 77 miles (124 km) of that highway, leading to St Peters, is a scenic drive paralleling the river.

The area is serviced by buses. The closest airport is in Quincy, Illinois.
Map ref: page 379 J8

HERMANN

German immigrants settled this part of the Missouri River area in 1836. They kept their German culture and skills, including winemaking. Leatherworkers, weavers, potters, and other artisans can still be seen working at the Deutsche Schule in the German School of Arts and Crafts. Hermann, population 2,800, also has craft and antique shops.

Visitors can learn more about the town's German heritage at the Deutschheim State Historic Site, as well as at the Historic Hermann Museum and Information Center. The latter's displays are more wide-ranging, and even include a piece of the Berlin Wall.

Several area wineries, including the Stone Hill Winery and the Hermannhof Winery, welcome visitors year-round. A good time to visit is during one of its German festivals, in May or October.

The area, midway between Jefferson City and St Louis, is serviced by trains.
Map ref: page 378 J10

Hermann has a number of picturesque wineries producing quality red and white wines; most are open to the public for tastings.

Missouri schoolchildren are among the many visitors to take a tour of Kansas City's impressive State Capitol building.

INDEPENDENCE

Lying just east of Kansas City, this town of 112,300 people is best known as the hometown of President Harry S. Truman. But that is not its only claim to fame; it was also the starting point of the Santa Fe Trail in 1821, and the Oregon and California Trails in the 1840s.

The Harry S. Truman Library and Museum documents Truman's career and the country's history during his two terms, from 1945 to 1953. Truman's office is replicated inside the museum. His grave is in the courtyard. The Harry S. Truman National Historic Site, the Victorian house where Mr and Mrs Truman lived when not in Washington, is full of their furnishings and other possessions. Tickets for the guided tours of the house are distributed from the Truman Home Ticket and Information Center on a first-come, first-served basis for that day's tours. In summer, visitors should plan to arrive early in order to assure a place.

Guided walking tours of the Truman neighborhood are conducted from Memorial Day to Labor Day. Brochures describing a self-guided walking tour of the Harry S. Truman Historic District, with its Civil War era and Victorian houses, can be picked up or ordered from the Independence Department of Tourism.

The National Frontier Trails Center has informative displays on the mid-1800s westward-heading pioneers and the trails they followed.

Other attractions worth a look include the Bingham-Waggoner Estate, whose interior has been restored to its Victorian look. The 1859 Marshal's Home and Jail Museum complex includes a Civil War-era jail, a local history museum and a one-room schoolhouse. There is also a Mormon Visitor Center that has information about the sect whose founding members lived in Missouri before eventually migrating to Utah's Great Salt Lake basin.

The area is serviced by trains. The nearest airport is located in Kansas City.

Map ref: page 382 B2

JEFFERSON CITY

Missouri's capital city (population 35,500) was named after the president who signed the Louisiana Purchase, which brought this land under United States control. Thanks to its location on the banks of the Missouri River in the middle of the state, Jefferson City also thrived as a river trading port in the 1800s. Jefferson Landing State Historic Site features three buildings that stood at the center of this trade. One of them, the 1839 Lohman Building, has a small museum about the landing site and Jefferson City's history. The Jefferson City Area Chamber of Commerce has information about walking tours of the city's historic attractions.

The original State Capitol building burned down in 1837; its replacement was also destroyed by fire. The current State Capitol was built in 1918 of Carthage stone and overlooks the Missouri River. Its interior is graced by paintings by such notable artists as Thomas Hart Benton and N.C. Wyeth. Also within the building is the State Museum, which has exhibits on Missouri's ecological and cultural heritage.

The Runge Conservation Nature Center has exhibits and nature trails that showcase a variety of Missouri habitats, from wetlands to prairies and caves. Native fish can also be viewed in its 2,400-gallon (91 hl) aquarium.

Jefferson City is serviced by the nearby Columbia Regional Airport. It can also be reached by bus or train.

Map ref: page 382 F3

KANSAS CITY

Hard against the Kansas border, Kansas City is in fact divided between the two states. But despite its name, the commercial heart of Kansas City lies on the Missouri side. The city began as a trading post in 1821 then flourished as an outfitting station during the great westward migrations in the mid-1800s, thanks to its position on the Missouri River and at the head of the Santa Fe and Oregon trails. It fell on hard times in the prelude to the Civil War, as slavery supporters and abolitionists clashed trying to ensure Kansas entered the Union under their preferred classification. After the war, Kansas City benefited from a new rail link to Chicago. It soon became the nation's biggest cattle-trading center, and a major grain market.

Today Kansas City, with a population of 435,100, is still a top wheat market and agricultural distribution center. But it is also the headquarters of several big commercial concerns, including Hallmark Cards. It also boasts the nation's first shopping center, and prides itself on its civic improvement drives, which have introduced many statues and parks to the city. More significant to visitors, Kansas City has a rich and deservedly famous tradition of jazz and barbeques.

Kansas City has a number of art museums that are well worth a visit. The Kansas City Museum explains the city's role in the country's westward migration and gives visitors a sense of frontier life on the plains. The museum complex

Science City is located in the Union Station building in Kansas City.

includes a 50-room mansion, a natural history hall, and a planetarium. The Kemper Museum of Contemporary Art's diverse collection features works by such well-known artists as Georgia O'Keeffe and William Wegman. The Nelson-Atkins Museum of Art is renowned for its Oriental collection. Its 58 galleries and 11 period rooms also feature Egyptian and classical sculptures, European and American paintings, and English pottery. Its

Henry Moore Sculpture Garden displays a dozen large bronze sculptures, the largest American collection of Moore's works. Elsewhere in the city is the Thomas Hart Benton Home and Studio State Historic Site, celebrating this twentieth-century Missouri artist.

The Museums at 18th and Vine include the American Jazz Museum and the African-American Leagues Baseball Museum. They are in a neighborhood well known for its jazz and blues scene in the 1920s and 1930s. The complex's Horace M. Peterson III Visitor Center screens a video about the local African–American community.

The Arabia Steamboat Museum displays items recovered from a steamboat that sank in the Missouri River in 1856. There is also a working preservation lab on the site.

Greeting card enthusiasts can visit the Hallmark Visitor Center, which has a dozen exhibits about the company and the manufacture of its products. Other Kansas City attractions include the John Wornall House Museum, an 1858 Greek Revival plantation house; the Kansas City Zoo; an IMAX theater; casinos; and the Toy and Miniature Museum of Kansas City, which displays a large collection of antique toys.

A fun day out can also be enjoyed at two popular theme parks. The 175-acre (71-ha) Worlds of Fun boasts one of the world's tallest, longest, and fastest roller coasters. It is open from mid-April to mid-October. Nearby Oceans of Fun is a 60-acre (24-ha) water park with slides, a wave pool, and other water playgrounds. It is open from Memorial Day to Labor Day.

Year-round recreation is offered at over 300 parks. The most notable among them are Loose Park, Swope Park, and Fleming Park. Popular activities include bicycling, cross-country skiing, ice skating, hiking, and boating. Visitors can even ride horses along part of the Santa Fe Trail, at Benjamin Ranch.

More passive entertainment is available at Kansas City's many professional sporting events. Visitors can watch the Kansas City Royals playing baseball or the Kansas City Wizards playing soccer in the spring and summer; the Kansas City Chiefs playing football in the fall; and the Kansas City Blades playing ice hockey in the winter.

Kansas City is also renowned for its 55-acre (22-ha) Spanish and Moorish-style shopping complex, Country Club Plaza, the country's first completely planned shopping center. It has more than 150 shopfronts including well-known retail chains, as well as specialty stores, nightclubs, and restaurants. The city also has about a dozen other shopping centers, including Westport Square, once a Santa Fe Trail outfitting station. Antiques hunters should check out the State Line Antique and Art Center.

Cultural events include performances by the Lyric Opera of Kansas City and the Kansas City Symphony. The restored 1912 Gem Theater hosts a variety of multicultural events. For an old-fashioned evening out, there is the Martin City Melodrama and Vaudeville Co. In the summer, visitors can choose among the Music in the Parks outdoor concert series, the Theater Under the Stars, or the Swope Park Starlight Theater

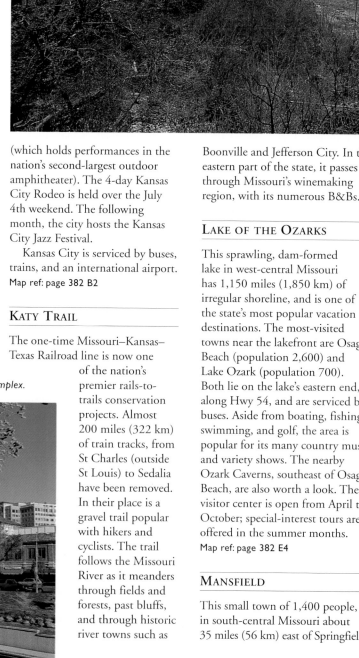

(which holds performances in the nation's second-largest outdoor amphitheater). The 4-day Kansas City Rodeo is held over the July 4th weekend. The following month, the city hosts the Kansas City Jazz Festival.

Kansas City is serviced by buses, trains, and an international airport.
Map ref: page 382 B2

KATY TRAIL

The one-time Missouri–Kansas–Texas Railroad line is now one of the nation's premier rails-to-trails conservation projects. Almost 200 miles (322 km) of train tracks, from St Charles (outside St Louis) to Sedalia have been removed. In their place is a gravel trail popular with hikers and cyclists. The trail follows the Missouri River as it meanders through fields and forests, past bluffs, and through historic river towns such as

Boonville and Jefferson City. In the eastern part of the state, it passes through Missouri's winemaking region, with its numerous B&Bs.

LAKE OF THE OZARKS

This sprawling, dam-formed lake in west-central Missouri has 1,150 miles (1,850 km) of irregular shoreline, and is one of the state's most popular vacation destinations. The most-visited towns near the lakefront are Osage Beach (population 2,600) and Lake Ozark (population 700). Both lie on the lake's eastern end, along Hwy 54, and are serviced by buses. Aside from boating, fishing, swimming, and golf, the area is popular for its many country music and variety shows. The nearby Ozark Caverns, southeast of Osage Beach, are also worth a look. The visitor center is open from April to October; special-interest tours are offered in the summer months.
Map ref: page 382 E4

MANSFIELD

This small town of 1,400 people, in south-central Missouri about 35 miles (56 km) east of Springfield,

Brush Creek flows gently past Kansas City's appealing Country Club Plaza shopping complex.

Part of the scenic Current River winds through the Ozark Mountains.

was once home to Laura Ingalls Wilder. Wilder wrote her popular *Little House* books after she and her family moved from the Dakota Territory to Mansfield in 1894. The family home is preserved with its original furnishings. The on-site museum has family pictures, articles about the books, and assorted memorabilia.

Springfield Regional Airport services the area.
Map ref: page 382 E7

OZARK MOUNTAINS

The Ozark mountain chain, which stretches from northern Arkansas and southern Missouri to northeast Oklahoma, is one of the oldest in North America. It is known for its hardwood forests, isolated hollows, and caves. Culturally, the area is associated with hardscrabble farming and fiddle music.

The Mark Twain National Forest encompasses 1,473,000 acres (596,565 ha) of woodlands, in more than half a dozen unconnected patches. Its highest point is 1,772-foot (540-m) high Taum Sauk Mountain. Popular recrea-

tional activities within its borders include hiking, fishing, canoeing, camping, hunting, and scenic drives. Hiking trails range from short lakeside rambles to more challenging paths over steeper terrain. Water sports are available at several recreation areas. The Forest Supervisor's office in Rolla, at the Forest's northern end near I-44, has more information.

Also in this area are the Ozark National Scenic Riverways, which include portions of the Current and Jacks Fork Rivers. They are especially popular for float trips (floating on inflatable inner tubes). Their mostly forested shorelines are home to a range of wildlife. There are also more than 60 springs in the area. The Riverways headquarters is in Van Buren.

The closest airports to the Ozark Mountains are in Springfield, Rolla, and Poplar Bluff.
Map ref: page 382 F7

ST JOSEPH

Founded as a fur trading post in 1826, St Joseph is a city of 71,900 people, about an hour's drive north

of Kansas City. The town became a major wagon-staging area and supply depot during the Western gold rushes of the mid-1800s. It then secured its place in history when it became the starting point of the legendary Pony Express, which launched its mail service in 1860. Riders spent 10 days in the saddle between St Joseph and Sacramento, California.

St Joseph was also home to the outlaw Jesse James, who was killed in a shootout in 1882. The mark left by the bullet that killed him can be seen inside his restored home. The building is in the grounds of the Patee House Museum, one of the finest hotels west of the Mississippi during the mid-1800s. The museum also houses a re-created Pony Express office and artifacts, among other things relating to the area's frontier history. Elsewhere in town is the Pony Express National Memorial, whose exhibits tell the story of the operation.

More area lore, also covering Native American culture and natural history, can be explored at the St Joseph Museum. Bison, longhorn cattle, burros, and other animals roam Krug Park.

One of the town's more unusual attractions is the Glore Psychiatric Museum of St Joseph State Hospital, which recounts the history of psychiatry.

The area is serviced by buses, and the town has its own airport.
Map ref: page 378 C8

ST LOUIS

French fur trader Pierre Laclede founded the first settlement on the site of St Louis in 1764, near the point where the Missouri River flows into the Mississippi River on the state's eastern border. The mighty Mississippi brought trade and settlers from the directions of both New Orleans and Canada. As a major port in what was then French territory, the area

This dramatic memorial in St Joseph commemorates the famous Pony Express.

developed a European character. After the United States acquired the Louisiana Territory, explorers Meriwether Lewis and William Clark set off from nearby Camp Wood in May 1804 on their 28-month journey of discovery through the western half of the continent. Thus Missouri became known as America's "Gateway to the West."

Not everyone who came to Missouri was just passing through though; St Louis today has 396,700 residents. A rail link to the East Coast, completed in 1857, brought many of their ancestors from Germany, Ireland, and other parts of Europe.

St Louis was almost destroyed by fire, flood, and a cholera epidemic in the 1840s, but survived to become a thriving industrial city. The 1904 Louisiana Purchase Exposition in St Louis lasted seven months and introduced the nation to ice-cream cones, iced tea, and hot dogs, among other things.

St Louis has always looked east as well as west, and eagerly supported native son Charles A. Lindbergh in his bid to fly solo across the Atlantic Ocean. In gratitude he named his aircraft *Spirit of St Louis.* The city has also been home to many influential ragtime, blues, jazz, and rock and roll musicians, including Scott Joplin, Miles Davis, and Chuck Berry.

One of the nation's most recognized landmarks,

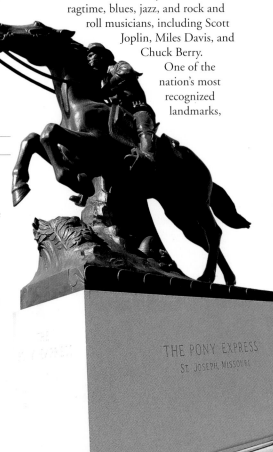

the Gateway Arch, commemorates St Louis' role in the nation's western expansion. The stainless steel structure, designed by Eero Saarinen and built in the 1960s, towers 630 feet (192 m) above the riverfront, near the site of the area's first trading post. Mechanical trams take visitors to an observation deck at the top. The visitor center at the base screens short films about the construction of the arch, and western settlement. Beneath the arch is the Museum of Westward Expansion, whose exhibits tell the story of western exploration and migration.

The Old Courthouse nearby was the site of the landmark Dred Scott slavery trial. It features the story of St Louis' development through the years. Also nearby is Laclede's Landing, site of the city's first settlement. Now restored to an early twentieth-century look, with cobblestone streets, it is a popular place to shop, eat, and work.

Residents and visitors alike flock to the 1,293-acre (524-ha) Forest Park, both for its recreational activities (including ice skating, roller skating, and golf) and for the well-respected St Louis Science Center, which has hands-on exhibits, an OMNIMAX theater, and a planetarium. Another popular spot is the Missouri Botanical Garden,

The Gateway Arch in St Louis symbolizes Missouri's role as the "Gateway to the West."

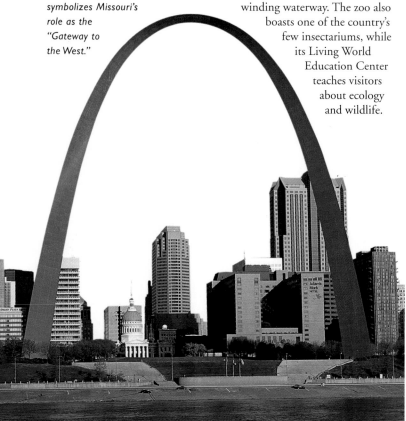

one of the nation's oldest. Its grounds include a Japanese garden, English woodlands, rose and herb gardens, and a fragrance garden for the visually impaired. More than 20 thematic residential gardens accent the Kemper Center for Home Gardening. Plants from different climate zones are displayed in several structures, including a geodesic dome known as the Climatron.

The excellent St Louis Art Museum is housed in the fine arts pavilion of the 1904 World's Fair. A mounted statue of St Louis the Crusader guards its entrance. Inside there are some 30,000 works of art from around the world, representing a variety of periods. Major touring shows are also displayed on a rotating basis.

Anheuser-Busch, one of the major corporations headquartered in St Louis, offers tours of its brewery. The company also operates the unusual Grant's Farm, open from April to October. The 281-acre (114-ha) site contains a cabin built by Ulysses S. Grant a few years before he left to help the Union win the Civil War. It also has a Clydesdale stable, animal feeding area, a deer park, and animal shows.

The St Louis Zoo showcases thousands of animals in a range of natural settings that include a tropical rainforest for apes. A new exhibit gives visitors an opportunity to see animals from a winding waterway. The zoo also boasts one of the country's few insectariums, while its Living World Education Center teaches visitors about ecology and wildlife.

Visitors to the small town of Stanton enjoy an inexpensive meal at a local bar.

Other St Louis attractions include the Eugene Field House and St Louis Toy Museum; the Scott Joplin House State Historic Site; the American Kennel Club Museum of the Dog, whose collections include a library of instructional videos that can be viewed in its theater; the International Bowling Museum; riverboat cruises on the Mississippi; and the 96-acre (39-ha) Laumeier Sculpture Park. The restored Union Station is a popular indoor marketplace.

The St Louis Symphony is one of the nation's oldest symphony orchestras. Forest Park's Muny outdoor theater stages 11 weeks of popular theater every summer. One of the nation's largest July 4th celebrations is also held in St Louis, with a three-day fair along the riverfront.

St Louis is serviced by buses, trains, and an international airport.
Map ref: page 383 K3

SPRINGFIELD

Southwestern Missouri's only city is home to 140,500 people and serves as a regional hub. Thanks to its location, it served an important role in the country's westward migration. Union and Confederate forces fought to control the city during the Civil War; the legacy of that battle can be seen at Wilson's Creek National Battlefield, 10 miles (16 km) southwest of Springfield. After the war, the city was home to James Butler Hickok, also known as Wild Bill Hickok, who once killed a man in the public square.

The following century, the nation's first transcontinental highway, Route 66, passed through Springfield, and parts of the old route can still be seen. Springfield is a good place to shop for antiques, especially at the Bass Country Antique Mall and the Commercial Street Historical District.

A more contemporary and very popular attraction is the Bass Pro Shops Outdoor World. The store is part theme park, part retail outlet, and part ode to the outdoors lifestyle. Its highlights include a 140,000-gallon (5,292 hl) game fish aquarium, a fishing and hunting museum, and a trout pond. Springfield's new Wonders of Wildlife, the American National Fish and Wildlife Museum, also appeals to outdoors enthusiasts.

Springfield has its own airport and is serviced by buses.
Map ref: page 382 D7

STANTON

This small settlement, about 45 miles (72 km) southwest of St Louis on I-44, is home to the Jesse James Wax Museum. But most visitors come to the area to see the nearby Meramec Caverns. Apart from its natural attractions—there are five floors of unusual formations—the cave complex boasts a rich history. Discovered in the early 1700s, it was later used by Union forces to store powder kilns during the Civil War. An outlaw band of Confederate irregulars, including Jesse James, seized their supplies. James later used the cave as a hideout. Modern visitors can take guided tours around the caves, which are now well-lit.
Map ref: page 383 H4

OHIO

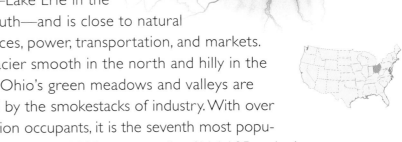

Because its north-central location makes it a strategic crossroads of the nation, Ohio attracted settlers from all parts of the country, and has developed a culture significant for its diversity. It is known as "The Buckeye State" because of the buckeye trees in the forests that once covered the land.

Ohio is important agriculturally; it sits between two principal waterways—Lake Erie in the north and the Ohio River in the south—and is close to natural resources, power, transportation, and markets.

Ohio farming land, between Millersburg and Berlin. The state is home to many food processing businesses (as well as producing a wide variety of agricultural produce)—from yogurt and pizza to soup, soybean oil, and ketchup.

Glacier smooth in the north and hilly in the south, Ohio's green meadows and valleys are dotted by the smokestacks of industry. With over 11 million occupants, it is the seventh most populous state. It is 44,828 square miles (116,105 sq km) in area, making it the 35th-largest state in size.

Ohio's name is taken from the Iroquois word meaning "great river," and it has produced many great men, including inventor Thomas Edison, astronauts John Glenn and Neil Armstrong, and eight presidents—William Harrison, Grant, Hayes, Garfield, Benjamin Harrison, McKinley, Taft, and Harding.

The earliest inhabitants built more than 10,000 mounds, many of them striking-looking effigy mounds. More recent architecture is eclectic. Ohio ranks third in the country for the number of sites listed on the National Register of Historic Places.

Ohio's industries carry across the eight major cities in the state, and include the construction of motor vehicles and equipment, steel and metal products, and tires and other rubber goods. Ohio is also a leader in the manufacturing of business machines, business tools, and road-building and earthmoving equipment.

Potteries are important to eastern Ohio. Lime, sand, gravel, and coal have figured prominently in Ohio's industrial capacity. There are plenty of cows, too, as well as soybeans, wheat, corn, vegetables, fruit, and greenhouse and nursery products.

State motto With God, All Things Are Possible
State flag Adopted 1902
Capital Columbus
Population 11,353,140
Total area (land and water) 44,828 square miles (116,105 sq km)
Land area 40,953 square miles (106,068 sq km)
Ohio is the 35th-largest state in size
Origin of name From the Iroquois word meaning "great river"
Nickname The Buckeye State
Abbreviations OH (postal), O.
State bird Cardinal
State flower Scarlet carnation
State tree Buckeye
Entered the Union March 1, 1803 as the 17th state

STATE FEATURE

Cincinnati

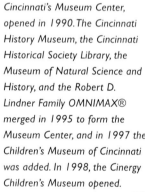

"Swine Lake" (sponsored by the Cincinnati Ballet), part of the Big Pig Gig Public Art Project, is set up at the Aronoff Center in Cincinnati. The five Miss Piggies, created by T.A. Boyle, are named Odile and Odette (from the ballet Swan Lake), Hoofanova, Porkiskaya, and Swine-Hilda.

Cincinnati's Museum Center, opened in 1990. The Cincinnati History Museum, the Cincinnati Historical Society Library, the Museum of Natural Science and History, and the Robert D. Lindner Family OMNIMAX® merged in 1995 to form the Museum Center, and in 1997 the Children's Museum of Cincinnati was added. In 1998, the Cinergy Children's Museum opened.

Cincinnati is a city between north and south, located on the border of bluegrass and mint julep Kentucky, brushing up against the east, but decidedly belonging to the Midwest. It is located at midpoint of the 981-mile (1,578-km) course of the Ohio River in the southwestern corner of Ohio, at an elevation of 540 feet (165 m). It is conservative, friendly, unpretentious—known for small-town charm and a cosmopolitan flavor. Winston Churchill called it "the most beautiful of America's inland cities," Charles Dickens described it "as a place that commends itself…favorably and pleasantly to a stranger," *Places Rated Almanac* rated it "America's most livable city," and poet Henry Wadsworth Longfellow immortalized it as "the Queen City."

City limits squeeze 364,000 people into roughly 78 square miles (202 sq km). But Greater Cincinnati encompasses three states, eight counties, and dozens of smaller cities, towns, and villages that take up 3,866 square miles (10,013 sq km) and include 1.7 million people; it is the 23rd largest city in the country.

Downtown is a basin surrounded on three sides by rolling hills—the geographic layout is often likened to an amphitheater. Fountain Square, with its elaborate bronze Tyler-Davidson Fountain—the Spirit of Water—is the heart of the city. A multi-million dollar redevelopment of downtown has built a skywalk that connects major hotels, stores, office complexes, restaurants, and entertainment centers. The riverfront has been renovated into an entertainment and recreation center.

Residents and visitors are flocking again to the middle of the city after a bleak period of withdrawal.

Early settlers battled smallpox, insects, floods, and crop failures. After General Anthony Wayne broke the resistance of the Ohio Indians, a large influx of German and Irish immigrants settled the area. In 1811 the first steamboat arrived, the *New Orleans*. The construction of the Erie and Miami Canals in the late 1820s gave farmers transport to the city and a market for their products. In the 1840s and 1850s Cincinnati boomed as a supplier of produce and goods to the South. After the Civil War, prosperity brought art, music, a new library, and one of the first professional baseball teams, the Cincinnati Red Stockings (now called the Cincinnati Reds). Late nineteenth-century political corruption led to the establishment of a city-manager form of government that has earned Cincinnati the title of America's best-governed city.

Cincinnati's skyline indicates its corporate power. Twin towers on the eastern edge are the world head-quarters for Proctor & Gamble, the consumer prod-ucts giant. Five other local businesses are on the Fortune 500 list of largest industrial companies—Chiquita Brands International (bananas); Cincinnati Milacron (robots and machines that make other products); Eagle-Picher Industries Inc. (industrial manufacturing); General Cable Corp. (electrical, automotive, and telecommunications wire and cables); and E.W. Scripps (media). The city also houses ten of Fortune 500's largest service companies.

Cincinnati is home to several colleges and uni-versities, including the University of Cincinnati (largely a commuter school), with 34,000 students, and the Jesuit Xavier University, with 6,000 students.

This is an active city, offer-ing festivals, music, one of the best zoos in the

country, excellent museums, opera and ballet, and outstanding professional sports teams.

Tall Stacks, a nationally renowned event that occurs in October every three or four years, goes back to the days when Cincinnati was one of the largest cities in the country. *Belle of Louisiana, The Delta Queen, Mississippi Queen*, and dozens of other paddlewheelers line the banks of the Ohio with their calliopes tooting, as they did a hundred years ago. Flatboats like the ones that carried settlers before steamboats pull into a landing set with hay bales, old storefronts, and people in period costumes. This event draws two million visitors.

The Flower Shower, run on the last weekend every April, is the best-known open-air flower and garden festival in the country, and the only North American flower show endorsed by the Royal Horticultural Society of Great Britain.

The Riverfest, held each Labor Day (the first Monday in September), brings 500,000 people to the waterfront to enjoy fireworks and watch musical performances. Another big annual event is Oktoberfest Zinzinnati: during mid-September, more than half a million people in six downtown blocks sing, dance, and enjoy beer, sausages, and sauerkraut. Seven stages, 50 food vendors, and a children's area make this the country's largest Octoberfest.

The Cincinnati Zoo is renowned for its collection of 100 endangered species and its birth programs for such exotic animals as Malaysian tapirs, okapis, white tigers, and gorillas. More than 100 white tigers have been born here. The Zoo Babies event, held each June, is especially popular. Jungle Trails is a mock African and Asian rainforest that exhibits flora and fauna. The Festival of Lights, held during the winter holidays, strings more than 1.5 million light bulbs above ice skaters, hayrides, and ice carvings, and the premises in general.

Since the early nineteenth century Cincinnati has had a distinguished cultural life. William H. McGuffey's *Eclectic Readers*, which were textbooks for many US primary schools, and Lyman Beecher's religious writings and sermons were printed in local publishing houses. Harriet Beecher Stowe, who used the area as a setting for parts of *Uncle Tom's Cabin*, lived in Cincinnati for 18 years.

The Cincinnati Symphony Orchestra was founded in 1894. It was the first US symphony orchestra to tour Europe, and regularly sells out venues such as Carnegie Hall in New York. Guest conductors and performers over the years have included Vladimir Horowitz, Beverly Sills, Benny Goodman, Marian Anderson, Sir Thomas Beecham, Enrico Caruso, Pablo Casals, Artur Rubenstein, Itzhak Perlman, Yo Yo Ma, and Ezio Pinza.

The Cincinnati Opera Company is the second-oldest opera company in the country—it gave its first performance in 1920 in a converted band shell at Cincinnati Zoo. It continued to perform at the zoo until it moved to the Music Hall in 1972. The company performs four operas a year.

The Cincinnati Pops performs indoors and outdoors, presenting top entertainers such as Ray Charles, Doc Severenson, and Roy Clark, and combining symphonic music with lasers, projections, fireworks, fire and water, and hot-air balloons.

The city has a grand cultural showcase, the US$82 million Aronoff Center for the Performing Arts. It opened in 1995, and has three performance halls. The Cincinnati Ballet, one of the top 10 in the country, plus dance theaters and Broadway shows are among its occupants.

The Cincinnati Art Museum's 118 galleries contain the world's largest collection of miniature art, several Picassos, a 300 BC Egyptian mummy, Andy Warhol's *Pete Rose* painting, a large collection of Frank Duveneck paintings, Rockwood pottery, Persian architecture dating back to 480 BC, marble carvings dating back to 2500 BC, Nabataen art, and Jin dynasty wood carvings. It is one of the oldest American art museums, having operated since 1876.

Professional baseball began in Cincinnati in 1869, and the first night game was played here when President Franklin Roosevelt threw a switch at the White House to turn on the ballpark lights. Former Cincinnati Reds player Pete Rose is baseball's all-time hit leader. The Reds, who have won five World Series, play on artificial turf at Cinergy Field.

The Cincinnati Bengals have reached two Super Bowls. They play in Paul Brown Stadium, which opened in 2000. The Cincinnati Cyclones play in the International Hockey League, a step below the major leagues, at Firstar Center, next to Cinergy Field. Cincinnati University has a strong basketball team, and has one of the famous names in college and pro basketball history—"the Big O," Oscar Robertson.

Cincinnati may be reached by car on I-74 and I-75 and by bus. The Greater Cincinnati/Northern Kentucky International Airport is located across the Ohio River in Kentucky.

The Roebling Suspension Bridge across the Ohio River. The bridge was designed by John A. Roebling, and the bridge was completed in 1866. Its central span was the longest in the world at that time, and the bridge was the first to use vertical suspenders and diagonal stays from both towers. It was largely rebuilt in the 1890s, and has been changed several more times—in the 1920s, 1950s, and in 1998.

Places in OHIO

AKRON

Akron, known as the "Rubber Capital of the World," and also as the "Home of Breakfast Cereal," is a city of 223,000 located 35 miles (53 km) south of Cleveland and the St Lawrence Seaway in the northeastern part of the state. Covering 54 square miles (140 sq km), it commands the highest point on the Ohio and Erie Canal. The name Akron is derived from the Greek word for "high."

Simon Perkins, promoter of the Ohio and Erie Canal, laid out the town in 1825. The canal opened in 1827 and Akron flourished. Benjamin Franklin Goodrich opened a rubber factory here in 1870; it aroused little interest. It took the "horseless carriage" to spark the future of Akron—its rubber industry boomed between 1910 and 1920. Other thriving nineteenth-century businesses included iron manufacturing, farm implements production, pottery, flour milling, and cereal.

In 1854 Ferdinand Schumacher began selling his homemade oatmeal, later founding Quaker Oats. Today's Quaker Square Mall and Entertainment Complex, in downtown Akron, is carved from the original Quaker Oats cereal mill. The Akron Hilton Inn is converted from the Quaker Oates silos, 120 feet (37 m) tall and 24 feet (7 m) in diameter; they once housed more than 1.5 million

Amish communities farm the area around Berlin and Millersburg. Their religion stresses humility, community, and family.

bushels of grain. The 196 hotel rooms are perdectly round and contain 450 square feet (43 sq m) of space–50 percent more than the average hotel room

Akron once led the world in the production of rubber goods. Local production is now minimal, but Akron is still the corporate home of Goodyear, Genic, and Uniroyal Goodrich. The Goodyear World of Rubber museum depicts the history of rubber, with exhibits of a rubber plantation, tires, memorabilia of Charles Goodyear, and a reproduction of his workshop. There is a videotape describing the tire production process, and a self-guiding tour.

The Stan Hywet Hall and Gardens were built between 1911 and 1915 by Frank A. Seiberling, founder of the Goodyear and

Dr Bob Smith and Bill Wilson founded Alcoholics Anonymous in this Akron house.

Seiberling Rubber companies. The 65-room house is a fine examples of Tudor Revival architecture. The furnishings include Tudor and Stuart furniture, antique silver, pewter, and sixteenth and seventeenth-century Flemish tapestries. The 70-acre (28-ha) grounds include a fully restored English garden, lagoons, scenic vistas, and a Japanese garden.

The Simon Perkins Mansion, the estate of Simon Perkins Jr, son of Akron's founder, is a stone Greek Revival structure, built in 1835. It is furnished with glass, Victorian costuming, and pottery. Across the street is the John Brown House. Brown was a sheep farmer and liberator of slaves who was hanged. His farmstead contains period clothing and firearms. The Hower House is a handsome Second Empire-Italianate mansion, built in 1871 for industrialist John Henry Hoover. It has a lavish interior and original family furnishings.

Today Akron is a center for scientific research. The Firestone and Goodyear Laboratories focus on rubber and plastics research. The original spacesuits worn by US astronauts were made and fitted by B.F. Goodrich. The University of Akron's Institute of Polymer Science is renowned for its work.

The Akron Museum of Art is an 1899 Italian Renaissance-style post office that has been has been transformed into an exciting modern facility. Then there is Dr Bob's Home, where Alcoholics Anonymous was founded in 1935.

Memorabilia and a library that belonged to Dr Bob Smith and his wife Anne are housed here.

Inventure Place is a dramatic contemporary building in downtown Akron, designed by architect James Stewart Polshek. It pays homage to great men and women inventors. It's a fun place, where potatoes are clocks, eggs fly, the sky can be plucked, and a person can take off in a bath tub.Hands-on exhibits, displays, and workshops help visitors appreciate the contributions of great thinkers. The building's centerpiece is a soaring stainless-steel sail, which houses five tiers of National Inventors Hall of Fame exhibits.

The Akron Civic Theatre has a lavish design, and a ceiling with blinking stars and floating clouds —it is one of the last "atmospheric" theaters. The Carousel Dinner Theatre is America's largest professional dinner theater.

The All-American Soap Box Derby has been held at Derby Downs each August since 1934. Boys and girls aged nine to 16 who have won local championships all over the world compete in their homemade gravity-propelled vehicles. The soap box idea was developed by Dayton, Ohio news photographer Myron Scott, who covered a race of cars built by boys in his hometown and created a national program.

Akron may be reached by car on I-76, I-77, and Hwy 8, or by bus or plane.

Map ref: page 381 N2

BERLIN

Berlin is a village of 3,100 located in the heart of Amish country, 33 miles (53 km) southwest of Canton in the northeastern part of the state. The Amish live without electricity, motors, or engines of any kind, maintaining a simple rural way of life. The country roads here are traveled by Amish horse-drawn buggies. The Amish sell crafts, antiques, and homemade foods at roadside stands and in shops.

Behalt, a 265-foot (81-m) cyclorama, illustrates the heritage of the Amish and Mennonite people. At Schrock's Amish Farm, a guided tour and videotape present Amish life in the surrounding area.

Two miles (3 km) north of Berlin is the Rolling Ridge Ranch. A ride through 80 acres (32 ha) of woods and meadows passes among 350 domestic and exotic animals, including zebras, Watusi cattle, and water buffalo.

The Wendell August Forge is 4 miles (6 km) north of Berlin. Forged aluminum, bronze, pewter, and silver items are on display. Visitors can watch artisans, explore a museum, and take a tour.

Berlin may be reached by car on US-62 and Hwy 39.
Map ref: page 381 M3

CANTON

Canton joins with Massillon 20 miles (32 km) south of Akron in the northeastern part of Ohio. Canton, with a population of 84,161, and Massillon, with 31,000, lie on the edge of a "steel valley" where three branches of Nimishillen Creek come together. The area is one of the largest producers of specialty steels in the world. Canton is also well known as the home of the Pro Football Hall of Fame, and of former US President William McKinley.

First settled in 1805, Canton was bypassed by the Ohio and Erie Canal, but emerged as an important steel center by the end of the nineteenth century. William McKinley, born in nearby Niles in 1843, came to Canton in 1867 to set up a law practice. He then became active in politics, serving in Congress for 14 years and as governor for four years. In 1896 McKinley conducted his "front porch campaign" for the presidency. He was elected, and then was reelected in 1900, but in 1901, while visiting Buffalo, NY, he was assassinated.

The McKinley Complex honors the former president. It includes a National Memorial, a Museum of History and Industry, and Discover World. The memorial, in which McKinley is interred with his wife Ida and their two daughters, is a large circular mausoleum with two domes that are made of pink granite from Massachusetts.

The Museum of History goes back two centuries. It contains a pioneer kitchen, historic toys, the Street of Shops, and an exhibit of nineteenth-century interiors, including a lawyer's office and a print shop. Other features are a 1908 Martin glider and displays concerning important local industries, such as the production of steel and roller bearings. An operating HO-gauge model train complex represents the Pennsylvania Railroad tracks that pass through many towns in the area.

A life-sized robotic allosaurus roars in the nearby Discover World. Fossil remains, a massive mastodon skeleton, prehistoric Native American cultures, and outer space are on display. Space Station Earth shows how air reacts under pressure and examines light waves and lasers.

Pro football began in Canton in 1920, which resulted in the building of the Pro Football Hall of Fame here. A four-building complex offers exhibition areas, a movie theater, and research library. A 7-foot (2-m) bronze statue of Jim Thorpe, an early football hero, greets visitors. A 52-foot (16-m) dome in the shape of a football encases the Professional Football Today displays, in which all current

Berlin is renowned for its Amish handicrafts.

National Football League teams are represented. Features include an art gallery; the Leagues of Champions Rooms, which chronicle the histories of the American Football League, the NFL, and the Super Bowl; and a historical tribute to early African-American players in Pro Football. The week-long Pro Football Hall of Fame Festival takes place during July. Visitors can meet football greats, and participate in a range of activities include a hot-air balloon invitation, a food festival, fireworks, a ribs burn-off, a drum corps contest, the induction of newly enshrined members, and a football game.

In next-door Massillon, the Massillon Museum lies behind the facade of a renovated 1931 Art Deco building on historic Lincoln Highway. Contemporary art, photography, textiles, and local glass are featured. The modernistic display cases may be opened, but artwork may not be touched. Some 2,620 miniature pieces make up the complete Immel Circus.

At the Canton Classic Car Museum, more than 40 models from 1904 through 1981 are presented among the fashions and antiques of their eras. The 1937 "Bandit Car," for instance, was purchased by the Canton Police Department to retaliate against mobsters. It has gun ports in the windows, bulletproof tires, and trunk and rear-seat arsenals.

Canton is known as a place to play golf, as 40 golf courses are located with a 50-mile (80-km) radius of the town.

Canton may be reached by car on I-77, US-30 and US-62, as well as by bus.
Map ref: page 381 N3

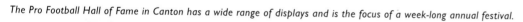

The Pro Football Hall of Fame in Canton has a wide range of displays and is the focus of a week-long annual festival.

A paper mill in Chillicothe. Forestry products have long been big business in Ohio.

CHILLICOTHE

Chillicothe is on the west side of the Scioto River Valley, 45 miles (72 km) south of Columbus. It is an industrial city of 21,923; Mount Logan, just east of town, is pictured on the state seal.

This part of the valley was once a major center of the Hopewell Culture, which flourished from 200 BC to AD 500. The wealth of ancient sites in this area inspired two local residents, Ephraim S. Squier and Edwin H. Davis to investigate and map many of them. *Ancient Monuments of the Mississippi Valley*, their 1848 book, was the first publication of the Smithsonian Institute.

Chillicothe is named for Challagawtha, the Shawnee Indian village that previously occupied the site. The town was the capital of the Northwest Territory, and the state capital from 1803 to 1810 and 1812 to 1816. In the 1830s and 1840s Chillicothe thrived as a port before rail traffic superseded the inland waterways.

The Ross County Historical Society houses its collections in three houses. Antiques, period furnishings, pioneer crafts, Indian artifacts, and exhibits pertinent to Ohio statehood are found at the McClintock Residence, built in 1838. The McKell Library, also built in 1838, houses books and manuscripts. Exhibits related to nineteenth-century women are displayed in the 1901 Franklin House.

The Adena State Memorial is a Georgian stone mansion built in 1806–07. It was designed by Benjamin Latrobe, who directed the reconstruction of the Capitol in Washington DC after the British burned it in the War of 1812. A tenant house, smokehouse, washhouse, barn, and springhouse now occupy the site.

The *Chillicothe Gazette*, first published in 1800, is the oldest continuously published newspaper west of the Allegheny Mountains. On display here are two cases with written matter from Babylonian times, wooden printing blocks from Asia, and a page from the Gutenberg Bible.

The drama "Tecumseh" is presented at Sugarloaf Mountain Amphitheatre, about 6 miles (10 km) northeast of Chillicothe, from mid-June to early September. The play traces the struggle of Tecumseh to preserve a home for the Shawnee Nation.

Chillicothe may be reached by car on US-35, US-50, US-23, and Hwy 159, as well as by bus.
Map ref: page 381 K6

CLEVELAND

Cleveland is an old steel, railway, and oil city on the banks of Lake Erie in northeast Ohio. It is jokingly referred to as "the Mistake on the Lake," but is actually quite a nice place, particularly rich in culture and parkland. A population of 2.9 million makes Greater Cleveland the largest city in Ohio.

The city skyline is highlighted by the 52-story Terminal Tower, which once housed the Union Railroad Station. Now a three-level mall called The Avenue fills the space. The Society Center on Cleveland's Public Square, which opened in 1992, stands at 948 feet (289 m)—it is the tallest structure in Cleveland and one of the tallest 25 buildings in the world.

The 10-acre (4-ha) Public Square is dominated by the Cuyahoga County Soldiers and Sailors Monument, which commemorates men who served in the Civil War. Completed in 1894, it is a stone building surrounded by a 125-foot (38-m) granite shaft that holds aloft a 15-foot (4.5-m) Statue of Liberty. Bronze sculptures representing the four armed service branches adorn the structure. The finest architectural expression of Cleveland's industrial might is the Cleveland Arcade, two nine-story office buildings joined by a five-story skylighted court, with ornate iron galleries, stairs, and balustrades.

Since 1950, the population within city limits has declined by nearly one-third as residents have moved to the suburbs. But in recent decades Cleveland has attracted new enterprises and jobs. It is the nation's 12th largest consumer market, and headquarters for many industrial corporations and smaller companies.

Cleveland's earliest settlers included British and Scottish New Englanders. These were followed by Irish, Germans, Bohemians, Hungarians, and Poles, eager to farm or build canals, as well as Italian and Eastern European craftspeople. Today the city also includes African-Americans, Greeks, Asians, Puerto Ricans, Czechs, Slovaks, Slovenes, Croats, and Serbs, providing a wide variety of cultural festivals and cuisine.

Despite its industrial bent, Cleveland also knows how to appreciate life. It has almost 19,000 acres (7,695 ha) of metropolitan parks, and rivers, streams, and lakes, including 90 miles (145 km) of scenic Lake Erie and

The Cuyahoga River, Cleveland—legislation after a 1969 river fire has seen this once badly polluted river return to life.

Cleveland lakefront; Cleveland was once known as "Forest City." The Cuyahoga River Valley, where refineries, oil tanks, and steel mills once made fortunes, is now known for the entertainment and dining area along the river called the Flats. Cleveland is also home to many universities, including Case Western Reserve, John Carroll, and Cleveland State.

Shaker Heights, a scenic area of woods, lakes, and winding boulevards, is a classic example of the early twentieth-century "garden city" ideal. Shaker Square boasts Georgian Revival buildings around a traffic circle.

The Cleveland Museum of Art is one the world's top art museums. Its collections include more than 48,000 items, ranging from ancient Egyptian art to twentieth-century works. The museum is especially noted for its medieval collection and Asian art. Well-known paintings here include Caravaggio's "Crucifixion of St Andrew," John Singleton Conley's portrait of Nathaniel Hurd, and Albert Pinkham Ryder's "Death on a Pale Horse." The American painting collection is particularly noted for its nineteenth-century landscapes by Frederick E. Church, Thomas Cole, George Inness, and Winslow Homer. The museum

displays one of America's most popular sporting images, George Bellow's 1907 boxing scene "Stag at Sharkey's."

The excellent Cleveland Museum of Natural History features the Gallery of Gems and Jewels, which showcases more than 1,500 rare and precious stones, jewelry, and lapidary artworks. Astronomy and geology are integrated in the Reinberger Hall of Earth and Planetary Exploration.

The Great Lakes Science Center, located on the section of Lake Erie known as North Coast Harbor, contains 50,000 square feet (4,750 sq m) of hands-on exhibits. Center highlights include an indoor tornado, a bridge of fire, and the Polymer Fun House. Other Cleveland attractions include the Health Museum of Cleveland, which dramatizes the workings of the human body with the likes of Juno, the Transparent Talking Woman, and the Giant Tooth; and the Rock and Roll Hall of Fame and Museum, which presents film clips, photos, animation, and a retrospective of music videos from MTV's beginnings to the present.

The Cleveland Orchestra performs mid-September through May at the Severance Hall in the University Circle Area, and at the open-air Blossom Music Center from July 4 through early September. Cleveland has outstanding theater groups and the renowned Cleveland San Jose Ballet.

With one of the largest concentrations of parkland per capita in the nation, hiking, biking, picnicking, horseback riding, golfing, swimming, and many other water sports and winter sports are popular here. Spectator sports are big, too—the Cleveland Indians in baseball, football's Cleveland Browns, and basketball's Cleveland Cavaliers.

Cleveland may be reached by on I-90, I-77, and I-71, and by bus. The city has two separate airports —Booth Hopkins International, and Burke Lakefront Airport.
Map ref: page 381 N1

COLUMBUS

Columbus is the state capital and home of Ohio State University. Located nearly exactly in middle of the state, its city population of 632,910 makes it the largest in

Throughout the year, Columbus hosts many arts, music, and food festivals and fairs.

Ohio, but as a metropolitan area it is far smaller than Cleveland or Cincinnati. Columbus is a city on the cutting edge of scientific and technological progress. It has broad tree-lined streets and parks as well as impressive modern buildings designed by many of the country's leading architects.

In 1812 residents of Franklinton, a county seat along the Ohio River, offered the state 1,200 acres of land and $50,000 to erect a Capitol building and a penitentiary on the opposite bank of the Scioto River. The offer was accepted, and the capital was built on the new site, which was named Columbus. Within decades Columbus began to overshadow Franklinton, drawing its people and business.

Known as the "Hat Box Capitol" because of its distinctive rotunda, the Capitol building, built by penitentiary inmates, is one of the country's finest examples of Greek Revival architecture, called by Frank Lloyd Wright "the most honest of state capitols." It is constructed of Columbus limestone and is one of the few that doesn't have a dome. It is decorated with 24-carat gold leaf, and took six architects 22 years to complete— it finally opened in 1857. Tours and displays are available.

The Ohio Agriculture and Mechanical College (now Ohio State University) opened in 1873. The university developed the forerunner of the computer, the xerography process, and many advances in the medical treatment of the

physically impaired. One of the largest universities in the country, Ohio State has 19 colleges, a graduate school, more than 120 departments, a medical center, libraries with more than four million volumes, 58,000 students, and a famous football team.

Columbus ranks with Washington DC as a center of science and technology. More than 150 high-tech companies are located here. Columbus was one of the first areas offering city-wide cable television and the 24-hour banking machine. It is also a center for retail banking, insurance, and real estate, and has become a leading convention city.

Because Columbus is so representative of America, many products are tested here, among them the fast-food menus of food chains. The city is nicknamed "Test Market, USA."

Columbus has a number of annual events and festivals. The OSU Jazz Festival takes place in April at the university; in June there is a Columbus Arts Festival, with music, dance, and theater performances, arts, crafts, and food; and in August there is the Ohio State Fair, one of the largest state fairs in the nation, held at the Ohio Expo Center. Octoberfest is held in September, and the Columbus International Food Festival in November mixes ethnic foods, cultures, and souvenirs while musicians and dancers of many different nationalities continuously perform on several stages.

There's a lot to do in downtown Columbus. Probably the most popular place to visit is German Village, said to be the largest restored neighborhood in the United States. The brick-lined streets, slate roofs, ironwork, and flower boxes go back to the 1800s. The Octoberfest is held here, and a house and garden tour is offered. The Golden Hobby Shop, in the village's 125-year-old brick schoolhouse, offers many needlepoint items, and has a toy room and outdoor gallery.

The new Center of Science and Industry Columbus (COSI), covering 300,000 square feet (28,500 sq m), exhibits Learning Worlds, or high-tech displays. It offers an unusual 3-D space show and presentations in four theaters, while it celebrates achievements in technology and gadgets that have molded our lives.

The Columbus Museum of Art exhibits American and European art from 1850 to 1950 as well as traveling shows. At the Columbus Zoo, 650 animal species from all over the world are on display, including Coco, the first gorilla born in captivity. The Martin Luther King Jr Performing and Cultural Arts Complex features African-American art in two galleries, and its 440-seat theater offers plays, dance, and music.

The old-fashioned North Market features 30 merchants and weekend entertainment at a location that has operated since 1876. The Civil War era is re-created at the Ohio Village and the Ohio Historical Center. A museum-quality replica of the *Santa Maria*, the sailing vessel that brought Christopher Columbus (for

The old and the new—a history of aviaton—at Dayton's US Airforce Museum.

whom the city is named) to America from Spain, is docked downtown on the Scioto River, in Battelle Riverfront Park. The house of comic writer James Thurber and the Motorcycle Hall of Fame Museum are among other Columbus attractions.

At the Franklin Park Conservatory and Botanical Garden, changing exhibits provide in-depth exploration of the seven climatic zones. Just north of the city, in Westerville, 92-acre (37-ha) Inniswood Metropark Gardens presents nine garden areas, along with natural woodland trails and running brooks.

Columbus may be reached by car on I-70 and I-71, as well as by bus. Its airport is Port Columbus International.
Map ref: page 381 K5

Columbus' city skyline rises behind an old bridge over the Scioto River.

CUYAHOGA VALLEY NATIONAL RECREATION AREA

The 33,000 acres (13,365 ha) of this park run along a 22-mile (35-km) section of Cuyahoga River between Akron and Cleveland. The river flood plain, streams, and creeks move into forested valleys and upland plateaus. Bicycling, hiking, picnicking, horseback riding, cave exploration, and visits to waterfalls are popular summer activities. Canal lock demonstrations are given on weekends by park service staff and volunteers wearing period costume. One of the visitor centers is in a canal history museum that once was a hotel, general store, tavern, and dance hall.

The Cuyahoga Valley Line Railroad takes passengers on a 52-mile (84-km) park trip with stops at Hale Farm and Village or Akron. A 90-minute fall-color train excursion is offered in October.

Winter activities include ice skating, cross-country skiing, sledding, and snowshoeing. The park has two downhill ski areas—Boston Mills Ski Resort (seven slopes, six chair lifts, and two surface tows); and Brandywine Ski Resort (one triple chair, four quad lifts, three handle tows, and a vertical drop of 250 feet [76 m]).

Cuyahoga Valley National Recreation Area may be reached by car on I-80 and I-271, and by bus. Cleveland and its two airports, Hopkins International and Burke Lakefront, are nearby.
Map ref: page 381 N2

DAYTON

Dayton is an industrial city of 182,000 people 55 miles (88 km) north of Cincinnati in the south-western part of the state. It is on a fork of the Miami River, which curves into the Stillwater River. Mad Creek and Wolf Creek join these rivers—the city has 28 bridges. Dayton was settled in 1796 and named for General Jonathan Dayton. Today Dayton is home to more than 830 high-tech companies.

Many original buildings stand in the 12-block Oregon Historic District, the location of one of the city's first communities. Courthouse Square is the center of downtown and the venue for concerts and street entertainment.

Dayton was the home of Orville and Wilbur Wright, who in 1903 in Kitty Hawk, North Carolina became the first men to fly an airplane. Dayton has a number of memorials and sites dedicated to these aviation pioneers. Their home is open to visitors. At 65-acre (26-ha) Carillon Historical Park, a museum of history, transport, and invention, the Wright Flyer III—the plane in which Orville and Wilbur taught themselves to fly—is on display. Also at the museum are antique autos, a plush railroad car, and a replica of the Wright Brothers' bicycle shop. The Wrights' 1905 airplane, a 1930s print shop, and a nineteenth-century schoolhouse are other museum exhibits.

The Wright Cycle Company and Hoover Block are where the brothers combined their printing and bicycle businesses. While working there they began their early work in aviation. The bike shop has historic photos and artifacts, and was declared a National Historic Landmark in 1990. The nearby Hoover Block building once housed their business, "Wright and Wright Printing," which printed the work of another Dayton luminary, poet Paul Laurence Dunbar.

The Dayton Heritage National Historical Park honors the Wrights and Dunbar with historic buildings and an Aviation Trail through the Convention and Visitors Bureau.

Women of aviation are not forgotten here. The International Women's Air and Space Museum is located in a nineteenth-century limestone house in Centerville, a Dayton suburb. This small museum honors women aviators such as Amelia Earhart and Jacqueline

Loudonville farming land. Ohio's biggest industry is agribusiness—raw produce (from soybeans to celery), food processing, forestry, and the nursery/horticulture industry.

Cochran, women astronauts, and women who participated in Desert Storm, the US war against Iraq. A special display honors Katharine Wright, who inspired the efforts of her brothers.

Dayton's connection with flying continues at the US Air Force Museum, the oldest and largest military aviation museum in the world. Aviation films are shown on a gigantic screen with dynamic sound. Ten acres (4 ha) of exhibits span the history of flight from hot air balloons to the B-1 bomber. The World War I Sopwith Camel, an original Wright wind tunnel, an XB Valkyrie, and the original Apollo command module are on display. Discovery Hangar Five explains the hows and whys of flight, and different types of planes, their parts, and how they work.

The city's biggest annual event is the Dayton Air Show, held each July at the city's airport in Vandalia. Jets, aerobatics, barnstormers, sky divers, air racers, balloons, and pyrotechnics contribute to the show. This air show attracts a quarter of a million spectators and 150 types of aircraft.

Dayton has many other attractions, including the Aullwood Audubon Center and Farm. This 350-acre (142-ha) wildlife sanctuary features a nature center and an educational farm. More than 200 examples of animal, bird, and plant life are on display, and there are trails through streams, woodland, and meadows.

The Boonshoft Museum of Discovery houses natural history exhibits including animals common in Ohio. Its Philips Space Theater has a planetarium with a state-of-the-art Digistar system that takes visitors on computerized star treks through the universe. On display are tools, jewelry, and other artifacts of the peoples who inhabited the Miami Valley 14,000 years ago, as well as an Egyptian tomb.

Sun Watch Thirteenth-Century Indian Village explores the life of a group of Ohio's early farmers, the Fort Ancient Indians. They settled along the Great Miami River, and after 20 years of excavation constructed a thatched village and stockade. Sun Watch is a National Historic Landmark.

The Dayton Art Institute, built in 1930, has a collection of African, American, Asian, and European art, including photographs, sculpture, furniture, and decorative art. It has more than 10,000 items, spanning 5,000 years. Its Experiencenter is a participatory center with thematic shows. Its library contains books and periodicals about art and architecture.

The Citizens Motorcar Company, America's Packard Museum is located in a restored dealership. About 20 Packard models dating from 1899 to 1956 are displayed in an Art Deco showroom that has a working service department.

The Cox Arboretum and Gardens is a 175-acre (71-ha) preserve with nature trails, a shrub garden, water garden, edible landscape garden, plant collections, and a butterfly house. The Arboretum Visitor Center has a horticultural reference library, an auditorium, and seasonal art exhibits.

Dayton may be reached by car on I-75, US-35, and Hwys 48 and 35, and by bus and plane.
Map ref: page 381 H5

FORT HILL STATE MEMORIAL AND NATURE RESERVE

This prehistoric earthwork, believed to have been built by the Hopewell Indians, is 70 miles (113 km) east of Cincinnati. An earthen and stone wall, ranging from 6 to 15 feet (1.8 to 4.6 m) in height and 30 to 40 feet (9 to 12 m) at its base, encloses 48 acres (19 ha) at the summit of a steep hill. The earthworks lie at the center of a 1,186-acre (480-ha) nature preserve that is an isolated pocket of Appalachia flora and fauna. A deep gorge cut by the Baker's Fork of Brush Creek borders the area on the north and west. The museum has exhibits about the prehistoric earthwork and Fort Hill's natural history. Picnic facilities and 11 miles (18 km) of hiking trails are within the grounds.

Fort Hill is located on Hwy 41.
Map ref: page 381 H5

LOUDONVILLE

Located 10 miles (16 km) east of Mansfield in the north-central part of Ohio, Loudonville is the birthplace of Charles F. Kettering, the engineer who invented the electric automobile starter. Loudonville, population 2,900, has many beautiful streams and rivers—it is called the "Canoe Capital of Ohio."

Mohican State Park is in Mohican State Forest. At the upper edge of the forest is the 113-foot (34-m) Pleasant Hill Dam, the highest dam in the Muskingum Conservancy. The Mohican River forms a gorge 1,000 feet (305 m) wide at the top and 200 to 300 feet (61 to 92 m) deep; it is popular for canoeing. Mohican Country Stables, which offer horseback riding, are also in Loudonville.

Loudonville may be reached by car on Hwys 39 and 3.
Map ref: page 381 M3

MANSFIELD

Mansfield, population 50,600, is 75 miles (121 km) southwest of Cleveland. It was laid out in 1808 by the Surveyor General of the United States, Jared Mansfield, for whom it is named. A pioneer log blockhouse, built as protection against the Indians in the War of 1812–14, still stands in South Park, in the city's western district.

As the surrounding lands were cleared and cultivated in the 1820s, Mansfield became a center of trade and commerce. In the late 1840s and 1850s the railroads and telegraph drew industries such as Ohio Brass Co. and Aultman and Taylor. Today Mansfield is a diversified industrial center.

John Chapman, better known as Johnny Appleseed, planter of apple seeds and pruner of apple trees, lived and traveled in Richland County for many years. Pulitzer-Prize winning novelist Louis Bromfield was born here. John Sherman, brother of General William T. Sherman and author of the Sherman Anti-Trust Act, is also from Mansfield.

Mansfield is well known for its artists—their paintings, watercolors, photographs, quilts, and weavings can be seen at the Mansfield Art Center.

Kingwood Center covers 47 acres (19 ha) and has landscaped gardens and trails through woodland to ponds with waterfowl, and greenhouses filled with flowers and other plants. The gardens have a large display of tulips, plus other perennials—irises, daffodils, peonies, day lilies, and roses—and an herb garden. Kingwood Hall, a

An Ohio barn with the right attitude.

Amish farmers, Ohio. They use only old-fashioned farming methods that tie in with their belief in separating from the world .

French Provincial-style mansion, has an excellent horticultural reference library.

The Living Bible Museum has two museums. The Life of Christ contains 21 life-size dioramas, with an audiovisual accompaniment. Miracles of the Old Testament presents 19 dioramas, providing a close look at the Old Testament. Also on display are a collection of rare Bibles, immigrant American religious folk art, and woodcarvings.

Richland Carousel Park, with its hand-carved carousel, is located in a restored downtown area.

Mansfield may be reached by car on I-71 and US-30, and by plane. Map ref: page 381 L3

MARIETTA

Marietta is 100 miles (160 km) southeast of Columbus, across from West Virginia. The beautiful treefilled town of 15,000, sits at the confluence of the Ohio and Muskingum Rivers. Now a producer of oil, plastics, rubber, paints, glass, dolls, safes, and concrete, it is the oldest settlement in Ohio and the Northwest Territory.

In 1788, a venturesome group of New England investors called the Ohio Company and Associates purchased 1.5 million acres (607,500 ha) in the southeast corner of what is now Ohio. Surveyors, carpenters, and artisans led by General Rufus Putnam, a Revolutionary War veteran who served on George Washington's staff, floated down the Ohio River and founded Marietta. The name Marietta was chosen to honor Queen Marie Antoinette, in recognition of the aid rendered to the colonies by France during the Revolutionary War. Many of the settlers who followed were soldiers who received land in place of cash for their service in that war.

Putnam and the settlers constructed a fortification overlooking the river and named it Campus Martius ("Field of Mars"), for the military camp where the legions of ancient Rome trained. The Campus Martius Museum of the Northwest Territory recreates the founding and early development of Marietta. It has exhibits of Native American crafts and costumes, original furnishings, tools, agricultural implements, and decorative art. One wing contains the Rufus Putnam house, the only structure from the historic stockade still standing on its original foundation. The 1788 two-story house is built

of planks and posts. Also on the site is the plank-and-clapboard Ohio Company Land Office, from which land grants were made and the territory surveyed and platted.

The Ohio River Museum touches on a broad spectrum of Ohio River history with exhibits that focus upon the natural history and early exploration of the river and the age of steamboat travel. Visitors may board the *W.P. Snyder Jr*, which is moored alongside the museum and is the last surviving example of a steam, stern-wheeled towboat. The museum displays scale models of nineteenth-century riverboats, pictures, whistles, and a calliope. The theater presents a videotape, "Fire on the Water." Also on the grounds are a replica of the flatboat, the river conveyance that carried eighteenth and nineteenth-century settlers into Ohio before the steamboat arrived, and the pilot house and river steamboat *Tell City*.

The *Valley Gem*, a replica of a sternwheeler, offers summer and fall cruises along the Muskingum and Ohio Rivers.

The Castle, in the heart of the historic district, is an 1855 mansion—an outstanding example of Gothic Revival architecture.

Ohio Company settlers found many prehistoric earthworks on the river bluff. The earthworks

were surveyed and mapped, and some became public squares. Conus Mound, built by the Adena Indians between 800 BC and AD 100, stands 30 feet (9 m) tall in Mound Cemetery; many early settlers, including Rufus Putnam, are buried here.

Harmar Village, across the Putnam Bridge by car or the Harmar Bridge by foot, began as a fort in 1785. It now contains four museums. Butch's Cola Museum goes through the history of colas. Harmar Station has a large collection of electric toy trains. The 1847 Fearing House displays period furnishings, and there is a Children's Toy and Doll Museum.

Marietta may be reached by car on Hwys 7 and 60; it is just west of I-77. It can also be reached by bus.
Map ref: page 381 N6

MILLERSBURG

Millersburg, population 3,100, is located 34 miles (55 km) southwest of Canton. Four blocks to the south of Courtyard Square stands a 28-room Queen Anne-style house that was built in 1902. It has parquet floors, elegant windows, hand-painted ceilings, a third-floor ballroom, a 1920s steam bath, and a summer kitchen.

Millersburg may be reached by car on US-62 and Hwys 241, 39, and 83.
Map ref: page 381 M3

NEWARK

This industrial city with 44,400 residents, located 28 miles (45 km) east of Columbus, is known for its large prehistoric mounds.

Newark was founded in 1802 by a man who named it for his New Jersey home town. Like its namesake, Newark became a center of trade and industry after the completion of the Ohio and Erie Canal in 1832 and the arrival of railroads in the 1850s.

A monument commemorating the opening of the canal by New York Governor Dewitt Clinton in 1825 stands 3 miles (5 km) south of town on Hwy 79. On nearby Buckeye Lake is Cranberry Island, a sphagnum bog that was formed at the end of the Ice Age. It contains alder bush, sundew, poison sumac, and other plants.

The Licking County Historical Society exhibits three restored houses: the Sherwood-Davidson House, a frame structure built around 1815, contains eighteenth- and nineteenth-century furnishings and collections; the 1835 Buckingham House and Webb House focus on the early twentieth century. Louis Sullivan's Old Home Bank, a square stone building completed in 1914, is downtown.

The Newark Earthworks was a rich assortment of earthen structures—circles, parallel embankments, a square, an octagon—scattered over a terrace overlooking the tributaries of the Licking River. They were built by the Hopewell Culture, between 200 BC and

AD 500. Many of the earthworks have been destroyed by agriculture and the encroaching city, but some on the western edge of Newark have been preserved or restored.

Octagon State Memorial is the major site. The earthworks here enclosed 50 acres (20 ha) of the 138-acre (56-ha) tract of land. The 66-acre (27-ha) Mound Builders Memorial encompasses a large circular wall known as the Great Circle Earthworks—it is 1,200 feet (366 m) in diameter, and encloses 26 acres (11 ha) of land; its grass-covered walls vary in height from 8 to 14 feet (2.5 to 4.3 m). The effigy mound in the circle may represent a bird in flight.

The Ohio Indian Art Museum on the memorial grounds is devoted to prehistoric Native American art, with the cultures of Ohio represented in various media.

The National Heisey Glass Museum has a collection of 5,000 pieces of glassware made at A.H. Heisey Co. from 1896 to 1957.

Newark may be reached by car on Hwys 16, 13, and 79.
Map ref: page 381 L5

SANDUSKY

Located midway between Toledo and Cleveland on Lake Erie, Sandusky is the second-largest coal-shipping port on the Great Lakes and a center of industry. The city of 29,764 stretches for more than 6 miles (10 km) along 18-mile (29-km) Sandusky Bay, a natural harbor formed by the Cedar Point and Marblehead peninsulas.

Sandusky was visited by French explorer Robert LaSalle in 1679 and later by English trader George Crogham in 1760, but it wasn't until 1816 that the town was settled and given the Wyandot Native American name Sandouske, which means "cold water."

With lakeside resorts, wineries, fishing, and access to Lake Erie Islands, Sandusky became a summer tourist center in 1882.

Cedar Point is a 364-acre (147-ha) amusement/theme park and resort that opened in 1870. Of its 68 rides, 14 are roller coasters. The Millennium Force, the 310-foot (95-m) roller coaster that opened in 2000, gives its riders a 92-mph (148-kmph) plunge. Other rides are the Mantis, whose passengers must stand; the Raptor; the wooden Mean Streak; and the magnum XL-200. There are also three water rides and a 300-foot (92-m) Power Tower.

Musical shows, Camp Snoopy, a sandy beach, and miniature golf are other attractions. Soak City, on the northeast corner of Cedar Point, has water slides and pools.

The Follett House Museum is an 1834 Greek Revival mansion built by businessman Oran Follett, who fought against slavery and helped establish the Republican Party. It contains items from early times to the present, including possessions of Confederate officers imprisoned on Johnson's Island.

Sandusky may be reached by car on Hwys 101 and 4, and on US-250 and US-6, as well as by bus.
Map ref: page 381 L1

A marina at Sandusky. The Bayfront Corridor and the town's many marinas provide great public access to its long waterfront.

SERPENT MOUND STATE MEMORIAL

The earth snake from which this area takes its name rises about 5 feet (1.5 m) above the ground, is about 20 feet (6 m) wide, and writhes through a distance of 1,348 feet (411 m). The tail is coiled and the mouth seems to be clenching a large oval. The form was marked on the ground with stones and lumps of clay, and baskets filled with earth were then piled on top.

The memorial is located 62 miles (100 km) east of Cincinnati and 5 miles (8 km) west of Locust Grove. Investigations suggest it was built by the Adena people, between 800 BC and AD 400. The site was first excavated by Frederic Ward Putnam, who in 1887 raised money to save it from destruction. In 1888 the Ohio legislature passed the nation's first law protecting archeological sites.

The memorial has an observation tower, a gorge, and a museum, which contains a diorama showing how the mound was built, a replica of an Adena burial mound, and artifacts excavated by Putnam.

Serpent Mound State Memorial may be reached by car on Hwy 73.

SOUTH BASS ISLAND, PERRY'S MEMORIAL

One of the most famous messages in American history, Oliver Hazard Perry's "We have met the enemy, and they are ours," is engraved here.

The park and museum commemorate Perry and the Battle of Lake Erie, on September 10, 1813. The 27-year-old stationed his flotilla at Put-in-Bay, and awaited the British Navy. When they were sighted, Perry advanced in his flagship, the *Lawrence*. The British destroyed it, and Perry and four men transferred to the *Niagara*, broke through the enemy line and defeated them during an intense 15-minute barrage. After the British surrendered, Perry sent General William Henry Harrison his terse line of triumph. Perry's victory gave America control of Lake Erie.

The towering Peace Memorial, erected between 1912 and 1915, is a 352-foot (107-m) Doric column of granite with a bronze urn. Its observation deck gives visitors a view of the battle site 10 miles (16 km) to the northwest. The museum exhibits weapons and equipment from the War of 1812, and tools and materials used to construct the memorial.

The memorial may be reached during summer by car and passenger ferry from Catawba Island, 10 miles (16 km) from Port Clinton, and by plane from Port Clinton and Sandusky.

Map ref: page 381 L1

TOLEDO

Toledo is a railroad center, one of the world's busiest freshwater ports, and renowned for its glass. The city of 332,900 is located where the

Trophies—and sauces—from Toledo's RibFest.

Maumee River flows into Lake Erie, on the northwest edge of Ohio near the Michigan border.

The French first explored the area in 1615. The present city was incorporated in 1837 following the Toledo War, a political battle between Ohio and what became Michigan for rights to the port.

In the 1840s the Wabash and Erie Canal linked Toledo to Indiana; the Miami and Erie Canal connected it with Cincinnati and the Ohio River. Mills and factories sprang up, and Germans and Poles poured into the city to work in them. Railroads followed—in the 1880s Toledo was the third-largest rail center in the country. Natural gas was cheap and abundant, and in 1895 the discovery of oil led to a local oil-refining industry.

Edward Libbey started the glass industry here in 1888, with crystal and lamp globes. Glassblower Michael Owens joined him and invented a machine that turned molten glass into bottles by the thousands. Today Toledo has four large glass manufacturers, and more than 1,000 manufacturing plants in total, producing jeeps, spark plugs, chemicals, and other products.

Toledo has many Metroparks. Promenade Park is good for viewing the boats on the Maumee River. Sidecut Park has picnic grounds beside canal locks. Raceway Park offers horse racing.

COSI Toledo, located on the riverfront, is an interactive science learning center where visitors can ride a high-wire cycle above an atrium, design a roller coaster, and apply aerodynamics to creating the perfect baseball pitch. In addition to hundreds of hands-on exhibits, demonstrations are given.

The Toledo Zoo has more than 525 species of animals, plus an African savanna alive with animals in their natural habitat. There are also large freshwater and saltwater aquariums, a conservatory, and botanical gardens. An underwater view of a hippopotamus family is presented at the Hippoaquarium.

The Toledo Museum of Art has 700 paintings, including works by El Greco, Rembrandt, Peter Paul Rubens, and Van Gogh; there are also books, manuscripts, prints, sculptures, medieval ivories, glass items, tapestries, decorative art, and a glass collection.

Wildwood Manor House is the former home of Champion Spark Plug founder Robert A. Strannahan Sr. It is eighteenth-century Georgian in style, and has 16 fireplaces and more than 50 rooms with period furnishings.

At International Park, the *Willis B. Boyer* has been refurbished—it was the biggest and, at the time, most modern ship on the Great Lakes. A museum depicts freighter history on the Great Lakes.

The Brukner Nature Center (165 acres [67 ha]) consists of a swamp, prairie, pine forest, flood plain, hardwood forest, and the Stillwater River. It has 6 miles (10 km) of trails, and the interpretive center displays flora and fauna.

Toledo may be reached by car on I-75, I-475, I-90/80, and I-280, as well as by bus and plane.

Map ref: page 381 J1

Serpent Mound State Memorial contains the best-known prehistoric Indian effigy mound in the Ohio Valley.

A house near Wilmington. The town prides itself on its ability to maintain small-town values—including peaceful living—while being as modern as its larger neighbors.

WARREN

Warren is a city of 50,800 people, located 66 miles (106 km) southwest of Cleveland. It was the first US city to light its streets with incandescent bulbs.

The city is named for territorial surveyor Moses Warren. It was an early iron and coal producer, and first capital of the historic Connecticut Western Reserve.

William Doud and James Ward Packard established the Packard Electric Co. here in 1890, leading to production of the first Packard car in the city.

The 1807 John R. Edwards House is maintained by the Trumbell Historical Society. The W.D. Packard Music Hall, built in 1955, stages concerts, lectures, and other programs. Mosquito Lake Park is popular for outdoor activities.

Warren may be reached by car on Hwys 82, 45 and 5, and US-422, as well as by bus and plane.
Map ref: page 381 P2

WILMINGTON

Wilmington, 30 miles (48 km) southeast of Dayton, is a town of 11,199 with three state parks, a museum, and Wilmington College.

The 10,771-acre (4,362-ha) Caesar Creek State Park is popular for fishing, swimming, boating, camping, hiking, and horseback riding in summer, and snowmobiling and ice skating in winter. Its Pioneer Village has many examples of early log architecture.

Cowan Lake State Park (1,775 acres [719 ha]) has swimming, fishing, boating, camping, cabin rentals, and hiking. Little Miami Scenic State Park (452 acres [183 ha]) offers hiking trails, paved bicycle trails, and canoeing.

Rombach Place, Museum of the Clinton County Historical Society, was the home of General James W. Denver. On display are furniture, Quaker clothing, tools, implements, and kitchenware, plus paintings and sculptures by Eli Harvey, and early 1900s' photographs of Indian chieftains by Carl Moon, a Wilmington native.

Wilmington may be reached by car on US-68, US-22 and Hwy 134, as well as by plane and bus.
Map ref: page 381 J6

WILMOT

Wilmot is the home of what may be the world's largest cuckoo clock. It stands more than 23 feet (7 m) tall, at the Alpine-Alpa Swiss Village Market. The market also features a life-size mural and a large collection of cuckoo clocks.

Wilmot is a town of 300 located 18 miles (29 km) southwest of Canton. It has a 573-acre (232-ha) wilderness center consisting of forests, prairies, and marshlands with winding trails. Its Interpretive Building offers nature displays and an observation room.

Wilmot may be reached by car on US-62 and US-250.
Map ref: page 381 J6

YOUNGSTOWN

Youngstown lies 5 miles (8 km) from the Pennsylvania border in northeast Ohio. It is a coal and steel town, and is the seat of Mahoning County.

Its first coal mine opened in 1826 and its first steel plant began operating in 1892. The industry of this city of 95,700 has become more diversified recently—rubber goods, light bulbs, aluminum and paper goods, office equipment, clothes, rolling-mill equipment, vans, autos and parts, paint, electronic equipment, and plastics.

The city is known for Warner Theatre, built in 1929, and Youngstown University, which has 12,500 students and was established in 1908.

The Arms Family Museum of Local History exhibits arts and crafts of the early twentieth century, and the history of the Mahoning Valley.

The Butler Institute of American Art, built in 1919, was one of the first built specifically to house American artworks. The permanent collection includes works by Mary Cassat, John Copley, Thomas Eakins, Adolph Gottlieb, Winslow Homer, Frederic Remington, Charles Sheeler, Robert Vonnoh, Andy Warhol, and Benjamin West.

Mill Creek Metropark is a 2,500-acre (1,012-ha) park with a long gorge, foot trails, three lakes, and Lanterman Falls.

The Youngstown Historical Center of Industry and Labor chronicles the local iron and steel industry, using artifacts, videotaped interviews with steelworkers and executives, and full-scale reproductions of the places where the steelmakers lived and worked.

Youngstown may be reached by car on I-680, US-62 and US-422, and Hwys 18 and 193. It can also be reached by plane and bus.
Map ref: page 381 P2

WISCONSIN

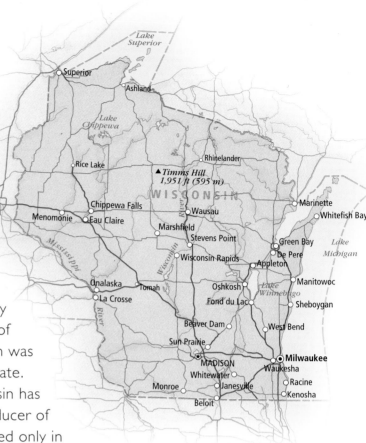

Known as "The Badger State," Wisconsin covers 65,500 square miles (169,645 sq km) and has a population of just over 5.3 million. Its nickname reflects the early settlers' practice of burrowing into the sides of hills for warmth, much like badgers. Wisconsin was admitted to the Union in 1848 as the 30th state.

Also known as "The Dairy State," Wisconsin has over 27,000 dairy farms. It is the leading producer of cheese in the world. Famous cheeses produced only in Wisconsin include Limburger and Colby which is named for a local town. Fans of the famous local football team the Green Bay Packers reflect the state's identity by enthusiastically endorsing the term "cheeseheads" as their moniker.

While corn, potatoes, and hay are major crops, most people are surprised to find that Wisconsin is the leading grower of cranberries in the country. Gravel, copper, and limestone are mined, while paper products, especially toilet paper, represent major sources of income for the state.

An angler fishes beside Hyde's Mill near Spring Green in Wisconsin.

Wisconsin is all about nature and the great outdoors. Trout and salmon fishing are immensely popular in this state, while deer hunting is a favorite yearly ritual. The cold temperatures and abundant snowfalls of winter provide some excellent opportunities for snowmobiling, as Winsconsin has over 25,000 miles (40,225 km) of trails.

The capital is Madison, while the largest city is Milwaukee, on the shores of Lake Michigan in the southern part of the state. Major attractions include Circus World in Baraboo, the House on the Rock near Dodgeville, Taliesin, the Wisconsin home and studio of renowned architect Frank Lloyd Wright in Spring Green, and the Wisconsin Dells.

Wisconsin is bordered on the south by Illinois, on its north by Lake Superior and the Upper Peninsula of Michigan, on its east by Lake Michigan, and on its west by Iowa and Minnesota.

State motto Forward
State flag Adopted 1913 (modified 1981)
Capital Madison
Population 5,363,675
Total area (land and water) 65,500 square miles (169,645 sq km)
Land area 54,315 square miles (138,085 sq km)
Wisconsin is the 26th-largest state in size
Origin of name From the Cheppewa word *Ouisconsin* meaning either "Gathering of the Waters" or "Grassy Place"
Nicknames The Badger State, The Dairy State
Abbreviations WI (postal), Wis.
State bird Robin
State flower Wood violet
State tree Sugar maple
Entered the Union May 29, 1848 as the 30th state

Places in
WISCONSIN

APOSTLE ISLANDS

Wisconsin's northernmost tip is a group of 22 islands that juts out into Lake Superior off Bayfield Peninsula. Known as the Apostle Islands National Lakeshore, this area offers some of the state's most awe-inspiring natural beauty, both in summer and winter.

Although some islands are inhabited, they are largely unspoiled, with groves of virgin timber as well as several endangered plant species. Over 100 species of birds, including blue herons, live here and there are even a few bears. Anglers can have a field day as there is an abundance of pike, lake trout, and perch.

There is much to explore for each island has its own personality and charm. All but two—which are flora and fauna preserves—can be visited. To get to the islands, visitors can take a water taxi or island shuttle. For those with sufficient stamina and a sense of adventure, canoes and kayaks are available for rental.

Madeline Island—the only island in the chain that is inhabited year-round—is the largest. Its village of La Pointe has places to stay as well as some very good restaurants. The area has much to offer lighthouse enthusiasts, with Sand Island having one of the most beautiful examples, a brownstone structure built in 1881.

Some of the islands are tiny. Gull Island, for example, is only 3 acres (about 1 ha). Others such as Stockton Island are quite large, covering 10,000 acres (4,050 ha). Some have conveniences including camping sites and boat docks. They all display a rugged beauty, from the deep ravines of Oak Island to the eerie caves of Devil's Island.

Hwy 13 from Superior and Ashland is the major road going to Bayfield Peninsula.
Map ref: page 371 L7

APPLETON

Appleton (population 70,087) is less than an hour south of Green Bay on Hwy 41. Located on the northern shores of Lake Winnebago, it is the major city in this area, which is known as the Fox River Valley. Like several of the other cities here, Appleton is a leading manufacturer of paper products.

One of the biggest attractions in town is devoted to Appleton's most famous resident, Harry Houdini. This illusionist/magician, who captivated America in the early twentieth century with his incredible escape acts, spent his boyhood years here after his family moved from Budapest. The Houdini Historical Center houses a collection of information about him from posters to the actual handcuffs he used in some of his performances.

The Fox Cities Children's Museum has interactive exhibits that cover a wide range of topics, from wildlife and health to other cultures. Baseball fans, both young and old, will enjoy minor league baseball in Appleton at Fox Valley Stadium, the home of the Wisconsin Timber Rattlers, the only A club of the big league Seattle Mariners.
Map ref: page 376 A3

ASHLAND

Ashland has a population of 8,620 people and is the largest town in the far northern region of Wisconsin. It sits at the southern end of Chequamegon Bay, an extension of Lake Superior. Although it is a frozen outpost in the depths of winter, Ashland turns into a thriving port when the weather allows ship traffic.

It is home to the Sigurd Olson Environmental Institute. Named for the ecologist from Ashland, the Institute is a tribute to Olson's work in this field. Nature photographs and other informative exhibits detailing the school's part in advancing ecology are the focus here. The institute is part of Northland College, located about 12 miles (19 km) south of town.

If docks interest you, then be sure not to miss the distinctive iron ore dock in Ashland. This concrete structure is made of hundreds of thousands of tons of stone and juts out a distance of some 1,800 feet

A sculpture dedicated to Houdini, in Appleton.

(550 m) into the bay. It is the largest structure of its kind in the United States.

Another attraction in Ashland is the Soo Line Depot, a nineteenth-century building which has been restored and is now home to a restaurant, microbrewery, and nightclub. You can enjoy your meal here amid beautiful mirrors and other furnishings over 100 years old.

Buses are available to Bayfield Peninsula to visit the Apostle Islands; by car they can be reached via Ashland and US-2.
Map ref: page 371 L8

DOOR COUNTY

Door County combines stunning natural coastline with miles of caves and forests, and acres of orchards. Located on a long peninsula jutting out into Lake Michigan, it is bordered on the west by Green Bay and on the east by the lake. There are over 250 miles (400 km) of shoreline carved by glacial activity. As a result, there are more lighthouses here—many of them well over 100 years old—than anywhere else in the country.

One of the county's most remarkable lighthouses, the Sturgeon Bay Ship Canal Lighthouse, stands almost 100 feet (30 m) tall and can be visited in May during Door County's Museum Lighthouse Tour.

At the northern end of Door County are the islands, the best-known being Washington Island. Ferry rides are the main way of reaching this island, where hiking and bicycle trails abound. Bicycles can be rented for a small fee.

To reach Door County, take I-43 north from Milwaukee, or Hwy 29 out of Green Bay. Cherryland

Acres of orchards characterize much of Door County. The month of May is a good time to see cherry trees in blossom.

Sturgeon Bay is the main town in Door County, which has miles of picturesque coastline and pretty villages to explore.

Airport in Sturgeon Bay has flights to Chicago, while the airport in nearby Green Bay is served by several major airlines.
Map ref: page 372 D10

EAU CLAIRE

French for "Clear Water," Eau Claire (population 61,704) is in western Wisconsin at the junction of the Chippewa and Eau Claire Rivers. Once an early lumber and wheat town, today the major products manufactured here include tires and paper products, while cranberries and the dairy industry also strengthen the local economy.

Major attractions include the Paul Bunyan Logging Camp, a restored 1890s' lumber camp, as well as the Chippewa Valley Museum with exhibits on the history of the local Chippewa people, and the lives of the early settlers who came to this region.

Ten miles (16 km) west is the Beaver Creek Reserve, home to a nature center and the Hobbs Observatory. Bears, deer, and a few

A customer chooses a new snowmobile for the winter season in Fond du Lac.

wild turkeys can be seen here, while the observatory offers visitors views of the heavens on Saturday nights.

Eau Claire can be reached by car via I-94 or by US-53 or US-12.
Map ref: page 375 J4

FOND DU LAC

Fond du Lac (population 42,703), meaning "At the far end of the lake," is a small town on the southern tip of Lake Winnebago some 40 miles (64 km) northwest of Milwaukee.

Just outside Fond du Lac is Kettle Moraine State Forest, which at 27,000 acres (10,935 ha) is one of the largest forests in the state. All sorts of outdoor activities from boating and waterskiing to horseback riding and hiking can be enjoyed here in the summer. There are over 300 campsites available. In the winter, cross-country skiing and snowmobiling take over.

In town, it is worth visiting the Galloway House, a restored 30-room Victorian mansion complete with a museum of Native American artifacts, and the Octagon House,

built originally as a fort and later used as a stop on the Underground Railroad, which harbored slaves during the Civil War. Interesting period pieces from dolls to antiques are on display here.

Fond du Lac can be reached via US-41 and US-45 from Milwaukee or US-191 out of Madison.
Map ref: page 376 A4

GREEN BAY

Located in northeastern Wisconsin along the body of water from which it takes its name, Green Bay (population 102,313) is the seat of Brown County. Originally discovered by the French explorer Jean Nicolet in 1634, it was Wisconsin's earliest settlement. It was named for the greenish color of the water at certain times of the year.

A fur-trading post in its early history, today Green Bay is a major manufacturer of paper products. Its location makes it a leading port, with millions of tons of cargo passing through each year.

Above all, this town is best known for its football team, the beloved Green Bay Packers. This is the only team in football owned by its local community, and as a result its fans' allegiance is unrivaled. In season, from August to December, this town knows only football. Off-season, football devotees can tour Lambeau Field, the team's home stadium. The Packer Hall of Fame is open year-round.

Other attractions include the National Railroad Museum, which features dozens of locomotives and diesels. Also of interest is the Oneida National Museum. This building tells the story of the Native

American tribe that purchased land in Wisconsin in the mid-nineteenth century. Today, the Oneida tribe also operates one of the state's most popular casinos. As well as gambling, many big-name musical acts are major attractions here.

Green Bay's airport, Austin Straubel Field, is served by several major airlines. I-43, US-41, and Hwy 29 are the major access roads.
Map ref: page 376 B2

KENOSHA

Just across the Illinois border, Kenosha (population 90,352) is one of Wisconsin's major industrial cities. It is the home of Jelly Belly gourmet jelly beans, Jockey International, makers of undergarments, and the location of the local cranberry processing plant for Ocean Spray. Two colleges, the University of Wisconsin-Parkside and Carthage College, are based in Kenosha.

Native Americans gave the city its original name, Mas-ke-no-sha, meaning "Place of the Pike." Kenosha is on the shores of Lake Michigan, and as the city owns over three-quarters of its lakefront, there are large tracts of public parkland that overlook the lake. One

An exhibit in the Packer Hall of Fame, Green Bay, a must for football fans.

of these parks—Harbor Park—encompasses 69 acres (28 ha) on the site of a former auto plant. This pleasant area has bike and jogging trails, as well as sculptures to enhance the views.

A great way to see Kenosha is on one of the newly refurbished electric streetcars. Covering 2 miles (3 km) of the city, the five streetcars are color-coded to indicate their routes and offer very afford-able rides.

Other attrac-tions include the Frank Palumbo Civil War Museum on the campus of Carthage College. This is one of the largest private Civil War collections in the country with weap-ons, uniforms, and private papers on display. The Kenosha Public Museum in Harbor Park focuses on the geological history of Wis-consin and has exhibits of stone tools and bones from ancient ani-mals. Free tours are available of the Harmony Hall, a mansion in the Tudor style that is the headquarters for the Society for the Preservation and Encouragement of Barber Shop Quartet Singing in America.

Just south of the city is the Bris-tol Renaissance Fair, a re-creation of a sixteenth-century marketplace, complete with entertainment in the form of musicians, jousters, and swordsmen. This venue comes to life on summer weekends, begin-ning on the last weekend in June.

Kenosha is served by trains from downtown Chicago and a bus ser-vice. If traveling from Chicago by car, take I-94 north right into town. The same highway connects the town with Milwaukee to the north.
Map ref: page 376 B7

LA CROSSE

La Crosse (population 51,818) is located in the southwest on the Mississippi River, which separates this part of the state from Minne-sota. Its name comes from lacrosse, a version of which, called *baggata-way*, was played by local Native Americans in the 1800s.

The town is best known for the G. Heileman Brewery, which pro-duces Old Style Beer. Although there have been several ownership changes over the last 30 years, the brewery is still going strong. Visi-tors can tour the brewery and see, among other things, the world's largest six-pack.

Riverboat cruises are offered by two paddlewheelers, the *La Crosse Queen* and the *Julia Belle Swain*. The former offers a 90-minute sightseeing cruise, while the latter has excur-sions of various durations from a few hours all the way up to two-day trips. Some 500 feet (153 m) above La Crosse, Grandad Bluff provides sweeping vistas of the city and valley. La Crosse can be reached by car on Hwy 35, and is served by both buses and trains.
Map ref: page 375 K6

One of Kenosha's claims to fame—the ubiquitous jellybean.

LAKE GENEVA

Only 10 miles (16 km) north of the Illinois border, Lake Geneva (population 7,148) began its life as a desirable summer retreat for wealthy Chicago residents in the 1850s. Today, the area is a desti-nation for golfers, skiiers, boaters, and other sports enthusiasts.

The Wrigley family of chewing gum fame built a spectacular sum-mer home called Green Gables, and soon after, other well-to-do Midwesterners built showy retreats here as well. Most of these houses are hidden from sight along the main roads. Take a boat tour of the lake to catch a glimpse of them.

Golfers have a choice of several world-class golf resorts, including the Americana Resort and Geneva Lakes. Wilmot Mountain, the area's best ski resort, is close by.

The US Snow Sculpting Cham-pionships are held in Lake Geneva every February. For a different look at things, the Yerkes Observatory, located at the north shore of Lake Geneva, houses one of the world's largest telescopes. Free tours are available on Sunday.

Lake Geneva can be reached by driving south from Milwaukee on I-43 and then east on US-12. From Chicago, take I-94 to US-12 west.
Map ref: page 376 A7

MADISON

Wisconsin's capital city is located in the south-central portion of the state, about 60 miles (97 km) west of Milwaukee. Running roughly northwest to southeast, the city lies between two lakes: Lake Mendota on the north and Lake Monona to the south. Settled in 1837, it has a population of 208,054. The Uni-versity of Wisconsin is here.

The most striking building here is the State Capitol. Patterned after the Capitol in Washington DC, it is the second tallest capitol in the country and the only one whose roof is made of granite. Free tours are available daily.

One of Frank Lloyd Wright's most unusual designs is located in Madison. The First Unitarian Meeting House has a triangular spire, which Wright said he used because it reminded him of hands outstretched in prayer. Tours are offered every day.

Wright's famous home and studio, Taliesin, is located about 40 miles (64 km) west of Madison in the town of Spring Green, via US-14. Built into the side of a hill (*taliesin* is Welsh for "shining brow"), the studio was burned to the ground twice, but immediately rebuilt. Wright lived and trained his students here off and on from the 1920s to his death in the late 1950s. He is buried a few miles away; a simple tombstone marks his last resting place.

An entirely different architectur-al style is evident in the House on the Rock, 9 miles (14 km) south near the town of Dodgeville. Wis-consin's single most visited tourist attraction, this famous building was built atop a 60-foot (18-m) rock by Alex Jordan, a recluse who had a passion for collecting things. Just as fascinating as the look of the exterior is the intriguing melange of art and toys inside. There is a charge to tour the house, which is open most of the year, except for the winter months.

Madison can be reached by bus, by car from Chicago on I-90/94, and from Milwaukee on I-94.
Map ref: page 375 N8

The graceful proportions of the impressive State Capitol Building in Madison.

MILWAUKEE

Wisconsin's largest city (population 596,974), Milwaukee is 50 miles (80 km) north of the Illinois border along the shores of Lake Michigan. German immigrants played an important role in the formation of Milwaukee in the mid-to-late 1800s, which no doubt led to the influx of breweries at that time.

Known as the "Beer Capital of America," Milwaukee was once a major brewing city in the twentieth century (the local baseball team, mindful of this, is named the Brewers). Schlitz, Pabst, and Miller's breweries were all headquartered here, although Miller's is the only major one still operating today (there are a few microbreweries here as well). Free tours are available every day except on Sundays.

Milwaukee also has some beautiful museums, most notably the Milwaukee Art Museum, downtown on the lakefront. Designed by Eero Saarinen, who created the Gateway Arch in St Louis, this museum has a nice mix of paintings

One of the grander houses in downtown Milwaukee, settled in the 1840s.

from the last 500 years as well as an exhibit honoring Frank Lloyd Wright. The Mitchell Park Conservatory, a striking complex of three glass domes, is visible to drivers coming downtown on I-94. The domes represent different environments and are open every day for a small fee.

The city's zoo, a few miles west of the city on I-94, is one of the finest in the country. Many of the animals live in areas similar to their natural habitats, with no bars. There are many walks, so allow plenty of time for a visit.

Two of Wisconsin's biggest annual attractions are held in or near Milwaukee. In July, the 10-day Summerfest at the city's lakefront attracts close to a million people to hear some of the most popular musical groups of today

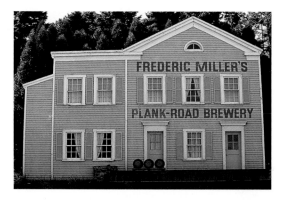

Miller's, the sole remaining big-name brewery in Milwaukee.

and yesterday. In August at nearby West Allis, the state fair is one of the country's biggest. It features livestock competitions, carnival rides, and food stands.

Milwaukee is served by Mitchell International Airport, and there are trains and local and long-distance buses. Main routes into the city are I-90/94 and I-43.
Map ref: page 376 B6

OSHKOSH

Oshkosh (population 62,916) is in northeastern Wisconsin on the west shores of Lake Winnebago. Named for the chief of the Menominee tribe, Oshkosh was once nicknamed "Sawmill City," reflecting the number of sawmills here in the 1840s when huge forests were cut down to provide timber for construction. Unfortunately, the many wooden buildings in the city burned down in a fire in 1875. Because of this catastrophe the town was largely rebuilt with stone.

Today, the city of Oshkosh is familiar to millions as the home of Oshkosh B'gosh, the well-known manufacturer of bib overalls and children's clothing. Although the plant is no longer open for tours, there is an outlet store at the Horizon Outlet center, which is just south of town.

Aviation fans know Oshkosh for its Experimental Aircraft Association Museum (EAA). This has over 90 aircraft on display with items from home-built planes to spacecraft. In July there is a fly-in featuring experimental aircraft and historic planes which brings in thousands of visitors from all over the United States and Canada.

The free Oshkosh Public Museum is in a 1907 English-style home, and filled with all sorts of fascinating memorabilia including

Tiffany glass, antiques, model trains, fire equipment, and the Apostles Clock, one of the state's icons.

Nature and art-lovers will enjoy the Paine Art Center. Set in a Tudor Revival home from the 1920s, American and European paintings from several different eras are on display. Outside, an arboretum has six different gardens displaying hundreds of flower varieties and a remarkable collection of roses.

Oshkosh can be reached via US-41, US-45, and Hwy 44.
Map ref: page 375 P6

RACINE

Located between Milwaukee and Kenosha along Lake Michigan, Racine (population 81,555) is known for manufacturing such products as farm machinery, lawn mowers, and electrical motors. The largest number of Dutch descendants in the United States live here, and their specialty pastry known as a kringle (a coffee cake filled with fruits and nuts) has given the city its nickname of "Kringleville."

Racine's most recognized landmark is the S.C. Johnson Wax Administration Center. In 1936, the company asked Frank Lloyd Wright to design its new headquarters. He obliged by producing one of his most striking and original designs. Huge columns in the shape of lily pads are the dominant interior features, giving the building a delicacy unknown in most office architecture. Tours of the facility are available from Tuesday through Thursday and are free, although reservations are required.

Wright also designed a home for the company's Herbert Johnson the following year. Named Wingspread, this is an eye-catching brick structure that hugs a bluff overlooking Lake Michigan. Now a conference facility, public tours are available when the building is not in use.

A notable part of the complex is the Golden Rondelle Theater, a circular building that was designed for the New York World's Fair of 1964. Three short documentary films are shown daily.

Another free attraction is the Racine Zoological Gardens with several hundred animals on display, including a rare white tiger.

Racine can be reached by bus or train, or by car on I-43.
Map ref: page 376 B6

Lighthouses are a feature of much of Wisconsin's coastal scenery. Here, the Racine lighthouse provides a beacon for the area's commercial and recreational watercraft.

SHEBOYGAN

Sheboygan is on the shores of Lake Michigan, about halfway up the state. The town is the seat of Sheboygan County, and has a population of 50,792. It is famous for making traditional bratwurst. These popular sausages, enjoyed by millions of Americans around the country at summertime barbeques, bring many visitors to the city for Bratwurst Days, a festival held here in early August.

The town of Kohler, adjacent to Sheboygan, is the headquarters of the well-known Kohler Company, one of the world's most successful manufacturers of bathroom sinks and fixtures. Tours of the plant are available to visitors.

In the 1980s, company man Herbert Kohler, also a keen golf player, commissioned famous architect Pete Dye to build two golf courses nearby. Known as Blackwolf Run, they are renowned for being two of the finest courses in the country, and the resort here is spectacular. As their fame spread, golfers came from around the world to play these courses, so Kohler decided to expand the facilities and commissioned Dye to design two more courses. Known as Whistling Straits, it sits on the shores of Lake Michigan and is reminiscent of a Scottish links course, even down to the use of sheep instead of mowers to trim the fairways.

The major road in and out of Sheboygan is I-43, which connects the city with Milwaukee, some 40 miles (64 km) to the south.
Map ref: page 376 B4

SUPERIOR

While Lake Michigan is the dominant feature of the eastern boundary of Wisconsin, Lake Superior borders the state at its northernmost points, tucked between Minnesota and the Upper Peninsula of Michigan. The city of Superior (population 27,368) sits at the far northwestern point of the state, just opposite the much larger city of Duluth, Minnesota.

The city of Superior is the busiest port on Lake Superior and much of the shoreline here is dotted with grain elevators, warehouses, and shipyards. The harbor is on a small inlet known as the St Louis Bay that leads out into Lake Superior. The city was the departure point for the *Edmund Fitzgerald*, an ore boat that sunk in a storm in 1975 shortly after leaving port. That

One of the attractions at Big Chief Theme Park in Wisconsin Dells.

fateful trip became the inspiration of a famous song by Canadian singer Gordon Lightfoot.

A major attraction here is the Fairlawn Mansion, a Queen Anne style residence built for a former mayor of the town. Now restored to its original glory, it is a museum with exhibits on Native Americans as well as information on shipping in this area.

The nearby Patison State Park is worth a visit as it is one of the state's most beautiful parks. Those who love waterfalls should see the Big Manitou Falls which, at 165 feet (50 m), is one of the highest waterfalls west of the Mississippi. Wisconsin Point, just south of the city, is an isolated preserve that provides a close-up look at the famous Superior entry lighthouse. This is a dramatic spot to be during wild winter weather.

Car access is via I-35 or US-53.
Map ref:
page 371 J7

WISCONSIN DELLS

Ask most people to pick the state's most popular attraction and the answer will be the Wisconsin Dells for its blend of regal natural beauty and cornball entertainment.

For those in search of scenic wonders, take a boat ride on this stretch of the Wisconsin River. Both Upper and Lower Dells tours are available (the Upper is the more picturesque of the two) and give the visitor an excellent view of the beautiful sandstone formations along the river. Tours run for one or two hours. Smaller vessels known as DUKs, which maneuver at a faster pace, also offer river tours.

The late showman and talk-back radio pioneer Tommy Bartlett was the man largely responsible for the presence of glitzy entertainment in Wisconsin Dells. One example is an aquatic show that features a mind-boggling combination of waterskiing and acrobatics.

There are several golf courses in the Wisconsin Dells area, including Trapper's Turn, co-designed by Wisconsin native architect Andy North.

Hotel rooms can be difficult to obtain during the summer but nearby camping sites offer a cheap alternative. Located about 50 miles (80 km) north of Madison at the intersection of US-12, Hwy 16, and I-90/94, the Dells can be reached by car and train.
Map ref: page 375 M7

Northern Minnesota • Northwestern Wisconsin

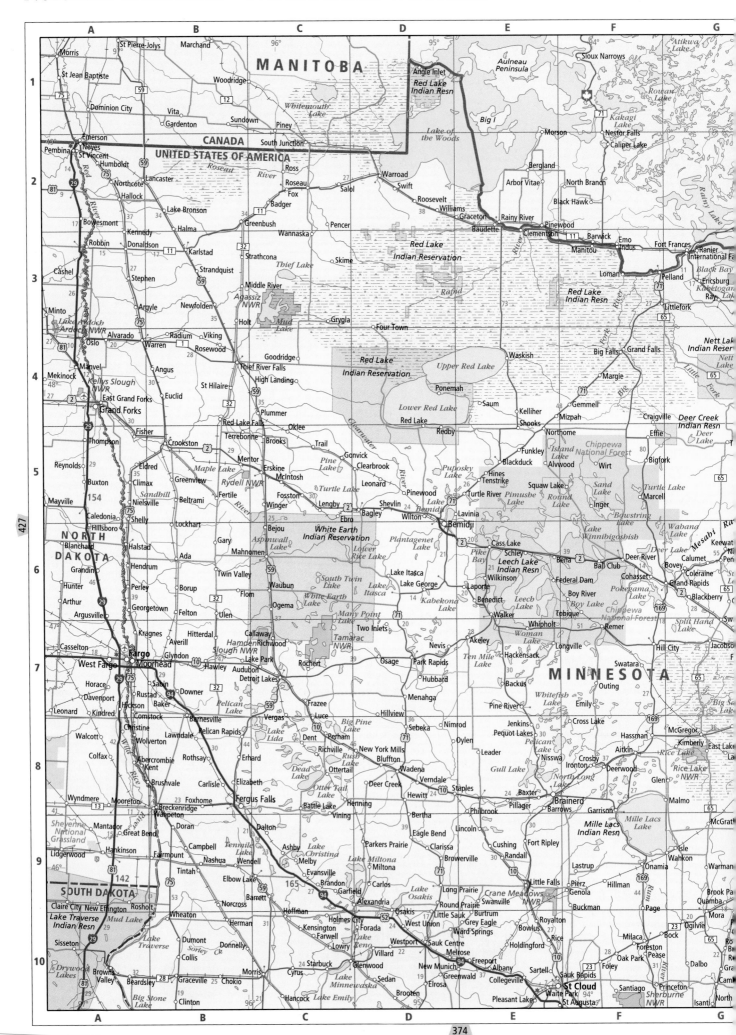

Northern Michigan • Northeastern Wisconsin

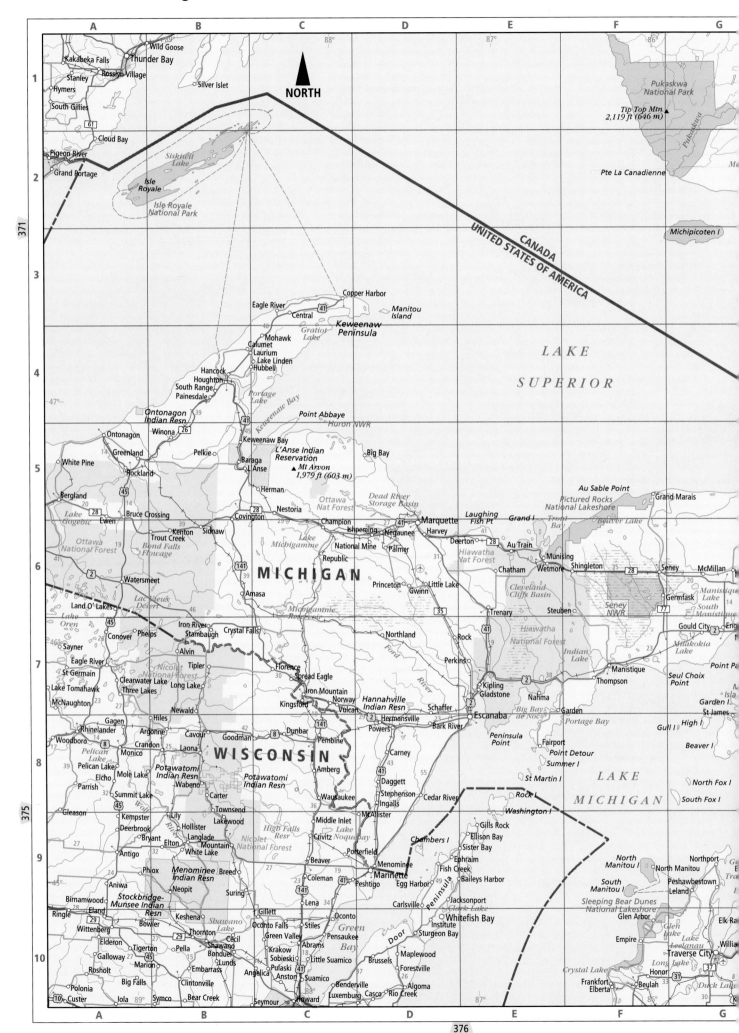

NORTH

Kakabeka Falls
Wild Goose
Thunder Bay
Rosslyn Village
Stanley
Hymers
Silver Islet
South Gillies
61
Cloud Bay
Pigeon River
Grand Portage

Pukaskwa National Park

Tip Top Mtn 2,119 ft (646 m)

Pte La Canadienne

Siskiwit Lake

Isle Royale

Isle Royale National Park

CANADA
UNITED STATES OF AMERICA

Michipicoten I

Copper Harbor
Eagle River
Central
41
Manitou Island
Keweenaw Peninsula
Gratiot Lake
Mohawk
Calumet
Laurium
Lake Linden
Hubbell
Hancock
Houghton
South Range
Painesdale
Portage Lake
Keweenaw Bay
Point Abbaye
Huron NWR

LAKE SUPERIOR

Au Sable Point
Pictured Rocks National Lakeshore
Grand Marais

Ontonagon
Ontonagon Indian Resn
Winona
26
Greenland
White Pine
Pelkie
Keweenaw Bay
Baraga
L'Anse
L'Anse Indian Reservation
▲ *Mt Arvon 1,979 ft (603 m)*
Big Bay
Herman
Dead River Storage Basin
Ottawa Nat Forest
Laughing Fish Pt
Grand I
Beaver Lake
Trout Bay
Munising
Shingleton
28
Seney
McMillan

Bergland
Rockland
Lake Gogebic
28
Ewen
Bruce Crossing
Kenton
Sidnaw
Nestoria
Covington
Champion
Ishpeming
Negaunee
Marquette
Harvey
Deerton
28
Au Train
Wetmore
Chatham
77
Hiawatha Nat Forest
Cleveland Cliffs Basin
Seney NWR
Germfask
Manistique Lake
South Manistique

Trout Creek
45
National Mine
Palmer
Ottawa National Forest
Bond Falls Flowage
141
MICHIGAN
Republic
Princeton
Gwinn
Little Lake
Watersmeet
2
Amasa
Michigamme Reservoir
Lac Vieux Desert
Land O' Lakes
Lake Oren
Trenary
Steuben
Gould City
2
Milakokia Lake
Hiawatha National Forest
Indian Lake
Manistique
Thompson
Point Pa
Seul Choix Point

45
Conover
Phelps
Iron River
Stambaugh
Crystal Falls
Sayner
Eagle River
St Germain
Clearwater Lake
Alvin
Tipler
Florence
Spread Eagle
Northland
Rock
41
Perkins
Kipling
Gladstone
Nahma
Hiawatha National Forest
23
Point Pa
Garden I

Nicolet National Forest
Three Lakes
Long Lake
Iron Mountain
Norway
Vulcan
Hannahville Indian Resn
Schaffer
Ford River
2
Big Bay de Noc
Garden
St James

McNaughton
Newald
Kingsford
Hermansville
Escanaba
Portage Bay
Gull I
High I
Beaver I

Gagen
Hiles
Powers
2
Bark River
Peninsula Point
Fairport
Point Detour
Summer I
North Fox I
South Fox I

Rhinelander
Argonne
Cavour
Goodman
8
Dunbar
Pembine
Carney
Daggett
St Martin I

Woodboro
8
Crandon
Laona
42
Stephenson
Ingalls
Rock I
Washington I
LAKE MICHIGAN

Monico
Pelican Lake
Pella
Potawatomi Indian Resn
Wabeno
Carter
Amberg
Wausaukee
55
Gills Rock
Ellison Bay
Sister Bay

Pelican Lake
Elcho
Mole Lake
Potawatomi Indian Resn
36
Middle Inlet
McAllister
Cedar River
Chambers I
Ephraim
Fish Creek

Parrish
Summit Lake
45
Townsend
Lakewood
Lake Noquebay
Crivitz
Washington I
North Manitou I
North Manitou
Northport

Gleason
Kempster
Lily
Hollister
Langlade
Mountain
White Lake
Beaver
Porterfield
Menominee
Marinette
Peshtigo
Egg Harbor
Baileys Harbor
South Manitou I
Sleeping Bear Dunes National Lakeshore
Glen Arbor
Peshawbestown
Leland

Deerbrook
Bryant
Elton
Antigo
32
Phlox
Menominee Indian Resn
Breed
Neopit
Suring
Lena
34
Coleman
41
Oconto
Carlsville
Door Peninsula
Jacksonport
Clark Lake
Lake Leelanau
Lake Michigan
Empire
Honor
Beulah

Birnamwood
Aniwa
Stockbridge-Munsee Indian Resn
141
Gillett
Pensaukee
Sturgeon Bay
Institute
Crystal Lake
Frankfort
Elberta
31
Duck L

Ringle
29
Eland
Wittenberg
Keshena
Shawano Lake
Cecil
Stiles
Green Valley
Abrams
Oconto Falls
Whitefish Bay
Sturgeon Bay
Empire
Traverse City
37

Elderon
Tigerton
Pella
Bonduel
Krakow
Sobieski
Little Suamico
Brussels
Maplewood
Forestville
Algoma
Green Bay
William

Galloway
45
Marion
Embarrass
Lunds
Angelica
Pulaski
Anston
Suamico
Benderville
Luxemburg
Casco
Rio Creek

Roshalt
Big Falls
Clintonville
Seymour
Howard
Polonia
10
Custer
Iola
Symco
Bear Creek

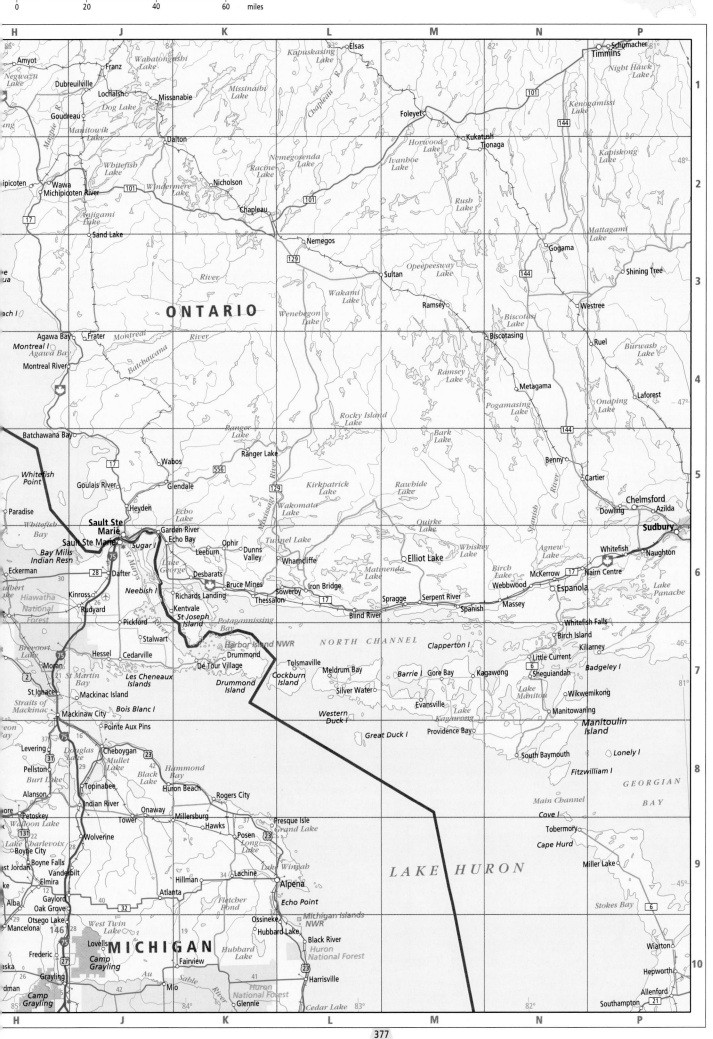

0 20 40 60 80 100 kilometers
0 20 40 60 miles

H J K L M N P

Amyot
Franz
Negwazu Lake
Dubreuilville
Lochalsh
Missanabie
Goudreau
Dalton

Wabatongushi Lake
Missinaibi Lake
Missinaibi R.
Chapleau R.
Kapuskasing Lake
Elsas
Foleyet
Kukatush
Tionaga
Timmins
Schumacher
Night Hawk Lake

101
144
Kenogamissi Lake
Kapiskong Lake

82°
81°

ipicoten
Wawa
Michipicoten River

101
Windermere Lake
Nicholson
Racine Lake
Nemegosenda Lake

Horwood Lake
Ivanhoe Lake
Rush Lake

Anjigami Lake
Sand Lake

17
Chapleau

129
Nemegos
Sultan
Opeepeesway Lake
Gogama
Shining Tree

144

48°

Mattagami Lake

ONTARIO

River
Wakami Lake
Wenebegon Lake
Ramsey
Biscotasi Lake
Westree

Agawa Bay
Frater
Montreal R.
Biscotasing
Ruel
Burwash Lake

Montreal I
Agawa Bay
Montreal River
Batchawana River
Ramsey Lake
Metagama
Laforest

Onaping Lake

47°

Pogamasing Lake

Batchawana Bay
Ranger Lake
Rocky Island Lake
Bark Lake

144
Benny
Cartier

Whitefish Point
17
Wabos
556
Ranger Lake
Mississauga R.
Kirkpatrick Lake
Rawhide Lake
Spanish R.
Chelmsford
Azilda

Goulais River
Glendale
129
Wakomata Lake
Dowling
Sudbury

Paradise
Heyden
Echo Lake
Quirke Lake
Agnew Lake
Whitefish
Naughton

Whitefish Bay
Sault Ste Marie
Garden River
Echo Bay
Tunnel Lake
Whiskey Lake
Birch Lake
McKerrow
17
Nairn Centre

Sault Ste Marie
Sugar I
Leeburn
Ophir
Dunns Valley
Wharncliffe
Elliot Lake
Matinenda Lake
Webbwood
Espanola
Lake Panache

Bay Mills Indian Resn
Dafter
Lake George
Desbarats
Iron Bridge
17
Spragge
Serpent River
Spanish
Massey
Whitefish Falls

Eckerman
28
30
Kinross
Rudyard
Neebish I
Richards Landing
Bruce Mines
Sowerby
Thessalon
Blind River
Birch Island

Hiawatha National Forest
Pickford
St Joseph Island
Potagannissing Bay
Killarney

Brevoort Lake
75
Stalwart
Harbor Island NWR
NORTH CHANNEL
Clapperton I
Little Current

Hessel
Cedarville
Drummond
Tolsmaville
Meldrum Bay
Barrie I
Gore Bay
Kagawong
Sheguiandah
Badgeley I

Moran
2
St Martin Bay
Les Cheneaux Islands
De Tour Village
Cockburn Island
Silver Water
Lake Kagawong
Wikwemikong

St Ignace
Mackinac Island
Drummond Island
Western Duck I
Evansville
Manitowaning

Straits of Mackinac
Bois Blanc I
Great Duck I
Providence Bay
Manitoulin Island

Mackinaw City
75
16
Pointe Aux Pins
South Baymouth
Lonely I

GEORGIAN BAY

Levering
37
Douglas Lake
Cheboygan
23
Fitzwilliam I

Pellston
31
29
Mullet Lake
Hammond Bay
Main Channel
Cove I

Burt Lake
Black Lake
42
Huron Beach
Rogers City

Alanson
Topinabee
Huron Beach
Tobermory

Petoskey
Indian River
Onaway
Millersburg
Presque Isle
Cape Hurd

Walloon Lake
131
22
Tower
Hawks
37
Grand Lake

Lake Charlevoix
Wolverine
Posen
23
Miller Lake

Boyne City
28
Long Lake
45°

Boyne Falls
Elmira
Hillman
34
Lachine
Lake Winyah
Alpena
Stokes Bay
6

Jordan
12
Atlanta
Echo Point

Gaylord
40
Fletcher Pond
82°
Wiarton

Oak Grove
32
Ossineke
Hubbard Lake
Black River
Hepworth

Otsego Lake
29
West Twin Lake
Michigan Islands NWR

Mancelona
146
28
Lovells
19
Hubbard Lake
Huron National Forest
Allenford

Frederic
75
27
Camp Grayling
Fairview
Au Sable River
Harrisville
21
Southampton

Grayling
26
42
Mio
41
Huron National Forest
Glennie
Cedar Lake
83°
82°

MICHIGAN
LAKE HURON

H J K L M N P

Southern Minnesota • Northern Iowa • Southwestern Wisconsin

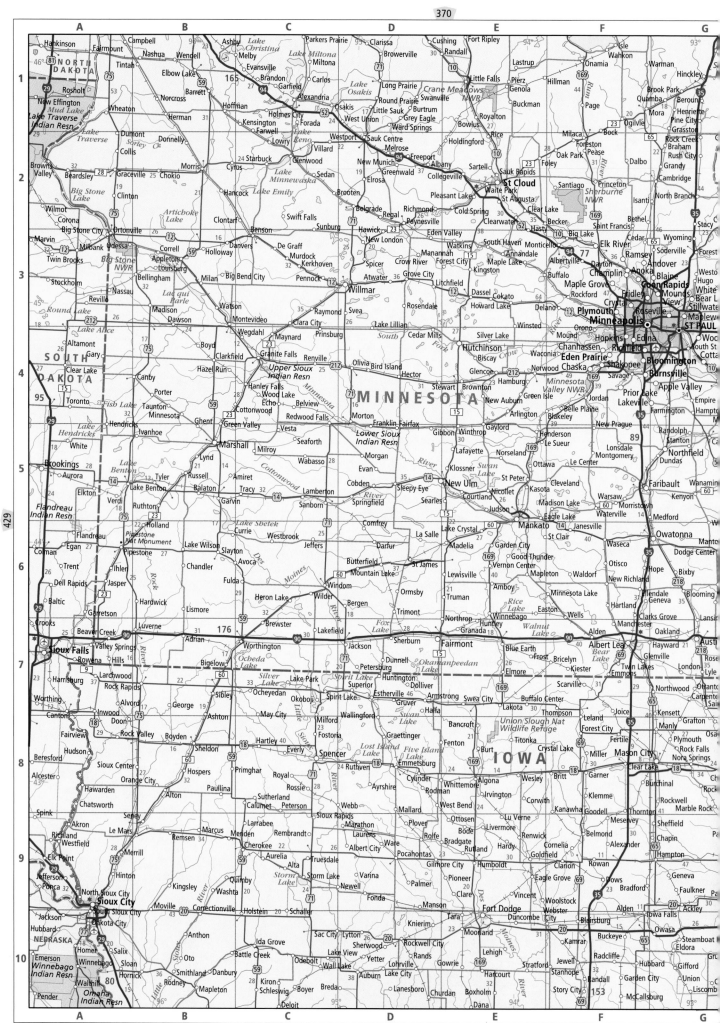

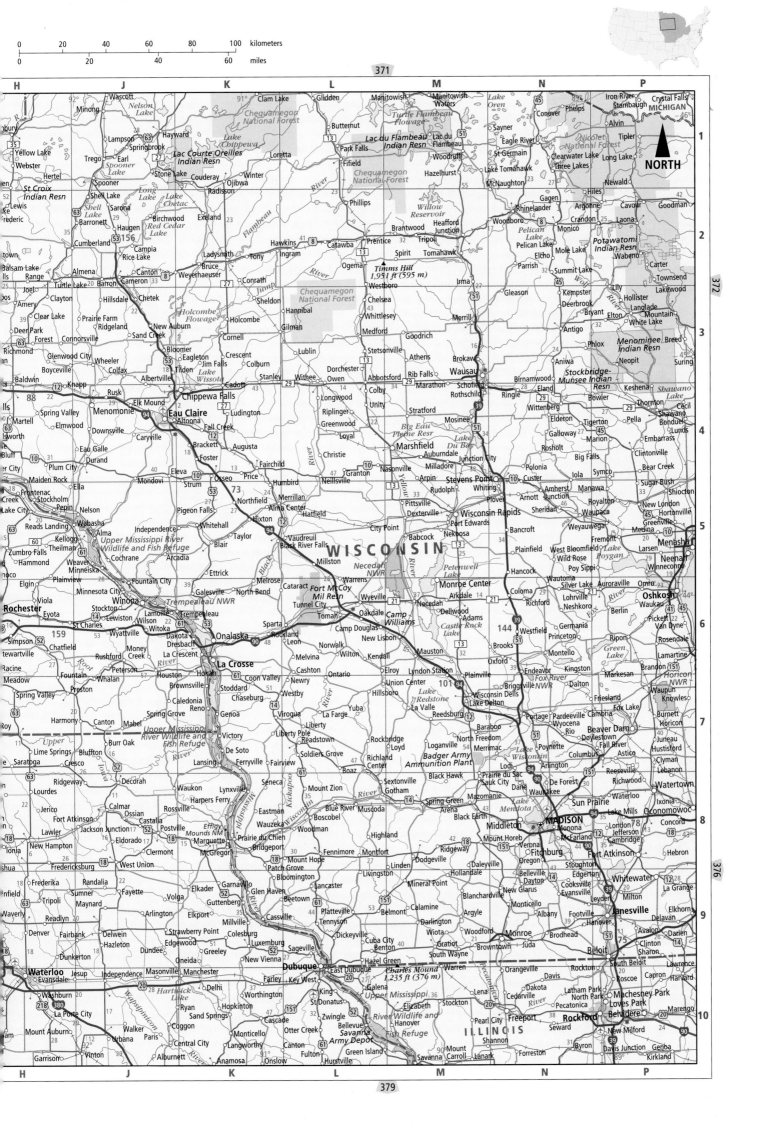

MIDWEST

Southern Michigan • Southeastern Wisconsin • Northeastern Illinois

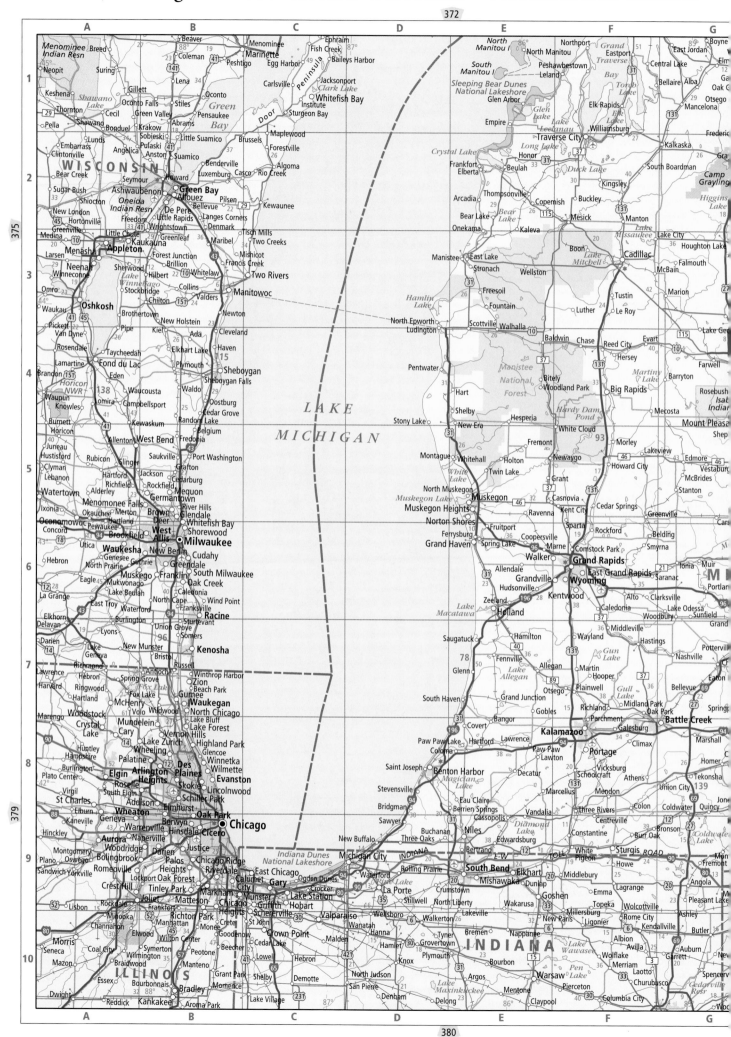

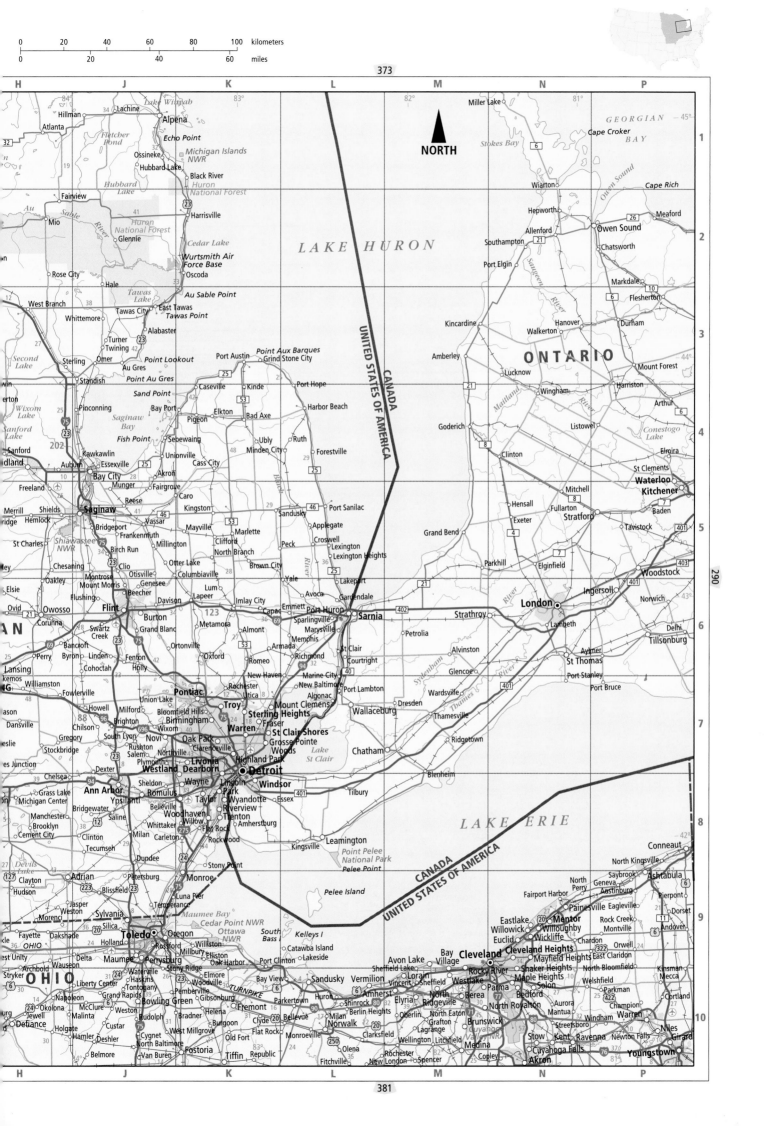

kilometers
miles

MIDWEST

Southern Iowa • Northern Missouri • Northwestern Illinois

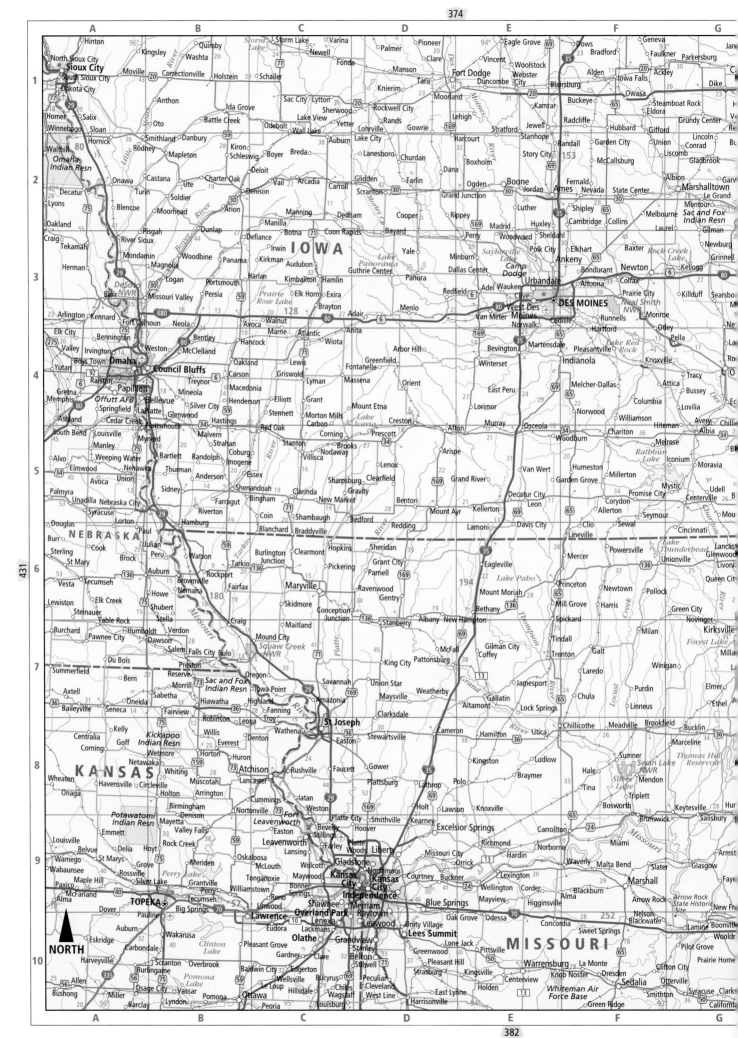

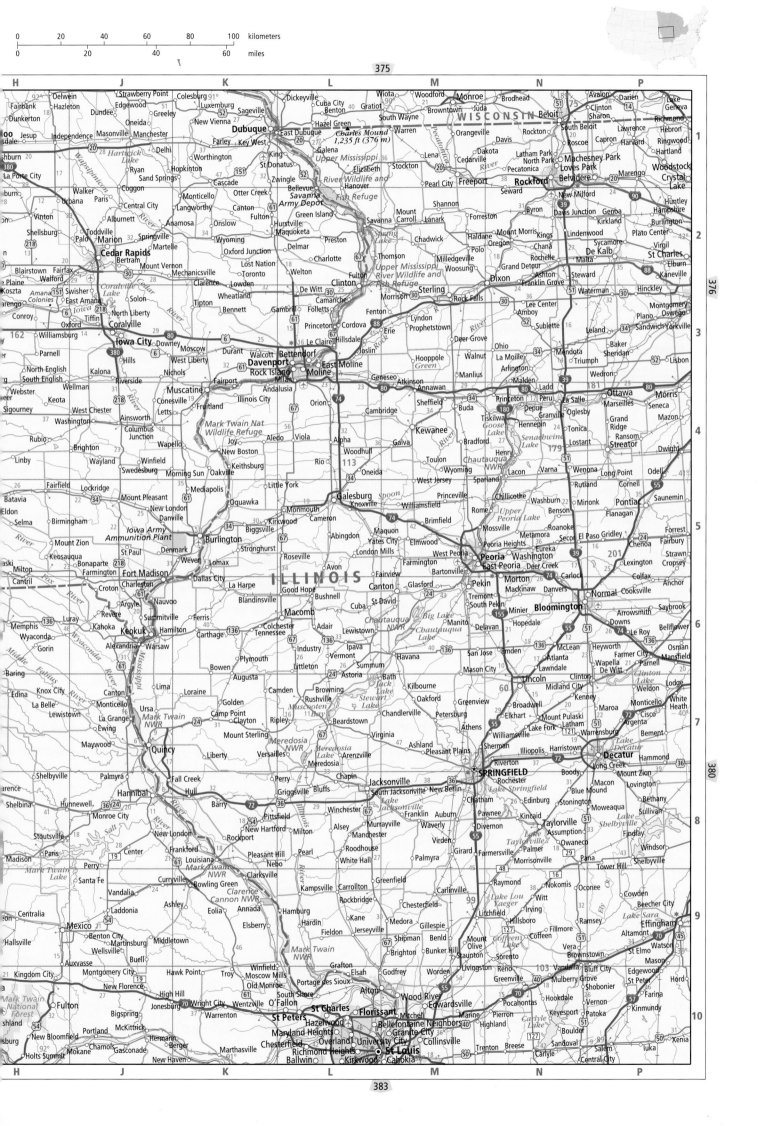

MIDWEST

kilometers
miles

Indiana • Ohio • Eastern Illinois

379

383

MIDWEST

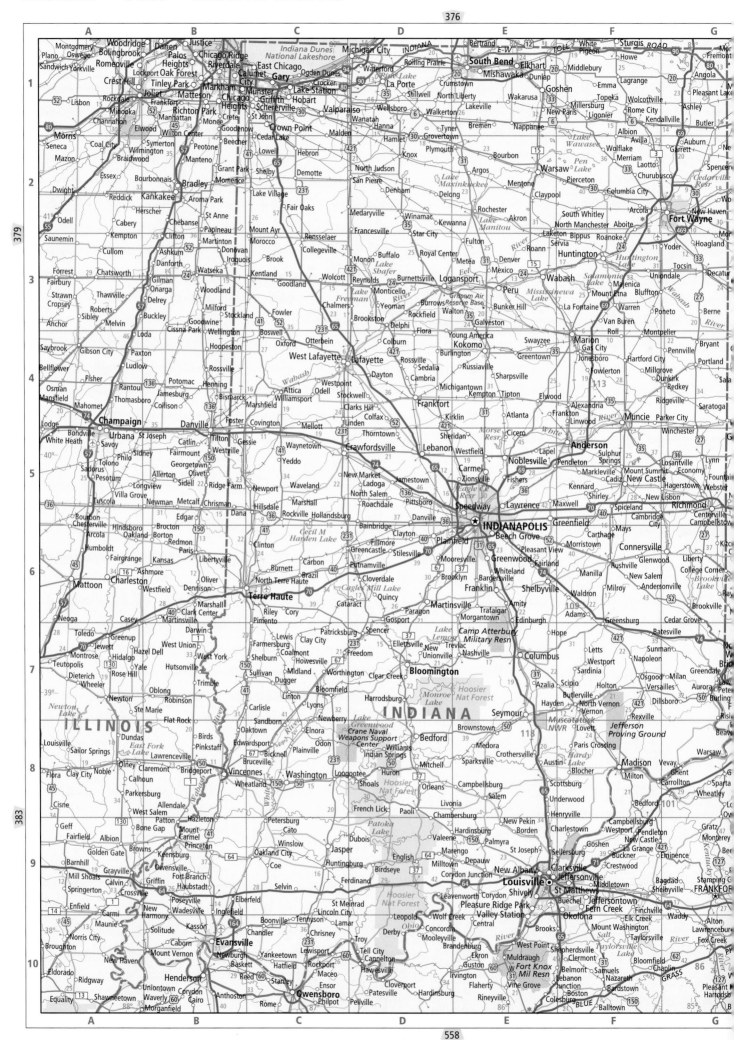

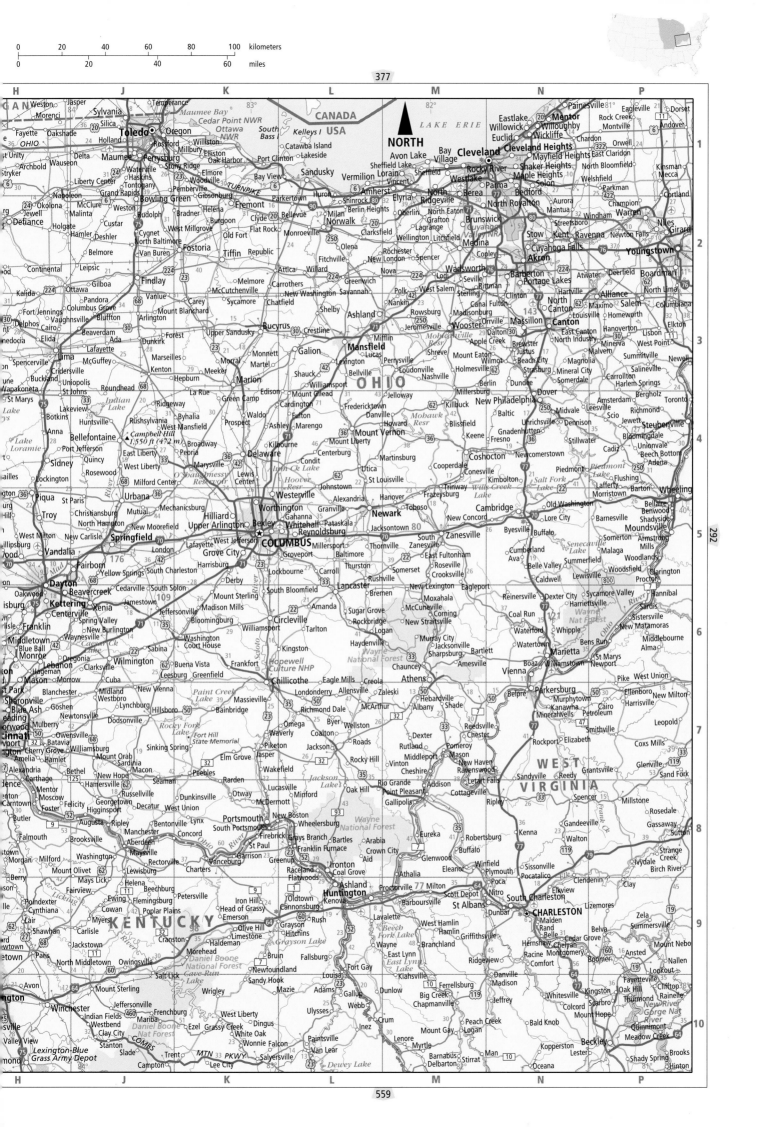

Southern Missouri • Southern Illinois

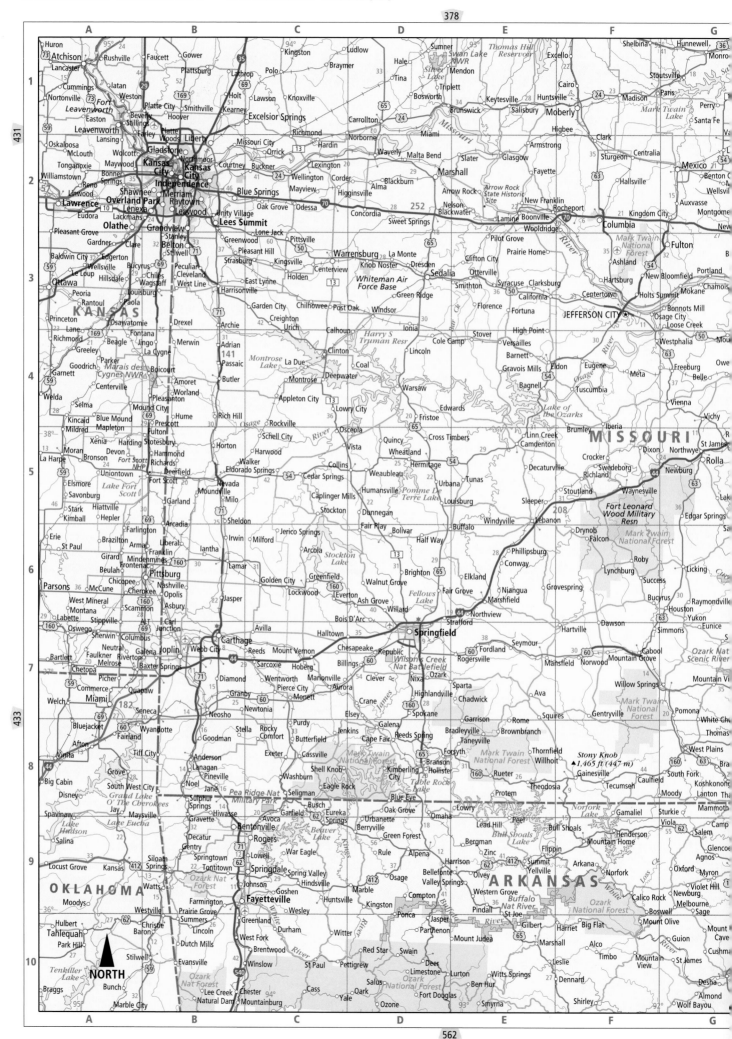

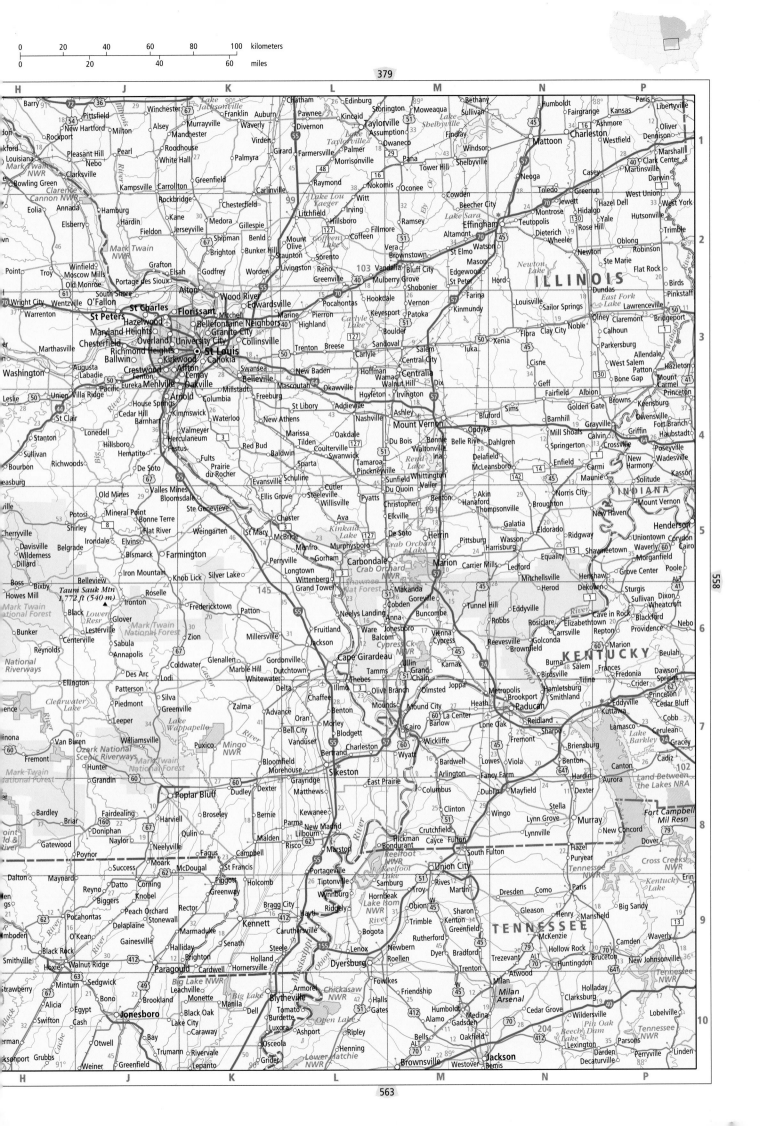

kilometers

miles

558

MIDWEST

THE GREAT PLAINS

NORTH

0	100	200	300	kilometers
0	60	120	180	miles

THE GREAT PLAINS

The Great Plains are often associated with Middle-American conservatism, geological flatness, and vast wheatfields interrupted by the occasional small rural center. While there is some truth to such generalizations, they gloss over the region's geological variety and its turbulent past. For while the area is now considered part of the Midwest it was once *the* West, and the terrain and history of the Great Plains region contributed much to the historical and mythical canvas that shaped America's self-perception.

The Great Plains is an enormous elongated band of semi-arid grassland extending north–south for over 2,500 miles (4,000 km) through the middle of the country. They sit on a plateau between the Rocky Mountains and the Central Lowlands escarpment. Usually associated with prairies, the area does have topographical diversity. It is broken up by the Platte, Arkansas, Missouri, Red, and Canadian rivers, by forests, and some spectacular eroded landscapes. Wildlife includes prairie dogs, opossums, raccoons, skunks, rattlesnakes, and weasels. Human habitation is fairly sparse, with the population progressively increasing as one heads south from North Dakota to Oklahoma.

Cold winters and warm summers are typical, with low rainfall and low humidity—although sudden climatic changes are quite common. Oklahoma, Kansas, and Nebraska are part of "Tornado Alley."

The economic focus is on agriculture and mining. Known as "America's breadbasket," this region is one of the world's most important wheat-growing areas. It is also the nation's principal oil-producing area.

Native Americans lived on the Plains for thousands of years, but were few in number, mostly in villages along waterways where land was conducive to agriculture. In summer they hunted bison on foot. When the Spanish explored here in the sixteenth century, they introduced horses, which allowed the Native Americans to pursue and live more intensively off the vast bison herds, leading to a more itinerant lifestyle.

The French began trading animal pelts with the Native Americans in the 1700s, but it was not until the 1840s that westward expansion drew settlers along the Oregon, Santa Fe, California, and Mormon Trails. The various migrant origins are reflected in the present ethnic diversity. Norwegian heritage is strong in the Dakotas, while Oklahoma has an unexpectedly strong African-American heritage. German, Irish, English, and Native American heritage is also pervasive. Mennonites from Russia introduced a strain of wheat that has enabled the Plains to flourish.

The intensification of settlement in the 1800s led to much bloody, savage, and unequal conflict between the indigenous inhabitants on the one hand, and, on the other, the European settlers and their ally, the US government. White settlement in the east also forced eastern tribes to move westward. From the 1820s many were forcibly relocated to the "Indian Territory" (now Oklahoma). The mixture of diverse tribes and languages led to Native American sign language development—but also to increased inter-tribal conflict. Ultimately, the obliteration of the bison herds by whites, together with disease, massacre, and forced relocation, devastated the cultures of the Plains tribes.

After the Civil War, railroads arrived and accelerated settlement, and farming and ranching. In the late 1800s, Texas cattlemen employed cowboys to drive huge herds of cattle north along the Plains to railroad towns in Kansas. "Wild West" settlements like Abilene and Dodge City sprang up. This era is associated with legendary frontier figures like Wyatt Earp, Buffalo Bill, Kit Carson, George Custer, Calamity Jane, Wild Bill Hickok, Crazy Horse, and Sitting Bull. The Wild West is preserved in pioneer trail markers, cavalry forts, battle sites, museums, and theme parks. There are also archeological sites, and quirky places such as Corn Palace and Carhenge.Scenery includes the Black Hills, badlands, lakes and canyons of South Dakota, rock formations such as Chimney Rock and Scotts Bluff, and the colossal sculpture of Mount Rushmore.

A herd of dairy cows makes its way to a delightful red milking shed in South Heart, North Dakota.

Cattle being driven through the town of Kiowa, Kansas. The beef cattle industry is the main source of income for many Kansas farms.

KANSAS

*T*he Wizard of Oz, *The Little House on the Prairie*, plains full of wheat, fields of sunflowers, oil rigs, tornadoes, cattle drives, and the westward expansion associated with the Oregon and Santa Fe Trails—Kansas is home to all these images and, thanks to its sometimes wild past, it is also inextricably linked with cowboys, brawls, shoot-outs, and the likes of lawmen such as Wyatt Earp and Wild Bill Hickok.

Covering an area of 82,282 square miles (213,110 sq km), "The Sunflower State" is the geodetic center of the United States, giving a new meaning to the term "Middle America." These days the Wild West, the so-called "Indian Wars," and other episodes of the frontier are safely confined to museums and re-creations of the past. A darker side of the state's history is its association with slavery, which led to a violent conflict in 1854–56 that earned it the title of "Bleeding Kansas," and probably pushed the Civil War forward. Now the nation's leading producer of wheat, it was once part of the Dust Bowl, and suffered severe land erosion in the 1930s as a result of drought and over-cultivation.

In recent years the histories of the state's Native Americans, African-Americans, and Mennonites are being depicted in museums.

The sunflower (Helianthus annuus) is the state flower of Kansas, and gives the state one of its nicknames, "The Sunflower State."

With 23 state parks, Kansas offers visitors plenty of natural recreation areas. Topographically, most of the state is rolling plain. The northeast is fertile, green, and hilly and scattered with woods, streams, rivers, and lakes, while the rugged sparsity of the northwest is evoked by its tumbleweed and buffalo grass.

Although 90 percent of the state is still covered by farmland, two-thirds of Kansans live in urban areas with manufacturing and service industries now dominating the economy. Topeka, settled by anti-slavery colonists in 1854, became the state capital in 1861. Kansas tends to have cold winters and warm summers although it is prone to sudden climatic changes and dramatic phenomena such as tornadoes, blizzards, thunderstorms, and hail.

State motto *Ad Astra Per Aspera* (To the stars through difficulties)
State flag Adopted 1927 (modified 1963)
Capital Topeka
Population 2,688,418
Total area (land and water) 82,282 square miles (213,110 sq km)
Land area 81,823 square miles (211,922 sq km)
Kansas is the 14th-largest state in size
Origin of name From a Sioux word meaning "people of the south wind"
Nicknames The Sunflower State, The Jayhawk State, The Breadbasket of America
Abbreviations KS (postal), Kans., Kan.
State bird Western meadowlark
State flower Sunflower
State tree Cottonwood
Entered the Union January 29, 1861 as the 34th state

Places in
KANSAS

ABILENE

Abilene is a historic settlement of 6,000 people on the I-70, 83 miles (133 km) west of Topeka in east-central Kansas. While the town is remembered for its associations with the much-celebrated Wild West, these days its tone is more closely allied to the moderate conservatism of President Eisenhower, who grew up there.

Abilene's heyday began in 1867 when the arrival of the railroad prompted Texas cattlemen to send their stock along the Chisholm Trail to Abilene in order to access eastern markets. The action peaked in 1871 with 700,000 cattle and 5,000 cowhands. With a town full of transients and cowboys determined to enjoy themselves, some vice and unruliness was endemic. One of the elected marshals was Wild Bill Hickok. In his brief term of office he killed a gambler and, mistakenly, a policeman, and was criticized for his violent treatment of rowdy drunks. However, things calmed down after 1875 when the newly established Western Trail made Dodge City a more attractive market center for Texas cattlemen. Abilene is still a railroad shipping center of importance but these days the produce is regional crops.

Old Abilene Town (open March to September) replicates the settlement as it was during the cattle boom. Paying more heed to myth than reality—only 45 people were killed in all of the Kansas cattle towns between 1867 and 1885—"gunfights" break out on weekends. There are also cancan dancers in the saloons, and stagecoach rides.

Abilene's most famous son is Dwight D. Eisenhower who spent his childhood years in Abilene, although he was born in Texas. The Eisenhower Center includes the family's nineteenth-century clapboard home with original furnishings, tombs of Eisenhower, his wife Mamie and son Doud, the Eisenhower Library, and Eisenhower Museum which displays photographs, memorabilia, papers, and a film about his life.

Abilene is also home to the American-Indian Art Center which showcases the works of artisans from 30 regional tribes. Museums worth seeing include: Dickinson County Historical Museum, which has exhibits relating to the Plains Indians, the cattle boom, and frontier life and offers rides on the 1900s hand-carved "Carry-Us-All" carousel; Vintage Fashion Museum, a display of clothing from the 1870s to the 1970s; and the Patent Medicine Museum, housed in the Georgian Seelye Mansion. Trips can be enjoyed on the historic Abilene and Smoky Valley Railroad. To the northeast is Kansas' largest lake, Lake Milford, where visitors can enjoy fishing and boating.

Bus services connect Abilene to Topeka, Lawrence, Kansas City, and Denver.
Map ref: page 431 K9

COLDWATER

This small town of almost 1,000 people in southwestern Kansas is the seat of Comanche County. It sits at the intersection of US-160 and US-183. Comanche County Historical Museum has items of local history and an outdoor mural by renowned crop artist Stan Herd. However, the main attraction in the area is Coldwater Lake which is famous for its camping, fishing, boating, and waterskiing. There are designated swimming areas and the camping facilities are very good. On-site cabins, available year-round, offer excellent views of the lake shore. There are no bus or train services, though there is a small interstate airport.
Map ref: page 620 F4

DODGE CITY

Once known as the "Wickedest Little City in the West," Dodge City's name is likely to be forever associated with the Wild West. These days, the link is maintained in the annals of history, popular mythology, and the town's tourist attractions. Dodge City is now an agricultural and commercial center with a population of some 20,000.

Traders began passing through this area west of Wichita on the Arkansas River on the Santa Fe Trail in 1821. In 1865 Fort Dodge was established to protect travelers on the Trail. In anticipation of the establishment of a railroad in the early 1870s, a settlement emerged 5 miles (8 km) west of Fort Dodge.

Wheat silos at Coldwater.

Cattlemen from Texas soon forged the Western Trail to Dodge City. It also attracted cowboys and, inevitably, drifters, vice, and rowdiness. Two of the town's law officers in this period were the legendary Wyatt Earp and Bat Masterson.

The Bad Old Days are the subject of Boot Hill Museum, which re-creates the city's main street circa 1880. Cancan dancers perform every evening at the saloon where "gunfights" break out regularly. There are also stagecoach rides. Further up the hill is a re-creation of Boot Hill Cemetery, named after the tradition of burying cowboys with their boots on. Dodge City Roundup Rodeo is held during the Dodge City Days festival.

The Home of Stone focuses on pioneering women by re-creating an 1880s domicile, complete with contemporary domestic memorabilia. It is situated in the oldest surviving house (1879–81) in Dodge City. Nine miles (14 km) west along US-50 is the 140-acre (57-km) Sante Fe Trail Tracks Reserve where visitors can still see the ruts once created by the wagons moving along the Santa Fe Trail. Other attractions are Old Fort Dodge Museum, the Clyde Tombaugh Astronomy Center, and the Gunfighters Wax Museum. The Dodge City Trolley takes visitors on a narrated tour of historic sites.

Access is via the highway system (the town sits at the intersection of Hwys 283, 56, and 50), bus services from Wichita, and the regional airport.
Map ref: page 620 D3

The countryside around Coldwater is idyllic, and Coldwater Lake is perfect for water sports such as boating and waterskiing.

EL DORADO

El Dorado is off the I-35 northeast of Wichita. The Butler County Oil Museum commemorates the fact that an oil discovery was made near El Dorado in 1915, starting a boom of historic importance to the settlement. Coutts Memorial Museum of Art includes works by Renoir, Thomas Hart Benton, Frederic Remington and others. Local artworks are housed in the Gallery of the Hills Atrium. Of historic interest is the Missouri Pacific Railroad Depot. At El Dorado State Park there are extensive trails for cycling and walking.

Bus services connect El Dorado with Wichita and Topeka.
Map ref: page 621 K3

FORT SCOTT NATIONAL HISTORIC SITE

Fort Scott National Historic Site lies on Old Fort Boulevard within the town of Fort Scott in southeast Kansas, south of Kansas City. The Fort was built in 1842 as a frontier cavalry outpost in Native American territory. During the Civil War, Kansas' first all-African-American regiment was mustered here. The nine restored buildings include a hospital, guardhouse, barracks, living quarters, stables, and officers' quarters. There is also a museum. A sense of daily life at the Fort is evoked by regular reenactments. "Living history" events, such as the Civil War Encampment in April

and Frontier Garrison Days in both May and September, are also held at the Fort. In the Good Ol' Days Festival (held in June) there are more fascinating reenactments at the Historic Site. On Independence Day (July 4) visitors can enjoy traditional games, a 30-gun salute and artillery demonstrations at the Fort. American-Indian Heritage Weekend is held here at the Fort every September.

There are bus services to Kansas City, Springfield, and Tulsa and a municipal airport but no direct international services.
Map ref: page 621 P3

GREAT BEND

Great Bend is an area in central Kansas with historic sites associated with the Santa Fe Trail such as Walnut Creek, which was once a significant crossing point, and Pawnee Rock, a well-known natural landmark along the trail.

The Barton County Historical Museum and Village feature nine historic buildings dating back to 1871 and two museums. Other attractions are the Kansas Oil and Gas Museum, the child-oriented Fantasy Village, and the Shafer Memorial Art Gallery. The Kansas Quilt Walk features the patterns of seven historic quilts built into the sidewalk in Lafayette Park on Main Street. The Brit Spaugh Zoo features more than 100 different mammals and birds ranging from North American bears and cats to

birds of prey and waterfowl. There are also recreational facilities such as a swimming pool, softball diamonds, and playground equipment. Cheyenne Bottoms Wildlife Area is an important wetlands ecosystem where hunting, fishing, hiking, and birdwatching are popular.

Just 27 miles (43 km) southwest of Great Bend is the meticulously preserved Fort Larned National Historic Site. Fort Larned was established in 1860 to protect travelers on the Santa Fe Trail. Today visitors can explore the barracks, officers' quarters, a museum, the history/nature trail, and watch a video that presents an unvarnished account of the Fort's past.

Great Bend is located near the intersection of Hwys 56, 96, 156, and 281. There are no rail or bus services, but there is a small airport just outside town.
Map ref: page 620 G2

HAYS

Hays (population 18,000) in central-west Kansas was settled in 1867 around the new Union Pacific Railroad, and the nearby Fort Hays (1865). At times the Fort was home to the 7th US Cavalry, commanded by General Custer, and the African-American 9th and 10th US Cavalry, known as the Buffalo Soldiers. Other visitors to the Fort were Buffalo Bill Cody, who supplied bison meat to

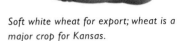

Soft white wheat for export; wheat is a major crop for Kansas.

railroad workers and acted as a civilian scout for the military, and Wild Bill Hickok, who scouted for Custer. In 1869 Hickok was elected sheriff of Ellis County, spending most of his time at Hays, which was then an unruly frontier town. By the mid-1870s the railroad had moved on and Hays settled down. It became a point of arrival for immigrants, most notably a group of Germans who built homes and beautiful churches of limestone. Fort Hays was closed in 1889.

Today, the town is home to Fort Hays State University. Of the Fort, the original stone blockhouse, guardhouse, and two officers' quarters remain. The visitor center has historical exhibits, and living history demonstrations are presented on weekends during summer. The Ellis County Historical Society Museum in Hays features the reconstructed Volga-German House as well as an 1873 church.

A major attraction is Sternberg Museum of Natural History where walk-through dioramas re-create Kansas in the Late Cretaceous period. Hays is also home to the original Boot Hill Cemetery; a small herd of endangered prairie bison; the Plymouth Stone Schoolhouse, built in 1874 by German settlers; 25 historical markers that denote significant sites in the downtown area; and Rattlers 'N' Relics, a museum which examines the history of Paleo-Native Americans through murals and relics such as a Hopi Ceremonial Rattlesnake Pit and a saber-toothed tiger skull.

Hays is at the junction of Hwy 183 and I-70. Bus services connect it with Topeka, Kansas City, and Denver, and there is an airport.
Map ref: page 430 F9

KANSAS CITY

The metropolitan area of Kansas City sprawls across the Kansas–Missouri state border. It is the second-largest city in the state,

Workers carrying out maintenance on an oil well; the discovery of oil near El Dorado started an important boom in the district.

with a population of 150,000. The portion that falls within Kansas lies on hilly countryside adjacent to the Kansas River. Most of the attractions lie over the border, but Kansas City, Kansas, does have historic interest.

Before the arrival of Europeans, the Kansa people inhabited the area. They left in the 1920s, after signing a treaty with the government and later, in 1873, sold their remaining lands, moving to a reservation in Oklahoma. In 1818 the US government made the area a reservation for the Delaware people. In the 1830s tribes such as the Wyandot and Shawnee, who had been forced off their lands to the east, began to settle in the area. The Shawnee Indian Mission was established in 1839 at 3403 W. 53rd Street by the Methodists to teach the English language and trade skills to Native Americans. In 1843 the Delaware sold the land to the Wyandot tribe who established a community known as Wyandot City which had the first free school in the territory. In the 1850s, when the government opened the territory up, Europeans arrived and renamed the settlement Wyandotte.

In the elections of 1855 pro-slavery candidates won control of the Kansas territorial legislature (with the help of like-minded Missourians who poured across the border to vote in the elections). This "Bogus Legislature," as it is sometimes known, passed pro-slavery laws and wrote a pro-slavery constitution. The laws were passed in the East Building (1841) of the Shawnee Indian Mission which, like the North Building (1845), is now open for inspection. However, the national congress refused to admit Kansas as a slave state. It was here, in 1859, that a convention wrote the first successful state constitution. Local citizens played a significant role in the anti-slavery movement and a number of African-Americans settled here after the Civil War.

When a meat-packing company opened in 1868, the industry attracted many immigrants from Europe. By 1880, their numbers had swelled the population to 3,200 residents. Other towns in the region grew around different meat-packing houses and, in 1886, Wyandotte merged with them to become Kansas City. By 1900, 50,000 people had settled there.

Kansas City offers a wide range of leisure activities, including bowling.

Of historic interest is the Huron Indian Cemetery, a nineteenth-century burial ground preserved in downtown Kansas City. Visitors can also see Grinter Place State Historic Site, an 1862 farmhouse with period furnishings, and Strawberry Hill Museum, which has exhibits relating to German, Russian, Balkan, and Eastern European communities. The history of slavery is remembered at Quindaro, a "station" on the Underground Railroad—a route along which escaped slaves were smuggled to freedom in Canada. To see it, visitors must apply to the Kansas City Public Library.

Kansas City is at the intersection of I-35, I-70, and I-29. Bus services connect it with Lawrence, Topeka, Abilene, Denver, and Wichita. Just over the state border are a train terminal and international airport.
Map ref: page 431 P8

KIOWA

Kiowa is a small town of 1,160 people on the state border with Oklahoma in south-central Kansas. The old City Hall and fire station have been converted into a local history museum. Artifacts include a hatchet wielded by Carry A. Nation, a violent advocate of the temperance movement in the 1890s, who allegedly began her campaign in Kiowa. Nation traveled around Kansas taking the law into her own hands by smashing

up saloons which continued to operate, although technically illegal under state prohibition law.

Hwy KS-2 goes west from here to Hardtner and north and east to Hazelton and Anthony.
Map ref: page 620 G4

LAWRENCE

Lawrence is a charming college town on the Kansas River, with long-standing liberal traditions. It was established in 1854 by New England abolitionists who wanted to prevent the territory entering the Union as a slave state. They also used the site as a "station" on the Underground Railroad. As a center of Free State sentiment it became the target of pro-slavery hostility and in May 1856, pro-slavery advocates attacked and burned most of Lawrence. Two

days later, John Brown led a counter-attack at Pottawatomie Creek, brutally killing five pro-slavery settlers. Another raid occurred in 1863 at the hands of William Quantrill. He and his men burned most of the town, killing 150 people. Watkins Community Museum of History features exhibits on Quantrill's Raid, the turmoil of the 1850s, the Underground Railroad, and James Naismith, the inventor of basketball.

The University of Kansas has the state's largest library, as well as the Spencer Art Museum, the Natural History Museum, and the Museum of Anthropology. The Haskell Indian Nations University, established in 1884, has students from 150 tribes and houses the Hiawatha Visitor Center and the American-Indian Athletic Hall of Fame.

Visitors can explore the West Lawrence historic district; interesting old cemeteries; the scenic drive along the Kansas River Valley; and a number of trails, including the Santa Fe and Oregon Trails.

The Prairie Park Nature Center is a 71-acre (29-ha) park with a virgin prairie and the Baker Wetlands Area where bald eagles can be seen. Clinton State Park is based around Clinton Reservoir where all manner of water sports can be enjoyed.

Lawrence is on I-70 between Kansas City and Topeka; both have airports. It also has buses and trains.
Map ref: page 431 N9

Cattle being driven through the historic town of Kiowa, a scene reminiscent of the Wild West.

LEAVENWORTH

Leavenworth was the first city in Kansas and the first capital of the Kansas Territory. It lies in the northeastern corner of the state beside the Missouri River and has a population of 40,000 residents. Nearby are Fort Leavenworth and Leavenworth Prison.

Before white settlement, the area was inhabited by the Kansa and Osage peoples. In 1827, Fort Leavenworth was founded by Colonel Henry Leavenworth to protect white pioneers on the Santa Fe Trail. It was the first permanent white settlement in Kansas. In the 1840s through-traffic increased when settlers began following the Oregon Trail to the less crowded lands of the nation's west. The city of Leavenworth was founded in 1854 as a major stop along that route. Among the early pioneers was Buffalo Bill Cody's family who moved here in 1854 when he was eight. His parents are buried in Leavenworth. Cuts in the hillside made by wagons on the Oregon and Santa Fe Trails can still be seen in some places.

Attractions include the Carnegie Arts Center, located in the oldest library building in Kansas; the First City Museum, featuring a collection of early frontier memorabilia; and the Richard Allen Cultural Center in historic Bethel Church, which was once part of the Underground Railroad, the escape route for slaves fleeing the United States. The Center focuses on local and national African-American history.

The Carroll Mansion (1867) features beautiful stained-glass windows, some outstanding handcrafted woodwork, and 16

rooms elegantly furnished in mid-Victorian style, with antiques of the era and artifacts that honor distinguished local citizens. One room has been transformed into a general store, another into a barber shop. Several times throughout the year actors portray a Victorian family as they prepare for their daughter's wedding.

The Gothic-style Chapel of the Veterans (1893), with its intriguing gargoyles and stained-glass windows, has served US veterans from every war since the 1848 Mexican War. It is the only house of worship in the nation in which Protestant and Catholic services can be conducted simultaneously under one roof.

To the north is historic Fort Leavenworth, which is the oldest continuously operating army post west of the Mississippi. Established in 1827, it was for many years the most important post on the western frontier. Those who served there include General Custer. The school, founded in 1881, is now the US Army Command and General Staff College and became known as the "leadership factory" because so many students and instructors went on to achieve high military rank. They have included George Marshall, Douglas MacArthur, George Patton, "Ike" Eisenhower (who graduated first in his class of 275), and Colin Powell. Historic structures include the Main Parade Ground and the Rookery which was built in 1834 as the first permanent headquarters. It is the oldest house in Kansas. The Frontier Army Museum examines the army's role in Western expansion from 1817 to 1917. A tour of the historic sites begins at

the information center and follows a series of limestone pedestal markers.

Near the Fort is Leavenworth Prison, a federal penitentiary built from 1895 to 1906. Past internees in this maximum security institution include Machine Gun Kelly, Al Capone, and Robert Stroud, the "Birdman of Alcatraz."

Leavenworth is on Route 7, 21 miles (34 km) north of Kansas City, which has a major airport.
Map ref: page 431 P8

MANHATTAN

Manhattan is a pleasant college city of about 40,000 people in the northern Flint Hills of Kansas. Short-story writer and journalist Damon Runyon was born here.

A large Kaw Native American village was once situated on the present site of Manhattan. Fort Riley was established to the southwest of the present town site in 1853. In 1854 two white settlements were established nearby. These were soon consolidated under the name of Boston. When a large group of new settlers arrived, the name was changed to Manhattan, reflecting hopes that the "Little Apple," as it is now called, would become a trading center to rival Manhattan in New York. Kansas State University was founded here between 1859 and 1863.

Manhattan has many historic buildings and museums. Worth

seeing are Aggieville Moro, an old shopping district full of interesting retail outlets; and Goodnow House, a stone farmhouse built in the 1860s by Isaac Goodnow, a leader in the Free State movement and one of the town's founders. He later established the college which became Kansas State University. Visitors to the University can enjoy the Marianna Kistler Beach Museum of Art, and the beautiful botanic gardens. Adjacent is Riley County Historical Museum.

Located in Pioneer Park is Hartford House, a prefabricated one-room house brought to the area by early settlers on a steamboat. Also of interest is the Wolf House Museum, based in an 1868 limestone boarding house and furnished with nineteenth-century period pieces, as well as the American Museum of Baking, the only baking museum in the United States.

An untouched native tallgrass prairie can be seen at the Konza Prairie Research Natural Area. The Oregon, Santa Fe, and Old Military Trails provide hiking and birdwatching opportunities in the Flint Hills. Tuttle Creek State Park is popular with anglers, and Sunset Zoo features animals of Kansas, Australia, South America, Asia, and Africa including snow leopards, tigers, and sloths.

Fort Riley, to the southwest of Manhattan, is known as the "Cradle of the Cavalry" because

Native tallgrass prairies, like this one near Manhattan, once covered half of Kansas.

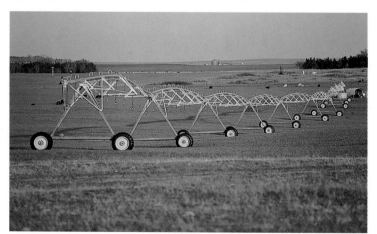

Irrigating farmland outside the historic frontier town of Leavenworth.

many cavalry regiments were formed here, including George Custer's 7th Cavalry, which suffered a dramatic defeat at Little Bighorn. The US Cavalry Museum, housed in the original 1855 hospital, features exhibits on American mounted forces from the Revolutionary War to 1950. The First Infantry Division Museum examines the Division's history from 1917 to the present. Custer House is an 1854 limestone structure that provides an insight into frontier life.

Also at the Fort is the First Territorial Capitol. The territory's first (pro-slavery) legislature met in this stone warehouse in 1855 before moving on to the Shawnee Mission (in Kansas City). It provides insight into the territorial and national conflict over slavery and into life on the Kansas frontier. In 1928 the building was rebuilt from its ruins. Visitors can also take a walk on the Kaw River Nature Trail which offers visitors outstanding views.

Manhattan is on the I-70 and has its own regional airport. Bus services connect Manhattan with Topeka, Kansas City, Denver, and Wichita.
Map ref: page 431 L8

NEWTON

Newton is a town of 17,000 people in Harvey County, south-central Kansas. It was established in 1871 by a group of Santa Fe Railroad stockholders in anticipation of the railway's arrival the following year and named after their hometown of Newton, Massachusetts. Newton's railroad service intersected with the Chisholm Trail which was a major stock route for Texas cattlemen and so the town experienced a period as an important cattle shipping center. As such, it was prone to the unruliness experienced by other early cattle towns such as Abilene and Dodge City.

Harvey County contains a significant Mennonite population stemming from the emigration of over 5,000 Mennonites from Russia between 1874 and 1884. They made an invaluable contribution to the community when they introduced a strain of winter wheat called Turkey Red which could be harvested in summer before it was ruined by heat and insects. As a result, by 1894, wheat had become the principal state crop, bringing vast wealth to Kansas. The Kauffman Museum, at Bethel College campus, has a good Mennonite display. The flour mill used to process the Turkey Red can still be seen. Built in 1879, Old Mill Plaza, as it is now known, was purchased in 1886 by Bernhard Warkentin, a young Russian refugee who did much to facilitate the Mennonite immigration. His home, Warkentin House, was completed in 1887. This 16-room Victorian house museum has retained about 80 percent of its original furnishings.

One rather unusual building in Newton is the railway station, built in 1929–30, which was modeled after Shakespeare's house in Stratford-on-Avon, England. Over the road is the historic and impressive Railroad Savings and Loan building, now known as 500 Main Place. Built of limestone, granite, marble, and brass, the entrance hall has 20-foot (6-m) high ceilings, tall arched windows, marble floors, decorative egg-and-dart plaster moldings, and beautifully finished birch woodwork. Goerz House (built in 1893), on Bethel Campus, was Bethel's first residence.

Other historic buildings include the Masonic Temple, which was the Harvey County courtroom from 1880 to 1883; the Queen Anne style S.A. Brown Home (1879); Neal House (1875); and Newton's oldest home, Muse House (1875). The Harvey County Historical Museum includes a Mexican Heritage room, and the Carriage Factory Gallery and Museum displays Kansas arts in an old carriage factory (1883–84).

Access is via Newton county airport, Hwys 50 and 81, and I-35. Train services extend west to Hutchinson and Dodge City and northeast to Topeka, Lawrence, and Kansas City, Missouri.
Map ref: page 621 J2

SALINA

Salina in central Kansas is home to the Kansas Wesleyan University. It has a population of 47,000. The region's history and heritage are explored at both the Smoky Hill Museum and the Central Kansas Flywheel Museum.

Downtown Salina displays a variety of period styles including Victorian homes and the Art Deco designs of the business district. The stained glass of Sacred Heart Cathedral is worth seeing because it illustrates the importance of wheat to the people of Kansas.

The Salina Art Center features regional, national, and international exhibits, a Discovery Area for children, and the new Art Center Cinema. Just north of Salina is Smoky Hill Vineyards and Winery. Hunting, fishing, hiking, and bird-watching can be enjoyed at nearby Lakewood Natural Area and Discovery Center. Just west of Salina is the Rolling Hills Refuge Wildlife Conservation Center, where 200 animals, including 61 endangered species, can be seen on the prairies. Inhabitants include an Indian rhinoceros, snow leopards, orangutans, white rhinos, giraffes, chimpanzees, and lemurs.

Salina is located on I-35 W. It is serviced by buses to a number of towns and by a regional airport.
Map ref: page 431 J9

The arrival of the railroad led to the establishment of many towns in Kansas, including Newton.

TOPEKA

The capital of Kansas, Topeka sits amid the gently rolling hills of the state's northeast. It is at the intersection of I-70 and I-35. The town has a population of 120,000 with 160,000 in the metropolitan area.

The area was originally occupied by members of the Kansa tribe. A ferry service was started on the Kansas River in 1842 to transport those traveling on the Oregon Trail. Topeka was established nearby in 1854 and it became the state capital in 1861. Significant historical buildings include the State Capitol; Cedar Crest, the Kansas governor's residence; and the First Presbyterian Church (1880s).

Kansas History Center is the state's largest historical museum. Its exhibits span 5,000 years. There is a Discovery Place for children and a nature trail. The beautiful Historic Ward-Meade Park features botanical gardens, a re-creation of an 1870s log cabin and brick-and-limestone residence, a one-room schoolhouse, and an early twentieth-century drugstore with working soda fountain. Gage Park is home to a carousel and Topeka Zoo.

History was made in this town in 1954 when Linda Brown, an African-American schoolgirl, challenged Topeka's Board of Education over the issue of racial segregation in public schools. She won the case, the US Supreme Court declaring segregation

Children playing basketball in Wichita.

inherently unequal and hence unconstitutional. The ruling gave African-Americans the leverage and encouragement they needed to challenge discrimination and sat at the very core of the civil rights movement which effectively began at Montgomery, Alabama, the following year. The school Brown attended, Monroe Elementary, is to become a National Historic Site.

Just outside Topeka, at Forbes Field, is the Kansas Air National Guard Air Park, with two hangars full of military aircraft dating back to World War I. Also worth taking a look at are the Kansas National Guard Museum and Mulvane Art Center at Washburn University. To the northeast of Topeka, fishing is popular in Perry Reservoir in Perry State Park. Lake Shawnee Recreational Area, built in the 1930s, is a large scenic park offering golfing, a botanical garden, an arboretum, camping, special events, and a vast lake for boating, fishing, and swimming.

Topeka has an international airport and is serviced by trains and buses.
Map ref: page 431 M9

WICHITA

With a population of 485,000, Wichita is the largest city in the state. It is in south-central Kansas at the confluence of the Arkansas and Little Arkansas Rivers. The city was the birthplace of jazz bandleader and composer Stan Kenton (1912–79) and the once reviled former American Communist Party leader Earl Browder (1891–1973). Wichita is now the world's largest

producer of general aviation aircraft. It has a lively arts scene, some very fine museums, and a number of public sculptures.

Plains Native Americans first occupied the area, and settlers entered the region in 1863 to trade with them. The next year, the government moved the Wichita tribe, after whom the city is named, to the area from Oklahoma. Wichita was incorporated in 1870. When the railroad arrived in 1872, it became an important cattle-shipping center. During this time famous frontiersman Wyatt Earp served as a law enforcement officer at Wichita. Earp later moved to Dodge City, then Tombstone, Arizona, where he was involved in the legendary gunfight at the O.K. Corral. During the land speculation of the 1880s the population grew from 5,000 to 24,000. In the early twentieth century, oil was discovered and the first airplane manufacturing plant was set up in 1919.

Wichita has many museums. The Indian Center and Museum features a 44-foot (13-m) statue of a Native American called *Keeper of the Plains* by Kiowa-Comanche artist Blackbear Bosin. The Old Cowtown Museum re-creates the Wichita of the 1870s cattle boom. The Wichita-Sedgwick County Historical Museum is in the old city hall (1892), a fine decorative stone building. The Museum has exhibitions on a vast range of local history subjects including the Wichita tribe, Victorian furnishings, and temperance crusader Carry A. Nation. The First National Black Historical Society of Kansas examines such subjects as the

Buffalo Soldiers, early African-American Wichitans and Kansans, and African-American art.

The Wichita Art Museum houses one of the nation's largest collections of American art. Art lovers should also visit the University's Ulrich Museum of Art in the McKnight Arts Center. One of its walls consists of an enormous glass mosaic by Joan Miro. The Corbin Education Center was designed by Frank Lloyd Wright, as was the Allen-Lambe House at 224 N. Roosevelt Street. Also at the University is the Museum of Anthropology which examines the diversity of ancient human cultures in various parts of the world.

Wichita's links with the aviation industry are reflected in the Kansas Aviation Museum in the old Art Deco air terminal, and Wichita State University's National Institute of Aviation Research, which features water tunnels and supersonic wind tunnels. Virtual-reality airplane flights are just one of the high-tech attractions at Exploration Place, a landscaped park with three theaters and hundreds of interactive exhibits.

Other attractions in Wichita are the Great Plains Transportation Museum, the botanical gardens, Sedgwick County Zoo, Wichita Center for the Arts, Omnisphere and Science Center, Lake Afton Observatory, and the Kansas Firefighters Museum. Maple Grove Cemetery, consecrated in 1888, is also well worth a visit.

Wichita can be reached via I-35. Train, bus, and air services are also available.
Map ref: page 621 J3

The State Capitol building is one of several significant nineteenth-century buildings in Topeka, the state capital since 1861.

NEBRASKA

Nebraska is known as "The Cornhusker State," reflecting its status as one of the nation's principal agricultural producers and the large proportion (95 percent) of its territory devoted to farmland. It is the 15th-largest and the 37th most populous member of the Union. Its inhabitants are chiefly of German, Irish, English, Czech, and Mexican descent. Omaha is its largest city, and Lincoln is the state capital.

One of the most popular activities for tourists is following the pioneers' footsteps along the Oregon, California, and Mormon Trails. Other historic attractions are the state's many museums and historic sites such as Fort Robinson, Homestead National Monument, Scotts Bluff, and Chimney Rock. Nebraska is also a state with many natural attractions, such as the forests and striking rock formations of Pine Ridge and the northwest badlands, its canoeable rivers, the bluffs along the Missouri River, paleontological sites such as Agate Fossil Beds, the wildlife refuges, and the Sandhills.

Father and son. Nebraska is a largely agricultural state, and farming is quite often a family affair.

In the colonial era the region was explored by the French and the Spanish, and both laid claim to it. At that time it was inhabited by the Omaha, Oto, Ponca, Missouri, and Pawnee peoples, although the Comanche, Arapaho, Cheyenne, and Sioux all hunted in western Nebraska. Until 1854 white settlement was forbidden. European visitation was limited to licensed fur traders, missionaries, Indian agents and, from 1843, settlers following the Oregon Trail to the nation's West. A land rush resulted from the combined effects of the declaration of the Nebraska Territory in 1854, the availability of free land under the 1862 *Homestead Act,* and construction of the railways from 1865.

Nebraska is the birthplace of Arbor Day (1872), the rodeo (1882), the United States' first and only unicameral (single chamber) legislature (1934), and such notable figures as Crazy Horse, Red Cloud, John J. Pershing, Willa Cather, Fred Astaire, Henry Fonda, Gerald Ford, Marlon Brando, Malcolm X, and Johnny Carson.

State motto Equality Before the Law
State flag Adopted 1925
Capital Lincoln
Population 1,711,263
Total area (land and water)
77,358 square miles (200,357 sq km)
Land area 76,878 square miles
(199,114 sq km)
Nebraska is the 15th-largest state
in size
Origin of name From an Oto Native
American word meaning "flat water"
Nicknames The Cornhusker State,
The Beef State, The Tree Planter State
Abbreviations NE (postal), Neb., Nebr.
State bird Western meadowlark
State flower Goldenrod
State tree Cottonwood
Entered the Union March 1, 1867
as the 37th state

Places in
NEBRASKA

AGATE FOSSIL BEDS NATIONAL MONUMENT

This national monument in north-western Nebraska contains world-famous deposits of ancient animal fossils, some dating back around 20 million years. An on-site museum displays such unusual remains as the antelope-like stenomylus, the dinohyus (a large tusked pig), a two-horned rhinoceros, and a creature with a horse-like head, rhinoceros-like forelegs, and bear-like hind legs.

Also on show are Native American artifacts and personal items that belonged to Red Cloud and James Cook. The former was a Teton Sioux chief who attacked white prospectors on Sioux land and then, in 1866, laid siege to three forts that had been set up to defend them. After two years the army agreed to abandon the forts and refrain from building any more roads through Sioux territory. He is thus considered the only Native American to ever win a war against the US government. Thereafter he lived peacefully with white people and settled on a reservation. Cook, a frontiersman, army scout, and cattle driver, discovered the fossil beds on his land.

The Agate Fossil Beds are located 23 miles (37 km) south of Harrison and 35 miles (56 km) north of Mitchell on US-29.
Map ref: page 428 B8

Cattle feed yards at Bridgeport. Cattle ranching has been a big part of Nebraska's economy since the mid-nineteenth century.

ALLIANCE

Alliance is the seat of Box Butte County in northwestern Nebraska. It is located 32 miles (51 km) north of Bridgeport via US-385, at the intersection with Route 2.

Two miles (3 km) north of town on US-385 is Carhenge, a Pop Art style assemblage of 36 junked Cadillacs, Chevys, and Plymouths painted gray and arranged at quite unusual angles to suggest an American-style parallel to England's ancient and venerable stone monument. Erected in 1987 by six local families during a family reunion, Carhenge attracts 50,000 tourists each year. However, its irreverent spirit and undeniable parallels with Stonehenge, widely held to have been a place of worship, have not met with universal approval. Fundamentalist Christians objected to its pagan connotations, while the Nebraska Department of Roads did its best to remove it. This action was avoided by the citizens of Alliance, who redrew the city boundaries in order to save Carhenge and the tourism it generates. On a nearby rise is another stark and haunting car sculpture known as The Four Seasons.

Also of interest at Alliance are the Carnegie Arts Center, which features works from Nebraskan artists; Dobby's Frontier Town, a re-creation of an early twentieth-century settlement; and the Knight Museum of the High Plains Heritage, which has interesting displays of pioneering and Native American artifacts from the region.

Anyone looking for a scenic drive would do well to investigate Route 2, a lengthy and solitary but exceptionally attractive drive through the Sandhills region which consists of a series of low hills and ridges formed of sand and covered with prairie grass. Cattle are plentiful but towns are small and scattered. This is a landscape of wildflowers, fish-filled rivers, lakes, streams, and ponds, the occasional farmstead, and some charming village churches. It is a longer but far more interesting alternative to I-80, the main east–west highway.
Map ref: page 428 C9

BEATRICE

Beatrice is located 38 miles (61 km) south of Lincoln on US-136. Gage County Historical Museum, in the 1906 Burlington Depot, has permanent exhibits on the County's industries, medical and dental history, and citizens, such as movie actor Robert Taylor. The Beatrice Big Blue Water Park is popular in summer. Two miles (3 km) south of nearby Filley is the largest limestone barn in the state, built in 1874. Rockford Lake State Recreation Area, 7 miles (11 km) east of Beatrice, centers around a 150-acre (61-ha) lake with 286 acres (116 ha) of land.
Map ref: page 431 K6

BRIDGEPORT

Bridgeport, in western Nebraska, is the seat of Morrill County. This likeable town is located 338 miles (544 km) northwest of Lincoln. Bridgeport sits on US-26, which follows the route of the Oregon Trail along the North Platte River. This historical association is celebrated at the town's Pioneer Trails Museum. Pioneers of the 1840s used various prominent natural landmarks to help keep them on track. Two such landmarks are the sandstone outcroppings known as Courthouse and Jail Rocks, located 4 miles (6 km) south of Bridgeport on Route 88. At Bridgeport State Recreation Area, visitors can enjoy the sandpit lakes and Wildcat Hills Nature Center.

Fifty-nine miles (95 km) southeast of Bridgeport and 3 miles (5 km) south of Lewellen is Ash Hollow State Historical Park. Interesting exhibits relate to the area's Native American and pioneering history. At Windlass Hill you can still see the ruts cut into the earth by the pioneers' wagons when they were lowered down the hill by rope.
Map ref: page 428 C10

Carhenge, an outstanding and controversial example of Pop Art, just north of Alliance.

CHIMNEY ROCK NATIONAL HISTORIC SITE

Chimney Rock is a striking and memorable rock spire that rises 500 feet (153 m) above the North Platte River. Visible 30 miles (48 km) away, it was used as an important landmark by pioneers on the Oregon Trail. It is 1 mile (1.6 km) south of the junction of Route 92 and US-26. A gravel road runs off Route 92 to within half a mile (800 m) of the Rock but rough terrain and rattlesnakes prevent closer access. A visitor center examines the history of the Oregon and other western trails.

Those wishing to further explore the pioneer lifestyle can take a trip on an original-style prairie schooner at Oregon Trail Wagon Train, 2 miles (3 km) south of Bayard.
Map ref: page 428 B10

FORT ROBINSON STATE PARK

Fort Robinson is Nebraska's largest state park. It is situated amid highly unusual rock formations and bluffs which sometimes rise to 1,000 feet (305 m) in the rugged White River Valley of Nebraska's northwestern Bad Lands. The preservation of the Fort Robinson site maintains crucial historical connections with the Indian Wars of the 1870s, which effectively obliterated an entire way of life.

Fort Robinson and an Indian Agency were established in the midst of ongoing conflict between white settlers and authorities on the one hand, and the Sioux, Cheyenne, and Arapaho peoples who were fiercely resisting the loss of their lands in western Nebraska. At that time some of the Sioux were living on a reservation under Chief Red Cloud. The US Army hoped to entice the rest of the Sioux to join him. In fact, in 1875 they ordered Crazy Horse and the rest of the Sioux to move onto the reservation but they refused.

In 1876, Crazy Horse led his warriors to famous victories over General Crook in the Battle of Rosebud and General Custer in the Battle of Little Big Horn. In 1877, to the bewilderment of many, he guided 900 of his men to Fort Robinson where he surrendered, demanding that the lands along the Powder River remain in Native American hands. However, a rumor spread that Crazy Horse planned to assassinate General Crook and an attempt was made to place him in jail on September 5. During the struggle he was stabbed by a soldier with a bayonet and died the following morning. It is unclear if this was a deliberate assassination or an incidental homicide. The site of the stabbing bears a stone marker.

The next year 300 Cheyenne fled their Oklahoma reservation and returned to their lands around the White River. A band of some 149 braves under Chief Dull Knife was captured and taken to Fort Robinson where the commanding officer denied them food in an attempt to subdue them. A group of young warriors escaped on January 9, 1879. They scaled the bluffs and remained at large without horses for nearly two weeks. Once located they refused to surrender, and a fight took place in which 64 Cheyenne and 11 soldiers died.

Today a fort complex retains the parade ground and the adobe officers' quarters, both dating from 1887. The Fort Robinson Museum has interesting displays that give a victor's viewpoint of the Fort's past, from the Indian Wars to World War II. The Trailside Museum focuses on Nebraska's natural history and includes a complete mammoth skeleton.

Close to the fort complex is the site of the Red Cloud Agency and a World War II prisoner-of-war camp for captured German soldiers. The Smiley Canyon Scenic Drive meanders through some of the Park's 22,000 acres (8,910 ha) of plains environment in which a herd of bison still roams. Separate tours highlighting the Park's history and natural environment depart from the Activity Center inside Sutler's Store, and an overview of the Park can be seen by taking a ride on the horse-drawn tour train. There are also 30 miles (48 km) of trails within the Park

Bison still roam Fort Robinson State Park.

which can be explored on foot, by mountain bike, or on horseback. Trail rides can be organized at the Fort's stables. Swimming, trout fishing, cross-country skiing, and hunting can also be enjoyed, depending on the season. Lodges, cabins, and camping are available.

Fort Robinson State Park is located on US-20, about 3 miles (5 km) west of Crawford and approximately 390 miles (628 km) northwest of Lincoln.

The awe-inspiring Chimney Rock, now a National Historic Site, was used as a landmark by travelers on the Oregon Trail. It can be seen from 30 miles (48 km) away.

FREMONT

Fremont, seat of Saunders County in eastern Nebraska, is 33 miles (53 km) northwest of Omaha. With 23,680 people, it is the state's sixth-largest city. Fremont was the birthplace of Harold Edgerton (1903–90), an American engineer and inventor who revolutionized high-speed photography with his electronic stroboscope.

The Louis May Historical Museum is a Victorian mansion that includes an 1868 log house, living history demonstrations, and re-created rooms of the nineteenth century. Visitors to Fremont can ride in vintage rail cars to investigate the Fremont and Elkhorn Valley Railroad, which takes in 15 miles (24 km) of lush river valley, and the historic town of Hooper. Fremont State Recreation Area offers 20 sandpit lakes, fishing, swimming, boating, camping, and picnicking.

Fremont is at the intersection of Hwy 30 and Hwy 77. There are also bus, train, and air services to the city.
Map ref: page 431 L3

GRAND ISLAND

With 40,000 people, Grand Island is Nebraska's third-largest city. The seat of Hall County in south-central Nebraska, it is an important manufacturing, food-processing, and distribution center. Grand Island is 86 miles (138 km) west of Lincoln and 4 miles (6.5 km) north of I-80, on US-281. It is the birthplace of movie actor Henry Fonda and of social-work pioneers Edith and Grace Abbott.

The Stuhr Museum of the Prairie Pioneer presents a restored 7-acre (3-ha) nineteenth-century railroad town with over 60 frontier

Loading seed for planting. In the 1860s, pioneers were enticed to farm the land that is now Homestead National Monument.

buildings, including the birthplace of Henry Fonda. An impressive and well-documented collection of Native American and pioneering artifacts can be seen in the rotunda, and there are some living history activities in the summer. Other attractions are the Heritage Zoo and Island Oasis Water Park. Grand Island is also the starting point of Route 2, a longer but far more scenic way of traveling westwards across the state than I-80.

Six miles (10 km) west of Grand Island is Crane Meadows Nature Center, which features 250 acres (100 ha) of wetlands and woodlands, with hiking trails and an interpretive center. Wildlife includes turtles, ducks, turkey, deer, coyote, and, from early March to mid-April, some of the 500,000 sandhill cranes that pause in the area during their annual migration. Camping, swimming, fishing, and a scenic lake can be enjoyed at Mormon Island State Recreation Area.
Map ref: page 430 G4

HASTINGS

Hastings, seat of Adams County, is located 90 miles (145 km) west of Lincoln on US-281. It is home to the substantial Hastings Museum which features exhibits on the Old West, the state's natural history, Native American history, vintage transportation, and antique firearms. Related films are screened in the IMAX theatre. The museum has a planetarium, and visitors can also view the universe at Hastings College Observatory. The Asmat Museum, located at the Crosier Monastery, features a rare collection of wood carvings and other display material relating to the Asmat tribe of New Guinea. Three miles (5 km) east of town is the largest World War II ammunition plant in the country, featuring bunkers, buildings, and covered walkways.
Map ref: page 430 G5

HOMESTEAD NATIONAL MONUMENT

Homestead National Monument commemorates the pioneers who rushed to the West to take up land under the 1862 *Homestead Act*. This legislation provided for one-tenth of the entire landmass to be issued in 160-acre (65-ha) allotments to individuals for free, provided they lived on the land for five years and improved it. By encouraging settlement in this way, the *Act* had a profound impact on patterns of land usage, migration, immigration, and agriculture, and on the lives of Native Americans.

Many of the Nebraskan pioneers who took up an allotment endured considerable hardship on the prairies in the days before irrigation and scientific farming. Aside from adverse seasonal factors such as drought, grasshopper plagues, and low produce prices, there was a general deficit of water and trees which meant that many farmers had to build homesteads from blocks of sod. For this reason they were known as "sodbusters."

However, this was not the case for all. Homestead Monument preserves a log cabin established in 1863 by Daniel Freeman who was one of the first to take up an allotment under the *Homestead Act*. The cabin, a nineteenth-century schoolhouse, and a museum foster understanding of the pioneer experience. Hiking trails pass through a field of tallgrass prairie, which re-creates the appropriate historical setting.

The Monument is 4 miles (6 km) west of Beatrice on Hwy 4 and 42 miles (68 km) south of Lincoln in the state's southeast.
Map ref: page 431 K6

KEARNEY

Kearney, seat of Buffalo County, is the state's fifth-largest city with 24,396 people. It is adjacent to I-80, 125 miles (201 km) west of Lincoln in south-central Nebraska. Because Kearney is a college town, it has a number of student bars and inexpensive restaurants.

Seven miles (11 km) southeast of Kearney is Fort Kearney State

Inspecting the railroad track. Grand Island is an important distribution center.

Historical Park. The Fort was built in 1848 to protect pioneers on the Oregon Trail from attacks by Native Americans. It was at this point that westbound trails merged. The Fort closed in 1871 when the trail was rendered redundant by the transcontinental railroad. Today the re-created buildings include a stockade, powder magazine, and blacksmith's. The Fort's role on the frontier is examined through interpretive displays, a walking tour of the extensive grounds, and an audiovisual presentation at the visitor center. Two miles (3 km) northeast is the Fort Kearney State Recreation Area which offers camping, a 5-mile (8-km) hiking–cycling trail along the Platte River, and, in the spring, thousands of migrating sandhill cranes.

Other attractions include the interactive displays of the Kearney Children's Museum; historic Frank House (1889) at the University of Nebraska; the Museum of Nebraska Art, which features works by or about Nebraskans; the Trails & Rails Museum, housed in a Union Pacific depot; and the eight-story Great Platte River Road Archway Monument, which spans I-80. The latter features a vast area of historical exhibits that examine the evolution of travel and communications along the Platte River Road from the Oregon, Mormon, and California Trails, and the Pony Express, to today's transcontinental superhighway and fiber optics.
Map ref: page 430 F5

LINCOLN

Lincoln is the state capital of Nebraska. With 192,000 people, it is the second-largest city in the state. Located 50 miles (80 km) southwest of Omaha on I-80, it is an educational, government, and retail shopping center with many fine parks and gardens, an active nightlife, and a reputation for a high standard of living. Lincoln is serviced by the highway system, a large airport, and trains and buses. The Nebraska State Fair, held in Lincoln, is one of the state's most important annual events.

White settlers were drawn to the area by the Salt Valley Lakes. The city was founded in 1859 and initially named Lancaster. With the bestowal of statehood in 1867, it was chosen as the state capital and

was renamed Lincoln to honor the recently assassinated President. The University of Nebraska was established in Lincoln by the state legislature in 1869, and the first railroad arrived in 1870.

Dominating the skyline of Lincoln and the surrounding plains is the State Capitol building which is an interesting departure, architecturally, from the usual Classical designs of such buildings. With its 400-foot (122-m) domed tower, it is the tallest building in the state. There are free tours of the beautifully detailed interior with its mosaic floor and murals representing the state's natural, social, and political development. Commanding views of the city can be had from the 14th floor. Visitors can also view the country's only unicameral (single chamber) legislature in action. The statue of Abraham Lincoln is attributed to Daniel Chester French, who created the sculpture of the Lincoln Memorial in Washington DC.

The Historic Haymarket District is the warehouse and farmer's market section of the city. Today it features galleries, restaurants, and antique shops in late-nineteenth-century buildings. The city's oldest building is Kennard House (1869), named for the first Nebraskan secretary of state. A more prominent political

The Historic Haymarket District, formerly Lincoln's warehouse and market area.

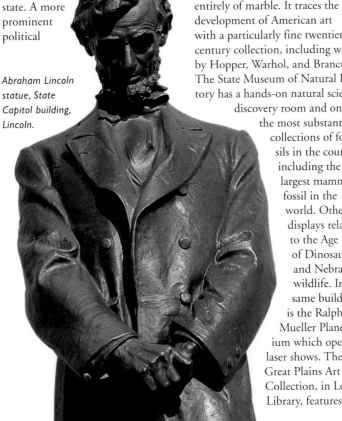

Abraham Lincoln statue, State Capitol building, Lincoln.

figure was William Jennings Bryan, an orator and unsuccessful presidential candidate on three occasions. He moved to Lincoln in 1887, and served Nebraska in the House of Representatives from 1891 to 1895. In the 1920s Bryan was seen as a hero or a fool, depending on one's beliefs, for aiding the prosecution in the infamous and highly public Scopes "Monkey" Trial, in which John Scopes was prosecuted for teaching Darwinian theory in a Tennessee school.

Not far north of the capital is the University of Nebraska, which is home to numerous attractions. The Sheldon Memorial Art Gallery and Sculpture Garden is made entirely of marble. It traces the development of American art with a particularly fine twentieth-century collection, including works by Hopper, Warhol, and Brancusi. The State Museum of Natural History has a hands-on natural science discovery room and one of the most substantial collections of fossils in the country, including the largest mammoth fossil in the world. Other displays relate to the Age of Dinosaurs and Nebraska wildlife. In the same building is the Ralph Mueller Planetarium which operates laser shows. The Great Plains Art Collection, in Love Library, features

western artworks, including sculptures by Russell and Remington, and works by Native American artists. Other attractions include the Larsen Tractor Museum; the International Quilt Study Center; the Lentz Center for Asian Culture; and the Robert Hillestead Textiles Gallery, which showcases fiber art, textiles, and apparel from a range of eras and locations. The college football team, the Cornhuskers, is enthusiastically supported at the 76,000-seat Memorial Stadium.

Lincoln also sustains several off-campus museums. The Museum of Nebraska History examines the state's anthropological history. There is a moving exhibit on the Native Americans of the Great Plains and a hands-on room for children. The National Museum of Roller Skating features skates, costumes, films, and other skating memorabilia dating back to 1819. Other attractions are the Frank Woods Telephone Pioneer Museum, the Lincoln Children's Museum, and a museum dedicated to preserving the culture and history of immigrants from Russia.

Folsom Children's Zoo and Botanical Gardens features 300 animals from 95 species as well as train and pony rides. On the western side of town is Nine Mile Prairie, where visitors can hike amid the natural landscape of the region. Pioneers Park and Nature Center has a range of wildlife, including bison, deer, and elk, as well as 5 miles (8 km) of trails. The Salt Valley Lakes are popular fishing and recreational areas, particularly Pawnee Lake and Branched Oak Lake.
Map ref: page 431 L5

Union Pacific rail reclassification yards, North Platte. The city is associated with railroads and Buffalo Bill Cody.

NORTH PLATTE

North Platte began in 1866 as a construction camp for railroad workers. It is the seat of Lincoln County in central Nebraska and the center of a farming and cattle-raising region. This city of 23,000 people is located at the intersection of I-80 and US-83, 213 miles (343 km) west of Lincoln. Nearby, North and South Platte Rivers meet to form Platte River. The largest mammoth fossil in the world was unearthed south of the city, near Wellfleet.

North Platte is a railroad town through which most of the transcontinental rail traffic passes. Bailey Yards, the world's largest rail reclassification yards, can be viewed from an observation deck. However, the city's main tourist attraction is the Buffalo Bill Ranch State Historic Park which is based around the former home of Buffalo Bill Cody. The 1886 ranch house and barn are full of memorabilia and nineteenth-century farm equipment. There are trail rides and screenings of Thomas Edison's film showing Cody's Wild West Show in action. The Buffalo Bill Rodeo is held in June as part of the city's Nebraskaland Days celebration.

At the Fort Cody Trading Post a replica of Cody's Wild West Show is displayed on the half hour. Lincoln County Historical Museum and Western Heritage Village, adjacent to the Buffalo Bill Ranch, displays tools, weapons, wagons, and other artifacts in a restored Old West Town.

Six miles (10 km) south of North Platte is Lake Maloney State Recreation Area which offers camping, fishing, boating, picnicking, and other outdoor activities. East of North Platte is the town of Gothenburg which retains an original Pony Express Station, used from 1860 to 1861.

US-83 heads north from North Platte. It offers fine views of the Sandhills' native shortgrass prairie and passes a section of Nebraska National Forest, near Halsey, which is the largest planted forest in the nation. Further north are the open country and trails of Valentine National Wildlife Refuge and the forests of Fort Niobrara National Wildlife Refuge, which shelters elk, bison, and longhorn cattle.

Fifty miles (80 km) west of North Platte is the town of Ogallala where Front Street is an 1880s re-creation with jail, barbershop, and wooden boardwalk. There is also the Cowboy Museum and the

Mansion on the Hill. Just north of Ogallala is Lake McConaughy. Known as "Big Mac," it is the basis of a State Recreation Area famous for its sandy beaches, fishing, and water sports.
Map ref: page 430 C4

OMAHA

Omaha is a substantial, prosperous, and essentially suburban city with a lively nightlife, many parks and natural recreation areas, a very good zoo, and an interesting history which is reflected in its numerous museums. With a total population of 640,000, it is the largest city in Nebraska. One-eighth of the population is African-American, with significant English, Irish, German, Italian, Polish, Swedish, and Mexican ancestries represented as well. Located on the eastern border of Nebraska, Omaha is one of the world's leading food-processing areas, an important national center for rail and insurance, and regional headquarters for the finance, industrial, trade, and service sectors.

The westward expedition of Lewis and Clark passed through this area in 1804 and a few years later a fur-trading post was established to the north of present-day Omaha. At that time the Missouri, Omaha, and Oto tribes occupied the land. Susan La Flesche Picotte (1865–1915), daughter of an Omaha chief and the first Native American woman to become a physician, was born on a local reservation.

In 1819 the US Army built Fort Atkinson on bluffs overlooking the river, about 8 miles (13 km) north of present-day Omaha. It became the site of the state's first school, library, sawmill, gristmill, and brickyard. The Fort was abandoned in 1827. A reconstruction forms the basis of Fort Atkinson State Historical Park.

Forced out of Illinois in 1846, 12,000 Mormons traveled to present-day Omaha where 4,000 stopped to recover before continuing on to Salt Lake City. The 600 followers who died during their stay are buried in the cemetery at the Historic Winter Quarters.

In 1854 a treaty gave most of the Omaha hunting grounds to the US government. This opened up the newly created Nebraska Territory for settlement. The city of Omaha was surveyed and laid out the same year. From this prairie outpost travelers prepared to embark upon the Oregon and Mormon Trails and the trek to the Colorado goldfields. Omaha was chosen by the Territorial legislature as the capital in 1855 and, by 1860, the population was 1,883. In 1865 Omaha became the base for the construction of the first transcontinental rail system and the western headquarters of Union Pacific. In 1867, the state capital was moved to Lincoln.

Fort Omaha was set up in 1868 as a staging post for soldiers heading west to counter Native American resistance. Ten years later, the Fort's commander was General Crook who led campaigns against the Sioux under Crazy Horse and the Apache under Geronimo.

In the 1880s Omaha became an important meat-processing center. The meat-packing plants drew

Omaha's Old Market District has become a popular downtown restaurant area.

thousands of immigrants from southern and central Europe. Consequently, the population had reached 191,000 by 1920, with manufacturing continuing to grow throughout the century.

In 1948, Offutt Air Force Base, south of Omaha, became the headquarters of the Strategic Air Command (SAC) which served as the United States' main deterrent against nuclear attack during the Cold War. The enormous Strategic Air Command Museum is located en route to Lincoln, adjacent to the very popular Mahoney State Park. Nearby is Simmons Wildlife Safari Park which is a drive-through park featuring North America's wild animals such as bison, pronghorns, elk, and waterfowl.

The outstanding Henry Doorly Zoo is the state's premier tourist attraction. It features a wildlife safari, an aquarium display with a 70-foot (21-m) underwater observation tunnel, a large open-air aviary, North America's largest wild cat complex, an excellent bear canyon, rare white Siberian tigers, an IMAX theater, and the Lied Jungle, a huge indoor rainforest populated by fauna of South America, Asia, and Africa such as howler monkeys, leopards, and exotic birds.

As with many American cities, malls are killing off the old downtown area, although the Old Market District is now a fashionable restaurant area. Nearby is

Heartland of America Park, which features a tall fountain with a colored light show, and boat rides.

The wonderful Joslyn Art Museum has a fine collection of works by American, European, and Native American artists, including El Greco, Monet, Degas, and Jackson Pollock. Karl Bodmer's watercolors and prints chart his journey to the Missouri River frontier in the early 1830s. Omaha Children's Museum offers engaging hands-on exhibits.

Other museums offer a range of specialized historical themes. The Great Plains Black Museum looks at the contribution of African-Americans to life on the prairies, as slaves, homesteaders, and cavalry outfits known as Buffalo Soldiers. El Museo Latino focuses on the art, culture, and history of the Latino people of the Americas, while Riekes Museum has displays on the history of synagogues in Omaha. Freedom Park is a naval museum which features a minesweeper, a training submarine, and an amphibious landing ship from World War II, and other military artifacts.

Visitors can also inspect the very different sites upon which stood the childhood homes of Malcolm X and President Ford. Both men moved to Michigan as children.

Civil rights leader Malcolm X was born in Omaha.

Omaha was also the birthplace of Marlon Brando, Fred Astaire, and Lawrence Klein, who won the Nobel prize for economics in 1980.

Neale Woods Nature Center preserves 550 acres (223 ha) of forests, prairies, and woodlands along the Missouri River. There are bird-feeding stations, a seasonal butterfly garden, and trails. Other recreational attractions are the Botanical Gardens, the four Papio Dam Sites, and Chalco Hills Recreation Area. South of Omaha, at historic Bellevue, is the Fontenelle Forest Nature Center which features 1,300 acres (527 ha) of forest and wetland, walking and hiking trails, and a boardwalk overlooking the forest floor.

Omaha is serviced by an airport, as well as trains, buses, and I-80.
Map ref: page 431 M3

SCOTTSBLUFF

The towns of Scottsbluff and nearby Gering are the commercial centers for the farmlands of western Nebraska. Scottsbluff is on US-26, 368 miles (592 km) northwest of Lincoln.

Two miles (3 km) west of Gering on Route 92 is Scotts Bluff National Monument, a famous clay and sandstone landmark of the Oregon and Mormon Trails, which rises 800 feet (244 m) above the North Platte River. The Monument is named for the fur trader Hiram Scott, who was found dead at the foot of the Bluff under mysterious circumstances in 1828. It was known to the Plains tribes as "meapate," meaning "hill that is hard to get around" and, initially, pioneers considered the Bluff too dangerous to cross. In the 1850s a single-file wagon trail was forged through the narrow confines of Mitchell's Pass and the wear and tear caused by the traffic can still be seen on the section of the trail that is preserved at the pass. Access from the visitor center is via the Oregon Trail Pathway.

From atop the Bluff visitors can experience the outstanding views that the trailblazers saw 150 years ago, and walk along the nature trails. The visitor center contains the fascinating Oregon Trail Museum, which is full of historic and geological material.
Map ref: page 428 B10

The road to Scottsbluff, a commercial center for the farmlands of western Nebraska. Scotts Bluff National Monument, a landmark of the Oregon Trail, is nearby.

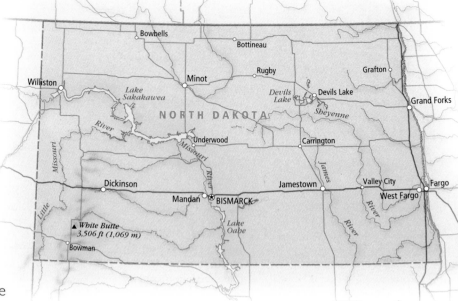

NORTH DAKOTA

North Dakota is located in the central-north of the United States, in the heart of the spring wheat belt, where wheat is planted in the spring and harvested in late summer. The state is surpassed only by Kansas in total wheat production.

North Dakota begins at Canada's Manitoba border. It is located on the 100th meridian at US-83, which divides the eastern United States and the arid western deserts. North Dakota is part of the Great Plains states, which are 2,500 miles (4,023 km) long and 600 miles (965 km) across at their widest point.

From north to south these states include Montana, Wyoming, Colorado, New Mexico to the east, and North Dakota, South Dakota, Nebraska, Kansas, and Oklahoma to the west. Texas is the most southern state. They are located 500 and 1,000 miles (805 and 1,609 km) inland from the Pacific Ocean, 1,000 miles (1,609 km) inland from the Atlantic Ocean, and 500 miles (805 km) inland from the Gulf of Mexico. Their western boundary is the Rocky Mountains.

The early residents of North Dakota were Native

The cool climate of North Dakota is perfect for the production of wheat crops.

Americans. The Cheyenne people occupied the Sheyenne River Valley, the Hidatsa moved to the Missouri River, and the Sioux moved onto the plains. In the late 1700s, Europeans, such as Lasalle and Henry Hudson, claimed territories and began fur trading. The first European settlement was established by Alexander Henry Jr near Pembina in 1801, when he moved his fur post there. By this time, fur trading was opened up with Canada and a trade route was established. After the Indian Wars ended and railroads were built, settlers moved in to take advantage of the area's rich farmlands. In 1861, when the region became a territory of the United States, it was named for the Dakota people who lived there. North Dakota's nickname, "The Peace Garden State," refers to the International Peace Garden on the border between North Dakota and Manitoba, Canada. It is also called "The Flickertail State," which refers to the flickertail ground squirrel common to central North Dakota.

State motto Liberty and Union, Now and Forever: One and Inseparable
State flag Adopted 1911
Capital Bismarck
Population 642,200
Total area (land and water) 70,704 square miles (183,123 sq km)
Land area 68,994 square miles (178,694 sq km)
North Dakota is the 17th-largest state in size
Origin of name From the Sioux word meaning "allies"
Nicknames The Sioux State, The Peace Garden State, The Flickertail State
Abbreviations ND (postal), N. Dak.
State bird Western meadowlark
State flower Wild prairie rose
State tree American elm
Entered the Union November 2, 1889 as the 39th state

Places in
NORTH DAKOTA

BISMARCK

Bismarck is located off I-94, halfway between Fargo and the Theodore Roosevelt National Park. Bismarck (population 50,000) was named for a wealthy European, the Chancellor of the German Empire, in order to make the state attractive to European investors and settlers. The ancestors of North Dakota emigrated from Norway, Germany, Russia, and Canada.

Bismarck is the capital city of North Dakota—one of the smallest capital cities in the United States. It is the administrative capital of North Dakota and is also a major commercial center.

The mean temperatures in Bismarck are representative for the rest of the state. January is the coldest month with an average temperature of just 9°F (–13°C), and July, which is the warmest month, with an average temperature of 70°F

Statue of Sacagawea, Bismarck.

(21°C). North Dakota is known for its hot summers and long, cold winters. It can also have extremes in temperatures with killing frosts.

Bismarck is a natural transportation junction because here the Missouri River is narrow enough to be easily crossed. Bismarck expanded following the building of the railroads, gold strikes and, more recently, the discovery of oil and synthetic fuels. It has thousands of parkland acres, well-preserved historical sites, and old-fashioned boat rides on the Missouri.

Washington and 9th Streets are the main streets running north–south, and Main Avenue, Divide Avenue, and Interstate Avenue run east–west.

The State Capitol building is nicknamed "Skyscraper of the Prairies." It is a 19-story, white, angular, Art Deco, limestone building. It can be toured for free daily. In the grounds is a statue of Sacagawea, the only woman to

travel with Lewis and Clark on their famed expedition.

The North Dakota Heritage Center houses an array of historical and cultural exhibits. There are treasures from the Lewis and Clark era—North Dakotans are proud of the fact that North Dakota is where the expedition spent most of its time. The center is open daily. It is free but it does accept donations.

There are many lively coffee houses and restaurants to choose from with a wide variety of cuisines on offer. There are hotels along US-83 and I-94. The visitor center has more information on dining and lodging and is open daily.

The Bismarck Municipal Airport is located on Airport Road 2 miles (3 km) southeast of the city. Buses also service the area. Map ref: page 426 G7

DEVILS LAKE

The town of Devils Lake has a population of 7,782. It is situated 85 miles (137 km) west of Grand Forks on the US-2. The nineteenth-century section of Devils Lake has

The Lewis & Clark paddleboat, Bismarck.

been painted and beautifully renovated to attract tourists. The town used to be a major stop for the educational group, the Chautauquas, that traveled across the country during the late nineteenth and early twentieth centuries.

The local visitor center is on US-2 at the southern end of town. The wetlands and water south of the town are one of the biggest tourist attractions in the state of North Dakota—Devils Lake is the largest natural salt-water lake in the state. It has bird-watching, hunting, and fishing opportunities.

Devils Lake Municipal Airport services the area, and Grand Forks has an international airport. Map ref: page 427 K4

Wheat farm with grain elevator, located near Devils Lake. The town of Devils Lake is a major trade and service center for the surrounding agricultural area.

The Superintendent's Residence at Fort Totten historic site, built in 1867.

FARGO

Fargo is located in southeastern North Dakota. It has a population of 62,000, making it the largest city in North Dakota. The city's greatest claim to fame is the recognition it received for the movie of the same name, which was made in 1996. Although very little of the movie was actually filmed in Fargo and the accent of the characters belongs more to Minnesotans, it brought the town notoriety. Fargo and Moorhead flank the Red River on the east and west. The sister cities are connected by a network of streets numbered from north to south with Maine Street as the central east–west thoroughfare.

One of North Dakota's leading newspapers, the *Forum*, is published here. Fargo is also home to 20,000 students who attend North Dakota State University, Moorhead State, and Concordia College. In the summer, Moorhead University rents dorm rooms to tourists. There are also plenty of motels along I-29 and 13th Avenue. Visitors wishing to camp can do so in Lindenwood Park at 17th Avenue and 5th Street. The park also offers many trails for hiking or mountain biking.

The predominant heritage in Fargo is Norwegian, and at the Heritage Hjemkomst Center visitors can enjoy its rich history and legends. It is also home to a 76-foot (23-m) Viking ship built by local, Robert Asp. In 1982, the ship sailed 6,100 miles (9,815 km) from Duluth, Minnesota, to Bergen, Norway. The Scandinavian Hjemkomst Festival is held each year in late June. It has music, dance, local food, and cultural exhibits. Throughout the summer months, Trollwood Park celebrates the Norwegian culture with similar festival weekends.

Hector International Airport is located in Fargo.
Map ref: page 427 N7

FORT TOTTEN

Historic Fort Totten is located on Hwy 57, 14 miles (23 km) south of Devils Lake. Fort Totten and Sully's Hill National Game Preserve are located on the 137,000-acre (55,485-ha) Fort Totten Sioux Indian Reservation. It is one of the country's best-preserved nineteenth-century military forts. Daily admission is free. There is also a theater where visitors can see productions during July and August. There is a central square with a museum and several shops. The last weekend of July is the Fort Totten Days observance. Here visitors can see a rodeo and a powwow with highly skilled Native American dancers.

Powwows were originally held in the spring to celebrate the new beginnings of life. The Native people would get together and sing, dance, renew old acquaintances, or make new ones. In the Sioux tradition, this celebration was a prayer to Wakan-Tanka, the "Great Spirit" or "Grandfather." Today, they are still important for many Native Americans, but when the Powwow announcer calls an "intertribal dance," everyone takes part—including any spectators.

Next door to Fort Totten is Sully's Hill National Game Preserve. This is a 1,600-acre (648-ha) refuge for elk, deer, bison, and other wildlife, which are visible from the hiking trails. Another big attraction is the Dakota Sioux Casino, which is one of North Dakota's largest. Apart from Nevada and New Jersey, casino-style gambling is only permitted on Indian reservations throughout the United States.

Devils Lake Municipal Airport services the area, and Grand Forks has an international airport.
Map ref: page 427 J4

GRAND FORKS

Grand Forks is located in eastern North Dakota. It has a population of 52,500 and is the oldest and second-largest community (after Fargo) in North Dakota. The heart of Grand Forks County, the city is at the junction of the Red Lake River and the Red River—it was named by the French fur trappers.

Grand Forks is the processing and shipping center of an accomplished agricultural region, which produces potatoes, sugar, beets, wheat, and livestock. The area was first settled in 1869 when settlers began arriving and the area grew as a river port for the shipbuilding industry. Today, Grand Forks is rated as one of the "Top Ten Most Livable Places" in the United States. Even after the devastating floods of 1997, the community quickly and energetically re-built itself as the cultural capital of the region.

Miraculously, the North Dakota Museum of Art survived the flood undamaged. It is home to dance and theatrical performances. It also holds the state's only contemporary art collection and is open daily.

Along the massive railroad yards north of De Mers Avenue is the 11,000-student University of North Dakota. Student activities from theater to festivals keep the community lively and youthful. A local

newspaper, the *Grand Forks Herald*, is a leading newspaper in North Dakota. The Chester Fritz Auditorium is the place to catch the big-name acts as well as a local venue for concerts and various stage performances. The auditorium is renowned for its great acoustics—even the great Tony Bennett was impressed when he performed here. Grand Forks sponsors its own community symphony orchestra.

Also close to the campus is the Center for Aerospace Studies, which is open for tours. There are many eateries in town. For information on lodging and activities, contact the Grand Forks visitor center.

Grand Forks International Airport services the area.
Map ref: page 427 N4

JAMESTOWN

Jamestown is in southeastern North Dakota on the James River, about 100 miles (161 km) west of Fargo on the I-94. It was founded in 1872 and today has a population of 16,000. It is a trade and transportation center for processed food, farm machinery, grain, and Aerospace equipment manufacturing, and Jamestown College is here.

Jamestown is located in the heart of buffalo country and here the legend of the American buffalo lives. The proud members of the community have formed the Jamestown Area Buffalo Association (JABA), which is a non-profit organization, dedicated to the preservation and promotion of the American buffalo, or bison.

Jamestown is home to the National Buffalo Museum, the world's largest buffalo, and "White Cloud," a rare albino bison. All along the plains surrounding Jamestown you will see the largest concentration of buffalo in the United States.

Another interesting attraction is the Annual Wagon Train. This adventure takes place for one week in June and starts at the historic Fort Seward, which overlooks the city. The wagon train consists mainly of canvas-topped, flare-boxed, wooden-wheeled wagons, much like the ones in Western movies.

Dairying is one of Mandan's most important agricultural industries.

The ride starts at dawn after breakfast. It averages 3–4 miles (5–6 km) per hour. The wagon train stops at historic sites along the way. Families and individuals are welcome, and visitors can rent pioneer clothing for the occasion.

Jamestown Municipal Airport is located here, and Hector International Airport is in Fargo.
Map ref: page 427 K7

MANDAN

Mandan is located in southern North Dakota, on the Missouri River opposite Bismarck and along the Heart River. Its population is approximately 16,000. It is named for the Mandan tribe and means "people of the riverbank."

The city has a large livestock market and is a center for farm-trade and transportation, and the manufacture of petroleum and construction materials. After 1882, when the Northern Pacific Railroad built a bridge from Bismarck, the city grew quickly to become a shipping and warehousing center.

There are two statues to see in Mandan—one of Teddy Roosevelt in front of the train station and one of a Native American carved from a cottonwood tree. For a truly American tradition, stop for a sandwich and milkshake at the Mandan Drugstore on Main Street.

South of Mandan, on Hwy 1806 along the Missouri River, is the sprawling Fort Abraham Lincoln

State Park. The park was originally a fur-trading post set by the Northwest Company in 1780. In 1872, it fell into the hands of the US Army and its name was changed to its current one. Soon afterward, General Custer took command of the post and, in 1876, it gained its national claim to fame as he and his 250 men left for Little Big Horn and their final demise. In 1891, the fort was abandoned and dismantled by the townspeople in order to build homes, and today almost everything is a reconstruction of the original. It is a beautiful park, which covers over 1,000 acres (405 ha). There are barracks, stores, stables, and even a replica of General Custer's house, which is open for guided tours. There is a museum, which covers the history of the region from prehistoric times until Custer's last stand. Most interesting of all is the "On-A-Slant Indian Village," which is an excavated Mandan village dating from the mid-seventeenth century. It consists of four full-scale earth lodges re-created to be exact replicas of Mandan dwellings. The park is open daily and there is a small entry fee. The Fort Lincoln Trolley, from Mandan, runs along the river to Fort Abraham Lincoln.

The Bismarck Municipal Airport is conveniently located on Airport Road, just 2 miles (3 km) southeast of Bismarck. Buses also service the area.
Map ref: page 426 F7

Grain being transported by truck from the major shipping town of Grand Forks.

The 100-year-old Assumption Abbey in Richardton is run by Benedictine monks. The church is surrounded by 2,000 acres (810 ha) of farmland and has a commercial wine cellar.

MINOT

Minot is a city in northern North Dakota, located on the Souris River at the junction of US-2 and US-83. The city has the nickname "Magic City" because of its quick rise to fame and fortune after the Northern Railroad came through in 1887. With a population of 34,544, Minot is a commerce center for agriculture, especially durum wheat. Also manufactured here are processed food, farm equipment, plastics, petroleum, and building materials. The city is also home to the Minot State University. The Minot Air Force Base has underground missile silos throughout the area. The Upper Souris and J. Clark Salyer National Wildlife Refuges are close by—it is a good idea to check opening times since they are not always open to visitors.

The most important event in Minot is the North Dakota State Fair. It is held annually in the third week of July and is a huge event that is visited by people from all over the state. It is held on the North Dakota State Fairgrounds and in the North Dakota State Fair Center. The fair is worth visiting and has livestock, entertainment, horse shows, rodeos, and fireworks. Visitors can camp close by or stay in one of many motels or hotels.

Another attraction, in the heat of summer, is Roosevelt Park, which is located between the fairgrounds and downtown Minot. It is full of huge and beautiful gardens along

Workers on a wheat farm near Sheyenne, taking a lunch break.

the banks of the Souris River and has a large swimming pool with a water slide. It is open daily with a small entrance fee. In October, visitors can attend "North America's Largest Scandinavian Festival"— the Norsk Hostfest, where the Scandinavian potato flatbread, *lefse*, is a significant part of the many festivities to be enjoyed.

There are many fast-food stands and restaurants in Minot. For night owls there are a few live honky-tonk bars that stay open late. There are many motels lining the exits off US-2 and US-83. Here visitors will also find bars and cafés.

Minot conveniently has its own international airport.
Map ref: page 426 F3

NEW SALEM

New Salem (population 900) is 3 square miles (9 sq km) in area. It is 32 miles (51 km) from Bismarck and is recognized as a leading dairy center in North Dakota.

The main reason for travelers driving to/and or through New Salem is to see the world's largest roadside attraction—a sculpture of a giant cow. Salem Sue is the world's largest Holstein cow. She is 38 feet (12 m) high and weighs around 12,000 pounds (5,448 kg). Salem Sue was built in 1974 for approximately US$40,000 by the local residents, dairymen, farmers, and businessmen. The local Lions Club maintains the site. The New Salem High School athletic teams are all

The Salem Sue roadside attraction, on School Hill in New Salem.

named Holsteins as a tribute to the area's main source of commerce.

The Bismarck Municipal Airport is located on Airport Road 2 miles (3 km) southeast of Bismarck. Buses also service the area.

Map ref: page 426 F7

RICHARDTON

Richardton is 78 miles (126 km) west of Bismarck on I-94. It is home to the Benedictine Assumption Abbey, a Bavarian Romanesque structure. It has lofty arches, 52 stained glass windows, 24 paintings of Saints on canvas, and a huge carved crucifix.

The nearest airport is Bismarck Municipal Airport, located on Airport Road 2 miles (3 km) southeast of Bismarck.

Map ref: page 426 D7

SHEYENNE

The population of Sheyenne is just 272, and the town is located 107 miles (172 km) northeast of the state capital, Bismarck.

The main destination in Sheyenne is the Sheyenne National Grassland. The grassland covers an area of 70,250 acres (28,451 ha), and is the largest tract of tall grass prairie in public ownership in the United States; it represents an important ecosystem for the future. Over 300 species inhabit the grasslands. The Endangered Species Act (ESA) has found the western prairie fringed orchid, the oak savannah, the greater prairie chicken, and the skipper butterfly in these grasslands. The Sheyenne River flows through the heart of the lands and provides

the area with diverse wildlife. Recreational opportunities include hunting, hiking, horseback riding, and fishing—and the fall colors in the forest are outstanding. It is home to the white-tailed deer, turkeys, and many non-game birds and animals. The Forest Service periodically cuts trees for firewood, but all useless cutting for farmland is prohibited. The largest threat to the grasslands is overgrazing by domestic cattle and the use of snowmobiles and other recreational vehicles. Ultimately, wilderness protection is the only way to protect the fragile ecosystem from damage.

Jamestown Municipal Airport is 75 miles (121 km) south on US-52/281, and Devils Lake Municipal Airport is 25 miles (40 miles) northeast of Sheyenne on US-281 and then Hwy 57.

Map ref: page 427 J4

WASHBURN

Washburn is 40 miles (64 km) north of Bismarck on the US-83, with a population of 1,500. It was once a busy place because it served as the Missouri River ferry crossing for steamboats from St Louis, which are now obsolete. At the base of the bridge there is a

mounted ferryboat. The 560-acre (227-ha) Cross Ranch State Park is full of cottonwood-shaded Missouri River bottomland. Here are the remains of Sanger, a "ghost town" full of hiking trails, camp sites, and a place to rent canoes. For a moderate fee visitors can sleep in an authentic log cabin. The annual Missouri River Bluegrass Festival takes place on the Labor Day weekend.

Along Hwy 1806 is the Cross Ranch Nature Preserve, one of the most plentiful surviving native Missouri River Valley ecosystems. There is a flood-plain prairie and riparian forest plus a herd of buffalo and some undisturbed Native American archeological sites.

Bismarck Municipal Airport is located on Airport Road 2 miles (3 km) southeast of Bismarck. Buses also service the area.

Map ref: page 426 F6

WILLISTON

Williston, on US-85, is in the northwest corner of North Dakota, about 20 miles (32 km) from the Montana border. Williston is a classic, all-American cliché of a one-horse town. It is the first settlement east of the Montana line. It is nicknamed "Champion City" although no one knows why the name was given. The town's economy used to be suppported by wheat growing and oil refineries, but now it is dependent mostly on tourism.

In May, the Rough Rider Art Show brings in artwork from all over the state. US-2 at the east edge of town is the traditional stop for good cafés along the Great Plains.

Sloulin Field International Airport is in Williston. Lewis and Clark State Park is southeast of town.

Map ref: page 426 B3

Oil well maintenance workers at one of the still-operating oil refineries in Williston.

STATE FEATURE

Theodore Roosevelt National Park

In 1883, when Theodore Roosevelt was 25 years old, he visited Medora, North Dakota, for the first time. He was on a buffalo hunting trip to breathe the clean air of the open country to alleviate his asthma. The following year, his mother and wife died within hours of each other. Roosevelt moved into his ranch in the Badlands for respite, mourning, and spiritual renewal. He ran 5,000 head of cattle on two ranches, hunted in the wild, and tracked thieves—living the rugged life of a cowboy. He later remarked, "I would have never been President if it weren't for my experiences in North Dakota."

Throughout his years as an up-and-coming politician, he commuted between New York and North Dakota frequently. He fell in love with the Badlands and invested over US$80,000 in the Maltese Cross Ranch and the Elkhorn Ranch. Upon subsequent visits, Roosevelt noticed the decline of wildlife and saw the damage of overgrazing. He began actively contributing to the conservation of the Badlands and the wildlife and natural resources.

In 1947, Congress established the North Dakota Badlands. Later, in November, 1978, the park's name was changed to Theodore Roosevelt National Park, which also placed all 30,000 acres (12,150 ha) of the park under the National Wilderness Preservation System. Roosevelt, the 26th head of the United States, was known as the "Conservationist President" and, during his presidency, he founded the US Forest Service, signed the National Monuments Act, and established the National Park Service.

The park is open year-round, although areas may close in winter due to snow and ice conditions. It is full of quiet caverns, secluded glens, and rocky outposts. Activities include visits to museums and the Maltese Cross Cabin, guided walks, driving scenic park roads, wildlife viewing, bird-watching, hiking and camping, backpacking, cycling, boating, cross-country skiing, fishing, snowshoeing, and stargazing It is noted for sightings of buffalo, elk, mule, white-tailed deer, pronghorn antelope, prairie dogs, coyote, and golden eagles, among other wildlife.

The park is split into two distinct regions. The southern (the South Unit) and the northern (the North Unit) are bisected by the border separating the Mountain and Central Time Zones. The South Unit has been shaped by wind, fire, and the Little Missouri River. The North Unit has taller buttes and is heavily forested. Driving distance between the North and South Units is 70 miles (113 km). Visitors should allow at least two days to visit both units. The topography and landscape of the two are entirely different.

When traveling west on I-94, the entrance to the South Unit is in Medora. There is a 36-mile (58-km) scenic loop with signs explaining some of the park's historical and natural features. Visitors should allow a minimum of four hours to explore and drive the loop road and need to add extra time if a hike or guided nature walk is planned.

The first attraction, before the main entrance, is the Painted Canyon Overlook, 7 miles (11 km) east of Medora. This overlook gives visitors the opportunity to view the magnificent panoramic view of the Badlands in its entire colorful splendor—and to watch in the distance for the wild horses. There are picnic tables and a visitor center open April to October. The Painted Canyon Trail is a 1-mile (2-km) walking loop through shaded areas and scorching buttes. There is no admission fee at Painted Canyon. Near the town of Medora is Demores State Historic Site where visitors can tour the 27-room chateau that the Marquis Demores built for his wife in 1884. The Marquis was a wealthy Frenchman who built the town of Medora with his beef and slaughterhouse business.

Continuing along the route, one reaches the main entrance. Here visitors can stop at the information desk, or visit the museum, theater, and bookstore. Also at this main entrance to the South Unit is Roosevelt's Maltese Cross ranch house, which is open to the public for self-guided tours.

Peaceful Valley Ranch is 7 miles (11 km) inside the park. During its heyday, in the 1880s, it was a cattle ranching site. Today visitors can go horseback riding or take a self-guided hike along the Ridgeline Trail. There are instructional signs pointing out the unique geology of the site. You can hike the Coal Vein Trail. Visitors can drive up to Buck Hill and then hike partway up the steep path to be rewarded with a 180-degree view of the Badlands landscape. The more adventurous visitor can ask a ranger for directions to the third-largest petrified forest in the United States, which is a day's hike into the park.

A familiar sight in the Badlands, the black-tailed prairie dog (Cynomus ludovicianus) inhabits colonies, or "towns," consisting of many closely spaced burrows, with an intricate network of interconnecting tunnels.

Although the feral horse, or mustang, is considered a pest in the area, the park retains and manages a herd of around 70 to 110 wild horses.

Boicourt Overlook has another spectacular view of the Badlands. At Scoria Point, you can see how the erosion and sun have transformed the landscape.

Elkhorn Ranch is Roosevelt's second ranch. It is accessible on a rather rough and obscure path leaving the South Unit—visitors should inquire at the visitor center before leaving for this trip.

The 36-mile (58-km) route accesses all the sights and trails. The summers are warm and sunny, and a hat for sun protection is highly recommended. The winters are cold and layers of clothing are suggested for this season—and rain gear is recommended for the spring. Once inside the park there is no food, but restaurants and stores are within a short drive. There is no lodging inside the park except camping with a permit and a fee. There are small entrance fees.

The North Unit is less frequented by visitors than the South Unit. It is 75 miles (121 km) from the South Unit on US-85. Visitors can drive the 14-mile (23-km) scenic drive from the entrance at the Oxbow Overlook. The North Unit is more conducive to trailblazing by foot—it is more forested and lush with greenery. Because there is less traffic, it is better for observing wildlife. Little Mo Trail (1 mile/2 km) is scenic and accessible, and Caprock Coulee Trail (2 miles/3 km) is level and walks hikers through prairie and dry-water ditches. The Caprock Coulee Trail connects with the Buckhorn Trail (11 miles/18 km) and takes hikers through a prairie dog "town." The 16-mile (26-km) Achenbach ("aching back") trail winds around the Missouri River with a series of vertical climbs and turns and is recommended for seasoned hikers.

Both the South and North Units are open year-round. If children between the ages of six and 12 are traveling, the park invites them to become junior rangers. They receive a booklet and pencil from the ranger with instructions for completing activities, attending a guided program, and going on a hike. They receive a junior ranger badge and certificate. It is a fun way to learn about the park and its natural resources.

There are air services available into Bismarck, Dickinson, and Williston. By car, the South Unit entrance is just off I-94 (exits 23 and 27) and is 135 miles (217 km) west of Bismarck. The North Unit is located 16 miles (26 km) south of Watford City along Hwy 85 and is 70 miles (113 km) from the South Unit. There is also a bus service along I-94. The bus stops in Medora just three blocks from the park's entrance. There is no public transportation service to the North Unit entrance.

In 1956, 29 American buffalo (Bison bison) were released in the park. Today the buffalo number 200 to 400 in the South Unit, and 100 to 300 in the North Unit.

The Little Missouri River course was formed during the ice age of the Pleistocene Epoch. Easily cutting through the soft sedimentary rock, its tributaries created the familiar, jagged topography of the Badlands.

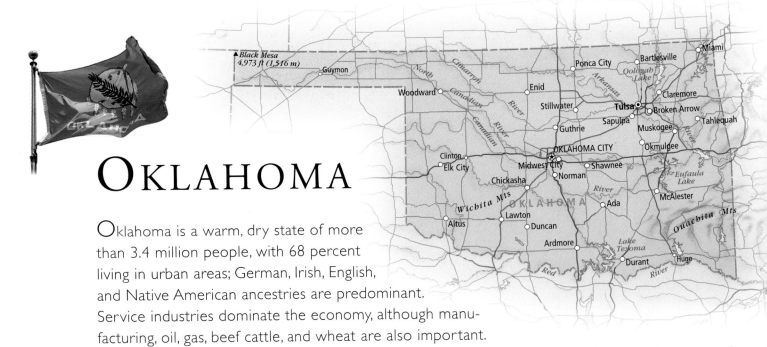

OKLAHOMA

Oklahoma is a warm, dry state of more than 3.4 million people, with 68 percent living in urban areas; German, Irish, English, and Native American ancestries are predominant. Service industries dominate the economy, although manufacturing, oil, gas, beef cattle, and wheat are also important.

Native Americans have always been an integral part of the state, and today their culture, art, and history are tourism drawcards. Prior to 1889, Oklahoma was set aside for Native Americans, namely the Seminole, Cherokee, Creek, Choctaw, and Chickasaw tribes. From 1830 to 1842, these tribes were driven from their lands in the Southeast and forced to march along the "Trail of Tears" to Oklahoma, in the course of which thousands died. The different tribes set up their own "nations" with their own governments, courts, laws, farms, and schools. Although the land was promised to them in perpetuity, it was later reclaimed and opened to general settlement. On April 22, 1889, the day the first land parcel was released, settlers, including about 10,000 African-Americans, assembled at the border. At the sound of a pistol shot they tore across the state to claim farms and town sites.

The Oklahoma National Stockyards situated in Oklahoma City contains the largest cattle market in the world.

Oklahoma became the 46th state in 1907. At that time there were more African-Americans in Oklahoma than there were Europeans and Native Americans combined—many had arrived as slaves and had established businesses and towns after slavery was abolished. In the twentieth century, oil and gas brought prosperity to the state, although the Great Depression saw many "Okies" fleeing unemployment, low produce prices, and a drought during the 1930s. The drought turned the farmlands into a "dust bowl," as famously depicted in *The Grapes of Wrath*, the songs of Oklahoman Woody Guthrie, and the photographs of Dorothea Lange.

The 1950s saw the rise of industrialization. Today, Oklahoma City has the largest cattle market in the United States, and Tulsa has world-class museums alongside world-class jazz. There are cowboys and rodeos, harvest festivals, and Native American powwows, all in a setting of stunning natural beauty.

State motto *Labor Omnia Vincit* (Labor conquers all things)
State flag Adopted 1911
Capital Oklahoma City
Population 3,450,654
Total area (land and water) 69,903 square miles (181,049 sq km)
Land area 68,679 square miles (177,879 sq km)
Oklahoma is the 18th-largest state in size
Origin of name From two Choctaw words meaning "red people"
Nickname The Sooner State
Abbreviations OK (postal), Okla.
State bird Scissor-tailed flycatcher
State flower Mistletoe
State tree Redbud
Entered the Union November 16, 1907 as the 46th state

Places in OKLAHOMA

ANADARKO

Anadarko is a town of 6,500. It is located 50 miles (80 km) southwest of Oklahoma City in the scenic Wichita River Valley. Modern-day Anadarko emerged overnight in 1901 when land was reclaimed from the Comanche, Wichita, and Kiowa people. Large numbers of Kiowa still live in rural communities nearby, along with six other tribes. Consequently, Native American culture is an attraction in the area, particularly during the annual Native American exposition in August.

The oldest building in Anadarko is the Riverside Indian School, which was built in 1871 and predates the town by 30 years. It is one of five remaining all-Native-American boarding schools in the United States and just one of 100 historic buildings in Anadarko.

Two miles (3 km) south is Indian City USA, which is located on the site of a massacre of Tonkawa people by a band of Shawnee during the Civil War. Indian City features authentic reconstructions of Seven Plains villages with artifacts, a museum, and activities such as tribal dancing and lectures. Dwellings include a Pawnee earth lodge, a Navajo hogan, along with a Wichita council house.

The Southern Plains Indian Museum exhibits and sells a diverse array of traditional and contemporary arts of the Arapaho, Caddo, Cheyenne, Comanche, Delaware, Fort Sill

Apache, Kiowa, and Wichita tribes. There is also a Delaware Tribal Museum and a National Hall of Fame for Famous American Indians, which features the stories and bronze busts of 40 distinguished Native Americans. More general in its focus is the Philomathic Pioneer Museum which preserves regional antiques such as railroad memorabilia, Native American dolls, military items, photographs, and period recreations of a country store and a physician's office.

Will Rogers World Airport, in Oklahoma City, is the closest major airport. There is also the Lawton Fort Sill Regional Airport in Lawton, about 35 miles (56 km) south of Anadarko.
Map ref: page 621 H10

ARCADIA

Arcadia is located 17 miles (28 km) north of downtown Oklahoma City in the state's center. The population is around 320. Arcadia's most famous landmark is the Round Barn, an icon of Route 66—America's most famous cross-country, pre-interstate highway drive. This heroically restored and unique barn has

Oil worker transferring crude oil from a truck to the main pipeline, Bartlesville.

a round roof 60 feet (18 m) in diameter. Built in 1898, it was used for dances and livestock. Also of interest is the old Tuton Drugstore, which is now the Old Country Store. To the east is Arcadia Lake where fishing, boating, camping, mountain biking, and hiking are popular recreational activities.

Will Rogers World Airport, in Oklahoma City, is the closest major airport to Arcadia.
Map ref: page 621 J8

BARTLESVILLE

Bartlesville is located 41 miles (66 km) north of Tulsa. The state's first substantial oil well was established here in 1897 and J. Paul Getty, who became one of the world's richest men, worked on these oil fields in 1909. Oil profits have provided the town with several

distinguished buildings and one of the state's best museums, the Woolaroc (from a shortened version of "woods, lakes, and rocks").

A major landmark is Frank Lloyd Wright's 1956 Price Tower, which contains an Arts Center. A private dwelling of note is the La Quinta Foster Mansion, a 32-room Spanish-style structure built by H.V. Foster, once considered the wealthiest man west of the Mississippi. It is now the centerpiece of Bartlesville Wesleyan College.

Another impressive building is the Frank Phillips Home, which was built in 1908. It is a 26-room mansion built by oilman Frank Phillips who also started the superb Woolaroc Museum, 13 miles (21 km) southwest of Bartlesville. Known as "the Smithsonian of the American West," the Woolaroc Museum has more than 60,000 items, including paintings by Frederic Remington and Charles Russell. It also has the world's finest collection of Native American blankets, a 95-million-year-old dinosaur egg, gun and rifle exhibits, saddles belonging to Theodore Roosevelt and Buffalo Bill, an oil history section, as well as scalps taken by Native Americans. There are extensive gardens and the 3,600-acre (1,458-ha) grounds are a refuge for various kinds of wildlife.

Tulsa International Airport is the closest major airport. Buses also service the area.
Map ref: page 621 M6

The historic Round Barn in Arcadia dates from 1898.

CHEYENNE

Cheyenne is 130 miles (209 km) west of Oklahoma City on I-40 then US-283. It is located among the rolling hills and pastureland of far western Oklahoma and is surrounded by both natural and historical landmarks. The town came into existence on April 19, 1892, when the land from a Cheyenne reservation was released to the general public for settlement.

Cheyenne is situated in the Black Kettle National Grassland. Cutting through Cheyenne is the California Road, which was once used as an immigration trail to California and a route to the northern markets for Texas cattlemen. North of town is the cluster of hills that form a horseshoe shape, aptly known as Horseshoe Hills. Boating can be enjoyed at nearby Dead Indian Lake.

Located 2 miles (3 km) east of Cheyenne is the Washita Battlefield National Historic Site. This "battle" took place in 1868 when Lieutenant-Colonel Custer launched a surprise attack on the camp of Chief Black Kettle, killing 100 Cheyenne, including women, children, and the Chief. Trail guides can be obtained at the Black Kettle Museum in Cheyenne, which displays artifacts from the battlefield and the settlement of the area by both the Cheyenne and whites.

Will Rogers World Airport, in Oklahoma City, is the closest major airport to Cheyenne.
Map ref: page 620 E8

CHICKASAW NATIONAL RECREATION AREA

Chickasaw National Recreation Area is 80 miles (129 km) south of Oklahoma City on I-35 then Hwy 7. It is Oklahoma's oldest National Park and draws 2 million visitors annually. It is located amid the Arbuckle Mountains in central-south Oklahoma, near the town of Sulphur. The Park headquarters are on US-177, just south of its intersection with Hwy 7.

Chickasaw is a surprisingly green area with spring-fed creeks, waterfalls, and cold mineral springs which were once sought out for their curative powers. The shallow waters of Travertine Creek are good for families with young children to swim in, while boating and fishing can be enjoyed at the Lake of the Arbuckles. Camping, hiking, and hunting are popular activities. Educational exhibits about the area's wildlife are offered at the Travertine Nature Center.

Will Rogers World Airport, in Oklahoma City, is the closest major airport. There is also the Lawton Fort Sill Regional Airport in Lawton, about 90 miles (145 km) west of Sulphur on Hwy 7.
Map ref: page 627 H2

DURANT

Durant is a college town of 14,000 residents. It is located in southern Oklahoma, 121 miles (195 km) southeast of Oklahoma City on

The waterways are the major attraction in Chickasaw National Recreation Area.

I-35 then US-70. Durant is home to the Choctaw Nation of Oklahoma, which numbers more than 100,000 and which graduates more college students than any other Native American tribe.

Three Valley Museum is housed in the basement of the Choctaw Nation headquarters. Artifacts relate to the Choctaw heritage and regional history. Stephens County Historical Museum focuses on the Plains Native Americans, cattle drivers, pioneers, and the oil boom. Six miles (10 km) north of town is Lake Durant, which offers fishing, walking trails, and a boat ramp. To the west is Lake Texoma, the state's most popular resort center and one of the country's best fishing spots.

Fort Washita Historic Site, 12 miles (19 km) northwest of Durant, features original and reconstructed elements of an 1842 army fort established to protect the transplanted Chickasaw and Choctaw people from indigenous Plains tribes. The reconstructed 1849 barracks, museum, and other buildings provide insights into pre-Civil War military life.

Dallas, Texas, is only about 90 miles (145 km) south on the US-75 and the Dallas–Fort Worth International Airport is the closest major airport to Durant. Buses also service the area.
Map ref: page 627 K4

GUTHRIE

Guthrie is located 30 miles (48 km) north of Oklahoma City on I-35. It was the capital of the Oklahoma Territory from 1890 and the state capital from 1907. When the capital was moved to Oklahoma City, in 1910, the wheels of progress slowed. Today, many original buildings have remained intact and 90 percent of the downtown buildings are of recognized historic importance. Guided tours are available of the Scottish Rite Masonic Temple, which engulfs a massive 268,000 square feet (25,460 sq m), making it one of the largest Masonic temples in the world. With a Greco-Roman design, it cost US$3 million in the 1920s.

Guthrie has several museums with diverse themes. The State Capitol Publishing Museum features printing and bookbinding equipment from 1889–1916. The Oklahoma Territorial Museum concentrates on the 1889 land rush and Guthrie's years as territorial and state capital. One exhibit concerns an African-American family

Tractor preparing the ground for spring planting on a wheat farm near the agricultural town of Cheyenne.

who made one of the first land claims near Guthrie. Next door is the 1902 Carnegie Library, the oldest library in the state. The Oklahoma Sports Museum focuses on athletes who have ties to Oklahoma, while the Oklahoma Frontier Drugstore Museum features a 1923 soda fountain and 1890s pharmaceutical memorabilia.

The National Lighter Museum has thousands of flame-producing objects from many eras and nations, and the National Four-String Banjo Museum has an excellent collection of vintage banjos. Each year, in May, well-known banjo players are inducted into the Museum's Hall of Fame prior to Guthrie's National Banjo Festival.

Will Rogers World Airport, located in Oklahoma City, is the closest major airport to Guthrie. Buses also service the area.

Map ref: page 621 J8

LAWTON

With over 80,000 people, Lawton is the state's fourth most populous city. Lawton is located 79 miles (127 km) southwest of Oklahoma City on I-44 in the state's southwest. Lawton was the last of the land-rush cities, emerging overnight in 1901. The Comanche, Apache, and Kiowa people jointly own about 4,500 acres (1,823 ha) in and around town.

The Museum of the Great Plains focuses on the cultural and natural history of the region. Adjacent is the Red River Trading Post, a two-story cabin, which replicates the trading posts of the 1830s and 1840s. The Lewis Museum has an international collection of items

and the Percussive Arts Society Museum has a diverse array of percussion instruments from around the world. Little Chapel, built in 1902, is believed to be Lawton's oldest building and now houses the Leslie Powell Art Gallery. Another fine old building of note is Mattie Beal Home, a 14-room Greek Revival building constructed in 1909.

Lawton serves Fort Sill, a military center 5 miles (8 km) north of town. It was established in 1869 to monitor the Comanche and Kiowa tribes. Apache chief, Geronimo, was moved to Fort Sill in 1894 after his resistance in the 1870s and 1880s. It is now the site of the US Army Field Artillery Center and School. The artillery museum consists of 26 historic buildings. It has exhibits on the frontier army, military weapons, and Native Americans—including a stone corral, the old guardhouse where Geronimo was held, and Geronimo's grave.

Just northwest of Fort Sill, Route 49 traverses the rugged granite peaks and prairies of Wichita Mountains National Wildlife Refuge—a fine spot for hiking, rock climbing, and wildlife watching. Walks to bald-eagle viewing sites depart from the visitor center. A road leads to the summit of Mount Scott where there are outstanding views of southwest Oklahoma. Also at the Refuge is the Chapel of the Holy City, which was built in 1936. It was founded by Reverend Anthony Wallock who thought the Wichita Mountains resembled the peaks of the Holy Land. Other attractions in the area are the Museum of the Western Prairie, Quartz Mountain State Park, Lake Ellsworth, and Lake Lawtonka.

Blacksmith mending a horseshoe in readiness for the State Prison Rodeo, McAlester.

Lawton is serviced by a regional airport and Will Rogers World Airport, in Oklahoma City, is the closest major airport. Buses also service the area.

Map ref: page 626 F2

McALESTER

McAlester is 90 miles (145 km) south of Tulsa on US-270. It is home to the state penitentiary and, in true Western fashion, every Labor Day weekend the inmates are pitted against professional cowboys at the State Prison Rodeo. In the late nineteenth century, coal mining around McAlester attracted many southern European immigrants whose descendants still populate the area. McAlester's famous progeny include poet John Berryman and Reverend Mark Sexson who founded the "Rainbow for Girls," an international organization linked to the Masons.

McAlester has a number of museums with diverse themes. The collection at Tannehill Museum includes firearms, dolls, antique tools, Civil War documents, Coca Cola memorabilia, and items associated with Oklahoma State Penitentiary. Visitors interested in the

latter can get their fill at the Oklahoma Prisons Historical Museum. The Oklahoma Trolley Museum has a display of restored trolley cars from McAlester's street-car line (1907–1933), while county history is explored at the Pittsburgh County Historical Society Museum and the Garrard Ardeneum.

Outdoor recreation can be enjoyed at Talawanda Lakes and Lake McAlester. Forty miles (64 km) east of town is Talihina, which is the start of Route 1, a beautiful drive through the northern section of scenic Ouachita National Forest.

Tulsa International Airport is the closest major airport. Buses also service the area.

Map ref: page 621 M10

MUSKOGEE

Muskogee is an attractive town with a fascinating history reflected in its historic sites and museums. It is located 45 miles (72 km) southwest of Tulsa in eastern Oklahoma. Historically this area was known as "Three Forks" because this is where the Verdigris, Grand, and Arkansas Rivers meet. It is named after the Muskogee tribe (more commonly known as the "Creek"), who

Car service at one of the many drive-in diners along I-44, Lawton.

established the town as a meeting place for the "Five Civilized Tribes" (the Seminole, Cherokee, Creek, Choctaw, and Chickasaw).

Ten miles (16 km) east of Muskogee is Fort Gibson, established in 1824 to prepare for the arrival of the Five Tribes. It later served as an administrative and supply center for those Native Americans who survived the march to Oklahoma. The commissary and stone barracks on Garrison Hill date from the mid-nineteenth century and the stockade from the 1930s. The fort preserves important aspects of Oklahoma's past as an Indian Territory. It illuminates pioneer life, military life, the attitudes and policies of the white majority regarding Native Americans, and the largely unrecognized presence of African-Americans in frontier history.

Further information regarding African-American history and the legacy of Native Americans in Oklahoma is available from the Oklahoma Creek Freedman Association and Shrine. One of the first Civil War battles involving African-American soldiers took place near Muskogee, in July 1863. The Battle of Honey Springs was also the first Civil War battle won with the help of African-American soldiers who were runaway slaves. Though outnumbered two to one, Union forces defeated Confederate troops, which included Native American regiments from the Five Civilized Tribes. The Battle effectively ended Confederate resistance in the Indian Territory and laid the groundwork for the capture

of much of Arkansas. Today, Honey Springs Battlefield is a state park to the south of Muskogee, where re-enactments are held.

The Muskogee area was opened up to white settlement in the late nineteenth century and oil was discovered locally in 1903. In 1905, the leaders of the Five Civilized Tribes held a constitutional convention at Muskogee, with white participation. A constitution was drawn up for the Indian Territory to become the state of Sequoyah and it was approved in an election. However, Congress refused ratification as it wanted the Indian Territory incorporated into the larger proposed state of Oklahoma.

The Five Civilized Tribes Museum is housed in the 1875 Union Indian Agency building on Honor Heights Drive. It preserves aspects of Five Civilized Tribes history and culture, focusing on the "Trail of Tears" and the ensuing period in which the tribes set up their own nations. A fine collection of Native American art can also be found at the Ataloa Lodge Museum on the Bacone College campus. Other historical artifacts are displayed at the historic Thomas-Foreman House, which was built in 1898, and the Three Rivers Museum.

The USS *Batfish* and War Memorial Park Museum exhibits include a World War II submarine, an army tank, cannons, missiles, and other military memorabilia.

Tulsa International Airport is the closest major airport. Buses also service the area.
Map ref: page 621 N8

The raised viewing platform at the stockyards in Oklahoma City.

NORMAN

Norman, the home of the University of Oklahoma, was founded in 1890. The third-largest city in the state, it has some fine museums, numerous private art galleries, and is close to an excellent state park. Norman has over 80,000 people and is located on I-35, south of Oklahoma City, in central Oklahoma.

Norman was created by the 1889 land run. It is the birthplace of artist David Salle, who came to prominence in the 1980s, and of engineer Karl Jansky who, in 1931, became the first person to detect radio waves emanating from outside the solar system, precipitating the development of radio astronomy.

Norman has a historic district, which includes the Santa Fe Depot and the Sooner Theater. The Cleveland County Historical Museum, built in 1900, is located in a Queen Anne-style house. The rooms are furnished to represent an upper-middle-class family residence in Territorial Oklahoma. The museum display focuses on the history of the county from the 1889 land run to statehood in 1907.

In Monnet Hall, at the University of Oklahoma, is the Western History Collection, which is one of the country's largest assemblages of material documenting the socio-economic development of the western frontier. There are 65,000 books, along with manuscripts,

periodicals, microfilm, oral histories, photographs, and maps, among other artifacts. Also on campus is the Oklahoma Museum of Natural History, which crams 6 million items into 195,000 square feet (18,525 sq m). Among the natural and cultural exhibits are the world's largest Apatosaurus, rare Native American artifacts, and a Discovery Room for children.

Will Rogers World Airport, in Oklahoma City, is located 19 miles (31 km) north of Norman. Buses also service the area.
Map ref: page 621 J9

OKLAHOMA CITY

Oklahoma City is the state capital, is one of the largest cities in the United States (647 square miles/ 1,676 sq km), and is Oklahoma's most populous city (population 463,200). Forty percent of the population of the city live in the metropolitan area.

Oklahoma City is one of the main centers of oil production in the United States. It is a commercial and manufacturing center and has the largest cattle market in the world—over 100 million animals have been sold since 1910. Visitors can observe the fascinating old-time auctions from a raised platform at the stockyards.

Oklahoma City is situated on the North Canadian River in the middle of the state. The downtown

The Five Civilized Tribes Museum in the Union Indian Agency Building, Muskogee.

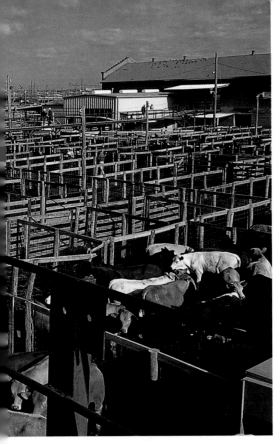

area remains surprisingly quiet, even sluggish, in this easy-going city, which has a superabundance of museums and art galleries and some pleasant parks and gardens.

On one single day (April 22, 1889) the population of the future Oklahoma City increased from zero to more than 10,000 as settlers staked out claims around the railroad tracks on land previously granted to the Seminole and Creek peoples. By 1910, when it became the state capital, it was Oklahoma's largest city with 64,205 people.

The huge and vastly prosperous Oklahoma City oil field was established in 1928, initiating a boom as the city became the center of the US petroleum industry. Major industrial expansion commenced in the 1950s and an urban renewal scheme began in the 1960s. Water taxis now ply a canal that flows beside restaurants, shops, and quaint cafés in the historic Bricktown entertainment district.

In 1995, a federal government building was blown up in Oklahoma City by three right-wing extremists, killing 168 people, including 19 children. It was the worst single terrorist act to occur within the United States. On May 3, 1999 the costliest tornado in US history struck, killing 36 people.

Nothing could be more symbolic of Oklahoma's economy and history than the fact that its State Capitol building, built in 1917, has working oil wells on its grounds. Across the street is the Oklahoma State Mu-

seum of History and nearby is the Heritage Hills area, which is home to the Victorian-style Overholser Mansion, built in 1903, the Oklahoma Governor's Mansion, and the Oklahoma Heritage Center.

One of the city's most popular attractions is the enormous complex known as the National Cowboy and Western Heritage Museum. Here the focus is on the Old West, taking in everything from Bob Wills' fiddle to John Wayne's collection of kachina dolls. Within the complex visitors can find the Western Entertainment Gallery, which focuses on western figures from movies and radio; the American Rodeo Gallery; the American Cowboy Gallery; the Frontier West Gallery, with displays on the African-American Buffalo Soldiers, a library of Western history, and a 14,000-square-foot (1,330-sq-m) re-creation of a western town circa 1900. The art collection includes paintings by Charles Russell, Frederic Remington, Albert Bierstadt, and contemporary works by Native Americans.

Nearby is the astounding Enterprise Square USA, within Oklahoma Christian University—a monument to free enterprise.

The Omniplex on 52nd Street houses a variety of museums and exhibits such as a planetarium, the Kirkpatrick Galleries, an IMAX theater, the Red Earth Indian Center, the Hands-On Science Museum, the Air Space Museum, and the International Photography Hall of Fame, which displays the world's largest Grand Canyon photomural. Adjacent to the Omniplex, in Lincoln Park, is the Oklahoma City Zoo, considered one of the 10 best in the United States.

Oklahoma City's other museums include the 45th Infantry Division Museum, the country's largest state military history museum; the Harn Homestead and 1889er Museum, where early twentieth-century life is illustrated by means of a historic buildings collection; the Oklahoma Firefighters Museum, with equip-

ment dating back to the eighteenth century; and the 99s Museum of Women Pilots, which features exhibits about early female pilots such as Amelia Earhart and Oklahoman Bessie Coleman, the first licensed female pilot in the world.

Oklahoma City also has many art galleries. The oldest gallery is the Oklahoma City Art Museum, which has 3,000 works, with an emphasis on nineteenth- and twentieth-century American art.

The achievements of African-Americans, both locally and internationally, are celebrated at the Freedom Center.

At Myriad Botanical Gardens the highlight is Crystal Bridge, a seven-story glass conservatory, 70 feet (21 m) in diameter, which contains a skywalk, a 35-foot (11-m) waterfall, and an international flora collection.

Oklahoma City is serviced by Oklahoma's largest airport, the Will Rogers World Airport, and by trains and buses.
Map ref: page 621 J9

OKMULGEE

Okmulgee is located on US-75, 40 miles (64 km) south of Tulsa. Twenty blocks of the downtown area have been designated as a National Historic District. The jewel in the crown is the Creek Capitol, from whence the Creek ruled their nation until it was abolished by the US Congress in 1906. This two-story sandstone building was erected in 1878. Upstairs are the two houses of the legislature, the House of Kings, and the House of Warriors. Today the Capitol is a center for the preservation of the Creek language and a museum of Creek history and culture.

From culture to nature, visitors to Okmulgee can inspect both the multi-million dollar Reynolds Technology Center, at Oklahoma State University, and Okmulgee State Park, which has

two lakes—Dripping Springs, which is a trophy bass lake, and Okmulgee. There are boat ramps, playgrounds, swimming areas, hiking and nature trails, a public hunting area, and campgrounds.

Tulsa International Airport is the closest major airport. Buses also service the area.
Map ref: page 621 M8

PONCA CITY

Ponca City is in central-north Oklahoma, 88 miles (142 km) north of Oklahoma City. It was established during the land rushes of the 1890s. The town later benefited from oil discoveries, as did the oilman and state governor E.W. Marland, whose two mansions are now open to the public. The first, which was built around 1916, had one of the state's first indoor swimming pools, early air conditioning, and a built-in vacuum system. A Native American museum is located on the grounds. More impressive is his second mansion, the 55-room "Palace on the Prairie." Built in the 1920s, it was the home of E.W. Marland and his second wife, Lydie.

In 1928 Marland commissioned the town's 17-foot (5-m) statue honoring pioneer women. Adjacent to the statue is a museum with

Oklahoma City National Memorial, Oklahoma City.

Oil well maintenance crew at a Ponca City refinery.

related displays. At the southern end of town, in a prairie park, is a 22-foot (7-m) statue honoring the civil rights endeavors of Ponca Chief, Standing Bear. His story, and the seals of the area's six Native American tribes, are displayed in the adjoining plaza.

The Ponca City Art Center features the works of local and state artists while the oriental and western art of the Matzene Art Collection is displayed at the Ponca City Library. The city is decorated with 10 public murals depicting the first 100 years of its history.

Outdoor recreation can be enjoyed to the east of town at Lake Ponca and the much larger Kaw Lake. The latter features the Five Fingers Equestrian Trail and the Eagle View Hiking Trail (12 miles/ 19 km), which, in winter, affords excellent views of bald eagles roosting and feeding.

Ponca City has its own Municipal Airport. The closest major airports are the Tulsa International Airport or the Will Rogers World Airport in Oklahoma City. The area is also serviced by buses.
Map ref: page 621 K6

STILLWATER

Stillwater is located in central Oklahoma, 50 miles (80 km) north of Oklahoma City. It was here that Oklahoma State University was established in 1890.

Stillwater has three museums. Airport Memorial Museum has pictures and artifacts dating from 1918, when the first plane landed in Stillwater. The Sheerar Museum has a 4,000-strong button collection, and focuses on regional history. The Museum of Higher Education is

located in Old Central, which was built in 1894 and was the first permanent building on the Oklahoma State University campus. It features artifacts of higher education in Oklahoma from 1880 to the present. Also at the campus are the excellent Oklahoma Botanical Gardens and Arboretum. Outdoor recreation is available at Stillwater Cycle Park (which is 500 acres/ 203 ha in size), Sooner Reservoir, Lake Carl Blackwell, Boomer Lake, and Lake McMurtry.

Silverwater is about midway between airports at Oklahoma City and Tulsa. Buses service the area.
Map ref: page 621 K7

TAHLEQUAH

Tahlequah is a peaceful college town of 10,000 people located 66 miles (106 km) east of Tulsa on Hwy 51, in the Ozark hills of northeast Oklahoma. Tahlequah was established in the late 1830s as the capital of the Cherokee nation, which established the first higher education school for women west of the Mississippi. The 1889 seminary is now located in Northeastern State University which has the highest number of Native American students in the United States.

The Cherokee Capitol building, built in 1870, still stands in the center of town on Cherokee Square. Other tribal government buildings include the Supreme Court and the Cherokee National Prison. Free maps of major downtown sites can be obtained from the visitor center.

Three miles (5 km) south of town is the Cherokee Heritage Center. It includes Tsa-La-Gi, a re-creation of a seventeenth-century Cherokee village with actors in period costume and demonstrations of basket weaving and flint knapping. There are also museums, farm exhibits, the Cherokee Genealogy Center, and craft centers. There is also the "Trail of Tears" play, which presents the Cherokee story from the "Trail of Tears" to Oklahoma statehood in 1907. It shows nightly from early June to Labor Day, and it is held in the Tahlequah amphitheater.

With its elevated bluffs, huge sycamores, camps, and resorts, the Illinois River is considered a fine stream for fishing, canoeing, kayaking, and rafting.

The nearest major airport is Tulsa International Airport.
Map ref: page 621 P7

TULSA

Tulsa is located on the banks of the Arkansas River in the state's northeast. With 375,000 people and over 700,000 in the metropolitan area, it is the second-most populous city in Oklahoma. Tulsa has an active cultural life, reflected in its many galleries and institutions such as the Tulsa Philharmonic, the Tulsa Opera, the Tulsa Ballet, and the Performing Arts Center.

Tulsa is also a major administrative center of the US petroleum industry, the state's busiest port, and its principal manufacturing center. It was the birthplace of country music mega-star Garth Brooks, motion-picture director Blake Edwards, noted US Democrat Senator Daniel Patrick Moynihan, and novelist S.E. Hinton.

The land on which Tulsa sits became the site of a Creek village in 1836 after the tribe was removed from its homelands in Tallassee, Alabama, and forced to march to Oklahoma. They named their new village Tallassee but, in time, this evolved into "Tulsa." According to legend, the 75-foot (23-m) Creek Council Oak at Cheyenne Avenue and 18th Street became the site of tribal councils.

The Creek culture was overturned by white settlement during the 1889 land rush. By 1900 Tulsa was a small trading center, rail depot, and

Sculpture, Oral Roberts University, Tulsa.

cattle-shipping center with 1,390 people. After oil was discovered at Red Fork, in 1901, Tulsa became one of the fastest-growing settlements in the United States. Declared a city in 1908, it had a population of 141,000 in 1930, by which time it was known as the "Oil Capital of the World."

The Greenwood Cultural Center celebrates the state's African-American pioneers. Also here is the Oklahoma Jazz Hall of Fame which honors jazz musicians who were born in Oklahoma (Jimmy Rushing); lived there (Charlie Christian); played in Walter Page's Blue Devils (Count Basie and Lester Young); or toured the state (Cab Calloway and Dizzy Gillespie). Musicians are inducted into the Hall of Fame during the African-American Juneteenth jazz celebrations. At the D & R Western Heritage and Rodeo Ranch, visitors receive an African-American perspective on the American West and history of Oklahoma. The University's North Conference Center has a photographic exhibit of 44 prominent African-American Tulsans.

Some of Tulsa's impressive architectural monuments are included in a walking tour, and a leaflet is available from the Chamber of Commerce. They include the Art Deco Union Railroad Depot and the 255-foot (78-m) Art Deco Boston Avenue Methodist Church, which has great views from the 14th floor.

One of Oklahoma's premier attractions is the Gilcrease Museum, which holds the world's largest collection of artworks and historical documents associated with the American West. It includes 250,000 Native American artifacts, about

The Art Deco Boston Avenue Methodist Church in Tulsa was built in 1924. It is considered the first church to be built in a strictly American style of architecture.

10,000 paintings, and thematic gardens offering fine views of the Osage Hills. The Philbrook Art Center is housed within an opulent Italian Renaissance-style villa. Inside are paintings dating back to the Renaissance, collections of Chinese art and jade, African sculpture, and Native American artifacts.

One of Tulsa's more unusual drawcards is the Oral Roberts University, established in 1965 after the Oklahoman televangelist claimed God commanded him to "build me a university." In 1987 God spoke again, saying that Roberts would not be taken to heaven unless he could raise US$4.5 million. To give his devotees a taste of his absence Roberts retreated to his 200-foot (61-m) glass Prayer Tower. Fittingly, when the deadline arrived, a lightning bolt struck the tower. Today a heavenly choir provides the aural backdrop to an exhibition, which celebrates Roberts' life. There is a multimedia presentation of the Bible's first eight books and an 80-foot (24-m) pair of hands raised in prayer. More historic religious material is on display at Tulsa's International Missionary Center, including manuscript bibles from the twelfth century, an original page of the 1452 Gutenberg Bible, a first edition of the 1611 King James Bible, and a full-scale working replica of the Gutenberg press.

Tulsa's other museums include the Tulsa Air and Space Center, which examines the history and future of aviation and Tulsa's aerospace pioneers; the Ida Dennie-Willis Museum of Miniatures, Dolls and Toys; Mac's Antique Car Museum, which includes the 1948 Hudson from the film, *Driving Miss Daisy;* the Sunbelt Railroad Museum; the Tulsa Historical Society Museum; and the Elsing Museum, which features a collection of rare and beautiful gems, including a 4-foot (1-m) jade sculpture.

Tulsa is serviced by its own international airport and by buses.
Map ref: page 621 M7

VIAN

Vian is a town of 1,400 people on the Arkansas River, 149 miles (240 km) east of Oklahoma City, off I-40. Three miles (5 km) south of Vian is Sequoyah National Wildlife Refuge, where visitors can find bald eagles, migratory waterfowl, and terns. Hiking, scenic drives, and wildlife observation are all popular activities. A satellite of Sequoyah is the Oklahoma Bat Cave National Wildlife Refuge, which is home to the endangered big-eared bat and gray bat.

Just northeast of Vian is Gore where visitors can pick up Route 10, which follows the rivers north

through the Cherokee Nation to Wyandotte. To the north is the former log cabin of Sequoyah, the man who invented the Cherokee alphabet. Also in the area are Lake Tenkiller and Tenkiller Ferry Dam where fishing, camping, boating, scuba diving, hiking, rock climbing, bird-watching, swimming, and waterskiing can be enjoyed. There is a nature center and a marina with boat rentals and pro-diving shops.

Tulsa International Airport is the nearest major airport. The area also has a limited bus service.
Map ref: page 621 P8

WILL ROGERS MEMORIAL

The Will Rogers Memorial, in Claremore, 30 miles (48 km) northeast of Tulsa on Route 66, honors the life of humorist and social critic Will Rogers (1879–1935) who is buried at the site. Rogers started his career in 1898 as a cowboy in Texas and later traveled to Argentina, South Africa, Australia, and New Zealand as an entertainer with Wild West shows and circuses. He returned to the United States in 1904 and launched a vaudeville career as a humorist and trick roper.

Rogers became internationally famous as a columnist, author, and lecturer and a star of radio and motion pictures.

Rogers died in a plane crash in Alaska. On his death, his life was honored with a nation-wide 30-minute silence and a statue in the US Capitol in Washington DC. A statue at the Claremore Memorial features the statement with which he was most famously associated, "I never met a man I didn't like." Northwest of town (2 miles/3 km east of Oologah) is Will Rogers' birthplace—a two-story log-and-clapboard home built in 1875.

Tulsa International Airport is the closest, and buses also service the Claremore area.
Map ref: page 621 M7

The historic Indian Smoke Shop in Vian.

SOUTH DAKOTA

South Dakota is located in the central-north of the United States—it has only 10 people per square mile (4 people per sq km), the highest ratio of sites-to-people in the Great Plains. South Dakotans' ancestors include the Lakota people who followed the buffalo across the Plains; German, Norwegian, and Czechoslovakian immigrants; miners who looked for gold; and farmers and ranchers who endlessly worked the land. This state has a rich and varied history.

South Dakota is home to the Sioux Nation of Plains Native Americans, which is made up of the Dakota, Lakota, and Nakota tribes. Names like Crazy Horse, Laura Ingalls Wilder, Calamity Jane, Sparky Anderson, George McGovern, Lewis and Clark, Wild Bill Hickok, and Sitting Bull make up the rich heritage of this state.

South Dakota has a diversity of commerce and resources such as farming, ranching, industry, lumbering, manufacturing, and mining. The chief crops are corn, oats, wheat, sunflowers, soybeans, and sorghum. The main source of income for the state is tourism.

Until the early 1600s, the land was home to the Paleo, Arikara, Cheyenne, and Sioux Native Americans, whose descendants still live in South Dakota today. In 1868, the Fort Laramie Treaty was signed, which led to the Great Sioux Reservation (which occupies nearly all of present-day South Dakota). However, gold was discovered in the Black Hills in 1874 and, by the end of the nineteenth century, thousands of European and American pioneers moved into the region and their dreams clashed with those of the Native Americans. They built fences and towns, and both the Native American culture and the great herds of buffalo were confined and diminished.

Today, South Dakota offers visitors a variety of spectacular sites, including the forested granite caves of the Black Hills, the glacial lakes of the northeast, the colossal Mt Rushmore and the Crazy Horse Memorial, the Badlands, the National Caves, state parks, and buffalo roundups.

The area around Buffalo, in the northwest of the state. South Dakota is a state of wide open plains and stark, ancient rock formations.

State motto Under God the People Rule
State flag Adopted 1909 (since modified)
Capital Pierre
Population 754,844
Total area (land and water) 77,121 square miles (199,743 sq km)
Land area 75,896 square miles (196,571 sq km)
South Dakota is the 16th-largest state in size
Origin of name From the Sioux word meaning "allies"
Nicknames The Mount Rushmore State, The Coyote State
State bird Ring-necked pheasant
State flower American pasque flower
State tree Black Hills spruce
Entered the Union November 2, 1889 as the 40th state

Places in
SOUTH DAKOTA

BLACK HILLS NATIONAL FOREST

The Black Hills are in western South Dakota, southwest of Rapid City. They are the oldest mountains in the United States dating back 2.5 billion years. Here is a 1.2 million-acre (486,000-ha) oasis of pine-covered mountains that offers two scenic drives, waterfalls, 1,300 miles (2,092 km) of streams, abundant wildlife, 353 miles (568 km) of recreation trails, 30 campgrounds, trout fishing, golf, gaming, and shopping.

The hills were named for the dark-green needles of the Ponderosa pines and Black Hill spruce trees, which cover the hills in a thick mass such that, from a distance, they look black. Most of the land in Black Hills is part of the national forest and all activities are monitored.

The Black Hills have four major features: the Central Area, Limestone Plateau, Red Valley, and Hogback Ridge. The Central area is mainly sedimentary and igneous rock and granite—Mt Rushmore is carved from granite. The Limestone Plateau is mainly Paleozoic limestone with sandstone and dolomite. The Red Valley is red shales, clays, and sandstone from the Triassic and Jurassic periods, and the Hogback Ridge is mainly lower Cretaceous sandstone.

Of the 1,585 different plants found in South Dakota, 1,200 species are in the Black Hills. The Norbeck Wildlife Preserve, which was established in 1920, covers about 35,000 acres (14,175 ha) and is home to elk, deer, and mountain goats, to name but a few animals.

Along the hiking trail, visitors can see granite formations and small lakes. In the Norbeck Wildlife Preserve is the Black Elk Wilderness. This 9,824-acre (3,979-ha) wilderness was named for Black Elk, an Oglala Sioux holy man. Harney Point is the centerpiece of this wilderness and is the highest point in the Rockies, at 7,242 feet (2,209 m). The national forest's visitor center is at the Pactola Reservoir and offers nature trails and an exhibit on the Black Hills'

natural history. It is open from Memorial Day to Labor Day and visitors can find out about the best fishing spots and information on renting a boat. Hiking is especially good here along the Centennial and the George Mickelson Trails.

The I-90 is the best east–west route and US-85/385 is the best north–south connector to the Black Hills. Nearby Rapid City has an airport and buses service Rapid City. Organized tours are available.
Map ref: page 428 B4

CUSTER STATE PARK AND WIND CAVE NATIONAL PARK

Custer State Park is 83 square miles (215 sq km) in southwestern South Dakota, about 30 miles (48 km) south of Rapid City. It was established in 1919. The most astonishing attraction in the park is the herd of more than 1,500 buffalo, which roams freely here and, consequently, there are more buffalo jams than traffic jams. A favorite hiking trail is Needles Highway (Route 87) within the park and great care must be taken because it is especially narrow and winding.

Perhaps the most exciting event to take place in the park is the annual October Buffalo Roundup. The buffalo are herded into corrals along the Wildlife Road. Some of the animals are kept and are auctioned

Crazy Horse Memorial, in Black Hills National Forest, shows the chief astride his horse. Still in progress, the statue is a memorial to all Native Americans.

off—the funds from the auction go back into the park. This also serves to control the numbers of buffalo in the park. The event is coupled with the annual Buffalo Roundup Arts Festival, which, among other things, hosts a chili cook-off.

The park has more wildlife and natural resources than anywhere else in the state and there are four resorts, one in each corner of the park, and many camping facilities.

The park offers everything from lakeside lodging to paddleboats, canoes, and mountain bikes. There are trips through the Needles Eye and the Cathedral Spires. The spires are pure granite towers rising out of the forest floor and are a registered National Landmark.

Wind Cave National Park is at the southern border of Custer State

Park. It is 28,000 acres (11,340 ha) of wildlife preserve above a long cave. The park is home to elk, deer, buffalo, and antelope. Visitors can enter the 91-mile (145-km) cave, which is considered to be the seventh-longest in the world. Tom Bingham discovered Wind Cave in 1881 when he heard the wind coming from its opening and then felt the breeze as it blew his hat off. When he returned, the cave sucked his hat inside. There are five tours of the cave and each includes more than 150 stairs. The Wind Cave National Park Visitor Center takes reservations for tours and offers other activities and services.

Visitors can fly into Rapid City and buses also service the city.
Map ref: page 428 B5

Even though lumber is a major industry in South Dakota, logging is closely regulated in national forests such as the Black Hills.

DEADWOOD

Deadwood (population 1,734) lies in the middle of the Black Hills National Forest, about 45 miles (72 km) northwest of Rapid City on US-85. In 1989, limited gambling was approved in Deadwood. It is hoped that the increased revenue will provide funds to maintain its Wild West legends and character. Deadwood is the town where gunslingers Wild Bill Hickok and Martha "Calamity" Jane lived and died. The story goes that in 1876, when gold was discovered in Deadwood, 6,000 gold diggers from all over the country came to find their wealth. James Butler, also known as Wild Bill Hickok, and Calamity Jane, came to town in the hope of winning some of the new wealth at the gambling tables.

Wild Bill had a reputation as a good gunman because he worked as a sheriff in Wyoming. The town of Deadwood hoped he could help bring order to a town out of control by the gold rush. Unfortunately, as he played cards in Saloon #10, he was shot in the back of the head by a Jack McCall. (When he fell forward and spilled the cards he was holding they were black aces and eights. This combination has

Wild Bill Hickok's burial site, Mount Moriah Cemetery, Deadwood.

since been called dead man's hand.) McCall was found guilty, hanged, and buried in an unmarked grave. Hickok's body lies with his fellow legends of the west, Calamity Jane, Deadwood Gulch, Preacher Smith, and Madam Dora Du Fran. Lawlessness continued for 10 more years until millionaire George Hearst (father of William Randolph Hearst) came to Deadwood with two other investors. They bought mines and built businesses and buildings, many of which are still standing.

Every summer the shooting of Wild Bill Hickok is re-enacted at Saloon #10 at 657 Main Street. Walking the streets of Deadwood, visitors encounter random shoot-outs all along Main Street. There are many places to gamble, some with names such as "Silverado," and "Miss Kitty's."

The Homestead Gold Mine Surface Tour and the Black Hills Mining Museum, both on Main Street, are places to learn more about the history of the gold rush in Deadwood.

Nearby Sturgis and Spearfish are serviced by buses and Rapid City has air and bus services.
Map ref: page 428 B4

HOT SPRINGS

Hot Springs (population 4,132) is 50 miles (80 km) south of Rapid City. In 1890, wealthy businessmen turned the springs into a spa.

Today, visitors can enjoy the springs by visiting Evans Plunge, the world's largest natural warm-water swimming pool. It maintains a constant temperature of 87°F (30.5°C) and is 50 × 200 feet (15 × 61 m) complete with three water slides, exercise equipment, water volleyball, and basketball. The Angostura Recreation Area has four campgrounds and 175 campsites, cabins, fishing, picnic areas, sandy beaches, hiking, paddleboats, and more. It is open year-round.

The Mammoth Site, just west of Hot Springs is the largest paleontological find of its kind in the world. Here are the fossils of nearly 50 mammoths found on this land as

A gold mine near Deadwood. Gold was discovered here in 1876, bringing huge changes to the area.

well as fossils from other species, which lived on these grasslands 26,000 years ago. There are guided tours, mini digs, and a bookstore. A 20,000-square-foot (1,900-sq-m) building is dedicated to research and is open for tours. Also worth visiting is the Black Hills Wild Horse Sanctuary where hundreds of mustangs run wild on a private preserve. This is the first privately owned wild horse preserve in the United States.

Rapid City is the nearest airport.
Map ref: page 428 B6

JEWEL CAVE NATIONAL MONUMENT

Jewel Cave is the world's fourth longest cave. It is in the Black Hills National Forest, about 16 miles (26 km) west of Custer, off US-16. It was established as a National Monument in 1908. It is a labyrinth, which twists and turns for 80 miles (129 km) beneath the Black Hills. It started millions of years ago when the mountains created faults in the Earth. The slightly acidic groundwater seeped into these crevices and dissolved the Pahasapa Limestone, which, over several million years, hollowed out the passages within Jewel Cave. The formations within the cave are breathtaking. Millions of particles of mineral calcite from millions of drops of water make up each formation. Jewel Cave got its name from the jewel-like crystals, known as dog-tooth spar and nailhead spar, which line the rooms and passages. The cave contains some very rare formations in unusual shapes.

The rooms have names such as "Contortionist's Delight," "The Club Room," "The Miseries," and "The Formation Room." Herb and Jan Conn spent 21 years of their life exploring the cave and retired

when they had discovered 65 miles (104 km). They are credited with the naming of the rooms and pioneering the exploration of the cave, which is now caved to about 80 miles (129 km). They discovered rooms 150 × 200 feet (46 × 61 m) and passageways as long as 3,200 feet (976 m). There is a place in the cave where the wind blows up to 32 miles (51 km) per hour, and there are 18-inch (45-cm) high passages, and holes narrower than a man's shoulders. One room is 600 feet (183 m) long and eight stories high with boulders the size of houses. It is a truly amazing sight and worth seeing. Visitors should be sure they are not claustrophobic, wear a heavy sweater, and bring along enthusiasm and nerve. The park rangers can set up visitors' tours.

Rapid City is the nearest airport.
Map ref: page 428 B5

MITCHELL

An hour west of Sioux Falls, on I-90, visitors can see a church steeple in the distance—then they know they are near Mitchell, a small midwestern town of 14,000 people. Mitchell has a reputation for attracting the road-weary, the unusual, and also the notably famous, to its city. The main town consists of three or four storefronts, which house the law offices, the jeweler, and the bars. What attracts the visitor to Mitchell is that it is home to the world's only Corn Palace, nicknamed the world's biggest bird feeder. It was built in 1892 to celebrate the agricultural richness of the area and to encourage settlers to the area. Each fall there was a festival, which grew larger and larger until they had to add newer and larger structures until, in 1937, the final turrets and Moorish-inspired details were added. It is decorated with 3,000 bushels of corn, grain, and native grasses. Much like a float, the corn, grain, and grasses are used to create murals of the South Dakota landscape, history, and harvest scenes. Inside is an auditorium, which has hosted every big band in the 1930s, 1940s, and 1950s. Even Andy Williams and Bob Hope have performed at the Corn Palace. Each summer the murals are stripped off and new ones take their place—this costs about US$35,000. All this preparation is for Corn Palace Week held in mid-September that features country-and-western bands, and carnivals.

Oscar Howe, a Yanktonai Sioux painter, has six panels inside. Visitors can also visit the Oscar Howe Art Center. His art depicts Native American life and has earned him international acclaim. The Art Center is a National Historic Site. The Friends of the Middle Border Museum also has Howe's work, that of other American artists, and Native American exhibits.

The Mitchell Prehistoric Indian Village is just north of town. This is a National Archeological Landmark of a town from 900 BC, when it is believed that the people were devastated by drought. There is a hunter's lodge, a museum, and a visitor center offering guided tours.

Mitchell is serviced by buses and Sioux Falls Regional Airport is the closest airport.

Map ref: page 429 L5

MT RUSHMORE NATIONAL MONUMENT

Mt Rushmore stands as the gateway to the West, 25 miles (40 km) southwest of Rapid City. It is surrounded by the Black Hills National Forest, Custer State Park, the Wind Cave National Park, and the Black Elk Wilderness Area.

It took sculptor Gutzon Borglum and his crew 14 years to carve the 60-foot (18-m) tall faces of the four presidents. George Washington, Thomas Jefferson, Theodore Roosevelt, and Abraham Lincoln are exposed on granite to embody the spirit of the foundation, preservation, and expansion of the United States.

Visitors can see the Sculptor's Studio and learn about the construction of the monument. Presidential Trail leads to the base of the mountain where visitors are treated to spectacular views of the faces. It is open daily, depending on weather conditions.

Borglum had to change the sculptures nine times because of fractures in the granite. Then the nearly completed face of Thomas Jefferson had to be blasted off the right side of Washington, because of insufficient granite, and re-carved to the left. Almost 90 percent of the carving was done with dynamite. Gutzon made several other works in his lifetime, including the remodeled torch for the statue of Liberty, a seated Lincoln in Newark, and an oversized Lincoln bust for the US Capitol. US President Calvin Coolidge dedicated the memorial in 1927. The Washington head was formally dedicated in 1930, Jefferson was dedicated in 1936, Lincoln in 1937 and Roosevelt in 1939. Borglum died in March 1941.

Borglum's son, Lincoln, supervised the completion of the heads after his father's death. All carving ceased in October 1941, on the eve before the United States entered World War II. All federal funds went to the war fund and the carvings were never completed.

The best time to to view the giant faces is in the warm light of early day. Besides the Presidential Trail and Borglum's Studio, during the summer the Mt Rushmore Memorial Amphitheater hosts a monument-lighting ceremony. The visitor center and the information center have films and tours.

Major airlines and bus routes service Rapid City.

Map ref: page 428 B5

Mt Rushmore. Gutzon Borglum and his crew took 14 long years to chisel and blast the faces of four beloved Presidents.

The State Capitol building, Pierre.

PIERRE

Pierre, with a population of 13,422, is the state capital of South Dakota. It is the second-smallest and easily the sleepiest state capital in the United States. It is part river town, part farm town, and part railroad town. One reason as to why the city was chosen for the capital is because it is nearly in the very center of the state. No interstate passes through Pierre and it is serviced only by commuter airlines. For nine months of the year it is without legislators.

For such an unobtrusive place, the South Dakotans have built one of the most impressive Capitol buildings in the country. The building has mosaic floors, stained-glass skylights, and marble staircases. It is full of early nineteenth-century artwork, murals, and Roman designs and stenciling. The foundation is granite and the dome is solid copper.

A not-to-be-missed stop is the South Dakota Cultural Heritage Center. It is built into the side of a hill and designed in the style of a traditional Native American dwelling. Inside are historical displays of Native American cultures and the history of the pioneers. The Cultural Heritage Center presents the annual Red Cloud Indian Art Show. In 1743, two sons of the French explorer, Pierre Gaultier de Varennes, Sieur de La Verendrye, became the first whites to enter South Dakota. They climbed to a bluff, above what is now Fort Pierre,

Crazy quilt, by Dora Smith, 1889, hung in the state's Cultural Heritage Center, Pierre.

and left an inscribed plate, claiming the land for Louis XV. In 1913, some children playing found it after 170 years and it is on view at the Cultural Heritage Museum.

At 303 E. Dakota is the South Dakota Guard Museum, which houses General Custer's dress sword as well as other military memorabilia. For nature at its finest, La Framboise Isle Nature Center is a perfect spot for walking, sightseeing, or picnicking.

Buses and the Pierre Regional Airport service the area.

Map ref: page 428 G4

PINE RIDGE AND PINE RIDGE INDIAN RESERVATION

There are over 70,000 Lakota (Sioux) Native Americans living in South Dakota. Over 75 percent of these live on either Rosebud or Pine Ridge Reservations. These two reservations cover over 2 million acres (810,000 ha). Most of the Native Americans live here part-time or make frequent visits to maintain family ties and keep cultural traditions, but go to work and school in the urban communities.

Pine Ridge Indian Reservation covers about 1.8 million acres (729,000 ha) and is the second-largest in the United States. Two thirds of the reservation is in Shannon County, which is consistently marked as the poorest in the United States. Alcoholism and infant mortality are very high, with unemployment at 85 percent.

Most activities center around the town of Pine Ridge, which is at the very southern edge of the

reservation. Everything comes to life the first week of August for the Oglala Nation Powwow and Rodeo. This is a three-day rodeo and a four-day powwow with drummers and dancers, softball, golf, and horseshoe pitching. The Red Cloud Indian Mission School, on US-18, has an art show with over 300 works from 30 different tribes. There are also Indian Star quilts and a gift shop in which to buy authentic bead and quill work.

Wounded Knee is east of the town of Pine Ridge and is marked as a National Historic Site. This is where, according to the Sioux, the soul of their nation is buried. The Wounded Knee Massacre marked

a major turning point in world history—it symbolized the end of almost 400 years of unrelenting war against the indigenous people of the Americas. Years after the Black Hills were given to the US Government, the Sioux leaders resisted relocating to the reservations as the treaty dictated. Big Foot was a respected chief and encouraged his people to perform the Ghost Dance, a ritual which the Sioux believed would restore their old way of life. In 1890, Sitting Bull, a great spiritual leader of the Sioux, was killed on his reservation in central-north South Dakota. Chief Big Foot decided to journey to Pine Ridge to see Red Cloud, another Sioux chief, to discuss the mounting tensions among the people. There were 350 men, women and children in the group, and one bitterly cold morning, on December 29, 200 members of the Seventh Cavalry caught up with them and around 200 men, women, and children were massacred.

Major airlines and bus routes are available from Rapid City, the nearest center to the reservation.

Map ref: page 428 C6

RAPID CITY

Rapid City is the home base for all excursions to the Badlands and the Black Hills. In summer its population is 60 times more than usual, (67,652). It averages 3 million

tourists a year. Downtown has a commercial historic district, including 38 buildings built between 1881 and 1930. The Buell Building, the Firehouse Brewing Company, and the Prairie Edge have been restored to their original grandeur. The West Boulevard Historic District is 18 blocks of Queen Anne and early twentieth-century Colonial homes. The Journey is a US$12.5 million museum, which opened in 1997. It has 48,000 square feet (4,560 sq m) dedicated to artifacts, memorabilia, and artwork of the history of the Black Hills. The Museum of Geology narrates the history of the Badlands and houses the most comprehensive collection of prehistoric mammal fossils in the state.

The Black Hills Stock Show and Rodeo is in late January and early February. In August is the Central States Fair. The Rushmore Plaza Civic Auditorium holds concerts and Broadway shows.

For excursions to Black Hills or Badlands, the Rapid City Chamber of Commerce and Visitor Information provides information and services. Visitors intending to drive into the hills need to know what the road conditions are like. There are buses, which service the sites. West of town, on the scenic Hwy 44, there are many lodging and restaurant options.

Major airlines and bus routes are available from Rapid City.

Map ref: page 428 B4

Pine Ridge Indian Reservation is at the southern edge of the Badlands National Park. In 1976, the park doubled in size with the addition of 133,300 acres (53,986 ha) of the Pine Ridge Reservation, in an agreement with the Oglala Sioux Tribe.

SIOUX FALLS

Sioux Falls, with a population of 116,762, is easily the cultural and commercial leader in the state. It is in the southeast corner of South Dakota, at the junction of I-90 and I-29. The city was named for the rapids at Falls Park, which is just north of downtown.

The Sioux River Greenway Recreation Trail is a good way to see the area. It circles the city from Falls Peak to Elmwood Golf course.

Sioux Falls has many art galleries, a symphony orchestra, dance companies, and playhouses. There are 62 parks, boutiques, five golf courses, a zoo, and more than 150 different kinds of restaurants.

The St Joseph's Cathedral Historic District is dedicated to the preservation of the Queen Anne style homes, which were built before the depression of the 1890s. One of these homes belonged to US Senator Richard Pettigrew. He collected art from his world travels and donated the house and its belongings to the people of Sioux Falls upon his death. The Pettigrew Home and Museum provides an insightful tour of the senator's life as well as a tour of exhibits covering the natural and cultural past of Sioux Falls and Minnehaha County. The Old Courthouse Museum also features history of the area but adds special events to enhance the experience, such as sheep shearing, tin smithing, and weaving.

Held in September, the Tribal Arts Festival attracts Native American artists and visitors from around the world. The Old Courthouse was built in 1890 with Sioux quartzite. Inside there are murals of scenes from Sioux Falls' history. Inside the Courthouse there are two museums, the Minnehaha County Historical Society and the Sioux Valley Genealogical Society Library. Historic walking tours are available of the courthouse and there is a museum store selling related merchandise, including books on local history. These are both National Historic Landmarks and are full of the history of the Sioux land region. The USS *South Dakota* Battleship Memorial is dedicated to the most decorated US battleship in World War II.

Sioux Falls has its own regional airport and is serviced by buses.
Map ref: page 429 N6

Old buildings in historic Belle Fourche, just north of Spearfish.

SPEARFISH

Located in the quiet hills in the northwest edge of the Black Hills, just south of Belle Fourche, is the idyllic town of Spearfish (population 8,851), which was founded in 1876. Spearfish makes a short and pleasant stop on the way in or out of the Black Hills.

Visitors can take the Spearfish Canyon Scenic Byway (US-14A) and wind through 18 miles (29 km) of forest featuring views of the Black Hills, picnic places, and waterfalls. The marked site where the movie *Dances With Wolves* was filmed is very attractive.

Spearfish first got onto the map because of gold, which was discovered in the Black Hills by a band of men who were all—except one—killed by Native Americans. Ezra Kind escaped and lived to tell his tale, which he etched onto a piece of rock, later to be called the Thoen Stone. The Adam's Memorial Museum has a display on the stone.

Spearfish has always been considered one of the most civilized of the Black Hills communities. The Matthews Opera House opened in 1906 and for 55 years, performances of the Passion Play have been held in a 6,000-seat amphitheater.

The Spearfish Ranger Station provides hiking advice and maps. The Chamber of Commerce also sets up tours and has visitor information. Spearfish is serviced by buses. Rapid City is the nearest airport.
Map ref: page 428 B3

WATERTOWN

Watertown (population 19,909) is on I-29 near the Minnesota border. It was home to the last and the first governor of South Dakota, Arthur Calville Mellette. He left his house, built in 1883, and all his assets to the people of Watertown.

The restored Mellette House is available for touring. The US$10 million Redlin Art Center at the intersection of I-29 and US-212 holds a planetarium, and 92 artworks by the acclaimed wildlife and American painter Terry Redlin. Visitors can visit the Bramble Park Zoo, which is home to 400 birds, mammals, and reptiles from all around the world.

The Dakota Sioux Casino is open 24-hours a day, it is run by the Sisseton-Wahpeton Sioux Tribe.

Watertown has a small airport and is serviced by buses.
Map ref: page 429 M2

YANKTON

Yankton (population 14,325) is in the southeastern corner of South Dakota. It is home of the Yankton Treaty of 1858, which stated that the Native Americans would sell 14 million acres (5.67 million ha), between the Big Sioux and the Missouri River, for 12 cents per acre. This city, lying on the banks of the Missouri River, claims to be the Mother City of South Dakota and its heritage is in the steamboat captains and railroad tycoons.

General Custer stopped here and took nearly 20 years to settle his debts with the merchants. It was named for the Yankton Sioux tribe that once ruled the area. Now it is a college town, supporting Yankton College. This old-fashioned town boasts Fourth of July Parades. The Charles Gurney Hotel is the site of the trial of Jack McCall for the murder of Wild Bill Hickok. The Carnegie Library was built in 1902 and is in its original condition. The Crime-Kenyon Heritage House has a beautiful garden and furnishings from the 1870s. The African Methodist Episcopal Church was built by slaves and is the oldest African-American church in the Dakotas. The Excelsior Mill houses the Gurney Seed and Nursery and has been in business since 1894.

There is a small regional airport just west of Yankton and buses service nearby Sioux Falls.
Map ref: page 429 M7

STATE FEATURE

Badlands National Park

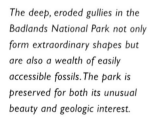

Jackrabbit, Badlands National Park, South Dakota. They are fast runners and powerful jumpers.

Badlands National Park is about 50 miles (80 km) east of Rapid City on I-90 in central-south South Dakota. This 244,000-acre (98,820-ha) park protects large tracts of prairie and stark rock formations. There are chiseled spires, ridges, and deep canyons. The land has been ravaged over the years by wind and rain and these ridges, spires, and knobs are reminders of the powerful forces of nature.

The Badlands are the result of a natural history that began around the time the dinosaurs vanished, about 65 million years ago. The Pierre Sea, which divided the continent, drained away and made North America whole again. From 37 million to 23 million years ago, the climate became cool and dry. Flooding over the years left layers of volcanic ash and mud. Between floods, plant-eating mammals lived off the vegetation. The meat-eating mammals left behind the bones of their prey, which became fossils and sediment. These fossils are the best and most complete record of the Oligocene Epoch, the Golden Age of Mammals, that took place after the dinosaurs. About a half million years ago, erosion sliced through the prairie and the layers of mudstone, creating a landscape both chaotic and spectacular.

The French fur traders referred to the land as "les mauvaises terres a traverser," or "bad lands to travel across." The Lakota Indians named it "mako sica," or "land bad." The word "badlands" became the generic geologic name for all barren, eroded landscapes in South Dakota, Montana, Mongolia, on the Moon, and on Mars. In 1939, President Franklin D.

The deep, eroded gullies in the Badlands National Park not only form extraordinary shapes but are also a wealth of easily accessible fossils. The park is preserved for both its unusual beauty and geologic interest.

Roosevelt proclaimed the Badlands a National Monument "to preserve the scenery, to protect the fossils and wildlife and to conserve the mixed-grass prairie." In 1978, Congress elevated the area to National Park status.

There are many activities in the park, no matter what time of year. The Ben Riefel visitor center at Cedar Pass is 5 miles (8 km) inside the park, on Hwy 240, and offers a video of attractions, history, camping, and other information. The White River Visitor Center is 55 miles (88 km) southwest of Route 27 in the park's southern section. These centers are helpful because most roadways in the park are unpaved and are accessible only by 4WD vehicles, foot, or horseback.

The Sage Creek Wilderness Area was set aside in 1976 by Congress for no further development. It is open for hiking, backpacking, and other activities. The buffalo created the only trails here. There is a campground just south of the Ben Riefel Visitor Center. For back-country camping, visitors must contact a ranger for detailed instructions.

The most popular activity in the park is hiking. Visitors can pick up trail guides from a visitor center. Hiking is permitted throughout the park but climbing on the formations is not encouraged. Visitors should always plan their route with a park ranger and have a compass, a map, and plenty of water. It is advisable to wear long pants and boots to avoid the poison ivy and being bitten by the venomous prairie rattlesnake.

The Door Trail winds through rocks and crevices and provides great views of the landscapes. The Window Trail is short but offers a spectacular view. The Cliff Shelf Nature Trail is through the woods and is unpaved. The Notch Trail is for the more experienced hiker—it involves climbs around narrow ledges and some sure footing up a 45-degree embankment. The end is an unbelievable view of the Cliff Shelf and White River Valley. The Saddle Pass Trail is also suited to the experienced hiker. It climbs very steeply to the top of the Badlands Wall and then connects with the Castle and Medicine Root Trails. To see wildlife, visitors can try the Sage Creek Rim Road

to see herds of buffalo and antelope. Hikers should always check with a ranger for details before beginning.

The Badlands are one of the last of the world's great grasslands. These grasslands are home to thousands of species of plants and wildlife. Year-round they are brimming with life—all together there are 50 different grasses and about 200 different wildflowers. Throughout the drastic temperatures, from summer to winter, many animals call the Badlands home. Prairie dogs, badgers, bobcats, foxes, coyotes, antelope, Rocky Mountain bighorns, mule deer, cottontails, and jackrabbits, the venomous prairie rattler, bull snakes, cliff swallow, and golden eagles are just a few. It is also home to 500 head of buffalo.

The landscape in the Badlands National Park is so stark that it has been described as "hell with the fires burned out." It is savagely beautiful.

For a stunning drive, visitors can take Route 240/ the Loop Road to see the park. It is a winding road through the colored bluffs and provides views of the many different Badlands terrain.

Other attractions are helicopter tours and the Badlands Petrified Gardens, located at Exit 152 off the I-90. Here are the largest petrified trees and logs ever found in the Badlands. There is a museum, which holds prehistoric fossils and an exhibit of minerals, agates, and crystals. There are also about a dozen horseback-riding trail outfits, and guest ranches offer one-hour, two-hour, and two-day rides.

Located just south of the Ben Riefel Visitor Center is an inn and a lodge, which rents cabins—lodging is also found in nearby towns, such as Wall. There are two campsites situated inside the park. Badlands National Park has a modest entrance fee. Buses leave daily from Rapid City.

Bull snakes are found in Badlands. A bull snake feeds mainly on rodents and is a large, nonvenomous snake of the genus Pituophis.

North Dakota • Northern South Dakota

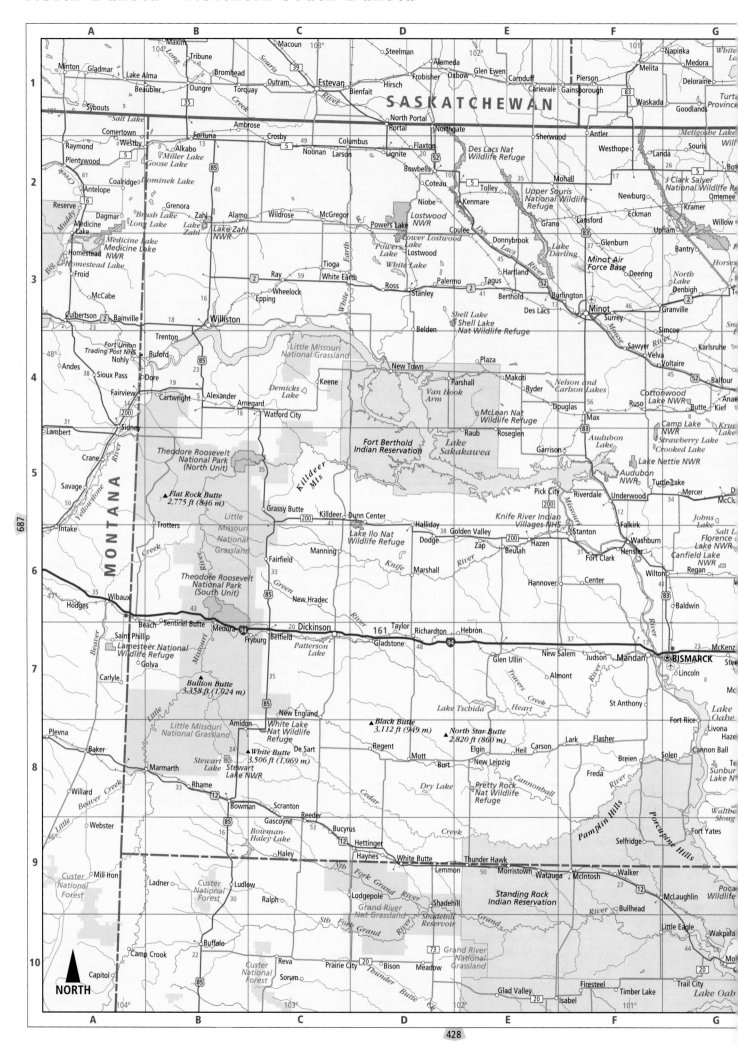

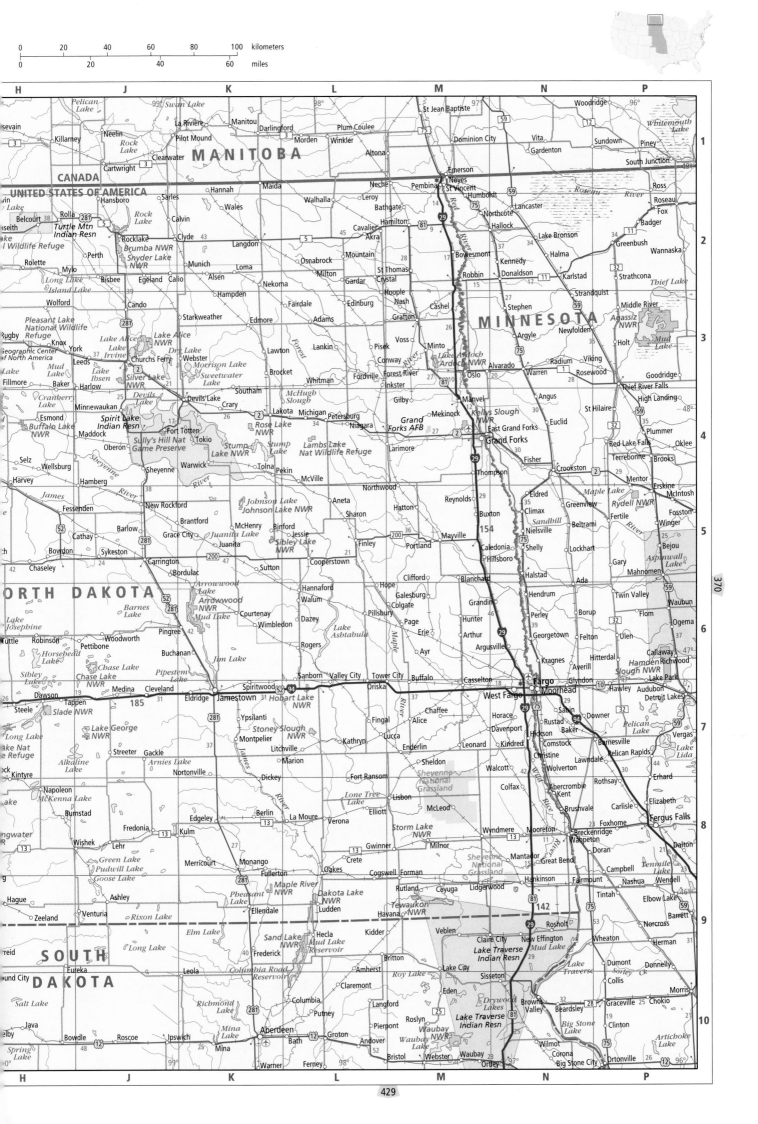

0   20   40   60   80   100 kilometers

0   20   40   60   miles

H   **J**   **K**   **L**   **M**   **N**   **P**

Pelican Lake
Swan Lake
Killarney   Neelin   Rock Lake   La Riviere   Manitou   Darlingford   Plum Coulee   St Jean Baptiste   Woodridge
991
Whitemouth Lake

MANITOBA   Pilot Mound   Clearwater   Pilot Mound   Morden   Winkler   Altona   Dominion City   Vita   Gardenton   Sundown   Piney

1

sevain   Cartwright   Clearwater   75   Neche   Emerson   Neyes   59   South Junction
CANADA
UNITED STATES OF AMERICA   Hannah   Maida   Walhalla   Leroy   Bathgate   Pembina   St Vincent   Humboldt   Ross   Reseau

win Lake   Belcourt   Rolla   281   Hansboro   Sarles   Wales   Bathgate   29   Noyes   Northcote   Lancaster   Fox   Badger
38   5   Calvin   Cavalier   Akra   Hamilton   81   9   Bowesmont   Kennedy   Halma   Greenbush   Wannaska
Turtle Mtn Indian Resn   Rocklake   Clyde   43   Langdon   45   28   Mountain   St Thomas   Crystal   17   Robbin   Donaldson   11   Karlstad   32   Strathcona   2
Brumba NWR   Munich   Loma   Osnabrock   Milton   11   Stephen   15   Middle River
Snyder Lake NWR   Rolette   Mylo   Perth   Egeland   Calio   Alsen   Nekoma   Gardar   Hoople   Nash   Cashel   Newfolden   Agassiz NWR   Mud Lake
Wolford   Bisbee   Hampden   Fairdale   Edinburg   Grafton   26   **MINNESOTA**   Argyle   Holt
Pleasant Lake National Wildlife Refuge   Starkweather   Edmore   Adams   Voss   Minto   Stephen   75   3
Rugby   Knox   York   Lake Alice   Lawton   Lankin   Pisek   Conway   Lake Ardoch NWR   Alvarado   Radium   Viking   Goodridge
Geographic Center of North America   Leeds   Lake Irvine   Churchs Ferry   Webster   Brocket   Whitman   Fordville   Forest River   Oslo   Warren   1   Rosewood   Thief River Falls
Mud Lake   Baker   Harlow   Silver Lake NWR   Southam   McHugh Slough   Inkster   Gilby   Mekinock   Manvel   Angus   St Hilaire   High Landing   4
Cranberry Lake   Minnewaukan   Devils Lake   Devils Lake   Crary   Lakota   Michigan   Petersburg   Niagara   Grand Forks AFB   East Grand Forks   Euclid   Plummer
Esmond   Spirit Lake Indian Resn   Fort Totten   Tokio   Rose Lake NWR   Larimore   Grand Forks   Fisher   Crookston   2   Mentor   Erskine   McIntosh
Buffalo Lake NWR   Maddock   Oberon   Sheyenne   Warwick   Stump Lake NWR   Lambs Lake Nat Wildlife Refuge   Northwood   Reynolds   Thompson   Red Lake Falls   Terrebonne   Brooks   Oklee
Selz   Sully's Hill Nat Game Preserve   Pekin   McVille   Hatton   Buxton   Eldred   Greenview   Rydell NWR   Fosston   Winger
Harvey   Wellsburg   Hamberg   Sheyenne   River   Aneta   Sharon   Mayville   Climax   Sandhill   Nielsville   Fertile   Maple Lake
James   Fessenden   New Rockford   Johnson Lake   Johnson Lake NWR   Finley   200   Portland   Caledonia   Shelly   Beltrami   Lockhart   154   5
52   Cathay   Barlow   Brantford   McHenry   Binford   Jessie   Sibley Lake NWR   Cooperstown   21   Hillsboro   Halstad   Ada   Gary   Bejou   25
Bowdon   Sykeston   Grace City   Juanita Lake   Juanita   Sutton   Hope   Clifford   Blanchard   Hendrum   Twin Valley   Aspinwall Lake   Mahnomen
Chaseley   Carrington   24   47   Galesburg   Colgate   Grandin   Perley   39   Borup   Flom   Waubun
NORTH DAKOTA   Bordulac   52   Arrowwood Lake   Hannaford   Walum   Pillsbury   Page   Hunter   Georgetown   Felton   Ulen   Ogema   6
Barnes Lake   Arrowwood NWR   281   Courtenay   Dazey   Lake Ashtabula   Erie   Arthur   29   Kragnes   Averill   Hitterdal   Hamden Slough NWR   37
Lake Josephine   Pingree   42   Mud Lake   Wimbledon   Rogers   Ayr   Argusville   Callaway   Richwood   47
Robinson   Pettibone   Woodworth   Buchanan   Jim Lake   Sanborn   Valley City   Tower City   Buffalo   18   Casselton   Fargo   Glyndon   10   Lake Park
Horsehead Lake   Chase Lake   Pipestem Lake   Spiritwood   52   94   Oriska   37   West Fargo   Moorhead   Hawley   Audubon   Detroit Lakes   7
Sibley Lake   Chase Lake NWR   Medina   Cleveland   Eldridge   Jamestown   31   Hobart Lake NWR   Ypsilanti   Chaffee   Horace   Sabin   Downer   32
Dawson   Tappen   185   Stoney Slough NWR   Fingal   Alice   Davenport   Rustad   Baker   94   Pelican Lake   Vergas
Long Lake   Slade NWR   Lake George NWR   Montpelier   Litchville   Kathryn   Lucca   Enderlin   Leonard   Kindred   Hickson   Comstock   Barnesville   Lake Lida
Lake Nat Refuge   Steele   Streeter   Gackle   Arnies Lake   Nortonville   Dickey   Marion   Fort Ransom   Sheldon   Walcott   Christine   Wolverton   Pelican Rapids   Erhard   44
Kintyre   Alkaline Lake   Fredonia   Edgeley   Berlin   La Moure   Verona   Elliott   Storm Lake NWR   Sheyenne National Grassland   Colfax   Abercrombie   Rothsay   8
Napoleon   Burnstad   13   Kulm   Lehr   Merricourt   Monango   Gwinner   Milnor   Wyndmere   Mooreton   Kent   Brushvale   Carlisle   Elizabeth
McKenna Lake   Wishek   Fullerton   Oakes   Crete   Cogswell   Forman   Mantador   Great Bend   Breckenridge   Wahpeton   Doran   Foxhome   Fergus Falls
ngwater   Green Lake   Pudwill Lake   Goose Lake   281   Maple River NWR   Dakota Lake NWR   Rutland   Cayuga   Hankinson   Fairmount   Campbell   Nashua   Dalton
Hague   Ashley   Pheasant Lake   Ellendale   Ludden   Tewaukon NWR   Lidgerwood   142   Tintah   Elbow Lake   59   9
Zeeland   Venturia   Rixon Lake   Elm Lake   Havana   Veblen   Rosholt   Wheaton   Herman   Norcross   31
reid   **SOUTH**   Sand Lake NWR   Hecla   Kidder   Claire City   New Effington   Mud Lake   Dumont   Donnelly
Salt Lake   **DAKOTA**   Eureka   Frederick   Mud Lake Reservoir   Britton   Lake Traverse Indian Resn   Lake City   Sisseton   Collis   Morris
Java   Long Lake   Leola   Columbia Road Reservoir   Amherst   Roy Lake   Eden   Claremont   Drywood Lakes   Brown Valley   Beardsley   Graceville   Chokio   10
elby   Spring Lake   Bowdle   Roscoe   Ipswich   Richmond Lake   281   Putney   Pierpont   Roslyn   Langford   25   Lake Traverse Indian Resn   Big Stone Lake   Clinton
12   Mina Lake   Aberdeen   12   Groton   Andover   Bath   Warner   Ferney   Waubay NWR   Waubay   Bristol   Webster   Ortley   Big Stone City   Artichoke Lake

GREAT PLAINS

370

Central and Southern South Dakota • Northern Nebraska

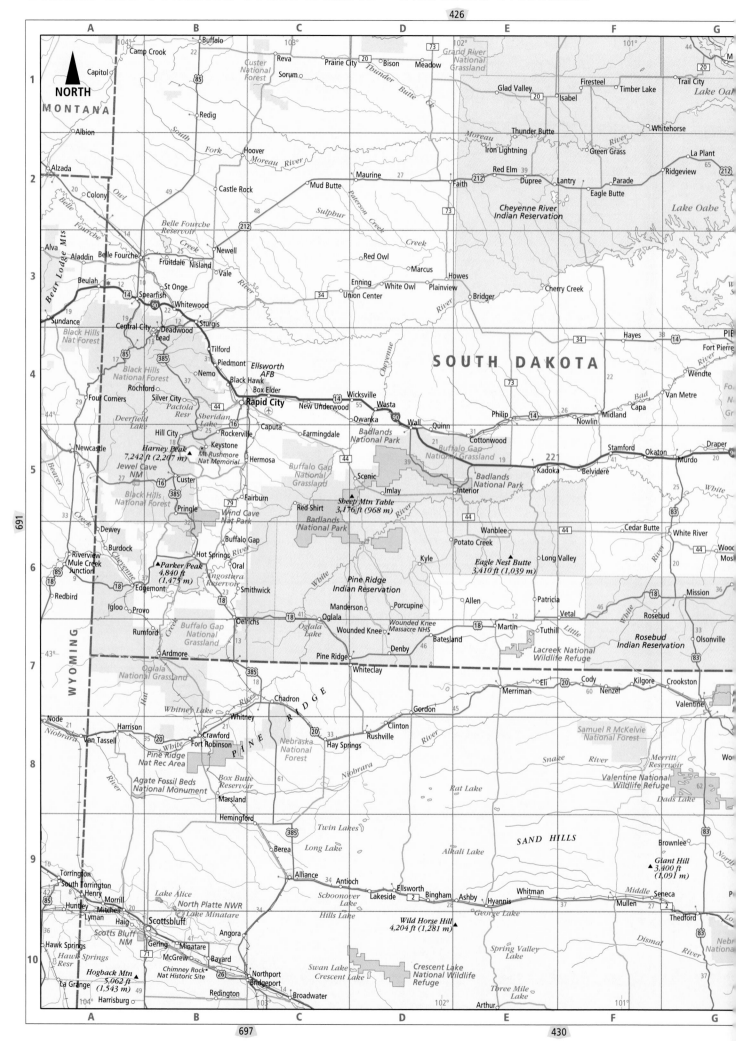

GREAT PLAINS

691

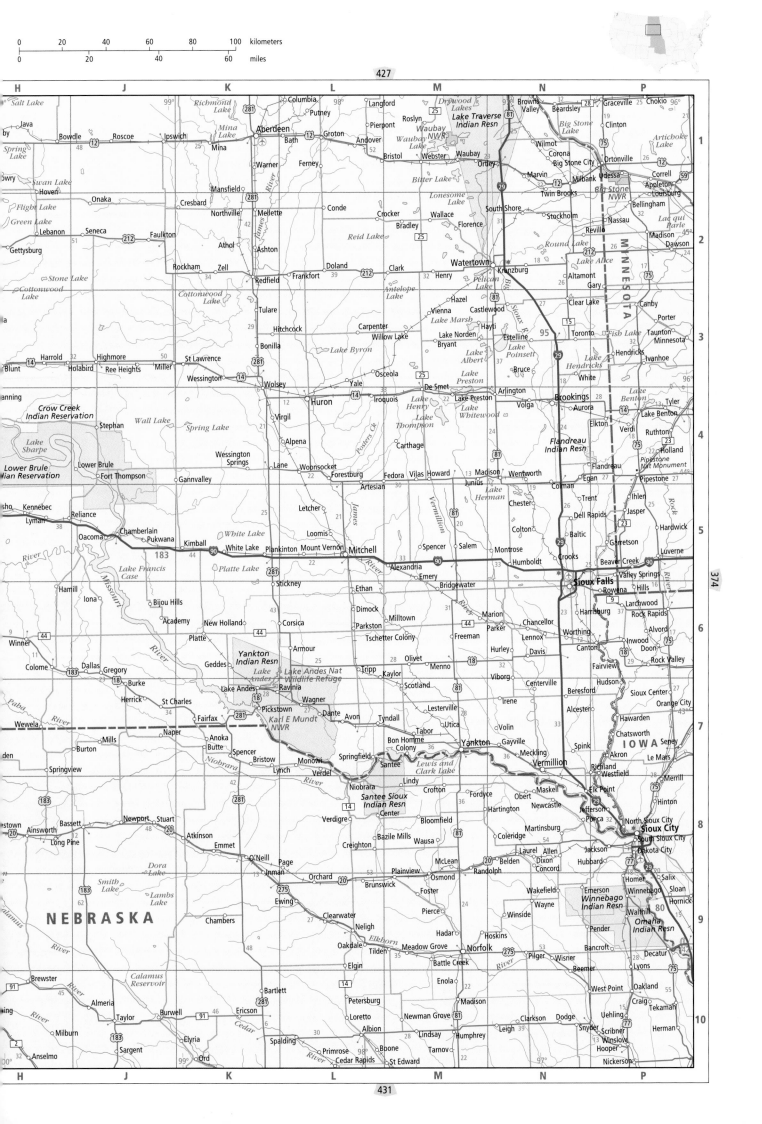

0 20 40 60 80 100 kilometers
0   20   40   60 miles

GREAT PLAINS

374

H J K L M N P

Salt Lake
Spring Lake
Java
by
Bowdle Roscoe Ipswich
Richmond Lake Columbia Langford Drywood Lakes Browns Valley Beardsley Graceville Chokio
Putney Roslyn Lake Traverse Indian Resn Big Stone Lake Clinton
Swan Lake 12 Mina Lake 281 Aberdeen Groton Pierpont Waubay Wilmot Corona Ortonville 12
Hoven Onaka Mina Bath Andover Bristol Webster Waubay NWR Ortley Big Stone City Odessa Correll 59
Flight Lake Mansfield Warner Ferney Ortley Marvin Milbank Appleton Louisburg
Green Lake Cresbard Northville Bitter Lake South Shore Twin Brooks Big Stone NWR Bellingham
Lebanon Seneca Faulkton Conde Crocker Wallace Florence Stockholm Revillo Nassau Lac qui Parle
Gettysburg Athol Ashton Reid Lake Bradley 25 Madison Dawson
Stone Lake Rockham Zell Doland Clark Henry Watertown Kranzburg Altamont Gary 75
Cottonwood Lake Redfield Frankfort 212 Pelican Lake 81 18 Lake Alice 17
Harrold Highmore St Lawrence Tulare Hitchcock Carpenter Willow Lake Hazel Castlewood Clear Lake Canby Porter
Blunt Holabird Ree Heights Miller Wessington Bonilla Vienna Lake Norden Hayti Toronto Taunton Minnesota
Crow Creek Indian Reservation Wolsey Yale Osceola Bryant Lake Albert Estelline 15 Fish Lake Hendricks Ivanhoe
Stephan Virgil Huron Iroquois De Smet Lake Preston Arlington Volga Brookings White
Lake Sharpe Alpena Carthage Lake Henry Lake Whitewood Aurora Elkton Verdi Ruthton
Lower Brule Indian Reservation Wessington Springs Lane Woonsocket Forestburg Fedora Vilas Howard Madison Wentworth Flandreau Indian Resn Flandreau Holland
Fort Thompson Gannvalley Artesian Junius Lake Herman Colman Egan Pipestone Nat Monument
Kennebec Reliance Letcher Loomis James R Chester Trent Ihlen Jasper
Lyman Chamberlain Pukwana Kimball White Lake Plankinton Mount Vernon Mitchell Spencer Salem Montrose Colton Baltic Garretson Luverne
Oacoma 183 90 Platte Lake 281 Alexandria Emery Bridgewater Humboldt Crooks Beaver Creek
Hamill Iona Bijou Hills Academy New Holland Corsica Dimock Milltown Marion Parker Chancellor Harrisburg Rock Rapids Alvord
Winner 44 Platte Parkston Tschetter Colony Freeman Hurley Lennox Worthing Canton Inwood Doon Rock Valley
Colome 183 Dallas Gregory Burke Geddes Yankton Indian Resn Armour Olivet Menno Viborg Davis Fairview Hudson Sioux Center Orange City
Herrick St Charles Lake Andes Ravinia Wagner Tripp Kaylor Scotland Centerville Beresford Alcester Hawarden
Fairfax 18 Pickstown Dante Avon Tyndall Lesterville Utica Irene Volin Chatsworth Seney IOWA
Wewela Naper Anoka Butte Spencer Bristow Monowi Verdel Niobrara Bon Homme Colony Yankton Gayville Meckling Vermillion Spink Akron Le Mars
Springview Burton Lynch Santee Lewis and Clark Lake Richland Westfield Merrill
Mills Naper Springview Bassett Newport Stuart Atkinson Emmet O'Neill Page Inman Orchard Brunswick Osmond Randolph Concord Dixon Jackson Hubbard North Sioux City Sioux City
Ainsworth Long Pine Dora Lake Smith Lake Lambs Lake Chambers Elgin Clearwater Neligh Tilden Meadow Grove Norfolk Pilger Wisner Beemer
NEBRASKA Ewing Plainview Foster Pierce Wayne Winnebago Indian Resn Omaha Indian Resn
Calamus Reservoir Bartlett Petersburg Madison Enola West Point Oakland
Brewster Almeria Taylor Burwell 91 Ericson Loretto Newman Grove 81 Clarkson Dodge Uehling Craig Tekamah
Milburn Sargent Elyria Ord Spalding Albion Lindsay Humphrey Leigh Snyder Winslow Herman
Anselmo Cedar Rapids St Edward Boone Tarnov Hooper Nickerson

H J K L M N P

Central and Southern Nebraska • Northern Kansas

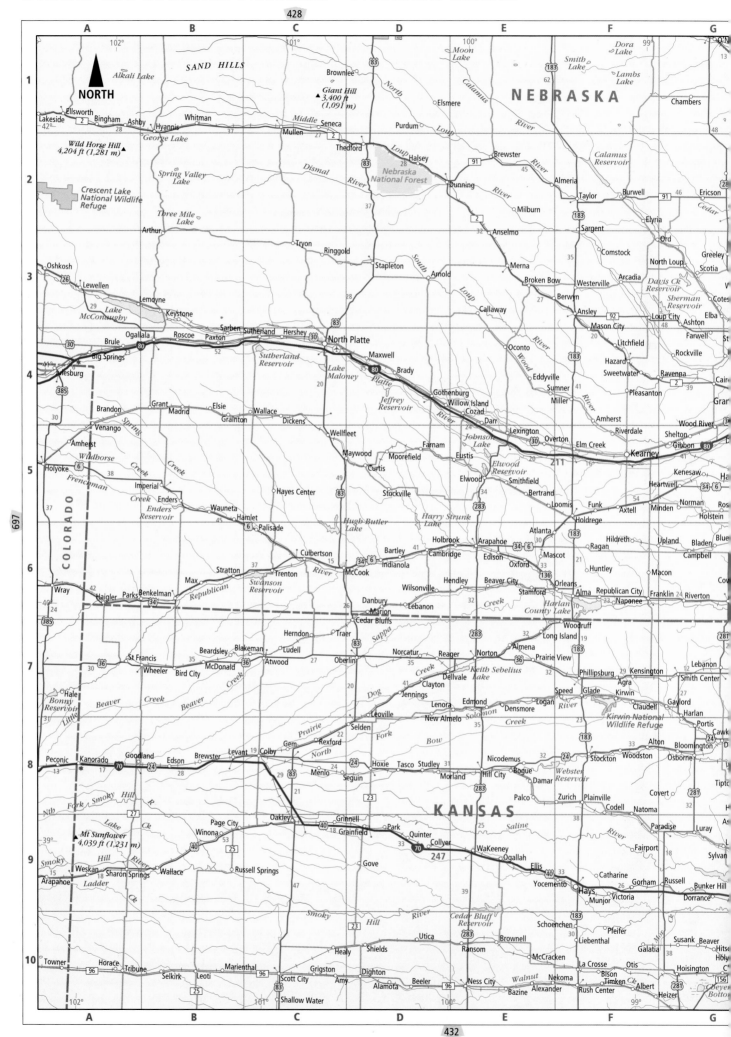

GREAT PLAINS

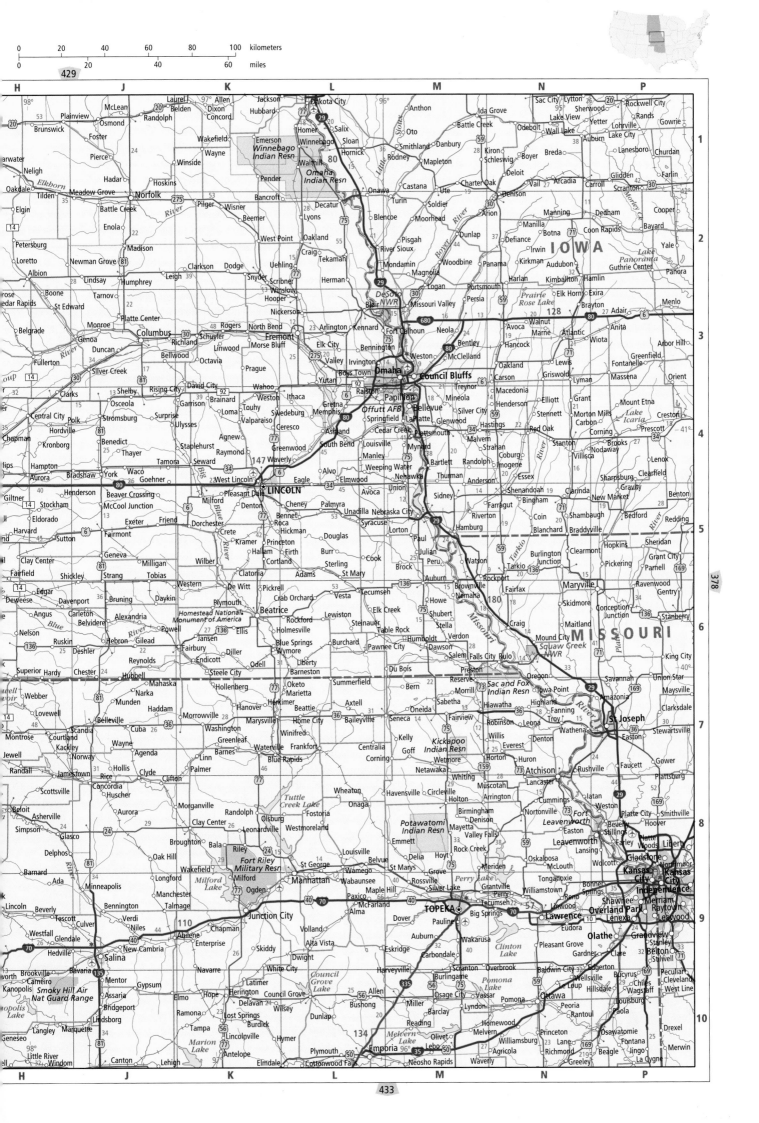

kilometers
miles

IOWA

MISSOURI

Omaha

Council Bluffs

Lincoln

TOPEKA

Kansas City

Winnebago
Indian Resn

Omaha
Indian Resn

DeSoto
NWR

Offutt AFB

Homestead National
Monument of America

Squaw Creek
NWR

Sac and Fox
Indian Resn

Kickapoo
Indian Resn

Potawatomi
Indian Resn

Fort Riley
Military Resn

Fort
Leavenworth

Smoky Hill Air
Nat Guard Range

Southern Kansas • Northern Oklahoma • Central-Northern Texas

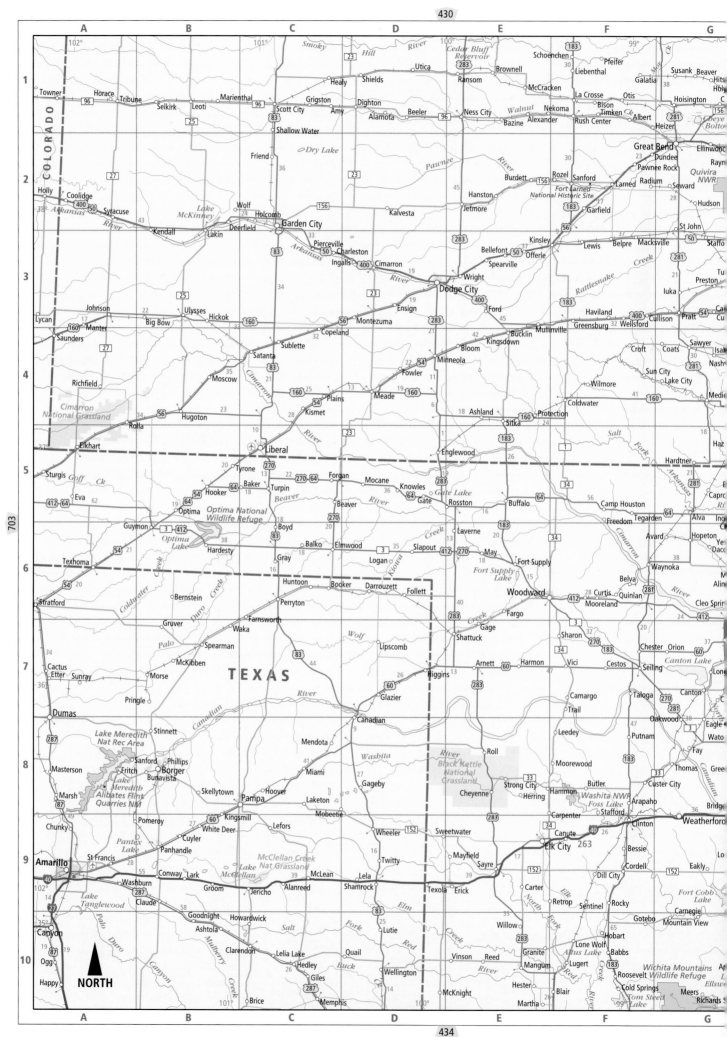

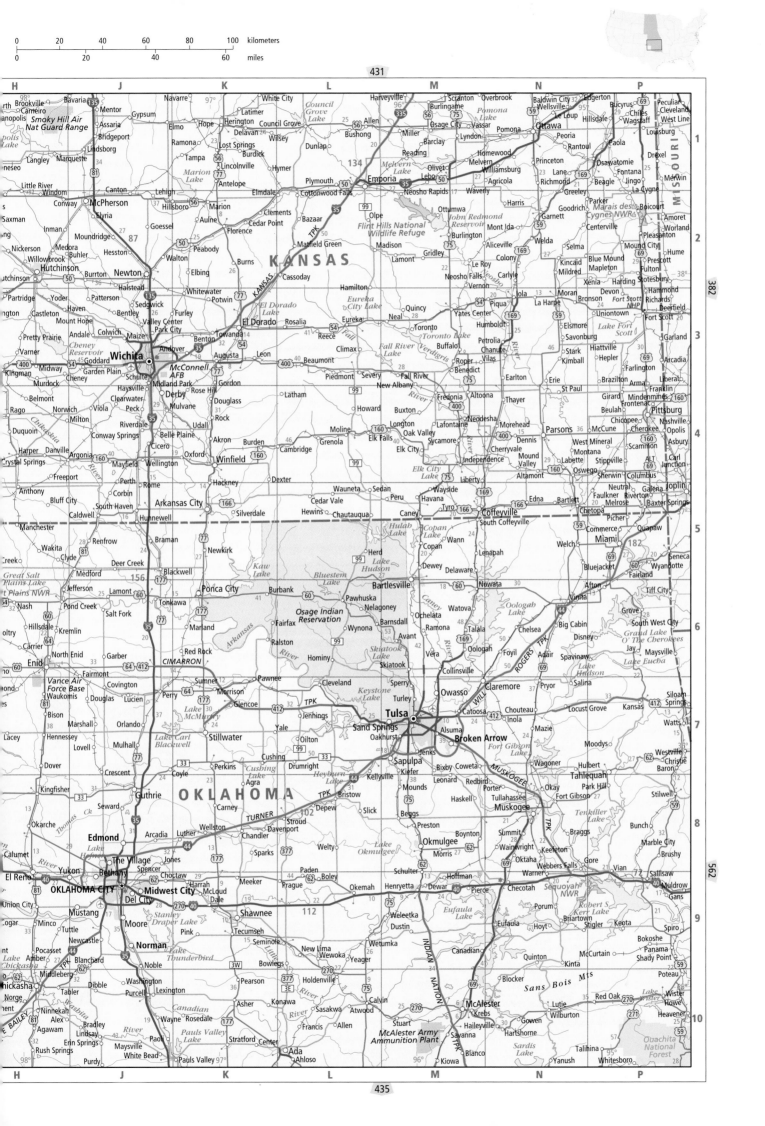

GREAT PLAINS

382

562

Southern Oklahoma • Northeastern Texas

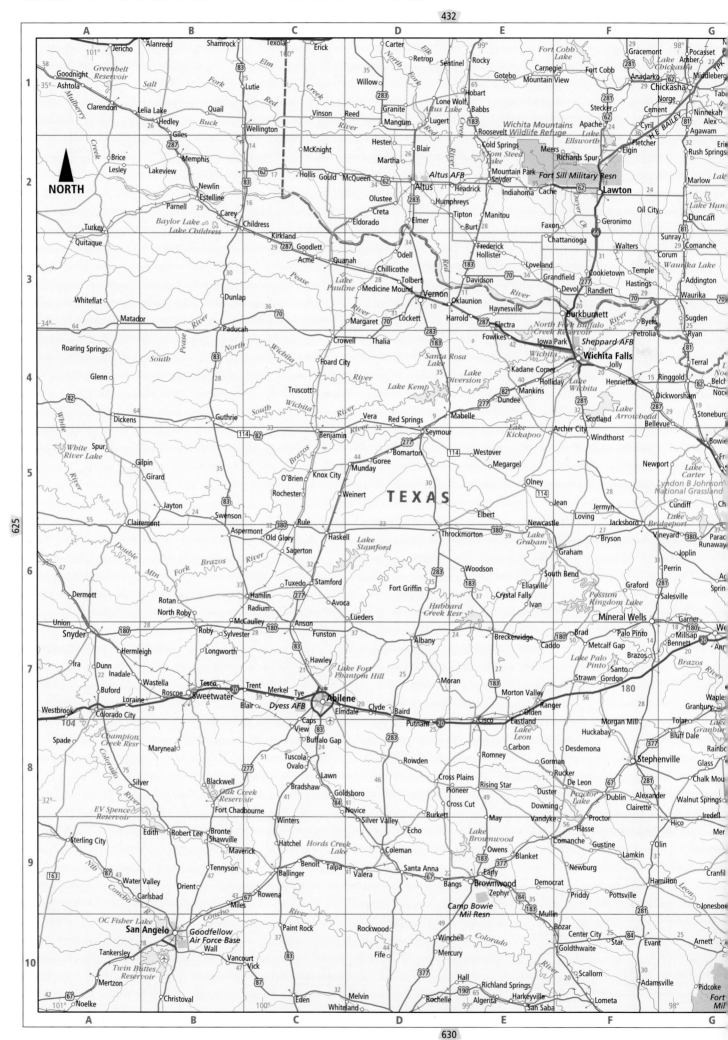

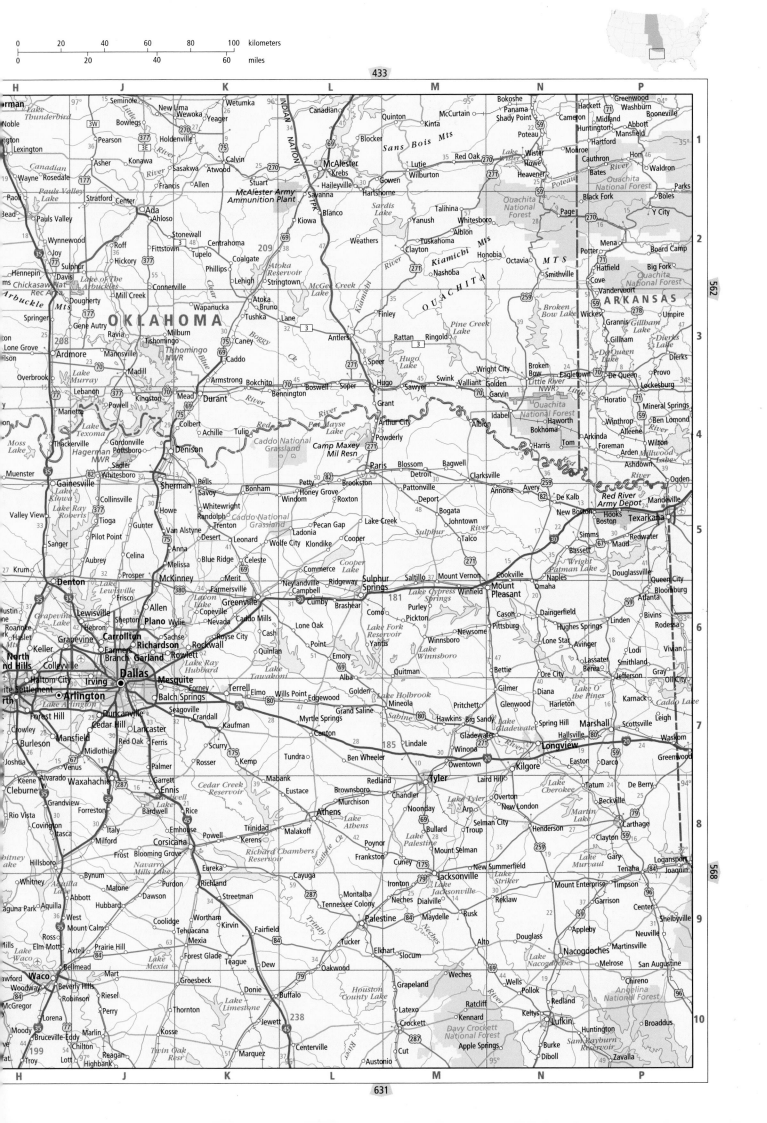

GREAT PLAINS

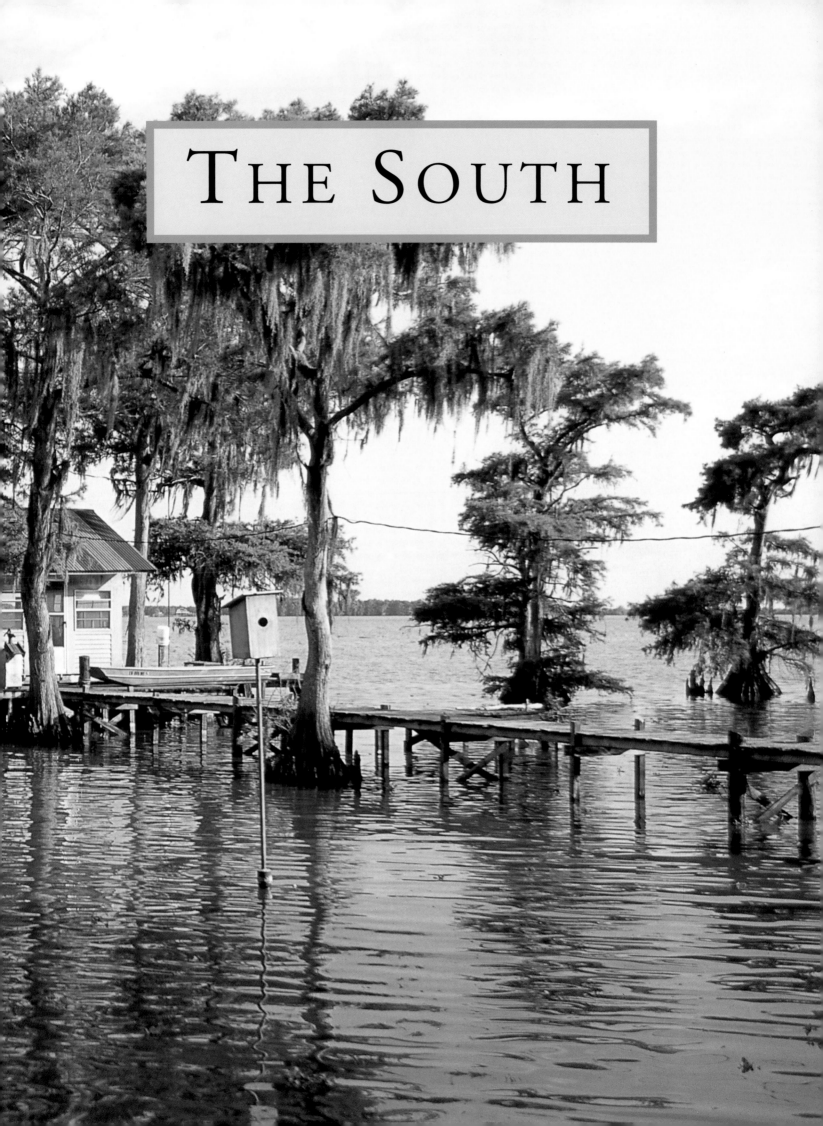

THE SOUTH

438

THE SOUTH

No matter where you drive south of the Mason–Dixon line, countless battle commemorations and the ever-present Confederate flag never let you forget where you are. The South may have been beaten in the Civil War, but it was certainly not emotionally defeated. In recent times, the Civil War has become the South's foremost money-spinner— some 140 years after the first artillery shot was fired in Virginia in 1861.

The Amish are not usually associated with the South, but there is a thriving community near Cynthiana, Kentucky.

Though much of the South's recovery was slow during Reconstruction, by the mid-twentieth century the region rose to become one of the most significant economies in the country, producing chemical, lumber, and petroleum products, as well as continuing its success in agriculture. The New South has retained its relaxed, unhurried pace and continues to entice thousands of tourists to visit its sweeping antebellum plantations with gardens of magnolia blossom, or to stroll along its famous sandy-white beaches.

The region has a rich musical heritage with Memphis and Nashville sitting at the fork of gospel, country, bluegrass, rockabilly, and blues. And, of course, there's New Orleans jazz. Just a few of the many great performers who hail from this section of the country are Louis Armstrong, BB King, Patsy Cline, Elvis Presley, and Johnny Cash.

A big part of the South's culture is centered around its waterways: the Mississippi River, and its tributaries; the bayous of Louisiana; and the Delta region of West Tennessee and Mississippi. The southern terrain consists of undulating coastal plains and gently sloping mountains rich with coal, whitewater rivers, and dense seasonal forests.

By presenting an array of distinct regions, the South has formed a composite of fiercely independent states and unique personalities. Louisiana, Mississippi, Tennessee, and Alabama constitute the region known as "The Deep South." Other states that fall within the South of the United States include Arkansas, Florida, Georgia, Kentucky, North Carolina, South Carolina, Virginia, and West Virginia.

Before the French, Spanish, and British came to the New World, the South was home to a number of Native American tribes, including the Seneca, Delaware, Cherokee, and Osage peoples. Virginia was first settled in 1607, and the new colony's economy depended heavily on an enslaved labor force to work the plantations. The coastal agricultural states of the Carolinas likewise prospered from slavery. Despite the thriving slave trade from Africa's Gambia region— which continued midway into the nineteenth cen-

tury—many generations of African-Americans were born on Southern plantations. Many African-Americans, however, moved west into Tennessee and Kentucky, and settled in the remote wilderness regions of West Virginia and Arkansas. The debate over slavery escalated quickly during the northern industrial revolution of the 1840s, eventually dividing the nation into Union and Confederate states.

After the Civil War the South was in ruins. The inception of the Ku Klux Klan in Tennessee, in 1865, triggered off a new level of white supremacy and racial discord. During the 1950s and 1960s, as the nation watched the non-violent black rallies and boycotts spearheaded by Dr Martin Luther King and the National Association for the Advancement of Colored People (NAACP). Demonstrations in Montgomery, Selma, Birmingham, and the Freedom March to Washington were perhaps the civil rights movement's most determined events that helped to magnify the need for racial equality.

While the South still struggles at times with its conscience, it has never lost its hospitality and serene beauty, and what writer Eudora Welty has described as "a sense of place."

Wherever you visit in the South, you're sure to meet an interesting character with a spellbinding story to tell.

ALABAMA

Alabama, named after a Native American tribe, is known as "The Heart of Dixie" because it was here that the Confederate States of America were established and the Constitution of the Confederacy drawn up in 1861. Die-hard Southern sentiments were still evident 100 years later in the state's violent resistance to desegregation. Race relations have improved since then, although levels of literacy and infant mortality are issues that still need addressing.

Ironically, it is the past that attracts tourists to the museums and sites associated with the Indian Wars, the plantation system, the Civil War, and the civil rights movement. Other points of interest include Alabama's many archeological sites, its musical heritage, and its profusion of historic buildings, homes, and gardens. The state's diverse natural resources are yet another drawcard, particularly the state parks and national forests, the Tennessee River, and the sandy beaches of Mobile Bay and the Gulf of Mexico.

Alabama was once occupied by the Cherokee, Creek, Chickasaw, and Choctaw tribes. The Spanish explored the area in the sixteenth century, but the first permanent European settlement was established by the French in 1702. The land they came to occupy, around Mobile Bay, was passed to the British in 1763, the Spanish in 1783, then seized by the US government in 1813.

When the Creek tribe was defeated by US forces in 1814, nearly half of the present state passed to the US government. Alabama became the nation's 22nd state in 1819. By this time it was economically dependent on cotton production and slavery. After the Civil War, and the decline in cotton production, Alabama became one of the first Southern states to begin industrializing. However, its fortunes waxed and waned during the twentieth century.

Sitting on a porch is a great way to watch the world go by. Alabama and other southern states have a more relaxed lifestyle than the states to the north.

State motto *Audemus Jura Nostra Defendere* (We dare defend our rights)
State flag Adopted 1895
Capital Montgomery
Population 4,447,100
Total area (land and water) 52,237 square miles (135,294 sq km)
Land area 50,750 square miles (131,443 sq km)
Alabama is the 29th-largest state in size
Origin of name May come from the Choctaw word meaning "thicket-clearers" or "vegetation-gatherers"
Nicknames The Camellia State, The Cotton State, The Heart of Dixie, The Yellowhammer State
Abbreviations AL (postal), Ala.
State bird Yellowhammer
State flower Camellia
State tree Southern longleaf pine
Entered the Union December 14, 1819 as the 22nd state

Places in
ALABAMA

ANNISTON

Anniston is a town of 27,000 people located in northeastern Alabama, 57 miles (92 km) east of Birmingham. It was established in the late nineteenth century around blast furnaces and textile mills.

One of the town's major attractions is the Anniston Museum of Natural History. A little further along Museum Drive is the Berman Museum, which houses a large collection of artworks and weapons. Nearby Talladega National Forest has numerous hiking trails, notably the 102-mile (164-km) Pinhoti Trail. There is an observation tower at the top of Cheaha Mountain which, at 2,407 feet (734 m), is the highest point in the state. The 26-mile (42-km) Talladega Scenic Drive is a good introduction to this beautiful area of Alabama. It com-

mences near Heflin and ascends Cheaha Mountain, taking in some fine lookouts.

Anniston is connected to the outside world by train, bus and the highway system (it is just off I-20). The nearest airports are located at Birmingham and Atlanta.
Map ref: page 564 D5

AUBURN

Auburn is quite a prosperous and pleasant university town, 50 miles (80 km) northeast of Montgomery in east-central Alabama. Two-thirds of the population of 35,000 attend the state's largest educational institution, Auburn University, which is the city's most significant employer. It is also a local attraction in its own right, with Samford Hall, Langdon Hall, and the chapel all dating from 1880.

Football is immensely popular in Auburn, in part because the University fields one of the country's best gridiron teams. Sports fans will enjoy the Lovelace Athletic

Children playing under a hose in Birmingham's Metropolitan Gardens.

Museum. On the city's southwestern boundary is the delightful Chewacla State Park.

Access to Auburn is via bus or the highway system (it is just off I-85). The nearest airports are at Montgomery and Atlanta.
Map ref: page 564 E8

BIRMINGHAM

Birmingham is the largest and most cosmopolitan city in Alabama; it has a population of 908,000 residents. Situated at the foot of Red Mountain in north-central Alabama, Birmingham offers evening entertainment, quality dining, cultural activities, and opportunities for open-air recreation.

The city is situated on land once occupied by the Cherokee, Creek and Choctaw tribes. Its genesis was related to the discovery, in the Jones Valley, of the three major elements of steel production—iron ore, limestone, and coal. Birmingham was founded by bankers and investors at the intersection of two new railroads in 1871. The first blast furnace was constructed in 1880. Demands for iron led to rapid growth and Birmingham soon became a major industrial center, swelling its population from 3,000 in 1880 to 132,000 in 1910.

As Birmingham grew, it developed a strict and punitive system of racial discrimination and implemented "Jim Crow" segregation laws. By the 1950s it had earned a reputation as the South's most segregated city. This became apparent

in May 1961 when activists riding desegregated buses through the South were savagely beaten by a Birmingham mob.

In 1963 civil rights leaders led silent marches of African-American citizens through the city to protest local conditions. Police Chief "Bull" Connor met the peaceful protesters, including women and young children, with cattle prods, fire hoses, police dogs, and mass arrests. Television broadcasts caused a national outcry and the combination of pressure from above and mass protest from below ultimately bore fruit. However, reactionaries resorted to a terror campaign which eventually culminated in the bombing of the 16th Street Baptist Church. Since that time African-American enfranchisement and political power has become a reality and race relations have greatly improved.

The Birmingham Civil Rights Institute is affecting. It attempts to explain the hatred, violence and discrimination that necessitated the civil rights movement by means of historical footage, photography, audio aids, and artifacts such as the burned-out bus firebombed in Anniston by whites in an attempt to kill African Americans who refused to adhere to segregated seating arrangements. Nearby is the 16th Street Baptist Church which was, in the civil rights era, a center of African-American community life and a rallying point for demonstrations. A shrine at the church commemorates the four young

Heading into the prosperous university town of Auburn in east-central Alabama.

African-American girls killed in the 1963 bombing. Over the road is Kelly Ingram Park where "Bull" Connor turned fire hoses on peaceful demonstrators. The event is commemorated by sculptures and inscriptions.

The visitor center has a brochure outlining a walking tour of the historic 4th Avenue African-American business district. Nearby is the Alabama Jazz Hall of Fame where there are exhibits relating to jazz figures with links to Alabama, such as W.C. Handy, James Reese Europe, Nat King Cole, and Dinah Washington. The Alabama Sports Hall of Fame has a similar focus on the state's sportspeople, such as Jesse Owens, Willie Mays, Carl Lewis, "Satchel" Paige, and Joe Louis. The distinguished Birmingham Museum of Art is the largest municipal museum in the Southeast.

To the east of downtown are the chimney stacks of Sloss Furnaces National Historic Landmark which supplied pig iron to the city's steel foundries from 1882 until 1971. It is now a museum of industry. A 10-minute audiovisual program outlines the history of Birmingham steel, and displays focus on such issues as poor working conditions of ex-slaves, unskilled immigrants, and prisoners. Other attractions include Arlington mansion (1840s), the Birmingham Zoo, and the McWayne Center, which is a new interactive science museum.

Five Points South is the most lively and interesting section of downtown Birmingham, boasting bars, restaurants, nightspots, shops, Art Deco buildings, and the Breck-enridge Brewery. To its south, atop Red Mountain, is the world's largest cast-iron statue, which depicts Vulcan, the Roman god of fire and blacksmiths. Standing a massive 55 feet (17 m) high, on a 124-foot (38-m) pedestal, it is a testimony to the importance of steel manufacture to the town's history. The views are outstanding, especially in the evening. About 2 miles (3 km) southeast of Five Points is the Birmingham Botanical Garden.

Birmingham is located at the intersection of I-65, I-59 and I-20. Other access is via daily trains, bus and an airport.
Map ref: page 564 B5

BRUNDIDGE

Brundidge is a small town of 2,500 people in southeast Alabama. It became economically reliant on the humble peanut when the Johnston Peanut Butter Mill opened in 1929, producing over two million jars a year as a Depression-era staple. The mill, located in Church Street, is occasionally open to visitors. It houses 1930s artifacts such as labels, photographs, equipment, and memorabilia from the annual Peanut Butter Festival, which is still held in October.

The town has, of late, become known as "Antique City," owing to the proportionally high number of antique stores. There are seven shops and an antique auction on the first Saturday of the month.

Brundidge is located just off Hwy 231, 52 miles (84 km) southeast of Montgomery.
Map ref: page 564 D10

The Industrial Gas Factory is an unusual backdrop for these cornfields near Decatur.

COURTLAND

This small and historic town is located in northwest Alabama, west of Decatur and just south of the Tennessee River, off Hwy 72/20. The first white settlers were cotton planters from the Carolinas who found good soil and water here around 1818.

The wealth produced by the plantation system has left a concentrated legacy of grand historic planters' and merchants' homes. The town's historic buildings are listed on a driving-tour brochure available for free from the Courtland town hall.

To the east of Courtland is Wheeler Plantation, which features 12 historic buildings and hosts a Civil War re-enactment in the fall. This property was once owned by nineteenth-century military figure "Fightin' Joe" Wheeler.
Map ref: page 564 B3

DAUPHIN ISLAND

At 14 miles (23 km) in length, Dauphin Island is Alabama's largest coastal island. A resting place for migrating birds, it is located at the western entrance to Mobile Bay in the southwestern corner of the state. Dauphin Island is a very popular summer attraction, offering visitors 40-foot (12-m) sea bluffs, low sand dunes, attractive beaches, plenty of fishing, boating, cycling, camping, and historical attractions.

The first Europeans to fly a flag there were the French. Briefly the capital of French Louisiana, it was subsequently ruled by the English, the Spanish, the Republic of Alabama, the Confederacy, then the United States.

One of the island's main attractions is Fort Gaines. It was built to defend Mobile Bay, and it fell to Admiral Farragut's Union forces in August 1864, during the Battle of Mobile Bay, and ceased operations in 1946. A museum displays military items and a brochure outlines a self-guided walking tour. During January there is a re-enactment of the Fort's seizure by Confederate forces in 1861.

The 160-acre (65-ha) Audubon Bird Sanctuary is situated near the ferry landing on Bienville Boulevard. It features a series of walking trails. The Estuarium at the Dauphin Island Sea Lab is a huge hall that displays the four principal habitats of Mobile Bay. Outside is the Living Marsh Boardwalk, which features interpretive signage explaining the geological history of the bay's islands and swamps. A shell mound, constructed by Native Americans, is located adjacent to Cadillac Street.

There is an 850-foot (260-m) pier behind the dunes at Bienville Boulevard and Penalver Street. The East End Pier is near the ferry landing at the mouth of Mobile Bay. Deep-sea fishing charters and island cruises operate out of the marina. The largest one-day sailing regatta in the United States is held at the island on the last weekend in April.

There are two means of access to Dauphin Island. From the east, a

The struggle for desegregation is commemorated in Kelly Ingram Park, Birmingham.

ferry departs from Pleasure Island's Fort Morgan, or visitors can simply drive onto the island via a bridge.
Map ref: page 569 M7

DECATUR

Decatur is a town of some 50,000 people located 76 miles (122 km) due north of Birmingham along I-65. Its situation, on the south bank of the Tennessee River, is central to its history and its attractions. The town site was chosen for its water access in the early 1820s and named after heroic naval commodore Stephen Decatur. The settlement prospered with the establishment of the Old State Bank in 1833 (still standing) and the arrival of the railroad.

During the Civil War the town was considered of strategic importance and was thus virtually destroyed, though it was soon reconstructed. An iron and steel works was established in the 1880s. However, it was the creation of Wheeler Dam and Reservoir that drew the chemical and textile companies that, along with agri-businesses, still underscore the local economy.

The creation of the dam also led to the emergence of wetlands on the lake shore. A portion of the wetlands, between Huntsville and the Eck River, is now the Wheeler National Wildlife Refuge where, from mid-December to mid-February, over 100,000 ducks, geese, and other migratory birds join the permanent inhabitants to make their winter home. The information center has a wetlands observation tower.

The Decatur Visitor Center has a brochure detailing walking tours of the town's two historic districts, New Albany and Old Decatur, which feature buildings dating back to 1829. Cook's Natural Science Museum contains fossils, stones, corals, birds, insects, and other animals, interactive exhibits, and unusual thematic displays.
Map ref: page 564 B3

DOTHAN

Dothan is a city of some 56,000 people located in the southeastern corner of Alabama, and is 96 miles (155 km) southeast of Montgomery. It has a fine museum and it serves as a good base for exploring the abundant natural attractions of the entire region.

The surrounding area was formerly inhabited by the Alibamu and Creek tribes. The first Europeans in the area were loggers. Cotton plantations followed, and Dothan was incorporated in 1885. When the boll weevil wreaked havoc on southern cotton, planters switched to peanuts and Houston County now supplies about a quarter of the nation's ground nuts. The National Peanut Festival starts on the first weekend in November.

The Dothan Visitor Center supplies a brochure outlining the many gardens of distinction to visit during the Azalea–Dogwood Trail and Festival in March. The town's cultural centerpiece is the Wiregrass Museum of Art. Three miles (5 km) north of town is Landmark Park where visitors will find a demonstration farm depicting a working day in the 1890s, wildlife exhibits, and hiking trails that lead into the woods. Northwest of Dothan is Fort Rucker. Its Army Aviation Museum houses the world's largest collection of helicopters.

Situated at the intersection of Highways 431, 84, and 231, Dothan has a small airport and a bus station.
Map ref: page 570 D3

FLORENCE

Florence is located on the northern bank of the Tennessee River in the northwestern corner of Alabama 102 miles (164 km) northwest of Birmingham. This area is home to the picturesque Wilson Dam, which brought electricity to the area, thus facilitating the development of local industry.

Florence was laid out in 1818. Since 1855 it has been home to the University of North Alabama. The university features a lovely campus on Wesleyan Avenue designed by Frederick Law Olmsted who was responsible for Manhattan's Central Park. Florence is also the birthplace of W.C. Handy, the self-proclaimed "Father of the Blues." Handy did much to bring the blues to wider public attention and he also wrote such early and famous tunes as "St Louis Blues" (1914) and "Beale Street Blues" (1916). The basic two-room wood cabin in which he was born and raised is now a museum.

Rosenbaum House (1940) is the only building in the state designed by famous architect Frank Lloyd Wright, while the 300-foot (91-m) Renaissance Tower provides the city's best views of the Tennessee River, the Shoals, and Wilson Dam. The Indian Mound Museum is situated adjacent to a 42-foot (13-m) high pre-Colombian ceremonial mound. It houses artifacts drawn from the mound and the surrounding area. Some date back over 10,000 years.

Florence is connected to Muscle Shoals, Tuscumbia, and Sheffield by Hwy 133. In the 1960s Muscle Shoals became a major music-recording center where the likes of Aretha Franklin, Percy Sledge, the Staple Singers, Etta James, Sam and Dave, Wilson Pickett, Duane Allman, the Rolling Stones, J.J. Cale, and Paul Simon all recorded their hit songs. Tuscumbia is home to the excellent Alabama Music Hall of Fame, which honors the music and artists of Alabama. Memorabilia includes the stage clothes of Emmylou Harris and Jimmy Buffet, Jim Nabors' Gomer Pyle uniform, and Toni Tenille's bell-bottom jeans. One of Tuscumbia's most famous daughters was the remarkable Helen Keller. Her childhood home, "Ivy Green," is now a museum.

A regular shuttle service connects Florence with Huntsville International Airport.
Map ref: page 563 P5

"Father of the Blues" W.C. Handy lived in this house in Florence. It is now a museum.

GADSDEN

Gadsden is a city of some 53,000 people situated on the Coosa River in northeast Alabama, 57 miles (92 km) northeast of Birmingham via I-59. It was founded as a riverside township in the middle of the nineteenth century. In 1899 it became the site of the first hydroelectric plant in the United States and, in 1929, of the world's largest tire and tube plant. Gadsden is still economically reliant on heavy industry. However, it is a good jumping-off point for the many state parks and scenic attractions of the region. Guided sightseeing cruises of the river and the terrain about the city are conducted on a replica paddleboat, *Alabama Princess*. Noccalula Falls Park, which centers on a 90-foot (27-m) waterfall, includes a miniature train, pioneer village, botanical garden, and campground.

Lookout Mountain Parkway is the access road that heads northeast from Gadsden out past the exceptional Little River Canyon, 16 miles (26 km) long and up to 700 feet (213 m) deep. Further north is De Soto State Park, which features endangered flora, 15 waterfalls, unusual geological formations, and a maze of hiking trails. Just north of the park lodge are De Soto Falls, which drop 100 feet (30 m) into the gorge.

Gasden has a bus service, and the nearest airports are at Atlanta and Birmingham.
Map ref: page 564 D4

HORSESHOE BEND NATIONAL MILITARY PARK

Horseshoe Bend National Military Park is located 12 miles (19 km) north of Dadeville in east-central Alabama. It marks the site of the Battle of Horseshoe Bend on which future US President, Andrew Jackson, and 2,000 men marched. They confronted, then killed, about 800 men of the Creek tribe.

The Battle occurred in a context of ongoing conflict between the Creek people and white settlers which had led, in 1813, to a massacre of several hundred whites at Fort Mims, near present-day Mobile. Widespread panic struck the South and General Jackson took charge of a volunteer force and embarked on a campaign to

subdue the Creek. On March 27, 1814, he came upon a Creek village at a bend in the Tallapoosa River. Jackson permitted the women and children to cross the river to safety before a numerically and technologically uneven fight in which almost all of the Creek men were killed. Consequently the Creek were forced to surrender 23 million acres (93 million ha) of land in what is now Alabama and Georgia. The Park has a 3-mile (5-km) interpretive roadway, a museum, and hiking trails.
Map ref: page 564 E7

HUNTSVILLE

Huntsville is a prosperous high-tech city in the Tennessee Valley boasting some fine attractions and an active nightclub scene. With a population of over 300,000, it is 83 miles (134 km) north of Birmingham in the Appalachian foothills of north-central Alabama. Huntsville is known as "Rocket City" because Redstone Arsenal, a rocket, satellite, and spacecraft research center, was established nearby in 1941. Scientists, led by Wernher von Braun, architect of the Nazi V-2 missile, designed the first US guided missiles at the center in the 1950s. In the 1960s they then went on to develop the *Saturn V* system that powered the first successful moon mission.

John Hunt of Virginia established Huntsville in 1805 on land formerly occupied by the Cherokee and Chickasaw tribes. In 1819 the settlement hosted Alabama's first constitutional convention and it

Joe Wheeler State Park has great campgrounds—perfect for getting back to nature.

served as the first state capital from 1819 to 1820, at which time it was Alabama's largest settlement. Despite destruction and looting in the Civil War, it grew throughout the nineteenth and early twentieth centuries as a cotton-trading center. In the 1950s aerospace-related business and industrial growth led to a dramatic population increase. Computers, computer software, and electronic equipment provide much local employment today.

A good way to explore the downtown area is by a trolley ride, which takes in the beautifully landscaped Huntsville Botanical Gardens and the US Space and Rocket Center. This excellent museum—theme park features an IMAX cinema, spacesuits, space simulators, full-scale models of Sky-

lab and the Space Shuttle, a moon rock from *Apollo XII*, the "Space Shot" which propels passengers into a condition of weightlessness, an International Space Station display, and the remarkable Rocket and Space Shuttle Parks where superannuated space vehicles (including the four-story *Saturn V*) adorn the grounds.

The Huntsville Depot Museum focuses on aspects of local history. A combination pass also allows entry to the Alabama Constitution Village. Guides in period costume illustrate pioneer life and take visitors around reconstructed buildings from the early nineteenth century, including the cabinet-maker's shop where the first state constitution was drawn up. History buffs may also enjoy the Twickenham Historic District, which features the state's largest collection of antebellum homes. The adjacent Old Town Historic District features Victorian-era homes. There is a daily tour of the district by motorized trolley and guided tours of some homes are conducted in April and December.

Weeden House, built in 1819, was the lifelong home of Maria Howard Weeden who, from 1898 to her death in 1905, gained international acclaim for her portraits of African-Americans. The house is now a museum displaying some of her works. Others are featured in the Burritt Museum on Round Top Mountain, which affords outstanding views of the city. The historic park has some renovated

Enjoying refreshments at one of Huntsville's many delightful outdoor cafés.

nineteenth-century log buildings set amid a large nature park. There are numerous woodland trails including one that leads to Monte Sano State Park where there are lookouts, waterfalls, rock-climbing walls, a 2-acre (0.8-ha) Japanese garden, 15 miles (24 km) of hiking trails, an amphitheatre, and a campground.

Access is via bus, an international airport and the highway system. (Huntsville is at the intersection of Hwys 231, 431, 53, 72, and I-565.) Map ref: page 564 C2

JOE WHEELER STATE PARK

This attractive resort park surrounds Wheeler Lake and straddles the Tennessee River in northwestern Alabama. It is named after Joseph Wheeler whose former plantation is located nearby (see entry on Courtland, page 442). Activities in the Park center around the lake which is a vast reservoir created by Wheeler Dam. To gain access to the southern section, head west of Courtland along Hwy 72/20 for about 5 miles (8 km) then turn right onto Hwy 101. It is on the left just before crossing the river. It has cabin lodging, hiking trails, a boat ramp, playgrounds, and also some tennis courts.

To access the main area, near Rogersville, head across the river, over Wheeler Dam, then turn right onto Hwy 72. This section, overlooking Wheeler Lake, has tennis courts, boat rentals, a marina, a golf course, and resort lodge. A pleasant wooded campground is located near the golf course. A

special day-use area near the campground boasts a beach, facilities, and 5 miles (8 km) of hiking and nature trails. A third area, on nearby Elk River, has fishing-boat rentals, a bait-and-tackle shop, and a group lodge.

MOBILE

Only a small section of Alabama touches on the coast and this occurs in the Mobile Bay area, which borders the Gulf of Mexico in the southwest of the state. This area is known as the "American Riviera" owing to the many vacationers drawn to the fine beaches of Gulf Shores, and the fishing opportunities. At the northern tip of Mobile Bay are the swamps and bayous of the Mobile River delta. Situated on the Bay's northwest, adjacent to the river estuary, is the port city of Mobile.

Mobile is a lively and elegant city. The state's second-largest center, it has a population of 480,000. With its diverse heritage, Mobile is atypical of Alabama. The European influences are reflected in the colonial buildings, plazas, wide boulevards, fine trees and parks, Creole cuisine, and the country's oldest Mardi Gras which dates back to 1704. These elements bring a saner and less commercialized New Orleans to mind. Mobile's historic districts are replete with oaks, dogwoods, magnolias, and azaleas. The latter are best seen in March and April when visitors can follow the well-marked Azalea Trail for 27 miles (44 km) around Mobile.

Mobile's ideal location has long rendered it of interest to colonial powers. The first European in the area was the Spanish explorer Alonso de Pineda who sailed into Mobile Bay in 1519. In 1559 Tristan de Luna organized small short-lived settlements on the Bay. A French Canadian settlement, known as Fort Louis de la Mobile, was founded just north of the Bay in 1702 by Pierre and Jean Baptiste Le Moyne. It served as an outpost for trading

and defense. The first permanent European settlement in Alabama, it served as the capital of French Louisiana until 1722. Owing to river floods the settlement was moved south to the site of present-day Mobile in 1711. When the French gave most of their Louisiana colony to Britain in 1763, the Mobile area became part of British West Florida. It was ceded to Spain in 1783, taken by US forces in 1813, and incorporated as a US city in 1819. Mobile became vital to the economy of Alabama as a major shipment point for cotton producers. It was also a crucial Confederate port in the Civil War, and the Battle of Mobile Bay (1864) was Alabama's most important Civil War battle.

An on-site reconstruction of Fort Conde (demolished in 1820) now functions as a museum and the Mobile Visitors' Center. There are guided tours and daily demonstrations of musket and cannon fire. The USS *Alabama* is permanently moored in Battleship Park, which also features the submarine USS *Drum* and an interesting indoor aircraft pavilion.

During the Historic Mobile Homes Tour in March, private homes are open for tours. To the north of the Fort is the Church

Signs like this one mark historic homes in Mobile.

Street Historic District, which includes two museums: the Phoenix Fire Museum; and the Museum of Mobile where resplendent Mardi Gras costumes, historic armaments, maritime artifacts, and Civil War memorabilia are housed.

Also within the city are the interactive child-oriented diversions of the fascinating Exploreum Museum of Science, the Mobile Museum of Art, and the National African-American Archives and Museum. Yet another activity that is highly recommended is a tour through the Delta swamps on a passenger boat, which departs from Chickasaw Marina.

To the south of Mobile are the outstanding Bellingrath Gardens. Southeast of Mobile, along the shores of the Gulf of Mexico, are the very popular beaches of the resort town of Gulf Shores. To its east is Gulf State Park and to its west are Bon Secour National Wildlife Refuge, Pleasure Island and Fort Morgan, which was built in 1834 to defend Mobile Bay. The Fort is the departure point for thoroughly enjoyable ferry trips to Dauphin Island.

Mobile sits at the intersection of I-65 and I-10 and is serviced by an airport, and trains and buses. Map ref: page 569 N8

One of Mobile's beautiful historic homes displays the elegance and grandeur of times gone by.

MONTGOMERY

Montgomery, the state capital since 1846, is known as the "Cradle of the Confederacy" because the Confederate States of America was established here in 1861 with Montgomery as its first capital. It was also in Montgomery that the Constitution of the Confederacy was drawn up. It is ironic, given this heritage, that Montgomery's African-American citizens made it a mainspring of the civil rights movement, and hence of nation-wide change, during the 1950s.

Montgomery is located in central Alabama at the intersection of I-65, I-85, and Hwys 80 and 231. It spreads out across several hills adjacent to the Alabama River. Although it has a population of 320,000, Montgomery retains something of a small-town feel. It has its own airport and a bus depot. Two of the city's most famous sons are research chemist Percy Julian and singer/pianist Nat King Cole.

The land hereabouts was formerly the preserve of the Alibamu and Creek tribes. Two independent but proximate European settlements were set up in 1817 and 1818. In 1819 the two were united and named after Richard Montgomery, a hero of the Revolutionary War. This township became an important riverport for the shipment of cotton south to the seaport at Mobile. In 1865 General Wilson led the Union's largest Civil War raid into Alabama, winning a victory at

The Civil Rights Memorial in Montgomery records significant events in the civil rights movement.

Montgomery. In 1910 Orville and Wilbur Wright constructed an airfield at what is now Maxwell Air Force Base where two students undertook the first night flights in aviation history.

A key moment in the history of both Montgomery and the US civil rights movement was the boycott of the Montgomery bus system by local African-American citizens. Martin Luther King, who was serving in his first posting as a minister, became the main spokesperson for the protesters. The boycott started in 1955 with the arrest of Rosa Parks for refusing to surrender her seat to a white person. Despite intimidation (King's home was bombed) and jailings, the Supreme Court eventually ruled the seating system unconstitutional and, after a year's grueling struggle, the bus

The State Capitol building in Montgomery.

companies yielded. The tactics, ideas, organizational methods, and impetus that developed during the boycott became a model for and a tremendous encouragement to others across the nation, and challenges to the Southern "Jim Crow" laws soon spread.

However, attitudes did not rapidly change in the "Cradle of the Confederacy." In May 1961 a group riding desegregated buses through the South were met by a huge mob of whites in Montgomery who brutally beat the riders and onlooking journalists and set an innocent African-American teenage bystander on fire. That night whites surrounded the church where the African-American community had gathered. With violence building, they were only stopped at the doors of the church by the last-minute arrival of the National Guard. Eventually the "Freedom Rides" continued with an escort of 42 vehicles (mostly highway patrol cars), National Guardsmen aboard the bus and an understanding that the riders would be arrested upon arrival in Mississippi!

In downtown Montgomery is a moving civil rights memorial, designed by Maya Lin who created the Vietnam Memorial in Washington. The King Memorial Baptist Church was the organizational and social center of the 1955 bus boycott. The former pulpit of Martin Luther King remains in the sanctuary and a civil rights mural adorns the basement.

The Montgomery Visitor Center is the starting place for a tour of Old Alabama Town. This re-created nineteenth-century Alabama village features 40 period buildings moved in from around the state. Another 20 nineteenth-century buildings can be found down in Montgomery's Old North Hull Street Historic District.

An architectural highlight of Montgomery is the State Capitol (1851), which has a beautiful and ornate interior with a rotunda and a magnificent spiral staircase designed by Horace King, a former slave. A bronze star on the steps commemorates the spot where Jefferson Davis took office as President of the Confederacy. It was on these same steps, in 1963, that Alabama Governor George Wallace made his famous "Segregation Forever!" inaugural speech. In 1965 the Selma to Montgomery march (see entry on Selma, page 447) ended here with Martin Luther King making a speech against segregation.

Montgomery has several museums of interest. The F. Scott and Zelda Fitzgerald Museum is based in a house briefly rented by the couple in 1931–32 while he worked on *Tender Is The Night*. Zelda was born in Montgomery. The Hank Williams Museum is dedicated to the country music legend who was born south of Montgomery near Georgiana in 1923. His funeral was held at Montgomery in 1953 with 25,000 fans in attendance, and his grave and large marble headstone can be found in Montgomery's Oakwood Cemetery Annex. The Montgomery Museum of Fine Arts features American paintings, regional art, and a hands-on studio for children. It is located within the grounds of the beautifully landscaped Wynton Blount Cultural Park where the Carolyn Blount Theater hosts the Alabama Shakespeare Festival, which is held each year.

Map ref: page 564 C8

OZARK

Ozark (population 13,000) is located in southeast Alabama, about 73 miles (118 km) southeast of Montgomery. Nearby Fort Rucker is home to the US Army Aviation Museum, which features an extensive collection of military airplanes and helicopters. The town's finest public recreation area is Ed Lisenby Lake, considered one of the state's best bass fishing spots. It is situated in a beautiful 390-acre (158-ha) park with a 3-mile (5-km) walking trail and boat rentals. KIDZONE is an impressive community playground for children located in Steagall Park. Ozark's historic buildings include Claybank Church (1852). Once the center of local community life, it retains its original wooden pulpit and church benches.

Ozark is on Hwy 231, and has bus and train services. The nearest airport is at Dothan, 18 miles (29 km) away.
Map ref: page 570 D2

RUSSELL CAVE NATIONAL MONUMENT

Russell Cave National Monument is a 310-acre (125-ha) site in the extreme northeastern corner of Alabama, 7 miles (11 km) north of Bridgeport. It centers on a small limestone cave that features tools and other evidence of continuous human occupation from about 7000 BC to AD 1650. There are ranger-guided tours, an informa-

An Alabama train driver. Rail is vital for freight transport.

tion center and a museum with displays of archeological artifacts. For larger groups there are demonstrations of prehistoric weapons and tools, food preparation, and cooking methods. The short trail near the cave features plants used by the inhabitants and there is a 1-mile (2-km) trail through the surrounding forest which provided them with their food. There is also a 6-mile (10-km) nature trail, but it is quite difficult.
Map ref: page 564 E2

SCOTTSBORO

Scottsboro is a town of over 14,000 people situated on the northern side of the Tennessee River in the northeast corner of Alabama, 26 miles (42 km) east of Huntsville. Because of its riverside location, Scottsboro is a popular place for recreational activities.

The area around Scottsboro was occupied by the Cherokee and Creek tribes until they were forcibly removed in 1838. Robert Scott, a state representative and the founder of Scottsboro, moved to the future town site in the early 1850s. In 1856 he was able to get a railway line constructed across his property. The origins of the town lay in a railway depot, which was erected nearby. It was initially called "Sagetown" but then changed to "Scott's Station." Scottsboro's name is most likely to be forever associated with the Scottsboro Case when the state's legal system was used to unjustly persecute and punish nine African-American youths. The legal farce surrounding the case focused attention on the absence of civil and legal rights for Southern African Americans, the centrality of racism to the Southern way of life and, more widely, on the problem of race relations in the United States. It is widely considered to have stirred consciences and awareness and to have provided impetus to the nascent civil rights movement, albeit at the expense of nine African-American men.

The Scottsboro–Jackson Heritage Center is a cultural and historical

museum that focuses on the history of Jackson County. It includes the antebellum Brown-Proctor house, the pioneer village "Sagetown," and the 1868 Jackson County Courthouse. A more unusual attraction is the Unclaimed Baggage Center, which is the nation's largest purchaser of lost and unclaimed luggage. Goose Pond Colony is a recreational area bounded on three sides by Guntersville reservoir, and visitors can pat and feed domestic and exotic animals at Old Mac-Donald's Petting Zoo.
Map ref: page 564 D3

SELMA

Selma is a small tidy town of 27,000 people located in central Alabama, 43 miles (69 km) west of Montgomery on Hwy 80. It is notable principally for its historic buildings, memorials and its role in the civil rights movement of the 1960s.

In 1865 General Wilson led the Union's largest raid into Alabama, winning a victory at Selma which was a major target owing to its shipbuilding plant, foundry, and munitions plant. Most of the town's buildings were burned to the ground by Union troops. A re-enactment of the Battle of Selma is held each year in April.

Another war of sorts commenced in Selma in February 1963 when the Student Non-Violent Coordinating Committee (SNCC) commenced a project to get local African-Americans registered to

The Alabama River, Selma. The Selma to Montgomery march in 1965 brought the world's attention to the disenfranchisement of the African-American population.

Playing a game of dominos in the open air. The citizens of Selma enjoy being in the outdoors.

vote. Though they made up half of the local population, only 1 percent of African-Americans in the area were registered, compared to 65 percent of whites. SNCC's efforts saw Sheriff Clark and other white authorities resort to intimidation, blackmail, beatings, harassment, and jailings to forestall legal registrations. In January 1965 Martin Luther King traveled to Selma to join the campaign, thereby bringing international attention to the disenfranchisement. Over the next two months well over a thousand African-Americans were arrested, including 800 children, and three people were murdered. Many were beaten, bullied or humiliated.

On March 7, known as "Bloody Sunday," 600 African-Americans and white sympathizers commenced a march to Montgomery to draw attention to their cause. As they knelt to pray on Edmund Pettus Bridge, television cameras recorded the group being attacked, gassed, shocked with electric cattle prods, and brutally beaten by state troopers. The outcry prompted by the international broadcast caused President Johnson to intervene and two weeks later the trip successfully took place complete with 25,000 marchers, including celebrities such as Dr King, Harry Belafonte, Lena Horne, Joan Baez, Sammy Davis and Mahalia Jackson. These events helped push the crucial *Voting Rights Act* through Congress in 1965.

The National Voting Rights Museum, located beside the Edmund Pettus Bridge, relates the story of the Selma civil rights struggle. The "I Was There Wall" records the testimonies of those who participated in the Bloody Sunday march. An anniversary march across the

Bridge is held each year in March. The Brown Chapel African Methodist Episcopal Church claims to be the first such church in the state, being founded in 1866. It served as the campaign headquarters of the local civil rights struggle in 1965 and the starting place for the Montgomery marches. An inner room has mementos of the movement. Outside are a bust of Dr King and a memorial to those who died in Selma. The Martin Luther King Jr Street Historic Walking Tour takes in 20 sites associated with the local voting rights movement.

A highlight of Selma is the Old Depot Museum. It displays an interesting assortment of artifacts including Geronimo's quiver, army muskets found wrapped around the skulls of disinterred Native Americans, historic photographs of African-Americans living and working on a local plantation, Civil War-era musket balls made at the Selma munitions plant, and letters from President Johnson pardoning Confederate soldiers. At the Old Live Oak Cemetery there is a substantial Confederate monument and the headstones, which date back to 1829, include that of Vice President William Rufus King (1786–1853).

Some of Selma's antebellum buildings survive in the Water Avenue business district. The Historic Selma Pilgrimage is an annual three-day tour of the town's historic homes, held on the third weekend in March. One such home is elegant Sturdivant Hall (1852), which features paintings by Nicola Marschall who designed the Confederate flag. Adjacent is the Heritage Village where tours

take in five relocated historic structures from the area. Also of interest are Grace Hall (circa 1857), the Selma Art Guild Gallery (circa 1900), and the Smitherman Historic Building (1847), built as a school for indigents and orphans.

Selma has a bus depot; the nearest airport is located at Montgomery.
Map ref: page 564 B8

TALLADEGA

Talladega is a town of 18,000 people located 35 miles (56 km) east of Birmingham on the western side of the beautiful Talladega National Forest. The Talladega Super Speedway hosts two of the fastest NASCAR Winston Cup Series races each season. The International Motorsports Hall of Fame has more than 100 racing vehicles and memorabilia dating back to 1902, while the Talladega Texaco Walk of Fame is a tribute to NASCAR's top drivers.

In 1813 the Battle of Talladega took place on the future town site between members of the Creek tribe and the forces of Andrew Jackson. A pyramid-shaped monument in Bradford Street marks the spot where the bodies of 17 Tennessee Volunteers fell. In the 1830s the government forced the local Creek people to abandon their lands and undertake a grueling march to Oklahoma, thus enabling the establishment of Talladega in 1835.

Talladega College was Alabama's first integrated institution of higher learning. It has 32 buildings listed on the National Register of Historic Places, including Swayne Hall which was built by slaves. Talladega's other historic buildings include: the courthouse (1836), the oldest in continuous use in Alabama; and the Alabama Institute for the Deaf and Blind, which features Manning Hall (1850), Grace Hall (1878), and Jemison House (1898). The Silk Stocking District also has a range of residential buildings from the period 1835 to 1910.

Talladega's other attractions include the Jemison–Carnegie Heritage Hall, which exhibits

historic photographs and works by national and local artists, and Bryant Vineyard.
Map ref: page 564 D6

TUSCALOOSA

Tuscaloosa has a population over 150,000 and is a university city and a lumber and manufacturing center. Located in west-central Alabama it has many natural, cultural, and historical attractions.

Prior to European settlement the area was occupied by the Choctaw and Creek tribes. The city was named after a Choctaw leader whose warriors ambushed Spanish explorer Hernando De Soto south of present-day Montgomery in 1540. The township was founded in 1816 and became the state capital from 1826 to 1846. Tuscaloosa's famous progeny include Robert Van de Graaff, the inventor of the Van de Graaff electrostatic generator; Coleman Young, the first African-American mayor of Detroit; and singer Dinah Washington.

Tuscaloosa is the home of the University of Alabama's original campus, established in 1831. It was rebuilt after much was destroyed by Union troops in 1865. In June 1963 Governor George Wallace personally stood in the doorway

of Foster Auditorium in order to prevent the first two African-American students from enrolling, thereby prompting President Kennedy to call out the National Guard to enforce the registrations. Gorgas House (1829) and President's Mansion (1841) remain from the antebellum days. The former is the oldest structure built by Alabama authorities still standing. Other highlights are the 60-acre (24-ha) arboretum, the Natural History Museum, and the Paul W. Bryant Museum, dedicated to the most successful college football coach ever. The local team, known as the Crimson Tide, are a local obsession.

Free tours are available of the outstanding private art collection at the Gulf States Paper Corporation. Another portion of the collection is located in the Mildred Warner House, built as a two-room cabin in 1822. The Murphy African-American Museum presents the material life of an African-American household of the early twentieth century.

The Mercedes Benz Visitor Center is located east of town. Further afield are: Moundville Archeological Park, 16 miles (26 km) south, the site of 26 pre-Colombian temple mounds; Deerlick Creek Park, 12 miles (19 km) east; and Lake Lurleen State Park, which is 12 miles (19 km) northwest.

Tuscaloosa is connected to the outside world via the highway system, bus, and train. The nearest airport is at Birmingham, 47 miles (76 km) to the northeast.
Map ref: page 563 P9

TUSKEGEE

Tuskegee, in east-central Alabama, is a rather small town with a remarkable African-American history. Located 35 miles (56 km) east of Montgomery, just south of I-85, it is home to the Tuskegee Institute National Historic Site, which draws attention to the historical importance of the Tuskegee Normal and Industrial Institute. It was started in 1881 as a vocational school by former slave Booker T. Washington, who was undoubtedly the most influential and famous African-American leader and spokesman of his day, exerting much influence in determining which racial theories and practices reached public consciousness.

The George Washington Carver Museum honors the contributions of African-Americans to the nation's history, particularly those of George Washington Carver who developed a reputation as a leading agricultural scientist through his work at the Tuskegee Institute. He researched and promoted improved crop production and also discovered a vast range of new uses for sweet potatoes and peanuts. A man of many talents, Carver was also an artist, inventor, and humanitarian.

Making hay in Alabama, a rural industry state.

Across the street is "The Oaks," a Queen Anne style house, built in 1899 as the home of Booker T. Washington. It was a rarity in its day for its usage of electric lights, its five bathrooms, and shower. Students at the Institute made the bricks and furnishings. A reproduction of the cabin where Washington was born is located at Taska Recreation Area, 5½ miles (9 km) east of Tuskegee on Hwy 80.

Tuskegee University campus is located on Old Montgomery Hwy. Many of the original buildings were designed by R.R. Taylor, the first African-American graduate of MIT (the Massachusetts Institute of Technology). The Booker T. Washington Monument, at the University, is a striking statue depicting Washington lifting the "Veil of Ignorance" from another African-American.

Tuskegee also deserves a place in history as the "Cradle of African-American Aviation" because it was here in 1941 that the US government created the all-African-American 99th Pursuit Squadron at Tuskegee Army Air Field. The unit destroyed 261 enemy aircraft in North Africa and Italy. Squadron commander Benjamin Davis earned the Distinguished Flying Cross and later became the first African-American major general. Another Tuskegee World War II pilot, "Chappie" James, became the first African-American four-star general and the Chappie James Center at the University is a museum that honors the aviators. Another important figure in African-American history, Rosa Parks (see entry on Montgomery, page 446), was born at Tuskegee in 1913.

A less salubrious aspect of Tuskegee history entails a shameful medical experiment that commenced at Tuskegee in 1932. Federal, state, and county authorities, in collusion with private medical practitioners, left a group of African-American men with syphilis untreated and in ignorance of effective treatment. The intention was to scientifically study the "natural" course of the disease. Remarkably, the experiment continued until it was exposed in 1972.
Map ref: page 564 E8

Tuscaloosa is one of Alabama's major lumber-producing areas. The logs are prepared and cut, then transported by rail.

ARKANSAS

Arkansas is an ancient land uplifted by tectonic shifting and patterned by unsullied woodlands and rivers. It is also a state of rich frontier heritage and wilderness attractions. Though Arkansas sat in the hub of the westward expansion, the state largely remained unpopulated—so much that until the mid-twentieth century pocket communities lay isolated around the Ozarks.

The Ozark Mountains are the state's natural wonder and main tourist draw, with the preservation of its mountain folk traditions and homespun lifestyle attracting the interest of most travelers. A century earlier, it was the natural spring waters that lured eastern gentry to its thermal baths.

The Arkansas territory was first explored by French fur trappers and inhabited by Osage, Quapaw, and displaced Cherokee Native Americans. It ceded in 1803 to the American government by the French as part of the Louisiana Purchase and was first settled in the 1820s. Cotton became the state's mainstay economy along the Mississippi Delta while west of Little Rock was reliant on the Arkansas River trade.

After the Civil War, the railroads jump-started the state's agricultural economy, and the short oil boom of the 1920s in the southwestern region added to its newfound prosperity. Then the Great Depression depleted Arkansas' riches and the state is now one of the poorest in the United States. Lumber, cotton, and agriculture still remain the economical lifeline, though manufacturing industries have since set up base in key cities.

Arkansas is resolutely Southern in tradition. A state of the Confederacy, it became the arena for bloody conflicts west of the Mississippi, its eastern boundary. Racial tensions escalated during the civil rights movement, with the state capital, Little Rock, taking center stage in the argument over racial integration in schools.

Renewed interest in the state grew during former President Bill Clinton's incumbency.

Central Avenue, Hot Springs. Many believe the thermal waters here have recuperative properties. The town offers many eateries, art galleries, music shows, hiking trails, and three lakes.

State motto *Regnat Populus* (The people rule)
State flag Adopted 1913
Capital Little Rock
Population 2,673,400
Total area (land and water) 53,182 square miles (137,741 sq km)
Land area 52,075 square miles (134,874 sq km)
Arkansas is the 27th-largest state in size
Origin of name From the Quapaw word meaning "south wind"
Nicknames The Land of Opportunity, The Natural State
Abbreviations AR (postal), Ark.
State bird Mockingbird
State flower Apple blossom
State tree Pine tree
Entered the Union June 15, 1836 as the 25th state

Places in ARKANSAS

ALTUS

The quiet town of Altus straddles Hwy 64 at the fringe of the Ozark National Forest, near the Arkansas River. Though the town of just 817 residents missed out on its chance of development when the I-40 whizzed by, the area itself offers some impressive back-country scenery, with miles of hiking trails on former Osage and Cherokee hunting grounds. Just west of Altus near Charleston lies the Cherokee Prairie Natural Area, which during spring becomes carpeted in wild-flowers and a very large expanse of unplowed tall-grass prairie.
Map ref: page 562 C4

ARKADELPHIA

Home to two universities, the town of Arkadelphia lies in the forested area of the White River in south-western Arkansas. Its youthful population of 10,912 tends to focus heavily on the great outdoors —and there's plenty of it around— from the scenic byway to the hilly region of the Ouachita Mountains and swift waters of the Ouachita River. Arkadelphia's De Gray Lake Resort boasts everything the local folks enjoy—golfing, fishing, and boating, along with 207 miles (333 km) of pleasant shoreline.

Being a college town, the place takes pride in hosting a wealth of sporting entertainment, while older residents partake in the more trad-itional mountain crafts known to the area. The Festival of Two Rivers, held in April, hosts an array of folk music, crafts, and canoe races. To the south of town at Gurdon, the county celebrates the Forest Fes-tival in October by showcasing wood-chopping contests.

Voted as "one of the 50 places to raise your family," Arkadelphia has painstakingly preserved its his-toric district, which predates the Civil War. Several buildings, in-cluding the Harris Fanigan Law Office, are listed on the National Register of Historic Places.

In the course of the Civil War, the town served as a Confederate supply depot, along with producing munitions for the war effort. There are several sites around the town that commemorate the town's battle with the invading Union army at Okolona in 1864.

In 1997, Arkadelphia sat right in the direct path of a massive tor-nado that significantly damaged a number of places in this town, including the United Daughters of the Confederacy Monument.

Arkadelphia is 63 miles (101 km) northeast of Little Rock and is serviced by train.
Map ref: page 562 D7

BATESVILLE

Located in the pleasant foothills of the gently rolling Ozark Moun-tains, Batesville lies on Hwy 167 at the nexus of the White River and Poke Bayou in north-central Arkansas. Though the highway leading to town winds past tiny Ozark villages such as Possum Grape, Batesville is actually a worldly community, one that was formerly settled by eastern gentry.

Batesville's original inception as a riverport in 1808 created the state's second oldest city after the territory was ceded by the Osage Native Americans. Upon changing its name from Poke Creek to Bates-ville—for Judge James Bates, who first represented the territory as a member of Congress—the town became a leading trade center for fur trappers and pioneers. Now sit-ting in the heart of prime cotton and dairy country, Batesville's population of 9,445 residents also revolves around a strong poultry industry and Lyon College, the oldest Christian liberal arts college.

The town has quite a handsome historic district, with much use of stone and marble masonry that today remains its architectural talking point. Batesville's former marble quarry also furnished Pio-neer Cemetery, where markers date back to the 1830s. Independence County correspondingly harbors the oldest gristmill found in the Ozarks, at Spring Hill.

A short drive northwest is Blan-chard Springs Cavern. This is a fossilized limestone bedrock and it features an underground river that flows out from the cavern walls. Not far away from the caves is the town of Mountain View and the Ozark Folk Center.

The nearest commercial airport is located 90 miles (145 km) west at the state capital, Little Rock.
Map ref: page 562 G3

See also Mountain View, page 456

A home in Altus—this town lies in the major Arkansas wine-producing region.

The Flying Saucer Bar and Restaurant in Little Rock, which lies between Arkadelphia and Batesville, in the center of the state.

BENTON

Turning off the I-40 at the city of Benton, visitors will get a sense of yesteryear America, with its Ma and Pa-style Royal Theater, Candy Shop, and Old Fashioned Soda Shoppe—all owned by actor, Jerry Van Dyke. Only 20 minutes from Little Rock, Benton also has a burgeoning manufacturing industry that sustains its economy.

This city of 21,009 people largely fashions itself around outdoor lifestyle and events including the folksy Saline County Fair during September and the Annual Old Fashion Days, held at the historic town square in October. There's even a rodeo for the cowboys in May. Benton also has three unspoilt rivers (Arkansas, Ouachita, and Saline) along with several lakes that all suffer from overload with anglers along with numerous recreational boats.

Very close to the famed spas of Hot Springs, Benton is an alternative rest stop if you want to enjoy the Ozarks and surrounds without spending too much money.

The nearest commercial airport is east at the city of Little Rock.
Map ref: page 562 E6

River Road Park at Hot Springs, near Benton, an area famed for its thermal waters.

BUFFALO NATIONAL RIVER

One of Arkansas' most beautiful recreation areas, Buffalo National River was created as a national park in 1972 after conservationists had lobbied extensively in Washington DC to prevent its flawless streams being dammed. Their efforts were certainly well worth it.

Tucked down into a 135-mile (217-km) pocket of unsullied terrain at the confluence of the White River, the park offers one of America's premier canoeing and whitewater locations. During the peak spring and summer seasons, kayakers and canoeists vie for water space on the upper Buffalo, making the river heavily congested.

All that aside, there are numerous nature trails embracing the steep limestone bluffs and caverns that trace the river's serpentine shape. A favorite haunt for many locals is at Hemmed-in-Hollow, the highest waterfall found midway between Appalachia and the Rockies to the west. Shaded by woodlands of oak, hickory, and pine, Buffalo National River nurtures an abundance of bird species. If you're visiting the area in fall, the region will be a profusion of color.

The main access to Buffalo National River is on the scenic byway along Hwy 7; its park headquarters are at Harrison. There is a scattering of privately owned farms around Boxley Valley, within the park boundary. One of the oldest Buffalo River homesteads, dating back to the 1830s, is the Parker-Hickman Farmstead, just north of Jasper.

Several outfitters also offer float trips (floating down the river on an inflatable inner tube) at the lower river, and rent out canoes and kayaks.
Map ref: page 562 E2

EUREKA SPRINGS

The mountain resort of Eureka Springs lies within the state's very rugged northwestern corner. Little has changed from its inception in 1879, when the town was regarded as a principal health retreat. Surrounded by over 60 natural springs from the neighboring caverns in the Ozark Mountains, visitors then flocked to the town hoping to cure a malady with a shot of the "Indian Healing Spring," as the waters were known at that time.

The Cherokee and Osage Native Americans had long enjoyed the region's thermal waters before they were driven out from the territory. When a former governor relocated to the town, he had persuaded the railway to follow suit.

Upon the arrival of the railroad in 1883, Eureka Springs enjoyed a new era of prosperity. The entire Historic District where the "Indian Healing Spring" was located is now listed on the National Register of Historic Places. Carefully preserved, Eureka Springs' handsome Victorian structures stand gracefully on hilly streets that thread into the steep hillside backdrop.

As the town continued to flourish, its architectural lines became giddier toward the end of the nineteenth century. The most flawless example is the Queen Anne style Rosalie House, located on Spring Street, with its ornate arbors and plaster-cast motifs.

Downtown is lined with grand hotels. Dozens of palatial hotels were built over the next 30-year boom cycle including the Palace Bath House, the Basin Park Hotel, and the flamboyant Crescent Hotel which was the height of Eureka Springs fashion in the early 1900s.

Though its population of 2,278 is fairly small, the influx of tourists to the town creates the illusion that the town is far larger than it is. Nevertheless, Eureka Springs remains a place for romantics and those who like to clop along city streets in horse-drawn carriages. Just taking a stroll through its historic district is a sweet delight. There are countless spas, galleries, trinket stores, and fudge shops lining the sidewalks. And in strong competition with the novelty boutiques are several religious establishments plugging the "Good Book" to the point of distraction.

No matter what your religious denomination, the Bible Museum, housing the world's largest biblical volumes and ancient manuscripts, presents a fascinating exhibition. Located in the multistoried Christ of the Ozarks building on Statue Road, the Museum's benefactors collectively gathered artifacts from the war-torn Middle East. Visitors can embark on a New Holy Land excursion to a small-scale exhibit of the River Jordan and the Sea of Galilee and a display of photographs in the Sacred Art Center.

Eureka Springs' water is collected and bottled locally.

But the religious overtones do not end there. Every year the locals put on the Great Passion Play, performed with a cast large enough to sink Noah's Ark. For over three decades, the play has been staged in a massive amphitheater, and it depicts Christ in the final days before his crucifixion.

Another enjoyable place to take a peek is the Hatchell Home. It was once the domicile of Carrie Nation, a crusader of sobriety who fervently pursued the closure of downtown's thriving saloons.

On Main Street is the Eureka Springs Historical Museum, which is located in Califf House. Constructed in 1889, the building served both as a general store and residence. Visitors can delve into Eureka Springs' regional history and enjoy an exhibit of Victorian dolls and period costumes. A bit further down the road is the Bank of Eureka Springs, which has been restored with period furniture, machines, and a classic pot-bellied stove. The Eureka Springs Trolley Service takes in all of the major points of interest.

Eureka Springs sits right at the crossroads of Hwys 65, 62, and 23 not far from Missouri's state line. The town is serviced by Fayetteville's regional airport.

Map ref: page 562 C1

FAYETTEVILLE

Historic Fayetteville, which lies in the northwest pocket of Arkansas, was settled as early as 1828. Now a burgeoning city of 58,047 residents, it is also home to the University of Arkansas and nearby wilderness attractions.

For people heading through the Ozarks, this town is a good place to bunk down for the night and soak up the area's rich Civil War and pioneer heritage. It boasts quite a handsome downtown square block that showcases the Classic Revival-style Old Post Office building and the adjacent courthouse, which features octagonal corner towers.

Fayetteville suffered a similar fate to other Southern towns during the Civil War. Some of the buildings still bear the scars including Headquarters House on East Dickson Street, which acted as center stage in a battle that took place in April 1863. Bullet holes are still present in a couple of the doors. Occupied by both opposing armies at different stages of the war, Headquarters House has since been transformed into a Civil War museum. On the fringe of the city is the Prairie Grove Battle Site, scene of another engagement in 1862.

Another particular attraction in the town is the Arkansas Air Museum, based at Drake Airfield. What makes this museum different from others is that most of the exhibits actually fly. Everything from 1920s racing planes to a carrier fighter are on display. The build-

ing itself at one time served as the headquarters for a World War II air training post.

More recently, Fayetteville's University of Arkansas has come under siege—it was under the media spotlight during the 1992 presidential campaign. Arkansas' native son, Bill Clinton, taught constitutional law at the college in the mid-1970s, and married his bride Hillary on campus.

Map ref: page 562 B2

FORT SMITH

Straddling the Oklahoma state line on the I-40, Fort Smith began as a military outpost for the Indian Territory in 1817. Built around the Arkansas River, it became a bustling thoroughfare for river traders, prospectors, and fur trappers on the journey west. Now a large city of 80,268, Fort Smith serves as the gateway city to western Arkansas' Ozark Mountains.

In the 1800s the city remained the quintessential frontier town complete with an unsavory reputation for lawlessness—so much that over 60 deputy sheriffs were murdered over a span of 21 years. Following occupation by both Union and Confederate troops during the Civil War, Fort Smith eventually matured into a city of respectability and became the principal commercial center

for manufacturing firms upon the discovery of viable regional natural gas and coal reserves.

The Belle Grove Historic District in Fort Smith is reminiscent of the nineteenth century with its painstakingly restored homes. The best place to delve into the town's local history is the Fort Smith National Historic Site at Rogers Avenue. This museum holds a fine collection including the relics of two frontier forts, Native American artifacts, and a courthouse with its chambers and jail. According to lore, the courtroom was kept busy when the town's "hanging judge," Isaac C. Parker, sentenced 79 men to the gallows. The site also chronicles the history of the Federal Native American policy and the subsequent removal of the Osage tribe and the already displaced Cherokee. Perhaps the most poignant tale is of the Trail of Tears—many tribe members perished along this route.

In town, city trolleys rattle along Main Street to the various points of interest including Miss Laura's Visitors Center, housed in a former brothel on B Street. Every year in April, the town stages a re-enacted Civil War Weekend.

Fort Smith has a municipal airport and is serviced by bus from Oklahoma City and Little Rock along the I-40.

Map ref: page 562 A4

The rustic Branding Iron restaurant and bar in the one-time river port of Fort Smith.

HELENA

More than any other community in Arkansas, the Mississippi river-port of Helena reflects the legacy of the Deep South. Only an hour's travel from Memphis on Hwy 49, Helena was, for a spell, a thriving shipping dock for transporting the state's cotton crops. However, after the railroads arrived, Helena's fortunes soon dwindled. With a shrinking population of 6,432 people, the town now focuses its energy on singing the blues.

In the 1940s, the company King Biscuit Flour sponsored legendary recording artist "Sunshine" Sonny Payne's "King Biscuit Time" slot on KFTA Radio. Along with playing a mean harmonica, Payne would advertise Sonny Boy's Biscuit Meal. Still an institution on the airwaves, the show is broadcast live from the foyer of the Delta Cultural Center on Missouri Street. The center also has a solid collection of the region's blues heritage along with snippets from the civil rights movement. The Phillips County Museum focuses on the region's Civil War history and features an assortment of documents and letters written by Samuel Clemens (also known as Mark Twain) and eminent Confederate general, Robert E. Lee.

The King Biscuit Blues Festival attracts an elite group of musicians and draws the crowds from across the Mississippi Bridge.
Map ref: page 563 J6

HOT SPRINGS AND HOT SPRINGS NATIONAL PARK

Famous for its mineral springs and bathhouses, Hot Springs serves as both a resort town and gateway to its national park. Located 50 miles (80 km) west of Little Rock on Hwy 70, Hot Springs is flanked by the densely forested Ouachita Mountains and is nestled in a valley that produces well over 850 gallons (3.2 megalitres) of springwater a day from the ground at a temperature of 143°F (62°C).

Since its inception in 1851, its famous thermal waters have shaped Hot Springs into a cosmopolitan community, attracting luminaries and former presidents. Former President Bill Clinton went to school there. During Prohibition, racketeers moved into town to run illicit gaming houses for the rich

A hot mineral spring bubbles over rocks in the Hot Springs National Park.

and not so savory, including the Chicago mobsters, Bugsy Malone and Al Capone. After World War II, however, the proclaimed healing waters of Hot Springs never reached their zenith in popularity again.

During the 1980s the town went into overdrive to preserve its historic downtown together with Bathhouse Row found on Central Avenue. Correspondingly there was renewed interest in Hot Springs after Bill Clinton was elected to the White House in 1993. The former President moved to Hot Springs with his mother in 1953, attending Hot Springs High School and the Park Place Baptist Church.

There are many points of interest in the historic district, and the best way to view them is to hop

aboard the city trolley. The visitor center at Central Court provides a wealth of information on the entire district, along with some detailed brochures on all of the area's grand hotels, bathhouses, and, of course, the favorite boyhood hangouts of the former President.

Shaded by a park of billowing dogwood and magnolia trees, Bathhouse Row features some of the nation's most resplendent European-style spas from the turn of the last century. The most opulent is the Fordyce Bathhouse, where the National Park Visitor Center and Museum is located. No expense was spared during its construction—from mosaic-tiled floors to a stained-glass ceiling. At the north end of Bathhouse Row is Arlington

Lawn, the town's local haunt and a very popular thermal spring.

Hot Springs is unique in retaining a national park within its city limits. Behind Bathhouse Row, a scenic road begins to zig-zag past dense groves of pine, oak, and hickory, leading to Hot Springs Mountain Tower. From its summit, a panorama of the city and the enfolding Ouachita Mountains comes into view. Remote and rugged, the Park is a patchwork of mesas and rolling valleys carpeted with hardwood.

Over 26 miles (42 km) of hiking trails wind and coil through Hot Springs National Park. The drive to Ouachita Lake is a pretty one, especially in fall when the leaves blaze in a spectacle of crimson and burnt-orange hues.

Hot Springs heats up in the spring with a series of folk and craft shows. The Hot Springs Music Festival, in June, and the Taste of Downtown Festival, cover everything from pie-eating contests to mountain-style crafts. Gamblers also come to Hot Springs to bet on the best thoroughbreds at the Racing Festival of the South at the Oaklawn Jockey Club. Hot Springs Memorial Field Airport has commuter services from Dallas, Fort Worth and St Louis. The nearest commercial airport is at Little Rock. A train stops daily at Hot Springs and the Hot Springs–Little Rock Airport Shuttle has a door-to-door service.
Map ref: page 562 D6

JONESBORO

The city of Jonesboro lies in the northeastern region of the state, 64 miles (103 km) from Memphis, Tennessee. Now a college town of 55,515 residents, its recreational focus is centered around the area's multiple state parks and also its wildlife refuges. Every outdoor sport is on offer here, from seasonal fishing to bird watching.

The Big Lake National Wildlife Refuge—the "Great Swamp of Arkansas"—is a haven for a variety of birds that nest in the cypress marsh. There are also numerous hiking trails at Lake Frierson and Crowley worth exploring, together with the Military Road Trail, once the pioneer thoroughfare between Memphis and Little Rock.

Upon the arrival of the railroad, Jonesboro became a leading supply and lumber center and the site of the Arkansas State University, the state's agricultural school. It has the ASU Museum, which has a superb collection of ancient Native American artifacts and pioneer annals.

For the roughrider, Jonosboro hosts the Northeast Arkansas District Fair and Rodeo. Located on Hwy 63, the city is served by bus and Jonesboro Municipal Airport.
Map ref: page 563 H3

KNOXVILLE

The "City of Knoxville" is actually a town of 460 people. But its feisty disposition and location make it a popular resting place on Hwy 64, in the heart of the Arkansas River Valley. Exceptional recreational areas, all within a half-hour's drive, surround Knoxville and include Cabin Creek Recreation Area and Lake Dardanelle. Many of these areas are a quiet sanctuary for a host of native and migrating birds. West of the lake, and along Hwy 309 is Magazine Mountain, the highest point in Arkansas with an elevation of 2,753 feet (840 m).

If you're in town during spring, be sure to mix with the folks at their Annual Fish Fry.
Map ref: page
562 C4

LITTLE ROCK

The city of Little Rock is famous for three reasons. First, for three terms it became the domicile of former President, Bill Clinton, during his 12-year incumbency as Arkansas' governor. Second it is recalled for Marilyn Monroe and Jane Russell's performance when they crooned about being "two little girls from Little Rock," in the musical *Gentlemen Prefer Blondes*. No matter that they weren't, people still remember the song.

The third reason has a more somber note. In the fall of 1957, Little Rock was in the world spotlight when nine African-American students enrolled at Central High School. Though the Supreme Court had ruled in favor of integration, Arkansas Governor Orval Faubus refuted the Court's decision and prohibited their admission. Despite an injunction served on the Governor, Faubus sent in the state troopers to prevent the students from attending school. His actions sparked a series of violent demonstrations that lasted for nearly a month until President Eisenhower sent in paratroopers and the National Guard to restore order to the school and to protect the students. Capitalizing on the public's mood, Faubus closed all of Little Rock's public schools the following school year and was duly elected for a second term.

This citadel of the civil rights movement is located on S. Park Avenue. Directly across from the school is a preserved 1950s Mobil gas station, now a visitor

A Knoxville farmer checks his tractor before taking it out to work the fields.

center. Its museum has quite an excellent exhibit of the crisis that tested the very foundation of the Supreme Court's earlier ruling of *Brown* v. *Board of Education*, which prohibited segregation in schools of the United States.

Little Rock has always played a pivotal role in Arkansas' development and it remains the political and commercial nucleus of the state. Its key riverside position has likewise assured the city of a continuation on its present prosperity.

The French first explored the area as early as 1722, and the settlement became an important junction and outpost for fur traders along the Southwest Trail. By 1812, the settlement evolved into a town overlooking the Arkansas River; it became the territory's capital in 1821. Its fortunes continued to boom until the occupation of the Union army during the Civil War. Following reconstruction and the westward expansion, Little Rock enjoyed

Little Rock Central High School, the scene of racial confrontation in 1957.

renewed prosperity, which is reflected in the city's line-up of grand and splendid old mansions.

Downtown's growing yet rather unimpressive skyline, together with the city's flourishing population of 183,133 people, give the visitor the impression that Little Rock is on the move. Nevertheless, the city's appeal largely remains largely with the visual reflection of its pioneer and Civil War heritage.

The Old State House Museum, located on Markham Street, served as Arkansas' capital until 1911. Tours to its legislative chambers showcase its handsome architecture and desks with brass spittoons. The Museum also contains excellent historical displays including period costumes and pioneer utensils.

Other grand Colonial Revival and Queen Anne-style buildings are located in Little Rock's historic Quapaw Quarter, primarily along Louisiana and Scott Streets. The State Capitol, which was modeled on the architectural lines of Washington's famed building, is located on the intersection of Capitol Avenue and Woodland Street.

The River Market District on Markham Street is Little Rock's main haunt and it is well worth taking a stroll here. The district is teeming with newly sprung restaurants and cafés, along with the city's traditional farmer's market. The city also has the fine Arkansas Arts Center, the Museum of Discovery, and the Children's Museum, located in the Union Station building. Also in the area is Riverfront Park, an unspectacular yet pretty inner city parkland that leads to the enshrining "little rock," after which the city is named. One of the more

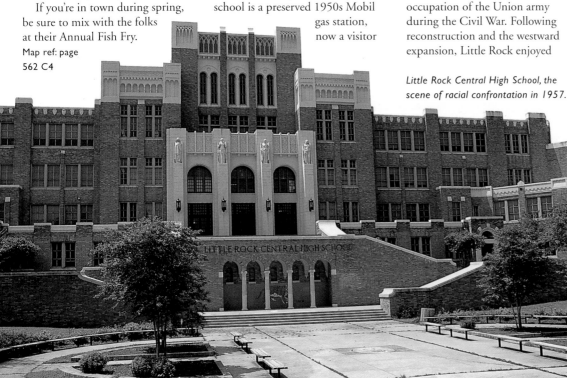

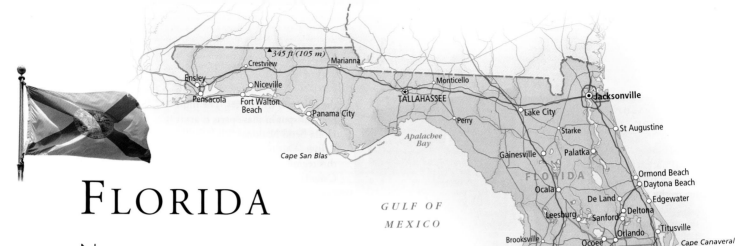

FLORIDA

GULF OF MEXICO

No state has more nicknames than Florida—"The Sunshine State," "The Peninsula State," "The Everglade State," and "The Orange State." Florida, the southeast-ernmost state, is primarily a large, low-lying peninsula surrounded by the Atlantic Ocean to the east and the Gulf of Mexico to the west. Circling the southern tip from Biscayne Bay out to the Dry Tortugas is a string of islands, or Keys, as they are known. Cape Sable is the southernmost point on mainland United States, and Key West is the southernmost city in the nation. The northwest part of Florida, bordering Alabama and Georgia, is known as the Panhandle.

Florida has the longest marine coastline of all states after Alaska, and an extremely inviting climate, which is one of its most valuable assets. Most of Florida is humid and subtropical, and the southern tip of the peninsula is tropical. Much of the state is protected wilderness, both on land and in the surrounding waters. The Everglades National Park is one of the United States' largest national parks, and there are dozens of others in the state, including undersea preserves.

Florida has a rich and colorful history; it has passed from its original Native American inhabitants into Spanish, French, British, and American hands. Historic forts, districts, and sites, such as Juan Ponce de León's Fountain of Youth, are popular tourist attractions. Tallahasee is the state capital and the near-by cities of Pensacola and St Augustine are of historic and cultural interest—St Augustine is the oldest city in the United States. Jacksonville is Florida's city with the largest population but many millions visit Orlando each year, most notably for Walt Disney World. Theme and amusement parks are as common as wilderness preserves in this part of Florida. From alligators in the swamps to the rockets soaring through space, Florida is truly one of the most unique places in the world.

The Suwannee River provides swimming, snorkeling, and fishing through several organized tours.

State motto In God We Trust
State flag Adopted 1900 (modified 1985)
Capital Tallahassee
Population 15,982,378
Total area (land and water) 59,928 square miles (155,214 sq km)
Land area 53,937 square miles (139,697 sq km)
Florida is the 22nd-largest state in size
Origin of name From Spanish, meaning "feast of flowers"
Nicknames The Sunshine State, The Peninsula State, The Everglade State, The Orange State
Abbreviations FL (postal), Fla.
State bird Mockingbird
State flower Orange blossom
State tree Sabal palm
Entered the Union March 3, 1845 as the 27th state

Places in
FLORIDA

BIG CYPRESS NATIONAL PRESERVE

Covering the northern section of the Everglades swampland, between Fort Lauderdale to the east and Naples to the west, this 729,000-acre (295,245-ha) preserve was established in 1974. Route 41, the Tamiami Trail, runs east-west along the southern section of the preserve and I-75, Alligator Alley, or the Everglades Parkway, runs east-west along its northern boundary. Big Cypress Seminole Indian Reservation and Miccosukee Indian Reservation adjoin the preserve at its northeastern corner. Fakahatchee Strand State Preserve and Collier Seminole State Park are on the park's western fringes. This subtropical swampland is made up of wet and dry prairies, coastal plains, mangrove forest, sandy pine forests, and mixed hardwood hammocks. The swampland is vital to the preservation of the Everglades—to the wildlife, and the watershed.

The Miccosukee Indian Village is on Route 41, 25 miles (40 km) west of the Florida Turnpike. It has a restaurant and offers handcrafted baskets, beaded jewelry, and traditional patchwork clothing as well as more commercial souvenirs.

Facilities are limited to a visitor center with restrooms on Route 41 between Shark Valley and Everglades City, picnic areas at roadside parks, nature trails, and six campgrounds. Some campgrounds accommodate motor homes, though none has full motor-home facilities. Fishing, canoeing, cycling, hiking, and horseback riding are popular activities. Airboat and swamp buggy rides are also available. Lodging and dining options are extremely limited.
Map ref: page 557 E7

BISCAYNE NATIONAL PARK

Ninety-five percent of this park, which covers 172,924 acres (70,034 ha), is under the Biscayne Bay and the Atlantic Ocean in southeastern Florida. Dry land acreage is spread across a line of 44 islands that make up the northern

Florida Keys. The most significant of these is the 29-acre (12-ha) Boca Chita Key. This isle is a popular stop for boaters. Elliott Key has a visitor center, hiking trails, and a campground. Adjoining the southern tip of the park is the Key Largo National Marine Sanctuary.

The Convoy Point Visitor Center is at the park's main gate, 9 miles (15 km) east of Homestead. Entrance is free, but transportation to Boca Chita or Elliott Key requires a modest fee—the only way to enter the park is by boat. Homestead Bayfront Park offers a boat launch, as does Elliott Key. Mooring buoys are generally available. Overnight docking fees at Boca Chita and Elliott Keys are modest. The Intracoastal Waterway spans the Biscayne Bay and its undersea preserve from Miami in the north to Key Largo in the south.

The park's greatest attractions are underwater and are best appreciated by snorkeling or scuba diving. A glass-bottom boat tour is the next best option. Canoeing, kayaking, fishing, hiking, swimming, and

Thinly distributed dwarf, or stunted, cypress trees (Taxodium spp.), Big Cypress National Preserve.

windsurfing are popular activities. There are camping sites on Elliott Key and Boca Chita and, since they are not accessible by land, are recreational-vehicle free. They offer state-of-the-art facilities and are generally not crowded. There are also many budget motels in Homestead. Take precautions against the sun, especially when in the water. Swimmers should wear protective footgear and watch for spiny sea urchins and coral. Mosquito spray is essential. With murky, irregular waters and strong currents, nautical charts are highly recommended even for the most experienced seafarers.

Miami International is the nearest major airport. Miami is 35 miles (56 km) to the north. Everglades National Park is around 21 miles (34 km) to the west.
Map ref: page 557 G8

Addison Mizner-designed fountain, Mizner Hotel, Boca Raton.

BOCA RATON

On the Atlantic Coast in southeastern Florida, the town of Boca Raton (population 68,800) is a renowned beach resort and polo center. It is midway between Palm Beach in the north and Hollywood in the south. "Boca," as it locally known, is the winter home for many wealthy Americans—it is a wealthy American, architect Addison Mizner, who originally dreamed up the city. The name is Spanish for "rat's mouth" in reference to jagged rocks at its narrow ocean inlet.

Seasonal tourism and computer and communications manufacturing support the local economy.

Cultural attractions include the Boca Raton Museum of Art, which features nineteenth-century oil paintings and local and international exhibits. Also of interest are the Children's Museum, the Morikami Museum, and Japanese Gardens in nearby Delray Beach, and the International Museum of Cartoon Art, which features 52,000 square feet (4,940 sq m) filled with prints, frames, books, and memorabilia of the world's top cartoonists. Florida Atlantic University offers concerts, dance, theater, and an art gallery. Each Sunday, from January to April, the Royal Palm Polo Sports Club hosts polo games.

The Gumbo Limbo Environmental Complex is a 20-acre (8-ha) complex protecting a coastal hammock (forest island) with an elevated boardwalk and a 40-foot (12-m) observation tower. Children love the snakes, sea turtles, crabs, and scorpions. Spanish River Park, located 2 miles (3 km) north of Boca's Palmetto Park Road, is a huge oceanfront picnic ground with nature trails, volleyball nets, and a 40-foot (12-m) high observation tower. Red Reef Park is a 67-acre (27-ha) oceanfront park with plenty of shallow water for swimming and snorkeling. Boating, scuba diving, golf, and shopping, particularly at Mizner Park and Town Center Mall, are also popular activities. Nearby Delray Beach is a good place to stay and eat if you are on a budget.

Palm Beach International and Hollywood International Airports are closest. Trains also serve the area.
Map ref: page 557 G6

CAPE CANAVERAL

Cape Canaveral, or the "Space Coast" as it is locally known, with the Kennedy Space Center (on Merritt Island) at its core, is located in northeast Florida on the Atlantic Ocean. Melbourne is the nearest large city, but the much nearer Cocoa Beach is a better point from which to explore the Cape.

In 1958 NASA took over more land than it required and, by 1964, turned over the balance to the Cape Canaveral National Seashore and the Merritt Island National Wildlife Preserve. Before NASA, the area was popular only with locals hoping to escape city life. Now thousands of tourists come to visit the John F. Kennedy Space Center each year, and to enjoy more than 72 miles (116 km) of beaches.

The Space Center on NASA Parkway, Hwy 405, is NASA's primary space launch facility and offers an impressive array of tours, displays, and activities just for children. Visits begin at the Kennedy Space Center Visitor Complex. From

here, shuttle buses take visitors on a two-hour tour of the complex. You should plan on spending the whole day if you want to see everything here. Spaceport USA has a Rocket Garden with rockets on display from each stage of America's space program—it is still the site of weather and communications satellite launchings. Full-size models of a lunar rover and the Viking Mars Lander and original spacecraft are on display inside the Gallery of Space Flight.

Shorebirds, waterfowl, reptiles, and alligators call Merritt Island National Wildlife Refuge home. The preserve is 140,000 acres (56,700 ha). It features the 6-mile (10-km) Black Point Wildlife Drive plus several nature trails—and the admission is free.

The Canaveral National Seashore is a pristine 13-mile (21-km) stretch of beach and marsh. It encloses

Mosquito Lagoon, where dolphins and manatee play. Herons, egrets, ibis, willets, sanderlings, turnstones, and terns are some of the bird species that live here and, between May and August, giant sea turtles also nest here. Camping with a permit is allowed here in winter, and a canoe trail is set in along the marshes of Shipyard Island.

Melbourne International Airport is to the south and Orlando International Airport is to the east. The only way to explore this area is by car. Local bus routes on the Space Coast Area Transit are very time consuming. Deep-sea fishing and charter boats depart from Port Canaveral. Cruise ships, bound for the Caribbean, depart frequently from Jetty Park in Port Canaveral.
Map ref: page 571 P10

CAPE CORAL

Cape Coral (with a population of 76,200) is in southwestern Florida on the Gulf of Mexico. It was first settled in 1958 and has the second largest area of all Florida's cities. Water sports, strolling along the canals, and golfing are popular recreational activities here. The area is a great base for exploring Fort Myers (just across the Caloosahatchee River), Sanibel and Captiva Islands (just outside Charlotte Harbor), and Bonita Springs (to the south).

Fort Myers offers the Calusa Nature Center and Planetarium, the Edison and Ford Winter Estates, Fort Myers Historical Museum, and the Imaginarium Hands-on Museum and Aquarium. Together with Captiva, the islands make up the Sanibel National Wildlife Preserve. More than 200 species of birds are found here, and the J.N. Ding Darling National Wildlife Preserve offers a 5-mile (8-km) scenic drive, as well as hiking and canoe trails. There is also good fishing here.

Dining and lodging are available to suit everyone's budget. The Southwest Florida International Airport serves the area and trains and buses serve Fort Myers.
Map ref: page 557 C5

One of eight rockets on view in the Rocket Garden, at the John F. Kennedy Space Center, Cape Canaveral.

DAYTONA BEACH

Daytona Beach (population 62,700) is a resort city on the Atlantic coast, 54 miles (87 km) northeast of Orlando. The beach is 500 feet (153 m) wide, 23 miles (37 km) long, and consists of hard-packed sand on which cars can drive. Since the early 1900s it has been used for car racing—it was here that the 1903 world's automobile speed record of 68 miles (109 km) per hour was set.

The 480-acre (194-ha) Daytona International Speedway opened in 1959 with the first Daytona 500; it has grandstands that can accommodate 125,000. Most events take place in February, March, July, October, and December. There is an IMAX film and interactive displays on the history of racing plus a virtual pit stop in a virtual stock car. From May to October there is also the opportunity to ride three times around the track at an average speed of 115 miles (185 km) per hour.

The Halifax River runs parallel to the beach and separates it from downtown. South of downtown Daytona Beach, at Ponce Inlet, there are archeological remains and the ruins of old plantations. The Ponce de León Inlet and Lighthouse is a National Historic Landmark with the second tallest lighthouse in the nation as its main attraction. The Halifax Historical Museum is housed in a former bank building, and features historic photographs and Native American artifacts.

Charter boats make deep-sea-fishing expeditions at offshore reefs and river fishing in inland waters. There are 25 golf courses including two of the nation's top-rated links for women golfers at the LPGA International.

The beach alone attracts close to 8 million visitors per year. Plan ahead for lodging and dining. Daytona Beach has an international airport, and nearby Orlando International Airport is a much larger facility. Cars are highly recommended for exploring Daytona, though the city offers a very convenient network of buses.
Map ref: page 571 N8

DE SOTO NATIONAL MEMORIAL

De Soto National Memorial is in Bradenton, 15 miles (24 km) north of Sarasota on I-75. It

Fort Lauderdale Beach Promenade offers an uninterrupted stretch of cafes, hotels, and stores.

commemorates the site where the Spanish explorer Don Hernando de Soto landed in 1539. De Soto led the first expedition to reach the southeastern United States.

De Soto National Memorial is on 75th Street, where the Manatee River meets the gulf. The visitor center offers displays of weapons, armor, a restoration of de Soto's original campsite, and depictions of sixteenth-century Spanish life. A self-guided interpretive nature trail follows the footsteps of de Soto and his men along the beach and through mangrove swamps and gumbo-limbo trees.

Bradenton is on the Gulf of Mexico and sits at the southern entrance to Tampa Bay. It offers a wide variety of dining options, but lodging is limited. More options exist near the Sarasota-Bradenton Airport and along the freeways.

The Sarasota Bradenton and St Petersburg Clearwater Airports serve the area, though fares into nearby Tampa International Airport are notably lower. Trains serve Tampa and there are bus connections to St Petersburg. Map ref: page 557 B3

Dry Tortugas National Park

Dry Tortugas National Park comprises a 7-mile (11-km) long archipelago made up of 27 coral keys with a magnificent fortress as a centerpiece. It covers approximately 65,000 acres (26,325 ha) with only 85 acres (34 ha) of land. One hundred square miles (259 sq km) is protected as a sanctuary for bird and marine life, as well as healthy coral keys. The park is teeming with tropical ocean birds, and fish are visible through crystal clear water. Spanish explorer Ponce de León,

in 1513, named the islands "Tortugas," meaning "turtles." The "Dry" in the name came later and refers to the total lack of fresh water.

Fort Jefferson, on the 10-acre (4-ha) Garden Key, is the largest fortress in the Western Hemisphere. This 16-million-brick fortress was never completed and it never saw battle. It was built in the 1800s and its perimeter encompasses the entire 10 acres (4 ha) of land. The Army abandoned the fort in 1874 and it was subsequently used as a naval base; the USS *Maine* launched here and was blown up on its way to Havana, setting in motion the Spanish–American War. In 1935 it was permanently preserved as a National Monument.

Allow at least a day to explore Garden Key. At a minimum, allow one hour to visit the fortress and visitor center. Garden Key has 10 camping sites but registration is required and they fill up quickly. They offer no facilities and no fresh drinking water. Loggerhead and Bush Keys are open for day use, though Bush Key is closed during the migratory tern's nesting season from March to September. There are no public boat moorings or slips, and private boats must anchor in designated areas. Bring water and food, and prepare for occasional rough seas.

Dry Tortugas National Park is 68 miles

(109 km) west of Key West in the Gulf of Mexico and is accessible by boat or seaplane. Key West International is the nearest airport. From Key West, a seaplane ride is around 40 minutes; the trip is three hours by boat. Map ref: page 557 A10

Fort Lauderdale

Known as the "Venice of America" because of the waterways that crisscross the city, Fort Lauderdale (population 154,200) is on Florida's famed Gold Coast, 23 miles (37 km) north of Miami. It has attracted college students on spring break and winter-weary Americans looking for warmth and sun since the 1950s. Today, commerce, high-tech industries, and tourism support the local economy of the city.

With around 23 miles (37 km) of beaches, 300 miles (483 km) of navigable waterways, and numerous rivers, canals, and inlets, this is a boater's paradise. All types and sizes of craft frequent the waters here, and in numbers up to 40,000 at one time. This is the yachting capital of the world and many homes have private slips along the waterways. Port Everglades is the deepest harbor in the state, and is the world's second-largest passenger cruise port. More than 1 million passengers sail from here each year.

All types of watercraft are available for rent and public fishing piers and boat ramps are easy to find. Dive shops line the beaches; a popular dive site is the *Mercedes I*, an intact ship sunk 97 feet (30 m) to provide an artificial reef.

Cruises are available down the New River on a Mississippi-style steamer. There are first-class sporting facilities including tennis, swimming, fishing, canoeing, and nature trails. There is also horse racing at the state's only track, Pompano Harness Track, and betting on Jai-Alai (a Spanish-style indoor lacrosse). Butterfly World is a 3-acre (1-ha) tropical garden with over 150 butterfly species. Bonnet House is a 35-acre (14-ha) historical plantation home, and the Stranahan House, built in 1901, is the city's oldest standing structure and a museum of South Florida pioneer life.

The Fort Lauderdale Beach Promenade offers low and high-rise hotels, bars, and shops as well as a crowded beach. This area is the hub for tourists. Cruising along the strip is a main event each night, whether in a car or on foot. The 3-mile (5-km) Hollywood Beach Boardwalk attracts people from all walks of life and offers a more pristine beach. Lodging and dining options exist in every category.

Nearby Miami International Airport offers domestic and international flights. Fort Lauderdale/ Hollywood International Airport offers limited services. Trains serve Fort Lauderdale and nearby Hollywood. The best ways to explore are by car and boat, though a free and convenient network of trolleys navigates the downtown area. Map ref: page 557 G6

Intricately sculpted sand castles on the beach at Fort Lauderdale, a popular vacation area in Florida.

FORT MATANZAS NATIONAL MONUMENT

This monument is in the northeast corner of the state. The park covers 298 acres (121 ha) across the Matanzas River from downtown St Augustine including the southern tip of Anastasia Island, and the site of the Fort, Rattlesnake Island.

"Matanzas" is the Spanish word for slaughter—Spanish explorer Pedro Menendez de Aviles arrived here in 1565, and slaughtered the French soldiers after their surrender. In 1740 the Spanish built Fort Matanzas to permanently control the Matanzas River inlet, which provided access into St Augustine. After a volatile history it was finally transferred to the United States in 1821. In 1916 the masonry fort was stabilized, and in 1924 it became a national monument.

Rattlesnake Island is rich in wildlife and is a sanctuary to endangered species such as the manatee. From March to April turtles nest on the ocean beach, including two species that are endangered.

The entrance to the island is 15 miles (24 km) south of St Augustine off US-1; the entrance is via ferry. There are tours of the island (including flashlight tours) and visitors can take a ½-mile (1-km) boardwalk trail through coastal maritime forest. There is a visitor center that includes a short video.

The entrance to the fort and the ferry boat tour (which takes about 45 minutes) are free. The fort is open every day, except Christmas Day. It is closed during thunderstorms for fear of lightning strikes; the ferry service is suspended until the storm has passed.

Daytona International Airport is about one hour south and Jacksonville International Airport is about one hour north, on the I-95.
Map ref: page 571 N6

GAINESVILLE

Gainesville (population 86,700) is in the northern interior and is primarily a university town. It was first settled in 1830.

Gainsville's main attraction is the Florida Museum of Natural History at the University of Florida. Here you will find a Mayan Palace, a Sioux Indian exhibit, a fossil study center, and a collection of rare seashells. The Object Gallery has fossilized sharks' teeth and live reptiles. This is the largest museum of natural history in southeastern United States. Also at this university are the Lake Alice Wildlife Preserve with alligators, turtles, and birds, and the Samuel P. Harn Museum of Art.

The Devil's Millhopper State Geological Site is a giant 5-acre (2-ha), 120-foot (37-m) deep sinkhole formed when the roof of an underground cave collapsed. A wooden walkway leads down into the hole and offers views of waterfalls, lush vegetation, and indigenous wildlife. The Fred Bear Museum is a tribute to avid hunter Fred Bear who made his conquests only with bow and arrow. Archery and bow hunting artifacts are on display here along with buffalo, caribou, elephant, and bear he felled. Native American, Eskimo, and African relics are also on display. Archery equipment manufacturing helps the local economy.

Downtown Gainesville is charming, with cobblestone streets and plazas, restored storefronts, and sidewalk cafes. Dining and lodging options are available in the low to medium range. Nearby Starke is a popular day trip from here. Visit the Camp Blanding Museum, a former training site for nine Army divisions during World War II.

Gainesville Regional Airport serves the area, while Jacksonville and Orlando International Airports both offer a much wider selection of flights.
Map ref: page 571 K7

JACKSONVILLE

Jacksonville, with a population of 670,000, is the insurance and banking capital of the south. It is located in northernmost Florida, 36 miles (58 km) south of Georgia, on the Atlantic coast, on the mouth of the St John's River. It is named for General Andrew Jackson who, in 1882, forced Spain to cede Florida to the United States.

Jacksonville is one of the largest cities, by area, in the United States. Its unusual combination of skyscrapers and southern hospitality, white sandy beaches and fine art museums, renovated old neighborhoods and military fortifications, and two riverfronts, attracts visitors from all over the world.

Jacksonville Landing is a glass and steel arts and entertainment complex on the north shore of the river and is similar to Boston's Faneuil Hall. This is the hub of downtown activity, with restaurants, shops, festivals, and concerts. Southbank Riverwalk is a 1-mile (2-km) boardwalk which is popular for jogging, strolling, or sitting on a bench and looking at the skyline. Other attractions on the Southbank Riverwalk include the Friendship Fountain, the nation's largest self-contained fountain, and the Museum of Science and History of Jacksonville, a children's interactive museum. The Timucuan Ecological and Historic Preserve covers around 46,000 acres (18,630 ha) within the city, and offers a look into the lives of the Timucuan Indians, who were the original inhabitants of Central and North Florida.

Jacksonville has an abundance of parks and community centers and an impressive zoo. Other activities include fishing, swimming,

The crystal-clear water at Juniper Spring Landing draws swimmers to the area.

Pedro de Aviles invaded Fort Matanzas in 1565.

sailing, horseback riding, golfing, cruising the river on the *Annabelle Lee*, and watching a game of baseball at the Alltel Municipal Stadium in the huge sports center. Camping with hookups and a sump station is available at the Little Talbot Island State Park. Amelia Island is 45 minutes by car from Jacksonville. It is a barrier island that offers 13 miles (21 km) of beaches, two luxury golf courses and tennis resorts, a quaint Victorian town—Fernandina Beach— and plenty of moderately priced lodging is available.

Conveniently, Jacksonville has its own International Airport.
Map ref: page 571 M5

JUNIPER SPRING LANDING

Juniper Spring is in the heart of the 430,000-acre (174,150-km) Ocala National Forest in Florida's northern interior.

An estimated 20 million gallons (76 million l) of crystal clear water bubble out of these natural springs. An old wheel-powered stone mill sits at the edge of the springs. The park offers a spring-fed cement swimming pool surrounded by a sandy "beach." Facilities include picnic areas, restrooms, showers, canoe rentals, and snack bars. There are 79 campsites—60 offer recreational vehicle access but no hookups—and the fees are modest.

Cars are recommended to get around the forest. Ocala, Daytona Beach, and Orlando each offer air services into the region. Orlando is the largest airport, but is the furthest away.

KEY LARGO

This is the longest, largest, and the most developed of the Florida Keys. It is approximately 2 miles (3 km) by 30 miles (48 km), and is connected to the mainland by the Overseas Highway. Key Largo is the self-proclaimed fish and diving capital of America and it is as popular with South Floridians as it is with the rest of the world. It has a population of 12,200. Tourism and fishing support the local economy.

For such a highly developed tourist spot, the area hosts several tributes to nature. John Pennekamp Coral Reef State Park, a huge nautical park named for former *Miami Herald* editor and conservationist, is considered the Keys' premier natural attraction.

This sanctuary is the nation's first underwater preserve and lies just off the east coast of Key Largo. It extends 3 miles (5 km) out into the Atlantic Ocean and, with Key Largo's portion of the Florida Keys National Marine Sanctuary, encompasses a spectacular, undersea coral reef garden. The park offers glass-bottom boat and snorkeling tours, certified scuba instruction, as well as motorboat and canoe rentals, nature trails, and camping. Other nature-oriented attractions include the Crocodile Lakes National Wildlife Refuge, the Florida Keys Wild Bird Rehabilitation Center, and the Key Largo Hammocks State Botanical Site. Cannon Beach and Far Beach are both popular snorkeling sites, and Wild Tamarind and Mangrove Trails offer a close-up look at local flora. The Maritime Museum of the Florida Keys offers exhibits of rare artifacts and treasures recovered from various sunken Spanish galleons.

One of the most unusual, as well as one of the most expensive, hotels in the world, sits on pillars on the ocean floor, and accommodates up to six in its one bedroom suite. It is popular with divers, and delivers room service and whatever else you may require in waterproof containers.

Buses run between Miami International Airport and Key Largo.
Map ref: page 557 F9

KEY WEST

Key West (population 26,400) is the southernmost city on mainland United States, the oldest city in South Florida, and the last of the inhabited Keys in the chain. It is connected to the mainland by the Overseas Highway.

Bahamians, Cubans, British, New Englanders, and Southerners followed the original visits by Calusa Indians and, later, Spaniards. In the 1800s, the city thrived as a commercial port and center for fishing, cigar manufacture, and sponge making. Cubans named the island "Stella Maris," or "Star of the Sea," and came here in droves to escape oppressive Spanish Colonial rule. The economy was lively and the island bustling until the early twentieth century when it went bankrupt. The opening of the Overseas Highway and a train route brought the city back to life. Tourism, commercial fishing, a Junior College, and US Navy and Coast Guard installations support the economy. The area also has a thriving artist's colony.

An angler casts a net into the waters of Key Largo, in search of the elusive bonefish.

Bird expert and artist John J. Audobon lived here in the frontier days and many of his original engravings are on display at the former home of Sea Captain John Geiger, now known as the Audubon House and Tropical Gardens. This well-preserved nineteenth-century house is furnished with eighteenth- and nineteenth-century furnishings, historical photos, and a lush garden.

The East Martello Museum and Gallery, housed in a fort built in 1861, offers a look into the history of the Keys. The Ernest Hemingway Home and Museum is one of the most popular attractions. The prolific writer purchased this Spanish Colonial home in 1931 and wrote many of his best works here. The Key West Aquarium offers displays of dozens of varieties of fish and crustaceans, and a touch tank for children includes sea cucumbers, sea anemones, horseshoe crabs, sea urchins, and conchs.

The Sunset Celebration on Mallory Pier occurs every evening from two hours before, to two hours after sunset. Acrobats, magicians, jugglers, and sword swallowers entertain the crowds. Fishing, diving, and sunbathing at Smathers, Higgs, or Fort Zachary Beach are popular recreational activities.

Lodging and dining options are plentiful. Nearby Dry Tortugas National Park is a popular day trip. Just west is the Key West National Wildlife Refuge, encompassing 2,019 acres (818 ha) of mangroves in the Marquesas Keys.

Key West International Airport offers limited services. Bus services are available between Miami and Key Largo. Cars are useful for getting to and from Key West but once

Citrus fruit is one of the mainstays of Lakeland's economy.

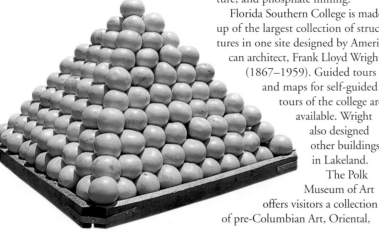

The busy port of Miami receives cargo and fishing vessels, as well as cruise liners.

you are there you may prefer to hire a moped or bicycle to more easily get around the congested streets.
Map ref: page 557 C10

LAKELAND

Lakeland (population 74,700) is in Florida's highland region between Tampa, on the Gulf of Mexico, and Orlando to the east. It was settled in the 1860s and is named for the 13 lakes within its city limits. Citrus groves are a common sight and citrus packaging and processing supports the local economy along with tourism, other agriculture, and phosphate mining.

Florida Southern College is made up of the largest collection of structures in one site designed by American architect, Frank Lloyd Wright (1867–1959). Guided tours and maps for self-guided tours of the college are available. Wright also designed other buildings in Lakeland. The Polk Museum of Art offers visitors a collection of pre-Columbian Art, Oriental,

and decorative art. The Orange Cup Regatta, a hydroplane race, is held the first weekend each April.

The closest airport to Lakeland is at Winter Haven, but Tampa International Airport is only about 30 miles (48 km) east on I-4.
Map ref: page 557 C2

MELBOURNE

This city is located on the Indian River, a lagoon, and the Atlantic Ocean in central Florida and is approximately 55 miles (88 km) southeast of Orlando on the I-95. It has a population of 70,100.

Melbourne was settled in the 1860s and was named for Melbourne, Australia. High-tech industries, aerospace equipment, as well as citrus processing support the economy as well as tourism dollars from its popular beach resort.

Melbourne's most popular attraction is the Brevard Art Center and Museum. It is set on beautifully landscaped grounds overlooking the Intracoastal Waterway and offers displays of modern art, primitive African works, and pre-Columbian art as well as hosting touring art collections from around the nation.

The Florida Institute of Technology and its Florida Tech Botanical Garden, with rare and exotic palms, is a popular attraction. Long Point and Wickham Parks offer, between them, more than 600 acres (243 ha) of parkland and lakes, with fishing, camping, and a free Archery Range (this is at Wickham). Fishing is a prime activity and is allowed from the causeways and in the rivers, Lake Washington, and the Atlantic. Boating, sailing, windsurfing, jet skiing, and water-skiing are also popular activities.

Buses and a small airport serve Melbourne. Larger facilities are available in Orlando.
Map ref: page 557 F2

MIAMI

Miami is in the southeastern corner of Florida on the Atlantic Coast. It is the southern anchor of the Gold Coast area and the last major city on Florida's Turnpike. The population of 371,000 includes a large concentration of Hispanics, Cubans, and, since the 1970s, Haitians; the city has a Little Havana and Little Haiti. In little Havana Spanish is more common than English, and street signs are in Spanish and English. Salsa music and the aroma of cigars fill the air, and affordable bistros line the sidewalks. With its warm, dry winters and generally mild climate, Miami grew rapidly as a resort area. An increasingly diversified economy today is based on tourism, international banking, and finance (especially with connections to Latin America), manufacturing, fishing and, recently, information technology.

There are many museums, art galleries, and theaters; other attractions include the elaborate

Italian Renaissance-style Vizcaya Museum and the Seaquarium on Virginia Key where visitors can swim with dolphins and watch them perform; there are also whales and sea lions in this 35-acre (14-ha) oceanarium.

South Miami has the Parrot Jungle and gardens, 18 acres (7 ha) of performing birds, including roller-skating cockatoos, jungle trains, an Everglades exhibit, tortoises, as well as an albino alligator.

The climate and coastline allow a wide variety of athletic activities from golf to roller blading to swimming and diving. Parks, beaches, and recreation areas line the coast—including Miami Beach.

Miami is the hub of the cruise industry; the port of Miami is always busy with both passenger and cargo ships.

Miami International Airport is one of the largest in the nation with more than 80 commercial airlines.
Map ref: page 557 G7

MIAMI BEACH

Miami Beach (population 95,800) is on an island in southeastern Florida. The island is 10 miles (16 km) long by 1–3 miles (2–5 km) wide and sits between Biscayne Bay and the Atlantic Ocean, just across from the city of Miami. Causeways connect it to the mainland.

The long, narrow island and adjacent islets were settled in 1870 and, at that time, the area was a swampland. In 1907, businessman John Collins dredged sand from the bay and transformed it into solid ground. Dredging created a yacht basin and islets. He built the longest wooden bridge of that time and starting selling plots of land. During the boom of the 1920s, many Art Deco structures were built. Today in South Miami Beach over 800 Art Deco buildings make up the Art Deco Historic District. Year-round tourism aided by a large convention center drives the local economy.

South Miami Beach is America's Riviera, and is known as "SoBe." Packed into these 40 blocks are refurbished, streamlined, and modern hotels and apartment complexes, shops, restaurants, and the area's best beaches and nightclubs. No other area in the nation is such a melting pot of cultures. A typical evening here is to enjoy a leisurely dinner followed by club hopping until dawn. Models and movie stars come here for the atmosphere, many celebrities own homes in the area, and it has a thriving gay community.

Ocean Drive, Collins Avenue, and Washington Avenue from 6th to 23rd Streets are the heart of the Art Deco Historic District. In 1979 the area was granted a listing on the National Register of Historic Places. The most convenient way to explore this district is on foot.

Ocala National Forest has a number of popular campgrounds, hiking trails, and swimming holes.

Miami Beach attractions include beaches, parks, swimming pools, museums, theaters, golf courses, and recreation areas such as the North Shore Recreation Area, a 40-acre (16-ha) sand-dune preserve.
Map ref: page 557 G7

OCALA

Ocala (population 45,000) is in Florida's central highlands about 35 miles (56 km) south of Gainesville on the I-75. It was settled in 1827, and its mineral springs were believed to be "fountains of youth." It is a major citrus-processing and shipping center.

Ocala has over 500 thoroughbred horse ranches; many of these welcome visitors. Racehorses thrive in this environment of sunshine and mineral spring water—Ocala was the birthplace of Needles, who won the 1956 Kentucky Derby.

The Appleton Museum of Art has pre-Columbian, African, Oriental, and European art spanning 5,000 years of culture. This is the collection of Chicago industrialist and local thoroughbred trainer Arthur Appleton. The Historic District has over 200 homes in the Gothic, colonial Italianate, and Queen Anne Revival styles.

Silver Springs nature park—a 350-acre (142-ha) national landmark—is the site of the largest limestone artesian spring formation in the world. Silver Spring is believed to be over 100,000 years old and its output is an average of 800 million gallons (3,000 million l) of water per day. It is 65 feet (20 m) by 12 feet (4 m). Glass-bottom boats, jungle cruises, jeep safari trams, and the World of Bears exhibit are popular.

The Ocala National Forest has 430,000 acres (174,150 ha) of preserved wilderness with gurgling springs including Salt Springs, Juniper Spring, and Fern Hammock.

Lodging and dining options are limited here. Small airports serve the region, and Orlando International Airport is nearby.
Map ref: page 571 L8

The bright sunshine and fine, white sand of Miami Beach in southeastern Florida attract vacationers from all over the United States.

With 50 acres (20 ha) of beautiful grounds, the Harry P. Leu Gardens in Orlando is a popular location for wedding ceremonies.

ORLANDO

Orlando (population 187,000) is a citrus-growing region in central Florida—at the heart of Florida's lake district—50 miles (80 km) from Cape Canaveral. Orlando's economy relies on theme parks, a massive convention center, and the manufacture of aerospace equipment and electronic components.

The three major theme parks are Walt Disney World, Sea World, and Universal Studios Florida. Walt Disney World is made up of Magic Kingdom, Animal Kingdom, EPCOT (Experimental Prototype Community of Tomorrow), Disney

The Disney–MGM Studios at Walt Disney World, Orlando.

MGM Studios, golf courses, water parks, campground facilities, a 7,500-acre (3,038-ha) conservation/wilderness area, hotels, restaurants, and nightclubs, and covers around 28,000 acres (13,340 ha). Sea World is a 150-acre (61-ha) marine park, and Universal Studios Florida is a 444-acre (180-ha) lot featuring sound stages, street sets, shows, rides, and an entertainment complex with a nightclub. Universal opened a second park in 1999, the 110-acre (45-ha) Islands of Adventure amusement park.

Parks, lakes, and rivers throughout the area offer plenty of outdoor activities, as well as sporting venues,

museums, and cultural activities. Every April the Orlando Shakespeare Festival takes place.

Avoid peak commuting hours when possible and make arrangements in advance for theme parks and lodging for better deals. Walt Disney World offers a Fastpass program, devised to reduce the time spent standing in line.

Nearby Kissimee has motels for those on a budget. Orlando International Airport is a major international hub. Trains and buses serve the area, however, cars are recommended for exploring this region.
Map ref: page 571 M9

PALM BEACH

This glitzy town in southeastern Florida—65 miles (105 km) north of Miami—sits on the northern

tip of a 14-mile (23-km) long barrier island. It is 1 mile (2 km) at its widest point, and sits between a lagoon (Lake Worth) and the Atlantic Ocean. The climate is subtropical, and the area has long attracted a wealthy crowd to its luxurious resort life. Palm Beach was settled in 1861. Coconuts from a shipwreck in 1878 floated ashore and took root, creating the famous tree-lined beach that gave the town its name. In 1890, Henry Flagler, developer of the Florida East Coast Railroad, built the Royal Poinciana Hotel and laid out the community as a resort. Palm Beach is home to 10,300 people.

The Kennedys, Rockefellers, Pulitzers, and Trumps are among the elite crowd that spends their winters here. Shopping on Worth Avenue is a major pastime. The island also has the unique honor of having all three of the Florida's AAA Five-Diamond rated resorts. Spas and restaurants are above average. Golf, tennis, scuba diving, sailing, jet skiing, water skiing, parasailing, kayaking, cycling, and bird watching are popular outdoor activities.

Henry Morrison Flagler Museum is a 55-room marble palace Flagler called home. It is a monument to the Gilded Age, the industrialization of America, and its accompanying newly created wealth, in the late 1800s after the Civil War. Porcelains, painting, silver, glass, dolls, and Flagler's private railroad car are on display. There are some museums of interest as well, such as the Norton Museum of Art in West Palm Beach that hosts American, French, and Chinese galleries, and the Hibel Museum of Art, which is a nonprofit museum dedicated solely to the works of Edna Hibel. Palm Beach also has many amusement parks and activities for children.

Palm Beach International Airport and trains serve the area. Cars are recommended, although some attractions are accessible by public transportation.
Map ref: page 557 G5

The solemn and dignified St Augustine National Cemetery contains the graves of more than 2,500 American soldiers who died in battle since the early 1800s.

PANAMA CITY

Situated in northwest Florida's Pan-handle, Panama City (population 37,100) is a deepwater port on St Andrew Bay, which was settled during the Revolutionary War. In 1888 founders named it in the hopes of attracting traffic from the Panama Canal. Tourism, fishing, the manufacture of paper and chemicals, an Air Force Base, and a US Navy Coastal Systems Center support the economy.

The Junior Museum of Bay County offers science and nature exhibits. Deer Point Dam offers fresh and saltwater fishing and a public boat ramp—Panama City offers some of the best fishing in the state. Nearby Panama City Beach attracts retirees and vacationers from the Deep South. Panama City Beach attractions include 23 miles (37 km) of white sand and turquoise water plus amusement parks and museums.

Shell Island is state owned and has 7 miles (11 km) of undeveloped beach. Glass-bottom boats offer shelling tours to Shell Island. Saint Andrews State Recreation Center is a 1,063-acre (431-ha)

wilderness preserve of sand dunes and white sand beaches. Jetties and boat ramps, a nature trail, and overnight camping facilities are available. Golf, scuba diving, and snorkeling are all popular activities here.

Nearby Apalachicola is a wilderness area which has long beaches, bays, and estuaries—it is considered to be the oyster capital of the state.

Commuter flights serve Panama City/Bay County International Airport. Trains serve Chipley, 45 miles (72 km) to the north.
Map ref: page 570 D5

PENSACOLA

Pensacola (population 62,100) is the last outpost on Florida's Pan-handle and 10 miles (16 km) east of the Alabama border. It rivals St Augustine as Florida's oldest town. Pensacola Bay is the largest land-locked deepwater harbor in the state. Over its colorful history, Native Americans, Spanish, French, British, and Americans struggled back and forth to control this harbor. Pensacola is a commercial, manufacturing, and military center; it is also the home to the Pensacola Naval Air Station.

Attractions include the Historic Pensacola Village, the Civil War Soldiers Museum, and the Natural Museum of Naval Aviation. The downtown Palafox Historic District is the site of the Pensacola Museum of Art and Pensacola Historical Museum. This area recalls life from an earlier era with buildings housed in original Spanish Renaissance and Mediterranean structures. North Hill Preservation District is listed in the National Register of Historic Places. It includes hundreds of architecturally significant homes covering 50 blocks north of the Palafox Historic District.

Gulf Islands National Seashore is a 1,742-acre (706-ha) wildlife preserve of sand dunes and white sand beaches. It provides sanctuary for over 280 species of birds. There is swimming, fishing, boating, scuba diving, nature trails, and camping, and includes Fort Barrancas and Fort Pickens. Nearby Milton is known as the "canoe capital of Florida," and Blackwater State Park is another popular day trip.

Lodging and dining options are plentiful. Pensacola Regional Airport and trains service the area.
Map ref: page 570 A5

ST AUGUSTINE

America's first city, St Augustine is 39 miles (63 km) south of Jacksonville. It is an important port, commercial, and distribution center for the surrounding agricultural region, and a popular year-round resort.

This city of 14,100 is the oldest permanent European settlement in the nation. In 1565 Spanish explorer Pedro Menendez de Aviles established St Augustine and destroyed the French Huguenot community. Later, railroad magnate Henry Flagler established the headquarters for his Florida East Coast Railroad.

Attractions include the Cathedral of St Augustine, the Castillo de San Marcos National Monument, Fort Matanzas National Monument, and the National Cemetery. The Fountain of Youth is a 21-acre (9-ha) tropical park and tribute to the Spanish explorer Ponce de León. Anastasia State Recreation Area offers 1,722 acres (397 ha) of sand dunes and coastal scrub, with swimming, fishing, and camping.

St Augustine is serviced by Daytona International or Jacksonville International Airports.
Map ref: page 571 M6

ST PETERSBURG

St Petersburg is 20 miles (32 km) southwest of Tampa on US-92 and covers the Pinellas Peninsula between Tampa Bay and the Gulf of Mexico and a string of barrier islands on the Gulf. Causeways link the islands, and bridges connect to Tampa and Bradenton across Tampa Bay. With a population of 239,000, St Petersburg is Florida's fourth-largest city, and it is second only to Miami in its popularity with winter vacationers and retirees. The community was first settled in 1834, and the railway arrived in the 1880s; a railroad official named the city after his childhood home in Russia. Rapid growth occurred during the land boom of the 1920s and, in the 1950s, the population doubled as retirees began to move here in droves.

The downtown area along the bay is one of Florida's most pleasant spots. There is a waterfront promenade, a five-story inverted pyramid-shaped pier complete with shops, restaurants, an aquarium, an observation deck, as well as the St Petersburg Museum of History.

The Pinellas Trail, along an abandoned railroad bed, is popular with roller bladers, cyclists, and hikers. From St Petersburg Beach along Gulf Boulevard are the Holiday Isles of Treasure Island, Madeira Beach, Indian Shores, Belleair Beach, and Clearwater Beach. The Suncoast Seabird Sanctuary on Indian Shores has native cormorant, white heron, brown pelican, and snowy egret. South of St Petersburg Beach, at the mouth of Tampa Bay, is Fort

The elegantly restored Old Capitol building in Florida's capital city, Tallahassee.

de Soto Park, a 900-acre (365-ha) flora and fauna sanctuary covering five connected islets.

St Petersburg Beach area is fully developed and very crowded in winter months. Make your plans well in advance. The lodging and dining options are plentiful here.

St Petersburg Clearwater International and Tampa International Airports, and trains serve the area.
Map ref: page 557 A2

SARASOTA

Overlooking Sarasota Bay, this city in west-central Florida, with a population of 52,500, is a popular resort and cultural, residential, and commercial center. From 1927 through the 1960s, Sarasota served as the winter base for the Ringling Brothers and Barnum and Bailey Circus. John Ringling built the causeway to St Armands and Lido Keys.

Of the 35 miles (56 km) of beaches, Siesta Key Public Beach, Turtle Beach, and North Lido Beach are three of the most popular. The Sarasota Polo Club offers weekly polo matches during winter. The Ringling Museum of Art includes John Ringling's residence, "Ca'd'zan," a 32-room Venetian-Gothic mansion (which was built to resemble the Doge's Palace in Venice), the Art Gallery, and Circus Galleries.

Nearby Myakka River State Park is a 35,000-acre (14,175-ha) wildlife area and breeding ground with hundreds of species of birds and plants. It also has alligators, deer, and raccoons. Lodging and dining options are available at all price levels.

Sarasota Bradenton International Airport serves the area. However, fares are less expensive into Tampa International Airport.
Map ref: page 557 B3

TALLAHASSEE

The state capital, Tallahassee (population 140,100) is more dependent on agriculture, science, and education than on tourism. Located midway between Pensacola to the west and St Augustine to the east, the area has more of a feeling of the Deep South than

a beach resort. Georgia is just 20 miles (32 km) north of the city. The name "Tallahassee" is thought to be an Apalachee term for "old town" or "abandoned fields."

Tallahassee is the seat of Florida State University (since 1851). The University supports an extensive array of ongoing archeological sites and projects. Mission San Luis de Apalachee, set up in 1656, is the most impressive of these.

The New Capitol Building, a skyscraper, is a stark backdrop for the restored Old Capitol, built in 1845. Historic districts including Adams Street Commons and the Park Avenue and Calhoun Street areas are popular, as are many museums. The Black Archives Research Center and Museum is one of the world's most extensive collections of African–American artifacts and history archives.

Outdoor enthusiasts enjoy the Alfred B. Maclay State Gardens, Natural Bridge State Historic Site, San Marcos de Apalache State Historic Site, Edward Bell Wakulla Springs State Park, and the Saint Marks National Wildlife Refuge.

Quite near to Apalachicola National Forest is a 557,000-acre (225,585-ha) preserve with pine and hardwood forests, swamps, rivers, streams, springs, and sinkholes. Camping, canoeing, bird watching, hunting, and hiking are popular in these parks. Dining and lodging options are available here, though they are more limited as you enter the wilderness areas.

Tallahassee Regional Airport offers limited service and it is serviced by trains. Cars are convenient for exploring the area, though a free Old Town Trolley is the best way to see historic downtown.
Map ref: page 570 F5

TAMPA

This city on the Gulf coast is the state's second-largest metropolitan area and is a major industrial, commercial, financial, and cultural center. Tampa (population 280,500) is at the mouth of the Hillsborough River at the head of Tampa Bay. The downtown area is the central business district, and the southern part of the city sits on a peninsula with Old Tampa Bay to the west and Hillsborough Bay to the east. The Port of Tampa is one of the nation's busiest seaports. It is the

Green iguana (Iguana iguana), an introduced species to Florida, pictured at Lowry Park Zoo, Tampa.

Roller blading along one of the boulevards just outside the campus of the University of Tampa. The city's name came from "tampa," a Calusa word meaning lightning.

closest deepwater port to the Panama Canal and is a popular stop for cruise lines. Tampa is also home to the MacDill Air Force Base, headquarters of US Central Command.

Spanish explorer Panfilo de Narvaez arrived here in 1528 and Hernando de Soto in 1539. By 1823 white settlers had established a plantation. In 1883, the discovery of phosphates, used to make fertilizer, gave the economy a boost and in 1884 Henry Plant, a Georgian industrialist, brought the railroad here. In 1886, Cuban tobacco processor, Vincente Ybor, brought cigar-making to the city of Tampa.

The climate here is humid subtropical, and the area records more days of thunderstorms than any other location in the nation. The Calusa word for lightning, "tampa," gave the city its name.

Busch Gardens brings more tourists here than any other attraction. It has one of the top-ranked zoos in the country containing several thousand animals, and is a massive amusement park—it was built before Walt Disney World. Adventure Island is a 25-acre (10-ha) outdoor water park. The Florida Aquarium and Lowry Park, with a zoo and a section of fairy tale and nursery rhyme character statues, are also

popular family attractions. MOSI Science Center (Museum of Science and Industry), Henry B. Plant Museum, Tampa Museum of Art, and Tampa History Center are popular attractions, and the Tampa Bay Performing Arts Center offers theater and concerts performances.

Ybor City, a colorful historic district and destination, was named after Vincente Ybor, the Cuban cigar maker. As in Havana, in Tampa there are cigar rollers to be seen everywhere. The Ybor City Brewing Company offers microbrews, and the district comes alive at night with jazz and blues music. Hyde Park is a popular tourist destination for shopping and dining. Fishing, golf, and tennis are popular and Bayshore Boulevard attracts joggers, walkers, cyclists, and roller bladers to its 7-mile (11-km) promenade. Day trips to St Petersburg are also popular.

The city is serviced by Tampa International Airport, and trains.
Map ref: page 570 B2

TARPON SPRINGS

This city (population 19,800) is north of St Petersburg on the Gulf of Mexico. It is a major sponge-fishing center and a resort. It is

situated between the Gulf to the west, Lake Tarpon to the east, and the Anclote River bayous to the north. It was founded in 1886 and named for the abundant local game fish, tarpon. Many Greeks from the Dodecanese Islands settled here in the 1890s to follow the tradition of sponge diving. The area is known as Florida's "Little Greece."

Attractions include the Downtown Historic District, the Sponge Docks, Spongeorama, the Coral Sea Aquarium, St Nicolas Greek Orthodox Church, the Unitarian Universalist Church, Inness Paintings, and Noell's Ark Chimpanzee Farm.

In Sponge Docks, fishing and sightseeing boats moor along the docks and riverside boardwalk, which are as popular with visitors as the shops and restaurants along the adjacent Dodecanese Boulevard. Boating, fishing, swimming, hiking, and diving are popular recreational activities, and Tampa and St Petersburg are close enough to visit in a day. The lodging and dining options are limited here.

The nearests airports to service the area are Tampa International and St Petersburg Clearwater International Airports.
Map ref: page 557 A1

Sponge-fishing boat moored in the harbor, Tarpon Springs.

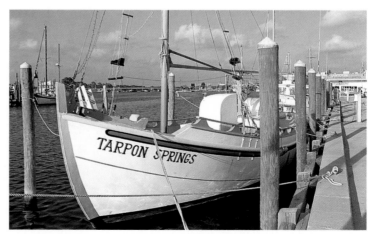

Everglades National Park

America's largest subtropical wilderness is located on the southern tip of Florida's peninsula in the vast Everglades. The Everglades cover 5,000 square miles (12,950 sq km) of freshwater marsh, swamp, savanna, and virgin forest. The northern part is a prairie covered by shallow water and by sawgrass, which can grow to 12 feet (4 m). Toward the south coast the Everglades become marshes and mangrove swamps.

Within this wilderness an area has been set aside as the Everglades National Park. This unique park has been designated a World Heritage Site, an International Biosphere Reserve, and a Wetland of International Significance.

During the early 1900s, parts of the Everglades were drained for farming land, and the area around Miami grew rapidly. Canals from Lake Okeechobee supplied water to the surrounding area. The channeling of the Kissimme River (the main supply of water to Lake Okeechobee) in the 1960s, and the huge growth of southern Florida since the 1970s has put considerable strain on the Everglades. The reduction of water to the Everglades, coupled with the use of harmful agricultural chemicals, greatly affected the plant and animal life of this extraordinary place. Water became polluted with fertilizer run-off, and wildlife and fish populations subsequently dwindled.

In 1947, 15 percent of the Everglades preserve was granted National Park status. In 1996 the federal government passed a bill to restore natural water flow and to further protect the environment of the park.

The Everglades National Park, the principal National Park in Florida, is at the south end of the Everglades, and protects around 1,507,850 acres

The turkey buzzard, or turkey vulture (Cathartes aurea), is often to be found roosting on the branches of trees growing in Everglades National Park.

Red mangroves (Rhizophora mangle), with their distinctive, stilt-like roots, line the winding channels and rivers in the park, and are home to a variety of bird life, which nests among the trees.

(610,679 ha) of wetlands. This area extends from Everglades City, in the northeast near the Gulf of Mexico and encompassing many of the Ten Thousand Islands, to near Fiesta Key in the Florida Keys and includes Cape Sable, the southernmost point on the United States mainland.

The character of the Everglades is determined by many factors. One of them is climate. Key West lies just about 1 degree from the Tropic of Cancer, which marks the beginning of the tropics. Thus the climate here has two, not four distinct seasons. From May to November the area is warm and wet, typically with short, heavy rain showers and the occasional hurricane. Hurricanes come up from the tropics, gaining power from the warm, moist, oceanic air. Though they can be destructive, their torrential rains replenish the water supply. Flooding from the ocean opens new channels and brings wildlife in from the Caribbean. From December to April the climate is dry and cool. Occasionally, a northern cold front makes its way this far south and causes frost. Trade winds from the southeast moderate the climate and, along with hurricanes, bring seeds from the West Indies.

The marsh lies in a large limestone basin formed by centuries of surplus water from Lake Okeechobee. Limestone is the only form of rock found here. Sinkholes, or natural depressions in the limestone, fill with water and act as reservoirs. These reservoirs provide water for Miami and nearby towns and some is piped to Key West, which has no fresh water of its own.

The Everglades is covered with dense vegetation and is referred to as "River of Grass," or "Pa-hay-okee" in Native American. Freshwater and saltwater areas teem with wildlife including alligators, crocodiles, turtles, manatees, frogs, snakes, aquatic weed, a lily-covered marsh, sea trout, tarpons, largemouth bass, garfish, panfish, mangrove snapper, dolphins, and sharks. Open sawgrass prairies, six species of palm, bay trees, gumbo-limbo trees, live oak, pine, stands of dwarf cypress, and mangrove thickets provide habitat for black bears, bobcats, cougars, and deer. Bird species finding sanctuary here include the heron, kingfisher, black vulture, pelican, ibis, snowy egret, wild turkey, Anhinga, white-banded teal, brown mallard duck, and shorebirds such as limpkins and the roseate spoonbill.

Though the Everglades and Keys may have been inhabited for thousands of years, records go back only about 3,000 years. When the Spanish explorers arrived, they found the Calusa Indians. This powerful tribe controlled the region south of Tampa, including the Keys and the Everglades, and the area along the Atlantic coast as far north as Cape Canaveral. The Calusa lived in small bands of 20 to 30, hunting, fishing, and gathering wild plants. They built open canoes and traveled as far as Cuba. When the first

Spanish vessels ran aground in the keys in the early sixteenth century, Calusa warriors attacked the crew and looted the ship. By 1567 the Spanish had established missions in Calusa territory and had allied with them against the French and British.

In the meantime, the British had allied with the Creek tribe, the Seminoles. The Seminoles pushed south and forced the Calusa into the heart of the Everglades. In 1763, when Spain ceded Florida to Great Britain, many Calusas moved to Havana, Cuba, and they eventually disappeared from the area.

By 1813, the Seminoles had established around 100 villages across the state and their population reached 5,000. They were eventually displaced and many were moved to Indian Territory (Oklahoma) and the rest—only about 300—took refuge in the swamps of the Everglades. They adapted to the wet wilderness, building "chickees" (adaptable stilt houses) as shelters, fishing, and building canoes. In the late nineteenth century they bartered for cotton cloth and sewing machines and created the bright, multi-colored Seminole costume that is still worn today. The population increased slowly, and had reached 1,000 by the mid-twentieth century. In 1962 the Seminoles resumed official relations with the United States. Today, about 2,000 Seminoles live in two separate groups on reservations. Three-quarters live near Alligator Alley, on Hwy 84, halfway between Fort Lauderdale and Naples. A smaller tribe, the Miccosukees, live in villages along the Tamiami Trail, or Hwy 41. These original inhabitants are now recognized as a vital component of the wilderness preserve and community.

Everglades National Park Headquarters is in Homestead. The Ernest F. Coe Visitor Center is at the Homestead entrance. Three miles (5 km) down the road is the Royal Palm Visitor Center and Nature Museum. The Flamingo Lodge Resort, with its Marina and Outpost, is the only option for in-park lodging, equipment rentals, and tours of the park.

The most popular activities are hiking and cycling, as well as camping, boating (including houseboating), bird watching, and guided tours in airboats, motorboats, or trams. There are five canoe trails, including Wilderness Waterway, a 100-mile (160-km) trail from Everglade City to Flamingo.

Do not interact with the wildlife, and take extra precautions when traveling through areas with alligators. Sunscreen and mosquito repellent are essential. The best time to visit Everglades National Park is from November to May. Homestead or Miami are good bases for exploring the park. Nearby attractions include the Miccosukee Indian Village, Big Cypress National Preserve, the Fakahatchee Strand State Preserve, and the Collier Seminole State Park.

The park is 35 miles (56 km) southwest of Miami, which is serviced by Miami International Airport, as well as buses and trains. From that point onward a car is essential. There are four entrances; the main entrance is in Homestead, south of Miami. The Shark Valley entrance is on the Tamiami Trail, Hwy 41, on the park's northern border and is west of Miami. The Chekika gate is also on the Tamiami Trail, on the way to Shark Valley. There is a modest entrance fee per car for a seven-day permit (this is the only option). There is a small fee for pedestrians and cyclists at Shark Valley.

The slough is the deep, fast-flowing center of the marshy river, which is covered in saw-grass (Cladium jamaicense), and other low-lying plants. Trees such as gumbo-limbo trees (Bursera simaruba) and live oaks (Quercus virginiana) grow on the small islets that interrupt the river's passage.

The gopher tortoise (Gopherus polyphemus) lives in the southwestern section of the park, Cape Sable, in branching burrows up to 30 feet (9 m) long.

GEORGIA

Georgia's popular image is one that is largely inseparable from the idealized and romantic pastoral scenes of cotton plantations and the Civil War. It brings to mind the images conjured up by that most famous of films, *Gone With the Wind*, which was, after all, written by Georgia's Margaret Mitchell. However, after the decline of the cotton industry other industries grew after the Civil War.

Georgia today is now the South's leading

The antebellum homes of Georgia conjure images of southern belles and their gentlemen sipping mint juleps on their porches in summer.

manufacturer and can perhaps be more aptly described as a modern state with a bit of pace, a little urban sophistication, industrial muscle, economic might, and cultural and social diversity. Present-day Atlanta contains 40 percent of the state's total population of over 8 million people. In fact, 63 percent of Georgians now live in urban areas, and it has been over 50 years since the majority worked on the land, although large sections of the state are still devoted to agriculture.

Nonetheless, it is Georgia's fascinating past that is one of the major attractions for the modern visitor. Pre-Colombian archeological sites, such as Ocmulgee; colonial stockades like Fort Frederica; former plantations; the extraordinary nineteenth-century architecture and historic atmosphere of a city such as Savannah; Civil War sites, like Andersonville and Chickamauga; places associated with the civil rights movement, such as Atlanta; and many fine museums are found throughout the state.

Georgia also boasts a great many natural attractions, and the state exhibits quite a diversity in its topography. These distinctive differences are encapsulated in some outstanding places such as Chattahoochee National Forest. This state also boats the Appalachian Mountains in the north and the rolling hills in central piedmont. Okefenokee Swamp is located in the southeast, and on the coast there are the beautiful Golden Isles of the eastern seaboard.

State motto Wisdom, Justice, and Moderation
State flag Adopted 2001
Capital Atlanta
Population 8,186,453
Total area (land and water) 58,977 square miles (152,750 sq km)
Land area 57,919 square miles (150,010 sq km)
Georgia is the 21st-largest state in size
Origin of name Named for King George II of England
Nicknames The Peach State, The Empire State of the South
Abbreviations GA (postal), Ga.
State bird Brown thrasher
State flower Cherokee rose
State tree Live oak
Entered the Union January 2, 1788 as the fourth state

Places in GEORGIA

ALBANY

Albany is 150 miles (241 km) south of Atlanta in southwest Georgia. Birthplace of Ray Charles (who sang the famous rendition of the song "Georgia on My Mind"), its population is 78,591. The Creek tribe first occupied the area but conflict in the early nineteenth century ended in their massacre and deportation from the area. Albany was founded in 1836 at the navigable head of the Flint River. Cotton plantations soon emerged, with the town's fortunes boosted by steamboat shipments from 1837. By 1900, it was a major rail center, stimulating local industry. Today, it serves as the principal center of southwest Georgia.

Albany's Mt Zion Albany Civil Rights Movement Museum commemorates the important role played by southwest Georgia, and the African-American church in the Civil Rights Movement. It is in the old Mt Zion Church where Martin Luther King Jr preached in 1961. The Thronateeska Heritage Museum has three sections: the Science Discovery Center, the Wetherbee Planetarium, and the Heritage Center, which focuses on local and regional history. The main cultural attraction is the Albany Museum of Art, with the largest collection of traditional African art in the Southeast.

Of Albany's historic buildings, Smith House (1859–60), was the first brick home. It has Masonic symbols in its gardens and a self-contained waterworks. The first bridge across the river and the Bridge House were built in 1857, to the slave Horace King's design. St Teresa's is the oldest Catholic church in continuous use in Georgia. Built in 1859, it served as a hospital during the Civil War.

Lake Chehaw is located a little beyond the city limits. Boardwalks and walking/cycling trails traverse 100 acres (41 ha) of piney woods, providing glimpses of both native and exotic animals.

Albany has its own airport and sits at the intersection of US-19 and US-82.
Map ref: page 565 H10

The 13,000 Union soldiers who died in the Confederate prisoner-of-war camp are buried in Andersonville National Cemetery.

ANDERSONVILLE

Andersonville National Historic Site marks the spot of the Civil War's most notorious prisoner-of-war camp. During the war about 400,000 men were detained in 60 such camps. An inability or unwillingness to provide adequate care meant overcrowding, malnutrition, and disease. The problems were especially acute in the South due to shortages that prevented the Confederate government from maintaining its soldiers and citizens.

Overt abuse, sullied water, and poor sanitation compounded the problems at Andersonville. Up to 33,000 at a time were crammed into a log stockade of only 16 acres (6.5 ha). Although operating for just 14 months (1864–65), 45,000 soldiers were interned there. After the war the graves of 13,000 troops were uncovered. These graves are now part of the adjacent Andersonville National Cemetery, which is still in use today. Henry Wirz, the officer in charge, became the only Confederate soldier to be tried and executed for war crimes.

In establishing the Site, Congress declared that its purpose was "to provide an understanding of the overall prisoner-of-war story of the Civil War, interpret the role of prisoner of war camps in history, commemorate the sacrifice of Americans who lost their lives in such camps, and to preserve the monuments located within the site." Visitors can see restored portions of the stockade, earthworks, and remnants of escape tunnels. The National Prisoner of War Museum looks at the American prisoner-of-war experience from the Revolutionary War to Vietnam.

Andersonville now has a population of 280 people. It is located about an hour southwest of Macon (I-75 south to Route 49 and follow the signs). It is roughly equidistant from Columbus, to the northwest.
Map ref: page 565 H9

ATHENS

Athens is famous for the rock bands REM and the B-52s. In northern Georgia, this small, attractive city amid green hills is 56 miles (90 km) east of Atlanta. Essentially a college town, its 86,000 residents include the 30,000 students that attend University of Georgia. In 1785, it became the first state-chartered university in the United States.

The streets of Athens are home to a number of classic antebellum mansions. The oldest building (1820) houses the town's Welcome Center. It has information on self-guided tours of historic homes, the university, and downtown. It is also the departure point for a daily driving tour. Artsy downtown boasts plenty of book stores, bars, restaurants, clubs, outdoor cafés, quaint shops, and a lively music scene.

In the University's Performing and Visual Arts Complex is the excellent Georgia Museum of Art. The Founders Memorial Garden is also at the University. This fine State Botanical Garden is located 4 miles (6.4 km) south of the town center, by the Oconee River.

Athens has a few curiosities. One, a failed Civil War invention, the double-barrel cannon, is in front of the city hall. There is the Tree That Owns Itself, so named because a professor was so fond of its shade that he ensured the tree ownership of its land. Morton Theater (1910) was the first in the country to be owned by African-Americans.

Athens has an airport and is connected by bus with Savannah, Atlanta, Augusta, and Charleston.
Map ref: page 565 J4

ATLANTA

Atlanta is the state capital and its largest city. Two-thirds of its total population of 405,000 are African-American. A major trade, transportation, business, communication, and service center, it contains the headquarters of such giants as Coca-Cola, CNN, and BellSouth. A principal crossroads for air, road, and rail travel, it is the hub of a cosmopolitan cultural scene with museums, galleries, historic sites, performing arts events, and nightlife. It has one of the nation's highest economic growth rates.

Atlanta emerged in 1837 and was initially called, unimaginatively, Terminus. It blossomed and was given the more poetic name of Atlanta in 1845. It served as a major Confederate center during the Civil War. General Sherman had it virtually burned down. Quickly rebuilt, it became the state capital in 1868, and was Georgia's largest city by 1880. Atlanta continued to expand throughout the twentieth century, particularly with the arrival of war industries in the 1940s.

In the 1950s and 1960s, Atlanta became a center of the Civil Rights Movement under pastor Martin Luther King Jr. In the 1960s it gained a reputation as one of the most racially progressive cities in the South. Unusually for the Deep South, the public schools were peacefully integrated and, in 1973, Maynard Jackson became the first African-American Southern mayor.

Looking down Atlanta's Peachtree Street to the Bank of America.

Atlanta's Capitol building sits side-by-side with the Coca-Cola center—Coke was invented in Atlanta in 1886.

City walking tours reveal the oldest parts, which disappeared below street level as bridges and viaducts were built to raise traffic above the railway lines. This underground maze of brick streets, gas lighting, and storefronts, restored to their original appearance, is now incorporated into Underground Atlanta. Also in the downtown area are Centennial Olympic Park (site of the 1996 Olympics); the CNN Center (tours are regularly held); the State Capitol (1889), with its gold-leaf dome; the Atlanta Public Library (which houses *Gone With the Wind* memorabilia); and the High Museum of Art, Folk Art & Photography Galleries.

East of downtown's Five Points intersection is an area known as "Sweet Auburn," once the city's most distinguished African-American neighborhood. Several blocks of Auburn Avenue now incorporate the Martin Luther King Jr Historic Site, including his restored birthplace, the King Center for Non-Violent Social Change, his sepulchre (behind the Center) and the Historic Site Museum and Visitor Center. Also here is the Ebenezer Baptist Church where King, his father, and grandfather were all pastors and where King Jr delivered his first pulpit oration. Further west the APEX Museum showcases African-American history and culture. Northeast is the Jimmy Carter Library and Museum on 30 acres (12.2 ha) of gardens set on a hill.

Further south are the extravagant funerary monuments of Oakland Cemetery (where Margaret Mitchell, Bobby Jones, and five Southern generals are interred) and Grant Park, which incorporates both Zoo Atlanta and the Cyclorama, a rotating platform surrounded by a huge circular oil painting completed in 1886. Forty-two feet (12.8 m) high and 358 feet (109 m) around, it depicts the 1864 Battle of Atlanta.

West End is an African-American area and Atlanta's oldest neighborhood. Herndon Home is a beaux-arts mansion, erected in 1910 by African-American artisans for ex-slave Alonzo Herndon who became one of the country's first African-American millionaires. Further south is Wren's Nest, former home of Joel Chandler Harris (author of the Brer Rabbit stories), which is now a museum. Hammonds House Galleries displays African-American art in one of the oldest surviving buildings. The Fox Theater is an extravagant Art-Deco movie palace opened in 1929. Margaret Mitchell House and Museum is where Mitchell lived while writing *Gone With the Wind*. The Fernbank Science Center is the largest museum of natural history in the southeast, next to 65 acres (26 ha) of forest. North of Piedmont Park is the High Museum of Modern Art, a remarkable building housing a large collection of American, European, and African exhibits.

The Governor's Mansion and the outstanding Atlanta History Center are both in Buckhead. The center's 32 acres (13 ha) includes a museum, an 1840s farmhouse with outbuildings, and a gracious 1928 mansion set amid gardens, woodlands, and walking trails.

About 16 miles (26 km) east of downtown is the wooded parkland of Stone Mountain Park. It has a lake, a paddlewheel riverboat, a petting Zoo, a scenic railroad, the Antique Car and Treasure Museum, and a restored antebellum plantation with assistants in period costume. Walking trails and cable-car rides lead to the top of Stone Mountain, which is at 825 feet (252 m) and which has a 90- × 190-foot (27.5- × 58-m) bas-relief carving of Confederate war heroes Jefferson Davis, Robert E. Lee, and Stonewall Jackson.

Northeast of town is Lake Sidney Lanier, which has an aquatic park and campground complex. To its north is the charming town of Dahlonega, which was, in 1828, the site of the first US goldrush. The events are commemorated in the Dahlonega Gold Museum.

An international airport, trains, and buses service Atlanta.
Map ref: page 564 G5

AUGUSTA

Augusta (population 41,783) is on the South Carolina border, 136 miles (219 km) east of Atlanta on I-20/520. Closely associated with the US Masters golf tournament, Georgia's most famous event is in April at the Augusta National Country Club. It is birthplace of soul singer James Brown.

Augusta was Georgia's second colonial settlement. It was established on the Savannah River in 1736 as a fur-trading center at the behest of James Oglethorpe, who had recently founded Savannah. It served as the state capital from 1786 to 1795 and, owing to its riverside location, it was, until the mid-twentieth century, the United

States' second-largest inland cotton market (after Memphis). During the Civil War it served as an ordnance center. Augusta's 41,783 residents are a part of a wider metropolitan population of 415,000. The enormous US-army training center, Fort Gordon, is 15 miles (24 km) southwest of the city.

The Cotton Exchange Welcome Center and Museum, built in 1886, features exhibits about the early cotton industry, and they have a brochure that outlines a driving tour of the historic sites. They include Meadow Garden House Museum, the home of George Walton, a signer of the Declaration of Independence, as well as the beautifully restored Ezekiel Harris House, built in 1797, the Appleby House (circa 1830), Old Government House (1801), the boyhood home of President Woodrow Wilson, the Augusta Museum of History, and also the Lucy Craft Laney Museum of Black History.

The beautiful Riverwalk Augusta follows the Savannah River from 5th to 10th streets, past a marina, a range of eateries, the Morris Museum of Art, the vast Georgia Golf Hall of Fame, and the National Science Center's Fort Discovery.

Buses service the area, and the nearest trains and international airport are in Atlanta.
Map ref: page 565 M5

BAINBRIDGE

Bainbridge is a modest town with a population of 11,255. It is in the southwestern corner of Georgia, 53 miles (85 km) southwest of Albany and 197 miles (317 km) south of Atlanta on US-84. The Information Center is the unusual McKenzie-Reynolds House on the riverbank at the Earl May Boat Basin Park. The Firehouse Center and Art Gallery is located in the town's Historic District. Southwest of Bainbridge is Lake Seminole, which is a popular fishing spot. To the northwest is Kolomoki Indian Mounds State Historic Park, which centers on ceremonial mounds built over 1,000 years ago by the Creek and Weeden Island Native Americans. A museum at the site has exhibits relating to prehistoric Native American culture.

Buses service Bainbridge, and the closest airport is in Albany.
Map ref: page 570 F4

BRUNSWICK AND THE GOLDEN ISLES

Brunswick (population 15,525) is a vital fishing port on the Atlantic coast. Located 243 miles (391 km) southeast of Atlanta, it is the only major settlement south of Savannah, which lies 64 miles (103 km) to the north, on I-95. Brunswick has Victorian buildings and good beaches but it is best known as a gateway to the Golden Isles.

The Hofwyl-Broadfield Rice Plantation (1807) provides a good insight into plantation slavery and rice cultivation. Fort King George State Historic Site at Darien was the first colonial British garrison in Georgia and the most southerly outpost of English forces in the British Empire (1721–1727). There are the brick ruins of an early sawmill, a graveyard, a reconstructed triple-story blockhouse, and also a museum with interpretive displays.

Offshore from Brunswick are the Golden Isles, best in spring. After the Civil War some of these islands were given over to emancipated slaves but these impoverished agricultural communities have virtually disappeared.

St Simons Island is the most developed of the group. Its palms, oaks, salt marshes, and Spanish moss were explored by the Spanish in the 1700s, and it was the site of conflict between missionaries and Native Americans. In 1736, James Oglethorpe began building Fort Frederica here as a defensive outpost. Today it is best known for its resorts and golf courses. The village of St Simons features a pier and a lighthouse (1872). The Museum of Coastal History is in the lighthouse-keeper's cottage. Bicycle rentals, dolphin-watching cruises, and fishing charters are available. The eastern side has good beaches.

Jekyll Island is 10 miles (16 km) south of Brunswick. Entry incurs a small fee. At its northern end are the ruins of Horton House, built circa 1740 of lime, sand, and oyster shells by William Horton, one of James Oglethorpe's officers. The island was purchased in 1886 by a group of millionaires, including the Vanderbilts, William Rockefeller, the Macys, the Astors, Joseph Pulitzer, J.P. Morgan, and the Gould brothers, forming the Jekyll Island Club. They built plush residences, now open to the public, and the southeastern area is now a Historic District. Tours of the mansions are run out of the museum orientation center, which also has exhibits relating to the history of the island. The original millionaires' club is now an opulent resort (there are other lodgings along Beachview Drive and a campground further north, near the nesting grounds of

Peaches from the Bainbridge region.

loggerhead turtles). The island has extensive cycle tracks, golf courses, beaches, and a large water park.

Cumberland Island is a wildlife refuge of marshes, lakes, semitropical forests, beaches, and wild horses, and includes Thomas Carnegie's Dungeness estate. Access is by ferry from St Marys. The National Park Service manages the island and runs history and nature tours. Only residents may drive cars here.

Bus services connect Brunswick to Savannah and Jacksonville.
Map ref: page 571 M3

A farmer picking squash on his property near Bainbridge. Georgia's soils and climate provide ideal growing conditions.

CHATTAHOOCHEE NATIONAL FOREST

The outstanding Chattahoochee National Forest sprawls out across much of northern Georgia. This hardwood forest incorporates a diversity of terrain including lakes, streams, mountains, valleys, the piedmont plateau, 10 wilderness areas, Tallulah Gorge, a portion of the Chattooga River, the state's highest mountain—Brasstown Bald at 4,784 feet (1,459 m)—and the outstanding Anna Ruby Falls. This variety engenders a wide range of flora and fauna throughout the forest. There are also some nineteenth-century historic sites as well as archeological sites.

The Forest is open year-round and over 500 campsites are available from May to September. Visitors can enjoy fishing, sailing, boating, hiking along 50 miles (80 km) of trails, whitewater rafting, kayaking, scenic drives, and swimming. Rafting packages and hiking supplies are available in Helen. Also in the area is the Unicoi State Park and a portion of the Appalachian Trail.

Atlanta is the nearest center with an international airport and bus and train services.

Map ref: page 565 H2

CHICKAMAUGA AND CHATTANOOGA NATIONAL MILITARY PARK

Chickamauga and Chattanooga National Military Park features two major Civil War battle sites. Covering 8,119 acres (3,288 ha), it spills over from northwest Georgia into southwest Tennessee. It was established in 1890 and is the nation's first and largest Military Park.

Chickamauga Battlefield was the site of the first battle on Georgian soil and the last significant Confederate victory. In September, 1863, General Rosencrans, with 60,000 Union soldiers, closed in on Chattanooga, Tennessee, which was a vital rail center and gateway to the South. Confederate General Bragg, with 43,000 men, was forced to retreat south into Georgia. Bragg received reinforcements by rail, so he had 66,000 men at his disposal when Rosencrans followed him south. A major battle took place at Chickamauga Creek, causing a Union retreat to Chattanooga. Following a Confederate siege of

Georgia license plate. Hoagy Carmichael's "Georgia On My Mind" is the state song.

Chattanooga, the north received reinforcements and, with the Battle of Chattanooga, allowed Union forces to move into Georgia and Alabama and so split the Confederate forces in two. The two battles and the siege led to the deaths of over 30,000 men.

Fortifications, weaponry, battlements, monuments, and interpretive markers are scattered about the Park, which can be explored by means of a 7-mile (11-km) self-guided auto tour. The park's main visitor center is located just south of Fort Oglethorpe on US-27, in the northwestern corner of Georgia. It is open daily and features a multimedia show on the battles, along with books and memorabilia.

Atlanta is the nearest center with an international airport and bus and train services. Chattanooga also has an airport and bus services.

Map ref: page 564 E2

COLUMBUS

The second-largest city in Georgia, Columbus has a population of 182,828 residents. An industrial and military center (Fort Benning lies just to the south) it is located 95 miles (153 km) south of Atlanta on the Chattahoochee River, which forms much of the state's western border. The use of hydraulic power from the river helped make Columbus the South's first industrial center; hydroelectricity still powers the city's factories. Columbus has several fine museums, some excellent antebellum homes, and is a good base for exploring the district.

Columbus was established in 1827 by the Georgia legislature as a defensive outpost against the Native Americans who occupied that land. The settlement's first cotton mill was established in 1838 and it

had become a substantial cotton-milling center by 1845. During the Civil War it manufactured swords and shoes for Confederate forces. Columbus fell to the Union in one of the last battles of the war. Later, General Wilson launched a damaging attack on the city, unaware that the South had surrendered.

The Columbus Visitor Center offers brochures outlining self-guided tours of the Black Heritage Trail, the downtown area, and the National Historic District. The latter, located at the southern edge of the town center, covers 28 blocks, incorporating some fine antebellum homes. These include Pemberton House (1840), once owned by the inventor of Coca-Cola, an 1820s log cabin and farmhouse, the 15-sided "Folly" (1862), and the 1871 Springer Opera House, which has housed such notable figures as Oscar Wilde and humorist Will Rogers.

Columbus has three museums of interest: the Columbus Museum, focusing on local history; the Confederate Naval Museum, displaying an iron-plated Civil War vessel; and the National Infantry Museum, which is located 5 miles (8 km) south of the city at Fort Benning. It fills three floors with military paraphernalia from the sixteenth century to the present.

Columbus is serviced by plane and bus.

Map ref: page 564 F8

FORT FREDERICA NATIONAL MONUMENT

Located on St Simons Island in southeastern Georgia, 69 miles (111 km) south of Savannah and 5 miles (8 km) east of Brunswick, the construction of the town of Frederica and its associated fort commenced in 1736 at the behest of James Oglethorpe. He had recently established Savannah as Georgia's first English colony. His intention was to defend the new British territory against potential threats from the Spanish, in Florida, who had prior claims to the land. It was, at the time, the largest British fort and the southernmost British post in North America.

In 1739, Britain declared war on Spain, prompting Oglethorpe to launch a failed attack against St Augustine, Florida. In 1741, the Spanish ventured north with 2,000 men. Although they went ashore at St Simons Island largely unscathed, Oglethorpe dispatched a column from the Fort and, after a series of ambushes, the Spanish retreated and returned to Florida.

When Britain and Spain signed a peace treaty in 1748 the garrison became redundant and was largely abandoned. In 1758 a major fire burned most of the fort and town to the ground. Subsequent archeological digs have turned up a large amount of historical material. The

Georgia's antebellum houses are typically symmetrical and have porches.

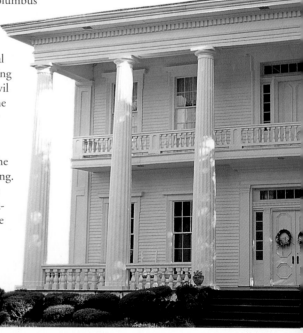

atmospheric ruins of the encampment, covering 241 acres (98 ha), are now a National Monument, complete with an informative visitor center. The park is noted for its remarkable beauty.

Bus services connect Brunswick to Savannah and Jacksonville. Savannah, to the north, has an international airport and bus and train services. Jacksonville, in Florida, also has an international airport.
Map ref: page 570 M3

MACON

Macon is one of the largest cities in Georgia. A pleasant place with fine historic buildings and museums, it is home to 114,336 people with over 322,549 in the metropolitan area. A trade and manufacturing center, it is on the Ocmulgee River at the southern end of the Appalachian Trail. Macon is known as "the Heart of Georgia" because it sits in the middle of the state, 78 miles (126 km) southeast of Atlanta on I-75. The Cherry Blossom Festival, in March, is a tribute to the more than 100,000 Japanese cherry trees, which adorn the city.

Thomas Jefferson established Fort Hawkins at the future townsite in 1806 on land then occupied by the Creek tribe. The city was chartered in 1823. Macon became a major railroad, river transport, and cotton center. It served as a supply depot and gold depository in the Civil War. Sherman's Union forces fired on the city in 1864 but moved on when fire was returned. The town's surrender in 1865 saved it from destruction.

Downtown Macon was revamped in the 1980s and the city has six historic districts that feature antebellum buildings in a diversity of styles. Further information is available from the visitor center, which offers customized tours of the city. Historic buildings include the outstanding mansion known as Hay House (1855–59), which features a three-story cupola and trompe l'oeil effects. It was built by William Johnston, a treasurer of the Confederacy. Another is the cottage where poet Sidney Lanier was born in 1842. It has Lanier memorabilia. Old Cannonball House (1853) gained its name from a Union cannonball, which hit the house in 1864, rolling into the hallway, where it is on display today.

The Georgia Sports Hall of Fame is being constructed and nearby is the Georgia Music Hall of Fame. The latter features thematic interactive displays relating to the state's musical progeny, including Ray Charles, James Brown, Joe Williams, the B-52s, REM, and two of Macon's most famous African-American sons— Otis Redding and Little Richard. Two former members of the Allman Brothers band (Duane Allman and Berry Oakley), who also hail from Macon, are buried in Rose Hill Cemetery. Both were killed in Macon, in motorcycle accidents.

Children enjoy the fine Museum of Arts and Sciences while the excellent Tubman African-American Museum has a diverse collection of material.

Seventeen miles (27 km) north of Macon is the Jarrell Plantation, near Dames Ferry. Twenty original structures remain, including the first dwelling, built in 1847. Twelve miles (19 km) north of Macon is Clinton where, in April, local Civil War battles are fiercely re-enacted.

A quiet day can be spent fishing for perch on the Ocmulgee River near Macon.

The Ocmulgee River between Macon and Jackson was once a transport route.

Twelve miles (19 km) north of Clinton is Piedmont National Wildlife Refuge.

Due north of Macon is Eatonton, the home, until 1864, of Joel Chandler Harris who popularized the folk tales of Brer Rabbit. A statue of the trickster sits on the courthouse lawn and a replica cabin of Uncle Remus holds Harris memorabilia. Five miles (8 km) north of town is the Rock Eagle Center, a 6,000-year-old mound of opalescent quartz in the shape of a large bird. It is 102 feet (31 m) long, 120 feet (37 m) wide and 10 feet (3.1 m) high. It is believed to have been was used by Native Americans for religious rituals.

Macon is at the intersection of two major highways—I-75 and I-16. It is serviced by buses, and the Spring Street bus station is allegedly where Little Richard wrote "Tutti Frutti" while washing dishes. Macon also has its own airport.
Map ref: page 565 J7

MARIETTA

Marietta (population 48,263) is in northwestern Georgia, not far beyond Atlanta. The centerpiece is Marietta Square in the downtown area. With a turn-of-the-century appearance it offers the visitor specialty boutiques, antique shops, restaurants, and coffee shops, all set around a lushly landscaped park.

The Historic Marietta Walking-Driving Tour is a self-guided tour of five registered historic districts full of Victorian and Greek Revival architecture. Information is available from the Welcome Center.

Marietta has several museums, covering fire, history, and art. It is home to two substantial Civil War cemeteries: the Marietta Confederate Cemetery, with graves of 3,000 Confederates; and the Marietta National Cemetery, where 10,000 Union soldiers lie.

Nearby Atlanta has an international airport, trains, and buses.
Map ref: page 564 G4

It is worth making a trip to Marshallville to see some of its many delightful antebellum houses.

MARSHALLVILLE

Marshallville is a small rural town and has a population of 1,488. It began shifting its agricultural focus from cotton to fruit after the Civil War. It is about 40 miles (64 km) southwest of Macon in central Georgia. In the 1930s, its 5-mile (8-km) floral corridors of camellias, crepe myrtles, and daffodils were created. The Crepe Myrtle Festival is held at Marshallville in July and Massee Lane Gardens, just outside of town, hosts the Camellia Festival each year in February.

A Historic District Driving Tour takes in a series of buildings along Main Street. Many downtown buildings date from 1870–1914. Of particular note are the substantial homes built by wealthy land-owners in the nineteenth and early twentieth centuries. The Frederick-Minnich House was built in town during the Civil War to safeguard the owners against fears of a slave uprising. The Slappey-Liipfert House was constructed by slaves, and the John Donald Wade Home (1845) was originally the center-piece of a plantation, which was moved to the present site by mule teams. It is said that the famous poet Robert Frost passed an evening here as a guest.

Also of interest in this town is the extravagant Rumph-Meyers Home, which was built in 1904 by Samuel Rumph, who invented a peach-shipping refrigerator that expanded the market for local fruit. There are many other noteworthy buildings for visitors to explore.

Marshallville has a limited bus service, but nearby Atlanta is serviced by an international airport, trains, and buses.
Map ref: page 565 J6

MILLEDGEVILLE

Milledgeville is 29 miles (47 km) northeast of Macon and it has a population of 17,982. It was the state capital from 1807–68 and has some stately buildings in the Historic District, including the former Governor's Mansion, built in 1838; the lovely Stetson-Sanford House, circa 1820; St Stephen's Episcopal Church, and the former State Capitol, built in 1807, which is now part of the Georgia Military College. A tour of the historic buildings is available from the tourist office.

Just south of town, at 1534 Irwinton Road, is Lockerly Arbor-etum where a guide leads visitors along the serene wooded trails of this 50-acre (20-ha) site.

Milledegville has a somewhat limited bus service, but nearby Macon is serviced by buses and also has its own airport.
Map ref: page 564 J7

A farmer, near Monticello—one in six Georgians work in agriculture.

MONTICELLO

Monticello (population 2,305) is just north of Macon. The Chamber of Commerce has material on the Historic District, which is formed by the commercial district in the center with residential neighborhoods radiating outwards. The Monticello Historic District Driving Tour highlights 86 historic homes as well as the downtown business district. The entire city has been listed on the National Register of Historic Places.

In the area is the Charlie Elliott Wildlife Center, as well as Oconee National Forest. Sinclair Recreational Area is located on Lake Sinclair and there are two boat-access recreational areas on Lake Oconee. Colonies of the rare red-cockaded woodpecker can be found in the forest.

There are no bus services but nearby Macon is serviced by buses and has its own airport.
Map ref: page 565 H6

OCMULGEE NATIONAL MONUMENT

On the eastern side of Macon, at 1207 Emory Highway, is the Oc-mulgee National Monument. This 700-acre (284-ha) archeological site, overlooking the Ocmulgee River, contains the most important prehistoric mounds of the South-east. Some ruins date back 12,000 years. Rising from the plateau are eight large ceremonial mounds built of sand and clay, which were once, it is thought, topped by tem-ples. The site also has an under-ground earth lodge. Within this is a bird-shaped dais and a ring of molded seats. The visitor center museum has a 17-minute film on the mounds, along with dioramas, graphics, and artifacts such as stone tools and pottery.

From Macon follow I-16 then US-80. Macon is serviced by buses and has its own airport.
Map ref: page 564 J7

OKEFENOKEE SWAMP

Located in southeastern Georgia, Okefenokee has 660 square miles (1,709 sq km) of land, stretching east–west for 20 miles (32 km) and south for about 45 miles (72 km) from just south of Waycross to a point across the state border. It is located 30 miles (48 km) south-west of Brunswick.

The Okefenokee Swamp is probably the largest, most primi-tive swamp in the United States. Its importance lies in its diversity of ecosystems and its significance as a refuge for native flora and fauna, including many threatened, rare, and endangered species.

This area is a vast peat bog fil-ling a huge, saucer-shaped sandy depression that was once part of the ocean floor. Swamp forests of bald cypress, tupelo, and bay cover about 80 percent of the area. Vast expanses of freshwater marshes occupy 60,000 acres (24,300 ha), principally on the eastern side of the site. There are about 70 scat-tered, elevated islands in the swamp and 60 lakes dot the swamp forests. The northern end is abutted by pine forests and dense vegetation, the west by cypress forests. The area's watersheds are clean, un-spoiled, nutrient-rich, and very beautiful. The swamps were once used as a hunting ground by the Creek and Seminole tribes.

The protected status, the un-spoilt nature of the environment, and the diversity of ecosystems has ensured a vast array of plant and animal life. The refuge contains 621 plant species (including the carnivorous hooded pitcher plant),

49 mammal species, 30 types of amphibians, about 50 fish species, 234 types of birds, and 54 reptile species. Among the fauna are black bears, a large population of endangered American alligators, bobcats, deer, otters, pumas, snakes, turtles, tortoises, opossums, and raccoons, and also kingfishers and hawks.

There are three main entrances to the swamp and each is associated with a recreational park. The northern entrance is at Okefenokee Swamp Park, 8 miles (13 km) south of Waycross, which is especially good for families with young children. On the western side is

The historic Tybee Island lighthouse.

Stephen C. Foster State Park, situated 17 miles (27 km) east of Fargo. On the eastern side is Suwanee Canal Recreation Area, 7 miles (11 km) southwest of Folkston. All offer a range of facilities and activities designed to ensure safe interaction with the swamp environment, such as boardwalks, observation towers, guided boat tours, and lodgings. All involve a small admission charge and access to all three is by car. There is no public transportation. Those wishing for more personal independence in the swamp can simply hire a motorboat, canoe, or kayak. The more adventurous may wish to undertake an overnight canoe trip into the swamp. However, reservations are quite difficult to obtain. Interested parties should first obtain a copy of the indispensable and comprehensive "Wilderness Canoeing" pamphlet.

Jacksonville, in Florida, is the closest center with an international airport and bus services.
Map ref: page 570 K4

TYBEE ISLAND

Tybee Island (population 2,949) is a very popular vacation spot on the Atlantic coast. Boasting 5 miles (8 km) of charming and untainted beaches, it has a visitor center, a marina, seafood restaurants, and lodgings. Tybee is located 17 miles (27 km) east of Savannah in southeast Georgia.

Once known as the "Playground of the Southeast," Tybee Island has quite a long and varied history, attracting Native Americans, pirates, the Spanish, the French, and the English, as well as the Confederacy. It is still possible to visit the clearing where Methodist founder John Wesley declared his faith upon American soil in the eighteenth century. Late in the nineteenth century, the island attracted Southern gentlemen who were disposed to dueling, and, in the 1930s, some of the country's most famous jazz bands.

The island features several historic attractions at the northern end including the 154-foot (47-m)

Trees covered in ivy in the Oconee National Forest, which is not very far from Monticello.

Tybee Lighthouse at the mouth of the Savannah River. It is the third-oldest lighthouse in the nation. The original tower was built by James Oglethorpe, in 1742. The current structure, which dates from 1773, was destroyed by Confederate forces in 1862 and restored in 1867. Visitors can ascend the 178 steps to the top. Over the road is the Tybee Museum with displays relating to the island's history. The museum is housed in a former section of Fort Screven, which was established in 1897.

Also on Tybee Island is Tybee Marine Center, which features a range of aquatic creatures, in particular those found along the coastline of southern Georgia.

There are no bus services to Tybee Island, but nearby Savannah has an international airport and bus and train services.
Map ref: page 564 P9

VALDOSTA

Valdosta (population 41,846) is located in southern Georgia, on US-84, 155 miles (249 km) southwest of Savannah.

It has several buildings of interest including the Converse-Dalton-Ferrell House (1902), Crescent House (1898), and the neoclassical Ola Barber Pittman House, which was built by E.R. Barber who owned the world's second Coca-Cola bottling works outside of Atlanta. The Lowndes County Historical Society and Museum features memorabilia and artifacts dating back to 1825, and the Valdosta Cultural Arts Center is also of interest. Langdale Park is good for birdwatching and nature walks along the Withlacoochee River.

Valdosta has a bus service as well as its own airport.
Map ref: page 571 J4

Tybee Beach on Tybee Island, a popular vacation spot on the Atlantic coast.

STATE FEATURE

Savannah

An interesting historic city with an old-world graciousness and distinctly Southern aura, Savannah has become a popular drawcard in recent years, especially for exploring the delights of the restored inner city and waterfront.

With a population of 136,262 and a wider metropolitan population of 293,000, Savannah is Georgia's third-largest settlement. It is located in the southeast of the state on the Savannah River, which forms the state border with South Carolina. Savannah is 223 miles (359 km) from Atlanta. It is connected to the Atlantic Ocean by an 18-mile (29-km) deepwater channel and is one of the South's major ports.

The first colonial settlement in Georgia and the first planned city in the United States, Savannah was established in 1733 by James Oglethorpe and 114 English Protestants. Oglethorpe originally envisaged the settlement as a utopian alternative to English society and a haven for those from English debtors' prisons. The problems of English society, as Oglethorpe saw it, were overcrowding and cankerous social practices. Savannah was intended as a fresh start based on a new model. His idea was to construct an environment ensuring spaciousness, comfort, beauty, and order. To this end a generous town plan was designed around 24 town squares, an orderly commercial area and a series of ameliorative strictures: no slaves, Catholics, alcohol, or lawyers! Although Oglethorpe's credo ensured the city an outstanding spatial environment, few debtors were resettled and the weight of history soon overtook his ideals. Savannah's natural harbor drew a motley bunch of immigrants and traders and it rapidly became a thriving port town, a major exporting center, and the principal city of the new colony. Savannah was the state capital until 1783. During the Revolutionary War the English took Savannah in 1778 and held it until driven out of Georgia in 1782.

The cotton gin, which led to the economic dominance of cotton in the South, was invented near Savannah, in 1793, by Eli Whitney. In 1819 the SS *Savannah* became the first steamship to cross an ocean when it sailed from Savannah to Liverpool.

During the Civil War, General Sherman ended his scorched-earth march across Georgia at Savannah, presenting the city as a Christmas gift to President Lincoln. It was spared the decimation handed out to so much of Georgia, since Confederate troops were evacuated before the arrival of the Union forces. With the decline of cotton after the war, the economy slumped, although this decline probably helped save the historic buildings from the bulldozer of progress. Savannah is now the commercial center for a wider farming district, a manufacturing center, and a major tourist attraction.

Visitors can enjoy the best weather, and the city's gardens, in March and April, the most popular times to visit, so prices are higher and lodging is booked out in advance. The weather is good year-round except in summer when it can get very humid.

Since the mid-1950s a concerted and very successful effort has been made to restore old structures in the city's original center, known as Old Savannah. This beautiful historic area covers 2½ square miles (6.5 sq km), making it the largest National Historic Landmark District in the nation. Taking in the riverfront, it features over 2,000 historic buildings of diverse architectural styles and 20 of the expansive, serene, Spanish moss-draped town squares included in the elegant 1733 town plan. It was on a bench in Chippewa Square that Forrest Gump related his life story. The picturesque and historic qualities of the town and area have also been captured in many other films, including *Cape Fear* and *Glory*. The Victorian District features a distinguished array of late nineteenth-century, two-story homes.

The Historic District is best explored on foot, but take care at night. Excellent walking tours are outlined at the Savannah Visitor Center. There are organized tours by foot, horse and carriage, riverboat, and bus. The most gracious lodging is in the restored historic homes of this area.

Savannah has a number of fine museums, including the Savannah History Museum, which is housed in a restored train shed from the old railway station; the Ships of the Sea Maritime Museum, which has a large collection of replica model boats covering the entirety of maritime history; and the Savannah Science Museum, which has a planetarium, an amphibian and reptile display, and hands-on exhibits relating to astronomy, natural history, and science. The Massie

River Street, with its cobbled walkway, plaza, old cotton warehouses, and City Market, is now geared to the thriving tourist trade, with plenty of specialty shops, boutiques, excellent seafood restaurants, bars, galleries, museums, and music venues. A festival unfolds on the first Saturday of each month along River Street, while the St Patrick's Day celebrations are an annual event.

Heritage Interpretation Center features a series of children's exhibits that relate to Savannah, while a variety of model and toy trains of all eras can be found in the River Street Train Museum. The Colonial Park Cemetery, used from 1750 to 1853, holds some of the city's earliest and distinguished residents.

Some of the beautiful historic buildings are open. Green-Meldrim Home (1850s) was used as General Sherman's headquarters in 1864, and there are two homes of Juliette Gordon Low, founder of the US Girl Scouts. Literary buffs will enjoy the childhood homes of Flannery O'Connor and Conrad Aiken. At Mercer House, outrageous local identity Jim Williams shot and killed his lover Danny Hansford, which is at the center of the popular book, *Midnight in the Garden of Good and Evil*. Also near Savannah, is "Bethesda," built in 1740, the oldest orphanage in the nation.

African-American heritage is featured at several venues, including the Ralph Mark Gilbert Civil Rights Museum, the Beach Institute, and the King-Tisdell African-American Cultural Center, and many historic churches, particularly the First African Baptist Church. Founded in 1773 the latter claims to be the oldest continuously active, autonomously developed, African-American congregation in North America. The present church building, which dates from 1861, was the seat of the local civil rights movement in the 1950s. At the Second African Baptist Church, Martin Luther King Jr first preached his "I Have a Dream" sermon and General Sherman read the Emancipation Proclamation to the newly freed slaves in 1864.

Exploration beyond the Historic District is best conducted by private vehicle although there are good bus services to many sites. The charming Bonaventure Cemetery contains the graves of Conrad Aiken and

his parents, who both died in 1901 when Conrad Sr killed his wife and himself. Songwriter Johnny Mercer is buried in the same plot as the Aiken parents.

Three Civil War forts are nearby: Old Fort Jackson (1808), the Confederate Headquarters; Fort Pulaski (1829–47); and Fort McAllister, a Confederate structure built 1861–1862. Its fall to a bayonet charge represented the culmination of General Sherman's destructive march across Georgia.

Just over the river is the Savannah National Wildlife Refuge, home to a large range of fauna including deer, otter, feral pigs, bald eagles, and alligators. It attracts hikers, naturalists, cyclists, and canoeists. Fishing and hunting is permitted but with strict conditions. South of Savannah are the Wormsloe State Historic Site and the Isle of Hope, with its carefully restored homes, fine views, oaks, and Spanish moss.

Savannah has an international airport and bus and train services.

Fort Pulaski, now a National Monument, was complete with moat and drawbridge (top). It was taken by Confederate forces in 1861, then recaptured after Union bombardment in 1862. The latter was a significant moment in military history as it proved, for the first time, that long-range artillery (bottom) could overcome masonry fortifications. Projectiles remain in the battered walls. A young Robert E. Lee served as an engineer at the fort before the Civil War, and it was used as a POW camp for Confederates after the war.

KENTUCKY

Kentucky is known as "The Bluegrass State" for the blue blossoms that spring from a type of grass that grows around Lexington. The term "bluegrass" also reflects the state's links to one of America's most distinctive musical forms, masterminded by Kentuckian, Bill Monroe, in the 1940s. However, Kentucky's most potent symbol is the horse—the state remains a major breeder of thoroughbred horses and is the site of America's premier horse race, the Kentucky Derby. The Bluegrass State is also noted for its tobacco and bourbon whiskey, as well as

The prime land in Kentucky's lush northern bluegrass region is a scene of rolling green hills criss-crossed with the white-railed pens of horse paddocks.

Kentucky Fried Chicken and the nation's only home-grown racing car, the Corvette. It is also home to Fort Knox, where most of the nation's gold reserves are stored. Visitors will find many recreational facilities, historic homes and sites, such as its Civil War battlefields, and some of the most popular scenic attractions in Cumberland Gap, Daniel Boone National Forest, and Mammoth Caves.

"Kentucky" is a Native American term and it serves as a reminder that the state was once occupied by the Cherokee, Iroquois, and Shawnee tribes, which fiercely resisted colonization, beginning with the repulsion of Daniel Boone's first group of settlers in 1773. Boone returned in 1775, blazing the "Wilderness Road" through the Appalachians and into Kentucky's heart. Among the thousands who followed in his wake were the family of Abraham Lincoln.

In 1792, Kentucky became the nation's 15th state with Frankfort as its capital. Agriculture prospered with the introduction of steamboats, which opened up markets along the Ohio River (the state's northern boundary) and the Mississippi (the western boundary). During the Civil War, Kentucky stayed in the Union although its citizens, and sometimes members of the same family, fought on both sides. Tellingly, the Union and Confederate presidents were both born in Kentucky. After the war, railroads allowed the state's natural resources to be exploited and today, Kentucky is still a major coal producer.

State motto United We Stand, Divided We Fall
State flag Adopted 1918
Capital Frankfort
Population 4,041,769
Total area (land and water) 40,411 square miles (104,664 sq km)
Land area 39,732 square miles (102,906 sq km)
Kentucky is the 37th-largest state in size
Origin of name From the Iroquoisan word *ken-tah-ten* meaning "land of tomorrow"
Nickname The Bluegrass State
Abbreviations KY (postal), Ky., Ken.
State bird Kentucky cardinal
State flower Goldenrod
State tree Coffee tree
Entered the Union June 1, 1792 as the 15th state

Places in KENTUCKY

ABRAHAM LINCOLN BIRTHPLACE NATIONAL HISTORIC SITE

This National Historic Site honors the birthplace of President Abraham Lincoln, on February 12, 1809. His parents, Thomas and Nancy, had bought a farm here in 1808. A Classical-style memorial shrine designed by John Russell Pope— who also designed the Jefferson Memorial in Washington, DC— marks the location.

The shrine is approached by 56 steps, one for each year of Lincoln's life. Inside is a log cabin similar to the one in which Lincoln was born. A visitor center has exhibits and a video on Lincoln's Kentucky years. It is located in a beautiful 116-acre (47-ha) park and provides some insight into frontier life.

In 1811, the Lincolns moved to another farm 10 miles (16 km) away, at Knob Creek, which is now occupied by the Lincoln Boyhood Home, a replica of the cabin. It is 8 miles (13 km) east of Hodgenville on US-31E; the town has a statue of Lincoln sitting ponderously outside the Lincoln Museum, which has dioramas tracing the course of Lincoln's life, plus art collections, an audiovisual room, and an interpretive children's area.

There is no public transportation to the site, 3 miles (4.8 km) south of Hodgenville via US-31E and Hwy 61. Hodgenville is about 90 miles (145 km) southwest of Lexington, which is serviced by the Blue Grass Airport and also by bus.
Map ref: page 585 F5

BARDSTOWN

Bardstown is the seat of Nelson County, 34 km (55 km) south of Louisville on US-150. It is sometimes known as the "Bourbon Capital of the World" because 90 percent of America's bourbon comes from Kentucky and of that, 60 percent is distilled in Nelson County and neighboring Bullitt County. Visitors can investigate Heaven Hill Distillery, America's largest family-owned distillery, and the Oscar Getz Museum of Whiskey History, which examines

the history of bourbon with old advertising posters, stills, rare historic documents, cooperage, and antique bottles.

As the second-oldest city in the state, Bardstown also has much to offer in the way of historic buildings and sites. The visitor center offers a self-guided walking tour of downtown or narrated tours on horse-drawn carriages.

Attractions include many historic homes: McLean House (1814) which served as Bardstown's first post office and a Civil War hospital; the elegant Colonel's Cottage, which was built in 1850 and is decorated with early nineteenth-century antiques and furniture; and Wickland, the "Home of Three Governors," which was built in 1817 and features fine architectural details and antique furniture.

The Talbott Tavern is where Jesse James and France's King Louis-Phillippe have stayed. Built in the 1780s, it is considered the oldest stagecoach store in America. Unfortunately, it was damaged by fire in 1998. St Joseph's Proto-Cathedral (1816–1819) was the first Catholic cathedral west of the Allegheny Mountains. It features

Patrons relax and have a chat over a soda and fast food at Hirst's Drug Store in Bardstown.

paintings donated by King Louis-Phillippe. The Abbey of Gethsemani was founded in 1848 and is home to America's largest and oldest order of Cistercian Monks. The public can attend vespers in the lay balcony. Spiritual writer and monk Thomas Merton is buried here.

At Old Bardstown Village, a frontier community is re-created with nine log cabins dating from the first half of the nineteenth century, crafts from the late eighteenth century, and a 52-minute multimedia presentation about Kentucky's history and culture. The Civil War Museum features the state's largest collection of artifacts from the war's western theater. The Women of the Civil War Museum examines the contributions of women to the causes of both the North and the South.

An old plantation house, Federal Hill (1818), is the focal point of My Old Kentucky Home State Park. The site's name celebrates its connection with Stephen Foster who, it is alleged, was inspired to write "My Old Kentucky Home" after visiting his cousins at this house in 1852. It is furnished in period style with tour guides in period costume. On summer evenings there is a performance of the popular show, "The Stephen Foster Story."

The nearest airport, train, and bus services are at Louisville.
Map ref: page 558 G4

A distiller takes a bourbon sample from a barrel.

BOWLING GREEN

Bowling Green, located 94 miles (151 km) southwest of Louisville, on the US-68, is a lively city. This may reflect the fact that it is the only place where alcohol can be purchased between Louisville and Nashville. The principal settlement of southern Kentucky and fifth-largest city in the state, it is home to around 41,000 people.

There are a number of interesting historic attractions in the area but Bowling Green is best known for America's only homegrown sports car, the Corvette. There are 1-hour tours of the General Motors Corvette Assembly Plant and, nearby, the National Corvette Museum, which takes in the car's history from the chrome and steel of 1953 to futuristic concept cars. Fifty models are displayed, including the famous "Stingray." There are also exhibits on motor racing, automobile culture, and Corvette advertising.

Bowling Green is also home to Western University where the Kentucky Museum examines state history. Also of interest is Riverview, at Hobson Grove, which is a historic house and museum built between 1860 and 1890.

Eleven miles (17.7 km) west of Bowling Green, in South Union, is a restored settlement established in 1807 by the Shakers, an ascetic sect noted for its emphasis on simplicity, hygiene, celibacy (men and women even entered the buildings through different doors), pacifism, communal ownership, and the high quality of their architecture and furniture. This was the very last of 19 Shaker villages set up in America. The community was disbanded in 1922. Only six out of 200 buildings remain—three are open to the public and one is now a B&B. The Center Family Dwelling House, which was built in 1824, is now a museum with displays of Shaker textiles, tools, crafts, and furnishings.

A Civil War Driving Tour takes in 10 Civil War sites, including forts, a cave, homes, a monument, markers, and a museum. Although Kentucky was officially neutral in the war, Confederate General Simon Bolivar set up headquarters at Bowling Green in 1861.

There is an airport in Bowling Green and buses service the area.
Map ref: page 558 E6

Riverboats are a great way to explore the Ohio River. Dinner, sunset, Sunday jazz, and full-day cruises are available at Covington.

CLERMONT

Clermont is a small town located on Hwy 245, 25 miles (40 km) south of Louisville, in bourbon-rich Bullitt County. Jim Beam's American Outpost is a center for the Jim Beam Distillery. Displays examine the history of the family, the world-famous company, and the bourbon-making process.

The 16,000-acre (6,480 ha) Bernheim Arboretum and Research Forest includes an arboretum of 250 acres (101 ha) with over 2,800 labeled trees and shrubs. It also includes a fishing lake, biking and picnic facilities, a nature center, over 35 miles (56 km) of hiking trails, numerous public programs and tours, and an exquisitely colorful display of azaleas and rhododendrons during spring.

The nearest airport, train, and bus services are at Louisville.
Map ref: page 558 F4

Clermont has a Jim Beam center.

COVINGTON

Covington is Kentucky's fourth-largest city. It is a lively, attractive, and charming settlement of some 43,000 people at the junction of the Ohio and Licking Rivers. It is connected to Cincinnati by a suspension bridge erected in 1866 to the design of John Roebling who also designed the Brooklyn Bridge. The area was settled as farmland in the early nineteenth century but later became a manufacturing center. Incorporated in 1834 it was named for General Leonard Covington, a hero of the War of 1812.

Riverboat cruises explore an extensive floating entertainment complex called Covington Landing. The city has several historic districts, notably Riverside where there are some fine nineteenth-century houses in a variety of styles. MainStrasse Village, a five-block commercial area with cobbled walkways, is the old German quarter. It is home to the Carroll Chimes Bell Tower. This Gothic structure has a 43-bell carillon, which sounds hourly. The Roman Catholic Cathedral Basilica, which was built in 1895, is a major landmark, modeled for the Cathedral of Notre Dame in Paris. It has one of the world's largest stained-glass windows. Also of interest is the Behringer-Crawford Memorial Museum, which examines 450 million years of both natural and human history.

Adjacent to Covington is Newport, which has an aquarium with 11,000 animals, and the World Peace Bell Exhibit Center, with the world's largest free-swinging bell, weighing a mighty 66,000 pounds (29,964 kg). The ring is heard each day at noon.

Buses service Convington. Cincinnati–Northern Kentucky Airport is near Covington, and buses and trains service Cincinnati.
Map ref: page 559 H1

CUMBERLAND GAP NATIONAL HISTORICAL PARK

Cumberland Gap is a natural break in the Appalachian Mountains, once a major barrier to westward expansion. Native Americans discovered the gap by following bison. It is essentially a notch 600 feet (183 m) deep in the Cumberland Mountain at about 1,600 feet (488 m) above sea level, near the point where Kentucky, Tennessee, and Virginia all meet.

Pioneer scout Thomas Walker and his party used the Gap in 1750. In 1769 Daniel Boone and John Findley passed through Cumberland Gap together. Boone was impressed with what he found, and remained exploring for two years.

In 1775, Boone returned with a party of 30 to blaze a trail through Cumberland Gap and into the center of present-day Kentucky by connecting up a series of Native American trails and bison paths. The resulting route, known as the "Wilderness Trail," opened up Kentucky to general settlement. Tens of thousands soon followed in Boone's wake. Thus the Gap became an essential element of a major commercial and transportation route. It was controlled alternately by both Union and Confederate forces during the Civil War.

The horse farms of Kentucky's bluegrass country have bred many a champion.

At 20,000 acres (8,100 ha) this is one of the country's largest historical parks. Fifty miles (80 km) of hiking trails lead to Sand Cave, White Rocks, and the Hensley Settlement—an attempt to establish a self-sufficient community atop Brush Mountain in the early 1900s. Three of its original 12 farmsteads have been restored.

The visitor center, in Middleboro, has a slide show and film on the Gap's history. Four miles (6.4 km) east of the center sees outstanding views of three states from Pinnacle Rock, at an elevation of 1,000 feet (305 m). Activities include camping, picnicking, fishing, hiking, and scenic drives.

There is no public transportation to the park—it can be reached using the US-25E. The nearest bus service is in Richmond, about 90 miles (145 km) northwest on US-25E then I-75. Lexington, a little further to the northwest, has an airport and a bus service.
Map ref: page 559 K7

CYNTHIANA

Cynthiana boasts the dubious record of Kentucky's lowest ever state temperature, −34°F (−36.6°C). It is 26 miles (42 km) north of Lexington in central Kentucky. Harrison County Museum has historical displays while Quiet Trails State Nature Preserve offers wildlife.

Ten miles (16 km) south is Paris, which is home to the Hopewell Museum. Housed in the old post office, it features exhibits on the art and history of Bourbon County and central Kentucky. The Duncan Tavern is a three-story stone tavern built in 1788. Daniel Boone is alleged to have frequented the establishment. Lexington has an airport and buses service the area.
Map ref: page 559 J3

DANIEL BOONE NATIONAL FOREST

Daniel Boone National Forest essentially occupies a long, narrow strip of land in southeastern Kentucky, extending from the Tennessee border almost all the way to the Ohio border. It has vast tracts of lush virgin woods full of pine, hemlock, and oak. It has two wilderness areas and superb Appalachian mountain scenery of sandstone cliffs, steep slopes, narrow valleys,

A classic Georgian-style home, at Cynthiana, in central Kentucky.

beautiful lakes, waterfalls, native vegetation, and unusual rock formations. A good way of exploring the forest is via the superb 254-mile (409-km) Sheltowee Trace National Recreation Trail, which links many of the forest's recreational sites. Most campsites are open from April to November.

Red River Gorge and Natural Bridge are located in the Stanton Ranger District, which is split by Mountain Parkway into the lavish Natural Bridge State Park, on the south side, and Red River Gorge Geological Area, to the north. Natural Bridge, off Hwy 11, is

a massive sandstone arch which is one of many interesting geological features in the area. It is 24 feet (7.3 m) wide. A trail leads to the top with panoramic views. Natural Bridge State Park has nine hiking trails plus a nature center detailing the area's flora and fauna.

The Red River Gorge Area can be explored via a loop drive on Hwy 77, near Slade. It features the area's richest and most varied terrain. There are winding mountain roads, bison, a historic log cabin, an old country railroad tunnel, 36 miles (58 km) of trails, and outstanding rock formations. The

beautiful Rock Bridge was created by 70 million years of wind and water, and Sky Bridge offers panoramic views of the green gorge.

Eighteen miles (29 km) southwest of Corbin, on Route 90, are Cumberland Falls. Known as the "Niagara of the South," they drop 125 feet (38 m) into the Cumberland River. Visitors can go to the falls at night during a full moon to see the famous "moonbows," created by the mist and moonlight. The falls are surrounded by a lovely state park. Brochures and maps are available from DuPont Lodge and there are several good nature trails, camping, and rapids for rafting.

Close to the falls, in the London Ranger District, is Laurel River Lake, which offers fishing, boating, hiking, marinas, camping, and a visitor center. The Morehead Ranger District features Cave Run Lake and Forest Development Road 918, which is a 9-mile (14.5-km) National Scenic Byway near Morehead. Also in the park is the Big South Fork Scenic Railway, which snakes through beautiful forests and down a 600-foot (183-m) gorge to Blue Heron, a former mining town, where a guided tour is available.
Map ref: page 559 H6

Children from the Amish Community around Cynthiana—the Amish have their own schools and educational system.

Horse farms dot the rich bluegrass country found around Frankfort.

DANVILLE

Danville, founded in 1775, is in a historic region, 31 miles (50 km) south of Lexington, in central Kentucky. Transylvania Seminary, the first institution of higher learning west of the Allegheny Mountains, opened at Danville in the 1780s. It later moved to Lexington where it has become Transylvania University.

In 1785, Danville became the seat of what was then the county of Kentucky, within the state of Virginia. During 1784–92, 10 conventions were held here to discuss statehood. Kentucky's first constitution was adopted in 1792 at Central Constitution Square, now a State Historic Site. It has replicas of log-cabin meeting houses, a courthouse, jail, and post office. There is also an art gallery and historical society museum.

There are many attractions in the Historic Downtown Area. McDowell House and Apothecary Shop is in the home of Dr Ephraim McDowell who made medical history by removing a 22-pound (10kg) tumor from the ovary of a 46-year-old woman, without anesthesia, in 1809. This is considered the start of successful abdominal surgery. McDowell's house (circa 1800) retains some original furnishings. Antiquated medical instruments are on display in the shop.

The Kentucky School for the Deaf opened in 1823 and its oldest surviving building is Jacobs Hill, constructed in 1855–57. Currently it houses the superintendent's office and a museum about the school. Also of interest is the Ida Crow Inn, the oldest stone house west of the Alleghenies. This 23-room manor house was built between 1776 and 1792. The landscaped grounds include walking trails, native plants, and wildlife.

Ten miles (16 km) west of Danville is Perryville Battlefield State Historic Site, where Kentucky's most significant and bloody Civil War battle took place on October 8, 1862. Confederate troops finally retreated, marking the end of the Southern campaign to win Kentucky. There were over 6,000 casualties, with 70 percent of them on the Union side. Visitors can take self-guided walking and driving tours and visit a burial ground, monuments, and a small museum.

Nine miles (14.5 km) northwest is Harrodsburg, the oldest permanent settlement west of the Allegheny Mountains and the site of the state's first law court, school, and religious service. Pennsylvania's James Harrod founded it in 1774. Old Fort Harrod State Park has a re-creation of the original fort with period cabins and blockhouses, the oldest cemetery west of the Alleghenies, and actors in eighteenth-century period costume demonstrating quilting, blacksmithing, and other frontier crafts. On summer evenings there is an outdoor drama about Daniel Boone's life. Also on the site is the cabin where Abraham Lincoln's parents were married in 1806, which has been relocated from its original site at Elizabethtown. The 1830 Mansion Museum, just below the Fort, displays items covering the period from 1774 to the Civil War, including a cast of Lincoln's face and hands. Downtown Harrodsburg is the historic district featuring various architectural styles dating back to the late nineteenth century. Historical walking and driving tours are available. Morgan Row, the oldest row house in Kentucky, is the headquarters of the Harrodsburg Historical Society and contains pioneer displays.

Nearby Lexington has Blue Grass Airport and is serviced by bus.
Map ref: page 559 H5

ELIZABETHTOWN

Elizabethtown is located 38 miles (61 km) south of Louisville in central Kentucky. An attractive settlement, with gracious homes, landscaped gardens, and tree-lined streets, it was settled in 1779. Its historic buildings and sites are covered in historic tours, with a choice of driving or walking.

Abraham Lincoln's parents, Thomas and Nancy, lived at Elizabethtown for the first 18 months of their marriage. Their first child,

The Old Governor's Mansion at Frankfort was built in 1798.

Sarah, was born here in 1807. The Lincoln Heritage House is a log structure crafted in part by Thomas Lincoln. The family moved on in 1808 but, after the death of his wife in 1818, Thomas returned to Elizabethtown in 1819 and married Sarah Bush Johnston. The Brown-Pusey House, built in 1825, is a Federal-style building, which was once an inn that housed General George Custer and his wife in the 1870s. Also of interest are the Black History Gallery, Swopes Cars of Yesteryear, and Schmidt's Museum of Coca-Cola Memorabilia.

Louisville has an international airport, and train and bus services.
Map ref: page 558 F4

FRANKFORT

Frankfort lies between Lexington and Louisville and was made Kentucky's state capital in 1792. This historic, well-preserved, and charming town has a multitude of historic attractions. It is located at the intersection of US-127, 421, and 60, in central-north Kentucky among the hills of the Kentucky River Valley. It has a population of 26,000, and its major industry and employer is the state government, although whiskey distilling and manufacturing are also important.

The first white person in the area was Christopher Gist, in 1751. The first land survey was carried out in 1773 and the town was established in 1786 by Revolutionary War general, James Wilkinson, and named for pioneer Stephen Frank.

The town's oldest district is known as the "Corner of Celebrities" because its residents have included Supreme Court justices, cabinet officers, ambassadors, politicians, and governors. Its historic homes include the Georgian-style Liberty Hall, built in the 1790s by Kentucky's first senator, John Brown. Also here is the Greek Revival Orlando-Brown House, built by Brown's second son in 1835, and designed by Kentucky's most distinguished architect, Gideon Shryock, who also designed the Old State Capitol. The latter is a Greek Revival building with a cupola and a remarkable self-supporting stone spiral staircase. It was completed in 1831 and used until 1910. Now a museum, it has been restored to its original and most charming antebellum decor.

Frankfort's State Capitol building.

Next door is the Old Governor's Mansion. It housed 33 governors and hosted seven presidents until it was replaced in 1914. The oldest official US executive residence still in use, it is now the lieutenant-governor's residence. The New State Capitol (1905–1910) overlooks the Kentucky River. It is a limestone and granite Beaux Arts structure with Ionic columns and a lantern cupola. The interior was modeled for Napoleon's tomb, with a 402-foot (123-m) columned nave, murals, stained glass, sculptures, and marble floors. The grand State Reception Room was inspired by the palace at Versailles. Outside is an enormous working clock with a face made of thousands of plants. The hour-hand weighs 420 pounds (191 kg) and the minute-hand is 530 pounds (241 kg). The present Governor's Mansion, built in 1914, is a Beaux Arts limestone building modeled for the Petit Trianon— Marie Antoinette's villa at Versailles. Guided tours of both are available. Also of interest are the early nineteenth-century Vest-Lindsey House and Zeigler House, designed in 1910 by Frank Lloyd Wright.

The Kentucky Military History Museum is located in the former state arsenal, while the Kentucky History Center features a number of interactive exhibits. Frankfort Cemetery has a large war memorial and the graves of both Daniel and Rebecca Boone. The names of the state's Vietnam casualties are in-scribed in granite beneath a memorial sundial which overlooks the city on Coffee Tree Road. The ingenious gnomon's (pointer's) shadow touches each veteran's name on the anniversary of his death.

There are several historic bourbon distilleries here. The Buffalo Trace Distillery is in Frankfort while Lawrenceburg, to the south, has Seagram's and Wild Turkey distilleries. The latter is one of the country's oldest and largest bourbon distilleries. At Versailles, to the southeast of Frankfort, is the Labrot and Graham Distillery, established in 1812.

Buckley Wildlife Sanctuary has hiking trails, a nature center, and a bird blind. Kentucky Department of Fish and Wildlife Game Farm is a 132-acre (53-ha) recreational complex, which features two fishing lakes, a songbird area, a small wetland, picnic areas, and the Salato Wildlife Education Center. The Kentucky River Campground has campsites, a boat ramp, fishing, and a playground while the Old Frankfort Pike, from Frankfort to Lexington, passes through some typical bluegrass countryside.

Capital City Airport is in Frankfort; the area has limited buses.
Map ref: page 559 H3

HOPKINSVILLE

Hopkinsville is on the US-68 in western Kentucky, and 134 miles (216 km) southwest of Louisville. A population of just over 30,000, it is Kentucky's sixth-largest city. The Trail of Tears Commemorative Park is situated on a portion of the campground used by the Cherokees during their forced march from their homelands in the South to Oklahoma, during which thousands died. Indeed, Chiefs White Path and Fly Smith are buried in the park grounds and there is a Heritage Center in the grounds.

The Pennyroyal Area Museum examines the history of southwestern Kentucky. It has displays on the Trail of Tears and the Black Patch War of 1904–1909 during which a group of western Kentucky farmers resorted to violence to break the monopoly of a small number of tobacco firms.

Bowling Green, about 70 miles (113 km) east of Hopkinsville on Hwy 80, has an airport, and buses service the area. An international airport and bus and train services are found at Louisville.
Map ref: page 558 C6

LAND BETWEEN THE LAKES

The Land Between the Lakes is an uninhabited 40-mile (64-km) peninsula of land that sits between the Kentucky and Barkley Lakes in western Kentucky. It is used for recreational purposes and as a demonstration project in environmental education and resource management. It features a living history farm, a bison herd, a nature center, audiovisuals, a planetarium, and observation areas. Hiking, camping, boating, and fishing are all available here. Kentucky Lake is a reservoir formed by Kentucky Dam, which was built across the Tennessee River and completed in 1944. It is the largest dam of the Tennessee Valley Authority. A canal connects Kentucky Lake with Lake Barkley, a reservoir on the Cumberland River about 1 mile (1.6 km) to the east. The nearest air and bus services are at Hopkinsville—about 30 miles (48 km) east.
Map ref: page 558 B7

LEBANON

Lebanon is on US-65, 55 miles (88 km) southeast of Louisville in central Kentucky. Its National Cemetery was built in 1863 to bury the dead from the Perryville Battlefield and has since buried Kentucky veterans of twentieth-century wars. Guided tours are available with advance notice. Lebanon Civil War Park has a memorial to Major-General George H. Thomas, the "Rock of Chickamauga," who led Union forces from Lebanon to the first major Civil War battle in Kentucky, at Mill Springs, in January, 1862.

The Historic Homes and Landmarks Tour takes in historic sites, particularly homes to do with the Civil War. William Clark Quantrill Driving Tour features sites relating to Quantrill who led a Confederate guerilla force that conducted savage raids on pro-Union communities in the border states.

Closest public transportation is at Louisville, which has an international airport, trains and buses.
Map ref: page 558 G5

See also Lawrence, Kansas, page 391, and Danville, page 486

The fertile soils of the bluegrass region are legendary—locals boast you can plant a nail at night and it'll be a spike by morning.

The Samuels have made bourbon in Maker's Mark Distillery, Loretto, since 1840.

LEXINGTON

Lexington is situated in a part of central Kentucky known as "Bluegrass Country," a lush area of rolling hills where the mineral-rich grass and water has fostered many famous horse farms, earning the city the nickname, "Horse Capital of the World." It is the state's second-largest settlement with about 226,000 people. Lexington is one of the nation's principal tobacco-trading centers and, although it has much industry in the metropolitan area, it somehow conspires to maintain a semi-rural atmosphere.

Lexington was established in 1775 in Shawnee territory. It was allegedly named because some pioneers were building the settlement's first cabin when news arrived of the Battle of Lexington, which marked the outbreak of the Revolutionary War. It briefly served as the state capital in 1792 until Frankfort was selected. Lexington Public Library (1795) is the oldest circulating library found west of the Allegheny Mountains, and the first teacher-training school in the United States opened in Lexington in 1839. It is home of the University

Horses are big business in Lexington, and there are hundreds of horse farms in the area.

of Kentucky and Transylvania University. The latter was the first institution of higher learning west of the Alleghenies. Students included Confederate President Jefferson Davis. Its architectural centerpiece is the Old Morrison Building, designed by Gideon Shryock.

The visitor center has a brochure outlining a historic buildings walk. The oldest historic district, which surrounds Gratz Park, attracted the town's leading families. One of its most impressive residences is the Hunt-Morgan House, an 1814 Federal-style mansion built by John Wesley Hunt, Kentucky's first millionaire. Later occupants were John Hunt Morgan, a Confederate general, and his grandson, Thomas Hunt Morgan, who won a 1933 Nobel prize. The house retains family furnishings and portraits, an unusual cantilevered staircase, and a Civil War display. The Bodley-Bullock House is another 1814 Federal mansion. It served as headquarters for Union and Confederate generals during the Civil War.

Ashland Museum was the home of leading American statesman and orator Henry Clay who was central to the settling of several major national disputes over slavery. He lived here from 1806 until his death in 1852. Almost all of the furnishings are original and the gardens and outbuildings remain. Clay is buried in Lexington Cemetery, along with other significant public figures such as John Hunt Morgan.

Pope Villa was designed in 1810–11 by Benjamin Latrobe for Senator John Pope and his wife, Eliza, who was the sister-in-law of future President John Quincy Adams. America's first important professionally trained architect, Latrobe, introduced the Greek Revival style to the United States and established the Neo-classical style for the new federal government buildings in Washington (notably the US Capitol) where he

worked with Jefferson on the White House. The Pope Villa is considered his best surviving domestic design and among the most important buildings of Federal America.

Abraham Lincoln's wife lived with her parents at the Mary Todd Lincoln House from 1832–1839, prior to her marriage. It was built in 1803 as a tavern. Little remains of the original furnishings but it has a good collection of personal effects and family portraits. Waveland State Historic Site preserves land purchased by Daniel Boone's nephew, Daniel Boone Bryan, and allegedly surveyed by Boone himself. Bryan established a plantation and his son built the Greek Revival mansion, which houses exhibits on Kentucky history.

The area around Lexington has hundreds of horse farms. Situated in beautiful countryside of rolling hills, they have vibrant green grass, trim lawns, white plank fences, grand barns, elegant houses, and, of course, remarkable horses. The Lexington visitor center has a list of those few farms that accept tours. They include the Kentucky Horse Center, which is a working thoroughbred training facility.

The main equine attraction, however, is the Kentucky Horse Park. It offers a daily parade of 40 different horse breeds, tours of a working horse farm, demonstrations of riding and equipment, rides, films, carriage tours, and campgrounds. It also has a statue over the gravesite of the famous racehorse Man o' War and the International Museum of the Horse, which examines the science of horse breeding and the historical role of horses as aids in hunting, transport, warfare, and sport.

In April, the beautiful and tasteful Keeneland Race Track hosts the final preparatory race for the Ken-

tucky Derby. Red Mile, established in 1875, is the state's oldest harness-racing track. Plenty of stables offer trail rides through the countryside. Six miles (9.7 km) from Lexington is the Raven Run Nature Sanctuary with scenic hiking trails that run through the rugged forested hills of Kentucky River Palisades.

Lexington is serviced by the Blue Grass Airport and buses.
Map ref: page 559 H4

LORETTO

Loretto, located 53 miles (85 km) southeast of Louisville, is home to Maker's Mark Distillery, a National Historic Landmark situated in very pretty countryside. Whiskey is still produced manually in attractive red, black, and gray plankhouses.

Older still is the beautiful Holy Cross Church, which was established in the 1780s by a group of Catholic families from Maryland. It was the site of the first Mass in Kentucky and the site of first Catholic Church west of the Allegheny Mountains.

Closest public transport is at Louisville, which has an international airport, trains, and buses.
Map ref: page 558 G5

LOUISVILLE

Louisville is home of the nation's most famous racing event, the Kentucky Derby. A lively cosmopolitan industrial city in central-north Kentucky, Louisville is the state's largest settlement with a diverse community of 270,000 people and an extensive metropolitan area. It is one of the country's largest manufacturers of tobacco and bourbon, and is a major river port.

Louisville has a vibrant cultural scene, an active nightlife, and excellent public parks designed by

Frederick Law Olmstead who was responsible for Manhattan's Central Park. The city is adjacent to the Falls of the Ohio. River tours are available on the paddlewheeler *Belle of Louisville,* which, with its calliope and quaint decoration, is one of the oldest stern-wheelers that is still in use.

Louisville was established in 1778 by a group of settlers from Pennsylvania, led down the Ohio River by George Rogers Clark, a frontiersman who played a major role in the defense of the early settlements from Native American attacks. He named the new village for King Louis XVI to honor the assistance of France during the Revolutionary War. In 1800, the first ocean-going ship reached Louisville which, thereafter, became an important river port. During the Civil War, Louisville was a supply depot for Union troops. After the war, trade with the South resumed, ushering in a period of prosperity.

Several public figures of note were born in Louisville. They include President Zachary Taylor, who is buried in the Zachary Taylor National Cemetery; noted justice of the US Supreme Court, Louis Brandeis; and vibraphone virtuoso Lionel Hampton. John Unitas, one of the United States' greatest quarterbacks, attended the University of Louisville.

Yet another famous son of this city is the "Louisville Lip," Muhammad Ali. The Muhammad Ali Center, scheduled to open early this century, will celebrate the values, influence, and life of the famous boxer.

The highlight of Louisville's calendar is the Kentucky Derby. The nation's oldest continuously run horse race, it dates back to the opening of Churchill Downs racecourse in 1875. Derby Day is held on the first Saturday in May when tickets can be purchased for standing-room-only spots on the infield, where there is virtually no view. There is a one- to 10-year wait for better tickets. Around 130,000 spectators gather for the principal race, the Run for the Roses, which offers almost US$1 million in prize money. Millions view the 1-mile (1.6-km) race on television. Around 500,000 visitors arrive for the pre-race celebrations associated with the Kentucky Derby Festival, which is said to be the country's largest civic celebration. It runs for two weeks, and commences with North America's largest fireworks display.

Churchill Downs racetrack is an impressive and elegant sight, most notable for its sheer scale, gardens, and twin spires. A good way to see this beautiful track is the "Dawn at the Downs" program. The Kentucky Derby Museum, at the Downs, offers tours of the facilities, three floors of horseracing exhibits, footage of every Derby recorded, and a 360-degree viewing screen of the entire track.

Just north of the racecourse is the University of Louisiana. It contains the J.B. Speed Art Museum, which is Kentucky's largest and oldest art institution. The university is at the southern edge of Old Louisville, which is the most gracious of the city's old neighborhoods. Downtown Louisville

also has many historic sites and buildings, built in the mid-1800s, such as the Jefferson County Courthouse, the Cathedral of the Assumption and the diminutive St Charles Hotel, built before 1832. Recent distinguished additions are the American Life and Accident Building, designed by Mies van der Rohe, and Michael Graves' post-modern Humana Building. The West Main Street Historic District has one of the country's finest collections of nineteenth-century cast-iron storefronts. Heading down along the riverfront, the Louisville Falls Fountain ejects a 375-foot (114-m) gusher in the shape of a fleur-de-lis, which is the city's symbol.

Locust Grove is a 1790 plantation home, which housed the city's founder, George Rogers Clark, in his retirement. Visitors to the house included Presidents Taylor, Jackson, and Monroe, and Clark's youngest brother William, who stopped at the mansion in 1806 after returning with Meriwether Lewis from a now-famous ground-breaking exploration of the Northwest. William Clark is but one of the historic figures buried in Cave Hill Cemetery.

Whitehall is an 1855 Classical Revival mansion and Thomas Edison House is an 1850s residence

The Louisville Slugger Factory and Museum.

where Edison rented a room while he worked as a telegrapher for Western Union from 1866 to 1867. There are displays of his inventions but no personal effects. Farmington is based on a design by Thomas Jefferson. Completed in 1816, it features two octagonal rooms and a large hidden staircase.

Also of interest are the Conrad-Caldwell House Museum, the Brennan Historic House and Medical Office Museum, the Farnsley-Moremen House, the Kentucky Art and Craft Gallery, and the Embroiderers' Guild of America, which features needlework displays and is located inside the historic Camberley-Brown Hotel.

The Louisville Slugger Factory and Museum presents a film and also exhibits relating to the manufacture and usage of their famous baseball bats and the batters who used them, including Babe Ruth. Outside is a 120-foot (37-m) slugger leaning on the wall. The Harland Sanders Museum at KFC (Kentucky Fried Chicken) International Headquarters has kitsch value while the Louisville Science Center holds a vast array of exhibits in a nineteenth-century warehouse, including an Egyptian mummy, hands-on activities for children, and an IMAX theater. Family entertainment is also available at Six Flags Kentucky Kingdom Amusement Park and the Louisville Zoo.

Louisville is serviced by an international airport and by buses.

Map ref: page 558 F3

The West Main Street historic district in Louisville stands out against the backdrop of modern office blocks.

MAMMOTH CAVE NATIONAL PARK

Mammoth Caves are located about 85 miles (137 km) south of Louisville, 85 miles (137 km) north of Nashville and 9 miles (14.5 km) northwest of I-65.

Established on July 1, 1941, Mammoth Cave National Park contains the world's longest known cave system. One of the country's superior natural wonders, it is a United Nations World Heritage Site and the heart of an International Biosphere Reserve. Mammoth Cave National Park features hundreds of enormous subterranean chambers full of spectacular and colorful limestone formations. They are conjoined by the world's longest network of cavern corridors and 340 miles (547 km) have so far been mapped.

The park occupies a ridge in central Kentucky. Above ground is 52,830 acres (21,396 ha) of beautiful forested hill country full of wildlife. Beneath the woodlands is a layer of sandstone and shale and below that is the limestone. During the course of millions of years, the mildly acidic water leaked through sinkholes in the upper rock layer, carving out the chambers and the spectacular rock formations below. Some of the corridors were formed by underground rivers, and visitors can see these, along with the lakes and the waterfalls.

The remains of mummies, plus simple tools, fire torches, and moccasins, testify to the fact that the cave system was known to prehistoric Native Americans as far back as 2500 BC. Early Kentuckian settlers stumbled across the cave system in the late eighteenth century and it was eventually opened to the public in 1816. A young slave, Stephen Bishop, became an early guide for spelunkers (cave explorers), accurately describing what he found as "grand, gloomy, and peculiar." He died in 1857 and is buried in the Guides Cemetery near the park entrance.

Six hundred thousand people a year take guided tours by rangers who explain the area's geology and tell stories, real and apocryphal, about the caves. Wear sturdy shoes and bring a jacket, as the temperature is cool. Twelve miles (19.3 km) of corridors on five levels are open to the public with the lowest level delving 360 feet (110 m) into the bowels of the Earth. Tours are conducted year-round but a greater range is available in summer. They vary from the short and easy Travertine Tour (75 minutes) to the gruelling 6-hour Wild Cave Tour, which involves crawling and wriggling through narrow spaces, and also climbing. Some tours exclude children and some have strenuous ascents. Rangers can suggest the tour that is most suitable to your level of interest and stamina.

For a good introduction to the cave system try the two-hour Historic Tour, which includes "Booth's Amphitheater," the "Bottomless Pit," "Fat Man's Misery," "Great Relief Hall," and two spectacular sites, the massive 192-foot (59-m) tall "Mammoth Dome," and the "Ruins of Karnak," which has limestone pillars reminiscent of an Egyptian temple.

The Introduction to Caving Tour provides some experience in spelunking (cave exploring). Participants have to stoop and crawl through narrow passages, climb, and walk above precipices. The tour ends at the "Frozen Niagara," where seeping water has created the impression of a flowing waterfall.

The 4-hour Grand Avenue Tour passes through "Cleveland Avenue" and lunch is taken 267 feet (81 m) below the surface in the "Snowball Dining Room."

There is a display of the Native American artifacts found underground, ruins of an experimental tuberculosis hospital (1842–43), Lake Lethe, and Echo River, which varies in width from 20–60 feet (6.1–18.3 m) and reaching a depth of 25 feet (8 m). It is inhabited by unusual eyeless, colorless fish and crayfish. Blind beetles and bats are also found in the caves.

Above ground there are 70 miles (113 km) of walking trails around Green River. The River Styx Spring Trail starts near the Historic En-

trance. It takes in the River Styx Spring where the water bubbles up from the caves below and into the Green River. Above-ground ranger-guided tours are available from the visitor center, which has good maps of the park's trails. Mammoth Cave Ferry Road leads to Maple Springs Campground where a gravel road leads to Good Springs Church, founded in 1842. From here there is a 10-mile (16-km) trail leads directly through reclaimed forest.

A scenic one-hour boat trip heads along Green River. Ferries have carried people (and now cars) across since the nineteenth century. Other activities include a children's exploration program, an evening program, fishing, horseback riding, and cycling. The visitor center also has maps outlining 30 miles (48 km) of canoeing along the Green and Nolin rivers.

Camping is possible year-round although there is a 14-day limit and reservations are required at some campgrounds. Tent and recreational vehicle sites are also available. Free camping permits can be obtained from the visitor center. There is also a hotel in the park with motels in Cave City, Park City, and Bowling Green. Be wary of signs declaring privately owned "mammoth" caves.

Buses go as far as Cave City. The nearest airport is at Bowling Green.
Map ref: page 558 E6

The Museum of the American Quilter's Society in Paducah exhibits the artistry of quilts, holds workshops, and sells supplies.

OWENSBORO

Owensboro is Kentucky's third-largest city with 54,000 people. It is located on the south bank of the Ohio River about 80 miles (129 km) southwest of Louisville in northwest Kentucky. Home to Brescia and Kentucky Wesleyan colleges, Owensboro is sometimes known as Kentucky's Festival City as it hosts several major riverfront festivals, notably the popular International Bar-B-Q Festival in May and a bluegrass festival in September. Bluegrass fans can also investigate the International Bluegrass Music Museum. Owensboro was founded in the late 1790s with the name "Yellow Banks" but it was renamed to honor Colonel Abraham Owen who died in the 1811 Battle of Tippecanoe.

The Owensboro Area Museum of Science and History houses exhibits on natural, cultural, and

Native American history, while the Owensboro Museum of Fine Art features nineteenth- and twentieth-century European paintings and sculpture, as well as decorative arts dating back to the sixteenth century. It is the only fine art museum in West Kentucky. Local natural attractions include Diamond Lake Resort and also Ben Hawes State Park, which offers an extensive range of sporting facilities.

Owensboro has its own airport and buses service the area.

Map ref: page 558 D4

PADUCAH

Paducah is at the confluence of the Ohio and Tennessee Rivers in western Kentucky, 175 miles (282 km) southwest of Louisville, on the Illinois border. Among the brick-lined streets and late 1800s architecture of downtown Paducah are six blocks of live music, museums, galleries, restaurants, and antique and specialty shops. Horse-drawn carriages are available and Paducah's history is depicted on flood-wall murals and interpretive panels.

During the Civil War, General Ulysses S. Grant moved south from his headquarters in Illinois in order to occupy Paducah when he learned that Confederate forces planned to seize the town. In 1864, Confederate Generals Nathan Forrest and John Hunt Morgan led a series of cavalry raids into Union territory, destroying communication and supply lines as far north as Paducah. The tourist office has maps that outline both Civil War sites as well as the historic features of Paducah's downtown area.

One of the buildings in the preserved Shaker town at Pleasant Hill, once a farming community of up to 500 residents.

The Museum of the American Quilter's Society is the largest quilt museum in the world. The National Quilt Show is held here in April. William Clark Market House is a museum with displays including the complete interior of the List Drug Store (1877), Native American artifacts, and Paducah's first motorized fire engine (1913).

The Tilghman Heritage Center examines the Civil War in West Kentucky while the River Heritage Museum focuses on the histories of the Cumberland, Tennessee, Ohio, and Mississippi Rivers. Paducah Railroad Museum features a collection of railroad artifacts and memorabilia. Also of interest are the Yeiser Art Center and the Paducah Railroad Museum. The Classical Revival Whitehaven Mansion,

built during the 1860s, is now the town's visitor center. Metropolis Lake has beaver, five species of rare fish, and bald eagles in winter. Hiking, birdwatching, and nature studies can all be enjoyed.

Barkley Regional Airport is just 10 miles (16 km) west of Paducah and buses also service the area.

Map ref: page 558 A6

PLEASANT HILL

Pleasant Hill is 25 miles (40 km) southwest of Lexington on US-68. Its main attraction is the country's largest restored Shaker Village, set up circa 1805 by a group of Shaker missionaries from New York. They supported themselves by selling cloth, tools, packaged garden seeds, and fruit preserves. The village peaked in the 1830s with about 500 people and closed in 1910 with the death of the last member.

This large farm sits on a plateau above the Kentucky River. It has 27 original buildings (1805–1859). Demonstrations show traditional activities such as weaving and making quilts, brooms, barrels, and apple butter. Visitors can sleep in a room with Shaker-inspired furnishings but modern amenities. The *Dixie Belle* riverboat has excursions on the Kentucky River and there is a restaurant. Music, hiking trails, and horseback riding can also be enjoyed in the area.

The Blue Grass Airport is at Lexington, also serviced by buses.

Map ref: page 559 H4

RICHMOND

Richmond is on US-421, just off I-75, about 30 miles (48 km) south of Lexington. Downtown has one of the state's finest restored nineteenth-century commercial districts including over 100 historic buildings; a walking tour covers 70 of these. In 1862 Confederate forces won a battle at Richmond and visitors can take the Battle of Richmond Driving Tour. Confederate President Jefferson Davis was reinterred at Richmond after his original burial at New Orleans in 1893. A site honors frontiersman Kit Carson (1809–1868), born in a small log cabin in the county.

Fort Boonesborough State Park is the site of Boonesborough, established in 1775 by Daniel Boone. It features a re-creation of the original fort, samples of eighteenth-century crafts, a small museum, riverside trails, films about the area's pioneers, and campsites. Wilgreen Lake, a fishing spot, also has camping.

To the north is White Hall State Historic Site. It is based around a 44-room brick mansion owned by abolitionist, reformer, politician, and newspaperman Cassius Marcellus Clay, who was the cousin of famous senator Henry Clay. The house was reconstructed by Cassius around his father's 1798 home. It contains Georgian, Italianate, and Gothic Revival elements.

Richmond is served by buses and the nearest airport is in Lexington.

Map ref: page 559 J4

Shaker farmland at Pleasant Hill. The Shakers were admired for their orderly farms.

LOUISIANA

Steeped in French, Spanish, African, and Acadian heritage, Louisiana celebrates its ancestry in numerous ways, especially through its festivals, music, and cuisine. Named for the French king, Louis XIV, Louisiana encompasses 49,651 square miles (128,596 sq km) of swamps, prairies, and the Mississippi delta. Sitting at an average elevation of 90 feet (27 m) above sea level, the state is susceptible to the elements, especially hurricanes. Louisiana is a survivor, however, always overcoming bad times to rejoice in the good.

First discovered by the Spaniards in 1530, the region remained uninhabited until the French settled Louisiana in 1682. Switching between French and Spanish ruling, the territory was finally sold to the Americans in 1803, under the Louisiana Purchase, and in 1812 the state was admitted to the Union. Divided into parishes instead of counties, Louisiana's law is based on the old Napoleonic Code of France.

Much of southwestern Louisiana was settled by French-speaking Acadians (Cajuns), who migrated from L'Acadie (now Nova Scotia) in the

Voodoo is still practiced in Louisiana. It combines elements of Roman Catholicism with elements of various African tribal faiths.

mid-eighteenth century, bringing with them a unique dialect and a love of music and spicy food. The Creoles, a hybrid of Spanish and French, socially ruled New Orleans' French Quarter in the late seventeenth century.

After the Union occupation of Louisiana from 1862 to 1865, Louisiana struggled to ignite its economy. Re-admitted into the Union in 1868, the state continued to languish until the new century. The 1920s marked a generation of populist politics and renewed prosperity. Louisiana now boasts a population of over 4 million people. The petrochemical, tourism, and gaming industries have contributed to the state's re-invigorated fortunes. Moreover, New Orleans, a busy seaport and Louisiana's largest city, remains one of the most desirable places to visit in North America.

State motto Union, Justice, and Confidence
State flag Adopted 1912
Capital Baton Rouge
Population 4,468,976
Total area (land and water) 49,651 square miles (128,596 sq km)
Land area 43,566 square miles (112,836 sq km)
Louisiana is the 31st-largest state in size
Origin of name Named for Louis XIV of France
Nicknames The Pelican State, Sportsman's Paradise, The Creole State, The Sugar State
Abbreviations LA (postal), La.
State bird Eastern brown pelican
State flower Magnolia
State tree Bald cypress
Entered the Union April 30, 1812 as the 18th state

Places in
LOUISIANA

ABBEVILLE

Located in the heart of Vermilion's regional wetlands is the historic town of Abbeville, founded by a Catholic priest in 1843. Though only a small city of approximately 11,000 people, it offers quite a few attractions for visitors, and all are accessible on foot.

With its downtown district focused around St Mary Magdalen Square, it is not uncommon to see a festivity in the making under a canopy of shaded oak. The square is often home to local fairs as well as the natural stage to the Abbey Players, a local theater group. The Abbey Theater, listed on the National Register of Historic Places, serves as their residence.

From the center of the square, the steeple of St Mary Magdalen Church, together with the Vermilion Parish Courthouse, acts as the city's celestial skyscraper. A stroll across Main Street leads to the Steen's Syrup Mill, the state's largest open-kettle syrup plant. The pungent smell of the boiling sugarcane is most prevalent from October to December. Several blocks down is the Riviana Rice Mill, Louisiana's oldest that dates back to the nineteenth century.

The Abbeville Culture and Alliance Center is worth a glance, if only to get an insight into the swampland culture. Just 6 miles (10 km) east of town is the drowsy village of Erath, home to the Acadian Museum and its excellent exhibits of the Prairie Bayou Acadians, recounting the history of their expulsion from Nova Scotia. Though the town is mostly

Sugarcane syrup is big business in Abbeville.

French-speaking, the museum has English interpreters on staff.

In October, Abbeville plays host to the Louisiana Cattle Show, with an added touch of Cajun barbeque. The following month the town showcases the Giant Omelet Festival, where omelet-tossing contestants end up either with egg on their face or are duly knighted into the Worldwide Fraternity of the Omelet. Abbeville also has some of the region's best oyster and shrimp eateries, including Dupuy's Oyster Shop.

Abbeville is located west of New Iberia along Hwy 14. It is serviced by Lafayette Regional Airport, 22 miles (35 km) northeast of town.
Map ref: page 568 D8

ALEXANDRIA

The central-Louisiana city of Alexandria was once a lively French and Spanish trading center before two merchants from Philadelphia decided to build a permanent settlement on the banks of the Red River in 1792. Becoming a bustling river port alongside neighboring Pineville, Alexandria built its economy around cotton, lumber, and sugarcane. During the Civil War, the city became a prime target for the invading Union Army during the Red River Campaign of 1864. In May of that year, Union troops torched most of the city, leaving only a few buildings, including Mount Olivet Church in Pineville, a Gothic-Revival Church that features Tiffany windows. The Alexandria National Cemetery on Shamrock Street has graves dating back to 1824 and those of over 1,500

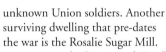
This Abbeville home on the bayou has real southern charm.

unknown Union soldiers. Another surviving dwelling that pre-dates the war is the Rosalie Sugar Mill.

Known as the "Crossroad City," Alexandria's population of 49,000 has seen its city lose the impetus it enjoyed during World War II. The downturn of the lumber industry, together with the closing of the England Air Force Base (which was the region's largest employer) has greatly impeded its economy. Nevertheless, Alexandria is slowly transforming its downtown region into a cultural attraction, with emphasis placed on the city's mid-twentieth century military history, together with its cotton, sugar, and African-American heritage.

Some of the town's attractions include Kent House, the finest example of surviving French and Spanish colonial architecture, which was built in 1800. During the Union occupation, its owner used his influential Masonic order membership to save the house from destruction. Elevated on brick pillars for protection against dampness and flooding, Kent House features a collection of outbuildings including slave cabins, a blacksmith shop and a sugar mill. The estate also has a fine museum, housing artifacts and old farming equipment. Open-hearth cooking demonstrations are held at the estate from October to April.

Alexandria's cultural exhibits are largely confined to three museums, including the superior and quite fascinating Arna Bontemps

African-American Museum and Cultural Center. The former home of Harlem Renaissance author Arna Bontemps has been transformed into a gallery featuring exhibits of the writer's works together with documents, photographs, and traveling art displays. The Alexandria Museum of Art on Main Street features a solid collection of contemporary folk art while the River Oaks Square Art Center displays a range of works by local artisans.

Radisson Bentley Hotel houses the richest history of Alexandria. During World War II, the parish of Rapides was used for the country's largest military maneuvers under the command of Generals George Patton, Dwight Eisenhower, and George Marshall, who was later instrumental in tailoring the post-war economic recovery under the "Marshall Plan." Over half a million troops were deployed to the area. Radisson Bentley Hotel was used as the main base for the generals. In the Mirror Room, several strategic battles were mapped out on hotel napkins.

Northeast of Alexandria, near the Mississippi state line, is the tiny town of Ferriday. This delta town has long been Louisiana's best kept secret, with its classic juke joints and gospel music. Ferriday was the birthplace of the 1950s singer Jerry Lee Lewis, whose first hit was "Great Balls of Fire."

Alexandria also has a fine zoo, but some would argue that the best attraction in the city is the neighboring "Hokus Pokus Liquors" sign, a classic American neon that depicts a phantom advertising its "house of many spirits." The Alexandria Visitor Center can give directions to the sign, as well as providing interesting local lore about Governor Earl Long. "Uncle Earl", as he was known, was governor in the 1940s and 1950s. His penchant for whiskey and strippers (including the famous Blaze Starr) was legendary.

Alexandria is connected by I-49, midway between Baton Rouge and Shreveport, and offers a regional airport along with bus services.
Map ref: page 568 B5

The Old State Capitol in Baton Rouge is now a museum complex.

BATON ROUGE

When French explorer, Pierre le Moyne, Sieur d'Iberville traced the Mississippi River in 1699, he came across two Indian villages that had marked their territorial boundaries by staining a tall cypress pole with animal blood. The Frenchman named the spot Baton Rouge, or "red stick." Amazingly, he recommended the river bluff as a perfect spot to develop a settlement. By the 1760s, Baton Rouge was on its way to becoming a leading river-port to the surrounding cotton, indigo, and rice plantations.

Though Britain was ceded the territory in 1763, the city retained a French influence. Baton Rouge also came under Spanish occupation following the First Battle of Baton Rouge in 1779 between England and Spain, and remained part of the Spanish dominion for the next 20 years. Baton Rouge returned to French rule, but the treaty's authenticity was soon in dispute by the Spanish. At that time, the French awarded America

the territory in the Louisiana Purchase of 1803. Seven years later an American militia stormed Baton Rouge's old Spanish Fort and drove the Spanish out of the city at the Second Battle of Baton Rouge.

Thirty-two years after Baton Rouge was founded as a town, it became the state capital in 1849. Though largely destroyed by the Civil War, Baton Rouge quickly rebuilt its city and river-based economy. By the 1920s, the city entered its most flamboyant years of populist politics under Huey Long, who served as governor from 1928 until he entered the senate in 1932. His administration built many of Baton Rouge's highways and bridges, along with the elaborate, beautiful, Art Deco Louisiana State Capitol, a 34-story skyscraper constructed in 1932. It was on the steps of the building that Long was assassinated in 1935. His grave, marked by a monument, rests in the grounds of the Capitol. Facing the river is the Gothic-style Old State Capitol, used from 1850 to 1932. Also part of the Old Capitol

complex is the Arsenal Museum, which houses interesting exhibits of Louisiana's history.

World War II brought renewed prosperity to Baton Rouge as petrochemical and aluminum industries established large plants in the area. It also marked a new era of politics with Huey Long's brother, Earl, becoming a three-term governor of the state throughout the 1940s and 1950s.

Baton Rouge is now the state's second-largest city with a population of approximately 575,000 residents. The city is also headquarters for all divisions of parish, state, and federal governments, which sustains nearly one-fifth of Louisiana's employment.

Thankfully, visitors to the city can distance themselves from the chemical plants and ramshackle districts that hug the Mississippi riverbank, and soak up the city's riverfront attractions. These include the Louisiana Arts and Science Center, which features an Egyptian tomb and fine arts gallery; the Riverside Museum; and Redstick Plaza. Also worth viewing are the Nautical History Center, and USS *Kidd*, a former World War II destroyer. Additionally, visitors can tour the Mississippi on a paddle-steamer, or stay moored on a gaming boat.

The Rural Life Museum and Windrush Gardens at Louisiana State University (LSU) features a fine collection of nineteenth-century plantation buildings as well as period artifacts and slave quarters. LSU also houses the Museum of Art, and the Museum of Natural Sciences. The Southern University, the country's largest college for African-American students in the nation, features its fabulous Jazz Institute as well as the Gallery of Fine Arts.

Close to LSU's campus is the state's oldest plantation, Magnolia Mound, which dates back to 1791. Overlooking the Mississippi, the meticulously restored estate features period furnishings along with a grove of oak and magnolia trees.

Visitors are also encouraged to drive the River Road, which traces the Mississippi River to New Orleans. The 70-mile (113-km) drive along Hwy 44/48 links many of Louisiana's

graceful river plantations including Nottaway, the largest enduring antebellum home in the South, and Oak Alley at Vacherie. The circa-1839 estate was featured as the home to Anne Rice's immortal characters, Louis and Lestat, in *Interview With The Vampire*.

Baton Rouge is serviced by most major carriers through its metropolitan airport, located off I-110. Bus services connect the city to New Orleans along I-10.
Map ref: page 568 F7

BOSSIER CITY

Bossier City, with a population of 53,000, is situated close to the Texas border in the state's northwestern region on the Red River, a natural boundary that separates the city from neighboring Shreveport. A major transportation route, Bossier City sits at the junction of I-20 and I-49.

For a city that started out as a cotton plantation in the 1830s, Bossier City does not reflect its nineteenth-century beginnings. In 1925, a terrible fire largely destroyed its downtown district; however, Bossier City's oil-based

The State Capitol in Baton Rouge.

Caddo Lake, the largest freshwater lake in the South. Caddo Lake State Park is a wildlife sanctuary featuring alligators, turtles, and white-tailed deer.

economy remained intact. In 1928, a National Air Guard squadron set up camp, expanding into Barksdale Air Force Base. The Air Force is now the primary focus of the town.

Bossier City's downtown region straddles the riverfront. The district features several modest attractions and recreational gaming at its three gambling riverboats. It is a pleasant area to stroll around and an interesting one to watch, including the blazing neon that splashes the Texas Street Bridge. Of all its attractions, the Ark-La-Tex Antique and Classic Vehicle Museum offers the most fun, with its collection of fast cars and vintage roadsters. The somewhat tamer Spring Street Museum displays Bossier City's local artifacts. If you are a science buff, the Sci-Port Discovery Center is the place to check out.

Both Bossier City's local colleges contribute their fair share to the city's cultural attractions. The liberal arts school of Centenary College houses the Meadows Museum of Art, and the Louisiana State University features a fascinating living history museum.

Greater Shreveport Airport and buses service bustling Bossier City.
Map ref: page 568 A2

CADDO LAKE STATE PARK

Caddo Lake is the largest freshwater lake in the South. The Park encompasses nearly 484 acres (196 ha) of bayous across from Louisiana into East Texas, with four watershed pockets that supply the lake: Little Cypress Bayou, Big Cypress Bayou, Black Cypress Bayou, and Jeems Bayou.

There is some debate about the origin of Caddo Lake. It is believed to have been created by the New Madrid earthquakes of 1811–12 (the epicenter was near the Missouri–Tennessee state line), though the age of the cypress trees that inhabit the waters indicate that the Lake had formed 500 to 600 years prior to the earthquake.

Caddo Lake was once inhabited by the Kadohdacho Native Americans ("Caddos") who sold this tract of water to the US government for US$80,000 in 1835. The region was soon infested with highway

robbers, makeshift brothels, and saloons around Old Monterey on the Texas side. During the Civil War, the Lake was used to transport military supplies to both armies.

By the end of the nineteenth century, Caddo Lake's water levels had dropped and its boat industry gave way to oyster farming and pearl harvesting. Oil was discovered, and the Gulf Oil Company erected the first offshore drilling platform in the country on Caddo Lake's waters.

Caddo Lake State Park was purchased in 1931; three years later it was opened to the public. The environmental expansion of the Lake continues today, with the Wildlife Management Area linking onto the Park's operation. The Lake's mass of dark misty waters and moss-laden cypress swamp has been its major appeal to many visitors, together with its wildlife habitat of alligator, white-tailed deer, turtle, and water-lily pads that support various species of frogs. Several self-guided nature trails traverse the bayous, and there are campgrounds and fishing spots.

The main park entrance is about 15 miles (24 km) northeast of Marshall, Texas, on Hwy 43. From Louisiana, Hwy 1 through Oil City will lead you directly to Lake Caddo's eastern entrance.

DELCAMBRE

Delcambre is a tiny inland Cajun port in the heart of south-central Louisiana located east of Abbeville on Hwy 14.

Delcambre is an entanglement of shrimp trawlers, nets, and seafood-packing plants, since the entire economy of this town of nearly 2,000 residents is centered around the shrimp business. Known as the "Shrimp Capital of Louisiana," the town exports millions of pounds of shrimp to the nation's markets.

The Delcambre Shrimp Boat Landing is a hub of activity. The main shrimp seasons extend from April to June and from August to October. The Delcambre Shrimp Festival, held each August, offers plenty of family fun.
Map ref: page 568 E8

The nature trails of Fontainebleau State Park offer plenty of bird-watching opportunities.

FONTAINEBLEAU STATE PARK

This backyard waterway to New Orleans also features one of the state's most beautiful parklands. Covering 2,800 acres (1,133 ha), Fontainebleau State Park is bordered by the shoreline of Lake Pontchartrain, along with Bayou Cane and Bayou Castine.

Accessible from Hwy 190 near Mandeville, the Park is a haven for boaters and campers, and hikers can enjoy the numerous nature trails that offer great bird-watching opportunities. Lake Ponchartrain's sandy beach is a popular spot for families, and a nearby swimming pool is framed by a pavilion on either side of the pool's bathhouse.

An old railroad track also runs the course of the Park. Recently the track was converted into the Tammany Trace, part of the new 32 mile (51 km) "Rails to Trails" program which starts in Mandeville.

One of the attractions in Fontainebleau State Park is the historic ruins of a sugar mill built in 1829. Bernard de Marigny de Mandeville, who founded the town of Mandeville, maintained the sugar plantation, Fontainebleau, until 1852.

The campgrounds within the Park have been divided into three groups that can accommodate different numbers of people. All of the group camps feature designated dormitories with fully equipped kitchens. The Park correspondingly houses the Fontainbleau State Park Lodge. Visitors are advised to make their reservations at Fontainebleau State Park's campsites, lodge, and picnic pavilion.

HOMER

Named for the Greek poet, this town of 4,500 people nestles in the attractive scenic hill country of northwestern Louisiana near Lake Claiborne. The first thing visitors should do when jumping off Hwy 79 is to go for a leisurely walk around the town square. The town's centerpiece is the Claiborne Parish Courthouse, which is one of four pre-Civil War courthouses in the state that is still in use. Built in 1860, the Courthouse was used as the official send-off location for the area's Confederate soldiers during the course of the Civil War.

Homer's H.S. Ford Museum, located in the Hotel Claiborne on Main Street, preserves the town's history together with the culture of its Scots-Irish and African-American settlers of the North Louisiana hill country. Another exhibit featured in this eccentric museum is an old doctor's buggy that was used as a prop in the John Wayne movie, *The Horse Soldiers*.

The best attraction of the town, however, is actually out of town, just 30 minutes away. Travel south on Hwy 9, then across I-20 to Hwy 154, to reach the small community of Gibsland, famous for its annual Bonnie and Clyde Festival and the Authentic Bonnie and Clyde Museum, which provides an insight into the couple's life of crime. Every year, on the second-last weekend of May, the town re-enacts one of their famous robberies and hosts a vintage car parade. Just a few miles south from Mount Lebanon along Hwy 54 stands a simple marker that reads: "At this site, May 23, 1934, Clyde Barrow and Bonnie Parker were killed by Law Enforcement Officials."

Greater Shreveport Airport is the nearest hub, located 50 miles (80 km) west of Homer.
Map ref: page 562 D10

HOUMA

Southwest of New Orleans lies the city of Houma, with a population of 39,000 people. It is set amid the dark shadowy water of Louisiana's alligator-infested swamps. Because of the surrounding water, Houma is often referred to as the "Venice of Louisiana."

The city's sugar, oil, and medical industries have been overshadowed by a newer source of revenue—tourism. Over the past 10 years, travelers from New Orleans have been flocking to Houma to embark on a Cajun swamp tour. The "gator dollar" is now big business, with as many as nine outfitters taking visitors on a journey through a world of alligators and Spanish moss-covered cypress trees. The swamplands are also a natural habitat for egrets, herons, cranes, and pelicans, which nest in the bulrush, together with turtle and snakes. Tours are mostly led by French-speaking Cajun guides so the emphasis is not on listening, but on viewing. The sudden emergence of a snapping and thrashing alligator is what most visitors hanker for.

Houma dates back to 1822, when the area was first settled by displaced Acadians from Nova Scotia. Of interest in Houma's historic district is the Terrebonne Museum, located in a former antebellum plantation home on Museum Drive. Featuring the region's history and artifacts, the Museum also houses the plantation's original slave quarters.

On Park Avenue is the Bayou Terrebonne Waterlife Museum, more appropriate for children and those interested in the region's flora and fauna. The visitor center also arranges guided land and cultural tours, in addition to providing information on the swamp boat tours. Of the best is "A Cajun Man's Swamp Cruise," hosted by Black Guidry, a singing, French-speaking Cajun who charms the local alligator population with his favorite song "Jambalaya."

Houma is serviced by New Orleans International Airport, which is 57 miles (92 km) north of town.
Map ref: page 568 G9

JEAN LAFITTE NATIONAL HISTORICAL PARK AND PRESERVE

The headquarters of the Jean Lafitte National Historical Park and Preserve is located on Canal Street in New Orleans. This unique park was established to preserve the natural history and cultural resources of the lower Mississippi Delta region. It is composed of six separate sites scattered throughout southeastern Louisiana. The Park illustrates for the visitor the region's evolution and cultural influences.

A squirrel in Fontainebleau State Park.

A Lake Arthur house—a reminder of days gone by.

The most popular visitor center is located in the heart of the French Quarter and Garden District on Decatur Street, where walking tours trace the city's Creole and American heritage. Another site covers the 1815 Battle of New Orleans at Chalmette. The Acadian Unit, with cultural centers located at Eunice, Lafayette, Thibodaux, Charenton, and Marksville, highlights the Acadian culture of Louisiana's swamps and prairie. The Barataria Preserve Unit near Marrero displays the natural and cultural history of the marshlands.

At the Prairie Acadian Cultural Center in Eunice, visitors can view a photographic exhibit of the history of the Cajun population, and at the same time enjoy some lively zydeco music, which features the sounds of accordions, washboards, and guitars, with lyrics sung in vernacular French Cajun. The Center explains the area's Creole lineage (a hybrid of Spanish and French), and offers cooking demonstrations of delicious Cajun dishes such as gumbo and jambalaya. There is no admission fee to the Center.

Eunice hosts the World Championship Crawfish Etouffeé Cookoff in late March, as well as the lively Cajun Prairie Folklife Festival in October each year.
Map ref: page 569 H8

LAFAYETTE

Exiled Acadians from Canada's Nova Scotia first settled the city of Lafayette on the Vermilion River in 1763. Originally inhabited by the Attakapas tribe, Lafayette existed for nearly 58 years before the foundations of a town were laid out by early pioneer and cotton planter, Jean Mouton. He donated land at the Bayou Vermilion for a church site and courthouse, and in 1836 the city was incorporated as Vermilionville. After the arrival of the New Orleans–Houston Railroad in 1884, the city's name was changed to Lafayette in honor of the French hero of the American Revolution, Marquis de Lafayette, who was passing through Louisiana at the time of the war.

Located along I-10, 134 miles (216 km) west of New Orleans, Lafayette sits in the center of the Cajun heartland, offering a strong financial, medical, and educational economy to Vermilion parish. Though its oil industry is now on the wane, Lafayette has not wallowed in the downturn. There is a future in tourism, with a focus on the Acadian culture.

Its unremarkable downtown region is compensated by its bustling college-town energy and wealth of cultural activities and museums. The Acadian Cultural Center on Fisher Road chronicles the history of the Acadians who settled in southern Louisiana's bayous, prairies, and marshlands. Close to the Center is the living museum of Vermilionville, set on 23 acres (9 ha) on the Bayou Vermilion. The Cajun folk museum at the Acadian Village is a good introduction to life on the bayous. Lafayette's University of Southwestern Louisiana is unique for its resident swamp, featuring alligators and several species of water birds. The college also displays a collection of contemporary and folk art at its University Art Museum. Military aficionados will relish the Louisiana Museum of Military History and its collection of weapons.

Of the city's architecture, St Johns Cathedral and the adjacent cemetery are of particular interest, along with the grave of Lafayette's founder, Jean Mouton. Lafayette Museum, now housed on Lafayette Street, features local artifacts and nineteenth-century editions of the city's newspaper, *L'Impartial*.

The Festival International de Louisiane celebrates all the French-speaking people of the world. The Acadia Symphony Orchestra is also worth hearing.

Lafayette has a regional airport, and is serviced by buses on I-10.
Map ref: page 568 E7

LAKE ARTHUR

The Attakapas Native Americans were the first people known to have settled the area of Lake Arthur before Arthur LeBlanc came to the region in the eighteenth century. Now a quiet lakeside community of over 3,000 people, Lake Arthur's old homes, as well as the town's park, pavilion, and boardwalk, are reminiscent of a bygone era.

Lake Arthur's backdrop of forests attracted lumber companies to the area. Rice-growing has also contributed to the economy, with the first rice mill established in 1876. By 1908, Lake Arthur was incorporated as a town upon the building of a library and schoolhouse.

The Lake is a popular spot for water sports. The park serves as the location for the town's annual festivities including the Spring Sailboat Regatta and the Lake Arthur Fourth of July Festival.

From Baton Rouge, visitors can travel along I-10 to exit 64, and then head south along Hwy 26 to Lake Arthur.
Map ref: page 568 C2

Boating is popular on Lake Arthur.

The Claiborne Parish Courthouse in Homer was built before the Civil War.

LAKE CHARLES

Lake Charles is often referred to as the "Festival Capital of Louisiana" with good reason. The city of approximately 70,000 people hosts more than 75 events each year. Lined by palm trees, this Cajun Riviera is also the only white sand inland beach on the entire stretch of the Gulf Coast.

Most of the area was largely settled by the mid-1800s and was serviced by the paddlewheeler, the *Borealis Rex*, between Lake Charles and the Gulf Coast, bringing both freight and passengers to the shores. Now three riverboat casinos have taken the paddlewheeler's place, attracting hordes of crowds to their gaming rooms.

You don't have to be a gambler to enjoy Lake Charles—there are plenty of other attractions. The city is proud of the Charpentier Historic District, an area covering 20 blocks of unique Victorian residences. Many of the homes were constructed before architects came to the region, so there is an eclectic range of designs with individual exterior features.

The most impressive gallery is the Imperial Calcasieu Museum, built on the original site of a cabin belonging to the town's namesake, Charles Sallier. The Museum chronicles the history of the Lake Charles region in a series of realistic exhibits together with Civil War paraphernalia, period costumes, and documents. The Children's Museum on Enterprise Boulevard allows children to participate in a number of different activities. They can even broadcast their own news from the studio.

An antebellum home in Monroe. The city is home to the University of Louisiana, and has a strong French and Cajun heritage.

Lake Charles was once an area inhabited by pirates; the most famous was Jean Lafitte, who stashed his booty around the present-day city's shorelines. Two weeks of festivities known as Contraband Days celebrate the buccaneer's legacy. The highlight event of the festival is walking the plank.

Thirteen miles (21 km) west at Sulphur is the Brimstone Historical Society Museum, located in the Southern Pacific Railway Depot. The Museum chronicles the history of the sulphur mines, and has photographs of the old mining town and regional exhibits. From Sulphur, Route 27 travels south to the Sabine National Wildlife Refuge in the heart of Louisiana's marshlands. The highway also is part of the Creole Nature Trail, a 105-mile (169-km) byway that provides excellent hiking trails as well as ample opportunities to spot various species of birds as well as

alligators. Looping around to Lake Charles after traveling to the Gulf Coast, the trail intersects several other wildlife refuges together with some wonderful bayou scenery.

Located 125 miles (200 km) west of Baton Rouge along I-10, Lake Charles is serviced through its regional airport; bus services are also available.

Map ref: page 568 B7

MONROE

Monroe has a French history that goes back to 1780, when a small band of settlers made a permanent camp by the Ouachita River. Three years later, the French soldier Don Juan Filhiol was granted 1,680 acres (591 ha) from the King of Spain, who built an outpost known as Fort Miro. Renamed "Monroe" after the first steamboat to arrive in the area, the town soon evolved into a major river hub and cotton-producing center during the nineteenth century. In 1916, the first drilling of natural gas took place, and for a time Monroe was a leading producer in this field.

Though not an especially tantalizing city to look at, as it spreads west across the river into an urban sprawl, Monroe definitely warrants a stopover. Monroe is now home to the Uni-

versity of Louisiana (and the Miss Louisiana Pageant). This city of nearly 56,000 people focuses on the arts and culture, and has some worthwhile museums. These include the Aviation Historical Museum of Louisiana, and the Louisiana University Monroe Museum of Natural History, which features many Native American artifacts. The Northeast Louisiana Delta African-American Heritage Museum studies the lives of nineteenth-century slaves and displays interesting artifacts from slave cabins. Visitors to Monroe can also visit the Louisiana Purchase Gardens and Zoo, or cruise the Ouachita River on the *Twin City Queen* riverboat.

The Emy-Lou Biedenharn Foundation is on Riverside Drive. Emy-Lou was an opera singer, and her father, Joseph Biedenharn, was Coca-Cola's first bottler. The heiress returned home to America from Europe at the outbreak of World War II to establish several formal gardens at her family's estate. Strolling through the serene grounds is pleasant enough; however, most people who visit come to see the Bible museum and Coca-Cola memorabilia.

The Black Heritage Parade held annually in February is a classic venue for gospel music, while the Louisiana Folklife Festival features a wide selection of Cajun arts, crafts, and music.

Located along I-20 at the junction of I-65, Monroe is serviced by buses, and by Monroe Regional Airport on Hwy 80.

Map ref: page 568 D2

A riverboat cruise is a good way to explore the Ouachita River, near Monroe.

MORGAN CITY

Located between New Orleans and Lafayette along Hwy 90, Morgan City is best known for its jumbo shrimps and Cajun heritage. Though it is only a small city of approximately 14,000 people, Morgan City has a solid economy backed by its location as headquarters to the off-shore gas and oil industries.

Described as a "gumbo city"—a melting pot of French, Spanish, German, and Dutch citizens—Morgan City was settled by Kentucky planter Walter Brashear. During the Civil War, its strategic river location along the Atchafalaya made Morgan City an important garrison for the Union army, who occupied it from 1862 to 1865. Union troops planned their assault of Texas from the city's Fort Starr.

Following the war, shipping and railroad entrepreneur Charles Morgan began draining the Atchafalaya Bay Channel, using Brashear as his company base. He also turned the city into a thriving fishing and cypress-lumber center, as well as establishing a boat building industry. In 1876, Brashear was renamed Morgan City in his honor and continued to flourish when off-shore oil was drilled in the late 1940s.

The twentieth century was marked by city development, and many churches and handsome mansions were constructed. Among those residences were the Norman-Schierer House, Cotton Top, and the Turn-of-the-Century House; the latter features paneled rooms, antique furniture, and a collection of Mardi Gras costumes. In 1997, Morgan City's Main Street Program expanded, and now its restoration efforts have been extended well beyond its nine-block historic district.

Morgan City's surrounding swamps were used as the setting for the early silent *Tarzan* features, which starred Elmo Lincoln. Since Hollywood's initial foray, Morgan City has been used periodically as the backdrop for several mainstream movies.

The Louisiana Shrimp and Petroleum Festival is the city's oldest and largest event, held every Labor Day weekend. The festival nurtures the tradition of the "blessing of the fleet," to ensure a safe return and a generous harvest.

Located along Hwy 90, Morgan City is serviced by airports at New Orleans or Lafayette.

Map ref: page 568 F9

NATCHITOCHES

The oldest permanent European settlement in the territory has been called the "New Orleans to the North." Explorers first came to the area as early as 1700 and 15 years later, the French constructed Fort Saint Jean Baptiste (now on Jefferson and Mill Streets), where they traded with the Natchitoches Native Americans.

After the Louisiana Purchase of 1803, the Americans soon inhabited the settlement, turning Natchitoches into a vibrant trade center for the shipment of livestock, tobacco, and indigo to New Orleans. When the Red River began to change its course, the river trade dried up with it. The remaining body of water, now called the Cane River Lake, separates the city's massive historic and commercial center along Front Street from the residences on the eastern bank.

Natchitoches has a population of approximately 16,600 residents. The wonderful architecture of Front Street rivals that of New Orleans' French Quarter. The townhouses, including Lucky Store, which was built in 1843, feature magnificent cast iron lace and

French and Spanish influences are evident in Cajun and Creole cuisines.

motifs. Other townhouses feature stately carriage houses at the rear of the buildings and have delightful views of the lake at the front. A walking tour is the best way to enjoy the area, starting at Front Street, within the boundaries of Rue Lafayette and Rue Touline.

Some of the stately buildings include the Natchitoches Parish Old Courthouse, which recently opened as a regional museum, and the Museum of Historic Natchitoches, which features an assortment of Civil War and French colonial artifacts. The downtown trolley links all of the major attractions within the Historic District including the American Cemetery, where many of the city's pioneers are laid to rest.

The St Denis Walk of Honor was designed to commemorate Natchitoches' most famous guests. In 1988, the town was the setting for the movie *Steel Magnolias* starring Julia Roberts, Sally Field, and Dolly Parton.

Although Natchitoches has become more prosperous (largely due to tourism), it has retained its old-world character. The city is surrounded by former plantations—many of them are along the Cane River Lake. These plantations are among the finest estates in the South and are fine examples of Creole architecture.

Natchitoches has a number of churches, bookshops, arts and crafts stores, and restaurants, and is home to the liberal arts college of Northwestern State University. And to keep the visitors' heels snapping, the Bayou Pierre Gator Park is located at the city's fringe.

There are airports 60 miles (100 km) on either side of Natchitoches at Shreveport and Alexandria. There are also bus services along I-49, but the city itself has no public transportation.

Map ref: page 568 C3

Louisiana has an abundance of lovely waterways, attracting tourists from around the globe.

Pastoral land near Shreveport. Along with oil and lumber, raising livestock and growing crops contribute to the local economy.

NEW IBERIA

The city of New Iberia (population 32,000) was first settled on the Bayou Teche by the Spanish in 1779 and remains the only permanent Spanish colony in the state. Sugar cane was the city's mainstay crop, although the production of hot spices also became a large enterprise when Acadian settlers moved into the region.

Avery Island (which is actually a salt dome) is home to McIlhenny Tabasco, a leading exporter of tabasco sauce, which has been in the McIlhenny family for four generations. Neighboring the tabasco plant is Jungle Gardens.

New Iberia's Main Street has several buildings of interest including the Church of the Epiphany, once used as a hospital during the Civil War; Broussard House; and the neighboring Mintmere Plantation House, which dates back to 1857. The loveliest structure overlooking the bayou and shaded by a canopy of live oak is Shadows-on-the-Teche, a plantation home built in the 1830s. The French colonial home features early Victorian period furnishings as well as a Pandora's box of 17,000 letters, photographs, and plantation receipts which surfaced during the

house's restoration. Later occupied by the Union Army during their Red River Campaign of 1863–64, the house fell into disrepair and has since been restored. It currently features a museum. The oldest rice mill in the nation is on Ann Street at Konriko, now on the National Register of Historic Places.

Each fall, the city holds the Gumbo Cook-off and the Louisiana Sugar Cane Festival. New Iberia is serviced by Acadiana Regional Airport, and there are bus services along Hwy 90/I-10.
Map ref: page 568 E8

NEW ORLEANS

See New Orleans, State Feature, pages 502–503

OPELOUSAS

The third-oldest city in the state was first inhabited by French traders in 1690, who traded with the local Opelousas people for several decades before the region was settled in 1782. Opelousas was incorporated as a town 18 years after the Americans acquired the territory under the Louisiana Purchase of 1803.

The surrounding farmlands of Opelousas supported a large agri-

cultural and livestock industry. Many cattle drives took place along the stretch of the Old Spanish Trail, from the present-day city to New Orleans. By the Civil War, Opelousas was flourishing from the additional cash crop of cotton, making the town a well-suited state capital during the Union Army's occupation of Baton Rouge of 1862–63. Opelousas did not engage in heavy fighting until October 1863, where the city lost and regained control from Union troops, only to succumb once again to Union occupation until the remainder of the War.

Now a city of nearly 23,000 residents, Opelousas is renowned as the Zydeco Capital of the World and birthplace to zydeco's king, Clifton Chenier. Opelousas also boasts some of the best zydeco dens in Louisiana. The Southwest Louisiana Zydeco Music Festival is held in nearby Plaisance on Hwy 167 every Labor Day weekend.

The Opelousas Museum and Interpretive Center presents an exhibit of the city's regional history together with a cultural overview. The city itself is centered around the well-preserved nineteenth-century Courthouse Square where some of the brick pavement dates back to 1838. Opelousas was also

the boyhood home of Jim Bowie, famous for his design of the Bowie Knife, who died at the Alamo in Texas. His home on Landry Street serves as both the Opelousas Tourist Center and Jim Bowie Museum, and features a collection of documents and firearms.

The Cajun prairie is an interesting place to explore, especially 6 miles (10 km) north of the city at the old steamboat port of Washington; its Acadian cottages and antebellum estates, along with a mixture of Cajun and Creole residents, make the town colorful and unique.

An 80-minute drive east of Opelousas near St Francisville is the Angola State Penitentiary, and its museum. Visitors will find the museum and the history of the electric chair known as "Old Sparky" grim but fascinating. The museum also houses the script from the movie, *Dead Man Walking*, which was based on the life of an Angola inmate.

Opelousas is serviced by Baton Rouge's airport, 52 miles (84 km) east along Hwy 90.
Map ref: page 568 D6

POVERTY POINT NATIONAL MONUMENT

Located 54 miles (87 km) east of Monroe is a collection of ancient Native American ruins dating back to 1700 BC. A complex of mounds and ridges, the largest construction at Poverty Point is shaped like a bird and spans 700×640 feet (213×195 m) at its base, rising to 70 feet (21 m) at its highest point.

The earthworks were arranged to accommodate ceremonial and burial mounds on what was previously the Mississippi River, which once flowed through the area. Its series of ridges reputedly served as a foundation for the village, though nothing has been recovered to support the claim. Some of the artifacts found in the village came from as far away as Appalachia and the Ohio Valley.

Stretching across some 1,500 acres (607 ha), Poverty Point was designated a national historic landmark in 1962. The visitor center, 15 miles (24 km) from Delhi on Hwy 577, can provide detailed information on the six mounds scattered over the site.
Map ref: page 568 F1

Sarah Albritton is one of Ruston's most talented and best known folk artists.

RUSTON

The college city of Ruston, with a population of 23,000, sits in the heart of Louisiana's peach country, 35 miles (56 km) south of the Arkansas state line.

Ruston's historic district dates back to its inception in 1884, when land mogul Robert E. Russ donated acreage to the Vicksburg, Shreveport, and Pacific Railroad in order to develop a depot center on his land.

Ruston eventually became a leading education base and home to Grambling State University and Louisiana Tech University. But it was the founding of the Louisiana Chautauqua Society in 1890 that gave academic credibility to the city, with its members playing host to the country's most noted philosophers, writers, and politicians. The Lincoln Parish Museum at North Vienna Street is the best place to delve into the town's history as well as the roots of the Chautauqua Society.

Although there are no significant attractions to the town, Louisiana Tech University does offer a sideline attraction for children at its museum, The Idea Place, which also has an art gallery, planetarium, and arboretum.

The Louisiana Peach Festival is held each June, and the celebrated Jimmie Davis Tabernacle, an annual homecoming parade, takes place in October. Former Ruston resident and two-term state governor (1944-48 and 1960-64), Jimmie Davis was also a country music artist who recorded "You Are My Sunshine." Not surprisingly, his vocals won him both elections.

Ruston has a regional airport, and I-20 and Hwys 80/87 link Ruston to Shreveport, Louisiana and Vicksburg, Mississippi.
Map ref: page 568 C2

SHREVEPORT

Once a prosperous city dominated by cotton crops, Shreveport became the state's third capital during the Civil War. Incorporated as a town on the banks of the Red River in 1839, Shreveport was also the last Confederate capital to surrender to the victorious Union Army, seven weeks after the defeat of the Confederacy at Appomattox.

Shreveport (population 200,000) is proud of its Southern heritage. The economy was based around oil, lumber, and agriculture; the introduction of river casinos to the city has largely turned its foundering economy around. Together with its sister city, Bossier City, which nestles on the river's eastern shores, Shreveport is redeveloping its combined six historic districts (see entry on Bossier City, page 494) including the Riverfront. Since the mooring of the river casinos, the Red River entertainment district has begun to transform itself into a funky nighttime venue, covering the spectrum of jazz, Cajun and, of course, the blues.

Shreveport offers very little in the way of cultural appeal. Aside from the Ark-La-Tex Antique and Classic Vehicle Museum, and the Sci-Port Discovery Center and IMAX Dome Theater, there's not a feast of attractions on the city's entertainment menu. But there is a little piece of Elvis Presley trivia worth noting. The Municipal Auditorium was once the venue for the "Louisiana Hayride" show, where the young Elvis Presley made his first radio appearance in 1954. After that there was no stopping him.

Greater Shreveport Airport services the city; buses are available.
Map ref: page 568 A2

THIBODAUX

This traditional Cajun city of 15,000 was once a thriving trading post in the late 1700s, when transportation from New Orleans was limited to the bayous. Named for one of the early settlers to the region, the city today is still surrounded by sweeping plantation estates including the Laurel Valley Plantation, built in the 1840s. Featured in the Laurel Valley Village, a massive restoration project has brought back to life the plantation's former slave quarters, barns, and a schoolhouse. Guided tours of the quarters are available.

Downtown is rather deserted and lacks the liveliness found in other bayou towns in the Cajun Wetlands. Nevertheless, Thibodaux has preserved its courthouse, built in 1861, together with Saint John's Episcopal Church, one of the oldest churches west of the Mississippi River. Efforts are now being made to re-create the city's historic district and promote its French heritage through the Jean Lafitte Acadian Wetlands Cultural Center (see entry on Jean Lafitte National Historical Park and Preserve, page 496).

Thibodaux is served by New Orleans International Airport and bus services along Hwy 1/90.
Map ref: page 568 G8

A potential star of the future on the way to a performance. Louisiana has a strong tradition of support for the performing arts.

STATE FEATURE

New Orleans

Music is a way of life in New Orleans, and street musicians can be found on many corners.

New Orleans is an intoxicating fusion of cultural diversity, reflected in its music, festivals, and cuisine, and is affectionately known as the "Big Easy." The city has a population of some 500,000 residents (nearly 1.2 million in the greater metropolitan area) comprising people with Creole, Cajun, Anglo, and African backgrounds. There is a sense of timelessness about the place, especially in The French Quarter— formerly known as the Vieux Carré—where mule-drawn carriages set the pace of its streets.

Positioned at the crescent of the Mississippi River, 105 miles (169 km) upstream from the Gulf of Mexico, the city's elevation drops to 10 feet (3 m) below sea level in some area points. Though protected by levees and enormous pumps that drain excess water into Lake Pontchartrain and the surrounding bayous, New Orleans remains susceptible to floods.

The historic district was first settled in 1718 by Jean Baptiste and named in honor of the Regent of France. During both the French and Spanish rules, New Orleans served as the territory's capital and became part of the United States under the Louisiana Purchase of 1803. When Louisiana was admitted to the Union in 1812, New Orleans served as the state's first capital until 1830 and again from 1831 to 1849. The city was also center stage to the conflict with Britain in 1815 at the Battle of New Orleans.

When the steamboats arrived along the Mississippi in the first half of the nineteenth century, New Orleans entered the "Golden Age" as a leading river port and commercial center. Its prosperity came to a halt during the Civil War (1861–65), as the city was under Union occupation. Cut off from the world markets, New Orleans' isolation came with dire financial and racial consequences during Reconstruction (1865–77). The demise of its river trade and traditional plantation economy together with civil rights for former slaves led to increasing racial discord.

New Orleans was reinvigorated at the beginning of the twentieth century when the city gave birth to the sound of jazz. Jazz is as energetic today as it was when Buddy Bolden led jazz funerals with his cornet, and Jelly Roll Morton first brought the sound of Dixieland to the once-flourishing bordellos.

The New Orleans "Jazz Age" spawned many noted musicians including Sidney Bechet, Edward Kid Ory, as well as Joe "King" Oliver. The city's undisputed crown prince, however, was Louis "Satchmo" Armstrong, who first entertained people on the streets as a teenager when he was a resident at the Jones Colored Waifs' Home.

The best place for authentic Dixieland Jazz is at the decayed dwelling of Preservation Hall on St Peter Street. There are no seats and little ventilation, but the atmosphere makes up for the lack of creature comforts.

Anywhere along gaudy Bourbon Street, in the heart of the French Quarter, is an assortment of Cajun,

The French Quarter of New Orleans is a busy, exciting area, bristling with restaurants, bars, galleries, and shops.

blues and jazz bars. Other nighttime revues are also located within a six-block stretch.

The only way to explore the historic French Quarter is on foot. Bordered by the river and Canal Street, the Quarter remains the city's main attraction.

Many of the early nineteenth-century townhouses feature secluded rear gardens and cast-iron galleries. Starting from Jackson Square's Saint Louis Cathedral, which was rebuilt in 1794, many of the street names disclose French influence: Bourbon, Chartres, Toulouse, and Burgundy. The most resplendent is Royal Street, an avenue brimming with antique shops, galleries, and fine restaurants. Off Royal is St Louis Street, the site of Antoine's, the city's oldest family-owned restaurant.

A tour of historic places should also include the Old Pharmacy Museum, which preserves the original La Pharmacy Française dating back to 1823; the Inn on Bourbon (formerly the French Opera House); Napoleon House; Beauregard-Keyes House; the Old US Mint (part of the Louisiana State Museum); and the Old Ursuline Convent, the oldest surviving Creole dwelling in the city. Other architectural landmarks along Royal Street include the Court of the Two Sisters, the Cornstalk Hotel, and the notorious Haunted House at 1140 Royal Street.

Voodoo, a belief system based on African spiritualism, was practiced in New Orleans in the nineteenth century. At the Voodoo Museum at 724 Dumaine Street, visitors can delve into the origins of voodoo.

The Historic New Orleans Collection on Royal Street exhibits the documents of the Louisiana Purchase together with artifacts, Civil War paraphernalia, and a host of cultural and historic heirlooms. Off Royal Street at Pirates Alley is the Faulkner House, where novelist William Faulkner wrote his first essay, "A Soldier's Pay," in 1926.

At the edge of the French Quarter is the old French Market and Warehouse District. Along with the garish casinos, the Riverwalk Marketplace complex is the city's major shopping area. Here visitors can jump aboard the steamboat *Natchez* or visit several museums and attractions including Jackson Brewery, the Aquarium of the Americas, the Confederate Museum, the Louisiana Children's Museum, and the Piazza d'Italia, which was featured in the opening scene of the movie, *The Big Easy*. The open-air pavilion of Café du Monde has also been a favorite to locals for over a century.

Bordered by Iberville, St Louis, Robertson, and Basin Street, Storyville's legalized brothels flourished for 20 years until the US Navy closed down the district in 1917. It is unwise to stroll these streets or Armstrong Park after dark. Within the park is the Mahalia Jackson Theater for the Performing Arts, home to the New Orleans Ballet and Opera.

Old Congo Square—now Beauregard Square—was the actual birthplace of jazz. In the eighteenth and nineteenth centuries, slaves were allowed the freedom to gather in the square every Sunday, where they would sing and dance. The rhythm and instruments used in these rituals, historians believe, are part of the origins of jazz.

The wide boulevard of Poydras Street is home to New Orleans' Superdome, where the annual Sugar Bowl football game is played. On Rampart Street is Our Lady of Guadeloupe Church, formerly the Mortuary Chapel for yellow-fever victims, built in 1826.

Canal Street, which separates the Quarter from the Garden District, sits in the very heart of New Orleans' commercial area and is the terminus of the St Charles Streetcar, leading to the neighborhood established by wealthy Americans after the Louisiana Purchase. Many of the Greek Revival-style houses feature lush landscaped gardens with ornate cast-iron gates. Examples include Payne-Strachan House, the landmark Pontchartain Hotel, Bultman House, which was the inspiration for Tennessee Williams' drama, *Suddenly Last Summer*, and Brevard House, the private home of author Anne Rice. Along Magazine Street are numerous Creole cottages and faded Victorian mansions now housing New Orleans' premier antique galleries.

New Orleans nurtures many unique cemeteries, also known as the "Cities of the Dead." Because of the city's low elevation by the river, interred residents are buried in mausoleums and above-ground tombs. Row upon row of crypts feature elaborate marble monuments, adorned with crosses, angels, and the occasional voodoo charm.

New Orleans' cultural life is centered on festivals such as the Jazz and Heritage Festival (known as Jazz Fess) each April, and the Carnival Season, which starts 12 days after Christmas, culminating in the world-famous Mardi Gras, the day before Ash Wednesday. Mardi Gras is a festival of masked balls, street parties, and float parades which draws visitors from around the world.

If you miss the Carnival, Mardi Gras World across the Mississippi River at Algiers tells the complete story, and features massive giant figures, floats, and props.

New Orleans is famous for its Cajun and Creole restaurants. The selection of food includes jambalaya, crawfish bisques, mudbugs, andouille, and gumbo.

New Orleans International Airport is located west of the city, off I-10. There are also numerous train and bus links.

The novelist William Faulkner lived for a time in this house in Pirates Alley.

New Orleans' French heritage is evident—Joan of Arc was from Orléans in France.

MISSISSIPPI

More than any other Southern state, Mississippi embodies the very spirit of the "Deep South." Nicknamed "The Magnolia State," it cradles a legion of antebellum mansions, haunting Civil War battlefields, and vast fields of cotton.

One-third of Mississippi's population of 2,844,658 is African-American, with large numbers living in the Mississippi Delta, a region also known as the "Cotton Belt." During the 1960s, Mississippi fought bitterly against integration of its schools and colleges in a struggle marked by violence and murder. However, times have changed, and evidence of racial reform is reflected in the appointments of African-American representatives in state politics.

Tourism is becoming part of Mississippi's mainstay economy. Although cotton remains king, the harvesting of rice, wheat, and soybeans has expanded the state's agricultural base. Mississippi's economy also relies on livestock, such as poultry, and live-

Stately cypress trees line the edges of the Mississippi Delta.

stock products; as well as the manufacturing of textiles, paper, and processed foods. In recent years gaming centers moored along the Delta and Gulf of Mexico shorelines, as well as land-based centers, have re-energized the state's coffers.

Mississippi is the home of the blues. Some of America's most famous bluesmen (BB King, Robert Johnson, Muddy Waters, and John Lee Hooker) came from the state, and it is also the birthplace of rock and roll legend Elvis Presley.

The 46,914 square miles (121,507 sq km) of lowlands, and coastal and river plains were once the territory of the Choctaw and Chicasaw peoples. The area was charted in 1540 by Spanish explorer Hernando de Soto; the first European settlement, nearly 160 years later, was by the French. Mississippi became a state in 1817, but seceded to join the Confederacy in 1861.

State motto *Virtute et Armis* (By valor and arms)
State flag Adopted 1894
Capital Jackson
Population 2,844,658
Total area (land and water) 48,286 square miles (125,061 sq km)
Land area 46,914 square miles (121,507 sq km)
Mississippi is the 32nd-largest state in size
Origin of name Possibly from a Native American word meaning "father of water" or "great river"
Nickname The Magnolia State
Abbreviations MS (postal), Miss.
State bird Mockingbird
State flower Flower of the magnolia or evergreen magnolia
State tree Magnolia
Entered the union December 10, 1817 as the 20th state

Places in
MISSISSIPPI

BILOXI

Settled in 1699 by the French, Biloxi is the nation's second oldest city and arguably Mississippi's most progressive metropolis. It is steeped in both Spanish and English heritage and, with a population of 56,403, sprawls around the shores of the Gulf of Mexico. Each year thousands flock to its casinos and sandy beaches.

Ignoring the heavy oil and chemical industries that foul the air, Biloxi remains focused on boating and fishing along the barrier islands which fringe the coast 12 miles (19 km) offshore. The Gulf Islands National Seashore preserves this waterway and four of Biloxi's islands. Most popular is West Ship Island, part of Ship Island which was split in half by Hurricane Camille in 1969. The island's main attraction is Fort Massachusetts, built by the Confederacy and which later served as a Union base and POW camp. West Ship now shelters alligators and marshland birds and attracts hordes of day-trippers who come for the sand, sun, and swimming. The Gulf islands' main wilderness treasure is Horn Island, 3,650 acres (1,480-ha) of sanctuary to nearly 260 bird species and unsullied marsh forests. There are numerous hiking trails along with mosquito-infested campgrounds. Both islands can be reached from Biloxi by ferry services.

Exhibits at Biloxi's Maritime & Seafood Industry Museum bring to life Biloxi's pirate past and fishing history as well as the devastating hurricanes that have whipped through here. At the Marine Education Center and Aquarium children can ogle the assortment of marine life in an enormous 42,000-gallon (159,000 l) fish tank. Keeping company with the aquarium on Beach Boulevard are six off-shore casinos with gaudy gaming rooms that would give their Las Vegas cousins a run for their money. The Ohr-O'Keefe Museum of Art, possibly the city's most unusual attraction, showcases the works of artist George Ohr, also known as the "Mad Potter of

Biloxi," who produced innovative pottery along with a brood of children with equally creative names; Clo, Flo, Geo, Ojo, Oto, and Zio. The museum also exhibits pieces by local artists.

Nineteenth-century Biloxi was a resort town and principal center to the Gulf's fishing industry. Today most of its historic buildings are either private residences or restaurants, and so not open to the public. Nonetheless they are well worth viewing, even if only from the street. Start your self-guided tour at the 1895 Brielmaier House, now the visitor center, then check out the architecture of the Old French House and the Old Spanish House (both private residences). The historic Magnolia Hotel, a grand estate dating back to the 1830s, now houses the Mardi Gras Museum and its colorful displays chronicling the history of the festival along the Gulf Coast. Biloxi's Civil War connections are fostered at Beauvoir, the former summer home of Confederate president, Jefferson Davis. Davis's widow left the home and grounds to Confederate veterans and it has since been turned into a museum featuring personal and Confederate artifacts.

Biloxi is served by Gulfport-Biloxi Regional Airport through the major carriers, trains, and bus services along the I-10.
Map ref: page 569 L7

Clarksdale is not only a center for the blues, it is also a thriving farming area.

BRICES CROSS ROADS
NATIONAL BATTLEFIELD SITE

One of the most strategic battles in Mississippi was fought here towards the end of the Civil War. In attempt to cut off crucial Union supplies to General William T. Sherman's troops along the Tennessee railway line, Confederate General Nathan Bedford Forrest out-maneuvered General Samuel Sturgis's invading regiment at Brices Cross Roads in June, 1864. Though outnumbered by five to one, the Confederate army out-flanked the opposing troops, thereby forcing them back into Tennessee. The victory unfortunately was short-lived, however, as the battle failed to stop Sherman in his march across the South to the Atlantic.

The site features several interpretive signs along with two cannons used in the combat. Brices Cross Roads is located west from Baldwyn off Route 370.
Map ref: page 563 M6

CLARKSDALE

Vast fields of cotton stretch across the rich alluvial plains that surround Clarksdale, a northern Delta town of 19,717 people that lives and breathes the blues. Located on "The Blues Highway"—Hwy 61—Clarksdale was the birthplace of bluesmen Muddy Waters and John Lee Hooker. The Delta Blues Museum in the Old Freight Depot in the Blues Alley district downtown houses an eclectic collection of blues memorabilia. These include recordings, photographs, and rock group, ZZ Top's "Muddy Wood" guitar— a guitar built from remnants of Muddy Water's home at the Stovall Plantation, 7 miles (11 km) north-west of town. The Depot is the also location for the Sunflower River Blues Festival each August.

Riverside Hotel, on Sunflower Avenue, was a hospital when blues singer, Bessie Smith, died there in 1937 after being hurt in a car crash.

Clarksdale has seen other revered folk, and institutions, pass on, including the first African-American DJ in the South, "Soul Man" Wright, who hosted blues music on WROX 1450 AM from 1947 until his death in 1999. Walton's Barber Shop, home for years to Clarksdale's blues-singing barber

Fishing is big business in Biloxi, which is centrally located on the state's coastline.

The back streets of Tutwiler, near Clarksdale. It was near here that W.C. Handy first heard the sound of the blues.

Wade Walton, now sits idle. Also gone is Rooster Records, together with their once-famous guide the Delta Blues Map Kit.

But all is not lost. Every October the town hosts the Tennessee Williams Festival. The playwright lived most of his childhood at the St George Episcopal Church, where his grandfather was pastor.

To soak up more of the Delta region's character, drive north along Route 1 to the Mississippi crossing to Helena, Arkansas. Another blues diversion is south along Hwy 49, to the village of Tutwiler, in Tallahatchie County. It was near a cheerless railroad crossing here that W.C. Handy ("Father of the Blues"), overheard a drifter singing a mournful song while waiting for the train. Handy took this blues sound with him to Memphis, where he composed a series of mainstream songs. The mural near the tracks which features this tale also points visitors in the direction of the Whitfield Church graveyard, where Helena's famous DJ and harmonica player, Sonny Boy Williamson, is buried.

Continue south along Hwy 49 to Parchman Penitentiary, where Vernon Presley (Elvis's father) and thousands of other inmates were forced to work in the Mississippi cotton fields. The chain gangs were immortalized in producer and writer Alan Lomax's "Southern Journey" recordings and also in the Miles Davis song "Going on Down to Parchman Farm."

Clarksdale's many juke joints include the legendary Smitty's Red Top Lounge, renowned for its line-

up of musicians capable of converting the uninitiated into blues aficionados. Those who wish can visit the Tallahatchie Bridge, which was immortalized in singer Bobbi Gentry's ballad, "Ode to Billy Joe" as the place where Billy Joe McAllister plunged into the river.

Clarksdale is at the crossroads of Hwy 61 and Hwy 49. Buses travel Hwy 61 (the Blues Highway) from Memphis to New Orleans.
Map ref: page 563 J7

COLUMBUS

The pretty antebellum city of Columbus sits close to the Alabama state line off Hwy 82. Despite its small population of 23,799, Columbus packs in a lot of attractions, starting right on Main Street with the Victorian building that was the birthplace of playwright Tennessee Williams. Now a Mississippi Welcome Center, it's the place for visitors to scoop up walking tour maps and information on the town's history.

Columbus grew from a trading post in the late-eighteenth century into a center for a wide range of agricultural industries before becoming a place of higher learning. After establishing the state's first free public school in 1821, Columbus turned its attention to developing Mississippi's first college for women in 1847. Now the Mississippi University for Women, it is an interesting faculty, only admitting men since 1982 and also offering a degree in culinary arts. Writer Eudora Welty is the university's most famous alumnae.

Around Third Avenue are a host of Gothic and Greek Revival buildings as well as a number of ornate townhouses built by wealthy nineteenth-century planters and their families.

Although Columbus was not involved in any battles in the Civil War, its buildings became hospitals for soldiers from both armies. The town's Decoration Day dates from 1866 when a group of local matrons meeting at Twelve Gables initiated the practice of laying flowers on the graves of Union soldiers, in addition to Confederate graves of their own family members at Friendship Cemetery. As the story of this "Blue and the Gray" gesture became widespread, Decoration Day evolved into the nation's official Memorial Day. The highlight of this event in Columbus takes place after dark, with costumed guides directing a candlelight tour around Friendship Cemetery, complete with tales of the interred residents.

Columbus opens the doors to a number of its historic homes, including the circa 1838 Twelve Gables, during its Spring Pilgrimage tours. Several churches that served as Civil War field hospitals are also included. Waverley Plantation, located off Route 50 near the Tombigbee River, is open all year-round. Once the largest estate in the area with more than 1,000 slaves working its fields, the plantation lay in deserted ruin until the 1960s. Now painstakingly restored to its former magnificence, it has obligingly produced an apparition of a young girl in period bedclothes.

Columbus lies on the Tennessee-Tombigbee Waterway— that is known as Tenn-Tom—a channel lined with nature trails, marinas, and campgrounds on its 234-mile (275-km) journey to the

Gulf. It is served by the Golden Triangle Regional Airport between the cities of West Point and Starkville.
Map ref: page 563 N8

DE SOTO NATIONAL FOREST

Named for the Spanish explorer Hernando de Soto, who blazed through here in 1541, this national forest in southeastern Mississippi is the state's largest. Hwy 49 runs north/south through the forest, and Hwy 26 runs east/west, dividing the north from the south. From the town of Laurel, you can head east to the northern section, in the Chickasawhay region, where slow-moving streams cut a winding swath through thick woodlands. The district office—in the southern section, at Wiggins, on Hwy 26—provides a wealth of information on the various recreational pursuits available, including float trips, canoeing, fishing, hunting, and hiking.

The most popular area of the national forest is the Black Creek district, in the south. Hikers to the forest usually negotiate the much-favored, 41-mile (66-km) Black Creek Trail, which is also a haven for woodpeckers, owl, blue herons, and wild turkey. The trail meanders past aging oak and overhanging cypress, occasionally traveling parallel to Black Creek. Some 21 miles (34 km) of this waterway has been designated a national scenic river. This is the best place in the forest to find native beaver and deer.
Map ref: page 569 L5

Log truck, near De Soto National Forest.

GREENVILLE

The largest city in this state on the Mississippi River, Greenville (population 40,648) sits at the junction of Hwy 82 and Route 1. Though its economy remains based around its river port, the sea of fading neons along Route 1 seem to exemplify the sweltering fatigue of this tired city.

Rising from the ashes of three devastating fires, Greenville has received a shot in the arm since the introduction of gaming. Casinos now lap in the Old Muddy's waters alongside river barges and a replica of a nineteenth-century stern-wheeler that serves as the River Road Queen Welcome Center.

The hometown of Civil War historian, Shelby Foote, Greenville had liberal views on black integration in the 1940s that set the city a league apart from the rest of staunchly segregated Mississippi. In 1946 Greenville came under the national spotlight when Hodding Carter from the *Delta Democrat-Times* won a Pulitzer Prize for his essay on racial reform. The city now hosts the Greenville Writers Exhibit, celebrating its rich literary heritage, which also includes Walker Percy and Ellen Douglas.

At Warfield Point Park, 5 miles (8 km) south of the city, an observation tower provides a panoramic vista of life on the Mississippi River. Leland, east of Greenville on Hwy 82, was the childhood home of Muppet maestro, Jim Henson; the whimsical Birthplace of the Frog Museum on South Deer Creek Drive features Kermit and other Muppet memorabilia.

Visitors will need a car to travel Route 1 to Greenville.
Map ref: page 563 H9

GREENWOOD

Greenwood's sad record of racism has earned it an infamous place in civil rights history. In 1954 Emmett Till, a 14-year-old black boy was murdered. The haunting image of his corpse in national newspapers, and the subsequent trial and shameful acquittal of his killers, galvanized the civil rights movement into action. A decade later Greenwood was again in the spotlight when white supremacist and local resident Bryon de la Beckwith was acquitted of the

1963 murder of civil rights activist Medgar Evers (see entry on Jackson).

Formerly Choctaw Indian land, the city (population 18,906) is named for Greenwood Le Flore, who made his fortune from cotton crops and slave labor on property he acquired by negotiating the treaty of Dancing Creek. The pact saw the Choctaw tribe exiled to Oklahoma. Greenwood is the South's leading cotton exchange outside of Memphis. Visitors to the Florewood River Plantation State Park can stroll around a recreated 1850s plantation home, smokehouse, and blacksmith shop, while the Cottonlandia Museum, to the west, has cotton industry artifacts, Civil War documents and a news clipping of President Lincoln's assassination in 1865. The best time to visit Greenwood's famed Cotton Row is the annual CROP Day Festival, held in August.

Greenwood features genteel Victorian buildings and Lusco's, one of Mississippi's most popular restaurants during Prohibition. Legendary bluesman Robert Johnson died in a boarding house here; his memorial is located at Mt. Zion Missionary Church, though the Zion Church, off Money Road, is rumored to be his resting place.

Greenwood is located just off Hwy 82.
Map ref: page 563 J8

GULFPORT

A sister city to Biloxi, Gulfport's population of 64,829 differs little from other industrialized cities along the Gulf of Mexico. Scattered around its fringes, however, are fishing villages and artist colonies. You'll also find a couple of lavish casinos, which channel cash into the city's economy.

The Navy's long association with Gulfport dates from the Civil War, when Union gunboats moored at Fort Massachusetts. The port is now home to the Naval Construction Battalion Center, the Navy's construction force which is known as the Atlantic Fleet Seabees. Tours highlighting the history of the Seabees are available through their Gulfport Public Affairs Office.

One of the prettiest estates in Gulfport is Grass Lawn, overlooking the Gulf off Route 90. The former summer home of a plantation owner, it showcases a seaside garden and 1840s cypress and pine house. Exhibits in the Gulfport Centennial Museum allow the visitor to delve into Gulfport's development since the Civil War.

Gulfport is served by Gulfport-Biloxi Regional Airport through the major carriers, along with trains, and buses along the I-10.
Map ref: page 569 K7

Jefferson Davis Library, Gulfport.

HATTIESBURG

Hattiesburg (population 41,882) is a good place to stop en-route to the De Soto National Forest, to the city's east. Located off the I-59 in the state's southeast, Hattiesburg is home to the University of Southern Mississippi and is involved with campus and cultural activities.

Fishing boats at Greenville, Mississippi's largest city on the Mississippi River. The port is an important part of the local economy.

Hattiesburg's pleasant historic district encompasses 115 acres (63 ha) of late-Victorian and early-twentieth-century house, shops and churches, including the Tally House, a classic inn with a wrap-around porch. For many visitors, however, the city's main attraction is board game champion Robert Walker's International Checkers Hall of Fame, located in Petal, just to the east on Hwy 11. Here visitors can view the largest checkerboard in the nation as well as an eclectic collection of checkerboard paraphernalia (you must make an appointment to visit here).

A short drive south finds the Armed Forces Museum at Camp Shelby, with more than 6,000 exhibits covering every aspect of the US Military, from the Civil War to the Persian Gulf War (admission free).
Map ref: page 569 K4

HOLLY SPRINGS

The old tobacco and cotton-producing town of Holly Springs is steeped in Civil War heritage. Nestled at the junction of Hwy 7 and Hwy 78, its population of 7,261 is today focused on promoting the town's traditions.

Every April Holly Springs hosts a three-day Spring Pilgrimage, when the doors to a number of its 90 or so antebellum estates are opened to the public.

Start a visit here with a stroll around the tree-lined streets surrounding the town square, taking in the Marshall County Historical Society Museum, four pre-Civil War churches, and the antebellum houses showcased along Salem Avenue. Perhaps the most splendid structure in town is Montrose, built in 1858 by wealthy landowner and slave-holder Alfred Brooks and now home to the town's Holly Springs Garden Club.

During the Civil War, Union General Ulysses S. Grant made Holly Springs his camp base during the preparation for his Vicksburg invasion of 1862. During his occupation, General Grant moved his family into Walter Place on Chulahoma Avenue, an address that later also became a refuge for Confederate spies. The town is believed to have changed hands over 50 times during the Civil War. A more poignant attraction is Hillcrest Cemetery, which contains the graves of Confederate soldiers and victims of the town's 1878 yellow fever epidemic.

The oddly fascinating Graceland Too, on E. Gholson Avenue, is somewhat at odds with the rest of genteel Holly Springs. Here two local residents have turned their home into a shrine to the King of Rock and Roll, Elvis Presley, with all sorts of memorabilia on display.
Map ref: page 563 L5

INDIANOLA

In the heart of the Mississippi Delta's prime cotton country, Indianola (population 11,809) began as a lumber-mill settlement in 1886. Today the town's blues heritage is its primary attraction. B.B. King (born Riley B. King) began life in neighboring Itta Bena. A stroll through downtown Indianola is full of constant reminders of the bluesman's association with the town, including a street and park named for him and the imprints of his hand and foot embedded into the sidewalk at the corner of Second and Church Streets. Music fills Indianola in the first weekend of June during B.B. King's Homecoming festival. The town was also home to civil rights activist, Fannie Lou Hamer.
Map ref: page 563 H9

The original State Capitol in Jackson was built in 1833.

JACKSON

Jackson, in the state's mid-region, has its origins in a trading post built late in the 1600s by French-Canadian Louis Le Fleur. Known first as Le Fleur's Bluff, it was renamed for the nation's seventh president, Andrew Jackson, and in 1821 was appointed Mississippi's second capital—Natchez (see entry) was the first. With a population of 202,062, Jackson is Mississippi's largest city. Recently, however, many businesses have relocated to the suburbs, leaving the downtown district a mere shell of its former glory. But there are still numerous points of interest.

Jackson flourished during the antebellum era and the expansion of the southern railroad to the key cities of Vicksburg and New Orleans, and today is the spiritual bastion of Confederacy. During the Civil War it was occupied, then torched (in 1863) by General William T. Sherman's Union troops. The original 1833 State Capitol was one of the few of Jackson's buildings to be spared; it now houses the State Historical Museum, where displays include an impressive collection of Civil War artifacts. The New Capitol, built in 1903, is on High Street.

Jackson is home to three African-American colleges, including the prestigious Jackson State University. The Smith-Robertson Museum and Cultural

Cotton farming at Indianola, in the heart of the Mississippi Delta. Cotton is still Mississippi's most important crop.

Center (Bloom Street), originally the first public school for Jackson's black population, pays homage to Mississippi's rich African-American culture as it chronicles local history from slavery to the mass migration north following the Civil War. The State Historical Museum, as well as Jackson State University feature extensive exhibits focusing on civil rights.

The most telling event of Jackson's racial conflict during the 1960s was the murder in June, 1963 of Mississippi NAACP (National Association for the Advancement of Colored People) branch leader Medgar Evers, in the driveway of his home. Located at 2332 Margaret Walker Alexander Drive, the house remains sheltered from the public; however, a bronzed memorial in honor of the slain activist has been erected on Medgar Evers Boulevard at Sunset Drive. It took 30 years for Evers's killer, Byron de la Beckwith, to be successfully convicted of his assassination.

The Agriculture & Forestry Museum on Lakeland Drive provides a living-history exhibit of a recreated 1920s Mississippi community and a pre-Civil War homestead. Adjacent is the Mississippi Sports Hall of Fame.

The Eudora Welty Library is Jackson's cultural jewel and, with the Mississippi Writers Room, showcases the works of Mississippi literati such as William Faulkner, Tennessee Williams, Richard Wright, and Shelby Foote. Eudora Welty still lives in the Jackson suburb of Belhaven in the house across from Belhaven College Campus where she has spent most of her long life.

Jackson's quirkiest attraction is probably the Dixie National Rodeo and Livestock Show, held mid-February, complete with bronco-busters and a covered-wagon parade. Other notable events include the annual Martin Luther King Day in January and the Mississippi State Fair in October.

Jackson is the Mississippi's transport hub, linked by road to all major centers in the state. Jackson Airport is off the I-20, 10 miles (16 km) from downtown. Buses link the city with Memphis and New Orleans, and there is also a rail service.
Map ref: page 569 H2

MERIDIAN

One of the important industrial and railroad centers during the Civil War, Meridian still keeps a firm grip on manufacturing as its principal economy. Today its most important business is Peavey Electronics, the largest manufacturer of amplifiers to the music industry. With a population of 40,835 the city is now the state's third largest.

Though Meridian is primarily used as a pit-stop at the junction of the I-20 and I-59, the Peavey Visitor Center and Museum is worth a look for those with a desire to road test the company's highly regarded guitars, keyboards, and drums. You can also visit the Jimmy Rodgers Museum, dedicated to country music's "Singing Brakeman," where an exhibit features an outdoor locomotive and various railroad paraphernalia along with Rodgers' guitar.

The town of Chunky, 10 miles (16 km) west on the I-20 is host to the Chunky Rhythm and Blues Festival, held every July. There are bus, rail, and road links.
Map ref: page 569 L2

NATCHEZ

Natchez's graceful architecture and spectacular natural setting—high on a bluff overlooking the Mississippi River—combine to make it one of the prettiest antebellum towns in the state. Unlike most Southern towns under Union occupation, Natchez remained unscathed during the Civil War. Now with a population of 19,460, it is a remarkably preserved gem

Gardens like this add charm to rural properties all over the state of Mississippi.

reflecting the South's Golden Age. Allow the best part of a day to visit the antique shops and the stately buildings in the historic district.

The town was originally home to the Natchez Indians. Initially they coexisted peacefully with the French who established Fort Rosalie trading post here in 1716. However the Natchez soon became disenchanted with the arrangement, and in 1729 made a brutal attack on the outpost; in retaliation the tribe was subsequently banished from their ancestral land. Visitors can view the Grand Village of the Natchez Indians, a reconstructed and archeological site that depicts the tribe's unique infrastructure.

Natchez was the capital of the Mississippi Territory from 1798 until 1822, when Jackson took on the role. In the 1820s Natchez's port began welcoming the steamboats that plied the Mississippi

during the river's grand days as a major transport route. It was during this period that many wealthy planters moved to town, establishing magnificent estates close to the banks. The riverboat landing at Natchez Under The Hill was once a notorious den for unsavory folk, littered with saloons and brothels, and called "Sodom of the Mississippi" by residents. Now the luxurious Lady Luck casino is perched at the landing. There are numerous opportunities here to catch a classic Mississippi River vista of the *Delta Queen* or *Mississippi Queen* riverboats making their way slowly upstream from New Orleans.

The town's well-restored and maintained buildings are attributed in large part to the work of two local organizations—the Natchez Garden Club and Natchez Pilgrimage Garden Club. Both are based at Stanton Hall on Pearl Street. Notable mansions (and their delightful, old-fashioned gardens) now on show to the public include Linden, Monmouth, Auburn, Stanton Hall, and Longwood. The 84-acre (34-ha) plantation home, Melrose, operated by the National Park Service, features the original slave quarters behind the main house. The Historic Natchez Foundation can provide visitors with lots of interesting information on local historic estates.

Natchez is served by Jackson Airport, 155 miles (250 km) to the east, and by Baton Rouge in Louisiana.
Map ref: page 568 F4

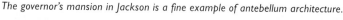

The governor's mansion in Jackson is a fine example of antebellum architecture.

NATCHEZ TRACE PARKWAY

The Natchez Trace Parkway is a scenic road following ancient Indian paths that once linked present-day Nashville, Tennessee, with the Mississippi River at Natchez. It enters the state near Tupelo, continuing southwest to Jackson, then on to its southern end, 10 miles (16 km) north of Natchez.

For more than 8,000 years the Natchez Trace was the main thoroughfare for the Choctaw and Chickasaw tribes. In the late-1700s colonists attracted to the frontier by land grants took the same route, turning the Trace into a busy highway. The Natchez Trace was designated as US land under an 1801 treaty; five years later Congress appropriated funds to develop the trail for commercial trade. In 1812, during the war with England, it served as a military road. But by the 1820s steamboats along the Mississippi became the main source of transportation, and so the Natchez Trace returned to wilderness.

The efforts of the Daughters of the American Revolution saw the Trace restored as an historic pathway by 1909. Today's trail mainly follows the original highway and has been operated by the National Park Service since 1934. Only a two-lane highway, the Natchez Trace Parkway is marked by numerous entrances, historic markers, plantation ruins, Indian burial grounds, and towns.
Map ref: page 563 M7

OCEAN SPRINGS

Ocean Springs is primarily a dormitory town for the nearby centers of Biloxi and Gulfport, with its tranquil setting a pleasant respite from the industrial bustle of its neighbors. A community of nearly 15,000 residents, it has a large artist colony, and many art galleries line the downtown sidewalks.

It is worth seeking out the Walter Anderson Museum of Art which showcases the work of a twentieth-century local painter known for his striking canvasses of Gulf plants and animals. Also on view in Ocean Springs is the striking architecture of Louis Sullivan, whose young protégé was Frank Lloyd Wright.

Though Biloxi is often considered the landing point and site of first settlement in Mississippi, this honor actually belongs to Ocean Springs. French explorer Pierre Le Moyne, Sieur d'Iberville, who was commissioned by King Louis XIV to settle the Louisiana Territory, arrived at present-day Ocean Point in 1699.

Ocean Springs is served by Gulfport-Biloxi Regional Airport, along with buses along the I-10, and trains.
Map ref: page 569 L7

William Faulkner's home, Rowan Oak, near Oxford, is a mecca for lovers of literature.

OXFORD

Situated in the northwest of the state, in the gentle rolling foothills of the Holly Springs National Forest, is the graceful town of Oxford. The life of the town is focused around its town square, the location of the handsome Lafayette County Courthouse. Although the scene of much devastation during the Civil War, Oxford's tree-lined streets, white clapboard homes with wraparound porches, and grand antebellum estates today present a picture of tranquility. With a population of 9,984, Oxford is also home to "Ole Miss" (the University of Mississippi) and author John Grisham, who currently lives in a colorful farmhouse west of town. For some 32 years it was the base of writer and Pulitzer and Nobel Prize winner William Faulkner.

Oxford shaped the imagination of Faulkner, providing the basis for his fictional Yoknapatawpha County, and its idiosyncrasies and decadence were captured works such as *Sanctuary*, *Light In August*, and *A Green Bough*. Faulkner purchased Rowan Oak, his rambling 1840 estate, in 1930. Surrounded by lofty trees at the end of a long pathway off Old Taylor Road, it has changed little since Faulkner's passing in 1962. Visitors

Rico's fishing supplies, Mississippi River.

to the writer's unassuming office can see his typewriter and, on the wall, the outline of his prize-winning novel, *A Fable*. Faulkner's grave is in the local cemetery, not far away on Jefferson Avenue. Regular book readings at the re-vered Square Books, a mecca for literary disciples, together with the celebrated Faulkner and Yokna-patawpha Conference, and the Oxford Conference for the Book, draw many visitors.

The University of Mississippi is an attraction in itself. The 1848 Lyceum, built four years after the founding of the university, is one campus building that remained after the Union invasion. Other surviving antebellum structures include the Barnard Observatory, housing the Center for the Study of Southern Culture, and the 1853 Old Chapel. "Ole Miss" also over-sees the most extensive collection of blues heritage artifacts, records, and photographs at the Mississippi Blues Archive. The personal papers of William Faulkner and James Meredith, both former alumni, are on exhibition at the John D. Williams Library. James Meredith's enrolment in 1962 ignited local hostility over black integration, resulting in a riot in which two people died.

Oxford is serviced by buses along Hwy 9 and chartered flights to University Oxford Airport.
Map ref: page 563 L6

PASCAGOULA

The city of Pascagoula lies along Mississippi's heavily industrialized coastline, close to the Alabama state line. A former Spanish settlement, it is the location of the oldest structure in the Mississippi Valley—the Old Spanish Fort built around 1718. A cypress and pine edifice rather than a citadel, the fort now houses a museum display-ing Pascagoula Indian artifacts. The Pascagoula River, which runs west of the city, is subject of an Indian legend. It is called the "Singing River" for the eerie sounds that come forth from its waters; locals believe the sounds are the chanting souls of the Pascagoula tribe, who linked hands and walked to watery graves rather than be captured by invading Biloxi Indians.

Located within 15 minutes of Biloxi along Hwy 90, Pascagoula is

The humble home in Tupelo that is the birthplace of rock star Elvis Presley.

served by Gulfport-Biloxi Regional Airport through the major carriers, by Greyhound buses along the I-10, and by trains.
Map ref: page 569 M7

TUPELO

Tupelo nestles in the state's north-east, near the boundary of the Natchez Trace. Headquarters for the Natchez Trace Parkway (see entry), are just to the north. But visitors do not visit this city of 36,000 people for its surrounding rural beauty alone. Tupelo's greatest claim to fame is as birthplace and hometown of the King of Rock and Roll, Elvis Presley.

Numerous signs direct visitors to the Elvis Presley Birthplace and Museum. What comes as a shock to the uninitiated is the small size of the home where Elvis and his stillborn twin, Jesse, were born in January, 1935. His father Vernon Presley—a poor sharecropper—built the two-room shack for a borrowed $180; however he, wife Gladys, and young Elvis were evicted two years later when the loan was foreclosed. The family remained in the town until 1948. When he became nationally famous, Elvis returned to Tupelo amid great fanfare for a charity concert. With the proceeds, Elvis purchased the 15-acre (6-ha) park that now includes the humble house where he was born. The museum now located directly behind his birthplace features a host of Elvis accoutrements, ranging from records and Elvis clocks though to a few of the

singer's personal possessions. The visitor center on Main Street can provide a map of the former haunts of the King. These include the still-trading Tupelo Hardware, where Elvis bought his first guitar.

Civil War buffs can visit the Tupelo National Battlefield, where in 1864 a 14,000-strong Union force overwhelmed Confederate troops under the command of General Nathan Bedford Forrest. The modest Tupelo Museum on W. Main Street features a small display of Civil War paraphernalia, Indian artifacts, and a one-room schoolhouse. Along the Natchez Trace Parkway are numerous campgrounds and hiking trails, as well as a mound site of the Chickasaw ancestors.

West of Tupelo along Hwy 45 is the tiny and pretty community of Ponotoc, and on Hwy 9, the

outlandish Westmoreland, where owner Mrs Westmore has collected a medley of scrappy quilts, farming instruments, and an odd assort-ment of clothing and furniture.
Map ref: page 563 M6

VICKSBURG

The fall of the river port of Vicksburg to Union General Ulysses S. Grant marked the turning point in the Civil War and the start of the Confederacy's spiral into defeat. Having de-stroyed railroads in the South during the first two years of war, the Union army began a cam-paign to cut off the South along the Mississippi River. The strategic target of Vicksburg remained under siege for 47 days until its eventual surrender on July 4, 1863. Formerly one the South's busiest commercial ports, at the close of war it lay in ruins.

First settled in 1790 by the Spanish and named Nogales, it was renamed Vicksburg for the Reverend Vick, who purchased 1,120 acres (455 ha) of land here and in 1820 developed the town along a bluff overlooking the river. Vicksburg's fortunes grew around the shipping of cotton bales and during the late 1800s it grew into largest city in the state. Now with a population of 27,056, Vicksburg is a living monument to its Civil War legacy. Every July it hosts a Civil War Reenactment Siege as well as its Memorial Day Reenactment, which features both Union and Confederate costumed soldiers and camp tents.

An unusual book sculpture at the corner of Troy and Spring Streets in Tupelo.

Floating casinos like the *Ameristar* have become a major part of Vicksburg's economy.

Downtown, an easy-to-navigate walking tour takes in several antebellum buildings. Included is the 1858 Old Court House Museum with its white-marbled portico climbed by General Grant to survey Vicksburg after its surrender; the building today houses an extensive archive of the battle and military weapons. Duff Green Mansion, on First East Street, served as both a Union and a Confederate hospital; its mistress fled the house during the conflict. Balfour House, on Crawford Street, was the location of the city's famed Confederate Christmas Ball of 1862, when the merriment was interrupted by the announcement of advancing Union gunboats. The city relives the event, complete with period regalia, every December.

Several homes in Vicksburg's Garden District, around Washington Street, open their doors to the public during the Spring and Fall Pilgrimages. The area is also rich with antique shops and interesting galleries. Worth a look is the Biedenharn Candy Company and Museum of Coca-Cola Memorabilia housed in the premises where the drink was first bottled; exhibits include a restored 1890 candy store (with stock for sale) and soda fountain.

Without boubt one of the most eye-popping places on show is Margaret's Grocery on Hwy 61— a food market that doubles as a bible-thumping hideaway. Its extra-ordinary ensemble of patchwork brick, pillars, and archways was built by Margaret's husband, Reverend Dennis. Apart from a dose of the Good Book and a can of beans, visitors can view the Reverend Dennis's version of the Ark of the Covenant. One of the impassioned sermons delivered to customers concerns the "evil of the gambling boats," yet callers to Vicksburg readily succumb to temptation at the floating casinos that dot the shoreline. Since its introduction in the 1990s, gambling has made a major contribution to the economy of Vicksburg.

Another nearby attraction, some 10 miles (16 km) west of Port Gibson, is the structural skeleton of Windsor Castle. The mansion survived the siege of Vicksburg, but it was burnt down in 1890; leaving 23 Corinthian columns.

Buses service Vicksburg from Jackson along the I-20 and from Memphis on Hwy 61.
Map ref: page 568 G2

VICKSBURG NATIONAL MILITARY PARK

A somber sanctuary comprising 1,800 acres (730 ha) of the Civil War battleground, Vicksburg National Military Park is lined with monuments and markers chronicling the battle and subsequent defeat of the Confederate Army. Begin your visit at the park center, located near the main entrance, on Clay Street to pick up detailed information along with audio tapes for touring the park. On exhibit in the park is the USS *Cairo*, a Union gunboat that was sunk in the Yazoo River by a Confederate mine, and raised from its watery grave just over 100 years later. Also within the park is the haunting Vicksburg National Cemetery, which holds 17,000 Union graves—nearly two-thirds of the markers read "unknown." The park is west of Vicksburg on I-20.
Map ref: page 568 G2

YAZOO CITY

Located 40 miles (64 km) northwest of Jackson, in Mississippi's "catfish corridor," medium-sized Yazoo City (population 12,427) exists largely on the of catfish farms that surround the town.

Vicksburg National Military Park.

The city's historic district is picture-perfect in the spring with colorful blooms spilling onto its sidewalks. Yazoo City is also known for its Mississippi Cheese Straw Factory along with the Oakes African-American Cultural Center, a regional museum that chronicles Yazoo City's black heritage.

A further attraction is the Witch Way to Yazoo Festival, a springtime event that milks a local legend concerning an alleged witch who lured fishermen to their deaths, only to die herself in a swamp filled with quicksand. The old woman was buried in Glenwood Cemetery from where, in 1904, she was believed to rise from her grave to cause a fire which wreaked havoc on Yazoo City.

Yazoo City is on Hwy 49.
Map ref: page 563 J10

This mighty bridge spans the Mississippi River at Vicksburg. During the Civil War, Vicksburg was of great strategic importance.

NORTH CAROLINA

With over 8 million people, North Carolina is the nation's 11th-most populous state and the largest producer of tobacco, textiles, and wooden furniture. The state's most compelling attraction is its still largely undeveloped natural beauty, particularly its mountain ranges, rivers, waterfalls, lakes, parks, and its scenic coastline. Its historic houses, battlefields, and gardens are also major drawcards.

The Sarah P. Duke Gardens, Durham, is especially attractive in fall when the foliage is most colorful.

The Atlantic Coastal Plain dominates the state's east, while the hilly center is known as the Piedmont. This region contains most of the population, as well as manufacturing industries, the famous Research Triangle, and the popular sandhills area. In the west of the state are the southern Appalachians, featuring some of the most spectacular scenery in the southeast, especially in Great Smoky Mountains National Park and along the Blue Ridge Parkway.

The first European in North Carolina was Giovanni da Verrazzano who, in 1524, explored the Cape Fear area for France. The first English colony in the United States was established on North Carolina's Roanoke Island, but it completely disappeared . between 1587 and 1590. Migrants from Virginia settled on Albemarle Sound in around 1650. North Carolina became the 12th US state in 1789 with Raleigh as the capital.

Before the Civil War (1861–65), North Carolina tried to preserve the Union but, once it had joined the Confederacy, it dedicated itself to the cause, losing about 40,000 soldiers. The post-war economy recovered, with cotton and tobacco leading the way, although discrimination prevented African-Americans from capitalizing on their liberation and joining in the prosperity.

Two historical events associated with North Carolina are the Wright brothers' first airplane flight in 1903, and the birth of the Civil Rights sit-in movement at Greensboro in 1960.

State motto *Esse Quam Videri* (To be rather than to seem)
State flag Adopted 1861
Capital Raleigh
Population 8,049,313
Total area (land and water) 52,672 square miles (136,420 sq km)
Land area 48,718 square miles (126,180 sq km)
North Carolina is the eighth-largest state in size
Origin of name Named for King Charles I of England
Nickname The Tar Heel State
Abbreviations NC (postal) N.C.
State bird Cardinal
State flower American dogwood
State tree Pine
Entered the Union November 21, 1789 as the 12th state

STATE FEATURE

Great Smoky Mountains National Park

The Great Smoky Mountains are among the highest and most rugged mountains in the Appalachian Range and are one of the world's oldest mountain groups. They are named for the bluish haze in which they appear to be constantly enveloped. This humidity is produced by the transpiration of water and hydrocarbons from the dense forests, although since the 1950s air pollution has thickened the mist.

The national park that protects the Smokies is America's most popular, attracting around ten million visitors a year. It sprawls across the state border with Tennessee, incorporating 800 square miles (2,072 sq km) of largely unspoilt mountainous terrain, which includes 16 craggy peaks over 6,000 feet (1,830 m). The flora and fauna of these eastern forests is so diverse that the Smokies have been designated an International Biosphere Reserve. There are 1,500 species of flowering plants, including some found only in the Park, 150 species of trees, and the most extensive virgin hardwood and red spruce forests in the United States. Sadly, pollution is affecting the stands of red spruce. The park's wildlife includes 200 bird species, plus cougars, groundhogs, white-tailed deer, black bears, raccoons, bobcats, and eagles.

Activities within the park include scenic drives, hiking, horseback riding, fishing, canoeing, white-water rafting, and mountain biking. Most visitors drive along the major scenic roads that traverse the mountains. On summer weekends there may be 60,000 people on the bitumen. There are 270 miles (434 km) of roads and 800 miles (1,287 km) of walking trails, including a 68-mile (109 km) portion of the Appalachian Trail, a footpath 2,000-miles (3,218 km) long for hikers and campers that traverses the Appalachian Mountains from Georgia to Maine.

A garden near the Oconaluftee Visitor Center in the Great Smoky Mountains National Park. From April to October, employees at the Visitor Center demonstrate traditional farming practices.

The Trail follows the ridgeline of the Great Smoky Mountains through the park.

The park is open year-round although some visitor centers close from November to April and some roads are closed in winter. The tourist season is from late May until late August. In summer the weather can be hot and humid at the lower elevations. The transition to the beautiful fall colors is best seen from mid-to-late October at the lower elevations.

The Park is effectively bisected north–south by Newfound Gap Road (US-441). It passes from lowland hardwood forests at 2,000 feet (610 m) up to spruce-fir forests at 5,000 feet (1,525 m). At such altitudes, rain, mist, fog, and icy cold can come suddenly at any time of the day or year, even if the sun is beaming below, so be prepared.

At the southern end of Newfound Gap Road, near the Park's North Carolina entrance, is the Oconaluftee Visitor Center, open year-round; further north is Mingus Mill (1886) which still grinds wheat.

Continuing north along Newfound Gap Road past Smokemont Camping Area, there are picnic facilities and a nature trail. Further north is the 5,048-foot (1,540 m) Newfound Gap. From the overlook it is possible to see Mt LeConte, 6,593 feet (2,011 m), and Clingman's Dome, at 6,643 feet (2,206 m) makes it the highest point in the Smokies. A spectacular seven-mile (11.3-km) spur road heads southwest from this overlook to the start of a short steep paved trail that leads to the top of Clingman's Dome where there is an observation tower.

Return to Newfound Gap Road and continue north. It is not far to an overlook which is the start of an easy-going 2½-mile (4 km) loop trail that follows a wooded creek to Arch Rock—a natural tunnel carved out by erosion. A steep three-quarter-mile (1.2 km) offshoot leads up to Alum Cave Bluffs, which in the nineteenth century was the site of an alum mine and a source of saltpeter for Confederate gunpowder. It is a further 2½ miles (4 km) to the summit of Mt LeConte although this is a very difficult and exceedingly steep trail requiring good health, a high level of fitness, good weather, and caution in an oxygen-thin environment. At the top is LeConte Lodge where basic lodging is available for those with advance reservations.

Further north again is a stop associated with the vertical cliffs known as Chimneys. There are two tracks: the Cove Hardwood Nature Trail and the steep Chimney Tops Trail, which reaches up 1,335 feet (407 m) to the sheer cliffs. It is possible to drive to Chimney Tops Overlooks from whence there are views of the twin peaks known to the Cherokee as "Duniswalguni", meaning "forked antlers."

Another major driving route is the Cades Cove Loop Road, which can be accessed from the Sugarlands Visitor Center by heading west along Laurel Creek Road and Little River Road. Cades Cove is situated within a scenic valley, which was cleared after 1819 when a treaty was signed with the Cherokee. An 1850 census revealed 680 people living there. These pioneers left behind many structures, which form an open-air museum.

There are also several churches: the Primitive Baptist Church and Graveyard, which closed in the Civil War because the congregation was Union-oriented amid a Confederate majority; the Methodist Church, which had separate doors and pews for men and women; and the Missionary Baptist Church, formed in 1839 by members expelled from the Primitive Baptist Church which was also closed due to divided sentiments during the Civil War.

At the Cades Cove Visitor Center there is a collection of buildings relocated from elsewhere in the Park, such as a cantilever barn, a smokehouse, and a blacksmith's.

The easiest climbing trail in the Park is the Balsam Mountain Trail—this loop track departs from Balsam Mountain Campground. Laurel Falls Trail, the park's most popular waterfall trail, commences on Little River Road near Elkmont Campground.

Ten campgrounds are available in the Park. Smokemont, Elkmont, and Cades Cove are open all year-round. They have a seven-day limit from mid-May to the end of October, at which times reservations are recommended. The limit is extended to 14 days the rest of the year.

The Great Smoky Mountains National Park has densely packed areas of shrubland, streams, and some of the world's oldest mountains.

The Mountain Farm Museum consists of farm buildings relocated from other sites within the park.

Places in
NORTH CAROLINA

BLUE RIDGE PARKWAY

The Blue Ridge Parkway, in the west of the state, is hewn into the side of the Blue Ridge Mountains. Considered one of America's finest scenic highways, it offers spectacular views of the forest-clad mountains from an average elevation of 3,000 feet (915 m). The Parkway winds its course through 459 miles (739 km) from Virginia's Shenandoah National Park to North Carolina's Great Smoky Mountain National Park. The Parkway, which attracts more than 16 million visitors a year, is used only for vacation travel and is off-limits to commercial vehicles. In spring the route is marked by mountain laurels, azaleas, and dogwoods, while fall sees a colorful display of reds, oranges, and yellows. Along the route are visitor centers, hiking trails, camping areas, whitewater rafting and canoeing opportunities, historic sites, and superb vistas.

The Parkway's mileage is numbered from north to south,

The Blue Ridge Parkway, carpeted in autumn leaves

beginning in Virginia. Stops within North Carolina include Cumberland Knob (Mile 217.5), Doughton Park (241.1), where there is a popular walk to the isolated Brinegar Cabin, and Blowing Rock (291.8), near the town of Boone. The actual Blowing Rock, at 4,000 feet (1,220 m) above Johns River Gorge, is named after the strong winds that climb up the cliff face returning light objects to those who throw them over the edge. At 294.1 is the Parkway Craft Center, which is set amid the 3,600-acre (1,440-ha) grounds of the Moses H. Cone Memorial Park. At 305.1 is the turnoff onto US-221 which leads to the 5,964-foot (1,819 m) Grandfather Mountain. Entry is costly but there are great views, hang-gliding opportunities, a natural history museum, and a small animal exhibit. A 228-foot (70 m) long, suspension bridge swings over 1,000 feet (305 m) above the chasm below. At 316.4 is the Linville Falls Visitor Center. It is a short hike to the picturesque double-level falls, which plunge into a rugged 2,000-foot (610 m) gorge. At 355.5 is Mt Mitchell State Park where it is possible to drive to the top of Mt Mitchell, which at 6,684 feet (2,039 m) is the highest peak east of the Mississippi. At 382 is the Folk Art Center.

Another 5 miles (8 km) west is Asheville, a New Age center with "alternative" activities, shops, and an active night life. Asheville's downtown and its opulent architecture are meticulously preserved. Its principal attraction is Biltmore Estate. A fine example of the excess associated with the Gilded Age,

One of the many historic homesteads in Ashville, on the Blue Ridge Parkway.

it features 250 rooms, a 70-foot-high (21 m) vaulted ceiling, a bowling alley, an indoor swimming pool, a medieval banquet hall, and a 10,000-volume library. Outside is a winery and 75 acres (30 ha) of outstanding gardens masterminded by Frederick Law Olmstead, who designed Central Park in Manhattan. The largest private home in America, it was designed in the style of a French chateau by Richard Morris Hunt for George Vanderbilt, the grandson of railroad baron Cornelius Vanderbilt. The house is furnished with artworks by Renoir, Durer, and Whistler, Flemish tapestries, opulent furnishings, and Meissen porcelain. It was built from 1889 to 1895. On the estate is Biltmore Village, a group of specialty shops, galleries, restaurants, and cobbled walkways.

The boyhood home of novelist Thomas Wolfe, which inspired "Dixieland" in his 1929 novel *Look Homeward, Angel*, is now a State Historic Site. Both Wolfe and short-story writer O. Henry are buried in Riverside Cemetery. The Pack Place Center houses the Asheville Art Museum (featuring twentieth-century American paintings), the YMI Culture Center (displaying African-American art), and Colburn Gem and Mineral Museum. Just southwest of Asheville is the North Carolina Arboretum, which features south Appalachian flora.

Chimney Rock Park, 20 miles (32 km) southeast of Asheville, is based around an unusual rock formation which offers panoramic views of the Blue Ridge Mountains and Lake Lure where the movie

Dirty Dancing was filmed. A 26-story elevator leads to the top from whence there is a clifftop walk to Hickory Nut Falls, one of the highest waterfalls in the eastern United States. Some of *The Last of the Mohicans* was filmed here. Beyond Asheville, the Parkway traverses the beautiful Pisgah National Forest.

Map ref: page 559 K10

See also Virginia, page 543

BOONE

Named after frontiersman Daniel Boone, this town of 13,000 people is located 83 miles (134 km) northwest of Charlotte, amid spectacular high-country scenery in the upper region of the Blue Ridge Mountains.

Boone is a good stopover for those traveling along the Blue Ridge Parkway. There are antique shops and opportunities for golf, swimming, fishing, hiking, mountain biking, canoeing, and whitewater rafting. The district also features the largest concentration of alpine ski resorts in the southeast. Appalachian folk musician Doc Watson was born at Deep Gap, east of Boone, in 1923.

In the Daniel Boone Theater, from late June to mid-August, *Horn in the West* dramatizes the efforts of southern Appalachian citizens to gain independence during the Revolutionary War (1775–83). Adjacent are Daniel Boone Native Gardens, and Hickory Ridge Homestead, which recreates eighteenth-century mountain life. The Appalachian Cultural Museum covers everything from the natural history of the region to stock-car racing.

Boone sits at the intersection of US-321, US-421, and Route 105, and is accessible by train.
Map ref: page 559 P8

BURLINGTON

Burlington is located off I-85 and has strong associations with several historic battlefields, such as the Alamance Battlefield Site where 2,000 farmers called the Regulators were defeated by 1,000 troops led by Royal Governor William Tryon on May 16, 1771. The farmers were rebelling against the taxes and dishonest officials imposed upon them by wealthy eastern planters.

Three markers denote the sites of local battles that occurred in 1781 during the Revolutionary War. Pyle's Defeat Marker commemorates the slaughter of about 100 loyalists by rebel forces. At the Clapp's Mill Marker, rebel forces retreated under fire from the British forces of General Cornwallis and, at Lindley's Mill Marker in Graham, over 250 soldiers were killed or wounded.

Burlington's Historic District dates back to the 1880s. The Captain James White House is an 1871 Queen Anne-style mansion that has been converted into an art gallery, while at the restored Cedarock Historical Working Farm, nineteenth-century farming techniques are demonstrated. The Alamance County Historical Museum is the nineteenth-century home of textile pioneer Edwin

The University of North Carolina at Chapel Hill is the oldest state-chartered university in the country.

Michael Holt. Also of interest is one of only 14 Dentzel Menagerie Carousels in existence; it was made in 1910 and it is now the centerpiece of City Park.
Map ref: page 566 G1

CHAPEL HILL

Chapel Hill is a college town of 39,000 people in the state's central Piedmont area. It is located at the southwest corner of the Research Triangle, which is completed by two other proximate university towns: Durham in the north and Raleigh 25 miles (40 km) to the southeast. The Research Triangle is a regional identity that expresses the local emphasis on, and the relationship between, research, industry, and federal government agencies. President Gerald Ford once taught physical education at a naval base in Chapel Hill.

The University of North Carolina is the country's oldest state-chartered university (1789). Visitors can enjoy the historic Old East building, the Ackland Memorial Art Center, and the outstanding Morehead Planetarium, a 68-foot (21 m) dome where NASA astronauts trained until 1975.
Map ref: page 566 F1

CHARLOTTE

Charlotte is the largest city in the Carolinas with nearly 440,000 people. It is located in the southern Piedmont near the South Carolina border on the I-85 and

I-77. A successful major financial and wholesaling center, Charlotte's city center is marked by concrete and skyscrapers, strip malls, and clubs.

European settlement of Charlotte began around 1748 with Scottish–Irish families from Pennsylvania. The city was incorporated in 1768 and named after Queen Charlotte, the wife of King George III. In 1799 a gold boom commenced and the Piedmont region remained the nation's leading gold producer until the 1849 California rush. In the twentieth century Charlotte industrialized and rapidly expand-ed from a small city of 18,000 in 1900 to 200,000 by 1960. It was the birthplace of African–American visual artist Romare Bearden, and evangelist Billy Graham was born near Charlotte in 1918.

The main uptown attraction is the Discovery Place, a hands-on child-oriented science museum. The Charlotte Museum of History examines local European settlement while the Museum of the New South explores the post-Reconstruction era with themes ranging from sharecropping to the local music scene with a focus on

There's an architectual mix in downtown Charlotte, with classic buildings sitting beside skyscrapers.

the ground-breaking 1930s' gospel group, the Golden Gate Quartet. The African-American Cultural Center has films, performances, and temporary exhibits.

The Mint Museum of Art is a reconstruction of the building that served as the first branch of the US Mint, which operated in Charlotte from 1837–1861 and 1867–1913. Costumed guides conduct tours of the Hezekiah Alexander Homesite, a 1774 stone dwelling, and the city's oldest.

To the south of Charlotte is Carowinds (a Paramount Pictures and Carolinian history theme park) and Pineville, the 1795 birthplace of the 11th US President, James Polk.
Map ref: page 566 C3

CHEROKEE

Cherokee, located on US-19 in western North Carolina, lies at the center of a 56,000-acre (22,400-ha) Cherokee Reservation at the foot of the Great Smoky Mountains. It is the home of about 11,000 Native Americans who are descendants of several hundred Cherokee who managed to evade a forced march to Oklahoma in the 1830s by hiding in the harsh terrain of the Blue Ridge Mountains.

The reservation relies on income generated by tourism, so the town has a number of tourist attractions, gift shops, motels, fast-food outlets, and a casino.

For something more genuine examine the Museum of the Cherokee Indian. It has archeological exhibits and a focus on Cherokee arts and history, including the Cherokee alphabet devised by Sequoyah. Over the road is Qualla Arts and Crafts, a tribal cooperative that sells traditional handicrafts.

Nearby is Oconaluftee Indian Village, a living-history complex with a replica of an eighteenth-century Cherokee village offering demonstrations of basketweaving, pottery, blowpipe hunting, and how arrowheads, beads, and dugout canoes are made. There are lectures on aspects of Cherokee life and, in summer evenings, performances of the play *Unto These Hills*, which tells the moving story of the Cherokee people from their first contact with Europeans

This Cherokee man is wearing a tradional headdress.

Sculpture guarding the entrance to the Indian Museum in Cherokee.

in the 1520s to the forced migration of 1838. Fishing is also popular on the reservation—there are 400,000 trout in the streams.

Access is by car only.
Map ref: page 559 L10

DURHAM

Durham, the home of Duke University, is part of the Research Triangle, and is located on I-85, 22 miles (35 km) northwest of Raleigh. The population of 137,000 includes an active African-American community that takes pride in their city's heritage.

American businessman and philanthropist James Buchanan Duke, who was born near Durham, set up the immensely profitable American Tobacco Company here in 1890. This allowed him to bestow a $40 million endowment upon Trinity College, which expanded to become Duke University. One of its students was US President Richard Nixon who was President of the student law association.

Duke has one of the most beautiful Southern campuses with Gothic and Georgian architecture, venerable trees, and sprawling lawns. Duke University Chapel features the 5,000-pipe Flentrop Organ and one million pieces of stained glass in 77 windows, depicting nearly 900 figures. Other campus highlights are the beautiful Sarah P. Duke Gardens and Duke Museum of Art, which features European, African, Asian, and pre-Colombian items.

Duke Homestead and Tobacco Museum is where Duke started his tobacco business. It features the 1852 homestead, a reconstruction of the first tobacco factory, a curing barn, a museum covering the social history of tobacco farming, and other outbuildings.

The Museum of Life and Science has hands-on exhibits, animatronic dinosaurs, NASA artifacts, and live animals. At Bennett Place State Historic Site, Confederate General Johnston surrendered to Union General Sherman on April 26, 1865, thus ending the war in the Carolinas, Georgia, and Florida.

Durham is serviced by buses, trains, and an international airport.
Map ref: page 566 F1

EDENTON

Edenton is a small coastal town on Albemarle Sound—the first area of North Carolina to be permanently settled by Europeans. Founded in 1712 it was incorporated in 1722 as a colonial capital, which it remained until 1743. In the eighteenth and early nineteenth centuries it was an important regional center of politics, commerce, and culture, with early citizens including signatories of the US Constitution. In 1774, 51 local society women staged an "Edenton Tea Party" by swearing off tea to protest English taxation. An interesting historical and literary footnote concerns Harriet Jacobs, an African-American slave who hid in her grandmother's Edenton attic for seven years before escaping to Boston. Jacobs' *Incidents in the Life of a Slave Girl* (1861) became one of the best-selling slave narratives of the nineteenth century.

Edenton faded from prominence in the mid-nineteenth century but retained a fine legacy of historic buildings, particularly on Edenton Bay. A self-guided walking brochure is available from the Edenton Visitor Center. It is possible to inspect the Jacobean-style Cupola House and Gardens (circa 1725), St Paul's Episcopal Church (mid-eighteenth century), the Georgian-style Chowan County Courthouse (1767), and the James Iredell House State Historic Site, which was the home of a justice of the first US Supreme Court. Broad Street, with its Victorian facades, 1950s chrome signs, and old-fashioned drug stores, is also interesting.

Edenton is accessible via US-17, bus services, and a regional airport.
Map ref: page 567 K1

FAYETTEVILLE

Fayetteville (population 124,000) is located on I-95, 52 miles (84 km) south of Raleigh. Hiram

The tobacco museum at Durham includes Duke's original 1852 homestead.

Rhodes Revels (1822–1901), the first African-American to serve in the US Senate, was born free at Fayetteville, and the first major African-American fiction writer, Charles Waddell Chesnutt (1858–1932), moved there at the age of eight.

Fayetteville has numerous museums, galleries, and historic buildings. The Fayetteville Independent Light Infantry Armory and Museum honors the oldest southern militia unit in continuous existence (1793). The Museum of the Cape Fear Historical Complex explores regional history. The Airborne and Special Operations Museum reflects the town's proximity to Fort Bragg, 9 miles (14.5 km) to the northwest. The Fort houses the Special Warfare Center, the US Army's airborne combat units, along with the 82nd Airborne Division War Memorial Museum and the John F. Kennedy Special Warfare Museum.

Three historic buildings can be found at Heritage Square, which includes Sandford House (1800), the Oval Ballroom (1818) and the Baker-Haigh-Nimocks House (1804). Also of historic interest are the unique Market House (1832), the First Presbyterian Church (1832) and Saint John's Episcopal Church (1833).

Fayetteville is accessible via bus and train services and an airport.
Map ref: page 566 F3

GREENSBORO

Greensboro, founded in 1808, is full of museums, historic sites, art galleries, and outdoor recreation areas. This commercial and industrial city (population 184,000) is located 68 miles (109 km) west of Raleigh, at the intersection of I-85, I-40, and US-29.

Six miles (9.7 km) northwest of Greensboro is the Guilford Courthouse National Military Park, the site of a major battle on March 15, 1781, between British forces under General Cornwallis and American rebels under Nathanael Greene, after whom the city is named. Although the rebels were forced to retreat, the British army took such a battering that it was forced to rest at Wilmington. The visitor center displays military memorabilia. Tannenbaum Historic Park in

A spectacular display of fall color entices many people to the numerous walking trails in North Carolina.

Greensboro preserves the site of a staging area for British troops.

On April 11, 1865, Confederate President Jefferson Davis met at Greensboro with Union General Joseph Johnston to discuss the surrender of the entire Confederacy. However, the Union victory proved hollow for African-Americans.

As part of the attempt to overturn 100 years of postbellum segregation and discrimination, four black students took their seats at a whites-only Woolworths lunch counter in Greensboro in 1960. African-Americans all over the South followed suit, thereby providing a crucial impetus to the Civil Rights Movement.

Historical figures born in or near Greensboro include short-story writer O. Henry, broadcaster Edward R. Murrow, and Dolley Madison, the wife of the fourth US president. Famous jazz saxophonist and composer John Coltrane was born nearby.

Arguably Greensboro's finest historic home is Blandwood Mansion (1844), the former home of North Carolina Governor John Motley Morehead. Now a National Historic Landmark it depicts life in the mid-nineteenth century. The

Old Greensboro Historic District is a turn-of-the-century commercial and industrial district.

Family fun is available at the Children's Museum and the Natural Science Center, which includes a hands-on museum, zoo and planetarium, and interactive exhibits. South is Asheboro's North Carolina Zoological Park, one of the largest zoos in the world.

Greensboro has a wide variety of art galleries. African artworks and artifacts from 35 countries are on display at the Mattye Reed African Heritage Center; African-American works are presented at the Atelier Gallery. ArtQuest, at the Green Hill Center is an art gallery for children.

The city is serviced by trains, buses, and an international airport.
Map ref: page 566 E1

GREENVILLE

Greenville is located on the Atlantic Coastal Plain, 72 miles (116 km) east of Raleigh at the intersection of Hwy 264 and US-13 and US-11. It is home to East Carolina University where the Ledonia Wright Cultural Center houses a collection of African and

African-American art. Other attractions are the East Carolina Village of Yesteryear, which consists of 19 historical buildings housing over 2,000 artifacts from early North Carolina history. River Park in North Greenville features ponds, bottomland forest, and open grassland areas. Greenville has a municipal airport and can be reached by interstate bus services.
Map ref: page 567 J2

OUTER BANKS

Outer Banks is a lengthy and almost continuous chain of barrier islands that flank much of the North Carolina coast. These islands are essentially low sand dunes with long sandy beaches on the eastern side and salt marshes and lagoons to the west. They help shield the coast from Atlantic squalls and hurricanes. Six hundred vessels have foundered on the southern shores of Outer Banks, which are known as the "Graveyard of the Atlantic." The wrecks are now a drawcard for scuba divers.

Thinly populated until a network of roads, bridges, and ferries was developed, the islands are now popular vacation destinations. No

The Cape Hatteras lighthouse situated on the Outer Banks is the tallest lighthouse in North America.

launch is now marked by the Wright Brothers National Memorial (a white granite monolith atop a hill adjacent to US-158) and a visitor center. Further south, at Nags Head, is Jockey's Ridge. At 138 feet (42 m), it is the tallest sand dune in the eastern United States and an excellent site for kite-flying and hang-gliding.

At Nags Head it is possible to head west along US-64/264 across a bridge to Roanoke Island and onto the mainland. It was on Roanoke Island that the earliest attempts at English settlement in the United States were made. Unfortunately the colonists had disappeared without trace by 1590. Three miles (4.8 km) north of Manteo (the main town on Roanoke Island) is Fort Raleigh National Historic Site, a partial reconstruction of the original colony's earthen fort. From June to August there are performances at the beachside amphitheater of *The Lost Colony*, which is the longest-running outdoor drama in the United States. Adjacent to the fort are some Elizabethan Gardens. In Manteo harbor is a full-size 69-foot (21 m) recreation of a sixteenth-century sailing vessel, the *Elizabeth* II, which evokes the realities of early transatlantic voyages. Three miles (4.8 km) north of Manteo is the North Carolina Aquarium, which has a 180,000-gallon (6,813 hl) ocean tank with a variety of reef fishes.

Cape Hatteras National Seashore extends south for 75 miles (121 km) from Nags Head through Hatteras to Ocracoke Island. At the northern end of Hatteras Island

The Wright Brothers National Memorial, on the northern end of the Outer Banks.

is the Pea Island National Wildlife Refuge, which has a visitor center, walking trails, and observation platforms to view the extensive birdlife. At the elbow of Hatteras Island is Cape Hatteras, which has North America's tallest lighthouse—208 feet (63 m). In summer visitors can climb the 268 steps of the 1870 lighthouse for outstanding island views; a visitor center and museum feature historical displays. South at Frisco is a Native American museum.

At the southern end of the island is Hatteras, which has a popular fishing pier and a car ferry across to beautiful Ocracoke Island where Hwy 12 follows the largely secluded 15-mile (24 km) beach southwards. The island's former isolation made it a useful hideout for Blackbeard the pirate who terrorized the coast from 1717 until local planters killed him during an offshore battle in 1718. The stocky Ocracoke Lighthouse (1823) is the oldest operating lighthouse in the state. Toll ferries depart from Cedar Island and Swanquarter for the crowded

village of Ocracoke, at the southern end of the island.

South of Ocracoke Island is Cape Lookout National Seashore, which extends 55 miles (88 km) southwards along three remote and uninhabited sand islands to Shackleford Banks. Feral horses have roamed here for centuries At the northern tip, and only accessible by foot, are the picturesque ruins of deserted Portsmouth Village. Access to the northern end is via ferry from Ocracoke or Atlantic. At the southern end is the Cape Lookout lighthouse, accessible via ferry from Harker's Island.

To the west of Cape Lookout is the island of Bogue Banks. At its eastern tip is Fort Macon, which is the state's most popular state park. Its central feature is a masonry fort built between 1826 and 1834 to guard Beaufort Inlet. In 1862, 11 hours of Union bombardment led to a Confederate surrender. Further south again is unspoiled Bear Island, which is home to the outstanding Hammocks Beach State Park.

Map ref: page 567 M4

public transportation is available but Hwy 12, which tends to be packed in summer, follows the beach along most of the island chain.

At the northern end of Outer Banks are the rapidly developing—and now overlapping—beach resort towns of Nags Head, Kill Devil Hills, and Kitty Hawk. It was at Kill Devil Hills, on December 17, 1903, that the Wright brothers changed the world when they successfully completed an 852-foot (260 m), 57-second motorized flight in the 605-pound (275 kg) *Flyer*. The site of the

RALEIGH

Raleigh is the state capital and, being home to North Carolina State University, it is part of the Research Triangle. With 208,000 people, it is the state's second-largest city.

Founded by the state legislature in 1792, Raleigh was named after Sir Walter Raleigh of England. It rapidly expanded after World War II, especially with the opening of the Research Triangle Park in 1959.

The Student Nonviolent Coordinating Committee, a vitally important civil rights organization, was founded at Raleigh in 1960.

Ocracoke Harbor at the southern end of the Outer Banks; Ocracoke Island was once the hideout of Blackbeard the pirate.

At the town's center is Capitol Square, which showcases the handsome Neoclassical State Capitol (1833–1840) where Confederate President Jefferson Davis lay in state in 1889. Close by is the enormous North Carolina Museum of History and directly opposite, on Bicentennial Plaza, is the North Carolina Museum of Natural Sciences which is popular with both adults and children.

South of the Capitol is the four-block City Market and the North Carolina Museum of Art, one of the South's finest art museums.

Mordicae Historic Park in Oakwood recreates nineteenth-century plantation life. It includes the Greek Revival Mordicae House (circa 1785). The tiny hut that served as the 1808 birthplace of the 17th US President, Andrew Johnson, has been relocated to the Park north of the Capitol.

Located in central North Carolina at the intersection of I-40, US-1, and US-64, Raleigh is serviced by an international airport, trains, and buses.
Map ref: page 566 G2

WILMINGTON

Wilmington has a population of 92,000 and is located on the Cape Fear River and is the major deep-water port on the North Carolina coast. A principal trade, manufacturing, and retail center, it is an attractive town with many carefully preserved historic buildings. This has made it a popular movie setting in films such as *Blue Velvet, Teenage Mutant Ninja Turtles,* and television's "Dawson's Creek."

The city was incorporated in 1739 and was the state's largest town by 1780. During the Revolutionary War it was a major center of rebel activity. In the Civil War it served as the South's last port of exchange with the outside world. The racial issues that under-scored the Confederate cause were still running strong in 1898 when a white mob killed dozens of blacks during a race riot. President Woodrow Wilson moved with his family to Wilmington in 1873, although he soon took up studies at Princeton. Basketball legend Michael Jordan is another former resident.

Wilmington has numerous extravagant, antebellum houses, churches, and public buildings that

There are many interesting old homes in Raleigh.

testify to its former importance and wealth. Of interest is the Cotton Exchange building, now an interesting waterfront shopping center and the Georgian Burgwin-Wright House (1770), which briefly served as the 1781 headquarters of England's General Cornwallis.

The 44,000-ton (39,908 tonne) USS *North Carolina* is birthed at Eagle Island in the Cape Fear River. This 2,300-man battleship took part in every major offensive in the Pacific during World War II.

St John's Museum of Art includes a rare collection of prints by Mary Cassatt while the Cape Fear Museum examines the region's natural, cultural, and social history.

South of Wilmington are Carolina Beach State Park and the generally uncrowded Kure Beach. Nearby is Fort Fisher State Historic Site, overlooking the ocean and the mouth of the Cape Fear River. It preserves 10 percent of the earthworks associated with this earth-and-sand Civil War fort that protected ships running the Union blockade, thus allowing the Confederate forces

to retain a trading harbor. The fort fell after a major Union assault in 1865 which was allegedly the largest land-sea battle prior to World War II. A museum displays war relics from sunken Confederate blockade runners. Adjoining is the North Carolina Aquarium, showcasing local marine fauna.

Some 23 miles (37 km) northwest is Moores Creek National Battlefield where, in February 1776, colonists defeated a band of Highland Scots during the Revolutionary War, thus ending royal rule in North Carolina.

Wilmington is linked to the outside world by the highway system (I-40, US-17, US-117, US-421, US-74/76), an airport, and bus, and train services.
Map ref: page 567 H5

WINSTON–SALEM

It is no coincidence that the settlements of Winston and Salem are inextricably associated with cigarette brands, as Winston–Salem has one of the largest tobacco-manufacturing plants in the world. Salem was founded as a communal town in

1766 by and for Moravians fleeing religious persecution in Europe. They still have one of their two US headquarters at Winston–Salem. The town's name comes from "shalom", meaning "peace". The demand for their highly valued crafts helped to form Winston, founded in 1849; the two towns were consolidated in 1913.

The city's main tourist attraction is "Old Salem". This 20-block area features about 90 eighteenth- and nineteenth-century buildings. Some buildings are open to the public including Mikisch Tobacco Shop, thought to be the oldest tobacco shop in the United States, Salem Tavern, and Winkler Bakery (a restored Moravian bakery).

The Reynolda House Museum of American Art is housed within the former mansion of tobacco merchant R.J. Reynolds. The outbuildings are now a series of upmarket stores known as Historic Reynolda Village. Nearby is the Southeastern Center for Contemporary Art and the Museum of Early Southern Decorative Arts. At Winston–Salem State University is the Diggs Gallery, which has an emphasis on African-American art.

Ten miles (16 km) west of Winston–Salem is the small town of Flint Hill, the birthplace of bluegrass banjoist Earl Scruggs. Further west is Stone Mountain State Park, which centers on a 600-foot (183 m) granite dome.

A city of 144,000 residents, it is 105 miles (169 km) west of Raleigh on the I-40 and is serviced by buses and an airport.
Map ref: page 566 D1

Capitol Square at Raleigh showcases the Neoclassical State Capitol built between 1833–1840.

SOUTH CAROLINA

Although it is the Deep South's smallest state, South Carolina has much to offer: sublime mountain scenery, beaches, forests, spectacular waterfalls, beautiful rivers and lakes, an abundance of animal and plant life, fine gardens, a remarkable array of colonial and antebellum architecture, historic forts and battlegrounds, and many fine museums.

South Carolina's coastline forms an almost continuous beach in the north, known as the Grand Strand, breaking into a tortuous pattern of bays, rivers, islands, and saltwater marshes further in the south. The terrain ascends from southeast to northwest, from flat coastal plain through the hilly piedmont in the center to the Blue Ridge Mountains in the northwest.

About 55 percent of the state's 4 million inhabitants live in urban areas, with Columbia doubling as the largest city and state capital. Thirty percent of the citizens are of African-American heritage, while German, Irish, British, and Native American backgrounds also common. South Carolina is an important manufacturing and farming state and principal producer of textiles and tobacco. Many are employed in service industries that feed off a profitable tourism sector.

Fishing is a very popular pastime in South Carolina, and there's no shortage of fishing spots for enthusiasts.

Prior to European settlement, over 30 Native American tribes lived in here. The French and Spanish attempted to establish permanent settlements in the sixteenth century, but colonization truly began with the British at Charleston in 1670. During the Revolutionary War, South Carolina was the scene of some crucial battles. It became the eighth US state in 1788 and the first state to secede from the Union in 1860. In fact, the Civil War began when Confederate forces took the Federal stockade at Fort Sumter Harbor.

The post-war years were marked by the violent subordination of African-Americans and fierce resistance to their push for equality after World War II.

State motto *Animis Opibusque Parati* (Prepared in mind and resources)
State flag Adopted 1861
Capital Columbia
Population 4,012,012
Total area (land and water) 31,189 square miles (80,780 sq km)
Land area 30,111 square miles (77,987 sq km)
South Carolina is the 40th-largest state in size
Origin of name Named for King Charles I of England
Nickname The Palmetto State
Abbreviations SC (postal), S.C.
State bird Carolina wren
State flower Carolina yellow jessamine
State tree Palmetto
Entered the Union May 23, 1788 as the eighth state

Places in
SOUTH CAROLINA

BEAUFORT AND THE SEA ISLANDS

Established on a small peninsula in 1711, Beaufort is the second-oldest town in South Carolina. With a population of 10,000 it is located at the intersection of US-21 and US-280, 49 miles (79 km) south of Charleston in the state's southeast. This old seaport grew to prosperity in the eighteenth century on the back of Sea Island cotton and slavery. The old wealth has left the city a legacy of attractive colonial and antebellum houses that, along with its excellent seafood restaurants and interesting African-American heritage, make it a popular tourist attraction. In 1779 Beaufort was the site of a Revolutionary War battle in which William Moultrie defeated the British who were occupying the city.

The town's small historic district, with its narrow streets, eighteenth-century buildings and huge live oaks, can be explored by means of a self-guided walking tour available from the visitor center. They can also tell you where scenes from the films *The Big Chill, The Prince of Tides,* and *Forrest Gump* were shot. Highlights include Thomas Hepworth House (circa 1717), the oldest building in town; John Mark Verdier House (1802); and Henry McKee House, which was purchased by Robert Smalls (1839–1915) who had previously

worked there as a slave. Smalls, born at Beaufort, became something of a Union hero in the Civil War when he guided his steamship out of Charleston Harbor and into the hands of Union forces. Later, he was the state's first African-American congressman.

It is said that the grave slabs from St Helena's Episcopal Church (circa 1720) were employed as operating tables by surgeons in the Civil War. A far more substantial burial ground is the National Cemetery created by Abraham Lincoln in 1863 for those killed in Southern battles. It includes the graves of 9,000 Union soldiers and 122 Confederates, as well as British officers from the Revolutionary War. More history is located in the Beaufort Museum, housed within a 1798 Gothic-style arsenal. It displays decorative arts, Native American pottery and artifacts from prehistory, early industry, and the Revolutionary and Civil Wars.

Just east of Beaufort is Parris Island Marine Corps Recruit Depot, established in 1891. This institution trains most marine recruits east of the Mississippi River. The harsh regime was allegedly the inspiration for the first half of Stanley Kubrick's *Full Metal Jacket.* The Depot has a museum that covers the history of the Marine Corps and its training methods. Displays here include weapons, uniforms, and exhibits

on the European history of Parris Island which dates back to a French Huguenot settlement attempted in 1564. Driving tour maps of the area are available from the Parris Island Visitor Center.

The principal attraction in the area is Saint Helena Island, also to the east of Beaufort. Probably one of the least environmentally degraded of the Sea Islands, it has a truly gorgeous landscape. There are strong African-American shrimp and oyster-fishing communities in this area, descended from slaves freed when the island was taken by Union troops who granted them allotments here.

The Island's Penn Center has its origins in a school for freed slaves that opened in 1862. It was used as a retreat in the 1960s by civil rights leaders such as Martin Luther King. The Center houses a museum with interesting exhibits about the Center and about Gullah culture. Gullah is a "Creolized" form of English that retains words and grammatical features from West African languages, reflecting the origins of the communities that use this patois among the Sea Islands and coastal regions of South Carolina, Georgia, and northeastern Florida. The Gullah Institute has recordings of the dialect, along with other examples of Gullah culture such as the

Nearly one-third of South Carolina's citizens are African-Americans.

intricately woven local sweet-grass baskets that also stem from West Africa. Photographs from the turn of the century capture African-American farmers and fishermen, and their antiquated tools, rattlesnake skins, and shrimp nets.

A bridge leads over to Hunting Island State Park. Just nine miles (15 km) beyond the museum is the area's main beach. The island is popular and, at times, crowded but it is quite a beautiful prospect with its fine white sand, warm water, salt-marsh boardwalk, fishing pier, birdlife, deer, nature trail, shrimp boats, sea oats, and dense forests. The visitor center has good exhibits on the island's history, its beach habitats, and its lighthouse (1875). There is a campground or, if you have booked two years in advance, some appropriately weather-worn cabins.
Map ref: page 566 C10

CHARLESTON

Charleston is one of America's most historic, elegant, and well-preserved cities. With its stately antebellum mansions, old plantations, cobbled and tree-lined streets, picturesque courtyards, relaxed subtropical climate, outstanding gardens, historic sites, fine restaurants, and lively bars, it is an exemplary Southern city full of old-world charm, character, and atmosphere. Yet it has the added benefit of functioning as a town rather than a museum piece.

Charleston is scenically located on a peninsula at the place where the Ashley and Cooper River estuaries meet. It is a manufacturing center, a major East Coast port,

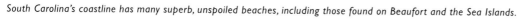

South Carolina's coastline has many superb, unspoiled beaches, including those found on Beaufort and the Sea Islands.

and is the second-largest city in the state, with a population of roughly 507,000 people.

Charleston was the first European settlement in South Carolina and one of the United States' earliest planned cities. The first British colonists arrived in 1670. They moved on to the present townsite in 1680 and named the settlement Charles Town, which became the colonial capital. The colonists repelled French, Spanish, and Native American assaults during Queen Anne's War (1702–1713) and, in the 1710s, Charleston was harried by pirates such as Blackbeard who blockaded Charleston in 1717, and seized ships in the harbor.

Charleston's enormous rice and indigo plantations, driven by slave labor, soon made it the wealthiest city in the South and a lively cosmopolitan social center. By 1775 it was the fourth-largest settlement in the colonies with around 12,000 people. During the Revolutionary War, as the South's major port, it became a British target. Attempts to capture it in 1776 and 1779 were repelled; the

Charleston's distinctive architecture is one of its many attractions.

city fell in 1780 and was occupied until 1782. The surrender and capture of the defending army was a major blow to the Rebel cause.

In 1822 Charleston nearly endured a very substantial slave uprising. It was planned and organized by an African-American named Denmark Vesey who worked as a carpenter at Charleston after purchasing his freedom. However, the plan was exposed as the day of the revolt approached and Vesey was hanged. The incident led to greater restrictions on the movements, occupations, and education of African-Americans.

Charleston also lay at the heart of the Civil War's outbreak as it was the Confederate attack on the Federal stockade of Fort Sumter, in Charleston Harbor, that precipitated the outbreak of hostilities. The subsequent Union blockade there ruined the state's economy. In 1863, Fort Wagner in the Harbor was stormed by the first Northern African-American troops to fight for the Union as an organized regiment. Their courage did much to gain acceptance in the North for the idea of using African-American soldiers.

The combination of a long history and remarkable wealth has left Charleston with one of the coun-

try's finest collections of over 1,000 antebellum homes, including 73 built prior to the Revolutionary War. Not surprisingly Charleston is a superb place for walking tours exploring such themes as the city's architecture, Civil War sites, and African-American history.

During the Festival of Houses in spring many historic homes are open to public inspection. For the rest of the year only a small number welcome visitors. They include Nathaniel Russell House (1808), which has a free-standing, three-story spiral staircase and formal gardens; and Calhoun Mansion (1876), with an opulent interior featuring hand-painted porcelain and etched-glass chandeliers. The Aiken-Rhett House (circa 1817), which served as the headquarters of General Beauregard in the Civil War, retains its slave quarters and an intact workyard.

George Washington was entertained in 1791 at the Heyward-Washington House (1772). Later the home of Thomas Heyward Jr, a signatory of the Declaration of Independence, it was also used by Du Bose Heyward as the setting for his 1925 novel about African-American life on the city's waterfront, *Porgy*. He later worked with Ira Gershwin on the libretto for George Gershwin's *Porgy and Bess*.

One of the city's most important buildings is the Palladian-style Old Exchange and Provost Dungeon. It dates from the early eighteenth century and features a portion of the original brick seawall. The building above it was constructed by the British in 1771 as an exchange and customs house.

An elegant Charleston home.

Charleston has 180 historic churches, earning it the nickname "the Holy City." They include the Kahal Kadosh Beth Elohim Synagogue (1840); St Michael's Episcopal (1761), the city's oldest surviving church; the Gothic Revival Huguenot Church, built in 1845 on the site of the 1687 original; and the First Baptist Church, the oldest in the South.

The Charleston City Market dates back to the eighteenth century, although the current buildings were constructed in the 1840s. By the river is the beautiful Waterfront Park, with boardwalks that extend over the river, and the White Point Gardens are at the tip of the peninsula. The now symbolic Battery was established to protect the city from British armies. Pirates such as Stede Bonnet were publicly hanged here in the 1710s. The South Carolina Aquarium is also beautifully situated overlooking Charleston Harbor.

Just north of the Historic District is the Charleston Museum, established in 1773. It features displays relating to anthropology and to colonial history including slave badges, a duelling contract, hands-on exhibits for children, and a replica of the 1864 Confederate submarine *Hunley* which, in Charleston Harbor, became the first submarine in the world to sink a ship.

The Old Slave Mart Museum serves as a grim reminder that the Charleston waterfront was once an enormous slave market through which one-third of all the nation's slaves passed. The history and heritage of Lowcountry African-

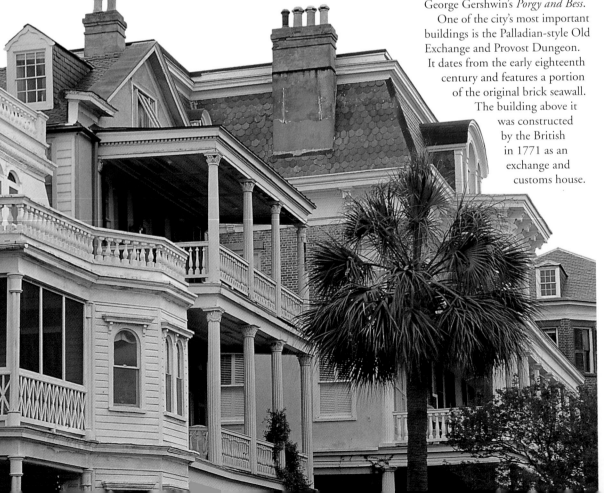

Americans is also documented in the Avery Research Center at the College of Charleston. At the Lowcountry Legends Music Hall, traditional songs and spirituals are interwoven with stories of Sea Island and Gullah culture.

The Gibbes Museum of Art specializes in portraits of South Carolina's aristocracy, while the Wallace Exhibit replicates eight rooms from historic American buildings. The American Military Museum displays artifacts from all branches of the American military forces and from each of the major international conflicts.

On the east side of Cooper River is the Patriot's Point Naval and Maritime Museum where visitors can explore a submarine, a destroyer, a Coast Guard cutter, the world's first nuclear-powered merchant ship, a re-created Vietnam-era naval support base and the 888-foot (271-m) aircraft carrier USS *Yorktown* which features more than 20 World War II aircraft on its flight deck.

A major event on the Charleston calendar is the Spoleto Festival, a cultural celebration of music, dance, drama, and art from around the world. Performances and exhibits are held around the city in May. Visitors to Charleston should also sample a vital aspect of local culture, she-crab soup.

Charleston is connected to the rest of the world via I-26, US-17, the state's largest airport, and also by trains and buses.
Map ref: page 566 D9

CHARLESTON AREA (PLANTATIONS, SEA ISLANDS, AND GARDENS)

The area around Charleston is also replete with wonderful historic and scenic attractions. Just 8 miles (13 km) north of Charleston is Boone Hall Plantation, which was used for background shots in *Gone with the Wind*. The estate was established in 1681, although the present house is a 1935 reconstruction. The eighteenth-century brick cabins were built for the domestic slaves and skilled artisans. The driveway features a wide avenue of oaks planted in 1743.

To see other Charleston plantations, head west from Charleston along Route 61, which follows the Ashley River. Nine miles (15 km) from Charleston is Drayton Hall (1738–1742), considered one of the nation's finest examples of Georgian Palladian architecture.

It is another 2 miles (3 km) to one of Charleston's finest attractions, the 50-acre (20-ha) ornamental gardens of Magnolia Plantation, which has been in the Drayton family since the 1670s.

The Gardens were established in 1865 and feature flower and tree species from around the world, including 900 types of camellia. Although they are beautiful all year, they are in full bloom in March and April. There is also a herb garden, a sixteenth-century hedge maze, a topiary garden, a children's petting zoo, a waterfowl sanctuary, a cabin and rice barge from the antebellum era, tram tours of the property, and 500 acres (202 ha) of wildlife trails. The simple eighteenth-century house replaced an earlier home which was burned down by Union troops in 1865. Also on the property is the independently operated 60-acre (24-ha) Audubon Swamp Garden, which is a preserved blackwater cypress and tupelo swamp full of alligators, otters, and waterbirds, as well as lush flowers.

Four miles (6 km) north is Middleton Place Gardens. The oldest landscaped gardens in the United States, they were created between 1741 and 1751 by 100 slaves at the behest of rice planter Henry Middleton who was the president of the First Continental Congress. The guest wing is all that remains of the original 1755 mansion after the rest was torched by Union troops. The story of the African-American is explored at Eliza's House.

On the other side of the Ashley River is Charles Towne Landing, a state park centered on the area where South Carolina's first permanent English settlement was established in 1670. The park attempts to re-create the area as it would have appeared to the original settlers. It includes a full-size

Magnolia Plantation near Charleston boasts over 900 different types of camellia.

replica of a seventeenth-century colonial trading ship, a living history re-creation of a seventeenth-century colonial village, a wild animal enclosure, a seventeenth-century crop garden, English Park Gardens, marshes, enormous oaks, freshwater lagoons, and also hiking and biking trails.

To the east of Charleston, on the Atlantic coast, are the popular beaches at Isle of Palms and Sullivan's Island. Wild Dunes Resort has two championship golf courses and it can organize deep-sea and inshore fishing trips.

To the south is a series of small marshy Sea Islands. Folly Island has a popular beach, a county park and a 1,045-foot (319-m) fishing pier. Wadmalaw Island lies 15 miles (24 km) south of Charleston and features the Charleston Tea Plantation, established in 1799. It grows American Classic, the only American tea that is served at the White House.

Further south is Kiawah Island, which has a beach, marshes and forests, two resort villages, golf courses, a tennis resort, fishing opportunities, and canoeing on the Kiawah River.

Further south again is Edisto Island, a largely unspoiled resort with excellent beaches and plenty of birdlife. Edisto Island Museum has exhibits on Sea Island plantation life, the Civil War, and Native Americans. Campsites, cabins, and hiking trails are all available at Edisto Beach State Park. Colleton State Park is the headquarters of the scenic 56-mile (90-km) Edisto River Canoe and Kayak Trail.

South Carolina's historic buildings range from opulently furnished mansions to quaint old sheds.

The University of South Carolina is located in Columbia, the state's largest city.

Bronze star on Columbia's Capitol.

COLUMBIA

Columbia is the state capital and South Carolina's largest settlement with a population of over 450,000. It is a trading, banking, and manufacturing center located in the middle of the state on the Congaree River. It has a strong arts community, its own symphony orchestra and an entertainment district by the river.

The Congaree tribe lived in the area until farms and cotton plantations were established in the eighteenth century. With statehood approaching, tension arose between coastal planters and upcountry farmers concerning the location of the state capital so, in 1786, the South Carolina legislature decided on a compromise. They selected a new site in the center of the state, named it Columbia and met there for the first time in 1790. During the Civil War the city was burned and looted by Union troops.

In 1870, the future President Woodrow Wilson moved to the capital when his father was appointed a professor in the Presbyterian theological seminary. The Tuscan style home which he inhabited between the ages of 14 and 17 is preserved. It includes the bed in which he was born in Staunton, Virginia.

Columbia has many other historic buildings such as the Robert Mills Historic House (1823), designed by Robert Mills who was responsible for the Washington Monument in Washington DC.

Right across the road is the rather elegant Classical Revival style Hampton-Preston Mansion (1818), which served as Union headquarters in the Civil War. It retains family furnishings of the distinguished Hampton family. The original owner of the Mann-Simons Cottage was former Charleston slave Celia Mann who walked to Columbia after purchasing her own freedom with money earned as a midwife. It is now a museum of African-American culture. The Governor's Mansion has housed a number of state governors since 1868.

It was at the city's First Baptist Church (1859) that the Secession Convention met a few days before deciding to leave the Union, thus putting the state on course for war. The consequences of this action are inscribed on the walls of the 1855 Capitol (known as the State House) where bronze stars denote former pockmarks left by Union cannonballs. Adjacent is a very large Episcopal church. Modeled after England's York Minster, it was consecrated in 1847. Six governors are buried in its churchyard.

Across Sumter Street from the State House is the Horseshoe, a parklike space surrounded by the stately buildings of the University of South Carolina. Also found in this area is the McKissick Museum, which examines the folklore of America's Southeast through music, art, history, and science; as well as the Confederate Relic Room and Museum, which houses Civil War artifacts.

On the waterfront is the South Carolina State Museum, which has four floors of displays on natural history, human history, art, science, and technology. It is housed in an 1894 textile factory building, which was one of the first electrically powered mills in the world. There is a hands-on discovery center for children. A somewhat more specialized museum is the South Carolina Criminal Justice Hall of Fame, which examines the history of law enforcement in America and honors those who died in the process.

Six miles (10 km) east of town is the Fort Jackson Museum. This garrison, established in 1917, became a facility which trained 500,000 military personnel in World War II. Displays focus on the history of military training. A collection of memorabilia celebrates the life and times of President Andrew Jackson, after whom the Fort is named.

The Columbia Museum of Art is South Carolina's largest fine arts museum. It retains one of the Southeast's strongest collections of Italian Renaissance and Baroque paintings. Botticelli, Monet, and Remington are all represented. Art of a different kind is featured on the wall of the Federal Land Bank Building where artist Blue Sky has created the illusion of a tunnel passing right through the building. The Riverbanks Zoological Park and Garden is considered one of the country's top ten zoos and it has over 2,000 animals. Those who like the outdoors may also wish to examine the excellent South Carolina State Botanical Garden on the university campus. Memorial Park honors 980 South Carolinians who lost their lives in Vietnam.

There are also many attractions in the area around Columbia. To the north of town is Lake Wateree State Park and 20 miles (32 km) southeast is Congaree Swamp National Monument, which features the oldest and largest trees east of the Mississippi River.

Thirty two miles (51 km) northeast of Columbia is the Battle of Camden Historic Site, which features reconstructions relating to both a crushing defeat of Rebel forces by the British in August 1780, and the 1730s trading post that formed the foundation of Camden, South Carolina's first inland town.

Columbia is serviced by an airport, train, and bus. Visitors traveling by car can reach Columbia via I-26, I-77, and I-20.

Map ref: page 565 N4

The State Capitol Building in Columbia was built in 1855.

FORT MOULTRIE

Fort Moultrie is a historic American stockade located on Sullivan's Island at the main entrance to Charleston Harbor. It was crucial to the defense of the South's principal port during the Revolutionary War and is now part of the Fort Sumter National Monument. British ships first attempted to take Charleston on June 28, 1776. They hoped to make it a base for future operations. However, they first had to sail past Fort Moultrie (then Fort Sullivan). The British fired on the Fort but the Rebels returned fire damaging several warships. Consequently the British withdrew. The Fort was renamed to honor Colonel William Moultrie who led Charleston's defense.

By 1780, with the French involved in the War, the British shifted their attention to the South. They took control of Georgia then, on May 7, 1780, British troops under General Sir Henry Clinton took Fort Moultrie and hence Charleston. A force of 5,500 surrendered and were taken prisoner.

After the Revolutionary War, Fort Moultrie was expanded into a five-sided, earth-and-timber structure with 17-foot (5-m) walls. One of the troops who served here in the late 1820s was author Edgar Allan Poe. He later set his short story, "The Gold Bug" on the island. In 1837 the Seminole Native American leader Osceola was imprisoned at Fort Moultrie as part of a campaign to move the Seminole out of their homelands in Florida. He was arrested after he approached US troops under a flag of truce and died in 1838 at Fort Moultrie where he is buried.

After South Carolina's secession from the Union in 1860, the Fort was abandoned by Major Robert Anderson who transferred his personnel to Fort Sumter. The Confederates took control of Moultrie and used it as headquarters during the bombardment of Fort Sumter in April 1861. It was reactivated during World War II.

Today Fort Moultrie features a stockade of palmetto logs, completed in 1809, and a visitor center. Visitors can explore the ramparts and passageways. There are excellent views of Charleston Harbor, Fort Sumter, and the city.
Map ref: page 567 D9

Fort Moultrie, located at the entrance to Charleston Harbor, played an important role during the Revolutionary War.

FORT SUMTER

Fort Sumter was built between 1829 and 1860 on a small artificial island in Charleston Harbor. It is a national monument, as it was the site of the first shot fired in the American Civil War. The background to this event was the secession of South Carolina from the Union on December 20, 1860. With Federal forces now deemed the enemy, Rebels regarded the presence of a Federal fort in one of their harbors as a provocation. With a mere 79 troops the Fort was hardly a meaningful threat, but became a symbolic focus of the attempts of the two sides to assert claims to having right on their side.

On December 26, 1860, a small garrison of Federal troops was transferred to Fort Sumter. South Carolina demanded the immediate withdrawal of the Federal troops, but this was refused. The garrison was running short of supplies, so an attempt to relieve it was made. South Carolina batteries fired on the supply ship, forcing it to quickly withdraw. President Buchanan did not wish to hand a national conflagration to incoming President Lincoln, and refused to view the attack as an act of war.

Lincoln needed to decide whether to resupply the Fort or abandon it.

Because Buchanan had already relinquished so many forts to the Confederacy, it had become something of an election issue, and Lincoln had pledged to "hold, occupy and possess" all Federal properties in the South. This made it hard to compromise over Fort Sumter. He attempted a couple of maneuvers that would allow him to surrender the Fort in return for the reinforcement of Fort Pickens in Florida or the loyalty of Virginia to the Union. However, both plans were frustrated so Lincoln sent off a force to resupply the Fort.

Meanwhile, South Carolina had been joined by six other states that had established the Confederate States of America. All moves were now crucial and Lincoln's decision to resupply the Fort was deemed unacceptable by many. At the same time Confederate President Jefferson Davis was placed under much pressure from extremists, notably state governor Francis Pickens,

who threatened to personally authorize an attack on the Fort. Davis ordered the Confederate troops under General Beauregard to bombard Fort Sumter on April 12, 1861. Major Anderson surrendered and on April 14 US troops withdrew. Nobody had been killed, but Lincoln called for 75,000 volunteers to put down the "insurrection" in the South. The Confederacy declared a state of war now existed. Union forces did not retake the fort until February 1865.

As the Fort was bombarded by the Confederacy in 1861, then by the Union from 1863 to 1865, much was reduced to rubble. Some original fortifications and gun emplacements remain. The concrete defenses were added later. Today there is an excellent museum with artifacts from the siege. The Fort is accessible from Charleston Harbor. Tours depart from the City Marina.
Map ref: page 566 D9

Lake Moultrie canal, a peaceful and scenic diversion for visitors to Fort Moultrie.

GEORGETOWN

Georgetown is a leading seaport of 10,000 people on Winyah Bay. The Spanish attempted to establish North America's first settlement on Winyah Bay in 1526, but it failed because of a hurricane and Indian attacks. The English arrived in 1726 and named the settlement after George II. It was occupied by British forces during the Revolutionary War. Once an important international port serving the area's rice plantations, it features a beautiful waterfront where the old docks have been converted into an array of restaurants and shops.

The town's historic district is full of attractive eighteenth- and nineteenth-century homes and churches and has a very pleasant main street. Walking, driving, tram and horse-drawn carriage tours as well as water excursions are available. Historic buildings include Harold Kaminiski House (1760s) and Prince George Winyah Episcopal Church, established in 1721. The latter's grounds contain the graves of soldiers from the Revolutionary and Civil Wars. On the northern side of town is the Belle W. Baruch Plantation, which retains the wooden shacks that served as slave quarters. The main home was once owned by influential financier and statesman Bernard Baruch who advised

A buggy, in the foothills of the Blue Ridge Mountains, north of Greenville.

presidents Wilson, Harding, Coolidge, Hoover, Roosevelt, Truman, and Eisenhower.

A walking tour of the historic district is available from the visitor center. Next door, in the old market building (1842), is the Rice Museum, which uses dioramas, tools and maps to examine the history of rice cultivation that flourished here with the expertise and labor of African slaves. For a time Georgetown was the world's biggest exporter of rice.

Twelve miles (19 km) south of Georgetown is the Hopsewee Plantation, which retains the large 1740 mansion where Thomas Lynch Jr was born in 1749. A signatory of the Declaration of

Independence, he served in the state's first General Assembly and Second Continental Congress. The perfectly manicured grounds feature an abundance of Spanish moss; mosquitoes from the nearby river are in plague proportions in summer, however, leading one to contemplate what the working conditions were for slaves on this former rice plantation.

A further 5 miles (8 km) south is Hampton Plantation State Park which is based around an exceptional Neoclassical mansion visited by President George Washington in 1791. It was erected by Huguenots during the mid-eighteenth century. The Park is located within Francis Marion National Forest. This area is largely African-American and is quite famous for traditional African sweet-grass baskets. At the northeastern corner of the forest, off US-17, is the Santee Coastal Reserve, which incorporates 11 miles (18 km) of beach. This reserve is home to waterfowl, wading birds, deer, alligators, snakes, and raccoons. There are nature trails for walks, and also canoe and bike trails. Further south along the coast is the wilderness terrain of the Cape Romain National Wildlife Refuge, which encompasses a stretch of barrier islands and also salt marshes.

Georgetown is located at the intersection of US-521 and US-17, 56 miles (90 km) north of Charleston. It is serviced by Georgetown county airport and Myrtle Beach International Airport.
Map ref: page 566 E7

GREENVILLE

With 60,000 people, Greenville is one of South Carolina's largest cities. Established in 1776, this textile-producing center has a beautiful orderly downtown with plenty of parks, trees, and public artworks. Served by train and located at the intersection of I-85, I-385 and I-185 in the state's northwest, it offers entertainment and historic, scenic, and family attractions. Greenville's distinguished citizens have included psychologist John Watson (1878–1958) who developed an influential movement in psychology called behaviorism; Charles Townes, who shared the 1964 Nobel prize for physics for his work on masers and lasers; and distinguished African-American civil rights activist Jesse Jackson.

Different aspects of Greenville's history are represented in two of its museums. The Greenville Cultural Exchange Center is a museum and resource center dedicated to African-Americans. Displays relate to Jesse Jackson and early Greenville. The 16th South Carolina Volunteers Museum of Confederate History is located in the Pettigru Historic District. It houses a collection of Confederate artifacts, both military and personal, and a research library.

Bob Jones University is a training ground for the fundamentalist right. It features a large collection of religious paintings while the Greenville County Museum of Art is particularly strong on Southern art. It includes works by Jasper Johns and Georgia O'Keeffe. Cultural programs are offered at the Nippon Center, which is in the style of a fourteenth-century Japanese mansion and features a lotus pond, some cherry trees, and also a rock garden.

For outdoor entertainment try the Greenville Zoo; the test gardens of the Park Seed Company, which are at their best from May to July; and the Reedy River Falls Historic Park, which occupies the downtown site upon which

The majestic Washington oak, Hampton Plantation State Park near Georgetown.

A young African-American boy living in South Carolina.

Greenville was first established in 1776. The latter features walking paths, picnic spots, two waterfalls, and six landscaped garden areas. Another place of interest is the Roper Mountain Science Center, an educational center that features a living history farm, a Discovery Room, a Sealife Room, an observatory, a health education center, chemistry/physics shows, and also a planetarium.

To the north of Greenville is Paris Mountain State Park and 25 miles (40 km) northwest is Mountain Bridge State Natural Area where the spectacular Blue Ridge Mountains suddenly drop nearly 2,000 feet (610 m) to the piedmont, forming an escarpment which furnishes excellent views of the foothills to the south. Here Raven Falls, the highest falls in the state, drop 420 feet (128 m) into the gorge below. Also to the northwest is Table Rock State Park, which is one of the state's oldest and most popular parks.
Map ref: page 565 L2

HILTON HEAD ISLAND

Once occupied by local Native Americans, this beautiful barrier island is the largest Sea Island between New Jersey and Florida, covering some 42 square miles (109 sq km). It has about 29,000 permanent inhabitants and attracts around 500,000 visitors annually. Located on the Intracoastal Waterway, about 65 miles (105 km) south of Charleston via US-17 and US-278, it was settled by cotton planters in the eighteenth century then divided into allotments for freed slaves as a result of the Civil

War. Now Hilton Head is a sophisticated and luxurious vacation and retirement resort with upmarket lodging, shops, restaurants, nightclubs, marinas, and extensive recreation facilities. However, quite unlike Myrtle Beach, Hilton Head seeks to maintain a sense of balance between commercialism and the environment, limiting buildings to tree height and banning billboards. The Gulf Stream and the temperate subtropical climate keep the water and air warm for a great deal of the year.

The main attractions are the truly outstanding beaches; Forest Beach is the most popular one. Covering 12 miles (19 km) on the eastern side of the Island, they are fringed with palms, and the rolling sand dunes with their firm sand makes them ideal for cycling, jogging, hiking, and beach games. Bicycles, beach gear, and watersport equipment are available for rent with kayaking, parasailing, sailing, windsurfing, and waterskiing all proving popular.

Hilton Head Island has around 25 miles (40 km) of cycling paths and 22 golf courses. Some of the championship courses are open to the public. The Island is also considered one of the country's better resorts. It boasts more than 300 tennis courts and 19 tennis clubs, seven of which are open to the public. Visitors can also undertake nature cruises to the resorts of Daufuskie Island, dolphin-watch cruises, and sunset dinner cruises. Deep-sea fishing excursions offer the chance to catch sharks, king mackerel, and barracuda. Offshore fishing is best from April to October and inland waterways fishing from September to December. Crabbing is also popular on the island.

Nature preserves such as Audubon-Newhall Preserve and Sea Pines Forest Preserve offer fine walking possibilities. Sea Pines features white-tailed deer, alligators, and a 3,400-year-old Native American shell ring. Guided tours are available when the flowers are in bloom. Several stables facilitate horseback riding through the preserves and forests.

The Coastal Discovery Museum features aquariums, historical and ecological exhibits, and seashell collections. It also organizes nature walks and guided tours of the Island that take in its beaches, marshes, plants and animals, and

sites associated with Native Americans, former plantations and old forts. The Self Family Arts Center is a large complex that combines state-of-the-art facilities for both performing and visual arts, including the Hilton Head Playhouse Theater and an art gallery with changing exhibits.

West of Hilton Head Island is Pinckney Island National Wildlife Refuge, which covers 4,000 acres (1620 ha) of salt marsh and small islands. It has 14 miles (23 km) of walking and cycling trails for wildlife observation; no cars are permitted beyond the parking lot.
Map ref: page 565 P8

MYRTLE BEACH AND THE GRAND STRAND

Myrtle Beach is a popular coastal spot 98 miles (158 km) north of Charleston on a 55-mile (88 km) stretch of almost unbroken beach known as the Grand Strand, which extends from the state's northern border to Winyah Bay, which is near Georgetown. In 1999 it was ranked the second most popular tourist destination in the country, attracting twice as many visitors as Hawaii. Myrtle Beach has a regular population of 28,000 but in summer that can soar to 350,000. However, its extreme clutter and commercialization is not everyone's

Greenville is surrounded by many beautiful, wild places, such as Mountain Bridge State Natural Area, northwest of the city.

Spartanburg, once famous for its cotton, is now known for its delicious peaches.

idea of paradise although, for the young, particularly students in mid-term vacations, it is unmitigated seaside fun.

Myrtle Beach is marked by its high-rise developments, countless motels, fast-food outlets, neon signs, an amusement park with enormous roller coasters, a water park, family-oriented country music variety shows, t-shirt shops, ice-cream parlors, video-game parlors, mini-golf courses, mini-Grand Prix tracks and other carnival-style amusements, bars, clubs, sidewalk cafes, restaurants, and numerous factory outlets. The attractive albeit jam-packed beaches, beach-party scene, fashionable resort hotels, temperate climate, and golf courses (more than 50 of them) attract visitors all year round.

Some specific attractions at Myrtle Beach are a wax museum; Ripley's Aquarium, which features the world's longest underwater observation tunnel; the Children's Museum of South Carolina, which offers hands-on science and technology exhibits for young children; the South Carolina Hall of Fame, which pays tribute to distinguished South Carolinians through interactive video displays; and Alligator Adventure, which houses rare albino alligators, dwarf crocodiles, giant snakes and a number of other exotic species.

Other possibilities offer some escape from the commercial brouhaha. The Hobcaw Barony Visitors' Center features terrariums, aquariums, and displays on the

nature research of the Baruch Institutes; while Myrtle Beach State Park offers 312 acres (126 ha) of sandy beach and pine forest with nature trails, a fishing pier, and campsites. The Grand Strand is traversed by US-17. To the north of Myrtle Beach are Windy Hill Beach, Atlantic Beach, Crescent Beach, Ocean Drive Beach, and Cherry Grove Beach. To the south are Murrells Inlet, a small and quiet fishing port with fine seafood restaurants and fishing boats for hire; Litchfield Beach; and secluded Pawleys Island, which was once favored by plantation owners. Visitors can try one of the island's hammocks, which have been made by hand since 1880.

On US-17, between Murrells Inlet and Litchfield Beach, is Brookgreen Gardens, which was

Mobile homes near Spartanburg.

developed by sculptor Anna Hyatt Huntington and her husband. The land was once occupied by four rice and indigo plantations. It features azaleas, lily ponds, dogwoods, mossy live oaks and other state flora, a wildlife area with deer and alligator, a 90-minute boat tour of the area, and over 500 figurative sculptures in landscaped settings including works by Frederic Remington and Daniel Chester French. Across the road is Huntington Beach State Park, which was also once the property of the Huntingtons. It has 3 miles (5 km) of beautiful beach, attractive campsites, nature trails, a bird-filled freshwater lagoon, dense forest, a saltwater marsh with boardwalk, and the Huntingtons' Moorish style Atalaya House.

Thanks to the Gulf Stream, the offshore waters ensure good fishing opportunities for most of the year. There are a number of piers and jetties along the Grand Strand and fishing and sightseeing excursions depart from North Myrtle Beach and Little River by the northern state border.

Myrtle Beach is serviced by bus and it has an international airport.
Map ref: page 566 F7

SPARTANBURG

Spartanburg is an increasingly industrialized city of 46,000 people in a major peach-growing area. Established in 1785, it prospered before the Civil War on the back of slavery, cotton, and an ironworks. After the War it became a railway hub. General William Westmore-

land, who commanded US forces in the Vietnam War from 1964 to 1968, was born in Spartanburg County in 1914.

Spartanburg County Museum of Art has changing exhibits and the Regional Museum of Spartanburg County has local history exhibits including one of the state's oldest European artifacts: an etched stone trail marker used by the Spanish in 1567. The beautiful Hatcher Gardens have more than 10,000 plants and plenty of birds and other wildlife, along with dams, ponds, and trails.

Twelve miles (19 km) southwest of Spartanburg is the Walnut Grove Plantation, which is based around a vernacular two-story log house with plank floor, which was built around 1765. Powder horns and hunting rifles hang at the ready inside the front and back doors and there are bloodstains on the second-story floor where it is alleged Loyalists stabbed a Rebel soldier to death during the Revolutionary War. South of Spartanburg is Croft State Park which is ideal for horseback riding. It offers equestrian facilities, a large swimming pool, a 160-acre (65-ha) fishing lake, rental boats, tennis courts, and nature trails.

Two rather crucial battles that turned the tide of the Revolutionary War also took place in the area around Spartanburg. The first was at Kings Mountain National Military Park, to the northeast of town, off I-85, not very far from Blacksburg. Here the left wing of the British Southern army (which was made up of American

A fine example of antebellum (or pre-Civil War) architecture, located in Walhalla.

Loyalists) was surrounded and captured by rough-shod mountain Rebels, causing British leader General Cornwallis to withdraw his forces from North Carolina and refocus on South Carolina. Today the battle is explored by means of dioramas, artifacts, and a video at the visitor center. A marked, self-guided trail traverses 1½ miles (2.4 km) through the dense woods and hilly terrain. Adjoining the Military Park is the Kings Mountain State Park.

To the north of town, near Chesnee, is Cowpens National Battlefield Site where a small Rebel army under Daniel Morgan defeated a much larger, more experienced, and better trained British force under Banastre Tarleton. Morgan, pursued by Tarleton, dug in and prepared for battle in this cattle-grazing area and, on January 17, 1781, his sharpshooters killed and captured most of the on-rushing British troops. The site is explored by means of an auto tour, a walking trail, and a slide show at the visitor center.

Taken together, these two victories, after devastating losses at Charleston and Camden, proved pivotal to the course of the War. They did much to restore battered morale and proved that Britain did not control the Carolinas. More importantly they limited

Cornwallis' capacity to move on from South Carolina to secure other states.

Access to the Cowpens site is via the Cherokee Foothills Scenic Highway (SC-11), which follows the course of an old Cherokee path. It leaves I-85 at Gaffney and traverses 130 miles (209 km) of beautiful countryside, taking in the foothills of the Blue Ridge Mountains, villages, peach orch-

ards, state and county parks, Lake Keowee, Salem, Walhalla and Westminster, rejoining I-85 at the Georgia border.

Spartanburg is in the northwest of the state at the intersection of US-176, US-221 and US-29.
Map ref: page 565 M2

WALHALLA AND THE SCENIC NORTHWEST

Walhalla is a gateway to the scenic delights of the state's northwest corner, which is dominated by the beautiful forest-clad Blue Ridge Mountains and dotted with attractive lakes and waterfalls. The town of Walhalla, just north of US-76, is located on the Cherokee Foothills Scenic Highway (SC-11) which offers a gorgeous scenic drive through the area. There are several parks in the area, most of which have excellent picnic areas, walking trails, and camping areas. The lakeside parks offer fishing, swimming, boating, and canoeing. Some of these have a park store and canoe rentals.

Five miles (8 km) north of Walhalla is the sublime 200-foot (322-m) cascade of Issaqueena Falls, which is connected to Stumphouse Mountain Tunnel Park by a nature trail. Further north, beyond Salem, are Devils Fork State Park on the shores of bracing Lake Jocassee, and the two

Whitewater Falls that straddle the border and drop 400 feet (644 m) over rocky terrain.

To the northwest of Walhalla, near the settlement of Mountain Park, is Oconee State Park. The lakes and stonework were created by the Civilian Conservation Corps in the 1930s.

To the west of Walhalla is the tumultuous Chattooga River which constitutes 40 miles (64 km) of the Georgia state border. It drops in altitude an average of 49 feet (15 m) per mile as it makes its way through Sumter National Forest. Its rapids, which make it ideal for rafting, canoeing, and kayaking, were made famous in James Dickey's novel *Deliverance* (and filmed in the award-winning movie starring Jon Voight).

To the southeast of Walhalla is Lake Hartwell State Park, at the intersection of I-85 and SC-11. To the east of Walhalla, on the shores of Lake Keowee is Toxaway State Park, a forest-clad oasis that features some of nature's most beautiful lakes and rivers.

It was just to the south of this site that European explorers found Keowee, the capital of the lower Cherokee nation, and the Keowee River. The Cherokee people are remembered through artifacts and exhibits in the Park's interpretive center.
Map ref: page 565 K2

The crystal-clear waters of Lake Jocassee, in South Carolina's scenic northwest, are especially popular with visitors to Walhalla.

TENNESSEE

Tennessee is imbued with a rich frontier heritage, Civil War history, and America's homespun sound of blues, country, bluegrass, and rockabilly music. Tennessee was once the ancestral homeland of the Cherokee and Chickasaw people. It was also home to the nation's music king, Elvis Presley.

Although Tennessee joined the Union in 1796, the state was divided—in the east the inhabitants largely supported the dissolution of slavery, while the slave-holding plantation owners of middle and west Tennessee did not. By only a marginal vote, the state was the last to join the Confederacy in April 1861, and the first to rejoin the Union in 1865. Tennessee was the site of several major Civil War battles including Shiloh and Franklin.

Tennessee abolished slavery in 1865, but in that same year a group of former Confederate officers established the Ku Klux Klan as a political club. The club was soon abandoned by its founding members, but the Klan movement, wrapped in secrecy, evolved into a powerful fraternity of bigotry and violence. During the 1960s, Nashville, the state's capital, was at the forefront of the civil rights movement.

Window display in Mr Handy's Blues Hall in Memphis, the birthplace of Memphis blues.

Nashville today is synonymous with country music, while Memphis, Tennessee's largest city, is home to the blues. Each year, thousands flock to the honky-tonk shows of The Grand Ole Opry or pay homage to Elvis at Graceland. Nevertheless, Tennessee's Great Smoky Mountains remain its number one attraction, with over 9 million visitors to the region each year.

Tennessee covers 42,146 square miles (109,158 sq km) of varied terrain, from the Appalachian ranges in the state's east, to the Delta flatlands, which border the Mississippi River. The Tennessee River slices through the Cumberland Plateau, dividing the state into west, middle, and east Tennessee. President Roosevelt's *New Deal* during the Depression saw the creation of the Tennessee Valley Authority in 1933, and the transformation of the state's agricultural economy into an industrial one.

State motto Agriculture and Commerce
State flag Adopted 1905
Capital Nashville
Population 5,689,283
Total area (land and water) 42,146 square miles (109,158 sq km)
Land area 41,219 square miles (106,757 sq km)
Tennessee is the 34th-largest state in size
Origin of name The word is of Cherokee origin, however, the exact meaning is unknown
Nickname The Volunteer State
Abbreviations TN (postal), Tenn.
State bird Mockingbird
State flower Iris
State tree Tulip poplar
Entered the Union June 1, 1796 as the 16th state

Places in
TENNESSEE

BIG SOUTH FORK NATIONAL RIVER AND RECREATION AREA

This area lies about 120 miles (193 km) northeast of Nashville. The 113,000-acre (45,765-ha) Big South Fork National River and Recreation Area winds its way across 500-foot (153-m) gorges and sheer sandstone cliffs into neighboring Kentucky. It has Pickett State Rustic Park at its western boundary.

Until the early 1960s, the area was being stripped of its timber and heavily mined for coal. It was due to the extensive lobbying of political patriarch to the state, Senator Howard Baker of Watergate fame, that the region was designated a national recreation area. Dense in hardwood, some of Tennessee's premier nature trails and whitewater rapids are found here, without the usual accompanying crowds.

Located west of Onieda, on Hwy 287, the Big South Fork features several trailheads that follow the river and connect to an old railroad trestle, once linking Oneida to Jameston. Another popular trail is Twin Arches, which starts near Bandy Creek Visitor Center on Hwy 297.

Hundreds of bird species, along with deer, raccoon, and wild boar, are found in Big South Fork's wilderness. Hunting is permitted during two weeks in November, so it is recommended that visitors check in with the park ranger and wear bright clothing or avoid the woods that have been marked for the seasonal sport. As well as being a haven for anglers, the Big South

Fork River is also a perfect spot for kayaking and white-water floats. Cycling, camping, and horseback riding are likewise permitted within its boundaries.

Nearby, 10 miles (16 km) north of Jamestown, is the family gristmill of World War I hero, Sergeant Alvin York. A quaint community straddling the recreation area's southern boundary is the town of Rugby, founded in 1880 by English author Thomas Hughes, of *Tom Brown's School Days* fame. Designed to be a genteel utopia in the rugged farming land of East Tennessee, the town's few residents all but disappeared after a typhoid epidemic. Over 20 buildings have been restored, including the Christ Episcopal Church and the Thomas Hughes Free Public Library, containing the most extensive collection of Victorian literature in the nation. The School House now serves as Rugby's visitor center.

Knoxville, about 60 miles (97 km) southeast of the area, is the closest center with an airport and bus service.
Map ref: page 559 H7

CHATTANOOGA

This industrial city of 144,776 is known nationally for the lyrical train, the Chattanooga Choo-Choo, made famous by bandleader Glenn Miller, as well as for the

The famous haze of the Great Smoky Mountains, a day trip from Chattanooga.

devastating Battle of Chattanooga and Chickamauga, one of the last victories for the Confederacy.

Chattanooga is now the state's fourth-largest city, built around the banks of the Tennessee River. It was this very river that changed Chattanooga's fortunes when, during the 1930s, the federal government established the Tennessee Valley Authority to conserve and develop the resources of the Tennessee River Valley. The Authority directed its massive power plants from the city, and controlled the floodwaters of the Tennessee River. Chattanooga grew from a strategic military prize for the Union during the Civil War to become a leading agricultural and rail center.

Its progress as a city came at a great cost to the Cherokee people, who had lived in the Tennessee Valley. Driven from their land in 1838, on the site of Chattanooga's Ross's Landing, the Cherokee were moved west to the Oklahoma territory on what is now known as "The Trail of Tears."

Chattanooga's downtown region has the Tennessee Aquarium at Ross's Landing, the Tennessee Valley Railroad Museum, and also the Chattanooga Regional History Museum. The Chattanooga African-American Museum showcases the life of jazz priestess, Bessie Smith, who came from the city. Her life is also celebrated

during the annual Riverbend Festival's "Bessie Smith Strut" party. Chattanooga is also home to the International Towing and Recovery Hall of Fame and Museum, homage to the city-founded, tow-trucking industry.

The best attraction is out of town at Lookout Mountain, the site of the city's theater of war. The Battles for Chattanooga Museum, formerly known as Confederama, profiles Chattanooga's surrounding battlefields, including neighboring Chickamauga, in Georgia. From Point Park, visitors can view the 8,000-acre (3,240-ha) Chickamauga–Chattanooga National Military Park and gain an extensive view of Chattanooga—all from the same location where, in 1863, Union General Ulysses S. Grant opened fire on the Confederate fortification at Lookout Mountain. The park's main visitor center is at Park Point on East Brow Road, off Route 148.

Chattanooga is serviced by the Chattanooga Metropolitan Airport and also by buses.
Map ref: page 564 E1

CLARKSVILLE

Located at the confluence of the Cumberland and Red Rivers, near the Kentucky border off I-24, this vital city of 103,455 people is one of Tennessee's oldest, dating back

The area around Chattanooga is a leading agricultural center.

to 1784. Clarksville became a major tobacco port during the nineteenth century and, in 1806, home to the Rural Academy, established on the present-day site of Austin Peay State University. During the Civil War, the city attempted to defend its western boundaries at nearby Fort Donelson, now a national battlefield. The capture of the fort in February 1862 marked the first victory for the Union Army as well as for Ulysses S. Grant.

After the war, Clarksville grew as a leading agricultural hub and by World War II was a military base. In 1950, Fort Campbell became the largest army base in Tennessee. Covering a massive 108,068 acres (43,768 ha), it is home to nearly 28,000 military and civilian personnel. The fort features numerous maneuver and artillery ranges and an assault landing strip. Its paratroopers were the first to land in France during the D-Day Invasion and, today, it has the world's only air assault division. The fort is also a base for the army's Green Berets and home to the 101st "Screaming Eagles," whose history is showcased at the Don F. Pratt Memorial Museum.

A gentler attraction is Clarksville's homespun Plummer's Store and Museum, on Hwy 76. The sign near a weighing scale that says, "No fancy grub, Just plain vittles," pretty much sums up its display of rural accoutrements.

Clarksville has become a leading communications and technological center. However, in its rush for modernization, the city has retained some yesteryear charm. There are several interesting sites downtown, including the Clarksville–Montgomery County Historical Museum, and Seiver Station on Walker Street, which was built in 1792 and is the city's oldest stone structure. Nearby is Fort Defiance, built by Clarksville's residents during the Civil War to ward off the Union troops.

A stroll downtown takes in Clarksville's historic Franklin Street district, complete with restored Victorian architecture and period lighting along the tree-lined brick sidewalk. There is also the Cumberland Riverwalk and a paddle-wheeler that churns along the river for the benefit of tourists. The city's most-photographed structure

An abundance of delicious fresh fruit for sale at the markets in Clarksville.

is the Customs House Museum and Cultural Center, an 1898 building that showcases the city's tobacco trade.

The most interesting story associated with Clarksville is the legend of the Bell Witch. In 1804, at the nearby town of Adams, the Bell family purchased land from an old woman who claimed she was swindled in the transaction. In retaliation, the woman stated she would haunt the family upon her death—and did. Though never sighted, her apparition caused havoc by moving furniture and turning objects into projectiles. Upon John Bell's death, the Bell Witch ceased its ghostly activities and the family's homestead soon burnt to the ground. Close to Adams is the Bell Witch Cave, famous for the eerie noises within. Today, visitors can hear the sounds of bluegrass and country music at the Bell Witch Opry.

There are no buses servicing Clarksville, but Nashville is only 49 miles (79 km) south, on I-24. Nashville is also serviced by an international airport, as well as trains and buses.
Map ref: page 558 C7

COLUMBIA

This quaint town of 32,043 residents sits right in the heart of Tennessee's Antebellum Trail, 45 miles (72 km) south of Nashville, on Hwy 31. Columbia was the ancestral home of the 11th President of the United States, James K. Polk.

Settled on the former hunting grounds of the Cherokee and Chickasaw peoples in 1812, Columbia grew around the Duck River and developed into a major mule-trading center.

The town boasts wonderful antebellum architecture and remains one of the state's wealthiest cities. Visitors can either embark on a self-guided tour or book a tour through the Maury County Convention and Visitors Bureau. Either way, Columbia's magnificent array of antebellum estates and pre-Civil War homes is, for most visitors, its main attraction.

Columbia's Court House Square remains the dominant feature of the town, with many of its buildings listed on the Historic Register. There is also the James K. Polk home on West Street, which is Columbia's most visited property. Built in 1816 by the father of the future president, many of the original furnishings are still on show. The Gothic mansion, The Athenaeum, built for the nephew of James Polk later became a ladies' academy. Another link to the Polk family is St John's Episcopal Church—built in 1839, it served as a plantation church.

There are several interesting events in Columbia, including the Spring Garden Plantation Pilgrimage in April. Mule Day, held on the first weekend of April, features a gathering of mules and fiddlers, and a liar's contest is one of its major highlights.

Columbia is serviced by buses. Nearby Nashville is serviced by an international airport, as well as trains and buses.
Map ref: page 558 D10

DAYTON

This rather unassuming college town of nearly 6,000 people is located just 35 miles (56 km) northwest of Chattanooga, on Hwy 27. Its main claim to fame is the Scopes Museum and Rhea County Court House, where the famous "Monkey Trial" took place in 1925, attracting worldwide attention and bringing thousands of visitors to Dayton.

The trial involved the school teacher John Thomas Scopes, who was accused of violating the controversial Tennessee law that prohibited the teaching of evolutionary theory in schools. The lawyers in the case were Clarence Darrow (defence), a famous criminal lawyer, and William Jennings Bryan (prosecution), famous for running for US President three times. Scopes was found guilty and fined—a conviction that was later reversed due to a legal technicality. The law prohibiting the teaching of evolution in schools was not overturned until 1967, 42 years later.

The Scopes Museum and Rhea County Court House now form a National Historic Landmark. The restored, third-floor courtroom is open to visitors and the Scopes Museum houses a detailed account of the trial. William Bryan died five days after the closing of the trial; Dayton's Bryan College was named in his honor.

There are no buses to Dayton, but nearby Chattanooga has air and bus services.
Map ref: page 564 F1

ELIZABETHTON

Elizabethton is located not far from the Cherokee National Forest, and this town is nestled at the foothills of the Appalachian Mountains in northeastern Tennessee. It is the perfect place for visitors wishing to soak up some of Tennessee's rural beauty. One of the loveliest features of the town is the Doe

River Covered Bridge, a 134-foot (41-m) wide clapboard bridge built in 1882, which stands at the fringe of the business district.

Elizabethton has a population of 13,000 people and was settled as Fort Watauga in 1769, at the Sycamore Shoals river crossing. Living beyond colonial protection, the settlers negotiated a land deal with the Cherokee in 1775, the largest exchange of land at that time.

The Sycamore Shoals State Historic Area, at West Elk Avenue, features a replica of the old fort used by the Overmountain Men at the Battle of King's Mountain in South Carolina during the Revolutionary War. Also located in the area is the oldest frame house in the state. The John and Landon Carter Museum, at Broad Street, dates back to 1775 and features Revolutionary-period furnishings.

Close to Elizabethton is a series of hiking trails, including the Appalachian Trail, a 2,100-mile (3,379-km) trek that follows the ranges to Maine. The scenic trail starts near Watauga Lake, on Roan Mountain, 15 miles (24 km) from town. It features numerous cabins and camping grounds along the way. Other stunning vistas are provided along the Laurel Fork Falls trail, together with Blue Hole Falls, 10 miles (16 km) north of town off Hwy 91.

One of the most popular events in Elizabethton is the Slagle's Pasture Bluegrass Festival, which is held over several days in June and features Appalachia's premier bluegrass musicians.

Johnson City is serviced by buses and is about 45 miles (72 km) west of Elizabethton. The Tri Cities Regional Airport is to the north of Elizabethton, between Johnson City and Kingsport.
Map ref: page 559 N8

FRANKLIN

Nestled in the heart of Middle Tennessee's lush pastoral farmlands, the city of Franklin is one of the nation's wealthiest communities—its economy is based on tourism and agriculture. Franklin (population 20,098) has a staunch Confederate history, reflected in the town's antebellum architecture and genteel customs.

Founded in 1799 as a leading plantation center, the city pros-

T-shirts with historical themes for sale in Gatlinburg.

pered until the Civil War, when it was occupied by Union troops for nearly three years. Hostilities eventually culminated in the Battle of Franklin, in November 1864, which is often referred to as the "Last Hurrah" because of the devastating casualties suffered by the Southern army.

Franklin's restored town square is one of the best you'll find in the South, with its classic Court House and buildings of a bygone era lining the sidewalks. The best way to explore the area is by foot, taking in the tree-lined residential avenues that branch off the square. Worth viewing is the Lotz House Museum on Columbia Avenue, showcasing an extensive display of rare Confederate and Union army artifacts, as well as the McPhail Office, used by Union Generals Schofield and Stanley as their headquarters during their military occupation. Many other houses of historic note are now private residences along Third Avenue.

On the fringe of the town are two of the best Civil War attractions in Middle Tennessee. Across the town's old railroad tracks is the plantation home of Historic Carnton, which was used as a field hospital during 1864. Within its grounds, the estate has the nation's largest private Confederate cemetery. The inside of the house has recently been restored to look as it would have during the battle—in the area used as an operating

room, blood stains still remain in the floorboards.

The other attraction is the Carter House, which was built around 1820. Besieged by opposing armies during the Battle of Franklin, its outhouses remain riddled with bullet holes. The Carter House has one of the best museums in town, featuring a detailed account of the battle along with military paraphernalia.

Winstead Hill Lookout, south of town, on Hwy 31, is where Confederate General Hood launched his ill-fated attack at the Battle of Franklin. During the first weekend of May, the Heritage Foundation Town and Country Tour of Homes takes in all the town's National Register estates for viewing.

There are numerous B&Bs in and around the city. In nearby Nashville, which is about 20 miles (32 km) north of Franklin, there is an international airport, as well as train and bus services.
Map ref: page 558 D9

GATLINBURG

Originally settled as White Oak Flats in 1835, Gatlinburg is located in a deeply wooded valley that is framed by the mist-shrouded mountain peaks of the Great Smoky Mountains. The town has a population of some 3,500 residents and it plays host to approximately 4 million people each year as the gateway to Great Smoky Mountains National Park (see entry on Great Smoky Mountains National Park, page 536).

Rather less well known, Gatlinburg is also the most popular honeymoon spot found outside of Las Vegas. Over 20,000 people "tie the knot" annually at one of Gatlinburg's 15 wedding chapels. Visitors can also get spiritually blessed at the Christus Gardens on River Road, a parkland that features life-size figures of Christ in a series of dioramas including Leonardo da Vinci's "Last Supper." Understandably, the park is host to numerous Christian bus tours that frequent this site.

The town has a trolley that links the foot-weary traveler to all of the major attractions including Ripley's Believe It or Not and the Guinness World Records Museum.

In the winter months, the Ober Gatlinburg Ski Area lures both locals and visitors alike to its moderate slopes and eight trails. The Gatlinburg Aerial Tramway travels over 2 miles (3 km), from downtown up to the resort, providing a beautiful vista of the town. In summer, the area transforms into a hive of activity, with everything from bungee jumping to alpine slides.

Gatlinburg is 45 miles (72 km) east of Knoxville's McGee-Tyson Airport via I-40. Knoxville is also serviced by buses.
Map ref: page 559 K9

Taffy maker working to supply tourists in the Smoky Mountains town of Gatlinburg.

GREAT SMOKY MOUNTAINS NATIONAL PARK

America's most visited region, this World Heritage Site has 9 million visitors each year. The park is 800 square miles (2,072 sq km) of dense woodlands and sharp-ridged mountains straddling the eastern boundary of Tennessee into North Carolina. It was designated a national park in 1934.

The park's topography is as diverse as its scenery; elevations range from 800 feet (244 m) to 6,643 feet (2,026 m) at Clingmans Dome, the highest peak in Tennessee. But it is the bluish haze that shrouds these ancient mountains—produced by hydrocarbons and moisture from the profuse vegetation—that gives them their mystical appearance.

Along the numerous trailheads throughout the park, many species of wildflowers carpet the forest floor and over 120 varieties of trees can be found—from pine-oak in the drier ridges to the spruce-fir at the higher elevations. Wildlife includes deer, bobcats, skunks, chipmunks, otters, and black bears, the park's mascot. Over 120 varieties of birds are found here, including hawks, turkey vultures, blue jays, and swallows.

The Sugarlands Visitor Center, near Gatlinburg on Hwy 441, is the Tennessee side's main entrance. The center offers ranger-led programs and a 20-minute orientation film. Other park entrances in Tennessee are at the Townsend Visitor Center on Hwy 321 and the Smoky Mountain Visitor Center off Hwy 66. The 11-mile (18-km) loop circuit around Cades Cove is the most popular thoroughfare for drivers and cyclists. There are 10 camp sites within the park, though only Cades Cove and Smoketrout are open year-round. Admission to the Park is free.
Map ref: page 559 K10

GREENEVILLE

Greeneville is situated to the west of the Appalachian Mountains, about 30 miles (48 km) southwest of Johnson City, on Hwy 321. Greeneville was first settled in 1783, and was temporarily the capital of the pioneer state of Franklin from 1785–88. The Nathanael Green Museum, which

Grotto Falls, one of the beautiful sights in Great Smoky Mountains National Park.

is located on McKee Street outlines the town's history and its somewhat colorful beginnings.

During the Civil War, Greeneville was of divided allegiance. The town's Green County Courthouse pays tribute to both armies by featuring two monuments, one Union and one Confederate. A fragment from a Union cannon remains embedded in the Greeneville Cumberland Presbyterian Church.

For many visitors to Greeneville, the main attraction is the fact that it was home to the ill-fated Andrew Johnson, successor to Abraham Lincoln. His time as President was marked by turbulent politics, and he was the first president to be impeached by Congress, though he was later acquitted in a Senate trial.

The visitor center, now the Andrew Johnson National Historic Site, has a museum with exhibits of Johnson's life, along with his tailor shop and residence, dating back to 1830. A few streets away is the Homestead, Johnson's home from 1851 until his death 24 years later. He was buried at the Andrew Johnson Cemetery, at the town's edge.

Greeneville is serviced by buses. The nearest airport is the Tri Cities Regional Airport, 50 miles (80 km) northeast, located between Johnson City and Kingsport.
Map ref: page 559 M8

JACKSON

Jackson is about 90 miles (145 km) northeast of Memphis on I-40. It is a college city of nearly 49,000 with an economy based on medical and agricultural industries. In 1819, Jackson was settled by soldiers from Andrew Jackson's one-time regiment, on what was the ancient tribal land of the Cherokee and Chickasaw Native Americans. After the arrival of the railroad in 1858, Jackson flourished as an agricultural and commercial center. The start of the Civil War saw the town become headquarters to Confederate General P.G.T. Beauregard before the Union Army took control of its rail depot. Union troops burnt the downtown region to the ground.

Jackson's most noteworthy buildings include the 1950s Greyhound Station and the South Royal Depot, once the center of the railroad industry. One of Jackson's four colleges, Lambuth University, houses the M.D. Anderson Planetarium.

The most significant building in Jackson is the Madison County Courthouse, where pioneer Congressman Davy Crockett made his famous announcement, following his 1836 re-election defeat, "The rest of you can go to hell, for I am going to Texas."

Jackson was the birthplace of "Blue Suede Shoes" Carl Perkins, and legendary blues artist Sonny Boy Williams. It is also the last home of railroad legend Casey Jones, showcased at the Casey Jones Village, off I-40. The Casey Jones Home and Railroad Museum chronicles the life of the Illinois Central Railroad engineer, John Jones (the "Casey" comes from his hometown in Kentucky—"KC"). It also features Casey Jones' heroic death, in 1901, when he chose to ride out a track collision in his train to prevent further fatalities. There is other railroad paraphernalia, including the famous ballad of Casey Jones.

Buses, and a regional airport southeast of town, serve Jackson.
Map ref: page 563 M3

JOHNSON CITY

With a population of 54,000, this is the sixth largest city in Tennessee. It lies in the heart of frontier country in the Cumberland Valley —Daniel Boone was among the first frontiersmen to blaze a trail through the area in 1760.

Always independent, the region chose to break away from the South by remaining loyal to the Union and defiantly published *The Emancipator*, the first abolitionist paper in the nation.

Johnson City's downtown region boasts little in the way of attractions with the exception of the Hands On! Regional Museum, which is a gallery of arts and sciences for inquisitive children.

However, within its city limits there are a number of places of interest. Perhaps the most intriguing is located at Rocky Mount, the oldest territorial capital in the nation, now a living history museum where guides dressed in period costume reenact life in the territory in the late eighteenth century. Another home worth viewing is the Tipton-Haynes Historic Site owned by John Tipton, a member of the 1776 Constitutional Convention. Later purchased by a Confederate Senator, the house has been restored to its 1860s splendor.

West of Johnson City is Tennessee's oldest town, Jonesboro, featuring a meticulously restored downtown region, now on the Historic Register.

Located off I-181, Johnson City is serviced by Knoxville's International Airport. Johnson City and Knoxville have bus services.

Map ref: page 559 M8

KINGSPORT

The city of Kingsport (population 41,300), located on the Holston River, lies in the northeastern corner of Tennessee near the borders of Virginia and North Carolina. Nestled in historic frontier country, Kingsport saw pioneers Davy Crockett and Daniel Boone trail the Wilderness Road into Kentucky around 1775.

The town muddled along until the arrival of the railroad in 1909. Kodak's founder, George Eastman, was one of the industrialists who founded the Eastman Chemical Company, together with Kingsport Press, now the largest bible manufacturer in the United States. Though lauded as America's "Model City," Kingsport was one of the nation's most polluted cities until the 1970s.

Several buildings provide the visitor with a glimpse of Kingsport's former frontier. The Exchange Place, housed on a former plantation, was once a resting point on the Great Stage Road, as well as an important place for exchanging colonial currency. Its eight outbuildings include a granary, store, smokehouse, and the cabin quarters of the plantation's slaves. Restored to its original condition is the Netherland Inn, dating back to 1818, which operated as a tavern

BB King's Blues Club in Memphis.

and inn for nearly 100 years. On the fringe of the city is Allandale Mansion, a 50-year-old edifice once dubbed Kingsport's "White House." Bequeathed to the city by its owner, it has some beautifully landscaped gardens.

Close to the city is Bays Mountain Park, a 3,000-acre (1,215-ha) parkland that features many species of birds, mammals, and a wealth of outdoor activities including a river barge ride. The park also has a planetarium and a natural wolf environment.

Kingsport is serviced by the Tri Cities Regional Airport and also by buses along I-81.

Map ref: page 559 M7

KNOXVILLE

With a population of 165,121, Knoxville is one of the largest cities in Tennessee. Built as a fort in 1794, it emerged as the new territory's capital and it is home to Blount College, now the University of Tennessee.

The region's natural resources allowed Knoxville to build its economy on lumber and coal. Knoxville also became a "New Deal" town under President Roosevelt's Tennessee Valley Authority program. Now headquarters to the Tennessee Valley Authority, Knoxville also serves as a gateway town to the Great Smoky Mountains National Park.

The city's only National Historic Landmark, Blount Mansion, was built in 1792. The former territorial governor, William Blount, drafted the first Tennessee State Constitution there. Close by is the remodeled version of James White's Fort, the city's first house, which was built in 1786.

Listed on the National Register of Historic Places is the Mabry-Hazen House, located on Dandridge Avenue, occupied by both Union and Confederate troops in 1863. The Confederate Memorial Hall is housed in a Victorian estate that was once occupied by

A trolley service takes in the attractions found along Main Street in Memphis.

Confederate General James Longstreet during the 1863 siege.

Norris is 30 miles (48 km) north of Knoxville, on I-75, and is a community founded around the Tennessee Valley Authority. Norris features the brilliant, 75-acre (30-ha) Museum of Appalachia, a collection of pioneer artifacts and buildings transported there from several nearby counties by its owner, John Rice Irwin. The author of *Roots*, Alex Haley, lived in Norris until his death in 1992.

The area is serviced by buses and Knoxville International Airport.

Map ref: page 559 K9

MEMPHIS

Named for the Egyptian city on the Nile, Memphis sits on a bluff overlooking the Mississippi River on Tennessee's southwestern boundary. From Riverside Drive, which runs parallel to the river, the city's most distinctive landmark, the Pyramid, rises above the otherwise unremarkable skyline.

Memphis is Tennessee's largest city—it has a population of 1,163,015. It was first settled in 1819 and became the cotton capital of the South. Its prosperity was shattered during the Civil War when Union forces controlled the city after the Battle of Memphis in 1862. It took another 30 years for Memphis to recover from the ravages of war and several yellow-fever epidemics.

The downtown district of Memphis is small, with Beale Street and

the new Peabody Center being the main focus. One hundred years ago, Beale Street was the birthplace of Memphis Blues, and later became a melting pot for blues musicians and the migrating African-American population.

On Union Street is the modest Sun Studios building, the music industry's most revered recording studio and birthplace of Rock 'n' Roll. Founded in 1950, legends such as BB King, Johnny Cash, Jerry Lee Lewis, Roy Orbison, U2, and Elvis Presley have passed through its doors. Other noted music venues are the Smithsonian's Rock 'n' Soul Museum and the Memphis Music Hall of Fame Museum, which showcases rare recordings and vintage footage of rock musicians.

Graceland is the place most tourists want to visit. Located on Elvis Presley Boulevard, the antebellum home was purchased by Elvis for his mother in 1957. The interior—upgraded three years before his death in 1977—is a delicious concoction of 1970s style, complete with green shag carpet (floor to ceiling) and yards of vinyl. His grave is located in the Meditation Garden. Across from the house is a museum selling a complete collection of Elvis memorabilia.

Memphis was center stage during the civil rights movement. In 1968, Dr Martin Luther King was assassinated on the second-floor balcony of the Lorraine Motel, now sheltering the Civil

Nashville is blessed with many natural recreation areas. One of these is the Cumberland River, which flows right through the city's downtown area.

Rights Museum. Visitors can ride the Montgomery bus to freedom, view exhibits of the movement and Dr King's room.

A walkway and a monorail link visitors to Mud Island, where the Mississippi River Museum is located. Also in the vicinity is the infamous World War II B17 bomber, *Memphis Belle*. Another way to explore the city is to catch a trolley to the downtown attractions. Visitors can also cruise the Mississippi on a stern-wheeler.

Henning, located 35 miles (56 km) north, was Alex Haley's boyhood home and the birthplace of *Roots*. Haley grew up at his grandparents' house on South Church Street, now the Alex Haley State House Museum, where he heard the ancestral tales of Kunta Kinte's clan. Several family members are buried at Henning's local cemetery, including Will and Cynthia Palmer and family patriarch, Chicken George.

Ten miles (16 km) away is Memphis International Airport. The city is also serviced by buses and trains.

Map ref: page 563 K4

MURFREESBORO

At the outbreak of the Civil War, the quiet rural community of Murfreesboro was largely known for being the former capital of Tennessee. After the state legislature relocated to Nashville in 1826, the town's focus is on its three state colleges.

This city is on US-41/70S, 30 miles (48 km) southeast of Nashville and is one of Tennessee's fastest growing cities (population 59,506). Its new economic focus is the local Nissan car plant, plus medical and high-tech industries.

Nashville busker Boots Roots.

Strategically positioned on the Nashville and Chattanooga Railroad, control of Murfreesboro was vital during the Civil War. After engaging in several clashes throughout 1862, the Union army was determined to recapture the town. An enormous earthwork fort was dug at its city limits and, during the following winter, 83,000 combined forces fought at Stones River. Over 23,000 men lost their lives in the bloodiest battle west of the Appalachians.

Stones River National Battlefield covers 570 acres (231 ha) of parkland and has over 6,000 Union graves in its cemetery. It also has the oldest Civil War Monument in the nation. Much of the battlefield lies on private land off Old Nashville Hwy in Murfreesboro. Every July, the city hosts a Civil War Encampment, in full period regalia, at Stones River National Battlefield.

The Pioneer Village of Cannonsburgh is a collection of reconstructed frontier buildings. Other places worth exploring include the plantation estate of Oaklands, and Fortress Rosecrans,

an earthwork built by African-American Union troops to protect Murfreesboro's depot and supplies.

The nearest airport is Nashville International, where train and bus services are also available.

Map ref: page 558 E9

NASHVILLE

This city of 488,374 people, at the junction of I-40, I-24, and I-65, prides itself on being the country music capital of the world. Nashville was founded on the banks of the Cumberland River in 1779 as Fort Nashborough and became the state capital in 1843.

Before the start of the Civil War, Nashville was a flourishing city, with its economy centered around agriculture and the railroad, which made it a key target for invading Union forces. From 1862–65, Nashville's handsome streets were transformed into army barracks, with much of the city destroyed during the Battle of Nashville in December, 1864. Even the elegant Tennessee State Capitol building, erected between 1845 and 1859, saw cannons placed on its steps.

After the Civil War, the state of Tennessee was the first to rejoin the Union, with its one-time governor and senator, Andrew Johnson, succeeding Abraham Lincoln as President. Nashville's geographic position guaranteed its return to prosperity, and the city quickly rebuilt. With the founding of Vanderbilt University in 1873, Fisk University, and Central Tennessee College, Nashville became the "Athens of the South."

In homage to its image, Nashville constructed a replica of the Parthenon for the city's centennial exposition in 1897. Rebuilt in 1931, the massive building now houses an art museum.

By the 1920s, Nashville's title of "Athens of the South" was replaced by "Music City." Nashville had long had a reputation for hosting everything from the classics to pure bluegrass. In 1925, the local radio station WSM hit the airwaves, featuring a regular Saturday night slot called "Barn Dance." Every fiddler jumped on board, including barnyard bands such as "The Dixie Clodhoppers." WSM's Barn Dance announcer christened his show "The Grand Ole Opry" as a telling jibe at Nashville's smart set, and a show was born in 1927. It is now the longest running radio show in the nation—it is broadcast live every Friday and Saturday night.

By World War II, The Opry was a national institution and musicians and songwriters flocked to "Music City." Legendary performers such as Roy Acuff,

The elegant Tennessee State Capitol building in Nashville was completed in 1859.

Hank Williams, Jim Reeves, Patsy Cline, and Loretta Lynn were all part of The Opry's lineup, followed by Willie Nelson, Dolly Parton, Tammy Wynette, and George Jones. Artists such as Elvis Presley and Bob Dylan used Nashville as a base to record their hits in the studios along Music Row.

Many big-name singers now play to massive crowds at the Nashville Arena, the city's new sports and entertainment center.

Mural in the lobby of the Country Music Hall of Fame in Nashville.

The Arena also has to the week-long Fan Fair, held for country music enthusiasts each June.

A city built on hills, Nashville's downtown district, with the Cumberland River flowing through it, is best discovered on foot. A walking trail covers the pioneer and Civil War sites along the city's riverfront. Visitors can also take a trolley downtown, to Music Row and Music Valley.

The downtown area, known as The District, is Nashville's entertainment heart, with most venues located on Broadway. The recently restored Ryman Auditorium oozes nostalgia, and features a small country music museum. The Wildhorse Saloon on Second Avenue, and the cobblestone laneway of Printers Alley between Third and Fourth Avenues, have the best live entertainment in town.

Of historic note are the replica of Fort Nashborough near the Cumberland River, and the Tennessee State Museum, which features an excellent presentation of Tennessee's pioneer and Civil War history. The Country Music Hall of Fame exhibits an extensive array of country music mementos.

Fifth Avenue is where the famous "lunch counter sit-ins" during the civil rights movement

took place, organized by Fisk University students. The majestic Hermitage Hotel is noted for its lineup of legendary guests, including Gene Autry.

Broadway leads to Music Row in the West End District and Studio B, famous for producing the "Nashville Sound," created by Chet Atkins. The area is home to a host of recording labels. The most colorful place in the West End is Manuel's, Nashville's legendary tailor to the stars.

Music Valley, 10 miles (16 km) north of the city, off Briley Parkway, is home to Opryland. The massive building features the Grand Ole Opry House, a 4,400-seat contemporary auditorium that hosts the Friday and Saturday night show of "The Grand Ole Opry," together with other live performances throughout the week. There's nothing "country" about this complex—it's just pure rhinestone glitz.

Other attractions here include a paddle-steamer trip along the Cumberland River, the Tennessee Performing Arts Center, and Ernest Tubb's Record Store Midnight Jamboree at the Texas Troubadour Theater, which hosts a lineup of artists for a radio show every Saturday at midnight.

The Andrew Jackson Visitor Center features a small museum dedicated to the nation's seventh president. A stroll across the estate leads to the graves of "Old Hickory" and his wife, Rachel. Marking the beginning of Middle Tennessee's Antebellum Trail is Belle Meade, Nashville's finest plantation-era mansion, constructed in 1853. The handsome Travelers Rest, built in 1799, is another historic home that has been meticulously restored to its former glory.

Nashville has numerous recreational areas, the most beautiful being the serene woodlands of Radnor Lake Natural Area on Otter Creek Road off Hillsboro. There are numerous nature trails and scores of wildlife at the lake, especially at dawn.

Visitors can use Nashville as a base for exploring the battlefields and mansions of Franklin (see entry on Franklin, page 35), together with Lynchburg, home to the Jack Daniel's Distillery. Located 70 miles (113 km) southeast of Nashville, the nation's oldest distillery dates back to 1866. A free tour features a viewing of the whiskey-making process—but be warned—sipping any samples is totally prohibited, because Lynchburg lies in a dry county.

Nashville is serviced by Nashville International Airport, 8 miles (13 km) east of the city, as well as by buses and trains.

Map ref: page 558 D8

PIGEON FORGE

Located 33 miles (53 km) southeast of Knoxville, the sleepy town of three decades ago has become Tennessee's major attraction. What was at one time Cherokee hunting grounds in this lush Appalachian valley is now a town of 3,975 people, which has been made famous by Dolly Parton. The town's fortunes changed when the lure of the Great Smoky Mountains National Park enticed people into the area. However, it was the singer's signature theme park, Dollywood, which opened in 1986, that turned its former economy of iron forging into pure mountain gold.

Pigeon Forge now houses more than 50 family-themed attractions together with theaters, shopping malls, and numerous specialty shops selling homespun crafts. During summer, it is not uncommon to have 40,000 people crowding downtown's streets.

Pigeon Forge is a town for pure frolic. Visitors can find corn-on-the-cob anytime at a downtown hoedown venue or hear live entertainment at Dollywood, which is open from April to October. Go-cart tracks, miniature golf courses, and water slides are just some of the attractions, as well as Dolly's Splash Country—a 25-acre (10-ha)

Billboards on a hillside outside Pigeon Forge.

water park. Other attractions include the Elvis Museum, which houses the largest private collection of Elvis paraphernalia, Smoky Mountain Car Museum, and the offbeat Carbos Police Museum.

Pigeon Forge is linked to Knoxville by I-40, Hwy 66, and Hwy 321, and is serviced through Knoxville's McGee Tyson Airport.

Map ref: page 559 K9

PULASKI

The gentle town of Pulaski, which sits in Middle Tennessee's southern region, about 80 miles (129 km) south of Nashville, was named for an exiled Polish count, who died fighting for American independence in 1779. Founded in 1809, Pulaski flourished as a center servicing the surrounding plantations.

Now a town of 9,181 people, Pulaski's most popular attraction is the Sam Davis Museum. The Confederate hero, Sam Davis, was executed by Union troops for spying, and the museum is located at the site of his execution. Other attractions are the Giles County Historical Museum, and Milky Way Farm, built by Mars Candy Co founder, Frank Mars, 8 miles (13 km) from Pulaski.

Pulaski is the birthplace of the Ku Klux Klan, formed as a social club in a law office off Madison Street in 1865. Shrouded in white sheets and secrecy, the KKK built up momentum and created a wave of terror over the South.

In more recent times, Pulaski is remembered for taking a dramatic step against the Klan with great success. The town's people, both white and black, had had enough of the hate-filled rhetoric that they witnessed each year during the KKK's annual march, so in 1989, the entire town, including the commercial center, shut its doors as the Aryan Nation and KKK marched through the

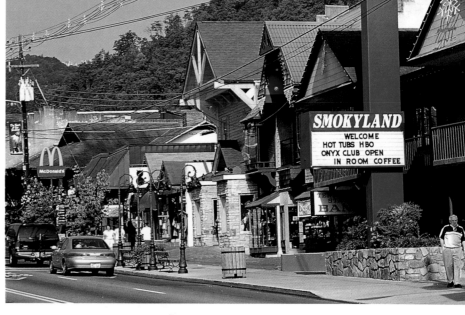

One of several motels in the busy downtown tourist area of Pigeon Forge, home of Dollywood.

deserted streets. Every January, the town celebrates Martin Luther King Day with the Brotherhood Parade, a united gathering that declares that racism is no longer tolerated on the town's streets.

Located at the junction of Hwy 64 and Hwy 31, Pulaski is 21 miles (34 km) from Lawrenceburg, one-time home of Davy Crockett and Tennessee's Amish community.

Map ref: page 564 B1

SEVIERVILLE

The area surrounding the Little Pigeon River was first settled by an Indian trader in 1780. Sevierville was established as a town 15 years later. Archeologists believe a Woodland Native American culture existed in the region around 2000 BC.

Named for the first governor of the state, Sevierville (population 8,700) grew around trade. Much of the town was destroyed by a fire in 1856, but by 1896, when the Sevier County Courthouse was built, the town had been restored to its former glory.

Surrounded by the unspoiled backdrop of the Great Smoky National Park, tourism is now the town's mainstay, replacing the traditional agricultural trade.

Every year during April, Dolly Parton, Sevierville's honorary resident, returns to town to kick off neighboring Pigeon Forge's Grand Opening at Dollywood, her signature theme park.

Sevierville's rustic downtown center soon melts into a strip of motels, amusement parks, and outlet malls. The main attractions are the Sevier County Heritage Museum, featuring local frontier artifacts, Wilson's North American

Wildlife Museum, which has a 15,000-foot (4,575-m) cave gallery showcasing some of North America's animals, and Floyd Garret's Muscle Car Museum.

Sevierville is linked to Knoxville by I-40 and Hwy 66, and is serviced through Knoxville's McGee Tyson Airport.

Map ref: page 559 K9

SHILOH NATIONAL MILITARY PARK

The tranquil woodlands of Middle Tennessee, which surround Shiloh, are a far cry from the bloody battle that took place here in April, 1862. In 1894, the 4,000-acre (1,620-ha) Shiloh National Military Park was established to preserve the memory of this two-day battle.

Six weeks after his victorious engagement at Fort Donelson, General Ulysses S. Grant camped along the Tennessee River at Pittsburg Landing to wait for Union reinforcements. In an attempt to surprise Grant, Confederate General Albert Johnson led a disastrous charge, which saw nearly 20,000 men slaughtered or wounded. By the second day, Grant had replaced his weary troops with fresh reserves, forcing the Confederates to retreat.

The Shiloh National Military Park's visitor center provides information on numerous sites including the Union defense point of Hornet's Nest, and Bloody Pond, where the blood of soldiers trickled into the water, causing it to go the color of blood.

Shiloh National Military Park is located off Route 22, 110 miles (177 km) east of Memphis.

Map ref: page 563 N4

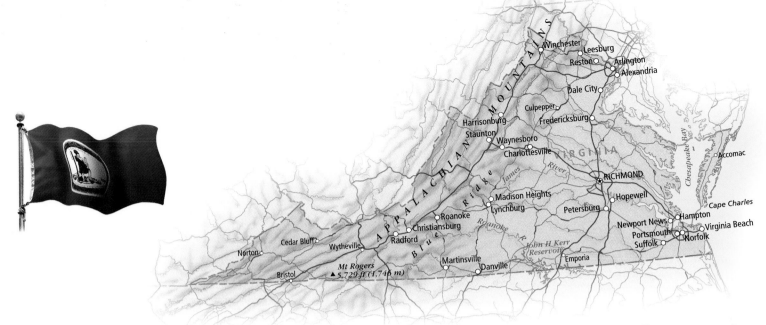

VIRGINIA

Virginia's diverse landscape is bordered by a tidewater coastline and the radiant Blue Ridge and Allegheny mountains; nestled midway is the pastoral tranquility of the Shenandoah Valley. Known as "The Old Dominion State" and "Mother of Presidents," Virginia was the birthplace of seven presidents including George Washington, Thomas Jefferson, and Woodrow Wilson. The state was also involved in the story of Native American princess Pocahontas and Captain John Smith.

Virginia's heritage goes back to the first permanent settlement at Jamestown in 1607, where 105 colonists came from England to make their fortunes in the New World. Originally home to the Powhatan and Algonquian Native Americans, Virginia was declared the first of 13 colonies in America in 1776. After drafting the *Declaration of Independence*, Thomas Jefferson became Virginia's second governor and was instrumental in relocating its capital from Williamsburg to Richmond in 1779.

A horse-drawn carriage in colonial Williamsburg. Virginia's heritage can be seen in an array of antebellum estates, national battlefields, and historic places like Williamsburg, Richmond, and Charlottesville.

The state flourished despite the growing dissension over slavery in the state's west, and Virginia seceded from the Union to join the Confederacy. The break divided its citizens, creating the state of West Virginia in 1863. During the Civil War Virginia's soil saw many bloody battles, with the commander of the Confederate Army, General Robert E. Lee, surrendering the Confederacy on Virginian soil in April 1865.

Virginia's proximity to Washington as well as to the Atlantic seaboard kick-started its economy, with US naval bases and viable coal, lumber, rail, and shipping industries. Virginia remained defiant in its standing on segregation and, though its transformation was slow, by 1989 Virginia was the first state in the nation to elect an African-American governor.

State motto *Sic Semper Tyrannis* (Thus always to tyrants)
State flag Adopted 1861
Capital Richmond
Population 7,078,515
Area (land and water) 42,326 square miles (109,624 sq km)
Land area 39,598 square miles (102,559 sq km)
Virginia is the 36th-largest state in size
Origin of name Named for Elizabeth I, Virgin Queen of England
Nicknames The Old Dominion State, Mother of Presidents
Abbreviations VA (postal), Va.
State bird Cardinal
State flower American dogwood
State tree Flowering dogwood
Entered the Union June 25, 1788 as the 10th state.

Places in VIRGINIA

ALEXANDRIA

The old river port of Alexandria is the official gateway to the South from Washington DC. Hugging the Potomac River, which acts as a natural border to the state, this city of 120,000 people is steeped in a rich heritage preceding the Revolutionary War (1775–83). Established as a major tobacco port in 1749, most of its Federal-era buildings are fully restored in Alexandria's historic Old Town District.

A walking tour may include George Washington's townhouse, and Carlyle House, which was used as a meeting house in the French and Indian War (1754–63). Captain's Row features the original cobblestone road constructed around the 1790s, and along Gentry Row, Old Town's most handsome Georgian dwellings line the streets. Further south on Fairfax is the Old Presbyterian Meeting House, where the funeral for George Washington was held in 1799. The church here also holds the Tomb of the Unknown Soldier of the Revolutionary War in the adjacent graveyard. George Washington along with his band of patriots once frequented the now-restored Gadsby Tavern Museum,

The restored Boyhood Home of Robert E. Lee was occupied by this war hero's family periodically from 1811 to 1825. An earlier dwelling belonging to Lee's family is at the Lee-Fendall House Museum, displaying personal artifacts and a period-dollhouse collection. Alexandria's history is chronicled at The Lyceum, an 1829 Greek Revival building that served as a hospital during the Civil War.

Other points of interest are the Torpedo Factory Art Center, which built torpedoes during World War II, and Fort Ward Museum and Historic Site, used from May 1861 to September 1865 by the Union Army to protect the capital from possible Confederate attack.

Alexandria is served by Ronald Reagan National Airport and train services from Washington DC. Drive in via the George Washington Memorial Parkway.
Map ref: page 561 J3

APPOMATTOX COURT HOUSE NATIONAL HISTORIC PARK

Just 16 miles (26 km) east of Lynchburg is Appomattox Court House National Historic Park, which witnessed the surrender of the Confederate Army, led by General Robert E. Lee, to General Ulysses S. Grant's Union forces on April 9, 1865. The hushed ceremony was brief as the two generals laid down their arms to sign the documents inside the McLean House parlor.

The house itself was not without bitter irony. Its owner, Wilmer McLean, moved to Appomattox from Manassas, to avoid further conflict after his house was shelled at the battle of Bull Run in 1861. McLean witnessed the first battle of the war and was present to watch the Confederacy surrender at the close of the war.

Created by Congress in 1935, the National Historic Park has restored the region's beautiful village including 13 of the original buildings. The original Courthouse still sits amid rolling green hills. After the surrender, the two-story McLean House was at the mercy of souvenir scavengers and a devastating fire that destroyed the home. The current site was reconstructed from the original bricks. following the old plans.

Changing guards, Arlington National Cemetery. The cemetery covers 612 acres (248 ha).

Located only a short distance from Hwy 24, the Appomattox Court House National Historic Park is a commemorative memorial of a war that once bitterly divided the country.
Map ref: page 560 F7

ARLINGTON

Designed to become the nation's capital, Arlington (population 189,453) evolved into a medley of high-rise buildings and urban sprawl, and is just a short commute to Washington DC across the Potomac River. The George Washington National Parkway connects the capital to two rather important national landmarks: the Pentagon and Arlington National Cemetery. Located adjacent to the Memorial Bridge (that was built as a symbolic connection to link the South to the North), the cemetery spreads over 612 acres (248 ha) of green and tranquil grounds that were once the ancestral home of General Robert E. Lee's wife, Mary Custis.

Though the war hero's land was actually confiscated during the Union Army's occupation from

The Arlington cemetery has graves of soldiers from every American war. It was once the home of Robert E. Lee's wife, Mary Custis.

May 1861 to September 1865, his home, Arlington House, was spared from destruction and today sits within the cemetery, gazing toward Washington. At the outbreak of war in April, 1861, Lee declined a commission with the Union Army, returning to his native Virginia to take command of the Army of Virginia. In an act of malice, Union troops buried their dead in the fields surrounding Lee's home so that he would nevermore be able to feel comfortable at his estate. He died in Lexington in 1870, never to return to Arlington House. Many original furnishings and the family portraits remain on display.

From Arlington House's portico, row after row of plain, white headstones dot the gentle acres of grassy knolls. Since the first burial took place in May 1864, over 220,000 soldiers have been buried here under simple markers.

Along with the grave of Washington DC's city-architect, Pierre L'Enfant, visitors usually seek out the newly erected memorials—Challenger Space Shuttle and Women in the Military Service, together with The Tomb of the Unknowns. Guarded by ramrod soldiers, the shrine commemorates the many nameless Americans who fought in World Wars I and II, and the Korean and Vietnam wars. The most visited grave site, is that of John F. Kennedy, in addition to the sites of former First Lady, Jacqueline, and Robert F. Kennedy, Arlington National Cemetery has tourmobile excursions for a nominal fee through the visitor center.

North of the center is the grand 78-foot (24-m) bronze statue of Iwo Jima, showing four marines struggling to raise the American flag.

A stone's throw from Arlington National Cemetery is the Pentagon, the largest single-structure office in the world, which houses 20,000 Department of Defense employees. Near the Potomac River, it has 17 miles (27 km) of corridors and covers over 6 million square feet (570,000 sq m). This complex, completed

halfway through World War II, was designed for easy access to all of its 17 buildings during any emergency. Tour passes to a maze of several unrestricted areas are available to the public, though the area called "Ground Zero" is still shrouded in mystery.

South of Arlington is Manassas Battlefield National Park. The Battle of Bull Run, as the major conflict was originally named, took place here on July 21, 1861 at Henry Hill, signaling the first engagement of the Civil War. Though 20,000 Union troops outnumbered their opponent, the Confederate Army led by General Thomas Jackson out-maneuvered the Union charge, thwarting their attempt to control the Virginia railroads on their march to Richmond. It was the Battle of Bull Run that earned the Confederate General his nickname, "Stonewall." In August 1862, the Second Battle of Manassas was fought.

Prince William County is also home to the world's largest outlet mall, as well as Quantico Marine Corps Base and Marine Corps Air-Ground Museum. The museum provides an excellent overview of life as a US Marine. The base still trains the nation's combative forces.

Looping around Lovers Peak, Blue Ridge Parkway leads to Mabry Mill, a water-powered gristmill.

Down a stretch is the legendary FBI Building, nestled in Quantico's wooded terrain.

Arlington is accessible by car, or by plane, train, and bus via adjacent Washington DC.

Map ref: page 561 J3

BLUE RIDGE PARKWAY

The two-lane Blue Ridge Parkway runs 469 miles (755 km) from the Shenandoah National Park in Virginia's southern Appalachian region to the Great Smoky National Park in North Carolina. With numerous lakes, cascading waterfalls, and forests overlapping the Parkway, there are plenty of opportunities to take a hike on one of the well-marked trails. Rising to 6,000 feet (1,830 m), the Blue Ridge Mountains are shrouded

in a blue-tinged mist. In the fall the forest foliage turns a fiery hue. A region of ancient land formations, the land was once the Cherokee's before they were forced in the early nineteenth century along "The Trail of Tears," in their journey to the Oklahoma territory.

Anyone traveling the Blue Ridge Parkway should not be in a hurry. The area provides a stunning panoramic backdrop for a number of outdoor activities such as camping and hiking to cycling and kayaking.

Built around the Shenandoah Valley and Norfolk & Western Railroads, Roanoke is a pleasant commercial center with a historic downtown region. Along with the old farmer's market, visitors should also see the Virginia Museum of Transportation and the History Museum of Western Virginia.

The natural beauty of the parkway's serene blue ridgelines can be best enjoyed around Floyd County, where pocket towns nuture the traditions of Appalachia's mountain people. From Roanoke, detour across to Fairy Stone State Park on US-57, known for its fortuitous "fairy" stones. The town of Ferrum features the Blue Ridge Institute and Farm Museum, which highlights the region's German heritage.

Bluegrass music fills the mountain air at Galax each August when the region's best fiddlers pack in the crowds at the Old Fiddlers Convention. The Blue Ridge Parkway is open year-round, except when there is heavy snow on the roads in the winter months.

Map ref: page 560 F5

See also North Carolina, page 516

Bikers enjoy a stop at Larry's Antiques and Secondhand Shop on Blue Ridge Parkway.

Charlottesville's downtown area is filled with cafés, bookshops, and antique malls.

CHARLOTTESVILLE

The university city of Charlottesville sits in the pastoral tranquillity of the Piedmont Plateau, midway across Virginia, about 71 miles (114 km) from Richmond on the I-64. Founded in 1762, the city largely grew around Thomas Jefferson's estate, Monticello, and the University of Virginia. With a population of 38,000, this city has a number of stately buildings set against a backdrop of the moody Blue Ridge Mountains.

Of interest is the Virginia Discovery Museum, which exhibits a late 1700s log cabin. "Jefferson's Corner" here chronicles this former President's life's work and has various regional artifacts.

The foremost attraction of the city is Jefferson's magnificent estate, Monticello, designed by the man himself. While work first began on this Palladian-style villa in 1768, Jefferson was constantly tinkering with the villa's construction over a 40-year period. After spending five years in France, Jefferson adopted the old country's beautiful architectural lines and assembled a dome atop of his mansion. An eccentric intellectual, he kept a wealth of artifacts in his own personal museum. He also designed a rather ingenious bedroom. Jefferson positioned the bed in an alcove so he could either step out into his study or dressing room, without ever getting out of bed on the "wrong side." A passage from the kitchen leads to the remains of Mulberry Row, the estate's former slave quarters—where he fathered a child with one of his slaves. Though only the first floor is opened to visitors, the estate looks similar to how Jefferson left it upon his death on Independence Day, 1826— exactly 50 years to the day that the

Declaration of Independence was signed. He is buried at the end of Mulberry Row, marked by a plain headstone.

Near to Monticello is the historic Michie Tavern, dating back to 1784. Still in operation as an inn, the tavern is in close proximity to the Federal-period Meadow Run Gristmill.

The University of Virginia, founded in 1819, is one of the nation's most liberal colleges. Recognized for its architectural splendor and designed by Jefferson, the neoclassical campus features a beautiful white-domed rotunda along with splendid seasonal gardens. Visitors should view former student Edgar Allan Poe's room in the West Building.

Charlottesville is surrounded by no less than 40 vineyards and pastures filled with thoroughbred horses. Many estate owners are of old money pedigree, where fox hunts and barking hounds are part of the social course. At Thanksgiving, the traditional Blessing of the Hounds occurs at the old Grace Episcopal Church, 16 miles (26 km) east of the city on US-231. North of Charlottesville is the Barboursville Winery and the ruins of Governor James Barbour's mansion, now a historic landmark. Seven miles (11 km) northeast on Hwy 20 is the town of Orange; its attraction is the James Madison Museum, which commemorates Jefferson's presidential successor and has exhibits of regional history.

Southwest of Charlottesville is the region that inspired the 1970s homespun television series, "The Waltons." The Waltons' Mountain Museum in Schuyler takes a trip down memory lane to Ike Godsey's store and John-Boy's bedroom.

There are several festivals worth catching including the Virginia

Festival of the Book, held in October, and the Virginia Film Festival. During Christmas, Charlottesville is lit up like a Christmas tree and celebrates the holiday with a number of events, including A Merrie Olde England Christmas Festival. The city also brims with some of the region's most beautiful B&B establishments.

Charlottesville is serviced by jet flights from Washington DC, New York, and Richmond through Charlottesville–Albermale Airport, as well as by rail and bus services.
Map ref: page 560 F5

CHESAPEAKE

Located right in the swamplands of Virginia's tidewater, 105 miles (169 km) southeast of Richmond, this city of 204,470 is steeped in colonial heritage. It was at the forefront of the colonialists' battle with the British at Great Bridge (where the Chesapeake Municipal Center is now located), during the

Revolutionary War in December 1775. Eighteen years later, the construction of the Dismal Swamp Canal began—it is now the oldest artificial waterway still in operation in the country.

Later occupied by Union troops during the Civil War, the city bounced back with a buoyant economy largely due to its natural resources by the water. While the focus is more on industry than tourism, there are several points of interest worth a glance. Visitors can take a walk along the trails at Chesapeake Arboretum or do some local stargazing at the Chesapeake Planetarium. An interesting museum, it features a sky theater in a dome ceiling, complete with some fascinating special effects that bring to life the phenomenon of our vast and fascinating solar system.

Located in an area known as Hampton Roads—the crossroads of four cities—Chesapeake also sits within the beltway of the I-64 and is serviced by Norfolk Regional Airport. Chesapeake can also be accessed by rail at Newport News railway, only 10 miles (16 km) away.
Map ref: page 561 K8

Paths along the Chesapeake and Ohio Canal were redesigned for recreational use.

Shells for sale at the remote and peaceful seaside town of Chincoteague.

CHINCOTEAGUE

This quaint fishing village nestles south of the Maryland border as a barrier island on the eastern shore. Chincoteague (population 3,572) is Virginia's only resort island and is a sanctuary to many migrating shorebirds and waterfowl. This town also features some beautiful shoreline nature trails.

Windswept and remote, the village is gateway to the Chincoteague National Wildlife Refuge, famous for its lovely beaches, bird-watching, and wild ponies. Established in 1943, it has many trails that trace the shoreline to Swan Cove and Snow Goose Pool. Every July, the ponies are herded across Assateague Channel for their annual swim to Chincoteague Memorial Park.

In the village, the Refuge Waterfowl Museum recounts the move to save these once-endangered birds. Further down the boulevard, the Oyster and Maritime Museum displays maritime life and chronicles the history of its local industry.

From Virginia Beach to Chincoteague, take the US-13 across the lengthy Chesapeake Bay Bridge. Access is only by car.
Map ref: page 561 M5

DANVILLE

The industrial city of Danville at the foothills of the Blue Ridge in the Piedmont Region, is 160 miles (257 km) south of Richmond. It makes a pleasant overnight stop before crossing the North Carolina state line on Hwy 29.

It was once refuge to President Jefferson Davis when he fled Richmond in April 1865. The Sutherlin House, briefly used for his cabinet, called the last "Confederate White House" by the locals. Its museum showcases Jefferson's one-week occupation including the dining room, which served as the council room for his staff. Visitors can view Virginia native Nancy Astor's birthplace at Broadstreet and learn about the woman who swept through English society by becoming the first lady to serve in the British House of Commons. Appropriately enough, Danville (population 50,000) also boasts the National Tobacco–Textile Museum, highlighting the city's traditional economy.

The Danville Regional Airport services Danville, which is not accessible by bus or train.
Map ref: page 560 E9

FREDERICKSBURG

Fredericksburg (population 20,000) was founded in 1723 as a major tobacco port along the Rappahannock River. A pretty place with a rich historic district, the exit off I-95 brings into view narrow streets lined with white picket fences and Federal-style buildings.

Halfway between the opposing capitals of Washington and Richmond, Fredericksburg's rolling green fields were bloody battlefields during the Civil War. There are reminders of the Union artillery shells that bombarded the town. In Fredericksburg's Old Town area, the Presbyterian Church features indented shrapnel from a cannonball in its walls. The Rising Sun Tavern was built in 1760 by George Washington's brother. The Old Town Hall and Market House, built in 1816, is the one of oldest continually used community halls in the South. Other Federal-era buildings include the James Monroe Museum, where the former President practiced law from 1786 to 1789, and the estates of Kenmore, Belmont, and the Mary Washington House, built by George for his mother in 1772. The Freemasons have a solid collection of artifacts from the colonial years at the George Washington Masonic Museum, while the Fredericksburg Area Museum and Cultural Center has Native American, Colonial, and Civil War collections. An interesting display of medicinal procedures used two centuries ago is exhibited at the Hugh Mercer Apothecary. A Scottish doctor who was killed in battle during the Revolutionary War owned the shop.

The boyhood home of George Washington is at Ferry Farm in Falmouth, while west of the river from Fredericksburg is Chatham Manor, a Georgian structure dating back in the 1770s. Of the many dignitaries who were entertained its parlors are Abraham Lincoln; General Joe Hooker, who used the house as his headquarters; and Clara Barton, founder of the Red Cross.

The serene Fredericksburg and Spotsylvania National Battlefield Parks present a solid insight to the four battles that saw Confederate sharpshooters under the command of General Robert E. Lee rip apart the Army of the Potomac. Though the battles of Fredericksburg (1862), Chancellorville (1863), the Spotsylvania Court House (1864), and the Battle in the Wilderness (1864) were largely Confederate victories, the fight over the control of the Virginia railroads saw over 100,000 casualties, including Confederate General "Stonewall" Jackson at Chancellorville.

Within 17 miles (27 km) of each other, the battlesites have been preserved including Confederate cannons at Hazel Grove, plus 5 miles (8 km) of trenches and fortifications The remains of 15,000 Union troops are buried at Fredericksburg National Cemetery.

The National Park Service provides self-guided touring maps that cover the 75-mile (121-km) area. The pass to the Fredericksburg and Spotsylvania National Battlefield Park is valid for 10 days.

Fredericksburg is serviced by buses, trains, and planes.
Map ref: page 561 H5

Fresh summer foliage graces the forests on the Blue Ridge Parkway, near Danville.

HAMPTON

The university city of Hampton is famous for its pirate history and also for being the oldest English-speaking community in America. A heritage city of 134,000 residents, it is located at the wind-swept point of Virginia's tidewater in the Chesapeake Bay region of Hampton Roads.

Built as a fort in 1609, Hampton was troubled by invading pirates. According to local lore, the notorious buccaneer Blackbeard (aka Edward Teach) had attacked numerous cargo vessels along the Virginia coastline. But his fateful attempt to outrun two British sloops cost him his head in 1718. Returning with the bloody prize, the sailors placed Blackbeard's head at the point of the Hampton River as warning to other pirates.

Though Hampton saw its city largely destroyed by the British during the War of 1812 and again during the Union occupation of the Civil War, several noted buildings survived including St John's Church (1728). The oldest continuously used church in America, it has a stained-glass window of Pocahontas. The nation's largest stone-constructed fort is located south of Buckroe Beach at Old Point Comfort. Built in 1819, Fort Monroe became an impenetrable bastion for the Union Army

and refuge for escaped slaves. Harriet Tubman, who helped many of the slaves travel north along the Underground Railroad, served as a matron at the fort's colored hospital. After the war, the army incarcerated Jefferson Davis for a year on a trumped-up charge of plotting Abraham Lincoln's assassination. Along with Castmate Museum, visitors can view Davis' cell and Fort Monroe's white stone lighthouse, which is still in use for Atlantic mariners.

Overlooking the Hampton River is the Hampton University, the nation's first African-American college established by the Freedman's Bureau in 1868. The college now houses a museum featuring Native and African-American artifacts along with a brief history of its students, including Booker T. Washington. The city's architectural feat is the Virginia Air and Space Center and its two museums: the Air and Space Center and the Hampton Roads History Center. Both gallery exhibits run the gamut of Hampton's history to the present day space program at Langley Air Force Base and NASA facilities.

Hampton has focused on rejuvenating its old downtown waterfront, adding a sentimental touch by restoring the 1920 Hampton Carousel, once part of the now defunct Buckroe Amusement Park

Insignia for the independent Washington and Lee University in Lexington.

that entertained wide-eyed children for 60 years. Buckroe Beach is still the city's favorite haunt in the summer, along with the Grandview Nature Reserve, a great place for bird-watching. A restored trolley car travels from the visitor center to the downtown spots.

Hampton is serviced through The Newport News and Williamburg International Airport, which is 10 miles (16 km) north off Hwy 17/143 and it is also accessible by rail at nearby Newport News.
Map ref: page 561 K8

HARRISONBURG

This reserved city nestles in the lush Shenandoah Valley, about 131 miles (211 km) northwest of Richmond. Featuring a traditional economy

based on agriculture, Harrisonburg also has a strong Mennonite population with the Eastern Mennonite University located in town together with the James Madison University and Bridgewater Community College.

A city of 36,730, Harrisonburg has numerous nearby attractions. In winter, the Massanutten Ski Area offers reasonable terrain and miles of pristine winter scenery while the Endless Caverns, north of the city on US-11, feature colorful cave formations.

The Shenandoah Valley also witnessed bitter fighting in 1864 at New Market. Just off the I-81 on US-211 is the New Market Battlefield State Historic Park, which reenacts the charge of nearby Virginia Military Institute's cadets against the 5,000-strong Union troops. The battle was fought over the control of the supply depot at nearby Staunton. The Hall of Valor, located in the visitor center of the New Market Battlefield State Historic Park, remembers the battle and its hero cadets from the Virginia Military Institute.

Shenandoah Valley Regional Airport services the area, but there are no trains or buses.
Map ref: page 560 F4

LEXINGTON

Picturesque Lexington sits west of the Natchez Trace along the I-81 about 138 miles (222 km) west of Richmond. A town of about 7,000 people, it grew around Washington University, founded in 1749. The visitor center provides maps of self-guided tours to Lexington's attractions and the location where the film *Sommersby* was shot. Horse-drawn carriages clop downtown's streets, which are lined with meticulously restored Federal and Victorian buildings.

Lexington's main attractions start with the Washington and Lee University, the nation's sixth-oldest college. When the President donated stock to the college, its founders bestowed Washington's name; further adding "Lee" at the end of the Civil War. Setting up home on campus, General Lee became the college's president from 1865 until his death in 1870. Lee is buried in Lee Chapel,

Luray Caverns in the Shenandoah Valley not far from Harrisonburg are impressive caves featuring white calcite columns.

Along with meticulously restored Federal and Victorian buildings, Lexington houses the Rockbridge County Vietnam Memorial.

which now houses a museum; his horse, Traveler, is buried in the campus yard.

Nearby is the Virginia Military Institute (VMI). Stonewall Jackson taught artillery tactics and physics before he took a posting with the Confederate Army in 1861. But it is the celebrated Battle of New Market of 1864 that saw 257 cadets gain glory. Using skills learned in the classroom, the cadets won the battle with only 10 deaths, including the son of Thomas Jefferson. The VMI Museum features a host of military regalia including the coat Jackson wore when he was mortally shot at Chancellorville. Another graduate from VMI was the Nobel Peace Prize-winner General George Marshall, who was instrumental in designing the *Marshall Plan*—the post-World War II reconstruction blueprint of Europe. George C. Marshall Museum features his life's work.

Stonewall Jackson's unpretentious townhouse, built in 1801, now showcases personal mementos belonging to the general. On South Main Street is the Stonewall Jackson Memorial Cemetery. Along with Lee, Jackson was the South's most revered commander who led the Confederate Army's first victorious charge at Bull Run, in 1861. Lexington features over 35 historic B&B establishments. An airport is at Roanoke, 50 miles (80 km) south on the I-81 and there are buses to Washington DC.
Map ref: page 560 D6

MOUNT VERNON

A monument to the nation, Mount Vernon was the country estate of George and Martha Washington. Constructed in 1754, the architect of American independence lived at Mount Vernon from 1759 to the outbreak of the Revolutionary War

in 1775. In 1797, after completing two terms as the nation's first President, Washington returned to the rambling property, and died two years later. Overlooking the Potomac River, 16 miles (26 km) from downtown Washington DC, Mount Vernon showcases Washington's life, as a farmer rather than the legendary politician. Visitors can view various colonial furnishings and personal artifacts together with the estate's slave-quarters and manicured gardens.

Nearby is the Georgian estate of Woodlawn Plantation and Pope-Leighey House, a wedding gift to Martha Washington's grand-daughter by the President. Exhibits feature Nancy Custis Lewis' late eighteenth-century needlepoint and a more recent collection of furnishings designed by Frank Lloyd Wright at Pope-Leighey.

Another colonial estate in Fairfax County just shy of Mount Ver-

non is Gunston Hall, once owned by George Mason, the *Bill of Rights* architect. Built in 1755, the estate features original boxwood gardens and furnishings. Visitors should also take in the beautifully reconstructed George Washington Gristmill. Mount Vernon is an easy train ride from Washington DC By car, take the George Washington Memorial Parkway.
Map ref: page 561 J4

NEWPORT NEWS

Newport News is located in the Chesapeake Bay region of Hampton Roads in the southeastern corner of the state on the I-64/664. With a population of 171,000 people, the city's economy is based around its huge shipyards together with the building of the US Navy's nuclear submarines and aircraft carriers. The lineup of attractions in this town caters to both sea dogs and military aficionados.

The Mariners' Museum is one of the city's superior treasures, displaying everything from model period vessels to the great luxury liner era of the *QE2*, while The War Museum covers North America's major battles from the Revolutionary War to Operation Desert Storm. Children can view native animals and fish, or even take a peek at the stars, at the Virginia Living Museum. A more curious exhibit is the US Army Transportation Museum, where everything from khakis to mud flaps is on display.

Newport News has a regional airport. It is also accessible by bus and rail.
Map ref: page 561 K8

George Washington's country home at Mount Vernon was constructed in 1754. Both he and his wife Martha are buried in the estate's beautifully maintained grounds.

Fishing and crabbing are popular in the seaport of Norfolk. Fishing gear can even be rented at the local pier.

NORFOLK

The seaport of Norfolk has always been the eastern seaboard's busiest trade center because of its prime location at the mouth of the Lafayette River at Chesapeake Bay. Linked to the coast by the Hampton Roads, this city of 261,500 residents oozes energy. Most of Norfolk's historic buildings dating back to the 1680s were either torched during the Revolutionary War or destroyed by Union bombardment during the Civil War but two that survived are the 1792 Moses-Myers House and the Willoughby-Baylor House, which dates back to 1794.

Norfolk's commerce is bustling with the largest US naval base in its port. You can watch naval cruisers slicing through the waters to the base at the International Pier.

Norfolk also boasts the massive Douglas MacArthur Center Shopping Mall. Near the harbor, the Douglas MacArthur Memorial features the noted World War II general's military life in news reels and personal papers. MacArthur was instrumental in turning the tides of victory from Japan in the Pacific, along with commanding the UN forces in Japan. He fell from grace during the Korean War over his desire to bomb China. His tomb is located here under the rotunda.

Norfolk's maritime pride, Nauticus: The National Maritime Center is housed within a battleship. It has fascinating virtual reality exhibits— a sonar submarine hunt and a search for the Loch Ness monster.

Adjacent to the center is the new Tugboat Museum. Within the Nauticus complex, the Hampton Roads Naval Museum delves into both Revolutionary and Civil War history.

A casual atmosphere is enjoyed at the Waterside Festival Marketplace. Next door is Town Point Park, the center of Norfolk's year-round festivities, and the poignant Armed Forces Memorial. Also close by is the esteemed Chrysler Museum of Art, housing the titans of canvas including the eclectic work of Andy Warhol. Additionally the museum has a superb collection of Tiffany glassware.

The city is on the I-64. It has an International Airport; buses and trains are at Newport News.
Map ref: page 561 K8

PETERSBURG

Petersburg, 18 miles (29 km) south of Richmond, witnessed the Confederacy's last desperate attempt to keep the South from collapsing while trying to protect its railroad junction.

An old city of 38,500 people, Petersburg began as a trading post in the 1640s. Before it succumbed to the Union Army after a 10-month siege in April 1865, the British army overcame Petersburg during the Revolutionary War. In 1993, the city's historic Old Towne district received a direct hit from a tornado, destroying a large number of Federal and antebellum buildings.

Fortunately many Petersburg buildings have been restored to their former grandeur. These estates include the Center Hill Mansion and the historic 1735 Blandford Church, now a Confederate memorial.

South of the city is Pamplin Historical Park, the site where Union troops broke through the Confederate lines, forcing Lee to retreat from Petersburg. Along with its Interpretive Center, the park features the brilliant National Museum of the Civil War Soldier, where camp and trench life is vividly showcased.

The best place to understand the strategic moves of both opposing armies during the siege is north of the city at Petersburg National Battlefield. Its 2,650-acre (1,073-ha) park provides interpreters dressed as soldiers, reenacting the rudiments of the ongoing attack.

The Petersburg National Battlefield preserves four miles (6.4 km) of entrenchment, muzzle-loading cannons, and strategic markers, including a tunnel that was dug directly under the Confederate line by Union troops. With the aim of creating a gap in the Confederate fortification, army engineers planted explosives in the underground passage. The massive blast created a 170-foot (52-m) crater, and killed hundreds of soldiers.

Visitors can purchase a "Petersburg Campaign Pass," which covers all of the battlefield sites and some Civil War attractions in Old Towne. The city is serviced by Richmond International Airport. Bus services link the city to the state capital.
Map ref: page 561 H7

PORTSMOUTH

West of Norfolk on the Elizabeth River is Portsmouth (population 103,500), the oldest and largest shipyard in the nation, dating back to 1620. Located in the Hampton Roads, the city saw its naval yards bombarded and later burnt during the Civil War by Union troops.

The tranquil countryside outside towns throughout Virginia belies their history as the site of many battles.

The commanding George Washington statue in front of Richmond's State Capitol.

Visitors can cruise by the naval dockyards on the paddlewheeler, *Carrie B.* This is possibly the best tour to learn about the Battle of the Ironclads, which took place in the Chesapeake waters between the newly deployed steel battleships, USS *Virginia* and USS *Monitor.* It was this conflict that singularly ended the use of the navy's wooden fleet and moved its fleet into the era of massive steel warships. The Portsmouth Naval Shipyard Museum chronicles the navy's development of warships.

The Elizabeth River Ferry Service links Portsmouth to Norfolk, and the city is serviced by Norfolk International Airport and the I-64.
Map ref: page 561 K8

RICHMOND

Serving as the capital of both Virginia and the Confederate States from 1861 to 1865, Richmond was first settled as a trade and mill center in 1737. With the arrival of the railroad, and tobacco and wheat manufacturing, it was flourishing as a leading commercial center by the outbreak of the Civil War. Its key position along the James River also saw its exporting industry thrive.

Today, Richmond (population 203,000) has an economy centered on tobacco, papermaking, and chemical manufacturing. Its cityscape is a mixture of high-rise office blocks and drab warehouses but there are several areas within town that reflect its antebellum era.

The Church Hill Historic Area features quite a host of antebellum houses and colonial dwellings, including St Johns Episcopal Church (1794), where one-time Virginia governor, Patrick Henry, called for the independence from Britain in his famous "Give me liberty or death!" rhetoric. The oldest building in the city is The Old Stone House, featuring the Edgar Allan Poe

Museum together with a display of personal papers and artifacts.

The neoclassical Virginia State Capitol, designed in part by Thomas Jefferson, features a rotunda that frames the statue of George Washington and busts of seven Virginia presidents. It was in this building that Robert E. Lee took command of the Virginia Army upon the outbreak of war. The Museum and White House of the Confederacy has in-depth accounts of the contribution of African–Americans to the war and a brilliant exhibit of Confederate history.

The oldest mercantile district, now fully restored, is Shockoe Slip. Much of this area was destroyed by Union artillery during the army's occupation. Another interesting area to explore is The Canal Walk, tracing the James River's restored waterfront district and the 60-acre (24-ha) park at Belle Isle, which served as a Union prison camp during the war.

The elegant tree-lined boulevard of Monument Avenue features the city's well-heeled estates plus many statues of the South's revered war heroes, including Robert E. Lee on horseback. In Hollywood Cemetery are the graves of war hero J.E.B. Stuart, President Monroe, and Jefferson Davis.

Richmond's "Little Africa," a National Historic Landmark, features the African-American History Museum and Cultural Center of Virginia. The Maggie Lena Walker National Historic Site chronicles the life of the former slave and first woman to become president of the St Luke Penny Savings Bank. African-American people first began their public education at Leigh Street's Ebenezer Baptist Church.

The aim to capture and control Richmond saw several campaigns fought in and around the city in 1862 and 1864. The Richmond Battlefield Park preserves 11 sites scattered across three counties. The park's visitor center provides detailed information of the various battle sites around the city.

Richmond is served by Richmond International Airport and by rail. Buses run along the I-95.
Map ref: page 561 H6

SHENANDOAH NATIONAL PARK

The brilliant blue tinge of the Blue Ridge Mountains serves as a backdrop to Skyline Drive. Dissecting what is arguably one of the nation's most beautiful national parks, the 105-mile (169-km) byway weaves around deeply wooded forests. The Shenandoah National Park begins in the north at Front Royal off the I-66; its southern boundary lies near Rockfish Gap.

Established as a national park in 1935, the area was first settled nearly 300 years ago by pioneer homesteaders. By the 1930s the government was slowly encouraging the Shenandoah region to return to its natural state; since then wildlife has flourished in its back country.

Mile markers identify each area along Skyline Drive including the highest summit at Skyland, which sits at an elevation of 3,680 feet (1,122 m).

Visitor center at Dickey Ridge and Byrd along with ranger stations can assist travelers with maps and information on park lodging, camping, and nature trails, along with points of interest.
Map ref: page 560 G4

*White-tailed deer (*Odocoileus virginianus seminolus*) in Shenandoah National Park.*

STAUNTON

This quiet hillside college town of 25,000 residents rests in the Shenandoah Valley off the I-81, about 130 miles (209 km) northwest of Richmond. Settled in 1732, it became the seat of government for the frontier territories. During the Revolutionary War it was also used as an interim state capital. George Washington held a council of war at Hale-Brynes House before engaging in a battle with the British in Pennsylvania.

Along with the Mary Baldwin College (founded in 1842), two other attractions are worth seeking out. The best is the Museum of American Frontier Culture on Richmond Road, a living museum depicting early seventeenth- and eighteenth-century pioneer homesteads. The Statler Complex is a gallery dedicated to the country music singers, the Statler Brothers. The town was also the birthplace of World War I President, Woodrow Wilson. The Birthplace and Museum comprises an exhibit of his life's achievements through documents and photographs.

Staunton is serviced by the Shenandoah Valley Airport, 15 miles (24 km) to the north, and is not accessible by train or bus.
Map ref: page 560 E5

VIRGINIA BEACH

A fast-growing coastal metropolis of 431,000 people, Virginia Beach runs along 6 miles (9.7 km) of sandy beaches. The Virginia Marine Science Museum has hands-on exhibits and the 300,000-gallon (11,355 hl) Norfork Canyon Aquarium. The museum also has dolphin-watching tours aboard *Miss Virginia Sea*. The Old Coast Guard Station Museum recounts tales of Virginia Beach's shipwrecks, and displays a collection of model ships. The 1680 brick dwelling Adam Thoroughgood House was named for a Virginia plantation owner who came to the colonies as an indentured servant. North of the beach at Cape Henry Memorial, a cross marks the first landing of the Jamestown settlers in 1607.

Virginia Beach is ideal for fishing, boating, scuba diving, and surfing.

Along the Boardwalk in June, the Contemporary Art Center of Virginia hosts the annual art show. That same month sees the Viva! Elvis Festival followed by the Blues at the Beach and Neptune Festivals.

This city is served by Norfolk International Airport, and by bus and rail through Newport News.
Map ref: page 561 L8

Burnishing a spoon in historic Williamsburg.

WILLIAMSBURG

Williamsburg lies on the fork of the James and York Rivers, 51 miles (82 km) southeast of Richmond. Settled in 1632 as Middle Plantation, it became the state capital in 1699. Renamed Williamsburg, it flourished. In 1780 Thomas Jefferson designated Richmond as the new capital so Williamsburg reverted to a quiet town, later surrendering to the Union army after a minor battle in 1862. It remained a bygone place until the 1920s, when John D. Rockerfeller funded a $70 million restoration project which turned part of the town into a living theme park known as Colonial Williamsburg.

The College of William and Mary, (circa 1693), where Jefferson was an alumnus, is the second oldest university in the nation, and the Sir Christopher Wren Building, (circa 1695) is the nation's oldest continuously used academic building.

The town is serviced by the Williamsburg-Jamestown Airport, 45 miles (72 km) west, and a railway, with bus services on the I-64.
Map ref: page 561 J7

WINCHESTER

Winchester (population 24,000) is the "apple center of the world;" it hosts Shenandoah's Apple Blossom Festival in May and the Apple Harvest Festival in September. It was the birthplace of novelist Willa Cather and the childhood home of country music's Patsy Cline.

Nestled in the hills of the Shenandoah Valley, Winchester was settled in 1732 on Shawnee land by Quakers and German farmers. The town was ravaged by the Civil War, with many battles and 72 changes of military occupation.

Winchester was headquarters to Confederate General Stonewall Jackson and Union General Philip Sheridan's Northern Virginia campaigns of 1862, 1863, and 1864. There are many Civil War sites here and The Olde Town Welcome Center guides visitors to the locations, including Sheridan's headquarters, now a private home. The Stonewall Jackson Headquarters Museum was used by the General during his 1862 campaign. A Quaker's home built in 1754 is now the Abram's Delight Museum, and Glen Burnie was at one time the splendid abode of the town's founder, Colonel James Wood.

Revolutionary War heroes are buried near the Old Lutheran Church ruins in the Mt Hebron Cemetery. Both Stonewall and National cemeteries have the graves of nearly 7,000 soldiers.

Winchester is served by buses. The nearest international airport is 66 miles (106 km) east at Washington-Dulles International Airport.
Map ref: page 560 G2

The six miles of Virginia Beach are often crowded, especially during the long summer vacation from June to September.

WEST VIRGINIA

A vast ribbon of blue highways winds through a landscape of former coal-mining communities and perpetual rolling highlands, dense with forests and glorious mountain streams. This is West Virginia, a rugged region with four distinct seasons, a patchwork of farmlands, and mist-shrouded hills and valleys with countless back-country trails. West Virginia is largely dominated by the Allegheny Mountains, one of the most isolated wilderness areas within Appalachia. Westward the Alleghenys' foliage rivals New England in its spring and fall glory, yet it remains one of North America's best-kept secrets.

A topography of ancient landforms provides an unspoiled backdrop for recreational sports from whitewater rafting and hiking to skiing. But it is the classic John Denver song, "Country Road," that takes the visitor on a journey into a provincial region inhabited by mountain people, with their penchant for folk crafts, haunting bluegrass music, and a little moonshine on the sly.

In the heart of whitewater country, Hawks Nest State Park is home to the New River, leading to Hawks Nest Lake. The narrow canyon above the lake has the most challenging waters.

West Virginia is steeped in frontier and Civil War history. The Civil War began at Harpers Ferry, and the state was the scene of many other battles. A constituent of the Virginia colonies when it was settled in the late seventeenth century, West Virginia was once the home of the Seneca, Shawnee, and Delaware Native Americans, and birthplace of Confederate general Thomas "Stonewall" Jackson. Sectionalism divided Virginia in 1860; the region was not admitted into the Union until 1863.

One of America's poorest states, its economy is based around coal mining, glass-making, and lumber industries. Tourism has gained momentum, with an array of outdoor attractions, but the brilliant scenery is the main appeal.

State motto *Montani Semper Liberi* (Mountaineers are always free)
State flag Adopted 1929
Capital Charleston
Population 1,808,344
Total area (land and water) 24,231 square miles (62,758 sq km)
Land area 24,087 square miles (62,385 sq km)
West Virginia is the 41st-largest state in size
Origin of name Named for Elizabeth I, Virgin Queen of England
Nickname The Mountain State
Abbreviations WV (postal), W. Va.
State bird Cardinal
State flower Big laurel
State tree Sugar maple
Entered the Union June 20, 1863 as the 35th state.

Places in
WEST VIRGINIA

BABCOCK STATE PARK

The swift-flowing trout streams and natural beauty of Babcock State Park stretch to the boundary of the New River Gorge National River. The park is located in the heart of the New River/Greenbrier Valley. Aside from recreational pursuits, its main attraction is the recently reconstructed Glade Creek Gristmill, assembled from old gristmill parts from the neighboring counties. Currently providing cornmeal, as well as whole-wheat and buckwheat flour, the gristmill is now a working museum and a testament to a bygone time when grinding grain by a stream was a common practice in West Virginia.

The park also provides boating and fishing excursions at Boley Lake, and numerous horseback riding and hiking trails that zigzag across 4,127 acres (1,671 ha) of rugged mountain back country.

Several lookouts capture a picturesque panorama of boulder-strewn canyons and the region's highlands. In the winter, Babcock State Park offers the perfect terrain for cross-country skiers. Quite unique to the area is the rustic Camp Washington Carver—a family-style compound that offers weekend dinner theater productions and dances. The park also offers several cabin-style lodgings and a campground.

Just a short drive east of the park, heading along Hwy 60, is the former headquarters of Confederate General Robert E. Lee, at Big Sewell Mountain.

CHARLESTON

The capital of West Virginia is among the state's most progressive cities and is located at the crossroads of three major Interstates (64, 77, and 79). Additionally, the city's close proximity to the Appalachian Mountains at the confluence of the Kanawha and Elk Rivers perhaps makes Charleston the perfect introduction to the wonders of West Virginia.

More of a leading manufacturing city than a mainstream tourism town, Charleston does offer a modest selection of attractions and cultural events. Moreover, the city has the Kanawha Forest at its back door and is within a reasonable driving distance to the state's domestic ski village of Snowshoe Mountain Resort.

Decidedly, Charleston's initial attraction is its historic district, which dates back to the 1790s. Built as a fort along the Kanawha River, which flows through the downtown district, Charleston became a central trading post for the pioneers who had begun to migrate into the Ohio Valley and neighboring Kentucky. One of the earliest settlers to Charleston was frontiersman Daniel Boone.

Though the area remained largely untouched by the Civil War, Charleston fought another battle—that of recognition as the state's capital—with Wheeling in 1863, upon West Virginia's admittance into the Union.

The debate raged on for 14 years with each city highlighting its own agenda until a referendum finally settled the issue. Charleston became the official capital in 1885.

Cass Gilbert, the architect of Washington's US Supreme Court and Lincoln Memorial, designed West Virginia's State Capitol—the second to be constructed after the original building was destroyed by fire. Completed in 1932, the marble and limestone building features a massive 293-foot (89-m) gold dome and a 10,000-piece, hand-cut Czechoslovakian chandelier weighing 2 tons (1.8 tonnes). Also honoring the city's allegiance to the Union, and on the Capitol's grounds, is a commemorative bust of Booker T. Washington and a statue of Abraham Lincoln. Adjacent is the West Virginia Capitol Center, a complex that houses the region's history along with pioneer artifacts and an ever-changing art exhibit. The center's theater is undoubtedly the main highlight with its weekly broadcast of the Mountain Stage Show, a composite of bluegrass, jazz, and classical music. The center likewise hosts the folksy Vandalia Festival every Memorial Day. A statewide event, the Festival showcases an array of bluegrass melodies from around the region.

On the banks of the Kanawha River is the Haddad Riverfront Park, featuring a 2,000-seat amphitheater and the *P.A. Denny Sternwheeler*.

Around Charleston's Historic East End District is a selection of interesting Victorian buildings and a gentle mix of cafés and galleries including the Sunrise Museum, which features a planetarium, children's museum, and 16 acres (6 ha) of lush garden trails.

Within a short driving distance from Charleston on Hwy 119 is a small selection of provincial mining towns. A detour onto Route 44 will take you into the Hatfield and McCoy territory and the rustic community of Sarah Ann, where the Hatfield Family Cemetery is located.

Charleston is serviced by Yeager Airport, with daily flights to the major eastern US cities, and by bus and train.

Map ref: page 559 P3

Made from parts of old mills, the Glade Creek Gristmill in Babcock State Park produces freshly ground cornmeal and buckwheat.

Charleston is on the Kanawha River; the city holds a festival in August with contests, dancing, parades, and paddlewheeler races.

CLARKSBURG

Located in West Virginia's mountaineer country, Clarksburg is a small city with folksy attractions and a splendid background landscape. First settled in 1774, the city grew around the surrounding coal and oil industries, along with the Baltimore and Ohio Railway. Now with a population of 18,059 people, the city has taken on a new line of economic growth with its burgeoning, 800-acre (324-ha) business and technology center as well as several state and federal agencies including the FBI Fingerprint Identification Center. Headquarters to all of the nation's digital fingerprints, the FBI agency houses the latest technology on criminal investigation processing. Disappointingly, the complex is not open to the public.

Visitors should leave the car in favor of a walk through Clarksburg's downtown historic district, largely built by West Virginia's immigrant laborers. Now on the National Register of Historic Places, the area features a good selection of Italianate- and Renaissance-style buildings from the late Victorian era, along with the site of Thomas "Stonewall" Jackson's birthplace on W. Main Street. The Confederate general, who later mastered the South's first victory at Bull Run in Virginia, went to live with relatives at Jackson's Mill near Weston, upon the death of his parents.

The city is never short of active pioneer museums. The Watters Smith State Park is a good example of nineteenth-century farm life in rural West Virginia, featuring its own blacksmith shop and smokehouse. But the best exhibit is at Fort New Salem, a reconstructed eighteenth-century Appalachian pioneer settlement. Guides roam the settlement in period costume, demonstrating the daily activities that once took place at these somewhat remote homesteads.

One of several covered bridges near Clarksburg is the red-roofed Philippi Covered Bridge on Hwy 250, currently the longest sheltered bridge in use on a US highway. Pre-dating the Civil War, the Bridge was used as a temporary Union barrack in 1861.

Not everything is history-related in this town. Clarksburg is famous for its Pasta Cook-Off at the Italian Heritage Festival, which is held each year on the Labor Weekend. In contrast is the African-American Heritage Festival, which occurs each year during August.

For something more quirky, visitors should take a quick drive east of the city on US-50 to Grafton, famous for its International Mother's Day Shrine. This is where the Maytime tradition of Mother's Day started and was duly declared a national holiday in 1914 by then President Woodrow Wilson. Once an important rail center, Grafton is now featured as part of the Civil War Discovery Trail. The town's national cemetery cradles the graves of 1,251 soldiers, including the first Union recruit killed by the Confederate army.

Located at the junction of I-79 and US-50, Clarksburg is also served by Benedum Airport via commuter aircraft from Pittsburgh and Washington DC.
Map ref: page 560 C2

FAIRMONT

The college town of Fairmont lies between Clarksburg and Morgantown in the gentle rolling hills of the state's north-central region. Though Fairmont's fortunes did flounder with the surrounding coal mines, the city once prospered when the Baltimore and Ohio Railroad turned the place into a viable trade center. Now with a population of 20,600, Fairmont's economic base primarily revolves around technology in addition to its Fairmont State College, which was West Virginia's first teacher-training school.

The city's pioneer heritage is commemorated at Prickett's Fort State Park, a reconstructed trading post that showcases a medley of artifacts in an interpretive display along with 16 log cabins and a storehouse. Situated about 2 miles (3.2 km) off I-79 from Fairmont, the original fort was built in 1774 to protect the governor of Virginia's own fur trading interests.

During the Civil War, the town became a supply center for the Union army, however the city luckily largely remained free from wartime destruction. Despite being listed on the National Register of Historic Places, its downtown historic district lacks noteworthy attractions with the exception of the Marion County Courthouse and a relocated 1871 schoolhouse that now serves as a museum at Fairmont State College.

As a form of compensation to its cityscape, Fairmont boasts some great kayaking courses on three river tributaries—and all within a 10-mile (16-km) radius. At Valley Falls State Park, sightseers can get out of the car and hike then get back behind the wheel to view several of Marion County's covered bridges including the second-oldest structure at Barrackville.
Map ref: page 560 C2

The nation's largest State Capitol dome sits above the Kanawha River in Charleston.

A visitor at Harpers Ferry—a place of history, bloodshed, and natural disasters.

HARPERS FERRY NATIONAL HISTORIC PARK

At the confluence of the Potomac and Shenandoah Rivers up in the state's northeastern promontory lies the historic town of Harpers Ferry. Considered a pioneer corridor to the west from Washington DC since 1733, this town also served as a Federal armory for George Washington's administration.

In October 1859, abolitionist John Brown and 16 members of his renegade band attempted an ill-fated raid on the armory, in the hope of instigating a general slave revolt. Inevitably overpowered by armed forces under General Robert E. Lee's command, Brown was captured in the armory's engine room and sentenced to death at Charles Town, about 14 miles (23 km) west of Harpers Ferry.

By the outbreak of war, Harpers Ferry became a strategic bastion for both opposing armies and played a crucial role in the Battle of Antietam (across the border of Maryland), one of the bloodiest battles ever fought during the conflict. The armory itself was destroyed by Union troops before 12,000 of its men were captured by the Confederate army under General "Stonewall" Jackson, in 1862.

Even though Harpers Ferry was largely destroyed by war and a disastrous flood, its surviving buildings and cobblestone streets have been meticulously preserved. The town today remains one of the few living historic sites that has maintained a healthy respect for its past. Harpers Ferry is now a 2,600-acre (1,053-ha) National Historic Park that extends from the town's historic center of just 400 people, across to the pocket corners of Maryland and Virginia. Passes are required to enter any of the town's museums and are available from the visitor center on US-340.

From the visitor center you can also catch a shuttle to the town's historic district and major sites including the Stage Coach Inn (now a bookshop), the John Brown Museum, and the Master Armorer's House. The latter gives an orientation exhibit of the town's volatile history and of the events that led to the Civil War, 16 months after John Brown's hanging. Another worthwhile exhibit is at the Storer College on Filmore Street, which was once a teacher's college for liberated slaves.

In Charles Town is the Jefferson County Museum on East Washington Street, which exhibits several of Brown's personal weapons and also his wagon, which carried him to the gallows. A historic marker here identifies the actual site where the abolitionist was executed.

There are numerous hiking trails within the park that take in the panoramic scenery of the three states, along with a dozen or so B&B establishments.

Only an hour-and-a-half's drive from Washington DC, Harpers Ferry is also an easy drive from the town of Martinsburg.
Map ref: page 560 H2

LEWISBURG

The pretty town of Lewisburg is primarily a tourist center of 4,500 people, nestled in the Greenbrier Valley at the edge of the Monongahela National Forest and the Greenbrier River. Lewisburg also connects intrepid travelers to the southern boundary of the Greenbrier River Trail, an adventurous 75-mile (121-km) trek that takes in the tiny community of Hillsboro (birthplace of novelist Pearl S. Buck) before terminating at Pocahontas County, the home of the narrow-gauge Cass Scenic Railroad.

Now on the National Register of Historic Places, Lewisburg covers 236 acres (96 ha) of historic sites including the circa 1796 Old Stone Presbyterian Church and the log structure of The Barracks, built in 1770 and used during the British War of 1812. Though the Battle of Lewisburg was fought near the town center in 1862 under Union General George Crook's command, the town remained unscathed. In contrast, at the time of its inception in 1763, the settlement fought numerous conflicts with the Shawnee tribe, culminating in the Battle of Point Pleasant nine years later.

Located off I-64, Lewisburg is 9 miles (14 km) west of Greenbrier Resort and is serviced by its own commercial airport which has regular connections to Pittsburgh and Washington DC.
Map ref: page 560 C6

MARTINSBURG

The town of Martinsburg lies on the Cumberland Trail, which was a major thoroughfare for pioneers and fur traders in the late 1700s. Located 30 miles (48 km) west of Harpers Ferry and about a half-hour drive across the border from Antietam National Battlefield

At Harpers Ferry, ghost tours of its historic buildings are available on weekend evenings.

Park in Maryland, it is also the commercial and judicial center of West Virginia's eastern Panhandle region.

Along with a classic historic Main Street and the usual dose of other historic sites, Martinsburg showcases the progressive Boarman Art Center. Having just recently acquired the city's landmark buildings of the Old Post Office and Federal Building, the center is also expanding its art program and its range of regional exhibits.

Another attraction of interest is the General Adam Stephen House, dating back to 1774. A former Native American and Revolutionary fighter, the General was the founding town planner of Martinsburg, which developed as a result of the arrival of the Baltimore and Ohio Railroad in 1837. The town's railway was also a coveted prize to the Confederate army during the Civil War. Miles of track were destroyed and the city saw many of its buildings ruined.

Eight miles (13 km) east of Martinsburg is the picturesque community of Shepherdstown,

overlooking the Potomac River, off Hwy 45. The oldest existing town in West Virginia, Shepherdstown dates back to 1730 and was the site where the first steamboat was launched in 1787. Another attraction in town is the 1738 Shepherd Gristmill featuring the largest waterwheel in the country. One aspect to this quaint town that is undoubtedly appealing is its numerous antique shops and cafés.

West of Martinsburg, located on Hwy 9, is the spa resort of Berkeley Springs. Its natural warm springs are still in use at Berkeley Springs National Park and were once the region's most popular recreational area for the new colony's gentry. George Washington first frequented its baths in 1748, when he was working as a surveyor for the grandson of Virginia's governor.

Perched on a hill overlooking Berkeley Springs' tree-lined town square is the elaborate circa 1885 Berkeley Castle, in addition to several B&B establishments.

Located at the crossroads of two major Interstates, I-81 and I-70, Martinsburg is serviced through Eastern Regional Airport by private aircraft and commuter services.
Map ref: page 560 G2

MATEWAN

Cradled in the isolated mountain region of Tug County and sitting snug alongside the Kentucky border is the historic coal-mining community of Matewan. This town was recently designated a National Historic Landmark.

Matewan was at one time center stage to an extremely bitter struggle that occurred between West Virginia's coal-mining management and the town's fledgling union movement back in 1920.

Founded in 1895 as a coal-mining center, the poor mining town was soon represented by United Mine Workers of America in the fight to obtain better working conditions and pay.

In May 1920, as the Union began to recruit new members, detectives from the coal-mining industry's Baldwin-Felt Security Agency were sent to evict the "defectors" from their company homes. Eventually a shoot-out ensued at the Matewan Train Depot, the resulting chaos leaving nine men dead.

Fields of summer wildflowers flourish in the region around Martinsburg.

Matewan's rather calamitous events triggered a reform and ended the coal companies' taut control over mining towns right across North America.

Visitors to Matewan will get another dose of bloodstained folk history in addition to the Battle of Matewan. The town was once a backdrop to one of Appalachia's bloodiest family feuds. This dispute occurred during the 1880s between the Hatfields and McCoys. A falling-out between the two families started over an alleged theft of a hog and triggered off a 15-year feud that led to several fatalities. The Hatfield Family Cemetery is located on Hwy 44 near the village of Sarah Ann.

Visitors should stroll around Matewan's historic district to soak up a classic West Virginia mining town. The Tug River Valley also stages several events throughout the year including the Hatfield and McCoy Festival and Matewan Homecoming. Understandably, the use of firearms is not encouraged at either festival—even to shoot the occasional turkey buzzard.

Matewan is located at the junction of Hwys 65 and 49, and the town is accessible only by road.
Map ref: page 559 N5

MORGANTOWN

A city of 26,809 people, Morgantown is home to West Virginia University and a burgeoning economy centered around glass manufacturing, regional government, and health care. Located off the I-76 along the Pennsylvania border at the Monongahela River, Morgantown's seemingly prosperous infrastructure gives it a commercial edge over many other West Virginia cities.

Unfortunately, the city's attractions remain somewhat limited. Once the commercial thoroughfare upon its inception as Fort Morgan in 1772, the diversion of the Baltimore and Ohio Railroad to neighboring Fairmont saw the old town languish until the Civil War turned the community into a leading iron-manufacturing center.

Not far from Morgantown is the Henry Clay Iron Furnace, which once produced nails for the Union army.

Morgantown has a few notable historic buildings, including the Old Stone House built in 1795, and the more recent Monongahela County Courthouse, constructed a hundred years later.
Map ref: page 560 D1

The New River Gorge Bridge is the longest single-arch steel bridge in the United States

NEW RIVER GORGE NATIONAL RIVER

Covering a 52-mile (84-km) tract through West Virginia's southwestern region, the New River Gorge National River's swift waters swirl past canyon walls and deep gorges, plunging to 1,000 feet (305 m) near Hinton. There are over 20 major rapids in this 15-mile (24-km) stretch.

The Gorge remained relatively isolated until 1873, when the railroad was built parallel to the river. Communities flourished within the Gorge area when local mines had an easy way of transporting coal from the mountains. The railroad brought other economic opportunities to the area, such as farming, especially during the downturn of the coal-mining industry. Now a refuge for many species of migrating birds, the National River covers 70,000 acres (28,350 ha).

In 1977, the canyon's boundaries were linked by the New River Gorge Bridge, the country's longest steel arch span covering 1,700 feet (519 m), and the second highest, at 1,900 feet (580 m). Next to the Bridge is the Canyon Rim Visitor Center, which advises on hiking trails and equipment outfitters.

The most spectacular vistas within the New River Gorge are close to the Grandview Visitor Center and at Sandstone Falls Lookout. The park also protects 40 miles (64 km) of the New River Gorge's tributaries, Bluestone National Scenic River, and Gauley River National Recreation Area.

Map ref: page 560 B5

SPRUCE KNOB–SENECA ROCKS NATIONAL RECREATIONAL AREA

The Monongahela National Forest is a beautiful woodland dense with oak, sugar maple, and birch. Its remote trails are a mecca for hikers.

In the heart of the National Recreational Area is Spruce Knob. The state's highest peak at 4,861 feet (1,483 m), it towers over the Canaan Valley. The Shenandoah Mountain ranges and Potomac River sit directly at its eastern corridor along with numerous trails that traverse the Allegheny Mountains to Seneca Rocks. Dramatic limestone cliffs plunge 1,000 feet (305 m), and Seneca Rocks offers rock climbing along its hiking trails. There are camping and cabin facilities; details are available at the visitor center.

Map ref: page 560 D3

THURMOND

Located 7 miles (11 km) off US-25 near the New River Gorge National River, a winding road from Beckley leads to Thurmond Depot, a boom town that once made its fortune transporting coal along the Chesapeake and Ohio Railway. By the 1920s the mines had taken a nosedive, and the thriving population of this once-flourishing town trickled to a mere handful.

The revival of Thurmond's steam locomotives has rejuvenated this rustic town, with the Thurmond Depot remaining the highlight. It is open from May to September.

Map ref: page 560 B5

WHEELING

Wheeling (population 32,000) lies 68 miles (109 km) west of Pittsburgh, Pennsylvania. The Wheeling Suspension Bridge (1849) is the oldest standing cable suspension bridge in the country. The view from nearby Point Overlook Museum takes in a stunning vista of Ohio and Pennsylvania.

The town survived several Delaware Native American uprisings to become a major fort during the final years of the Revolutionary War. When West Virginia broke rank with Virginia in 1861, Wheeling harbored a desire to become the new state's capital. Dissension heightened when Charleston made a claim. A referendum was held and the issue was resolved 14 years after the state entered the Union.

Wheeling is listed under the National Register of Historic Districts, and its downtown region has Civil War-era edifices. A Victorian House walking tour takes in several period buildings including Wymer's General Store Museum and the West Virginia Independence Hall, where Wheeling denounced Virginia's secession to the Confederacy. The Challenger Learning Center highlights space technology, with a narrative of the ill-fated launch of the space shuttle *Challenger*.

Ohio County Airport offers a regional runway for chartered flights, with Pittsburgh's national airport remaining the city's main commercial airport hub.

Map ref: page 381 P5

WHITE SULPHUR SPRINGS

White Sulphur Springs (population 2,779) has always been considered a healing place by locals. During the 1830s, the resort town was the Southern domain of pampering, culminating in the construction of the White Sulphur Springs Hotel in 1858.

During the course of the Civil War, the town became headquarters to both the Confederate and Union armies, while the resort's courtly dining room was transformed into a hospice during the Battle of White Sulphur Springs in 1863. In 1910, it was renamed the Greenbrier Resort, and it is now one of the main getaway spots in the region.

The surprise of the resort is its underground bunker—a top-secret facility built during the height of the Cold War by the Eisenhower administration. The former Government Relocation Facility was to accommodate members of Congress under the code name "Greek Island." Unveiled by the *Washington Post* in 1992, the bunker was phased out three years later; its 25-ton (23-tonne) steel door a telling reminder of the fear and secrecy of the Cold War era.

White Sulphur Springs is 5 miles (8 km) from the state border on I-64. Greenbrier Community Airport has charter flights to White Sulphur Springs and Lewisburg.

Map ref: page 560 C6

Rafting is popular in the New River Gorge near Thurmond.

Southern Florida

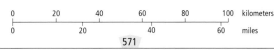

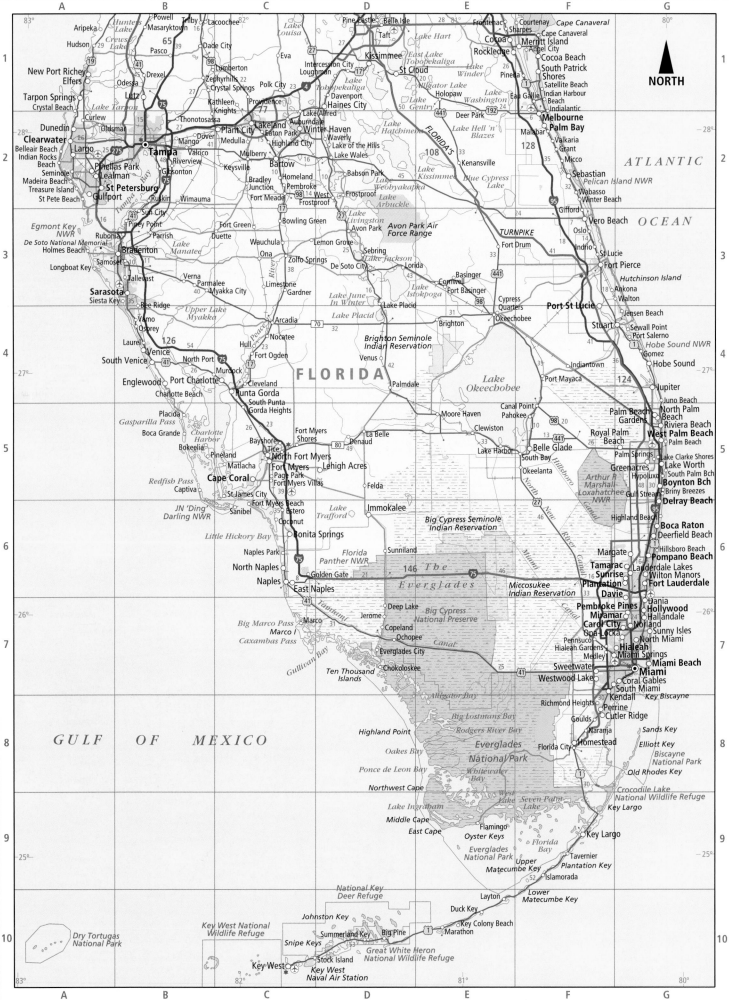

Kentucky • Northern Tennessee
Western Virginia • Western North Carolina

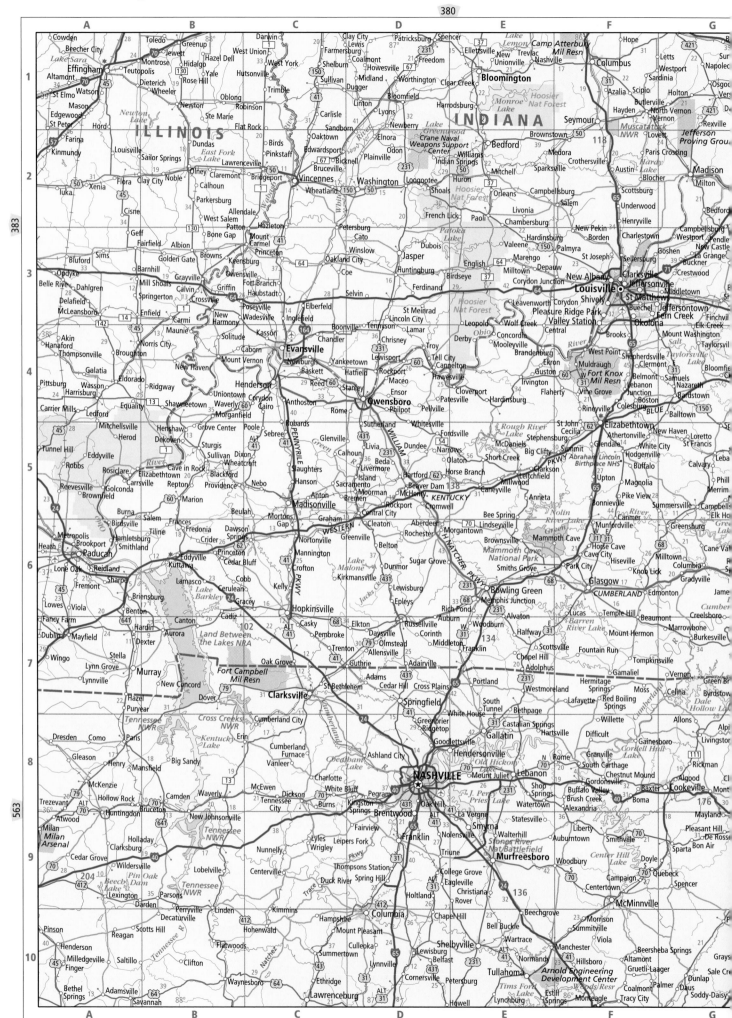

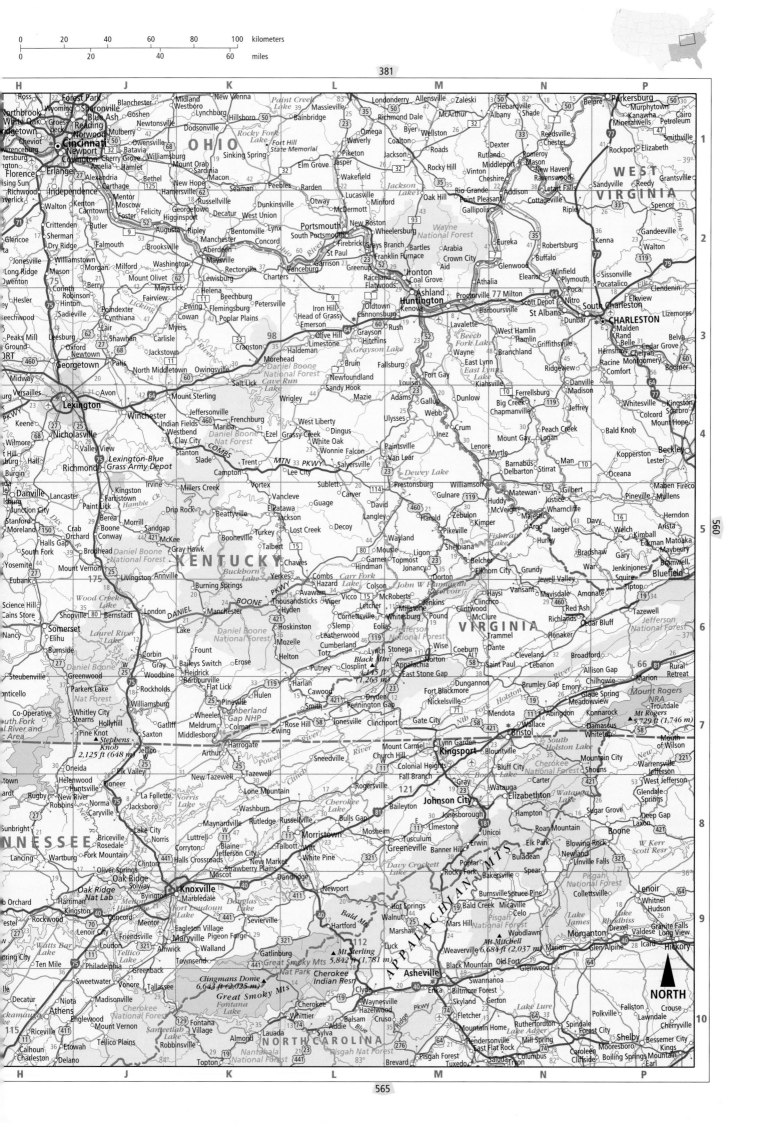

NORTH

West Virginia
Eastern and Central Virginia • Northern North Carolina

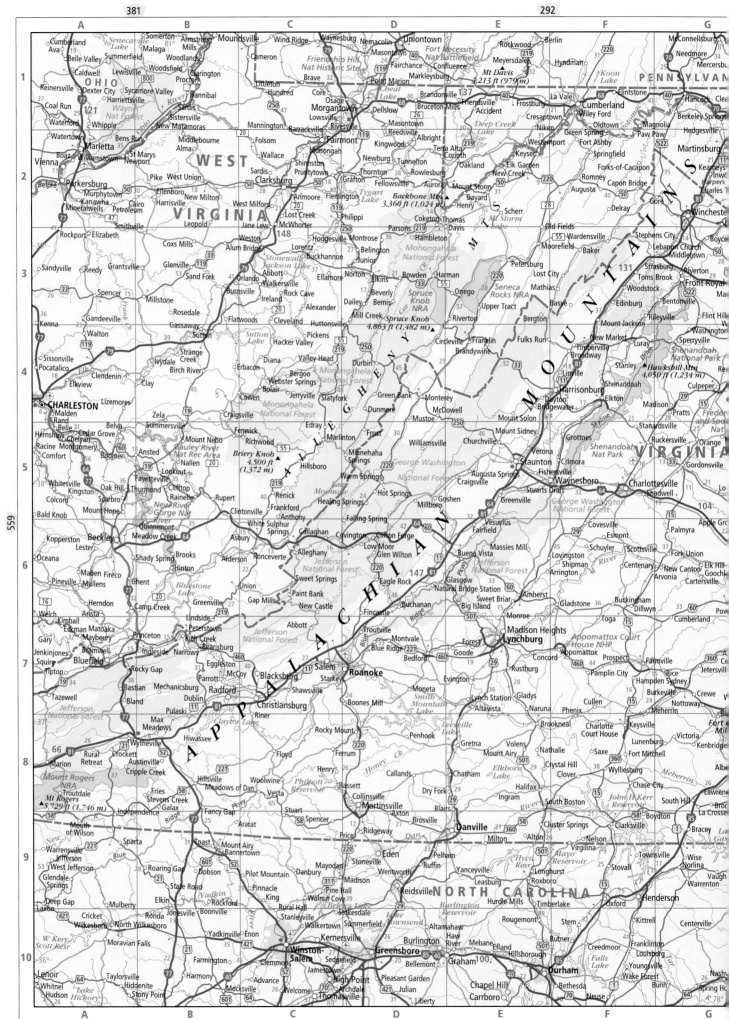

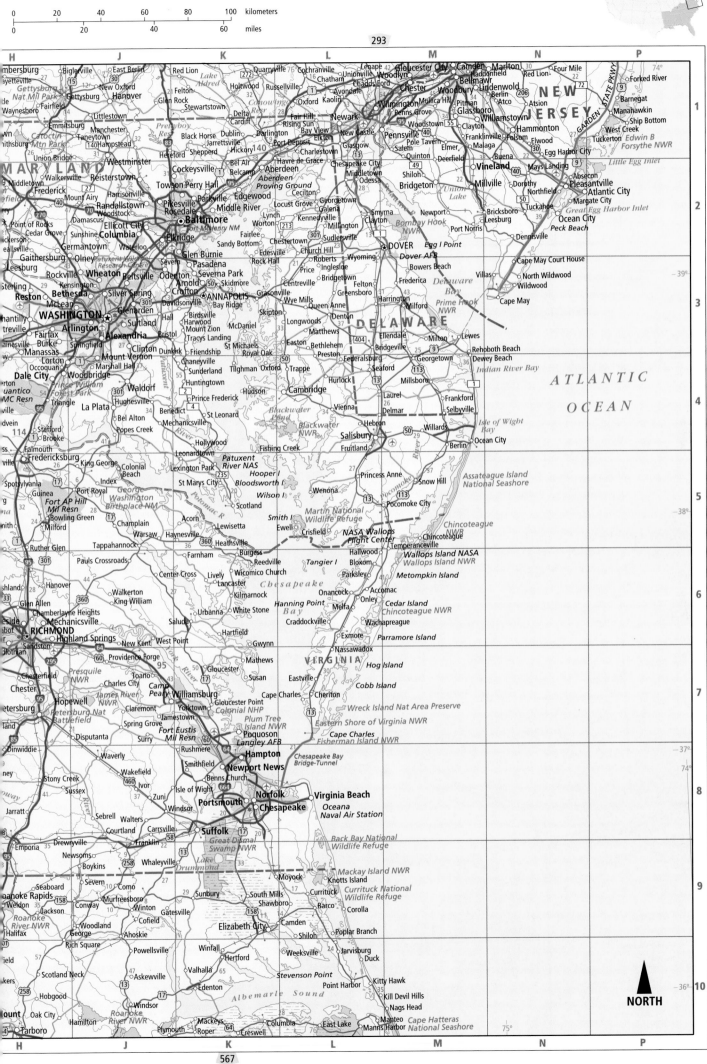

Arkansas • Northern Mississippi • Western Tennessee

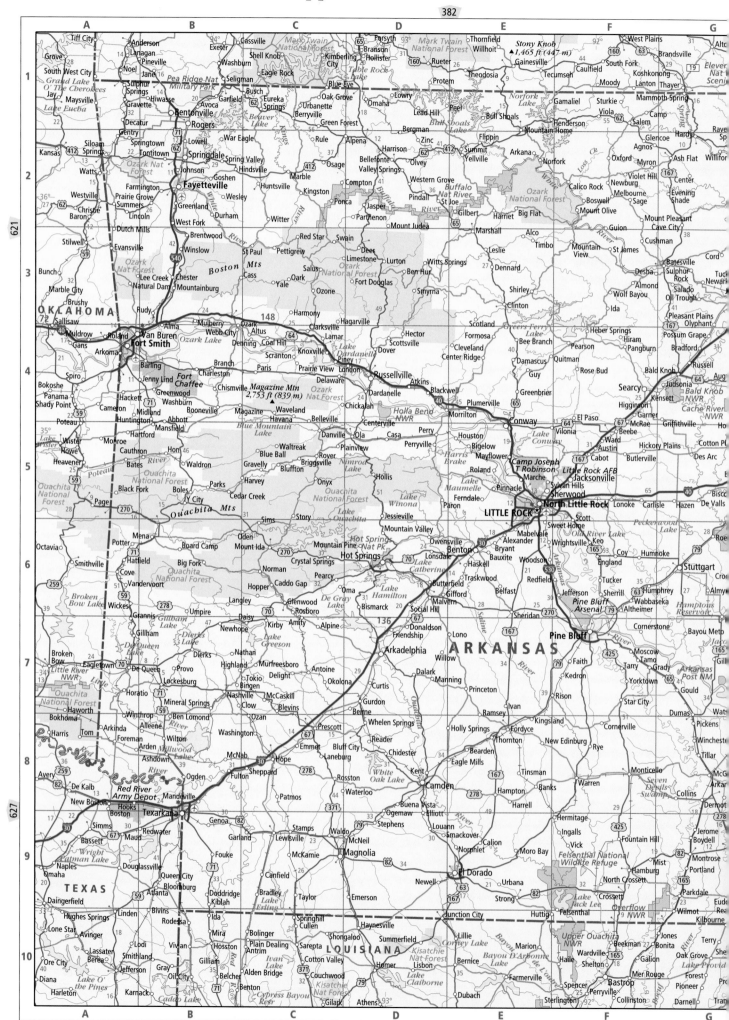

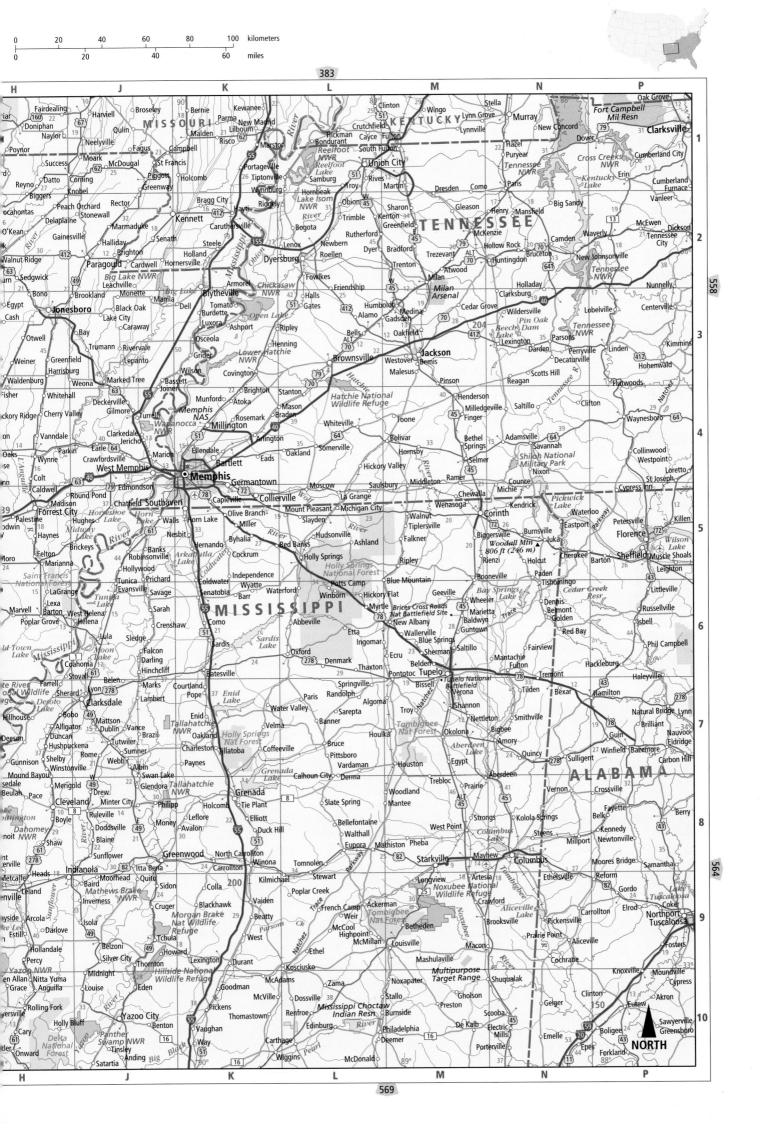

Northeastern Alabama • Northern Georgia • Western South Carolina

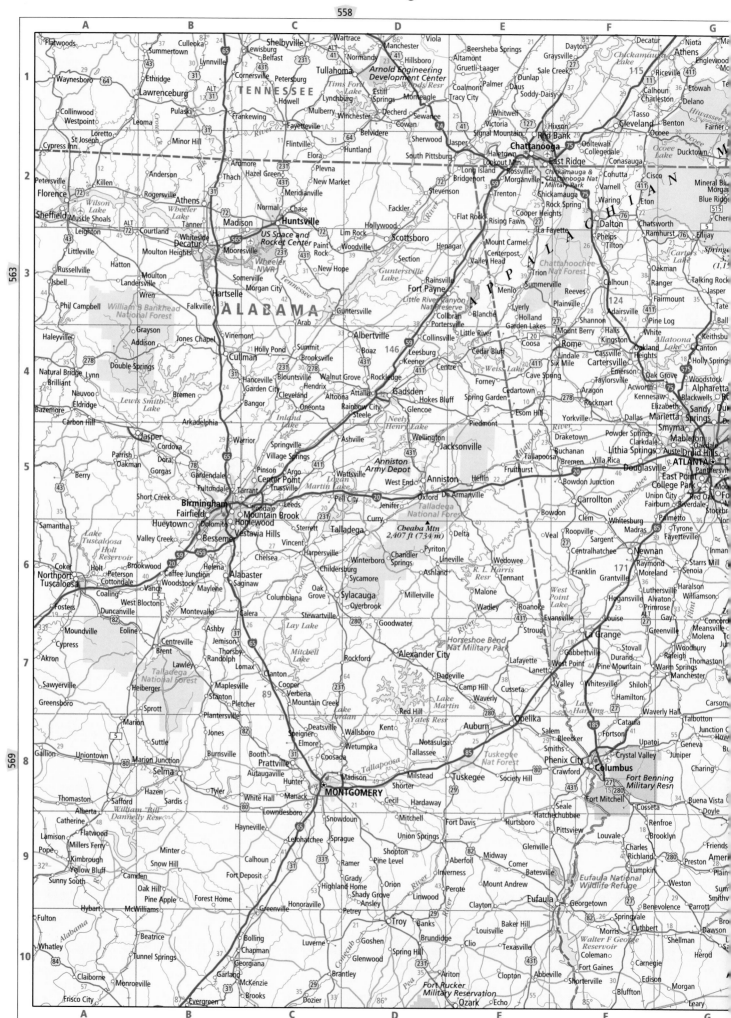

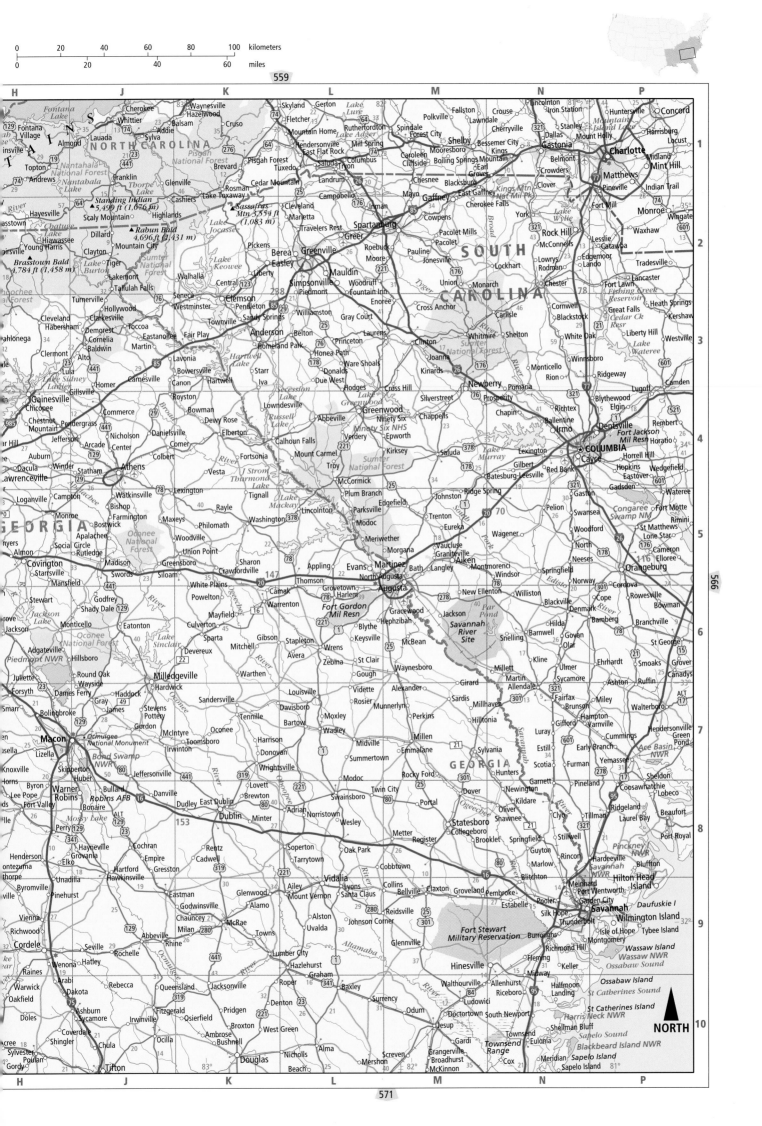

566

THE SOUTH

0   20   40   60   80   100   kilometers
0   20   40   60   miles

H   J   K   L   M   N   P

NORTH CAROLINA

SOUTH CAROLINA

GEORGIA

Fontana Lake
Cherokee
Fontana Village
Whittier
Waynesville
Hazelwood
Cruso
Skyland
Gerton
Lake Lure
Polkville
Fallston
Crouse
Lincolnton
Iron Station
Huntersville
Concord
Harrisburg
Locust

Standing Indian ▲ 5,499 ft (1,676 m)
▲ Sassafras Mtn 3,554 ft (1,083 m)
▲ Rabun Bald 4,696 ft (1,431 m)
Brasstown Bald 4,784 ft (1,458 m)

Charlotte
Gastonia
Spartanburg
Greenville
Anderson
Columbia
Augusta
Macon
Savannah
Hilton Head Island
Wilmington Island

Gainesville
Athens
Warner Robins
Robins AFB
Dublin
Statesboro
Vidalia

Cordele
Tifton
Douglas
Hinesville

NORTH

Sapelo Island
Blackbeard Island NWR
Ossabaw Island
St Catherines Island
Wassaw Island

10

Southeastern North Carolina • Central and Eastern South Carolina

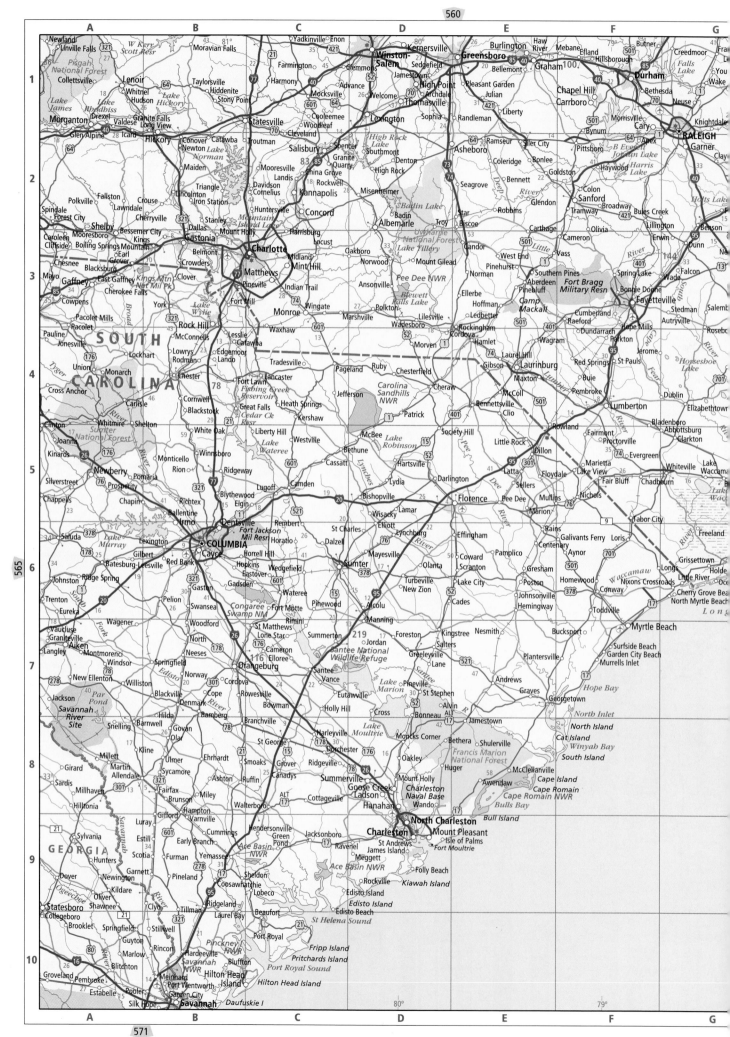

0   20   40   60   80   100   kilometers

0   20   40   60   miles

NORTH

561

NORTH CAROLINA

Whitakers, Scotland Neck, Askewville, Valhalla, Stevenson Point, Point Harbor, Kitty Hawk, Kill Devil Hills, Nags Head, Rocky Mount, Hamilton, Windsor, Edenton, Albemarle Sound, Columbia, East Lake, Manteo, Manns Harbor, Cape Hatteras National Seashore, Sharpsburg, Tarboro, Parmele, Robersonville, Williamston, Plymouth, Roper, Mackeys, Creswell, Wanchese, Oregon Inlet, Elm City, Pinetops, Bethel, Jamesville, Roanoke River NWR, Alligator River NWR, Wilson, Saratoga, Greenville, Pocosin Lakes NWR, Phelps Lake, Pungo Lake, Pocosin Lakes NWR, Stumpy Point, Pea Island National Wildlife Refuge, Ludama, Stantonsburg, Farmville, Grimesland, Pinetown, Pike Road, Alligator Lake, Kilkenny, Sandy Point, Rodanthe, Fremont, Winterville, Chocowinity, Washington, Pantego, Mattamuskeet NWR, Long Shoal Point, Salvo, Pikeville, Ayden, Washington Park, Belhaven, Fairfield, Lyn Point, Cape Hatteras National Seashore, Snow Hill, Bath, Pamlico Beach, Swan Quarter, Lake Mattamuskeet, Long Point, Belfast, Hookerton, Grifton, Pamlico River, Bluff Point, Avon, La Grange, Vanceboro, Aurora, Lowland, Swanquarter National Wildlife Refuge, Pamlico Sound, Kinston, Fort Barnwell, Ernul, Hobucken, Hatteras, Buxton, Cape Hatteras, Seven Springs, Dover, Cove City, Vandemere, Bayboro, Bay Point, Cape Hatteras National Seashore, New Bern, Bridgeton, Florence, Cherry Point US Military Range, Ocracoke, Pink Hill, Trenton, James City, Arapahoe, Oriental, Ocracoke Inlet, Portsmouth Island, Kenansville, Pollocksville, Cedar Island, Cedar Island NWR, Outer Banks, Beulaville, Maysville, Cherry Point Marine Corps Air Station, Atlantic, Richlands, Great Lake, Havelock, Sealevel, Chinquapin, Jacksonville, Newport, Otway, Davis, Core Banks, Bogue, Salter Path, Beaufort, Marshallberg, Rose Hill, Midway Park, Morehead City, Cape Lookout National Seashore, Wallace, Swansboro, Emerald Isle, Atlantic Beach, Maple Hill, Bogue Inlet, Cape Lookout, Camp LeJeune Marine Corps Base, Dixon, Sneads Ferry, New River Inlet, Holly Ridge, Surf City, Topsail Beach, Hampstead, ONSLOW BAY, Hayne, Rich Inlet, Wilmington, Wrightsville Beach, Carolina Beach, Kure Beach, Sunny Point Army Terminal, Bald Head Island, Cape Fear

ATLANTIC OCEAN

Louisiana • Southern Mississippi • Southwestern Alabama

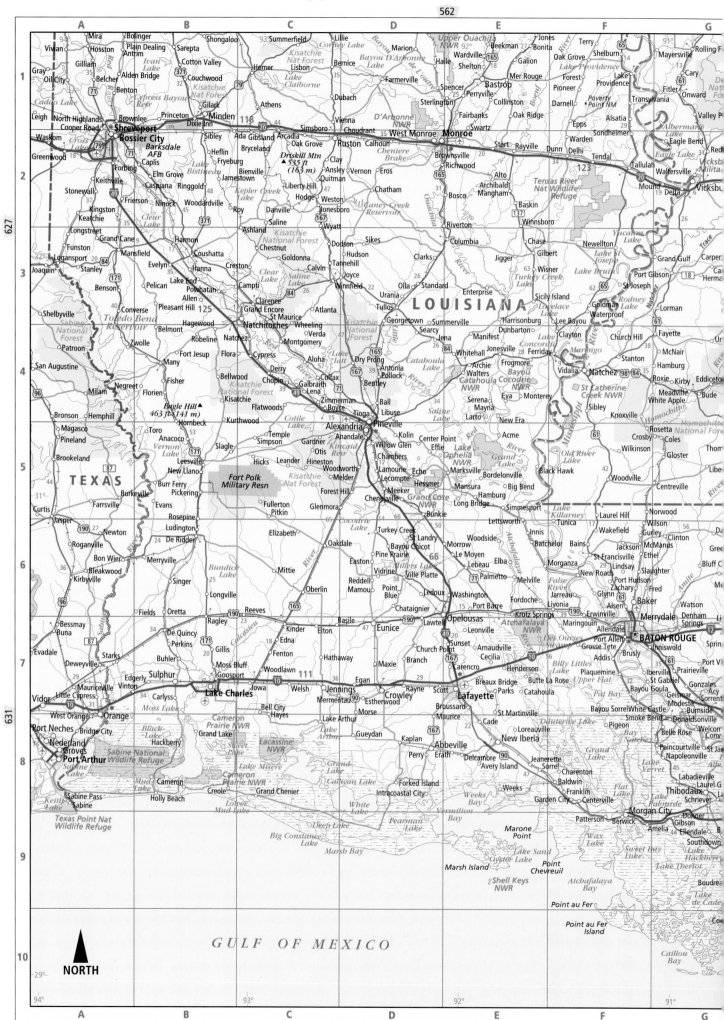

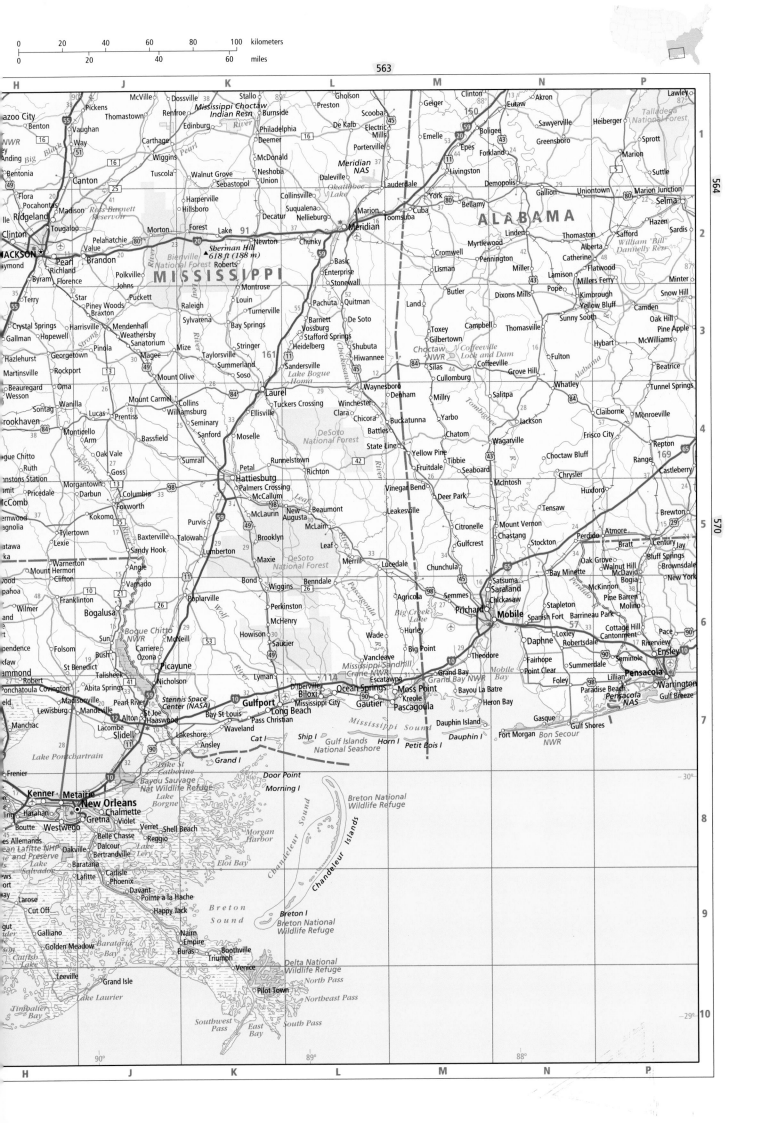

Northern Florida • Southeastern Alabama • Southern Georgia

THE SOUTH

GULF OF MEXICO

NORTH

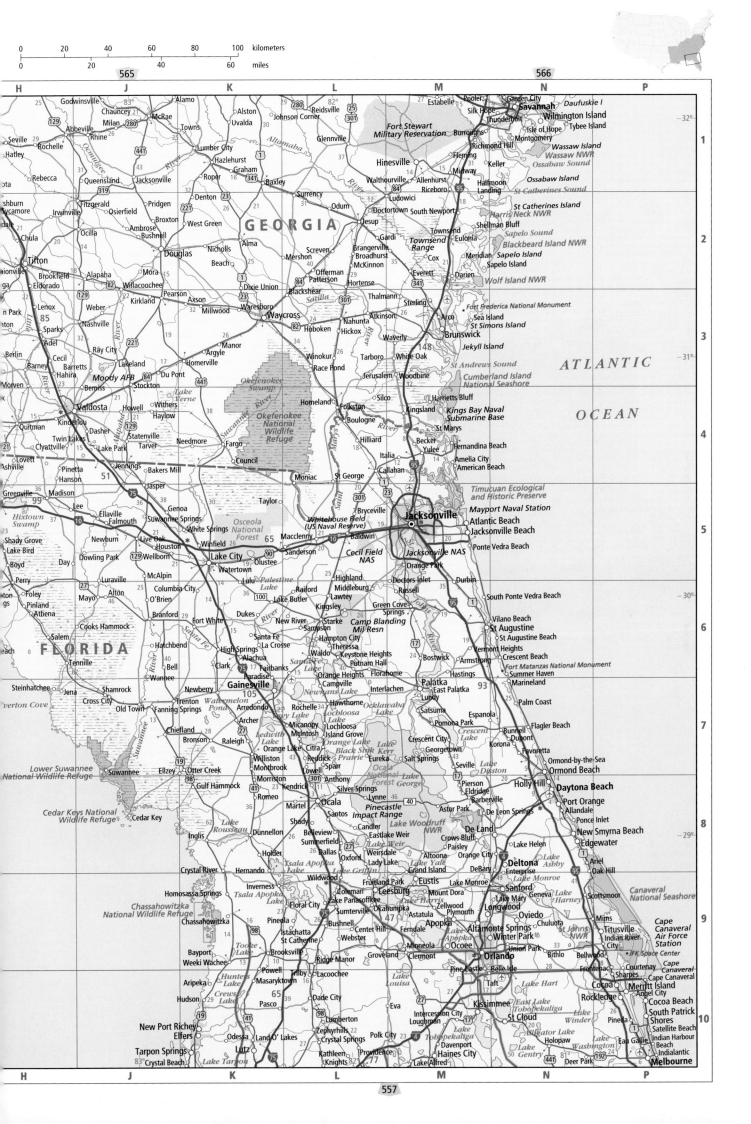

THE SOUTHWEST

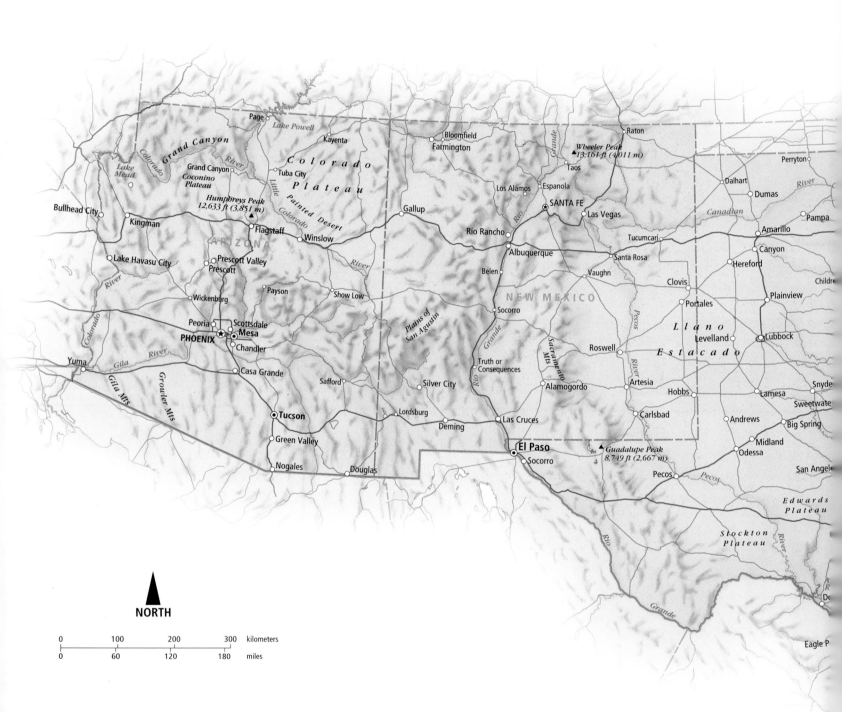

NORTH

| 0 | 100 | 200 | 300 | kilometers |
| 0 | 60 | 120 | 180 | miles |

THE SOUTHWEST

Texas, New Mexico, and Arizona cut a broad, vast, mostly dry and dusty swath across the top of Mexico, running from Louisiana and the Gulf of Mexico to temperate southern California. Although this is largely lowland territory, it has plenty of high mountains, too. Part of the Grand Canyon falls within its treasure trove of earth and rock configurations, hilly and forested retreats, and two big rivers (the Rio Grande and Colorado) that have been imperative to civilization.

The natural wonder of the Southwest, as magnificent as it is, is only a small part of what makes this area so magnetic to visitors from around the world. There is a cultural diversity and energy here that is quite unlike anywhere else in the country.

The Spanish came in the sixteenth century, building missions that still dot the landscape, and christening places with such musical-sounding names as Guadalupe, San Antonio, and Casa Grande.

All three states share Mexico as a southern neighbor. The adobe architecture emulates Mexico's style. Southwestern cuisine has its own Mexican tang, as tasted in the delicious flavors of Tex-Mex. New Mexican food, the basis of all Southwestern cuisine, originated with the Pueblo Indians and their harvests of blue corn, beans, pinon nuts, and green chili.

Before the Spaniards and Mexicans, the Native Americans lived in Arizona and New Mexico, and they continue to have a strong presence. The Pueblo, Apache, Navajo, Paiute, Hopi, Mohave, and many other peoples are keeping alive the traditions, which were very nearly destroyed by the new settlers.

Artists, writers, and spiritual seekers are drawn to such places of special beauty as Taos and Santa Fe in New Mexico, and Sedona in Arizona.

Texas conjures up images of size, wealth, and, of course, cowboys. Oil and cattle were once the basis of the state's economy—today it is manufacturing, research, the space program, and high-tech industries.

In the glorious Southwestern outdoors, snow skiing, river rafting, horseback riding, golf, and hiking are all popular pursuits.

Understandably, Arizona, Texas, and New Mexico attract people from all over the world who come to enjoy the delights that the Southwest has to offer.

The Conoco truck stop on the I-40 in New Mexico. Long-distance truckers transport agricultural products, oil, and manufactured goods across the resource-rich Southwest.

The completion of the transcontinental railway in 1881 linked the Southwest to the rest of the country. Restored steam trains still run today.

ARIZONA

Arizona is renowned for its spectacular scenery, which encompasses deserts, mountains, valleys, plateaus, and canyons, including the Grand Canyon. Here in the Southwest, Native Americans, Spanish explorers, settlers, outlaws, and twentieth-century dam-builders have written some of the American West's most memorable history.

Archeological evidence dates human occupation of what is now Arizona back 20,000 years. Spanish explorers were the first non-indigenous people to see Arizona, whose name is thought to derive from a Pima Native American word, *ari-son*, meaning "little spring." The expedition led in 1540–42 by Francisco Vasquez de Coronado in the vain search for the fabled Seven Golden Cities of Cibola was the first major exploration of Arizona and the Southwest. Spain ruled the vast New Mexico region until 1821, when Mexico took control after winning independence. The war with Mexico in 1846 resulted in the American annexation of the area in 1848 under the Treaty of Guadalupe Hidalgo.

In 1863 President Abraham Lincoln approved the establishment of the Arizona Territory, hoping its gold mines would bolster the war-depleted Federal treasury. After years of sometimes violent frontier conflict that included the shootout at the O.K. Corral and the war against the Chiricahua Apache tribe, Arizona was granted statehood on February 14, 1912.

Mission San Xavier del Bac was built by Spanish missionaries in 1700 near present-day downtown Tucson.

For much of the twentieth century, Arizona's economy was dominated by its "five Cs:" cattle, copper, cotton, citrus, and climate. In the northwest is Hoover Dam, one of the nation's greatest concrete works, and in the northeast is the Navajo Indian Reservation. The warm, dry climate that the state enjoys almost year-round has helped make it the wintertime home of large numbers of retirees from colder areas.

Visitors should note that Arizona is in the Mountain Time Zone, but (with the exception of the Navajo Reservation) the state does not observe daylight saving time.

State motto *Ditat Deus* (God enriches)
State flag Adopted 1917
Capital Phoenix
Population 5,130,632
Total area (land and water) 114,006 square miles (295,276 sq km)
Land area 113,642 square miles (294,333 sq km)
Arizona is the sixth-largest state in size
Origin of name From the Pima Native American word *ari-son* meaning "little spring" or "young spring"
Nickname The Grand Canyon State
Abbreviations AZ (postal), Ariz.
State bird Cactus wren
State flower Flower of the saguaro cactus
State tree Palo verde
Entered the Union February 14, 1912 as the 48th state

Places in ARIZONA

AGUA FRIA NATIONAL MONUMENT

Just 40 miles (64 km) north of central Phoenix, amid a mosaic of semi-desert wildland and pristine streamside forests, are some of the most significant late-prehistoric Native American sites in the Southwest. At least 450 sites are protected within the boundaries of 71,000-acre (28,755-ha) Agua Fria National Monument, proclaimed by President Bill Clinton in January 2001.

Between AD 1250 and 1450, many Pueblo dwellings throughout the Southwest were abandoned by their occupants, who then congregated in a relatively small number of densely populated areas. Agua Fria has four such settlements consisting of stone pueblos, or villages, some with at least 100 rooms. The monument also protects an extraordinary record of the vanished culture's agricultural practices, including extensive terraces bounded by rocks, and numerous rock art sites.

The rugged, undeveloped monument encompasses two mesas—Perry Mesa and the adjacent, smaller Black Mesa—and the canyon of the Agua Fria River. For visitors seeking a backcountry experience not far from the heavily urbanized Phoenix area, Agua Fria provides opportunities for hiking, mountain biking, camping, and fishing as well as viewing cultural and historic sites.

It can be reached by taking I-70 north to exit 244 at Black Canyon City, or exit 256 to Badger Springs. Map ref: page 622 F3

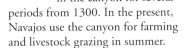

Road sign for the I-10, near Chiricahua.

CANYON DE CHELLY NATIONAL MONUMENT

Set amid the Navajo Indian Reservation in northeastern Arizona is 83,840-acre (33,955-ha) Canyon de Chelly (pronounced "d' Shay") National Monument. The 26-mile-long (42-km) canyon is famous for its magnificent red-hued sandstone cliffs, which rise up to 1,000 feet (305 m) above the canyon floor. The monument's namesake canyon is joined by 25-mile-long (40-km) Canyon del Muerto. In both are found pictographs—ancient figures painted on rock surfaces—dating from the canyons' earliest inhabitants to the current Navajo culture. Prominent among the centuries-old structures and dwellings remaining in the canyon are White House, occupied from 1060 to 1275, and Mummy Cave, in which well-preserved human remains have been found.

Indian occupation of the canyon dates back to AD 348. Ancestral Pueblo peoples, commonly called Anasazi, built multi-room homes and shelters in caves and alcoves above the canyon floor. Hopi Indians lived in the canyon for several periods from 1300. In the present, Navajos use the canyon for farming and livestock grazing in summer.

Activities include scenic drives with views of most major ruins, hiking, pictograph viewing, interpretive talks, horseback riding (by prior arrangement), picnicking, and photography. Lodging is available, and camping is free. Guided trips in off-road vehicles are available from the visitor center.

Visitors who wish to drive through the canyon in their own 4WD vehicles must have a Park Service permit and an authorized Navajo guide. Hiking in the canyon also requires a permit and authorized Navajo guide, except along the 2.5-mile (4-km) White House Ruins Trail. There is no entrance fee.

The visitor center is located 3 miles (4.8 km) from US-191 in Chinle. There is no public transportation available. Map ref: page 617 N7

CASA GRANDE RUINS NATIONAL MONUMENT

When the first Europeans arrived in south-central Arizona, they found the remains of an ancient culture whose people had farmed much of the region for more than 1,000 years. The local Pima Indians called them the Hohokam, meaning "those who are gone." What is left of their civilization includes villages, irrigation canals, and artifacts. Most impressive are the ruins of Casa Grande (Big House). The four-story structure, built in the mid-1300s, is one of the largest prehistoric structures ever built in North America. It was named in 1694 by a missionary, Father Eusebio Francisco Kino. The 472-acre (191-ha) park is the nation's first archeological preserve.

The park is in Coolidge, off Arizona Hwy 87/287, between Phoenix and Tucson. There is no camping or lodging. Map ref: page 622 G6

CHIRICAHUA NATIONAL MONUMENT

Twenty-seven million years ago, a volcanic eruption 1,000 times more powerful than the 1980 eruption of Washington's Mt St Helens rocked the region of today's 12,000-acre (4,860-ha) monument. The eruption laid down 2,000 feet (610 m) of ash and pumice, which fused into rock. It offers interestingly eroded volcanic geology. Over time, the rocks have eroded into the spires and monoliths that visitors see today.

The monument is located in the Chiricahua Mountains south-

The Spider Rock monolith, in Canyon de Chelly, is 800 feet (244 m) tall.

east of Willcox and south of I-10, in the southeastern corner of Arizona. It occupies a region where the Chihuahuan and Sonoran deserts intersect with the Rocky Mountains and the northern Sierra Madre Mountains. An outstanding panorama of the region can be seen from 7,000-foot (2,135-m) Massai Point, 8 miles (13 km) from park headquarters via a scenic paved mountain road.

The land within the monument was once part of the region occupied by the Chiricahua Apaches. A historic attraction is the Faraway Ranch, a pioneer homestead and later a working cattle and guest ranch. The house is furnished with a range of interesting artifacts that trace the development of technology during the first half of the twentieth century.

There is a campground in Bonita Canyon, (no wilderness camping is permitted) and the park maintains 17 miles (27 km) of trails. There is a small entry fee per vehicle. The visitor center is open year-round. The park is closed on Christmas Day. Peak season is from March through May.

About 29 miles (47 km) north of the park, off Apache Pass Road, is Fort Bowie National Historic Site. For more than 30 years Fort Bowie and Apache Pass were the center of bitter fighting between the US military and the Chiricahua Apaches. These hostilities culminated in the surrender of the Apache Chief Geronimo in 1886 and the banishment of the Chiricahua Apaches to Florida and Alabama.

Map ref: page 623 L8

CORONADO NATIONAL MEMORIAL

Spanish explorer Francisco Vasquez de Coronado may never have set foot in this place during his journey through the Southwest in the sixteenth century but the park, on the international border with Mexico at the southern end of the Huachuca Mountains, does overlook the San Pedro River Valley, the route his expedition is believed to have taken. Consisting of 1,400 soldiers and Indians and 1,500 animals in search of the gold of the fabled Seven Cities of Cibola, it was the first major European expedition through the Southwest. After five months, the expedition found not cities of gold, but the stone and earth pueblos (villages) of the Zuni Indians near Zuni, New Mexico. The expedition traveled as far north as central Kansas, and a member of the expedition made the first recorded sighting of the Grand Canyon.

The memorial is dedicated to interpreting the expedition, memorializing the ties between the United States, Mexico, and Spain, strengthening international friendship and cultural understanding, and protecting the area's unique natural and cultural resources.

Visitors can take in a vista of the region from 6,575-foot (2,005-m) Montezuma Pass, about 3½ miles (5.6 km) west of the visitor center. East Montezuma Canyon Road

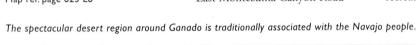

A common sight in a state renowned for its arid deserts.

is paved from Hwy 92 to 1 mile (1.6 km) west of the visitor center, where it becomes a narrow, unpaved mountain road to the scenic overlook on the pass. The dirt road continues west into Coronado National Forest.

The memorial is open for day use only all year except for Thanksgiving (fourth Thursday in November) and Christmas Day. It is located 22 miles (35 km) south of Sierra Vista and 5 miles (8 km) off state Route 92. Entrance to the memorial is free.

Map ref: page 623 K10

FLAGSTAFF

In a state known for its deserts, the town of Flagstaff sits amid pine forests and lofty mountain peaks at an elevation of 6,905 feet (2,106 m). Flagstaff was settled in 1871 and named on July 4, 1876 when a ponderosa pine from the region served as a flagstaff during the Independence Day celebration. Since then it has grown to a population of over 55,000 people. The forest is the basis of Flagstaff's wood products industry and it is the seat of Coconino County, the second-largest county in the nation. It is ideal as a base for exploring the nearby Grand Canyon National Park and several other national monuments.

In February the city hosts Winterfest, a festival that celebrates the area's abundant wintertime recreational opportunities with more than 100 events, including dog-sled races, sleigh rides, snowboard events, and Nordic and alpine ski racing. Visitors can head for the Arizona Snowbowl, a year-round resort that is one of the country's 10 oldest continuously operating ski resorts. It is located in the San Francisco Peaks about 14 miles (23 km) north of Flagstaff via US-180. The Coconino Center for the Arts and the Museum of Northern Arizona organize the Festival of Native American Arts from mid-June to early August. In July and August, Northern Arizona University is the venue for the Flagstaff Festival of the Arts.

Other places of interest include the Museum of Northern Arizona, which contains exhibits on the archeology, anthropology, geology, and art of northern Arizona, and Riordan State Historic Park, with the 40-room Riordan Mansion, built in 1904, as its centerpiece.

Flagstaff is located at the intersection of I-40 and I-70. Tour buses are available to the Grand Canyon, Sedona, Lake Powell, and other attractions. Commercial airlines fly to and from Flagstaff Pulliam Airport. A regular bus service is also available.

Map ref: page 617 J9

GANADO

Located on the Navajo Indian Reservation in northeastern Arizona, the Ganado area has been used as a Native American gathering place for many centuries, beginning with the long-vanished Anasazi and continuing with the Navajo people. It has about 1,300 residents.

One mile (1.6 km) west of Ganado, on state Route 264, is Hubbell Trading Post National Historic Site, the reservation's oldest continuously operating trading post. It was purchased by John Lorenzo Hubbell in 1878, and the Hubbell family operated it until it was sold to the National Park Service in 1967.

The still-active trading post is operated by a non-profit organization. The site consists of the original 160-acre (65-ha) homestead, the trading post, family home, and visitor center. It is open year-round except for Thanksgiving (fourth Thursday

The spectacular desert region around Ganado is traditionally associated with the Navajo people.

in November), Christmas Day, and New Year's Day. There is no entrance fee. Some travel restrictions apply to reservation visitors. There is no public transportation.
Map ref: page 617 N8

GLEN CANYON NATIONAL RECREATION AREA

The power of both nature and humans to transform a vast landscape can be seen at Glen Canyon National Recreation Area in northern Arizona and southern Utah.

Over millions of years, geologic and erosive forces have created a spectacular array of red-rock canyons, buttes, towers, cliffs, and arches along the Colorado River. Prehistoric Native Americans, from Archaic people to the Anasazi, occupied the region for thousands of years before the Spanish Dominguez-Escalante expedition of 1776 made the first written record of Glen Canyon, followed by Colorado River explorer John Wesley Powell in 1869.

In the early 1950s, the US Bureau of Reclamation proposed building a hydroelectric dam and storage reservoir on the Colorado River that would inundate Glen Canyon, most of which lies in Utah. The canyon, one of the Southwest's most beautiful, was relatively little-known and seldom visited at the time.

Environmentalists, led by the Sierra Club, which was founded in 1892 with pioneering conservationist John Muir as its first president, were more focused on blocking the construction of a dam at Echo Park, in northern Utah's Dinosaur National Monument, and Glen Canyon was sacrificed in a compromise that saved Echo Park.

The Bureau began construction of Glen Canyon Dam, on the Arizona side of the state line near Page, in 1956. It was completed in 1962, but the reservoir didn't fill until 1980. Today, the Colorado's waters are backed up for almost 200 miles (322 km), most of it in Utah, forming Lake Powell, one of the Southwest's most popular recreation destinations.

Glen Canyon Dam's crest is 1,560 feet (476 m) long, and rises 583 feet (178 m) above the original river channel. Boaters can explore 96 major canyons as well as

Grand Canyon National Park has an abundance of wildlife, including deer.

Rainbow Bridge National Monument which protects the world's largest natural bridge, a sandstone arch that is 290 feet (88 m) high and spans 275 feet (84 m) from end to end.

Glen Canyon NRA covers more than 1 million acres (405,000 ha) along the Colorado River, extending from the northern reach of Grand Canyon National Park to Utah's Canyonlands National Park. It offers a wide range of recreational opportunities, from houseboating to backroad four-wheel driving, water skiing, fishing, hiking, and camping. Visitors can also explore countless side canyons by boat.

Summers are extremely hot in the Glen Canyon National Recreation Area, with little or no shade available. Winters are moderately cold with nighttime lows often below freezing. Spring weather is variable and windy. Fall weather is usually mild.

At the NRA's southern end is the Navajo Bridge Interpretive Center. Located on Hwy 89A near Lees Ferry, it has a pedestrian walkway across the old Navajo Bridge over the Colorado River in Marble Canyon. The center shows an interactive video,

and there is a small bookstore. There is a small entrance fee per vehicle, which is good for seven days. Commercial and charter flights are available at Page. Bullfrog and Hite, in Utah, have landing strips. Cal Black Memorial Airport is located about 10 miles (16 km) from Halls Crossing, Utah.
Map ref: page 617 K5

GRAND CANYON NATIONAL PARK

Few sights in the world rival northwestern Arizona's Grand Canyon of the Colorado River which lies just south of Utah and east of Nevada. The colorful, eroded gash in the Earth's crust is 277 miles (446 km) long and an average of 10 miles (16 km) wide.

The breathtaking vista of the Grand Canyon.

At its deepest, it plunges 6,000 feet (1,830 m) from rim to river. So deep is the sheer-walled canyon, where the rock strata reveal 250 million to 2 billion years of the Earth's history, that getting to the bottom and back (on foot or by mule) takes two days. A trip through the canyon by river raft can take two weeks, and experienced backpackers can spend weeks in the more remote areas of the canyon. The park's elevation and climatic variations encompass multiple life zones, from canyon-bottom desert of cacti and creosote bush to woodlands of pinyon pines and junipers and, at the higher elevations, conifer forests.

As geologic forces lifted the Earth's crust to form the high Colorado Plateau, the Colorado River slowly eroded its way downward through thousands of feet of rock. Split-twig figurines found in caves have dated human habitation to at least 2000 BC. Havasu Canyon, a tributary of the Grand Canyon, is part of the Havasupai Indian Reservation.

The first recorded view of the canyon was by a member of the 1540–42 expedition of Spanish explorer Francisco Vasquez de Coronado. In 1869, Major John Wesley Powell's expedition down the Colorado River was the first to explore the canyon's full length.

Kayenta, in northeastern Arizona, is often called "The Gateway to Monument Valley."

Today, an average of 5 million visitors annually keep the park crowded most of the year, making advance planning and reservations for campsites, lodging, mule trips, and back-country permits essential. Visitor numbers are heaviest in spring, summer, and fall, and lowest from November through February, when winter conditions prevail. Day visitors are encouraged to arrive early due to limited parking.

The South Rim, more than 7,000 feet (2,135 m) above sea level, is open year-round, 24 hours a day. Winter can bring snow, and even summer nights are cool. In the canyon, however, summertime temperatures can reach 120°F (49°C). The North Rim, at 8,000 feet (2,440 m), can receive snow almost any time of year, and heavy snow closes roads in winter; the weather is changeable in spring and fall. The North Rim is open from mid-May to mid-October.

There is a park entrance permit per vehicle, good for seven days. There are information centers at South Rim and North Rim.

Commercial flights are available at Las Vegas in Nevada, as well as at Phoenix, Flagstaff, and Grand Canyon Airport in Tusayan, south of the park. South Rim's Grand Canyon Village is 60 miles (97 km) north of I-40 via state Route 64/US-180, and 80 miles (129 km) northwest of Flagstaff via US-180.

A variety of lodging choices and campground facilities are available for overnight stays.
Map ref: page 616 F7

GRAND CANYON–PARASHANT NATIONAL MONUMENT

In contrast to adjacent Grand Canyon National Park and Lake Mead National Recreation Area, where millions of tourists each year find a range of lodgings and amenities, this new national monument is notable for its remoteness and lack of development.

It is located in the far north-western corner of Arizona, in a region north of the Grand Canyon and south of St George, Utah, known as the Arizona Strip. It preserves more than 1 million acres (405,000 ha) of wildland north of the Grand Canyon's North Rim, and encompasses many of the same features as the Grand Canyon, including deep canyons, mountains, isolated buttes, colorful vistas, and biological, archeological, and historical resources. Scattered throughout the park are signs of ancient Native American inhabitants.

Visitors will find no paved roads and no visitor services or facilities, and thus should prepare for a remote back-country experience. A 4WD vehicle with two spare tires is recommended. Although some roads are graded, they can still become impassable after heavy rain—even for those with a 4WD. Spring and fall are generally the best times to visit.

The monument, with its headquarters in St George, is managed by the National Park Service and the US Bureau of Land Management. The most popular access is via Main Street Valley Road from St George. There is no entrance fee, but officials do recommend calling ahead for current road conditions. The nearest airports are at St George, and Las Vegas, Nevada.
Map ref: page 616 F7

KAYENTA

Kayenta is a good base from which to explore nearby Navajo National Monument, Keet Seel Ruin, and Betatakin Ruin. It is in Monument Valley on US-163 just north of the junction with US-160, on the Navajo Indian Reservation in northeastern Arizona.

Kayenta began as a trading post established in 1910 by John Wetherill, who called it Oljeto. Uranium mining has been important to the town, which has about 4,400 residents. Scenic US-163 continues north from Kayenta, through the spectacular Monument Valley and into southern Utah.
Map ref: page 617 M5.

LAKE HAVASU CITY

If long, sparkling, man-made bodies of water aren't enough of an oddity in the desert of the Arizona–California border, then perhaps the sight of historic London Bridge is.

In 1968 the British government decided that London Bridge, built in 1831, could no longer handle the volume of traffic crossing the River Thames, and put the span up for sale. Oil industry executive Robert P. McCulloch Sr, founder of this recreation-oriented city of 24,400 residents, bought the bridge for US$2.46 million, dismantled it and transported it to Lake Havasu City, where it was reconstructed. It was dedicated anew on October 10, 1971, a date the community celebrates during the annual London Bridge Days.

Lake Havasu City began as a World War II rest camp for the US Army Air Corps. The 45-mile-long (72-km) lake, 3 miles (5 km) across at its widest point, is created by the impounded waters of the Colorado River. It provides a full range of aquatic recreation. Hiking, camping, and four-wheel driving in the publicly owned desert lands surrounding Lake Havasu are popular, as 2.5 million visitors a year can attest. Lake Havasu State Park offers camping, boating, picnicking, and restrooms complete with showers.

Temperatures are mild in winter, spring, and fall, but in summer they soar to over 100°F (37°C). A wide range of lodgings is available.

Lake Havasu City is located 23 miles (37 km) south of I-40. Commercial flights go to Lake Havasu Airport, as well as to Laughlin–Bullhead City International Airport to the north. Buses run between Lake Havasu City, Las Vegas and Laughlin in Nevada, and Needles in California.
Map ref: page 622 B2

LAKE MEAD NATIONAL RECREATION AREA

Shared by Arizona and Nevada, Lake Mead NRA occupies one of the hottest and driest places in

Lake Mead is the largest man-made lake in the United States.

the American Southwest, an extraordinary environment where three of the nation's four great deserts—the Mojave, the Great Basin, and the Sonoran—meet. The area is formed primarily from the impounded waters of the Colorado River, and stretches for 140 miles (225 km) along on the Arizona–Nevada border just east of Las Vegas. Its namesake reservoir is 115 miles (185 km) long, with 550 miles (885 km) of shoreline. The National Recreation Area reaches from the boundary of Grand Canyon National Park to a point 67 miles (108 km) below Hoover Dam, taking in both Lake Mead and Lake Mojave to form one of the Southwest's most popular year-round aquatic playgrounds. Visitors come to this area for boating, camping, fishing (largemouth and striped bass as well as catfish), hiking, and scenic driving.

The Lake Mead National Recreation Area charges an entry fee per vehicle, good for five days. It is open seven days a week.

Lake Mead is about 25 miles (40 km) from Las Vegas International Airport.

Hoover Dam, begun in 1931 and completed in 1936, was built as a flood control and hydropower project. Today, the 726-foot-tall (221-m) monolith across Black Canyon is still among the highest in the world. The 4 billion kilowatt-hours of power it generates goes primarily to meet the electricity needs of Arizona,

Nevada, and Southern California. Guided tours of the dam are offered daily except Thanksgiving (fourth Thursday in November) and Christmas Day. US-93 runs across the top of Hoover Dam.
Map ref: page 616 D7

MESA

Arizona's third-largest city, Mesa, occupies a plateau 12 miles (19 km) southeast of Phoenix on US-60, hence its name, which is the Spanish word for "tabletop." Since its founding in 1878, it has become one of the state's fastest-growing cities, with an economy fueled by at least 30 Fortune 500 companies, and manufacturers of electronics products, automotive safety and aerospace products, and heavy equipment. It is the retail center for Maricopa County. In winter, its population soars by an estimated 135,000 part-time residents who come south to enjoy the milder climate.

Residents find a range of recreational opportunities in the five large lakes that lie an hour's drive away, as well as in the mountainous national forests to the north. The Arizona Museum for Youth lets children view, create, and explore a range of art forms. The Champlin Fighter Museum, at Falcon Field, is home to the American Fighter Aces Association, with exhibits covering the history of fighter pilots and aircraft from World War I.

Commercial flights to Mesa are available at Phoenix Sky Harbor International Airport; rail and bus services go from Phoenix.
Map ref: page 622 F5

MONTEZUMA CASTLE NATIONAL MONUMENT

As the National Park Service readily admits, this is not a castle, and Montezuma never set foot in what is today an 840-acre (340-ha) site that protects the best-preserved Native American cliff dwellings in North America. (The reason for its name is that early settlers assumed the structure was associated with the Aztec ruler Montezuma. However, he was born a century after the structure was abandoned.)

Montezuma Castle is an impressive, five-story, 20-room dwelling built by the Sinagua

Fans of Western films will recognize the towering monoliths of Monument Valley.

more than 600 years ago. It is set inside a large alcove in the limestone cliffs above Beaver Creek, in the Verde Valley along I-17 between Flagstaff and Phoenix.

Spring and fall are the best times of the year to visit. Summers are very hot, though winters are mild.

There are no camping facilities, but campgrounds and RV (recreational vehicle) parks are available elsewhere in the area. The park has a picnic area as well. Overnight lodgings are available in Camp Verde, which is about 5 miles (8 km) south of the park.

The park is located 3 miles (5 km) off I-17. Access is by car. There is no public transportation, but commercial tours are available from Flagstaff and some surrounding communities.
Map ref: page 622 F2

MONUMENT VALLEY

Spread across northeastern Arizona and southeastern Utah lies the vast red desert of the Colorado Plateau. It is famous for its isolated sandstone buttes, towers, and monoliths, some reaching 1,000 feet (305 m) in height. So many classic Western movies, television commercials, and landscape photographs have used this majestic expanse as a backdrop that it has become one of the quintessential images of the Southwest.

The valley is near the Four Corners area, where Arizona, Utah, Colorado, and New Mexico

meet. It is actually a vast desert expanse rather than a valley, and the famous rocks are mere remnants of a great layer of sedimentary rock that has eroded away over millions of years. It is traversed by scenic US-163.

Straddling the Arizona–Utah border is Monument Valley Navajo Tribal Park, part of the Navajo Indian Reservation, the nation's largest. The park helps to preserve the Navajo way of life as well as the inspiring landscape. The most famous rock landmarks are concentrated around the small Native American town of Goulding, just across the state line in Utah. A visitor center 4 miles (6 km) southeast of US-163 provides information on self-guided and guided tours by horseback and 4WD vehicle, park lodging, camping, and picnicking.

Visitors can drive themselves along a 14-mile (23-km) dirt loop road from the visitor center through the park, but you need a guide to drive or hike elsewhere in the park.

The park and visitor center are open daily except for Christmas Day and after noon on Thanksgiving (fourth Thursday in November). A small entrance fee is required. Visitors should not photograph the Native Americans or their property without permission. If permission is granted, a gratuity is usually appropriate. Check at the visitor center for additional restrictions.
Map ref: page 617 M4

NAVAJO NATIONAL MONUMENT

Located on the Shonto Plateau in northeastern Arizona, this small national monument preserves three of the most intact cliff dwellings of the ancestral Pueblo people known as the Anasazi. It overlooks the Tsegi Canyon system of the Navajo Indian Reservation.

There is a visitor center and museum, two short self-guided mesa-top trails, a campground, and picnic area. In summer, park rangers take visitors on tours of the Keet Seel and Betatakin cliff dwellings via trails over difficult terrain with steep switchbacks, sand hills, quicksand, and other back-country hazards.

The park charges no entrance fee. It is closed on Thanksgiving (fourth Thursday in November), Christmas, and New Year's Days. The campground is open year-round, weather permitting. The park lies at the end of state Route 564, which branches off US-160 at Black Mesa. Summers are hot, and thunderstorms are common in July and August. Spring and fall can be pleasant, but windy. Winters can be snowy and cold. Map ref: page 617 L5.

NOGALES

Nogales, Arizona, shares the international border with Nogales, Sonora, in Mexico, and the long-standing cultural and trade ties between the two cities have grown under the North American Free Trade Agreement. The cities are the site of one of the largest clusters of cooperative manufacturing plants (known as maquiladora) along the United States–Mexico border.

Located an hour south of Tucson via I-19, Arizona's Nogales serves as the seat of Santa Cruz County, the state's smallest county. In addition to being a major border crossing point for tourists, Nogales is the largest port of entry for winter fruit and vegetables in the United States.

The valley that extends to the north has for thousands of years served as a trading route and mixing area for various cultures. In the seventeenth and eighteenth centuries the valley was part of Spain's El Camino Real (Royal Highway) which ran from Mexico

Chilies, like these in Nogales, are an essential part of Southwestern cuisine.

City, Mexico, to Santa Fe, New Mexico, USA. In the nineteenth century raids on travelers by bandits and Apache Indians earned it the gruesome nickname of "Blood Highway." Nogales was founded in 1880 by Isaac and Jacob Isaacson as a border trading post. In 1882, American and Mexican railroads met for the first time here to serve the growing cross-border trade. It was incorporated as a city in 1893. Nogales served as an arms supply center for the forces of Francisco "Pancho" Villa, one of the heroes of the Mexican Revolution early in the twentieth century.

Pimeria Alta Historical Society Museum, which includes a library and archives on the history of southern Arizona and northern Sonora, is located in Old Nogales City Hall (1914).

Commercial flights are available at Nogales International Airport and buses run there.

International visitors intending to go to Mexico should carry a passport but Mexican officials will also accept a certified birth certificate, a voter's registration card, or a notarized affidavit of citizenship. American and Canadian visitors to Mexico must carry proof of citizenship. (Be aware that driver's licenses and baptismal certificates are not considered proof of citizenship.) Anyone intending to visit Mexico for longer than 72 hours must also obtain a Mexican government tourist card, called a *tarjeta de turista*. Map ref: page 623 H10.

ORGAN PIPE CACTUS NATIONAL MONUMENT

The 330,689 acres (133,929 ha) of Organ Pipe Cactus National Monument highlight the life and landscape of the Sonoran Desert. Amid a wilderness of plants and animals and dramatic mountain and plains scenery, one can drive a lonely road, hike a back-country trail, camp, or just enjoy the warmth of the Southwestern sun.

The park is on state Route 85, southwest of Phoenix. It has abundant examples of its namesake, the organ pipe cactus. From October through April days are typically sunny, with temperatures in the 60s and 70s°F (15°C–21°C), with occasional light rains. May through September temperatures often exceed 105°F (40°C), and brief, violent thunderstorms occur. Nights are considerably cooler than days year-round.

The visitor center is open all year except Christmas Day.

There is a small entrance fee per vehicle. Overnight back-country permits are available for a small fee. The park has two campgrounds, with sites available on a first-come, first-served basis. Map ref: page 622 D8.

PAGE

Page, at the southwestern end of Lake Powell, was founded in 1957 in the heart of northern Arizona's canyon country as a temporary camp for workers building Glen Canyon Dam. It was named for the 1930s' Bureau of Reclamation Commissioner John C. Page. Today, it is a planned community of more than 9,200 people.

Perched atop Manson Mesa, overlooking Lake Powell's Wahweap Bay, Page has become a major resort area centered on Glen Canyon National Recreation Area. Besides being the site of NRA headquarters, it benefits from employment opportunities at the

*Saguaro cacti (*Carnegiea gigantea*) in the Superstition Wilderness, near Phoenix.*

In Petrified Forest National Park, visitors can view the remnants of ancient trees that have been turned to stone.

nearby Salt River Project's Navajo Generating Station. Many visitors use Page as a base for visiting the wild and spectacular canyon country of northern Arizona and southeastern Utah.

Page is near the Utah state line, on US-89 and state Route 98. Page Airport has a service from Phoenix.
Map ref: page 617 K5

PETRIFIED FOREST NATIONAL PARK

East of Flagstaff, northeastern Arizona's 93,533-acre (37,881-ha) Petrified Forest National Park features one of the world's largest and most colorful concentrations of petrified wood, as well as multi-colored badlands known as the Painted Desert. In addition to its 225-million-year-old fossils, the park protects historic structures and archeological sites.

Few places in the world have a fossil record as diverse and complete as that found at Petrified Forest National Park. During the Triassic Period (250 million to 200 million years ago), the Colorado Plateau area of today's northeastern Arizona was located near the equator, creating a forested tropical environment. Petrified wood is the fossil evidence of this period, exposed now in sediments known as the Chinle Formation. There are heavy penalties for the theft of petrified wood, which is a serious problem. Recreational collecting for personal use is allowed on public lands managed by the US Forest Service and the US Bureau of Land Management.

Petrified wood collected on private lands can be purchased at shops outside the park.

Summer days are generally hot, with temperatures in the 90s°F (30°C+) and occasionally low 100s°F (around 38°C). Average winter daytime temperatures vary from the 40s to 50s°F (4°C–10°C). Temperatures can sometimes dip below zero and high winds can occur anytime. There is no public transportation in the park. Wilderness camping is allowed with a free permit, but there are no campgrounds or lodging facilities.

The park is open year-round except Christmas Day, and charges a small fee per private vehicle, good for seven days. It stretches between I-40 and US-180, which are connected by a road through the park.
Map ref: page 617 N10

PHOENIX

Nicknamed "the Valley of the Sun," the seat of Maricopa County and the centrally located capital of Arizona is a fast-growing southwestern melting pot of different cultures. With over 1.2 million residents, it is the state's largest city, and the sixth-largest city in the nation. It is the commercial and transportation hub of the rapidly growing Southwest, and the heart of a metropolitan area that is home to almost two-thirds of the state's population.

Founder Jack Swilling formed a canal company in 1867 that channeled water from the Salt River for irrigation. By 1879 Phoenix had become a supply

center for the mines of northern Arizona. The key to the desert city's growth in the early twentieth century was the completion of Theodore Roosevelt Dam in 1911, which stabilized the city's water supply. Modern air conditioning, and water supplied by the Salt River Project and the Central Arizona Project, have helped support and fuel the area's growth.

The city, named for the mythical bird symbolic of rebirth, was built on the ruins of the Hohokam Indian civilization, whose farmers dug irrigation canals that remain in use today. They mysteriously disappeared about 1450.

Phoenix's generally reliable weather has long played a role in its growth. Rapid expansion began during World War II, when the area's favorable climate led to the establishment of military airfields and then defense industries. Nearby Luke Air Force Base remains a major training center for fighter pilots.

Manufacturing, particularly electronics, and tourism are major economic forces. Many large companies have made Phoenix their headquarters, including U-Haul and Phelps Dodge. But the city's rapid growth and development since the 1960s has led to a serious air pollution problem for the Phoenix metropolitan area, created by industries

such as copper smelting and the large number of automobiles. Pollution was significantly reduced by the early 1990s following enactment of more stringent emissions standards.

Downtown is the locale of the Phoenix Civic Plaza, a sports, convention, and meeting complex; the Phoenix Symphony Hall, home of the Phoenix Symphony Orchestra; the Arizona Science Center, which has hands-on displays in aerospace, geology, computers, biology, psychology, and physics; and the Phoenix Museum of History, which has exhibits depicting the city's growth from desert town to modern metropolis.

The Heard Museum, opened in 1928, highlights the Southwest's native cultures with 75,000 artifacts. The Phoenix Zoo exhibits more than 1,300 mammals, birds, and reptiles on 125 acres (51 ha). Waterworld USA offers 20 acres (8 ha) of water slides and wave pools. South Mountain Park is the world's largest municipal park.

There are flights from Phoenix Sky Harbor International Airport, as well as rail and bus services. The metropolitan area is easily reached by car via I-8, I-10, and I-17.
Map ref: page 622 F5

Phoenix's State Capitol has an appealing façade.

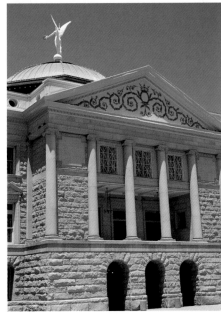

Wolves can be found along the Arizona–Mexico border region.

PIPE SPRING NATIONAL MONUMENT

This small gem is located off state Route 389 on the Kaibab Indian Reservation south of the Utah state line, in northwestern Arizona. It is rich in the history of Native Americans, early explorers, and Mormon pioneers.

The waters of Pipe Spring have long sustained a variety of desert plants and animals as well as humans. Ancestral Pueblo and Kaibab Paiute gathered grass seeds, hunted animals, and farmed near the springs for at least 1,000 years. In the 1860s Mormon pioneers brought cattle to the area, and by 1872 the Mormon Church built a fort over the main spring. Called Windsor Castle (for the first ranch manager), the fort was the headquarters of a large cattle ranch.

The outpost was a way station for people traveling across the Arizona Strip, the part of Arizona separated from the rest of the state by the Grand Canyon. Although their way of life was greatly affected, the Paiute Indians continued to live in the area owned by Pipe Spring Ranch. In 1923 the ranch was purchased and set aside as a national monument. Today, a visitor center, tours of Windsor Castle, summer "living history" demonstrations, an orchard and garden, and a half-mile (1 km) foot trail offer glimpses of Native American and pioneer life.

The park is open all year except Thanksgiving (fourth Thursday of November) and Christmas and New Year's Days. In summer, expect daytime temperatures above 90°F (32°C), and nighttime lows near 60°F (15°C). Summer afternoons often bring sudden thunderstorms. Winter daytime highs are around 40°F (4°C); nighttime lows drop to near 20°F (–6°C). Expect occasional snow. A small entrance fee is charged. There is no camping or lodging available in the immediate area of the park.
Map ref: page 616 G5

PRESCOTT

Prescott lies amid the largest stand of ponderosa pines in the world. The discovery of gold in the Prescott area northwest of Phoenix led to the establishment of Arizona Territory in 1863, in the midst of the Civil War. Prescott, the seat of Yavapai County, was founded in 1864 and named after historian William Hickling Prescott. It was the capital of Arizona Territory from its founding until 1867, and then again from 1877 to 1889. It was made a city in 1881.

Government employment and spending have always been dominant factors in its economy. Prescott is also a copper mining, ranching, and nineteenth-century Western-style resort center. Manufacturing, including firearms, plastics, and aerospace equipment, has been the fastest-growing sector of the economy. Thirty church-affiliated camps and a private summer camp also contribute to the economy.

The Bead Museum exhibits beads from ancient and ethnic cultures. Sharlot Hall Museum and the Smoki Museum display an array of pioneer and Native American artifacts. The John C. Fremont House (1875) was the home of the famous explorer during his term as territorial governor. The 1.2-million-acre (486,000-ha) Prescott National Forest, headquartered in Prescott, provides a full range of outdoor recreation opportunities.

There are several annual events in Prescott, including Arts and Crafts Shows and the Folk Art Festival in June. The Frontier Days Celebration and Rodeo, first held in 1888, is held during the week of the July Fourth celebrations. The Prescott Bluegrass Festival is held in the third week of July. Prescott Downs offers thoroughbred races Thursday through Saturday from Memorial Day weekend (last Monday in May) through Labor Day weekend (first Monday in September). Dog races are broadcast Mondays and Wednesdays.

Prescott can be reached by car via state Route 69 from I-17, or state Route 89 from I-40. Commercial flights are available at the Ernest A. Love municipal airport. A bus service is also available.
Map ref: page 622 E2

The state flower of Arizona is the bloom of the saguaro cactus (Carnegiea gigantea).

SAGUARO NATIONAL PARK

The long, upward-reaching arms of the giant saguaro cactus (*Carnegiea gigantea*) may be the most readily recognized symbol of the Southwest. Saguaro grow only in the desert of southern Arizona, along the Colorado River in southern California, and in the northern Mexico state of Sonora. Its blossom, which appears in May and June, is the state flower. Native Americans use the fruit as food. Giant saguaro, which are unique to the Sonoran Desert, sometimes reach a height of 50 feet (15 m) and live as long as 200 years in the cactus forest of Saguaro National Park, outside of Tucson. This area has been protected by the National Park Service since 1933, first as a national monument and then, since 1994, as a national park.

The park is comprised of two detached districts: the Rincon Mountains District (Saguaro East) is east of Tucson and the Tucson Mountain District (Saguaro West) is west of the city. The latter also features many Native American rock art sites.

Both districts are open daily, sunrise to sunset. Both have visitor centers, which are open daily except Christmas Day. Winter days are mild, with temperatures in the 60s and 70s°F (15°–21°C). Summers can be very hot, with daytime temperatures of 100°–115°F (38°–46°C) in the shade. Both districts have miles of trails, but even short hikes require lots of water, a hat, and sunscreen. Scenic loop drives are available as well. Back-country camping is permitted in Saguaro East with a free permit, available at the visitor center.

There is a small entrance fee at Saguaro East per private car, good for seven days. There is no fee at Saguaro West. Major airlines and a bus service are available at Tucson.
Map ref: page 623 H8

Historic Route 66, near Seligman, draws visitors from all over the world.

SEDONA

This upscale, artistic community lies amid the spectacular red-rock scenery of Oak Creek Canyon and is surrounded by Coconino National Forest. One of Arizona's premier tourism, recreation, resort, and art centers, it has become the state's second most heavily visited place after the Grand Canyon. Clear skies and mild temperatures are the norm here. and because of its elevation of 4,500 feet (1,370 m) Sedona escapes the extremes of both low desert and high mountains. Many residents and visitors are drawn here by the belief that their creativity is enhanced by psychic energy caused by "energy vortexes" said to be focused on Bell Rock, Table Top Mountain, Cathedral Rock, and Boynton Canyon.

Native Americans had lived in the area for thousands of years before John James Thompson settled in Oak Creek Canyon in 1876. A petition in 1902 to have a post office established in the canyon was granted to Theodore Schnebly, who named the postal station after his wife, Sedona.

Originally known for its fruit farms, tourism has since become the town's economic mainstay, and many artists have been drawn to its rugged beauty. Many specialty shops and boutiques are found in Sedona and in the Mexican/Spanish-style village of Tlaquepaque.

Other attractions include swimming, horseback riding, fishing, hiking, mountain biking, and scenic drives through the dramatic red-rock country. 4WD outings into the back country are offered by a number of tour operators. Golf and tennis are available virtually year-round.

Sedona is on state Route 89A west of I-17, about 30 miles (48 km) south of Flagstaff. Charter services fly between Sedona Airport and Phoenix Sky Harbor International Airport.

Map ref: page 617 J10

SELIGMAN

Seligman lies at the junction of historic Route 66 and I-40 in northwestern Arizona. Early settlers arrived in 1886.During its early railroad period it was known as Prescott Junction. It is named after Jesse Seligman, a prominent New York banker responsible for financing railroad construction. Its post office was established in 1886. The town now relies on nearby ranches and tourism to survive.It remains unincorporated, and has about 940 residents.

In 1987 Arizona dedicated the longest remaining stretch of Route 66, between Seligman and Kingman, as Historic Route 66 to help preserve it and to boost tourism. The community's motels, restaurants, and service stations are the main attractions for visitors.

Map ref: page 616 G9

SONORAN DESERT NATIONAL MONUMENT

Sonoran Desert National Monument's 486,000 acres (196,830 ha) of undeveloped wildland include forests of saguaro cacti and an array of plants and animals, as well as numerous archeological sites.

This new national monument, established in January 2001, ranks among the most unspoiled examples of a Sonoran desert ecosystem. Endangered Sonoran pronghorn, desert bighorn sheep, mountain lions, endangered bat species, desert tortoises, Sonoran green toads, and more than 200 species of birds are among the many inhabitants of the monument.

Vekol Wash is believed to have been an important prehistoric travel and trade corridor between Hohokam villages and tribes living in what is now Mexico. Evidence of villages and permanent habitations is found throughout the monument, which also takes in portions of the historic Juan Bautista de Anza Trail, the Mormon Battalion Trail, and the Butterfield Overland Stage Route.

Sonoran Desert National Monument lies just east of US-85. It is bisected by I-8.There are no visitor facilities, and no entrance fee is charged.

Map ref: page 622 E6

SUN CITY

Sun City is the quintessential retirement community. It began as a partnership between builder Del Webb and cotton farmer J.G. Boswell, who owned the land. Their intention was to create an attractive retirement community and to this end deed restrictions require that at least one resident per household be 55 or older. It opened on New Year's Day, 1960, and home sales were immediately brisk.

Located 12 miles (19 km) northwest of Phoenix, within its metropolitan area, Sun City boasts 350 clubs, seven recreation centers, 1,200 acres (486 ha) of golf courses, the nearby Lake Pleasant Regional Park, and plenty of sunshine.

Sun City is serviced by Phoenix Sky Harbor International Airport, Glendale Municipal Airport, and Phoenix–Goodyear Airport.

Map ref: page 622 F4

Saguaro (Carnegiea gigantea) are popular in the desert-style gardens of Sun City.

TEMPE

Tempe lies in the center of the Phoenix metropolitan area. It is bordered by the capital city to the west, Scottsdale to the north, Mesa to the east, and Chandler to the south. From its beginnings as Hayden's Ferry in 1872, it has grown into an urban community of about 164,000 residents. It was renamed in 1878 for ancient Greece's idyllic Vale of Tempe. Now it is a manufacturing city, producing semiconductor devices, metals, machinery, communications equipment, and other products. It has also seen the growth of software and bio-tech companies, and financial services.

Each New Year's Day the city kicks off with the Fiesta Football Classic, one of the nation's largest college bowl games, at ASU (Arizona State University). The city is also the home of the NFL's Arizona Cardinals, and host to the Tostitos Fiesta Bowl and the Anaheim Angels for spring training. Downtown Tempe, where historic buildings mingle with modern architecture, has become a regional entertainment center with live music, restaurants, boutiques, cafes, theaters, and cinemas. The annual spring and fall Festival of the Arts, the largest events of their kind in the Southwest, draw thousands to the area.

The ASU Art Museum, in the Nelson Fine Arts Center at 10th Street and Mill Avenue, exhibits American and European prints from the fifteenth through to the twentieth centuries, and American paintings and sculptures from the nineteenth and twentieth centuries. The university's Museum of Geology, in building F near the intersection of University Drive and McAllister Street, has one of the world's largest meteorite collections.

With more than 44,000 students, Arizona State University in Tempe is the fourth largest public university in the country. Its Gammage Center for the Performing Arts, designed by Frank Lloyd Wright and completed in 1964, seats 3,000 people.

Phoenix Sky Harbor International Airport provides domestic and international flights. Both rail and bus services are available.
Map ref: page 622 F5

TOMBSTONE

It wasn't violent events like the bloody 30-second gunfight at the O.K. Corral that earned this old mining town the moniker "The Town Too Tough To Die," but rather its survival of falling silver prices, the loss of the Cochise County seat to Bisbee, and the Great Depression.

Its unusual name derives from the warning that prospector Ed Schieffelin was given when he set out to find his fortune: that he'd find only his tombstone in what was then considered the "Apache-infested" San Pedro Valley. Thus, when he defied the doom-mongers and found silver in 1877, he jubilantly named his claim Tombstone, and the rough-and-tumble boom town that followed was given the same name.

On October 26, 1881, Tombstone forever entered the history books as the site of the shootout at the O.K. Corral. On one side were lawmen Wyatt, Virgil, and Morgan Earp, and John "Doc" Holliday. On the other were suspected cattle-rustlers and outlaws Joseph "Ike" Clanton, Billy Clanton, Frank and Tom McLaury, and Billy "the Kid" Clairborne. When the gunfire ended, Virgil and Morgan Earp and Holliday were wounded and Billy Clanton and the McLaurys were dead.

Tombstone, with 1,655 residents, occupies a mesa (plateau) between the Dragoon and Huachuca mountains. Once notorious for saloons, gambling houses, and general lawlessness, it was for a time one of the most prominent cities in the West. However, massive underground flooding in the silver and gold mines and depressed silver prices ended its heyday by 1904.

In 1962 the US Department of the Interior designated Tombstone a Registered Historical Landmark.

The flower of the torch cactus (hybrid *Trichocereus*).

Tourism is the city's economic mainstay today. The Tombstone Courthouse (1882) is now a state park. Other historic attractions include Boot Hill Graveyard, which has 300 marked graves that include those of early settlers and outlaws; St Paul's Episcopal Church (1882), the oldest Protestant church in Arizona still standing at its original site and still used for its original purpose; the luxurious Crystal Palace Saloon (1879); the Bird Cage Theater (1881), reputed to have been one of the 20 wildest nightspots in the Wild West; and the O.K. Corral. The town's early years are recalled during three days in October, dubbed Helldorado Days. Shootouts are staged daily. Tombstone has a wide range of lodgings and restaurants.

Tombstone is located one hour south of Tucson via I-10 and state Route 80. Regional commercial flights are available at Sierra Vista Municipal Airport, which is 29 miles (47 km) southwest of Tombstone.
Map ref: page 623 K9

Boot Hill Graveyard is the final resting place of many Tombstone legends.

TONTO NATIONAL MONUMENT

Tonto National Monument, on state Route 99 east of Phoenix near Theodore Roosevelt Dam, protects well-preserved cliff dwellings that were occupied by people of the Salado culture during the thirteenth, fourteenth, and early fifteenth centuries. The Salado Indians farmed in the Salt River Valley, and supplemented their diet by hunting and gathering native wildlife and plants. They also produced some of the highest-quality polychrome pottery and woven textiles in the Southwest. (This can be seen in the visitor center museum.)

Tonto National Monument was established by President Theodore Roosevelt in 1907 and was among the first national monuments to be proclaimed under the Antiquities Act of 1906.

The monument is open daily except Christmas Day. Note that Lower Ruin Trail closes to uphill travel at 4 p.m. There is a small park entrance fee per car. While winters are mild, summer temperatures can exceed 110°F (43°C). January through February, and July through September are the rainy season months.

There are no lodgings or campgrounds at the monument, although they are available elsewhere in the area.
Map ref: page 623 H4

Magnificent mountains overlook the outskirts of Tucson; to the north of Tucson is 9,157-foot (2,793-m) Mount Lemmon.

TUCSON

"Old Pueblo" (meaning "old village"), as Tucson is affectionately nicknamed, is Arizona's oldest city and, with about 468,500 residents, its second-largest. Located in southeastern Arizona beside the Santa Cruz River, in a high desert valley surrounded by mountains, its human history reaches back to the Native Americans who occupied the area as long as 12,000 years ago.

Father Eusebio Francisco Kino first visited the valley in the late 1600s, and in 1700 he established several missions in the area. Tucson was founded in 1775 as a Spanish presidio, or military garrison, to protect settlers from Apache raids. It was Spain's northernmost outpost in the New World.

Its name is an Pima Native American word meaning "water at black mountain." An unruly but growing frontier town, it was governed by Mexico from 1821 until 1854, when the Gadsden Purchase made it part of the United States. In February 1862, during the Civil War, Captain Sherod Hunter briefly seized the city for the Confederacy. It served as the capital of Arizona Territory from 1867 to 1877. The city is noted for its mix of cultures.

Tucson was incorporated in 1877, and serves as the seat of Pima County. It is famous for its mild winters, although summers are hot. With an average of 3,800 hours of sunshine and only 11 inches (28 cm) of rain annually, it is one of the nation's sunniest cities.

The University of Arizona is the largest single employer in Tucson, with more than 10,000 employees. Davis–Monthan Air Force Base has more than 8,000 military and civilian employees. High technology has grown in importance to the economy as companies like Raytheon, Allied Signal, Sargent Controls, and others have located operations here. Tourism is also a dominant economic force.

Among the local attractions are Mission San Xavier del Bac (1700); Saguaro National Park; Old Tucson Studio and Park, the set for many Hollywood Westerns; and the Arizona State Museum, an anthropology museum with exhibits depicting the history of Southwestern cultures from prehistoric mammoth hunters to today's Native Americans.

The primary access route by car is east–west I-10. Commercial flights go from Tucson International Airport. Both rail and bus services are available.
Map ref: page 623 H8

TUMACACORI NATIONAL HISTORICAL PARK

This park, located in the Santa Cruz River Valley in southern Arizona, shows evidence of the first Europeans who came to southern Arizona and of the native people who lived here then. It consists of three separate areas (or units) with ruins of three early Spanish colonial missions. The oldest, San Jose de Tumacacori, was built on the site of a Pima village, and is one of the earliest of the Southwest's missions. Jesuit missionary Father Eusebio Francisco Kino came to the area in 1691. In 1767 the King of Spain expelled the Jesuits, and replaced them with Franciscans. Construction of the adobe church at the site began about 1800, but it was never finished. Visitors can tour the church, the cemetery, and outlying structures and grounds.

Winters are moderate in the Tumacacori National Historical Park, but summer temperatures often exceed 100°F (38°C). Thunderstorms typically occur in July and August.

The park is open daily except Thanksgiving (fourth Thursday in November) and Christmas Day. There is a small entrance fee per adult (aged 17 and older), good for seven days. The park is located off I-19 about 18 miles (29 km) north of Nogales and the Mexican border.
Map ref: page 623 H9

TUZIGOOT NATIONAL MONUMENT

Tuzigoot National Monument protects an ancient pueblo, or village, located on a desert hilltop 6 miles (10 km) northeast of Clarkdale.

The village was built by the Sinagua Native Americans, an agricultural people who traded over a region extending hundreds of miles, then mysteriously disappeared around 1400.

The pueblo includes two and three-story structures and consists of 110 rooms. The first buildings were constructed around AD 1000. Adjacent to Tuzigoot is Tavasci Marsh, one of the few freshwater marshes in Arizona.

The small entry fee is good for seven days. The park is open all year except Christmas Day.
Map ref: page 617 J10

A large collection of old planes is on show at the Davis–Monthan Air Force Base in Tucson.

VERMILION CLIFFS NATIONAL MONUMENT

This newly designated national monument includes 293,000 acres (118,665 ha) of remote, unspoiled wildland on the Colorado Plateau in northern Arizona, west of Page between US-89A and the Utah state line. It includes the majestic Paria Plateau, the colorful Vermilion Cliffs, and the spectacular Paria River Canyon–Vermilion Cliffs Wilderness amid elevations that range from 3,100–7,100 feet (946–2,166 m) above sea level.

Human presence in the area has been dated as far back as 12,000 years. The area still contains a large number of ancestral Puebloan (Anasazi) sites, including remnants of villages with intact walls, granaries, burial sites, and camps.

Many historic expeditions crossed through the area including the Spanish Dominguez–Escalante expedition of 1776, Antonio Armijo's 1829 Mexican trading expedition, and Mormon exploring parties in the 1860s led by Jacob Hamblin. Major John Wesley Powell also passed through here during a scientific survey in 1871.

The region is known for its biological diversity, which includes 20 species of raptors, desert big-horn sheep, mountain lions, and California condors. Activities include hiking, camping, sight-seeing, and back-country driving.

The monument has no paved roads, and visitors should prepare for a back-country experience. 4WD high-clearance vehicles are recommended. One campground is available. Spring and fall are the best seasons to visit. Some areas of the monument require reservations and a small per-person fee. Headquarters are in St George, Utah.
Map ref: page 617 J5

WALNUT CANYON NATIONAL MONUMENT

This park, located just east of Flagstaff, off I-40, preserves more than 300 prehistoric Native American dwellings thought to have been built by ancestors of today's Hopi people and abandoned 700 years ago.

Before the eruption of nearby Sunset Crater Volcano in AD 1064–65, natives of the region lived in pithouses—clay or stone-lined holes in the ground—and farmed the open meadows. It appears they sensed the impending eruption and relocated to settlements in Wupatki, Walnut Canyon, and Verde Valley. Those who moved to Walnut Canyon took advantage of ledges in the canyon that formed natural shelters.

There is a small entrance fee per person to the park, good for seven days. Be prepared for abrupt weather changes in any season.
Map ref: page 617 K9

WINDOW ROCK

Located in northeastern Arizona near the New Mexico state line, Window Rock (population 3,300) is the capital of the Navajo Nation and the seat of tribal government. Also located here is the US Bureau of Indian Affairs, Navajo Area Office.

The Navajo Tribal Museum, in the Navajo Arts and Crafts Enterprises building, displays items related to the history and culture of the Navajo and the prehistoric cultures of the Four Corners region.

From Wednesday to Sunday during the second week of September, visitors crowd into the fairgrounds at Window Rock for the Annual Navajo Nation Fair.
Map ref: page 617 P8

At sunset, the Vermilion Cliffs become a brilliant scarlet streak across the Arizona horizon.

Navajo woman, Arizona.

WUPATKI AND SUNSET CRATER NATIONAL MONUMENTS

The hundreds of pueblos (villages) and cliff dwellings protected by 35,253-acre (14,277-ha) Wupatki National Monument, off US-89 north of Flagstaff, are so well-preserved that visitors may find it hard to believe that their Native American builders, thought to be ancestors of today's Hopi people, left the site seven centuries ago.

Sunset Crater National Monument is south of Wupatki. The two monuments are linked by a paved road. Sunset Crater Volcano is a 1,000-foot (305-m) high cone named by Colorado River explorer Major John Wesley Powell in 1892. Camping is available at the US Forest Service's Bonito Campground. It is generally open from late May through mid-October. Be prepared for abrupt weather changes in any season. Expect wind most of the year. During summer, the days are warm, with afternoon thunderstorms likely from July through September. In winter, snow and freezing temperatures alternate with mild weather.

Both parks are open year-round except Christmas Day. Note that Sunset is often confused with Meteor Crater, 35 miles (56 km) east of Flagstaff on I-40. Meteor Crater is 500 feet (153 m) deep and 1 mile (1.6 km) wide.
Map ref: page 617 K8

YUMA

Yuma (population 68,000) occupies the banks of the Colorado River in the far southwestern corner of Arizona, near the California state line and Mexican border, and south of the Colorado's confluence with the Gila River. It is named for the Yuma Indians. Fort Yuma, built in 1851 provided travelers and settlers with a safe southern route into California. Prior to being called Yuma in 1873, it was first Colorado City and then Arizona City.

In contrast to the high plateaus of northern Arizona, Yuma lies just 138 feet (42 m) above sea level. It is the commercial, political, and population hub of Yuma County, Arizona's largest agricultural area. Its location along I-8 continues the city's history as a way station for food and lodging (and now fuel) for modern cross-country travelers as it did in bygone times.

The Fort Yuma Quechan Museum has exhibits depicting Native American culture, the early military era, and Spanish expeditions through the Southwest. Yuma Territorial Prison State Historic Park, on 4th Street, was built in 1876 and served until 1909.

There are flights from Yuma Airport, as well as bus services.
Map ref: page 622 A7

NEW MEXICO

New Mexico, located in the Southwest of the United States, is the fifth-largest state in area. Its vast space contains wide geographic variety, from the broad eastern deserts joining with Texas, to the low Navajo lands in the northwest corner, the peaks of Gila National Forest, and other preserves in the Southwest, and the gorgeous alpine country to the north.

This "Land of Enchantment," as it is known, is very diverse. It has Native American pueblos and cliff dwellings, adobe architecture and other influences of the Spanish occupation, fantastic and colorful rock shapes, and light that attracts artists. It also features extensive cattle ranching, scientific discovery and research, and exceptional outdoor recreation. Today, thanks to damming of rivers and irrigation, the fertile Mesilla Valley produces many crops, including New Mexico's staple, the chili. The Spanish explorer Coronado arrived in 1540, searching for gold that he never found. The Spanish established the first settlement in 1598, founded Santa Fe as the capital in 1609, and formed villages all along the Rio Grande. In 1821 Mexico won independence from Spain and ruled the

The Rio Grande, which is Spanish for "big river," carves through the entire length of New Mexico, past Albuquerque and Las Cruces.

area. After the Mexican War of 1846, New Mexico became a US territory, and then a state in 1912.

In 1945 the first atomic bomb was detonated northwest of Alamogordo. Scientific research at Sandia Laboratories, in Albuquerque, and Los Alamos National Laboratory, and new computer chip and other electronics plants led to a great population increase in the last half of the twentieth century.

Albuquerque, located near the center of the state and with a population of 600,000 people—about a third of the state's population—is the largest city and the state's business center. However, the state capital of Santa Fe, 60 miles (97 km) further north, has a special atmosphere and unusual style that sets it apart as an exclusive destination like Aspen in Colorado, and Sun Valley in Idaho.

State motto *Crescit Eundo* (It grows as it goes)
State flag Adopted 1925
Capital Santa Fe
Population 1,819,046
Total area (land and water)
121,598 square miles (314,939 sq km)
Land area 121,364 square miles (314,333 sq km)
New Mexico is the fifth-largest state in size
Origin of name Named for the country of Mexico
Nickname The Land of Enchantment
Abbreviations NM (postal), N.Mex., N.M.
State bird Roadrunner
State flower Yucca flower
State tree Nut pine
Entered the Union January 6, 1912 as the 47th state

Places in
NEW MEXICO

Grass tree (Nolina bigelovii) growing in the wide open spaces found around Alamogordo.

ACOMA PUEBLO

Acoma Pueblo is about 60 miles (97 km) southwest of Albuquerque on I-40, then Hwy 22. Acoma Pueblo, also known as "Sky City," was built some time between AD 600 and 1150, making it one of the oldest continually inhabited settlements in the United States.

The homes here are built of adobe and rock on top of a 70-acre (28-ha), 365-foot (111-m) high multi-colored sandstone mesa. They were built here as a safeguard against raiding tribes. Acoma Pueblo was once home to thousands of people, although only several hundred remain today.

The Spanish explorer, Francisco Vasquez de Coronado, in 1540, was the first white man to enter the Acoma Fortress.

In 1598, most of New Mexico's Pueblo people had surrendered to the Spanish. However, the nephew of Spanish colonial leader Juan de Onate was killed when he went to Acoma to demand tribute. Onate sent a party of 70 soldiers to exact revenge and Acoma was nearly destroyed. The Acomas are well known for their pottery, which is displayed at the Sky City Visitor Center.

Between 1629 and 1640, the San Esteban del Rey Mission was built here under the direction of Friar Juan Ramirez. Legend has it that Ramirez was allowed into the pueblo after miraculously saving an Indian infant who had fallen off a cliff. San Esteban is one of

The rattlesnake is found in the deserts and grasslands of the Southwest.

the most beautiful mission churches in New Mexico, which is more impressive because all the materials, including earth for the 2,000-square-foot (190-sq-m) cemetery, had to be carried up the mesa. Visitors today are greeted by the white-washed walls that contrast starkly with a wooden altar painted in bright reds, blues, yellows, and greens. Each year the walls are painted with traditional yucca and sheepskin brushes prior to San Esteban's Feast Day on September 2. The paint is ground from pink and white sandstones from a nearby mesa.

After the Mexican War of 1846 when New Mexico was granted to the United States, the Acoma and six other Pueblo tribes applied for land rights. Their requests were ignored but President Abraham Lincoln listened to tribal representatives and gave each tribe an inscribed silver-headed cane. Acoma governors consider this cane to be a badge of office and pass it on to their successors after each election.

Today, the pueblo and the mission are designated Registered National Historical Landmarks

The Enchanted Mesa, which is 400 feet (122 m) high, rises a few miles east of Acoma. According to legend, this was an ancestral dwelling but access to it was wiped out by a violent storm, leaving an old woman and her granddaughter to starve on the mountaintop.

Today, about a dozen families reside at the pueblo. It has never had running water or electricity but there is an antenna attached

to a generator-driven television. Most of the tribal members live in nearby villages. The only way to visit this village is through a tour, which begins at the visitor center at the bottom of the mesa. A van takes visitors up a narrow road, which was financed in 1941 for the shooting of the movie *Sundown*, when fake trees and real ostriches turned the pueblo into a jungle city.

Albuquerque International Airport is the closest and Albuquerque is serviced by trains and buses. Grants, which is 30 miles (48 km) northwest, is serviced by buses.
Map ref: page 624 B1

ALAMOGORDO

This desert town has a population of 29,000 and is located on US-70 in central-south New Mexico. It is beneath the western slope of the Sacramento Mountains, which rise to 8,650 feet (2,638 m) in Lincoln National Forest. Just west is White Sands National Monument and, in town, is the International Space Hall of Fame. In 1945 a huge mushroom cloud rose 40,000 feet (12,200 m) over the Trinity Site in Tularosa Basin, northwest of Alamogordo—it was the first ever atomic explosion.

Folsom Man is thought to have hunted in this area 10,000 years ago and a cave, between Alamogordo and Cloudcroft, known as "Fresnal Shelter," housed Native Americans 3,500 years ago. These are

good examples of the prehistoric sites located in this area. Pit houses and adobe pueblos also figure in local history. Huge cattle ranches occupied the Tularosa Basin in the late nineteenth century, when feuds led to sieges and gunfights that gained national attention. Charles Eddy built a "model city" on the Alamo Ranch that attracted 4,000 residents between 1898 and 1902. After that, railroad and lumber industries helped the town grow.

Today, Alamogordo, which means "fat cottonwood," is a large ranching and farming center, and the home of Holloman Air Force Base, which tests guided missiles and aircraft without pilots. It is also the location of a branch of New Mexico State University, where 1,500 students take the first two years of college before finishing at the campus in Las Cruces.

The International Space Hall of Fame is a US$2-million, four-story gold cube set against the foothills of the Sacramento Mountains— it has exhibits of the world's space programs. Displays include models of the Apollo Command Module and NASA's planned space station, samples of "space food" (such as dehydrated corn beef, cheese spread, and biscuits in cans), photos of Earth taken from the moon, the history of satellites, and a study of early rocketry.

Next to the Space Hall of Fame is the Clyde W. Tombaugh Dome Theater and Planetarium, named for the man who discovered Pluto in 1930. The Omnimax theater shows films on a four-story, wrap-around screen that puts viewers into the middle of a space trip or in the Grand Canyon.

During the annual Rattlesnake Round-up, up to 1,500 pounds (681 kg) of desert rattlesnakes are trapped and sold to a restaurant.

About 15 miles (24 km) southwest of Alamogordo is the White Sands National Monument. It is 300 acres (122 ha) of white soft sand with dunes rising and changing with prevailing winds. The 16-mile (26-km) park loop passes through the dunes in their various stages. The spade-foot toads, hognose snakes, kangaroo rats, cactus wrens, ocotillo, cholla, and yucca that live in the dunes are presented at the visitor center.

The 180-acre (73-ha) Oliver Lee Memorial State Park is located 10 miles (16 km) south of Alamogordo in the mouth of Dog Canyon. Evidence shows that human beings have existed here for 6,000 years; Dog Canyon was the only year-round water supply in the area. "Frenchy" Rochas built a cabin here, in the early 1880s, and raised cattle and had an orchard and vineyard. He was found dead with three bullets in his chest, supposedly a suicide—although a water conflict was probably the reason. In 1905, Oliver Lee, who had worked with Frenchy on navigation systems, built the Circle Cross Cattle Company that controlled 1 million acres (405,000 ha) of the surrounding valley.

The park has a visitor center, hiking, and camping. Tours to the White Sands Missile Range Trinity Site, where the first atomic bomb was exploded, are offered every April and October.

A short, steep rise above Alamogordo is Cloudcroft, a village of 750 people surrounded by the 215,000-acre (87,075-ha) Lincoln National Forest and just a few miles from the 460,000-acre (186,300-ha) Mescalero Apache Reservation. It is a beautiful climb from the hot Tularosa Basin into cool air, pines, and aspen. Cloudcroft gets 75 inches (188 cm) of snow in winter, and has a popular ski area. Summer activities include camping, fishing, hiking, and golfing at 9,000 feet (2,745 m).

There is a bus service, and regional airport in Alamogordo with flights to Albuquerque.

Map ref: page 624 E6

ALBUQUERQUE

New Mexico's largest city has grown out, not up, covering 163 square miles (422 sq m) of high desert in a wide valley between the Sandia Peaks and the plateau country beside the Rio Grande. Albuquerque is just northwest of the geographic center of the state at the intersection of I-25 and I-40. With 600,000 residents, it has about a third of New Mexico's population.

It is the state's business center, with headquarters to companies ranging from banks to microchip manufacturers. Sandia Laboratories, with 7,000 workers, is one of the largest employers, as is the University of New Mexico. Kirtland Air Force Base is another big employer. In recent years, an active Asian community has joined the city's population mix of Indian, Hispanic, and Anglo residents.

In 1540, Pueblo people were living on the river banks of the Rio Grande when Spanish explorer Coronado passed through. Native Americans had farmed here for 15 centuries. In 1706, Spanish families established the town of Albuquerque. It was named for the Duke of Albuquerque and viceroy of New Spain. It became a stop on the extension of the Sante Fe Trail. Its river attracted settlers who lived in adobe houses around San Felipe de Neri Church, which was the central plaza, and today is the center of Old Town.

The city's emergence as a military outpost and railway transfer point between the East and Southwest gave it new importance in the last half of the nineteenth century. In 1899, the University of New Mexico was founded. Today, with 9,500 workers, it is the city's fourth largest employer and the state's most influential educator. In the early part of the twentieth century, many tuberculosis patients sought treatment in Albuquerque, which led to the construction of sanatoriums; this began the strong medical presence in the city.

Summer rainstorms bring dangerous flash floods to Albuquerque, when dry arroyos swell with water that rushes down hillsides onto streets. Floods as high as 3 or 4 feet (1 m) may rise up, and can vanish, with clearing skies, as quickly as they have formed.

Another unusual aspect of the city is the Sandia Peak Aerial Tramway, which rises about 3 miles (5 km), in just 18 minutes, to the Sandia Crest in the 10,678-foot (3,257-m) high Sandia Mountains. This is a quick trip from the cholla cactus and high desert heat to a windy, pine-covered summit with excellent views of the Rio Grande greenbelt and surrounding lands. Sandia Peak Ski Area is filled with downhill and cross-country skiers in the winter months. In warmer months mountain bikers, hikers, and sightseers ride the ski area's chairlifts. Dusk is the most spectacular time on Sandia Peak when the sun disappears behind West Mesa, casting a rosy glow across the city, before nightfall.

Old Town has a wide range of shopping opportunities, from cheap and gaudy to expensive. Visitors can take in the 1706 San Felipe de Neri Church, enjoy the grassy plaza, and explore the narrow back streets adorned with 300-year-old adobe houses.

The New Mexico Museum of Natural History and Science, a modern building set off by a life-size dinosaur, looks at the area's past and present, including the creation of the Earth, DNA, volcanoes, and dinosaurs. The Albuquerque Museum of Art, History, and Science features 400 years of New Mexico history, with maps, Spanish armor and helmets, blacksmith shops, and blankets. Also near Old Town is a Turquoise Museum and the American International Rattlesnake Museum, which claims to have the world's largest collection of live rattlesnakes.

The meeting of two worlds—bustling brand new suburbs of Albuquerque meet the ageless Petroglyph National Monument.

plex has structures and artifacts from the area, including a church, pueblo pottery, and a wooden oil-drilling rig from the 1920s.

Just north of Aztec is the Aztec Ruins National Monument, one of the largest and best-preserved Ancient Pueblo ruins in the Southwest. It has about 500 rooms and the only restored great kiva (large subterranean ceremonial building) in existence. It was excavated in 1921 and rebuilt in 1934. It was mistakenly thought to be part of Mexico's great Aztec empire, which is how it got its name. The monument was named a World Heritage Site in 1987. The visitor center has a short video as well as books and postcards, and a self-guided trail.

Four Corners Regional Airport at nearby Farmington has services to Albuquerque and bus services. Map ref: page 618 C5

BANDELIER NATIONAL MONUMENT

Bandelier National Monument is a 32,737-acre (13,258-ha) area of volcanic rock formations, mesas, canyons and prehistoric dwellings of the Ancestral Puebloan people. It is about 6 miles (10 km) south of Los Alamos. About 23,000 acres (9,407 ha) is wilderness. It was named for the nineteenth-century anthropologist, Adolph Bandelier.

The park is a unique mixture of fascinating archaeological, natural, and historical features and is under constant threat from outside interests in the area. The monument contains about 70 miles (113 km) of trails that lead to ancient cliff dwellings, a ceremonial cave, and remote camping areas. The main attraction is the Frijoles Canyon

Pueblo structures at Aztec Ruins National Monument near Aztec.

The 77-acre (31-ha) Balloon Fiesta Park is the site of the colorful nine-day international Albuquerque Balloon Festival.

The Indian Pueblo Cultural Center is a museum, gift shop, gallery, and restaurant that provides an in-depth look at the state's 19 Indian pueblos. It has displays on history, languages, pottery, clothing, tools, and art. The National Atomic Energy Museum is at Kirtland Air Force Base. It covers the development of atomic energy and displays replicas of bombs dropped during World War II.

Albuquerque's best-known and most popular event is the spectacular October balloon fiesta, in which more than 1 million people watch from the launch area as hundreds of brightly colored balloons fill the sky. The pilots and crews are from all over the world.

Albuquerque International Airport services the area, and train and bus services are available. Map ref: page 624 C1

AZTEC

Aztec, a village in the northwest corner of the state, is set on the blue-green Animas River. Unlike much of the Southwest, the area is green, hilly, and filled with trees, and its homes are made of wood and brick, not adobe.

Aztec has a number of buildings on the National Register of Historic Places. The Aztec Museum Com-

which contains ancient ruins and receives many visitors. Prehistoric life within the monument and on the surrounding Pajarito Plateau thrived for about 400 years, from 1150 to 1550. With the migration of the Ancient Puebloans from the Four Corners region, the small pueblos consolidated into larger villages ranging from around 100 to 1,000 rooms.

In 1916, the monument was named for anthropologist Adolph F. Bandelier, who, with his Cochiti Indian guides, descended into Frijoles Canyon in 1880 and found cliff dwellings and caves. Bandelier, at 40, gave up international banking to pursue his lifelong interest.

Frijoles Canyon, where the visitor center is located, was first excavated by Edgar Lee Hewett in 1907. Hewett and his School of American Research students excavated ruins at Tyuonyi, the large, oval-shaped pueblo built of volcanic tuff that may have had as many as 300 rooms and stood three stories high. Hewitt discovered a large, well-preserved kiva at Ceremonial Cave that is entered by climbing ladders 150 feet (46 m) above the canyon floor.

Santa Fe is 25 miles (40 km) southeast and it is serviced by an airport and buses. Albuquerque International Airport is about 65 miles (105 km) southwest.
Map ref: page 618 F8

CAPULIN VOLCANO NATIONAL MONUMENT

This 1,000-foot (305-m) cinder cone rises 27 miles (44 km) east of Raton in the northeastern corner of the state. Its volcano erupted 60,000 years ago but today, visitors can drive up the side of the volcano

Adobe brick houses have been built in New Mexico for thousands of years.

and hike down the inside. On a clear day visitors can see Colorado, Oklahoma, Kansas, and Texas. The visitor center exhibits the area's plant and wildlife and shows a film on volcanic activity.

In 1925, 10 miles (16 km) north at Folsom, a cowboy named George McJunkin was riding when he noticed bones sticking out of the ground. He also found flint spearheads that measured up to 3 inches (72 mm) long. The bones found with the spearheads were from animals that had been extinct for 10,000 years. The spear points had been used to kill mammoths, mastodons, four-toed horses, and giant ground sloths. This was an important discovery because, previously, it was thought the earliest occupation of the Western Hemisphere was shortly before 1 AD. It is now known that these

early people were ancestors of the people who continued their migration from the Bering Strait to South America. Those who stayed behind, known as Folsom Man, roamed the plains for food. Today, hunters pursue deer, pronghorn, quail and grouse in this area.

Nearby Raton is serviced by trains and buses.
Map ref: page 619 K5

CARLSBAD CAVERNS NATIONAL PARK

Twenty miles (32 km) from Carlsbad, in the barren desert of southeast New Mexico, is one of the most spectacular underground openings in the world. In the foothills of the Guadalupe Mountains, this national park consists of caves and rooms created by groundwater eating through limestone

250 million years ago when the area was under a sea. Fantastic formations made of limestone and calcite deposits fill giant chambers. Stalagmites tower 60 feet (18 m) from the cavern floor, and stalactites in a variety of different shapes—conical, narrow and long, distorted and twisting—hang from the ceiling. One particularly massive chamber is called the Big Room, and it is about 1,800 feet (549 m) long and 255 feet (78 m) high.

The fantastic, multi-colored recesses are inhabited by bats, which put on a tremendous show when they spiral out of the cave mouth, usually around sundown, during the summer months. Some 300,000 bats live about half a mile (0.8 km) inside the cave, and as many as 5,000 billow out, each minute, in dark clouds searching for insects to eat. They are migratory Mexican free-tail bats that weigh about half an ounce (14 g) and have 11-inch (28-cm) wingspans. They arrive in late April or early May and stay until October or November.

There is some evidence that prehistoric people lived in and around these caves. Faded pictographs and mescal cooking pits show that early Native Americans lived here. For the first 20 years of the twentieth century, guano was brought out from the caves in mine cars and sent to southern California to be used as fertilizer.

One of the miners, James White, who had been an area cowboy, went deeper into the caves with a lantern and came back with incredible tales about what lay inside. In 1913, following exploration by a mineral examiner and then a *National Geographic* article about the cave's exploration by geologist Willis T. Lee, President Hoover declared Carlsbad Caverns a national park.

The first visitors to the park were lowered in a large bucket and explored the cave on wooden stairways. Today, visitors follow a paved trail into the cave or take an elevator. A stone and concrete amphitheater is built right at the cave's entrance, where visitors sit and listen to a ranger's lecture before the nightly flight of bats.

Carlsbad has air services to Albuquerque and bus services.
Map ref: page 624 G8

Horses in a lush paddock near Cochiti. There are hundreds of guest ranches and horseback riding trails all over New Mexico.

COCHITI

The Cochiti Pueblo and Indian Reservation is located west of Santa Fe and north of Albuquerque. Its Church of San Buenaventura displays tin candlesticks brought from Chihuahua, Mexico, and a large painting of the patron saint above the altar. The pueblo is especially known for its pottery—red-and-black "storyteller dolls" show little children clinging to a grandmother or grandfather figure. Just north of the pueblo's water tanks, the Rio Grande backs up to Cochiti Dam, creating a reservoir for windsurfers, sailboats, and anglers fishing for bass, crappie, and pike.

Two other ancient pueblos, San Felipe and Santo Domingo, lie just south, on the Rio Grande. All are traditional pueblos and each has its own dialect. Only one of Santo Domingo's ceremonies, its August Corn Dance, is open to the public.

Nearby Santa Fe has a bus service and Albuquerque, which is about 50 miles (80 km) south on I-25, has an international airport, bus and train services.
Map ref: page 618 F8

EL MORRO NATIONAL MONUMENT

The Spanish called this mesa "El Morro," meaning "the bluff," or "the headland." It is 127 acres (51 ha) located 43 miles (69 km) southwest of Grants. This has been a stop for passengers since prehistoric times. In 1605, Juan de Onate, governor and colonizer of New Mexico, carved a message into the sandstone, as have many other visitors over the centuries, including settlers making their way west.

Two Ancient Puebloan villages once thrived on top of the mesa. There is a partial excavation of what may have been a 300-to-400-room dwelling in the thirteenth century. The views of distant mesas and mountains and of fields of wildflowers are exceptional and there is a visitor center.

Twenty miles (32 km) east of El Morro are the Bandera Volcanic Crater and Ice Caves. The cave is a chamber with perpetual ice on its floor and in its crevices. Ice from the floor was used by local farmers for refrigeration. There is a slab of green ice—green from the algae—of about 30 square feet (3 sq m).

Grants has bus services and Albuquerque is 80 miles (129 km) east of Grants on I-40.
Map ref: page 618 B10

FARMINGTON

Navajo Mine, one of the largest coal-mining operations in the world, fuels the adjacent Four Corners Power Plant. It lies near the town of Farmington, found in the northwest corner of the state, which has a population of 41,000. At an elevation of 1mile (2km), the town sits where the Animas and La Plata Rivers join the San Juan River.

In the late nineteenth century, Farmington was a cattle and orchard area, where peach and walnut trees were grown. It was an area of land disputes and gunplay and of outlaws and card sharks. Today it is the major industrial and retail center of the Four Corners region, where New Mexico, Arizona, Colorado, and Utah come together.

Some of the finest trout fishing in the state is found here in the San Juan River. Nearby Durango and Telluride, in southwest Colorado, offer terrific snow skiing and snowboarding.

Two miles (3 km) north of town, at Lions Wilderness Park, the Black River Traders present a historical play that shows the culture clash between Mexicans, Indians, and Anglos at the turn of the twentieth century. This is a summer show presented in a sandstone outdoor amphitheater.

Farmington has an Apple Blossom Festival in April, and the Four Corners Hot-Air Balloon Rally in May. The two-day Totah Festival in September celebrates Indian and pioneer contributions to the Four Corners area. Indian dancing, Navajo rug exhibits, and auctions are some of the highlights.

There are bus and air services, including flights to Albuquerque.
Map ref: page 618 C5

GALLUP

Gallup, (population 19,200), is 23 miles (37 km) from the Arizona border in the northwestern part of the state. It is chiefly a trading center for the Navajo and Zuni peoples. Gallup has more than 100 trading posts, shops, and galleries along old Route 66, which passes through town south of the I-40.

The town's four-day Inter-tribal Ceremonial, held in early to mid-August, brings in Navajo, Zuni Pueblo, Hopi, Crow, Kiowa, Comanche, and Cheyenne peoples as well as thousands of tourists for dancing, crafts shows, and a rodeo. Native American dances are held every night during summer.

Gallup was a stagecoach stop until the Atchison, Topeka & Sante Fe Railroad arrived in 1881. Large coal deposits in the area attracted miners, and the town was incorporated in 1891. In the early part of the twentieth century, Gallup was the center of Navajo wool and

The Cochiti dam and power station on the Rio Grande is a good spot for fishing and water sports.

pinon nut trading. Gallup continued mining coal and attracting immigrants from throughout Europe until oil replaced coal as the country's main heat and energy source, after World War II, and the mines closed down.

The 640-acre (259-ha) Red Rock State Park, 3 miles (5 km) east of Gallup, hosts the Intertribal Ceremonies. Towering red sandstone cliffs watch over the austere park. Ancient Puebloan sites include petroglyphs and pictographs. A museum displays area history, pottery, kachina dolls, Hopi baskets, Apache masks and clothing, paintings, tack, and saddles. The park has a rodeo area, a natural amphitheater, two nature trails, and stables and camping.

The Gallup campus of the University of New Mexico, located high on a bluff above town, has 1,500 students.

The Gallup Cultural Center looks at prehistory and history in the area, with exhibits including Native American contributions and the development of the railroad. It is in the restored railroad station.

Gallup has flights to Albuquerque and bus and train services.
Map ref: page 618 A8

GILA CLIFF DWELLINGS NATIONAL MONUMENT

This national monument is located 42 miles (68 km) north of Silver City in the Gila National Forest. It is a rough ride over desolate territory to seven natural cavities

that indent the face of a cliff about 175 feet (53 m) above the canyon floor. Five of the openings contain rooms constructed during the late thirteenth century by people of the Mogollon Culture, when about a dozen families lived here.

The Mogollon had lived in pithouses elsewhere in the area from about AD 500. At approximately AD 1000 they began building their homes on the surface. These caves have 42 rooms.

A visitor center offers detailed pamphlets on the construction of the homes and the Native Americans who made them. It also has a museum with pottery, baskets, and tools discovered in the area. From there, visitors drive to a trailhead where a 1-mile (2-km) round-trip hike leads to the cliff dwellings.

The Gila National Forest, in the 1870s, was the center of a mining boom, of which ghost towns and old mining structures are the only reminders. Stream and lake fishing, and big game hunting are popular.

Nearby Silver City has flights to Albuquerque and bus services.
Map ref: page 623 N5

LAS CRUCES

Las Cruces (population 70,000) is an hour north of the Mexican border. It is a leading producer of alfalfa, chilies, onions, corn, cotton, and pecan nuts. It is home to the New Mexico State University and, with a growing base of manufacturers, is the largest business center in southern New Mexico.

The Gila cliff dwellings were used by a dozen or so families for about 40 years.

The first Spaniards passed through the area in 1535. In 1630, the tribe of Native Americans that lived here was wiped out by smallpox, and other diseases, after a Spanish mission was established here. Las Cruces became a stopover for caravans on El Camino Real, or "The Royal Road." In 1787, Mesilla Valley travelers came upon oxcart drivers killed by Apaches and erected crosses at the site. In 1830, travelers from Taos were also killed by Apaches and crosses were erected for them as well. That led to the name "La Placita de las Cruces," or "Little Place of the Crosses," which became shortened to "Las Cruces."

The Organ Mountains were named for their pipelike spires and pinnacles. They rise up to 5,000 feet (1,525 m) from the valley floor just east of Las Cruces. White Sands Missile Range, over San Augustin Pass through the Organ Mountains, employs about 9,000 Las Cruces residents.

New Mexico State University, with 4,000 workers, is the second largest employer. The campus is one of the largest in the country and dates back to an 1880s land grant. Agriculture is the major area of study and the university has a highly respected computer science program, and one of the nation's largest planetary observatories.

The 3-million-acre (1.2-million-ha) Gila National Forest consists of spectacular canyons and mountains. The forest surrounds the Gila Cliff Dwellings National Monument.

The New Mexico Museum of Natural History runs exhibits such as "The Life of Caves," "Fire," "Dinosaurs," and "Jupiter and its Moons." At the Branigan Cultural Center, the work of local artists is exhibited, as well as photographs and historical artifacts from Mesilla and Las Cruces.

About 3 miles (5 km) southwest from Las Cruces, Mesilla is home to restaurants, galleries, gift shops, and museums. One of the oldest missions in the Mesilla Valley, San Albino Church, was built in 1851 and reconstructed in 1906. The Gadsden Museum displays artifacts from Indian, Mexican, and early Anglo settlers.

La Cruces air services to Albuquerque and bus services.

Map ref: page 624 C8

LAS VEGAS

"Las Vegas" (population 16,500) in Spanish means "the Meadows." It is located at an elevation of 6,415 feet (1,957 m) in the foothills of the Sangre de Cristo Mountains in the northern part of the state, about 100 miles (161 km) east of Santa Fe. Las Vegas has tree-lined streets, antique shops, galleries, a wide range of Victorian homes as well as old adobe buildings, and a central plaza going back to the nineteenth century. Recreational opportunities, New Mexico Highlands University, and the Las Vegas Medical Center are here.

In 1823, Luis C. de Baca received a grant from the Mexican government on the shores of the

Adobe houses, in the historic Mesilla Plaza in Las Cruces.

Gallinas River where he and his 17 sons would raise sheep. However, the Comanches kept him from occupying most of it. Another grant, in 1833 to another group of Spanish ranchers, was tied to their building a central plaza, from which they could defend themselves from raiding tribes. The plaza became a trading center for wagon trains on the Sante Fe Trail. In 1846, the United States claimed the land and built Fort Union five years later.

With the arrival of the railroad in 1879, Las Vegas became a prominent commercial center, and some of the West's most notorious outlaws galloped in, such as Tommy the Poet, Little Jack the Cutter, Stuttering Tom, Flapjack Bill, the Durango Kid, and Scarface Charlie. By 1852, townspeople, fed up with the wild shooters, routinely used the windmill in the town plaza for hangings. In the twentieth century, Las Vegas continued to be a transportation center for sheep, and cattlemen spread across Mora and San Miguel counties. Today it has more than 900 buildings on the Federal Register of Historic Places.

The elegant Plaza Hotel is one of the classic buildings of the old West. It was restored during to accurately reproduce it from a century before, when its guests included Billy the Kid, Doc Halliday, and Big Nose Kate.

Three self-guiding tours move through the central plaza, the railroad district, and Carnegie Park—the location of many old homes and the Carnegie Library, built in 1803 and modeled for Thomas Jefferson's Monticello. The Theodore Roosevelt Rough Riders Museum and City Museum

Las Vegas main street. This is a place of hilly streets and a variety of building styles.

commemorate the Rough Riders' campaign in the Spanish American War of 1898. More than 40 percent of Teddy Roosevelt's Rough Riders were from New Mexico, and many were from Las Vegas. In addition to military artifacts, the museum displays relics from local history, including pioneer and Native American weapons, household items, and newspaper stories.

The 18,000-acre (7,290-ha) Las Vegas Wildlife Refuge, just east of Las Vegas, is home to prairie falcons, golden eagles, mule deer, and coyotes. Migrating sandhill cranes, long-billed curlews, geese, and ducks also come through. Hiking and a 7-mile (11-km) driving tour run through prairie, marsh, forest, and steep canyonlands.

Montezuma Hot Springs is located 5 miles (8 km) north of Las Vegas. According to legend, this series of hot springs was visited in the early sixteenth century by Aztec Indian Chief Montezuma, and was also used by local Indians for its curing powers. Today it is open to the public.

Montezuma Castle, built where two other hotels had burned down, was a failure as a resort complex and given up on by its railroad investors in 1903. Over the next 70 years, the 77-room stone hotel, which was across the road from Montezuma Hot Springs, was used by the YMCA, as a Baptist College, and as a Jesuit Seminary. In 1981, the philanthropist Armand Hammer turned it into the Armand Hammer United World College of the American West — it was an unusual

experiment in international education. With a US$45-million grant, restoration of the main building, the student housing, and other buildings on a 110-acre (45-ha) campus, around 200 teenagers from 70 countries study together. Their rigorous two-year curriculum includes workshops that promote inter-racial harmony.

Storrie Lake State Park, 6 miles (10 km) north of Las Vegas, has a 1,100-acre (446-ha) reservoir that is excellent for windsurfing and trout fishing. Las Vegas is serviced by buses and trains.

Map ref: page 619 H8

LINCOLN

Famous Old West outlaw Billy the Kid practiced his handiwork in this preserved historical town. It is in the Lincoln National Forest area in central-south New Mexico, 130 miles (209 km) northeast of Las Cruces. The town is a "living historical museum" with about 40 buildings going back to its old gunslinging days, and no fast-food or franchise motels are allowed.

Lincoln was settled in the late 1840s by farmers who built stone fortresses to guard against Apache Indian raids. In the late 1870s, merchants Tunstall and Murphy went to war in an engagement that split the town into opposite parties. When Tunstall was murdered, William Bonney, known as Billy the Kid, swore to avenge the death by killing all those involved. The Lincoln County War followed, culminating in a 5-day gun battle that drew national attention.

Lew Wallace, the governor of the New Mexico Territory at that time, declared an amnesty. Billy the Kid submitted to arrest and testified in court. However, he escaped and, when Pat Garrett was elected

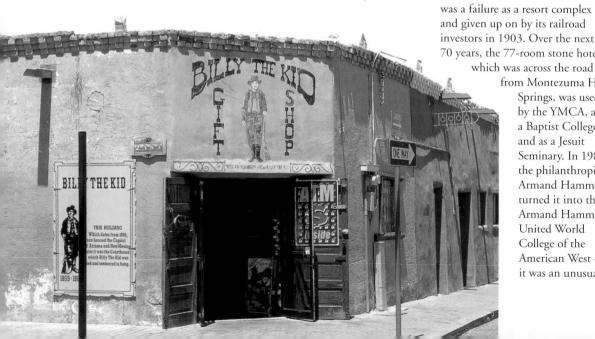

sheriff of Lincoln County, he arrested him, and yet again he escaped. Garrett tracked the Kid to Fort Sumner and shot him dead.

Old Lincoln Days are held from the first full Friday to the Sunday weekend in August. They include a parade, folk pageant, and living-history demonstrations.

Alamogordo, which is 65 miles (105 km) southwest of Lincoln, has bus and air services, including flights to Albuquerque.

Map ref: page 624 F5

LOS ALAMOS

This town, with a population of 19,000, is at an elevation of 7,410 feet (2,260 m). It is northwest of Santa Fe on the edge of the Sante Fe National Forest, and will always be famous for the development of the atomic bomb.

This was Ancient Puebloan territory, where thousands of ruins are hidden in the back country of the Pajarito Plateau. In 1918, the Los Alamos Ranch School was established by Detroit business-man, Ashley Pond. In 1942, the federal government selected the school for its top-secret maximum security site for the Manhattan Project, which, in a race with Germany and other countries, developed the first atomic bomb. In 1945, the first bomb was successfully tested at Trinity Site, 60 miles (97 km) northwest of Alamogordo. The flash could be seen as far away as Sante Fe, Gallup, and El Paso. Three weeks later, the bombs were dropped on Hiroshima and Nagasaki.

Los Alamos National Laboratory, where 3,000 civilian and military personnel worked on the bomb, has since grown into an organization of 9,000. Here they conduct research on nuclear weapons and other war technology, as well as research dealing with energy production, health, safety and environmental concerns, and astrophysics and life sciences.

The Bradbury Science Museum has displays on the Los Alamos National Laboratories, including the history of the Manhattan Project, displays on laser, geothermal, solar, and nuclear technology, and environmental studies.

At Fuller Lodge Art Center and Museum, the work of northern New Mexico painters and sculptors

The area around Los Alamos is dominated by mesas. Mesa is the name given to a small, isolated, flat-topped hill in the Southwest.

is exhibited. The log building is a National Historic Landmark.

The Los Alamos Historical Museum depicts the history of the Pajarito Plateau. Displayed are ancient axe heads, needles, potsherds, and arrowheads, as well as Manhattan Project items such as memos, pamphlets, and photographs. The Bandelier National Monument (see separate entry) is just south of Los Alamos.

There are bus and air services, including flights to Albuquerque.

Map ref: page 618 F8

PECOS NATIONAL MONUMENT

The extensive ancient pueblo found at this monument, located 29 miles (47 km) southeast of Santa Fe, thrived because of its location between the Plains and Pueblo peoples. The Franciscans established a mission in Pecos in 1620. A church built at the mission was destroyed during the Pueblo Revolt of 1680. When the Spanish recaptured the area, another church was built in 1717 on the same foundation, the ruins of which may be visited today. Between 1450 and 1600, the pueblo had 700 rooms built in a quadrangle around a plaza. The pueblo survived until 1838.

There are bus and air services, including flights to Albuquerque.

Map ref: page 618 G8

PETROGLYPH NATIONAL MONUMENT

This was the first national monument dedicated to prehistoric art.

Fifteen thousand petroglyphs, or prehistoric pictures, and five extinct volcanoes are found on this serpentine escarpment of volcanic rock located west of Albuquerque. White or gray lines are chipped into the dark rock. Petroglyphs here date from AD 700 to 1200. Between the fourteenth and seventeenth centuries BC, the Tiwa carved animals, birds, people, flute players, and kachina figures. They are reached by four short trails on the million-year-old lava flow.

Albuquerque has an international airport, bus and train services.

Map ref: page 624 C1

ROSWELL

With 50,000 residents, Roswell is the largest community in southeastern New Mexico. Its International UFO Museum and Research Center revisits the alleged crash of an alien spaceship near Roswell in 1947. The Roswell Museum and Art Center displays a huge array of arts and artifacts in its 17 galleries. Its Southwestern Collection of Paintings, Prints, and Sculpture displays works by Georgia O'Keefe, Stuart Davis, and John Martin.

Bottomless Lakes State Park, named for the seven sinkholes scattered about its grounds, offers fishing, windsurfing, camping, swimming, and hiking. Ten miles (16 km) northwest of Roswell, the 25,000-acre (7,625-ha) Bitter Lake National Refuge Area

has marshy grassland that provides refuge for migrating ducks, geese, and sandhill cranes.

Roswell has a small airport and bus services.

Map ref: page 624 G5

RUIDOSO

Ruidoso is a resort set in the White Mountain Wilderness Area of central-south New Mexico. Snow skiing, hiking, camping, fishing, cycling, hunting, and horseback riding are the activities in this town of 4,500, which is at 6,900 feet (2,104 m) where the hills are covered with pine, cedar, and aspen.

Ruidoso Downs Racetrack runs quarter horses and thoroughbreds from early May to early September. The Hubbard Museum of the American West focuses on the horse and its role in American history, and exhibits saddles, carriages, surreys, a Conestoga wagon, and 12-passenger stagecoach that goes back to 1866.

Ruidosa is serviced by buses.

Map ref: page 624 E5

Purple aster (Machaeranthera pinnatifida) at Petroglyph National Monument.

The Rio Grande Gorge bridge, west of Taos, is 650 feet (198 m) above the river.

SANTA FE

Santa Fe, founded in 1607, is the oldest capital city in the United States. It is where the vast desert meets the Rocky Mountains. Santa Fe has an ambience so strong that artists, photographers, and writers,

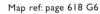

New Mexico seal, on the Capitol Building, Santa Fe.

and those in search of physical and spiritual healing, have been coming here since the early 1900s.

Brown adobe houses line narrow crooked streets in the foothills of the Sangre de Cristo Mountains. Centuries-old adobe churches overlook plazas, museums, and hotels. Some of the most highly prized art in the country is sold here, and the Santa Fe Opera has a wide following. Santa Fe not only has its own style, but it has many outdoor activities, such as wind-surfing, cycling, whitewater rafting, fishing, golf, and snow skiing.

Indians, Spaniards, and Anglos have contributed to Santa Fe's rich heritage but the Spanish influence dominates, as seen in street names, food, and architecture. Building codes preserve a look going back

three centuries. One of most traveled roads west was the Santa Fe Trail, a 1,000-mile (1,609-km) dirt track that ran from western Missouri into Santa Fe. In the 1860s, as many as 5,000 freight wagons a year took this road.

Mexico ruled New Mexico from Santa Fe until 1848, when the territory was claimed for the United States. In 1851, Santa Fe was given territorial status. The railroad arrived in 1879 and replaced the Santa Fe Trail in importance. Statehood came to New Mexico in 1912 and was met with a week-long fiesta in Santa Fe.

From early on, the sublime landscapes and inspiring skies attracted artists and painters. Later, scientists and their families moved in from Los Alamos, 35 miles (56 km) away.

Santa Fe has a number of first-rate museums, including the Museum of Fine Arts, where Southwestern art is displayed on a rotating basis.

Santa Fe's striking architecture starts with the state capitol, remodeled for US$34 million in 1992, and inspired by a Zia sun sign, which reflects the circle of life. The Cathedral of St Francis of Assisi, Mission San Miguel, and Loretto Chapel are among other stand-out buildings.

Santa Fe is well-known for its res-

taurant food that features tortilla chips with salsa or guacamole, fresh meat, and seafood grilled over mesquite or pecan-wood fires, and seasoned with green chilies.

Santa Fe is serviced by an airport and buses.
Map ref: page 618 G8

SILVER CITY

This town of 12,335 is in the foothills of the Pinos Altos Mountains at the southern edge of the Gila National Forest, about 125 miles (201 km) northwest of Las Cruces. Silver was discovered here in the late 1860s and cattle ranching took over when the bottom fell out of the silver market in 1893. Vast open-pit copper mines are seen at the Chino Mine and Phelps-Dodge mine. Western New Mexico State University, with 2,200 students, is located here.

Silver City's streets, sidewalks, and buildings maintain a Wild West mining feel. A short distance north the forested Mogollon Mountains provide some of the most beautiful scenery in the state.

Silver City has an airport with services to Albuquerque.
Map ref: page 623 N6

TAOS

Taos, with a population of 6,400, is on a plateau between the Rio Grande and Sangre de Cristo Mountains. It is about 80 miles (129 km) northeast of Santa Fe. Taos has lured writers and artists since the mid-nineteenth century. Galleries, studios, and shops occupy brown stucco buildings that surround the town plaza, which is the center of an original Spanish town.

San Francisco Street, Santa Fe, heart of the tourist area.

The Taos pueblo is the tallest in Southwest New Mexico, consisting of two five-story dwellings. It is a World Heritage Site and a National Historic Landmark. Nearby are the ruins of Mission San Geronimo de Taos, which was originally built in 1598. All that remain today are some sections of the massive walls and part of the original bell tower. Tours of the pueblo are available.

Also in Taos, in the third village, Ranchos de Taos, is the beautiful San Francisco de Asis mission church, built in 1772.

Taos Ski Valley is the best downhill ski area in the state. It has many good choices, which include one of the most formidable in the country. Above a Swiss-style village created in the wilderness, Taos displays a magnificent wall of "black" expert run verticals. Fifty-one percent is expert, 25 percent intermediate, and 24 percent beginner. The area rises from its 9,207-foot (2,808-m) base in a box canyon to 11,819 feet (3,605 m), and offers 1,094 acres (443 ha) of wide-open bowls, narrow trails, steeps, and gentle terrain. For the advanced powder hound, Taos Ski Valley and Telluride, Colorado, provide the most spectacular downhill ski challenges combined with the best ambience in the country.

Taos is known for its Mexican, New Mexican, and Southwestern food that is served at many different types of restaurants. Its Farmer's Market runs midsummer through October, offering fresh produce at the Taos Courthouse complex. It also has year-round recreational opportunities, such as snow skiing, rafting, camping, hiking, and cycling. There are bus services in Taos.
Map ref: page 618 G6

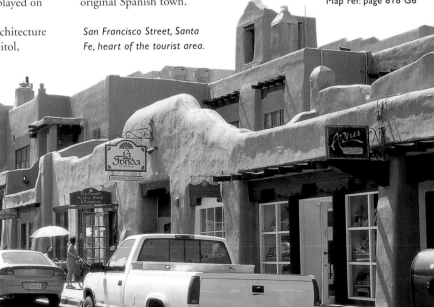

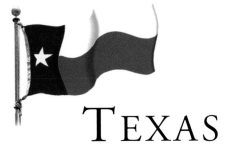

TEXAS

Texas is known, first and foremost, for its size. With a breadth and length of more than 700 miles (1,126 km), it's by far the largest of the lower 48 states, stretching from the Gulf of Mexico into the arid Southwest and high plains. The state's broad geographic range includes tropical swamps, beaches, desert, mountains, and broad grain fields, with Mexico stretching hundreds of miles across its southwest border. Much of Texas is dry, dusty, and brown until spring, when it is covered with a profusion of colorful wildflowers.

The west is desolate cactus and red rock territory. The north is cattle country on high plains. Central Texas has lovely rural scenery as well as high-tech and musical Austin, the state capital. South Texas is known for its Mexican heritage, the Latino cultural capital of San Antonio, and its vacation beaches and islands. East Texas has swamps, pine trees, bass fishing, and the nation's fourth-largest city, Houston, an international center for commerce, technology, and oil. The immense urban area of Dallas–Fort Worth joins on the north-central flats. Dallas is a modern city of corporate headquarters, while Fort Worth clings to Old West traditions.

Stetson-wearing cowboys have long been associated with Texas, especially in the cattle country in the north of the state.

The Spanish were the first European settlers. When Mexico, including Texas, became independent of Spain in 1821, Stephen F. Austin led an influx of settlers from the United States, who revolted against Mexican rule in 1835. The legendary defeat at the Alamo was followed by victory under Sam Houston at San Janice, and Texas enjoyed its independence for a decade before the republic joined the American Union in 1845.

Texas is a leader in oil production, agriculture, and manufacturing; it is also involved in the high-tech and space industries. It is home to President George W. Bush, as well as past presidents George Bush and Lyndon Baines Johnson.

State motto Friendship
State flag Adopted 1845
Capital Austin
Population 20,851,820
Total area (land and water)
267,277 square miles (692,247 sq km)
Land area 261,914 square miles
(678,357 sq km)
Texas is the second-largest state in size
Origin of name From a Native American word meaning "friends"
Nickname The Lone Star State
Abbreviations TX (postal), Tex.
State bird Mockingbird
State flower Bluebonnet
State tree Pecan
Entered the Union December 29, 1845 as the 28th state

STATE FEATURE

Big Bend National Park

The black-tailed jackrabbit (Lepus californicus) has oversized ears to allow body heat to escape easily in hot desert conditions.

Rugged, desolate, stark beauty characterizes Big Bend National Park, an 800,000-acre (324,000-ha) preserve located on the western "toe" of the state, 329 miles (529 km) from El Paso, 409 miles (658 km) from San Antonio, and 530 miles (853 km) from Dallas–Fort Worth. A state park was established here in 1933, and with the state donation of an additional 706,706 acres (286,216 ha), the United States established Big Bend as its 27th national park in 1944.

"Big Bend" is the course of the Rio Grande River, which marks the southern perimeter of the park and divides Texas from Mexico. It is here that the river dips for 100 miles (161 km) as it bumps into three mountain ranges and abruptly changes direction from southeast to northeast. Big Bend's wide range of geography, plants, and animal life, and the big river that curls through it, make it one of the country's top five national parks, although its remote location makes it far less-frequently visited than other national parks such as Yosemite, Yellowstone, and Glacier.

The park is situated in the Chihuahuan Desert, the largest in North America, which reaches west into New Mexico and south into four Mexican states. The squiggling ribbon of the Rio Grande flows through river cane and tamarisk vegetation, as well as mountain oases of conifer forests and shaded springs, providing amazing contrasts such as ferns and cacti living near each other. The dominant mountain range, the Chisos, consists of lava masses and peaks that climb to 7,835 feet (2,390 m). The unusual and sometimes unique plant and animal species found tucked away in the harsh desert secured for Big Bend the designation of International Biosphere Reserve from UNESCO, one of 250 such sites in the world.

The mountains and green valleys close to the Rio Grande are rich with birds that find refuge on this southern end of the central flyway and enjoy a diversity of habitat. The bird most often noted is the road runner, made famous by a cartoon of the same name, which, fueled by the moisture it extracts from snakes and lizards, tears along at 20 miles per hour (32 kph). Altogether, 430 species of birds live here— more than in any other national park in the United States or Canada. They range from small desert wrens, graybreasted jays, and hummingbirds to great blue herons, Mexican mallards, golden and bald eagles, red-tailed hawks, American kestrels, peregrine falcons, great horned owls, screech owls, and white-throated swifts. Two birds found only here in the United States are the colima warbler, a small yellow-and-gray song bird that nests in Boot Canyon and the Laguna Meadow, and the lucifer hummingbird. Cacti provide nests for the aptly named cactus wrens.

At least 75 species of mammals live in the park, including white-tailed and mule deer, foxes, prong-horns, coyotes, black bears, and mountain lions.

A common sight is the javelina, or collared peccary, which looks like a wild pig but is more closely related to tapirs and horses. Small herds feed in the early morning and late evening near campgrounds and the Chisos Mountain Lodge. Other small mammals include the black-tailed jackrabbit and kangaroo rat.

Ten species of amphibians and 56 species of reptiles also live here. And there are over 100 species of snakes, 22 of lizards, and four of turtles. The most venomous snakes include the Trans-Pecos copper-head, the western diamondback rattlesnake, the mottled rock rattlesnake, the Mojave rattlesnake, and the blacktail rattlesnake, none of which usually trouble visitors. Most commonly seen is the long, pink coachwhip snake, which is harmless.

Hairy tarantula spiders are commonly seen on roads in late summer and fall. Despite their repu-tation, they aren't poisonous or dangerous, and will bite only if threatened. Scorpions—15 species exist here—inject venom through the stinger on their tail, but none of the scorpions in the park are lethal.

The desert here can be colorful, with purple, blue, brown, orange, green, and yellow hues decorating the changing seasons. More than 70 species of cacti thrive here and produce splendid flowers, usually in early April. Cholla, prickly pear, southwestern barrel cactus, devil's claw, and strawberry cactus are well represented. At higher elevations, pinon pine, oak, and juniper cover meadows and hills. The Chisos Mountains reveal a bounty of pine, cypress, Douglas fir, maple, and quaking aspen.

Fishing is good in the park, with blue, channel, and flathead catfish. Anglers can also hook carp, small-mouth buffalo, longnose gar, river carpsucker, and freshwater drum. Mexican stoneroller, huahua shiner, and Big Bend gambusia are particular to the park.

This is a dry place, where the desert receives only 5–8 inches (125–200 mm) of rain a year, and the mountains around 15 inches (375 mm). June and August average temperatures rise over 90°F (over 32°C) and slip just beneath 70°F (21°C) at night. October to November and March to April are the best times to visit. Autumn, when water levels reach 4 feet (1.2 m), is best for river running, while spring is best for bird-watching and wildflowers. Summer rains make August the coolest summer month.

Because of vast distances between towns, park visi-tors should ensure the gas tank is filled when driving to the park. Entry to the park is from Alpine on the west or from Marathon on the east. Alpine is a retail center and shipping point for the huge ranching area, headquarters for mining companies, home of Sul Ross State University, and offers B&B lodgings in historic buildings. The name Marathon came from a sea cap-tain who said the area reminded him of Marathon in Greece. The historic Gage Hotel, with original pine

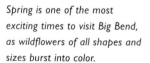

Spring is one of the most exciting times to visit Big Bend, as wildflowers of all shapes and sizes burst into color.

floors and woodwork and ranch-style furnishings dating back to the 1920s, is located here. A motel for visitors is found in Chisos Basin, just beneath Casa Grande, an impressive stack of rocks rising 7,325 feet (2,234 metres). The park headquarters and main visitor center are located at Panther Junction, in the northern central area of the park. The park has three drive-in camp sites and back-country camp sites that require permits. All camp sites and campgrounds are assigned on a first-come, first-served basis.

Paved roads, improved dirt roads and back-country dirt roads provide vehicle access within the park. The Ross Maxwell Scenic Drive, which runs west beside the Chisos Mountains to the historic farming settlement of Castolon Valley and to the mouth of the Santa Elena Canyon, is an outstanding route with diverse geography. The Rio Grande Village Drive, Maverick Drive, and Basin Drive are also popular. Keep the gas tank full because gas is available only at two widely separated park points—Panther Junction and Rio Grande Village. Drivers stuck in sand may free their vehicles by deflating the tires to 15 psi (103 kPa) and slowly accelerating. Car doors should be locked to prevent petty thievery.

The park has more than 200 miles (322 km) of trails that vary in distance from short walks to longer treks of 33 miles (53 km), and in elevation from 1,800–7,835 feet (549–2,390 m). The 1.7-mile (2.7-km) round-trip Santa Elena Canyon Trail, 5.6-mile (9-km) round-trip Window Trail, 4.6-mile (7.4-km) round-trip Lost Mine Trail, 4-mile (6.4-km) round-trip Pine Canyon Trail, and 14-mile (23-km) round-trip South Rim Loop are among those recommended for day hikes. Top back-country trails include the 14-mile (23-km) Cross Canyon Trail, the 32-mile (51-km) Outer Mountain Loop, and the 11-mile (18-km) Dodson Trail. Horseback riding is permitted on two trails for people who bring their own horses and supplies as there is no riding stable.

In 1899, Dr Robert Hill, assisted by a local trapper who knew the canyons, was the first to float down the Rio Grande, which skirts the southern edge of the park. He put in at Presidio, 55 miles (88 km) west of the park, and boated to the mouth of the Pecos River, near Langtry, taking a month to complete the trip. Unlike the tame upper reaches of the river, the current is strong and full through the park. Today it typically takes two weeks for a river runner to cover the 245 miles (394 km) of Rio Grande wilderness, which includes 118 miles (190 km) of park through Santa Elena, Mariscal, and Boquillas canyons. The Lower Canyons in the park, which extend for 83 miles (134 km), appeal to advanced river runners. Above the park, Colorado Canyon offers moderate rapids. The canyons offer spectacular scenery and good white water, so they are more popular than the entire river stretch.

Canoe, kayak and inflatable rafts are used to run the Rio Grande. People bring their own equipment or rent it at local outfitters, and must obtain a use permit from a ranger station. Another way is to sign on with licensed river outfitters in the area's towns that provide one- to nine-day trips through remote canyons. Guided tours for bird-watching, mountain biking, and horseback riding may also be arranged.

Immense ranches dominate this scenic part of the state, but hardy communities also offer a variety of recreation and entertainment facilities.

An unusual activity, said to be good for the skin, is to have a mud bath on the banks of the Rio Grande River.

Mesa, Big Bend National Park.

Places in TEXAS

ABILENE

This city of 117,061 people is located in an area of rolling, grassy hills known as the Prairies, at a point 180 miles (290 km) west of Dallas–Fort Worth. One of the first inhabitants were the nomadic South Plains Native Americans, who were drawn to the huge buffalo herds that migrated through the Callahan Divide, near Abilene, in late fall and early spring. In the 1870s came the Creek Native Americans as well as white buffalo hunters. When the buffalo were wiped out, the Comanches—the original inhabitants— lost their source of food, clothing, tools, and shelter. They departed, opening the door to farms, ranches, and railroads.

The Texas and Pacific Railroad established a railhead here in 1881, and the cattle-loading town was named after the prosperous Abilene, a town in Kansas. It was a tough, wild place that grew with ranching, agriculture, oil, and the military at Dyess Air Force Base. When the city celebrated its centennial in 1981, it set up a demonstration oil-drilling rig on the county fairgrounds to illustrate the techniques of "making hole." By accident it struck oil that was enough for a modest profit.

From its early days, circuit preachers held sway in this territory, leading the way for contemporary Christian fundamentalists. The city has been called "the buckle of the Bible belt," and its three universities are religious institutions—Abilene Christian University, Church of Christ (4,600 students); Hardin–Simmons University, Baptist (2,000 students); and McMurray University, Methodist (1,600 students).

The Abilene Zoo, one of the five largest in the state, is divided into three habitats—the Texas Plains, the African Veldt, and the Herpetarium. The Plains exhibits animals native to West Texas, such as bison, pronghorn, javelina, coyote, wild turkey, prairie dogs and road runners. The zoo's 10,300-square-foot (979-sq-m) Discovery Center compares life zones in the American Southwest and Mexico with similar areas in East Africa and Madagascar. Its comparative habitat displays include invertebrates, fish, reptiles, birds, and small mammals.

Dyess Air Force Base is the home of Air Combat Command's historic seventh wing, which during World War II bombed Japanese supply lines in Southeast Asia, including the Bridge over the River Kwai that became famous in a movie of the same name. During the Korean War in 1952, Dyess was a Strategic Air Command Base. Currently it flies B-1B Lancers and C-130H Hercules planes. A collection of 25 military aircraft from World War II and the Korean and Vietnam Wars are on display at the base.

Fort Phantom Hill, located 10 miles (16 km) north of Abilene, was one of four US Army forts built in the 1850s to protect traders and settlers against Comanches. Later, it became a way station for the Butterfield Overland Mail, and was used by Confederate forces in the Civil War. Chimneys and foundations are the principal ruins along with a stone commissary, guardhouse, and powder magazine. The site is open to the public and offers interpretative signs.

Grace Museum, housed in the 1909 Grace Hotel that is listed on the National Register of Historic Places, is a cultural center. Its local history museum presents controversial subjects such as the Ku Klux Klan, and the children's museum offers hands-on art and science exhibits. Its art museum features changing and permanent exhibits.

An Abilene Historic Landmark, the Paramount Theater, is a beautiful art deco building that inside displays slow, drifting clouds and twinkling stars on a blue sky. Neon and incandescent cove lighting alter the color and brightness of the sky beyond the archways and bell tower with twin domed turrets. Classic films, art films, plays, and concerts are presented here throughout the year. Abilene can be accessed by I-20, plane or bus.
Map ref: page 624 C7

AMARILLO

Amarillo, which means "yellow" in Spanish, is in the center of the Texas Panhandle, located at the edge of the Great Plains. It is a flat, windy city of 174,000 people situated 337 miles (542 km) northwest of Dallas–Fort Worth. Its cowboy reputation is evidenced by its jeans-and-Stetson clothes and the state's largest cattle auction, held every Tuesday morning at the Western Stockyards.

Amarillo began with a buffalo-hide tent camp for railroad workers in 1887 and came to be known as "the world's biggest truckstop" for catering to trucks streaming across the southern half of the nation. Its vast Panhandle Oil and Gas field struck in 1916 was the world's largest single petroleum deposit until the Arabian oil fields were discovered in 1930. The area is also the source for 90 percent of the world's helium, used in aerospace technology, welding, cryogenics, and as a leak detector.

Its cattle auction, where stockyards annually sell off more than 300,000 head of cattle, is open to the public. Auctions take place in a dirt-floor ring, where the auctioneer sits at a microphone, calling out prices to the audience. Cattlemen bring their animals in trailers to the stockyard; here they are routed through a maze of pens, one owner's lot at a time. Prospective buyers raise their hands or shout out their assent to a price; afterwards they load up the cattle they have bought to take home or to a slaughterhouse.

At the Amarillo Museum of Art, a broad range of paintings, prints, photographs, sculptures, and textures from twentieth-century artisans is displayed. The three-story building designed by Edward Stone is the cultural and fine arts center for West Texas. Its permanent collection includes the works of Georgia O'Keefe, Fritz Scholder, Franz Kline, Jack Boynton, and Elaine de Koonig. Changing exhibits feature a wide range of themes—everything from European masters to cowboy art.

Cadillac Ranch, a must-see for visitors to Amarillo, is a quirky tribute to the freedom of the open road.

Austin is acclaimed for its live music, with the city's large number of clubs attracting would-be stars from all over Texas.

Also in Amarillo, the American Quarter Horse Heritage Center and Museum features many interactive exhibits, video presentations, artifacts, and live demonstrations on the history and significance of this unique American breed. Special riding programs are presented in an outdoor demonstration area.

Amarillo can be reached by car on I-40, I-27, or by bus, and it has an international airport.

Map ref: page 620 A9

AUSTIN

Located in the south-central part of the state, 190 miles (306 km) south of Dallas–Fort Worth, Austin is much more than the state capital. The city of 575,000 people is also the state center of art and education, where academics, musicians, writers, sculptors, and artists gravitate for creative opportunities. It is the home of the esteemed University of Texas, whose 50,000 students enjoy a 357-acre (145-ha) campus with 120 buildings. In recent decades it has also become a booming high-tech metropolis, with a scientific base that includes Texas Instruments, Motorola, IBM, Dell Computers, and Apple Computers. The city's counterculture has spawned hippie musicians, "redneck rockers," and "cosmic cowboys", including Willie Nelson and Waylon Jennings, which has given birth to performance centers

and recording studios. Scores of restaurants and bars offer live music ranging from blues, folk, country, and jazz to zydeco, reggae, and rock.

Austin is a place of historic and modern architecture, splendid parks, oak trees, rolling hills, clear lakes, and the Colorado River that curls through its center. Barton Springs, a city swimming hole where artesian waters remain a cool 68°F (20°C) year-round, attracted Spanish priests in 1730, the start of settlement here. Traders built cabins and a stockade in what is now downtown Austin in 1838. When Mirabeau B. Lamar became President of the Republic of Texas in 1838, he chose the site as the republic's capital, and it was named after colonizer Stephen F. Austin. In 1883, the University of Texas was established, adding the town's educational dimension. Austin remained a college and government town until the Tracor Electronics Company arrived in the 1960s. Hundreds of other high-tech companies, attracted by the relatively low cost of living and high-quality work force, poured in. Austin's music industry is significant enough to place it with Nashville and New York on the national scene.

Preserving its nineteenth-century architectural history, Austin has designated nine different historic districts, and the city offers free guided-walking tours for several

of these. True to the Texas tradition of bigger is better, Austin's Capitol building stands 7 feet (2.1 m) higher than the national Capitol in Washington DC, and is the largest state capitol building in the country. Built in 1888, it is of Renaissance Revival style. It took enough pink granite to fill 15,000 railroad cars to construct it, and 85,000 square feet (8,075 sq m) of copper to cover its roof. The interior contains 7 miles (11.3 km) of oak, pine, cherry, cedar, ash, walnut, and mahogany wainscoting. The 500 doors and 900 windows are framed in oak, pine, and cherry. The magnificent structure has 392 rooms. Its 9-foot-tall (2.7-m) doors are supported by 8-pound (3.6-kg) brass hinges. The state's symbol, the Lone Star, is cast into the doorknobs, and the property's iron fence has 8,000 stars in its design. Free tours are given daily, and the entrance foyer and rotunda are always open for self-guided tours.

Austin has more than a score of small art galleries tucked away in its low-rent districts. Some are

co-ops, some are run by individual artists. The O. Henry Museum preserves the memorabilia of William Sydney Porter (O. Henry was his pen name), as well as period furnishings that go back to the late nineteenth century.

The Romanesque-style Driskill Hotel, layered like a fancy wedding cake, was once used for legislative meetings and gubernatorial inaugural balls. There is also an elegant Louisiana Bayou-style house built by the French delegation in 1841, featuring window glass and furniture imported from France, and hardware from England.

The Slaughter–Leftwich Vineyards produce an often-awarded Texas Chardonnay as well as excellent Cabernet Sauvignon, Sauvignon Blanc, and Chenin Blanc wines. The Cells Brewery has also won awards for its Belgian-style beers and ales, and the Hill Country Brewing and Bottling Company produces its own highly touted local beer.

Austin claims to have the largest bat population in the world. Between April and October up to 750,000 Mexican free-tail bats emerge at sunset from the Congress Avenue Bridge over the Colorado River, eating as many as 30,000 bugs a night.

Austin can be reached by I-35, by bus, and it has an international airport.

Map ref: page 630 F6

Austin's Capitol building was built using pink granite.

BEAUMONT

Beaumont, Port Arthur, and Orange form what is called the "Magic Triangle" in the southeast corner of the state, near the Louisiana border. All three cities have deep-water ports and oil refineries and, in their extensive rural surroundings, harvest rice and crawfish. This area has also been called the "Cajun Triangle" because of the great influence of Cajun culture, and "The Golden Triangle" because of the oil that brought wealth in the twentieth century.

Beaumont, with a population of 115,00, is 275 miles (442 km) southeast of Dallas–Fort Worth. About a third of the population is African–American, one of the largest percentages in the state. In 1901 the oil gusher at a salt-dome hill called Spindletop just south of town became the richest oil field in the United States, leading to the formation of contemporary oil giants such as Texaco, Chevron, Mobil, and Exxon. Beaumont is the state's fourth-largest port.

Beaumont's 36-block Old Town features historic houses that have been turned into shops. The Babe Didrikson Zaharias Museum celebrates the greatest female American athlete of the first half of the twentieth century, who was from Beaumont. The Spindletop–Gladys City Boomtown re-creates the world's first oil boomtown with typical clapboard buildings of the era, which include a photo studio, post office, saloon, livery stable, blacksmith shop, surveyor's office, and wooden oil derricks.

Beaumont also has steamboat, fire-department, and energy museums; the McFaddin–Ward restored beaux-arts colonial mansion; and a French historic pioneer settlement

Big Thicket Natural Preserve offers visitors the chance to see vast carpets of native flowers in bloom.

house. Bird sanctuaries owned by the Houston Audubon Society, and 500-acre (203-ha) Tyrell Park, which offers golf, archery, horseback riding, botanical gardens, and a cattail marsh, make for popular outings. At the Port of Beaumont an observation deck gives a good view of the city's shipping industry.

Beaumont may be reached on I-10, and by bus or plane.
Map ref: page 631 N6

BIG THICKET NATIONAL PRESERVE

This 100,000-acre (40,500-ha) preserve of virgin pines, underbrush, and marshland is located in the Piney Woods section of the state, a broad swath of territory running north from Beaumont on the eastern edge of the state all the way to Texarkana on the Arkansas border. Sabine, Davey Crockett, Angelina, and Sam Houston national forests also lie in this region, bringing the total parkland to 750,000 acres (303,750 ha); however, only Big Thicket is completely protected from timber harvesting, which goes back to the nineteenth century as the chief industry here.

Big Thicket is pierced by the bayous, creeks, and sloughs that feed into the Neches River, and swamps that become flood plains during rains. Forests, swamps, prairies, and deserts produce almost a hundred different soil types, which combined with 55–60 inches (1,375–1,500 mm) of rain a year produce more plant communities than any other area of comparable size in North America. The land is so thickly covered and laced with waterways that even the indigenous Caddo and Atakapa had trouble getting through.

The preserve boasts 85 species of trees, more than 60 species of shrubs and nearly a thousand species of flowering plants. Animals include deer, coyotes, bobcats, racoons, beavers, otters, gray foxes, armadillos, feral hogs, squirrels, rabbits, alligators, turtles, and snakes. More than 300 bird species are found here, among them the pileated woodpecker, wood ducks, and the yellow-billed cuckoo.

The main tourist office for Big Thicket is at its Turkey Creek Unit, 8 miles (12.9 km) north of Kountze. Eight hiking trails, ranging from less than 1 mile (1.6 km) to 18 miles (29 km), are maintained. Mosquito repellent is essential during the warm, wet months, and the weather must be considered—trails get flooded during downpours.

Canoeing is an excellent way to visit the park, assuming the possession of a good map, because this is an easy place to get lost in the rivers, sloughs, creeks, and bayous. A navigable 93-mile (150-km) course runs from Steinhagen Lake to Cooks Lake. Another 49-mile (79-km) route extends from Saratoga to Beaumont, and a 37-mile (60-km) paddle connects

Village Mills and the Neches River. Riverbank and sandbar camping is possible with the possession of a back-country use permit.

The 4,800-acre (1,944-ha) Alabama–Coushatta Native American Reservation lies adjacent to the preserve's Big Sandy Creek unit, and may be visited by the public. About 500 people live on the reservation, where pine-needle basketry, other arts and crafts, as well as outside jobs provide sustenance.

A number of state highways and US-69, US-190, and US-96 provide car and bus access to the Big Thicket Preserve. There is an airport at nearby Groves, while Houston to the south has an international airport. The greater Big Thicket region can be accessed by I-30 or I-20 by car or bus, or via Texarkana and Longview in the north, which both have airports.
Map ref: page 631 M5

BROWNSVILLE

This is the southernmost city of Texas, located about 500 miles (805 km) south of Dallas–Fort Worth and across the border from its Mexican sister city of Matamoros. Brownsville is a bilingual city with 134,267 residents; people from both sides of the border frequently cross the three international bridges to shop, visit, and work.

The city is known for its shrimp fleet and its dual-frontier *maquiladora* manufacturing program, which includes Fortune 500 companies among scores of firms operating on both sides of the border. A major seaport and railhead, Brownsville exports agricultural products from the Rio Grande Valley and Mexico.

This is a typical sunset silhouette in oil-mining towns such as Beaumont.

Texans are proud of their "Lone Star" state, a name symbolized in their state flag.

During the nineteenth century, Brownsville and Matamoros were enemies, engaging in war and banditry. A boundary dispute between the United States and Mexico led to the construction of a US fort across from Matamoros, which provoked the 1846–48 Mexican–American War. Mexican troops attacked the fort, killing Major Jacob Brown, for whom the town would be named. During the 1861–65 Civil War, Brownsville supplied Texas cotton to Europe, avoiding the Union stockade on the Texas coast. The last battle of the Civil War was fought five weeks after Robert E. Lee's surrender at Appomattox, at Palmito Ranch, east of Brownsville. Union troops attacked from Brazos Island and were defeated by Confederate forces led by Colonel Rip Ford.

Brownsville is popular with bird watchers, who have spotted more than 370 species in the refuges and

Adobe buildings are seen in towns along the Mexico border, such as Brownsville.

wild places around the city. The convergence of two major flyways brings an abundance of northern birds migrating for the winter. At the Sabal Palm Grove Sanctuary, the rare green jay, the chachalaca or Mexican pheasant, olive sparrow, white-tipped dove, green- and red-crowned parakeets, least grebe, buff-bellied hummingbird, kiskadee flycatcher, and black-bellied whistling duck may be seen. The 172-acre (70-ha) sanctuary protects the last remaining sabal palm grove in the delta. These trees reach heights of 20–48 feet (6–15 m) and are topped with a feathery crown.

Brownsville has scores of historic buildings of Spanish Colonial, Gothic, and Renaissance Revival architecture. Historic Brownsville Museum, housed in a 1928 Southern Pacific depot, displays the Spanish Colonial Revivalist style. It contains photographs, exhibits, and artifacts from the area, as well as local military history.

Brownsville visitors can easily walk across bridges to Matamoros and its gift shops, markets, night Brownsville has an international airport, and can also be reached by car on US-77, or by bus.
Map ref: page 632 J10

BRYAN–COLLEGE STATION

These towns join together in an agricultural area 165 miles (265 km) south of Dallas–Fort Worth, where their combined population is 125,000. Stephen F. Austin's colonists settled in this area between 1821 and 1831. Today, almost year-round hunting, fishing, and camping are popular at the nearby streams and woodlands. College Station is home to Texas

A & M University, the state's first public institution, established in 1876. The university is known for its Cadet Corps and ROTC (Reserve Officers Training Corps), whose graduates have served by the thousands in World Wars I and II, Korea, Vietnam, and Iraq. The town is noted for research in the areas of agriculture, animal pathology, saltwater and freshwater fisheries, engineering, and nuclear technology. The George Bush Presidential Library and Museum is located on the Texas A & M campus. The 69,000-square-foot (6,555-sq-m) building is dedicated to the preservation and exhibition of official records, personal papers, and memorabilia from the life and career of the former President, whose son George W. Bush became President in 2001.

Bryan–College Station is accessible by car on US-6 and US-21, and by plane or bus.
Map ref: page 631 H5

CORPUS CHRISTI

The deep-water port of Corpus Christi, located 377 miles (607 km) south of Dallas–Fort Worth, is a modern port city. Gutzon Borglum, the builder and sculptor of Mt Rushmore, built a 2-mile (3.2-km) seawall in the heart of this city's business district with steps leading into the water, joining urban structures with the sea. Much of the focus of this city of 275,000 people is on sand, sea, sun, and partying—college students throng here during spring break for the more than 100 miles (161 km) of beaches on nearby Padre and Mustang Islands, which have the best sand along the Texas coast.

The Texas State Aquarium is the largest in the country. It features close-up views of the Gulf of Mexico in a wide variety of marine habitats, including an artificial reef community created by the massive leg of an offshore oil rig, and other exhibits containing more than 250 species of marine life in 350,000 gallons (13,248 hl) of sea water. The aquarium is home to the only albino alligator in captivity. "The Wonderful World of Sherman's

Lagoon" features stars of Jim Toomey's comic strip who explain lagoons, barrier reefs, and the animals that inhabit them. The Conservation Pavilion has water turtles and Texas otters among its occupants.

Corpus Christi visitors can enjoy greyhound racing.

The Corpus Christi Museum of Science and History offers hands-on exhibits. Visitors may explore a 1554 Spanish shipwreck, identify local shells and birds, see live alligators and other South Texas reptiles, and walk among native plants.

Corpus Christi also has botanical gardens, a greyhound racetrack, and a zoo. Boat trips in Corpus Christi Bay visit dolphins in their natural habitat. Fishing is possible from municipal piers, jetties, beaches, and the seawall, as well as from charter boats. Anglers hook sheepshead, sand and speckled trout, redfish, flounder, catfish, whiting, drum, pompano, and Spanish mackerel. Deep-sea anglers cruising Gulf waters take tarpon, sailfish, wahoo, king mackerel, bonito, red snapper, and jewfish.

The USS Lexington Museum on the Bay is housed in a vintage wartime aircraft carrier that served longer and set more records than any other carrier in the US Navy. The Lefty Frizzell Country Music Museum is dedicated to a local boy who made it big in country music. And the 110-mile (177 km) Padre National Seashore is one of the last natural seashores in the nation.

Corpus Christi may be reached by car on I-37 and US-35, or by bus; it has an international airport.
Map ref: page 633 J5

The John F. Kennedy Memorial in Dallas was designed by architect Philip Johnson.

CRYSTAL CITY

This town of 8,224 people is located 110 miles (177 km) southwest of San Antonio on the South Texas Plains and is the seat of Zavala County. It is a primary center for packing, processing, and shipping vegetables, and the commercial hub for a large ranching area. This winter-garden area produces large quantities of onions, carrots, tomatoes, and peppers. But it is best known for its spinach crop, and its statue of Popeye, the cartoon character who devours spinach to gain incredible strength.

Crystal City may be reached by car on US-83 and by bus. The nearest airport is in San Antonio.
Map ref: page 632 D3

DALLAS

Dallas is the best-known place in the state. Its 1.1 million residents make it the ninth-largest city in the country and second after Houston in Texas. John F. Kennedy was assassinated in Dallas; the TV series "Dallas" was shot here; the Dallas Cowboy football team plays here; and big corporations such as J.C. Penney, and organizations like the Boy Scouts, have their headquarters here. Dallas has a spectacular skyline designed by top architects, sweltering summers, strong cultural interests, and many colleges. It's a conservative, white-collar, office metropolis of a commercial bent with more shopping centers and retail space per capita than any other US city. It also takes its religion seriously, as shown

by the Methodist and Baptist churches here, which are the largest in the world.

"If it doesn't sell in Dallas, it won't sell," say buyers who come to some 32 wholesale fashion and furnishing markets each year. Dallas is the Southwest's leading banking center, second in the nation in insurance company headquarters, third in the nation in "million-dollar" Fortune 500 companies, and number two nationally in convention business.

Dallas is also a place of originality. The nation's first convenience store, 7-Eleven, opened here in 1927. In 1958, engineer Jack Kilby invented the microchip at Texas Instruments. Door-to-door cosmetics sales leapt forward with the "house party" concept of Mary Kay, founded by Dallas housewife and widow Mary Kay Ash in 1963. The company now has hundreds of thousands of sales people in more than 20 countries and is listed on the New York Stock Exchange.

Balancing its business concentration, Dallas set aside a 60-acre (24-ha) downtown arts district, where historic buildings have been preserved, theater and concert performances are given, and museums and artwork mix past with present. The Dallas Museum of Art is the biggest draw, housing thousands of items ranging from prehistoric art to contemporary painting and sculpture. Permanent exhibits focus on pre-Cortisan, African, nineteenth-century

and early modern European, and eighteenth-century to post-World War II American collections. The Museum of the Americas displays North, Central, and South American art from pre-Hispanic times through the mid-twentieth century. A re-created Mediterranean villa presents top silver and European furniture collections, impressionistic paintings, and Chinese porcelain.

Like many American cities, affluent Dallas shops have moved out from downtown. The famous Nieman-Marcus department store is still located downtown, but others have relocated in malls surrounded by suburban housing. More than 200 restaurants and specialty shops are located below ground in a network of tunnels that provide refuge from hot summers and cold winter winds.

The world's largest steam locomotive, a 1903 depot, and 1930s passenger car are preserved at the Age of Steam Railroad Museum. The Biblical Arts Center features world art from the early biblical era. The Dallas Memorial Center for Holocaust Studies is dedicated to the Jewish experience in Europe during World War II.

The African-American Museum, founded in 1974 as part of the Bishop College Library, houses one of the largest collections of African–American art in the country. Artistic, cultural, and historic items are preserved, and there is a religious center and African–American women's archives.

The Reunion Tower in Dallas is a stunning example of modern architecture.

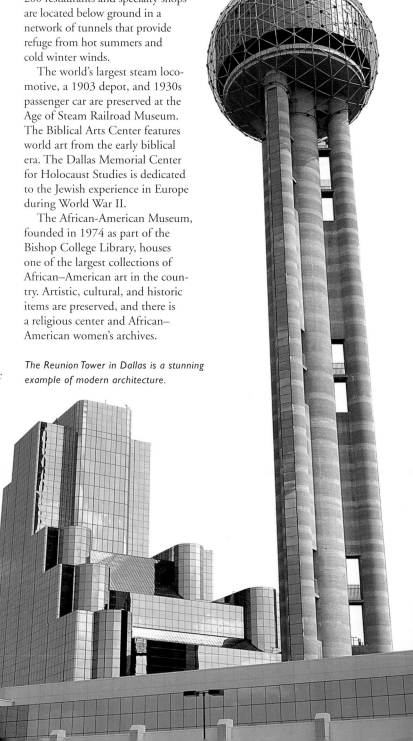

The Dallas World Aquarium, the Dallas Zoo, a 66-acre (27-ha) arboretum and botanical garden, and a firefighters museum that has an 1884 horse-drawn steamer and a 1936 ladder truck are among other Dallas attractions. Six Flags Over Texas is the city's theme-park answer to Disney World, while the State Fair of Texas held in the fall draws more than three million people to the 277-acre (112-ha) Fair Park.

Dallas is a big professional sports city. The Dallas Cowboys won National Football League

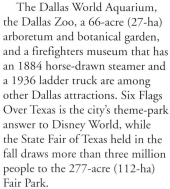

Super Bowls in 1993, 1994, and 1996. The major league baseball team, the Texas Rangers, play at the ballpark in Arlington, which relives earlier days with a red-brick façade, natural grass, and a pedestrian park in center field. It even has jogging paths. The Dallas Mavericks of the National Basketball Association, the Dallas Stars of the National Hockey League, and professional indoor and outdoor soccer teams also play here. Mesquite Championship Rodeo, with Friday and Saturday night weekly performances from April through September, began in 1958. Barbecue plates of spicy meat dishes are popular rodeo grub. And the New Year's Day Cotton Bowl is one of college football's big annual games.

Unlike many American cities, Dallas did not begin because of its port, or railroad, or fort, or discovery of gold. It began as one log cabin built in north-central Texas in 1840, and grew as a promotion, a place with fertile black farmland but no river connection to the sea, as claimed. Surrounding cotton fields led to its manufacturing of cotton gin machinery, dresses, and women's hats. Later, railroad lines and oil money helped it continue its ascent as the banking and commercial center of Texas.

Dallas has an international airport and may be reached by car on I-20, I-35, I-30, I-45, and by bus or cross-country train, which runs between Chicago and Los Angeles.
Map ref: page 627 J7

EL PASO

With 600,000 residents, El Paso is the largest US city on the Mexican border. Its sister city, Juarez, is the largest Mexican city on the US border, and together they have a population of about two million people. El Paso is situated in an ancient mountain pass, from which its name derives, and is surrounded by desert mountains. It is a Texas city that is out there by itself on the far western thumb of the state, closer to three other state capitals—Santa Fe, Phoenix, and Chihuahua City—than to Austin, and closer to Los Angeles than Houston. It is also in the mountain-time zone, unlike the rest of Texas. El Paso is 617 miles (993 km) from Dallas–Fort Worth.

El Paso is greatly influenced by Mexican culture, and its *maquiladora*, or twin plant industry with Juarez, which utilizes cheap Mexican labor and US management, is its driving economic force. Boots and jeans are two of the big products manufactured here. Downtown streets are paved with black cement squares, as in Mexico. The city has large shopping malls that cater to Mexican shoppers coming across the border, and to Mexican street vendors who have smuggled untaxed products across the line. Tourists shop in El Paso and gamble in Juarez.

El Paso receives only 8 inches (200 mm) of rain a year, and has very hot summers and mild winters. Air pollution from industry is heavy, except during spring and late fall. Long-time staples Egyptian cotton, Messilla Valley chili, and sweet onions make this a rich agricultural area.

El Paso del Norte ("The Pass of the North") was first discovered by Europeans in 1581 and later provided access for Spanish colonists. In 1598 Don Juan de Onate and several hundred conquistadors came looking for gold. Sixty-one years later a Spanish mission was founded in what is now Juarez. A village grew up around it that became an important stop on the Camino Real, or Royal Road, connecting Chihuahua City and Santa Fe, and later became the first road in North America—the Chihuahua–Santa Fe Trail.

Shoppers will find bargains galore in the markets of El Paso.

The US Army established Fort Bliss in 1848 to defend the area against Apache attacks. Two stage-coach lines were established during the California Gold Rush of 1849. In 1881 the Southern Pacific Railroad opened up trade when it reached El Paso from California. For the next 40 years El Paso was an important part of "The Wild West," where gunfighters, soldiers of fortune, banditos, cattle rustlers, and Texas Rangers fought. Among the famous marshals of that time were Wyatt Earp, Bat Masterson, and Pat Garrett. General Black Jack Pershing's campaign against Pancho Villa in 1916 strengthened the military presence at Fort Bliss and ended the lawless era.

Today Fort Bliss is a US Army Air Defense Center, which offers combat training for allied nations.

Its museums have displays and dioramas concerning the history of air defense, and a replica of the original adobe fort.

The El Paso Zoo exhibits more than 700 animals and 200 species, and is a major attraction for West Texas, southern New Mexico and northern Mexico. El Paso also has an auto racetrack, several graceful old Spanish missions, a fascinating science center, railroad museum, and the Tigua Native American Reservation—Ysleta del Sur Pueblo—which is the oldest community in Texas. Its Border Patrol Museum offers uniform, canine, and weapon displays, and commemorates agents killed while on duty.

El Paso may be reached by car on I-10, and by bus or via its international airport.
Map ref: page 624 D9

The United States–Mexico border, dividing El Paso and Juarez, is crossed by large numbers of workers and tourists every day.

Workers in Fort Worth take a break from repairing a building that was damaged by a tornado.

FORT WORTH

Fort Worth is the cowboy and oil sidekick to polished and refined Dallas, a city of 481,000 people right next door geographically to the "Big D" in north-central Texas. It has its own big industries like American Airlines, Lockheed, and Burlington Northern Railroad; millionaires who greatly contribute to its quality of life; the Stockyards National Historic District; and its Western-style nightlife. Fort Worth has one tavern for every 26 people, compared to one per 3,500 in Dallas. An adage says, "Dallas is where the east peters out; Fort Worth is where the west begins."

The city began with the establishment of Fort Worth, home of US Army Company F, Second Dragoons, after the 1846–48 Mexican–American War. A settlement grew up around the fort that became the present city. The Chisholm Trail, a main route for huge Texas cattle drives to Kansas between 1866 and the mid-1880s, ran right through Fort Worth, which became known as "Cowtown." Saloons, casinos, and brothels served the likes of Butch Cassidy and the Sundance Kid. The railroad arrived in 1876, making Fort Worth a shipping point for cattle. Meat-packing plants came at the turn of the twentieth century. Trucking brought the decline of the stockyards, as trucks could transport live beef north faster and in smaller lots. Of late, high-tech industries have come to town, including Tandy Corporation,

the parent company of Radio Shack, and Bell Helicopter, as well as the Chance–Vaught aircraft company. The city also has one of the main US currency plants outside of Washington DC.

Fort Worth calls itself "The Museum Capital of the Southwest." The Amon Carter Museum, established by newspaperman, oil mogul, and philanthropist Amon G. Carter, is particularly strong in western art. Works by Frederic Remington, Charles M. Russell, Georgia O'Keefe, Winslow Homer, Grant Wood, Laura Gilpin, and Ansel Adams are featured.

The Kimbell Art Museum possesses the collection bequeathed by Texas industrialist Kay Kimbell. Award-winning galleries designed by Louis Kahn display works by El Greco, Velazquez, Rembrandt, Cezanne, and Picasso. The Modern Art Museum of Fort Worth, not to be outdone, offers riveting works by Picasso, Rothko, Pollock, Warhol, and Stella. At the Sir Richardson Collection of Western Art, Remington and Russell get more exposure. There is even an airline museum—the American Airlines C.R. Smith Museum—through which visitors get to see the operation of an airline with films, videos, and hands-on exhibits.

The Fort Worth Stockyards became a National Historic District in 1976. Weekly cattle and hog auctions are still held here. The National Cowgirl Hall of Fame, Stockyards Hotel, Booger Red's Saloon and Restaurant, and the Stockyards Drugstore supply

colorful western history. Pioneer Days in September, the Chisholm Trail Roundup in June, and the Southwestern Exposition Stock Show and Rodeo in January fill the district with activity. Billy Bob's Texas is one of nearly two-dozen nightclubs in the area. It is the world's largest honky-tonk with a 4,800-foot (1,464-m) rodeo area, 600 feet (183 m) of bar rails, a 1,650-foot (503-m) stage for country-and-western entertainment, and shops, games, and restaurants.

Sundance Square, where the Sundance Kid disappeared between bank robberies, covers six historic city blocks. It includes the 1895 Tarrant County Courthouse, constructed of pink granite and marble in the Renaissance Revival style, and the turret roof of the Knights of Pythias Hall, erected in 1881 as the world's first Pythian Temple. The Plaza Hotel, constructed in 1908, was one of the city's last working brothels. The stunning Bass Performance Hall is located in the square. It is the permanent venue for the city's acclaimed symphony, ballet, and opera companies. Touring Broadway shows and special concerts are held here. The striking façade features two 48-foot-tall (15-m) heralding angels in Texas limestone. The building bears a beaux arts revival design, and is modeled after European opera

houses. Its interior features a 2,056-seat audience chamber in a tiered horseshoe style.

Unique to Fort Worth is the Southwestern Baptist Theological Seminary, which trains some 800 Southern Baptist preachers a year, including most of those presiding over pulpits in Texas, where Southern Baptists are the largest denomination. The Tandy Archeological Museum, which has items from the Holy Land uncovered at Tel Batash–Timnah, is located here.

The Fort Worth Museum of Science and History contains 100,000 artifacts and specimens for research and exhibition. The museum has a children's indoor discovery area, a planetarium, and three digging areas for amateur paleontologists.

Mammals, birds, and reptiles from around the world are housed at the Fort Worth Zoo. An African Savanna, Koala Outback, Herpetarium, Asian Falls, World of Primates, and Raptor Canyon are the main features.

The Texas Motor Speedway, the second largest sports facility in the country, hosts Indy-style and NASCAR (North American Stock-car Association) Winston Cup stock-car races. It has 150,000 seats and 194 skybox VIP suites.

Fort Worth may be reached by car on I-35, I-20 and I-45, or by bus, and it shares an international airport with Dallas.
Map ref: page 627 H7

Texans are proud of their "Wild West" heritage.

FREDERICKSBURG

This is a German stop in the middle of Texas. A town of 8,600 people, located 63 miles (101 km) northwest of San Antonio, it has German timber-worked walls, mansard roofs, lacy storefronts, waitresses in dirndls, and a number of German celebrations and traditions—Schuetzenfests (marksmanship tournaments), Octoberfest, Kristkindl, and Kinderfests. The delicious German bread and pastries made here are widely known.

The town was settled through the efforts of the *Adelsverein*, or Association of Noblemen, who brought more than 7,000 Germans to Texas, mostly between 1845 and

1847. The settlement area that they had arranged with Republic of Texas promoters was still ruled by the Comanches, so land at New Braunfels, 50 miles (80 km) south of Austin, and Fredericksburg was settled instead. To quiet her children one evening, a pioneer mother told of the Easter Rabbit who lit fires on the town's hillside to boil Easter eggs. In reality those were Comanche fires. The Easter Fire tradition is observed today with hillside fires that glow each Easter eve during a pageant that retells the story.

Chester W. Nimitz, Commander in Chief of the Pacific Fleet during World War II, was born in Fredericksburg of German parents in 1885. His grandmother opened the Nimitz Hotel, a handsome wood structure of columns, balconies, and a high-shingled tower with the American flag on top. The hotel now houses the Admiral Nimitz Museum, which chronicles the life and naval career of the admiral and the war's Pacific operations. The Plaza of Presidents recognizes 10 US Presidents from Franklin Roosevelt to George Bush who served in the military during World War II. And the George Bush Gallery of the Pacific War helps define the experience for those who lived through the campaigns in the Pacific War.

The Garden of Peace, a gift from the Japanese people, is located behind the museum. Found here are replicas of Admiral Togo's office and teahouse. East of the museum is the four-acre (1.6 ha) History Walk of the Pacific that displays war machinery used in Pacific battles.

Fredericksburg has a dulcimer factory, toy museum, herb farm, and Vereins Kirche Museum, which is a reconstructed "coffee-mill church" that was used as a public building for meetings and worship, and now holds archives, photos, and archeological items.

Enchanted State Park features a massive, solid granite dome of about 640 acres (259 ha) that is 500 feet (153 m) high. Native American legend pegs it as the site of human sacrifices. The park is popular for picnicking, hiking, and rock climbing.

At the Pioneer Museum Complex, an eight-room furnished pioneer home and store, built in 1849, shares space with a Victorian-style home, barn, and blacksmith shop,

The Michel B. Menard Home, built in 1838, is one of Galveston's finest museums.

smokehouse, log cabin, wagon shed, one-room schoolhouse, and fire station. Fredericksburg may be reached by car on US-87, or by bus. The nearest airports are in San Antonio and Austin.
Map ref: page 630 C6

GALVESTON

The city of Galveston, which has 65,000 residents, is located on an island 27 miles (43 km) long and less than 3 miles (4.8 km) wide at its broadest point. Named for a Spanish viceroy, Galveston is 51 miles (82 km) southeast of Houston in the Gulf of Mexico, and is known for its beaches, historical districts, and busy seaport.

Pirate Jean Lafitte established a colony called Campeachy on the island in 1871, and speculation continues about his buried loot. Texas navy ships that were docked at Galveston defeated a Mexican blockade off the coast in 1836, assisting the Republic of Texas' drive for independence. After the 1846–48 Mexican–American War, Galveston became the biggest and most modern city in Texas, acting as the banking center for the Southwest and operating the nation's third-largest port.

Galveston turned on the state's first electric lights and telegraph system, and established the first medical college that is now a branch of the University of Texas. It had the state's first post office, telephone service, public library, and streetcar system. During the Civil War of 1861–65, Union Navy forces captured the Port of Galveston, disembarked, and declared an end to slavery on

June 19, 1865. Following the war, migrating Europeans passed through the immigration station at Galveston en route to the Southwest, with many Greek, Italian, and Russian-Jewish descendants remaining in the port city.

The hurricane of 1900, the worst natural disaster in American history, killed 6,000 people, destroyed hundreds of buildings, and changed the destiny of Galveston. A massive 10-mile-long (16-km) seawall was built 17 feet (5.2 m) above low tide, as Galveston became a place to protect rather than a business leader. Much of the fuel used for World War II was shipped out of Galveston, and for many years after the war the beaches were soiled by oil from ships sunk by German U-boats. Chemicals from nearby refineries and Gulf oil-rig spills added to the pollution, all of which has since been cleaned up as an example of a big environmental comeback. Huge chunks of pink Texas granite, the same rock used

in the state capitol building in Austin, serve as a break for hurricane tides. The seawall has become a social and recreational hangout like those found in Atlantic City, New Jersey, and Los Angeles.

Galveston's historic districts preserve more than 1,500 nineteenth-century buildings, 550 of which are listed on the National Register of Historic Places. Among the most celebrated structures are the Ashton Villa, an 1859 Italiante house-museum; the Bishop's Palace, the only Texas building on the American Institute of Architect's list of the nation's 100 outstanding buildings; the 1894 Grand Opera House; the 1838 Michel B. Menard Home, Galveston's oldest house; and Moody Mansion and Museum, built in 1892, a prime example of traditional Victorian architecture.

The popular 156-acre (63-ha) Moody Gardens feature a subterranean pyramid that allows visitors to experience ocean waters; a rainforest pyramid that represents Asia, South America, and Africa; and a glass discovery pyramid that explores the wonders of space.

At the Ocean Star Offshore Drilling Rig and Museum, visitors learn how gas and oil are produced offshore. Replica 1900 trolley cars glide over 4 miles (6.4 km) of tracks between the seawall beach and the historic Strand/Bay area. The third-oldest ship afloat, the 150-foot, (46 m) square-rigged iron barque *Elissa*, is moored at Pier 21 in Galveston.

Galveston may be reached by car on I-45 or by bus. The closest international airport is in Houston.
Map ref: page 631 M8

Galveston's Seawall Boulevard is popular with family groups, especially in summer.

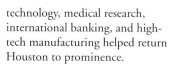

GUADALUPE MOUNTAINS NATIONAL PARK

The desolate outer slopes of the Guadalupe Mountains are not a reflection of what lies within. Magnificent highlands and rugged, majestic canyons characterize the 86,416-acre (34,998-ha) Guadalupe Mountains National Park, on the New Mexican border 87 miles (140 km) east of El Paso, and about 600 miles (965 km) west of Dallas–Fort Worth.

Park elevation ranges from 3,650 feet (1,113 m) to 8,749 feet (2668 m) at the summit of Guadalupe Peak, the highest point in Texas. Four of the state's highest peaks are in the park, as well as many other unnamed peaks over 8,000 feet (2,440 m). The park provides an excellent wilderness experience for hikers and backpackers, but does not have overlooks and roads into its splendid interior. For that reason, it is one of the least visited national parks in the United States, and a joy for those wishing to escape crowds.

Winds rip through between late fall and late spring, often reaching 60 miles per hour (97 kph) and sometimes topping 100 miles per hour (161 kph). Winter and summer temperatures are mild. Many visitors come for the fall foliage in October and spring color in April and May.

Desert, canyon, and highland zones provide a diverse community of animal and plant species. Chihuahuan Desert plants such as prickly pear, yucca, and creosote bush rise to ponderosa pine, Douglas fir, and quaking aspen. The red-skinned madrone tree, which produces white flowers and oval leaves that don't shed in winter, is found here.

Mule deer, elk, gray foxes, coyotes, black bears, bobcats, and mountain lions are among the 58 species of mammals. Birdwatching is a treat here. Road runners, doves, woodpeckers, quail, killdeer, hawks, eagles, falcons, and six species of hummingbird decorate the dry air. There are also six types of venomous rattlesnake, so it is best to be wary in rocky areas.

Perhaps the most special place in the park is McKittrick Canyon, because of its wonderful variety of foliage that lights up from late October to mid-November. Visitors may drive to near the mouth of the canyon and use easy hiking trails that lead to remarkable views. The McKittrick Canyon Visitor Center presents a geology program and slide show.

Two of the park's campgrounds are accessible by car, and nine designated wilderness camping sites can be reached on foot. The park has 80 miles (129 km) of marked trails. Guadalupe Mountains National Park headquarters is located at nearby Pine Springs, which had a station on the famous stagecoach run, the Butterfield Overland Mail Route, which was established in 1858 and is remembered by a tumble of stone ruins and a granite marker. The park may be reached by car on US-180 or by bus. The nearest airport is in El Paso.
Map ref: page 624 F9

This barren salt lake belies the beauty to be found among the nearby Guadalupe Mountains.

HOUSTON

Houston is the largest Texan city and the fourth largest in the nation, with 1.8 million people spread over 500 square miles (1,295 sq km). It is located in East Texas, where it is connected by ship channel to Galveston Bay and the Gulf of Mexico. Houston is known for its humid, rainy weather, for difficult driving on its many freeways, for its polluted air, and as the largest unzoned city in the country—meaning a high-rise can be built beside a farm shack, with a steel mill across the street next to a park. But it also has many fine museums and is strong in the performing arts. Well-known home of the National Aeronautics and Space Administration (NASA), Houston also has a notable medical presence with its Texas Medical Center, plus it has the eighth-largest port in the country and has two well-known universities.

Houston was launched from the maritime trading post of Harrington, founded in 1824 by John Harris. After Harris died, in 1936 his brothers Augustus and John Allen purchased a plot farther up the Buffalo Bayou, where they set up a trading post. They named it for General Sam Houston, who had just defeated the Mexicans at San Jacinto.

The conversion of Buffalo Bayou to a ship channel led to rapid industrial growth. At the turn of the twentieth century, timber and cattle followed cotton as big exports. The discovery of oil at nearby Spindletop in 1901 brought in the refining and petrochemical industries, as well as steel and synthetic rubber. With a decline in oil prices, Houston's economy suffered in the 1980s. Aerospace technology, medical research, international banking, and high-tech manufacturing helped return Houston to prominence.

Space Center Houston, a 183,000-square-foot (17,385-sq-m) educational and entertainment facility designed by NASA and Walt Disney Imagineering, employs 20,000 scientists and researchers. Visitors explore the manned space program through shuttle and space-module mockups, shuttle-landing simulators, low-gravity units, and a vault that houses lunar rocks. Tram tours visit Mission Control Center, the Skylab/Space Shuttle Training Facility, Rocket Park, and other areas of the Johnson Space Center. NASA spacesuits and Mercury, Gemini, and Apollo spacecraft are on display.

The Houston Astrodome is one of the country's best-known sports stadiums. Opened in 1965, it was the first air-conditioned domed sports arena and the first to use artificial grass, or Astroturf. Its major-league baseball team, the Astros, still play at the Dome, and the annual Houston Livestock and Rodeo is also held there, along with hundreds of conventions and expositions. The Houston Rockets of the National Basketball Association play at the Summit. Houston also has a new national football league team, the Houston Texans, who will enter the competition in 2002.

Rice University, often said to be a southern Ivy League school, educates 4,000 students at a picturesque campus in the center

Houston's complex system of freeways is notoriously difficult to negotiate.

of town. The University of Houston, which enrols 50,000 students through its various branches, has an open-admission undergraduate division and graduate schools in engineering, pharmacology, and optometry, as well as the Bates School of Law and Hilton School of Hotel and Restaurant Management. These are two out of 25 institutions of higher learning in Houston.

The Texas Medical Center became famous for its heart transplants. This immense complex of hospitals, medical and nursing schools, and research institutions coordinates health education, patient care, and research. Its more than 100 buildings occupy 650 acres (263 ha) in southwest Houston, and it offers free tours.

Houston has a natural science museum, its shining feature being its butterfly center. The Market Square Historic District is composed of 53 historic buildings, while the San Jacinto Museum of History chronicles regional history through statehood. Also in town are a 50-acre (20-ha) zoo; the Six Flags Astroworld/WaterWorld amusement park that has 11 roller coasters as well as Texas Tornado and Texas Cyclone rides; and a passenger excursion train that runs to Galveston, 51 miles (82 km) southeast in the Gulf of Mexico.

The revitalized Downtown Houston Theatre District has the Alley Theatre, one of the oldest residential theaters in the country.

The Ensemble Theatre is the oldest and most professional theater in the Southwest, and it is devoted to the African-American experience. As well as parks, there are also museums, symphony music, opera, and ballet.

Houston may be reached by car on I-10 and I-45, or by bus, and the city has an international airport.
Map ref: page 631 K7

KILLEEN

A town of 82,145 located 142 miles (228 km) south of Dallas–Fort Worth, Killeen is next door to the largest group of soldiers and war machines in the free world at Fort Hood. The 339-square-mile (878-sq-km) post is home to the Army's III Corps, 1st Cavalry, and 4th Infantry Division.

The 1st Cavalry Museum has more than 150 years of cavalry uniforms, equipment, and arms. Emphasis is placed on division combat during World War II, Korea, and Vietnam. On display are artillery, trucks, tanks, and captured foreign weapons.

The 4th Infantry Division Museum explores the history of the Division through a series of self-guided exhibits that use artifacts, text, and photography showing soldiers in three wars. A large number of historical vehicles are on display.

Both museums are open to the public. Killeen also has 10 city parks covering 250 acres (101 ha) that offer sports fields, tennis courts, swimming pools, picnic areas, and golf courses. Killeen may be reached by car on I-35 and US-190, and by bus or plane.
Map ref: page 630 F4

LAREDO

This city of 167,628 people, located 424 miles (682 km) south of Dallas–Fort Worth, is the major international crossing on the United States–Mexican border. *Maquiladora* industry, using cheap Mexican labor and US management, is big here. Laredo has the nation's biggest inland port. Petroleum and natural gas, feeds and fertilizers, brick and tile, are also important to the economy.

Fort McIntosh, which was in service from 1848 to 1946, the 371-acre (150 ha) Lake Casa Blanca International State Park that is known for bass fishing, and the Laredo Children's Museum are popular with visitors. Nuevo Laredo offers jewelry, crystal, onyx, metallic arts, handicrafts, baskets, hand-dyed cloth, serapes, clothing, leatherwork, and silver.

Laredo may be reached by car on I-35 and US-59 and US-83, or by bus. It also has an international airport.
Map ref: page 632 E6

LUBBOCK

Lubbock (population 194,000) is the major city of the South Plains and is located 322 miles (518 km) west of Dallas–Fort Worth. Cattle and ranching provided late nineteenth-century and early twentieth-century growth. Today industry, technology, oil, agriculture, warehousing, and medicine are the economic staples. Lubbock is one of America's largest cotton producers, and, in addition to that crop, it ships a lot of livestock and grain.

Rock 'n' roller Buddy Holly, a Lubbock native, is honored by the Buddy Holly Statue and Walk of Fame that celebrates West Texas entertainers. Mac Davis, Waylon Jennings, Roy Orbison, and Bob Wills are featured on plaques.

Texas Tech University is located here. Its museum covers a broad range of arts, humanities, social sciences, and natural sciences, with an emphasis on the study of arid and semi-arid lands, and environments and cultures that inhabit them.

At the Lubbock Lake Landmark State Historical Park, excavations have revealed remains of extinct mammoth, horse, camel, giant bison, and 6-foot-long (1.8-m) armadillos. The Robert A. Nash Interpretive Center exhibits fossils and artifacts from the site. Prairie Dog Town at Mackenzie Park preserves one of the few remaining prairie-dog colonies in the nation. Close-up views reveal the frisky little animals that once inhabited the plains by the millions. Windmills of all descriptions are found at the Wind Power Center.

Lubbock may be reached by car on I-27, US-82, and US-84, or by bus. It has an international airport.
Map ref: page 625 M4

Outside cities such as Lubbock, it's not unusual to find fields of colorful wildflowers.

McDONALD OBSERVATORY

The big mushroom caps of the McDonald Observatory are set on the 6,791-foot (2,071-m) peak of Mt Locke, located 19 miles (31 km) northwest of Fort Davis in west Texas, and about 500 miles (805 km) west of Dallas–Fort Worth. The clear air, cloudless nights, distance from artificial lights, and timber and shrubs that filter out radiation are the reasons the observatory was built here. It is owned by the University of Texas, Penn State University, Stanford University, and universities in Munich and Goettingen, Germany.

The US$13.5 million Hobby–Eberly Telescope positions 91 hexagonal mirrors over its 36-foot-wide (11-m) surface and is the third largest in the world. It was designed to specialize in spectroscopy, the technique astronomers use to break down light into component wavelengths. It is used to analyze light from other planets, satellites, stars, and quasars. Research astronomers from around the world also use the telescope for many different projects.

McDonald's 16-foot (4.9 m) wave dish is used for studying gas clouds and particles in the Milky Way. Its laser-ranging telescope is used to calculate lunar orbits and distances, and its 30-inch (75 cm) scope studies lunar occultations, when the moon passes in front of a star. A visitor information center offers exhibits, and guided tours are available year-round. The observatory may be reached by car on US-118, off I-10. Midland and El Paso have international airports.
Map ref: page 628 E3

Texas is cattle country, as this sculpture outside Marathon attests.

Odessa's economy has relied on the petrochemical industry since oil was found in the area during the 1920s.

MARATHON

Marathon is a tiny settlement 69 miles (111 km) north of Big Bend National Park. Highway 385, which runs through it, provides the eastern entry point for Big Bend. A sea captain suggested Marathon's name—he said the area reminded him of Marathon in Greece.

The historic Gage Hotel, with original pine floors and woodwork and ranch-style furnishings dating back to the 1920s, is located here. The guest rooms have separate themes, and Tarahumara pottery decorates the lobby. The bar has a Yaqui Native American altar and a Chusa, a Mexican marble game similar to roulette. Alfred Gage, who was a banker and cattle baron, built the yellow-brick hotel in 1927. It was refurbished in 1978.
Map ref: page 628 G4

MIDLAND

This town of 89,000 people got its name in 1880 for being halfway between Fort Worth and El Paso on the Texas and Pacific Railroad Line. It became more than a railroad stop and farming community with the discovery of oil in the Permian Basin in the 1920s. The vast basin also has tremendous quantities of anhydrite, potassium, salt, and natural gas. Although oil is king, huge cattle ranches and agricultural fields exist in the area.

The American Airpower Heritage Museum and Confederate Air Force headquarters here preserves World War II aircraft. An impressive array of US, British, German, and Japanese planes are on display. A four-day air show held every October features the Ghost Squadron.

The history of oil exploration and oil technology is presented at the Permian Basin Petroleum Museum. At the Museum of the Southwest Complex, art collections are displayed at a 1934 mansion on the National Historic Register. Works include those of the Taos Society of Artists, Texas regionalists, photographers, and sculptors.

Midland may be reached by car on I-20, US-349, and Hwy 158, or by bus or plane.
Map ref: page 625 M8

ODESSA

Russian railroad workers named Odessa in 1881 for their homeland, where the wide, flat prairies of the steppes also exist. Discoveries of oil and gas in the vast Permian Basin in the 1920s began Odessa's transformation from an agricultural railroad stop to a petrochemical giant. A town of 90,000 people, it is right next to Midland and 347 miles (558 km) west of Dallas–Fort Worth.

The second largest meteor crater in the United States is located 8 miles (13 km) west of the city. In town, the Presidential Museum offers exhibits and educational programs focusing on the American presidency. The Odessa College campus has the Globe of the Great Southwest, a replica of Shakespeare's original playhouse.

Odessa can be accessed by car on I-20 and US-385, or by bus. An airport is in neighboring Midland.
Map ref: page 625 M9

OZONA

This is the only city in Crockett County, a vast oil and ranching area of 3,000 square miles (7,770 sq km). It has a population of 3,500 and is located 82 miles (132 km) southwest of San Angelo and 334 miles (537 km) southwest of Dallas–Fort Worth. Ozona is one of the nation's top areas in wool production, marketing 2 million pounds (908,000 kg) annually. In the surrounding Edwards Plateau regions, hunters take white-tailed deer, javelina, and upland game birds. Ozona may be reached by car on I-10 or Hwy 163. The closest airport is in San Angelo.
Map ref: page 629 L3

PADRE ISLAND NATIONAL SEASHORE

The 110-mile (177-km) Padre Island, located south of Corpus Christi in the Gulf of Mexico and about 400 miles (644 km) from Dallas–Fort Worth, offers one of the last natural seashores in the nation and is the longest coastal-barrier island in the world. Each end of the narrow sand strip is developed with parks and resorts, but the 80 miles (129 km) between is untouched.

Seashells, driftwood, and glass floats from Portugal and Asia are sought by beachcombers. Sea turtles, snakes, and rodents are seen on the island. Dolphins, pelicans, and herons are also spotted. On the lagoon side of the island, there are flounder, sheepshead, redfish, blackdrum, skipjack, striped mullet, and speckled trout. On the gulf side, anglers cast for sand trout, pompano, mackerel, and tarpon. Further offshore are grouper, bonito, kingfish, red snapper, marlin, and sailfish. Oysters and crabs are also plentiful.

Padre Island may be reached by car on I-37 to Corpus Christi then Hwys 358 and 361, or by bus, or by plane to Corpus Christi. Map ref: page 633 J7

PORT ARTHUR

This town of 58,000 sits on the northwest shore of Lake Sabine, 9 miles (14 km) from the Gulf of Mexico on the southeastern edge of Texas, and about 300 miles (483 km) from Dallas–Fort Worth. Port Arthur and its sister cities Beaumont, 17 miles (27 km) east, and Orange, 22 miles (35 km) northeast, compose the "Magic Triangle," a petrochemical, shipbuilding, and papermaking complex.

Port Arthur's Museum of the Gulf Coast, located in a former bank building, focuses on the history and cultural diversity of southeast Texas and southwest Louisiana Gulf Coast. Relics from the Battle of Sabine Pass, a mortgage note issued by Santa Anna, and an Edison Talking Machine are among the many diverse items on display. Rock star Janis Joplin was from Port Arthur, and her painted psychedelic Porsche sits on top of a spinning gold record. Port Arthur may be reached by car on US-96, or I-10 and Hwy 73 and is serviced by the Southeast Texas Regional Airport; there is an international airport in Houston. Map ref: page 631 N7

SAN ANGELO

This city of 90,000 people, located at the bottom of the Texas Panhandle and 252 miles (405 km) west of Dallas–Fort Worth, is the nation's largest wool and mohair market. The Edwards Plateau is ideal for raising sheep and goats; four rivers join here, and lakes are on three sides of the city. San Angelo is the regional hub of cotton, grain, and pecan production. The city is known for Concho River pearls, found in mussels that live in the Concho River.

The International Water Lily Collection at Civic League Park has water lilies from around the world, including the "Victoria," which spans 8 feet (2.4 m) in diameter, as well as day- and night-blooming varieties. The Cactus Hotel, built in 1929, was one of the first Hilton Hotels. The city has a symphony orchestra, ballet, a jazz series at the Cactus Hotel, and a jazz and blues festival on its river stage.

Angelo State University is located here. Its planetarium is the fourth largest university planetarium and features a three-dimensional view of the universe with sparkling stars and celestial fireworks. San Angelo may be reached by car on US-277, US-67, and US-87, and by bus or plane. Map ref: page 629 M1

Visitors to San Antonio will enjoy the city's many cafés.

SAN ANTONIO

This is a favorite city of Texans and out-of-state visitors, too, because of its laid-back tempo, historical flourishes, river walk, and so many things to do. It's a city of flowers and festivals that is easy to relax in, and, with 1.1 million people, it's the largest US city with an Hispanic majority. San Antonio is the capital of South Texas, a huge area of gently rolling plains that extend west and south to the Rio Grande and Mexico.

San Antonio is about 250 miles (402 km) south of Dallas–Fort Worth and 200 miles (322 km) west of Houston, but Mexico is its real influence. The food, manner, color, architecture, dress, and pace represent the more affluent and stable Americanized version of south-of-the-border.

In 1681, the governor of the Spanish colonial territory met a group of Coahuiltecans on St Anthony's Day, and named the site San Antonio. A Franciscan priest established a mission on the San Antonio River, and Spanish soldiers founded a presidio there in 1718. Missions were built alongside the expanding civilian population, and the city of San Antonio became a part of Mexico after the Mexican Revolution of 1821 shed its Spanish ties. By 1836, 3,500 Anglos lived in San Antonio, when the city refused to recognize General Santa Anna's Mexican presidency. After winning independence from Mexico in 1836, many German settlers moved in. By 1860, when Texas was a part of the United States, San Antonio's population had risen to 8,000 people. Asians and Mexicans escaping Mexican tyranny flowed into the growing city. Today the Mexican consul, critical in cross-border trade, is as important as the San Antonio mayor.

The military plays an important part in San Antonio's economy, as it has since the founding of a presidio here nearly three centuries ago. Four air force bases—Brooks, Kelly, Lackland, and Randolph—and one Army base, Fort Sam Houston, are located in San Antonio. "The Home of Army Medicine," Fort Sam was established in 1845, and is a center for military medical training and care. The active military, civilian employees working for the military, and military retirees run into the hundreds of thousands. The city's 10 colleges and universities, and tourism prominently

White-tailed deer (Odocoileus virginianus seminolus) are found in abundance throughout the Edwards Plateau, near Ozona.

Cap Rock Canyon, near Silverton, is a breathtaking convergence of lush vegetation and sheer stony cliffs.

figure into the economic mix, as do regional manufacturers such as Pace Foods, the largest producer of salsa in the United States, and Pearl and Lone Star beers.

San Antonio has five missions built along the San Antonio River, around which the modern city developed, which can be visited on the 5¹/₂-mile (8.8 km) Mission Trail. The Alamo was the first mission, established in 1718, and is the biggest name and most visited site in Texas. Each year some three million visitors tour the remodeled plaza and building, which is operated by the Daughters of the Republic of Texas. The ochre stone mission is not as well-known for its architectural grace as it is for the courage of its 182 defenders in facing up to the siege of Mexican General Santa Anna in 1836. The gritty Texas band threw back two assaults of the vastly superior force before giving way, one by one, until all but a handful were dead. In finally overtaking the Alamo, Santa Anna lost 1,600 men, and with his forces decimated, he could not overcome the Texas insurgency. Two months later in Galveston, Santa Anna lost 650 troops, and the Texans suffered seven dead and 18 wounded at the Battle of San Jacinto, and Texas had its freedom to become a republic.

Native Americans call the San Antonio River "drunken old man going home at night," because of its meandering course through the city, which at one point, with the help of a concrete channel, becomes a water horseshoe. Along with the Alamo, the River Walk afforded by this spring-fed, dirt-bottom water thread is the city's best-known attraction. Its cobblestone and flagstone paths extend

Many people visit Texas in spring just to see its vibrant wildflowers.

for 21 blocks and almost 3 miles (4.8 km), and it is the center of downtown life. WPA (Work Projects Administration) crews built the pathways, the 35 bridges, and 31 stairways between 1935 and 1941. Lush trees and flowers decorate the way, which winds past restaurants, cafés, bars, and shops. Barges and river taxis carry passengers up and down the river, and

there are dinner cruises on flat-bottom boats. Summer theater and festivals take place along the river.

El Mercado, or Market Square, is a festive Mexican bazaar filled with stalls selling a broad range of items—crafts, food, housewares, silver, and ceramics. La Villita National Historic District is a restored limestone and clapboard neighborhood that attracts artists and is occupied by restaurants, gift shops, and art galleries.

At the 18-acre (7.3-ha), domed Aladrome, the city's National Basketball Association team, San Antonio Spurs, play. The 250-acre (101-ha) Sea World of Texas is the largest of four Sea Worlds in the United States and a popular attraction. The 200-acre (81-ha) Six Flags Fiesta Texas, which is set in a limestone quarry and surrounded by 100-foot (31 m) cliffs, highlights Texas music and culture in four themed areas.

San Antonio may be reached by car on I-10, I-37 and I-35, or by bus. It has an international airport.
Map ref: page 630 D8

SILVERTON

Silverton is a town of 3,261 people located in the middle of the Panhandle, 77 miles (124 km) southeast of Amarillo. It is the center of an immense farming and ranching area that includes some spectacular

scenery in Palo Drum County and Tule Canyon, and it is located at the edge of Cap Rock Canyon State Park. On scenic drives through the area, travelers see the startling contrast of the high plains and the colorful Tule and Palo Duro canyons. The town's Old Jail Museum was built in 1892 and has a restored windmill outside.

Silverton may be reached by car on Hwy 86 and Hwy 256. The closest airport is in Amarillo.
Map ref: page 625 P2

TEXARKANA

In Texarkana (population 33,250), you may place one foot in Arkansas and one in Texas. The state line runs through the center of town, which is located on the northeast edge of the Texas, 178 miles (286 km) northeast of Dallas–Fort Worth.

A downtown Scott Joplin mural colorfully depicts the life and accomplishments of the Pulitzer Prize-winning musical pioneer, known as "The King of Ragtime," who was from Texarkana. "The Ace of Clubs House", built in the shape of that card, was erected in honor of the winner of a huge poker pot who played the ace of clubs. The elegant 1884 Italianate–Victorian house is one several museums in this town.

It may be reached by car on I-30 and US-82, or by bus or plane.
Map ref: page 627 P5

TEXAS CITY

Twenty-six miles (42 km) southeast of Houston, Texas City (population 57,380) joins with La Marque to form a business and living area located on Galveston Bay, right next to the Gulf of Mexico. The local industries include a tin smelter, oil refineries, metal fabrication, and chemical plants. The port ships grain, cotton, sulfur, petroleum, and chemical products.

The Texas City Dike extends 5 miles (8 km) into Galveston Bay, with a 600-foot (183-m) fishing pier beyond the dike, providing the deepest water for pier anglers in the state. Speckled trout, redfish, flounder, and tarpon are hooked here.

Texas City may be reached by car on Hwy 146 and I-45 and by bus. There is an international airport in Houston.
Map ref: page 631 L8

TULIA

Tulia is a commercial center for a Panhandle Plains agricultural area that grows milo, wheat, and cotton, and has several large livestock feed operations. The Swisher County Museum in Tulia has an excellent collection of pioneer and ranch artifacts that includes home furnishings, tools, firearms, photos of early life on the plains, and Native American artifacts. It also has a replica blacksmith shop and tools, as well as the restored first log cabin of the area, and typical homes from the 1890 to 1930 era.

The town of 5,300 people is located 49 miles (79 km) south of Amarillo. It may be reached by car on I-27 or by bus. The nearest airport is in Amarillo.
Map ref: page 625 N2

TURKEY

Wild turkeys discovered along a creek led to the naming of this town of 553 residents, which is situated 123 miles (198 km) southeast of Amarillo in the Panhandle. On the last Saturday of April, the Bob Wills Reunion is held, drawing up to 15,000 people to the festival commemorating the "King of Western Swing," who grew up on a farm just north of town. A Main Street monument and museum honor Wills and the Texas Playboys, his band. The museum displays fiddles, boots, hats, music, and photographs. Turkey may be reached by Hwys 86, 70, and 256. The nearest airport is in Amarillo.
Map ref: page 625 P2

VAN HORN

Surrounded by the Van Horn, Sierra Diablo, and Apache Mountains, Van Horn sits in a mining and hunting area 107 miles (172 km) southeast of El Paso in west Texas. The town of 2,900 has the Culberson County Historical Museum, housed in the historic Clark Hotel, which displays Native American artifacts; antique ranch, farm, and home implements; and preserves a resplendent antique bar. Van Horn is also home to the Smokehouse Auto Museum, which displays restored vehicles from the early 1900s to the 1960s.

Van Horn may be reached by car on I-10 and US-90, or by bus. The nearest airport is in El Paso.
Map ref: page 628 D2

VICTORIA

This city of 61,320 people is located 78 miles (126 km) northeast of Corpus Christi on the Gulf Coast, and was named by the Spanish in 1824 for General Guadalupe Victoria, Mexico's first President. It was one of the first three towns incorporated by the Republic of Texas. A major industrial and agricultural crossroads, it is home to Victoria College and the University of Houston at Victoria. The McNamara Historical Museum, which deals with local history, and the Nave Museum, which displays paintings by Texas artist Royston Nave as well as contemporary art and sculpture, are both located here.

Victoria is at the intersection of US-59 and US-77, and is also accessible by bus or plane.
Map ref: page 633 K2

WACO

Waco (population 108,562) is located in the rich agricultural region of the Brazos River Valley, which produces cotton, cattle, and corn. It is 91 miles (146 km) south of Dallas.

The Armstrong–Browning Museum in Waco has the world's largest collection of works and memorabilia of poets Robert and Elizabeth Browning, including 56 stained glass windows, each depicting a Browning poem.

Turkey is proud of musician Bob Wills, a former resident.

The Dr Pepper Museum focuses on the soft drink, soda fountain, and bottling plant from which the well-known drink evolved in 1885. Waco has a number of other museums, including The Texas Ranger Hall of Fame, built at the original Texas Ranger fort established in 1837. Its Texas Sports Hall of Fame preserves sports memorabilia of nationally known Texas athletes, among them golfers Byron Nelson, Lee Trevino, Don January, and Babe Didrikson Zaharias; boxer George Foreman; and baseball pitcher Nolan Ryan. Waco may be reached by car on I-35, US-77, and Hwy 6, and by bus or plane.
Map ref: page 630 G3

WICHITA FALLS

Sheppard Air Force Base, oil processing, and manufacturing all drive the economy of this city of 98,160 people, perched on the Oklahoma border 136 miles (219 km) northwest of Dallas–Fort Worth. Sheppard is one of the five largest air-force bases in the nation and hosts the only NATO (North Atlantic Treaty Organization) pilot-training program in the world.

The city has 38 parks for outdoor recreation, a fire and police museum, a 54-foot-high (16-m) re-created waterfall, and Graham Central Station, an entertainment center with five different clubs under one roof. Midwestern State University's art gallery features the works of regional artists. The Wichita Theatre and Opry House presents the "Home of Texas Gold Country Music Show" every Saturday night, featuring old-fashioned family entertainment. Wichita Falls may be reached by car on US-287 and US-281, on I-44, or by bus. The nearest airport is in Dallas.
Map ref: page 626 F4

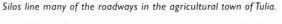

Silos line many of the roadways in the agricultural town of Tulia.

Northern Arizona • Southeastern Nevada • Southern Utah

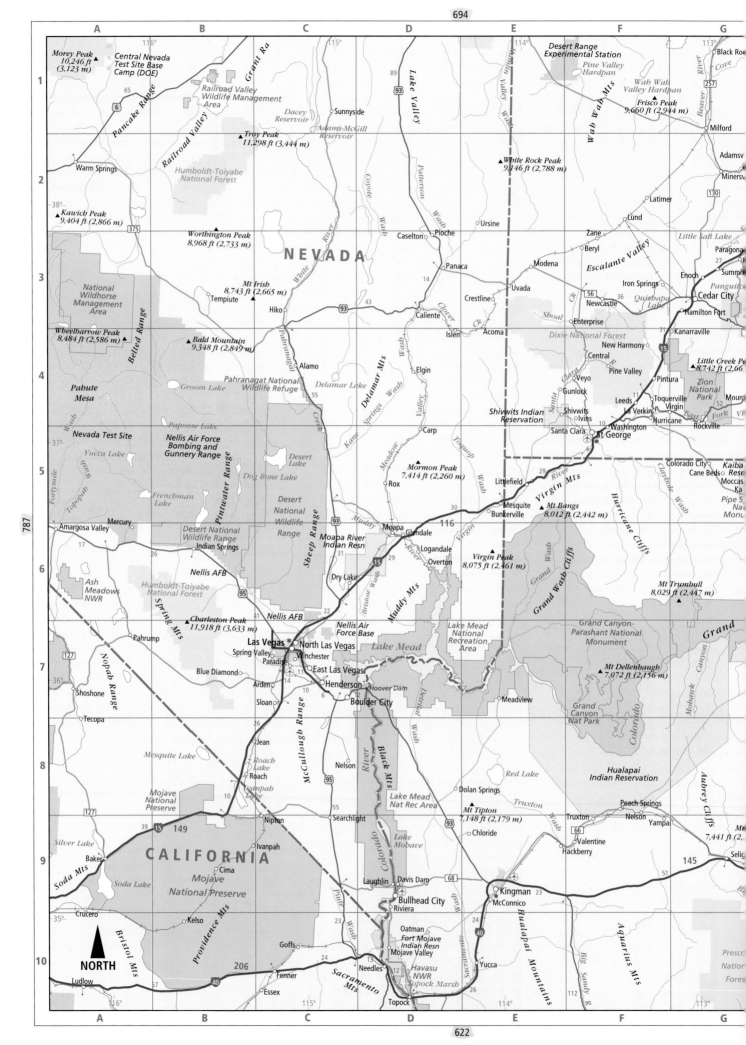

Morey Peak
10,246 ft
(3,123 m)

Central Nevada
Test Site Base
Camp (DOE)

Railroad Valley
Wildlife Management
Area

Desert Range
Experimental Station

Pine Valley
Hardpan

Wah Wah
Valley Hardpan

Black Ro
Cove

Pancake Range

Grant Ra

Dacey
Reservoir

Adams-McGill
Reservoir

Sunnyside

Frisco Peak
9,660 ft (2,944 m)

Milford

Warm Springs

Humboldt-Toiyabe
National Forest

Railroad Valley

Troy Peak
11,298 ft (3,444 m)

White Rock Peak
9,146 ft (2,788 m)

Adamsv

Minersv

Kawich Peak
9,404 ft (2,866 m)

Worthington Peak
8,968 ft (2,733 m)

N E V A D A

Coyote

Patterson

Wash

Wash

Ursine

Latimer

Lund

130

Zane

Beryl

Little Salt Lake

Paragona

National
Wildhorse
Management
Area

Mt Irish
8,743 ft (2,665 m)

Tempiute

Caselton

Pioche

Modena

Escalante Valley

Iron Springs

Enoch

Panguit

Cedar City

Belted Range

White River

Panaca

Cle

Newcastle

Summi

Wheelbarrow Peak
8,484 ft (2,586 m)

Bald Mountain
9,348 ft (2,849 m)

Mt Irish

Hiko

14

93

43

Crestline

Uvada

56

Hamilton Fort

Sboal

Kanarraville

Pabute
Mesa

Pahranagat National
Wildlife Refuge

Delamar Mts

Alamo

Delamar Lake

Caliente

Islen

Acoma

Enterprise

Dixie National Forest

New Harmony

Central

Pine Valley

Little Creek Pe
8,742 ft (2,66

Nevada Test Site

Nellis Air Force
Bombing and
Gunnery Range

Groom Lake

Papoose Lake

Kane

Springs

Wash

Carp

Meadow Valley

Santa Clara R

Shivwits Indian
Reservation

Veyo

Gunlock

Shivwits

Ivins

Pintura

Leeds

La Verkin

Virgin

Toquerville

Zion
National
Park

Mount

Rockville

Yucca Lake

Frenchman
Lake

Pintwater Range

Dog Bone Lake

Desert
Lake

Desert
National
Wildlife
Range

Mormon Peak
7,414 ft (2,260 m)

Rox

Littlefield

29

Virgin Mts

Mt Bangs
8,012 ft (2,442 m)

La Verkin

Santa Clara

St George

Washington

Hurricane

Colorado City

Cane Beds

Kaiba
Rese

Moccas

Pipe S
Na
Mon

Ka

Amargosa Valley

Mercury

Desert National
Wildlife Range

Indian Springs

Sheep Range

Moapa River
Indian Resn

Moapa

Glendale

Bunkerville

Mesquite

Virgin Peak
8,075 ft (2,461 m)

Grand Wash Cliffs

Hurricane Cliffs

Mt Trumbull
8,029 ft (2,447 m)

Ash
Meadows
NWR

Humboldt-Toiyabe
National Forest

Nellis AFB

95

Dry Lake

15

Logandale

Overton

Virgin River

Grand Wash

Grand Canyon-
Parashant National
Monument

Grand

Spring Mts

Charleston Peak
11,918 ft (3,633 m)

Nellis AFB

Nellis Air
Force Base

Muddy Mts

Bristow Wash

Lake Mead
National
Recreation
Area

Mt Dellenbaugh
7,072 ft (2,156 m)

Mohawk Canyon

Pahrump

Las Vegas

North Las Vegas

Winchester

East Las Vegas

Lake Mead

Meadview

Grand
Canyon
Nat Park

Colorado

Nopah Range

Spring Valley

Paradise

Henderson

Hoover Dam

Blue Diamond

Arden

Sloan

14

11

10

6

12

Boulder City

McCullough Range

Detrital Wash

Shoshone

36°

127

Tecopa

Jean

26

Roach
Lake

Nelson

Black Mts

River

Dolan Springs

Red Lake

Hualapai
Indian Reservation

Aubrey Cliffs

Mesquite Lake

Roach

Ivanpah Lake

95

Searchlight

55

Lake Mead
Nat Rec Area

Mt Tipton
7,148 ft (2,179 m)

Truxton

Peach Springs

Nelson

Yampa

Mojave
National
Preserve

10

Nipton

Chloride

93

66

Valentine

Hackberry

7,441 ft (2,

127

Silver Lake

39

15

149

Ivanpah

CALIFORNIA

Baker

Soda Mts

Cima

Mojave
National Preserve

Soda Lake

Laughlin

Davis Dam

68

Colorado

Lake
Mohave

145

51

Selig

Crucero

35°

Kelso

Providence Mts

Pittle Wash

Bullhead City

Riviera

Kingman

McConnico

40

23

Ludlow

NORTH

Bristol Mts

206

Fenner

Essex

Goffs

24

Sacramento Mts

Oatman

Fort Mojave
Indian Resn

Mojave Valley

Needles

Havasu
NWR

Topock Marsh

Topock

Yucca

Sacramento Wash

Big Sandy R

Hualapai Mountains

Aquarius Mts

40

Prescc
Natio
Fores

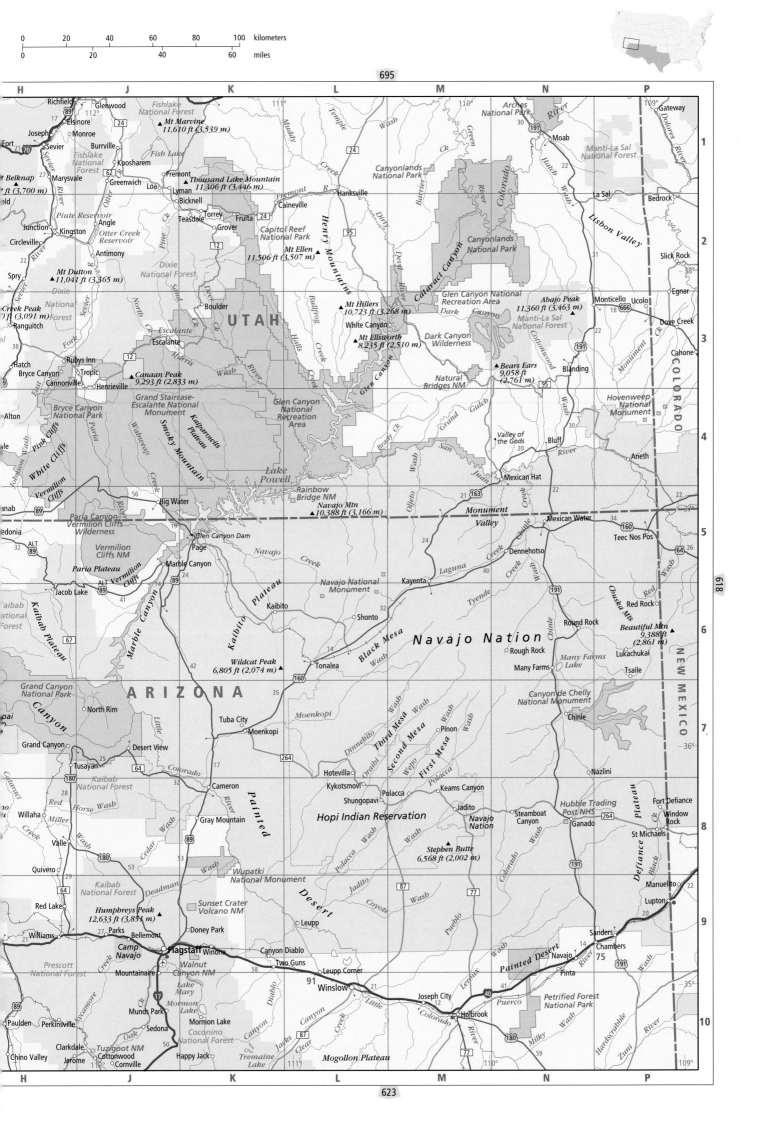

0 20 40 60 80 100 kilometers
0 20 40 60 miles

H   J   K   L   M   N   P

1

Richfield
Glenwood
89 112°
17 Elsinore
Joseph Monroe
Fort Sevier Burrville
21 70 Marysvale Kooosharem
27 ▲ Mt Marvine
Belknap 11,610 ft (3,539 m)
ft (3,700 m) 62
eld Greenwich
24 Loa ▲ Thousand Lake Mountain
Fremont 11,306 ft (3,446 m)
Burrville Lyman
Kooosharem Bicknell
Fishlake National Forest
Fish Lake
Temple
Wash
Green
River
Arches National Park
30
191
Moab
Manti-La Sal National Forest
Gateway

2

Junction Angle
Circleville Antimony
22 Mt Dutton
Spry ▲ 11,041 ft (3,365 m)
Creek Peak
ft (3,091 m)
Panguitch
Piute Reservoir
Otter Creek Reservoir
Teasdale Torrey
Fruita 12
Grover 24
Caineville
Capitol Reef National Park
Henry Mountains
95
Dirty Devil River
Hanksville
24
Muddy Creek
111°
Cataract Canyon
Canyonlands National Park
110°
Green River
Colorado River
31
Lisbon Valley
109°
La Sal
Bedrock
Slick Rock
38°

3

UTAH
Boulder
Escalante 12
Escalante
Canaan Peak
▲ 9,293 ft (2,833 m)
Henrieville
Dixie National Forest
North Ck
Sand Ck
Escalante
Mt Hillers
▲ 10,723 ft (3,268 m)
White Canyon
Mt Ellsworth
▲ 8,235 ft (2,510 m)
Glen Canyon National Recreation Area
Dark Canyon
Dark Canyon Wilderness
Bears Ears
▲ 9,058 ft (2,761 m)
Natural Bridges NM
95
Abajo Peak
▲ 11,360 ft (3,463 m)
Manti-La Sal National Forest
Monticello
18 666
191
22
Ucolo
Dove Creek
Egnar
Cahone
Blanding

4

Hatch
Bryce Canyon
Cannonville
Rubys Inn
Tropic
12
Bryce Canyon National Park
Alton
Pink Cliffs
White Cliffs
Vermilion Cliffs
Paria
Grand Staircase-Escalante National Monument
Kaiparowits Plateau
Smoky Mountain
Hall Creek
Glen Canyon National Recreation Area
Lake Powell
Brady Ck
San Juan River
Valley of the Gods
20
Bluff
Aneth
Mexican Hat
163
Hovenweep National Monument
22°

5

Kanab
89
Cedonia
ALT 89
Parla Canyon-Vermilion Cliffs Wilderness
Big Water
56
19
Rainbow Bridge NM
Navajo Mtn
▲ 10,388 ft (3,166 m)
Glen Canyon Dam
Page
Navajo Creek
Ojieto Wash
21 163
Monument Valley
Mexican Water
160
Teec Nos Pos
34
64 26
36°

6

Vermilion Cliffs NM
Paria Plateau
Jacob Lake
41
Kaibab National Forest
Kaibab Plateau
67
Marble Canyon
ALT 89
24
89
14
Kaibito Plateau
Kaibito
Shonto
32
Navajo National Monument
Laguna Creek
Kayenta
40
Black Mesa
Chinle Wash
Tyende Creek
191
Round Rock
Rough Rock
Many Farms Lake
Beautiful Mtn
▲ 9,388 ft (2,861 m)
Red Rock
Lukachukai
Chuska Mts
NEW MEXICO

7

Grand Canyon National Park
North Rim
Grand Canyon
Tusayan
180
Wildcat Peak
▲ 6,805 ft (2,074 m)
42
Tonalea
160
14
ARIZONA
Tuba City
Moenkopi
Desert View
64
32
Cameron
17
Little Colorado River
Moenkopi Wash
Dinnebito Wash
Oraibi Wash
Third Mesa
Second Mesa
Wepo Wash
First Mesa
Polacca Wash
Navajo Nation
Pinon
Canyon de Chelly National Monument
Chinle
Many Farms
Tsaile
36°

8

Willaha
Red Lake
Valle
180
29
64
Quivero
Kaibab National Forest
Gray Mountain
Painted
Desert
Hotevilla
Kykotsmovi
Shungopavi
Polacca
Hopi Indian Reservation
Keams Canyon
Jadito
Navajo Nation
Steamboat Canyon
Ganado
264
Hubbell Trading Post NHS
Defiance Plateau
Fort Defiance
Window Rock
St Michaels
Nazlini
Stephen Butte
▲ 6,568 ft (2,002 m)
191

9

Williams
21
Parks Bellemont
Camp Navajo
27
Humphreys Peak
▲ 12,633 ft (3,851 m)
180
53
53
Doney Park
Sunset Crater Volcano NM
Wupatki National Monument
Leupp
Jadito Wash
Coyote Wash
Pueblo Colorado Wash
87
77
Painted Desert
Sanders
Navajo
75
Chambers
191
Manuelito
Lupton
20
22
35°

10

Prescott National Forest
89
Paulden
Perkinsville
Chino Valley
Clarkdale
Jerome
Cottonwood
Cornville
Flagstaff
Winona
Mountainaire
17
Munds Park
Sedona
Tuzigoot NM
Oak Creek
Sycamore Creek
Walnut Canyon NM
Lake Mary
Mormon Lake
Mormon Lake
Happy Jack
Coconino National Forest
Tremaine Lake
Canyon Diablo
Two Guns
58
91
Leupp Corner
Winslow
21
Mogollon Plateau
111°
Little Colorado River
Jacks Canyon
Clear Creek
87
Joseph City
40
12
Holbrook
77
180
Puerco River
Milky Wash
Petrified Forest National Park
Zuni River
Hardscrabble Wash
59
110°
109°

H   J   K   L   M   N   P

Northern New Mexico • Northwestern Texas • Southern Colorado

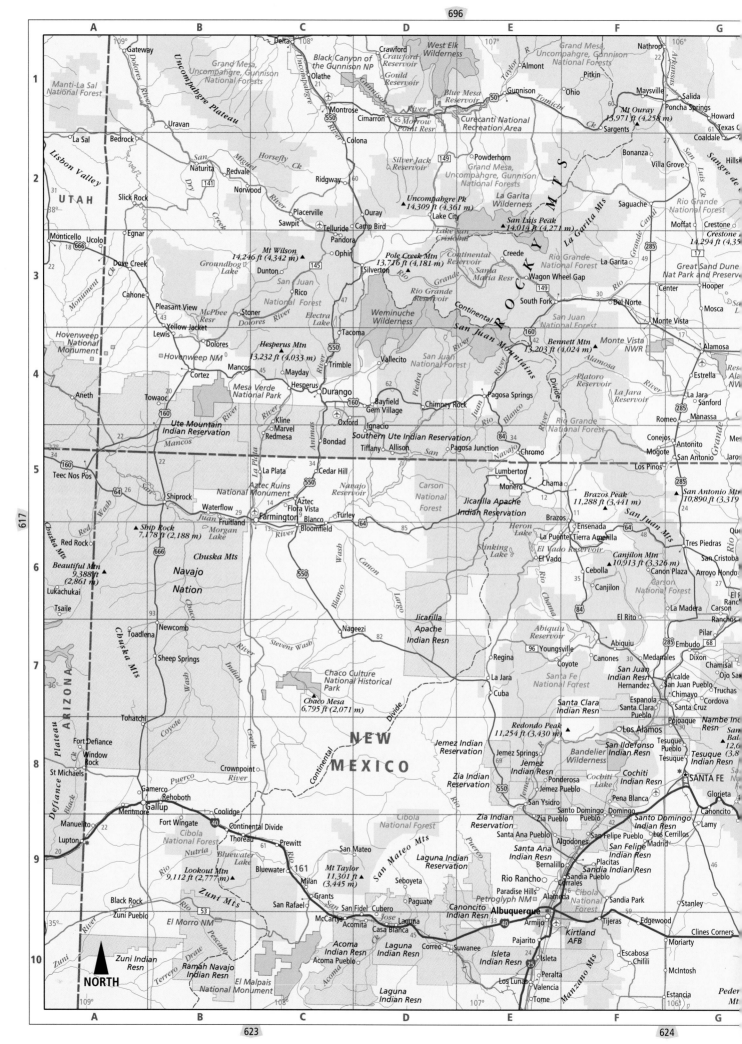

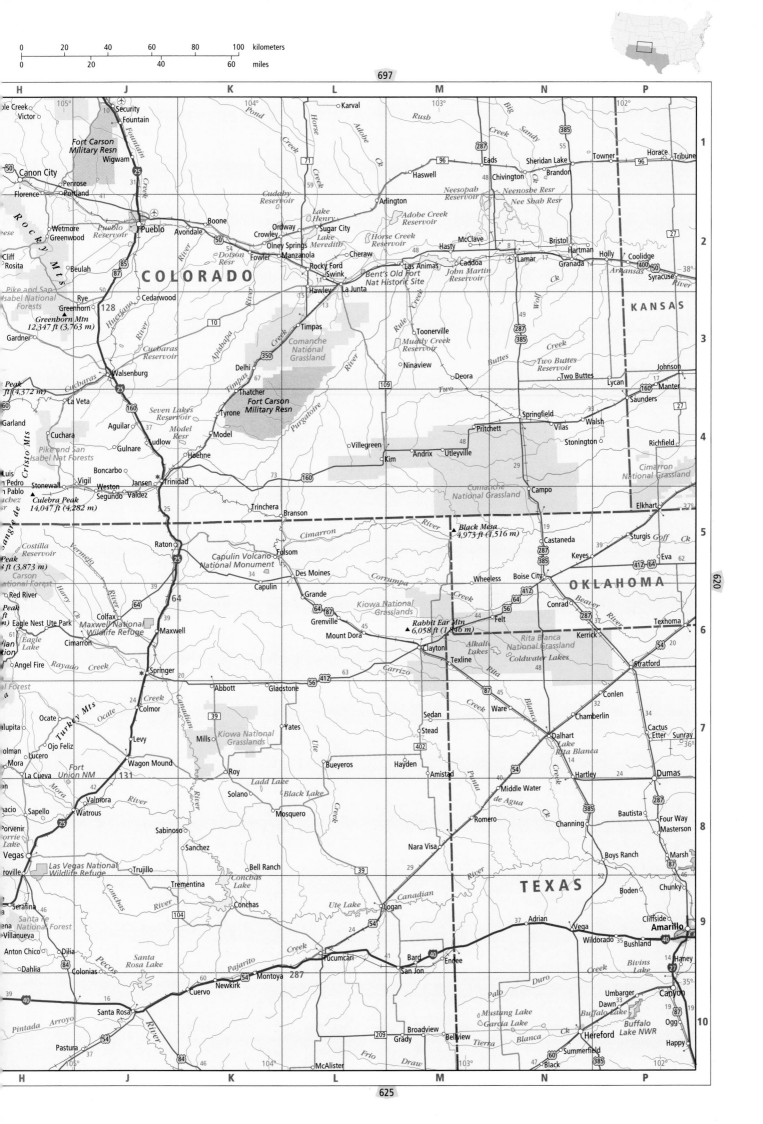

SOUTHWEST

Central-Northern Texas • Southern Kansas • Northern Oklahoma

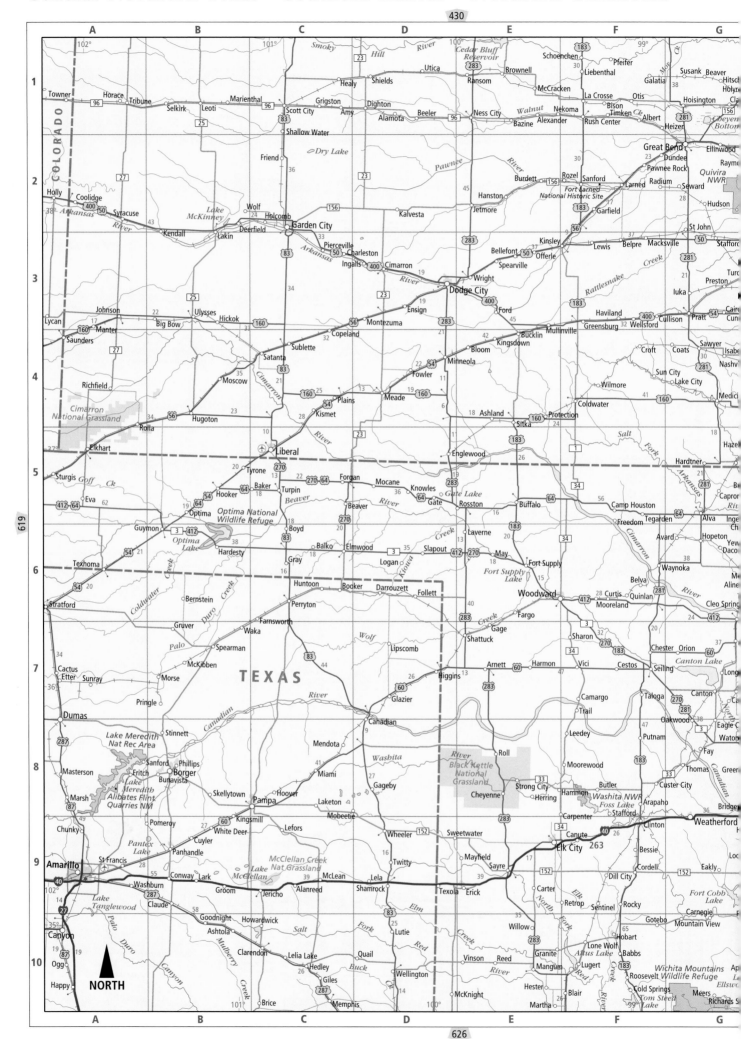

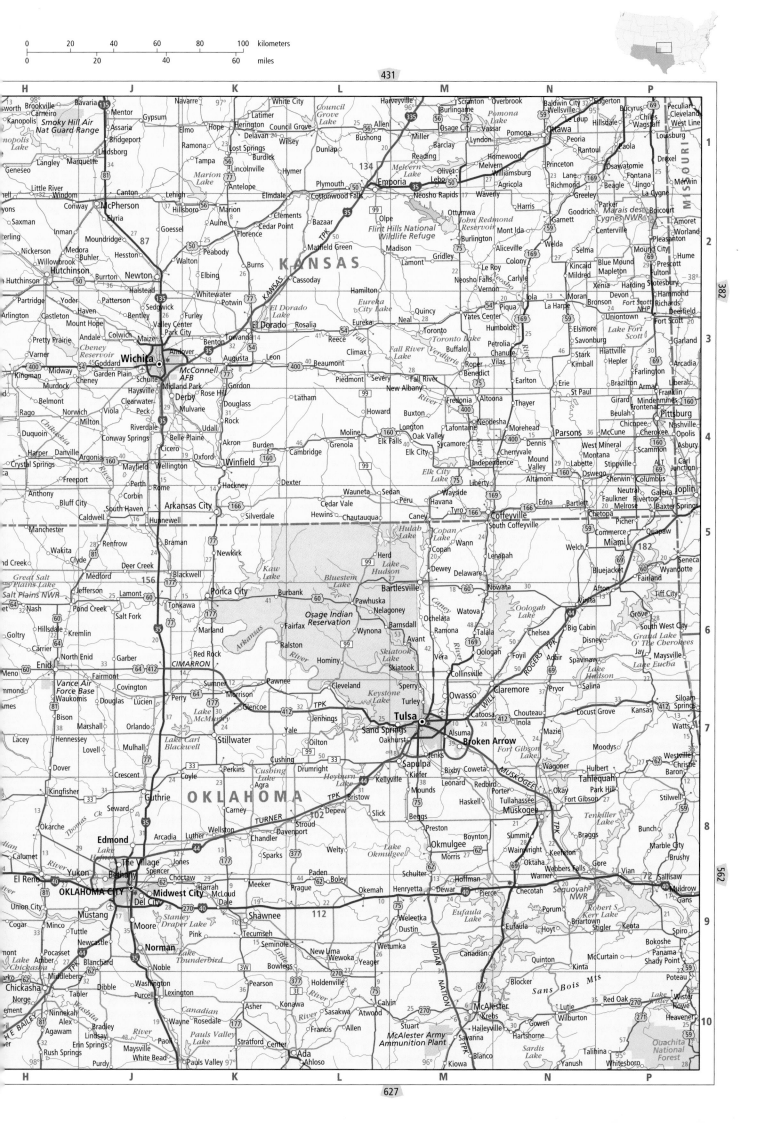

0 20 40 60 80 100 kilometers
0 20 40 60 miles

H J K L M N P

MISSOURI

382

SOUTHWEST

562

Southern Arizona • Western New Mexico

616

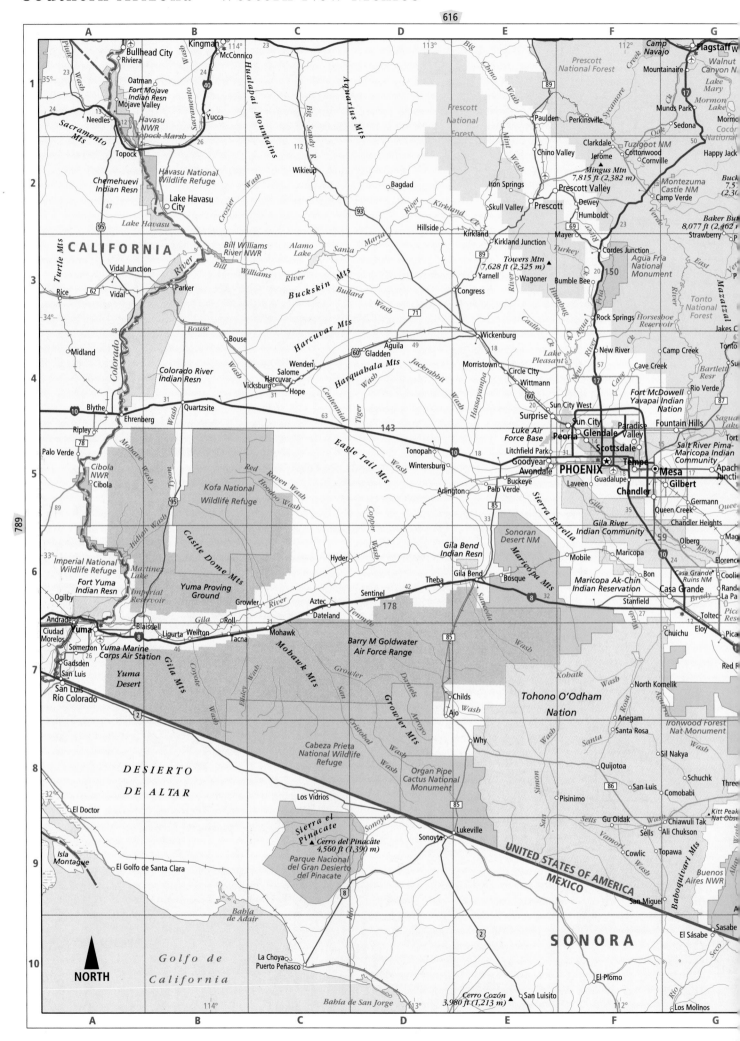

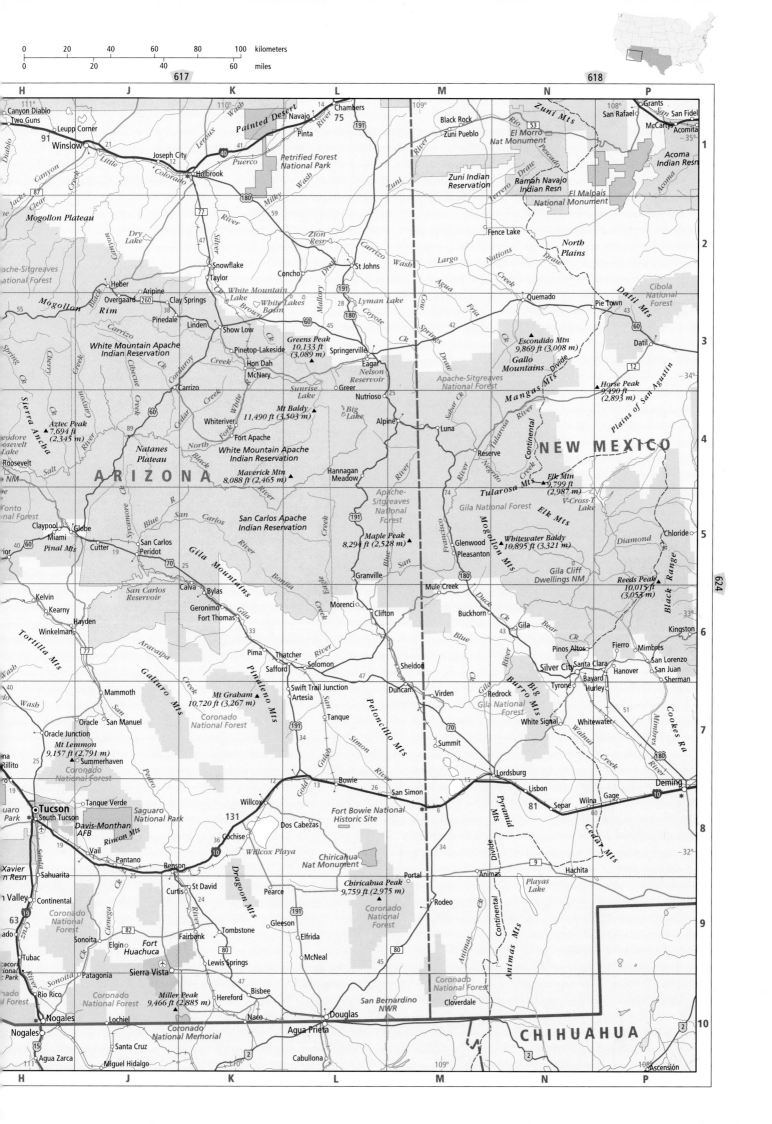

Southern New Mexico • Central-Western Texas

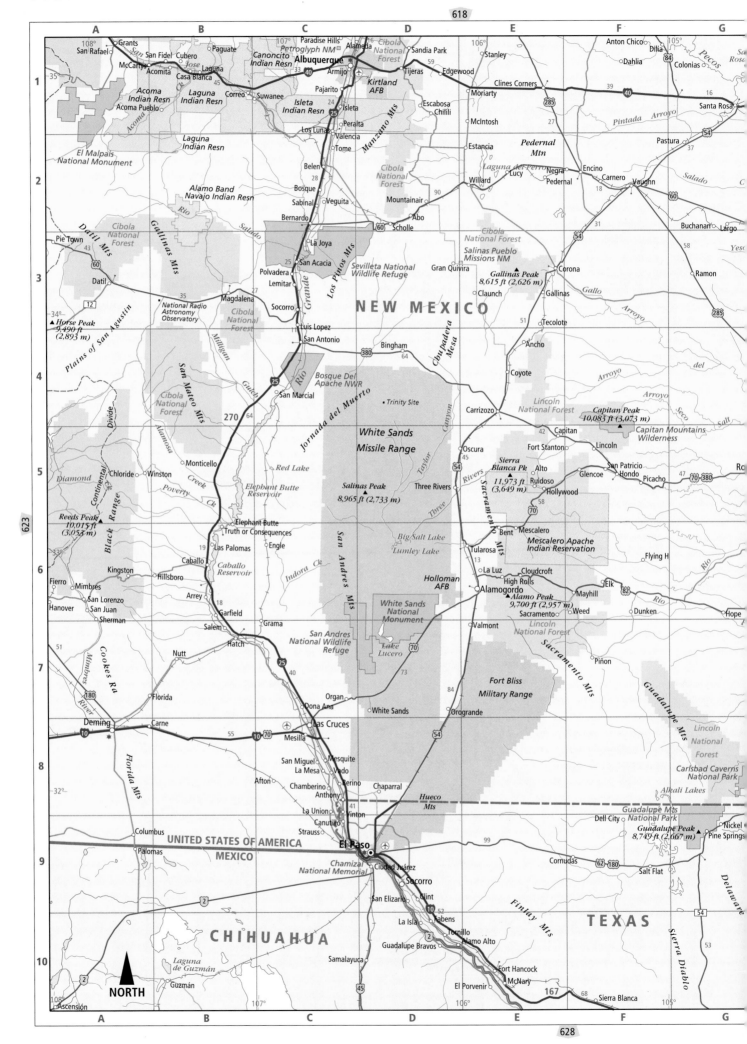

SOUTHWEST

NORTH

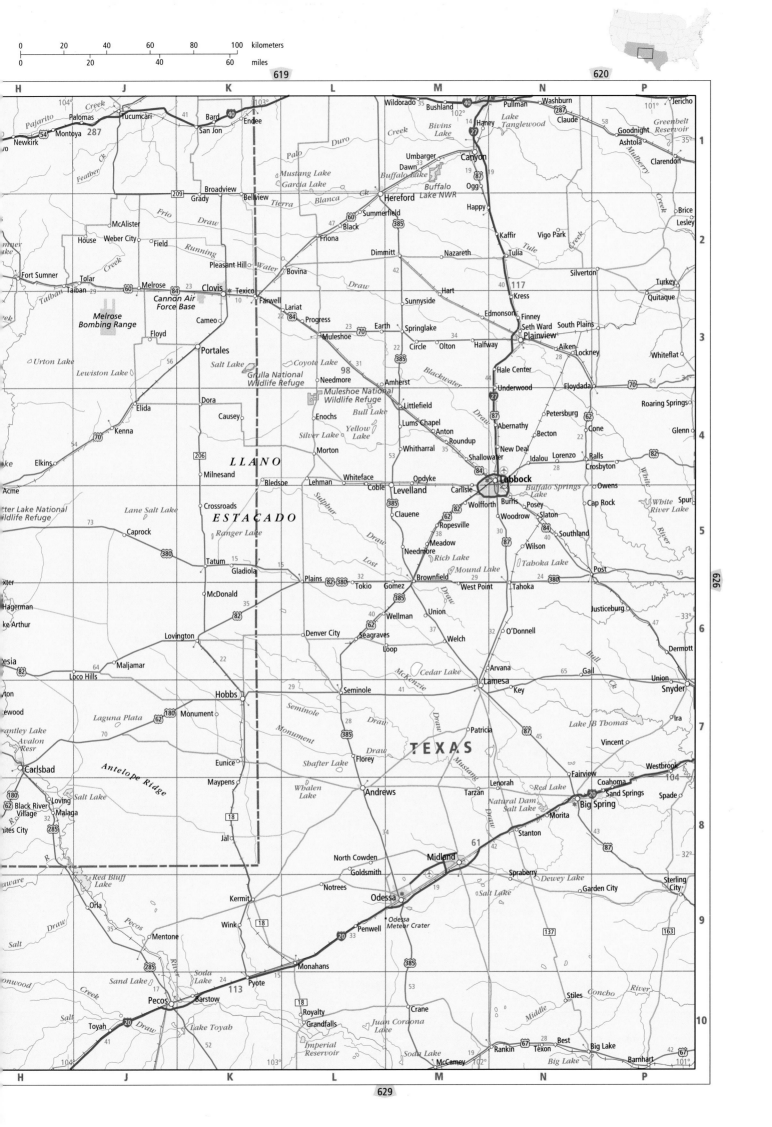

SOUTHWEST

Northeastern Texas • Southern Oklahoma

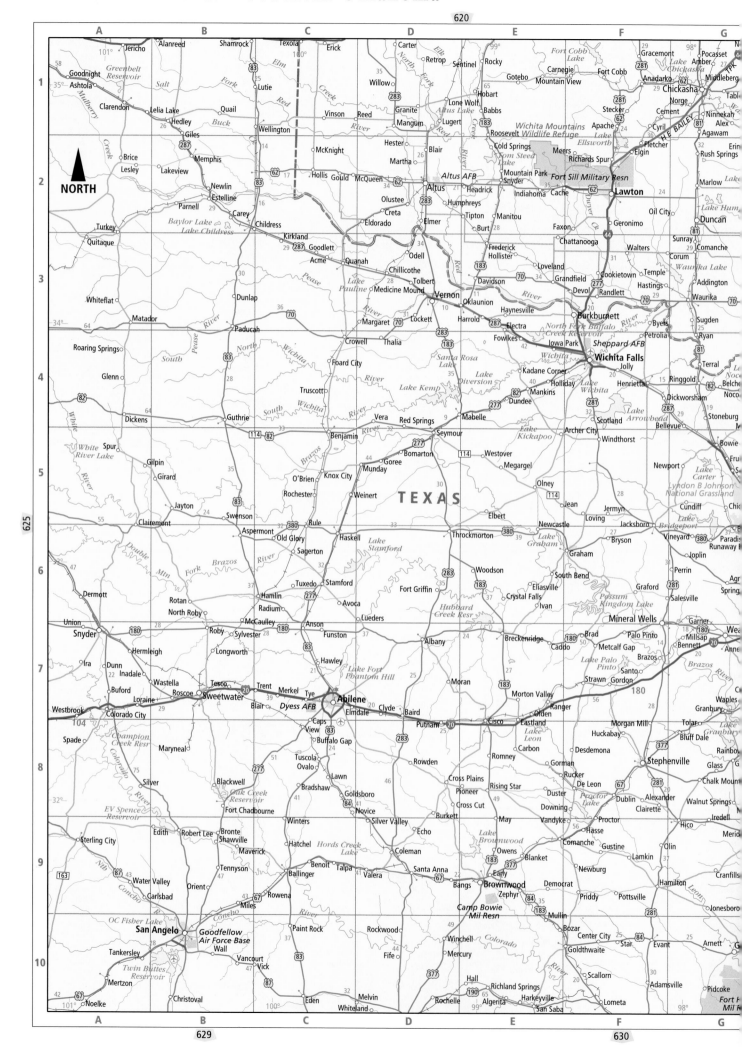

SOUTHWEST

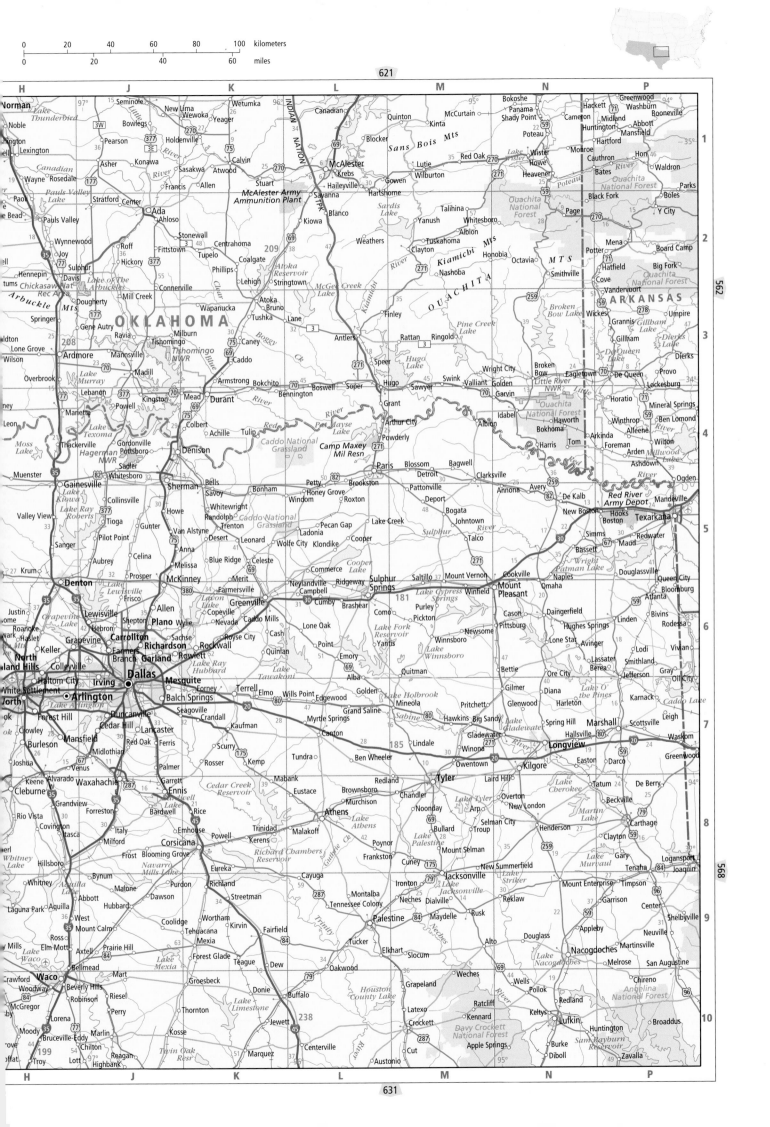

SOUTHWEST

Southwestern Texas

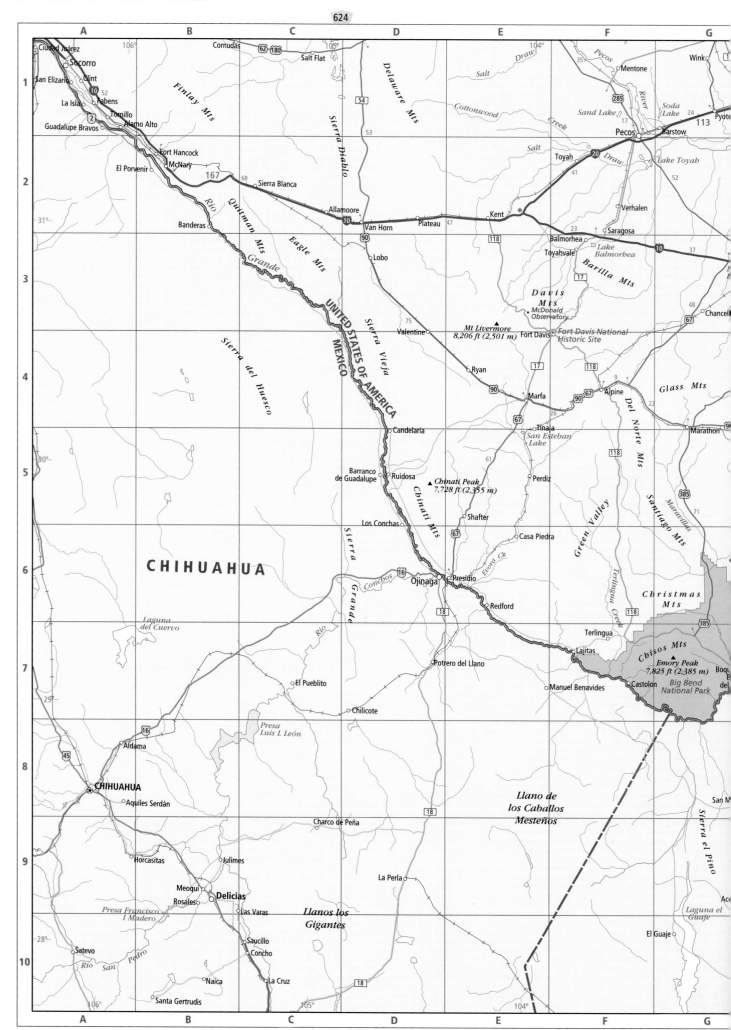

Ciudad Juárez
Socorro
San Elizario
Clint
La Isla
Fabens
Tornillo
Alamo Alto
Guadalupe Bravos
Fort Hancock
McNary
El Porvenir
Sierra Blanca
Banderas
Allamoore
Van Horn
Plateau
Lobo
Valentine
Mt Livermore
8,206 ft (2,501 m)
Fort Davis
Ryan
Candelaria
Barranco
de Guadalupe
Ruidosa
Chinati Peak
7,728 ft (2,355 m)
Los Conchas
Shafter
Casa Piedra
Ojinaga
Presidio
Redford
Terlingua
Lajitas
Potrero del Llano
Manuel Benavides
Castolon
El Pueblito
Chilicote
Aldama
CHIHUAHUA
Aquiles Serdán
Charco de Peña
Horcasitas
Julimes
La Perla
Meoqui
Rosales
Delicias
Las Varas
Satevo
Saucillo
Concho
Naica
La Cruz
Santa Gertrudis

Cornudas
Salt Flat
Delaware Mts
Salt Draw
Pecos
Mentone
Wink
Cottonwood Creek
Sand Lake
Soda Lake
Pyote
Pecos
Barstow
Toyah
Lake Toyah
Kent
Verhalen
Saragosa
Balmorhea
Lake Balmorhea
Toyahvale
Barilla Mts
Davis Mts
McDonald Observatory
Fort Davis National Historic Site
Marfa
Alpine
Glass Mts
Tinaja
San Esteban Lake
Marathon
Del Norte Mts
Perdiz
Green Valley
Santiago Mts
Christmas Mts
Emory Peak
7,825 ft (2,385 m)
Big Bend National Park
Terlingua Creek
Manzanillas
Llano de los Caballos Mesteños
Sierra el Pino
Laguna el Guaje
El Guaje

CHIHUAHUA

Finlay Mts
Quitman Mts
Eagle Mts
Sierra Diablo
Rio Grande
Sierra del Huesco
UNITED STATES OF AMERICA
MEXICO
Sierra Vieja
Chinati Mts
Sierra Grande
Rio Conchos
Evora Ck
Laguna del Cuervo
Presa Luis L León
Presa Francisco I Madero
Rio San Pedro
Llanos los Gigantes

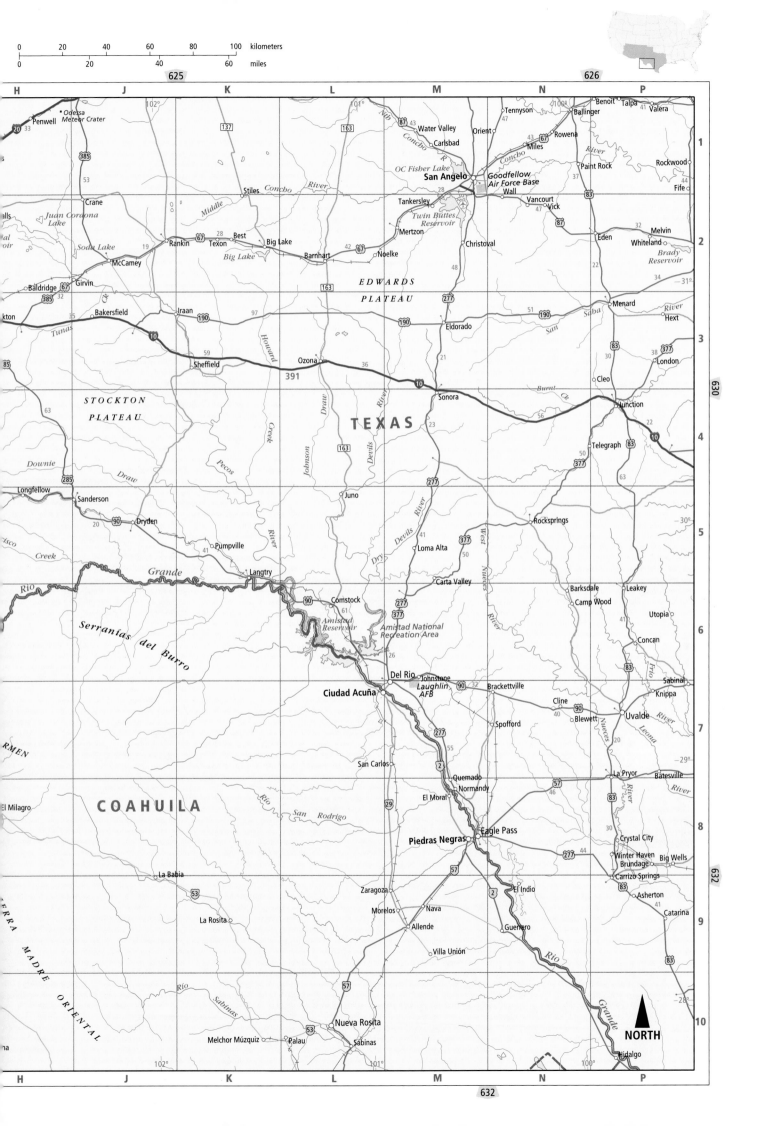

kilometers

miles

625
626
630
632

Penwell
Odessa Meteor Crater

Crane

Juan Cordona Lake

Soda Lake

Rankin
Texon
Best
Big Lake

McCamey

Baldridge
Girvin

Bakersfield
Iraan

Sheffield
Ozona

STOCKTON PLATEAU

Downie

Longfellow

Sanderson

Dryden

Pumpville

Langtry

Comstock

Serranías del Burro

Amistad Reservoir

Del Rio

Ciudad Acuña
Laughlin AFB
Johnstone

COAHUILA

San Carlos

El Moral

La Babia

Zaragoza

La Rosita

Morelos
Nava

Allende

Villa Unión

Melchor Múzquiz
Palau

Nueva Rosita

Sabinas

Hidalgo

NORTH

Stiles
Concho River

Middle

Concho River

Barnhart
Noelke

EDWARDS
PLATEAU

Mertzon

Tankersley

San Angelo
Goodfellow Air Force Base
Wall

OC Fisher Lake

Twin Buttes Reservoir

Water Valley
Carlsbad

Orient

Christoval

Eldorado

Sonora

TEXAS

Juno

Loma Alta

Carta Valley

Rocksprings

Barksdale
Camp Wood

Amistad National Recreation Area

Brackettville

Spofford

Cline
Blewett

Quemado
Normandy

Eagle Pass

Piedras Negras

El Indio

Guerrero

Benoit
Talpa
Valera

Tennyson
Ballinger

Miles
Rowena

Paint Rock
Rockwood

Fife

Vancourt
Vick

Eden
Melvin
Whiteland

Brady Reservoir

Menard
Hext

London

Cleo

Junction

Telegraph

Leakey
Utopia

Concan

Sabinal
Knippa

Uvalde

La Pryor
Batesville

Crystal City

Winter Haven
Brundage
Big Wells

Carrizo Springs
Asherton

Catarina

Rio Grande

SIERRA MADRE ORIENTAL

SOUTHWEST

Central-Eastern Texas

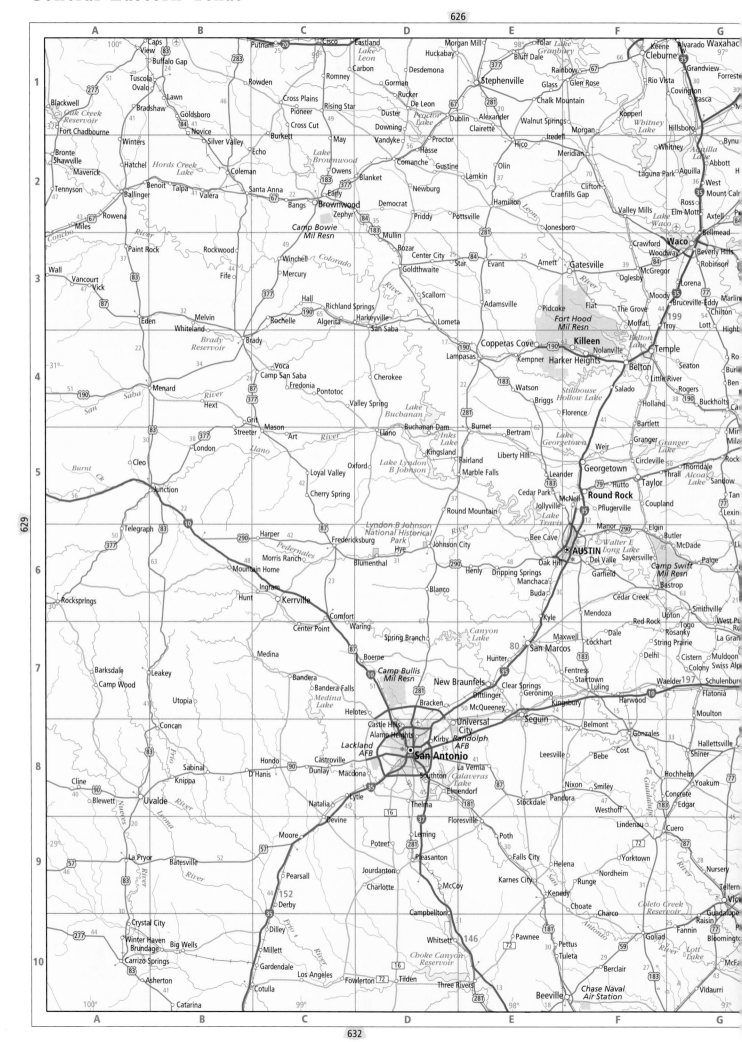

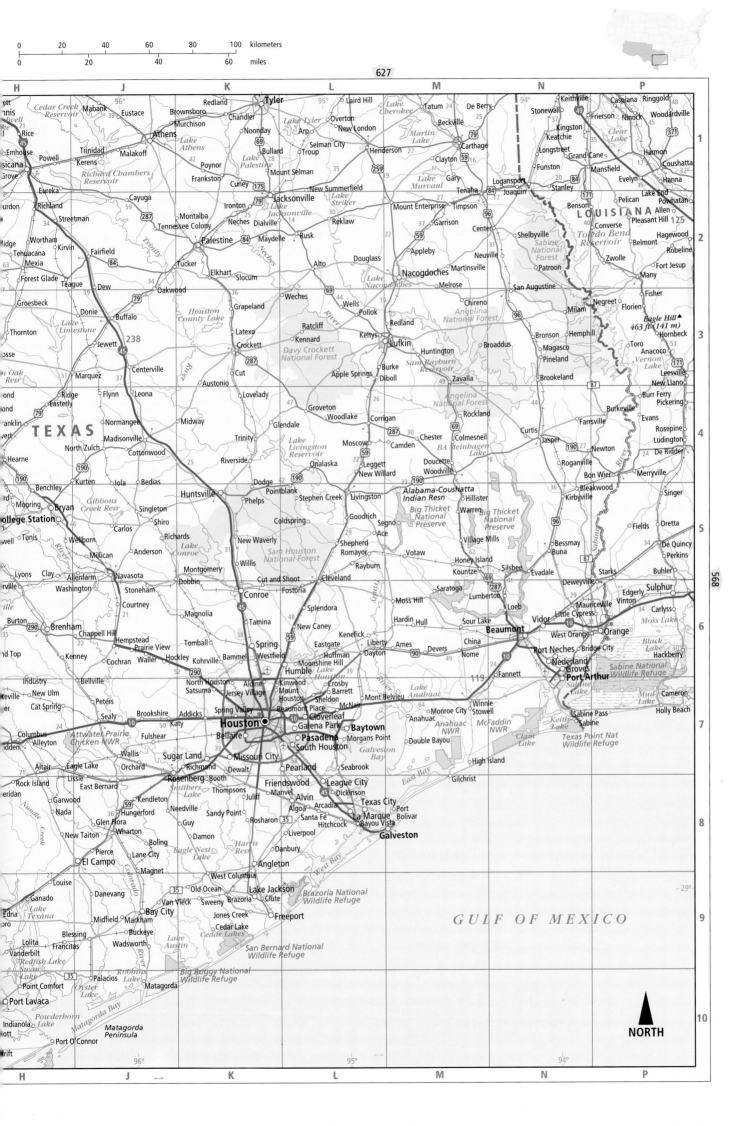

Southeastern Texas

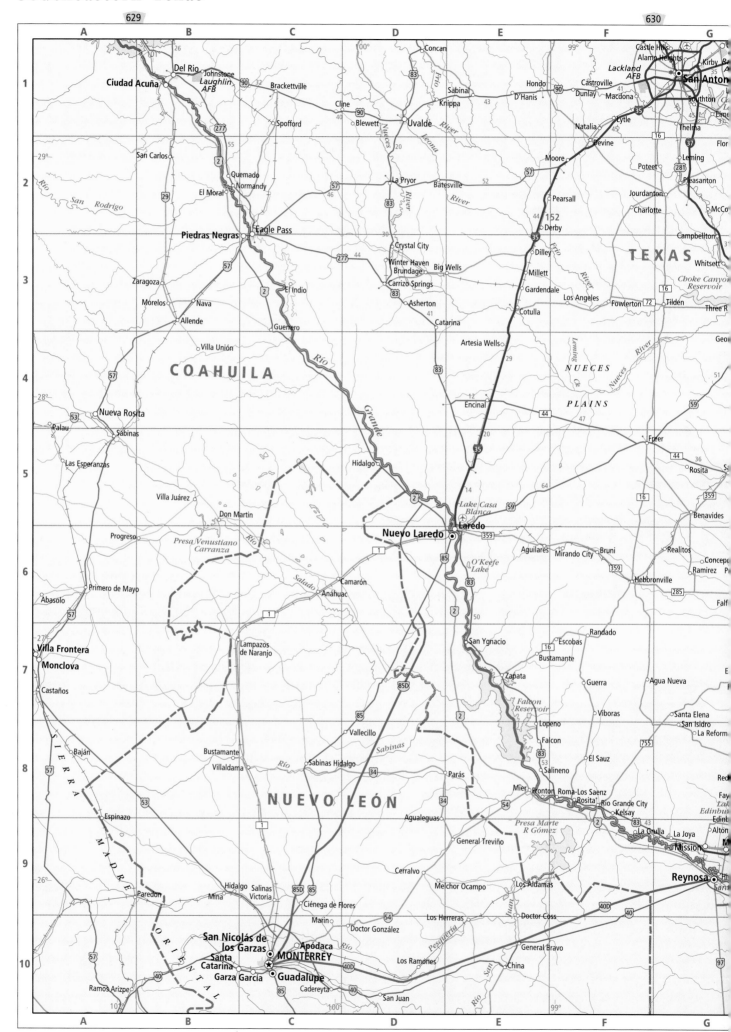

Map grid columns: A B C D E F G

Map grid rows: 1 2 3 4 5 6 7 8 9 10

Concan
Castle Hills
Alamo Heights
Lackland AFB
San Anton
Kirby

Del Rio
Johnstone Laughlin AFB
Brackettville
Sabinal
Hondo
Castroville
Dunlay
Macdona
Southton
Elme

Ciudad Acuña
Cline
Knippa
D'Hanis
Lytle
Thelma

Spofford
Blewett
Uvalde
Natalia
Devine
Poteet
Pleasanton

San Carlos
La Pryor
Batesville
Moore
Jourdanton
Charlotte
McCo

Quemado
Normandy
Pearsall
Derby
152

El Moral
Crystal City
Dilley
Campbellton

Eagle Pass
Winter Haven
Brundage
Big Wells
Millett
TEXAS
Whitsett

Piedras Negras
Carrizo Springs
Gardendale
Los Angeles
Fowlerton
Tilden
Choke Canyon Reservoir

Zaragoza
Asherton
Cotulla
Three R

Morelos
Nava
Catarina

Allende
Guerrero
Artesia Wells
Geo

Villa Unión
COAHUILA
NUECES
PLAINS

Nueva Rosita
Encinal
Freer

Palau
Sábinas

Las Esperanzas
Hidalgo
Lake Casa Blanca
Benavides

Villa Juárez
Rosita

Don Martin
Laredo

Progreso
Nuevo Laredo
Aguilares
Mirando City
Bruni
Realitos
Concepc

Presa Venustiano Carranza
O'Keefe Lake
Ramirez
P

Camarón
Hebbronville

Primero de Mayo
Anáhuac
San Ygnacio
Escobas
Randado
Falf

Abasolo
Bustamante

Villa Frontera
Zapata
Guerra
Agua Nueva

Monclova
Lampazos de Naranjo
Falcon Reservoir

Castaños
Viboras
Santa Elena
San Isidro
La Reforma

Vallecillo
Lopeno
La

Bajan
Bustamante
Falcon
El Sauz

Villaldama
Sabinas Hidalgo
Parás
Salineno

Espinazo
NUEVO LEÓN
Mier
Fronton
Roma-Los Saenz
Rosita
Rio Grande City
Fay
Edinbu

Agualeguas
Presa Marte R Gómez
Kelsay
Edinb
Alton
M

General Treviño
La Grulla
La Joya
Mission

SIERRA MADRE ORIENTAL
Cerralvo
Los Aldamas
Reynosa

Hidalgo
Salinas Victoria
Melchor Ocampo

Paredon
Mina
Ciénega de Flores
Doctor Coss

Marin
Doctor González
General Bravo

San Nicolás de los Garzas
Apódaca
Los Ramones
China

Santa Catarina
MONTERREY
Los Herreras

Garza García
Guadalupe
San Juan

Ramos Arizpe
Cadereyta

0   20   40   60   80   100   kilometers
0   20   40   60   miles

H   J   K   L   M   N   P

1

Belmont
Leesville
Bebe   Cost
Gonzales
Hallettsville
Sublime
Sheridan
Rock Island
Lissie
East Bernard
Booth
Thompsons
Friendswood
League City
Dickinson
Texas City
Port Bolivar

Stockdale
Pandora
Nixon   Smiley
Hochheim
Yoakum
Shiner
Concrete
Edgar
Cuero
Westhoff
Lindenau

Garwood
Nada
Hungerford
Glen Flora
Wharton
New Taiton
Pierce
Lane City
Boling
Magnet
El Campo

Kendleton
Needville
Guy
Damon
Sandy Point
Rosharon
Juliff
Manvel
Alvin
Arcadia
Algoa
Santa Fe
Hitchcock
Liverpool
La Marque
Bayou Vista
Galveston

Helena
Nordheim
Runge
Kenedy
Choate
Charco

Yorktown
Morales
Louise
Danevang
Van Vleck
Old Ocean
West Columbia
Lake Jackson
Sweeny
Brazoria
Clute
Angleton
Danbury
Freeport

2

Coleto Creek Reservoir
Nursery
Inez
El Toro
Edna
Telferner
La Salle
Vanderbilt
Blessing
Francitas
Midfield
Markham
Buckeye
Wadsworth
Bay City
Jones Creek
Cedar Lake
Cedar Lakes

San Bernard National Wildlife Refuge

Victoria
Guadalupe
Raisin
Fannin
Placedo
Bloomington
Goliad
Kamey
Port Lavaca
Point Comfort
Palacios
Matagorda

Oyster Lake
Robbins Lake
Big Boggy National Wildlife Refuge

3

Pettus
Tuleta
Berclair
McFaddin
Vidaurri
Long Mott
Tivoli
Indianola
Port O'Connor
Seadrift

Powderhorn Lake
Matagorda Bay
Matagorda Peninsula

Beeville
Chase Naval Air Station

Refugio
Woodsboro
Skidmore
Tynan
Papalote
Cranell
Lamar
Fulton
Rockport
Estes

Aransas National Wildlife Refuge
San Antonio Bay
Matagorda Island
Matagorda National Wildlife Refuge

4

Mathis
Saint Paul
Sinton
Edroy
Odem
Taft
San Jose Island

Orange Grove
Gregory
Portland
Ingleside
Aransas Pass
Port Aransas

5

Robstown
San Pedro
Corpus Christi
Corpus Christi Bay
Mustang Island
Corpus Christi Naval Air Station

Driscoll
Bishop
Chapman Ranch

6

Kingsville
Kingsville Naval Air Station
Ricardo
Riviera
Sarita

Laguna Larga
Baffin Bay

GULF OF MEXICO

7

Padre Island National Seashore

Cayo Grande
Armstrong
Norias
Cayo Soledad

Padre Island

8

Rudolph
Port Mansfield
San Perlita

Laguna Madre

9

La Sal Vieja
Lasara
Raymondville
Lyford
Sebastian
Delta Lake
Edcouch
Santa Rosa
Combes
Rio Hondo
Primera
Harlingen
La Feria
San Benito
Bayview
Los Fresnos
South Padre Island

Laguna Atascosa National Wildlife Refuge
Cayo Atascosa
Laguna Atascosa

Veslaco
Progreso
Los Indios
La Paloma
Olmito
Port Isabel
Bahia Grande

10

Bravo
Matamoros
Brownsville
Playa Lauro Villar

TAMAULIPAS
Valle Hermoso
Independencia

NORTH

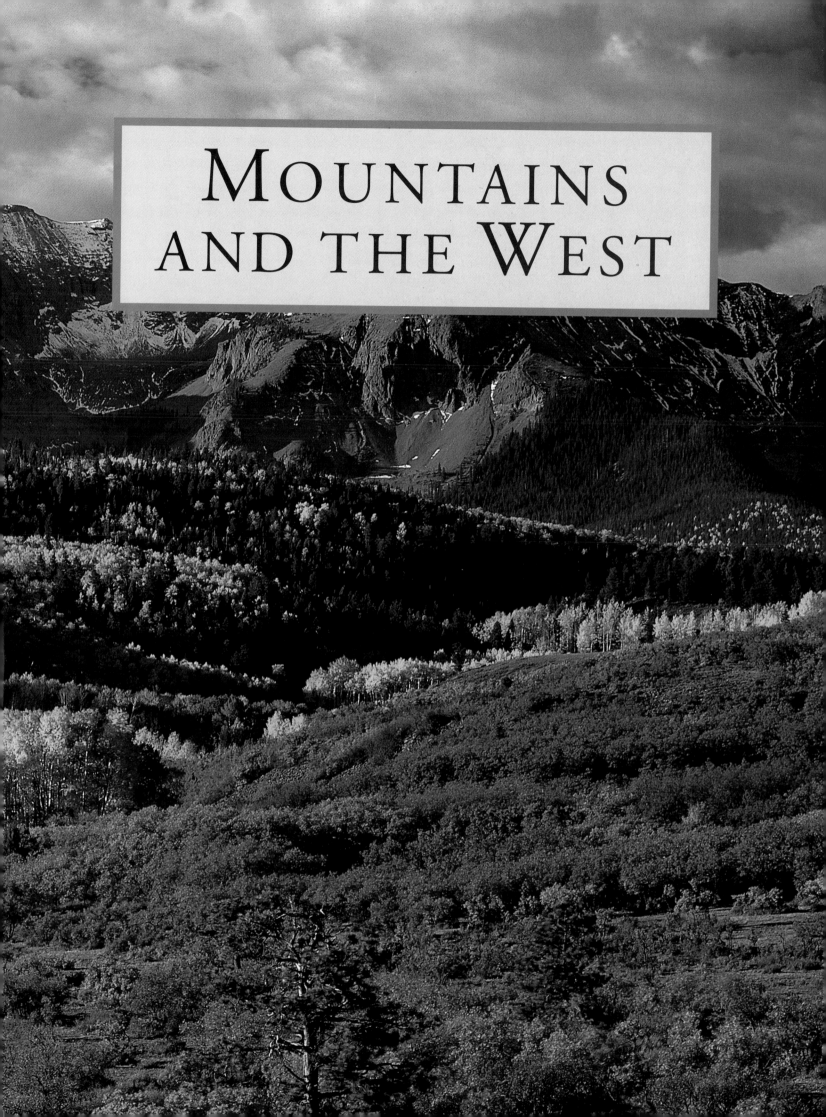

MOUNTAINS AND THE WEST

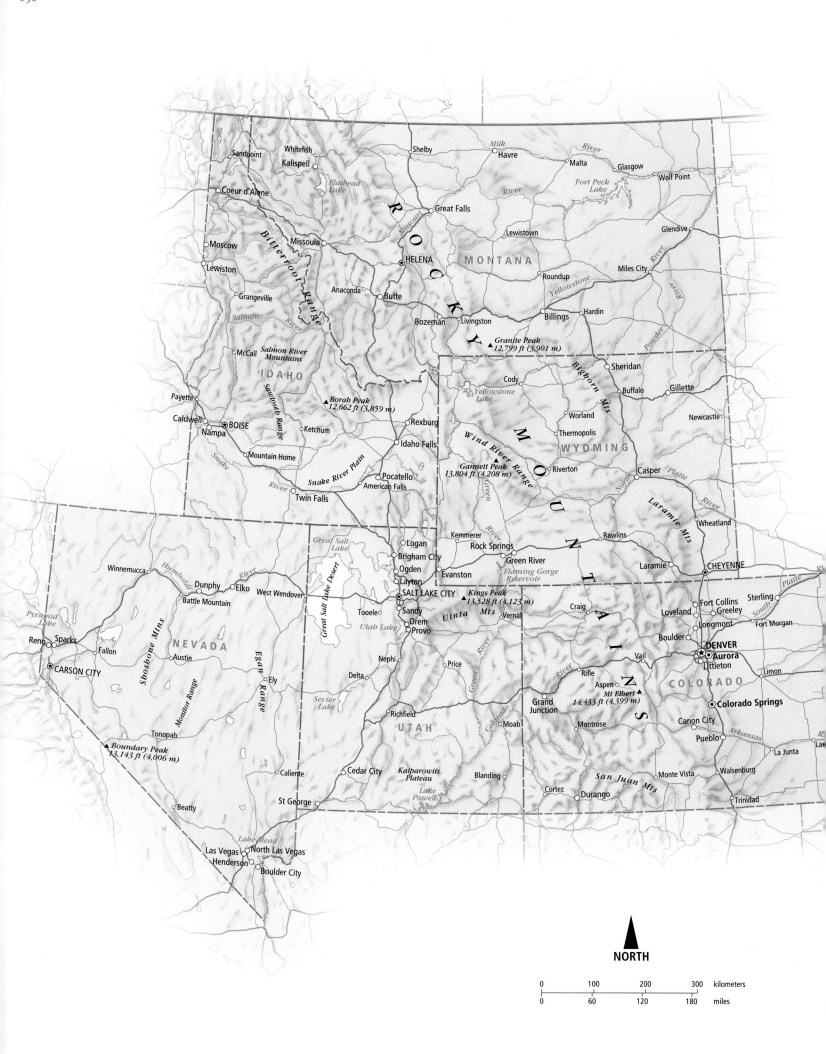

Sandpoint Whitefish Shelby Havre Milk River Malta Glasgow Wolf Point
Kalispell
Coeur d'Alene Flathead Lake Fort Peck Lake
Moscow Missoula Great Falls Lewistown Glendive
Lewiston HELENA MONTANA Roundup Miles City
Grangeville Anaconda Butte Yellowstone Billings Hardin
Salmon River Bozeman Livingston River
McCall Salmon River Mountains ▲ Granite Peak 12,799 ft (3,901 m)
IDAHO Cody Sheridan
Payette ▲ Borah Peak 12,662 ft (3,859 m) Yellowstone Lake Buffalo Gillette
Caldwell BOISE Ketchum Rexburg Worland Newcastle
Nampa Sawtooth Range Wind River Range MOUNTAINS Thermopolis WYOMING
Mountain Home Idaho Falls ▲ Gannett Peak 13,804 ft (4,208 m) Riverton Casper Platte
Snake River Plain Pocatello Green River North
River American Falls Kemmerer Rawlins Wheatland Laramie Mts
Twin Falls
Winnemucca Humboldt Great Salt Lake Logan Rock Springs Laramie CHEYENNE
Dunphy Elko River Brigham City Green River Flaming Gorge Reservoir Platte
Battle Mountain West Wendover Ogden Evanston Fort Collins Sterling
Pyramid Lake Layton Kings Peak 13,528 ft (4,123 m) Craig Loveland Greeley
Reno Sparks SALT LAKE CITY Uinta Mts Longmont Fort Morgan
Fallon Shoshone Mtns NEVADA Tooele Sandy Vernal Boulder
CARSON CITY Austin Orem Provo DENVER Aurora
Egan Range Nephi Price Vail Littleton Limon
Monitor Range Ely Utah Lake Rifle COLORADO
Sevier Lake Delta Aspen Mt Elbert 14,433 ft (4,399 m) Colorado Springs
Tonopah Richfield Grand Junction Montrose Canon City
▲ Boundary Peak 13,143 ft (4,006 m) UTAH Moab San Juan Mts Pueblo
Caliente Cedar City Kaiparowits Plateau Blanding Monte Vista Walsenburg
Beatty St George Lake Powell Cortez Durango Trinidad
Lake Mead La Junta
Las Vegas North Las Vegas
Henderson Boulder City

NORTH

| 0 | 100 | 200 | 300 | kilometers |

| 0 | 60 | 120 | 180 | miles |

MOUNTAINS AND THE WEST

The region known as "The West" stirs both the heart and imagination of anyone who traverses it. Wyoming, Montana, Utah, Nevada, Idaho, and Colorado are sprinkled with tight-knit communities, vast cattle ranches, and intriguing ghost-town remnants of communities that went bust after the silver and gold mines lost their luster. With its vast, open ranges and a fabled big sky, the area also represents the last piece of the American frontier and all its former glory.

Just over 150 years ago, the West was high-plains desert, impenetrable mountains, and rushing rivers, and bison and wolves roamed the land. The region still nurtures its timeless beauty, albeit not without struggle.

In the twentieth century, mining, ranching, and oil drilling each played a pivotal role in the economic expansion of the West, encouraging a swift population growth. But the influx of people and development came at a price: the land succumbed to overgrazing, and precious metals became fatigued. Conservationists, ranchers, corporations, and federal agencies still remain in conflict over the use of public land. Only in Yellowstone National Park has the ecosystem remained reasonably unchanged.

Following the Civil War, settlers began to blaze the emigrant route west. With the pioneers came the cowboys who herded thousands of longhorn cattle to cowtowns in Kansas, Wyoming, and Montana.

Land in the West has always been important. The Native Americans based their religion and survival around it; emigrants imbued it with their hopes and fortunes. After the government acquired the former French territory in the Louisiana Purchase of 1803, President Thomas Jefferson commissioned Captains Lewis and Clark in 1804 to investigate the uncharted territory west of the Mississippi, in search of a northwest passage to the Pacific Ocean. Their two-year trek paved the way for frontiersmen and fur-trappers.

Across the Continental Divide, an insatiable thirst for minerals and the promise of other fortunes initiated rapid settlement. By the 1860s, the boom years in the gold fields were the catalyst for the West's transformation. And with it came lawlessness, creating further discord between prospectors and indigenous tribes.

Army forts were established, and treaties were constantly violated; it was inevitable that the ensuing hostilities would end in bloodshed. The Indian Wars raged for over 20 years. By the late nineteenth century the Native American population was reduced to a mere 500,000, and the surviving tribes were forcibly moved to government reservations.

The linking of the Union Pacific, Southern, and Northern Pacific Railroads, and the cattle boom of the 1880s, made the West accessible for wealthy easterners. Buffalo Bill Cody's Wild West extravaganza similarly enticed a new wave of visitors.

As well as the enduring image of the cowboy, at every turn there are spectacular national parks and endless river tributaries—havens for grizzly bears, elk, moose, bison, bald eagles, and the fattest trout. Beyond the sheltered groves of forests are wild grouse, prairie dogs, and coyotes.

The region boasts some of the country's premier ski slopes. In the summer months, the diversity of the terrain provides plenty of outdoor activities from whitewater rafting and canoeing to horseback riding and hiking along picturesque trails.

Whether it's savoring its pristine wilderness, wandering through forgotten ghost towns, or exploring ancient cliff dwellings or fossilized dinosaur beds, the West is crammed with boundless adventures.

Small and wolf-like in appearance, the coyote (Canis latrans) is found in great numbers throughout the west.

The Grand Canyon of the Yellowstone is a remarkable ravine in Wyoming's Yellowstone National Park.

COLORADO

Colorado is a dramatic landscape of two contrasting climatic zones. The eastern plains are largely made up of agricultural farmlands, while the imposing Rocky Mountain Ranges are in the state's western region.

The Spanish first explored Colorado in the seventeenth century, and the Fremont Native Americans and the Anasazi, or Ancestral Puebloans (prehistoric ancestors of modern Pueblo peoples), once flourished in the Four Corners region, leaving a legacy of cliff dwellings and rock art.

During the early 1800s, French fur traders and American prospectors moved into Colorado's Rocky Mountains, while the Plains Native American tribes of the Ute, Cheyenne, Kiowa, Comanche, Pawnee, and Arapaho roamed the land in pursuit of migrating buffalo herds. Increased settlement and the discovery of gold in 1858 spawned many bloody battles between the Native Americans and the US Army. By the 1880s, Colorado's indigenous people had been relocated to Native American reservations throughout the state.

Colorado prospered when large deposits of minerals were discovered in the Rocky Mountains. Silver, gold, zinc, coal, and uranium remain a vital part of Colorado's economy today, as well as oil, natural gas, technology, and, more traditionally, ranching in the state's northeastern pocket. Tourism has further augmented Colorado's wealth, with the state boasting the nation's premier ski resorts and wilderness areas.

The Rocky Mountain ski slopes at Steamboat Springs boast one of the highest vertical drops in Colorado.

With a population of over 4 million, the state has seen incredible growth along the Front Range, from Colorado Springs to Fort Collins. The capital, Denver, is Colorado's largest city and has two-thirds of the state's population.

For the visitor, Colorado's alpine country is the primary attraction, as well as Mesa Verde and Rocky Mountain National Parks. With nearly 60 summits piercing the sky to more than 14,000 feet (4,270 m), there is never a shortage of summer and winter recreational activities in Colorado.

State motto *Nil Sine Numine* (Nothing without providence)
State flag Adopted 1911 (since modified)
Capital Denver
Population 4,301,261
Total area (land and water) 104,100 square miles (269,619 sq km)
Land area 103,729 square miles (268,658 sq km)
Colorado is the eighth-largest state in size
Origin of name From the Spanish word meaning "red"
Nickname The Centennial State
Abbreviations CO (postal), Colo.
State bird Lark bunting
State flower Rocky Mountain columbine
State tree Blue spruce
Entered the Union August 1, 1876 as the 38th state

Places in
COLORADO

ASPEN

The ritzy resort of Aspen lies in the high valley of Roaring Folk River, 156 miles (251 km) west of Denver. Once a weathered mining community, the town's population of 5,245 offers an astonishing selection of cultural events and, of course, its year-round mountain resorts. Surrounded by sheared glacial peaks and a forest dense with billowing aspen, oak, and pine, Aspen seizes every opportunity to promote its natural features. It is the ultimate playground for the rich.

Since its renaissance as America's golden ski resort, the town has lured many wealthy notables and celebrities into the valley. Its downtown area showcases razzle-dazzle at every turn, from its boutiques along Galena Street and Hyman Avenue to the Saabs driven by its

Fly-fishing in Maroon Lake, Aspen.

own police force. Aspen is a mishmash of Victorian and 1970s-style architecture. However, it is the construction of multi-million dollar mansions that leaves mouths gaping. Aspen's latest crop of migrating millionaires has contributed to a high-priced real estate boom—so high that many of the town's workers cannot live there and now reside in secondary communities along the US-82, the main artery that links Aspen to the I-70.

Although après-skiing is serious business to the town, Aspen also caters well to the general public by hosting a series of cultural events. In summer, the town lines up an incredible choice of concerts, with everything from jazz to the classics. The Aspen Music Festival, which

began in 1949, offers almost 160 concerts that run during high summer at the Aspen Music School.

The historic Wheeler Opera House on East Hyman Street hosts an array of operas during the summer season. Rebuilt in 1912 after being ravaged by fire, its interior reflects the height of Victorian fashion, complete with plush red chairs and a stage curtain featuring a mural of Brooklyn Bridge. The Aspen Art Museum, which is reached by a 90-year-old trestle, showcases some of the best contemporary exhibits outside of Denver.

It is by far, though, the natural beauty that outstrips all other attractions and there are several trails that surround the town. One of the most popular is the Maroon Bells-Snowmass Wilderness Area in the White River National Forest off US-82. Casting a shadow over Maroon Lake, the twin peaks of Mt Maroon and North Maroon soar to over 14,000 feet (4,270 m). The main trail leads to prime glacial country where gossamer air and jagged slopes harbor elk, moose, and bighorn sheep in its meadows. As cars are prohibited in the area, regular scheduled buses depart from the Ruby Park Transit Center to transport hikers.

The Aspen Center for Environmental Studies, on Hallam Lake Preserve, allows the visitor to delve into the Roaring Folk Valley's natural habitat. A sanctuary to golden eagles, owls, and red-tail hawks, the center offers programs that create a greater understanding of the environment, including a self-guided trek around the preserve's 25 acres (10 ha). As well as providing conservation guides to Maroon Bells, the center also offers summer hikes and snowshoe excursions to the summit of Aspen Mountain on its gondola. The 20-minute ride on the Silver Queen Gondola brings into view the town's fine Victorian architecture and a wondrous view

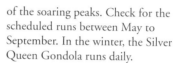

The twin peaks of Mt Maroon and North Maroon rising on either side of Maroon Lake in Aspen.

of the soaring peaks. Check for the scheduled runs between May to September. In the winter, the Silver Queen Gondola runs daily.

The Aspen Historical Society offers excursions throughout the summer. Guides dressed in period costumes take two-hour tours through Aspen, covering the Victorian landmarks and the town's illustrious mining history.

The Aspen Historical Society Museum, once the estate of Aspen magnate Jerome Wheeler, houses a collection of the town's artifacts. A partner in the famed Macy's Department Store, Wheeler moved to Aspen and became the town's benefactor. Along with the Wheeler Opera House, the silver baron also built the Jerome Hotel in 1889, still the town's finest. He was also influential in convincing the Denver and Rio Grande Railroad to extend its tracks to Aspen and invested heavily in several silver mines.

Aspen has always made its fortune from the ground. When businessman B. Clark Wheeler arrived by skis to develop a mining camp in 1880, never did he imagine that the town's long-term success would be made from powder snow. Aspen's silver mines produced in excess of US$6 million a year until the market bottomed 13 years later. The town's population of 12,000 faded to a mere 700. It would take another 56 years for the town to emerge from its slumber and strike gold with the marketing of its fine mountain slopes.

The four main ski areas in Aspen are Aspen, Aspen Highlands, Buttermilk, and Snowmass.

Elizabeth and Walter Paepcke became benefactors midway last century and they spearheaded the present-day Aspen Skiing Corporation. With the backing of investors, Paepcke started the Ajax Mountain chairlift in 1946 and completed his blueprint by hosting the prized Federation Internationale de Ski in 1950. It was this event alone that propelled Aspen's reputation as a world-class resort. The couple also nurtured Aspen's first Music Festival by attracting virtuosos such as Arthur Rubinstein and Dimitri Mitropoulos' Minneapolis Symphony. Years later, the late John Denver founded the acclaimed Rocky Mountain Institute. The subsequent development, in 1967, of Snowmass Village, located 12 miles (19 km) west on US-82, saw Aspen become a first-class resort.

There are four different ski areas at Aspen that offer superb downhill runs and cross-country tracks. The most advanced back-country skiing is on the 10th Mountain Trail, where

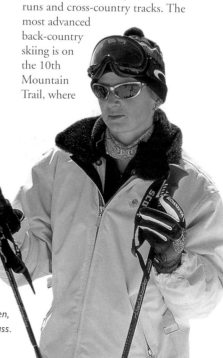

the famed US Army's 10th Mountain Division trained. Snowmass and Aspen Mountain both offer advanced and intermediate terrain while Aspen Highlands offers every type of ski run, from beginner slopes—Buttermilk/Tiehack is ideal for the uninitiated—to one of the steepest vertical drops in the country—for expert skiers only.

Aspen's appeal lasts into January for the five-day celebration of Winterskol. Using the mountains as a perfect crystal backdrop, the town unleashes a barrage of fireworks and hosts several fun-filled events, including the annual Bartender's Drink Contest. There is also downhill night skiing by torch light.

Even by resort standards, Aspen dishes up an endless menu of recreational sports from hiking, cycling, fishing, and skiing, to name only a few. There are also plentiful restaurants and bars, which dot downtown's star-studded streets.

The Aspen Chamber Resort Association provides entire listings of lodging facilities including budget motels and condominiums. The Aspen Skiing Company offers a reservation service at any of their resorts. The Aspen Chamber Resort Association provides seasonal maps and general information.

Aspen's Sardy Field Airport is just 4 miles (6 km) from town. Buses connect Snowmass to most resorts. Buses also serve Aspen from Denver International Airport. To drive from Denver, the 208-mile (335-km) journey along the I-70/US-82 takes approximately 4 hours but be aware of slippery road conditions and traffic jams.
Map ref: page 696 E8

BENT'S OLD FORT NATIONAL HISTORIC SITE

Located just near the Comanche National Grassland on Hwy 50, approximately 60 miles (97 km) southeast of Pueblo, Bent's Fort was once the most prominent trading post of the Old West. Servicing the newly opened Santa Fe Trail, the adobe structure was built in 1833 by brothers William and Charles Bent, on the western banks of the Arkansas River, which divided Mexico from the United States. The fort became the major trading post for fur trappers, immigrants, and the Plains Native Americans who traded buffalo robes for firearms.

The walls of Bent's Fort measured over 15 feet (4.6 m) high, and housed several living quarters, a trading room and dining hall, and a Native American council room.

Many luminaries of the West traded and hunted in the area, like frontiersman Kit Carson and explorer John C. Frémont. Bent's Fort also became a pivotal army post under the command of General Phil Kearney during the Mexican War in 1847.

During an outbreak of cholera, Bent blew up the adobe dwelling before building another makeshift fort, further along the river. Acting as an Indian agent on behalf of the government, Bent tried in vain to assist the Cheyenne as the encroachment of white settlers populated their traditional hunting grounds.

On a private piece of land on Hwy 96, near Brandon, is the site of the Sand Creek Massacre of

Cycling is a popular activity in Boulder.

1864, a massacre of Native American people, which was led by Colonel John Chivington. Bent's Old Fort National Historic Site was reconstructed on the original site. Interpreters, dressed in fringed buckskins and gingham frocks, provide visitors with an authentic look at frontier life.

Pueblo Memorial Airport is the closest regional airport, and Colorado Springs Municipal Airport is the closest major airport.
Map ref: page 619 L2

BLACK CANYON OF THE GUNNISON NATIONAL PARK

Located near Montrose, on Hwy 347, this untamed chasm is one of America's most mysterious yet pristine canyons. So impenetrable, the

Art Deco-style building at the University of Colorado campus in Boulder.

Ute people believed that anyone entering the gorge would simply vanish without a trace. Its sheer vertical cliffs shield the canyon from direct sunlight (hence the name) and trap the swift-flowing Gunnison River in a series of narrow escarpments. In front of Chasm View, its walls are only 1,100 feet (336 m) apart and, at Painted Wall, visitors can view the rushing water carving its way 2,300 feet (702 m) below, from a vertical drop—this is the longest precipice in Colorado.

Black Canyon's natural balcony provides a haven for a host of black ravens, swallows, and falcons which can be seen making death-defying swoops on small prey.

There are various trails within the canyon. The visitor center at Gunnison Point provides information on the best vantage points at the monument's north and south rims. Camping and rock climbing are permitted, though only the fittest should ever attempt to climb Black Canyon's sheer ledges.

Entrance fees for vehicles are small and the visitor center is open from May to September. Montrose Regional Airport is the closest.
Map ref: page 696 C10

BOULDER

The university city of Boulder is just 45 miles (72 km) northwest of Denver. It has a cityscape of evergreen parklands, bicycle tracks, and pristine suburbs. Boulder's cultural activities are generally through the esteemed University of Colorado. The city has soaring real-estate prices, with many of the residents working in the high-income fields of technology and medicine.

It is a beautiful city that provides a wealth of recreational pursuits—the Flatiron Ranges form a perfect backdrop to the city, and hiking the Flatiron's mountain trails is a very

popular activity. The most popular track is along the Mesa Trail, which brings into view the spectacular Eldorado Canyon and the National Center for Atmospheric Research—a good place to revive and check the Doppler screen for storms.

Founded in 1859 by gold prospectors, Boulder has evolved into a rather fashionable city of 91,000 people with the downtown district of Pearl Street Mall remaining the major drawcard. Other attractions in the area include the Boulder Historical Society Museum on Euclid Avenue and the Naropa Institute. It is here that the beat-Laureate, Ginsberg, co-founded the school's Jack Kerouac School of Disembodied Poetics.

In the summer, visitors can catch the University of Colorado's Shakespeare Festival, from June to August, and the Rocky Mountain Bluegrass Festival in early August.

Boulder Airport provides regular shuttle services to Denver International Airport.
Map ref: page 697 H6

Mail boxes, Colorado.

CANON CITY

To most visitors Canon City is promoted as the gateway town to Royal Gorge, home to the world's highest suspension bridge, which rises over the Arkansas River at 1,053 feet (321 m). Constructed in 1929, the bridge is a brilliant engineering feat that spans the world's steepest-incline railway, plunging at a 45-degree angle to the canyon floor.

The town's population of nearly 15,000 also caters to tourists who stop to visit the Colorado Territorial Prison Museum Park. Still used as a penitentiary, the prison has a museum in an adjoining cell block, including its famous gas chamber, which was last used in 1967.

Canon City's Main Street is characteristic of most nineteenth-century towns, with classic Victorian buildings framing the downtown sidewalks. Canon City was once a leading movie town during the silent picture era. Cowboy star Tom Mix lived periodically at the Hotel Saint Cloud while riding the celluloid range.

Located on Hwy 50, Canon City is serviced by buses.
Map ref: page 697 H10

COLORADO NATIONAL MONUMENT

Located west of Grand Junction off the I-70, Colorado National Monument rises abruptly along a fault to 2,000 feet (610 m) above the Grand Valley of the Colorado River. Several hiking trails take you through 32 miles (51 km) of sheer eroded

Quaking aspens (Populus tremuloides), Colorado Springs. The trees are so named due to the "quaking" of the leaves in a breeze.

sandstone escarpments dotted with sagebrush and juniper trees. There are camping facilities and numerous lookouts that provide perfect views of a land where dinosaurs once roamed. The visitor center at the park's northern entrance provides detailed information on the area's geological history, as well as information on the numerous back-country trails available.

The Walker Field Airport is in Grand Junction and provides regular services to Denver.
Map ref: page 696 B9

COLORADO SPRINGS

Colorado Springs, which sits at the basin of the Rocky Mountains' Front Range, serves as a gateway to Pikes Peak and Garden of the Gods—a spectacular formation of sandstone rocks and crimson turrets that has been preserved in a 1,350-acre (547-ha) city parkland, 6 miles (10 km) from downtown.

The old city of Colorado Springs was founded 5 miles (8 km) west, in 1859, during the Pikes Peak Gold Rush. Now merged with neighboring Manitou Springs, the prosperous city's population has grown to a staggering 346,000,

with a steady stream of newcomers arriving every year to work in the fields of technology or at one of the city's five regional military bases.

Downtown has all of the attractions of a city—shopping, bookstores, and a host of museums and galleries, including the Colorado Springs Pioneer Museum, the Fine Arts Center, the Western Museum of Mining & Industry, and the Pro Rodeo Hall of Fame and Museum of the American Cowboy. However, it is the famed US Air Force Academy, set against the backdrop of the Front Range, that most people come to visit. The Cadet Chapel, featuring massive 150-foot (46-m) spires, reflects a progressive, modern image. There's also a World War II B-52 bomber on display.

From the air, Colorado Springs is outlined with numerous military posts. In the boom years of the 1950s, the town used its natural-sanctuary status to pull in the Defense Force to safeguard its economy.

The Broadmoor Hotel is Colorado Spring's most famous landmark. Built in 1918, its lavish Italian-Renaissance style is complemented by the framework of Cheyenne

State line sign on Hwy 113.

Mountain. There are hiking and cycle paths, including the challenging North Cheyenne Canyon Trail.

The road to Pikes Peak twists around treacherous hairpin curves for 19 miles (31 km) and finally reaches the summit at a breathtaking 14,110 feet (4,304 m). There are views of Colorado Springs, the distant Denver Metro, and the rugged peaks of the Continental Divide. Another way to climb to the top is to hop aboard the century-old Pikes Peak Cog Railway from Manitou Springs.

The Colorado Springs Municipal Airport is located 67 miles (108 km) south of Denver on I-25. There are shuttle services between the cities.
Map ref: page 696 J9

CORTEZ

The town of Cortez, which is at an elevation of 6,201 feet (1,891 m) on Hwy 160/666, sits in the heartland of Colorado's southwestern region. It is a small town of 8,726 people, largely made up of Hispanic and Native Americans who cater to tourists traveling to the Four Corner region and Mesa Verde National Park. Cortez sits in a region steeped with Ancestral Pueblos, or Anasazi, heritage as well as the cultures of the Ute, Navajo, and Apache tribes.

At the Cortez Center, several cultural events are held throughout summer, including Native American dances, art, storytelling, cowboy poetry, and Mexican fiestas. The Anasazi Heritage Center, 10 miles (16 km) north, at Delores on Hwy 184, offers further insights into the culture of the ancient cliff dwellers, along with a collection of artifacts and tours to two ruins that date to the twelfth century.

South of Cortez is the Ute Mountain Indian Reservation and the Ute Mountain Casino, which is the region's main money spinner apart from tourism. Its tribal center conducts tours to the Ancestral Pueblos cliff dwellings as well as to the petroglyph sites.

Located 2 miles (3 km) from town, Cortez Municipal Airport operates daily flights to Denver.
Map ref: page 619 B4

CRESTED BUTTE

Nestled on the fringe of the Gunnison National Forest, on Hwy 135, is the former mining town of Crested Butte, now a first-rate ski resort. Its location, in the striking wilderness tracts of the Elk Mountains and Maroon Bells-Snowmass, is enough to excite any outdoor enthusiast to test the trails.

Crested Butte also has an interesting history of gunslingers. Some of the West's most disreputable characters passed through town, including Jesse James, Butch Cassidy and the Sundance Kid, and a young Billy the Kid, when he was just a young pup working in one of the region's sawmills.

Originally a supply center for the surrounding mining camps of the Rockies, Crested Butte became a prosperous coal-mining town when other camps failed with the gold bust.

In 1963, after its local coal mine ceased operation, the town focused on its natural resources to lure local skiers to Crested Butte Mountain. Today, with its resort located 2 miles (3 km) from the historic town center, Crested Butte has retained its Victorian appeal without the encroachment of condominiums.

Crested Butte has more than 85 trails, 13 mountain lifts, and plenty of spectacular downhill skiing for daredevil skiers. Snowboarding and cross-country skiing are also popular here and well catered for. In the summer, Crested Butte's rugged mountains offer hiking as well as mountain-bike trails.

The nearest airport is Gunnison County Airport. There is a shuttle service that takes skiers between Crested Butte with Crested Butte Mountain and regular round-trip services from Gunnison County Airport to Crested Butte.
Map ref: page 696 E9

DENVER

Denver (population 2.1 million) is Colorado's "Mile High City" (exactly 1 mile from sea level at 5,280 feet/ 1,610 m) and one of the fastest growing metropolises in the United States. Bordered by the snow-capped summits of the Rocky Mountains to its west and vast high plains to the east, Denver's economy has evolved from being a major cow town at the turn of the twentieth century to spearheading a healthy economy in oil, mining, technology, as well as federal branch agencies.

Gray squirrel (Sciurus carolinensis) *in city parkland, Denver.*

Located at the crossroads of the I-70 and 25, Denver is a city of perpetual gridlock. But the city itself is constantly on the move. The lower downtown region, which is known as "LoDo," is renowned for its excellent brewpubs, its new-age galleries and boutiques, and the restaurants along Larimer Square. The pedestrian mall in Denver extends to Writers Square where there is another selection of specialty shops to be found.

Denver is home to the major league basketball team, the Colorado Rockies, and the Denver Broncos football team—so enthusiastic are its supporters that everything comes to a halt during a big game.

Despite the urban progress, Denver's skyline remains characteristic of its mining and cow-town origins. Weathered Victorian buildings and drab streets frame the periphery of Denver's central business district. Denver's expanding wealth is reflected by its large-scale shopping at Cherry Creek Shopping Mall, on First Avenue, where dozens of boutiques and leading department stores have transformed this suburb into Denver's largest attraction. Opposite the complex is the highly revered, five-storied Tattered Cover Bookstore, which stocks every book currently in print. Each floor has a cluster of oversized reading chairs, creating the perfect environment to browse through the books, with the aroma of delectable coffee wafting from its first floor café.

The gold rush of 1859 at the confluence of the South Platte River and Cherry Creek brought prospectors and buffalo hunters to Denver's Front Range. Its bawdy reputation was cemented during the cattle-boom era when there were more brothels sprouting in the city's backstreets than there were gold nuggets in the nearby mines.

Tagged the "Queen City of the Plains," Denver continued to flourish with the expansion of the transcontinental railroad. By the turn of the twentieth century, Denver had

Cyclists entering Crested Butte. During the spring and summer months, mountain biking and hiking replace skiing in this popular ski resort town.

The Colorado State Capitol building in Denver was constructed in 1886.

evolved into a respectable city, weathering several economic "boom and bust" cycles.

Denver has numerous stately buildings, including the gold-domed State Capitol Building near the Civic Center and the resplendent Brown Palace Hotel, which was once the center of Denver society. Straddling the Capitol on Pennsylvania Street is the Molly Brown House Museum. A former clerk who struck it rich in the Colorado gold fields, Molly Brown was generally treated as an outcast by Denver society until she set sail on the *Titanic* in 1912. She survived the shipwreck and helped other survivors, becoming a national treasure and earning the name the "Unsinkable Molly Brown."

Forming part of Denver's "Museum Row" is the Colorado History Museum at Broadway, which provides a detailed insight into Denver's pioneer heritage. The museum also exhibits a wealth of Native American artifacts. On Colfax Street is the US Mint, which is the second largest gold repository outside of Fort Knox in Kentucky.

The Denver Museum of Natural History with its Planetarium and IMAX Theater is a great source of entertainment for younger children. The best of the museum's exhibits is the "Prehistoric Journey," where visitors go back to the time when dinosaurs roamed the Continental Divide. And for some stomach-wrenching fun, there's the Elitch Gardens Amusement Park, complete with a roller coaster ride aptly called "The Twister."

The Black American West Museum features superb artifacts and photographs of the "Buffalo Soldiers," cowboys and pioneers who resettled in the West after the Civil War. The Denver Public Library includes an extensive collection of the region's history.

Denver has gained a well-earned reputation for its dedication to the arts. The Denver Art Museum has the reputation of being one of the best galleries in the West. It exhibits Native American art, Hispanic, and Pre-Columbian paintings, along with works of the European and Western greats. Visitors can take advantage of the museum's free admission every Saturday.

A short distance from the city is the Buffalo Bill Memorial Museum and Grave, located at Lookout Mountain off the I-70W. The museum displays the frontiersman's life in a series of photographs and personal mementos. Heavily in debt at the time of his death, Buffalo Bill's estranged wife accepted money from a local carnival entrepreneur to have the body buried near Denver, though he had wished to be buried in Cody, Wyoming. Buffalo Bill's funeral procession in 1915 was the largest spectacle the city had ever seen.

The newly constructed Denver International Airport is located 24 miles (39 km) from downtown. Connecting bus and shuttle services are available and the area is also serviced by trains and buses.
Map ref: page 697 H7

DINOSAUR NATIONAL MONUMENT

Sharing its Jurassic boneyard with neighboring Utah, the Dinosaur National Monument features over 1,500 fossilized dinosaur bones in the world's largest quarry. Though its visitor center is near the town of Dinosaur on Hwy 40, the fossil bed is located on Utah's state line.

About 145 million years ago, many 70-foot (21-m) *Brontosaurus* roamed the countryside, with a host of lesser creatures. A treasure-trove for paleontologists, Dinosaur National Monument also offers three quarries for visitors to explore.

Dinosaur National Monument is open year-round and a small entrance fee is applicable. Park rangers provide walking interpretive tours of the monument.
Map ref: page 696 B5

FORT COLLINS

Largely a college and agricultural town of 104,000 people, Fort Collins is located 62 miles (100 km) north of Denver on the I-25. Home to Colorado State University, Fort Collins is usually regarded by motorists as a suitable place to pull over for gas before embarking on the next highway stretch across to the Wyoming state line.

Once an outpost along the Overland Trail, Fort Collins has preserved its Victorian heritage in the district of Old Town. Visitors can stroll along Mountain Avenue and Linden Street to view the handsome structures dating back to the 1880s. The most prominent landmark is the City Drug Store. The Fort Collins Museum, on Matthews Street, has a modest collection of pioneer artifacts and the first log cabin erected at the fort.

Fort Collins hosts the two-day Colorado Brewers Festival in late June, and Oktoberfest in mid-September. At any time of the year, visitors can mingle with the college kids at one of several downtown breweries or tour the Anheuser-Busch Brewery on Busch Drive.

There are shuttle services from Denver International Airport.
Map ref: page 697 H5

GLENWOOD SPRINGS

Glenwood Springs is a perfect place to take a dip at one of its natural hot springs. An unassuming town of 7,620 people, Glenwood Springs

Glenwood Springs offers rafting, hiking, and mountain biking as well as hot springs.

The area around Grand Junction is known as Colorado's "wine country." The Mediterranean-style climate here is ideal for grape cultivation.

has a backyard of hiking trails and great whitewater rafting at nearby Glenwood Canyon.

The handsome Hotel Colorado was the foremost spa resort for railroad barons as well as President Teddy Roosevelt, who was a frequent guest. In its heyday, the hotel's 10-acre (4.5-ha) grounds boasted a polo field, a 600-foot (183-m) long swimming pool, as well as a railway track.

Another attraction is "Doc" Holliday's gravesite at the Glenwood Springs Cemetery. The gunslinger who found fame at the OK Corral with Wyatt Earp, moved to town in 1887 to convalesce from tuberculosis until his death.

With a solid selection of budget hotels, the town is a great alternative to Apsen's high rates if you are traveling on a budget.

There are buses and trains to Denver and a bus service to Aspen.
Map ref: page 696 D7

GRAND JUNCTION

A city of 34,500 people, Grand Junction sits at the confluence of the Gunnison and Colorado Rivers off the I-70. In the agricultural heart of the Grand Valley, Grand Junction acts as the gateway-city to Colorado National Monument.

The city has several museums, which focus on its local heritage. The Museum of Western Colorado and the affiliated Dinosaur Valley Museum feature exhibits on pioneer farming and fossils found in the western region of the state. The outdoor museum of the Cross Orchards Living History Farm features a guided costume tour of its several restored period buildings and apple orchards.

Walker Field Airport is in Grand Junction. Denver International Airport is 100 miles (161 km) west.
Map ref: page 696 B9

GREAT SAND DUNES NATIONAL MONUMENT

The impenetrable Great Sand Dunes National Monument sits at the basin of the Sangre de Cristo Mountains, northeast of Alamosa. Visitors come here to tumble over 39 miles (63 km) of ivory sand, and to check out the tallest sand dune, which rises 700 feet (214 m) from the vast San Luis Valley floor. The visitor center is located 3 miles (5 km) from the monument's entrance off Hwy 150 and there is a small admission fee.
Map ref: page 619 G3

Map ref: page 696 B9

GREELY

Located in the high plains of Northern Colorado near the Wyoming border, around 80 miles (129 km) northeast from Denver, Greeley is largely a farming town and home to the University of Northern Colorado.

Greely was named for publisher Horace Greeley, who authored the famous line, "Go West Young Man, Go West." Greely had a vision of the town as a utopian settlement, and hoped to encourage other pioneers to head out west. Over the last century, he developed the area into a rich agricultural and livestock community.

Greely chose journalist, Nathan Meeker, to headline the town's development. However, his taking on the role of Indian agent for the government was a fateful one. Involved in a heated dispute with the

Great Sand Dunes National Monument, in the San Luis Valley, contains the highest sand dunes in North America.

Ute people over the irrigation of the land, Meeker and his family were massacred. His house, the Meeker Home Museum, is now listed on the National Register of Historic Places.

Near the Meeker home is the Centennial Village Museum, which houses an extensive collection of historical buildings, including a log cabin dating back to the 1860s. Both museums are closed during the winter season.

Denver International is the closest major airport, 40 miles (64 km) southwest of Greely.
Map ref: page 696 J5

HOVENWEEP NATIONAL MONUMENT

The 734-acre (297-ha) monument lies in the traditional land of the Ancestral Pueblo people, or Anasazi, who inhabited the area around AD 1000. Located west of Cortez, the monument was established in 1923 and has six sets of tower ruins, though only the Square Tower area is accessible to the public. Interpretative brochures and maps are

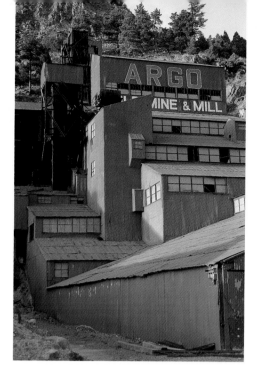

The Argo gold mine and mill, near Idaho Springs.

provided through the Park Service's Ranger Station and there are also several self-guided trails that bring into view the remaining ruins, along with a host of desert wildlife. There is a small entrance fee.

Cortez Municipal Airport operates daily flights to Denver.
Map ref: page 619 B4

IDAHO SPRINGS

Idaho Springs is a town from Colorado's great mining era. Nestled in the steep mountainside of the Rockies, Idaho Springs is now more popular for its fine selection of pioneer and Victorian antiques.

Visitors can discover many forgotten gold mines including the Argo Gold Mill. Its 22,000-foot (6,710-m) tunnel was used to transport ore between Idaho Springs and Central City.

Not far from the town are the Victorian mining communities of Georgetown and Silver Plume, and the famed Georgetown Loop Railroad. Every summer, the smell of burning cinders and plumes of smoke fill the air as the momentous steam-engine train chugs its way across steep iron trestles—some of which tower to 600 feet (183 m). Departing from Old Georgetown station, the journey takes a little over half an hour to reach Silver Plume.

Looming over Georgetown is Mt Evans, which rises through the clouds to 14,264 feet (4,351 m). There are several trails, including the celebrated Oh-My-God Road—the name summing up the mountain's natural challenges.

Traveling by car, Idaho Springs is located approximately 20 miles (32 km) west of Denver, just off the I-70.
Map ref: page 696 G7

LEADVILLE

This Victorian town of 2,612 people is known as "Cloud City" for good reason. At an elevation of 10,200 feet (3,111 m), Leadville is often shrouded in cloud.

Despite its origins as a mining center, Leadville has turned its attention to restoring many of its old Victorian structures, making it more tourist-friendly.

During its heyday, Leadville produced US$82 million worth of silver, and its downtown region still shows signs of that bygone prosperity. The Western Hardware Company and the Silver Dollar Saloon are just some of the buildings that were built during the late nineteenth century. The stately Tabor Grand Hotel and the Tabor Opera House, built by former US senator and Leadville's first mayor, are still the town's finest.

Visitors can stroll down to the local Chamber of Commerce for a map of the Route of the Silver Kings. This is located east of town

and covers the spectrum of mining structures, abandoned shacks, and old mine-shafts. Leadville's Heritage Museum showcases a wealth of mining artifacts, the most interesting being the replica of its famed Ice Palace. The splendid Healy House and neighboring Dexter Cabin reflect Leadville's blend of citizens. Operated by the Colorado Historical Society, tours are conducted by costumed guides.

Leadville offers a wealth of recreational opportunities including camping, hiking, and skiing. About 10 miles (16 km) north of town is Ski Cooper, which was once a training center for the famous 10th Mountain Division troops, who were trained to fight in mountain terrain. The surviving soldiers returned to the region after the war to help establish the new resorts of Aspen and Vail. Ski Cooper's terrain is perfect for the advanced or intermediate skier.

Leadville is located at the junction of Hwy 24/91. Renting a car in Denver is the best way to explore the mining town.
Map ref: page 696 F8

PUEBLO

The industrial city of Pueblo lies south of Colorado Springs along I-25. Once a major steel producer, the city's population now stands at 104,000. It was the arrival of both the Denver & Rio Grande Western and the Santa Fe Railroads that

Store owner selling second-hand toys at one of the popular antique stores in Leadville.

quickly turned Pueblo's fortunes around because this made possible the shipment of coal to its smelters, from nearby mines.

Today, Pueblo is used as a rest stop between Santa Fe and Denver although there are a few points of interest to visitors. The El Pueblo Museum is a large-scale replica of an original adobe fort, complete with pressed mud huts and Anasazi cultural exhibits from around Colorado.

The city's main attraction is the Rosemont Museum on Grand Avenue, which is an ornate Victorian mansion constructed with pink rhyolite stone and stained glass windows. The museum also features Rosemont's early twentieth-century travel collection, including an Egyptian mummy which he packed in his trunks.

Pueblo's regional claim to fame is its Colorado State Fair, which is hosted from mid-August until early September. This includes rodeos, live country music, and various barnyard entertainment.

Pueblo Memorial Airport services the area. There are buses to Denver.
Map ref: page 619 J2

ROCKY MOUNTAIN NATIONAL PARK

First created as a national park in 1915 to preserve the Rockies' dwindling wildlife, Rocky Mountain National Park remains one of Colorado's most popular and accessible wilderness areas. So much so that, in the summer, the human gridlock can outnumber the traffic along the I-25. The park is approximately 80 miles (129 km) northwest of Denver.

Rocky Mountain National Park offers some 355 miles (571 km) of picture-perfect trails and three different climate zones that contain abundant and varied flora and fauna. Connected by Hwy 34 (also known as Trail Ridge Road) park visitors are led through around 265,726 acres (107,619 ha) of coniferous forests, mountainous back country, and meadows showcasing a vibrant display of wildflowers. Coiling its way through the park is the Continental Divide, sending the Cache La Poudre, Big Thompson, and St Vrain Rivers to the Pacific, and the serpentine Colorado River, east to Grand Lake.

Deep glacial valleys and isolated alpine lakes create a refuge for wildlife including elk, moose, mule deer, black bear, and big horn sheep. The park's pristine beauty also features many beautiful summits, which loom at elevations of over 14,000 feet (4,270 m). Ponderosa pine, quaking aspen, and Douglas fir form thick canopies of forest and challenging trails for hikers.

The San Juan Mountains, near Silverton.

The most popular trail within the park is the Bear Lake Trail, though on the park's west side, the more challenging Lulu City Trail follows a pathway to the Colorado River and the former mining town of Lulu City. The 48-mile (77-km) Trail Ridge Road, the highest paved road in the nation, showcases striking views of Rocky Mountain National Park's fragile wilderness.

A small fee will get you a seven-day multiple entrance pass, and hiking permits are available, also for a small fee. The two eastern park entrances are located at Fall River on US-34 and Beaver Meadows on US-36 and the western entrance at the Grand Lake Station.
Map ref: page 696 G6

SILVERTON

The tiny town of Silverton sits at the heart of Colorado's high country. Once a rip-roaring town, which had a thriving red-light district, Silverton also had hills that produced over US$250 million dollars in silver, gold, copper, and zinc. When the Denver & Rio Grande Western Railroad started its services

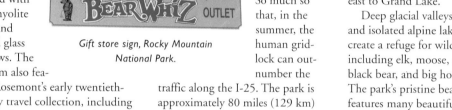

*Meadow with tansy asters (*Machaeranthera bigelovii*) and orange sneezeweed (*Dugaldia hoopesii*), Rocky Mountain National Park.*

Gift store sign, Rocky Mountain National Park.

to the town, Silverton had struck gold. It remains a classic Western town with false-fronted buildings complete with hitching posts that straddle its main street.

Though its population of 540 remains small, Silverton today is a town of respectability and sheer Victorian splendor—so much so that it was designated a National Historic Landmark over 30 years ago. Many of these buildings are located on Greene Street, including the Grand Imperial Hotel, the Town Hall, the San Juan County Courthouse, and the former county jail, now the San Juan County Historical Society Museum.

Following the same fate as other Western towns, Silverton went into perpetual slumber until 20 years ago, when the Durango & Silverton Narrow Gauge Railroad started bringing tourists up the mountain.

The recently restored Rio Grande Depot is where passengers climb aboard the train for the 45-mile (72-km) journey through the San Juan Mountains alongside the Animas River. Open from May to October, the old steam-engine train travels over steep trellises, canyons, and along hairpin tracks before reaching Durango, a town which grew around the railroad and now enjoys the overflow of tourists from the nearby Purgatory Ski Resort.

Durango's youthful population of 13,900 is largely made up of outdoor enthusiasts and has become the principal destination for serious mountain-bike riders. Durango's main street features cafés and restaurants, sports stores, art galleries, and bookstores. There are still real cowboys who frequent the older bars and the historic Strater Hotel.

Another interesting drive north from Silverton is the dramatic "Million Dollar Highway," which traces the San Juan Mountains at an elevation of around 11,008 feet (3,357 m). Known by that name because of the abundance of ore found along the route, the highway has also been called the most beautiful drive in the nation. The road wraps around narrow mountain passes that wind past a backdrop of brilliant razor-edged peaks. Though these craggy mountain ranges feature exposed granite escarpments, below its alpine line lies a carpet of jeweled meadows billowing in a profusion of color. The steep slopes of the San Juan

Mountains also provide refuge for scores of mule deer, bob cats, elk, and black bear. Though rarely sighted, mountain lions roam around the rocky ledges.

The nearest airport is located in Durango, which offers regular services to Denver, Dallas, and Phoenix. There are also bus services to Albuquerque and Montrose and trains from April to November.

Map ref: page 618 D3

VAIL

Vail is the quintessential resort town that was first conceived from a blueprint in 1952. Located 123 miles (198 km) west of Denver off the I-70, Vail remains a village for the wealthy, with its tree-lined streets crowded with multi-million-dollar condominiums and chalets. This is the largest ski resort in the country and has a year-round population of 3,900. The resort consistently ranks among the top five in surveys of American ski resorts.

Vail's main drawcard, Beaver Creek, offers exceptional powder terrain along with numerous downhill runs and ski-lifts. There is also a heart-pumping bobsleigh run and other winter sports including ice-skating and back-country and cross-country skiing.

In summer, mountain biking and playing golf on the 18-hole course are the main outdoor activities in Vail. There is also a host of activities incorporating wilderness hikes, whitewater rafting, and kayaking along the Roaring Folk River. The trail to Ten Mile Canyon over Vail Pass is one of the most

Springtime on the mountain in Vail, showing an example of the elegant ski lodges available.

popular hikes. The beautiful landscape of the Holy Cross Wilderness Area has a challenging 12-mile (19-km) trail, which incorporates its namesake granite peak.

The Colorado Ski Museum & Hall of Fame provides an insight into the mountain resorts of the Rockies and Vail's inception. During the first week of March, Vail

hosts the American Ski Classic. In July and August there is a series of symphonic concerts.

Vail's Eagle County Airport has many domestic services during winter. There are also many well-scheduled shuttle services from Denver International Airport, as well as bus services.

Map ref: page 696 F7

Mesa Verde National Park

Spanish explorers of the eighteenth century came close to discovering Mesa Verde, near Delores, 9 miles (15 km) north of Cortez. But it would be another 100 years before the treasures of Mesa Verde unfolded. In 1888, while searching for roving livestock, local ranchers Richard Wetherill and Charles Mason came across the ruins at Cliff Edge during a snowstorm. It is not known if disease, ruination of crops, or warfare caused the Ancestral Puebloans—formerly known as the Anasazi (Navajo, meaning "ancient enemies")—to abandon the cliff dwellings. Archeologists have never found traces of a major conflict, only natural burial sites. Regardless, their ancestors, the Ute tribe, never ventured into the area, deeming it sacred. The Navajo believed the land was haunted.

Interest in the discovery of Mesa Verde brought souvenir hunters to the area, where precious artifacts exchanged hands. It wasn't until 1891 that archeologists began to excavate the ruins. Ten years later, the Utes were granted an endowment in exchange for the land and, in 1906, Congress declared it a national park.

Mesa Verde National Park is America's only archeological site that has been designated by congress as a national park. Surrounded by the Dolores Plateau and Mancos and Montezuma Valleys, in Colorado's southwestern pocket known as the Four Corners region, Mesa Verde has an exceptional collection of Ancient Puebloan ruins. More than 4,000 sites have been excavated and preserved—many of them accessible on self-guided trails which loop around the park.

Mesa Verde comprises 81 square miles (210 sq km) of ancient landscape with red-tinged mesas that ascend to an elevation of 8,571 feet (2,614 m) at Park Point, before sloping down to 6,720 feet (2,050 m), south of the park headquarters. The park's only entrance is located off Hwy 160, just 10 miles (16 km) east of Cortez. A short distance from the gates is Mesa Verde's first trail, at Point Lookout, which brings into view the distant mountains of La Planta and Wilson, along with Delores Peaks. The Prater Ridge Trail, which heads south toward the Prater and Morefield Canyons, is a haven for mule deer, bighorn sheep, wild turkey, the occasional black bear, and golden eagles—also roaming the jagged tablelands are cougars.

Heading west, the road divides into a fork at Navajo Hill. Visitors to the national park can buy tour tickets and maps at the visitor center, at Far View. There are tours to the three major ruins and maps of the various relics and cliff dwellings. From Far View, it is an unbroken trail past ruins and gentle sloping hills covered in piñon and juniper trees.

The Ancestral Pueblo came to the region sometime in the Basketmaker stage (AD 450) to farm the land, gathering on top of mesas in small villages. Primarily hunters and basket makers, the Pueblo are believed to have been the only people inhabiting the land at the time. The Ancestral Puebloans rapidly cultivated a sophisticated social infrastructure. By around AD 700, they cast aside pit houses—dugouts featuring a slat roof and corner posts made from wood—and began making adobe structures.

In the park's southwestern corner is Wetherill Mesa, where the largest concentration of pit houses is located. It was this site's excavation that provided archeologists with the best insight into this lost civilization. Open from June to September, the National Park Service runs a tour to the mesa from Far View Visitor Center, which takes visitors on a laborious 12-mile (19-km) trail to the Step House. It was here that the pit houses were occupied during the Modified Basketmakers period (AD 450–750). Over the course of 400 years, they began to build multistory chambers into the cliffs.

This landscape of 1,000 years ago saw irrigated crops of corn, squash, and beans harvested and dams built to store precious water, with canals leading to the fields. Linked to each village were ceremonial kivas (ring-shaped pits used to worship the four elements—earth, water, wind, and fire). Multiple towers were built and likely used as a safeguard from any attacking enemies, with most connected by underground passages to a kiva. Around the last 200 years of their inhabitancy, the Classic Pueblo phase (AD 1100–1300), the Ancestral Puebloan's foundation was complete. A political structure gave the village parameters for everything from farming to social cohesion.

Picking up the trail from the Step House leads to the second-largest cliff dwelling. Visitors must descend over 50 steps to reach the main complex, which features 21 kivas and multiple rooms.

After the Puebloans vanished—possibly to the Zuni and Hopi villages of neighboring New Mexico and Arizona—the region lay uninhabited for almost

Numerous canyons cut through the cliffs at Mesa Verde. Millions of years of water erosion created the alcoves or niches in these canyons, where the Puebloans built their dwellings.

OPPOSITE: The Square Tower House, the ruins of a multi-storied structure which once contained more than 80 rooms. On top of the flat cliff are the juniper and piñon trees—this is the image that gave the area its name, Mesa Verde (Spanish for "green table").

Rose paintbrushes (Castilleja rhexifolia) and orange sneeze-weed (Dugaldia hoopesii), Mesa Verde National Park.

600 years. In addition to their cliff-side apartments, the Ancestral Puebloans abandoned scores of pottery, jewelry, weapons, and even bowls of corn.

Traveling the circuit back to the visitor center leads to the park's southern boundary at the Ute Mountain Indian Reservation. Midway through this loop is Far View Ruins and a trail, which leads to an impenetrable ruin atop a mesa. Exceptional in design, its walled complex features a circular tower, constructed between AD 900 and 1300.

One of the easiest trails within Mesa Verde starts at Spruce Tree House which, similar to Cliff Palace, was only occupied in the thirteenth century. Folded into the cavern of Spruce Canyon lies a composite of three-leveled structures that feature more than 100 rooms and eight kivas. One of the kivas has been reconstructed for visitors, to allow them to climb down a ladder and view a room supported by wooden beams and decorated in rock art.

Tours to sites are only led by park rangers in the winter but visitors can embark on a 2-mile (3-km) self-guided trek along the Spruce Canyon Trail which coils around red-rock cliffs before descending to the canyon floor. The Petroglyph Point Trail travels further south where it wraps around a cliff dwelling before reaching a prehistoric rock carving.

At the Park Headquarters, near the junction of Ruins Road, the Chapin Mesa Museum provides a wealth of information on the park's history, the indigenous people of the Southwest, and of the mesa-top villages that became cliff-dwelling communities.

The Chapin Mesa Trail leads to the lost city of Cliff Palace, the largest collection of ancient cliff dwellings in the world. Containing 217 rooms and 23 kivas, the dwellings are protected from frigid winds and snow by a protruding ledge. The trail from Mesa Top Drive, past early pit houses, brings into view the ruin's sheer majestic construction, which took place sometime between AD 1210 and 1273.

Overlooking the Soda Canyon is Balcony House, a 40-room complex that is cradled by its abrupt walls. To gain entrance, visitors must climb down a 32-foot (10-m) ladder and crouch down into a tunnel. It is an arduous trek but the timeless panorama is worth it.

Sitting at elevations from around 5,000–8,500 feet (1,525–2,593 m), Mesa Verde experiences dry, scorching daytime temperatures but cool evenings and biting winters. Camping within the park is permitted only at Morefield Campground from May 1 to October 31. Hiking permits are restricted to five trails. For lodging, Far View offers the Far View Lodge— located on top of a mesa. The lodge is not expensive but reservations are recommended. The lodge is open from mid April to late October. The towns of Cortez and Marcos offer a selection of budget hotels.

The visitor center at Far View is open daily from early spring to late fall. The Park Headquarters is open Monday to Friday and the Chapin Mesa Museum is open daily. Hiking outside of the main trails is prohibited and visitors must register with a ranger at the Park Headquarters.

IDAHO

Though Idaho is largely known for its pioneer heritage, the state boasts more than 28,000 miles (45,052 km) of pristine wilderness, with the northwest region the most mountainous.

Idaho's Federal land is protected from logging and its national forests are perfect for outdoor enthusiasts, who flock to the winter play-grounds and the summer trails of its craggy mountain ranges. With the Continental Divide running east of the state, over 3,100 miles (4,988 km) of rivers cut through the region, creating deep gorges and whitewater tracts. This area is also the natural habitat for a variety of animals and birds, including black bear, wolf, moose, elk, beaver, river otters, and osprey.

For over 15,000 years Idaho was home to the Shoshone, Bannock, and Nez Perce peoples. In 1805, Lewis and Clark were the first explorers to travel across the region's impenetrable terrain. Prospectors, during the 1860s gold rush, brought a flow of settlers to the region where, originally, only a small number of fur trappers and mountain men roamed. When the boom went bust, many of the mining camps languished until the railroad enabled the development of another flourishing industry. Idaho produces the largest crop of potatoes in the United States—and it produces grain, cattle, and sheep throughout the irrigated plains of the Snake River Basin.

Idaho remains free of urban encroachment, and each region's distinctive geographical elements influence its economic infrastructure. Nevertheless, all contribute equally to the state's vibrant economy, with the ski resort of Sun Valley alone generating millions of tourism dollars in the winter.

Cattle production is a major industry in Idaho. This is a typical scene in the Sun Valley region, with the soaring Pioneer Mountains in the background.

State motto *Esto perpetua* (Let it be perpetual/It is forever)
State flag Adopted 1907
Capital Boise
Population 1,293,953
Total area (land and water) 83,574 square miles (216,457 sq km)
Land area 82,751 square miles (214,325 sq km)
Idaho is the 13th-largest state in size
Origin of name An invented name
Nicknames The Gem State, The Spud State
Abbreviations ID (postal), Ida.
State bird Mountain bluebird
State flower Mock orange (*Syringa*)
State tree Western white pine
Entered the Union July 3, 1890 as the 43rd state

Places in
IDAHO

BOISE

Idaho's largest city and capital, Boise is a relaxed metropolis of outdoor revelers and university students. Though Boise has a population of only 164,000, it is one of the fastest growing cities west of the Rocky Mountains. The city's youthful population is largely centered around technology, with the giant corporations of Hewlett-Packard and Micron Technology making Boise their home.

The urban sophistication of Boise extends to the universities and artistic community. Boise has the open-air Idaho Shakespeare

The State Capitol Building, Boise.

Festival throughout the summer, and the Boise Opera Company, Boise Philharmonic, and Boise Art Gallery, which houses an American Realism collection. The Basque Museum and Cultural Center celebrates Idaho's Spanish migrant sheep-herders who settled in the region in the 1890s. They had a profound impact on Boise's culture, particularly music and dance.

Sixteen miles (26 km) north is the homegrown ski resort of Bogus Basin, which was originally a gold-mining camp. It boasts an 1,800-foot (549-m) vertical drop.

Over 60 lakes surround Coeur d'Alene. The area is rich with wildlife; recreational activities include water skiing, hiking, and cycling.

University towns often boast of fine cuisine and Boise is no exception—it has first-rate restaurants and trendy cafés flooding its main streets. But the city's real attraction is its geographical location and casual, Western flavor. Known as the "City of Trees," Boise rises 2,842 feet (867 m) above the alluvial plains of the Snake River and is framed by Boise National Forest.

From its inception as an army fort, Boise became a fully fledged town in 1890, when it turned its attention to federal irrigation projects along the Snake River. Many of its nineteenth-century buildings remain intact, including the graceful Capitol Building, which was built in 1905. Crowned by a large bronzed eagle, its stately Corinthian columns and Classic Revival lines mirror Washington's Capitol.

Idaho State Historic Museum has exhibits on the region's Native American heritage and Chinese laborers, who toiled in Idaho's gold fields and on the Utah & Northern Railroad. Adjacent to the museum is the Pioneer Village, housing two of Boise's earliest pioneer cabins.

In summer, the Boise Tour Train conducts city tours from a replica of an old steam engine with open-air passenger carriages. Main Street has a collection of Old Boise's late Victorian buildings.

Visitors can also delve into frontier prison life at the Old Idaho State Penitentiary, which operated for more than a century before permanently closing its doors in 1973. Tours of its chilling gallows and cells are available year-round.

Boise Municipal Airport services the area and and there are bus and train services, including a service linking Boise to Salt Lake City.
Map ref: page 688 C5

CALDWELL

The gateway to Idaho's vast southwestern plains, the agricultural and hi-tech town of Caldwell, with a population of 21,849, is fast becoming an alternative city to Boise because of its lower cost of living. Nearby Mountain Home is the base for the Air Force, and test exercises are regularly performed over the Owyhee Desert. Caldwell also boasts of the state's oldest college, Albertson.

Visitors can see this area in a number of ways, including guest ranches, and tours of the farms, vineyards, and orchards.

Caldwell is serviced by buses. Nearby Boise is serviced by buses and trains, as well as the Boise Municipal Airport.
Map ref: page 688 B5

COEUR D'ALENE

Characterized by a cerulean–blue lake, Coeur d'Alene evolved into a tourist town as early as 1910. It began as an outpost in 1878 when

Young people playing baseball, which is a national sport, and popular in Caldwell.

Civil War general, William T. Sherman, moved his army to Idaho's Panhandle following the Indian Wars. Today, with a population of only 31,000, Coeur d'Alene is a first-class resort.

In winter, the town serves as a refuge for local skiers at the nearby resorts of Schweitzer Mountain and Silver Mountain. The pocket village of Sandpoint and Pend Oreille Lake—the deepest lake in the Northwest—also offers many hiking trails and fishing charters. The remote waters of Priest Lake are paradise for trout anglers.

The outpost of Fort Sherman now serves as a museum. A display of documents and other military paraphernalia chronicles the army's mission in the Panhandle region. The former officers' barracks has been transformed into the Fort Sherman Chapel. The building served as the fort's first church and school for the early settlers.

The magnificent Coeur d'Alene Resort has replaced the city's once-thriving lumber mill. It now has a floating boardwalk, bowling alley,

The Craters of the Moon National Monument is a lava field that encircles 643 square miles (1,665 sq km) of lava flow.

and marina. Tourists also flock to this resort in high summer to tee off from an 18-hole golf course.

The downtown district includes early twentieth-century businesses and the Museum of North Idaho, which is a gallery that exhibits weapons of the early explorers and fur trappers, logging artifacts, and rare arrow tips.

Twenty miles (32 km) from town is the Cataldo Mission, which was built in 1850 by the Coeur d'Alene people who were converted by Jesuit priests, or "black robes." Constructed without nails, its adobe structure has an open room for worshipping and no pews.

The nearest airport is Spokane International, 33 miles (53 km) west in Washington State. Located on I-95, renting a car could be the best alternative from either Spokane or Missoula, Montana.
Map ref: page 684 B4

CRATERS OF THE MOON NATIONAL MONUMENT

The desolate terrain of Craters of the Moon National Monument, is in central Idaho, about 90 miles (145 km) west of Idaho Falls. It is believed to have formed around about 15,000 years ago after a series of volcanic eruptions. The largest of three cinder cones is located at Great Rift. Stripped of vegetation, with the exception of an eerie lone pine at Inferno Cover, visiting this area is an experience visitors do not forget. The whole area remains susceptible to further eruptions.

There are seven lookouts along the Crater of the Moon's 7-mile (11-km) loop road and several trails lead to desolate chasms and lava tubes that resemble underground tunnels. The Indian Tunnel is the largest, sprawling across 50 feet (15 m) of caustic terrain. Open late April to September, scorching temperatures often soar past 100°F

Hells Half Acre National Landmark is a lava flow 20 miles (32 km) from Idaho Falls. The area is great for hiking.

HELL'S HALF ACRE NATIONAL LANDMARK
GEOLOGISTS BELIEVE THAT ABOUT 4,100 YEARS AGO A LARGE CRACK, OR RIFT, OPENED IN THE EARTH ABOUT 5 MILES SOUTH OF HERE. HOT MOLTEN ROCK POURED OUT AND FORMED THIS LAVA FIELD. OVERALL THIS BARREN LANDSCAPE MEASURES 18 MILES EAST TO WEST AND 8 MILES NORTH TO SOUTH.

(37.7°C). The Big Lost River, flowing south from Arco, simply disappears into the abyss of the barren landscape.

East of Craters of the Moon is the Big Southern Butte National Natural Landmark, a 300,000-year-old formation, which jolts 2,500 feet (762 m) above the Snake River Basin. Once a natural marker on the Oregon Trail, the flat-topped hill offers the best vantage point for viewing Craters of the Moon National Monument.

Idaho Falls is the closest center to the monument. It is serviced by the Idaho Falls Municipal Airport and buses. There is an airport shuttle service to Salt Lake City.
Map ref: page 688 F6

HAGERMAN FOSSIL BEDS NATIONAL MONUMENT

Thirty miles (48 km) west of Twin Falls, on Hwy 30, lies one of the largest deposits of fossil horses. Hagerman Fossil Beds have been a national monument since 1988. These zebra-like horses from the Pleistocene Period were extinct by the time Native Americans inhabited the land. The monument has no facilities. Guided tours from June to September are available from a boardwalk located near the interpretative center.

On the way to the monument is the Archie Teater House, the only Frank Lloyd Wright stone house to be built in Idaho. Nearby Twin Falls has a re-

gional airport which connects the town to Salt Lake City and buses service the area, including a charter bus service to Ketchum in winter.
Map ref: page 688 E7

HAILEY

Hailey has a population equaling its elevation—5,342 feet (1,629 m). It has a long history of mineral prospecting and lays claim to being the first community to have electric lights and the first in the state to have a telephone system. The Hollywood actor, Bruce Willis, invested in Hailey's downtown to bring better entertainment facilities.

Many of Hailey's charming nineteenth-century buildings still stand, including the birthplace of the poet, Ezra Pound—his possessions are today exhibited at the Blaine County Historical Museum.

The Friedman Memorial Airport is just south of Hailey.
Map ref: page 688 F6

IDAHO CITY

During the state's gold rush of 1862, the mining camp of Idaho City developed into the region's largest town. Located just 38 miles (61 km) north of Boise, Idaho City built its fortune on strikes that yielded US$24 million in gold in just under five years. Though des-

troyed by a fire in 1867, the town was rebuilt in brick, including numerous gambling saloons and brothels. Of the town's population, almost half were Chinese.

Visitors can see various pioneer and gold-rush artifacts at the Boise Basin Museum and view Idaho's first State Penitentiary on Wall Street. On Centerville Road is the historic Pioneer Cemetery, where it is said that only a few of its interred residents died of natural causes.

Shooting is a popular recreational activity in Idaho; this is a gun club practicing near Idaho Falls.

Boise Municipal Airport services the area and and there are bus and train services, including a service linking Boise to Salt Lake City.
Map ref: page 688 C5

IDAHO FALLS

Idaho Falls, which is on I-15, is a perfect jumping-off point to the Craters of the Moon National Monument, Sun Valley, the West Grand Teton National Park, and the Snake River's rapids. With a population of 43,929, Idaho Falls is the largest city in Idaho. It is in the heart of ranching and fertile agricultural land.

Named "Eagle Rock" at the time of its inception, Idaho Falls was renamed in order to attract more settlers. Today, the city offers a wide selection of lodging and restaurants.

Idaho Falls is serviced by the Idaho Falls Municipal Airport and buses. There is a four-hourly, airport shuttle service to Salt Lake City.
Map ref: page 689 K6

LEWISTON

The twin city of Lewiston (Clarkston sits across the Washington state line) was named for the famed explorers who passed through the region in 1805. Straddling the Snake and Clearwater Rivers, the former gold-mining camp evolved into a city and the territorial capital, in 1863, on what was traditional Nez Perce land. Lewiston now with a population of 31,164, serves as an agricultural port from the Pacific Coast via the Columbia River.

Downtown's Pioneer Park features a typical 1860s log cabin and Luna House, the city's first hotel, showcases pioneer artifacts and photographs in its museum. The Lewiston Roundup, Idaho's oldest rodeo, pays homage to the West over three festive days which includes cookouts, carnivals, and Nez Perce tribal dancing. The Roundup takes place annually, the first weekend in September.

Lewiston is the gateway to Hells Canyon National Recreation Area. With cliffs 7,900 feet (2,410 m) above the deepest river gorge, the region is only accessible by jet boat or float, but there are many outfitters in the area.

Adjacent to the Clearwater and the Snake Rivers is the 20-mile (32-km) stretch of the Levee Parkway from Hells Gate State Park. Midway along the drive is the Lewis and Clark Interpretive Center that chronicles the explorers' trek along the Snake River, and the indigenous tribes who first populated the valley. The Old Spiral Highway, branching off Hwy 95, twists over hills that look down into the valley.

Lewiston is serviced by buses and there is a small airport just south of town.
Map ref: page 684 A8

The sign at the Idaho state line, on Route 26.

MONTPELIER

In 1864, Mormon leader, Brigham Young, settled the tiny town of Montpelier (population 2,656), which sits east of Bear Lake near the Wyoming border. Named for the capital of his home state in Vermont, the town is worth visiting for its Mormon pioneer heritage and outlaws, including Butch Cassidy, who robbed Montpelier's local bank of US$7,000 in 1896. Montpelier is one of the oldest cities in Idaho. The Daughters of Utah Pioneers Relic Hall, located in the Mormon Church, also provides a display of pioneer artifacts and photographs.

Nearby Bear Lake is 80,000 acres (32,400 ha) in area and has four species of fish unique to the lake. The Bear Lake National Wildlife Refuge has over 165 species of birds. Tours are available.

Pocatello Municipal Airport, which is about 90 miles (145 km) northwest of Montpelier, includes flights linking Boise and Salt Lake City. Buses also service Pocatello.
Map ref: page 689 L9

NEZ PERCE NATIONAL HISTORICAL PARK

The Nez Perce National Park stands alone among other parks because of its unique boundaries. Keeping in spirit with the Nez Perce's belief that there are no defining borders to their land, there are 24 park sanctuaries scattered around central Idaho. Along the Nez Perce National Historic Trail there are many significant tribal sites, including White Bird Canyon Battlefield. Located at the bottom of a gorge, this site commemorates the government's first battle with the Nez Perce people in 1877.

The Nez Perce National Historical Park's Visitor Center, at Spaulding on Hwy 95, has an interpretive center, outlining Nez Perce culture and leaders, including the notable Chief Joseph. Near Kamiah, is the Heart of the Monster, a stone connected to the mythological creation of the Nez Perce.
Map ref: page 684 B9

POCATELLO

Pocatello is Idaho's second largest city and is home to the Idaho State University. It began as a humble trading post along the Oregon Trail before the Union Pacific Railroad turned the town into the largest rail center in the West. Pocatellos was named for the Bannock Native

American chief. The region is famous for its potatoes, which can be the size of footballs.

A mix of settlers, including Idaho's first African-American community and Chinese, populated the city when it became a railroad junction in 1884. Its late Victorian architecture is still featured along Main Street. The Bannock County Historical Museum has railroad and Native American exhibits. There is also a replica of Pocatello's original Fort Hall at Ross Park.

Pocatello Municipal Airport has flights linking Boise and Salt Lake City. Buses also service Pocatello.
Map ref: page 689 J7

SAWTOOTH NATIONAL RECREATION AREA

The Sawtooth Mountains form the most dramatic backdrop to Idaho's wilderness. Established in 1972, the area stretches 1,100 square miles (2,849 sq km) across four mountain ranges carved by glaciers and four major rivers. Its steep jagged ridges separate into a myriad of crystal-blue alpine lakes and meadows where Bighorn sheep can be seen grazing with elk and deer, which forage on the lower slopes in dense forests. There are hiking trails that lead to peaks that tower over 11,000 feet (3,355 m).

With over 1 million visitors annually, the area caters largely to outdoor enthusiasts. Though it can snow in summer, an array of

Potato farm near Carey, just south of the Sawtooth National Recreation Area, with the Sawtooth Mountains in the distance.

activities is still on offer including hiking, horseback riding, rafting, and camping. During the winter months, snowboarding and cross-country skiing dominate the wilderness tracts. At Redfish Lake, a haven for sockeye salmon and anglers, charter boats are available through the local visitor center.

Along Hwy 75, the road curves into two valleys with three scenic byways linking the region. The Sawtooth Scenic Byway follows Hwy 75 while the Ponderosa Pine Scenic Byway follows Hwy 21 between Stanley and Boise. The Salmon River Scenic Byway picks up Hwy 75 between Stanley and Challis and intersects Hwy 93, to Salmon.

Visitors traveling on Hwy 75 will reach the highest point of 11,170 feet (3,407 m) at Galena Summit before descending into the Big Wood River Valley. A view of Boulder Mountains and its stark, rose-brown escarpment looms in the distance before the Sawtooth National Forest tumbles onto the plains of the Snake River.

The Sawtooth Valley offers some of the best whitewater rapids as it cuts through the Salmon River Canyon, a sanctuary for black bear, elk, and deer. There are pocket hot springs, including Sunbeam Hot Springs, just minutes from Sunbeam village. Guided rafting trips take in three sections of this wild river, including the aptly named, River of No Return. Just south is the Middle Folk, deemed one of the top-10 rapids in the world.

The rugged community of Stanley, at the junction of Hwy 75 and 21, is the main center of the Sawtooth National Recreation Area. It also takes in the Sawtooth Valley and Sawtooth Basin. There are campgrounds scattered throughout the region and motels in Stanley and Salmon. Passes are available for the Sawtooth Recreation Area and National Forest through the visitor center, 8 miles (13 km) north of Ketchum on Hwy 75.

Idaho Falls is the closest center to the monument. It is serviced by an airport and buses. There is also a small airport south of Hailey.
Map ref: page 688 E4

SILVER CITY

This mining town is Idaho's oldest. Founded in the 1860s, tiny Silver City still resembles a Wild West community. It can be reached from a dusty trail off Hwy 78, east of Murphy. Nestled in a hollow of the Owyhee Mountains, the town is a mixture of former saloons and brothels that spawned from the local mines. Its historic district boasts of an old courthouse and the Idaho Hotel, an original stagecoach outpost.
Map ref: page 688 B7

SUN VALLEY

Visitors to Sun Valley could mistake this town for a European ski resort but the chalets are a mere diversion to a community that is more Western in style than the Wild West ever was. A playground for the rich, billionaire businessman Averell Harriman, then chairman of Union Pacific Railroads, bought 4,300 acres (1,741 m) of prime ranch and commissioned an Austrian count to design the Sun Valley Resort in 1935. The Rocky Mountains' first ski resort lured many celebrities, including Gary Cooper, Clark Gable, and author, Ernest Hemingway. Sun Valley still attracts many of the smart-set though its elevation of 5,750 feet (1,754 m) makes the region warmer than other Rocky Mountain resorts—and less crowded.

The town's population of just over 1,000 inevitably swells during the winter when the ski runs of Dollar and Bald Mountains are in operation. Built by Union Pacific engineers, the Sun Valley ski area boasts first-rate downhill skiing with some slopes descending 3,400 vertical feet (1,037 m). During the summer, the region largely caters to outdoor devotees with hiking, horseback riding, kayaking, and golfing at Elkhorn Resort. Flyfishing is also highly popular at Silver Creek and the Big Wood River.

Ketchum is 1 mile (2 km) northeast of Sun Valley, on Hwy 75. The town began as a mining community in 1882 and today has a population of 3,280 residents. A regular visitor to town, Ernest Hemingway lived at the Sun Valley Lodge for a short time, where he wrote, in part, *For Whom the Bell Tolls.* Returning from Cuba in 1960, depression overcame him and he ended his life in July 1961. Buried at Ketchum Cemetery, a simple memorial salutes the author on Trail Creek, 1 mile (2 km) east of the lodge. His once-favorite drinking hole, now called Whiskey Jacques, is located on Main Street.

The Sun Valley region is serviced by airplanes through Hailey, with connections to Boise and Salt Lake City. There is a free shuttle service between Sun Valley and nearby Ketchum.
Map ref: page 688 F5

Guest ranches are a good lodging option in Idaho.

TWIN FALLS

Twin Falls, 6 miles (10 km) south of Sun Valley on I-84, is primarily a ranching community of 32,660 people. The construction of Milner Dam converted its arid terrain into 60,000 acres (24,300 ha) of farmland. Twin Falls is an excellent pit stop to Hagerman Fossil Beds National Park and Bruneau Dunes State Park, on Hwy 78, where North America's largest sand dunes rise to 470 feet (143 m).

Its airport connects to Salt Lake City and buses service the area.
Map ref: page 688 F8

WALLACE

The bygone mining town of Wallace is on the National Register of Historic Places. Also famous as the birthplace of actress Lana Turner, Wallace has a population of 954. It offers several unique expeditions for tourists, including a tour which takes visitors on a fascinating underground mine excursion. Wallace has converted its former railway line, once servicing the Silver Valley Mines across dangerous mountain passes, into a hiking and mountain-bike trail.

The nearest airport is in Spokane, 100 miles (161 km) west in Washington State. Wallace is serviced by buses.
Map ref: page 685 C5

One of the many quaint houses built on ranch land in the Sun Valley ski area.

MONTANA

Montana's popular name, "The Treasure State," was given with good reason. When gold was discovered in 1862, the state's yield was the biggest in the country; there were also huge deposits of silver and copper. Montana's economy still revolves around the gold and silver industries, as well as zinc, phosphate, oil, and ranching. However, to many thousands of tourists who visit Montana each year, the state is known as "Big Sky Country." Here the sky dominates the horizon, and miles of wilderness endure in a vast unpopulated expanse.

Bordered by Canada in the United States' northwestern pocket, Montana is a place of undulating prairies, high craggy mountains, and glacial lakes. The rushing waters of the Yellowstone and upper Missouri Rivers are associated with the legend of Lewis and Clark, who first explored the region in 1805. But it is the mountain rivers of the Gallatin and Madison that entice anglers and outdoor enthusiasts who hike many wilderness trails and cast a hook into trout-laden streams.

Montana's contrasting landscape provides refuge for a diversity of wildlife, including mountain lions, grizzly bears, moose, elk, and wolves. Golden eagles and hawks often swoop over the region's wilderness. Wildlife watching is becoming increasingly popular, with the National Bison Range and the Pryor Mountains Wild Horse Range offering total sanction. This vision extends to its population as well, with only 902,195 people living in 145,556 square miles (376,990 sq km) of land.

The settlement of Montana came at a price. The state's history is marked by bloody conflicts with the Cheyenne and Sioux native peoples—with the ghostly battlefields of the Rosebud and the Little Bighorn scarring the land.

The region's alpine beauty is the paramount attraction to visitors. In particular, Glacier National Park and Paradise Valley, which traverses the mountainous corridor of the Gallatin and Absaroka Ranges to Yellowstone Country. What the state lacks in population is made up in sheer wild splendor.

The National Bison Range, south of Lake Flathead. This was the first land US Congress purchased for the benefit of wildlife. The Range receives over 250,000 visitors every year.

State motto *Oro y plata* (Gold and silver)
State flag Adopted 1905 (modified 1981)
Capital Helena
Population 902,195
Total area (land and water) 147,046 square miles (380,849 sq km)
Land area 145,556 square miles (376,990 sq km)
Montana is the fourth-largest state in size
Origin of name Latinized Spanish word meaning "mountainous"
Nickname The Treasure State
Abbreviations MT (postal), Mont.
State bird Western meadowlark
State flower Bitterroot
State tree Ponderosa pine
Entered the Union November 8, 1889 as the 41st state

Places in
MONTANA

ANACONDA

The town of Anaconda, which is located 25 miles (40 km) west of Butte on Route 1, once housed the world's largest smelting operation. In the 1880s, the Anaconda Mining Company produced copper in vast quantities. But "Copperopolis," as it was dubbed, started to lose its luster when the demand for copper waned, eventually closing its plants in 1980. Former golfing champion, Jack Nicklaus, recently transformed Anaconda's smelters into the Old Works Golf Course.

Thankfully, the town's historic district remains a reflection of its boom years with a host of late-Victorian buildings and the Art Deco-style Washoe Theater crowding Main Street. There are some dramatic limestone cliffs and waterfalls worth exploring in nearby Lost Creek State Park.

Anaconda's modest population of 10,300 provides a regional pit stop to visitors who are exploring Montana's gold country.

The nearest airport is at Helena, about 20 miles (32 km) north on I-90 then about 30 miles (48 km) east on US-12. The towns of Missoula and Bozeman also have airports. Buses service the area.
Map ref: page 685 H8

BIG HOLE NATIONAL BATTLEFIELD

Big Hole National Battlefield is a memorial to those who died in the Battle of the Big Hole, one of four major battles that took place during the Nez Perce War. The battlefield is 10 miles (16 km) west from Wisdom on what is now Route 43. It is about 60 miles (97 km) south of Missoula.

In 1877, fleeing from Idaho in an attempt to escape being forced onto reservation land to make way for the settlement of the West, the Nez Perce clashed with General John Gibbon's Seventh Infantry at the Big Hole River. Though the Nez Perce's charismatic Chief Joseph led his warriors to victory in the first battle, they ultimately withdrew when realizing the futility of engaging in further clashes.

Attempting to continue their journey to the Canadian border, the Nez Perce were captured just a few miles from freedom during the following October.

In 1992, Big Hole National Battlefield was incorporated into the Nez Perce National Historic Park as one of 38 sites, in five states, that commemorate the culture and history of the Nez Perce.

Visitors can view the Nez Perce campsite and the battleground near the visitor center. There are self-guided trails, and guided tours during summer. The visitor center houses a small Nez Perce museum, a short video, and a sales area. There is a small entrance fee during summer only. The center is only closed for Thanksgiving, Christmas, and New Years Day. There is no public transportation in the park and the road to the battlefield is usually closed from late fall to sometime in April. There are no lodging or camping facilities in the park, the closest lodging is in Wisdom and there is more choice in Jackson, a little further away.

Grant-Kohrs Ranch National Historic Site is 75 miles (121 km) northwest. This ranch commemorates the history of cattle ranching in the West and is a working ranch.
Map ref: page 684 F10

BILLINGS

Billings is Montana's largest city with a population of 91,195. Its economy is firmly based around oil and farming and it is headquarters to many large banks and health-care enterprises that service much of northern Wyoming and the western Dakota states. Its central location, on the I-90 near the Crow Indian Reservation, the Little Bighorn Battlefield, and Red Lodge Mountain Ski Area, also makes the city an ideal base for visitors touring southern Montana.

Built around the fortunes of the Northern Pacific Railroad and the local ranching community, Billings has retained its cowboy appearance. Luminaries of the West frequently visited town, including Buffalo Bill Cody and artist, Charles Russell. At the Western Heritage Center on Montana Avenue, regional Native American artifacts and images of the Yellowstone River's early years are on display. The Moss Mansion, designed by Henry Hardenburg, who was the Waldorf-Astoria's founding architect is also worth a visit.

By far the most interesting site is Sacrifice Cliff, near the Black Otter Trail off Hwy 318. The legend has it that two Crow warriors, believing the gods were punishing their tribe during an outbreak of smallpox, picked two ponies and rode off the cliffs to celestial glory. The trail is pleasant for a stroll and provides a panoramic view of Billings and the distant mountain ranges.

On Lake Elmo Drive is Pictograph Cave State Park, preserving the remnants of a 5,000-year-old prehistoric culture. The site is open only from April to October.

Billing's Logan Airport is the official gateway to Montana and buses also service the area.
Map ref: page 686 E9

BOZEMAN

The town was named for trailblazer, John Bozeman, who led the first wagon train into the Gallatin Valley in 1864. Fifty years earlier,

fur traders were among the first to trample the region after the Lewis and Clark expedition. By 1883, the Northern Pacific Railroad brought a steady trail of settlers who were to develop the town.

Now the fastest growing city in Montana, with a population of 29,230, Bozeman sustains a youthful demographic, centered on Montana State University. Bozeman's prosperous community is also flourishing with artists, sports enthusiasts, and ranchers. A drive along Main Street features multiple sports stores selling every imaginable ware, and there are many bookstores and trendy cafés.

Worth viewing is the university's Museum of the Rockies, which chronicles everything from the evolution of the dinosaurs to foreign lights in space. It also has an excellent presentation of a Native American interpretation of the universe. The more generic Gallatin County Historical Museum features local history from an old county jail that only closed its doors in 1982. Bozeman's solid artistic community is represented at the Emerson Cultural Center while the most

Billings is an industrial city, with an economy that relies heavily on oil.

Bozeman is a jumping-off point for the Northern tip of Yellowstone National Park.

unusual gallery is at the American Computer Museum on Babcock Street. Everything from an abacus to slide rules and PCs are on display.

Bozeman's exquisite location, which is at the foothills of the Bridger Mountains and Gallatin River, is within striking distance of the Big Sky Ski Area as well as Yellowstone National Park. It remains Montana's revered base for fly-fishing at the Yellowstone, Madison, and the Gallatin Rivers. The latter, brimming with trout, was the location for the movie *A River Runs Through It*.

The town is 8 miles (13 km) east of Bozeman Hot Springs, once the sacred cleansing ground for local Blackfoot Native Americans, which now serves as a campground. There are numerous downhill ski runs at Bridger Bowl Ski Area and groomed cross-country ski trails at the Bohart Ranch, less than 1 mile (2 km) away from the resort.

Bozeman's has its own airport—the Gallatin Airport, and buses also service the area.
Map ref: page 685 L10

BUTTE

One hundred years ago, Butte sat on mines which produced unprecedented quantities of copper and silver. Today it remains one of the richest historic cities in Montana, where handsome Victorian edifices dominate the downtown district.

Though Butte's prosperity has diminished with the downturn in mining, its colorful legacy of copper kings who controlled the region has made it an interesting place to explore. It is also a city fueled by its once-vibrant migrant labor force comprising people of Irish, Chinese, and Mediterranean extraction. Their cultures are reflected in the number of bars and cafés downtown.

The Butte Historic District includes several mining museums and a curious statue of Our Lady of the Rockies, which became a symbolic shrine to unemployed miners. At night, the 90-foot (27-m) statue, perched on a hill east of town, can be seen illuminated by a blaze of lights.

The Bert Mooney Airport is in Butte and the other nearest airport is at Helena, about 40 miles (64 km) northeast on I-15. There are also airports at Missoula and Bozeman. Buses service the area.
Map ref: page 685 H9

DILLON

Dillon sits in the heart of Montana's gold country, 63 miles (101 km) north of the Idaho border off the I-15. Though it began as a terminus for the Utah and Northern Railroad, Dillon's population of 4,382 now supplies the pocket ranching community of Madison County and Western Montana College. While there are very few regional attractions outside of the parochial Beaverhead County Museum, Dillon offers easy access to a wealth of activities including camping and fishing in the Beaverhead National Forest. Undoubtedly Dillion's stellar event for the year is the frolicking Labor Day Rodeo, featuring a wild horse race and a Western barbeque.

The Bert Mooney Airport in Butte is the closest. Butte is about 40 miles (64 km) north on I-15.
Map ref: page 689 J2

The mineral-rich vicinity of Butte has produced gold, lead, zinc, and copper.

FORT BENTON

Fort Benton, 38 miles (61 km) north of Great Falls on Hwy 87, was one of Montana's significant outposts. The American Fur Company originally established the fort across the river in 1846 before relocating to its present site in 1848. Fort Benton became a thriving trade center, when the first steamboat arrived from St Louis in 1859, and continued to boom during the gold rush. The town harbored more than 120 saloons and countless brothels, along with an illicit whiskey trade. Worth a glance is the Fort Benton Museum across from the Lewis and Clark Memorial.

Ranches dot the area around Dillon.

Recreational activities have superseded gunfights and lynchings, which once were the town's customary pastimes. The most popular activity in the town, which boasts a population of 1,600, is a float trip along the "Missouri Breaks," bringing into view sheer cliffs and caves only visible from the water.

The closest airport is Great Falls.
Map ref: page 685 L4

GLACIER NATIONAL PARK

The jewel of Montana, Glacier National Park, features a myriad of dense forests, snow-capped peaks, and sparkling lakes—over 1,560 square miles (4,040 sq km) of ice-carved country. In 1995, the park was designated as a World Heritage Site, less than one hundred years after conservationist James Williard Shultz lobbied Congress to create the park in 1910. He called the park, "Crown of the Continent," with good reason. The grandeur of the mountains that thrust forward from the forests is testament to the majestic beauty of region.

Snowlines that blanket the mountains' apex form hundreds of cascading waterfalls and streams, creating lush meadows of vibrant wildflowers and a bounty of impenetrable hardwood.

The park's creation began over 1.5 billion years ago and has evolved through the constant shifting of the North American plate. Its mountain rocks, though relatively young in geological terms, have been carved into peaks and razor sharp ridges. Within Glacier National Park's patterned valleys, there are over 50 new glacial lakes fused into the mountain crevices that formed less than 3,000 years ago.

The landscape sustains an abundance of wildlife. Black bears straddle large logs in moments of respite and moose and mule deer forage the forest floor. Mountain lions are occasionally heard growling from boulders, and golden eagles and hawks swoop across timber tops looking for cottontails. In the alpine region, bighorn sheep and mountain goats perch on rocky ledges. In the marshland area, muskrats, geese, and beaver seek refuge behind tall reeds and gray-brown stones that lie along the shoreline of numerous lakes.

A labyrinth of hiking trails traverses the park, attracting more than 2 million tourists each year during the high summer season of July–August. The park also extends beyond the border into Canada where it merges with Waterton Lakes National Park, forming miles of unspoiled terrain.

The main entrance to the park is at St Marys, east on Hwy 89 with the most popular drive following the spiraling 50-mile (80-km) Going-to-the-Sun Road. Midway on the scenic route, the Continental Divide cuts vertically through

Mountain goat, Glacier National Park.

Avalanche Creek, Glacier National Park.

the park, creating three drainage systems to the Atlantic, Pacific, and Gulf of New Mexico near St Mary's Lake, creating a sweeping vista of sparkling water and serrated peaks.

Much of the park's dense groves of aspen and birch appear on the fringe of Logan's Pass, with an elevation of 6,646 feet (2,027 m). The deep gorges of Avalanche Creek bring into view a series of cascading waterfalls and a red sandstone ravine. Snow-covered peaks frame every corner of Lake McDonald, the largest body of water in Glacier National Park.

Apgar Village, at the west entrance at the junction of US-89 and Route 2, follows the southern course of the park. There are numerous budget and middle-range lodgings neighboring the area. However the Great Northern Railway's legacy of grand hotels and chalets remains the highlight for many guests.

The grandest is the imposing Glacier Park Lodge at the park's eastern frontier, which was built around 1913.

Campgrounds and rustic cabins are available in summer along with organized tours, which focus on Native American translations by

Blackfoot guides. Fishing, cross-country skiing, horseback riding, rafting along the Flathead River, and mountain-bike riding are available through outfitters at Apgar, and at the park lodges.

While the park is open year-round, most roads are closed from November to April. The park lodges likewise remain closed in the winter. However, winter lodging is available at both East and West Glacier. Glacier Park Inc. provides information on lodgings and activities. A seven-day pass is available for a small per-vehicle fee. There is also a slightly higher fee available that will gain entry to Waterton Lakes Park as well.

Glacier International Airport, near the town of Kalispell, services Glacier National Park, as do trains.
Map ref: page 684 F2

GREAT FALLS

Great Falls, the second-largest city in Montana, with a population of 57,758, sits in the heartland of agricultural and cattle country on the Missouri River. Explorers, Lewis and Clark, first stopped on the present site of Great Falls in 1805 and, by 1887, the city became a railway center for the Great Northern Railroad. Great Falls now promotes itself as Montana's gateway to Glacier National Park and Yellowstone National Park.

The vast open ranges surrounding Great Falls were immortalized in a series of sweeping paintings by one of the West's greatest artists and adopted son, Charlie Russell. A composite of the artist's personal memorabilia and life's work is showcased at the Charles Russell Museum Complex. It also houses

his 1903 log-cabin studio where he romanticized the West just as its legacy began to diminish.

Close to the city is the 7-mile (11-km) River's Trail Edge where visitors can explore the visual history of Lewis and Clark. The Lewis and Clark Interpretive Center exhibits historical presentations and films about the explorers.

Great Falls International Airport is to be found off the I-15.
Map ref: page 686 A5

HAVRE

The town of Havre sits 38 miles (61 km) south of the Canadian border on Hwy 2 (also known as the Hi-Line). Following the Great Northern Railroad tracks in Montana's desolate high plains, the agricultural community of 10,232 is surrounded by an endless expanse of wheat fields and cattle ranches.

It is also close to where the Nez Perce Indians made their last camp as unconstrained people in 1877, after fleeing from the army in Idaho. The Bears Paw Battlefield Monument marks the spot where the army engaged in battle with Chief Joseph's unsuspecting warriors who believed that freedom was only a day away from camp. They surrendered to General Nelson A. Miles four days later. About 16 miles (26 km) west of the battlefield is the tiny hamlet of Chinook where the Blaine County Museum chronicles the battle.

Tepee-style lodging, near Great Falls.

Havre itself is of little interest to passing tourists, although a subterranean tour of its historic Main Street's former brothels and opium dens is interesting.

Havre has an airport, and Great Falls is around 80 miles (129 km) southwest of Havre on US-87.
Map ref: page 686 D2

HELENA

Situated on the I-15, just east of the Continental Divide, like most Montana cities, Helena made its fortune on gold, building a prosperous city rich in architecture and commerce. Though the city remains small, with a population of 27,982, its late-Victorian downtown district hosts some of the state's most resplendent buildings, including the copper-dome State Capitol built in 1899, and St Helena Cathedral, which was modeled on a Viennese cathedral.

According to local lore, Helena, which became the state capital in 1889, almost never made the honor. A fierce competition took place with rivaling Anaconda, which largely monopolized the state's financial strings with its gold smelters. A vote took place giving Helena the green light but, years later, it was revealed that Anaconda was the rightful winner when the original voting documents were located and recounted.

By 1888, Helena was producing the second-largest yields of gold, turning its citizens into multimillionaires. An open-air train

conducts a one-hour tour of Last Chance Gulch (where gold was first discovered and which is now the main street), from the Montana Historical Society, bringing into view Helena's classic structures. The Historical Society showcases a peerless collection of art by Charles Russell, along with a host of photographs from its archives. Visitors can stroll Reeder's Alley, a narrow corridor filled with charming shops and restaurants that were once apartments providing housing during the 1880s.

Helena retains a strong cultural link to music and film. In June, Helena hosts the week-long Montana Traditional Jazz Festival. The former county jail on Ewing Street is now the Myrna Loy Center for the Performing Arts, showcasing the life of the Montana-born actress in photographs; it also has an in-house theater. Directly opposite is the Lewis and Clark County Courthouse, the State Capitol until 1902.

The temptation to go for a long walk is made easy by the number of hiking and mountain-biking trails surrounding Helena. As well as the Helena National Forest and the Big Belt Mountains, which cradle the city, the Continental Divide National Trail takes in the vast Rocky Mountain scenery. Several campgrounds are located in the Helena National Forest as well as a recreational vehicle park on Hwy 12, east of Helena. In February, the city hosts the longest dog-sled race outside of Alaska.

Helena Regional Airport, north of downtown, services the area.
Map ref: page 685 J7

KALISPELL

As the gateway to Glacier National Park, Kalispell's population of 15,678 revolves around tourism. Nestled in the Flathead Valley on US-93, Kalispell began as a trading post in 1881 and soon became the terminus and trade center on the Great Northern Pacific line to the local ranching and farming community. Today Kalispell remains the Flathead Valley's hub and rivals Whitefish, 13 miles (21 km) north, with budget lodgings and cafes.

An hour north of town is the region's largest ski resort, Big Mountain Ski and Summer Resort, 30 miles (48 km) from Glacier National Park. In summer, the

In Glacier National Park, near Kalispell, there are over 700 miles of walking trail.

resort has hiking, mountain biking, horseback riding, and a scenic gondola ride, which glides to Big Mountain's peak. There is a stunning view from the peak that takes in the Flathead Valley, Whitefish Lake, and the snow-capped peaks of Glacier National Park.

Flathead Lake is a major attraction, with many boating activities and wildlife-spotting opportunities available. Among the most popular activities around Polson and Whitefish are golfing and whitewater rafting along the Middlefolk or the Flathead Rivers.

Surrounded by a host of historic homes in Kalispell is the Conrad Mansion National Historic Site Museum. Its former owner, Charles Conrad, made his fortune as a commercial mercantile trader on the Missouri after marrying a local Blackfeet woman. The house is a resplendent feat of architecture, complete with Tiffany-glass windows and original furnishings. Conrad was an advocate of Blackfeet land rights and pursued the government for land. The Blackfeet Indian Reservation is located east of Glacier National Park.

Kalispell still honors its cow town heritage by hosting the Northwest Montana Fair and Rodeo in late August. Throughout the summer, on Saturday mornings, visitors can walk the Kalispell Farmers Market at the Kalispell Center Mall. Here local farmers sell an impressive array of harvested produce and homespun sweet bread.

Glacier Park International Airport services both Kalispell and Whitefish. An airport shuttle from both towns to the airport is available. There is also a train service from Whitefish.
Map ref: page 684 F3

LITTLE BIGHORN BATTLEFIELD NATIONAL MONUMENT

Little Bighorn Battlefield National Monument is about 45 miles (72 km) southeast of Billings on I-90. The US Army endured its greatest debacle on June 25, 1876 at the Little Bighorn River, on a high bluff near the town of Hardin. A detachment of 7th Cavalry led by General George Armstrong Custer clashed with the Sioux and Cheyenne—led by Crazy Horse—while trying to advance on their village. Custer had arrogantly miscalculated the number of Plains Indians in the encampment, which turned out to be the largest gathering of local Plains Indians ever assembled. Custer and 224 soldiers were soon outnumbered by a 1,800-strong war party and Custer's regiment was annihilated. Stone tablets now mark the spots where the entire regiment fell in the battle, though Custer's body was relocated to the military cemetery at West Point.

US cavalry stone markers, Little Bighorn National Monument.

A visitor center, on US-212, offers an interpretative display of the battle with a wealth of books and a narrative tour. A windblown pathway leads visitors to the site.

The nearest airport to Little Bighorn is the Billings-Logan International Airport, in Billings.
Map ref: page 690 G1

LIVINGSTON

The pretty town of Livingston nestles in Paradise Valley, 57 miles (92 km) north of Yellowstone National Park at the junction of US-89 and I-90. Essentially a pastoral town once frequented by Calamity Jane, Livingston's population of 7,500 largely retains a bygone lifestyle that is reflected in its downtown district. Old hardware and sporting stores, and farm equipment businesses trade alongside local diners. The ornate Depot Center, built in 1902, has been restored and transformed into a

noteworthy museum. Art galleries and restaurants have appeared on Park Street, and Hollywood blueblood and famous authors have purchased properties in the area.

Visitors can drive south beyond the town limits on US-89 and make camp at Chico Hot Springs, at the foothills of the Absaroka Ranges. Chico Hot Springs has been Livingston's best-kept secret for more than one hundred years. Chico also hosts dozens of hiking and horseback trails, along with rafting on the Yellowstone River.

On the July 4 holiday weekend, the Livingston Professional Cowboys Association Rodeo takes place. Later in the month the wild Yellowstone Boat Float regatta begins its 110-mile (177-km) path on the Yellowstone to Columbus.

There are bus services connecting Livingston to Missoula and Billings.
Map ref: page 685 M10

MISSOULA

Missoula sits at the confluence of the Blackfoot and Bitteroot Rivers. Conveniently centered on the I-90, the former goldrush town is home to the University of Montana and boasts a rich cultural life.

Montana's third-largest city, with a population of more than 51,000 people, Missoula thrives on its consolidation of the music and theatrical scene. The university has spawned some of America's greatest contemporary writers including William Kittredge and James Welch. Local writer, Norman McLean, captured the beauty of the region in his novella, *A River Runs Through It.*

The Grizzly Statue in the grounds of the University of Montana, Missoula.

Missoula also has several museums of note including the Missoula Museum of the Arts and the Fort Missoula Historical Museum, the base of the US Army during the Nez Perce War.

Plentiful hiking and cross-country trails surround Missoula including the Rattlesnake Wilderness Area in the Lolo Forest and the tamer Blue Mountain Recreation Area, 2 miles (3 km) west of town. Missoula's local ski resort, Snowbowl Ski Area, is located 17 miles (28 km) north on US-93. The best whitewater rafting is located near Alberton Gorge on the Clark Folk River.

A short drive northeast of town on Route 200 is the ghost town of Garnet, a cast-off from the 1860s gold boom. About 40 buildings remain intact as do several mine shafts and the Wells Hotel.

Missoula County International Airport and buses service the area.
Map ref: page 684 F7

NATIONAL BISON RANGE

South of Lake Flathead, on US-93 near the Flathead Indian Reservation, is the National Bison Range, which encompasses an 18,000-acre (7,290-ha) refuge for nearly 700 head of bison. Founded in 1908 to protect the endangered bison, it also features other wildlife such as mule deer and bighorn sheep.

The reserve is a mix of rolling prairie grassland, marshes, and jagged cliffs. This broad expanse also views the cycle of endurance each spring, with the calves perpetuating the myth of the bison and their spiritual connection to the Plains Indians. In October, visitors can view the thundering herd being rounded up by cowboys, a sound that was heard across the Western Plains 130 years ago.

The National Bison Range's headquarters is located at Moiese on Route 212.
Map ref: page 684 F5

The Yellowstone River is a fishing mecca to anglers from nearby Livingston, home to the International Fly Fishing Center.

NEVADA

The Spanish first explored Nevada in the seventeenth century, and it remained part of New Spain's territory until ceded by Mexico to the United States in 1848. When silver was discovered near Virginia City in 1859, prospectors blazed the pioneer trails in search of the mother lode. Nevada's modern nomads largely pursue the elusive jack-pots of Las Vegas. Along with Reno, another large gaming town, Vegas is a dazzling oasis in the desert panorama.

From the moment you cross the border into Nevada, endless gaming billboards erupt through the desert haze. Gambling is the largest form of commerce, followed by tourism, mining, and ranching.

"The Silver State" covers 110,567 square miles (286,369 sq km) of mostly uninhabitable desert plains and unsullied wilderness areas. In the Great Desert Basin, mountain rivers end their westward journey, forming a series of interior lakes. Near the capital, Carson City, the Sierra Nevada ranges spill across from California's forested border at Lake Tahoe. To the south, the Mojave Desert sits at the lowest point of the state in temperatures frequently above 120°F (48.9°C). Most of the desert remains under military command, including Nellis Air Force Base.

Snow-clad Santa Rosa Range in the north of Nevada rears behind a lone trailer.

Though an afternoon mirage projects a forlorn flatness to the landscape, there are over 300 jagged mountain ranges in the state, Boundary Peak rising to 13,140 feet (4,008 m). On the desert flatlands, cacti, sagebrush, and yucca plants flourish against a scattering of Joshua trees. Nevada is also a haven for deer, antelope, bobcats, jackrabbits, and rattlesnakes.

Once inhabited by Paiute, Washo, and Shoshone Native Americans, the state has a modern population of almost 2 million people. What it lacks in permanent residents is made up for by the nearly 40 million visitors attracted annually by the call of the slot machines and the promise of superb outdoor recreational opportunities.

State motto All For Our Country
State flag Adopted 1929 (modified 1987)
Capital Carson City
Population 1,998,257
Total area (land and water) 110,567 square miles (286,369 sq km)
Land area 109,806 square miles (284,398 sq km)
Nevada is the seventh-largest state in size
Origin of name From the Spanish word for "snow-capped"
Nicknames The Sagebrush State, The Silver State, The Battle-born State
Abbreviations NV (postal), Nev.
State bird Mountain bluebird
State flower Sagebrush
State tree Bristle cone pine and piñon
Entered the Union October 31, 1864 as the 36th state

STATE FEATURE

Las Vegas

A sign advertising one of the many popular wedding chapels on "the Strip."

Las Vegas is a cocktail of entertainment, on tap 24 hours a day. It was the Spaniards who first used this unique desert oasis as a pit stop on the Old Spanish Trail between California and Santa Fe. Now it is a resort oasis for millions of tourists. Its pleasure spots never cease to spin in the hotel palaces along Las Vegas Boulevard, known locally as "the Strip." The 6-mile (10-km) tract is a gambler's paradise where over US$10 billion is dropped annually into the gaming industry's coffers.

Framed by both the Sonoran Desert and the Great Basin Desert, Las Vegas is one of the hottest and driest cities in America. It is also one of the richest, where money flows without obstruction. The city's casinos are a creation of grandiose themes, with its skyline a variety of fanciful architecture. These structures and the miniature cities of Paris, New York, and Venice are a traveler's El Dorado. The cityscape is constantly evolving with magnificent, new hotel-casinos continually being built.

By day, the 210,000 residents of Las Vegas swelter in the desert heat but at night, they come out to gamble at the 52 hotels that dot the Strip.

A creation of the early twentieth century, Las Vegas grew around the Union-Pacific Railroad. In 1905 the community largely comprised makeshift tents. The promise of fast fortunes from the nearby gold mines of Tonopah lured many new settlers. However, it was the region of Black Canyon, now the location of Hoover Dam, that gave Las Vegas its solid economic foundation.

Coinciding with the construction of the Dam, gambling was legalized in 1931. With the roulette wheel came "the Mob" and endless greenbacks.

In 1946, notorious gangster Benjamin "Bugsy" Siegel opened the lavish Flamingo on old Hwy 91, introducing Las Vegas to a new level of luxury and vice. He became the neon city's custodian of gaming and prostitution and set a precedent for his successors. Following his death in a gangland "hit," the Mafia moved in and controlled the town for the next 20 years. But by 1967, things began to wane for the underworld. The FBI initiated raids and shut down the racketeers. Also, billionaire Howard Hughes unwittingly changed the dynamics of the city's respectability when he bought the Desert Inn. After that a battalion of corporations followed suit, and casinos and high stakes took on a new edge with the focus shifting to big-name entertainers to lure more conventional crowds. "The Rat Pack" (Frank Sinatra, Dean Martin, Sammy Davis Jr, Peter Lawford, and Joey Bishop) kicked off at the Desert Inn before making their way to the Sands and the Sahara.

The Las Vegas Hilton introduced Elvis to a new generation of fans in a series of electric shows. A sparkling Liberace shimmered in sequins over at the Riviera. By the late 1980s, entrepreneur Steve Wynn had built the opulent Mirage, bringing with it fantasy entertainment—from its incredible success came a host of visionary casinos rivaling Disneyland in themes. The Egyptian-designed Luxor, Caesar's Palace, New York, New York, and the medieval Excalibur fulfilled every gambler's whims.

By the late 1990s the Strip saw a new level of opulence soar into the next stratosphere. The newest, Mandalay Bay—where the House of Blues resides— is located south along the Strip. Further north is the neon fantasy of Excalibur and the MGM Grand, igniting a pedestrian frenzy at the intersection of Las Vegas Boulevard and Tropicana Avenue.

A large number of veteran properties remain nestled in with the new. Paris-Las Vegas, the Venetian, Bellagio, and Caesar's Palace lead the line-up of plush hotels, with standard trappings fit for a sultan.

A stay at New York, New York takes visitors on a roller-coaster ride through the Big Apple. The Manhattan Express races past 12 skyscrapers, the Statue of Liberty, and a more pedestrian-friendly Central Park.

A great view of Las Vegas is presented from the Eiffel Tower at Paris-Las Vegas. Its cobblestone streets also lead to the city's premier French restaurants—a welcome change from the endless hotel buffets. At the Venetian, gondolas in the canal add to the splendor of the hotel, with its plush guest suites and ornate casinos. Treasure Island, an annex of the Mirage, boasts a smoking volcano and a Buccaneer pirate show.

Shopping in Vegas is just as serious as gambling. Beneath the jaws of Bellagio's casinos lies Via Bellagio, a labyrinth of dazzling boutiques. The Bellagio Gallery of Fine Art and Conservatory features "the best of the best," with the masters Picasso and Monet leading the line-up in its US$350 million collection. The beauty of the Conservatory belies the glitz outside on the street. Covering over 12,000 square feet (1,140 sq m), the botanical garden features a lush collection of scented blooms underneath a glass canopy.

At Caesar's Palace, eye-catching centurions and toga-clad hostesses raise the casino's temperature while its ornate portico nurtures the titans of fashion in the Forum Shops. The Forum also houses the Omnimax Theater, which showcases the Race to Atlantis, a 3-D IMAX simulator ride.

The New York, New York casino complex and the MGM lion are prominent landmarks of the city.

At night, the Strip is a spectacle of fountains and flashing neon amid a valley of twinkling lights. The laser beams are reserved for the extravaganza performances that dazzle the Strip.

Siegfried and Roy have long entertained visitors at the Mirage with their line-up of big cats. Panthers, lions, and tigers perform alongside the masters but shelter during the day in the tropical enclave of the Secret Garden. Circus Carnival Midway goes one step further by scaling down the size of performing felines for their Housecats performance. Next door is the Canyon Blaster, which features a stomach-wrenching roller-coaster ride. And the suffering doesn't stop there. At Wet'n'Wild the tummy torture continues on a series of massive chutes and slides. The more congenial Star Trek Experience at the Las Vegas Hilton is ideal for land lovers wanting to blast off into space with other Trekkie fans.

The Imperial Palace Auto Museum has a fascinating collection of vehicles, including a Mercedes-Benz driven by Adolf Hitler and one of John F. Kennedy's presidential limousines. At the Sahara Speedworld, a 3-D simulator keeps racing-car buffs in good company with NASCAR drivers.

The best way to enjoy the city is to take a 30-minute helicopter tour from McCarran International Airport. The next best thing is to ride what can only be described as a G-force elevator to the top of the 1,149-foot (350-m) Stratosphere Tower. Offering panoramic views, the tower is the tallest building west of the Mississippi River.

Getting "hitched" in Las Vegas is part of the city's lore. For a modest fee, a wedding license can be purchased from Clark County Marriage License Bureau if the bride and groom are single and over eighteen. The variety of wedding chapels is endless. The best are the Little White Chapel, where lovebirds can "drive-in and drive-out," and the Graceland Wedding Chapel, where an Elvis impersonator can walk the bride-to-be down the aisle while singing "You Ain't Nothing But a Hound-Dog."

The Liberace Museum pays homage to "Mr Showman." Liberace's glittering costumes, over 30 pianos, and an elaborate candelabra are only part of the exhibit; there is also a musical toilet, which plays the melodies he once played.

Growth is expected to continue over the next 10 years. Currently accommodating 120,000 hotel beds, Las Vegas is expected to host a staggering number of new arrivals with primarily one thing on their agenda—to gamble. What will be Las Vegas's next flamboyant theme? One thing is certain, there will never be a shortage of Elvis impersonators along the Strip.

McCarran International Airport is located 4 miles (6 km) south from the Strip. Las Vegas is located at the intersection of I-15 and Hwys 93/95.

Las Vegas Boulevard ("the Strip") at night, the heart of Vegas' "phosphorescent oasis."

The Luxor Casino's glistening pyramid is fronted by a huge pharaonic mask.

Places in
NEVADA

The jagged heights of the Ruby Mountains near Elko open out to well-watered valleys where cattle graze.

BOULDER CITY

Located about 20 miles (32 km) southeast of Las Vegas, on Hwy 93, is the town of Boulder City. It was built during the construction of nearby Hoover Dam in the 1930s. Government-owned for 29 years, the city became an independent municipality in 1960 when its residents bought their houses at a federal sale. With the title deeds came the liberty to consume alcohol and to gamble, vices that were previously prohibited.

Now Boulder City is the official gateway to Lake Mead and Hoover Dam. Its 13,000 residents have maintained a unique stance on gambling—they have outlawed it within the city limits. Without the neon lights of the gaming towns and city gridlock at twilight, the town's sleepy streets are a picture of bygone America. This quiet town makes an excellent base from which to explore Lake Mead Recreational Area.

Boulder City's most famous landmark is the Boulder Dam Hotel. Once a refuge for Hollywood's golden-era celebrities, the hotel fell into a state of decline until 1993, when a huge restoration project rejuvenated the classic hotel. A short stroll away is the Boulder City Visitor Center on Arizona Street, where a visual exhibit of Hoover Dam's construction is on show. The structure contains over 7 million tons (6.3 million tonnes) of concrete and 840 miles (1,352 km) of steel pipes. There are also photographs and artifacts from the 1930s.

McCarran International Airport, in Las Vegas, is the closest.
Map ref: page 616 C7

CARSON CITY

The capital of Nevada, Carson City is situated 32 miles (51 km) south of Reno along Hwy 395 in the foothills of the Sierra Nevada ranges. First settled as a Mormon community, an entrepreneur bought the land and founded the city in 1858. Gold was discovered at nearby Six-Mile Canyon in 1859, and Carson City soon flourished with the arrival of the Virginia and Truckee Railroad in 1870.

Carson City has retained its Victorian-style architecture. Along Carson Street visitors can take the self-guided Kit Carson Trail to view the historic district. A blue stripe marker is painted on the sidewalk and city maps highlight the main attractions.

The best tour on offer is the Ghost Walk where a guide outlines the city's haunted sites dating back to the gold-rush era. At the northern end is the Nevada State Museum, formerly the old US Mint, which currently exhibits an array of pioneer artifacts, along with a nineteenth-century coin press which is now used for pressing silver and bronze medallions. A subterranean passage links visitors to a full-scale mine.

The 1871 Nevada State Capitol nestles in among the trees along Carson Street and houses an important archival library. The Nevada State Railroad Museum showcases a fine collection of vintage passenger and freight cars and locomotives that were once used on the Virginia and Truckee Railroad.

Buses connect Carson City to Reno, Los Angeles, and Las Vegas.
Map ref: page 693 J8

Indian paintbrush
(Castilleja augustifolia).

ELKO

Located on the massive northern stretch of I-80, Elko is the town that everyone drives through, but seldom stops in. But this town is worth stopping for. It sits right in the heart of the state's cowboy country amid a herd of pickups and a sea of Stetsons. This is how the West once was, and its 19,000 residents remain determined to preserve their heritage.

Elko is surrounded by some brilliant desert scenery and jagged mountain ranges. South of the town are the Ruby Mountains where horseback riding and hiking trails along the Humboldt River provide plenty of recreational opportunities. The town itself is a mixture of ranchers, Basque sheepherders, cattle barons, and the occasional dude from Reno.

In 1868, Elko was primarily a terminus for the Central Pacific Railway, which transported minerals from the surrounding mines. By the turn of the twentieth century, Elko harbored several brothels and saloons before the mines began to decline. Answering the call of Nevada's burgeoning casinos in the 1940s, Hollywood started to showcase glittering acts in town. Bing Crosby went further and purchased the Elko County Ranch, a rather sizable chunk of grazing land on the fringe of town.

The Northeastern Nevada Museum in Elko displays a host of regional pioneer artifacts, including a saloon bar and a dandy pair of boots owned by a notorious cattle rustler. Its industrious owner had the boots fitted with slick cow hooves so he could avoid detection when gathering a stolen herd. The Western Folklife Center carries on Elko's cowboy heritage at the annual Cowboy Poetry Gathering in January, where the ritual of campfires and singing cowboys preserves the myth of the Old

Nevada State Capitol building (1871) on Carson Street, Carson City.

West. Formerly the Pioneer Saloon and Hotel, the Center offers a fine selection of cowboy paraphernalia for sale while the J.M. Capriola Company on Fifth Street sells the best buckaroo outfits in the state.

Seventy miles (113 km) west along I-80, toward Winnemucca, is Battle Mountain, site of a major fight in 1861 between the Shoshone tribe and the settlers. The Trail of the 49ers Interpretive Center displays pioneer artifacts from their westward journey to the California gold mines. The National Basque Festival, a three-day festival, is held on the July 4 weekend.

Buses and trains connect to Reno and Salt Lake City.
Map ref: page 694 C4

GREAT BASIN NATIONAL PARK

Straddling the Utah border across the rugged Snake Range is Great Basin National Park in eastern Nevada. Created in 1986, the country's youngest national park covers 77,000 acres (31,185 ha) of unspoiled wilderness. Because of

Cirque at Wheeler Peak, Great Basin National Park.

its remote location on Hwy 50, the Great Basin National Park generally remains uncrowded.

The Park offers nine hiking trails along lush alpine meadows, a glacial icefield, and numerous streams that rush beside the tract of the mountains. The range of hiking varies but the most challenging climb is to an elevation of 13,063 feet (3,984 m) at Wheeler Peak, Nevada's second-highest mountain. The Bristlecone Pine Glacier Trail goes past several alpine lakes to the state's only glacier at Wheeler Peak Cirque. Its cool bristlecone forests, which date from 3,500 years ago, offer sanctuary to scores of deer, squirrels, and antelope.

The park is fused with the spectacular Lehman Caves. Guided 90-minute tours offer views of the serrated limestone caverns, some of the largest in the United States.

Ely, an unassuming town that developed around the copper and silver boom of the 1870s, lies 60 miles (97 km) to the west. Ely also served as the headquarters for the Nevada Northern Railroad.

Worth viewing is its railway museum, which houses a very well-preserved caboose, an assortment of railway equipment, and a collection of rolling trains. A 1910 Baldwin locomotive, known as "The Ghost Train of Old Ely," now hauls passengers on a bumpy track to the mining community of Keystone.
Map ref: page 694 E9

LAKE MEAD NATIONAL RECREATION AREA

Just 12 miles (19 km) south of Las Vegas, Lake Mead has long been a recreational spot for Las Vegas residents yearning for respite from the midnight neon.

Covering both the waters of Lake Mead and Lake Mohave, the 2,337-square-mile (3,760-sq-km) recreation area also sees the Colorado River cut along the desert border of Ari-

Lumber pines and rugged slopes are typical of many of the protected areas in Nevada.

zona, adjacent to the Grand Canyon National Park. The lake is a perfect spot for camping, its most popular point being the aptly named Boulder Beach, located near the Alan Bible Visitor Center on Hwy 93.

The massive Hoover Dam created Lake Mead and tamed the Colorado River and its tributaries. Taking four years to construct, Boulder Dam, as it was originally called, was completed in 1935 for US$165 million.

While this large artificial lake provides outdoor diversion for thousands, it is also a lifeline for the parched desert area. Measuring 110 miles (177 km) long and over 500 feet (152 m) deep, the reservoir irrigates hundreds of miles of land extending well into Mexico. It also supplies water and electricity to over 18 million people in the tri-state region that encompasses Nevada, Arizona, and southern California.

At the Hoover Dam Center, visitors can tour the dam's imposing basement as well as a subterranean station that houses the massive turbine pumps. The admission fee is quite high, but it includes a preview film of the dam's construction.

There are a host of activities available in the park, such as boating, scuba diving, and water-skiing. For anglers, the lake is laden with catfish and trout. Lake Mead also has many interesting treks, including treks to the old Mormon town of St Thomas and Wishing Well Cove. There are also many secluded coves suitable for mooring a boat.

The drive along Route 169 from the lake's northern boundary is the most scenic. Near the Muddy River is the Lost City Museum, which exhibits artifacts of the ancient Anasazi people who erected the Pueblo Grande de Nevada, or the Lost City, at the mouth of the Muddy and Virgin Rivers around AD 1000. Though the Lost City was excavated during the 1920s, remnants from the dig were tragically washed away after the Hoover Dam filled Lake Mead in the 1930s.

Just 6 miles (10 km) west of Overton are the ancient jagged rock formations and petroglyphs of the Valley of Fire State Park. Once an inland sea, the area has been patterned by wind and sun for over 140 million years. Its uplift of sand became solidified and in due time eroded into serrated ridges, which reflect a kaleidoscope of classic desert colors. By mid-afternoon, the sun extracts a stunning medley of scarlet, cinnamon, and magenta hues from the ancient sandstone.

The most spectacular trail lies quite close to the Valley's eastern entrance, where the road leads to a cluster of sandstone bunkers that sit precariously beneath looming boulders. These rough buildings were constructed in 1935 for the maverick travelers who first trekked to the Valley of Fire when Nevada declared the area as its first state park.

Further along the trail is the Petroglyph Canyon Trail, where hikers can view numerous rock carvings dating back to AD 500.

Organized park ranger tours take in many of the petroglyphs and native flora. From here the track moves on to Rainbow Vista with a sweeping panorama of the canyon.

At Overton a couple of motels cater to the passing traffic.
Map ref: page 616 D7

LAKE TAHOE

Located only about 25 miles (40 km) west of Carson City, chilly, sapphire-blue Lake Tahoe is one of the world's highest and deepest volumes of water. Created by ice flow, the largest alpine lake in North America has a shoreline circumference of 72 miles (116 km) and it spans 12 miles (19 km). Lake Tahoe is surrounded by the Sierra Nevada and Carson Ranges and California.

At an altitude of 6,235 feet (1,902 m), Lake Tahoe invariably attracts skiers and snowboarders to its backyard slopes in the winter. Driving can be hazardous at times with Hwy 89 remaining closed throughout the colder months. By summer, the region is exploding with water revelers, hikers, and hordes of gamblers. At times, the drive around the lake can amount to five hours of gridlock,

Billboard outside Las Vegas on I-15.

especially at the town of Stateline, where the roadside suddenly becomes neon-charged. South Lake Tahoe is crowded with people, pick-ups, and casinos packed with fervent gamblers. The area provides an abundance of great budget lodgings.

Straddling the southern boundary of Lake Tahoe is Incline Village, a popular gaming resort and, in winter, home to vacationers enjoying the Slide Mountain, Peak, and Mount Rose Ski Areas. For television fans of the popular 1960s western, "Bonanza," Incline Village is home to the Ponderosa Ranch Western Theme Park. Hoss and Little Joe key chains and the show's theme song are also available at the park.

Unsullied blue water fills a glacially eroded tarn in the Ruby Mountains, near Lamoille; the mountains are perfect for hiking.

From Stateline, an aerial tram at 8,250 feet (2,516 m) glides its way into the Heavenly Ski Area. Along with the spectacular view, Heavenly offers over 80 ski runs and nearly 30 lifts. The more popular resort of Squaw Valley, the site of the 1960 Winter Olympics, nestles on the California side. At Spooner Lake, on Hwys 50/28, there are numerous trails and plenty of lake viewing for cross-country skiers.

Not all lakeside activities require you to exert physical energy. Near Zephyr Cove, visitors can glide across the turquoise waters aboard a paddle-steamer. There are plentiful camp sites at Emerald Bay State Park, near the lake's southern boundary.

Lake Tahoe's weather is often unpredictable in early spring and late fall. The visitor center located at Incline Village provides daily reports of road conditions, as well as regional trail maps.

Buses serve Lake Tahoe at Stateline along Hwy 50 from Sacramento and San Francisco. Shuttle services connect the smaller shoreline communities.
Map ref: page 693 H8

LAMOILLE

Twenty miles (32 km) south of Elko, along Hwy 227, is the picturesque community of Lamoille, nestled at the basin of the lofty Ruby Mountains. From its summit

lookout can be seen the massive ranches in the valley and numerous hiking trails, which are often dusted in a blanket of snow. By winter, the Ruby Mountains are transformed into the ultimate thrill center where Heli-Skiing has become a popular yet expensive sport. The more sociable Swisher's General Store is the perfect place to browse and recover.
Map ref: page 694 C4

LAS VEGAS

See Las Vegas, State Feature, pages 662–63

LOVELOCK

With the Trinity Range to the north and Humboldt Range to the south, Lovelock sits on what was an old fur-trapper trail, which

traveled southwest from Salt Lake City to Reno. From its initial appearance, Lovelock doesn't promise to be any different from other highway towns, with its steady stream of fast-food outlets and rumbling gas stations. Nevertheless its very appellation and unique courthouse creates a sense of curiosity for passing motorists along I-80.

Downtown is the Pershing County Courthouse, an early twentieth-century edifice with a circular courtroom resembling the Roman Pantheon. Designed by a Reno-based architect, the courthouse remains one-of-a-kind.

The nearest airport is Reno–Sparks Cannon International, about 110 miles (177 km) southwest on I-80.
Map ref: page 693 L6

A picture-postcard view of the clapboard Lamoille Presbyterian Church.

RENO

Stretching into the urban sprawl of neighboring Sparks, along I-80, the "Biggest Little City in the World" is jammed with bustling casinos and Old West charm. On I-80 on the Truckee River, Reno–Sparks has a total population of 308,700.

Along with gambling, Reno has an assortment of drive-in wedding chapels. But divorce is the city's other main enterprise. With only a six-week residency requirement, disaffected matrons would file in to Reno, waiting out their time on nearby dude ranches. Upon the decree of their divorce, according to lore, many would hurl their wedding rings into the Truckee River and kick up their heels at Reno's roulette tables.

Despite Reno's lack of inherent glamor, the recent arrival of Circus Circus is a telling sign that Reno is on the move. Wayward gaming lounges, which once straddled Virginia Street, have given way to a little spit and polish. Noisy slot machines now drown out the reverberations of the freight trains which rumble along the city's tired railway tracks.

The Central Pacific Railroad first placed Reno on the map in 1868 as a terminus for the mines of nearby Virginia City. Reno also flourished from the sideline gaming rooms during the years gambling was outlawed in Nevada. In 1931, gambling was legally upheld and two industrious entrepreneurs, Raymond "Pappy" Smith and William Harrah, lifted the image of gambling by engaging women as dealers.

Though Reno's cityscape remains undistinguished, there are several noted attractions worth viewing. The Nevada Historical Society has an excellent exhibit on regional history while the National Automobile Museum is a must for vintage car aficionados. A nice touch to Reno is the Fleischmann Planetarium, which boasts a fantastic telescope for star-gazing.

Reno is served by Reno–Sparks Cannon International Airport, along with buses and trains.
Map ref: page 693 J7

VIRGINIA CITY

Virginia City, a town of around 900 people, remains a veritable

A casino reminiscent of days gone by, flanking Virginia Street in Reno.

link to the Wild West. Located off Hwy 341, the community once sat on a rich silver strike.

In 1859, two miners were swindled out of their fortune by Henry Comstock. Many soon heard of the "Comstock Lode" and the region was soon crowded with prospectors. Twenty years later, the arrival of the Virginia and Truckee Railroad cemented Virginia City's prosperity. Today visitors can stroll along the boardwalk past rows of late-Victorian façades housing gift shops and saloons, including the curiously named Bucket of Blood Saloon.

The best place to commence a walking tour of the town is at the Mark Twain Bookstore located on C Street—the town's main thoroughfare. Open year-round, the bookstore offers a vast range of

regional books as well as the works of the author, who first worked as a reporter for the *Territorial Enterprise* as Samuel Clemens. The Mark Twain Museum, located at the Territorial Enterprise Building, hosts a collection of Victorian printing presses, desks, and rustic paraphernalia. The Way It Was Museum is solely devoted to the history of the Comstock strike, and the Virginia City Radio Museum displays a massive collection of vintage radios. One of the most interesting tours is at the Best and Becher Mine, with treks to the mine starting at the rear of the rowdy Ponderosa Saloon.

By the 1870s, Virginia City's red-light district reached its peak, with the tidal surge of prospectors swelling the population to 30,000 accommodated by no less than

110 saloons and brothels. Upholding the city's colorful heritage, the Julia Bulette Red Light Museum commemorates the most famous town madame. A display of antiquated contraceptives and medicinal cures are on display, part of the history of prostitution in Nevada's mining towns.

In 1875, a fire consumed most of the city. It was rebuilt in brick, and several historic homes from this period still survive. The Mackay Mansion was built by John Mackay, the richest man in Virginia City and proprietor of the Big Bonanza mine.

On B Street is the Gothic mansion known as "The Castle," a treasure-trove of European fixtures dating back to 1868. Chugging past the Chollar Mine is the Virginia and Truckee Railroad, which was resurrected for tourists after its operations closed in 1950. The 35-minute ride is available throughout the summer, taking passengers though a series of twisting tunnels and over gravity-defying trestles.

There are more eternal residents in the graveyards of Virginia City than remain alive. At the Silver Terrace Cemetery, visitors can see many interesting graves. Housing crumbling headstones and weathered iron enclosures, the cemetery stretches over nine graveyards, with each area sectioned in different religions.

Virginia City is serviced through the Reno–Sparks Cannon International Airport.
Map ref: page 693 J8

Mackay Mansion (at back), once the Virginia City home of John Mackay, proprietor of the Big Bonanza mine.

UTAH

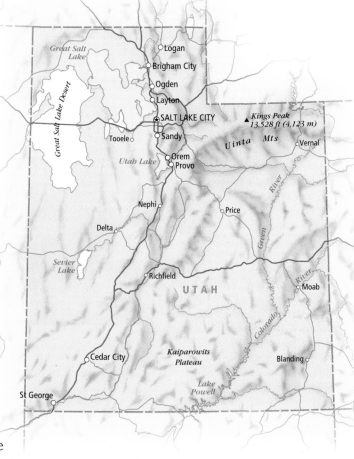

Utah is an incomparable terrain of dramatic visual contrasts, sculpted by water and wind over millions of years, and has the largest concentration of national parks in the country. Much of Utah experiences a high-altitude desert climate with very little rain.

Named for the Ute Native American tribe, Utah is split by the Wasatch Range which cuts a vertical swath through the middle. These lofty ranges are a haven to mountain lions, mule deer, moose, and elk. In the winter months, the snowy slopes are dotted with skiers.

The Colorado Plateau, stretching across the southeast corner, remains largely uninhabited. Its red-rock canyons and sagebrush flats are the pattern for most of Utah's wilderness corridor, a backyard of recreational delights for outdoor enthusiasts. Slicing directly through the plateau are the Colorado and Green Rivers, part of a landscape of eroded pinnacles, ancient arches, and narrow gorges.

Nestled in the northwestern desert basin is the state capital, Salt Lake City. It was here, in 1847, that Mormon leader Brigham Young led his persecuted band of religious pioneers to the region he named "Deseret"— a word from *The Book of Mormon* which means "honeybee".

Before the arrival of Spanish Franciscan friars in the seventeenth century, Utah was largely home to the Ute, Shoshone, and Paiute Native Americans. When the Mormons colonized the Great Salt Lake area, they turned the arid terrain into fertile farming land. In the 1870s an influx of new settlers arrived with the railroad, drawn by the gold and silver strikes in Utah's mountains. The discovery of copper, oil, silver, and uranium in the early twentieth century brought the state greater prosperity, and later, discord between environmentalists and federal agencies.

Mule deer (Odocoileus hemionus) foraging for winter feed in Bryce Canyon National Park in southern Utah.

State motto Industry
State flag Adopted 1913
Capital Salt Lake City
Population 2,233,169
Total area (land and water) 84,904 square miles (219,901 sq km)
Land area 82,168 square miles (212,815 sq km)
Utah is the 11th-largest state in size
Origin of name From the Ute Native American word meaning "people of the mountains"
Nickname The Beehive State
Abbreviations UT (postal), Ut.
State bird California gull
State flower Sego lily
State tree Blue spruce
Entered the Union January 4, 1896 as the 45th state

Places in
UTAH

BLANDING

Located on Hwy 191, 340 miles (547 km) south of Salt Lake City, in the sun-parched basin of the Abajo Mountains, Blanding serves primarily as a jump-off point to Hovenweep National Monument and Natural Bridges National Monument. It was on the fringe of town where the final conflict between the Native Americans and the US Army took place in 1923.

Though unspectacular as far as small towns go, Blanding does feature the impressive White Mesa Institute, which offers programs on the Southwest's indigenous people, wildlife, and archaeology. There are also outfitters who operate tours to the spectacular Anasazi, or Ancestral Puebloans (prehistoric ancestors of modern Pueblo people), ruins in the Four Corners region.

A self-guided trek along dusty Hovenweep Road takes in six ancient pueblos (villages), on what forms part of the Trail of the Ancients. Five of the sites are only accessible by hiking trails. The ruins at the Edge of the Cedars houses an enormous kiva (ceremonial building) and also features several square towers, which are not characteristic of their typical circular design. The outdoor treasury also displays a large collection of Anasazi pottery.

West of Blanding, off Hwy 95, is the Natural Bridges National Monument, a landscape of eroded sandstone bridges carved by the threshing waters of the Colorado River. A 10-mile (16-km) hiking trail traverses three bridges into an intractable landscape of ancient petroglyphs and rocky canyon country. Owachomo Bridge is the oldest, rising over 100 feet (30 m) and spanning 182 feet (56 m) across the sandstone escarpment. Rafting trips are available at Bluff, 25 miles (40 km) south of Blanding along the San Juan River.

Also near Blanding are the Ute Mountain and Navajo Indian Reservations. The Navajo Indian Reservation travels the course of Monument Valley into Arizona.

There are various types of lodgings available in Blanding, including guest houses and B&Bs, but make sure you book if you plan to travel during high season. Salt Lake City International Airport is the nearest major airport.
Map ref: page 617 N3

BONNEVILLE SALT FLATS

Located northwest in the Great Basin, the lunar landscape of Bonneville Salt Flats once formed part of the Great Salt Lake. Some 30,000 acres (12,150 ha) of leveled terrain off I-80 near the Nevada border, the flats are administered by the Bureau of Land Management and have been listed as an Area of Critical Environmental Concern. When visiting this area, stay on designated roads and do not drive when they are covered in water—not only do the roads become very slippery but the salt is extremely corrosive and can damage your car.

Bonneville Salt Flats has been used as a desert speedway for racing-car buffs since 1911. Here, drivers and their high-performance machines pursue records at speeds exceeding 500 miles (804 km) per hour over the bed of what was once an ancient lake. Every year, speed trials are held throughout the summer and fall months.

Temperatures reach extremes of high and low during summer and winter. The nearest place for lodging and other services is at Wending, which is just across the Nevada border. Salt Lake City International Airport is the nearest major airport.
Map ref: page 694 F4

Ruins at the Edge of the Cedars near Blanding, part of the Trail of the Ancients.

BRIGHAM CITY

Located north of Salt Lake City, in a basin of the craggy Wasatch Mountains, is Brigham City. Settlement of the area began in 1851 and eventually the town of Box Elder was established and later renamed in honor of Brigham Young. The Brigham City Mercantile and Manufacturing Association was created then, and the Baron Woolen Mills still barters using its homespun blankets.

This agricultural community has some of Utah's most resplendent Victorian buildings, including the Box Elder County Courthouse. The Box Elder Tabernacle, built over 25 years and completed in 1890, is a mixture of Victorian and Gothic set against a backdrop of snow-capped mountains. On West Forest Street is the recently restored Brigham City Railroad Depot, once a major terminus for the Union Pacific Railroad.

Brigham City is the gateway to an amazing bird sanctuary located 15 miles (24 km) west of the city. The Bear River Migratory Bird Refuge is a stopover for 200 species of bird each spring and fall, on nearly 73,000 acres (29,565 ha). Established in 1928 by Congress, the refuge features numerous interpretive boards which explain the birds' habitat.

At Thiokol Rocket Garden, located 5 miles (8 km) north of Golden Spike National Park, on Hwy 83, visitors can probe models of the test rockets which launch shuttles into space.

Throughout the summer a large stretch of Hwy 91, leading to the city, is lined with roadside fruit stalls, and the Peach Festival holds court the weekend after Labor Day.

The nearest major airport is Salt Lake City International. The area is serviced by buses and trains.
Map ref: page 693 J3

The Bonneville Salt Flats have been favored by racing-car buffs since 1911 as a site for setting speed records.

BRYCE CANYON NATIONAL PARK

Nothing along Route 12 prepares you for Bryce Canyon National Park's brilliant geological playing field. The sight of groves of ponderosa pines suddenly gives way to reveal an entanglement of dusty rose limestone pillars, curiously called "hoodoos," forming 14 immense amphitheaters, zigzagging over 20 miles (32 km) of eroded landscape. Dropping over 1,000 feet (305 m) into the Paunsaugunt Plateau, the hoodoos cast off a kaleidoscope of colors that makes Bryce Canyon the most colorful national park in America. Declared a national monument in 1923, Bryce Canyon was named for a Mormon farmer, Ebenezer Bryce, who grazed his cattle around the multihued rocks.

According to Paiute legend, the hoodoos were turned to stone by a disgruntled coyote. Geologically, the carving of Bryce Canyon began a little over 500,000 years ago, icy winters and summer rainstorms chiseling away around 16 inches (40 cm) of sandstone every 100 years. From Inspiration, Sunrise, Natural Bridge, and Rainbow Points, visitors can see the rock transform from desert cherry through to burnt orange and into shades of purple.

Bryce Canyon's 18-mile (29-km) road traces the precipice before coming to a dead-end at Rainbow Point. Other trails into the canyon traverse a landscape of old twisted trees and shifting rock. The visitor center is at the park's northern entrance, 1 mile (2 km) south of Fairyland Canyon.

Bryce Canyon offers sanctuary to over 150 bird species, including the white-crested eagle. In winter, the hoodoos are at their most beautiful when the tips are covered in a dusting of snow. Ancient bristlecone pines, dating back to the time of the birth of Christ, are found throughout the park.

The Bryce Canyon Visitor Center offers several slide and interpretive exhibits on the geological history of the park. There is a modest entrance fee for vehicles and a small fee for hikers and cyclists.

Cedar City is the nearest major airport, about 50 miles (80 km) west of the park.

Map ref: page 617 H4

A section of petroglyphs at Newspaper Rock, Canyonlands National Park.

CANYONLANDS NATIONAL PARK

So similar is it in appearance to Arizona's Grand Canyon that movie director Ridley Scott used Canyonlands National Park to film the closing scene in *Thelma and Louise* at Monument Basin. Canyonlands is a formidable place to navigate by road. It takes time to explore the the 527 square miles (1,365 sq km) of pristine wilderness, with its intricate pathways of ravines, arches, plateaus, and grottos.

At the confluence of the Green and Colorado Rivers, Canyonlands is the state's largest national park. The rivers divide its 337,258 acres (136,589 ha) into three regions, with Island in the Sky, off Hwy 191, the most popular and accessible. As it takes several days to cover all of the major sites, this is the best place to view the park if time is restricted. The visitor center has hiking trail information, including the popular trek along Mesa Arch Trail.

Entering the park off US-313 from Moab, a panorama of mesas, spires, and ravines descending over 2,000 feet (610 m) to the river's edge is unveiled. In the distance loom the snowcapped peaks of the La Sal Mountains.

Where the serpentine rivers converge, they erupt into whitewater and begin a fast-paced trip through Cataract Canyon before reaching Lake Powell. Experienced rafters ride the rapids on the 14-mile (23-km) stretch. The 5-mile (8-km) trail back to the nearest road leads through sagebrush and cottonwoods, sprinkled across a horizon of serrated cliffs and mesas.

Bryce Canyon turned into a winter wonderland by a fall of snow. The multicolored rocks make Bryce Canyon the most colorful national park in the United States.

The Green River carves its way through the Colorado Plateau in Canyonlands, Utah's largest national park.

Another panoramic view of the Colorado River, snaking its way through red-rock chasms, is at Dead Horse Point State Park, the spot where Thelma and Louise's 1966 Thunderbird became airborne. Cowboys used the table mountain to corral herds of mustang—its name derives from a group of horses left at the point which subsequently perished.

Off US-211 is a rugged trail, suited to 4WD vehicles, leading to Needles. Several hiking trails weave around the hoodoos and jagged canyons. One of the best vantage points is at Confluence Outlook, which takes in a bird's-eye view of Colorado and Green River tributaries. It is worth roaming around on foot to explore the colonnades of red sandstone pillars and canyons near the Colorado River, such as Lizard Rock and the Maze. At Newspaper Rock, petroglyphs weave an ancient story across the sandstone, antelope and bear featuring alongside soldiers with helmets—possibly the Spanish who blazed through the region nearly 600 years ago. The largest mass of ancient rock art is located near Horseshoe Canyon.

Inflexible entrance rules are in place to preserve the region's geological fragility. Only a limited number of visitors are permitted to camp. Backpacking permits must be purchased through the National Park Service Reservations at Moab. A small entrance fee is applicable between March to October and is valid for seven days at any of the entrances to Canyonlands.
Map ref: page 617 M2

CAPITOL REEF NATIONAL PARK

Off US-24, near Hanksville, is the radiant Capitol Reef, established as a national park 30 years ago. Native Americans named this region the "land of the sleeping rainbow" because of its brilliant display of color.

The park's name comes from Capitol Dome, a white sandstone bulge shaped like Washington DC's Capitol Building. Carved by 100 million years of geological activity, the unique landscape is marked by massive sandstone escarpments, arches, and deep red chasms that buckle and turn over a 100-mile (160-km) stretch. Many parts are only accessible by foot.

The highway leads to the lush Fremont River Valley, where the ancient Fremont tribespeople drew a series of animal petroglyphs on the sandstone cliffs.

At the heart of this oasis is the tiny town of Fruita where Mormon settlers irrigated the land and planted orchards. The visitor center at Fruita is the best place to begin the 25-mile (40-km) round trip that takes in Cassidy Arch and Capitol Gorge Trail. Near the trail is Pioneer Register, a boulder that features emigrant inscriptions.

Off US-24, the natural bridge of Hickman is Capitol Reef's most resplendent arch, 133 feet (41 m) across and towering to 125 feet (38 m). At the northern rim of Capitol Reef is Cathedral Valley, navigable only by hikers, horseback riders, and the best of 4WD vehicles. The sandstone monoliths appear like desert cathedrals.

Sandstone turrets rise again on the trail to Chimney Rock, a 400-foot (122-m) slab visible to the west from the visitor center. Another trail crosses Chimney Rock to a vantage point overlooking the snowcapped peaks of the Henry Mountains where bison roam the basins with snow egrets and deer.

Lodgings and restaurants are found at Torrey. The National Park has a small entrance fee and 4WD vehicles are highly recommended.
Map ref: page 617 K2

CEDAR BREAKS NATIONAL MONUMENT

One of Utah's loveliest outdoor amphitheaters, Cedar Breaks National Monument extends nearly 4 miles (6 km), a dazzling formation of turrets, deep chasms, and arches. Here, light dances on the sandstone escarpments, changing its colors from deep scarlet to burnt oranges and browns.

There are wildflowers, which add a profusion of color to the rocky edges in the spring and summer months. By winter, Cedar Breaks is transformed into a wilderness trail for cross-country skiers. Along the 2-mile (3-km) Alpine Pond Nature Trail, hikers will see ancient bristlecone pines along with thickets of purple lupine in bloom. At Alpine Pond, wildlife can be spotted.
Map ref: page 616 G3

CEDAR CITY

Located in Southwestern Utah, off I-15, this small university town of 11,000 people was a mining community during the 1850s boom. Its iron foundry was the economy's mainstay until the growth of tourism. A short driving distance to Bryce Canyon and Zion National Parks, Cedar City is a perfect starting point for desert travelers.

Cedar City's cultural events have also become a regional drawcard. It hosts the annual Shakespearean Festival and the Utah Summer Games. The Southern Utah University packs in the crowds on campus at Adams Memorial Theater, an excellent replica of a traditional Elizabethan playhouse.

Visitors can also view Iron Mission State Park, the site of the town's first iron foundry on Main Street. A series of pioneer artifacts is on display.

Cedar City Regional Airport services the area.
Map ref: page 616 G3

In afternoon light, Capitol Reef National Park is "the land of the sleeping rainbow."

A partially excavated dinosaur skeleton in Dinosaur National Monument Park.

DINOSAUR NATIONAL MONUMENT PARK

Designated as a national monument in 1909, Dinosaur National Monument is Utah's Jurassic Park. Located just east of the town of Vernal, on Hwy 149, and stretching 325 miles (523 km) across the Colorado border, this archeological antiquity features over 1,500 fossilized dinosaur bones in the world's largest quarry.

About 145 million years ago, gigantic apatosauruses roamed with a host of lesser creatures in a subtropical setting. A treasure-trove for paleontologists, Dinosaur National Monument Park also offers three quarries for visitors to explore.

Dinosaur National Monument is open year-round and there is a modest entrance fee.
Map ref: page 696 A5

GOLDEN SPIKE NATIONAL HISTORICAL SITE

For anyone interested in the history of America's first transcontinental railroad, Golden Spike National Historic Site is the place to delve into the West's greatest engineering achievement.

Located 32 miles (51 km) west of Brigham City, in the desert region of Promontory, the Golden Spike marks the place where the Union Pacific and the Central Pacific Railroads linked on May 10, 1869. Until the beginning of the twentieth century, the railroad

made Promontory important. By 1904, however, another section of easy-grade track had been completed at Ogden, taking that city closer to the commercial center of Salt Lake City. Many of the small railroad communities soon tapered off and, by 1940, the land along the tracks returned to parched desert and Promontory's glory days passed into history.

Every May 10, the Golden Spike Anniversary commemorates the historic event, including two steam-engine replicas in the ceremony. In August, during the Railroaders Festival, the smell of burning cinders fills the air as two reproduction steam engines race along the tracks to meet head-to-head at the Golden Spike.
Map ref: page 695 H2

LOGAN

Logan is in the north of the state, near the Idaho border, in the picturesque Cache Valley. First settled by Mormon pioneers around 1856, Logan's population of 38,132 is largely made up of a farming and university community.

Home to Utah State University, Logan provides a range of cultural activities in addition to showcasing modern art and photography at the Nora Eccles Harrison Museum of Art. During the summer, the Old Lyric Theater is worth visiting for a great musical performance. Logan's quiet streets are nice for a late afternoon stroll.

It is also worth embarking on a self-guided tour. The town is well-known for its splendid nineteenth-century architecture and the Logan Mormon Temple, which is a feature of the town's cityscape.

The Daughters of Utah Pioneers Museum, located at the Chamber of Commerce along historic Main Street, displays a collection of Mormon pioneer artifacts and vintage fiddles.

Many of Logan's domestic visitors come to visit the Cache Valley Cheese Plant, at the nearby hamlet of Amalga, and to traverse the 41-mile (66-km) scenic drive to Logan Canyon. The road traces the Wasatch-Chache National Forest and a series of steep cliffs before reaching Bear River Mountains where numerous hiking trails bring into view a blaze of aspen, maple trees, and ravines.

During the winter, the Beaver Ski Resort caters to the local population, who prefer to race downhill on its quieter powder slopes without the encumbrance of tourists. During summer, the area is transformed into pocket campgrounds and hiking trails.

Spring Hollow is the perfect base to begin some grueling hiking treks around Logan Canyon. At the summit of the canyon, a splendid vista brings into view Bear Lake and the impenetrable treetops of Caribou National Forest in neighboring Idaho.

Nestled at the base of Wellsville Mountain, to the west, are some challenging hiking trails that take in its summit of nearly 8,500 feet (2,592 m). Elk, deer, and hawks often search for food on the upper slopes. In winter, visitors can take a horse-drawn sleigh ride out to the elk herds, which gather at the Hardware Ranch, south on Hwy 165.

At the end of summer, Logan's population swells to over 90,000 during the eight-day Festival of the American West. At the American West Heritage Center every activity from goldpanning to a Wild West show is staged in a model frontier town. Also part of the center is the Jensen Historical Farm and the Man and His Bread Museum. People dressed as fur-trappers, woolly mountain men, and farmers act as interpretive guides and demonstrate what it was like to farm the land nearly 100 years ago.
Map ref: page 695 K2

MOAB

Fifty years ago, Moab was just a tiny ranching town on the edge of the Colorado River. First settled by Mormon farmers in 1852, the town is a verdant oasis of fruit trees encircled by sandstone cliffs, 238 miles (383 km) south of Salt Lake City on Hwy 191.

Moab's name was borrowed from the biblical kingdom at the edge of Zion. During the 1950s, the town became the very road to paradise with the discovery of uranium. But its fortunes did not last long when a few short years later, the boom went bust. Oil and potash mining soon replaced uranium as the town's mainstay natural resources, but they remain secondary to tourism, the largest revenue-spinner.

By virtue of its superb position, Moab is the gateway to the brilliant wilderness domain of Canyonlands National Park. Every summer, Moab's population of nearly 6,000 grows to a huge number as tourists, campers, and cyclists converge on the town to soak up the red-rock scenery and hot dry climate.

Hollywood producers similarly discovered Moab's natural charms and years ago transformed the independent community into the quintessential Western center. Its backyard of red-rock country has been used in numerous television commercials and movies.

Worth a visit is the Monument Valley Film Commission and Museum. Here visitors can glimpse the mystical West through the lens. Film location maps are provided for the curious hoping for a John Wayne look-alike to pop out from among the rocks, along with a collection of movie paraphernalia and photographs. There is also a tour that takes you to the region where epic features such as *Geronimo*, *Indiana Jones and the Last Crusade*, *Rio Grande*, and *Thelma and Louise* were shot on location.

Moab is the biking capital of the world, offering some of the region's most challenging treks and awesome scenery. Slickrock Bicycle Trail, Hurrah Pass Trail, and the Gemini Bridges Trail are the most popular tracks. The recently completed Kokopelli's Mountain Biking Trail, located between Moab and Grand Junction, attracts only the fittest cyclists.

There are countless back roads winding through barren canyons and across the rocky river bed, but you must obtain a permit before entering. Most of the land is controlled by either the Bureau of Land Management or the National Park Service.

For very fit hikers, Devil's Garden Trail traverses Arches National Park. Canyonlands National Park provides gentler hiking trails that take in the backcountry of the Islands in the Sky region. The most popular trail for 4WD vehicles is a 100-mile (160-km) track that leads past elegant arches and pocket canyons along the White Rim Trail. Heading south toward Needles is the formidable Elephant Hill Trail offering optional 4WD-vehicle treks or hiking.

Whitewater and flatwater rafting has long been Moab's other principal recreational pursuit. There are numerous outfitters offering guides and floats for rafting along the Colorado River into Cataract and Westwater Canyons. Also along the river is an 875-acre (354-ha) wetland reserve, which harbors a wealth of wildlife. Moab's reputation for providing great outdoor adventure extends to several rock-climbing sites at Fisher Towers and Castle Valley.

Moab is worthy of an evening stroll, even just to soak up its lively bars and Western hospitality under a canopy of brilliant stars. And if the summer sun is too hot for viewing Canyonlands during the day, visitors can embark on a nocturnal spotlight tour.

The town never lacks entertainment and outdoor festivities. Two popular attractions are the October Fat Tire Festival for cyclists, and the Labor Day Jeep Jamboree. During September, the Moab Music Festival utilizes the natural acoustics of its various outdoor venues.

The Moab Information Center, on Main Street, is the best place to become acquainted with the local touring companies and National Park services. General information, scenic maps, and recommended trails can all be obtained.

Salt Lake City International is the closest major airport. There are daily shuttle buses to Moab. Motels line Moab's Main Street, and reservations are recommended during the peak summer season.
Map ref: page 617 N1

MONTICELLO

The tiny town of Monticello nestles in the foothills of the Abajo Mountains on Hwy 191, 18 miles (29 km) from the Colorado border. With only 2,000 residents and a handful of budget motels, the town is primarily utilized as a pit stop for passing trade.

The main point of interest for travelers is the visitor center, which provides detailed information on

Mountain-bike riders on a challenging trek at Moab's Slickrock Bicycle Trail.

the Four Corners region and the scenic drives around the Abajo Mountains region.

North of town is Church Rock, a sunken boulder which was once used as a site for open-air prayers by local homesteaders.
Map ref: page 617 M3

OGDEN

Thirty-four miles (55 km) north of Salt Lake City is the university town of Ogden. Utah's third-largest city of 70,000 people, the city's heritage is unique, as it is one of a handful of settlements established prior to Mormon colonization.

Named for a fur-trapper who roamed the area in the 1820s, Ogden was founded as Fort Buenaventura in 1846 by Miles Goodyear. A year later, Brigham Young purchased the trading post to resettle his groups of disciples.

The town's fortunes did not take shape until the arrival of the transcontinental railroad in 1869, when Ogden became a major terminus in the West, within a decade being transformed into a major livestock, milling, and agricultural center.

In the late 1970s, the Hill Air Force Base further contributed to the city's economy. Its aerospace museum displays an impressive collection of aviation relics including an assortment of missiles and a massive B-52 bomber.

The best place to start a city tour is at the Ogden Union Station, which was rebuilt in 1924 after the original station was destroyed by fire. The railway depot's various galleries feature the Utah State Railroad Museum and a collection of vintage cabooses, automobiles, carriages, and engines.

As well as the Natural History Museum, the Myra Powell Gallery features some prized art collections throughout the year. But the most impressive is the John B. Browning Firearms Museum, which houses a staggering collection of Colts, Remingtons, and Winchester guns invented and manufactured by the Browning dynasty.

Ogden's 25th Street Historic District features a selection of interesting buildings, including the ornate London Ice Cream Parlor

A side road off Route 128, between the towns of Moab and Asco, arrows towards a group of red-rock mesas.

Salt Lake City is both the center of the Mormon faith and a thriving metropolis.

Building, which was once a brothel. On Grant Avenue is the Gothic-style Church of the Good Shepherd, and the Daughters of Utah Pioneers Museum. At the back of the museum is the Miles Goodyear Cabin, which was built in 1846 by the banks of the Weber River.

Students at the Weber State University make up some 13,000 of Ogden's residents. Like most college towns, Ogden emphasizes the arts. The city boasts both the Ogden Symphony and Ballet Association and a repertory theater at the Terrace Plaza Playhouse. Peery's Egyptian Theater, on Washington Street, is the most popular entertainment center. Built in 1924, and recently restored, the theater hosts an array of films, ballet performances, and the Sundance Film Festival.

Ogden's other recreational pursuits reveal a strong emphasis on the outdoors. Hiking, rock climbing, fishing, and camping are just some of the activities locals indulge in. Skiing is also popular, at the nearby resorts of the Wasatch Mountains, among them Snowbasin, home to the 2002 Winter Olympic athletes. The Ogden River Parkway is a favorite for cycling.

Salt Lake City International Airport services the Ogden region.
Map ref: page 695 J3

Statue of Chief Massachusetts, Capitol Building.

PRICE

The town of Price (population 10,000) sits halfway between Salt Lake City and Moab on Hwy 191 and caters to visitors to the Canyonlands region.

After refueling the car, take a peek at the College of Eastern Utah Prehistoric Museum, which houses a collection of bones from woolly mammoths and dinosaurs. There are also artifacts of the Fremont tribe on exhibit while, at nearby Nine Mile Canyon, many Fremont petroglyphs are visible on the red sandstone cliffs, which date back some 1,700 years.
Map ref: page 695 M7

PROVO

Provo is essentially a Mormon city. The state's second-largest city, with a population of 84,000, is nestled at the foothills of the Wasatch Front along I-15.

Provo was named after a fur-trapper and settled by Mormons in 1849. The city went on to become a strong agricultural community and college town by 1875, upon the construction of the Brigham Young University. Today, the university stands as a lasting legacy to the Mormon leader's

belief in clean and spiritual living, and is now the largest church-affiliated university in the United States. Each student must maintain an honor-code set by the Church of Jesus Christ of Latter-day Saints.

The university is never lacking in cultural events. There are four museums and numerous theatrical productions. Even the occasional Osmond Family performance has been given to packed houses.

Overlooking Provo from the Wasatch Ranges is actor Robert Redford's Sundance Resort. Since the inception of the Sundance Film Festival, the village has become a filmmaker's Mecca every January. Redford's Sundance Institute also conducts workshops and hosts outdoor theatrical productions throughout the summer.

Close to the resort, in the American Folk Canyon, is Timangogos Cave National Monument, with limestone caverns and hiking trails the main attractions. In contrast, Bridal Veil Falls, in Provo Canyon, has a brilliant spray of water cascading over 600 feet (183 m) from two cataracts.
Map ref: page 695 K6

SALT LAKE CITY

Since its inception in 1847, Salt Lake City has been both a hub of the West and the pivotal center of Utah, serving as the state capital and religious bedrock to the Church of Jesus Christ of Latter-day Saints. Framed by the snow-capped peaks of the Wasatch Mountains, and the Great Salt Lake, at an elevation of 4,330 feet (1,321 m), Salt Lake City has become one of the West's fastest growing metropolises, with its economy based around software and medical technology. As host to the Winter Olympics in 2002, Salt Lake City's population of 172,000 will multiply by thousands.

Its character recently has undergone a metamorphosis, with contemporary restaurants, shopping malls and a street beautification program luring businesses

and tourists back into the city. Despite the many changes, its cityscape remains faithful to church founder Joseph Smith's architectural plans. Characteristic of most Mormon cities, Salt Lake City's streets were designed as a simple grid leading from the Latter-day Saints Temple in four quadrants.

At the heart is Temple Square, with serene pathways lined by emerald lawns and majestic elms. It is home to the famous Tabernacle and its massive 10,857-pipe organ. During the Christmas season, a brilliant array of Christmas lights illuminates the Mormon Temple's six spires. The main attraction is the ethereal-sounding Tabernacle Choir, which daily attracts over 6,000 visitors.

At the north end of Temple Street is the Capitol Hill District where the beautiful State Capitol perches majestically over the city. On South Temple is the Beehive House, home and office to Brigham Young when he was the governor of the territory. The Family History Library on North West Temple is perhaps the city's most interesting building to visit. The library is the world's largest genealogical repository, where visitors can trace their family ancestors. Adjacent to the library is the Museum of Church History and Art, a short walk from the excellent Pioneer Memorial Museum on North Main.

Mormon Temple, Temple Square in Salt Lake City.

Ice fishing on one of the many frozen lakes along Route 40 near Vernal.

Salt Lake City is also home to the University of Utah, the oldest university west of the Missouri River and caretaker of the Utah Museum of Natural History.

Though the main attractions center around the Latter-day Saints Church, the city also offers some of America's premier ski runs, all within an hour's drive from downtown. The largest resorts of Alta, Snowbird, Brighton, and Solitude are all close by in Big Cottonwood Canyon.

Mountain-bike riding along the Lake Blanche Trail is equally as popular in the summer. This scenic corridor coils through to Little Cottonwood Canyon, revealing some of Utah's most breathtaking panoramas.

Five miles (8 km) from downtown is the Salt Lake City International Airport.
Map ref: page 695 K4

ST GEORGE

The orderly Mormon community of St George has a population of 35,000 and, because of its proximity to the gaming rooms of neighboring Nevada, has become one of the state's fastest growing cities.

Despite its haste to expand, the city has retained its handsome pioneer architecture and broad streets. Located off I-15, St George serves as a base for Zion National Park, catering also to vacationers wanting a taste of the year-round dry desert climate. Named for the Mormon missionary George Smith, who conscripted families to settle the region, St George was also named 'Dixie' because of its southern location and one-time cotton and tobacco enterprises. St George also served as the winter base of Brigham Young.

Basking in ample sunshine and offering high temperatures most of the year, a number of golf courses and spas have sprung up to cater to the burgeoning leisure market. Apart from this, St George has very little to offer visitors as a mainstay tourist town beyond a few notable attractions.

The St George Temple, which was constructed in 1871, is Utah's oldest Mormon temple in use. Costing over US$1 million to build, and reaching a height of 175 feet (53 m), the temple and adjoining Tabernacle remain the central focus of the city.
Map ref: page 616 F5

VERNAL

Known to many as the dinosaur capital of the world, Vernal sits a few short miles from Dinosaur National Monument at the junction of US-40/191. The town is also within an hour's drive of Flaming Gorge National Park, 49 miles (72 km) to the north.

Originally settled as a ranching community in the 1870s, the town's backyard of fossilized bones now dominates its economy.

The main attraction is the very polished Utah Field House of Natural History, complete with an outdoor Dinosaur Garden. Over a dozen dinosaur sculptures in a lush setting re-create the lost world of the Mesozoic period.
Map ref: page 695 P5

ZION NATIONAL PARK

Located in Southwestern Utah, Zion National Park is the state's oldest wilderness sanctuary. Named for the Mormon homeland of Zion in 1863, it is perhaps Utah's most striking region.

It is a landscape marked by dramatic shadows that swirl over gigantic rock formations and deep crevices carved by the Virgin River. Zion National Park is also characterized by colorful vegetation, which provides pocket canopies over sandstone walls and traces the Virgin River's embankment. The 6-mile (10-km) drive through the park also embraces distant views of the valley's desert floor and the formations of the Great White Throne, the Court of the Patriarchs, and Angel's Landing. From Zion Lodge, a trailhead leads through Hidden Canyon where torrents of water tumble off the rock face after a sudden cloudburst.

There are two main entrances to Zion National Park, with the Zion Canyon Visitor Center based at its southern gate near Springdale. The northern entrance takes in Kolob Canyons, incorporated as part of Zion National Park in 1956.

Open year-round, Zion National Park is very popular with tourists, especially during high summer. The best trail for camping and backpacking is at the Narrows, where compressed walls close in around you. The park has limited lodging facilities and reservations are required for Zion Lodge. Springdale offers budget lodgings.
Map ref: page 616 G4

Piñon pine dwarfed by the expanse of Checkerboard Mesa at Zion National Park, Utah's oldest wilderness sanctuary.

STATE FEATURE

Arches National Park

Created over 65 million years ago by freezing temperatures and wind, Arches National Park boasts the world's greatest expanse of natural sandstone arches. Though the park is relatively small by comparison to other Southwestern parks—73,379 acres (29,718 ha)—what it lacks in size, Arches makes up in sheer splendor. Located in the heart of the Colorado Plateau, at elevations of 4,000–5,400 feet (1,220–1,647 m), the park offers visitors an abundance of delicate rock formations.

The horizontal beds of sedimentary rocks date back to 175 million years ago. Once part of a great body of ocean that filled the Paradox Basin, the water began to evaporate during the Pennsylvanian period, leaving the salt and gypsum to crystallize in the searing heat. Over 1,500 arches were shaped by shifting salt deposits, cracking and thrusting the sandstone into vertical slabs which eroded into a series of domes and monoliths.

Erosion continues to reshape and strip away multiple layers of rock, while providing habitat for high desert vegetation and wildlife. Arches National Park averages just under 9 inches (22 cm) of rain per year, yet its flora flourishes in these conditions.

Tracing the rolling pattern of rocks is a variety of plant growth. Along the higher plateau, piñon pine and ghostly junipers form sparse groves, while prickly pear, blackbrush, and scrub take hold between rocky ridges and crevices. Columbine, monkey flower, and native cottonwood grow along the river's edge. In the park's Salt Valley, thickets of Indian rice grass, galleta, and snakeweed dominate.

Kangaroo rats, jack rabbits, and squirrels dart across the rocks, foraging for food. At dusk, an occasional coyote can be spotted looking for prey. But it is the golden eagle, gracefully circling a horizon of pale blue sky, which gives the visitor a sense of Arches National Park's unsullied remoteness.

Though the Mormons settled at nearby Moab in 1852, Arches was left largely unexplored. Eight hundred years earlier, the Fremont and Anasazi tribes farmed the land, their legacy a series of petroglyphs south of the park. By the time of the Mormons' arrival, Ute Indians inhabited the region.

The Denver and Rio Grand Railroad contributed to the new wave of communities being built around the mines of southwestern Utah. Renewed interest in Moab came after the relocation of the Ute tribe to a government reservation. In 1888, Civil War veteran John Wesley Wolfe built the first cabin in the sun-ravaged Salt Valley.

Prospector Alexander Ringhoffer first brought the Arches region to national attention, in 1923, with the realization that there was a fortune to be made from tourists. Arches became a national monument in 1929 and a national park in 1971. The individual arches were named in the 1930s by journalist Frank Beckwith, who led a year-long expedition through the newly created monument.

Until fifty years ago, the area remained largely unfamiliar to tourists—but then Moab's mining fortunes placed it on the map. Former park ranger and writer, Edward Abbey, wrote evocatively of the Arches National Park's isolation, and the importance of preserving it, in the fascinating and definitive book on the Southwest, *Desert Solitaire*.

Abbey's philosophy of safeguarding the park from "motorized tourists" has largely been carried on by the National Park Services today. The visitor center provides strict guidelines for Arches' many foot trails, and driving treks, and for camping.

The park entrance, just 5 miles (8 km) from Moab on Hwy 191, introduces the visitor to a prehistoric world. The dramatic panorama is broken only by a ribbon of asphalt—a road that carries over 500,000 tourists each year.

There are seven major trails through Arches National Park that provide superb vantage points, taking in the popular sites of Courthouse Towers, Balance Rock near the Windows, Delicate Arch, and Devil's Garden. Visitors can begin a 20-mile (32 km) drive through the park or use the visitor center as the starting point for the first of several hiking trails.

The main road spirals around steep rock along the Moab Fault for 18 miles (29 km), before finishing its course at Devil's Garden at the northeastern tip of the park. Forsake the excellent road, if you can, to follow in the footsteps of Edward Abbey, and explore the park by foot.

Park Avenue Trail follows an exposed escarpment with a skyline of fiery red and brown fins. Wedged in between jagged rocks are a sprinkling of junipers and desert shrubs. Just below the trail, Navajo Sandstone forms a secondary bed on the canyon floor, creating a natural esplanade. At the fringe of the trailhead is Courthouse Towers, where a lofty buttress known as the Organ thrusts vertically from a red sandstone bed.

Coyote (Canis latrans) in full winter coat considers the prospect before him.

OPPOSITE: *Delicate Arch is a popular frame for photographs of the distant La Sal Mountain.*

Park Avenue Trail passes below a colorful escarpment dotted with junipers.

Seven miles (11 km) north, in the heart of the park, lies the Window District and a sideline trail leading to another cluster of arches. Acting as road marker to the trail is the area's most precarious rock formation, Balanced Rock, a 50-foot (15-m) boulder that sits gingerly atop a narrow slab of stone. Double Arch Trail twists and winds through a series of narrow limestone pillars, or "hoodoos," and buttes to reach Double Arch, offering a superb vista of petrified dunes and the La Sal Mountains, which soar up to 12,000 feet (3,660 m) in the distance. (Double Arch was used as a location backdrop in *Indiana Jones and the Last Crusade*.) Although the arch is located at the highest point within the park, its trail is not especially ambitious.

Near Cove Arch, the fault lines of the Entrada and Navajo Sandstone have created a bedrock of fins, known as the Garden of Eden. Over time, this area will give way to further erosion, sculpting the fins into a framework of arches.

Back on the main road, visitors can take in Panorama Point before descending into the region known as Salt Valley. Sitting at the fork of the Delicate Arch Trail is the Wolfe Ranch, constructed by pioneer John Wesley Wolfe.

At the end of the trail is Delicate Arch, one of Arches National Park's most photographed sites. Spanning 45 feet (14 m) and standing 65 feet (20 m) high on a corner ledge, this dainty rock formation frames the canyon in an amphitheater of brilliant hues and sound. Looking beyond to the La Sal Mountains, a distant raven squawk can echo for miles.

From the Salt Valley Overlook, the road leads on to Fiery Furnace Viewpoint, a trail that takes in intricate passageways through narrow escarpments so tight that bodies brush past the walls.

Heading north, a series of trails connects visitors to the Devil's Garden region and over 60 of the park's natural arches. A 1½-mile (2.5-km) stroll takes you to the Sand Dune, Broken, and Tapestry Arches before the loop road winds around a collection that includes Double O, Navajo, and Landscape Arches. Perched near the top of a scrubby bluff, Landscape Arch, spanning 90 feet (27 m) and 291 feet (89 m) high, is the park's widest arch.

To the northwest, along a 9-mile (15-km) dirt road, is Klondike Bluffs and the least-used Tower Arch Trail. This section of the park attracts the hardier hiker and the avid 4WD-vehicle adventurer, with its series of dunes and abrupt inclines.

Arches National Park's only campground is located in Devil's Garden. Open year-round, there are only 53 sites available, including trailers. Backpackers can camp for free with a permit, but campsites must be a minimum of 1½ miles (2.5 km) from the trails and roads. Permits are available at the Arches Visitor Center year-round and cover a seven-day period. Entry fees are small for hikers and slightly higher for vehicles. Escorted ranger tours are available at Fiery Furnace for a small fee. Visitors should come prepared for the excessive heat in high summer.

WYOMING

A place of open ranges and honorary cowboys, Wyoming is as close as you can get to experiencing the Wild West. The least populated state, with only 493,782 citizens, Wyoming holds the West's richest history and nature's most resplendent scenery. Geysers percolate in the scalded grounds of Yellowstone, the nation's first national park. Devils Tower, the first national monument in the United States, fuses with the forests of the Black Hills, and the jagged peaks of the Grand Teton Mountains pierce the sky. East of the mountains, groves of aspen and cottonwood give way to grasslands that roll across miles of pioneer tracks—the Oregon, California, and Mormon Trails from the east and the Overland Trail from the south—leading to the former cow town of Cheyenne, the state's capital.

Wyoming has witnessed some of the bloodiest conflicts between the settlers and the Plains Native Americans and was refuge to some of the West's most colorful characters—Butch Cassidy and the Sundance Kid, Tom Horn, Wild Bill Hickok, Buffalo Bill Cody, and Calamity Jane. Interestingly, Wyoming is also known as "The Equality State." It was the first state to grant women the right to vote.

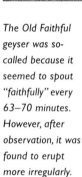

The Old Faithful geyser was so-called because it seemed to spout "faithfully" every 63–70 minutes. However, after observation, it was found to erupt more irregularly.

The state is a natural habitat for a number of animals, including grizzly bears, black bears, wolves, moose, and elk, as well as bald-crested eagles. Bighorn sheep graze on rocky ledges of the Bighorn Mountains, and coyotes howl in thickets of sagebrush on the Thunder Basin grasslands.

Wyoming's economy is centered on its resources—oil, coal, natural gas, and tourism—Yellowstone and Grand Teton National Parks are big tourist drawcards. It is perfect for activities such as skiing, whitewater rafting, dude ranching, and cattle drives—and it has some of the finest rivers for fly fishing. In Wyoming the sky is bigger and the landscape never ends—it is the perfect place to roam the Old West.

State motto Equal Rights
State flag Adopted 1917
Capital Cheyenne
Population 493,782
Total area (land and water)
97,818 square miles (253,349 sq km)
Land area 97,105 square miles
(251,502 sq km)
Wyoming is the ninth-largest state in size
Origin of name From a Native American word meaning "mountains and valleys alternating"
Nickname The Equality State
Abbreviations WY (postal), Wyo.
State bird Meadowlark
State flower Indian paintbrush
State tree Cottonwood
Entered the Union July 10, 1890 as the 44th state

Places in
WYOMING

The countryside outside Aladdin. Agriculture is the economic mainstay of the area.

ALADDIN

There are more cows than people along the frontage road of Hwy 14 where the town of Aladdin lies. Once a coal-mining community, historic Aladdin has only 10 residents. On the front porch of the general store rests the "liar's bench" where storytellers hatch colorful tales of the West. Stop to look through the store's second-story museum and its antiquated post office to see evidence of a by-gone era. Two miles (3 km) east are some wagon ruts from General George Armstrong Custer's Black Hills exploration of 1874.
Map ref: page 691 M3

BIGHORN MOUNTAINS

Along Hwy 14, a serpentine road follows 1 million acres (405,000 ha) of coniferous forests, leading to the summit of the Bighorn Mountains. In addition to snowmobiling, skiing at Antelope Butte Ski Area is becoming increasingly popular while on Hwy 16, High Park Ski Area and Meadowlark Lake, largely cater to the domestic market.

Craggy peaks rise above both highways, which frame the national forest. There are over 100 miles (161 km) of hiking and horseback trails in the Cloud Peak Wilderness Area where the lofty mountain, Cloud Peak, stands aloof in the distance at 13,175 feet (4,018 m). It is not uncommon to spot elk, deer, moose, and black bears foraging close to the road. However, the weather is changeable and the road often closes during a snowstorm.

Mule deer (Odocoileus hemionus), Bighorn Mountains.

Hwy 14 at Burgess Junction divides into a fork with Hwy 14A traversing a windswept mountain leading to the Medicine Wheel, 25 miles (40 km) east of Lovell. Shaped from limestone rocks with 28 spokes branching from its center, the site is believed to have been created by unknown Native Americans some 700 years ago.
Map ref: page 691 H5

BUFFALO

Buffalo's primary businesses are beef and oil, and its population of 3,900 caters mainly to the local ranches. Seated in the high plains of Johnson County at the junction of the I-90 and I-25, Buffalo was once the center of the West's most bitter disagreements between cattle barons and settlers, which led to the Johnson County War in 1892.

Buffalo is still a cow town. Main Street features many late Victorian façades. The Johnson County Courthouse, the Gatchell Drugstore, and the former Occidental Hotel are a reflection of the Old West. The hotel was also the setting of the climactic shoot-out scene in Owen Wister's novel *The Virginian*. The Jim Gatchell Museum on Main Street is also worth a visit.

Fifteen miles (24 km) north of the town is Fort Phil Kearny State Historical Site. Built in 1866 to protect settlers along the Bozeman Trail, today only a memorial and a cemetery stand with the charred remnants of the former outpost. North of Hwy 87 is the Fetterman Battle Site, a tribute to Captain William Fetterman's cavalry who were annihilated by the Sioux. Twenty miles (32 km) from

town is the less significant Wagon Box Monument, and the Hole-in-the-Wall, south along Route 190, where the sharp red-hued rocks served as the hideout for Butch Cassidy and the Sundance Kid.

Buffalo hosts the Bozeman Trail Days, a three-day historic, music and chuck wagon (mess wagon) venue held late June. Other events include Powder River Roundup (also in June) and the Johnson County Fair and Rodeo (in August). The nearest airport is in Sheridan, 32 miles (51 km) north on the I-90. An airport shuttle service is available.
Map ref: page 691 H4

CASPER

The oil town of Casper is Wyoming's second-largest city; its burgeoning population of 47,000 is spurred on by its natural resources and college crowd. The downtown region is quite contemporary with Casper's Nicolaysen Art Museum and Discovery Center on Collins Drive. Casper College hosts several museums, including its fossil exhibit at the Tate Mineralogical Museum and the Werner Wildlife Museum, where taxidermists proudly display their furry treasures.

Fort Caspar began as an outpost along the Oregon Trail. Landmarks, including Independence Rock and Ayres Natural Bridge, are within striking distance, along with the Wyoming Pioneer Museum, east at Douglas off the I-25. Historic Trail Expeditions provide wagon and horse treks along the Oregon Trail. Air services are available at Casper's Natrona County Airport.
Map ref: page 691 J7

CHEYENNE

Cheyenne is the capital of the "Cowboy State" and Wyoming's largest city of nearly 51,000 people. Located at the junction of the I-25 and I-80, Cheyenne sits on high

plains 17 miles (28 km) from the Colorado border. The city's orderly infrastructure belies its colorful inception as a cow town that grew around the Union Pacific Railroad. The town was ruled by the cattle barons and was frequently visited by Calamity Jane, Wild Bill Hickok, and Tom Horn. The Black Hills gold rush poured more money into Cheyenne's economy, making it one of the wealthiest cities in the United States by the 1880s. Today, Cheyenne's commerce is firmly established around federal and state departments along with its military base at Fort Warren Air Force Base, which features a small museum and missile simulator. Originally an outpost in 1867, Fort Warren became a missile site in 1958.

Chamber of Commerce, Cheyenne.

Cheyenne's historic district features the Governor's Mansion, the state Capitol, and a wealth of late Victorian and Queen Anne homes once owned by the cattle kings. The old Union Pacific Depot remains the granddaddy of buildings and at Holiday Park sits the Big Boy, the last and heaviest of the steam locomotives. Wyoming State Museum has reopened its doors to exhibit Plains Native American artifacts and an array of ranching apparatus. The Cheyenne Frontier Days Old West Museum features a collection of rodeo memorabilia, Western art, and of Old West history.

It is the frolicking romp of Cheyenne Frontier Days that remains the city's major drawcard. Hosting a week of rodeo events, chuck wagon races, and live country music, the oldest outdoor rodeo in America is held the last week in July. At the Terry Bison Ranch, located south of the city off I-25, wagon tours to grazing bison herds are available along with horseback riding and chuck wagon dinners. On Happy Jack Road lies the Drummond Ranch, complete with horseback rides and South American llamas.

Air services are available from Cheyenne and there is also a coach shuttle service which goes to Denver International Airport.
Map ref: page 697 J4

CODY

The tourist town of Cody sits at the western edge of the Bighorn Basin on the Shoshone River. Cody is the gateway to Yellowstone National Park's east entrance, 52 miles (84 km) west along Hwy 20.

Cody's attraction is its very name and the image of the Old West that goes with it. In 1895, William F. "Buffalo Bill" Cody and partners wanted to lure the Burlington & Quincy Railroad into the region to further develop the settlement and irrigate surrounding farmlands. The railroad arrived in 1901, turning the town into a tourism center for the park. Three years later oil was discovered and has since remained Cody's other principal income for its population of 7,000.

The historic Irma Hotel, named for Buffalo Bill's daughter, was built in 1902. Its dining room sports a handsome cherrywood bar presented to the showman by Queen Victoria during his Wild West tour of England. Old Trail Town, west on Hwy 14, is a collection of re-assembled territorial relics and token gravesites to frontier characters, including Jeremiah Johnson.

Cody's pride and joy is the Buffalo Bill Historic Center, known as "The Smithsonian of the West." Visitors need two days to explore the four galleries properly: the Plains Indian Museum, the Buffalo Bill Museum, the Cody Firearms Museum, and the Whitney Gallery of Art.

Each summer night in Cody, there is the Cody Nite Rodeo and Cody Stampede. The Buffalo Bill Festival is held in August.

Air services are available from Cody and there are shuttle coach services to Billings, Montana.
Map ref: page 690 D3

The fluted shape of Devils Tower was formed by the cracking of cooling volcanic rock.

DEVILS TOWER NATIONAL MONUMENT

The flat-topped, basalt mass of Devils Tower in northeastern Wyoming rises above the Belle Fourche River, 25 miles (40 km) northwest of Sundance on Hwy 24. Covering only 2 square miles (5 sq km), the ancient volcanic rock, which is 865 feet (264 m) high, became the country's first national monument and holds sacred importance to the Plains Indians. Lichens cover much of the tower and other vegetation grows on top. Devils Tower has inevitably become a popular recreational ground for camping, hiking, and rock climbing. It also featured as the site for the alien rendezvous in Steven Spielberg's film "Close Encounters of the Third Kind." The visitor center's hours of operation extend from May to September but the monument is accessible year-round if weather permits.
Map ref: page 691 L3

Black-tailed prairie dog (Cynomys ludovicianus), near Devils Tower.

FORT LARAMIE

Fort Laramie, two hours north of Cheyenne on Route 26, bore witness to the West's most important treaty between the Sioux and the US Government over their traditional hunting territory along the Bozeman Trail. Originally a fur trading post, Fort Laramie became a military post in 1841, protecting the pioneers along the Oregon Trail. Now, comprising 830 acres (336 ha), the reconstructed fort houses various buildings including the officers' quarters furnished with a wealth of military artifacts and photographs.

In the summer, Fort Laramie reenacts life at an outpost in a living history program, complete with period costumes. The Fort is open daily and houses a massive library of the pioneers who passed by.

At Guernsey, on US-26, the Oregon Trail Ruts National Historic Landmark features a deeply embedded wagon rut on a hill of sandstone. Nearly 2 miles (3 km)

away is Register Cliff, where thousands of emigrants carved their names and dates of passage into the limestone rock. East at Torrington is the Homesteaders Museum where a classic stagecoach and homestead stands adjacent to the museum.
Map ref: page 697 J1

FOSSIL BUTTE NATIONAL MONUMENT

Around 22 miles (36 km) from the mining town of Kemmerer near Route 30 is Fossil Butte National Monument. Over 50 million years ago, sea creatures lived in subtropical conditions around the lake. Fossilized fish, crocodiles, stingrays, and birds have been found on the lake's limestone bed. The Fossil Butte Visitor Center's museum houses many fossil models along with an interpretive trail that leads to a former fossil quarry. In Kemmerer, the J.C. Penney Homestead, which was once the home of the department store magnate, is the town's main attraction.
Map ref: page 695 M2

GRAND TETON NATIONAL PARK

The Grand Teton National Park encompasses the Jackson Hole valley at the foot of the Teton Mountains, and the majority of the Teton Mountains. Carved from glaciers, the mountains cradle pristine alpine

Villages in the Teton Mountains offer luxury lodging to skiers who flock to the slopes.

lakes and dense forests of birch and aspen. The park's wildlife includes moose and black bear, and, each winter, the largest migration of elk at the Elk Refuge, north of Jackson. The Snake River, which slinks around the park's valley floor, offers numerous outdoor activities in the summer including whitewater rafting, kayaking, and hiking.

French trappers who trampled the summits nearly 200 years ago called the Grand Tetons' sheer granite peaks *Les Trois Tetons* (which translates as "the three breasts"). Today, they are known as South, Middle, and the Grand Teton—

which puncture the sky at around 13,770 feet (4,200 m). Neighboring the trio is the less imposing Mt Moran and the serene Jackson and Jenny Lakes to the north.

First created as a national park in 1929 by benefactor, John D. Rockefeller Jr, the Grand Teton National Park's present-day boundaries include the ski resort at Teton Village and the hamlet of Wilson. Unlike Yellowstone, the park is open year-round pending winter road closures at some entrances. A multiple entry pass, for a modest fee, is available for a seven-day period—this covers both parks plus numerous camp sites and lodges.

Grand Teton National Park began as a gigantic fault block, raised from the Earth's core.

There are many excellent vantage points within the park. Less than 1 mile (2 km) from Moose's Visitor Center on Hwy 191 is the Chapel of Transfiguration, log-built with an ethereal altar window that frames a view of the Teton Mountains. In summer, Signal Mountain Road offers a superb view of the valley and is a great hiking trail. Photographers William Jackson and Ansel Adams took many of their wilderness shots from this spot. At Mormon Row, a cluster of weathered barns lies against a backdrop of the Grand Tetons and grazing bison. It is this singular scene that characterizes the region's rustic beauty.
Map ref: page 690 B5

JACKSON

Approximately sixty miles (97 km) south from Yellowstone is the town of Jackson. With a population of around 4,700, Jackson has evolved into the consummate ski resort and its economy is solely dependent on tourism. The rustic town has retained its rugged appeal, notwithstanding the million-dollar homes, since the homesteaders first settled the region in 1884. Its town square is a ribbon of wooded boardwalks, flanked by designer outlets and expensive art galleries. Crowning the square's corners are the Elk Antler Arches, built from naturally shed antlers from the nearby Elk Refuge.

At an elevation of 6,234 feet (1,901 m) and cradled in three directions by the Gros Ventre Range, East Gros Ventre Butte, and Snow King Mountain, the resort offers premier powder snow and the longest continual vertical ski run in the United States. The Jackson Hole Ski Area at Teton Village has an aerial tram that glides skiers to Rendezvous Mountain in 12 minutes. Snow King is Wyoming's oldest run and has a vertical drop of 1,571 feet (479 m). The Grand Targhee resort boasts the best powder with a base elevation of 8,000 feet (2,440 m) and a vertical rise of 2,200 feet (671 m), complete with a backdrop of Mt Moran.

The Elk Refuge on Hwy 191 offers sleigh rides from the National Museum of Wildlife Art. A stunningly designed sandstone building, the museum blends into the hills overlooking herds of migrating elk. The museum also displays a collection of Western wildlife on canvas by the American masters, Frederic Remington, Charlie Russell, and Carl Ringus. The Jackson Hole Historical Society and Museum on Mercill Avenue houses a collection of early Jackson town history. From Memorial Day to Labor Day weekends in summer, the town of Jackson stages a reenactment of a dastardly shootout in the square along with the Jackson Hole Rodeo at the fairground.

Restaurants in town are excellent and most are centered near to, or on, the town square. The Million Dollar Cowboy Bar on North Cache is the place to take a shot of

An antler arch stands at each corner of Jackson Square.

whiskey on a stool made of saddles. The bar displays a modest collection of Western paraphernalia including spurs, chaps, and a token bear behind a glass case. Around the corner at the Wort Hotel is the Silver Dollar Bar, where Jackson's real-life cowboys drink beer over a bar embedded with silver dollar coins.

Jackson has many outfitters who largely provide hiking and horseback guides in the Tetons. There are also whitewater trips along the Snake River through Barker Ewing Whitewater River Trips. Jackson features the gamut of lodgings from budget motels downtown to the ritzy resorts in Teton Village. There are also several B&Bs within two blocks of the town square.

Jackson Airport is 7 miles (11 km) north of town on US-191 in the Grand Teton National Park. Shuttles are also available from Salt Lake City to Jackson.
Map ref: page 690 A6

Killpecker Dune Fields, near Rock Springs, is an ancient landscape of eroded volcanoes, and huge sand dunes formed by high winds.

LARAMIE

Like most college towns, Laramie's population of 25,000 enjoys a buoyant economy and cultural life. Home to the University of Wyoming, Laramie sits at the foothills of the Medicine Bow National Forest and Snowy Range on the I-80. There are numerous hiking trails and campsites in the region plus a stretch of whitewater rafting at the North Platte River wilderness area. Laramie is also an excellent base for touring the smaller towns on the high plains together with Medicine Bow, a former Union Pacific Railroad town. Its only attraction is the Virginian Hotel, a period guesthouse that milks the legend of Owen Wister's famous book, *The Virginian.*

Laramie's historic district, dating back to the 1860s, features many handsome buildings including the old Union Pacific Depot. The University of Wyoming offers a number of museums including the American Heritage Center and the University Art Museum. Another good outing is guaranteed at the Wyoming Territorial Prison and Old West Park where Butch Cassidy served some time.

Laramie has daily flights and a coach service to Denver. By I-80, the city is only 55 miles (88 km) west of Cheyenne.
Map ref: page 696 G3

RAWLINS

The town of Rawlins sits halfway between Evanston and Cheyenne on the I-80. Its small population of 11,000 once catered to the Union Pacific Railroad and attracted many desperadoes including Big Nose George Parrot, a murdering train robber who ended up being lynched on Rawlin's main

The walking tour through Rawlins features 31 historic buildings.

street. Rawlin's main attraction is the Frontier Prison, which only closed its doors in 1982. Tours of the jail include its cadaverous gas chamber and "Death Row."
Map ref: page 690 G10

RIVERTON

Riverton cuts into the southeastern pocket of the Wind River Reservation, home to the Shoshone and Arapaho Indians. It was developed in 1906 after a pledge was made to irrigate their land.

Surrounded by acres of irrigated crops and dairy farms, Riverton's population remains modest at 9,200. While it offers the visitor very little in the way of attractions, the town is well positioned for exploring the Wind River Mountains and the stunning Wind River Canyon on Hwy 26. A 12-mile (19-km) stretch of narrow highway meanders along next to the swiftly flowing Wind River and 1000-foot (305-m) cliffs featuring ancient petroglyphs. There are numerous rafting tracts and hiking trails that also follow the river's course.

Over the summer, powwows are held on the reservation with exhibits of Shoshone and Arapaho arts and crafts from the Shoshone Tribal Cultural Center at Fort Washakie, which is now headquarters for the reservation. At nearby Ethete, the Arapaho Museum has a display of artifacts in the building of St Michael's

Episcopal Mission. Clothing and beadwork are featured at St Stephen's Mission, a former school building dating back to 1890.

The reservation marks the final resting place of the great Shoshone Chief, Washakie, who guided his people to live peacefully with the white settlers. On Route 287 is the gravesite believed to be of Sacajawea, the Shoshone scout who helped navigate the westward expedition of explorers Lewis and Clark.

The Riverton Museum focuses mainly on local history and exhibits a tipi with a buffalo robe and ceremonial drum. The town also hosts the Mountain Man Rendezvous and Music Festival the first weekend in July and the Cowboy Poetry Roundup in October. Riverton has its own airport with connections to Denver.
Map ref: page 690 E7

ROCK SPRINGS

Rock Springs is an unassuming town of 20,000 people that nestles in the red rock region of southwest Wyoming on the I-80. The town is the principal jumping-off point to Flaming Gorge National Recreation Area where, in 1868, explorer John Wesley Powell followed the tract of the Green River on his journey west. Also close to Rock Springs is the enormous sandy

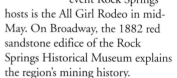

Petroglyph at White Mountain, Rock Springs.

expanse of the Dunes, which rise to more than 150 feet (46 m), and White Mountain, where petroglyphs of bison and horses are carved into the sandstone.

Rock Springs has remained a rough-and-tumble town on a seesaw of boom cycles of mining construction and natural resources. A stroll along its historic district brings into view an array of interesting buildings including a former butcher shop, at 422 Main Street, where outlaw Butch Cassidy worked and acquired his name. One interesting event Rock Springs hosts is the All Girl Rodeo in mid-May. On Broadway, the 1882 red sandstone edifice of the Rock Springs Historical Museum explains the region's mining history.

There is a bus service which connects Rock Springs to Salt Lake City and Denver.
Map ref: page 696 A2

SHERIDAN

The handsome town of Sheridan, at the foothills of the Bighorn Mountains, boasts a rich lineage tracing back to cattle barons and ranchers of the late nineteenth century. Though coal mining has become its mainstay economy, its heritage is reflected by the many late-Victorian homes and commercial buildings on its historic Main Street. The most resplendent is the Sheridan Inn, an intermittent home to Buffalo Bill Cody. Main Street also flaunts a classic neon sign of a cowboy on a bucking bronco, and the King's Saddlery, one of the finest Western-wear stores, houses a little cowboy museum at the rear of the store.

Also worth a glance is the Trail End Historic Center, which was the former summer home to John Kendrick, a cattle baron who became Wyoming's governor and long-term US senator. In the summer, Sheridan hosts the North American Cowboy Roundup and the Sheridan County Rodeo at the Sheridan County Fairgrounds.

Surprisingly, the town of Sheridan is quite gentrified, with polo games held most summer weekends near the Old West town of Big Horn. The village features the largest collection of original false-fronted edifices in the state including the Big Horn Mercantile Building and the Bozeman Trail Inn. Off Route 331 is the Bradford Brinton Memorial Museum at Little Goose Creek. Brinton's oriental-style Quarter Circle A Ranch features a collection of Western paraphernalia and art.

Sheridan has daily flights to Denver and there is also a bus service that travels between Billings, Montana, and Denver.
Map ref: page 691 H3

The 10,000-year-old Grand Canyon at Yellowstone is predominantly made of the light-colored, volcanic rock rhyolite.

Morning Glory Pool, Yellowstone National Park.

YELLOWSTONE NATIONAL PARK

Yellowstone is an anomaly among national parks. Established as the country's first in 1872, the park nurtures almost half the world's geysers and the largest number of wildlife including moose, black bear, and bison. Stretching about 3,457 miles (5,562 km) along the state's northwest, the Yellowstone spills over into Montana and Idaho.

Since the release of wolves into the park, Yellowstone's ecosystem reflects the wilderness of over 200 years ago when John Colter first explored the region.

Yellowstone was molded into a series of geysers and canyons resulting from cataclysmic volcanic activity more than 2 million years ago. Shaped by repeated eruptions, the park divides into three quadrants. On the western boundary lies a series of boiling-hot springs and steaming geysers in the Upper Geyser Basin, where over 180 of the park's 230 steaming geysers heat the ground. Its most famous is Old Faithful, which jettisons about 8,000 gallons (30,280 l) of boiling water to nearly 200 feet (61 m) high, almost every 70 minutes.

The northern tract extends from Mammoth Hot Springs in the Lower Geyser Basin where the steaming water, loaded with calcium carbonate, forms white travertine terraces. The oldest geothermal area is the magnificent Grand Canyon where the spectacular Upper Falls and Lower Falls cascade down into deep gorges. Yellowstone's southern tract encompasses deciduous forests and the Yellowstone Lake at an elevation of 7,000 feet (2,135 m). The Continental Divide cuts a swath through the region where the Yellowstone River flows northeast and the Snake River drifts southwest.

The length of the 142-mile (228-km) Grand Loop scenic drive can be done in a day but a minimum of three days to view the park is recommended. The park is always under threat of fire—the Yellowstone fires of 1988 destroyed some 793,000 acres (321,165 ha) in the Upper Geyser Basin.

The park has two entrances in Wyoming: north from Grand Teton National Park on Hwy 89/191/287, and east on Hwy 14/16/20 from Cody. There are three additional entrances from Montana with US-89 from Gardner open year-round to traffic. The other entrances are open from May to October. Snowcoaches transport visitors to the park in winter when Mammoth Hot Springs Lodge and Old Faithful Lodge are open.

Yellowstone National Park is serviced through Cody, Jackson, and Bozeman, Montana, which are all approximately one hour away. West Yellowstone's airport across the Montana border is seasonal—it only opens during summer. While there are bus services to the park from Jackson and Cody, it is recommended that visitors rent a car for touring the park. A seven-day pass is available for a modest fee, allowing multiple entry to both Grand Teton and Yellowstone National Parks. There are miles of cross-country ski trails along with outfitters offering horseback trips, chartered boats, and wildlife tours.
Map ref: page 690 B3

Northern Idaho and Northwestern Montana

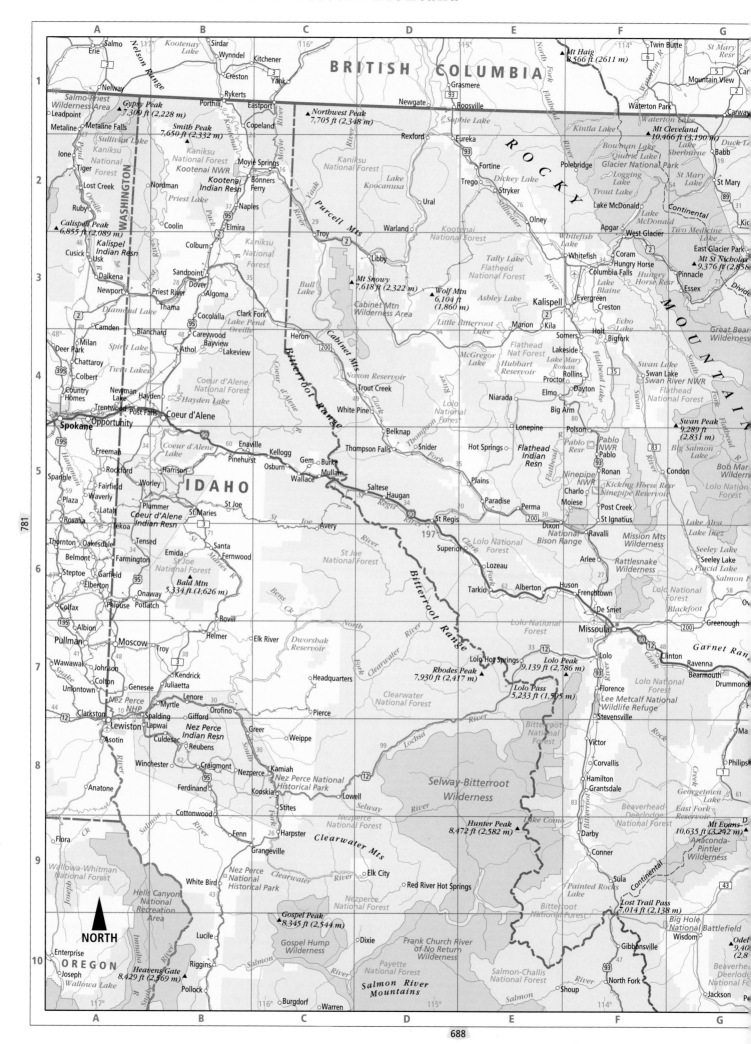

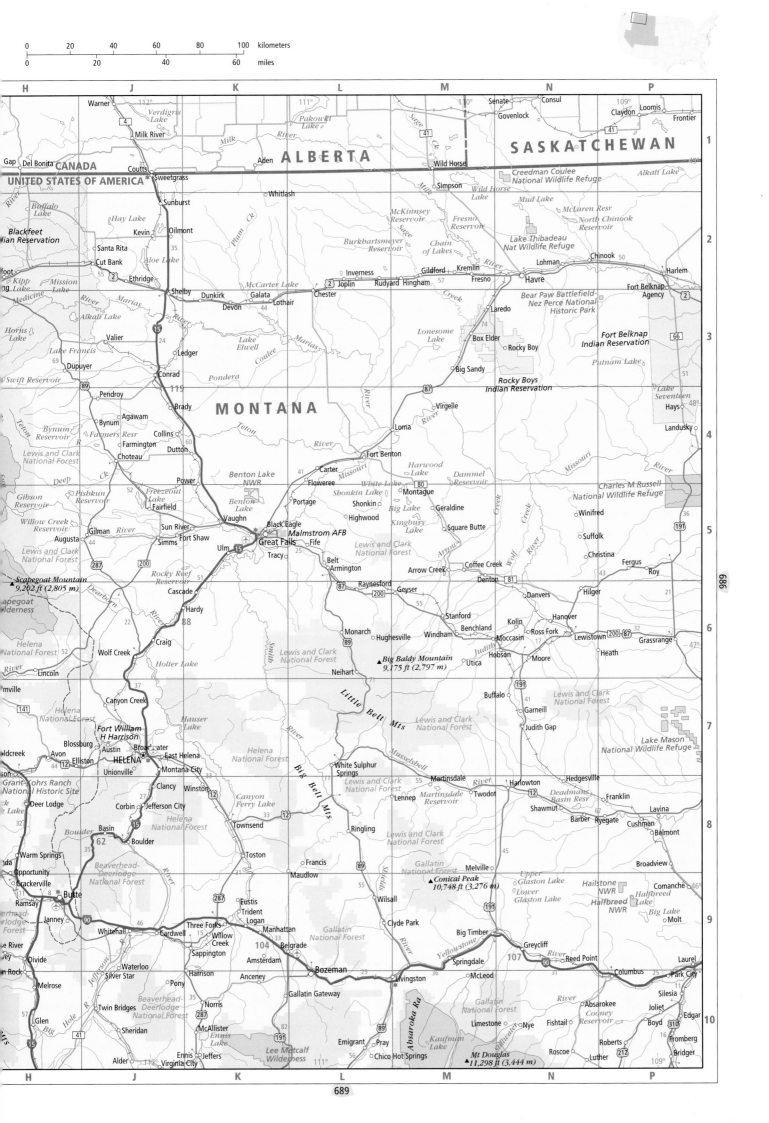

Central and Eastern Montana

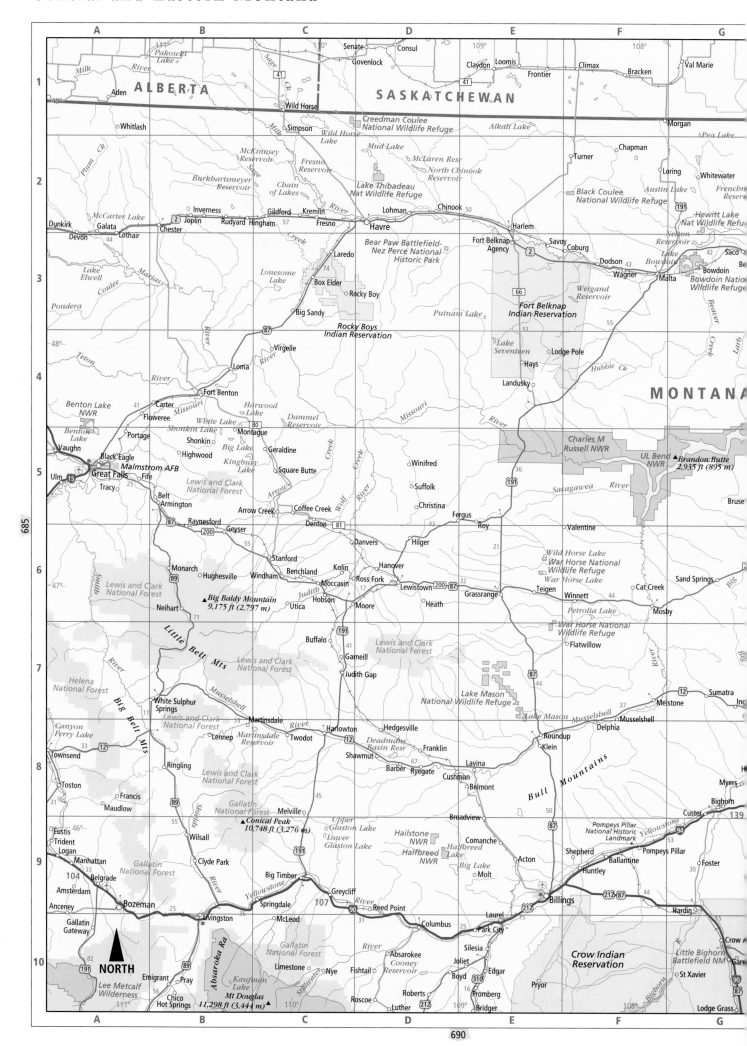

685

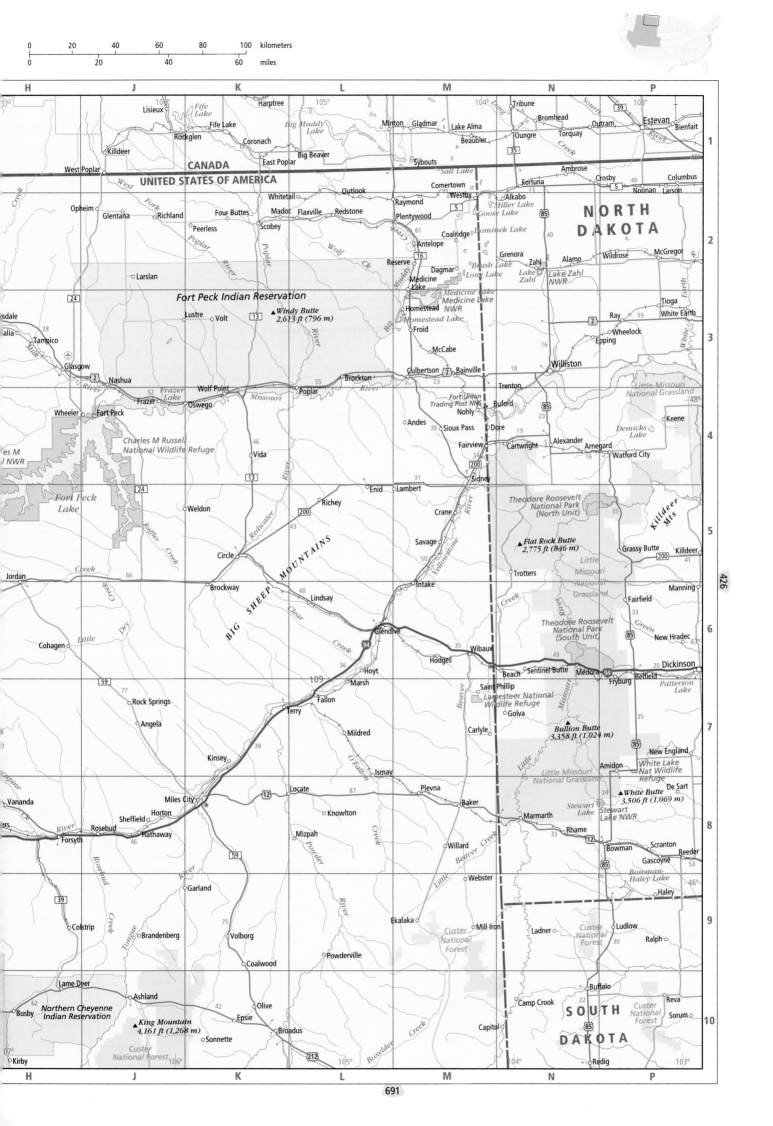

0   20   40   60   80   100 kilometers
0   20   40   60 miles

426

MOUNTAINS AND THE WEST

Southern Idaho • Southwestern Montana

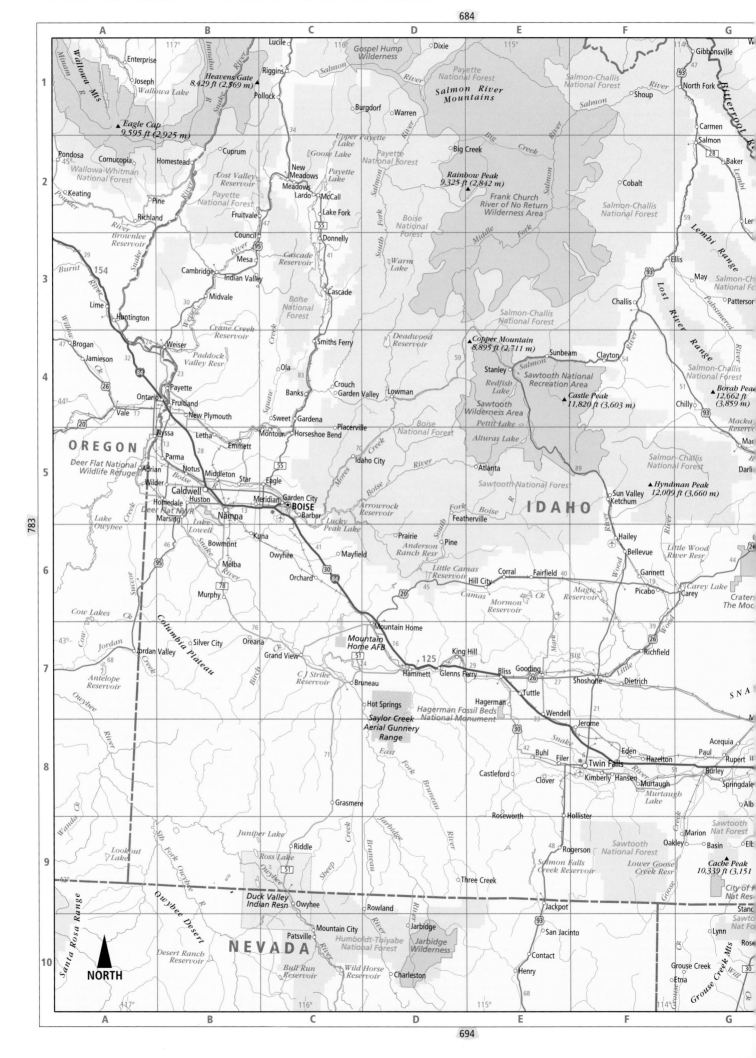

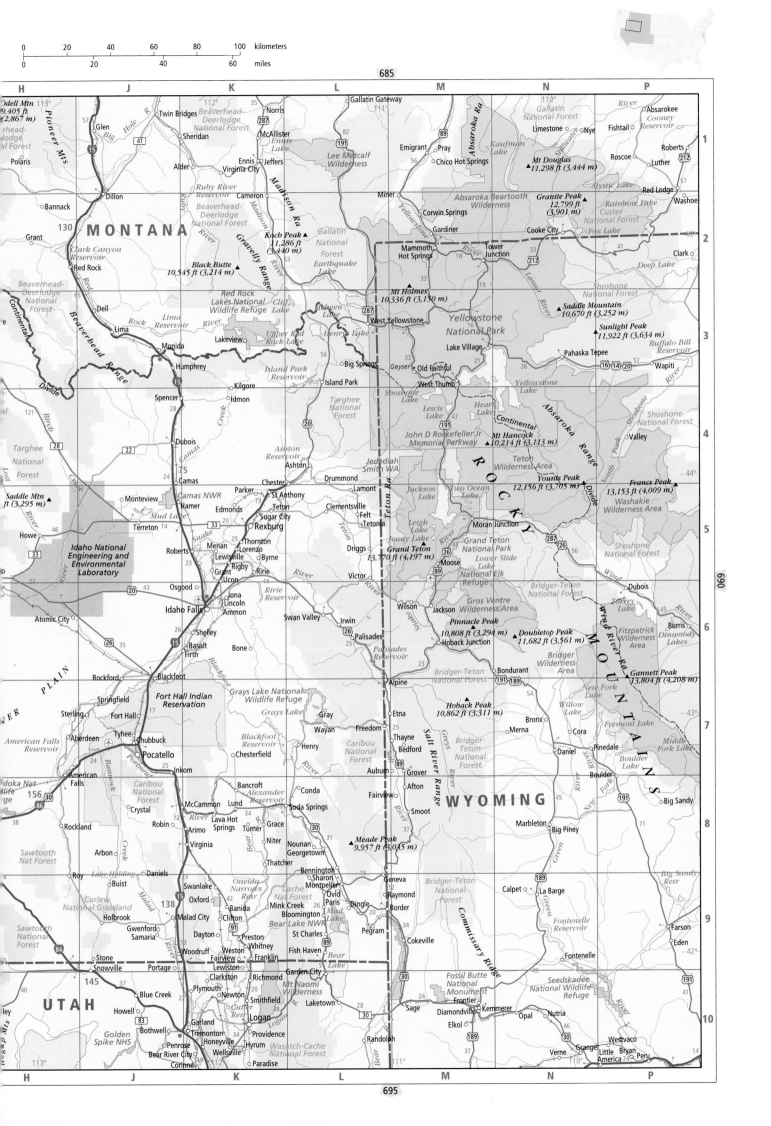

MONTANA

WYOMING

UTAH

ROCKY MOUNTAINS

690

0   20   40   60   80   100 kilometers
0   20   40   60 miles

Row 1
Odell Mtn 113° 9,405 ft (2,867 m)
Pioneer Mts
head-Lodge al Forest
Glen
Twin Bridges
Beaverhead-Deerlodge National Forest
Norris
Gallatin Gateway
Gallatin National Forest
River
Limestone Nye
Absarokee
Cooney Reservoir
57
Sheridan
McAllister
287
191
82
111°
89
Absaroka Ra
Kaufman Lake
Fishtail
110°

Polaris
Sheridan
Ennis
Jeffers
Emigrant Pray
Mt Douglas 11,298 ft (3,444 m)
Roscoe
Roberts
Luther
212
15
Alder
Virginia City
Ennis Lake
Lee Metcalf Wilderness
56
Chico Hot Springs
Washoe

Bannack
Dillon
Cameron
Ruby River Reservoir
Miner
Corwin Springs
Absaroka Beartooth Wilderness
Granite Peak 12,799 ft (3,901 m)
Rainbow Lake
Custer National Forest
Red Lodge
57

MONTANA
130
Red Rock
Beaverhead-Deerlodge National Forest
Koch Peak 11,286 ft (3,440 m)
Gardiner
Cooke City
Fox Lake
Washoe

Grant
Clark Canyon Reservoir
Red Rock
Gravelly Range
Black Butte 10,545 ft (3,214 m)
Madison River
Mammoth Hot Springs
Tower Junction
212
33
41
Clark
Deep Lake

Beaverhead-Deerlodge National Forest
65
Dell
Red Rock Lakes National Wildlife Refuge
Cliff Lake
Mt Holmes 10,336 ft (3,150 m)
18
19
Shoshone National Forest
Saddle Mountain 10,670 ft (3,252 m)

Continental Divide
Lima
Monida
Lakeview
Upper Red Rock Lake
Hebgen Lake
West Yellowstone
Yellowstone National Park
Sunlight Peak 11,922 ft (3,634 m)
Buffalo Bill Reservoir

121
Humphrey
15
Big Springs
Geyser Old Faithful
33
26
Pahaska Tepee
16 14 20
52
Wapiti

Spencer
Kilgore
Island Park
West Thumb
Shoshone Lake
Lewis Lake
Heart Lake
Continental
Absaroka Range
Valley
Shoshone National Forest

Targhee National Forest
28
Idmon
Island Park Reservoir
Yellowstone Lake
ROCKY

Saddle Mtn ft (3,295 m)
Dubois
22
Ashton Reservoir
20
John D Rockefeller Jr Memorial Parkway
Mt Hancock 10,214 ft (3,113 m)
Teton Wilderness Area
44°
Francs Peak 13,153 ft (4,009 m)

Targhee National Forest
75
Camas
Ashton
Drummond
Jedediah Smith WA
Younts Peak 12,156 ft (3,705 m)
Washakie Wilderness Area

Monteview
Parker
Chester
Lamont
Teton Ra
Jackson Lake
Two Ocean Lake
Divide

Montview
Camas NWR
Hamer
St Anthony
Teton
Clementsville
Felt
Tetonia
Leigh Lake
Moran Junction
287
Shoshone National Forest

Howe
46
Mud Lake
Edmonds
Sugar City
Rexburg
Driggs
Grand Teton National Park
Jenny Lake
26
56

33
Terreton
14
Thornton
Lorenzo
Byrne
Grand Teton 13,770 ft (4,197 m)
Lower Slide Lake
Wind

Idaho National Engineering and Environmental Laboratory
Roberts
Menan
Lewisville
Rigby
Ririe
Victor
Moose
89
National Elk Refuge
Bridger-Teton National Forest
Dubois

Atomic City
Osgood
20
43
Grant
Ucon
Ririe Reservoir
Wilson
Jackson
Gros Ventre Wilderness Area
Torrey Lake
45
Burris

33
Idaho Falls
Iona
Lincoln
Ammon
Swan Valley
Irwin
26
Hoback Junction
Pinnacle Peak 10,808 ft (3,294 m)
Bondurant
Fitzpatrick Wilderness Area
Dinwood Lakes
Gannett Peak 13,804 ft (4,208 m)

Shelley
Basalt
Firth
Bone
Palisades
25
Palisades Reservoir
Doubletop Peak 11,682 ft (3,561 m)
Bridger Wilderness Area
43°

26
35
Rockford
Blackfoot
Fort Hall Indian Reservation
Grays Lake National Wildlife Refuge
Gray
Alpine
23
191 189
Bronx
New Fork Lake
Fremont Lake

Springfield
Sterling
Fort Hall
17
Grays Lake
Wayan
Freedom
Etna
Hoback Peak 10,862 ft (3,311 m)
54
Cora
Boulder Lake

American Falls Reservoir
Tyhee
Chubbuck
Pocatello
Blackfoot Reservoir
Henry
Thayne
Bedford
Salt River Range
Merna
Daniel
Pinedale
Middle Fork Lake

doka Nat llife ge
156
American Falls
86
30
Inkom
Chesterfield
Auburn
Grover
89
Fairview
Afton
WYOMING
Boulder
191
Big Sandy

Aberdeen
Bancroft
Lund
Alexander Reservoir
Conda
Smoot
45
Marbleton
Big Piney
71

Rockland
McCammon
Crystal
Soda Springs
30
Meade Peak 9,957 ft (3,035 m)
Green

Robin
Arimo
Lava Hot Springs
Turner
Grace
31
37
La Barge
Big Sandy Resr

Arbon
Virginia
Niter
Nounan
Georgetown
Thatcher
Bennington
15
Geneva
Bridger-Teton National Forest
Calpet
189

Sawtooth Nat Forest
Roy
Buist
Daniels
Swanlake
Oxford
Oneida Narrows Resr
Cache Nat Forest
Montpelier
Sharon
Raymond
189
La Barge
Fontenelle Reservoir
Farson
42°

Curlew National Grassland
138
Holbrook
Malad City
Banida
Clifton
Mink Creek
Ovid Paris
Bloomington
Dingle
Border
Seedskadee National Wildlife Refuge
Eden

Sawtooth National Forest
Gwenford
Samaria
Dayton
91
Preston
Whitney
St Charles
Bear Lake NWR
Mud Lake
Pegram
34
Cokeville
Fossil Butte National Monument
191
Farson

ley
Mts
145
Stone
Snowville
Portage
Woodruff
Fairview
Franklin
Fish Haven
Bear Lake
Commissary Ridge
Frontier
Diamondville
Kemmerer
Nutria
41

UTAH
40
Bothwell
83
Howell
Blue Creek
Plymouth
Clarkston
Newton
Richmond
Mt Naomi Wilderness
Garden City
30
Sage
Elkol
Opal
Granger
Westvaco
Peru
14

Golden Spike NHS
Tremonton
Honeyville
Garland
Smithfield
Logan
Laketown
28
24
30
Randolph
189
30
Verne
110°
Little America
24
Bryan

Penrose
Bear River City
Corinne
Hyrum
Paradise
Logan River
Wasatch-Cache National Forest
111°
Providence
Wellsville
37
Bear

113°
112°

Northern and Central Wyoming

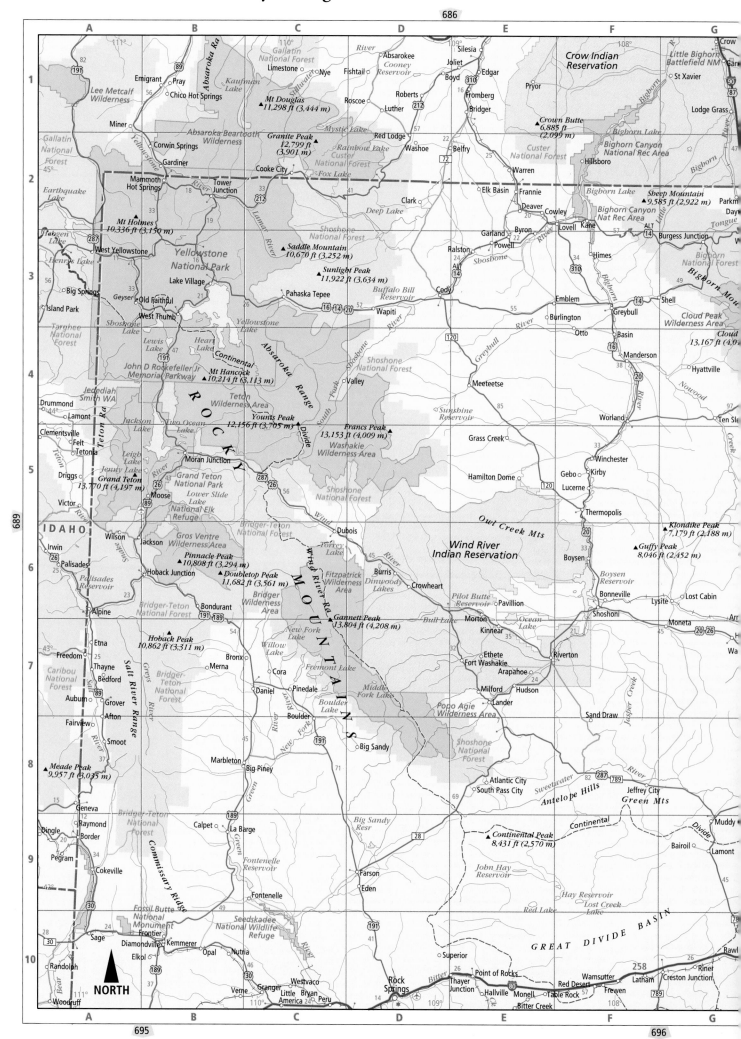

A B C D E F G

1 | 111° | 82 | 191 | Emigrant | 89 | Pray | Chico Hot Springs | Absaroka Ra | Kaufman Lake | 110° | Gallatin National Forest | Limestone | Nye | Fishtail | Absarokee | Cooney Reservoir | River | 109° | Silesia | Joliet | Edgar | Boyd | 310 | Fromberg | Bridger | Pryor | Crow Indian Reservation | St Xavier | Crow | 90 | Little Bighorn Battlefield NM | Gar

Lee Metcalf Wilderness | Miner | Mt Douglas 11,298 ft (3,444 m) | Roscoe | Luther | Roberts | Red Lodge | 212 | Warren | Crown Butte 6,885 ft (2,099 m) | Bighorn | Lodge Grass

NORTH

MOUNTAINS AND THE WEST

A B C D E F G

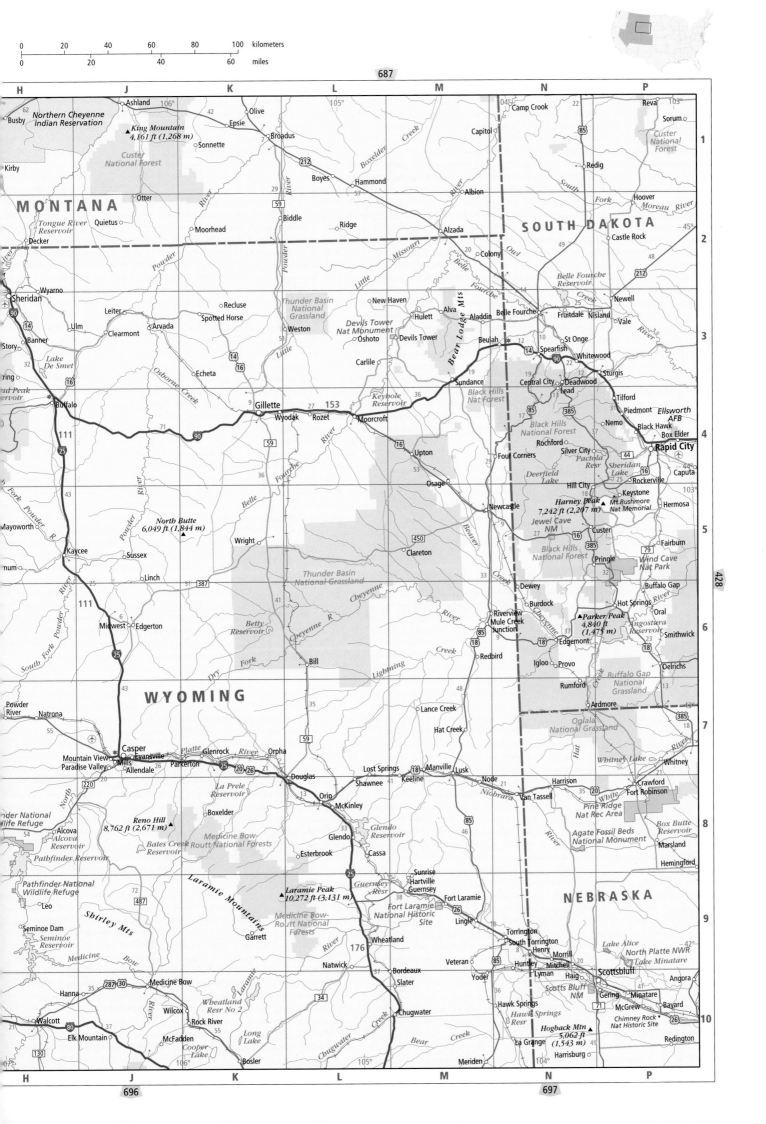

0   20   40   60   80   100 kilometers
0   20   40   60 miles

| H | J | K | L | M | N | P |

MONTANA

SOUTH DAKOTA

WYOMING

NEBRASKA

Northern Cheyenne
Indian Reservation

King Mountain
4,161 ft (1,268 m)

Custer
National Forest

Custer
National Forest

Busby
Kirby
Decker
Sheridan
Wyarno
Story
Banner
Ulm
Buffalo
Kaycee
Sussex
Linch
Midwest
Edgerton
Mayoworth
Natrona
Powder River
Casper
Mountain View
Paradise Valley
Mills
Allendale
Alcova
Seminoe Dam
Leo
Seminoe Reservoir
Hanna
Walcott
Elk Mountain
McFadden
Wilcox
Rock River
Bosler

Ashland
Olive
Epsie
Sonnette
Broadus
Boyes
Hammond
Otter
Moorhead
Biddle
Ridge
Quietus
Leiter
Clearmont
Arvada
Spotted Horse
Recluse
Weston
Echeta
Gillette
Wyodak
Rozet
Moorcroft
Wright
Bill
Edgerton
Douglas
Orin
McKinley
Glendo
Esterbrook
Cassa
Sunrise
Hartville
Guernsey
Fort Laramie
Lingle
Wheatland
Natwick
Bordeaux
Slater
Yoder
Medicine Bow
Garrett

North Butte
6,049 ft (1,844 m)

Reno Hill
8,762 ft (2,671 m)

Laramie Peak
10,272 ft (3,131 m)

Hogback Mtn
5,062 ft (1,543 m)

Parker Peak
4,840 ft (1,475 m)

Harney Peak
7,242 ft (2,207 m)

Thunder Basin
National
Grassland

Thunder Basin
National Grassland

Devils Tower
Nat Monument

Devils Tower

Bear Lodge Mts

Black Hills
Nat Forest

Black Hills
National Forest

Black Hills
National Forest

Medicine Bow
Routt National Forests

Medicine Bow-
Routt National
Forests

Shirley Mts

Laramie Mountains

Pathfinder National
Wildlife Refuge

Pathfinder Reservoir

Alcova
Reservoir

Bates Creek
Reservoir

La Prele
Reservoir

Glendo
Reservoir

Guernsey
Resr

Wheatland Resr No 2

Betty
Reservoir

Keyhole
Reservoir

Belle Fourche
Reservoir

Wind Cave
Nat Park

Buffalo Gap
National
Grassland

Oglala
National Grassland

Pine Ridge
Nat Rec Area

Agate Fossil Beds
National Monument

Scotts Bluff
NM

Chimney Rock
Nat Historic Site

North Platte NWR

Lake Alice

Lake Minatare

Box Butte
Reservoir

New Haven
Hulett
Alva
Aladdin
Beulah
Oshoto
Devils Tower
Carlile
Sundance
Upton
Osage
Newcastle
Clareton
Redbird
Riverview
Mule Creek Junction
Dewey
Burdock
Rumford
Ardmore

Colony
Belle Fourche
Fruitdale
Nisland
Spearfish
Whitewood
St Onge
Central City
Deadwood
Lead
Sturgis
Tilford
Piedmont
Nemo
Black Hawk
Box Elder
Rapid City
Rochford
Silver City
Hill City
Keystone
Mt Rushmore
Nat Memorial
Hermosa
Jewel Cave
NM
Custer
Pringle
Fairburn
Hot Springs
Oral
Edgemont
Smithwick
Igloo
Provo
Oelrichs

Camp Crook
Capitol
Reva
Sorum
Redig
Hoover
Castle Rock
Newell
Vale
Rochford
Caputa
Rockerville

Deerfield
Lake
Pactola
Resr
Sheridan
Lake
Angostura
Reservoir
Whitney Lake
Whitney

Lost Springs
Manville
Lusk
Node
Harrison
Crawford
Fort Robinson
Shawnee
Keeline
Van Tassel
Orpha

Torrington
South Torrington
Henry
Morrill
Mitchell
Lyman
Huntley
Scottsbluff
Gering
Minatare
Bayard
McGrew
Angora
Bardeaux
Haig
Hawk Springs
La Grange
Meriden
Harrisburg
Redington

Four Corners
Lance Creek
Hat Creek
Van Tassell
Harrison
Niobrara
White
Hemingford
Marsland

Powder River
Tongue River
Reservoir
Lake De Smet
Osborne Creek
Little
Missouri
River
Belle Fourche
Owl Creek
South Fork
Moreau River
Cheyenne R
Lightning Creek
Dry Fork
South Fork Powder River
North Platte
Medicine Bow
Laramie River
Chugwater Creek
Bear Creek
Cooper Lake
Long Lake
Sweetwater
Hawk Springs
Resr

106°
105°
104°
103°
45°
44°
43°

62
42
29
57
59
212
212
106°
32
14
16
16
14
16
90
25
111
90
59
27
153
9
71
387
51
59
35
6
43
25
25
220
26
20
26
18
21
13
72
487
176
287
30
35
34
130
80
37
55
46
21
49
38
37
37
49
79
18
16
44
385
385
32
27
85
17
18
10
14
13
19
22
12
14
20
85
48
25
24
18
9
33
37
20
21
23
35
85
71
13

**MOUNTAINS
AND THE
WEST**

428

Northwestern Nevada • Northern California

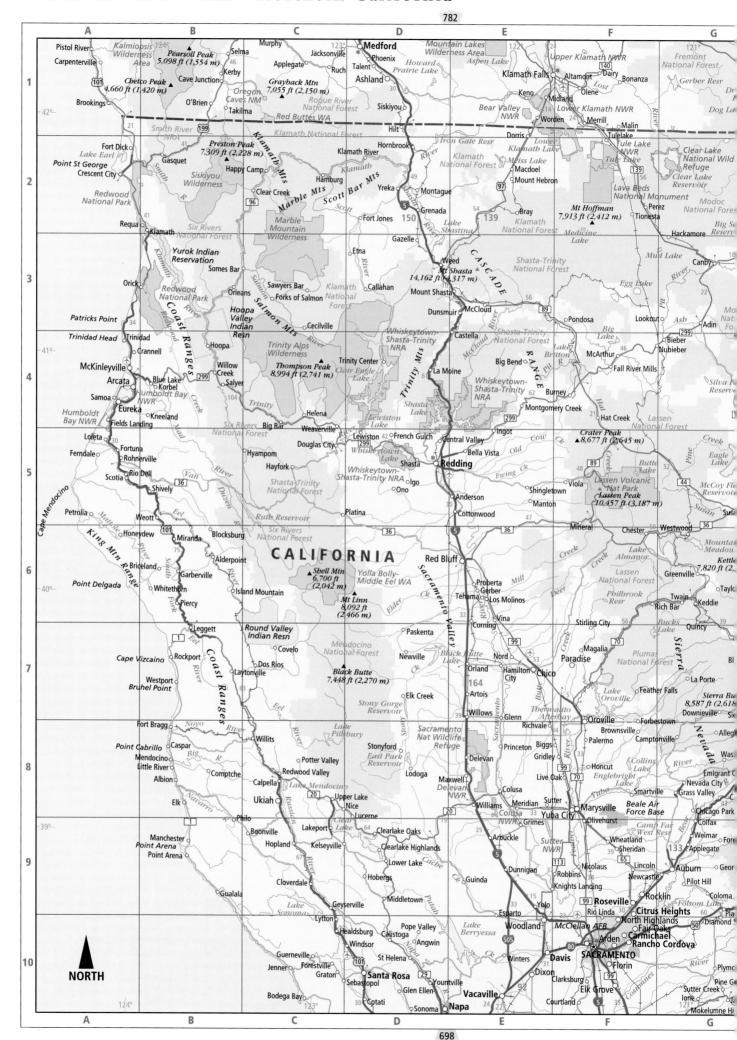

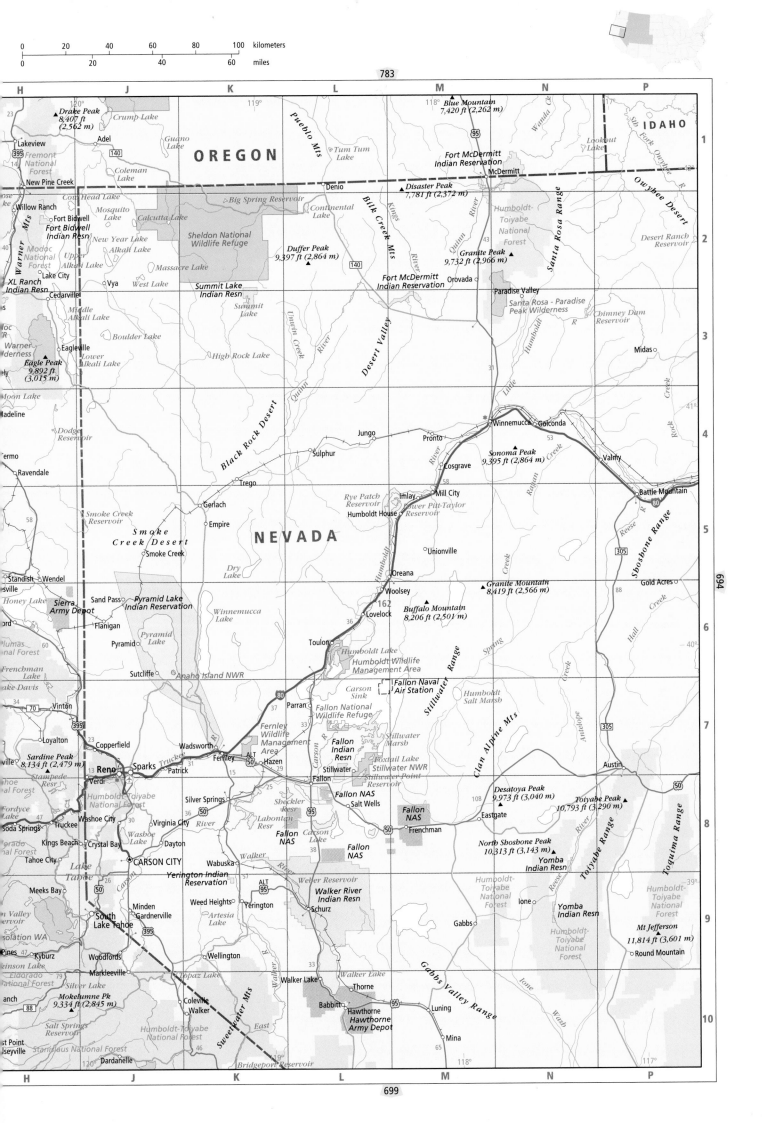

MOUNTAINS AND THE WEST

Northeastern Nevada • Northern Utah • Southwestern Wyoming

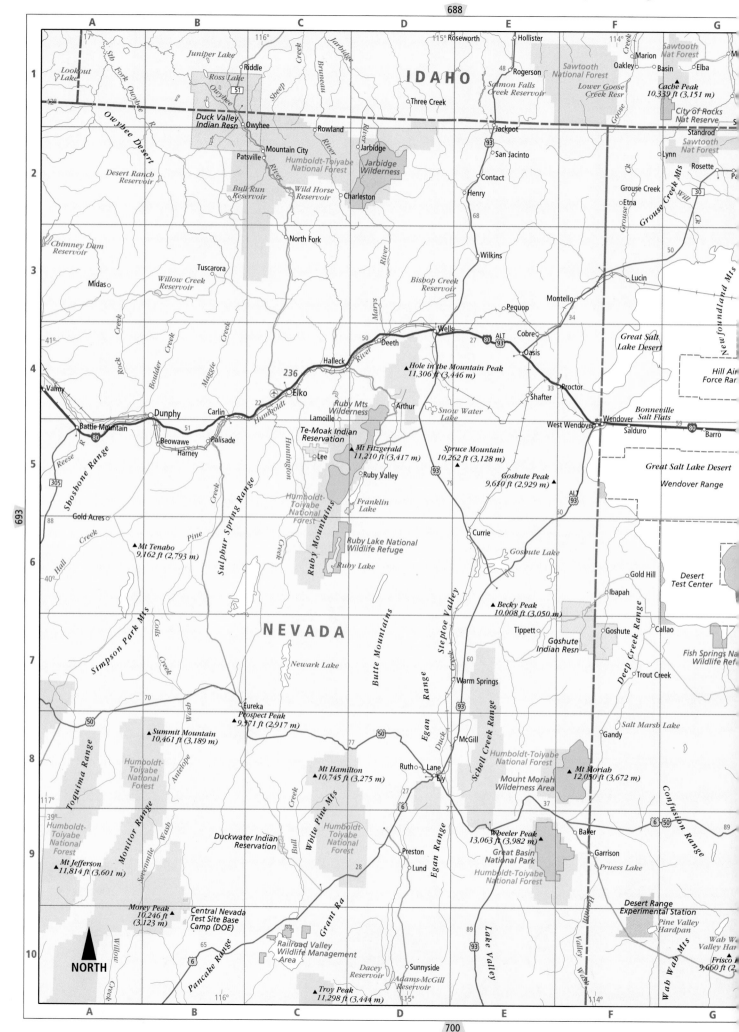

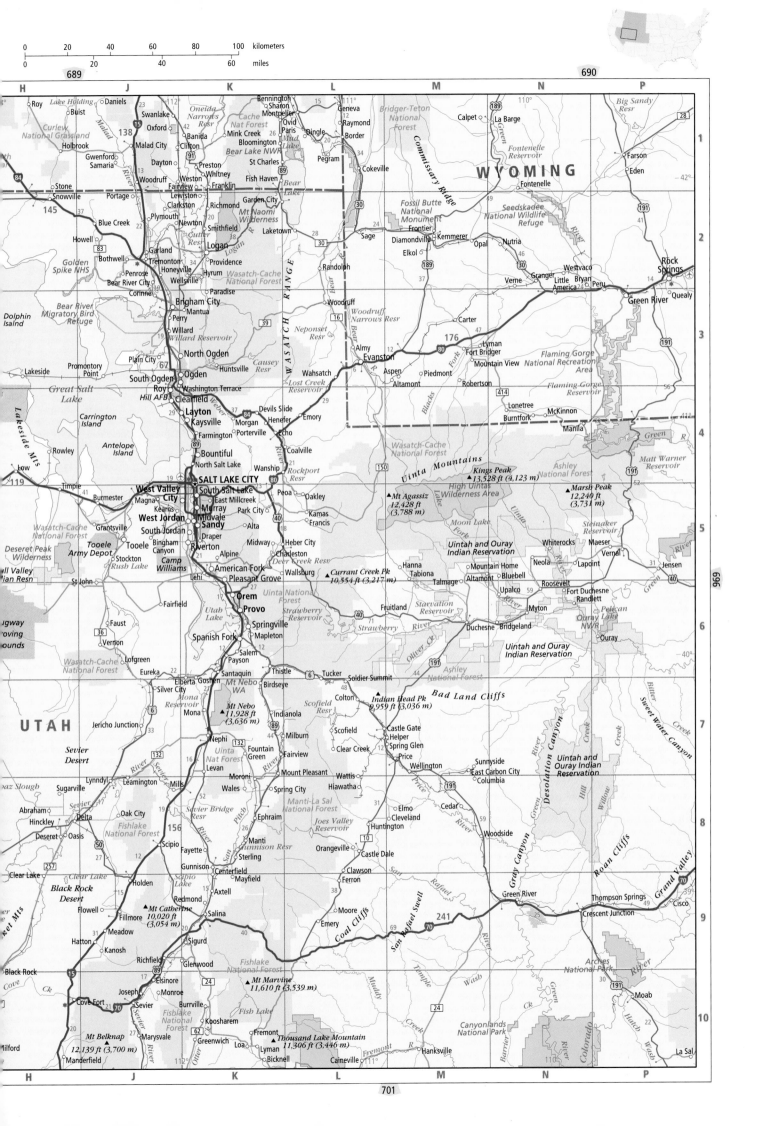

MOUNTAINS AND THE WEST

Southeastern Wyoming • Northern Colorado • Western Nebraska

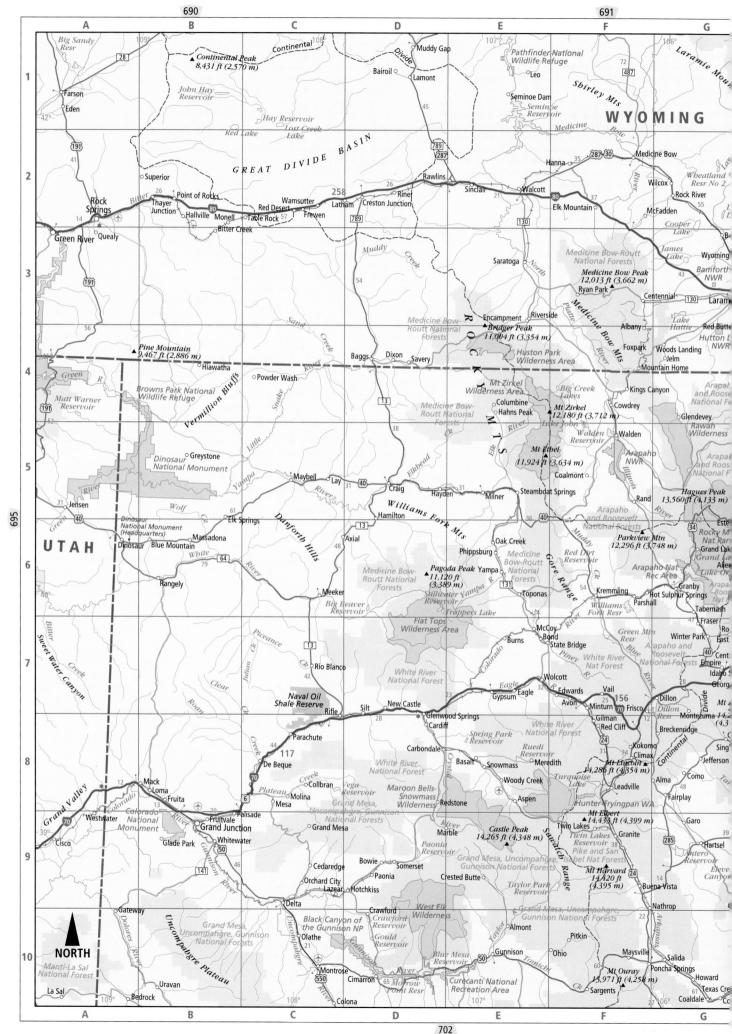

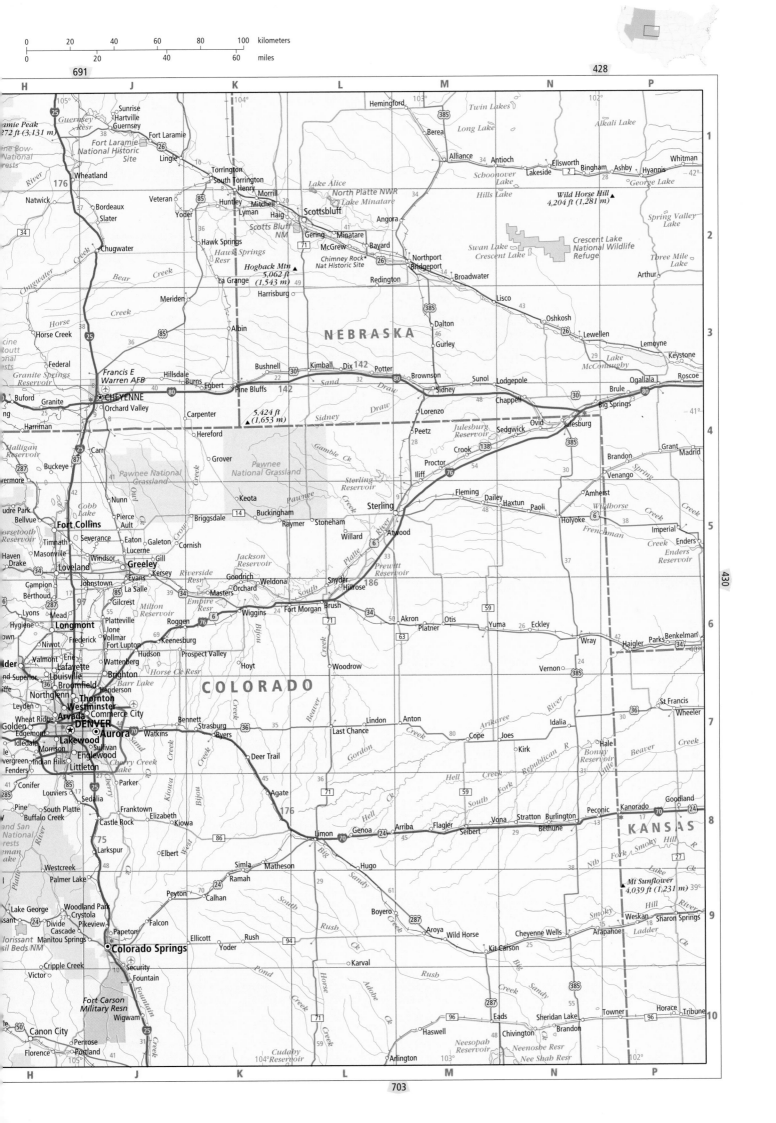

MOUNTAINS AND THE WEST

Southwestern Nevada • Central California

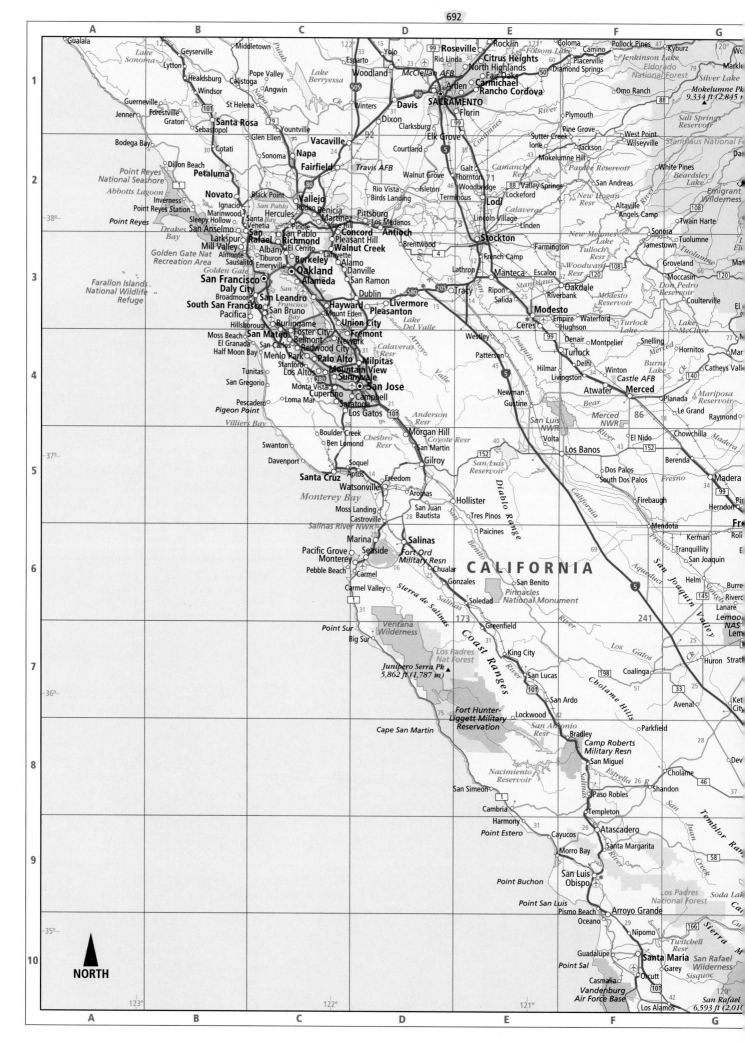

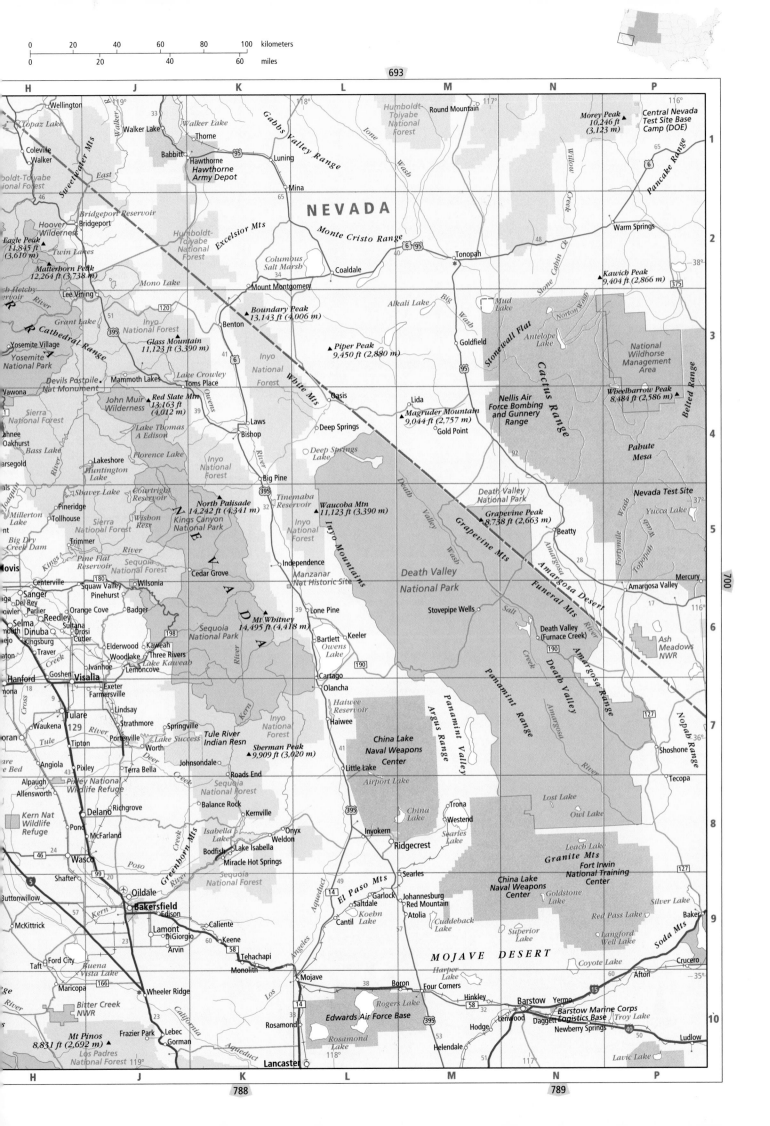

0 20 40 60 80 100 kilometers
0 20 40 60 miles

NEVADA

H J K L M N P

Wellington
Topaz Lake
Coleville
Walker
boldt-Toiyabe
ional Forest
Eagle Peak
11,845 ft
(3,610 m)
Twin Lakes
Matterhorn Peak
12,264 ft (3,738 m)
Hoover Wilderness
Bridgeport
Bridgeport Reservoir

Walker Lake
Thorne
Babbitt
Hawthorne
Hawthorne Army Depot
Luning
Mina
Coaldale

Humboldt-Toiyabe National Forest
Round Mountain
Morey Peak
10,246 ft
(3,123 m)
Central Nevada Test Site Base Camp (DOE)
Pancake Range
Warm Springs
Tonopah
Kawich Peak
9,404 ft (2,866 m)

Sweetwater Mts
East
Gabbs Valley Range
Excelsior Mts
Monte Cristo Range
Ione Wash
Stone Cabin Ck
Willow Creek

Yosemite Village
Yosemite National Park
Cathedral Range
Grant Lake
Lee Vining
Mono Lake
Inyo National Forest
Benton
Boundary Peak
13,143 ft (4,006 m)
Columbus Salt Marsh
Mount Montgomery
Glass Mountain
11,123 ft (3,390 m)
Piper Peak
9,450 ft (2,880 m)
Alkali Lake
Goldfield
Stonewall Flat
Antelope Lake
Mud Lake
Cactus Range
National Wildhorse Management Area
Belted Range
Wheelbarrow Peak
8,484 ft (2,586 m)

Devils Postpile Nat Monument
Mammoth Lakes
John Muir Wilderness
Red Slate Mtn
13,163 ft (4,012 m)
Lake Crowley
Toms Place
White Mts
Owens River
Oasis
Laws
Bishop
Deep Springs
Lida
Magruder Mountain
9,044 ft (2,757 m)
Gold Point
Nellis Air Force Bombing and Gunnery Range
Pabute Mesa

Sierra National Forest
Lakeshore
Huntington Lake
Shaver Lake
Courtright Reservoir
Big Pine
Deep Springs Lake
Death Valley
Nevada Test Site
Yucca Lake

Pineridge
Tollhouse
Trimmer
Wishon Resn
North Palisade
14,242 ft (4,341 m)
Kings Canyon National Park
Tinemaha Reservoir
Inyo National Forest
Waucoba Mtn
11,123 ft (3,390 m)
Inyo Mountains
Death Valley National Park
Grapevine Peak
8,738 ft (2,663 m)
Beatty
Grapevine Mts

ovis
Centerville
Sanger
Squaw Valley
Pinehurst
Big Dry Creek Dam
Pine Flat Reservoir
Sequoia National Forest
Cedar Grove
Independence
Manzanar Nat Historic Site
Death Valley National Park
Amargosa Desert
Mercury
Amargosa Valley

Del Rey
Parlier
Orange Cove
Badger
Kings River
Lone Pine
Mt Whitney
14,495 ft (4,418 m)
Stovepipe Wells
Death Valley (Furnace Creek)
Funeral Mts

Reedley
Sultana
Orosi
Cutler
Sequoia National Park
Bartlett
Keeler
Owens Lake
Ash Meadows NWR

Selma
Dinuba
Kingsburg
Elderwood
Kaweah
Three Rivers
Woodlake
Lake Kaweah
Lemoncove
Cartago
Olancha
Panamint Range
Amargosa Range

Hanford
Goshen
Visalia
Ivanhoe
Exeter
Farmersville
Haiwee Reservoir
Haiwee
Panamint Valley
Argus Range
Amargosa River
Nopah Range
Shoshone

Tulare
Waukena
Lindsay
Strathmore
Springville
Lake Success
Tule River Indian Resn
Sherman Peak
9,909 ft (3,020 m)
China Lake Naval Weapons Center
Tecopa

Tipton
Porterville
Worth
Terra Bella
Johnsondale
Little Lake
Airport Lake
Lost Lake
Owl Lake

Angiola
Pixley
Roads End
Balance Rock
China Lake
Trona
Westend
Searles Lake

Alpaugh
Allensworth
Pixley National Wildlife Refuge
Sequoia National Forest
Kernville
Inyokern
China Lake Naval Weapons Center
Leach Lake
Granite Mts
Fort Irwin National Training Center

Kern Nat Wildlife Refuge
Delano
Richgrove
Isabella Lake
Onyx
Weldon
Ridgecrest

Pond
McFarland
Bodfish
Lake Isabella
Miracle Hot Springs
Searles
El Paso Mts
Garlock
Johannesburg
Red Mountain
Atolia
China Lake Naval Weapons Center
Goldstone Lake
Red Pass Lake
Silver Lake

Wasco
Shafter
Greenhorn Mts
Sequoia National Forest
Saltdale
Koehn Lake
Cuddeback Lake
Superior Lake
Langford Well Lake
Baker

Oildale
Bakersfield
Edison
Lamont
DiGiorgio
Arvin
Caliente
Keene
Tehachapi
Monolith
Cantil
Mojave
MOJAVE DESERT
Harper Lake
Coyote Lake
Soda Mts
Crucero
Afton

McKittrick
Taft
Ford City
Buena Vista Lake
Wheeler Ridge
Maricopa
Bitter Creek NWR
Mt Pinos
8,831 ft (2,692 m)
Frazier Park
Lebec
Gorman
Los Padres National Forest
Aqueduct
Rosamond
Lancaster
Edwards Air Force Base
Rogers Lake
Boron
Four Corners
Hinkley
Hodge
Helendale
Barstow
Lenwood
Daggett
Newberry Springs
Barstow Marine Corps Logistics Base
Yermo
Troy Lake
Lavic Lake
Ludlow

MOUNTAINS AND THE WEST

Southeastern Nevada • Southern Utah • Northern Arizona

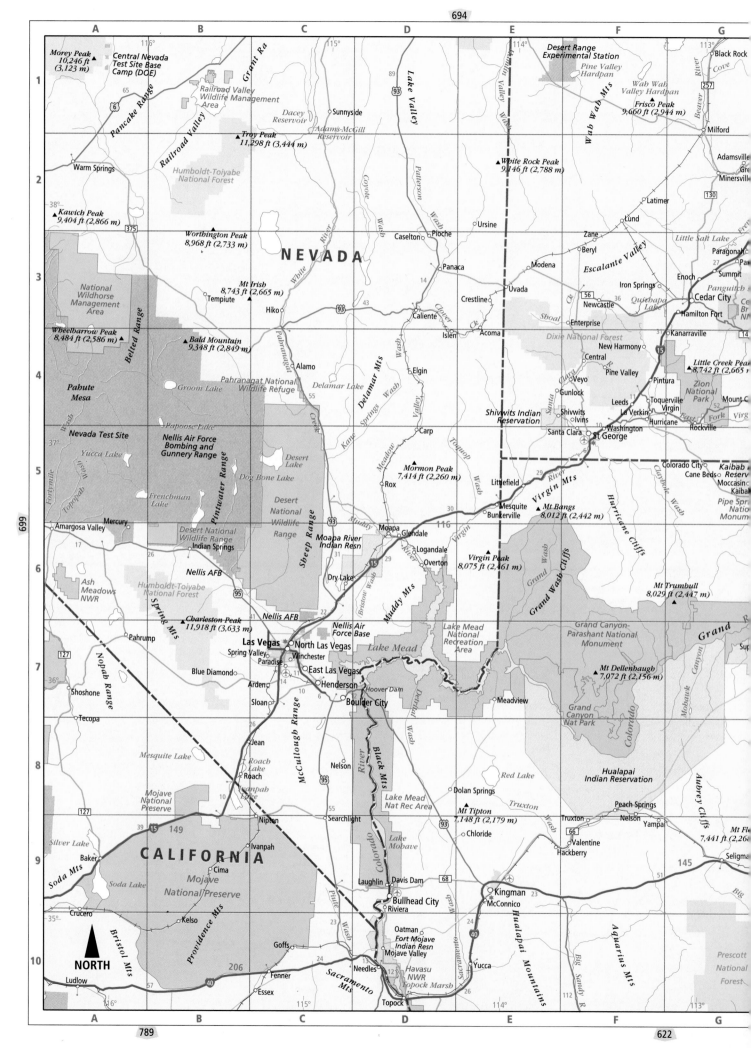

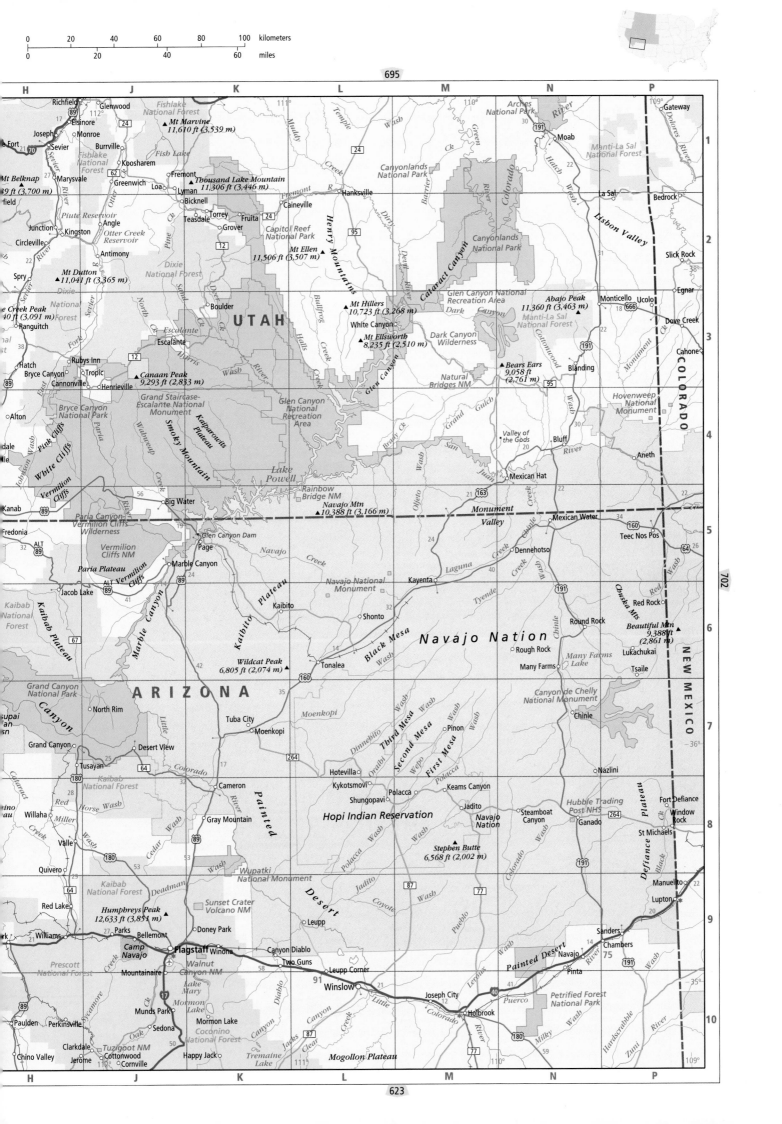

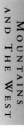

Southern Colorado • Northern New Mexico • Northwestern Texas

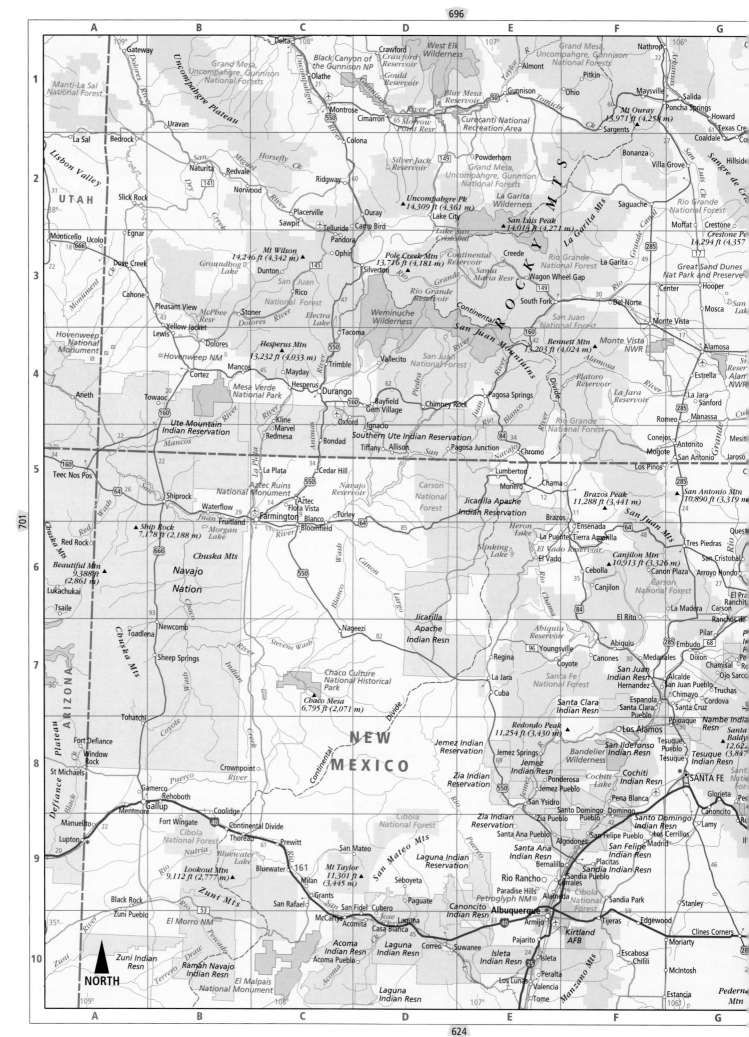

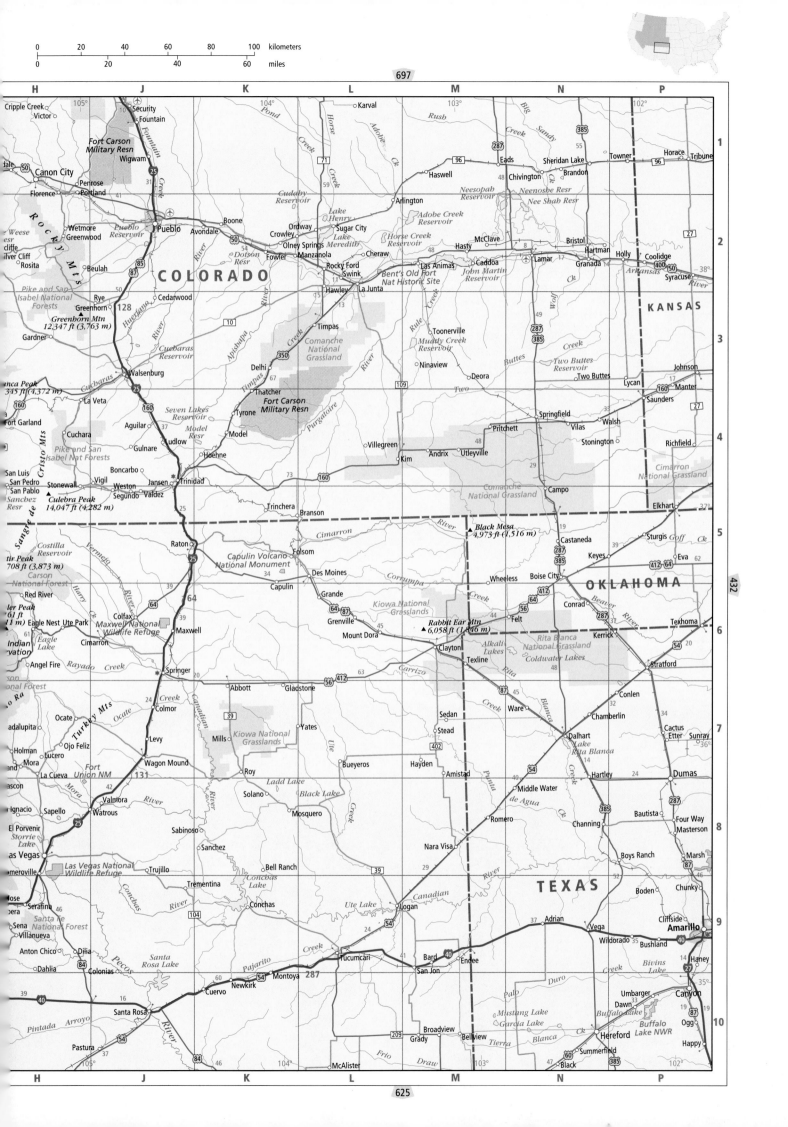

THE PACIFIC
STATES

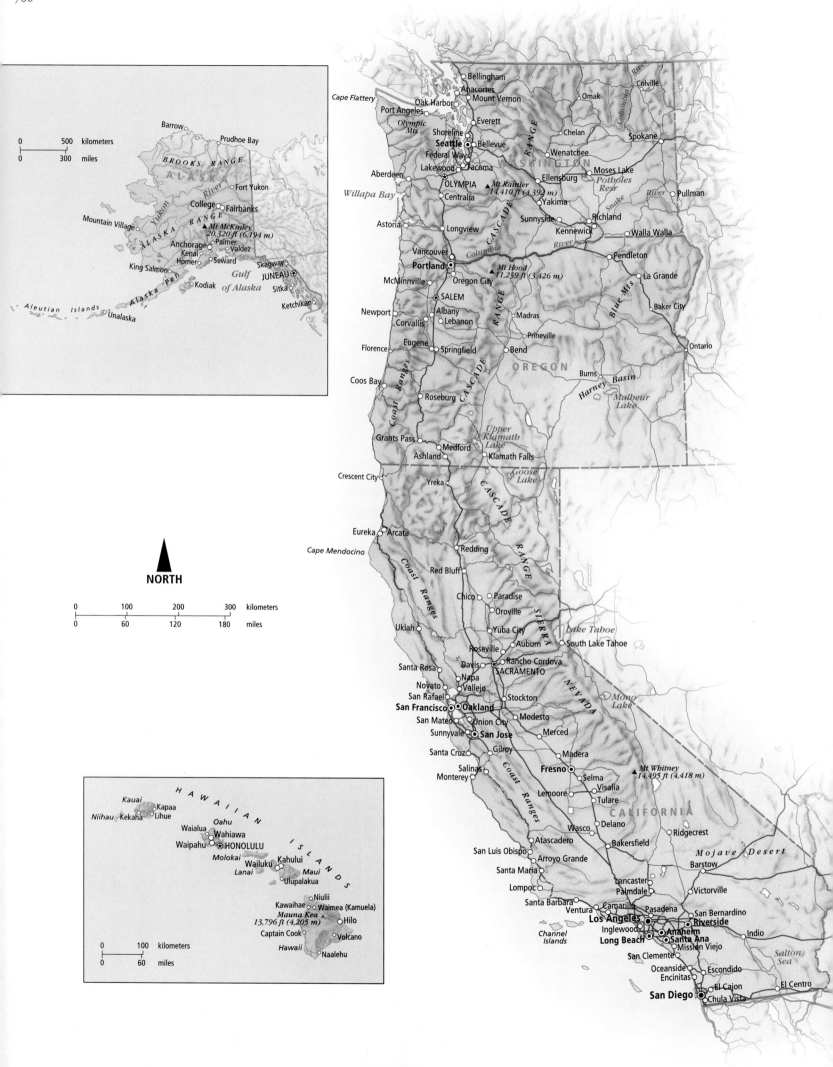

NORTH

| 0 | 100 | 200 | 300 | kilometers |
| 0 | 60 | 120 | 180 | miles |

Cape Flattery

Olympic Mts

Willapa Bay

Columbia River

Coast Ranges

Cape Mendocino

Coast Ranges

WASHINGTON

Mt Rainier 14,410 ft (4,392 m)

CASCADE RANGE

OREGON

Mt Hood 11,239 ft (3,426 m)

Blue Mts

Harney Basin
Malheur Lake

Upper Klamath Lake

Goose Lake

CASCADE RANGE

SIERRA NEVADA

Lake Tahoe

Mono Lake

CALIFORNIA

Coast Ranges

Mt Whitney 14,495 ft (4,418 m)

Mojave Desert

Salton Sea

Channel Islands

Alaska inset

| 0 | 500 | kilometers |
| 0 | 300 | miles |

BROOKS RANGE

ALASKA

Yukon River

ALASKA RANGE

Mt McKinley 20,320 ft (6,194 m)

Gulf of Alaska

Alaska Pen

Aleutian Islands

Hawaiian Islands inset

HAWAIIAN ISLANDS

Kauai
Niihau
Oahu
Molokai
Lanai
Maui
Hawaii

Mauna Kea 13,796 ft (4,205 m)

| 0 | 100 | kilometers |
| 0 | 60 | miles |

THE PACIFIC STATES

There is something undeniably appealing about the Pacific region. Each state in this region—Alaska, Washington, Oregon, California, and Hawaii—is a geological master-piece, with completely unique and dramatic natural features. No other region in the nation, perhaps even the world, expresses so vividly the raw, untamed power of nature, with its ancient volcanoes and violent earthquakes. Is this area the least developed in the nation? Perhaps, but that is a matter of opinion. For those who appreciate the beauty and bounty of earth, the Pacific States are, quite simply, paradise.

Alaska is the largest state in the nation, and the least populated. It is the only state with land in the Arctic Circle, and has more land in national parks, wilderness areas, and national wildlife refuges than all of the other states combined. Extremes of climate and topography combine to make this state "The Last Frontier." Because of its northern latitude, the variation in daylight hours between summer and winter is as great as that of Norway and Sweden. It has 50 active volcanoes, and 17 of the nation's 20 tallest mountains, including Mt McKinley in the Denali National Park and Preserve, the tallest peak in North America. The Yukon River, flowing across the interior, is one of the longest navigable rivers in the world. Fifteen percent of the human population is of Native American origin, and whales, bison, caribou, moose, reindeer, grizzly bears, black bears, and polar bears live here.

Washington, "The Evergreen State," is rich in un-usual natural contrasts. Western Washington is covered with dense forests and snow-covered mountains, and enjoys a temperate marine climate, while the eastern part, across the Columbia River and the Cascade Range, is arid, flat, and less temperate. Mt Rainier is the state's highest peak and is a dormant volcano, while Mt St Helens, also in the Cascade Range, erupted as recently as 1980. Eastern Washington produces more apples than any other state in the nation, and is begin-ning to make its mark as a top wine region.

Oregon has 11 national wildlife refuge areas, and is home to deer, elk, and antelope. Hells Canyon, carved out by the Snake River in northeastern Oregon, is the deepest gorge in America. One of the world's deepest and most strikingly beautiful lakes, Crater Lake, fills the caldera of the extinct Mt Mazama in the southwest. Mt Hood in the Cascade Range is a nationally recognized landmark, and Portland is the largest city. Oregon's significant agricultural zone is the Willamette Valley, which is a notable wine region recognized as a top producer of the varietal pinot noir. Oregon blackberries and raspberries are the finest in the nation.

California, "The Golden State," is the third-largest state in the nation, and has the largest population. It has the highest and lowest points on the United States mainland: Mt Whitney and Death Valley. Earthquakes are common due to the San Andreas Fault running through western California. The combination of coast-line and mountains in close proximity makes for an outdoor-lover's paradise. The nation's finest wine is produced here from grapes grown all along the coast and even from the inland Sierra Foothills. The varietal zinfandel is a specialty. San Francisco is an inter-nationally renowned culinary center.

Hawaii, "The Aloha State," is the southernmost US state and is the only island state. It is made up of an archipelago that extends across the central Pacific Ocean. The eight main islands—Niihau, Kauai, Oahu, Molokai, Lanai, Kahoolawe, Maui, and Hawaii (the Big Island)—are some of the least developed and most beautiful tropical destinations on the planet. The extinct volcanic craters Punch Bowl, Diamond Head, and Koko Head define Oahu's landscape. Maui was formed as the lava of two volcanoes, Haleakala and Puu Kukui, joined together in the sea. The Big Island is the youngest island and, with two active volcanoes and a hot spot, is still in formation, making Hawaii the only state in the nation that is growing physically.

Hawaii's beaches, particularly on the island of Oahu, draw surfers and boogie boarders from all over the world.

Designed by Joseph Strauss, San Francisco's Golden Gate Bridge is an enduring icon of this popular Californian city.

ALASKA

There is an overwhelming grandeur about this vast territory of 615,230 square miles (1,593,446 sq km) that can inspire feelings of both fear and euphoria. Although Alaska makes up a fifth of the United States (it is separated by western Canada from the Lower 48 states), its population is only 626,932. Its topography includes three million lakes, 1,800 islands, and 5,000 glaciers, including one glacier that is larger than Switzerland. Alaska has 17 of the country's 20 highest peaks, including the highest in North America, Mt McKinley, and nine national parks and preserves.

In most of Alaska, summers are a mixture of long days and short nights. In late June and July, even after the sun has set, dusk still allows for good visibility. Conversely, winter is locked in by the darkness of long nights and comparatively brief episodes of light.

Anchorage, located in the south-central part of the state, and Fairbanks, in the interior where McKinley rises, are the two largest cities. The rest of the state is made up of the southeast archipelago, with the state capital of Juneau; the Inside Passage; the Arctic to the north, home to the Inuit (Eskimo) culture; and the pristine and remote southwest, with its tundra, volcanoes, and Aleutian and Kodiak Islands.

An impressive wooden sculpture by artist Peter Toth commemorates Alaska's Native American history in Valdez.

During the ice age 30,000 to 40,000 years ago, nomads crossed the land bridge linking Siberia and Alaska. Their descendants are the five tribes of Native Americans that are still living here today. The Russians occupied the land for its tremendous bounty of fur for more than a century. Its purchase by the United States from the Russians for less than two cents an acre (0.405 ha) in 1867 may well be the best land buy of all time.

Natural resources and wildlife have always driven Alaska's economy, especially gold, oil, and salmon. In summer, tourism is the second-largest industry. Hazards include mosquitoes and bears which should be watched from a safe distance.

State motto North to the future
State flag Adopted 1927
Capital Juneau
Population 626,932
Total area (land and water)
615,230 square miles (1,593,446 sq km)
Land area 570,374 square miles
(1,477,269 sq km)
Alaska is the largest state in size
Origin of name From the Aleut word meaning "Great Land" or "that which the sea breaks against"
Nicknames The Land of the Midnight Sun, The Last Frontier
Abbreviation AK (postal), Alas.
State bird Willow ptarmigan
State flower Forget-me-not
State tree Sitka spruce
Entered the Union January 3, 1959 as the 49th state

There are few traffic jams to frustrate the visitor in Alaska, even here, near Anchorage, a city of a quarter of a million people.

Places in ALASKA

ANCHORAGE

With about 40 percent of the state's population, Anchorage is the metropolitan launching pad for Alaska's outdoor wonders. A city of 250,000 people, it is embraced by the Knik and Turnaggain arms of the Cook Inlet. A plain-looking collection of buildings, Anchorage is redeemed by its handsome mountain vistas. Most visitors to Alaska fly into the city for business or tourist itineraries, or pass through on wheels, as the city is the hub of the state's road system. A number of bus and van companies provide service to most places in the state that are accessible by road. The Alaska Railroad runs daily services to Fairbanks and Denali National Park, except for mid-September to mid-May, when it runs only on Saturdays.

Anchorage is relatively dry compared to much of the rest of the state as the Kenai Mountains north of the city protect it from heavy rainfall. The natural bowl in which Anchorage is located also excludes it from the extreme conditions of the interior so that average winter temperatures are freezing but well above zero degrees Fahrenheit (–17.8°C), and in the height of summer remain in the 60° to 70°F (15.5° to 21°C) range, whereas the interior can range from 90° to –60°F (32.2° to –51.1°C).

Visitors may be surprised to find that, despite being surrounded by wilderness, Anchorage is a sophisticated place, offering the comforts and attractions enjoyed by many larger US cities. It offers good lodging, cultural activities, and plenty of entertainment.

Sometimes the wilderness creeps in and wolves and moose are seen in the middle of the city. Nearby are glaciers, mountains, hiking trails, and whitewater rivers. The Kenai Peninsula as well as several state and national preserves offer many outdoor activities, such as camping, hiking, and fishing and are only a few hours away by car. Many local companies offer cruises, float, and air trips to nearby rivers, islands, glaciers, and bays, as well as railway visits to Denali National Park, 237 miles (381 km) away.

In 1778 Captain James Cook sailed up what would become known as Cook Inlet searching for the Northwest Passage. Later, with the arrival of the Alaska Railroad, a city was founded in 1914. Agriculture in the Matanuska Valley attracted farmers in the 1930s, and the population further expanded when military bases were set up here during World War II. The discovery of oil in Prudhoe Bay in 1968 also increased community numbers.

There were setbacks, such as the largest earthquake ever recorded in the Western Hemisphere—9.2 on the Richter Scale—which struck in 1964, devastating the entire city, but the oil boom revitalized the economy and Anchorage now wields rare political clout, often vying with its chief rival, Fairbanks, for favorable state budgets.

Anchorage is the starting point for the famous Iditarod Trail Sled Dog Race which begins the first Saturday in March. Husky dogs pull sleds driven by "mushers" from here over the Alaska Range and across frozen Norton Bay—a distance of 1,161 miles (1,868 km)— arriving in Nome nearly two weeks later.

The Alaska Aviation Heritage Museum displays 39 vintage aircraft, memorabilia, and photographs that chronicle the history of aviation in Alaska, a place where air transport is vital for everyday survival. A domed screen

at the Alaska Experience Center shows footage of the state filmed from planes, river rafts, and trains and there is an earthquake exhibit.

Located on a site of 26 wooded acres (10 ha), the Alaska Native Heritage Center presents information about the Native American groups who inhabit Alaska. There is a gathering place for storytelling, and dance and musical performances, as well as a theater for films. The Hall of Cultures focuses on traditions and customs such as moose-hunting, weaving, fishing, philosophy, and dancing, and displays replicas of different dwellings.

The outstanding Anchorage Museum of History and Art presents exhibits on the art, history, and cultures of Alaska. Objects in the Alaska Gallery date from prehistoric times through European exploration, Russian settlement, the Gold Rush, World War II, and statehood in 1959. Visitors can see drawings, paintings, and a display of the Alaska Pipeline. As well, full-scale dioramas illustrate an Athabaskan tent, Yupik, Tlingit, and Aleut houses, examples of a goldminer's cabin and a typical early Anchorage house, moose boats, and some Quonset huts from World War II.

Map ref: page 779 J6

Captain Cook explored Alaska in 1778.

BARROW

The town of Barrow (population 4,380) is a remote place 340 miles (547 km) north of the Arctic Circle. This far north, the sun does not go below the horizon for 82 days from early May to early August or rise above the horizon for 51 days between November and January.

Barrow is home to the largest number of Inupiaq people in the state, making it one of the largest communities in North America. The town is expensive to reach, being accessible only by plane and the flight from Anchorage is 700 miles (1,126 km). Although residents have embraced modern conveniences such as satellite TV, gas heating, and snowmobiles, traditional local customs such as the use of husky sleds continue to some extent and the spring whale hunts here remain popular.

Amateur softball is big in what would seem to be an unlikely and unnatural spot for the game. A styrofoam pad is placed over the infield at the $1 million Piuraagvik Park to prevent the frozen ground from turning into a quagmire, although players have to watch out for the occasional polar bear.

Point Barrow, a narrow spit about 12 miles (19 km) northeast of the city, divides the Chukchi Sea to the west from Beaufort Sea to the east. In winter and spring, polar bears hole up in dens there.

The Inupiaq Heritage Center in town houses a museum and library, and stages traditional dance performances. Museum exhibits focus on the Inupiaq culture, commercial whaling, and ice-age animals such as mammoths which once inhabited the area of Alaska and Siberia known as Beringa.

In late June, the Nalukataq Festival is held featuring whale dishes and sealskin blanket tosses. This can last for a few days to more than a week, depending upon the success of the spring whale hunt.
Map ref: page 779 H1

FAIRBANKS

With a metropolitan population of 83,770, the second-largest city in Alaska is low-rise and sprawling. Despite its somewhat ordinary appearance, it has a certain charm and many log cabins can be seen tucked into the trees, as well as a sizeable population of sled dogs.

Located at the center of the state, Fairbanks is the military, transportation, and market core of the interior. Prudhoe Bay, the oil gusher, lies 390 miles (627 km) north.

The Alaska Hwy was constructed in 1943 as an emergency passage for American troops following Japanese occupation of the Aleutian Islands during World War II. In

addition to troops, Native Americans, prospectors, and fur traders also worked on the road, completing it in just eight months. Later, 70 companies and 16,000 civilians labored to turn it into a year-round, all-weather route.

The highway is now much used as a scenic tour and provides travelers with spectacular views of the Alaskan wilderness starting in Canada at Dawson Creek, British Columbia, through the Yukon Territory and Delta Junction to Fairbanks. Spruce forests, mountain passes, lakes, rivers, and glacial ice formations, as well as bears, moose, and other wildlife, can be seen.

Fairbanks was founded in 1901 when Tanacross goldfield supplier E.T. Barnette became stranded by low rivers and set up a trading post. Shortly afterwards, an Italian prospector called Felix Pedro found gold nearby. The word spread and by 1908, more than 18,000 people had settled in the Fairbanks Mining District. The railroad arrived in 1923, reviving the flagging gold industry by bringing in much-needed dredges. Eventually, more than US $200 million in gold-sourced revenue was made here.

World War II attracted military construction and personnel, but with the 1973–77 construction of the Trans-Alaska Pipeline the city hit the economic jackpot. Subsequently it tumbled economically until tourism and the Fort Knox Gold Mine, just north of the city, provided a boost in the 1990s. In 1998 Fort Knox produced US$170 million worth of gold.

Part of Fairbanks' appeal lies in the independence and individuality of its residents. Compared to other Alaskan cities, it is a more affordable place to stay than Anchorage, if not as charming or as picturesque as Homer and Juneau, with their decorative mountains, glaciers, and seas. Summers here are pleasant but winters are cruel, with temperatures dropping to as low as –60°F (–51.1°C). The Northern Lights, a solar-powered light show in the upper atmosphere, appear here an average 240 nights a year.

Downtown Fairbanks features Golden Heart Plaza, a park on the river with a statue commemorating an Athabascan family. Historic buildings of interest include the log St Matthew's Episcopal Church and the Immaculate Conception

Fast-flowing, snow-fed rivers, stately trees, and impressive mountain scenery are abundant in Alaska's picture-postcard wilderness.

This saloon bar, near Fairbanks, harks back to Alaska's lively gold rush days when entertainment was much in demand.

Church, set off by its attractive stained glass windows. Early artifacts are displayed in the Fairbanks Community Museum.

Alaskaland, a pioneer theme park, is the city's largest attraction. Displays include the *Nenana*, a former sternwheeler in the Yukon River fleet, the railroad car that carried President Harding to the golden spike ceremony to celebrate the completion of the railroad in 1923, and a century-old carousel that still offers rides. Also on the premises are a gold rush town, the Pioneer Air Museum and a Native Village Museum. The Palace Saloon offers visitors entertainment and a noted salmon bake.

The University of Alaska, Fairbanks (UAF) is known especially for its research into agriculture and mining. It is worth visiting the campus not only for its impressive museum, but also, when weather conditions are favorable, for its extensive views across the Tanana Valley. The University Museum has interesting displays examining the geology, history, and special aspects of the area. Its most famous exhibit is Blue Babe, a 36,000-year-old bison preserved by permafrost. The university's Agricultural Experimental Farm produces enormous vegetables as well as researching crops that are able to thrive in the harsh conditions of the very short Alaskan growing season.

Eight miles (13 km) north of the city there is a viewing spot for the Trans-Alaska Pipeline, which carries a daily flow of 1.5 million barrels of oil to Valdez. The Alyeska Pipeline Visitor Center is located here. Other attractions include

panning for gold at Gold Dredge No. 8 and the El Dorado Gold Mine and three-hour trips on the sternwheeler *Discovery III* which navigates the Chena and Tanana Rivers. Guides discuss wildlife, history, anthropology, geology, and local customs. There is a stop at an Athabascan village, and impressive views of the surrounding wilderness.

Thirteen miles (21 km) northeast of Fairbanks on Steese Hwy is the National Oceanic and Atmospheric Administration Satellite Tracking Station, which has been important to the US space program. It tracks, commands, and receives telemetry and imagery data from polar-orbiting, Earth-observing satellites which are used to gather data for global environmental monitoring and weather forecasting. Guided tours are available to visitors here.

Fairbanks is the northern terminus of the Alaska Railroad and the 1,523-mile (2,450-km) Alaska Hwy, 360 miles (579 km) from Anchorage on the George Parks Hwy. It can also be easily reached by bus, train, or plane.
Map ref: page 779 K5

GATES OF THE ARCTIC NATIONAL PARK AND PRESERVE

Bob Marshall, a forester who came upon this uncharted region in the late 1920s and was struck by its wild and untouched character, gave this spectacular national park its name. The area possesses tundra and peaks so far away and relatively little-known that they still appear newly discovered. It is certainly a

long way from anywhere. The park is 200 miles (322 km) northwest of the city of Fairbanks, and extends 200 miles (322 km) from east to west, north of the Arctic Circle. It is a magnificent, challenging area of pristine wilderness that contains not a single campground, outhouse, or trail. Although it is undeniably austere in winter, in summer the landscape comes alive briefly with the emergence of a profusion of colorful wildflowers.

The rocky spine of the Brooks Range forms the backbone for this raw and sometimes forbidding landscape of sparse vegetation and jagged spires. The boreal forest or taiga, composed of spruce, birch, and poplar that clothes its slopes, meets the tundra that rolls down to the Arctic Ocean.

An abundance of wildlife may be seen here including caribou, moose, wolves, wolverines, dall sheep, and grizzly bears, which roam the 13,125-square-mile (33,994-sq-km) park in search of food. Anglers may find lake trout in the larger, deeper lakes, and grayling and arctic char can be hooked in the clear streams. Canoeing and rafting the lakes and rivers, along with hiking, are popular. The Dalton Hwy runs 100 miles (161 km) up the eastern edge of the park, maintaining a distance of about 5 miles (8 km) away, and is the closest roadway. To get here, most visitors use air charter services from Fairbanks or Bettles, a small airstrip village located just south of the eastern end of the park.

The park's visual magnets are Frigid Crags and Boreal Mountain, and the Arrigetch Peaks, which are reached by a floatplane trip to Circle Lake west of Bettles.
Map ref: page 779 J3

GLACIER BAY NATIONAL PARK AND PRESERVE

Glacier Bay National Park is a magnificent ice and water-scene, set off by a spectrum of different blues that lies beneath some of the tallest mountains in Alaska. The park is 3.3 million acres (1,336,500 ha), located 50 miles (80 km) west of Juneau and may be reached only by airplane or boat. It receives more than 300,000 annual visitors, of which 90 percent arrive aboard a cruise ship and never leave the boat. Tour groups, independent travelers, and kayakers can stay at the public campground, the park lodge, or at lodgings in nearby Gustavus.

Glacier Bay has changed dramatically and relatively quickly over the years, providing much interesting information for geologists and naturalists. Captain George Vancouver recorded his impressions of the glacier when he sailed through Icy Strait in 1774. When explorer John Muir arrived in 1879, he found that the end of the glacier had retreated 20 miles (32 km). Today, the glacier named after him has retreated a further 40 miles (64 km). This retreat has made it possible to observe the dynamics of plant succession, as lichens, mosses, and then grasses create soils eventually suited for more complex plants such as fireweed and blueberries.

The beauty and the diversity of the glaciers in Glacier Bay continue to attract visitors today. Blue-white ice flows from the snow-clad peaks of Fairweather Range to the fjord-like inlets of the park, making it

A modern building on the George Parks Hwy echoes a traditional shape.

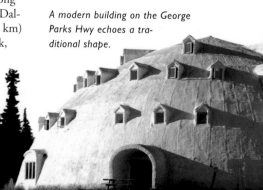

one of the most scenic spots in Alaska. The bay, beneath the mass of 15,320-foot (4,673 m) Mt Fairweather, is 65 miles (105 km) long and 2–10 miles (3–16 km) wide. Sometimes thunderous booms can be heard as icebergs crack off, or calve, from vertical ice cliffs, marking the continuing glacial retreat.

As impressive as the geology are the northern Pacific marine mammals—killer, humpback, and minke whales, sea otters and seals—and the land animals, which include moose, wolves, grizzly and black bears, mountain goats, black-tailed deer, lynx, mink, and beaver. The bay has more than 200 bird species and is also rich in fish such as halibut, Dolly Varden, and salmon. The scenery is a contrast of thick spruce and hemlock forests, bare shores exposed by glaciers, flat terrain around the village of Gustavus, and the inlet filled with icebergs.

Because of fears that ever increasing numbers of visitors in the area were causing a drop in the whale population, in 1978 the National Park Service reduced cruise ship visits. Congress then increased the number. As a result, the park service took further measures and designated Muir Island as wilderness water, off-limits to large boats.

The largest ever-recorded sea wave took place in the park in 1958 when a colossal water rise in Lituya Bay climbed approximately 1,740 feet (530 m)—the height of a 140-story building—up the side of Cenotaph and Spur Islands, stripping away the trees, plants, animals, and soil on their surface so that only slick bedrock remained.

Gustavus, a settlement of 400 people, is the service center for the park. It has lodges, inns, and B&Bs, as well as a landing strip for planes flying in from Juneau and elsewhere. The park has a campground and the 55-room Glacier Park Lodge. Hiking, kayaking, fishing, and the nine-hour trip up the West Arm on the *Spirit of Adventure*, a 220-passenger catamaran, are popular activities.

Map ref: page 779 M8

JUNEAU

The Alaskan capital is a beautiful enclave beneath massive rock and forest walls that cannot be reached by road but is accessible by plane and the Inside Passage vehicle ferries, which make regular stops here. Island-hopping on the ferryboats is a fascinating and inexpensive way to explore the Inside Passage, which

is a romantically rugged tongue of water filled with straits, channels, and sounds that writhes along about 1,000 miles (1,609 km) of coastline north from Puget Sound in Washington State to Skagway in southern Alaska.

Juneau has a population of 30,850 with a rare indigenous and cosmopolitan blend that makes it different to anywhere else in Alaska. Its high-rise buildings, cultural halls, legislative chambers, and shopping malls are enwrapped by sprawling glaciers and snow-capped peaks, and offset by the cold blue sea. Narrow streets run past a mixture of new and old buildings and houses with steeply slanting roofs, linked by staircases. Cruise ships, fishing boats, kayakers, and floatplanes fill an active waterfront. This is a city abundant in wildlife. Just a short distance from the Governor's Mansion, grizzly bears can sometimes be seen plucking berries.

Juneau began as a disorganized mining camp. In 1880 a couple of

itinerant miners discovered gold in a stream that runs through what is now the middle of town to Gastineau Channel. They staked out the area and others quickly followed. The town which sprung up was named after one of the two lucky prospectors, Joe Juneau, and prospered, producing enormous quantities of gold. In 1906, when Sitka began to lose its influence as its local industries of whaling and fur trapping went into decline, it was decided to move the capital of Alaska here. Nearly US$100 million worth of gold was mined here before the mines closed in 1944. Although small in population, Juneau is large in area. Its territory encompasses an area of 3,100 square miles (8,029 sq km) and reaches the Canadian border. The busy center of town includes the State Capitol and St Nicholas, a fabulous-looking Russian Orthodox church, established in 1894. The Juneau–Douglas City Museum has interesting displays of the town's gold-mining history. The Alaska State Museum focuses on Native American artifacts and Juneau's Russian history, as well as providing information on gold strikes around the state, and the Trans–Alaska Pipeline. The influential career of one of Juneau's eminent past residents, Judge James Wickersham (1857–1939), a collector of ivory carvings and Alaska's delegate to Congress, is presented at the Wickersham State Historical Site, where Wickersham lived.

Mining enthusiasts are well catered for in this area. Two miles (3 km) from the city center the Last Chance Mining Museum displays a collection of mining equipment. Visitors can also explore the Glory Hole Mineshaft, Treadwell Mine Ruins, and the Alaska–Juneau Mine.

Juneau is a good base for hiking. The 4-mile (7-km) Mt Roberts Trail leads to the peak above the city. Cruise ship visitors can take a tram there, where they will find a restaurant, theater, and alpine hiking trails. The Perseverance Trail, reached by walking up Basin Road

Statue at Juneau's State Capitol Building.

Juneau's waterfront on the Gastineau Channel is a busy marine highway for ferries, fishing boats, tankers, and cruise ships.

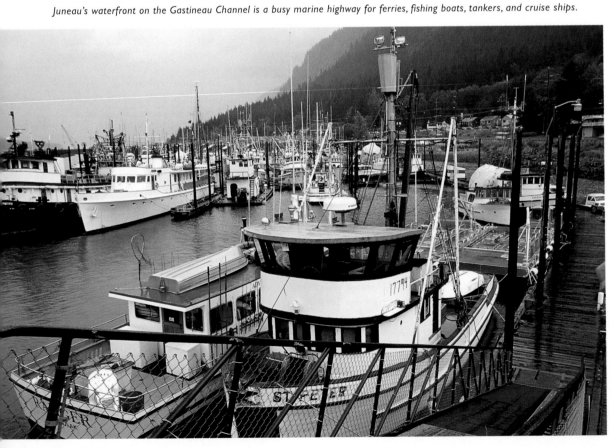

Awe-inspiring glaciers and icefields abound in southeast Alaska's magnificent scenery. This area, around the state capital, Juneau, is known as "Gateway to the Glaciers."

from the center of town, leads through a coastal rainforest of towering spruce and hemlock trees above lush ground cover and blueberries as it continues on to the 3,576-foot (1,091-m) Mt Juneau. Other trails exist in nearby Mendenhall Valley and on Douglas Island, across Gastineau Channel.

Juneau is famous for its glaciers and the nearest, Mendenhall Glacier, is only 13 miles north (21 km) from the city center. It extends 12 miles (19 km) from its source, the Juneau Ice Field. Luminous shades of blue can be seen within the glacier ice, backed by a panorama of snow-capped mountains. The US Forest Service Visitor Center nearby has exhibits, a large relief map of the area, and various film and slide presentations in its theater. Lemon Creek Glacier, Herbert Glacier, and Eagle Glacier also lie north of Juneau. It is possible to drive to Lemon Creek by car, and Herbert and Eagle Glaciers can be reached via hiking trails.

Map ref: page 779 N8

KATMAI NATIONAL PARK AND PRESERVE

Located 300 miles (483 km) southwest of Anchorage on the Alaska Peninsula, Katmai is famous for having the largest protected population of brown bears in the world —more than 2,000 live there. This 4.3-million-acre (1,741,500-ha) park and preserve is almost twice the size of Yellowstone, the largest national park in the Lower 48 states.

Its other claim to fame is a volcanic eruption of such power that it was estimated to be ten times greater than the explosion of Mt St Helens in Washington State in 1980. Following a week of severe earthquakes in 1912, the Novarupta volcano erupted with such force that the top of the mountain was blown off, firing huge amounts of pumice, ash, and rock across the landscape. It had a devastating and long-term effect on the immediate environment and its inhabitants. Nearby, a valley was completely buried in 700 feet (214 m) of

debris. The subsequent blasts of lava, gas, pumice, and ash filled the atmosphere with haze lasting for weeks and lowered the temperature by 2 degrees over the following year. Further afield, people from as far away as Vancouver, Canada (at least 1,000 miles or 1,609 km), reported that the acid rain from the blast had caused clothes to fall apart while drying on clotheslines.

Four years later, Robert Griggs explored the smoldering territory for the National Geographic Society, and named the primary scene of destruction The Valley of Ten Thousand Smokes. This valley is the centerpiece of the park, which has eight major river systems and 15 volcanoes within its boundaries. It includes glaciated volcanoes, lakes with many islands, and a coastline of bays, fjords, and beaches. As well as its famous bears, moose, sea lions, arctic foxes, and wolves live here. Katmai also has some of the best fishing in the state for grayling, northern pike, rainbow trout, and sockeye salmon.

Adult brown bears feast on the plentiful salmon in the park and may reach weights of more than 1,000 pounds (454 kg). They can be watched from observation platforms at Brooks Camp and nearby

Moose (Alces alces) live in Katmai NP.

The dramatic sweep of the Alaska Range can be seen across Cook Inlet, to the southwest of Kenai, in south-central Alaska.

Exit Glacier, which is easy to reach by car, receives many visitors. Also worth seeing is one of the largest ice fields in North America, Harding Ice Field, which is about 50 miles (80 km) long, 30 miles (48 km) wide, and as much as 16 feet (5 m) deep. Mountaineers equipped with skis, ice axes, and crampons can explore the field itself, while hikers can observe it from the edge. Around the area there are nature, glacier, and ice-field trails to take.

Seward (population 3,000) is the park's gateway. It's an attractive town flanked by rugged snow-capped mountains on one side and deep-blue Resurrection Bay on the other. In 1964 a tidal wave over 100 feet (30 m) high obliterated the town's seafront, which has since been nicely rebuilt with wood-frame houses and gardens. Despite its pretty location, Seward is notorious for its year-round harsh conditions. It is 127 miles (204 km) from Anchorage, and is accessible by car, bus, or ferryboat, and, May to September, by train.
Map ref: page 779 J7

McNeil River State Game Sanctuary. In July as many as 40 bears can be seen congregating along half a mile of the Brooks River, and up to 60 may gather at Brooks Falls and along the McNeil River.

Hiking and backpacking are good ways to see the park's unusual back country. There is excellent kayaking and canoeing in the area and to Bay of Islands, 30 miles (48 km) from Brooks Camp.

The park is only accessible by air, and commercial airlines fly into King Salmon, a village of some 500 people, most of them park service employees. The King Salmon Visitor Center, which has books, maps, and displays of the area, is located next to the terminal. From there it is a 47-mile (76-km) flight by amphibious aircraft to Brooks Camp, on the shores of Naknek Lake, the summer headquarters of the park. Camping reservations are taken by phone beginning on the first working day of January, and camp sites for the prime bear-viewing month of July are usually snapped up in the first three or four days. Within the park is Brooks Lodge, which offers cabins for rental and has a store for supplies.
Map ref: page 779 H8

KENAI

Established by Russian fur traders in 1791, this is the second oldest permanent settlement in Alaska. The town of 6,300 is located at the mouth of the Kenai River on Cook Inlet, 158 miles (254 km) from Anchorage, and can be reached by car, bus, or plane. It has excellent views of the Alaska Range and of active volcanoes across the inlet—Mt Redoubt and Mt Iliamna—at the head of the Aleutian Range.

Kenai has the largest oil industry presence outside of Prudhoe Bay. Across the inlet, 15 oil platforms pump out 42,000 barrels a day. The Kenai Peninsula is also known for its summer berry picking. There is an amazing variety, including Alaska blueberries, nagoonberries, cloudberries, salmonberries, crowberries, northern red currants, wild raspberries, and cranberries.
Map ref: page 779 J7

KENAI FJORDS NATIONAL PARK

This 587,000-acre (237,735-ha) stretch of land between Seward and Point Graham on the southeastern edge of the Kenai Peninsula is distinctive for its rocky narrow inlets, or fjords—a dream for those who love kayaking in rugged scenery. In the deep cold fjords lives an abundance of marine wildlife which includes sea otters, harbor seals, Pacific dolphins, harbor porpoises, sea lions, and killer, gray, humpback, and minke whales.

KETCHIKAN

Ketchikan is the first Alaskan city north of Canada. It is 90 miles (145 km) from Prince Rupert, and being accessible only by water, it is a regular ferryboat and cruise ship stop. Its population of 8,000 lives on the southwest of Revillagigedo

An old Ninilchik village on Cook Inlet, near Kenai, originally settled by Russians.

Floatplanes can reach areas not accessible by road in Alaska's rugged interior.

Island, separated from the mainland by Behm Canal. It is the wettest community in North America, with an average rainfall of between 156 and 162 inches (390–405 cm). To avoid floods, many businesses and homes rest on stilts or cling to hillsides. Winding staircases and wooden boardwalks provide access.

This is a fishing, canning, and logging town, though tourism is also important to the economy. It contains the largest number of Tlingit and Tsimshian people in the country and displays many totem poles. At the Deer Mountain Tribal Hatchery and Eagle Center, 150,000 king (chinook) and coho (silver) salmon are raised and released into the wild each year.

Misty Fjords National Monument, an area of 3,570 square miles (9,246 sq km), begins 22 miles (35 km) east of Ketchikan. It is famous for its sea cliffs, rock walls, and steep fjords, and is home to many marine mammals, black bear, Sitka deer, and bald eagles.
Map ref: page 779 P9

KODIAK

Kodiak is the largest commercial fishing port in Alaska, and Kodiak Island is the largest island in Alaska. The city of Kodiak (population 14,000) is located on the northeastern tip. Conditions in the Gulf of Alaska influence the weather here, and fog, rain, and winds are common. Rainfall can be as much as 80 inches (200 cm) a year.

Kodiak was the first capital of Russian America in 1784, and displays the blue onion-shaped domes of the Holy Resurrection Russian Orthodox Church from that era. The Baranov Museum, in the Erskine House on the harbor, exhibits early Russian and Alaskan artifacts, and American household furnishings from the early twentieth century. Going back earlier in time, the Alutiiq Museum and Archeological Repository showcases 7,000 years of native culture with displays, galleries, exhibits, and a diorama of typical village life.

The Kodiak National Wildlife Refuge occupies the southwestern two-thirds of the island and preserves the habitat of the giant Kodiak brown bear (*Ursus arctos*). About 2,400 of these huge animals, which can grow up to around 1,500 pounds (680 kg), live on the island, which is also inhabited by Sitka black-tailed deer, tundra voles, sea lions, and bald eagles. The refuge is accessible only by plane and boat. Visitors can take narrated tours of the island.
Map ref: page 779 J8

LAKE CLARK NATIONAL PARK AND PRESERVE

This park of nearly 4 million acres (1,620,000 ha), located 100 miles (161 km) southwest of Anchorage, is well-known to backpackers, river runners, and anglers. The Alaska and Aleutian mountain ranges meet here in this natural wonderland of coastal rainforests and alpine tundra, active volcanoes and serene fjords, high mountain lakes and saltwater estuaries. The park encompasses numerous glaciers, dazzling turquoise lakes, and three designated wild rivers.

Local wildlife includes beluga and killer whales, moose, wolves, grizzly and black bears, dall sheep, and caribou. The salt and fresh waters of Lake Clark National Park offer some of the best fishing in North America. The Newahlen River is famous for its red salmon, the Iliamna River for its rainbow trout; Lake Clark and nearby Lake Iliamna yield the largest runs of sockeye salmon in the world. These go to Bristol Bay where there is some incredibly productive commercial fishing.

The only access is by charter plane from Anchorage to Iliamna, an attractive village located on the north end of Iliamna Lake, the largest lake in the state. From the village, air taxis can be arranged to specific destinations.
Map ref: page 779 H6

NINILCHIK

This village of 680 people is located between Homer and Soldotna on the Kenai Peninsula, about 185 miles (298 km) from Anchorage. It is a scenic area with good facilities—there are four state campgrounds and beaches where clams can be found. Russian descendants of those who worked for the Russian–American Company, which set up here in the 1820s, make up most of the population. The town was largely rebuilt following the 1964 earthquake although the old Russian Orthodox church here, which dates back to 1901, survived intact. It stands on a wide bluff that has a sensational view of Cook Inlet and the volcanic mountains across the water.
Map ref: page 779 J7

NOME

Nome (population 3,600) is located on the Seward Peninsula beside the Bering Sea in northwestern Alaska, more than 500 miles (805 km) from Anchorage, and is accessible only by air. A century ago it was a gold-rush town; today, it is a judicial and commercial center that supplies nearby mining districts and Inuit (Eskimo) villages. The extremely arduous annual Iditarod Trail Sled Dog Race commencing in Anchorage ends here for a special reason. The race commemorates the courageous emergency mission of a dogsled team in 1926 which carried the vital serum that snuffed out a diphtheria epidemic in Nome. It is 1,100-mile (1,770-km) in length. The race begins in early March so competitors often have to battle through blizzards, treacherous ascents, and even river passages.
Map ref: page 778 F4

PRUDHOE BAY

Prudhoe Bay is the center of operations for the Alyeska Pipeline Company, which sends the oil drilled here south by pipeline to Valdez on the Gulf of Alaska, where it is carried away by oil tankers. The town is on the Beaufort Sea on the northern edge of the state, 484 miles (779 km) north of Fairbanks via the Elliott and Dalton Hwys, and 844 miles (1,358 km) from Anchorage. More people live here than in any other Arctic town, with the

The attractive town of Sitka was called New Archangel when it was owned by Russia. It was known as the "Paris of the Pacific" in the mid-nineteenth century.

population rising to as much as 10,000 with the influx of seasonal workers. Bus tours to the city from nearby Deadhorse are available.

In 1968 Atlantic Richfield discovered massive oil deposits beneath Prudhoe Bay. A consortium of oil companies built the 789-mile (1,270-km) Trans–Alaska Pipeline, which took three years and US$8 billion to construct. It was completed in 1977. At the time it was the most expensive private construction project ever undertaken. The risk paid off as the oil turned out to be a bonanza for the next decade for the state as well as the oil companies, accounting for as much as 80 percent of state revenues. However, Alaskan oil (and its associated revenue) is now running out.
Map ref: page 779 K2

Old totem pole in Sitka.

SITKA NATIONAL HISTORIC PARK

This 107-acre (43-ha) park, with its handsome forest by the sea, is located east of the town of Sitka in the band of islands that make up southeast Alaska. A circular trail winds around 15 totem poles that were displayed in St Louis at the Louisiana Purchase Exposition in 1905. The Tlingit people were defeated here by the Russians in 1804 after defending a wooden fort for a week. The visitor center displays Russian and native artifacts, and carvers demonstrate their traditional arts.
Map ref: page 779 N8

SKAGWAY

Skagway is rather windy and dry relative to most of the state, with only about 26 inches (650 mm) of rain a year. The Klondike Gold Rush National Historical Park encloses the period

buildings and restored façades of Skagway, which was settled in the late nineteenth century by gold prospectors. As many as 40,000 people subsequently left from here to travel to the Yukon over the Chilkoot or White Pass Trails.

Visitors come to Skagway to experience its old-fashioned charm and to walk its picturesque mountain and glacier trails. The Skagway Overlook, a scenic lookout near the town, provides an excellent view of the settlement, its waterfront, and the nearby peaks.

Located at the northern end of the Inside Passage in southeast Alaska, Skagway is about 750 miles (1,207 km) from the city of Anchorage. It can be reached by car, bus, plane, train, or ferryboat.
Map ref: page 779 N7

TALKEETNA

About 90 miles (145 km) north of Anchorage, the village of Talkeetna (population 300) was once an important supply station for goldminers from the late 1800s to 1940, and today is a staging area for outdoor enthusiasts. It is near the confluence of the Susitna, Talkeetna, and Chulitna Rivers. The village derives its name from a Tanaina word which means "River of Plenty."

Every spring Talkeetna is headquarters for those climbing Mt

McKinley. Climbers board fixed-wing aircraft here for the flight to Great Gorge, where they establish base camps prior to their ascents. In the big-game hunting season, which most years runs from late August through early October, the 4,000-foot (1,220-m) paved airport runway becomes particularly busy. There is excellent salmon fishing in nearby creeks and rivers. For those interested in history, the Talkeetna Museum, located in an old red schoolhouse, has displays relating to the area. Every mid-summer, the village hosts a bluegrass festival.

Visitors can reach Talkeetna by car, bus, and train.
Map ref: page 779 J6

VALDEZ

This town of 4,100 (pronounced "Val*eez*") is located in the middle of Prince William Sound, 25 miles (40 km) east of the Columbia Glacier and 304 miles (489 km) to the east of Anchorage, and is ringed by snowcapped mountains. It is best known as the southern terminus of the Trans-Alaska Pipeline and 30 percent of its population works in pipeline-related jobs.

In 1964 an earthquake demolished the town, which was rebuilt on more stable ground 4 miles (6 km) west. After the pipeline had been completed in 1977, it began loading tankers with oil. In 1989 the area suffered an environmental disaster when the tanker *Exxon Valdez* ran aground on a reef and spilled its cargo of millions of gallons of oil into the waters of Prince William Sound.

In the town center the Valdez Museum has a number of interesting displays that include historic charts and maps of the Valdez area, a model of the pipeline, a nineteenth-century saloon bar, an early twentieth-century steam engine, a glacier exhibit, and first-hand descriptions of the earthquake.

Valdez is accessible by car, bus, plane, and ferryboat.

Map ref: page 779 K6

WRANGELL–ST ELIAS NATIONAL PARK AND PRESERVE

About 150 miles (240 km) east of Anchorage lies this 13-million-acre (5,265,000-ha) park, which is the

Wrangell–St Elias National Park has 9 of the 16 highest peaks in North America.

largest in the United States. Its massive ice fields affect places as far far south as Chicago and the Great Plains by acting as giant cooling systems. People lived in the area long ago. The Ahtna Dene (meaning "People of the Copper River")

and other Native American tribes forged their tools of locally mined copper here. Lieutenant Henry Allen explored much of Alaska's interior in 1885 and verified this source of copper trading. Fifteen years later, two miners discovered

the malachite cliffs above Kennicott Glacier. As a result, it became one of the richest sources of copper in the world when mined by Kennicott Copper Company. The great wealth and development it spawned affected not only the state of Alaska but also the entire nation. The flow of wealth came to an end when the plummeting price of copper forced the mines to close in 1938. Now only ruins remain of this once huge enterprise.

The Richardson and Glenn Hwys follow the park's western boundary and offer visitors spectacular views of the 12,010-foot (3,663-m) Mt Drum, Mt Wrangell which, at 14,163-foot (4,320-m), is the highest volcano in Alaska, and 16,163-foot (4,930-m) Mt Sanford. Fishing, hiking, rafting, and watching wildlife, particularly the park's large number of dall sheep, are popular. Access is by road and charter plane.

Map ref: page 779 L5

Columbia Glacier in Prince William Sound, near Valdez, is 42 miles (68 km) long, 3 miles (5 km) wide, 300 feet (91 m) high, and 440 square miles (1,140 sq km) in area.

STATE FEATURE

Denali National Park

Denali National Park is the highest and one of the most spectacular preserves in the United States, offering eye-popping views of lakes, peaks, wildlife, and tundra. At 20,320 feet (6,198 m) Denali's Mt McKinley is the highest peak in North America. In 1794 explorer George Vancouver saw the distant mountain covered with snow from Cook Inlet near Anchorage. The ancient Athabaskan people called it Denali, "The Great One." Other princely peaks include 17,400-foot (5,307-m) Mt Foraker, 13,220-foot Silverthrone (4,032-m) and Mt Russell, at 11,670-foot (3,559-m). It would be more than a century after Vancouver's glimpse before the interior of Alaska became more than a mystery to the outside world.

In 1896 prospector William Dickey took out his transit and made some crude measurements from the headwaters of the Chulitna River. He was amazed to discover that the peak in his viewfinder climbed more than 20,000 feet (6,100 m), making it the highest mountain north of the Andes. Much speculation followed about the presence of precious metals in the vertical relief and uplift of this staggering geography. In 1906 gold was discovered and the Kantishna gold stampede brought more than 2,000 miners into the Moose Creek and Wonder Lake area. As a result, the goldminers and those who hunted big game exploited this immense natural wonderland with no thought of preserving it for the future until self-made millionaire and conservationist Charles Sheldon intervened to protect it. It took a decade of determination and tireless pursuit of his dream for the philanthropical Sheldon to persuade President Woodrow Wilson to sign a bill that in 1917 established the area as a national park.

Once little-known due to its remoteness, today the summit of Mt McKinley is a treacherous, mountain-climbing prize for crampon and ice-axe enthusiasts from around the world. Several attempts at reaching the summit were made at the beginning of the last century, including one in 1910 by four climbers who styled themselves the Sourdough Expedition. They managed to scale the 19,470-foot (5,938-m) North Peak and thought they had reached the top. However, three years later, another four-man team made up of Episcopalian minister Hudson Stuck, Robert Tatum, Walter Harper, and Henry Karstens passed the 14-foot (4-m) flagpole left by the Sourdoughs and reached the South Peak—the real summit.

In the 1930s, against the wisdom of its expert advisor, zoologist Adolph Murie, the park service embarked on a drastic program of exterminating wolves so that the numbers of dall sheep, moose, and caribou would increase. As a result, caribou populations initially soared, but the survival of their weak, infirm, and old members later reduced their strength drastically, a fate from which they're still recovering.

In 1980 the Alaska National Interest Land Act enlarged the park from 4,000,000 to its present 6,000,000 acres (1,620,000–2,430,000 ha) and changed its name from McKinley to Denali National Park and Preserve. The mountain itself is still officially known as McKinley, although it is commonly referred to as Denali. Hunting is prohibited except for subsistence hunting by Native Americans in outer portions of the park.

Complementing the exceptional scenery is an impressive variety of wildlife that is the northern equivalent to

A willow ptarmigan (Lagopus lagopus) in his spring plumage blends in with the tundra snowscape in Denali National Park.

The icy spine of the Alaska Range towers over the subarctic landscape of one of the world's most spectacular national parks.

Africa's bounty. Thirty-seven species of mammal live in this 9,375-square-mile (24,280-sq-km) wilderness, including wolves, brown and black bears, caribou, and moose. It is possible to see some of these from the shuttle buses that traverse the territory, or during hiking and backpacking expeditions. As well, lynx, marmot, dall sheep, foxes, and snowshoe hares cavort beneath the gaze of the soaring golden eagle, one of approximately 130 bird species that have been spotted here.

Black and white conifers parade the ridgelines, with thickets of dwarf birch on lower slopes and valleys, and boggy meadows are interspersed with twisted and stunted black spruce. Higher up, forests give way to vast stretches of wet tundra that support shrubby plants above the permafrost. Even higher, blankets of dry alpine tundra rise into the clouds.

From late June to late August, Denali National Park is a busy and popular place, regardless of the cool weather which can include long periods of overcast skies and drizzle. Despite its size, Mt McKinley is elusive because clouds hide the summit about 75 percent of the summer and 60 percent of the year: on average, only 20 percent of visitors are fortunate enough to actually see the peak, which is an overwhelming sight as it rises from an elevation of 2,000 feet (610 m), so that more than three vertical miles (5 km) of rock, snow, and glaciers are visible.

Denali can be reached by car, bus, or train but entry into the park itself is restricted to shuttle buses, tour buses, official park vehicles, and cars of property owners. It is necessary to make reservations in advance, because about 65 percent of the bus seats and camp sites are taken in advance. Without a booking during the high season, a minimum of four days is needed to obtain a bus ticket, and four to seven days for interior camping and hiking.

In early June and September visitor numbers are not such a crucial factor. As well, September is a good month to visit because the bugs are less prevalent and the autumn foliage colors of reds and yellows are spectacular. However, shuttle buses stop running in the middle of the month with the coming of snow, returning at the start of June.

Shuttle buses run through the park with drivers doubling as park guides and naturalists. The 66-mile (106-km) trip to Eielson Visitor Center is an eight-hour round-trip journey, and the 88-mile (142-km) trip to Wonder Lake is an 11-hour round-trip. Hikers can get off buses to walk around and then flag down other buses to continue their motorized journeys, although available seats may be scarce during the high season.

Backpacking permits are issued only a day in advance from the Visitor Access Center and may take several days to secure. Cycling is increasingly popular in the park, with bicycle rentals available in the park and in Talkeetna. A bus ticket is not necessary for entering the park by bicycle. However, the subarctic climate, rough road, the gravel flung by bus wheels, and an occasional grizzly bear can make this a tougher adventure than many anticipate.

A number of campgrounds exist inside Denali. The Environmental Education and Science Center at the entrance was once the park hotel but now only camp sites are available for overnight stays. At the western end of the park are three places that are closed to wilderness lodges.

Camp Denali is a resort-type retreat that offers wildlife observation, photography, rafting, fishing, gold-panning, and hiking. Kantishna Roadhouse has 28 cabins, and offers gold-panning, hiking, and photography. Denali Backcountry Lodge is at the end of the road. These need to be booked well ahead of time. People arriving at the park without reservations are given a list of private lodgings outside the park, which include recreational vehicle parks, campgrounds, cabins, B&Bs, inns, and houses.

A number of activities take place near the park and good hiking trails exist near the park entrance. A dogsled exhibition is given every day at the kennels for the Denali dogsled team near the visitor center. The Class Three rapids of the Nenana River are located near the park entrance, and are run by several concessionaires. Flightseeing tours, either by helicopter or fixed-wing aircraft, are operated from near the park entrance.

Running east from the park for 135 miles (217 km) between Cantwell and Paxson is the largely unpaved Denali Hwy, which parallels the Alaska Range. Along the way are trails, canoe routes, campgrounds, and several traditional roadhouses that provide food, lodging, and gasoline. This is a good road for stopping for picnics, taking photos of scenery and wildlife, and for observing geological features. It also provides an opportunity to see the Alaska Range without park restrictions. Caribou, moose, dall sheep, grizzlies, black bears, wolves, foxes, coyotes, lynx, golden eagles, and ptarmigan can all be observed here and, with the exception of Mt McKinley, the subarctic scenery is similar to the park's. Much of the area along the road is managed by the Bureau of Land Management, which has a multiple purpose philosophy, rather than the national park philosophy of preserving land and wildlife with minimum human interference.

Nenana (population 435) is the only town between Denali and Fairbanks and is accessible by car, bus, and train. It is home to the Alaska State Railroad Museum, restored in 1988 and on the National Register of Historic Places. Outside the visitor center, a log cabin with a sod roof that is planted with flowers in the summer, is the *Taku Chief*, a river tugboat that pushed barges up the Tanana River. In town, fish wheels, traditional fish traps, scoop salmon out of the river as they swim upstream.

Denali seen from the south, with Mt McKinley, the highest peak in North America, in the background.

In Alaska the ground is frozen for most of the year, so many animals survive the winter by hibernating. Here, the Arctic ground squirrel (Citellus parryi) forages for food during the brief summer to lay in stores before going to sleep for nine months.

CALIFORNIA

California is the third-largest state in the United States and has the largest population, 93 percent of whom live in urban areas. The largest cities, in order, are Los Angeles, San Diego, San Jose, San Francisco, and Long Beach. The state motto—"*Eureka!*"—refers, by some accounts, to gold, and by others to a popular sixteenth-century Spanish novel describing a fantasy island called California.

Spaniards, Mexicans, English, Russians, and the first explorer, Portuguese Juan Rodriguez Cabrillo, all helped to establish the state in the sixteenth century. Sir Francis Drake explored the north coast, and later Father Junipero Serra founded Catholic California, establishing the mission of San Diego in 1769, the first in a wave of Spanish missionary settlements that soon dotted much of southern California. Today these Catholic missions mark some of the most beautiful sites on the coast. By planting vineyards to produce their sacramental wine, these same missions gave birth to what is today one of the state's most vital and lucrative enterprises—the wine industry. The population increased after gold was discovered in 1848.

An example of California's spectacular landscape, Mono Lake, is east of Yosemite National Park. Shown here with California's Sierra Nevada mountains in the distance.

Today, California has some of the best dining experiences in the world, most notably in the San Francisco Bay area. Information technology, aircraft and missiles, entertainment, and agriculture are the largest industries. The combination of counterculture, plastic culture, and old-world culture makes it difficult to stereotype Californians.

The Golden State stretches from the Oregon border in the north to Tijuana, Mexico, in the south. It contains the highest and lowest points in the mainland United States: Mt Whitney and Death Valley. The state's natural beauty, combined with a temperate climate, encourages year-round outdoor activities. Famous landmarks of the Los Angeles area are Disneyland and the California Adventure, the Monterey Bay Aquarium, and San Francisco's Golden Gate Bridge.

State motto *Eureka!* (I have found it!)
State flag Adopted 1911
Capital Sacramento
Population 33,871,648
Total area (land and water)
158,869 square miles (411,471 sq km)
Land area 155,973 square miles
(403,970 sq km)
California is the third-largest state in size
Origin of name Named for Califia, a fictional earthly paradise in *Las Sergas de Esplanidian*, written by Garcia Ordonez de Montalvo in 1510
Nickname The Golden State
Abbreviations CA (postal), Calif.
State bird California valley quail
State flower Golden poppy
State tree California redwoods
(*Sequoia sempervirens* and *S. gigantea*)
Entered the Union September 9, 1850 as the 31st state

Places in
CALIFORNIA

BAKERSFIELD

Bakersfield has a population of 206,000. It is in central-south California, about halfway between Las Vegas, Nevada, and San Luis Obispo, on the Pacific coast. It marks the southern end of the vast San Joaquin River Valley, better known in the wine and other agricultural businesses as the Central Valley. Much of the state's bulk wine is produced nearby—the climate is too hot to produce grapes for premium wine. Arid flatlands, marked by a vast network of highways, combined with baking heat in the summer months keep tourist traffic to a minimum, though a drive east along Hwy 178 takes visitors to the Kern River and some gently rolling hills for hiking, camping, and fishing. The 969-acre (392-ha) Tule Elk State Reserve on Stockdale Highway is home to a small herd of native elk.

Originally inhabited by Native Americans, the area was settled by goldminers in the mid-nineteenth century. Colonel Thomas Baker, a pioneer from Iowa, settled the area, and Baker's field, which he had planted with alfalfa, became known to travelers as the place to stop to feed their animals. The name stuck when, in 1869, Baker was appointed to survey a formal township. The railroad, a vast irrigation system, another gold rush, and, in 1899, the discovery of oil, brought notoriety and new life to the sleepy town. Bakersfield remains an important trading center, especially for agricultural products such as fruits, nuts, and grains, and for refined petroleum.

Popular attractions include the Bakersfield Museum of Art and the California Living Museum, which is complete with its own zoo, botanical garden, and a natural history museum. The Kern County Museum has 60 restored and representational buildings, including a log cabin, a Queen Anne-style mansion, and an 1898 locomotive. Stock and sprint cars race at Bakersfield Speedway, and the Mesa Marin Raceway offers high-speed

Agriculture in the Bakersfield area has been made possible by extensive irrigation.

stock cars and NASCAR racing. Downtown, there are two huge, and very popular, antiques malls.

Bakersfield is a relatively short trip from Los Angeles (112 miles, 180 km) and San Francisco (288 miles, 463 km), and has its own tiny airport. Buses and trains also service the area.
Map ref: page 788 D2

BRIDGEPORT

The tiny town of Bridgeport, which has a population of only 500, lies in the High Sierras at an elevation of 6,473 feet (1,974 m). Located near the Nevada border, on US-395 and only 20 miles (32 km) northeast of Yosemite National Park, the best way to visit this isolated area is as a day trip from Yosemite National Park. The main attraction here is the nearby Bodie Ghost Town and State Historic Park, at an elevation of 8,200 feet (2,051 m), on Hwy 270. Snow may close the highway in winter and early spring, but the park remains open to those willing to enter on foot.

At the height of the gold rush, in the late 1800s, Bodie had a population of 10,000. Booze and bullets flowed freely until a series of fires destroyed almost everything. State Park status was granted in 1962 to preserve the town. Abandoned mine shafts, the mining village of Rattlesnake Gulch, a jail, an old mill, and the Miners Union Hall—now a museum—are easy to find with the help of a self-guided tour brochure, which is available at the park.

No food, drink, or lodging is available in Bridgeport, and the nearest picnic ground is ½ mile (800 m) away. There is a limited bus service and nearby Yosemite is serviced by trains.
Map ref: page 699 H2

Bodie, not far from Bridgeport, is an original gold-rush ghost town—the buildings contain 100-year-old everyday items.

Carmel Mission, in Carmel-by-the-Sea, is one of many missions founded by Father Junipero Serra.

CARMEL-BY-THE-SEA

The tiny seaside enclave Carmel-by-the-Sea overlooks the Bay of Carmel, an inlet of the Pacific Ocean along central California's ruggedly beautiful coastline. Carmelite monks were part of Spanish explorer Sebastian Vizcaino's expedition, in 1602, and they gave this inlet its name. Father Junipero Serra, founder of most of California's missions, is buried in nearby Mission San Carlos Borromeo del Rio Carmelo, more commonly known as Carmel Mission. This mission served as headquarters for his mission system across the state in the late 1700s and it can be easily reached by car from downtown.

The population is a mere 4,300, and locals fight vigorously against growth or change of any sort. For example, houses have names instead of numbers, and the long, wide, white sandy beach allows dogs, campfires, and camping. Residents passionately support quirky local ordinances, including severe hit-and-run penalties for hitting a tree with a vehicle.

Carmel has been a community of artists and writers since the turn of the twentieth century. Cultural walking tours are offered year-round and offer access to the homes of several famous writers, sculptors, and painters who lived and worked in the area. However, while the starving artist may take inspiration here, today the ultra-rich Carmel community is more known for its shopping, fine dining, and its fabulous beach mansions. Popular local celebrities, including former local mayor, Clint Eastwood, live in this quaint European-style village framed with pine and cypress forests and a long sandy beach. Residents get about town in classic two-seater sports cars or walk hand-in-hand window-shopping along the cobblestone streets. Each year, since 1935, a three-week Carmel Bach Festival is held at Sunset Center in July and August. The Monterey County Symphony performs here as well from September to May. Lodging in quaint European-style inns is plentiful but can be expensive.

GEORIS

awand i tat iest   fe tet t'mind.

ESTATE   BOTTLED
SINCE   1982
MERLOT
Tasting Room

Carmel Valley tasting room sign, near Carmel-by-the-Sea.

Nearby, and right on the bay, is Point Lobos State Reserve, a lovely place to hike out to the coast and watch sea lions and whales cavort. This is also a great place to photograph Bird Rock—a large rock close to the shore frequented by sea birds. Carmel Valley, about a 20-minute drive away, is home to a golf course and many local winery tasting rooms. The valley is warmer and sunnier year-round than coastal areas.

It is a two-hour drive (or three hours on Hwy 1, the scenic Pacific Coast Hwy) from San Francisco and is very easily accessible from the nearby Monterey Peninsula Airport.
Map ref: page 698 D6

CRESCENT CITY

Crescent City is on the Redwood Highway section of US-101, a section that stretches 387 miles (623 km) from San Francisco to the Oregon border, and gives access to 97 percent of the world's coastal redwoods. It is Del Norte County's largest city, which is not saying much—the local population is only about 4,900. With more than 70 inches (1,778 mm) of rain per year, this is the wettest spot in the state. Pirates and other treasure seekers discovered the harbor and crescent-shaped beach and, later, after the city's founding in 1852, steamships frequented the port.

Crescent City is not a major tourist destination. It is, however, a gateway to the Oregon border and nearby Smith River, with its plentiful salmon and trout fishing. It also serves as headquarters for trips to the nearby Redwood national and state parks (see separate entry). Attractions in the city itself include two lighthouses. The Battery Point Lighthouse, on a small island, is accessible only by walking across a tide pool at low tide and is open from April to September. The St George Reef Lighthouse, at 146 feet (45 m), is one of the tallest ever built.

Del Norte County Historical Society's Museum has Native American and pioneer exhibits, and Ocean World features a shark-petting tank and sea-lion show. Visitors also enjoy the North Coast Marine Mammal Center and the wreck of a side-wheel steamboat, the *Brother Jonathan*, at Point St George, along Pebble Beach Drive. Each President's Day weekend (usually the third weekend in February), the Del Norte County Fairground plays host to the amazing World Championship Crab Races and Crustacean Festival.

Traffic on US-101 is heavy even in these remote parts, especially on summer weekends. Buses stop here and the nearest major airport is Arcata Airport, just north of Eureka.
Map ref: page 784 A2

DAVIS

Davis is home to the University of California, whose school of viticulture and enology is internationally renowned for an interdisciplinary approach to all aspects of grape-growing and winemaking. About 48,000 people live in this former farming town located just north of Sacramento. It is less than one hour from San Francisco

Shiraz grape harvest, near the Davis area.

northeast on I-80. It was settled by early pioneer Jerome C. Davis, who planted grains and grapevines, and brought in herds of livestock. Today Davis is still an important agricultural hub as well as one of the most ecologically sensitive little cities in the world. Many homes are powered by solar energy and there are self-guided tours of the Village Homes solar community. Cycling is also a popular activity, and the city has more than 67 miles (108 km) of bicycle trails. The Sacramento International Airport is just north of Davis.

Map ref: page 786 D1

DEATH VALLEY NATIONAL PARK

Forty-niners, so named because they flocked to California during the 1849 gold rush, gave the valley its name because so many prospectors lost their lives in this brutal desert while seeking a shorter route to the gold fields. Death Valley was finally established as a national monument in 1933 and designated a national park in 1994. Deposits of gold, silver, copper, lead, and borax have been mined in the area since the mid-nineteenth century.

Covering 5,262 square miles (13,629 sq km) and enclosed by the Panamint and Amargosa Ranges, much of the valley is below sea level. Badwater Basin, at 282 feet (86 m) below sea level, is the lowest point in the Western Hemisphere. It is even more dramatic because towering over it is Panamint's highest point, Telescope Peak (11,049 feet, 3,370 m).

The Rhyolite Ghost Town contains the ruins of a prosperous town that once was home to 10,000 people. Among the few complete buildings is the restored Bottle House, built by a resident in 1906 from 50,000 beer and liquor bottles. The village of Stovepipe Wells offers great views of colorful Mosaic Canyon. The canyon's banded marble-like walls with their mosaic patches of water-polished rock fragments can be seen up close from a short, easy walking trail.

Badwater, in Death Valley, the lowest point in the Western Hemisphere.

Another park attraction is Scotty's Castle—a Mediterranean hacienda built in the 1920s as a winter retreat by an eccentric Chicago millionaire. Hiking and camping are popular activities in the valley.

Average summer temperatures are some of the hottest known—they frequently go over 120°F (49°C)—and dust- and sandstorms are common. Precautions against the sun, wind, heat, snakes, and tarantulas are necessary. Good maps, a compass, binoculars, plenty of food, water (extra water for the car's radiator), gas, and oil are essential. Four-wheel drive vehicles are recommended.

The park is on the Nevada border 290 miles (467 km) northeast of Los Angeles. Crossing steep mountain passes to get into the valley adds travel time. The visitor center is in Furnace Creek but conveniences are as rare as signage. Lodging is limited but Barstow, one hour away, has motels and restaurants. Las Vegas, Nevada, is the closest center with a major airport, bus, and train services.

Map ref: page 787 L5

Zabriskie Point, in Death Valley National Park, is a landscape of gullies and mud hills at the edge of the Funeral Mountains—the view is most beautiful at sunset.

DEVILS POSTPILE NATIONAL MONUMENT

Devils Postpile is a spectacular formation of columns of dark, dense, glassy basalt 40–60 feet (12–18 m) high. They formed nearly 100,000 years ago when a massive flow of basalt lava cooled and the inner portion cracked into post-like columns. These formations were uncovered 10,000 years ago during the last major ice age as glaciers carved out the valley. The monument is just east of Yosemite National Park, near Mammoth Mountain, and 56 miles (90 km) northwest of Bishop, off US-395.

The formation can be reached via an easy 10-minute walk from the ranger station, though a better view is available by climbing up a steep, but short, 60-foot (18-m) high rocky cliff. Rainbow Falls, where the San Joaquin River drops 101 feet (31 m) over a lava ledge, is a 2-mile (3-km) hike away. A short hike leads to Soda Springs, where the water is cold and carbonated. Camping and fishing are popular activities in the park. The monument is open from late June to late October and is accessible by shuttle bus from the Mammoth Mountain Inn. Bears live in the area, so precautions are necessary, especially with food.
Map ref: page 699 J3

EUREKA

Eureka (population 30,000) is a northwestern California city on Humboldt Bay, 270 miles (434 km) north of San Francisco on US–101. It has had a thriving lumber business since the mid-

1800s. Its large, protected port serves as a convenient point for redwood shipping and is home to California's largest fishing fleet north of San Francisco. Nine miles (15 km) north is the quaint little town of Arcata, home of Humboldt State University.

Along the waterfront, Old Town Eureka, designated a National Historic District, is 13 blocks of shops, restaurants, and hotels, many in preserved Victorian structures. The Carson Mansion, built for lumber baron William Carson in 1886, is a fine example of the Victorian structures built here in prosperous times. It is now a private men's club, so the interior is off limits, except to members, but visitors can photograph the exterior. The world-famous Carter House—a re-created 1884 San Francisco-style Victorian house—and the city's museums and zoo are also popular places to visit. There are horse and buggy rides, and harbor cruises on the *Madaket*, purportedly the oldest passenger vessel on the Pacific Coast. In fall, winter, and spring, the Humboldt Bay National Wildlife Preserve is home to as many as 100,000 migratory waterbirds.

Eureka is served by Arcata Airport, to the north, and buses.
Map ref: page 784 A4

FRESNO

"Fresno" is Spanish for "ash tree," and this central California city was named for the ash trees that grew along the banks of the Fresno River. At the heart of one of America's richest farming areas, the San Joaquin Valley, Fresno is known

as the "raisin capital of the world" and is home to the Sun-Maid Growers Cooperative and the world's largest raisin processing plant. At 185 miles (298 km) southeast of San Francisco, Fresno is a popular stop on the way to nearby Yosemite, Kings Canyon, and Sequoia National Parks and the Sierra and Sequoia National Forests. The local population has nearly doubled, to about 400,000, in the last 20 years. This is mostly due to many families from urban San Francisco and Los Angeles escaping high housing prices and seeking more space for less money.

Pulitzer Prize-winning playwright and novelist William Saroyan was born in Fresno in 1908, and the Fresno Metropolitan Museum of Art, History, and Science houses a gallery in his honor.

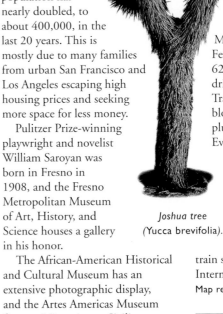

Joshua tree (Yucca brevifolia).

The African-American Historical and Cultural Museum has an extensive photographic display, and the Artes Americas Museum features Hispanic art. Sicilian immigrant, Baldasare Forestiere, spent 40 years carving out the Forestiere Underground Gardens. It is 10 acres (4 ha) of rooms, tunnels, grottoes and even an aquarium that is 20 feet (6 m) below ground. Today the underground gardens are a museum.

Chaffee Zoological Gardens in Roeding Park has a tropical rainforest, and tigers, lions, grizzly bears, tule elk, hooting siamangs, and a reptile house. Woodward Park is home to the Shin-Zen Japanese Friendship Gardens, opened in 1975 and dedicated to Fresno's sister city, Kochi, Japan. No tour of Fresno is complete without a stop at the Santa Fe Depot, a railway station built in 1896 in the California Mission Revival style. During February and March, the 62-mile (100-km) self-guided driving tour along the Blossom Trail is resplendent with blooming almond, apricot, plum, lemon, and peach trees. Even though fast-food outlets dot the landscape, the rich ethnic mix of the area means that almost any cuisine is available, from Armenian to Vietnamese. There is a bus service and a daily train service, and Fresno Yosemite International Airport is nearby.
Map ref: page 786 G5

JOSHUA TREE NATIONAL PARK

Early Mormons settlers gave the joshua tree its name, believing its upstretched arms resembled the biblical Joshua raising his arms up toward heaven. Up to 40 feet (12 m) high, these giant yuccas punctuate the desert landscape to this day, especially in this park in the Queen and Lost Horse Valleys. The park covers more than 1,236 square miles (3,201 sq km) and sits at a natural meeting point of two deserts, the high Mojave and the low Colorado Deserts. There are park gates 25 miles (40 km) east of Indio, on I-10, and near Joshua Tree and Twentynine Palms, both on Hwy 62. Joshua National Park is a popular day trip from nearby Palm Springs.

The Oasis of Mara, also called 29 Palms Oasis, is one of five fan palm oases in the park and draws visitors and wildlife alike. Hiking and rock climbing are very popular

Beautiful fields of flowers in bloom near Fresno, in the San Joaquin Valley, one of the most fertile agricultural areas in California.

activities in the park, and the Cholla Cactus Gardens, Hidden Valley, and the overlook at Key View are main attractions. Visitor centers are at Oasis, on the Utah Trail, and at Cottonwood. The park has no services, so it is necessary to carry plenty of water, and none of the park's nine campgrounds provide water or firewood. Motels are close by in Yucca Valley and Twentynine Palms.

Trains serve Indio and Palm Springs, buses serve Palm Springs, and the Palm Springs International Airport serves the area. Los Angeles is about a three-hour drive away.

Map ref: page 789 K5

KINGS CANYON NATIONAL PARK

See Sequoia and Kings Canyon National Parks, page 735

LASSEN VOLCANIC NATIONAL PARK

The 10,457-foot (3,189-m) volcanic Lassen Peak is the main feature and main attraction of this 106,372-acre (43,081-ha) park. Both the peak and the park are named for pioneer Peter Lassen, originally from Denmark, who used the peak as a landmark for the wagon trains of immigrants heading into the Sacramento River Valley in the mid-nineteenth century. The park, which sits in the lower Cascade Range in the northeastern section of the state, was established in 1907. It's 44 miles (71 km) east of Redding and 225 miles (362 km) northeast of San Francisco.

Lassen Peak is the southernmost peak in a chain of volcanoes that stretches south from British Columbia. It is dormant, but was active from 1914 to 1921, when numerous explosions caused, among other things, a devastating mudslide as hot lava melted snow on the mountain slopes. Other volcanic peaks are Cinder Cone at 6,913 feet (2,108 m), Prospect Peak at 8,342 feet (2,544 m), and Harkness Peak at 8,039 feet (2,452 m).

Volcanic activity is still evident today in the park's many geothermal features, including hot springs, bubbling mud pots, and steaming fumaroles, or vapor emitting vats. The Bumpass Hell Area, where features have reached temperatures as high as 284°F (140°C), was named for an explorer who lost a leg after falling into a boiling pool there. Visitors also enjoy the Sulphur Works, Boiling Springs, and Devil's Kitchen geothermal sites. At least 715 species of plants are found in the park's unusual environment. Hiking and camping in the lush forests, canoeing and kayaking on the park's 50 alpine lakes and, in winter, cross-country skiing and snowshoeing are very popular activities. There is a per-car entrance fee, and the largest visitor center is located just inside the northwest entrance. Besides campgrounds, the park has one lodge and several others are near by. Dining choices are limited. The nearest airport is Redding Municipal Airport.

Map ref: page 784 F5

LOS ANGELES

Los Angeles' city downtown area has never taken off. Instead, several independent communities (including Beverly Hills, Santa Monica, Hollywood, Pasadena, and Long Beach), covering 469 square miles (1,215 sq km) from cool coastal plains on the Pacific east into warmer foothills and canyons, have their own thriving centers. Neighboring Orange County is the home of Disneyland and Disney's new California Adventure. The ubiquitous freeway connects these disparate communities, so having a car here is essential. In fact, there are two cars per resident, and stop-and-go traffic is the norm.

With approximately 3.6 million residents, Los Angeles is the most populous city in the United States, after New York City. It is also California's biggest economic center, a thriving urban industrial center, a major importer and exporter of international trade goods, a gateway between Asia and the United States, and home to the nation's finest motion picture, television, radio, and musical studios.

In 1840, Los Angeles was the largest settlement in Mexican-ruled Alta California. The area was ceded to the United States in 1850 and the city was incorporated. A thriving cattle industry fed thousands of hungry prospectors on their way to the gold fields. Today the city is a rich cultural mix, as people from all over the world come to enjoy a buoyant economy and balmy climate. However, it is prone to major natural disasters, including earthquakes, fires, and floods, and limited water may hamper further growth.

At least three full days are needed to explore this city. One day could be spent along the coast, stopping in at famous beach communities such as Malibu, Santa Monica, and Venice Beach, and visiting the magical Santa Catalina Island. Another suggestion is for visitors to start out with a drive through Beverly Hills' residential areas to see where the stars live—and a walk along Rodeo Drive where the stars shop. Later, a drive up to Hollywood to visit Studio City and Universal Studios could be followed by a walk around Pasadena's Old Town. A third day could be spent at Disneyland and the California Adventure.

Aside from the traffic, normal precautions are necessary, as in any large urban area. Pickpockets are common, and women and children should not enter any park, at any time, unescorted. The central-south area of the city, near Los Angeles International Airport, is a center of gang activity.

Los Angeles is reached via train and bus, and by flights into Los Angeles International, Burbank-Glendale-Pasadena, Long Beach Municipal, or Orange County/John Wayne airports. It's also accessible by car from the north via the scenic Hwy 1, the quicker US-101, or the unpleasant but significantly shorter route, on I-5.

Map ref: page 788 E5

Los Angeles' famous "Hollywood" sign on the crest of the Hollywood Hills—it is 50 feet (15 m) tall and 450 feet (137 m) across.

Hollywood walk of fame, Los Angeles.

Just south of Monterey is the magnificent Pacific coastline of Big Sur. The name "Big Sur" came from the Spanish "El Sur Grande," meaning "the Large South."

MODESTO

One hour south of Sacramento and east of San Francisco, Modesto is known as a gateway to Yosemite National Park and the southern reaches of Gold Country. This small city (population 200,000) sits on the northern edge of the San Joaquin Valley, where it serves as a point of processing, shipping, and marketing for the agricultural riches of the Central Valley.

Film director George Lucas was born here, and the area is home to E. & J. Gallo, a family-owned firm that employs over 5,000 people locally to produce wine under one of the world's largest brand names.

The family of prominent local rancher–banker Robert McHenry has provided two of Modesto's main attractions, the McHenry Museum and the McHenry Mansion. The McHenry Museum building, originally the city library, was given to the city by the McHenry family and now houses a late eighteenth-century doctor's office,

general store, blacksmith, gold-mining paraphernalia, and a collection of cattle brands.

The McHenry mansion, built in the Victorian Italianate style, in 1883, is now on the National Register of Historic Places. Other attractions include the Caswell Memorial State Park and the Turlock Lake State Recreation Area.

Visitors to the area mostly fly into nearby Sacramento or San Francisco international airports and then drive in.
Map ref: page 786 E3

MOJAVE NATIONAL PRESERVE

This 1.4 million-acre (567,000-ha) preserve is part of the great eastern Mojave Desert. With elevations up to 8,000 feet (2,440 m), a cooler climate, and a varied plant and animal life, this park is drastically different from nearby Death Valley. It is located 180 miles (290 km) east of Los Angeles and reaches to the Nevada border—Las Vegas, Nevada, is only 75 miles (121 km)

to the northeast. The I-40 follows the southern boundary. This preserve exists under the California Desert Protection Act. What this means is that it is not as fully protected as a national park. Consequently, environmentalists continue with protests against grazing and mining within the boundaries.

There are no facilities in this remote preserve other than a few campgrounds. The adventurous enjoy the world's largest Joshua tree forest in the Cima Dome, the Mitchell Caverns historic mining sites, and the Hole-in-the-Wall—a rhyolite rock hole with iron rings to aid the descent of those wanting to hide away. The 11-mile (18-km) Wildhorse Canyon Road was America's first official back-country byway. Other attractions include the Kelso Dunes, the most extensive dune field in the West, and the nearby Kelso Depot, built by the Union Pacific Railway in 1924.

Appreciation of this arid region is definitely enhanced by visiting the Mojave Desert Information Center in Baker, the California Desert Information Center in Barstow, or the Information Center in Needles. Lodging can be found in nearby Barstow, Baker, or Nipton, or in Primm Nevada, which has three hotel–casinos and inexpensive food.
Map ref: page 789 K2

MONTEREY

Two hours south of San Francisco by car, Monterey offers small-town charm with an international flair. The city's population, about 33,000, enjoys an environment reminiscent of 1950s small-town America, alongside the unique combination of golf resorts, world-class race tracks, jazz festivals, an international language institute, and an aquarium.

Spanish explorers settled here in 1770, and the town became a Mexican administrative center before California was admitted to the United States in 1849. Whaling and sardines brought

notoriety in the 1800s and inspired works such as John Steinbeck's novel, *Cannery Row*. The Monterey Bay Aquarium on Cannery Row is world-renowned for its spectacular displays of 350,000 marine animals and plants along with a three-story, 335,000-gallon (12,884-hl) tank with a kelp forest, leopard sharks, sardines, and anchovies. The Outer Bay exhibit has a 1-million-gallon (37,850-hl) tank housing yellow-fin tuna, large green sea turtles, barracuda, soupfin sharks, giant ocean sunfish, and pelagic stingrays. The Maritime Museum and Customs House are also popular attractions. Cannery Row is a mecca for tourists—locals stay away unless visiting one of the top restaurants or the Taste of Monterey, a wine-tasting and educational facility on the bay.

Visitors enjoy kayaking, whale-watching, fishing, sailing, bird-watching, and hiking along the path at Lover's Point in charming Pacific Grove, which is known as Butterfly Town USA. It is the winter home of monarch butterflies as they migrate south from the Pacific Northwest. Jazz fans gather here for annual festivals, and Pebble Beach golf tournaments attract international visitors. The Monterey Peninsula offers 80 golf courses and a thriving wine industry—it is short drive to the Salinas Valley and Carmel Valley wine districts.

Monterey sits on the edge of one of the largest underwater canyons in the world, and its calm harbor is deceiving. Challenging and quick-changing conditions face those who venture out around the point and into the Bay where swells of 10–20 feet (3–6 m) are common in the afternoon, even when morning conditions have been perfectly calm. The water in the bay is icy and fog is common. Winds pick up quickly along the bay, especially during the warmer summer months, so jackets are essential. Stringent marine protection laws prohibit close approaches to sea lions, harbor seals, otters, or other sea life.

Bust of John Steinbeck, Cannery Row, Monterey.

The area is served by the Monterey Peninsula Airport and trains stop in nearby Salinas.

Map ref: page 786 D6

OCEANSIDE

Oceanside, 36 miles (58 km) north of San Diego on I-5, overlooks the Gulf of Santa Catalina. The city (population 142,000) is bordered by Camp Pendleton, a US Marine Base, to the north, and Carlsbad to the south. A wide, white sandy beach stretches 4 miles (6.4 km) from the harbor to the Carlsbad border. This beach boasts some of the world's best surfing. It hosts the Longboard Surf Contest and the World Bodysurfing Championships. Yachts, shops, and restaurants line the harbor.

Surfing, boating, fishing, and whale watching during migration season are the main activities in Oceanside. There are tram rides along the 1,954-foot (596-m) long pier, and the nearby Strand, a long, grassy park, is a favorite place to spend a sunny day. The 1798 Mission San Luis Rey de Francia, named for French King, Louis IX, is the largest of the state's 21 missions, and served as the backdrop for a film about Zorro. Other attractions include the Antique Gas and Steam Engine Museum and the California Surf Museum.

Oceanside has bus and train services, and nearby San Diego has and international airport.

Map ref: page 788 G7

OXNARD

This little town is halfway between Los Angeles and Santa Barbara, and is just a few minutes south of Ventura, on US-101. Oxnard has a population of approximately 154,000, of which many are of Mexican heritage.

Approaching Oxnard on the freeway, fast food restaurants, strip malls, and fields seem to stretch on for ever. The only thing to attract the visitor seems to be the promise of the Pacific Ocean, but Oxnard also hosts the annual California Strawberry Festival each May and is sometimes known as the Strawberry Capital. In town, Fisherman's Wharf is a charming New England style village with shops, eateries, and boat slips for small pleasure craft. The Channel Islands Harbor offers boating, fishing, beaches, barbecue and picnic areas, tennis courts, charter boats, and bicycle rentals.

Forty miles (64 km) offshore, the Channel Islands National Park encompasses five of the eight-island chain, including Santa Barbara, Anacapa, Santa Cruz, Santa Rosa, and San Miguel. The park protects the ocean one nautical mile offshore each island. In winter, elephant seals and, in spring, sea lions arrive in large numbers to breed, and many sea birds roost and nest on the islands. Camping is permitted but there are no facilities and precautions are necessary against wind and sun.

The visitor center in Ventura, about 10 miles (16 km) northwest of Oxnard, can help visitors plan trips to the islands. Boats are the most common form of transportation, but flights are available from nearby Camarillo or from Santa Barbara Airport.

Map ref: page 788 D4

Oxnard strawberries are exported around the world.

PALM SPRINGS

This resort area near Los Angeles has, for decades, been a destination for movie industry types looking for a break from the rigors of their work. It is recognized as one of the top three American destinations for gay travelers and is a retirement mecca. Today, its warm, arid climate, world-class golf courses, and top restaurants attract year-round residents in droves. The community has some quirky regulations. Former Mayor, Sonny Bono, passed an anti-thong swimwear ordinance in 1991, no billboards are allowed, and the word "motel" is not allowed to be visible. The local population has swelled to close to 45,000 since the town's founding in 1876. A Spanish explorer discovered the area in 1774 and named it "Agua Caliente," or "hot water," for its natural hot springs mineral pool. The Native American Cahuilla tribe is still a major landholder and, in cooperation with the United States Government, works to preserve their heritage.

Besides the warm, dry climate and wide-open spaces, golf is a major attraction. There are close to 100 golf courses, and tournaments are held year-round. The Palm Springs Aerial Tramway takes visitors on a breathtaking 2½-mile (4-km) ascent up Mt San Jacinto over terrain that changes from desert floor to alpine wilderness. The Palm Springs Desert Museum collections include twentieth-century and Mesoamerican Native American art, plus a natural science gallery. Hot-air ballooning and covered wagon tours are also available—the adventurous can skydive solo or in tandem. Other popular attractions include Moorten's Botanical Garden and the Oasis Waterpark.

Lodging and dining are available at all price levels, and Joshua Tree National Park is nearby, making it a popular day-trip destination from Palm Springs. Buses and trains service the area and Palm Springs has its own international airport. Los Angeles is only a two-hour drive to the west.

Map ref: page 789 J5

Teddy Bear Cholla (Opuntia bigelovii) gets its name from its soft and cuddly appearance, and is a feature of the Joshua Tree National Park near Palm Springs.

PASADENA

Founded in 1874, Pasadena is a 23-square-mile (60-sq-km) suburb of Los Angeles that sits at the base of the San Gabriel Mountains, in the San Fernando Valley. The Chippewa Native Americans named the area "Crown of the Valley" and, in 1771, the land here became part of the San Gabriel Mission.

Today, the population is approximately 134,800, many of whom are employed in the local NASA Jet Propulsion Lab, the California Institute of Technology, or the biotechnology, engineering, or environmental protection industries. By car—really the only practical manner of transportation here—it is reached either via I-110 north from downtown Los Angeles, Hwy 2 north from Hollywood, or Hwy 134 east through Glendale from Beverly Hills.

Each New Year's Day, crowds flock to the city's most famous landmark, the Rose Bowl, for the Tournament of the Roses, which is followed by a collegiate football game—a tradition since 1890. Nearby is the aquatic center, built with money left over from the 1984 Olympics, where visitors can watch Olympic hopefuls train. Old Town is a 14-block area combining traditional American small-town charm and tacky strip malls. Pasadena offers a free shuttle bus between Old Town and the Lake Avenue shopping area.

Pasadena's collection of clean, quiet residential areas, including La Canada, San Marino, and South Pasadena, attract Los Angeles residents looking for some respite from the big city. These areas are full of historic homes and grand old mansions, graceful tree-lined avenues, and roses, giving visitors a sense of the less frenetic lifestyle of yesteryear. Many examples of the California craftsman architectural style, in which the many elements were handmade by artisans, are open to the public. Other attractions abound, including the Norton Simon Museum of Art, Huntington Museum and Library,

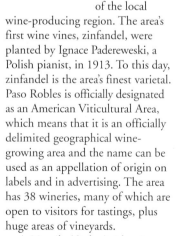

Pasadena, Los Angeles, police insignia.

Pasadena Historical Museum, the Huntington Botanical Gardens, the Pasadena Playhouse, and the Pasadena Civic Auditorium—site of the annual Emmy Awards ceremony. Lodging and dining options exist at all price levels.
Map ref: page 788 F5

PASO ROBLES

Franciscan fathers named this area "pass through the oaks," referring to the clusters of oaks located at the southern end of the Salinas Valley. Coastal breezes cool temperatures in the western region of the valley, while the eastern area is hotter and drier. Paso Robles was founded in 1870 by Drury James, uncle of the infamous outlaw, Jesse James. It is at the heart of the Central Coast wine country, (population approximately 19,200) and is 29 miles (47 km) north of San Luis Obispo, on US-101. Hwy 46 leads east and west off US-101, into the heart of the local wine-producing region. The area's first wine vines, zinfandel, were planted by Ignace Padereweski, a Polish pianist, in 1913. To this day, zinfandel is the area's finest varietal. Paso Robles is officially designated as an American Viticultural Area, which means that it is an officially delimited geographical wine-growing area and the name can be used as an appellation of origin on labels and in advertising. The area has 38 wineries, many of which are open to visitors for tastings, plus huge areas of vineyards.

A 38-mile (61-km) side trip to the coast leads to the Hearst Castle. This 165-room mansion, on a 127-acre (51-ha) estate, was built

Grape-picking season at the Arciero Estate Winery, in the heart of the Paso Robles viticulture area.

by newspaper publisher, William Randolph Hearst, on a 1,600-foot (488-m) promontory overlooking San Simeon and the Pacific Ocean. Four tours cover the estate. Visitors to Paso Robles can also enjoy the Sycamore Farm, a herb garden and nursery, and hot-air-balloon rides.

Temperatures often climb above 100°F (38°C) in summer months. Facilities at Paso Robles are plentiful near the freeway, but the landscape becomes rural very quickly. Many wineries provide pleasant

picnic areas, but the best place to find meals and lodging is the rustic downtown area near US-101. Paso Robles is about 100 miles (161 km) northwest of Bakersfield, which is serviced by buses and trains. The nearest major airports are in Los Angeles and San Francisco.
Map ref: page 788 A1

POINT REYES NATIONAL SEASHORE

One of the most beautiful preserves in the world, this area stretches 30 miles (48 km) along the Marin County coastline, 20 miles (32 km) north of San Francisco. In 1962, President John F. Kennedy signed legislation to protect forever these 70,000 acres (28,350 ha) of rugged coastline, alder and pine forests, canyons, and meadows. Tomales Bay and Dillon Beach mark the north end, while Stinson Beach and Bolinas mark the southern border.

The half-mile (800-m) Earthquake Trail near the Bear Valley Visitor Center clearly illustrates the damage caused during the 1906 earthquake—Point Reyes was shifted 20 feet (6 m) north. Geologically, Point Reyes rests on the Pacific Plate, and the rest of the state rests on the North American Plate. This meeting point is better known as the San Andreas Fault.

The preserve offers 140 miles (225 km) of hiking trails through canyons, forests, and grasslands, and down to rugged beaches. Mountain biking, horseback

The California state flower, the native golden poppy (Eschscholzia californica).

A stunning view, just southeast of Redding, of the Sierra Nevadas. Redding is close to many lakes and state parks.

riding, and kayaking are all popular activities in this area. The peninsula has several vantage points for viewing gray whales as they migrate to Mexico, peaking in mid-January, and back to Alaska, peaking in mid-March. Camping within the preserve is limited to four campgrounds and requires registration at the Bear Valley Visitor Center. More than 2.6 million visitors vie for these sites, making planning necessary.

Sea lions and mountain lions live in the preserve, as do countless other species including tule elk, albino deer, the rare rubber boa, the western territorial garter snake, owls, hawks, the peregrine falcon, the endangered snowy plover, and black oystercatchers.

Other major attractions in the preserve include the Point Reyes Bird Observatory in the Duxbury Reef area, the 1-mile (1.6-km) long shale inter-tidal Duxbury Reef, Limantour Beach in Olema, and the Point Reyes Lighthouse.

The Pacific Coast Highway (Hwy 1) gives easy access to most attractions. This area is very popular and winding roads through many small towns make for slow traveling, especially during summer weekends. Entrance to the park is free. Car camping and sleeping on beaches is prohibited. Facilities vary greatly depending on location. The best way to see this area is by car, San Francisco has all facilities.
Map ref: page 786 B2

REDDING

Redding is a gateway to Mt Shasta and the Cascade Range and marks the northern end of the Sacramento Valley. It was founded in 1872 as the northern terminus for the California and Oregon Railroad. Today, lumber and tourism are the major industries in this city of approximately 80,000 residents.

The Sacramento River flows through Redding, making fishing, and rafting popular. A 6-mile (10-km) trail follows the river and crosses on the first concrete stress-ribbon bridge in the country.

The Redding Museum of Art, located in Caldwell Park, features changing exhibits of contemporary art as well as displays of historical items and Native American art. The Carter House Natural Science Museum, also in Caldwell Park, has displays about the natural history of northern California.

Redding is full of motels and restaurants, and is a good base from which to explore the nearby Lake Shasta, Shasta Dam, the old mining town of Shasta, Trinity Lake, and the Whiskeytown-Shasta Trinity National Recreation Area (see separate entry on this area). Other nearby attractions are Lassen Volcanic National Park (see separate entry on this park), Castle Crags State Park, Shasta National Forest, Klamath National Forest, Ahjumani Springs State Park, Latour State Forest, and the William B. Ide Adobe Historic State Park.

The area is reached by car on I-5. Trains stop here, and the area is served by two small airlines into Redding Municipal Airport.
Map ref: page 784 D5

REDWOOD NATIONAL AND STATE PARKS

One national park and three state redwood parks—Redwood National Park, and the Jedediah Smith Redwoods, Prairie Creek Redwoods, and Del Norte Coast Redwoods parks—which are managed by the California Department of Parks and Recreation and the National Park Service, make up this 106,000-acre (42,930-ha) area in Humboldt County. In 1968, environmentalists won out against a logging industry that had managed to reduce redwood forests from 2 million trees down to 300,000, but old growth logging is still a point of contention and a

problem in the region. National park acreage begins in the Siskiyou and Klamath Mountains and continues out to the Pacific seashore.

The area is 336 miles (541 km) north of San Francisco and 40 miles (64 km) north of Eureka on US-101. The closest major airport is Eureka–Arcata. Orick is the southern gateway town, and Crescent City, near the Oregon border, the northern. Crescent City has plentiful and inexpensive lodging, gas, and supplies, and free maps are available at the Crescent City and Orick information centers. Entrance to the national park is free, and a day-use fee is good for entrance to all three state parks.

The Tall Trees Grove and Lady Bird Johnson Grove near Orick are favorites with visitors, and whale-watching, bird-watching, wildlife viewing, mountain biking, and camping are all popular activities with visitors to the park area. Scenic drives, including the Newton B. Drury Scenic Parkway, the Coastal Drive, and Howland Hill Road, offer spectacular views of these magnificent forests.
Map ref: page 784 A2

Towering, majestic redwoods can live for 2,000 years.

Freight train, near Sacramento, a major transport center.

SACRAMENTO

This is the state capital and the gateway to Gold Country. The area grew rapidly as a supply town during the gold rush and, when the gold was depleted, residents turned their attention to the bountiful fruit and vegetables of the Central Valley. The city is still a prosperous shipping and processing center, and is also known as the "camellia capital of the world."

In 1860, Sacramento was the western terminus for the Pony Express, and later four influential Sacramento businessmen financed building the Central Pacific Railroad from Sacramento through the Sierras to meet up with the Union Pacific Railroad, to be built west from the Missouri River. Today, the large metropolitan area has a population of approximately 1.9 million and growing fast. As the information technology industry grows, spillover from Silicon Valley continues at a dizzying pace.

Sacramento's main attraction is the state Capitol Building and grounds. The domed building is like a scale model of the nation's in Washington, DC. Hundreds of species of plants and trees are identified throughout the 40-acre (16-ha) grounds. The California State Railroad Museum, the largest interpretive museum of its kind in North America, displays 21 restored locomotives. Sutter's Fort Historic Park, Sacramento's earliest settlement (1839) features a cooper and blacksmith's shops, bakery, jail, dining room, and living quarters.

Outdoor enthusiasts enjoy river rafting on the America River and bicycling through Old Sacramento Historic District or along the 22-mile (36-km) American River Parkway. Lodging and dining options are plentiful. The port accommodates 20 ships per month from around the world. They enter through a 43-mile (69-km) channel from Suisun Bay in the upper reaches of San Francisco Bay. Sacramento is 90 miles (145 km) east of San Francisco on I-80. Trains and buses service the city, as does the Sacramento International Airport.
Map ref: page 784 F10

SAN BERNARDINO

San Bernardino, with a population approximately 170,100, is less than an hour's drive east of Los Angeles on I-10. This area received its name because missionaries came upon these mountains, valleys, and deserts in southern California in 1810 during the feast of San Bernardino of Siena. When the Mexicans secularized the missions in the 1830s, the settlement was granted by the government as a "rancho." In 1851, Mormons purchased Rancho San Bernardino and created a city modeled on Salt Lake City, Utah. Citrus farming is the main industry and, in spring, the wonderful fragrance of orange blossoms fills the air.

Nearby San Bernardino National Forest is popular for many outdoor activities and the Glen Helen Regional Park has water slides, nature trails, swimming, and camping. The Rim of the World Highway, (Hwy 18), runs through the national forest at elevations of up to 8,000 feet (2,440 m) along a ridge of the San Bernardino Range. The vistas are breathtaking, and it is sometimes possible to see to Palm Springs. From San Bernardino it is about a 45-minute drive to the Big Bear Lake, Snow Summit, Running Springs, Lake Arrowhead, Blue Jay, and Skyforest, and the Mountain High and Sugarloaf ski areas.

Buses and trains connect San Bernadino to nearby Los Angeles, and San Bernadino has its own international airport.
Map ref: page 788 G5

SAN DIEGO

Like Los Angeles, California's most southern city (Tijuana, Mexico, is only a 30-minute drive over the border) is made up of several communities spread out over a large area and connected by freeways. The greater San Diego metropolitan area includes Oceanside, Carlsbad, Encinitas, Del Mar, La Mesa, Coronado, National City, and Chula Vista along its 70 miles (113 km) of coastline, and the inland Escondido, Rancho Santa Fe, and El Cajon. The local population in San Diego alone is approximately 1.2 million and the greater metro area swells to approximately 2.6 million. The second-largest city in the state and the sixth largest in the nation, it covers 4,205 square miles (10,891 sq km).

San Diego was the first Spanish settlement in California, and was named by the Spanish explorer, Sebastian Vizcaino, in 1602, for the Spanish Franciscan saint, San Diego de Alcala.

Cool summers, warm winters, and one a fine natural harbor attract thousands to this city each year. The area is the West Coast base of operations for the US Navy, and has the largest percentage of military personnel in the nation.

Ornate sculpture on top of a San Diego fountain.

More cruise ships frequent this busy commercial port than any other on the West Coast. The sciences contribute to the local economy as well; the Salk Institute and the Scripps Institute of Oceanography are located here.

Balboa Park, a 1200-acre (486-ha) area downtown overlooking the Pacific Ocean, is home to many popular attractions. The world-famous San Diego Zoo is tucked into the park's canyons and mesas so that most animals are seen in surroundings that closely mimic their natural environments. The zoo's panda exhibit is a perennial favorite. Old Town, with buildings that date to the time of the early Spaniards, reflects the rich and colorful history of early California. The San Diego Civic Light Opera stages big-name musicals at the Starlight Bowl on most summer evenings. Other park attractions include the Museum of Man, the Museum of Photographic Arts, the Timken Museum of Art, the Natural History Museum, the Hall of Champions Sports Museum, the Globe Theatre, and two golf courses.

Charles Lindbergh built his famous *Spirit of St Louis* aircraft in San Diego and a full-size replica

"San Diego de Alcala," California's oldest mission, built in San Diego in 1769.

is a highlight at the San Diego Aerospace Museum. The 16-block Gaslamp Quarter is a national historic district at the heart of the downtown area. Here restored Victorian buildings, sidewalk cafes, and cobblestone streets give charm and character. Other popular attractions include the San Diego Wildlife Animal Park and the Mission Bay Aquatic Park/Sea World. Many lodging and dining options are available at all price levels. Parking, especially in the summer months and in Balboa Park, is limited.

The San Diego Trolley and Coaster Commuter lines service the area, but getting around to all of the attractions is easiest by car or, within districts, by bicycle. It is just under two hours' drive from Los Angeles via I-5. San Diego International Airport services the area, as do trains and buses.
Map ref: page 789 H8

SAN FRANCISCO

Not many cities in the world make the heart flutter the way this one does. The city is 47 square miles (122 sq km) in area, and covers the northern tip of a peninsula that is surrounded by the San Francisco Bay to the east and the Pacific Ocean to the west. San Bruno Mountain makes up the southern border and the Golden Gate strait and Marin County lie to the north.

The center of the city covers a series of steep hills, including Telegraph, Nob, Russian, and Rincon. Heights and peaks such as Potrero, Bernal, and Buena Vista dot the city's outer limits. Several islands—Alcatraz, Angel, Farallon, Treasure, and Yerba Buena—lie within the city limits. The population is approximately 810,000, although it is closer to 6,700,000 for the major metropolitan area including Oakland and San Jose.

In 1776, Spanish Officer Juan Batista de Anza founded a fort (presidio) here. Later that year, Father Junipero Serra established the nearby Mission San Francisco de Asis, now called Mission Dolores. By the time of the gold rush in the mid-1800s, San Francisco was a booming port and supply point, and was an early governmental and cultural center. By 1850 the city was incorporated. The destructive earthquake of

Cable car, with Alcatraz in the distance, San Francisco.

1906 slowed growth, but the city was quick to rebuild. Another quake destroyed much of the city's waterfront Marina district in 1989.

The city has a colorful history and culture, including the lawless Barbary Coast, a notorious saloon and red-light district along the piers in the gold-rush days; and North Beach, which is famous for its Beat Generation of the 1950s, Haight-Ashbury and the flower children of the 1960s and, since the 1970s, a thriving gay community. "The City," as the financial district is known, is the major financial trading center of the western United States. San Francisco is an international trade center and a home to apparel manufacturers and the information technology industry. Spillover from nearby Silicon Valley is changing the city's landscape as escalating rents force businesses, the arts, and even long-standing restaurants to relocate.

The city's most recognized landmark is the Golden Gate Bridge, which was opened in 1937 to reach Marin County to the north. Another landmark, the Bay Bridge, which opened in 1936 to connect San Francisco with Oakland, is one of the longest combination bridges (part suspension, part steel truss) in the world. The city is divided into districts, and the Marina, Cow Hollow, Pacific Heights, North Beach, Russian Hill, Nob Hill, Chinatown, Union Square, Mission, SoMa (South of Market), Japantown, the Castro (known as a gay neighborhood), and the Sunset

districts are popular destinations for visitors. There are ferries from Fisherman's Wharf to Alcatraz Island, the former maximum security prison that once held Al Capone and Robert Stroud, the "Birdman of Alcatraz." Alcatraz is now a popular recreation area with a self-guided trail, cellblock tour, slide show, and other programs.

Golden Gate Park has artificial lakes, riding trails, a golf course, tennis courts, and a Japanese tea garden. It is also home to the De Young Museum and the California Academy of Sciences, which includes the Steinhart Aquarium, Morrison Planetarium and the Natural History Museum. The Maritime National Historical Park displays a coastal lumber schooner, a ferry, a tugboat, and a sailing vessel. The Fort Mason Center is a World War II embarkation point that has been transformed into a regional cultural center which has theatres, museums, galleries, and craft studios. Some of the city's many other notable attractions include the Civic Center with its War Memorial Opera House and Louise M. Davies Symphony Hall, Cow Palace, the Exploratorium, the Palace of Fine Arts, the San Francisco Zoo, and the brand new Pacific Bell Ballpark.

Even more enticing than the shopping, which is some of the most interesting and unique in the nation, is the food. From freshly made tortillas served hot off the grill in the Mission to the most exquisite restaurant meal, San Francisco is a food-lovers paradise. Freshly baked bread and premium

San Francisco's tallest building, the Transamerica Pyramid.

specialty coffee is available just about every five blocks. Wine is equally as important, especially with America's premier wine-growing regions so close by. Berkeley, just across the east bay and home of chef Alice Waters and Chez Panisse, is by accounts the culinary seat of America.

The best way to explore San Francisco is on foot, walking up and down the hills in sturdy, rubber-soled shoes, or hopping on a cable car. The BART subway and MUNI buses run frequently and cover the entire region. Parking is extremely limited. It is advisable to dress in layers—the closer to the bay, the colder it gets, especially in the summer months when the temperature can vary as much as 20–30°F (11°–17°C) depending upon where you are in the city.

San Francisco International Airport and the smaller Oakland International Airport service the area, and San Jose International Airport is close—it is only about 45 miles (72 km) southeast of San Francisco. Trains and buses also service the area. It is six hours from Los Angeles on the US-101, or up to 12 hours on the more scenic Pacific Coast Highway (Hwy 1). It is about one hour from Sacramento on I-80.
Map ref: page 786 C3

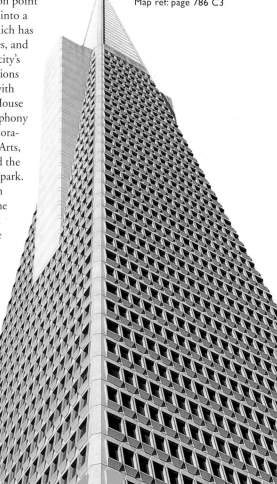

Roses and grapes at the picturesque Wildhorse Vineyard in San Luis Obispo.

SAN JOSE

Silicon Valley, San Jose's more popular name, is just 50 miles (80 km) south of San Francisco on US-101 or I-280. These 50 miles (80 km), however, often seem like 50,000 as traffic from rapid-growth technology businesses clogs the infrastructure. The city sits in the Santa Clara Valley, with the Santa Cruz Mountains to the east, the Diablo Range to the west, and the southern tip of the San Francisco Bay just 11 miles (18 km) from the city center. The greater metropolitan area covers 1,291 square miles (3,344 sq km); it comprises the Santa Clara County and includes Sunnyvale, Santa Clara, Mountain View, Cupertino, and Palo Alto. The population in San Jose itself is approximately 890,000—in the metro area it is 1,650,000 and growing rapidly.

The Native American Ohlone people inhabited the southern bay shore for more than 1,000 years before the arrival of white settlers. In 1777, San Jose became the first civil settlement in Spanish California, and was named El Pueblo de San Jose de Guadalupe for Saint Joseph, the husband of the Virgin Mary. The area quickly developed primarily as an agricultural center, and the state's thriving wine industry has its roots here. Concrete, strip malls, and housing developments now cover former orchards and vineyards, while areas

such as the Napa Valley have set up agricultural preserves to avoid the same fate given by rapid urbanization without long-term planning.

San Jose is the number one high-tech center in the United States, with specialties in aerospace and computer technologies. Apple, Intel, Hewlett-Packard, and IBM are all based here, as are Lockheed Martin's missiles and space divisions. The climate is mild year-round, crime levels are low, and the thriving economy has attracted hundreds of shops, restaurants, and other services that supply the newly wealthy residents.

The San Jose Museum of Art features local and national art exhibits, while the Tech Museum of Innovation is a hands-on technology museum. The Rosicrucian Egyptian Museum, architecturally inspired by the Temple of Amon at Karnak, houses a large collection of Egyptian artifacts, including objects from predynastic times through Egypt's early Christian era. The Peralta Adobe and Fallon House Historic Site is a history park with 27 original and replica homes, businesses, and landmarks highlighting periods of the Santa Clara Valley's past.

For those seeking something a little more exciting and an escape from the heat, Raging Waters has wave pools, inner-tube rides, waterfalls, and nearly a dozen types of waterslides. Other major attractions include the Children's

Discovery Museum, the Lick Observatory, the Cathedral Basilica of St Joseph, and the Winchester Mystery House.

Lodging and dining options range from roadside motels and fast-food restaurants to five-star resorts and restaurants. Fast-food prices are generic across the nation, but nothing else here is cheap. Even the economy motels are expensive—visitors on a budget should make this a day trip.

San Jose International Airport serves the area, as do rail and bus services from San Francisco.
Map ref: page 786 D4

SAN LUIS OBISPO

Halfway between San Francisco and Los Angeles, on US-101, and 10 miles (16 km) inland from the coast is the little college town of San Luis Obispo (population 43,200), or SLO to the locals. Father Junipero Serra established the mission here in 1772 and named it San Luis Obispo de Tolosa. The mission's thatched roof burned often and the tile roof that was finally added set the style for all future missions.

Agriculture, government, tourism, retail, and California Polytechnic State University are the base of the local San Luis Obispo economy.

The museum in the Mission San Luis Obispo de Tolosa, established in 1772, features exhibits and showcases local Chumash Native American culture as well as California's Mission Period. A Mozart festival in July and a wine festival in September are held in the surrounding Mission Plaza, overlooking the river. The University is worth visiting for its three art galleries, working livestock and farm units, horticultural displays, Performing Arts Center, and Shakespeare Press Printing Museum. The San Luis Obispo Art Center and the San Luis Obispo Children's Museum are also popular attractions.

Pismo Beach, with its pier and white beaches, is 15 miles (24 km) south on the US-101. Sea kayaking and fishing are popular activities there and at nearby Morro Bay. This region is a part of California's renowned Central Coast wine producing zone, with local wineries especially renowned for their pinot noir, chardonnay, and rhone

A marina in Santa Barbara, crowded with yachts and local fishing boats.

varietals. Dining and lodging options are limited in San Luis Obispo but there is a better selection on the coast.

The area is served by the tiny San Luis Obispo County Airport.
Map ref: page 788 A2

SANTA BARBARA

Santa Barbara, 92 miles (148 km) northwest of Los Angeles, sits between the Pacific Ocean and the foothills of the Santa Ynez Mountains just as the coastline jogs eastward. Directions can be confusing as the ocean now is to the south, not the west, but this is the calmest stretch of water along the state's coastline as a result. Chumash Native Americans lived here long before the European settlers arrived. Although Portuguese navigator Juan Rodriguez Castillo discovered the channel in 1542, December 4, is now celebrated as Santa Barbara Day—this commemorates the day Spanish explorer Sebastian Vizcaino entered the channel in 1602.

The city is a planned community and the current local population of about 87,200 now supports strictly enforced building codes preventing further development. Driving is the best way to get around the

The Santa Cruz boardwalk, amusement park, and beach—the water here is very cold and only the bravest actually swim.

whole area, but the best way to enjoy the downtown and waterfront areas is on foot.

Chase Palm Park, along the waterfront, hosts an arts and crafts show each Sunday. The Santa Barbara Museum of Art has nationally recognized collections of antiquities, nineteenth-century French, British, and American art, contemporary European, North American, and Latin American art, Asian art, photography, and works on paper. Other popular attractions include the Museum of Natural History, the Historical Museum, the Santa Barbara Courthouse, and the Zoological Gardens. Outdoor enthusiasts enjoy golfing at the municipal Santa Barbara Golf Course or at the 18-hole oceanside Sandpiper. Yachting, sailing, and fishing are serious sports here. World Cup hopefuls train in the waters. Sailing races around the Channel Islands take place from April to October. Rollerblading and bicycling along the waterfront are popular, as are the less strenuous eating, shopping, and whale-watching.

Up into the foothills from downtown is the Mission Santa Barbara, founded in 1786 and known as the "queen of the missions" for its magnificent architecture and sheer size—at one time it served as a beacon for passing ships. Further up into the foothills is the Santa Barbara Botanic Garden, as well as

romantic hideaways frequented by movie stars and tycoons.

The Santa Ynez Valley—the heart of Santa Barbara's wine country—is 30 minutes from downtown, and the local pinot noir is some of the best in the nation. Wineries ranging in size from little roadside shacks to huge estates are open for tasting.

Los Angeles residents make up a great part of the tourist traffic in Santa Barbara, and restaurants and hotels are geared to meet their demanding expectations for food and wine, but there are plenty of options in the middle and lower tiers as well. Like anywhere else along the coast, summer weekends are the busiest, and US-101 can turn into a parking lot.

Trains and buses serve downtown Santa Barbara. The Santa Barbara Municipal Airport offers a limited service.
Map ref: page 788 C4

SANTA CRUZ

Jagged mountains and steep, winding roads tend to keep the masses away from this fascinating beach town on northern Monterey Bay.

Northwest of Santa Barbara is the Santa Ynez Valley wine trail.

Located 76 miles (122 km) southeast of San Francisco via the scenic US-1 or the quicker US-101, Santa Cruz (population approximately 51,400) offers 29 miles (47 km) of public beaches, and includes the villages of Capitola, Soquel, and Aptos. The Santa Cruz Mountains rise quickly from the coast, providing natural shelter from the cooler San Francisco area. Father Junipero Serra built the Mission of the Holy Cross (Santa Cruz Mission) here in 1791. Later, in 1797, Spanish colonists founded a village nearby and named it Branciforte. However, the village lacked financial support and was eventually overtaken by the Mission.

Santa Cruz has a reputation as a center for counterculture, and a drive through the area is like a visit to the 1960s. Tie-dyes and dreadlocks are sported by even the newly wealthy young people that commute from here to Silicon Valley. The Santa Cruz Beach Boardwalk is California's only remaining seaside boardwalk and amusement park, and its Louff carousel and Giant Dipper roller coaster,

The J. Paul Getty Museum and the Getty Center, high above Los Angeles, in the Santa Monica mountains. It is built around a sunken garden designed by Robert Irwin.

which was built in 1924, have attracted crowds since the early twentieth century. Neptune's Kingdom, with a two-story miniature golf course, and the Casino Fun Center are also at the boardwalk.

At Lighthouse Point on West Cliff Drive, the Mark Abbot Memorial Lighthouse contains a surfing museum. The lighthouse overlooks Steamer Lane, the area's best spot for surfing, and the Santa Cruz Municipal Wharf—which is good for fishing, dining, shopping, or listening to sea lions yelp and bark—is just up the beach. The Natural Bridges State Beach, at the end of West Cliff Drive, has tide pools and hiking.

Near Felton, about 6 miles (10 km) north, The Roaring Camp and Big Trees Narrow-Gauge Railroad takes passengers up and down steep grades through giant redwood groves on authentic nineteenth-century steam locomotives. At Aptos, about 6 miles (10 km) east, is the Forest of Nisene Marks State Park, the epicenter of the 1989 earthquake. On Branciforte Road, the Mystery Spot is an area discovered in 1939 where laws of gravity are defied; trees grow sideways and balls roll uphill. Wineries are tucked away in

the mountains, and most have signs welcoming visitors. Several wine-tasting rooms are located downtown as well. The heart of downtown is along Pacific Avenue. The Pacific Garden Mall is a popular area for shopping and dining out, and many lodging options are available. Santa Cruz is serviced by trains and buses and San Jose, which is about 50 miles (80 km) north, has an International Airport.
Map ref: page 786 C5

SANTA MONICA

This seaside resort and city in southwestern California sits at the end of Los Angeles' famous Wilshire Boulevard. Tourism, aircraft, and aerospace manufacturing are the main industries here, though the city also collects fees from the movie industry for frequent filming along the palm-tree lined white sandy beaches. Spaniards came upon the area in 1769, and

in 1838 a Mexican Ranch was established by grant. The city was finally laid out in 1875 by land developers, and now has a population of 88,471 people.

The Santa Monica Pier is home to Pacific Park, a 2-acre (0.8 ha)

Street performer, Venice Beach, near Santa Monica.

amusement park, and to the UCLA Ocean Discovery Center, where interactive activities are used to introduce visitors to the basic concepts of marine environmental studies, marine biology, and oceanography. The Santa Monica State Beach is one of the best in the area and offers bike paths and volleyball courts in addition to plenty of surfing. Palisades Park covers 26 acres (11 ha) of coastline with paths and gardens. The Museum of Flying, at Santa Monica Airport, features a rare collection of World War II fighter aircraft, most of which are in flight-ready condition. The area is dotted with art galleries and artists' studios, and romantic beachfront hideaways and restaurants line the bay. Fine dining is an art form here, but the restaurants are much more innovative and less stuffy than the rest of Los Angeles.

Just a short distance to the south is Venice Beach, famous for its walking path lined with tattoo studios, street performers, magicians, fortune tellers, drug dealers, weekend rollerbladers, and the outdoor weightlifting center, Muscle Beach. visitors should be careful here—parking is expensive, and pickpockets are common.
Map ref: page 788 E5

SANTA ROSA

This vast residential and agricultural area with a population of 115,300, is about one hour's drive north of San Francisco. It is the county seat and the largest city in Sonoma County. The county is most famous for its local wine industry.

The Luther Burbank Home and Gardens, where the famous horticulturist created 800 new strains of plants, fruits, and vegetables at the turn of the twentieth century, is now open to the public. The greenhouse features changing exhibitions and includes a replica of his office which contains many of his tools. The Carriage House Museum has exhibits relating to the ongoing impact of Burbank's life and work.

Snoopy's Gallery is the world's largest collection of Snoopy memorabilia, thanks to the generous donations of "Peanuts" comic-strip creator Charles Schulz. The Sonoma County Museum offers displays on regional history and art exhibits. The life and work of the creator of the world famous "Ripley's Believe It or Not" comic strip, is featured at the Robert L. Ripley Museum, housed in the historic Church Built from One Tree, the largest building built from the lumber of a single redwood tree.

Santa Rosa is a good base for exploring the vast Sonoma wine country. Many of the area's nearly 200 wineries offer pleasant picnic areas in addition to tastes of their wares. Traffic is heavy in peak summer months, especially on weekends. Sonoma County Airport is just north of the city.

Map ref: page 786 B1

SEQUOIA AND KINGS CANYON NATIONAL PARKS

St Francis Winery, near Santa Rosa.

The towering granite peaks of the Great Western Divide and the Sierra Crest, alpine lakes and meadows, deep canyons, and giant sequoia groves attract more than 1.5 million visitors each year to these two adjoining national parks. The parks, which have a total area of 461,901 acres (187,070 ha), are located on the western slopes of the Sierra Nevada range in east-central California. At 14,494 feet (4,421 m), Mt Whitney in Sequoia National Park is the highest point in the contiguous United States. Kings Canyon Park has the highest canyon wall in the contiguous United States, rising 8,350 feet (2,547 m) from the south fork of the Kings River. Naturalist John Muir helped to establish these parks as well as that at Yosemite, 200 miles (322 km) to the north.

The parks were established independently but share their administration and a main highway, the General's Highway, which connects Hwy 180 in Kings Canyon to Hwy 198 in Sequoia. The drive is about six hours from San Francisco, and about five from Los

Stored wine casks at Ferrari–Carano Winery, a short distance north of Santa Rosa.

Ledson Winery, "Sonoma Castle" to the locals, Sonoma Valley, south of Santa Rosa. The climate in this area is perfect for growing the delicate grapes for premium wines.

Angeles. The parks are within easy access of Fresno, which is about 50 miles (80 km) east of the parks. The main park gates are at Ash Mountain on Hwy 198 and at Grant Grove on Hwy 180.

The visitor centers at Lodge-pole in Sequoia and at Grant Grove, in Kings Canyon, are the largest and most helpful. Grant Grove was known as General Grant's National Park from 1890 until Kings Canyon was designated a national park in 1940. It offers the 1-mile (1.6-km) Big Stump Trail as well as a ⅜-mile (600-m) trail winding past a 2,000-year-old sequoia called "General Grant" that is designated the country's official Christmas Tree. In Boyden Canyon, between Grant Grove and Cedar Canyon, visitors can take a 45-minute tour through Boyden Cavern to see its stalactites and stalagmites. Cedar Grove on the south fork of Kings River offers hiking, camping, and horseback riding through meadows or up to dramatic cliffs. At Road's End, on Kings Canyon Highway, the granite walls of the deepest canyon in the contiguous states drop an extraordinary 8,200 feet (2,501 m) to the Kings River.

In Sequoia National Park, Moro Rock, a granite monolith, rises 6,275 feet (1,914 m) from the edge of the Giant Forest. In the forest, the General Sherman Tree, which is the largest living thing on earth, has grown to 275 feet (84 m) high. It has a circumference of 103 feet (31 m), and is estimated to be between 2,300–2,700 years old. Nearby, 15 miles (24 km) from Ash Mountain, is Crystal Cave, where there is available a 50-minute tour of its splendid marble interior. At 14,495 feet, (4,421 m) high, Mt Whitney is the highest point in California. It is accessed from Hwy 395, on the far eastern border of Sequoia National Park. The 11-mile (18-km) hike to the top is best spread out over two days, and many climbers still suffer severe headaches from the high altitude.

Steep gradients in the mountain passes add travel time. Gas and groceries are limited, as are lodging and dining options. Camping is restricted to designated areas, and

Snow plant (Sarcodes sanguinea), Kings Canyon.

requires pre-registration and a small fee. Recreational vehicles and trailers are allowed at most sites, but visitors should be aware that space is limited. There are bears in the parks, so precautions are necessary, especially with food. Chains are required during periods of heavy snow, and road closures are common in winter months. Mosquitoes are prevalent during summer months.

The entrance fee can be used for both Sequoia and Kings Canyon National Parks and is good for seven days. Buses serve Fresno and Visalia, and Fresno Yosemite International airport is the closest.
Map ref: page 787 J6

SOLVANG

This little Danish village, 45 miles (72 km) north of Santa Barbara, on US-101, is one of the most popular tourist stops on the West Coast. Ornate buildings in the town center create the feeling of Denmark, and four windmills, cobblestone streets, wooden shoes, and horse-drawn streetcars complete the illusion. Busloads of tourists walk from shop to shop, comparing platefuls of sugar-covered fried dough that may at one time have had Danish origins.

The local population is around 4,920, two-thirds of whom are of Danish origin. The Elverhoy Museum showcases traditional Danish folk arts, including weaving, needlework, lace making, wood carving, and paper cutting. It also has an art gallery with rotating exhibits of regional art. Other attractions include the Motorcycle Museum, displaying motorcycles dating from 1906, and the Hans Christian Andersen Museum. Franciscan Fathers founded the Mission Santa Ines, a relatively plain-looking Spanish mission on the edge of town, in 1804. It is sometimes called the "hidden gem of the missions" because of its beautiful setting in the rolling hills of a lush, well-watered valley.

In summer, the open-air Festival Theater presents contemporary and classic plays. For those with an outdoor bent, Cachuma Lake is 12 miles (19 km) east of Solvang and offers hiking, fishing, and boating. Dining and lodging options in town are geared towards tourists. The nearest air, bus, and train services are in Santa Barbara.
Map ref: page 788 B3

Kings Canyon National Park, with the Sierra Nevada mountains in the distance, viewed from nearby Inyo National Forest.

STOCKTON

This mid-state city (population approximately 246,800), covering 53 square miles (137 sq km) and the seat of San Joaquin County, sits at the mouth of the fertile San Joaquin Valley on the eastern end of the Sacramento River Valley. A 78-mile (126-km) deepwater channel connects Stockton's inland port to San Francisco Bay, 80 miles (129 km) northeast, and the city's economy is based on its deepwater port. The Port of Stockton is the head of navigation on the San Joaquin River, and large ships have been loading ore, grain, and other products there since 1933. Warehousing, distribution, and processing of the agricultural bounty of the San Joaquin Valley are core businesses now, although electronics, lumber, plastics, and automobile products also contribute to the economy.

The town was named "Tuleberg" when Captain Charles M. Weber founded it in 1847. He later changed the name to honor Commodore Robert F. Stockton, a Naval officer who took part in the 1847 takeover of California from Mexico. During the gold rush, Stockton was a tent city. It grew as a supply center, and later, with the advent of the railway and the development of the port and the irrigation canals in the San Joaquin Valley, it became the agricultural hub it is today.

Micke Grove Park features a Japanese garden, the San Joaquin County Historical Museum, rides, and picnic areas in a beautiful oak grove setting. The Haggin Museum art galleries feature works by American and European artists. Its history displays focus upon the Stockton area's past and the accomplishments of its residents, such as Benjamin Holt, inventor of the Caterpillar track-type tractor. Other popular attractions include the Oak Grove Nature Center and Funderwoods Amusement Park. The Stockton Asparagus Festival takes place each April. The Sacramento-San Joaquin River Delta at the confluence of the Sacramento and San Joaquin rivers has numerous tributaries and waterways. Houseboat rentals are available north of Stockton off I-5. Famous residents include author Maxine Hong Kingston and singer Chris Isaak. Dining and lodging options are limited. Stockton Metropolitan Airport serves the area.
Map ref: page 786 E3

WHISKEYTOWN–SHASTA–TRINITY NATIONAL RECREATION AREA

This vast recreation area in the northern reaches of California covers the northern tip of the Sacramento Valley. The state's coastal and interior mountain

Belltower at Mission Santa Ines, in Solvang. The mission is set in a picturesque valley.

ranges—the Coast Range and the Sierra Nevada Range—converge at Redding just to the south, and the flat valley floor changes to lakes and mountains. To the northeast, the Sierras become the Cascade Range, and as the valley floor rises it forms the Trinity Mountains. To the west, the Klamath Mountains form the border of the area as they merge with the Coast Ranges. The area encompasses Clair Engle Lake, also known as Trinity Shasta Lake, and Whiskeytown Lake. The Shasta National Forest covers a vast portion of the recreation area.

Major attractions at Lake Shasta include the Shasta Dam—its overflow spillway is three times the height of Niagara Falls—and Lake Shasta Caverns, where caves have 20-feet (6-m) high stalactite and stalagmite formations. Lake Shasta offers 370 miles (595 km) of shoreline, and attracts 2 million visitors each year to its fishing, boating, and water sports activities. Houseboat rentals are popular.

Clair Engle Lake, known locally as Trinity Lake, offers 157 miles (253 km) of shoreline. Nearby Weaverville offers lodging and dining options, and its gold

mining heritage is captured at the Jake Jackson Memorial Museum-Trinity County Historical Park. At the same site is the Joss Historic House, the oldest continuously used Taoist temple in the state. To the north is the impressive Mount Shasta, a snowcapped mountain peak and former volcano with bubbling sulfur springs, downhill skiing in winter, and mountain climbing in spring and summer. The Mount Shasta region is on I-5 north of Lake Shasta. To the east are the McArthur-Burney Falls Memorial State Park and the Lassen Volcanic National Park.

Redding offers a wide variety of lodging and dining options and is a good base from which to explore this breathtaking region. Traffic can slow to a standstill during busy summer weekends. Temperatures can vary dramatically depending on elevation and proximity to the lakes so it is advisable to take a few layers of clothes.

Redding is the closest city, accessible by car on I-5 or Hwy 299 east from the coast. There is a train service, and the area is served by two small airlines into Redding Municipal Airport.
Map ref: page 784 D5

STATE FEATURE

Yosemite National Park

Yosemite National Park is located in the Sierra Nevada Range in central-east California. Open year-round, the park attracts close to 4 million visitors annually from every corner of the globe. Its unparalleled natural beauty includes the famous waterfalls and granite peaks of the Yosemite Valley and some of the world's tallest sequoias, in the Mariposa Grove of Big Trees. Covering 1,170 square miles (3,030 sq km), elevations in the park range from 4,000 feet (1,220 m) at Yosemite Valley to 13,114 feet (4,000 m) at Mt Lyell. With 80 species of mammals, 247 of birds, 24 of reptiles and amphibians, 37 of native trees, and 1,400 of flowers, the park is a nature-lover's paradise.

The Sierra Nevada Range was lifted out of the Earth's crust millions of years ago. The Merced River cut and defined the narrow, V-shaped Yosemite Valley. Later, ice-age glaciers widened the valley and formed its current shape of flat floors and sheer walls. Native American Miwok people first inhabited the area, and their culture is relatively well preserved in park exhibits. In 1849, however, the discovery of gold in the streams, rivers, and foothills of the Sierras led to the arrival of miners who fought the Miwok, eventually displacing them. Word began to spread about the area's spectacular scenery, and tourists followed. After preservationists voiced concerns about use of the area, President Abraham Lincoln granted much of the current park to the state of California in 1864 to ensure protection from development. Later, naturalist John Muir greatly influenced the decision of the US Congress in 1890 to establish Yosemite, the country's first national land preserve, as a national park. In 1984 Yosemite was designated a World Heritage Site by the United Nations Educational, Scientific, and Cultural Organization.

Many of the park's attractions are centrally located and easily accessible within the 1- × 7-mile (1.6- × 11-km) wide Yosemite Valley. El Capitan, Half Dome, Yosemite Falls, Bridalveil Falls, the visitor center, Ahwahnee Indian Village, the Indian Cultural Museum, Yosemite Fine Arts Museum, and the historic Ahwahnee Hotel are located here. The spectacular valley is sharply defined along its length by sheer granite cliffs, with towering sequoias and waterfalls softening the powerful impact of the mountain faces. Most imposing is El Capitan, the largest exposed granite monolith in the world—at 3,593 feet (1,096 m) high, it is twice the height of the Rock of Gibraltar. Rock climbers are drawn especially to the vertical front, thrust out from the valley rim. El Capitan is located on the valley's west side and is easily reached on foot, by shuttle, or by car. Half Dome, its west side fractured vertically, cut in two by natural erosion, is 4,733 feet (1,444 m) high. Rock climbers take the 17-mile (28-km) round-trip up the back face, which the local park service has fitted with steel cables.

Merced River tributaries and creeks spill over the cliffs surrounding the valley, creating dramatic waterfalls. Yosemite Falls is North America's highest waterfall and the fifth highest in the world. The upper falls (1,430 feet, 436 m), the middle cascades (675 feet, 206 m), and the lower falls (320 feet, 98 m) combine for a total of 2,425 feet (740 m). These falls are accessible by car with an easy ¼-mile (400-m) walk to the base. A strenuous 3½-mile (5.6-km) climb starting from Sunnyside Campground will take you above the upper falls. Nearby Bridalveil Falls, also a very short walk from parking, is 620 feet (189 m) high. It is known as "Pohono," or "Puffing Wind," by the Native American people because of the way the winds spread the mist up to 20 feet (6 m) in all directions.

Those less athletically inclined may choose to spend a day walking around Yosemite Valley Village, stopping at the visitor center for orientation slide programs and exhibits of geology and ecology, the Ahwahnee Indian Village, a reconstructed Miwok-Paiute village, the Indian Cultural Museum, or the Yosemite Fine Arts Museum. Inside the Ahwahnee Lodge, the high-ceilinged dining room is awe-inspiring, and the towering windows offer views of the powerful presence of the surrounding sheer mountain faces. Strolling the scenic hiking paths behind the property could fill a day.

Glacier Point, a 3,214-foot (980-m) high cliff 30 miles (48 km) south of Yosemite Valley, offers panoramic views of the valley and the High Sierra mountains, plus Nevada, Vernal, and Yosemite falls,

A giant sequoia (Sequoiadendron giganteum) in the Tuolumne Grove, Yosemite. Giant sequoias can be found in groves on the western side of the Sierra Nevada. Tuolumne Grove is one of three groves in Yosemite.

OPPOSITE: *El Capitan, in Yosemite Valley, is extremely popular with rock climbers. An average ascent takes about four days and there are over 70 routes up the rock.*

V-shaped Yosemite Valley, with El Capitan on the left. About 93 percent of the Yosemite National Park is wilderness.

The western white pine (Pinus monticola), which becomes stunted and wind-swept on Yosemite's granite domes.

A redwood forest within Yosemite National Park. These towering trees have to be experienced to be able to appreciate their sheer majesty and beauty.

and Half Dome and other peaks. The view here is accessible by a short walk from the parking lot, except during snow season when the access road is closed. Snow season is when the nearby ski area Badger Pass opens. A complimentary shuttle bus visits the various hotels and lodges in season—the ride is just short of one hour and is enjoyable in itself for the great wide-open vistas. Skiing and snowboarding here is geared for beginner and intermediate levels. The park offers nine short to medium-length runs and is not crowded, even in high season.

Thirty-six miles (58 km) from the valley, near Wawona and the south gate, is the Mariposa Grove of Big Trees, the largest of three giant sequoia groves in the park. Visitors can take the Big Trees Tram Tour or visit on foot. Out of 500 trees, the 2,700-year-old Grizzly Giant, 209 feet (64 m) tall, 32 feet (10 m) wide, and with single limbs 10 feet (3 m) thick, is a favorite. In the late 1800s, holes were cut through several mammoth trees and roads were built through them. Although no longer possible to drive through them, they are good sites for photographs.

Tioga Pass, on the eastern border of the park, is the gateway to Yosemite's high country, which is popular during summer for hiking, rock climbing, water sports, and camping. No other place rivals this part of the High Sierra, with the crystal-clear Tenaya Lake and the expansive subalpine Tuolumne Meadows. The highest point in the park, Mt Lyell at 13,114 feet (4,000 m), is here as well. Unlike the valley, cars are a necessity here.

The most spectacular places on the planet are usually the hardest to reach, and Yosemite National Park is no different. Steep winding grades, snow and ice in winter, and crowds in summer add to travel time. Park gates—there are four— are reached by car in four hours from San Francisco or six hours from Los Angeles, with another 30 minutes or so to reach a destination within the park. Most visitors enter through Arch Rock on Hwy 140. The National Park Service requires that automobile drivers carry chains throughout the snow season. The park is accessible by motor coach from gateway areas, connecting with the park's complimentary shuttles, so it is possible to navigate much of the park easily without a vehicle. Entrance fees are valid for seven days, and annual passes are available.

Summer months are the busiest, specifically between Memorial Day, May 30, and Labor Day, the first Monday in September. Park superintendents turn away thousands of cars annually. Summer activities include backpacking and camping. There are 800 miles (1,288 km) of hiking trails, with the option of going with guides specializing in nature or photography.

The Yosemite Mountaineering School offers rock climbing and backpacking classes. Water sports include fishing (a Californian license is required but can be purchased in the park), boating (no motors allowed), windsurfing, swimming, and river rafting on the Merced River. Bicycle riding, horseback riding, and a nine-hole golf course are also available. Winter activities include skiing, snowboarding, snow-shoeing, cross-country skiing, ice skating, and the annual Vintners' Holidays and Chefs' Holidays at the Ahwahnee Hotel each year from November to February. The Ahwahnee Hotel also hosts one of Yosemite's grandest traditions, the Bracebridge Dinner, which "transports diners to the splendor of a seventeenth-century English manor house celebration"—according to the Yosemite Concession Services literature. Tickets to this dinner, served at Christmas each year, are in such demand they are available only by lottery.

Year-round, the park hosts meetings and weddings, and holds spiritual re-awakenings. Artists find inspiration and city-dwellers find solace in this magnificent, isolated setting. Lodging ranges from upscale country inns to nature tents, cabins, and campgrounds, with family-style lodges in between. Motels and hotels are plentiful in gateway towns and cities, but the drive into the park is long. Yosemite National Park has a high number of fatalities and serious injuries each year. The park service advises visitors to stay on trails when hiking, and warns that many routes are often more difficult than they appear. They recommend that visitors approach rivers, streams, and waterfalls cautiously, and be aware of potential undercut banks and slippery rocks. The waters here are cold and fast currents are common.

Wild animals, including mountain lions and bears, live in the park, and it is not unusual for visitors to encounter them. Attacks are rare, but the park advises against hiking or running alone, and advises parents to keep children within sight at all times. Bears have grown fond of human food, and thorough precautions must be taken at all times. All edibles, plus sunscreen and anything else aromatic, should be removed from cars when parking, and following food storage regulations when camping is essential. It is illegal to feed or closely approach any of the wildlife, including birds, coyotes, deer, or squirrels.

Climbers preparing in Yosemite. The valley attracts rock climbers from all over the world.

The top of Vernal Falls is reached via the steep Mist Trail. From the top, visitors can view the spectacular Merced River plunging down the granite cliff face.

HAWAII

Hawaii, "The Aloha State," lies in the central Pacific Ocean. It is the southernmost part of the United States and the only island state, being a volcanic archipelago of 130 islands, islets, and shoals that extends for 1,600 miles (2,574 km). The eight main islands—Niihau, Kauai, Oahu, Molokai, Lanai, Kahoolawe, Maui, and Hawaii (the Big Island)—each have distinctive landmarks and geology. The Polynesian explorers who originally settled the islands called them "the land of raging fires." Captain James Cook of England discovered the islands in 1778. By 1900 Hawaii was a US territory, and in 1959 it became the 50th state of the Union.

The capital and largest city is Honolulu, on Oahu. The second-largest city is Hilo, on the Big Island. Honolulu is 2,400 miles (3,862 km) from the west coast of the US mainland. People from many different backgrounds live in Hawaii, including Native Hawaiian, Chinese, Japanese, Samoan, Filipino, African-American, Inuit, Tahitian, Tongan, European, Puerto Rican, and Korean.

The islands lie just south of the Tropic of Cancer and the climate is tropical, cooled in many parts by trade winds or higher elevations. Aside from the urban center of Honolulu, and coastal developments such as Waikiki and Kihei, most of the state is an unspoiled natural paradise, and tourism is a vital part of the economy. A strong military presence and agriculture, especially pineapple and sugarcane production, also contribute.

The islands are a gentle place, with a happy atmosphere. Locals are relaxed, friendly, and hospitable. The traditional flower lei greeting is just the beginning. Hawaiians share the welcoming aloha spirit quite easily with visitors. Those coming from frenetic urban lifestyles have the hardest time acclimatizing to the pace. *Akamai* (clever) *malahinis* (newcomers) sit on a *lanai* (porch or veranda) and unwind with some *ono* (delicious) *pupus* (appetizers).

Halona Cove in Koko Head Regional Park on the island of Oahu, part of an extinct volcanic crater.

State motto *Ua Mau Ke Ea O Ka Aina I Ka Pono* (The life of the land is perpetuated in righteousness)
State flag Adopted 1845
Capital Honolulu
Population 1,211,537
Total area (land and water) 6,459 square miles (16,729 sq km)
Land area 6,423 square miles (16,636 sq km)
Hawaii is the 47th-largest state in size
Origin of name The islands may have been named by Hawaii Loa, their traditional discoverer, or have been named for Hawaii or Hawaiki, the traditional home of the Polynesians. The word "Hawaii" may also be based on the native word for homeland, *Owhyhee*
Nickname The Aloha State
Abbreviation HI
State bird Nene
State flower Yellow hibiscus or pua aloalo
State tree Kukui
Entered the Union August 21, 1959 as the 50th state

Places in
HAWAII

HALEAKALA NATIONAL PARK

This Park in eastern Maui is made up of the world's largest inactive volcano, a massive structure covering 28,099 acres (11,380 ha) whose most dramatic feature is the barren stony waste of the Haleakala crater. The Park was established in 1916 and has a rich and colorful history. Native Hawaiians call Haleakala "House of the Sun" and find it to be a great source of spiritual power and cosmic energy. According to legend, power struggles between kahuna lapa'au, the healing practitioners, and kahuna ana'ana, the black magic sorcerers, took place here and at Kawilinau, "The Bottomless Pit," where Pele, the fire goddess, battled with a sibling.

Haleakala National Park extends from the summit of Mount Haleakala at 10,023 feet (3,057 m) down the volcano's southeast flank, out to Maui's eastern coast near Hana. Within the Park's boundaries are dry forests, rainforests, desert, and subtropical beaches. The Park is divided into two distinct sections that are separated by a scientific research center that is off limits to the public. Haleakala Summit is the larger western section, while Kipahulu on the eastern slope looks like a finger pointing down and touching the ocean. Kipahulu Valley has a rich tropical landscape, and Oheo Gulch with the Seven Sacred Pools

is near the coast. The Koolau, Hana, Kipahulu, and Kahikinui Forest Reserves flank the Park.

To reach the summit, drive 37 miles (60 km) from Kahalui on Hwys 37 to 377 to the winding 378, or take Haleakala Crater Road. Park headquarters are 1 mile (2 km) outside the gate. The visitor center is 11 miles (18 km) from the gate. Entrance fees apply per car or bicycle and the pass is valid for seven days. To reach Kipahulu from Kahalui, take Hwy 360 along the northern coast and continue about 40 minutes past Hana (Hwy 31). Treat the two Park areas as separate, and give at least a day to each, as no direct road connects them.

Sunrises and sunsets in the Park are spectacular, especially from Puu Ulaula Overlook, also known as Red Hill. Leleiwi Overlook faces into the crater, and Kalahaku Overlook is the best place to view the rare silversword plant. Sliding Sands, Halemauu, and Hosmer Grove nature trails are all popular hiking trails. Cycling down the volcano is easily arranged. Limited lodgings in the Park include campgrounds and cabins in the crater, and campgrounds at Hosmer Grove and Kipahulu. Camping permits and reservations are required—the demand is so high a lottery system is used. The nearest town for supplies is Pukalani. The weather can change suddenly and dramatically

Handmade silk leis are a popular tourist memento of Hawaii.

from cold wind, rain, and, in winter, snow, to hot and sunny conditions. Bring sunscreen and a hat, but also bring lots of layers and waterproof gear, wear comfortable, sturdy shoes, and carry plenty of drinking water.

Kahalui Airport services Maui with many direct flights from the US mainland. Cars are essential.
Map ref: page 791 L5

HAWAII

At an impressive 4,038 square miles (10,458 sq km), Hawaii is twice the size of all the other islands combined. It is more commonly (and less confusingly) referred to as the Big Island. Its other nicknames are Volcano Isle and Orchid Isle.

The island is triangular in shape. It is 76 miles (122 km) east to west, 93 miles (150 km) north to south, and has 266 miles (428 km) of scenic coastline. Formed by volcanic action, the landscape here is dramatic, with ash-covered volcanic peaks, lava ridges, and black lava-covered land and roads. There are also tropical rainforests, cattle ranches on wide, grassy plains, and spectacular waterfalls. At times

parts of the island are covered in vog (thick volcanic dust).

There are three volcanoes here, including the dormant Mauna Kea —at 13,796 feet (4,208 m), it is the highest—and the state's two most active volcanoes, Mauna Loa at 13,680 feet (4,172 m), and Kilauea. Kilauea projects from the side of Mauna Loa. Hawaii Volcanoes National Park encompasses Mauna Loa and Kilauea.

Tourism, the production of sugarcane, coffee, and pineapple, plus energy, aquatic, and astronomical research, support the economy. Hilo is the administrative center, largest community, and principal seaport. There are about 123,000 people on Hawaii.

Volcanoes rank as the number one attraction here, and the Puna Region is where all the action is. Kilauea erupts nearly every day. Much of the region has been covered in lava.

The town of Kalapana was destroyed in 1990, as was the Chain of Craters road leading down from Kilauea's crater to the coast. The Kona Coast is 70 miles (113 km) of black sand and blue water teeming with sea life. Sunbathing is as

Haleakala National Park on Maui contains the world's largest inactive volcano; its crater is a rugged landscape of scree slopes and jagged rocks.

popular as sports fishing. The town is developed but not too crowded. Kailua-Kona is a commercial center, and, Keauhou, a bit further south, is a hub of condominiums, hotels, and restaurants. The more rural South Kona Coast has macadamia farms and coffee plantations, and the little fishing village of Milolii. The marine-life preserve at Kealakekua Bay has the best dive-spot on the island.

The Kohala Coast on the northern tip overlooks the Alenuihaha Channel. Jetsetters sunbathe at Waikoloa, Mauna Lani, and Mauna Kea resorts, while cowboys and cattle roam the upcountry Parker Ranch, the largest working ranch in the state. The largest optical telescope in the world, the Keck, is at the Mauna Kea Observatory. Waipio Valley on the Hamakua coast is a lush, tropical valley leading out to a striking black-sand beach. Hilo, America's wettest city, is the gateway to Hawaii Volcanoes National Park.

Lodging options vary from plentiful B&Bs to campgrounds, with a few budget motels. Take precautions against the elements, most notably the sun.

Two airports, Kona International and Hilo International, service the island. Some international and many domestic airlines fly directly into Kona or there are inter-island flights from Honolulu to Kona. Cars are essential on Hawaii.

Map ref: page 791 N9

HAWAII VOLCANOES NATIONAL PARK

Covering some 209,695 acres (84,926 ha), this Park is on the island of Hawaii, the Big Island. It was established in 1916 and has two active volcanoes—Mauna Loa, the world's largest volcanic mass, and Kilauea, which has erupted almost every day since 1983.

With Hilo as a base, drive just 29 miles (47 km) south on Hwy 11 past Volcano Village to the Kilauea Visitor Center, where it is worth stopping to learn about the highly unusual surroundings and about Pele, the goddess of the volcano. Varying admission fees apply to vehicles, cyclists, and hikers, and a pass is good for ten days.

Mauna Loa rises 13,680 feet (4,172 m) above sea level, and its Mokuaweoweo crater has walls that reach a height of 600 feet (183 m). Kilauea projects from the eastern slope of Mauna Loa, rising to 4,090 feet (1,247 m). The heart of the Park is the Kilauea Caldera. It covers 4 square miles (10 sq km) and is the largest active volcanic crater in the world. The 11-mile (18-km) drive around the rim features sulfur banks, steam vents, and moon walks, and takes you through lush tree-fern and ohia forests. On the way is an observatory and a museum, which features exhibits explaining Hawaiian volcano history. Also en route is the Thurston Lava Tube—next to Kilauea Iki Crater—formed when a crust of lava developed a liquid core, about 400 years ago, leaving a 600-foot (183 m) long hollow space. Debris from the 1959 eruption can be seen along the paved Devastation Trail. The Hale-maumau Trail leads down to the home of the fire goddess, Pele. The Kau Desert is to the south and the lava freeway is at the end of Chain of Craters Road as it meets the ocean.

Not only is it a federal crime to remove anything from the Park, it may also be offensive to a greater power. The local post office regularly receives lava rocks from vacationers who have had bad luck ever since taking what they thought was a harmless souvenir. Do not touch moving lava or remove anything from the volcanoes, not even a lava chip. Also note the chilly conditions in the higher altitudes, and beware of too much exposure to volcanic smog and stinging vapor gases.

Volcano House is a hotel that overlooks the crater; this or limited camping are the only options within the Park, but plenty of other lodging options exist nearby. Remote B&Bs are more interesting than Hilo motels.

Two international airports service the island, however cars are essential in this Park.

Map ref: page 791 M8

Hibiscus feature among flowering plants in Hilo's Nani Mau Gardens.

HILO

On the eastern shores of Hawaii's Big Island, Hilo, with a population of 38,600, is one of the state's largest settlements. It is the seat of Hawaii County, and falls under the county's government. Despite a somewhat shabby appearance, Hilo is the most important commercial district on the island, has the principal seaport, and serves as a processing and shipping center for the surrounding sugarcane fields, fruit orchards, and macadamia nut fields (the Maunaloa Macadamia Nut Factory offers guided tours through its fields).

The United States' wettest city, Hilo was settled by missionaries in the 1820s. It is the gateway to the popular Hawaii Volcanoes National Park, and is serviced by an international airport.

Liliuokalani Gardens is a 30-acre (12.2-ha) formal Japanese Garden, while Nani Mau Gardens offers 2,000 varieties of flowering plants, a Japanese Garden, an orchid walkway, a botanical museum, and a butterfly house. Hilo Tropical Gardens and Gallery is also popular. Natural attractions near Hilo include the Rainbow Falls and the Boiling Pots in Wailuku River State Park. Legend has it that Hina, the mother of Maui, lives in the cave behind the 80-foot (24-m) falls. North of Hilo, the 420-foot (128-m) Akaka Falls are accessed by a 40-minute trail through a fern forest, while south of Hilo, Panaewa Rainforest Zoo is an outdoor zoo featuring a number of endangered Hawaiian birds.

Halemaumau Trail in Hawaii Volcanoes National Park leads to this crater, the home of the fire goddess, Pele.

A popular spot between resort and waterline on crowded Waikiki Beach in Honolulu. Waikiki is probably the best known of Hawaii's many beautiful beaches.

Hilo has several interesting museums. Volunteers at the Pacific Tsunami Museum recount personal experiences with devastating "walls of water." The Lyman Museum and Mission House once hosted literary luminaries Mark Twain and Robert Louis Stevenson. It has an excellent exhibition of missionary life, an Island Heritage Gallery, and an Earth Heritage Gallery. At the Mauna Kea Observatory, advance reservations will gain you a look through the eight major astronomical telescopes there.

A number of performances and festivals are held throughout the year at the East Hawaii Culture Center. The Naha Stone located in front of Hilo Public Library was involved in ancient rituals. One story is that babies were placed on the stone to see if they were part of the Naha clan. If they remained silent, they were considered true members of the clan. If they cried, they were not. Another story asserts that whoever could move the stone could conquer and unite the islands. A 14-year-old boy who had moved it later became King Kamehameha.

Beaches here are pockets of sand between lava flows. Coconut Island Park, reached by a footbridge, is a good place to swim.
Map ref: page 791 N8

HONOLULU

Honolulu covers 83 square miles (214 sq km) of southern Oahu. It occupies a narrow strip of land—12 × 26 miles (19 × 42 km)—and it stretches from Pearl Harbor in the west to Makapuu Point in the east, and from the shores of the Mamala Bay in the Pacific Ocean to the foothills of the Koolau Mountains. Its sheltered harbor, white sandy beaches at Waikiki, and imposing Diamond Head and Punch Bowl volcanic craters combine with the balmy weather and a slow, friendly pace of life to attract millions of visitors each year.

Honolulu is the capital city of Hawaii, and is under the governance of Honolulu County. It is the nation's eleventh-largest city, with a population of 861,000, and the leading economic center of the state. Military installations include Pearl Harbor Naval Base, Tripler Army Medical Center, and Hickam Air Force Base; manufacturing and tourism also support the economy.

British Captain William Brown discovered Honolulu Harbor in 1794. Honolulu was originally inhabited by Polynesians, but by the 1820s European and American missionaries had arrived and it became the main residence of the Hawaiian Royal Family. By 1898,

the area was annexed to the United States, and the city was incorporated in 1905. The surprise attack on Pearl Harbor by the Japanese in 1941 triggered the United States' entry into World War II, and throughout that war the area was an important Pacific hub for US forces. In 1959, when Hawaii entered the union, Honolulu became the capital.

Waikiki Beach is by far the main attraction here, and many vacationers never leave their pool or beachside perch. The strip is quite beautiful, but very crowded. White sand, clear blue water, palm trees swaying, and locals surfing make up for the wall of fast-food joints and hotels that line the beach. The west end has a few luxurious resorts. Each afternoon they offer local Hawaiian entertainment for the price of a cocktail. These oceanside verandas are a great place to sit and watch the sunset.

Ala Moana Beach Park, to the west of Waikiki, is more of a local's hangout, though tourists flock to the adjacent Ala Moana Shopping Center. Past Waikiki to the east, towards Diamond Head, is Kapiolani Park, home of the Honolulu Zoo and Waikiki Aquarium. Body builders and other locals congregate at Sans Souci Beach, or "Muscle Beach" as it is known locally.

Diamond Head and Punch Bowl are two extinct volcanoes. Visitors can walk from Kapiolani Park east to Diamond Head and visit the Diamond Head State Monument. Cultural attractions include the Queen Emma Summer Palace, former mountain home of the wife of King Kamehameha IV, and the Iolani Palace, the no-expense spared royal palace of King David Kalakaua. Museums include Honolulu Academy of Arts, Mission House Museum, and the Bernice Pauahi Bishop Museum.

Oahu is serviced by Honolulu International Airport, which offers frequent services to the mainland and outer islands. Buses and shuttles offer services to downtown, Waikiki, and most of Honolulu. Walking and cycling are good ways to explore. Cars are convenient, but parking is limited.
Map ref: page 790 G4

KAHALUI

Kahalui, with a population of just 18,100, is situated on Kahalui Bay on Maui's north coast. It is a residential and commercial hub and has the island's major seaport and airport. Agriculture is an important focus and Kahalui is a distribution point for pineapple and sugarcane. The Alexander and Baldwin Sugar

A breathtaking sunset glows behind the palm trees on the shores of Kaneohe Bay. Kaneohe is located at the southern end of the bay on Oahu's southeastern coast.

Mill Museum has good exhibitions on the history of Maui and sugar production. In the 1790s, Kamehameha I landed his war canoes here en route to the Iao Valley battle. It was an established sugar town by 1880, but in an attempt to control the plague, the whole town was burnt down and rebuilt in 1900. Nearby Wailuku, the county seat, is the largest community on the island.

The Kanaha Pond State Bird Sanctuary was once a royal fishing pond and now protects the endangered Hawaiian stilt, or ae'o, the Hawaiian coot, or alae ke'oke'o, and the Hawaiian Koloa ducks. Entrance to the Sanctuary is free. The Wailuku War Memorial Park and Center offers a football stadium, baseball field, swimming pool, and tennis courts, and the nearby Kahana Beach County Park has barbeque pits, restrooms, a pavilion, and is popular for sailboarding and outrigger canoeing.

Kahalui has an international airport and cars are essential here.
Map ref: page 791 K5

KAHOOLAWE

"Taking Away" is the translation of the name of this small Hawaiian island. And in fact, the US Navy took this uninhabited isle from 1941 to 1994 and used it for target practice. It was ceded to Hawaii in 1994, but the Navy controls access as long as unexploded bombs exist.

Kahoolawe has a rich history as a sacred place for Native Hawaiians; it was especially revered by the kahuna ana'ana, the black sorcerers. Protect Kahoolawe Ohana, a group that was formed to protect Native Hawaiian rights, played a role in the Navy's withdrawal.

The island is situated across the Alalakeiki Channel from Maui's southern shores. It is rocky and sparsely vegetated, with 29 miles (47 km) of coastline and a maximum elevation of 1,477 feet (450 m) at Moaulanui. Kahoolawe lies in Maui's rainshadow. It is 11 × 6 miles (18 × 10 km) and covers 45 square miles (117 sq km). Of the eight major islands, only Niihau is smaller than Kahoolawe.

In the winter months, whales and dolphins come here to mate and to calve their young.
Map ref: page 791 K6

KANEOHE

This residential community with a population of 37,100 is on Oahu's southeastern windward coast and overlooks one of the most beautiful bays in the Pacific, Kaneohe Bay. At the Bay there is a barrier reef, a hidden sand bar, and four islets, one of which appeared in the well-known 1970s television program "Gilligan's Island."

From the shoreline, Kaneohe extends westwards into the Koolau foothills. Kaneohe Bay Marine Corps Air Station is nearby, and the Hawaii Pacific University Hawaii Loa Campus is located here.

The Valley of the Temples, near Kahaluu, has a replica of Byodo-In Temple of Equality, a 900-year-old Buddhist temple in Kyoto, Japan. Hoomaluhia Botanical Gardens present an abundance of native flora and displays of the world's

tropical regions, featuring many rare and endangered plants. It has a lake, hiking trails, and a campground, and offers educational programs. Tram tours run through the five lush valleys of Senator Fong's Plantation and Gardens, which features tropical flowers, ferns, fruit and nut trees, and the option to learn lei-making. Sailboarding, surfing, and kayaking are extremely popular at Kaneohe Beach County Park, around Mokapu Point, and at Kailua Beach County Park. Snorkel or fishing charters depart from Heeia Boat Harbor.

The International Airport and downtown Honolulu are about 30 minutes by car along the Pali Highway. Several tour operators offer packages with transportation from Waikiki.
Map ref: page 790 G3

KAPAAU

Kapaau is a town along Hwy 270 on Hawaii's North Kohala Coast where macadamia-nut farming and small-scale tourism carry the local economy. This remote, quiet little town has one claim—the original statue of King Kamehameha the Great, in front of the Kapaau Courthouse. Commissioned by King Kalakaua in 1878, the original statue was thought lost in a shipwreck so the artist was commissioned to reproduce it. That copy stands across the street from the Iolani Palace on Oahu. The original was recovered from the sea not three months after the new statue was completed. Since Kapaau was the heart of Kamehameha's ancestral homelands, it was sent there. The bronzed sculpture gets a fresh coat of paint each year before Kamehameha Day, June 11. The Courthouse is a senior activity center and here town elders volunteer information, give Courthouse tours, and provide a free guide to North Kohala. The nearby Ackerman Gallery offers displays of crafts and fine art.

Kapaau is the last place to stop for supplies on the way to the Pololu Valley Lookout, one of the best scenic lookouts on the island and inhabited by the endangered Hawaiian hawk. On the way is Keokea Beach Park, a favorite with locals, where camping is allowed (by permit only).
Map ref: page 791 L6

The original statue of King Kamehameha the Great, Kapaau.

KAUAI

Kauai is the fourth largest in the chain of Hawaiian Islands. Like the others, it was formed by volcanic action and has a dramatic landscape of mountain peaks, valleys, sea cliffs, and spectacular beaches. The island is 90 miles (145 km) northwest of Oahu across the Kauai Channel. Mount Kawaikini, at 5,243 feet (1,599 m) above sea level, is the highest point. Waimea Canyon is 10 miles (16 km) long and half a mile (1 km) deep. Soil in the North Shore area is fertile, and the production of sugarcane and

tropical fruit, as well as tourism, supports Kauai's economy. The movie industry contributes regularly to the economy, with over 40 films showcasing this isle's wild, untamed beauty having been made to date.

Residents, of which there are approximately 52,200, live primarily in Lihue and Kapaa. Kauai remained independent from King Kamehameha and his desire to unite the islands in the late eighteenth century. Eventually—by 1810—the island was united with all the others, but the independent spirit lives on. Locals have resisted developing their "Garden Isle" just to support tourism. One ordinance restricts building heights to "no taller than a palm tree." Nature also participates—just when the

island seems too touristy, another hurricane wreaks havoc, and Kauai remains the least developed of the inhabited islands. Locals have survived strong forces of nature, yet they are some of the most hospitable, friendly people around.

The island is a natural paradise, with forest reserves, wildlife sanctuaries and state parks. Visitors can see the Spouting Horn, a lava-tube blowhole, at Poipu. Or they can take a riverboat journey, complete with Hawaiian legends and songs, to the lush Fern Grotto, with its cascading maidenhair ferns. Near Kapaa, the Sleeping Giant is a mountain said to resemble the face of a man. A little further on are Opaekaa Falls, while the morning-glory draped Wailua Falls are north of Lihue.

Outdoor-lovers seeking extreme adventure will find it here. Kauai offers a full range of outdoor activities, including freshwater and deep-sea fishing, boogie boarding, body surfing, water-skiing, kayaking, sailing, snorkeling, scuba diving, hiking, horseback riding, camping, hang-gliding, helicopter rides, birdwatching, whale-watching, golf, tennis, and stargazing.

There is a working lighthouse at Kilauea Point, which is a refuge for the enormous frigate birds and the red-footed boobies. Migrating

whales are frequently seen off the point during the winter months. At the Na Pali Coast State Park, the cliffs plunge directly into the ocean—here there are caves, waterfalls, and scallops of white sand. Lookouts at Kalalau and Puu O Kila, in Kokee State Park, give views above the peaks along the Na Pali Coast.

In Kauai, delightful public gardens abound, including Alberton Gardens, across from Spouting Horn; Lawai Gardens, with tropical native plants growing along pleasant streams; and the Limahuli Gardens, which feature ancient taro terraces.

Those with an interest in history can step back in time at the Grove Farm Homestead Museum, formerly a missionary's home, or visit the Kauai Museum, which shows how ancient Hawaiians lived. The remains of a Russian Fort in Elizabeth State Historical Park are also popular with visitors.

Lodgings—from luxury resorts and self-contained condominiums to camp sites—are plentiful. Seafood is a highlight here.

Lihue Airport offers direct service to Los Angeles as well as interisland services. Car rentals and a taxi service that offers some local color are available on the island.
Map ref: page 790 D2

Children frolic in the warm, gentle waters of a protected inlet on Kauai, a relatively undeveloped and unspoiled Hawaiian island.

The glorious blue waters of Kihei's beaches are irresistible.

KIHEI

Kihei is the most developed stretch of coastline after Waikiki. It is part of Maui's south coast and, with the exception of afternoon wind and sandstorms, offers some of the island's finest weather. The beachfront is crowded with hotels and condominiums, which offer the visitor plenty of lodgings but sadly have marred the area.

This region was an important landing spot for Hawaiian war canoes, and in 1793 Western navigator Captain George Vancouver anchored here. During World War II this was thought to be the likely sight for an amphibious attack.

From the numerous state and county beaches along the Kihei Coast visitors will have unobstructed views of Lanai, Molokini, West Maui, and Kahoolawe.

Natural attractions near Kihei include the Kealia Pond Wildlife Refuge, which safeguards the endangered Hawaiian stilt and Hawaiian coot; and the Ahihi-Kina'u Natural Area Reserve, which features shallow "bubble caves" near the shore and is excellent for snorkeling, swimming, scuba diving, kayaking, and viewing Hawaiian green sea turtles.

Kihei also has a number of golf courses, the Tedeschi Vineyards—Maui's only winery—and the science city, Maui Research and Technology Park. This 330-acre (134-ha) development sits on the slopes of Mt Haleakala.

From Kahalui International Airport, drive south on Hwy 311.
Map ref: page 791 K5

KOKO HEAD REGIONAL PARK

The island of Oahu has three signature landmarks: the extinct volcanic craters of Punch Bowl, Diamond Head, and Koko Head. Koko Head is the next piece of land that juts out from the coast after Diamond Head on Oahu's southern shore. From Waikiki, drive past Diamond Head, Maunalua Bay and Hawaii Kai on Hwy 72, the Kalinianiole Highway.

Hanauma Bay Beach Park is the major attraction in Koko Head Regional Park. This is one of the most popular—and crowded—snorkeling spots in the world. The parking lot fills up early. Public buses stop here, and the Hanauma Bay Shuttle offers a free service between the Park and Waikiki, but there is an entrance fee and the Park is closed on Tuesdays. The shallow inlet is only 10 feet (3 m) deep. Feeding out to the Kaiwi Channel, it is teeming with sea life. Hanauma Bay is a conservation district so human interaction with wildlife is prohibited.

Beyond the wide, shallow band at the shore is the dive site Witches Brew, accessed by diving through a reef opening. There are sharks and, as the Molokai Express causes strong currents out here, it is only for the experienced. Continuing down the highway you will come

across the Blowhole, a combination of rocks and water that sucks in water and spews it out with the tide. Sea Life Park is nearby.
Map ref: page 790 G4

LAHAINA

Like a bull's-eye, Lahaina, with a population of 10,100, is the dead center of West Maui's coastline. King Kamehameha I made this his residence, and later, in 1790, after he conquered most of the islands, he made it his capital. During the nineteenth century, Lahaina was a whaling port. Missionaries came to try and tame the debauchery and general chaos. Whaling declined, and was replaced with sugar production. In 1845, the location of the state capital was transferred to Honolulu.

The recent well-planned development of resorts at Kaanapali has re-invigorated Lahaina with the tourist dollar. The city has a thriving arts community, and each Friday night galleries open to the public and offer complimentary *pupus* (appetizers). To get to Lahaina, fly into Kahului International Airport, and then drive either around the north shore and then down, or cut across towards Maalaea Bay and drive up the coast.

Attractions in Lahaina include the famous Banyan Tree, whose trunks support a vast canopy shading almost 1 acre (0.4 ha). Behind the tree is the 1850s Courthouse, and in the pleasant boat harbor is the Fort as well as the square-rigged *Carthaginian II*, a floating museum dedicated to whales. Across the road is the Pioneer Inn, the island's first hotel. Also nearby is one of the oldest buildings in the town, Baldwin Home (circa 1850), now a museum, as well as an old

The clear waters of Hanauma Bay, Koko Head Regional Park, reveal volcanic rocks.

Pineapples were the mainstay of Lanai's economy until the late twentieth century.

prison, and numerous attractive parks and beaches.

Lahaina's restaurants are above average in quality, and there are plenty of choices in lodgings.
Map ref: page 791 K5

LANAI

At 140 square miles (363 sq km), Lanai is the sixth-largest island in the chain, and is across the Auau Channel from Maui. It is part of Maui County. Mount Lanaihale, at 3,336 feet (1,017 m), is its highest point. The island's name translates to "hump", and it is one of the best spots for whale-watching in the state. The population of 3,000 is concentrated in central Lanai City and at the port of Kaumalapau. It has 18 miles (29 km) of sandy shoreline. Every inch of cultivated land was used to grow pineapples until the late twentieth century. Two mega-resorts have changed the landscape and lifestyle dramatically.

Lanai City is the only area on the island that offers services. The town is a remnant from the 1930s, with Dole Town Square and a post office being the highlights. Nearby is Garden of the Gods, the Luahiwa Petroglyph Field, in Kanunolu Village. This national historic landmark features some of Hawaii's best-preserved ancient ruins and petroglyph carvings.

If you are not staying at the Lodge at Koele or the Manele Bay Hotel, your only options besides camping are in Lanai City. They include a hotel, a plantation house, and B&Bs. Make reservations well in advance. Upcountry from Lanai City is Koele with its magnificent English Tudor-style lodge. The weather is chilly here and many are drawn to the big fireplace in the Lodge's grand entrance and sitting room. Remote Shipwreck Beach is a popular beachcombing and whale-watching spot. Hiking or 4WD touring are the best (and at times the only) ways to explore the island.

Manele Bay Hotel is a popular Mediterranean-style beach resort. Hulopoe Beach is a protected marine preserve teeming with sea creatures, rated one of the best beaches in the world. Snorkeling and diving are popular: Cathedrals I and II are ranked in the world's top-ten dive spots. Hulopoe's lava-rock tide pools are another favored attraction here.

Reaching Lanai is challenging. Tiny Lanai Airport services the island with inter-island flights only via Honolulu. From the airport, drive or ride 10 minutes to Lanai City, or 25 minutes to Manele Bay. A ferry service runs between Maui and Lanai.
Map ref: page 791 J5

MAUI

Maui, known as the "Valley Isle," is the second-largest in the chain of Hawaiian isles, at 727 square miles (1,883 sq km). At its widest, it is 26 miles (42 km) from north to south and 48 miles (77 km) from east to west. Maui has 120 miles (193 km) of shoreline, and more than 80 beaches. Its climate ranges from desert conditions at Lahaina to humid subtropical in Hana. West Maui reaches an elevation of 5,788 feet (1,765 m) at Puu Kukui and is the smaller of the island's two sections. East Maui is made up of the mountain of Haleakala, a dormant volcano with a height of 10,023 feet (3,057 m). Its crater is 2,300 feet (702 m) deep and its circumference at the rim is 21 miles (34 km). It is also one of the tallest mountains on Earth but more than 20,000 feet (6,100 m) of it is under water. The island was formed when lava-flows from Puu Kukui and Haleakala met and formed an isthmus.

It is generally believed that Polynesians arrived in the islands from AD 500–800. Captain James Cook of England discovered the islands in 1778 but was killed in a battle after his return the following year. King Kamehameha rose to unite the islands, an astonishing feat he began in 1790 and finally accomplished in 1810. Missionaries and whalers followed but whaling abruptly declined from its mid-nineteenth century peak, and was replaced with sugar production. In 1959, Maui County joined the other islands to become the 50th state of the nation.

Today, pineapple and sugar production, cattle, construction, tourism, and scientific research all contribute to the economy. The population is approximately 101,600 and is concentrated in the communities of Wailuku and Kahalui.

The island of Maui is a resort destination. Many vacationers arrive at their beach-front hotels, which are concentrated in West Maui from Kapalua to Lahaina and at Kihei in South Maui, and remain there. Swimming, surfing, sailboarding, ocean rafting, ocean kayaking, parasailing, snorkeling, and diving expeditions to Molikini Crater can all be arranged without leaving the resort. Ferries to Lanai and a submarine dive are offered from Lahaina. Lahaina also has a historic district. From anywhere on the coast, whale-watching is prime from mid-December to April.

A number of world-class golf courses are nearby, some of them adjacent to the resorts themselves.

Haleakala National Park is Maui's premier attraction. Upcountry Maui is well worth a visit, especially the winding drive to Hana if you want to experience the "real" Maui, not just the manicured version. While you are there learn about the area's history at the Hana Cultural Center. Hiking and camping options are plentiful. Helicopter tours are a thrilling way to explore the island.

Kahalui Airport has direct flights from the mainland of the United States, as well as inter-island flights. Cars are essential.
Map ref: page 791 L5

MOLOKAI

The Friendly Isle of Molokai is across the Kaiwi Channel from Oahu to the west, and Lanai and Maui lie to its southeast. It covers 260 square miles (673 sq km) and has a population of about 6,700 residents. This island has the

Surfboards for rent at a beachfront resort in Maui.

highest population of Native Hawaiians, and remains a spiritual center. The hula dance was born here.

The island of Molokai measures 10 × 38 miles (16 × 61 km), and has resisted development. There is an old resort at Kalaukoi, and extremely expensive upscale camping at Molokai Ranch in "tentalows" built up on platforms overlooking the cliffs. At Kaunakakai you will find the ocean, budget condominiums and a few B&Bs, and free camping (no facilities). There are few shops and fewer restaurants.

What there is here, however, is raw natural beauty and miles of isolated beaches. Molokai has the world's tallest sea cliffs and Hawaii's highest waterfall. Its highest point is 4,961 feet (1,513 m).

The island was formed by three volcanic eruptions, and has a port at Kaunakakai on its southern coast. Kaunakakai is also the residential area and community center. Pineapple, coffee, and cattle all support the economy. Molokai coffee beans are highly sought after and are often used in Kona blends.

In 1873 a wealthy Belgian by the name of Joseph de Veuster came upon the Kalawao leper colony on the Kalaupapa Peninsula. He gave up his comfortable lifestyle and settled here, devoting his life to the lepers. He became a Roman Catholic missionary and was known locally as Father Damien.

The isolated peninsula is now the Kalaupapa National Historic Park. Mule rides are the best way to experience it.

Hoolehua Airport offers inter-island connections from Maui and Honolulu, and one small airline flies here direct from the US mainland. The *Maui Princess* also serves the area, sailing from Lahaina. Cars are hard to rent but taxis are sometimes available. The best way to see the island is on foot, bicycle, mule, or from a boat or kayak.
Map ref: page 791 J4

Sidewalk shopping is commonplace in Honolulu's Chinatown area, on Oahu.

NIIHAU

Known as the "Forbidden Isle," Niihai is 17 miles (27 km) west of Kauai across the Kaulakahi Channel. This privately owned island is 18 × 6 miles (29 × 10 km), and 70 square miles (181 sq km) in area. In 1864, King Kamehameha IV sold the island to Eliza Sinclair for US$10,000. Today her great-great grandson runs the ranch. Close to 300 people live here, in the main village of Puuwai. There is no indoor plumbing or electricity and, as on Molokai, Hawaiian native culture thrives.

Most of the residents are of native Hawaiian ancestry and still speak the language. Raising livestock, primarily cattle and sheep, and pleating mats from rush are the main activities. Niihau leis, strings of *pupu* Niihau shells, are another specialty and sell for several hundred dollars or more.

Visitors are not allowed on the island, but one dive operator offers a dive expedition from Kapaa in Kauai. It is a 90-minute ride, and is for experienced divers only. Waters here are challenging, and there is a healthy shark population.
Map ref: page 790 B2

OAHU

The Gathering Place island, Oahu, is the third largest in the chain. It covers a vast 600 square miles (1,554 sq km). The island is 44 miles (71 km) long, 30 miles (48 km) wide, and 112 miles (180 km) in circumference. It is cooled by constant trade winds and has a favorable climate. The great Koolau Range covers most of its eastern half, and the lesser Waianae Range covers part of the west. In between is a wide plain used for the production of pineapple and sugarcane. Oahu has three signature landmarks, the extinct

Traditional Hawaiian prints at the International Market Place in Honolulu, on Oahu.

volcanic craters of Punch Bowl, Diamond Head, and Koko Head.

Honolulu is the state capital and Oahu is the commercial center of the state, serving as the US Defense Base for the Pacific. Tourism supports the economy. Population is estimated at 1.1 million.

Honolulu is Hawaii's only major urban center. As a result, Oahu offers some of the best nightlife, restaurants, and cultural attractions in the state. Tourists congregate at Waikiki Beach. This is "the strip" and is considered one of the most famous beaches in the world.

Continuing along the south coast on Hwy 72, Diamond Head, Hanauma Bay at Koko Head, and the Halona Blowhole are popular stops. Just past Sandy Beach Park the coast juts out at Makapuu Point and then up to Waimanalo Bay and Kailua Bay. This is the windward coast, where water sports and fishing are especially good. Attractions include a rock formation called Crouching Lion, and the touristy Polynesian Cultural Center, which holds luaus and shows. The North Shore is remote and offers local color; the Banzai Pipeline is considered one of the best surf spots in the world. For the most part, the leeward coast is not recommended, as unfortunately the locals have been known to hassle visitors. In Central Oahu you can learn about pineapple diversity at the Pineapple Variety Garden, discover commercial pineapple cultivation at the Dole Plantation, or see native flora at the Wahiawa Botanical Garden.

Lodging is plentiful, and dining options are many, including Thai, Japanese, Chinese, Filipino, and Korean eateries. Oahu is served by Honolulu International Airport; buses and shuttles offer services to downtown, Waikiki, and most of Honolulu. Walking and cycling are good ways to explore.
Map ref: page 790 F4

PEARL CITY

Pearl City overlooks Pearl Harbor in south-central Oahu. Most visitors go directly to the USS *Arizona* National Memorial. Pearl Harbor is one of America's principal naval bases. The inlet is 6 miles (10 km) west of Honolulu on Hwy 1 and feeds out to Mamala Bay. In 1887 the US government was granted exclusive use of the inlet and used it as a repair and coaling station for ships. After the United States annexed the Hawaiian Islands in 1898, improvements were made. By 1911, a wide channel out to the ocean had been dredged through sand bar and coral reef. The channel is 35 feet (11 m) deep and the harbor is up to 60 feet (18 m) deep, allowing passage for even the largest naval vessels.

The surprise attack on Pearl Harbor by the Japanese in 1941 triggered the United States' entry into World War II. Japanese submarines and carrier-based planes attacked the US Pacific Fleet, sinking or damaging eight battleships and 13 other naval vessels. Two hundred American aircraft were destroyed, and 3,000 naval and military personnel were killed or injured. The USS *Arizona*, a 608-foot (185-m) battleship, sank in nine minutes. All 1,177 sailors and marines on board died. The deck of the ship lies 6 feet (1.8 m) below the water's surface. The memorial stands above the hull of the battleship. US Navy launches provide transportation to the memorial from the shore-side visitor center, which also offers a museum and a short video.
Map ref: page 790 G3

Frangipani (Plumeria species), one of the signature flowers of the Hawaiian Islands, is a common sight in the gardens of Wailuku.

The Hawaiian Islands often put on a spectacular show at sunset.

PU'UHONUA O HONAUNAU NATIONAL HISTORIC PARK

Located on the Big Island's Kona Coast, the west coast, this site is close to the town of Captain Cook and the beach where Cook was slain. The Pu'uhonua o Honaunau Heiau, or temple, is where *kapu* (law) breakers and vanquished warriors could come to find sanctuary, mercy, and forgiveness. In 1961, the National Park Service restored the abandoned temple grounds.

Strong Hawaiian heritage movements want to rename the Park "City of Refuge," its original name, though pu'uhonua translates to "temple of refuge." The compound sits on a 20-acre (8-ha) black-lava peninsula surrounded by water on three sides. A large stone wall built circa 1550, the Great Wall, marks the forbidding land-side entrance.

From Kona International Airport, drive south past Kailua-Kona on Hwy 11, the Hawaii Belt Road, until you reach Honaunau Bay. On the way, a popular stop is the working coffee mill at Captain Cook.
Map ref: page 791 L9

WAILUKU

Wailuku is the county seat of Maui and, together with nearby Kahalui, forms the largest community on the island. The name translates to "Bloody Waters" and refers to the battle between King Kamehameha I and Maui warriors in the Iao Valley in 1790. Apparently the massacre was so intense that the local stream ran red with blood. Missionaries settled here in the nineteenth century; many of their buildings still stand. Later, sugar production energized the economy and Wailuku became the hub of commerce, government, and population for the island. Since the 1960s decline of the sugar industry and the growth of tourism in other parts, Wailuku has faded into the background.

Attractions include the Bailey House Museum, a treasure trove of Hawaiian memorabilia. Past this is Iao Valley State Park, a rainforest and canyon in a caldera of the West Maui Mountains; a larger, lush oasis of waterfalls, pools, and hiking trails. The Hawaii Nature Center has many interactive exhibits on the Iao Valley's natural history.

Kahalui International Airport has flights to the US mainland and inter-island flights. Cars are essential. Wailuku has excellent restaurants but lodging is very limited.
Map ref: page 791 K5

WAIMEA

Waimea, or Kamuela, lies on the western slopes of Mauna Kea in the Big Island's South Kohala district. This is *paniolo* (cowboy) country and Parker Ranch, once the largest private ranch in America, is the hub. John Palmer Parker founded the enormous ranch (with 300 working horses, and 23 full-time cowboys) in the early nineteenth century. Major rodeo and "wild west" events are held in February, March, May, July, and September. The original homestead, Mana, is open for visits, as is the more recent Pu'uopelu mansion, with its huge art collection.

In Waimea's west, the Kamuela Museum has Hawaiian and other artifacts. In town country-style dining and lodgings are available.
Map ref: page 791 M7

STATE FEATURE

Hawaii's Volcanoes

Kilauea Caldera, part of Hawaii Volcanoes National Park on the island of Hawaii, is the world's largest active volcanic crater.

A volcano is a vent in the Earth's crust through which molten lava and gases are ejected when it is active. While the collision of tectonic plates created the explosive volcanoes in Alaska and South America, which feature violent eruptions, the Hawaiian volcanoes formed slowly into rounded mountain masses. These volcanoes are called shield volcanoes and they form over "hot spots," places of deep melting within the Earth's mantle, which enables the lava to move up to the Earth's surface.

Between 30 and 70 million years ago, the Hawaiian Islands were formed as molten rock flowed up from the Earth's crust, 20,000 feet (6,100 m) below the surface of the sea. Repeated volcanic eruptions spewed out vast quantities of lava, which hardened into rock as it cooled. These vast outpourings built up layer upon layer until they reached the sea's surface and slowly formed a landmass. Eventually the weight of the new island sealed the fissure below, forcing the molten lava and gases to seek a new outlet. The large

A small crater within the giant crater of Haleakala in Haleakala National Park, Maui. Haleakala is now inactive.

tectonic plate that forms much of the Pacific Ocean floor was shifting slowly to the northwest, riding over the stationary "hot spot," creating new volcanoes as older volcanoes eventually became extinct and formed islands. Eventually the remnants of these volcanoes formed the 130 islands, islets, and shoals that make up the Hawaiian Islands today. The archipelago is still shifting about 4 inches (10 cm) per year, with the Big Island being the current hot spot.

The islands came to their present shape through millions of years of earthquakes, erosion, uplifting of land, severe tropical storms, tidal waves, changes in sea level, and continuing eruptions of lava. As the volcanoes grew distant from the hot spot, they became dormant or extinct. Some sank back into the crust, submerging below the surface of the sea. Coral fringes and eventually barrier reefs formed. The caps of sinking volcanoes thus covered with coral eventually formed the atolls Laysan, Midway, and Kure in the northwest zone of the archipelago. The extinct vol-

canic craters Punch Bowl, Diamond Head, and Koko Head define Oahu's landscape. Kauai's deep Waimea Canyon and Molokai's towering waterfall echo the turbulent, formative stages and reflect nature's awe-inspiring dual abilities of destruction and creation.

Maui was formed as the lava of two volcanoes, Haleakala and Puu Kukui, joined together in the sea, creating an isthmus. Puu Kukui makes up West Maui. At East Maui's core is Haleakala, the world's largest inactive volcano. The area is protected now as Haleakala National Park. The name means "House of the Sun," and Native Hawaiians find the mountain to be a great source of spiritual power and cosmic energy. The US Air Force has a base here. Their research indicates that the natural energy forces—a combination of those coming from the Earth plus the high focus of radiation coming from outside the atmosphere—make this point the strongest configuration of natural energy forces in the USA. Haleakala, which covers 28,099 acres (11,380 ha), has as one of its most dramatic features the Haleakala Crater, an impressive 2,300 feet (702 m) deep with a circumference of 21 miles (34 km) at its rim. It is also one of the tallest mountains on Earth, with more than 20,000 feet (6,100 m) of it under water. The park extends from the summit of Mount Haleakala at 10,023 feet (3,057 m) down the volcano's southeast flank out to Maui's eastern coast near Hana.

The Big Island is the youngest island and, with two active volcanoes and a hot spot, is still in formation. Mauna Kea, at 13,796 feet (4,208 m), the highest of the island's three volcanoes, is dormant. The active volcanoes are Mauna Loa and Kilauea. Mauna Loa is 13,680 feet (4,172 m) above sea level, and its Mokuaweoweo Caldera has walls rising 600 feet (183 m). Lava from Mauna Loa covers about 50 percent of the Big Island, including parts of Kilauea. It has erupted approximately every four years since the early nineteenth century. Kilauea projects from the eastern slope of Mauna Loa and reaches a height of 4,090 feet (1,247 m) above sea level. The Kilauea Caldera covers 4 square miles (10 sq km) and is the largest active volcanic crater in the world. Since January 3, 1983, Kilauea has erupted nearly every day, and has greatly altered the Puna landscape in the longest-running eruption cycle in modern Hawaiian history. The volcano generates an average of 525,000 cubic yards (400,000 m³) of lava per day, and, since 1995, has added close to 500 acres (203 ha) of new land to the island. In 1989 Kilauea lava flowed over the park's Visitor Center, burning it down, and by 1990 it had destroyed over 65 homes in Kalapana as well as the Chain of Craters road leading down to the coast. There is nothing that compares to watching thick, black lava still red at its core flow across the path or road ahead and out into the ocean, smoldering and sputtering in its final fluid moment.

Hawaii is the only state in the nation that is growing physically. In addition to the daily expansion from Kilauea, a whole new island is forming just 30 miles (48 km) away. Loihi Seamount has been erupting frequently, and its mass is approaching sea level. It is still 3,000 feet (915 m) below the surface.

Hawaii is one of the few places in the world you can get close to the raw power of nature. This energy, known as mana, or spirit power, is felt most strongly where nature has been left untouched. It is not felt in Waikiki, yet just a few minutes away at Diamond Head, it is. Modern-day monitoring can actually register this unusual configuration of natural energy forces.

Hawaii's volcanoes were formed slowly and gently into domed masses, and their lava flows slowly enough to allow you to walk to its very edge. The urge to touch it is very strong. At Puna, many have suffered third-degree burns or worse as they try to make contact with the oozing molten lava.

Lava is much easier to observe in its hardened state. There are two types: pahoehoe and a'a. They are chemically the same, but pahoehoe is smooth and ropelike, with small holes formed by gas as it cools. It molds itself into fantastical shapes. A'a is rougher, pitted, and spiny. Gas escapes less regularly but more violently. A'a destroys the soles of your shoes quickly. The name is what native Hawaiians called out when they fell on it. Other lava features are "Pele's hair," clear white strands resulting from small particles of molten material thrown up into the air and spun about, and "Pele's diamonds," particles fused into tear-like drops of glass and peridot. "Hawaiian snow" is the name for the gray lichens that grow on the older flows.

Madame Pele, in Hawaiian mythology, is the fire goddess. The story goes that she had a bad childhood and wanted a home of her own to house her family and entertain her lover. When Namakaokaha'i, her sister the sea goddess, found out that the flirtatious Pele had seduced her husband, she flooded her out wherever she went. Pele finally took sanctuary in the Halemaumau Crater in Kilauea's south end. But her temperament never calmed down. In fact, every time she gets upset, she literally blows her stack. She is one of the most revered gods because her presence is so easily felt. She is also one of the most worshipped gods. In the past, pigs, dogs, sacred ohelo berries, and even the stray man (never a woman) were offered. These days, juniper berries distilled into gin and flower leis are offered to appease her. Perhaps Madame Pele and Mother Nature are in cahoots. Only time will tell.

Colonizing plants have established a foothold on a recent lava flow from the active Kilauea volcano on Hawaii, the Big Island.

OREGON

From the early years of white exploration Oregon's nickname has been "Beaver State." With fur hats fashionable in eastern cities and beaver abundant in Oregon's streams, trappers, known as mountain men, were the first Europeans to explore the region. After the rage for beaver hats passed, the trails taken by the trappers were used by the early pioneers and became the Oregon Trail, the corridor to the West. The rush to colonize Oregon's fertile valleys had begun. Today, its economy depends largely on timber and agriculture but electronics and tourism have broadened its base, with tourism now its third largest source of revenue.

The state's landscape is varied and dramatic—US-101 winds along the entire Pacific coast, showcasing Oregon's rugged coastline of rocky outcrops and soaring pinnacles.

The Cascade Range's volcanic peaks and vast forests of Douglas fir and Sitka spruce make it still possible to leave the crowds behind and gain a sense of isolation and discovery. The mountain peaks provide stunning backdrops to Oregon's urban centers—no better example being Mt Hood, silently and ominously presiding over the state's largest city, Portland.

Ponderosa pines (Pinus ponderosa) in Zion National Park. Throughout Oregon there are 35 wilderness areas and 14 national forests.

The Cascade Range slices north–south down the state's entire length. Many of its peaks exceed 10,000 feet (3,050 m) including Mt Hood, at 11,235 feet (3,427 m), the highest point in Oregon. Running roughly 100–150 miles (161–241 km) inland, the range separates the broad Willamette Valley and Oregon's coastal regions from the arid interior, producing two different climatic regions. Towards the coast a moist, maritime climate prevails with high rainfall and Douglas fir, Sitka spruce, and western hemlock the primary conifers. East of the Cascades, Oregon's high desert country fluctuates from scorching heat to bitter cold, with Ponderosa pine the dominant species.

State motto *Alis Volat Propriis* (She flies with her own wings)
State flag Adopted 1925
Capital Salem
Population 3,421,399
Total area (land and water) 97,132 square miles (251,572 sq km)
Land area 96,002 square miles (248,645 sq km)
Oregon is the 10th-largest state in size
Origin of name It is generally accepted that the name, first used by Jonathan Carver in 1778, was taken from the writings of Major Robert Rogers, an English army officer
Nickname The Beaver State
Abbreviations OR (postal), Ore., Oreg.
State bird Western meadowlark
State flower Oregon grape
State tree Douglas fir
Entered the Union February 14, 1859 as the 33rd state

Places in
OREGON

ALBANY

Albany is located in the Willamette Valley, one hour south of Portland, on I-5. Established in 1848 and with a population of 29,462, Albany—despite being a center for the manufacture of rare metals, food processing, and the timber industry—has never forgotten its Victorian beginnings.

The construction of I-5 by-passed Albany's older commercial and residential areas, leaving some 700 historic structures, both commercial and residential, intact. Albany now boasts representatives of every architectural style and form in the United States since 1850. One of its oldest homes is the Monteith House, built in 1849, and one of Oregon's oldest buildings. At various times a storehouse, residence, and trading post, it is now a museum. Albany's historic churches are also worth a visit, and Monteith Riverpark on the Willamette River is a reminder of the city's riverfront origins.

A short drive east from Albany is Scio, the 10th oldest town in Oregon and home to five covered bridges set among gentle hills, criss-crossing rich farmland with crops of mint, hazelnuts, blueberries, apples, and pears. A cycle tour is a great way to discover the area's delights. Scio makes a very pleasant day-trip from Albany.

Portland International Airport is one hour north of Albany on I-5, and there are train and bus services.
Map ref: page 782 C3

ASHLAND

Ashland, 15 miles (24 km) north of the California border on I-5, was settled in 1852 and used to be known as Ashland Mills for its sawmills and gristmills along the banks of Bear Creek, where they used its power to run the mills.

It is a small town with a population of 20,000 people. Ashland has the beautiful, 100-acre (40-ha) Lithia Park in the center of town. Filled with native, ornamental, and exotic plants, its 1-mile (2-km) trail makes for a leisurely walk.

Today, it is known throughout the United States as the home of the annual Oregon Shakespeare Festival, which first put the town on the map about 60 years ago. Performances take place throughout March at Ashland's outdoor Elizabethan Theater and the 600-seat indoor Angus Bowmer Theater. The 140-seat Black Swan Theater opened in 1977 and caters to more experimental theater. Soon more non-Shakespearean theaters opened, and there was an explosion

Crab pots in Astoria, the host of the annual Astoria-Warrenton Crab & Seafood Festival.

of B&B lodging in the area, several are in fine Victorian homes.

Ashland is within easy reach of Crater Lake National Park, the southern Oregon coast, and the headwaters of the mighty Rogue River. Skiing Mt Ashland is popular in the winter, with 23 ski runs and 80 miles (129 km) of cross-country skiing trails.

Visitors with an interest in mountain-biking can enjoy the 31-mile (50-km) Siskiyou Crest Mountain Bike Route, which provides spectacular views of the Siskiyou Mountains and Mt Shasta across the border, in California.

Medford/Jackson County Airport is about 12 miles (19 km) northwest of Ashland on I-5. Trains and buses service the area.
Map ref: page 782 D9

ASTORIA

Astoria (population 10,000) overlooks the Columbia River, a short distance from where it empties into the Pacific Ocean, in the extreme northwest corner of Oregon. Astoria is the oldest American settlement west of the Rocky Mountains and is rich in history.

Hundreds of Victorian homes cling to the wooded hillsides that tumble down to the city's waterfront, leading some to refer to Astoria as "little San Francisco." Its

maritime climate has its summers cool and its winters mild. Winter storms can be dramatic with winds of 100 miles (161 km) per hour on the ocean bluffs.

Immigrants from Scandinavia, Finland, and China have given Astoria its cultural richness. Its strong Scandinavian heritage is celebrated every year with the Scandinavian Midsummer Festival held in mid-June. Bonfires burn to destroy evil spirits, costumed locals dance the pole dance, and authentic Scandinavian cuisine, dancing, and crafts abound.

Attractions include the replica of Fort Clatsop at Fort Clatsop National Memorial. Community-built in 1955, to celebrate the 1805–06 encampment of the Lewis and Clark Expedition, the 50 feet (15 m) by 50 feet (15 m) hut is the focus of a 125-acre (51-ha) park. It is set among the coastal forests and wetlands of the Coast Range as it merges with the Columbia River Estuary.

Flavel House was built in 1885 by Captain George Flavel, Astoria's first millionaire. This magnificent example of Queen Anne style architecture covers an entire city block and is home to the Clatsop County Historical Society.

Another interesting site is the Astoria Column. Built in 1925, it is a 125-foot (38-m) column featuring a mural that depicts the history of the area.

Astoria has its own regional airport, or Portland International Airport is about 100 miles (161 km) southeast on US-30. Buses also service the Astoria area.
Map ref: page 780 B8

Albany has a huge variety of architectural styles; this home is in the Gothic Revival style.

BEAVERTON

Beaverton, with a population of 70,000, is the fifth largest community in Oregon. It is just 7 miles (11 km) west of Portland, off Hwy 217, in the heart of the Tualatin Valley, midway between Mt Hood and the spectacular Oregon coast.

Rolling hills, forests, rivers, and wetlands abound in the Beaverton area. The city has 185 parks covering 1,300 acres (526 ha). With 30 miles (48 km) of hiking trails and a 25-mile (40-km) network of cycle paths, Beaverton has more designated "green space" than most cities of its size.

First settled in the early years of the Oregon Trail, Beaverton was founded in 1883 and today is in the heart of Oregon's "Silicon Valley." It offers all the amenities of a big city and is known for its attractive, well-planned neighborhoods.

"A Taste of Beaverton" is the town's signature summer event. It brings 40,000 tourists to the town each year. It is a three-day festival in the town's Griffith Park featuring local food, music, hot-air balloons, and arts and crafts.

The mighty Columbia River, viewed from just outside Bonneville, forms part of the border between Washington and Oregon.

Beaverton's closest airport is Portland International. Buses and trains also service the area.
Map ref: page 780 D10

BEND

Located in the high desert area of central Oregon, and shielded by the Cascade Mountains, Bend receives only 12 inches (300 mm) of rainfall a year and its 51,000 inhabitants enjoy an abundance of recreational opportunities.

Although the timber industry and the production of wood-related products remain Bend's primary industries, tourism is its second largest. Kayakers and rafters can shoot the triple waterfalls of the Deschutes River and nearby Mt Bachelor, at over 9,000 feet (2,745 m), offers skiers some 3,200 acres (1,296 ha) of slopes.

Visitors can get a panoramic view of Bend, and the volcanic peaks that surround it, from Pilot Butte, a 511-foot (156-m) high volcanic cinder cone. The view of nine snowcapped Cascade peaks includes the Three Sisters, Broken Top Mountain, and Mt Jefferson, at 10,495 feet (3,201 m).

Twenty miles (32 km) south of Bend is the Newberry National Volcanic Monument, including 50,000 acres (20,250 ha) of lakes and lava flows. Here visitors find the 500-square-mile (1,295-sq-km) Newberry caldera (crater), which holds two sparkling alpine lakes full of trout and salmon. Its rim has a circumference of 21 miles (34 km) and can be hiked on a well-established trail.

Seven campgrounds lie within the crater, and Paulina Lake Lodge is the only visitor service open year-round. Newberry National Volcanic Monument is a must-see destination when visiting Bend.

The Redmond-Roberts Airport is 20 miles (32 km) north, in the town of Redmond. Trains and buses also service the area.
Map ref: page 782 F4

BONNEVILLE

Bonneville is on the Columbia River, 40 miles (64 km) east of Portland. The Bonneville Dam spans the river in four sections separated by Bradford, Cascade, and Robins Islands. The dam is 2,690 feet (820 m) long, 197 feet (60 m) high, and controls the flow of the lower Columbia River.

The Bonneville Dam was built between 1933 and 1937. Its glass-walled visitor center, on Bradford Island, features exhibits on the dam's operations and the maritime history of the river. When salmon are migrating, an underwater view of their spectacular ascent up the fish ladders can be enjoyed as they make their way to spawning grounds on the upper course of the Columbia.

Portland International Airport services the area. There are also train and bus services in Portland.
Map ref: page 780 E10

BROOKINGS-HARBOR

The twin towns of Brookings-Harbor boast the most temperate climate on the Oregon coast—and its own stands of giant redwoods. At first glance, Brookings-Harbor (population 9,000) seems more Californian than Oregonian. Located on the junction of the Chetco River and the Pacific Ocean, just 6 miles (10 km) north of the California border on the US-101, Brookings-Harbor has a Californian climate, with temperatures of 70°F (21°C) to 80°F (26.6°C) any month of the year.

Siuslaw National Forest, west of Beaverton, is one of the many forests near the town.

Brookings-Harbor has the distinction of being the only point in continental United States that was bombed by the Japanese in World War II. The bombsite is marked by a monument. Twenty years after the bombing, the Japanese pilot returned to present the town with his samurai sword, now on display at the Brookings Town Hall.

The pulse of Brookings-Harbor is centered around its port on the south side of the Chetco River. Charter boats are available for fishing and whale watching. Just walking along the marina and stopping at one of the many restaurants, seafood markets, or coffee shops is a popular activity.

Brookings-Harbor is famous for producing 90 percent of America's Easter lilies and a drive south, to Crescent City, California, in early summer is the opportunity for visitors to get a breathtaking view of fields of flowering lilies.

Giant redwood trees—more common to California—can be found in Loeb State Park, 8 miles (13 km) up the north bank of the Chetco River. The park is also home to Oregon's largest stand of coastal redwoods, reaching up to 350 feet (107 m) high and 25 feet (8 m) in diameter. The northernmost stands of redwoods in America are found in Loeb State Park, with the oldest trees between 300 and 800 years old. Loeb State Park also has 320 acres (130 ha) of myrtle wood, a tree that is found only in Oregon and the Middle East. The park has access to the Chetco River, and plentiful fishing and camping sites.

The quirky exterior of an ocean-front marine lighting store, "Sealines Nautical," situated just south of Cannon Beach.

The closest airport is in Crescent City, California. Medford and Jackson County Airport is about 80 miles (128 km) northeast. Buses service Brookings-Harbor.
Map ref: page 782 A9

CANNON BEACH

Cannon Beach has a population of 1,220 and is 25 miles (40 km) south of the Washington border, on US-101. It has a 3 ½-mile (6-km) sandy white beach, which is punctuated mid-way by Haystack Rock, the third largest coastal monolith in the world. The beach is vast and expansive, with rugged coastal outcroppings combining with superb ocean vistas to always provide a visual and sensory treat.

Cannon Beach also has a vibrant artistic community and is a town designed for walking. The exploration and discovery of its many art galleries, bookshops, and fine restaurants is a popular pedestrian activity. Strict building codes have helped Cannon Beach maintain its earthy, rustic appearance.

Haystack Rock is an inspiration for all visitors to Cannon Beach and for those who live there, ever changing with the seasons and always in the foreground of Cannon Beach's stunning sunsets. At 235 feet (72 m), it is the beach's centerpiece and one of the most popular attractions on the Oregon coast. A designated marine and bird sanctuary, its tidal pools are home to a diverse collection of starfish, crabs, anemone, and limpets. Several species of bird nest on Haystack Rock in the summer, including the colorful and unusual tufted puffin, which has a white face, orange bills, and tufts of feathers above the eyes.

Cannon Beach's status as a "Marine Garden" means the removal of any lifeforms within a 985-foot (300-m) radius is forbidden, as is climbing above the barnacle line onto the rock.

Ecola State Park is located just north of the city limits, offering fabulous views of the beach, Haystack Rock, and back along the coast north to Tillamook Rock Lighthouse. The park's magnificent scenery makes it a favorite spot for weddings and special gatherings

with its acres of forest, grass, and hiking trails. The park is open during the day only.

The world's tallest Sitka spruce is located in an old-growth fir and spruce forest a few miles from Cannon Beach, in Klootchy Creek Park. It is 216 feet (66 m) high and 52 feet (16 m) in circumference, and more than 700 years old.

Each November the Stormy Weather Arts Festival celebrates the more unpredictable winter storms and mists that swirl around Haystack Rock and sweep in off the coast. Writers, singers, composers, painters, sculptors, and magicians emerge from their homes and join together for a festival of theatre, poetry, and art.

Cannon Beach's famous Sandcastle Contest is held every June and draws competitors from all around the world. It is said to have begun when a tsunami washed out the bridge into Cannon Beach in 1964 leaving the residents stranded with little to do. It has grown to become one of the largest sandbuilding contests on the United States' West Coast.

There are many excellent restaurants in wonderful locations and after-dinner sunset walks on the beach are very popular.

Astoria Regional Airport is about 20 miles (32 km) north of Cannon Beach, on US-101, Portland International Airport is about 70 miles (113 km) southeast, and buses service the area.
Map ref: page 780 B9

Repairing fishing nets in Brookings. Fishing is a major industry in Brookings-Harbor.

The busy lumber port at North Bend, near Coos Bay.

COOS BAY

Coos Bay and the surrounding communities of North Bend and the old waterfront fishing village of Charleston are collectively known as Oregon's Bay Area, and together they form the largest urban area on the Oregon coast.

Coos Bay Harbor is one of the largest natural harbors between San Francisco, California, and Puget Sound, Washington, with the shipment of woodchips and other lumber-related products making it the second largest port in Oregon after Portland. Coos Bay is also the southern gateway to Oregon Dunes National Recreation Area, whose enormous sand dunes extend north along the Pacific Coast for some 50 miles (80 km).

Coos Bay's Shore Acres State Park offers visitors panoramic views of towering waves, rugged cliffs, and migrating whales (from December through June). The park's beautiful gardens feature trees and flowering plants from around the world.

The 134-acre (54-ha) Cape Arago State Park, located on a narrow coastal promontory jutting ½ mile (1 km) into the Pacific Ocean, has hiking trails that lead to numerous tidal pools along the beach. It is also a good place to view seals, sea lions, and whales.

Deep-sea fishing centers on Charleston harbor. Crab rings and baits can be rented for the trapping of Dungeness crab and the area is prospering from a growing demand for quality Oregon seafood. Charleston has served as a base for commercial fishing fleets for nearly 80 years, and today its bustling marina offers moorage for around 600 vessels.

The Oregon Bay Area is serviced by North Bend Municipal Airport and buses. Map ref: page 782 A6

CORVALLIS

Corvallis is a typical college town. Laid out in 1851 as Marysville and renamed Corvallis (Latin for "heart of the valley") in 1853. It has a population of 51,000 and is home to Oregon State University, the city's main economic asset.

Running and cycling are favorite pastimes in Corvallis, with cycle lanes on most of its wide streets and along the Willamette and Mary Rivers. Its location, in the heart of Willamette Valley, 85 miles (137 km) south of Portland, makes it an excellent base for exploring the coastal mountains.

It sits on a plateau 1½ miles (2.5 km) wide at the confluence of the Willamette and Mary Rivers, and possesses a wealth of historic commercial architecture, which can be seen on organized walking tours of the district. One of its finest examples is the Whiteside Theater, built in 1922, in the Italian Renaissance style. Once the second grandest movie palace in Oregon, its original layout is still intact and numerous decorative features remain from the 1920s.

The 500-acre (202-ha) Oregon State University campus is Oregon's oldest institute of higher learning, and the center of much of the town's activities. Its park-like campus features art exhibits, theater productions, and concerts.

Corvallis hosts the Da Vinci Days Festival. It is held each July and runs for three days and celebrates the arts, science, and technology.

Portland International Airport is 85 miles (137 km) north of Corvallis, on I-5. Trains and buses also service the area. Map ref: page 782 A6

CRATER LAKE NATIONAL PARK

Crater Lake is one of Oregon's scenic highlights and is often referred to as the "Gem of the Cascades." It is the deepest lake in the United States and the seventh deepest in the world. Around half a million visitors come each year to marvel at its deep blue waters and stunning natural setting.

About 7,700 years ago, the 12,000-foot (3,660-m) Mt Mazama erupted, falling in on itself and creating the bowl-shaped caldera (crater) of today. Following the eruption it took some 250 years of rain and snow for the caldera to fill to its present level.

Crater Lake is isolated from its surrounding streams and rivers. Its water level is maintained by a balance of rain and evaporation. With no incoming stream to bring organic materials, sediments, or chemicals into the lake, its water clarity is astonishing, measuring a record 134 feet (41 m) in 1994. A maximum lake depth of 1,996 feet (609 m) was measured in 1886 by a group of US geologic surveyors using piano wire and lead weights.

Studies still show a degree of hydrothermal activity with chemical analysis of the water indicating warm water entering from the lake floor. It therefore seems likely that Mt Mazama will erupt again.

The crater's "volcano within a volcano" is Wizard Island, a small volcanic cone rising from the crystal blue waters. Its 800-foot (244-m) high summit is worth the climb for the views of the surrounding rim. Wizard Island itself has a 90-foot (27-m) crater, and a trail leads to Fumarole Bay, an excellent spot for fishing, and swimming— but only if you can brave the water's icy 55°F (12.7°C).

Fish are non-native to the lake but were artificially introduced from 1888 to 1941. The two species in the lake are rainbow trout and kokanee salmon, and no license is required to fish.

The 33-mile (53-km) Rim Drive around the lake provides many stunning views but can be very crowded in summer. Open only from mid-June to mid-October, due to snow and ice buildup, it also provides access to many excellent hikes.

A 5-mile (8-km) trail to the 8,929-foot (2,723-m) Mt Scott, the highest point in the park, leaves the crowds behind and provide the best views of Crater Lake and the surrounding mountain peaks, including Mt Shasta in California. The Cleetwood Cove Trail on the north side is the only one that provides direct access to the lake. Boat tours depart Cleetwood Cove several times a day, from mid-June through mid-September, offering stunning close-ups of major formations such as Llao Rock, Phantom Ship, and Wizard Island. You can disembark on Wizard Island and take a later boat back.

Animals are seldom seen but a rich diversity exists including bears, pine marten, golden mantle ground squirrels, and deer. All are wild, and feeding is prohibited.

With an average of 529 inches (1,322 cm) of snow falling on Crater Lake each year, park rangers lead ecology walks through the eight-month winter. Strapping on a pair of snowshoes, the hour-and-a-half tour explains how plants and animals adapt and survive the

The beautiful Oregon State University is set in a huge area of parkland in Corvallis.

Looking across The Dalles to Washington State. The Dalles, with a population of 12,000, is the largest city and the primary center of trade in the Columbia River Gorge.

harsh conditions. Visitors can check at the park headquarters for the regularly scheduled walks—no experience is necessary.

Crater Lake is located in southern Oregon. Take Hwy 62 off I-5. Campsites are plentiful, or stay at the historic Crater Lake Lodge. Medford/Jackson County Airport and Klamath Falls International Airport are the closest.
Map ref: page 782 E7

THE DALLES

The Dalles is one of the oldest inhabited regions in North America. It has been a center of trade for Native Americans for over 10,000 years. The name "The Dalles" comes from the French words for "the trough," in reference to the trough of the Columbia River on which the town lies.

The Lewis and Clark Expedition camped at The Dalles in October 1805, at Rock Fort, a site that can still be visited today. Until the opening of the Barstow Trail around Mt Hood, The Dalles was the end of the Oregon Trail. From there, pioneers would load their belongings onto barges and make the treacherous trip through whirlpools and rapids down the Columbia River to Oregon City.

Today, The Dalles, with a population of 12,000, is the largest city in the Columbia River Gorge. It is still considered the gorge's primary center of trade, located on I-84 connecting the Midwest, West Coast, and Pacific Rim markets.

Its historic town can be seen on a walking tour, which includes Klindt's, Oregon's oldest bookstore. Established in 1870, it still has its original oak and plate glass display cases and wooden floors.

Fort Dalles Museum houses the only remaining building of the old Fort Dalles, the Surgeon's Quarters. The Fort was originally established

A mule deer (Odocoileus hemionus) in Crater Lake National Park.

in 1850 to protect immigrants and was then the only military post between the Pacific Coast and Wyoming. A collection of old military artifacts, household goods, and old medical equipment is housed in the museum.

Portland International Airport is the closest, and there are train and bus services in The Dalles.
Map ref: page 780 G10

DESCHUTES NATIONAL FOREST

Stretching for 100 miles (161 km) along the eastern crest of the Cascade Mountains, in central Oregon, the 1.6 million acres (648,000 ha) of Deschutes National Forest is home to 20 peaks over 7,000 feet (2,135 m). These include three of Oregon's five highest peaks, five wilderness areas, over 150 lakes, the largest variety of volcanic formations in the lower 48 states, and 500 miles (804 km) of streams, including six that are designated Wild and Scenic Rivers.

Huge tracts of undeveloped land help visitors leave the crowds behind. There are 1,338 miles (2,153 km) of trails to hike, ski, snowmobile, or mountain bike. Elevations within the forest range from 1,950 feet (595 m) at Lake Billy Chinook to 10,358 feet (3,159 m) of South Sister, the third highest peak in Oregon and in the Three Sisters Wilderness.

Many argue that the Three Sisters Wilderness has the finest diversity of landscape Oregon has to offer.

This area has 14 glaciers that provide the best examples of glaciation found in the Pacific Northwest, including Collier Glacier, the largest sheet of ice in Oregon.

Lava fields, waterfalls, alpine meadows, and streams full of fish, including brook and rainbow trout, fill its 286,000 acres (115,830 ha). Its 260 miles (418 km) of trails—including a 40-mile (64-km) stretch of the famous Pacific Crest Trail that winds from Canada to Mexico—are so popular that it is estimated that visitor numbers here will soon exceed any other wilderness area in the state. Eight million visitors come here each year. Mt Bachelor alone, with the largest downhill ski area in the Pacific Northwest, receives about 750,000 visitors annually and the forest has a total of 346 miles (557 km) of snowmobile trails, which are open during the winter months.

The diversity of recreational opportunities within Deschutes National Forest makes it one of the most popular forests in the Pacific Northwest. Camping season can start as early as mid-April and extends to late September.

Redmond-Roberts Airport, about 20 miles (32 km) north of Bend, is the closest airport. Bend is also serviced by buses.
Map ref: page 782 F4

EUGENE

Eugene is the second largest city in Oregon, with a population of 130,000. It is in central Oregon on the McKenzie and Willamette Rivers, 110 miles (177 km) south of Portland. The Pacific Ocean is to the west and to the east, the scenic McKenzie River Valley ascends into the Cascade Range. Settled in 1846, the city grew as a timber and agricultural center after the arrival of the railroad in 1871.

Eugene is rated as one of the top 10 cycling cities in the United States—the banks of the Willamette River and the town's many parks are covered in cycling, walking, and jogging paths.

A major attraction is Eugene's 250-acre (101-ha) University of Oregon campus with architectural landmarks dating to the 1870s.

Fern Ridge Lake, just outside town, offers anglers trout, bass, and catfish in the spring. The nearby McKenzie River, with Class II and Class III rapids, offers whitewater rafting to the more adventurous.

The historic Campbell House, built in 1892 has a view over the city and was rated one of the top 25 inns in the nation by American Historic Inns.

Mahlon-Sweet Regional Airport is northwest of Eugene. There are also bus and train services.
Map ref: page 782 C4

FLORENCE

Florence is a center for business, medical care, and education. Its restored Old Town offers shops, boutiques, and coffee houses as well as a picturesque marina along the banks of the Siuslaw River.

Florence (population 6,000) is ideally situated on the Oregon coast on US-101 at the northern tip of the National Dunes Recreation Area, which stretches down the Oregon coast to Coos Bay, 50 miles (80 km) to the south. The largest expanse of coastal dunes in the United States, these range up to 500 feet (152 m) high with banks up of to 3 miles (5 km).

Ten miles (16 km) north of Florence, along a dramatic stretch of Oregon coast, lies the Sea Lion Caves—an enormous grotto containing the only mainland rookery of Stellar's sea lions in the lower 48 states. Visitors descend a 208-foot (63-m) elevator carved through basalt cliffs and into the grotto itself, occupied by up to 200 sea lions during fall and winter.

Seventeen lakes surround this lovely seaside town, and activities include crabbing, fishing, clamming, and jet-boat trips up the Siuslaw River during the summer.

The American Museum of Fly Fishing, in the Old Town, includes thousands of hand-tied flies mounted in frames dating back to the 1800s. Dinner cruises are available on board an old-fashioned sternwheeler on the Siuslaw River.

North Bend Regional Airport is south and Mahlon-Sweet Regional Airport is east of Florence, on Hwy 126. Buses also service the area.
Map ref: page 782 B4

GRANTS PASS

Grants Pass (population 21,000) is in southern Oregon, 60 miles (97 km) north of the California border on I-5. It is named for Civil War hero—and later President—Ulysses S. Grant, and was recently

The breathtaking Heceta Head Lighthouse, north of Florence, on the 1,000-foot (305-m) high Heceta Head. The lighthouse also functions as a living history center.

Fishing is one of the many popular activities along the Hells Canyon National Scenic Byway.

given National Historic District status. Its downtown is a charming collection of historic buildings, ice cream parlors, and over 25 antique and collectable shops to explore.

The premier attraction of Grants Pass is the Rogue River. Protected under the Wild and Scenic Rivers Act, its collection of placid pools, narrow canyons, and thrilling stretches of whitewater provides a natural habitat for abundant wildlife including elks, otters, beavers, ospreys, and wood ducks.

Grants Pass offers rafting and jet-boating tours of nearby Hellgate Canyon and the Rogue River.

Twenty miles (32 km) north, on I-5, is the Wolf Creek Inn, the oldest continuously operating hotel in the Pacific Northwest. Built around 1883, it was a stagecoach stop on the 16-day journey from San Francisco to Portland. In the early days of Hollywood, it provided a retreat for Mary Pickford and Douglas Fairbanks Junior. Clark Gable, a good friend of the innkeeper in the 1930s, and Carol Lombard, danced the nights away in the inn's ballroom, fishing in the nearby Rogue River by day. Jack London completed his novel *Valley of the Moon* during an extended stay in 1913.

Medford/Jackson County Airport is in Medford, about 40 miles (64 km) southeast on I-5. Trains and buses service the area.
Map ref: page 782 C8

HELLS CANYON

Hells Canyon is the deepest canyon in the United States. Its adjacent ridges average 5,500 feet

(1,678 m) above the Snake River, which carries more water than the Grand Canyon's Colorado River.

The Hells Canyon National Recreation Area, established in 1975, is an area of 219,000 acres (88,695 ha) along the border of Oregon and Idaho. On the Idaho side, the Seven Devils Mountains tower 8,000 feet (2,440 m) above the river. Despite the canyon's width of only 10 miles (16 km), views from Hat Point, on the Oregon side, across to the Seven Devils and beyond, straight down to the Snake River below, combine to provide one of the grandest panoramas found in the United States.

The Hells Canyon National Scenic Byway is 314 miles (505 ha) of paved and gravel roads. The return trip from Imnaha to Hat Point, though only 23 miles (37 km), will take the better part of a day to negotiate along a steep, windy gravel road with few opportunities to turn around—it may not be to everyone's liking.

Fishing, camping, horseback riding, and jet boating are some of the many activities along the byway. Here, there are over 360 miles (579 km) of trails and a variety of campgrounds scattered throughout the wilderness. The alpine lakes of the Seven Devils is a major attraction during the summer months.

The extremes in elevation can cause unpredictable weather, with temperatures varying from lows of 30°F (–1°C), in the alpine areas, to over 100°F (37.7°C) at lower elevations along the Snake River.

Pendleton, La Grande and Baker City are all west of Hells Canyon

on I-84, and are all serviced by the Eastern Oregon Regional Airport, in Pendleton, and buses.
Map ref: page 781 P9

JACKSONVILLE

Jacksonville (population 2,000) is a short drive north of the Californian border and 5 miles (8 km) west of Medford, at the foothills of the Siskiyou Mountains.

Gold was first discovered at Rich Gulch in the Rogue Valley, in 1851, bringing settlers and miners seeking their fortune. Encampments sprang up alongside rivers and creek beds and were soon followed by saloons, trading posts, and banks. Jacksonville soon became the commercial center of southern Oregon, but when the railroad bypassed Jacksonville, in favor of nearby Medford, in 1884, many moved away and the town changed little for the next 50 years.

Thus the foundation was laid for the entire town of Jacksonville to be declared a National Historic Landmark in 1966. It has over 90 original brick and wooden buildings, dating to the 1850s, on the National Register of Historic Places. Jacksonville is recognized as one of the most historically significant communities in North America.

Peter Britt was Oregon's first photographer, arriving in Jacksonville on an oxen cart in 1852. In addition to being the first person to photograph Crater Lake, Oregon's only National Park, he also captured the architecture, landscape, and social life of Jacksonville. His 100-year-old images were used to restore many of the town's structures to their original state.

Grants Pass is considered to be the "whitewater rafting capital" of Oregon.

Jacksonville's annual Britt Festival features jazz, classical, bluegrass, and country music, and Broadway musicals in a series of about 40 concerts from June to September. It is the premier outdoor arts festival in the Pacific Northwest and is in its 39th year.

On North 3rd Street is an antique shop, open "by chance or appointment." California Street has a bookstore with 100-year-old issues of *Harper's Weekly* still for sale, and the 1856 Bella Union Saloon that still has its strawberry lemonades. Country Quilts on 5th Street has a fine selection of locally handmade quilts.

Jacksonville is an architectural treasure, with gems like the Nunan House, a Queen Anne-style mansion, built around 1892. It was purchased by Jeremiah Nunan as a Christmas present for his wife and was shipped to Oregon from Knoxville, Tennessee, in railroad cars. It took six months to reassemble the house.

Beekman House, circa 1876, was the home of C.C. Beekman, a Wells Fargo agent and banker. Actors dressed in period costumes give tours through the summer and by arrangement.

Medford/Jackson County Airport services this area, as do trains and buses.
Map ref: page 782 C9

Oregon Scenic Highway, just outside of La Grande, where a wide variety of crops are grown, including alfalfa, mint, and cherries.

JOHN DAY FOSSIL BEDS NATIONAL MONUMENT

Within the eroded volcanic deposits of the scenic John Day River basin, in remote far-eastern Oregon (about 120 miles, or 193 km, northeast of Bend), there exists a spectacular fossil record extending back from six to 54 million years, when Oregon was a lush, near-tropical forest with woodlands and savannas.

The John Day Fossil Beds National Monument was established by an Act of Congress in 1975 and is comprised of three units—the Sheep Rock, Clarno Unit, and Painted Hills Units. Together they make up a total of 14,000 acres (5670 ha). Priceless insights into plant and animal life have been uncovered among the valleys and bluffs of this region.

Near Dayville, the Sheep Rock Unit houses the monument's main headquarters and has a visitor center that is open daily

Bald eagles (Haliaetus leucocephalus) can be seen in Klamath Falls.

from March to October. It has a museum, which exhibits fossils from the area and a 3-mile (5-km) overlook trail climbs the rim of Blue Basin providing panoramic views of the valley's badlands. There are tours, talks, hiking trails, and films available.

In the Clarno Unit Beds, west of Fossil, more than 300 plant species have been uncovered, with the Clarno Nutbeds revealing hundreds of plant fossils—many new to science—containing seeds, fruits, leaves, branches, and roots, with cellular structures still visible.

The colors of the Painted Hills Unit, west of Mitchell, are remnants of volcanic ash producing colored rock layers. The Painted Cove Trail circles a crimson hill and views of the peculiar claystones that are representative of the Painted Hills.

The John Day Fossil Beds are famous for their sheer diversity. Entire communities have been preserved, reflecting rich ecosystems. The fossil beds are scoured regularly and are still giving up hundreds of specimens each year.

There is no camping or lodging in the park but there is plenty to choose from in the surrounding areas. The nearest airport is the Redmond-Roberts Airport in Redmond, northeast of Bend and buses service the area.

Map ref: page 782 H2

KLAMATH FALLS

Enjoying nearly 300 days of sunshine a year, Klamath Falls (population 19,000), on the southern shore of Upper Klamath Lake, lies 55 miles (88 km) east of Medford, nestled in the eastern foothills of the Cascade Range at an elevation of 4,100 feet (1,250 m). It is the largest body of fresh water in the Northwest.

Each February, Klamath Falls plays host to the annual Bald Eagle Conference, the nation's oldest birding festival. Many homes and businesses in Klamath Falls receive natural hot water from the many geothermal wells in the area. The Link River meanders through town, connecting Upper Klamath Lake to Lake Ewauna and originally providing the town with its name—Linkville—until renamed Klamath Falls in 1893 for the Klamath, a local Native American tribe.

Just 60 miles (97 km) south of Crater Lake National Park, Klamath Falls is the gateway to an extremely diverse geographic region, from the snow-capped Cascade Range to the west and the high desert country of the east, to Lava Beds National Monument just across the border in California.

Klamath Falls International Airport is at Kingsley Field, just a few miles southeast on Hwy 39 and trains and buses service the area.

Map ref: page 782 E9

LA GRANDE

La Grande is located in the northeastern corner of Oregon in the Grande Ronde Valley, nestled between the Blue Mountains to its west, and the rugged grandeur of the Wallowa Mountains to its east.

The discovery of gold at nearby Baker City in 1861 prompted settlement of the Grande Ronde Valley. The Oregon Trail passed through the valley, and at the Oregon Trail Interpretive Park at Blue Mountain Crossing, 12 miles (19 km) west of La Grande on I-84, you can walk beside the still-visible wagon ruts, and see how their iron-clad wheels scarred the trees. A paved, easily accessible trail takes visitors through forests and open ridges to some of the best-preserved traces of the historic Oregon Trail. Open from May to October, it offers picnic areas, hiking, restrooms, and water.

Today, La Grande has a population of 12,000 and is home to the Eastern Oregon University, the only four-year institute of higher learning east of the Cascade Mountains. The tree-lined streets of downtown La Grande shade turn-of-the-century architecture.

The surrounding national forests, lakes, and rivers contain some of the best hiking, fishing, and camping opportunities found anywhere in the state. Oregon's second-longest free-flowing river, the beautiful 180-mile (290-km) Grande Ronde River is home to rainbow trout and steelhead.

La Grande is serviced by the Eastern Oregon Regional Airport, in Pendleton, 75 miles (121 km) southeast on I-84. Trains and buses also service the area.

Map ref: page 783 M1

McMINNVILLE

McMinnville has a population of 23,000 and is 40 miles (64 km) southwest of Portland. It has acres of rolling farmlands, vineyards, and small towns, and a moderate, maritime climate. McMinnville was founded by William Newby, a pioneer from McMinnville, Tennessee, who came west in 1843, arriving in Oregon on the first wagon train. He built a gristmill at the west end of 3rd Street in 1853, the construction of which prompted the growth of the city.

Visitors to Medford during the fruit season can sample some world-class peaches.

The town's Historic District, which comprises 52 commercial buildings, has been transformed into one of the most charming areas in the state.

McMinnville is surrounded by more than 40 wineries and more than 100 vineyards, and the county is recognized as one of the premier Pinot Noir areas in the world, rivaling the best in Burgundy. It is Oregon's leading wine-producing area with over a third of the state's wineries and vineyards, most of which have tasting rooms.

McMinnville is also home to Howard Hughes' famous *Spruce Goose* aircraft, the largest wood-framed aircraft ever built. Flown only once on November 2, 1947, for a distance of only 1 mile (2 km), the *Spruce Goose* arrived in McMinnville in 1993 and is on display at the Captain Michael King Smith Evergreen Aviation Educational Institute, which features over 37 historic aircraft.

Portland International Airport is about 40 miles (64 km) north-east of McMinnville, buses also service the area.
Map ref: page 782 C1

MEDFORD

Medford is in southwestern Oregon. Originally named for Medford, Massachusetts, and founded in 1883, it is famous, in the United States, for its succulent peaches. Agriculture and lumber products are the town's main industries. It is the region's largest city and commercial hub, with a population of over 50,000 people.

Harry and David's Country Store, 1 mile (2 km) south of Medford, is one of the world's largest shippers of fruit and food gifts. Sample the area's harvests of berries, pears, and nuts before traveling ½ mile (1 km) south to see the roses at the 43,000-square-foot (4,085-sq-m) Jackson & Perkins Test and Display Gardens.

There are five covered bridges around Medford, including the Wimer Bridge, the only one in Jackson County open to traffic.

Upper and Lower Table Rocks, 10 miles (16 km) northeast of Medford, are giant sandstone-basalt mesas with lava caps. A 2-mile (3-km) trail to the top of Lower Table Rock affords views to the Siskiyou Mountains and the Rogue River. The Medford area is full with things to do—within an 80-mile (129-km) radius there are 153 stocked streams for fishing, 17 lakes, the Rogue River, and camping in 56 forest camps.

Medford/Jackson County Airport is in Medford and trains and buses service the area.
Map ref: page 782 D8

MT HOOD

Mt Hood is Oregon's highest mountain. It is off US-26, about one hour's drive east of Portland, where, at 11,235 feet (3,427 m), it dominates the city's skyline.

Eleven glaciers grace the slopes of this sleeping giant, which still has sulfurous steam escaping from vents on its upper southwestern sides. All its recent eruptions have been minor, though scientists believe Mt Hood could have a significant eruption within the next 75 years.

More than 10,000 people a year climb Mt Hood, making it the most-climbed mountain in the United States and the second-most-climbed in the world, after Japan's Mt Fuji. Its crevassed glaciers and inclement weather has led to one of the highest accident rates of any peak in the world.

The popular Timberline Trail encircles the mountain for 38 miles (61 km), winding through alpine meadows and creeks. Its heavily forested lower elevations consist of Douglas fir, with an undergrowth of Oregon grape.

Timberline Lodge lies nestled on Mt Hood's southern slope, mid-way to the summit, at 6,000 feet (1,830 m). Built in 1937, this National Historic Landmark is a fine example of Cascadian architecture with its interior use of local timbers and ornate carvings of animals on the doors and hand-rails. Massive internal beams and use of native stone make it one of the most architecturally significant structures in the Pacific Northwest.

The Timberline Lodge Ski Area has the only year-round ski season in North America, closing for only two weeks in late September. Most of the area's 150 inches (375 cm) of yearly rainfall falls as snow between October and April. The Mt Hood National Forest encompasses 1.2 million acres (486,000 ha), and includes over 1,200 miles (1,931 km) of hiking trails.

Portland International Airport is the closest to Mt Hood.
Map ref: page 782 F1

Douglas fir forest, Mt Hood. These trees are used in constructing buildings; the wood is said to be stronger than concrete.

NEWPORT

Tourism has enjoyed a long and successful history in Newport. Within four years of the Yaquina Bay oyster beds drawing the area's first settlers in 1862, Newport had its first resort. Built by pioneer Sam Case, he called the town Newport, for his favorite town in Rhode Island.

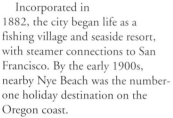
Busy workers at a Newport fish-processing company.

Incorporated in 1882, the city began life as a fishing village and seaside resort, with steamer connections to San Francisco. By the early 1900s, nearby Nye Beach was the number-one holiday destination on the Oregon coast.

Today, Newport has a population of 9,960, and its fashionable Bayfront, a 1-mile (2-km) long strip turned into a giant canvas for local and international artists, boasts turn-of-the-century store-fronts replete with art galleries,

seafood restaurants, and chowder houses. It is also home to Oregon's largest commercial fishing fleet.

Newport serves the area's lumber industry. Prior to World War I the world's largest spruce mill was constructed in this area, which supplied timber for the construction of the famous Howard Hughes *Spruce Goose* aircraft.

Newport's Oregon Coast Aquarium ranks among the top 10 in the nation with a submerged acrylic tunnel providing 360-degree views of Oregon's undersea world. Outdoor exhibits include sea otters, sea lions, and a giant Pacific octopus. The aquarium has one of the largest walk-through seabird aviaries in North America.

In 1980, Congress established the Yaquina Head Outstanding Natural Area, a headland of basalt rock formed from a lava flow some 14 million years ago. It is located

3 miles (5 km) north of Newport on US-101. Yaquina Head offers tidepooling, hiking, and bird watching. Seals can be seen year-round on Seal Rock, and migrating gray whales can be observed in early winter and spring.

Newport has an airport and is serviced by buses. Portland is about 120 miles (193 km) northeast.
Map ref: page 782 B3

OREGON CAVES NATIONAL MONUMENT

The Oregon Caves National Monument, though small in size, possesses one of the world's most diverse environments.

Calcite formations, with evocative names, such as the "Passage-way of the Whale," have been sculpted by the seeping waters and minute mushrooms grow along the roots of Douglas-firs.

The 480 acres (194 ha) of Oregon Caves was proclaimed a National Monument in 1909. The caves were first discovered by Elijah Davidson, in 1874, after chasing his dog into a cave and eventually finding his way out of the black-ness by wading along an ice-cold stream back into daylight. It was

the poet Joaquin Miller who first popularized the area after a visit in 1907, later writing of the "marble halls of Oregon."

All six of the world's major rock types and a multitude of calcite formations decorate the cave. Aboveground there are old growth forests rich in conifers, wildflowers, birds, and amphibians.

The National Parks Service has removed more than a 1,000 tons of rubble, the result of workers blasting passages in the caves during the 1930s. Thousands of formations have been uncovered.

There are daily tours with waiting times of up to 90 minutes during the summer. The route is 1½ miles (2 km) of often low and narrow passages, including some 500 steps and lasting 75 minutes.

The caves are at the end of a narrow and mountainous road 20 miles (32 km) south of Cave Junction in southwest Oregon. Lodging and food are available at the Chateau, a six-story hotel built in 1934 and listed on the National Register of Historic Places.

Medford/Jackson County Airport is about 75 miles (121 km) northeast of the monument.
Map ref: page 782 B9

Mural at the Newport historic dock area on Yaquina Bay—the heart of Newport is home to fishing fleets, seafood markets, restaurants, galleries, and gift shops.

Takhenitch Lake, in the Oregon Dunes National Recreation Area, is a popular fishing spot. The huge lake is undeveloped, and is bordered by vast areas of native forest.

OREGON DUNES NATIONAL RECREATION AREA

On the Oregon coast, between Coos Bay and Florence, lies the largest expanse of coastal sand dunes in North America.

Oregon Dunes National Recreation Area's geological foundation is a gently sloping terrace of solid marine sandstone called Coos Bay Dune Sheet, stretching 56 miles (90 km) from Heceta Head to Cape Arago. This contrasts with the steep headlands that characterizes most of Oregon's coastline. Its desert-like appearance, together with its lakes, rivers, and mature forests of conifer, combine to produce a diverse ecosystem.

The dunes are remnants of sedimentary rock from Oregon's Coast Ranges, uplifted 12 million years ago, carried downstream by rivers, and abraded into sand. Currents, tides, and wave action dredges sand from the ocean floor and deposits it on beaches where the wind sculpts it into the ever-changing shapes seen today.

Many types of dunes are present here, but the largest and most spectacular are called "oblique dunes." They can rise to nearly 500 feet (152 m) above sea level and move constantly, providing no opportunity for any vegetation to grow in them.

The Umpqua Dunes Trail provides access to the biggest and the best of these dunes. Its trailhead is found on US-101, about ¼ mile (1 km) north of the southern Lakeside exit. A 2½-mile (4-km) round trip provides spectacular views of a vast, unmarked expanse of sand 2 miles (3 km) wide and 4 miles (6 km) long. The trail takes you through coastal forest and past fragile plant communities.

The 65-foot (20 m) Umpqua River Lighthouse is at the entrance to Winchester Bay. It is available for tours from May to September.

Introduced grasses threaten the dunes of the Oregon Dunes National Recreation Area.

Thirty-two lakes punctuate the area here, some of which were once mountain streams dammed by sand, or ocean inlets cut off by the sand's relentless progress.

During winter, increased rainfall causes the water table to rise. As the sand grains become saturated and float, quicksand may result—usually in low-lying areas.

The Siltoos River is a wildlife hotspot with numerous campsites available, including the Waxmyrtle and Lagoon campgrounds. Geese and bald eagles may be seen on the river, which includes a lagoon and abundant wetlands containing a wide variety of plants and wildlife.

Only 10 minutes from Coos Bay, Horsfall Dunes has more than 1,000 acres (405 ha) of dunes, forested peninsulas, and wetlands. It is open only to hikers and horse riders. Campers can choose from two campgrounds.

The visitor center is in Reedsport, midway between Coos Bay and Florence, all three towns are serviced by buses. Access is off US-101, 7 miles (11 km) south of Florence.

Map ref: page 782 A5

The area around Pendleton, in northeast Oregon, is dotted with small towns and farming communities; it is considered by some to be the last of the wide open spaces.

PENDLETON

Pendleton, situated in northeastern Oregon, is a Wild West town. After humble beginnings in the early 1860's, when Moses Goodwin purchased land from a squatter for one span of horses, it was officially incorporated in 1880 with a population of 730 people.

Pendleton is well-known throughout the United States as the site of the annual Pendleton

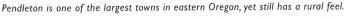
Pendleton is one of the largest towns in eastern Oregon, yet still has a rural feel.

Round-up. Established in 1909 and billed as the country's best rodeo, it is held in the second full week of every September. It includes an old-fashioned rodeo, parades, a country music concert, cowboy breakfasts, and a nightly pagent detailing the history of Native Americans and the early local pioneers.

The center of a large farming and ranching area, Pendleton is one of the largest towns in eastern Oregon. It has a population of 15,000 that swells to over 45,000 during the four days of the annual Pendleton Round-up.

The Confederated Tribes of the Umatilla Indian Reservation hold their largest powwow, the "Happy Canyon Pageant," in conjunction with the annual roundup. Prior to 1855, the Cayuse, Umatilla, and Walla Walla tribes inhabited 6.4 million acres (2.6 million ha) throughout northeastern Oregon and southwestern Washington.

The famous Pendleton Woolen Mills have been weaving blankets since 1909, and factory tours are popular, including a tour of the spinning machines and the automatic looms weaving the bright, geometric Pendleton designs.

Pendleton is serviced by trains and buses and the Eastern Oregon Regional Airport, in Pendleton.
Map ref: page 781 K9

PORTLAND

Portland is the largest city in Oregon with a population of 500,000 people. First settled in 1829, its name was decided on the flip of a coin by two of its early residents, and named for Portland, Maine, not for Boston, Massachusetts.

Situated 70 miles (113 km) from the Pacific Ocean on the confluence of the Willamette and Columbia Rivers, Portland is one of the United States' most beautiful cities, with plenty of lush greenery rarely found in urban areas.

Portland has over 200 parks, including Forest Park, the largest within a city in the United States, with 50 miles (80 km) of trails winding through 4,600 acres (1,863 ha), more than five times the size of New York's Central Park.

The city's steep western hills are home to many historic areas with architectural styles ranging from Queen Anne to Colonial Revival and Art Deco. Willamette Heights is the most intact of Portland's early twentieth-century neighborhoods, with almost every home being built prior to 1915. Portland's most famous home is Pittock Mansion, set in a 46-acre (19-ha) park and offering spectacular views across Portland to the icy pinnacle of volcanic Mt Hood brooding in the distance.

Downtown Portland is a mix of different architectural styles.

Its local pubs and brewhouses feature jazz and blues, while its various comedy clubs and art-gallery walks in the Pearl District contribute to an urban lifestyle envied by other cities.

Portland has its own international airport and is serviced by buses and trains.

Map ref: page 780 D10

ROSEBURG

First settled in 1851, Roseburg (population 20,000) lies in the midst of the Hundred Valleys of the Umpqua. These fertile, lush valleys yield a wide variety of crops and livestock, making agriculture the area's second largest industry after lumber.

Located 125 miles (201 km) north of the California border on I-5, Roseburg has an ideal climate. Extremes of heat and cold are rare, summer humidity is low and snowfall is rare on the valley floor. Its growing season is 217 days and it has one of the lowest average wind velocities in the United States.

The Umpqua occupied the area prior to the arrival of fur traders in the early 1800s. From 1865 to 1870 the population grew rapidly, largely due to an influx of soldiers engaged in the Rogue River Indian Wars. In 1864 it became a terminal on the stagecoach line between Sacramento and Portland, and 1872 brought the railroad to town.

There are only 19 people per square mile (2.6 sq km), and the valleys surrounding Roseburg are a playground of lakes, rivers, and reservoirs. The North Umpqua River is famous for being one of the world's only rivers that still has a run of summer native steelhead.

The area's covered bridges, restored homes, and the acclaimed Douglas County Museum of History and Natural History reflect its rich and varied history.

Roseburg is midway between Eugene and Medford Airports, about 70 miles (113 km) north or south, respectively, on I-5. Buses also service the area.

Map ref: page 782 C6

SALEM

Salem is the capital of Oregon, located 45 minutes south of Portland on I-5. It is in the heart of the fertile Willamette Valley and is the third largest city in Oregon, with a population of 120,000 people.

The city's early founders were Methodist missionaries who, in 1834, traveled west with the intention of converting the local Native Americans. In 1842, the first institute of higher learning west of the Rocky Mountains was founded by missionary Jason Lee. It was originally named the Oregon Institute and today is known as the Willamette University.

After tension between the United States and Great Britain over control of the region, a settlement in 1846 resulted in the Territory of Oregon being proclaimed in 1849, with Oregon City as its capital. When Oregon gained statehood in 1859, Salem was sanctioned as the official capital.

Points of interest include the John D. Boon House, built in 1847 and believed to be Salem's oldest family residence.

The Elsinore Theater reflects the city's close association with the arts. It was erected during 1925–26 and was designed to resemble Elsinore Castle, the setting for Shakespeare's *Hamlet*. The interior is Tudor Gothic with stained glass pieces acquired from a cathedral in Germany that was badly bombed during World War I.

Its Wurlitzer Organ has a bewildering 1,644 pipes and is one of the largest in the country. Performers such as James Earl Jones, Bernadette Peters, and the Glenn Miller Band have performed on its stage. Silent-movie nights are also very popular today, with classics such as Charlie Chaplin's 1917 *The Immigrant* being screened to large audiences.

Surrounding Salem are the wineries of the Willamette Valley, including Willamette Valley Vineyards, Oregon's premier landmark winery, known for its award-winning wines.

Silver Falls State Park lies 30 minutes east of Salem and is the largest park in Oregon at 8,700 acres (3,524 ha). Douglas Fir and Western Hemlock are the dominant vegetation with Giant Sword Ferns and Oregon Grape present along the miles of hiking trails. Deer are common and signs of beaver habitation can be seen in its creeks and waterways.

Portland International Airport is about 45 miles (72 km) north of Salem I-5. Trains and buses also service Salem.

Map ref: page 782 C2

Waller Hall, Willamette University, Salem. Built in 1867, this is the oldest building on campus. It was renovated in 1989.

STATE FEATURE

The Columbia River Gorge

The Columbia River begins its 1,240-mile (1,995-km) journey in the Canadian province of British Columbia, rising in Columbia Lake between the Continental Divide and the Selkirk Mountains.

Initially flowing northwest for 200 miles (322 km), through a narrow valley called the Rocky Mountain Trench, it turns south and picks up the Kootenay and Pend Oreille Rivers before crossing into the United States. Coursing southwest through Washington State it eventually turns east toward its junction with the Snake River, the Columbia's largest tributary which is more than 1,100 miles (1,770 km) long.

From here it heads westward, forming much of the boundary between the states of Oregon and Washington before ending its journey at the town of Astoria and emptying into the Pacific Ocean.

The river drains a 259,000-square-mile (670,810-sq-km) basin that includes territory in seven states (Oregon, Washington, Idaho, Montana, Wyoming, Nevada, and Utah) and one Canadian province. It is arguably the most significant environmental force in the entire Pacific Northwest.

The Columbia River Gorge is a particularly scenic portion of the river, cutting through the Cascade Mountain Range to create a 100-mile (161-km) long, 3,000-feet (915-m) deep gorge. It is the only sea-level river flowing through the Cascades.

While exploring the area during the early 1800s, Lewis and Clark noted that they had difficulty sleeping at night because of the amount of noise generated by the area's birdlife. In 1825, Britain's Hudson's Bay Company established a fur-trading post at Vancouver on the northern side of the estuary. Trappers and traders spread throughout the Columbia River

Basin and, in the 1840s, settlers began arriving in droves via the Oregon Trail.

In 1933 the Federal government began work on two giant dams—the Bonneville Dam on the lower river and the Grand Coulee Dam on the upper river. By 1975, 11 dams stood on the Columbia's main stream, and the original 1,290-foot (393-m) fall of the river within the United States had been reduced to a mere 80 feet (24 m) through the "stair-steps" of the 11 dams.

Prior to the age of dams and mass irrigation, the river plummeted over basalt cliffs. Today, the engineered Columbia provides a nearly sea-level pathway through the Cascade Range to the eastern regions of Oregon and Washington.

The most dramatic section of the Columbia River Gorge lies between the towns of Troutdale and The Dalles. Millions of years of geological upheaval has sculpted the gorge visitors see today, which exhibits columnar basalt, lava outcrops, and evidence of activity such as wind, water, and ice-age erosion, the uplift of tablelands, and giant mudslides.

Running parallel to the river and to I-84 is the Historic Columbia River Highway, US-30. Long considered to be one of the most beautiful roads in America, it provides panoramic views of the Columbia River Gorge as well as access to breathtaking waterfalls, rare wildflowers, and other flora found only within the gorge. This highway was built between 1913 and 1920 and, at the time, was considered an incredible architectural feat. Italian stonemasons were employed to construct stone guardrails, bridges, rock walls, and dry masonry, which appear along the highway's length. It was the vision of engineer Samuel Lancaster, whose goal was to reconcile nature and civilization and to "take the road to the beauty spots." Graceful bridges are in harmony with their surroundings, and virtually the entire length of this lovely highway is shaded.

The highway's western access point is exit 17 off I-84, near the town of Troutdale, 20 minutes east of Portland. Its first 5 miles (8 km) takes you through the towns of Springdale and Corbett, where the Portland Women's Forum State Park provides some of the panoramas for which the Gorge is famous.

Further on, at mile 24 (km 39), is Crown Point State Park and the igloo-shaped Vista House, providing another unforgettable view up and down the river. From this 733-foot (224-m) vantage point, one can view extinct volcanos in Washington and the spectacular eastern rim of the gorge.

There are many waterfalls along the Oregon side of the gorge, including Multnomah Falls. Continuing on from Vista House there is a descent of 600 feet (183 m) through a series of figure-eight curves, following Lancaster's decree that his road would have a maximum grade of five percent. Three state parks

The Historic Columbia River Highway, built along the cliffs of the Columbia River Gorge, is considered by many to be the greatest US scenic highway.

OPPOSITE: *The Multnomah Falls, Columbia River Gorge. There are 77 waterfalls on the Oregon side of the gorge, and Multnomah is the jewel of them all.*

One of a series of Columbia River dams, near The Dalles. The dams have harnessed the river for hydroelectric power, irrigation, and transportation.

The lush farming area around Hood River, near the Columbia River Gorge, where agriculture is thriving and cherries, pears, grapes, and peaches are grown.

appear along this stretch—Bridal Veil, Shepherd's Dell, and Latourell—and all offer many facilities including hiking trails and picnic areas.

At 620 feet (189 m), Multnomah Falls is the fourth-highest waterfall in the United States and one of the gorge's—and Oregon's—most popular sights. Early morning is the best time to visit, before the tour buses and crowds flock in. A trail leads to a bridge, at the 69-foot (21-m) lower falls, and from there it is a scramble to the top along a switchback trail.

Two miles (3 km) further east of Multnomah Falls is Oneonta Gorge—many of the Gorge's unique wildflowers are on display in the Oneonta Botanical Area. The many different elevations and water sources within the Gorge have encouraged a diverse range of wildflowers, including 14 species that are found nowhere else in the world.

The historic highway's eastern terminus is near Ainsworth State Park, set in the midst of fir, maple, and elder trees close by exit 35.

Heading further east on I-84 leads to Bonneville and the site of the massive Bonneville Dam. This features a multi-level visitor center with fish ladders and an underwater viewing room. The Columbia River Basin is the most hydroelectrically developed river system in the world; it generates a total of 21 million kilowatts. Since the 1950s, construction of the dam has combined with increased ocean fishing and the deterioration of stream and river habitats to endanger many species of fish. However, good fishing opportunities still abound, with small- and large-mouth bass, panfish, walleye, and shad still found in good numbers in the Columbia River. Lakes, such as Laurance Lake in the Washington section of the gorge, are good for rainbow and brook trout. River trout, salmon, and steelhead still fight the rapids in Wind River, Hood River, and White Salmon River, and the Sandy River is still one of the top 10 steel-head rivers in Oregon.

Hikers can walk the 13-mile (21-km) Eagle Creek Trail—perhaps the most scenic trail in the gorge—which visits more waterfalls than any other trail. The 35-mile (56-km) Columbia Gorge Trail is one of the more spectacular in the United States, taking you from the misty and mossy to the exposed and rocky. Currently a compilation of existing trails beginning at Bridal Veil, it will one day form a single trail stretching from Portland to the Hood River.

Continuing east along I-84, exit 44 takes visitors to Cascade Locks, home to the Cascade Locks Museum and Cascade Locks Sternwheeler riverboat cruises. The famous Pacific Crest Trail crosses the Columbia River here, and the impressive Bridge of the Gods toll bridge connects Oregon with Washington's Hwy 14.

Approaching Hood River from the west, it is possible to see the Gorge change from the moss-colored hues of Douglas fir to the yellowish greens of cottonwoods and alders. The township of Hood River is the windsurfing capital of the northwest. Hood River hosts the Apple Blosson Festival each spring.

The town of The Dalles marks the eastern extremity of the Columbia River Gorge National Scenic Area and has a historic district that includes Italianate, Gothic, and Queen Anne-style homes, as well as the original 1854 courthouse and Fort Dalles Surgeon's Quarters, established in 1847. Tours of The Dalles Dam are available. The Dalles marked the end of the overland portion of the Oregon Trail until the opening of the Barlow Road around Mt Hood in 1845. Up to that time, the only way to complete the journey westward to Oregon City was via one of two boats ferrying wagons down the Columbia River.

For a sensational place to stay while visiting the Columbia River Gorge, visitors cannot go past the majestic Columbia Gorge Hotel perched upon high bluffs just south of Hood River. Built in 1921 in the Spanish mission-style, its guests have included

Presidents Roosevelt and Coolidge, actresses Myrna Loy and Jane Powell, and, it is rumored, actor Rudolph Valentino. Steamer captains sounded the whistle on approach to the hotel—once for each guest they were carrying. Maids would then make up the beds required.

This Grand Hotel sits atop a 200-foot (61-m) waterfall and provides stunning views of the Gorge below. It has maintained a legendary reputation for hospitality for over 75 years.

Portland International Airport is the closest, and there are trains from The Dalles to Portland. The Dalles is also serviced by trains and buses.

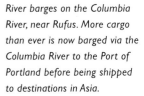

River barges on the Columbia River, near Rufus. More cargo than ever is now barged via the Columbia River to the Port of Portland before being shipped to destinations in Asia.

The awe-inspiring cascading Columbia River in the Columbia River Gorge National Scenic Area. This lush, wild area is literally swarming with life.

WASHINGTON

Washington is a state of amazing natural beauty whose mountains, thick forests, and coastline compete for attention. Occupying the northwest corner of the Lower 48 states, on the Pacific Coast, Washington (population 5.7 million) is the only state named for a US President. It borders the Pacific Ocean in the west, British Columbia, Canada, in the north, Idaho in the east and Oregon to the south—with which it shares the Columbia River Gorge.

Its nickname, "The Evergreen State," heralds the forests of fir, pine, and hemlock—the foundation of the lumber industry that helped establish port cities such as Seattle, Tacoma, and Aberdeen. While aluminum smelting, fishing, farming, forestry, and maritime trade remain important, companies like Boeing and Microsoft put Washington in the vanguard of aerospace and computer technologies.

Native Americans occupied Washington 11,500 years before British fur trappers arrived, the Chinook and Salish west of the Nez Perce, the Yakima to the east. The first white settlers came from the Midwest in the 1830s.

North Cascades National Park, in the north of the state near the Canadian border, has 505,000 acres (204,525 ha) of rugged mountain scenery, as well as over 300 glaciers.

Washington's highest point is the dormant, snow-capped Mt Rainier volcano; at 14,410 feet (4,395 m), it is the highest mountain in the Cascade Range which cuts Washington in two. West of the mountains is temperate, fertile, and well-watered, with up to 140 inches (3,500 mm) of rain annually on the Olympic Peninsula. Greater Seattle is the industrial, commercial, financial, and cultural capital, while Olympia is the political capital. In the two-thirds of the state east of the Cascades, rainfall in places averages only 10 inches (250 mm) a year, and the fertile farmlands depend on the Columbia Basin Irrigation Project. As well as providing much-needed irrigation, dams and reservoirs along the Columbia River also produce a third of the nation's hydroelectric power. Spokane is the region's center of commerce and transportation.

State motto *Al-Ki* (Native American word meaning "by and by")
State flag Adopted 1923
Capital Olympia
Population 5,894,121
Total area (land and water) 70,637 square miles (182,950 sq km)
Land area 66,581 square miles (172,445 sq km)
Washington is the 20th-largest state in size
Origin of name Named for George Washington
Nicknames The Evergreen State, The Chinook State
Abbreviations WA (postal), Wash.
State bird Willow goldfinch
State flower Coast rhododendron
State tree Western hemlock
Entered the Union November 11, 1889 as the 42nd state

Anacortes is one of the main ports for shipping in Puget Sound.

Places in
WASHINGTON

ABERDEEN

Aberdeen, with a small population of 16,600 residents, occupies the estuaries of the Chehallis and Wishkah Rivers, at the head of Grays Harbor. It is one of the most important ports of the Pacific Northwest and has long been a lumber town. It is just 49 miles (79 km) west of Olympia and, with its location on US-101, it is on a popular visitors' route—especially with its proximity to the Olympic National Park and a number of coastal state parks.

The Aberdeen Museum of History preserves the town's early history, from the days when it was founded around a sawmill in the 1880s. Grays Harbor Historical Seaport and Learning Center is a former shipyard and lumber mill. When it's in port, visitors can tour a replica of the *Lady Washington*, the tall ship of Captain Robert Gray, who discovered the harbor in 1792 while exploring the northwest coast and claiming the Oregon Territory for the United States.
Map ref: page 780 B6

Hoh River Valley, in the unspoiled Olympic National Park, near Aberdeen.

ANACORTES

Located on Skagit County's Fidalgo Island in Puget Sound, southwest of Bellingham, Anacortes (population 13,900) is an important port for shipping, and for ferries that shuttle among the sound's picturesque archipelago, the San Juan Islands, and Canada's Vancouver Island.

Anacortes offers boating facilities as well as saltwater and freshwater fishing. It can be reached on State Route 20 west from I-5.
Map ref: page 780 D2

BELLINGHAM

Bellingham (population 61,240) has the 10,778-foot (3,287-m) Mt Baker as a backdrop, numerous parks, three nearby lakes, and is close to Mt Baker-Snoqualmie National Forest and Mt Baker National Recreation Area.

The city was settled in 1852 and quickly grew into a coal-mining and lumber center. By the early 1900s, it had become a major center for salmon canning. Today, tourism and agriculture are the major economic forces.

Alaska-bound travelers board the ferries of the Alaska Marine Highway System. Ferries to Canada's Vancouver Island and the San Juan Islands are also available. Ships arrive and depart regularly at Bellingham Cruise Terminal, in the city's Fairhaven Historic District. Train and bus services are available.
Map ref: page 780 E2

BREMERTON

This city of 41,600 was created for, and remains sustained by, the huge Puget Sound Naval Shipyard on the western side of Puget Sound, west of Seattle. The shipyard is the largest and most diverse on the West Coast, and is the Northwest's largest naval shore facility. It is also Washington's second-largest industrial facility. The yard overhauls and repairs all types of Navy ships. It is also the home port of the nuclear-powered aircraft carrier USS *Nimitz*.

Bremerton Naval Museum portrays the history of the US Navy. The USS *Turner Joy* Naval Memorial Museum, a decommissioned destroyer, is an educational facility that highlights Navy history.

Bremerton is an hour from Seattle by ferry, and about 30 miles (48 km) by road from Tacoma on Route 16.
Map ref: page 780 D5

EVERETT

The turn-of-the-twentieth-century lumber port where Frederick Weyerhaeuser built a sawmill is now known for building Boeing 747s, 767s, and 777s. Visitors can take a popular one-hour tour of the Boeing plant, which is south of the city and west of I-5, on Route 526. Another addition to the city's economy is the Everett Naval Station, established in the early 1990s.

Everett, a city of 70,000 people, lies beside Port Gardner Bay, an inlet of Puget Sound 28 miles (45 km) north of Seattle, on I-5. The Mosquito Fleet offers marine wildlife cruises, including whale-watching tours, through the San Juan Islands. Train and bus services are available.
Map ref: page 780 E4

KENNEWICK

Christened with a Native American word meaning "winter heaven" because of its mild winters, Kennewick is a southeastern Washington town at the confluence of the Columbia, Snake, and Yakima Rivers. It grew slowly after it was settled in 1863. Irrigation arrived in 1892, transforming the region into productive farmlands.

In 1943, the 560-square-mile (1,450-sq-km) Hanford Engineer Works was established, bringing thousands of workers and scientists to the first large-scale production site for plutonium for nuclear weapons. Later known as the Hanford Site of the US Department of Energy, it began to produce electricity in the 1960s. It no longer produces plutonium and is the focus of the world's largest environmental clean-up effort.

Kennewick has been transformed from a farm town of about 2,000 residents in 1940 to a city of about 52,000 today, a growth fueled by the Hanford Site, the Richland-based Pacific Northwest National Laboratory, and hydroelectric dams on the Columbia River.

Kennewick is the largest of the Tri Cities, which include Pasco and Richland. It is also a port and a processing and distribution point for agricultural products.

Tri Cities Airport provides air services. Kennewick is reached by road on I-90 and I-84, and US-395.
Map ref: page 781 K8

MT RAINIER NATIONAL PARK

Mt Rainier, a dormant ice-capped volcano that soars to 14,410 feet (4,395 m) southeast of Puget Sound, is the highest point in Washington and in the Cascade Range. The summit was first reached in 1870. It has the largest single-peak glacier system in the contiguous states, with 25 named glaciers. Snow and ice cover more than 35 square miles (91 sq km).

The Park preserves an area of 235,625 acres (95,428 ha), almost all of it protected wilderness. It includes dense old-growth forest, subalpine meadows, and a diverse array of wildlife. Activities include camping, hiking, mountain climbing, fishing, horseback riding, snowshoeing, and cross-country skiing. It is generally cool and rainy, with summer highs of 60–70°F (15–20°C). July and August are the sunniest months but rain is possible any time.

There is a small entrance fee per vehicle that is good for seven days, but this does not include camping fees. Lodgings and restaurants are available at Longmire Historic District in the southwest corner and at Paradise.

The Park is open year-round, but various facilities are open seasonally. There is no public transport to or in the Park, but most roads are open from late May to early October— parking can be difficult to impossible on sunny summer weekends. Year-round access is on Route 706 to the Nisqually Entrance, in the southwest corner of the Park. Limited winter access is available on Hwy 123, in the southeast corner. The Carbon River/Mowich Lake area, in the northwest corner, is accessed on Route 165 through Wilkeson. Summer access is via Hwy 410 on the north and east sides of the Park. The main airport is Seattle–Tacoma International.
Map ref: page 780 F6

MT ST HELENS NATIONAL VOLCANIC MONUMENT

The Pacific Northwest will long remember the morning of May 18, 1980, when an earthquake, measuring 5.1 on the Richter scale, rocked 9,677-foot (2,951-m) Mt St Helens, triggering a massive volcanic eruption. The earthquake jarred loose the snowy volcano's north flank, which collapsed in a huge landslide that crashed into Spirit Lake, swept over Johnston Ridge and raced 15 miles (24 km) down the Toutle River Valley. Then a lateral blast tore out of the mountain and swept across the landscape. Trees were either leveled or left dead but still standing within a 150-square-mile (389-sq-km) region. A vertical ash column rose 17 miles (28 km) into the sky. Ash turned day to night, halted traffic, rained down on neighboring states, and circled the globe. Melting snow and ice created powerful mudflows. The nine-hour eruption ended 123 years of dormancy, left 57 people dead, and caused billions of dollars worth of damage.

The 110,000-acre (44,550-ha) Mt St Helens Volcanic Monument was established by Congress in 1982 and the environment has been left to recover naturally. The Cascade Range volcano remains active. Located in Gifford Pinchot National Forest, southeast of the Tacoma–Seattle area, the Monument offers the opportunity to view the collapsed volcano and the region devastated by the eruption. There are trails, interpretive talks, and visitor centers. Visitors can climb to the crater's rim but permits are required to go above 4,800 feet (1,464 m). Cross-country skiing and snowmobiling trails are open in winter.

The US Forest Service operates two information centers, at Pine Creek, 18½ miles (30 km) east of Cougar on Forest Road 90, and Woods Creek, 6 miles (10 km) south of Randle on Route 25.

Roads are open from late May or mid-June to late October. The Spirit Lake Memorial Highway (State Route 504) from I-5 is open year-round, although chains may be needed in winter.
Map ref: page 780 E8

NORTH CASCADES NATIONAL PARK

Established in 1968, this 505,000-acre (204,525-ha) preserve east of Bellingham contains spectacular alpine scenery, including mountain lakes, jagged peaks, lush forests, steep-walled valleys, waterfalls, and over 300 glaciers. It borders British Columbia, Canada.

The Park is one of three components of the North Cascades National Park Service Complex; the others

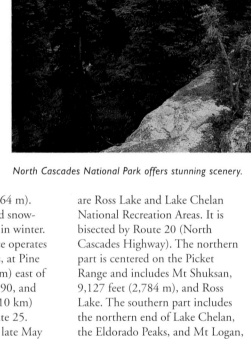

North Cascades National Park offers stunning scenery.

are Ross Lake and Lake Chelan National Recreation Areas. It is bisected by Route 20 (North Cascades Highway). The northern part is centered on the Picket Range and includes Mt Shuksan, 9,127 feet (2,784 m), and Ross Lake. The southern part includes the northern end of Lake Chelan, the Eldorado Peaks, and Mt Logan, 9,087 feet (2,772 m) high.

The Park offers backpacking, mountain climbing, camping, whitewater rafting, boating, fishing, biking, horseback riding, and cross-country skiing. North Cascades and adjoining areas are open year-round, although access is limited by snow in winter. Route 20 is partially closed from about mid-November to mid-April, the dates depending on the weather.

The best weather in the North Cascades is mid-June to late September. All but the highest hiking trails are usually clear of snow by July; summer storms are common. Expect heavy snow or rain (depending on elevation) from fall to spring.

The Park has no entrance fee but a Northwest Forest Pass (for a small monthly or modest yearly fee) is required to park in some places. Use of the Lake Chelan Dock also requires a pass. Lodging is available at Ross Lake Resort, June to October, and private lodgings in the Stehekin Valley.

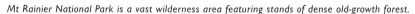

Mt Rainier National Park is a vast wilderness area featuring stands of dense old-growth forest.

Access to the North Cascades and Ross Lake area from the west is on State Route 20 from I-5 at Burlington. From the east, follow State Route 20 west from Twisp. A passenger ferry runs the length of Lake Chelan from the town of Chelan, on US-97, to Stehekin Landing. In the Lake Chelan National Recreation Area's Stehekin Valley, seasonal bus services are provided by the National Park Service (reservations are advised) and the Stehekin Adventure Company. The nearest major airport is Seattle–Tacoma International. Map ref: page 780 F1

OLYMPIA

Washington's capital is at Budd Inlet at the southern end of Puget Sound. The city of 39,000 is named for the Olympic Mountains. Olympia was the capital of Washington Territory until statehood in 1889, when it became the seat of state government. It is also an important commercial center and port. Wood products, processed foods, and mobile homes are produced here.

The city is the starting point for a loop drive around the Olympic Peninsula on US-101 (Olympic Highway). Popular sites are the Capitol Campus, and the State Capital Museum.

Olympia is located at the junction of I-5 and US-101, about 65 miles (105 km) south of Seattle and 115 miles (185 km) north of Portland, Oregon. There is a bus service along I-5 and rail services to Vancouver, British Columbia, Canada, and Eugene, Oregon, and a long-distance service to Los Angeles and Chicago. Map ref: page 780 D6

OLYMPIC NATIONAL PARK

On the Olympic Peninsula in northwestern Washington, Olympic National Park, which is 923,000 acres (373,815 ha) in area, encompasses glaciated mountains, over 60 miles (97 km) of wild Pacific coastline, and magnificent stands of old-growth and temperate rainforest.

Isolated for eons, the peninsula has a distinctive array of plants and animals. Elevations range from sea level to the 7,965-foot (2,429-m) summit of Mt Olympus. More than 600 miles (965 km) of trails course through virgin forests. Rainfall averages 140 inches (3,500 mm) a year in the western valleys, which makes them lush and green.

Park activities include alpine and cross-country skiing, hiking, whitewater rafting, and boating. There are 16 campgrounds and several lodges and resorts.

Hoh Rain Forest, on the western side, receives more than 12 feet (3.5 m) of rainfall a year, creating a world of huge trees and profuse greenery. It is reached via a 19-mile (31-km) paved road from US-101, 13 miles (21 km) south of Forks. Self-guided nature trails include the popular Hall of Mosses Trail.

Hurricane Ridge, almost 1 mile (2 km) above sea level, is reached on Hurricane Ridge Road, a steep drive from Port Angeles. At the end, Hurricane Lodge, for day-use only, provides sweeping views. Two of the Park's most accessible beaches, Kalaloch and Ruby Beaches, are reached on short trails from US-101 north of Queets. There is a campground at Kalaloch—recreational vehicles are discouraged.

There is a small entrance fee per vehicle or an annual park pass is available. Air services are available at Port Angeles' Fairchild International Airport. Map ref: page 780 C4

PASCO

With only 27,370 residents, Pasco is the smallest of the Tri Cities. These cities, which include Richland and Kennewick, occupy the confluence of the Columbia, Snake, and Yakima Rivers. Along with its two sister cities, Pasco is a transportation center and port. It is also a large irrigated agricultural area with productive farmlands and extensive vineyards.

Pasco, located about 190 miles (306 km) southeast of Seattle, can be reached by road via I-90 and I-84, and US-395. Tri Cities Airport provides air services to the city and surrounds. Map ref: page 781 K8

An imaginative rural mailbox near Twisp, in the north of the state.

PORT ANGELES

Located on the Strait of Juan de Fuca, on the Olympic Peninsula, Port Angeles is the gateway to the Olympic National Park. It serves as the port for ferries that make the 22-mile (36-km) trip across the strait to or from Victoria, on Vancouver Island, British Columbia.

With 18,600 residents, this Pacific Rim port is the largest city on the northern leg of US-101. Walkers, joggers, bicyclists, and inline skaters enjoy the paved Waterfront Trail, which runs 8 miles (13 km) from the site of the old Rayonier Mill to the end of the sandbar called Ediz Hook.

Fairchild International Airport services the city.

There are bus services to Port Angeles, Sequim, Seattle, Seattle–Tacoma (Sea–Tac) International Airport and points on the Olympic Peninsula. Map ref: page 780 C3

PORT TOWNSEND

Founded in 1851 on the Olympic Peninsula, this historic Puget Sound city of 8,700 is one of Washington's oldest. Its seaside location has made it a haven for artists and outdoor enthusiasts.

A shipbuilding and trade center in the late 1800s, it is well known for its Victorian buildings and is listed as a national historic landmark. The many guesthouses, shops, and inns make it a popular tourist destination.

North of Port Townsend is Fort Worden State Park, once part of a system of coastal defenses. It includes the Commanding Officer's Quarters, a restored Jeffersonian-style house. Old Fort Townsend State Park, south of the city, includes the site of an Army post built in 1856 to protect settlers. The fort burned in 1895, and is now a wildlife sanctuary. Also nearby is the Point Wilson Lighthouse (1879).

Port Townsend is on US-101. There is a ferry service to Whidbey Island and a passenger service to the San Juan Islands from mid-April to mid-October. Map ref: page 780 D3

Sunset backlights small offshore islands along the Pacifc coastline of Olympic National Park, near La Push.

The Space Needle, at 605 feet (184 m) in height, dominates the skyline of downtown Seattle, Washington's largest city.

RICHLAND

Richland is one of the Tri Cities located where the Columbia, Snake, and Yakima Rivers meet. With 37,445 residents, it is a commercial hub and the center of an agricultural region. Like its sister cities, Kennewick and Pasco, Richland's economy is heavily dependent on the US Department of Energy—their Hanford site headquarters and Pacific Northwest National Laboratory are here.

The town was settled in 1863. Points of interest include the Columbia River Exhibition of History, Science, and Technology; the Hanford Site's Plant 2 Visitor Center, which explains the operation of a nuclear power plant; and the Three Rivers Children's Museum, which has a variety of educational exhibits and activities for children aged two to 12 years.

Richland is reached by road on I-90 and I-84, and US-395. Tri Cities Airport provides air services.
Map ref: page 781 K8

SAN JUAN ISLANDS

Occupying the waters between mainland Washington and Canada's Vancouver Island, this picturesque archipelago of 172 islands at the entrance to Puget Sound is a premier summer travel destination. Ranging in size from rocky outcrops to the 57-square-mile (148-sq-km) Orcas Island, the San Juans are noted for their bays and wooded ridges. They offer wildlife viewing, sailing, relaxing ferry rides, swimming, hiking, bicycling, camping, fishing, and historic sites.

The largest and most populated islands are Fidalgo, Lopez, Orcas, and San Juan. Friday Harbor, on San Juan Island, is the principal town. San Juan Islands National

A grizzly bear (Ursus horribilis) at Woodland Park Zoo, Seattle.

Wildlife Refuge encompasses 48 of the islands. The islands are home to more bald eagles than anywhere in the country outside of Alaska. Offshore there are seals, whales, porpoises, and sea lions.

San Juan National Historical Park, at Friday Harbor, commemorates the peaceful resolution of the nineteenth-century dispute between Great Britain and the United States over ownership of the islands—it is open year-round.

At Moran State Park, on Orcas Island, a serpentine road leads to a parking area 100 yards (92 m) from the 2,409-foot (735-m) summit of Mt Constitution, the islands' highest point. An observation tower gives a 360-degree view.

Lime Kiln Point State Park, also on San Juan Island, is a favorite place for watching Pacific sunsets and some of the 80 or more orcas that make their home in the waters of Haro Strait in summer.

Weather in summer is typically sunny, with scattered showers and temperatures averaging 62–85°F (17–29°C). Winters are cloudy and wet.

Daily ferry services operate between the ports of Anacortes, Friday Harbor, Lopez, Shaw, Orcas, and Sidney (located in British Columbia). There are also seasonal ferries from mainland Washington and Canada.
Map ref: page 780 D2

SEATTLE

Washington's largest city has grown over the years from a small nineteenth-century port to a cosmopolitan Pacific Rim gateway. It is noted for its cutting-edge aerospace and computer industries.

Seattle sits on Elliott Bay, on a strip of land between Puget Sound and Lake Washington. During breaks in the 38 inches (9,500 mm) of precipitation that the "Emerald City" averages annually, residents can gaze west through a modern skyline (which includes the trademark Space Needle) to Puget Sound and the Olympic Mountains. Or they can look south to volcanic, snow-capped Mt Rainier and the Cascade Range. The greater Seattle area has over 2.3 million people, adding traffic congestion, suburban sprawl, and environmental problems to rapid economic growth.

The Duwamish and Suquamish Native Americans inhabited this area before European settlers landed in 1851. Seattle is named for the friendly Native American Chief Sealth. The city has undergone a number of economic surges and slumps since a steam-powered sawmill was fired up on the waterfront in 1853.

Seattle suffered a serious economic downturn when its employment mainstay, the Boeing Company, experienced no sales for a 17-month period in the early 1970s. The city began to recover in the 1980s and 1990s and became a center for finance, services, and high-technology start-ups led by Microsoft. It has grown into a major center for trade with Asia, and Asian immigrants have given the city ethnic diversity.

There is a bus and trolley service run by Seattle Metropolitan Transit System (Metro), in the city and suburbs, and the Monorail, serving the city center.

For a modest price the City Pass, good for nine days, provides access to the Space Needle, Pacific Science Center, Seattle Art Museum, Seattle Aquarium, Woodland Park Zoo, and the Museum of Flight in the Red Barn, where Boeing got its start in 1916.

Also of interest is the historic Pike Place Market, and the Pioneer Square Historic District, a large area of restored historic buildings, shops, restaurants, nightclubs, and sidewalk cafés. The International District is the shopping and cultural center for many Asian-American residents and the home of the Klondike Gold Rush National Historical Park.

North–south I-5, and east–west I-90 are the primary road routes to Seattle. Air services are provided through Seattle–Tacoma (Sea–Tac) International Airport. There are ferry services between Seattle and a number of Puget Sound locations.
Map ref: page 780 E5

SPOKANE

Spokane is located in the east-central part of the state less than 20 miles (32 km) from Idaho. With about 186,000 residents, it is the financial, commercial, transportation, and cultural hub of a region called the Inland Empire that encompasses eastern Washington, northern Idaho, western Montana, and northeastern Oregon. It is known for its irrigated wheat fields, hydroelectric plants, aluminum manufacturing, mining, forest products, and Fairchild Air Force Base.

In the heart of its business district is Spokane Falls, for which the city was originally named. "Falls" was dropped in 1891. The name "Spokane" derives from the name of the Native Americans who once fished for salmon at the falls—it means "children of the sun."

In 1974 Spokane became the smallest city to host a world's fair; the site of the event, Riverfront Park, is the city's centerpiece. It includes an opera house and convention center.

Cheney Cowles Memorial Museum has exhibits on the history of the Inland Empire region and Native American arts and crafts. Manito Park has a conservatory and flower gardens, and a Japanese garden. There are six local wineries and the Gothic-style Cathedral of St John the Evangelist.

Spokane is on I-90. Air services are available at Spokane International Airport. There is a rail service to Portland, Oregon, as well as Seattle and Chicago. There are also bus services.
Map ref: page 781 N5

TACOMA

This southern Puget Sound city on an excellent natural harbor has become one of the largest ports in the nation. Tacoma is also a lumber-producing center. Its name derives from the Puyallup Native American word for Mt Rainier, "Tahoma," the mountain that was God. Today, the city of 179,000 produces wood and paper products, textiles, machinery, processed foods, chemicals, computer products, ships, and aircraft. Its economy is also supported by nearby Fort Lewis, a major US Army base, and McChord Air Force Base.

Fort Nisqually, established on Point Defiance Park in 1833, by the Hudson's Bay Company, is today one of the oldest standing structures in the state. Here also, Washington State History Museum depicts the state's history and Native American culture.

Tacoma is located on I-5, south of Seattle. Between the cities is Seattle–Tacoma (Sea–Tac) International Airport. Motorists can reach the Olympic Peninsula via the Tacoma Narrows Bridge. There are also bus and rail services.
Map ref: page 780 E6

VANCOUVER

Established by the Hudson's Bay Company in 1825 as Fort Vancouver, this southern Washington city across the Columbia River from Portland, Oregon, is the oldest permanent non-Native American settlement in the Pacific Northwest.

The fort was named for British navigator George Vancouver, who surveyed the northern Pacific Coast in the late 1700s. For many years it was the center of British control over the Oregon Territory. Along with most of the Pacific Northwest, it came under United States' control in 1846.

The deepwater Port of Vancouver was established in 1912. Today, the city has a population of 135,100, and is seeing growth from high-technology industries and the aluminum industry.

Much of the area's history is recalled at Vancouver National Historic Reserve. Fort Vancouver National Historic Site was the center of the Hudson Bay Company's fur-trading region from 1825 to 1849. Officers' Row has 21 Victorian homes built between 1849 and 1906 to house US Army officers. Pearson Air Museum has exhibits on the history of aviation at Pearson airfield, the oldest operating airfield in the country and the place where three Soviet pilots landed in 1937, after completing the first non-stop flight from Russia to the United States.

Primary road access to Vancouver is via north–south I-5, or east–west I-84/US-30 along the Columbia River. Portland International Airport provides air services and bus and rail services are available.
Map ref: page 780 D10

WENATCHEE

Wenatchee is a central Washington city of 21,800 people, located on the east side of the Columbia River, at the eastern edge of Wenatchee National Forest. Irrigation has made it a major apple-growing area and a popular outdoor recreation area.

Among its attractions is the paved 11-mile (18-km) Apple Capital Recreation Loop Trail, popular with walkers, joggers, bicyclists, and inline skaters. It includes bridges to the east bank of the Columbia River.

Ohme Gardens County Park offers 9 acres (3.5 ha) of alpine gardens on a bluff overlooking the Wenatchee Valley and the Columbia River. The North Central Washington Museum has exhibits on pioneer and Native American life, including a replica trading post. An aviation exhibit commemorates the first non-stop flight across the Pacific in 1931.

Wenatchee is located on US-2. Air services are available at Pangborn Memorial Airport and there is a bus service.
Map ref: page 781 H5

WHITMAN MISSION NATIONAL HISTORIC SITE

The Whitman Mission National Historic Site, near Walla Walla, in southeastern Washington, preserves the site of Waiilatpu Mission, a Presbyterian mission to the Cayuse people from 1836 to 1847 and a stop for Oregon Trail pioneers.

The park is open year-round. The small entrance fee is good for seven days. Children under 17 are free. The visitor center is 7 miles (11 km) west of Walla Walla, off US-12 and Swegle Road.
Map ref: page 781 L9

YAKIMA

Named for the Yakima people, who occupy a reservation nearby, this city of 54,800 residents is on the banks of the Yakima River, in the heart of a relatively dry region that irrigation has turned into a highly productive agricultural area famous for fruit, hops, mint, vegetables, livestock, dairy products, and wine.

The Yakima Valley Sun Dome, or Washington State Agricultural Trade Complex, is an 85,000-square-foot (8,075-sq-m) multi-purpose facility that plays host to agricultural exhibits, trade shows, symposiums, conventions, concerts, track meets, and other events.

Yakima is at the junction of I-82 and US-12, southeast of Seattle. It is serviced by Yakima Airport, and there is a bus service.
Map ref: page 781 H7

The twin spires of the Gothic-style Cathedral of St John the Evangelist, in Spokane.

Alaska

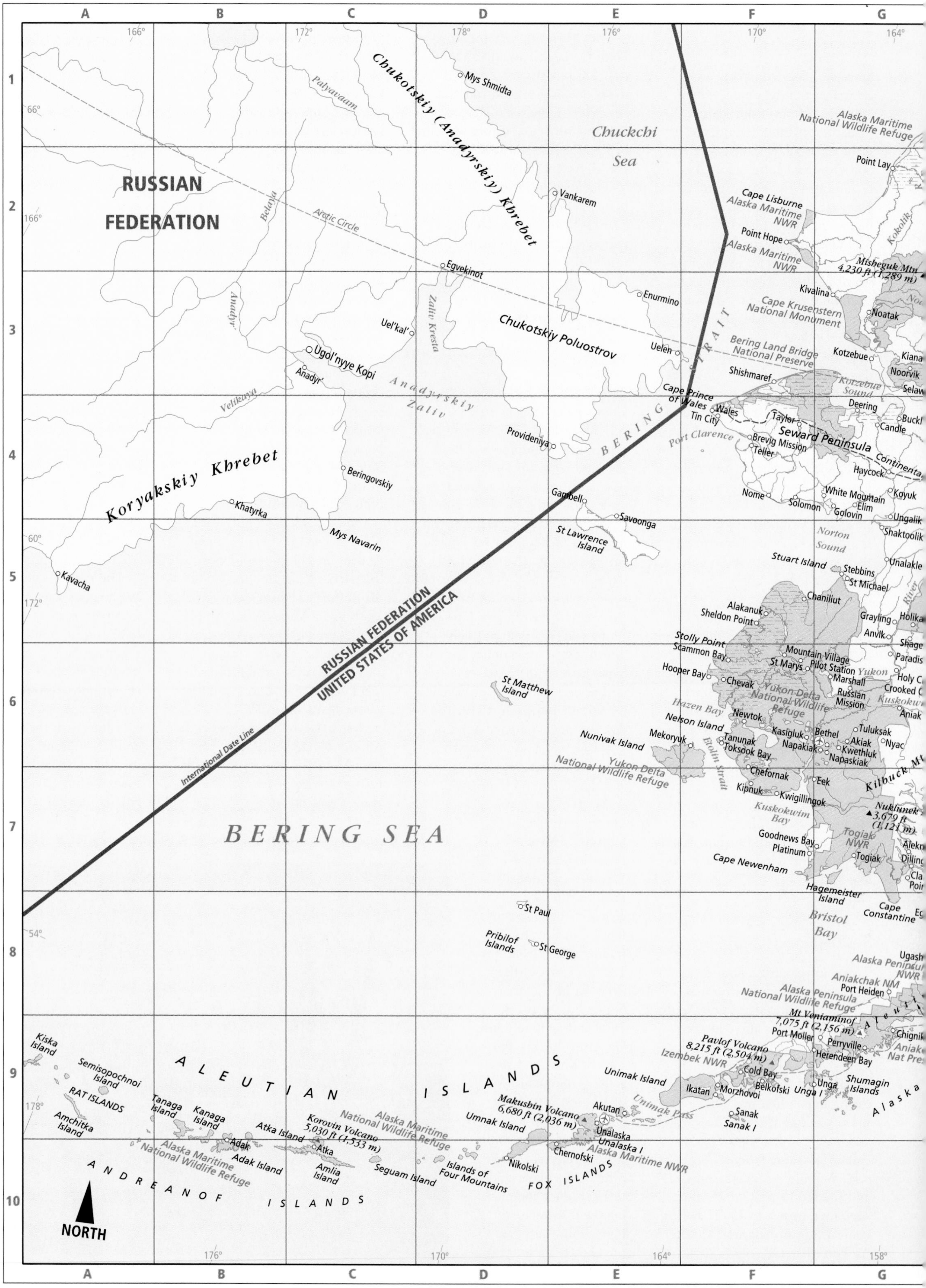

166° 172° 178° 176° 170° 164°

RUSSIAN FEDERATION

Chukotskiy (Anadyrskiy) Khrebet

Chuckchi Sea

Mys Shmidta

Vankarem

66°

Arctic Circle

166°

Belaya

Palyavaam

Egvekinot

Enurmino

Uel'kal'

Chukotskiy Poluostrov

Zaliv Kresta

Uelen

Ugol'nyye Kopi

Anadyr

Velikaya

Anadyrskiy Zaliv

Cape Prince of Wales

Alaska Maritime National Wildlife Refuge

Point Lay

Cape Lisburne
Alaska Maritime NWR

Point Hope
Alaska Maritime NWR

Misheguk Mtn
4,230 ft (1,289 m)

Kivalina

Noatak

Cape Krusenstern National Monument

Bering Land Bridge National Preserve

Kotzebue

Kiana

Noorvik

Selaw

Kotzebue Sound

Shishmaref

Deering

Buckl

Candle

BERING STRAIT

Wales

Tin City

Port Clarence

Taylor

Brevig Mission

Teller

Seward Peninsula

Providskiy

Providyenia

Haycock

Koyuk

Ungalik

Beringovskiy

Koryakskiy Khrebet

Khatyrka

Nome

White Mountain

Elim

Solomon

Golovin

Shaktoolik

Mys Navarin

Gambell

Savoonga

St Lawrence Island

Norton Sound

Stuart Island

Stebbins

St Michael

Unalakle

60°

Kavacha

172°

RUSSIAN FEDERATION

UNITED STATES OF AMERICA

Alakanuk

Sheldon Point

Chaniliut

Grayling

Holika

St Matthew Island

Stolly Point

Scammon Bay

Mountain Village

St Marys

Pilot Station

Yukon Delta National Wildlife Refuge

Anvik

Shage

Paradis

Hooper Bay

Chevak

Marshall

Holy C

Russian Mission

Crooked C

International Date Line

Nunivak Island

Mekoryuk

Hazen Bay

Nelson Island

Newtok

Tanunak

Toksook Bay

Kasigluk

Napakiak

Bethel

Akiak

Kwethluk

Napaskiak

Tuluksak

Nyac

Aniak

Kuskokw

Nuklunek
3,679 ft (1,121 m)

Kilbuck Mt

Chefornak

Eek

Kipnuk

Kwigillingok

Kuskokwim Bay

BERING SEA

Goodnews Bay

Platinum

Togiak NWR

Togiak

Alekn

Dilinc

Cape Newenham

Hagemeister Island

Cla

Poir

54°

St Paul

Pribilof Islands

St George

Bristol Bay

Cape Constantine

Eg

Ugash

Aniakchak NM

Port Heiden

Alaska Peninsula NWR

Alaska Peninsula National Wildlife Refuge

Mt Veniaminof
7,075 ft (2,156 m)

Port Moller

Perryville

Chignik

Aniak
Nat Pres

Kiska Island

Semisopochnoi Island

RAT ISLANDS

A L E U T I A N   I S L A N D S

Unimak Island

Pavlof Volcano
8,215 ft (2,504 m)

Izembek NWR

Cold Bay

Herendeen Bay

Unga

Belkofski

Unga I

Shumagin Islands

Alaska

Amchitka Island

178°

Tanaga Island

Kanaga Island

Atka Island

Korovin Volcano
5,030 ft (1,553 m)

Alaska Maritime National Wildlife Refuge

Makushin Volcano
6,680 ft (2,036 m)

Umnak Island

Akutan

Unimak Pass

Ikatan

Morzhovoi

Sanak

Sanak I

Adak

Adak Island

Atka

Amlia Island

Seguam Island

Islands of Four Mountains

Nikolski

Chernofski

Unalaska

Unalaska I

Alaska Maritime NWR

FOX ISLANDS

Alaska Maritime National Wildlife Refuge

A N D R E A N O F   I S L A N D S

NORTH

176° 170° 164° 158°

A   B   C   D   E   F   G
1 2 3 4 5 6 7 8 9 10

0 100 200 300 400 500 kilometers
0 60 120 180 240 300 miles

H 158° 72° J 152° K 146° L 140° −72° M 134° N 128° P 122°

ARCTIC OCEAN

Beaufort Sea

Point Barrow
Barrow
Peard Bay
Franklin
Dease Inlet
Smith Bay
Wainwright
Atqasuk
Harrison Bay
Meade River
Teshekpuk Lake
Colville River

Prudhoe Bay
Camden Bay
Kaktovik
Arctic National Wildlife Refuge

Banks I
Cape Lambton
Cape Bathurst
Liverpool Bay
Cape Dalhousie
Amundsen Gulf
Cape Parry
Franklin Bay
Darnley Bay
Paulatuk

Herschel I
Kugmallit Bay
Mackenzie Bay
British Mts
Lake Booker
Tuktoyaktuk
Inuvik
Sindgi Lake
Anderson River

NORTHWEST TERRITORIES

Aubry Lake
Colville Lake

BROOKS RANGE

Noatak Nat Preserve
Anaktuvuk Pass
Mt Chamberlin 9,020 ft (2,749 m)
Mt Sedgwick 2,956 ft (901 m)
Aklavik
Old Crow
Fort McPherson
Tsiigehtchic

Ambler
Kobuk
Shungnak
Als Mountain 6,905 ft (2,105 m)
Gates of the Arctic National Park and Preserve
Big Lake
Chandalar
Arctic Village
Venetie
Chalkyitsik
Fort Yukon
Porcupine River
Peel River
Red River
Mackenzie River
Fort Good Hope
Arctic Circle
Lac des Bois
Norman Wells

ALASKA

Hogatza
Kanuti NWR
Allakaket 11
Yukon Flats Nat Wildlife Refuge
Beaver
Stevens Village
Circle
Central
Circle Hot Springs

YUKON TERRITORY

Mt Klotz 5,900 ft (1,798 m)
Ogilvie
Yukon-Charley Rivers National Preserve
Eagle
Clinton Creek
Dawson
Keno Hill
Mayo
Stewart Crossing
Hess Mts
Selwyn Mountains
Mackenzie Mountains
Continental Divide
Logan Mts
Tungsten
Frances Lake

Huslia
Koyukuk NWR
Hughes
Bettles
Wiseman
Tanana
Rampart
Eureka
Livengood
Chatanika
Chena Hot Springs
Eielson AFB
Big Delta
Delta Junction
Boundary
Chicken
Sixtymile
Sulphur
Stewart
Pelly Crossing
Carmacks
Yukon Crossing
Faro
Ross River

Kokrines
Galena
Ruby
Long
Tofty
Manley Hot Springs
Standard
College
Fairbanks
Fox
Fort Wainwright Mil Resn
Aurora Lodge
Nenana
Anderson
Fort Greely Military Resn
Healy
Donnelly
Tanacross
Tok
Tetlin
Northway
Beaver Creek
Koidern
Aishihik
Big Salmon
Lake Laberge
WHITEHORSE

Nulato
Innoko NWR
Nowitna NWR
Nowitna Mts
Denali National Park and Preserve
Lake Minchumina
Cantwell
Summit
Colorado
Paxson
Tetlin National Wildlife Refuge
Nabesna
Wrangell-St Elias NP and Preserve
Burwash Landing
Kluane Lake

Takotna
Medfra
McGrath
Nikolai
Mt McKinley 20,320 ft (6,194 m)
Curry
Talkeetna
Chistochina
Gakona
Gulkana
Glennallen
Copper Center
Wrangell Mts
Mt Blackburn 16,390 ft (4,996 m)
May Creek
St Elias Mts
Haines Junction
Dezadeash
Tagish
Jakes Corner
Teslin
Johnsons Crossings
Watson Lake
Lower Post

Ophir
Sleetmute
Kuskokwim Mts
Montana
Skwentna
Susitna
Wasilla
Chickaloon
Tazlina Lake
Tonsina
Chitina
Chugach Mts
Bagley Ice Field
Mt Logan 19,551 ft (5,959 m)
Carcross
Bennett
Atlin
Atlin Lake
Swift River
Cassiar
McDame

Lime Village
Lake Clark Nat Park and Preserve
Houston
Palmer
Eagle River
Tyonek
Anchorage
Hope
Girdwood
Whittier
Ellamar
Valdez
Cordova
Katalla
Cape Yakataga
Yukutat Bay
Yakutat
Klukwan
Skagway
Haines
BRITISH COLUMBIA
Dease Lake
37

Redoubt Volcano 10,197 ft (3,108 m)
Kenai
Soldotna
Copper Landing
Kenai NWR
Seward
Chugach National Forest
Montague I
Kayak I
Glacier Bay Nat Park and Preserve
Gustavus
Elfin Cove
Funter
Thane
Hawk Inlet
JUNEAU
Telegraph Creek
Glenora
Coast Mountains
Stikine River

Fish Village
Nondalton
Iliamna
Newhalen
Iguigig
Kakhonak
Homer
Seldovia
Port Graham
Kenai Fjords National Park
GULF OF ALASKA
Sunnyside
Tenakee Springs
Chichagof Island
Angoon
Admiralty Island NM
Sitka
Baranof
Kake
Come
Petersburg
Wrangell
CANADA USA

Port William
Afognak Island
Chugach National Forest
ALEXANDER
Sitka National Historic Park
Kuiu I
Point Baker
Edna Bay

Port Lions
Kodiak
Cape Chiniak
Larsen Bay
Old Harbor
Kodiak Island
Kodiak National Wildlife Refuge
Baranof Island
Tongass National Forest
Prince of Wales I
Kasaan
Ketchikan
Metlakatla
Misty Fjords NM
Stewart

Karluk
Chignot
Akhiok
Trinity Islands
PACIFIC OCEAN
GULF OF ALASKA
ARCHIPELAGO
Bucareli Bay
Craig
Hydaburg
Dall Island
Dixon Entrance
Prince Rupert

Chirikof Island
Graham I
Masset
Port Clements
Hecate Strait
Queen Charlotte Islands
Skidegate
Moresby I
Sewell Inlet

UNITED STATES OF AMERICA
CANADA

H 152° J 146° K L 140° M N 134° P

Washington

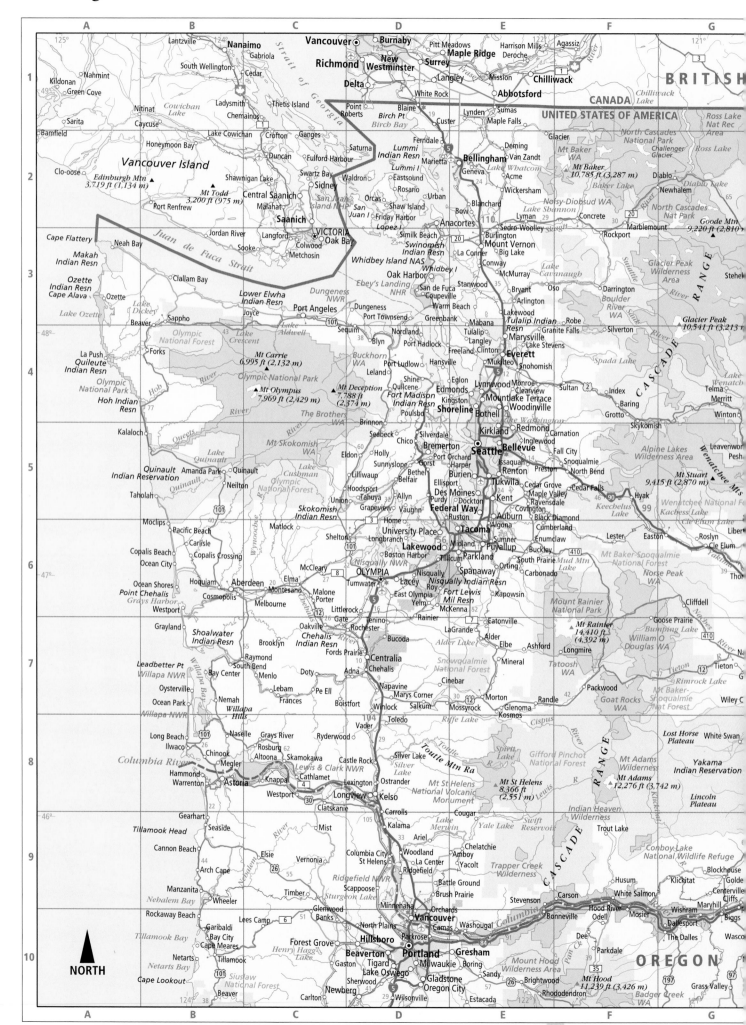

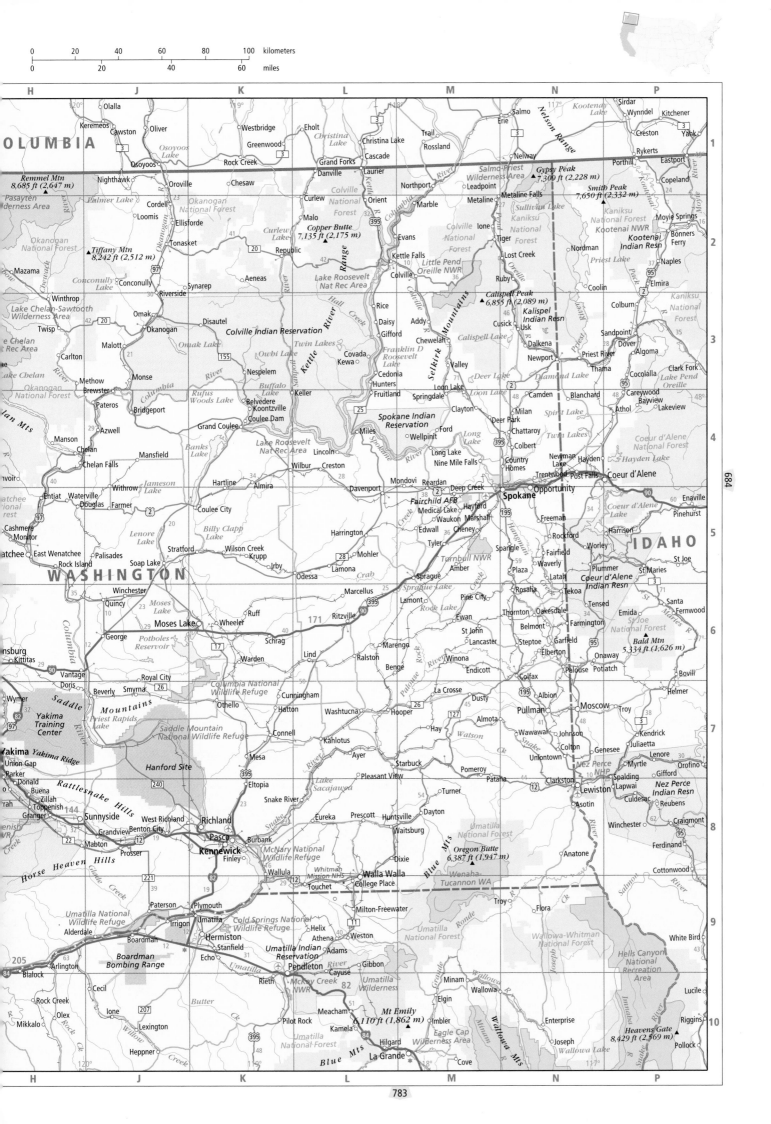

Oregon

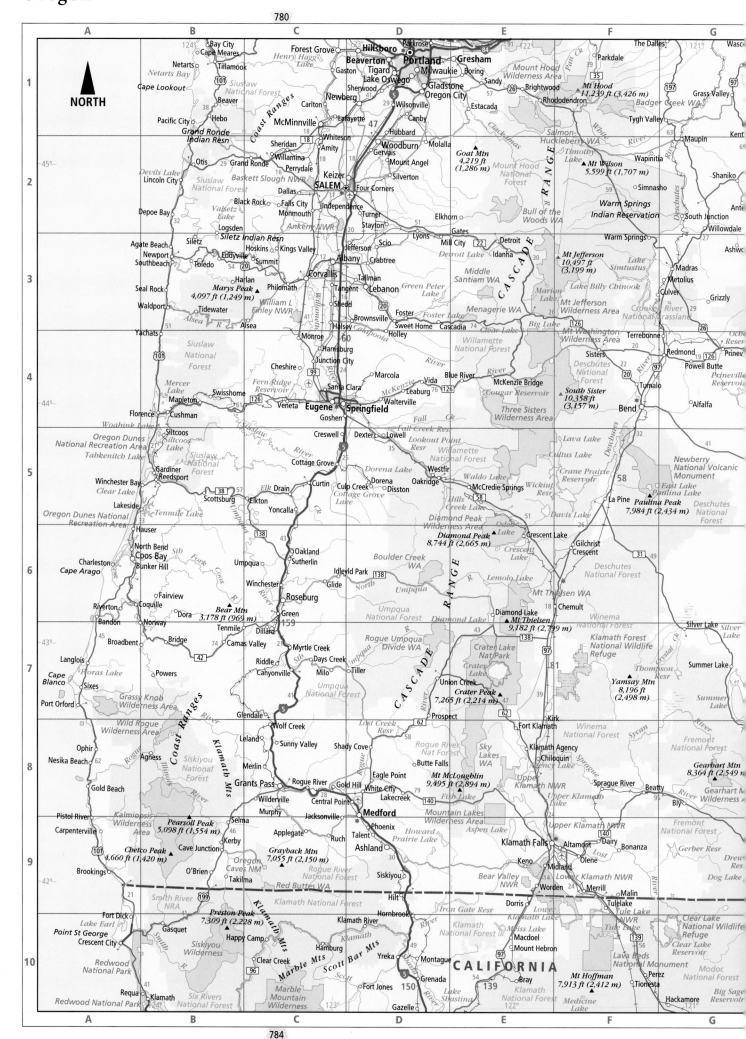

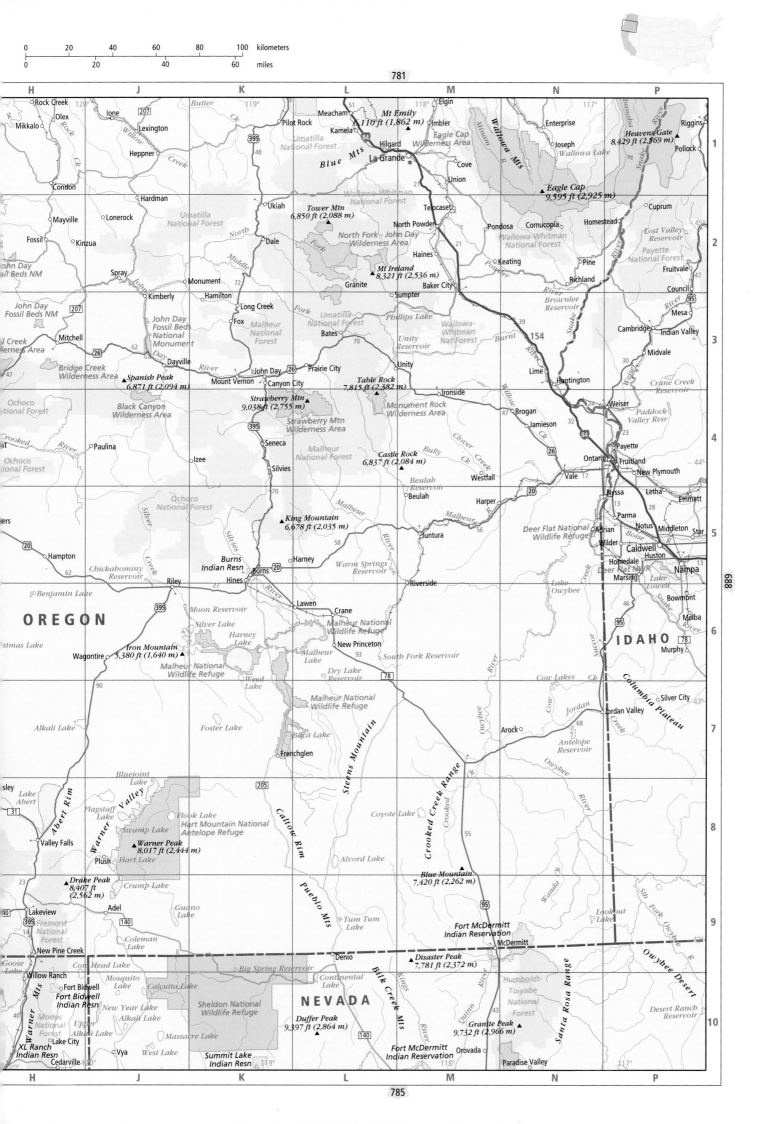

0 20 40 60 80 100 kilometers
0 20 40 60 miles

H J K L M N P

Rock Creek 120° **Ione** [207] **Butter** 119° **Pilot Rock** 51 **Meacham** **Mt Emily** 118° **Elgin** 117° **Riggins**
Olex Rock **Lexington** Ck **6,110 ft (1,862 m)** **Imbler** **Enterprise** **Heavens Gate**
Mikkalo Willow **Heppner** Creek **Kamela** **Hilgard** **Eagle Cap** **Joseph** **8,429 ft (2,569 m)** Pollock
[395] 48 724 **Wilderness Area** **Wallowa Mts** **Wallowa Lake** Snake

Condon **Hardman** **Umatilla** **Ukiah** **Blue Mts** **La Grande** **Cove** **Eagle Cap** **Cuprum**
National Forest **Union** **9,595 ft (2,925 m)**

Mayville **Lonerock** **Umatilla** **Tower Mtn** **Wallowa-Whitman** **Telocaset** **Pondosa** **Cornucopia** **Homestead** **Lost Valley** 45°
National Forest **6,850 ft (2,088 m)** **North Powder** **National Forest** **Reservoir**
Fossil **Kinzua** North **Dale** **North Fork-John Day** **Keating** **Pine** **Richland** **Payette**
John Day **Spray** Middle **Wilderness Area** **Haines** **Powder** **National Forest**
Fossil Beds NM [207] **Monument** 72 **Mt Ireland** 21 River **Lime** **Fruitvale** 47

Mitchell **Kimberly** **Hamilton** **8,321 ft (2,536 m)** **Baker City** **Brownlee** **Cambridge** **Council** [95]
John Day **Long Creek** **Granite** **Sumpter** **Reservoir** **Indian Valley** **Mesa**
Fossil Beds **Fox** Fork **Phillips Lake** **Wallowa-** 39
I Creek **John Day** **National** **Bates** Umatilla **Whitman** 154 **Huntington** 30 **Midvale**
rness Area [26] 62 **Fossil Beds** **Forest** **National Forest** **Unity** **Nat Forest** **Crane Creek**
47 **Dayville** River **John Day** [26] **Prairie City** **Reservoir** **Reservoir**

Bridge Creek 62 **Mount Vernon** **Canyon City** **Unity** Burnt **Weiser**
Wilderness Area [26] **Spanish Peak** **Table Rock** **Ironside** River **Payette**
Ochoco 6,871 ft (2,094 m) **Strawberry Mtn** **7,815 ft (2,382 m)** **Monument Rock** 47 **Brogan** [84] 23
ional Forest **9,038 ft (2,755 m)** **Wilderness Area** **Jamieson** 32 **Ontario** **Fruitland** 44°

Paulina **Izee** **Strawberry Mtn** **Castle Rock** Bully **Vale** 17 **New Plymouth**
Ochoco **Seneca** **Wilderness Area** **6,837 ft (2,084 m)** Ck Creek **Westfall** **Letha**
ional Forest **Silvies** **Malheur** **Beulah** **Harper** [20] **Nyssa** **Emmett**
National **Reservoir** **Parma** 28
Forest **Beulah** Malheur **Deer Flat National** **Adrian** **Notus** **Middleton**
King Mountain **Wildlife Refuge** **Wilder** **Star** 13
6,678 ft (2,035 m) River **Juntura** 56 **Caldwell** **Huston**
OREGON Silvies **Burns** **Harney** 58 **Homedale** **Nampa** 13
Hampton **Riley** **Indian Resn** [20] **Warm Springs** **Marsing** **Bowmont**
62 **Hines** **Burns** **Lawen** **Crane** **Reservoir** **Riverside** Lake **Deer Flat NWR** **Melba**
Benjamin Lake [395] **Moon Reservoir** **Crane** **Owyhee** **Murphy** 78

stmas Lake **Wagontire** **Iron Mountain** **Silver Lake** **Malheur National** **New Princeton** **IDAHO** 6
5,380 ft (1,640 m) **Harney** **Wildlife Refuge** **South Fork Reservoir** [78]
Malheur National **Lake** **Dry Lake** **Silver City** 43°
Wildlife Refuge **Weed** **Reservoir** **Columbia Plateau**
Alkali Lake 90 **Foster Lake** **Lake** **Malheur National** **Cow Lakes** Ck
Wildlife Refuge **Jordan** **Jordan Valley** 68
sley **Blueioint** **Baca Lake** **Antelope**
Lake **Lake** **Frenchglen** **Reservoir** **Arock** **Reservoir**
Abert **Warner** [205] **Steens Mountain** **Crooked** **Owyhee**
[31] **Valley** **Flook Lake** **Crooked Creek Range** River
Flagstaff **Hart Mountain National** **Coyote Lake** 55 **Ouybee Desert**
Lake **Antelope Refuge** **Calrow Rim**
Valley Falls **Swamp Lake** **Alvord Lake** **Blue Mountain**
Warner Peak **Hart Lake** **7,420 ft (2,262 m)** **Lookout** 120°
8,017 ft (2,444 m) **Lake**
Plush **Drake Peak** **Crump Lake** **Pueblo Mts** 95 **Sth Fork**
23 **8,407 ft** **Guano** **Tum Tum** **Wanda** Owyhee
40 **(2,562 m)** **Lake** **Lake** **Fort McDermitt**
[395] **Lakeview** **Adel** [140] **Indian Reservation** **Desert Ranch**
Fremont 14 **Coleman** **McDermitt** **Reservoir**
National **Lake** **Denio** **Disaster Peak**
Forest **New Pine Creek** 120° **Cow Head Lake** **Big Spring Reservoir** **7,781 ft (2,372 m)**
Goose **Willow Ranch** **Continental** **Humboldt-**
Lake **Fort Bidwell** **Mosquito** **Calcutta Lake** **Lake** **Bilk Creek Mts** **Toiyabe**
Fort Bidwell **Lake** **NEVADA** **National**
Indian Resn **New Year Lake** **Sheldon National** **Kings** **Santa Rosa Range** **Forest**
Warner Modoc **Alkali Lake** **Wildlife Refuge** **Duffer Peak** River **Granite Peak** 43
Mts National **9,397 ft (2,864 m)** **9,732 ft (2,966 m)** 117°
XL Ranch Forest **Lake City** **Massacre Lake** [140] **Fort McDermitt** **Orovada**
Indian Resn **Vya** **West Lake** **Summit Lake** **Indian Reservation** **Paradise Valley**
Cedarville 120° **Upper** **Indian Resn** 119° 118°

Northern California • Northwestern Nevada

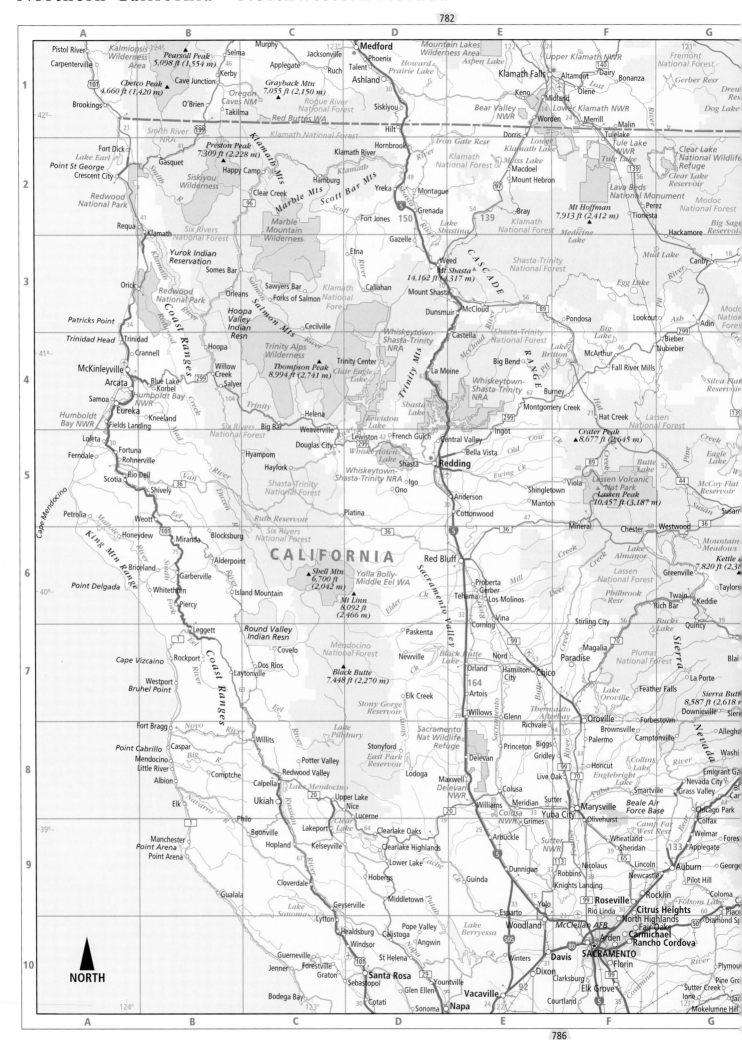

kilometers
miles

H J K L M N P

OREGON

IDAHO

Blue Mountain
7,420 ft (2,262 m)

Drake Peak
8,407 ft
(2,562 m)

Crump Lake

Lakeview
Fremont
National
Forest
Adel

Guano
Lake

Tum Tum
Lake

Wanda

Lookout
Lake

New Pine Creek

Denio

Fort McDermitt
Indian Reservation

McDermitt

Owyhee Desert

Goose
Lake
Willow Ranch

Fort Bidwell
Fort Bidwell
Indian Resn

Mosquito
Lake

New Year Lake

Calcutta Lake

Sheldon National
Wildlife Refuge

Continental
Lake

Disaster Peak
7,781 ft (2,372 m)

Humboldt-
Toiyabe
National
Forest

Desert Ranch
Reservoir

XL Ranch
Indian Resn

Modoc
National
Forest

Upper
Alkali
Lake

Alkali Lake

Massacre Lake

West Lake

Duffer Peak
9,397 ft (2,864 m)

Granite Peak
9,732 ft (2,966 m)

Santa Rosa Range

Lake City
Vya

Summit Lake
Indian Resn

Fort McDermitt
Indian Reservation

Orovada

Paradise Valley

Chimney Dam
Reservoir

Middle
Alkali Lake

Summit
Lake

Santa Rosa - Paradise
Peak Wilderness

Modoc
NWR

Boulder Lake

High Rock Lake

Desert Valley

th Warner
Wilderness
Eagleville

Midas

Likely
Eagle Peak
9,892 ft
(3,015 m)

Lower
Alkali Lake

Moon Lake

Madeline

Dodge
Reservoir

Black Rock Desert

Quinn River

Winnemucca Golconda

Termo

Jungo

Pronto

Ravendale

Sulphur

Sonoma Peak
9,395 ft (2,864 m)

Cosgrave

Valmy

Battle Mountain

Trego

Rye Patch
Reservoir

Mill City

Standish Wendel

Gerlach

Smoke Creek
Reservoir

Imlay

Lower Pitt-Taylor
Reservoir

Shoshone Range

Humboldt House

Honey Lake

Sierra
Army Depot

Empire

NEVADA

Dry
Lake

Smoke
Creek Desert

Smoke Creek

Unionville

Oreana

Gold Acres

Sand Pass

Pyramid Lake
Indian Reservation

Winnemucca
Lake

Granite Mountain
8,419 ft (2,566 m)

Flanigan

Woolsey

Milford

Pyramid
Lake

162

Buffalo Mountain
8,206 ft (2,501 m)

Plumas
National Forest

Sutcliffe

Lovelock

Frenchman
Lake

Pyramid

Anaho Island NWR

Toulon

Humboldt Lake

Humboldt Wildlife
Management Area

Stillwater Range

Humboldt
Salt Marsh

Lake Davis

Vinton

80

Carson Sink

Fallon Naval
Air Station

Loyalton

Copperfield

Wadsworth

Parran

Fallon National
Wildlife Refuge

Fernley
Wildlife
Management
Area

Sardine Peak
8,134 ft (2,479 m)

Reno Sparks

Fernley

Hazen

Fallon
Indian
Resn

Stillwater
Marsh

Clan Alpine Mts

Austin

Stampede
Resr

Verdi

Patrick

Stillwater

Stillwater NWR

Fordyce
Lake

Humboldt-Toiyabe
National Forest

Silver Springs

Fallon

Stillwater Point
Reservoir

Desatoya Peak
9,973 ft (3,040 m)

Toiyabe Peak
10,793 ft (3,290 m)

Soda Springs

Truckee

Washoe City

Virginia City

Sheckler
Resr

Salt Wells

Fallon
NAS

Eastgate

Kings Beach

Crystal Bay

Washoe
Lake

Dayton

Labontan
Resr

95

Fallon
NAS

Frenchman

North Shoshone Peak
10,313 ft (3,143 m)

Tahoe City

CARSON CITY

Wabuska

Carson
Lake

Fallon
NAS

Yomba
Indian
Resn

Lake
Tahoe

Yerington Indian
Reservation

Weber Reservoir

Humboldt-
Toiyabe
National
Forest

Meeks Bay

Minden

Weed Heights

Walker River
Indian Resn

Ione

Yomba
Indian Resn

Mt Jefferson
11,814 ft (3,601 m)

South Lake Tahoe

Gardnerville

Yerington

Schurz

Gabbs

Humboldt-
Toiyabe
National
Forest

Round Mountain

Kyburz

Woodfords

Artesia
Lake

Wellington

Ck Pines

Desolation WA

Markleeville

Mokelumne Pk
9,334 ft (2,845 m)

Topaz Lake

Walker Lake

Thorne

Gabbs Valley Range

Walker Lake

West Point
Wilseyville

Salt Springs
Reservoir

Stanislaus National Forest

Coleville
Walker

Babbitt

Hawthorne
Hawthorne
Army Depot

95

Luning

Mina

Dardanelle

Bridgeport Reservoir

PACIFIC STATES

Central California • Southwestern Nevada

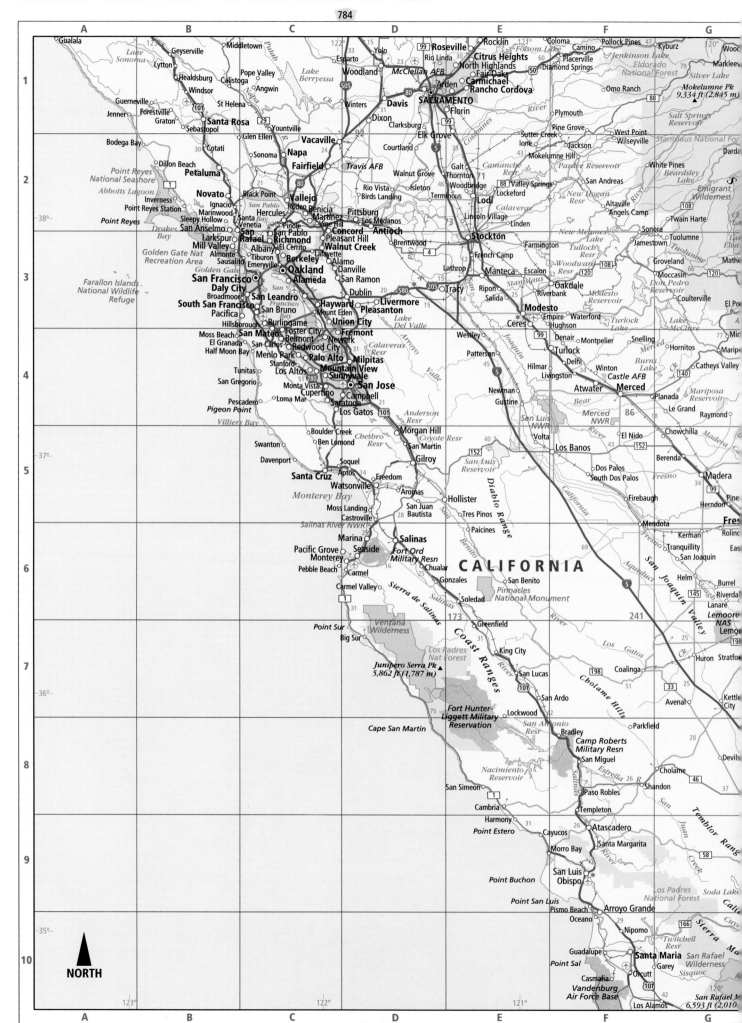

PACIFIC STATES

PACIFIC STATES

Southern California

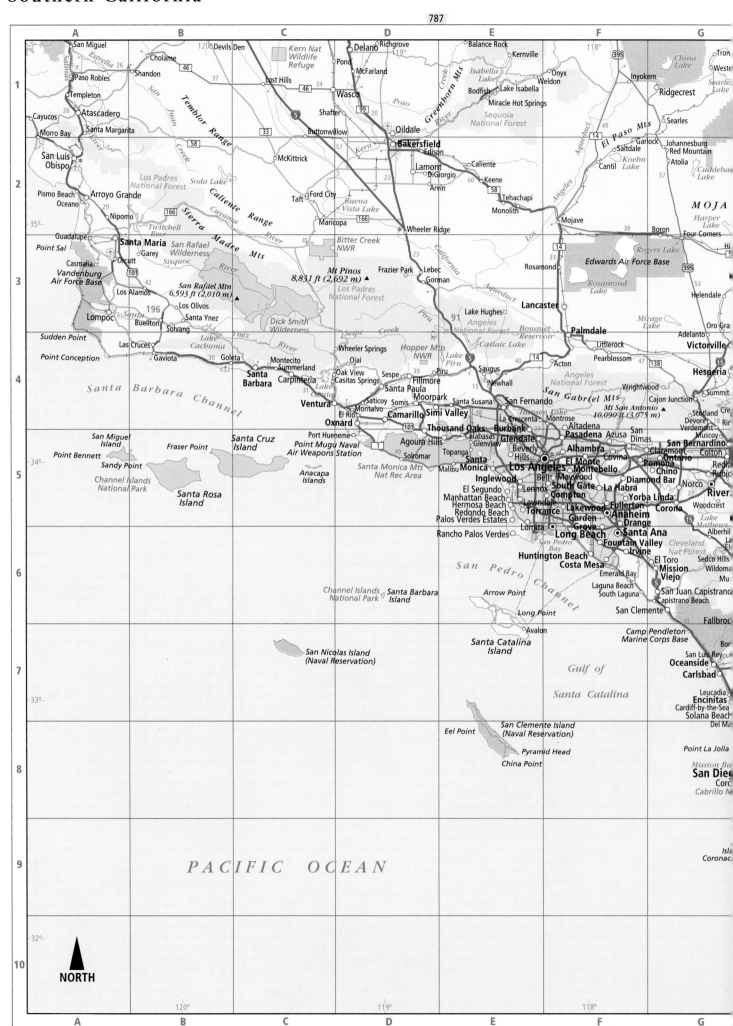

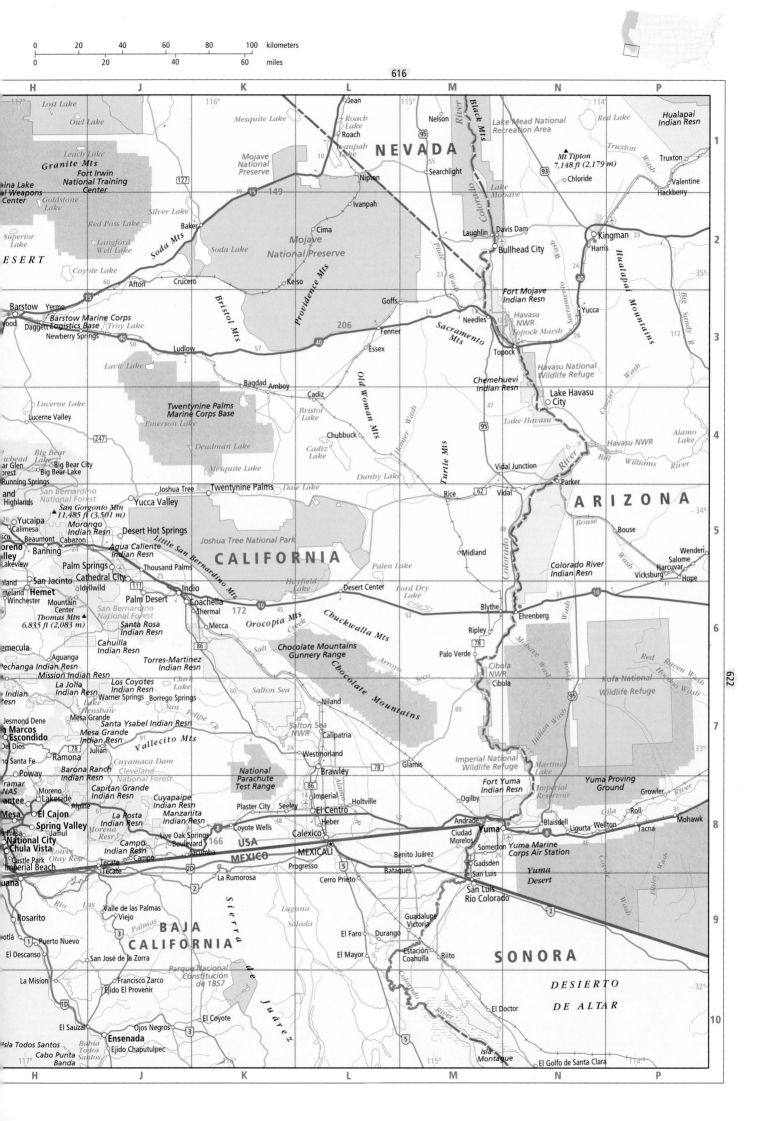

Hawaii

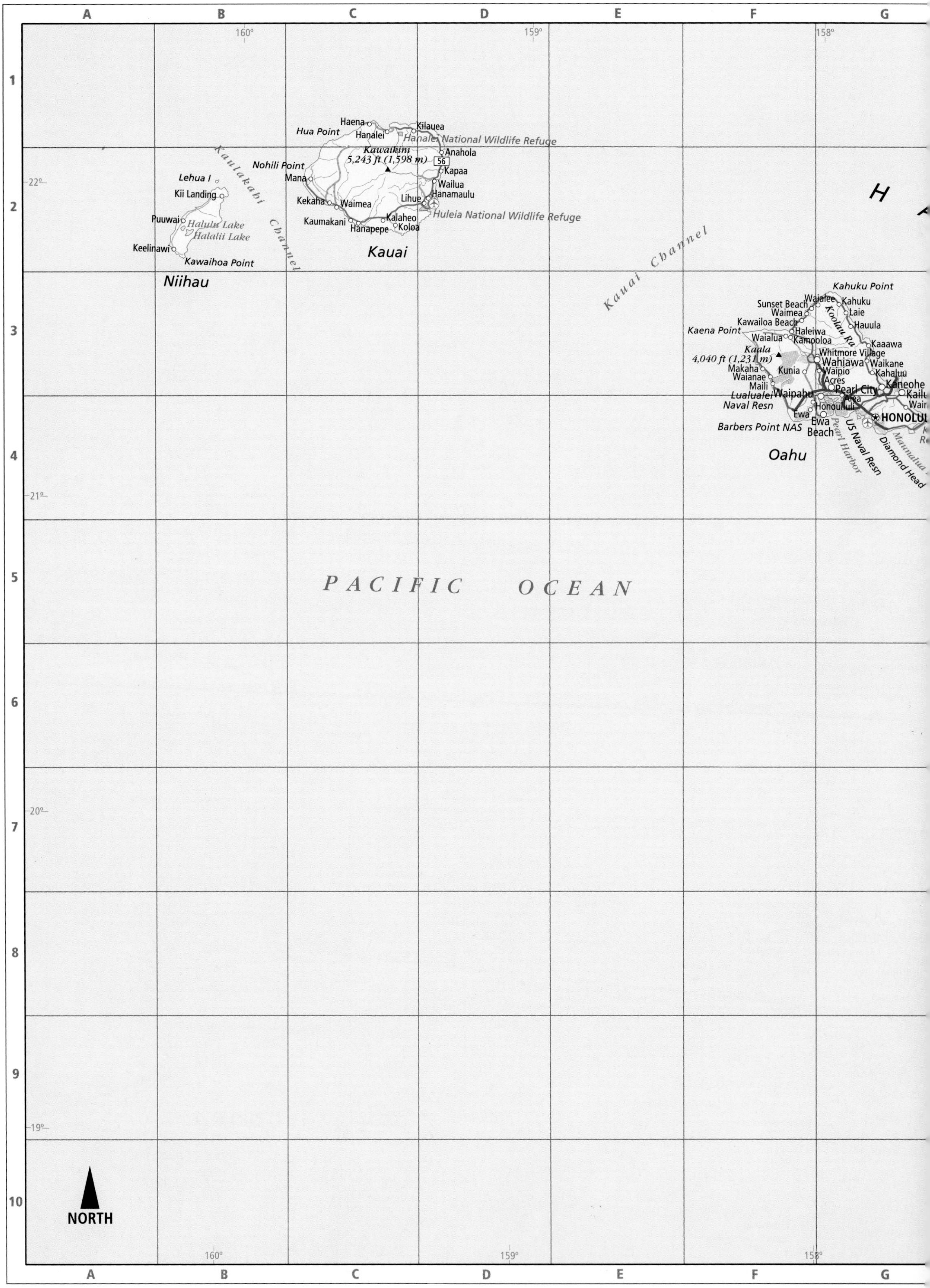

	A	B	C	D	E	F	G

1

160°   159°   158°

2

—22°—

Haena
Hua Point   Hanalei   Kilauea
Hanalei National Wildlife Refuge
Kawaikini
5,243 ft (1,598 m)
56   Anahola
Nohili Point   Kapaa
Mana   Wailua
Kekaha   Waimea   Lihue   Hanamaulu
Kaumakani   Kalaheo
Hanapepe   Koloa
Huleia National Wildlife Refuge

Lehua I
Kii Landing
Puuwai   *Halulu Lake*
Halalii Lake
Keelinawi
Kawaihoa Point

Kaulakahi Channel

Niihau   *Kauai*

Kauai Channel

H
A

Kahuku Point
Sunset Beach   Waialee   Kahuku
Waimea   Laie
Kawailoa Beach   Hauula
Kaena Point   Haleiwa
Waialua   Kamooloa
Koolau Ra   Kaaawa
Kaala   Whitmore Village
4,040 ft (1,231 m)   Wahiawa   Waikane
Makaha   Kunia   Kahaluu
Waianae   Waipio   Kaneohe
Maili   Acres   Pearl City   Kaili
Lualualei   Waipahu   Wair
Naval Resn   Honouliuli   Aiea
Ewa   *Pearl Harbor*   HONOLULU
Barbers Point NAS   Ewa   *US Naval Resn*
Beach   Diamond Head
Maunalua
Oahu

3

4

—21°—

PACIFIC   OCEAN

5

6

7

—20°—

8

9

—19°—

▲
NORTH

10

160°   159°   158°

	A	B	C	D	E	F	G

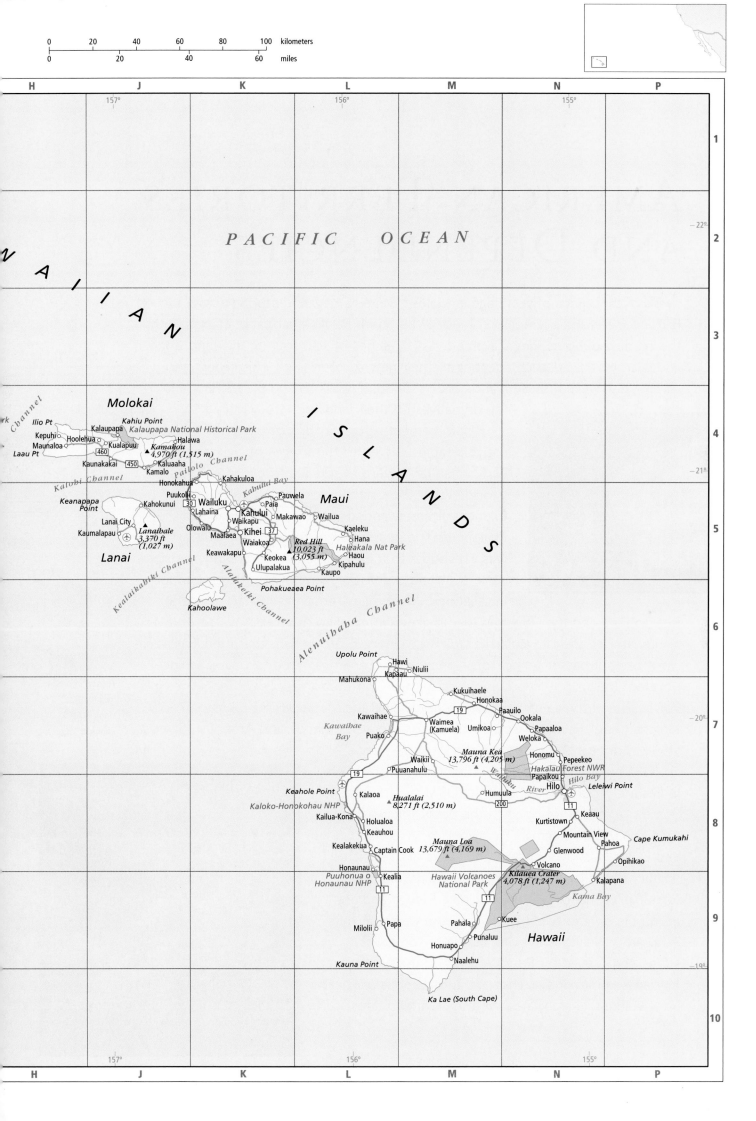

0   20   40   60   80   100   kilometers
0   20   40   60   miles

H   J   K   L   M   N   P

157°   156°   155°

PACIFIC   OCEAN

1

— 22°

2

3

Channel

Molokai

Ilio Pt
Kalaupapa
Kepuhi   Hoolehua   Kualapuu   Halawa   **Kalaupapa National Historical Park**   *Kahiu Point*
Maunaloa   ▲ *Kamakou*
Laau Pt   *4,970 ft (1,515 m)*
Kaunakakai   Kaluaaha   *pailolo Channel*
Kamalo
Kalohi Channel   Kahakuloa
Honokahua   *Kahului Bay*
Keanapapa   Puukolii   Pauwela
Point   Kahokunui   30   **Wailuku**   Paia   *Maui*
Lanai City   Lahaina   Kahului   Makawao   Wailua
Kaumalapau   Olowalu   Waikapu
▲ *Lanaihale*   Maalaea   Kihei   37   Kaeleku
3,370 ft   Waiakoa   Hana
(1,027 m)   Keawakapu   ▲ *Red Hill*   Haou
Lanai   Keokea   *10,023 ft*   Kipahulu
Ulupalakua   *(3,055 m)*   **Haleakala Nat Park**
Kaupo
Pohakueaea Point

4

— 21°

Kealaikahiki Channel

Kahoolawe   *Alalakeiki Channel*

ISLANDS

5

Alenuihaha Channel

6

Upolu Point
Hawi
Mahukona   Kapaau   Niulii
Kukuihaele
Honokaa
19   Paauilo
Kawaihae   Waimea   Ookala
Kawaihae   (Kamuela)   Umikoa   Papaaloa
Bay   Puako   Weloka
Honomu
▲ *Mauna Kea*   Pepeekeo
Waikii   *13,796 ft (4,205 m)*   **Hakalau Forest NWR**
19   Puanahulu   Papaikou
Humuula   *Waik River*   Hilo   *Hilo Bay*
Keahole Point   Kalaoa   *Hualalai*   *Leleiwi Point*
Kaloko-Honokohau NHP   ▲ *8,271 ft (2,510 m)*   200   11   Keaau
Kailua-Kona   Kurtistown
Keauhou   Mountain View   Pahoa
Kealakekua   *Mauna Loa*   Glenwood   *Cape Kumukahi*
Captain Cook   *13,679 ft (4,169 m)*   Opihikao
Honaunau   ▲   Volcano
Puuhonua o   Kealia   **Hawaii Volcanoes**   *Kilauea Crater*   Kalapana
Honaunau NHP   11   **National Park**   *4,078 ft (1,247 m)*   *Kama Bay*
Pahala   Kuee
Milolii   Papa   11
Punaluu   *Hawaii*
Honuapo
Kauna Point   Naalehu

7

— 20°

8

9

— 19°

Ka Lae (South Cape)

10

H   J   K   L   M   N   P

157°   156°   155°

American Territories and Dependencies

Tens of thousands of years ago, peoples from Asia began venturing across the Pacific Ocean and eventually colonized the South Pacific's habitable islands. With the crudest of boats they traversed vast stretches of sea, swamp, and sand. Speech and customs varied, each adapting to their new surroundings. Westerners and Asians "discovered" these islands and established missions and plantations, and forced natives off their land and into slavery.

Gracious colonial building and gardens in Old San Juan, Puerto Rico.

Reinforcement labor was brought in from Asia, and native peoples moved to the fringes of civilization. Most early inhabitants were eventually exterminated. During World War II, the United States captured dozens of extinct volcanoes and atolls between Hawaii and the Philippines. The possession of these Pacific outposts was irresistible to the American military. Landing strips were built, and eventually many of the islands had full installations. While many remain as military centers, Puerto Rico and the US Virgin Islands are of interest to travelers.

Territories are categorized as follows. "Unorganized" means that the US government has not passed an act to organize a government for the territory. "Unincorporated" means not all provisions of the US Constitution apply. US Territories in Polynesia and the Central Pacific are Midway Islands, Jarvis Island, Johnston Atoll, Kingman Reef, Palmyra Atoll, Baker Islands, Howland Islands, and American Samoa. US Territories in Micronesia, in the Western Pacific, are Guam and Wake Island. US Territories in the West Indies are Navassa Island and the US Virgin Islands. Some places are not open to the public: Midway, Johnston, Wake, Kingman, Palmyra, Jarvis, Howland, and Baker. Midway, Johnston, and Wake are restricted military bases. Jarvis, Howland, Baker, and Johnston form Pacific Islands National Wildlife Refuge and are accessible only to scientists or educators with permits. A commonwealth is the official title of some US states, and is used for Puerto Rico, and the Northern Marianas in Micronesia. They are autonomous political units voluntarily associated with the United States.

Yachts moored in tranquil Red Hook Bay, St Thomas, Virgin Islands.

AMERICAN TERRITORIES AND DEPENDENCIES

AMERICAN SAMOA

American Samoa is the most southerly of all lands under the jurisdiction of the United States and is 2,300 miles (3,701 km) southwest of Honolulu, Hawaii. It is a group of seven islands in the South Pacific Ocean covering some 77 square miles (199 sq km). They are Tutuila, Aunuu, the Manua Group—Tau, Olosega, and Ofu, and two coral atolls—Rose Island and Swains Island. With the exception of the two atolls, the islands are mountainous and of volcanic origin. Tutuila, at 55 square miles (142 sq km), is the largest and is the site of a US Naval Station. Rose Island is uninhabited and Swains Island is privately owned. The Three-Power Convention of 1899 awarded Eastern Samoa (Tutuila and Manua) to the US but it wasn't until 1926 that the accession was formally approved. Since the maintenance of the naval station at Pago Pago Harbor was the chief interest, the United States placed the administration in the hands of the US Navy. In 1951 the Department of the Interior took over. In 1960 a territorial constitution was approved, and in 1967 Samoa adopted a revised constitution. Today it is an unorganized and an unincorporated territory of the United States. The Secretary of the Interior appoints the governor, who has executive authority. The islands are divided into three districts. Each has a Samoan governor. The Secretary of the Interior appoints the Chief Justice and an associate justice. Four Samoan associate justices assist them.

The people of American Samoa are Polynesian. Samoa is believed to be the original home of the Polynesian race, and their dialect is thought to be the oldest form of the language. Most speak English as well. They are US nationals. Their constitution contains most of the guarantees of the US Bill of Rights. Population is an estimated 56,000, with 90 percent residing in

Tutuila and Aunuu. Pago Pago on Tutuila is the capital, and has one of the finest harbors in the South Pacific. A cable-car ride above the harbor offers spectacular views. Agriculture, tuna fishing, and tourism along with grants and appropriations by the US Congress support the economy. There are 30 public schools, six private schools, and a community college.

In 1988 the National Park of American Samoa, a 9,000-acre (3,642 ha) park, was established. It includes land on Tau, Tutuila, and Ofu, and preserves four types of rainforest, waterfalls, beaches and coral reefs. It provides sanctuary for the flying fox, a fruit bat with wingspans of up to 35 inches (90 cm). Unlike other national parks, the United States leases land from nine villages within the preserve. Villagers retain ownership of the land and they continue traditional activities including farming and fishing. This park has hiking trails and there are also guided trips to the volcanoes, and cruises to nearby islands.

Most tourists come for the white sandy beaches, waterfalls, and lush green forests. Fishing, diving, snorkeling, and surfing are popular here. Lodging options are extremely limited—there are no luxury resorts and there is a lack of dependable air transport. It is possible to stay overnight in Samoan homes. Pago Pago International Airport is an important stop on transpacific flights between New Zealand, Australia, Fiji, Tonga, Hawaii, and Los Angeles. Shipping services connect Samoa with mainland USA, as well as Hawaii, Fiji, Australia, New Zealand, and Japan.
Map ref: page 799 M10

BAKER AND HOWLAND ISLANDS

In 1936 the United States occupied these uninhabited mid-Pacific coral islands. Baker and Howland Islands are unincorporated territories under the authority of the Fish and Wildlife Services. Baker Island is just one square mile (2.6 sq km) and is 1,650 miles (2,655 km) southwest of Honolulu. The Howland Islands are treeless atolls covering $\frac{3}{4}$ square mile (1.9 sq km) with abundant seabird and fish populations. Guano, the powder-dry excrement of seabirds, covered the islands and was, during the mid-nineteenth century, sought after for its valuable phosphates and ammonium compounds.

Village set amid the lush mountains near Pago Pago, on Tutuila in American Samoa.

A lack of good soil and clean drinking water make these islands unsuitable for permanent settlements. They are situated about 1,620 miles (2,607 km) southwest of Honolulu, Hawaii. During World War II a landing strip here served military aircraft.
Map ref: page 798 F6

GUAM

Guam is the largest and southernmost of the Mariana Islands in the western Pacific Ocean, lying 3,700 miles (5,953 km) west of Honolulu. It is 209 square miles (541 sq km), 30 miles (48 km) long, and a maximum of 8 miles (13 km) wide. Agana, which is on the west coast north of Apra Harbor, is the capital.

In 1521 Portuguese navigator Ferdinand Magellan discovered the island—it was the first land he spotted after crossing the Pacific from South America. Later, in 1565, Miguel Lopez de Lagaspi, colonizer of the Philippines, annexed Guam for Spain. Spain ceded Guam to the United States in 1898 after its defeat in the Spanish–American War. Soon after Pearl Harbor was bombed in World War II, Guam became cut off from American aid by Japanese Micronesia. It fell into Japanese hands and was integrated into Japan's South Seas Empire. In 1944, Americans took it back. During the war, Guam was a strategic communications point en route to the Philippines and East Asia.

Under the US Navy, the Guamanian population doubled in 40 years, credited to public health and medical measures instituted by the Navy. Guam became an organized, self-governing, and unincorporated territory and its people were given citizenship status with the passage of the Organic Act in 1950. The US President appoints a governor, who has executive authority, for a four-year term. Guam sends one non-voting delegate to the US House of Representatives. The legislature is a 21-member single-house group elected biennially by the citizens. The citizens cannot vote in the US elections.

Guam has a tropical climate. Apra Harbor provides good anchorage. It is an important US Defense base with extensive naval, army, and air force installations. Petroleum refining, ship repairing, agriculture, fishing, and tourism support the economy. English is the official language but native Guamians, or Chamorros, speak Chamorro. Half the approximately 145,000 residents are of Micronesian heritage.

There is much of interest here for visitors. In the city of Agana, visit the Plaza de Espana with the Guam Museum and Cathedral, reminders of the Spanish colonial period. Prime hiking is possible in the Guam Territorial Seashore Park in the south, while Umatac is an unspoiled Chamorro village. Tagachang Beach Park in the north has views of the cliffs of east Guam. Guam is considered a premier destination for sea-lovers. Snorkeling and scuba diving are popular activities because of abundant reef life, excellent visibility, and numerous shipwrecks.
Map ref: page 798 B5

JARVIS ISLAND

In 1936 the US occupied Jarvis Island, a tiny uninhabited coral point in the central Pacific Ocean. It covers a mere 1.8 square miles (4.7 sq km) and is 1,300 miles (2,092 km) south of Honolulu. It is an unincorporated territory under the authority of the Fish and Wildlife Service.
Map ref: page 799 H6

JOHNSTON ATOLL

Johnston Atoll is a treeless atoll in the central Pacific Ocean covering 1 square mile (2.8 sq km). It is 700 miles (1,126 km) southwest of Honolulu, and has abundant seabird and fish populations. The island was covered with guano (the dry, powder-like excrement of seabirds); throughout the 1800s guano was a valued commodity because of its phosphates and ammonium compounds. There is no indigenous population. Lack of good soil and drinking water makes it unsuitable for permanent settlements. During World War II it was used as a major air-transport station. The United States acquired it in 1858, and it is now an unincorporated territory managed jointly by the Fish and Wildlife Service and the Defense Nuclear Agency.
Map ref: page 798 G4

Cemetario de Santa Magdalena, San Juan. Eighty percent of the population of Puerto Rico is Roman Catholic.

KINGMAN REEF

Kingman Reef covers $\frac{1}{5}$ square mile (1 sq km) and is in the middle of the Pacific Ocean about 1,075 miles (1,730 km) southwest of Honolulu, Hawaii. The United States acquired it in 1922, and it is an unincorporated territory under the authority of the Department of the Navy.
Map ref: page 799 H6

MIDWAY ISLANDS

The Midway Islands—a coral atoll consisting of Sand and Eastern Islands—cover 2 square miles (5.2 sq km). Named for their location near the geographic center of the Pacific Ocean, they are about 1,300 miles (2,092 km) northwest of Honolulu. An American sea captain discovered the atoll in 1859, and it was annexed to the United States in 1867. In 1903 the US Marines built a transpacific cable station on Sand Island. That same year President Theodore Roosevelt declared the atoll a naval reservation. In the 1930s a marine garrison, naval, and air defense bases were established. In 1942, during the Battle of Midway, US forces defeated a Japanese fleet. This is an unincorporated territory managed jointly by the Fish and Wildlife Service and the Department of the Navy. Around 35 military personnel plus 200 Thai and Sri Lankan contracters live here.
Map ref: page 798 F3

NAVASSA ISLAND

This tiny island in the Caribbean Ocean is only about 2 square miles (5.2 sq km) and is located 35 miles (56 km) west of Haiti. It is an unincorporated territory under the authority of the Department of the Interior, and was acquired in 1856.
Map ref: page 797 A2

NORTHERN MARIANA ISLANDS

The Commonwealth of the Northern Mariana Islands is in the western Pacific Ocean and is made up of 16 volcanic and limestone islands. It includes all of the Mariana Islands except Guam, and covers 179 square miles (464 sq km). The area is southeast of Japan and just across the Philippine Seas from the Philippines. It is about 100 miles (161 km) northeast of Guam. The principal islands are Saipan, which is 47 square miles (122 sq km), Tinian and Rota, which are each 32 square miles (83 sq km).

In 1521 Portuguese explorer Ferdinand Magellan sighted these islands, known as Ladrones Islands (Thieves Islands). In 1668 Spanish Jesuit settlers claimed them for Spain and renamed them after the regent of Spain, Mariana of Austria. In 1898 Spain ceded Guam to the United States and in 1899 Germany purchased the rest of the island group. Following the end of World War I, a League

of Nations mandate placed the German (Northern) Marianas under Japanese control. During World War II the United States captured the islands and produced sugar, copra (dried coconut meat), and other food for soldiers and laborers, as well as phosphate. After World War II the islands were placed under a trusteeship system of the United Nations, which in turn assigned the United States to administer them. They fell under the jurisdiction of the Department of the Interior. The Trust Territory of the Pacific Islands included the Northern Mariana Islands along with the Caroline and Marshall Islands. In 1975 Northern Mariana island inhabitants voted to become a US Commonwealth, and in 1978 they became self-governing. In 1986 US President Ronald Reagan proclaimed them a US Commonwealth and its residents (now approximately 51,000) became US citizens. In 1990 the United Nations Security Council formerly ended the trusteeship.

Agriculture, light manufacturing, and tourism support the economy of the Northern Mariana Islands. The beaches here are what attracts tourists, and its proximity to Japan makes it particularly popular with the Japanese. There is also good sailing and windsurfing. Saipan is the seat of the local government and has a busy seaport and an international airport.
Map ref: page 798 B4

PALMYRA ATOLL

The Palmyra Atoll consists of some 50 tiny islands in the central Pacific Ocean. They cover 4 square miles (10.4 sq km) and are located about 1,100 miles (1,770 km) south-southwest of Honolulu. In 1912 an American expedition visiting the area claimed this uninhabited island for the United States. During World War II it served as a major air transport station. From 1912–59 Palmyra was under the jurisdiction of the city and county of Honolulu and was separated when Hawaii became a state. It is a privately owned unincorporated territory under the authority of the Department of the Interior.

Map ref: page 799 H6

PUERTO RICO

The Commonwealth of Puerto Rico (*Estado Libre Asociado de Puerto Rico*) is the easternmost island—and also one of the largest—in the West Indies, and includes the satellite islands Culebra, Mona, Vieques, and several islets. It is the smallest of four islands that form the Greater Antilles. The other three are Cuba, Jamaica, and Hispaniola (Haiti and the Dominican Republic). A rectangular island, it covers 3,427 square miles (8,876 sq km), and is located about 1,000 miles (1,609 km) southeast of Miami, Florida. It offers 311 miles (500 km) of coastline.

Puerto Rico is a mountainous tropical island with fertile valleys. The climate is tropical and the island is cooled by constant trade winds. From August to October hurricanes are prevalent in the area. Manufacturing, commerce, tourism, and agriculture—most notably coffee bean and tobacco production—supports the economy.

The population, close to four million, is predominantly Hispanic. The largest communities are the capital city, San Juan, as well as Bayamon, Carolina, Ponce, Mayaguez, and Caguas. San Juan is the oldest capital city under the US flag. Eighty percent of the population is Roman Catholic. Spanish is the official language of the commonwealth, though English is also commonly used.

Tribal people inhabited the island as early as AD 1. They may have migrated from Florida, to Cuba, and then along the West Indian archipelago. By AD 300 Arawaks from the Orinoco Basin in Venezuela settled the island. Known by ethnologists as Saladoids, they were the first people in this area known to make and use pottery. Eventually this tribe became the Tainos. In 1493 Christopher Columbus claimed the island and called it "San Juan Batista." In 1509 Juan Ponce de Leon became the first governor, and by 1521 the city of San Juan was founded and the island took the name of "rich port," Puerto Rico. By this time, the Taino people had been almost completely exterminated. The Spanish controlled the island until its defeat in the Spanish–American War of 1898. During this time Puerto Rico was known as "The Island of Enchantment."

By an act of Congress in 1917, the people of Puerto Rico were made citizens of the United States and given a large degree of self-rule. On July 3, 1952, Congress passed legislation that changed Puerto Rico into a free commonwealth associated with the United States. Officially known as the Commonwealth of Puerto Rico, it is a self-governing, autonomous political unit voluntarily associated with the United States. Puerto Ricans cannot vote in the Presidential elections of the United States unless they move to the mainland. US Armed Forces members and federal employees are the only commonwealth residents obligated to pay federal income taxes. The people elect a governor, who has executive authority, to a renewable four-year term. The governor, with the consent of the bicameral Puerto Rico Legislative Assembly, appoints the heads of the commonwealth's executive departments. Puerto Rico does not have counties, but has 78 municipalities, "municipios," each governed by a mayor elected by the people. The people also elect a Resident Commissioner to represent Puerto Rico in the US Congress. This delegate has no voting privileges.

More than 3.5 million tourists visit this tropical destination each year. Popular attractions include the pristine beaches found along four coastlines. There is also El Yunque National Park, a 28,000-acre (11,340 ha) rainforest; the Rio Camuy Caves, carved by the world's largest underground rivers; the Taino Indian Cermonial Park; and the Arecibo Observatory. Puerto Rico has more than 20 forest reserves.

Las Cabezas de San Juan Nature Reserve is in the northeast corner of the island. It is surrounded on three sides by the Atlantic, and has 316 acres (128 ha) of beaches, cliffs, coral reefs, and forests. It protects sea turtles, fish, and shore and migratory birds. Condado and Isla Verde beaches are popular for snorkeling.

Old San Juan is a rich historic district offering the island's premier museums, churches, villas, and fortresses. San Juan nightlife is rich and varied, with shows, discos, salsa clubs, bars, theaters, and the very popular casinos. The Barrilito Rum Distillery and the Bacardi Rum Plant offer guided tours. San Juan is also the world's second-largest home US port for passengers on cruise ships.

Puerto Rico is three-and-a-half hours from New York and six-and-a-half hours from Los Angeles by air into San Juan's Luis Munoz Marin International Airport, the major transportation hub of the Caribbean. Driving is not recommended as car theft is high, interior mountain roads are often challenging, and locals have a reputation for driving aggressively. *Publicos*, public minibuses, serve the entire island and are a convenient means of transportation.

Map ref: page 797 C9

Puerto Rico has been called "The Island of Enchantment" because of its balmy climate and tropical beauty.

Charlotte Amalie Harbor, St Thomas, US Virgin Islands. The islands are favored tourist destinations with Americans, particularly from the East Coast.

US VIRGIN ISLANDS

The US Virgin Islands is about 90 small islands and cays in the West Indies. It is at the western end of the Lesser Antilles, which extends about 60 miles (97 km) from east to west. It is in the Anegada Passage, 40 miles (64 km) west of Puerto Rico, 1,110 miles (1,770 km) east of Miami, and about 1,500 miles (2,414 km) south of New York. The US portion of this island group consists of 65 islands and islets and it covers an area of 133 square miles (344 sq km). The three largest are St Croix, St Thomas, and St John. The islands are peaks of extinct volcanoes with miles of unspoiled tropical coastline.

The population is approximately 80,000, and many natives are descendants of the African slaves that

Carving of St Francis of Assisi at a church in St John, US Virgin Islands.

Europeans brought over to work the sugarcane plantations. Charlotte Amalie on St Thomas is the capital. Tourists come here for the beaches, water sports, fishing, and sailing.

Christopher Columbus "discovered" the islands in 1493, naming them *Las Once Mil Virgenes* for St Ursula's 11,000 martyred maidens. The original inhabitants were believed to have been the nomadic Ciboney Indians from mainland South America and later, the Arawak Indians from Venezuela. Arawaks dominated the islands for about 500 years until the arrival in the fifteenth century of the Carib Indians. The cannibalistic Caribs reportedly either ate or worked the Arawaks to death as slaves. European powers struggled over possession until 1917, when the United States purchased the Virgin Islands from Denmark for $25,000,000. The US Navy held authority over the islands. In 1927 the United States granted citizenship to the island residents. In 1936, the first Organic Act of the Virgin Islands passed under the Roosevelt administration, giving the islanders voting rights. In 1954 they came under the sovereignty of the Department of the Interior and were given a greater degree of self-government. They have no voice in the elections of the US. The President of the United States appoints the governor of the islands. Local legislature is a single body that consists of 11 senators who

are elected for two-year terms. Today the islands are an organized and unincorporated territory and remain under the authority of the Department of the Interior.

The Virgin Islands are rich in tropical vegetation including jasmine, hibiscus, orchids, ginger, bougainvillea, poinsettia, frangipani, cacti, acacia, fig, mango, coconut, and breadfruit trees. They enjoy constant trade winds, sunshine, and less humidity than other Caribbean islands. Northern shorelines are on the Atlantic Ocean, where the best beaches are protected from the surf by coral reefs. The southern shores are on the calmer Caribbean Sea—St Croix is entirely surrounded by the Caribbean.

St Thomas and St Croix are highly developed, and the harbors at Charlotte Amalie in St Thomas and Christiansted in St Croix are crowded with cruise-ship passengers from December to April, the high season. (Prices are lower in the slightly hotter off-season). St Croix has Carambola, the Virgin Island's top golf course. Snorkelers and scuba divers frequent Buck Island National Park because of its 100 feet (31 m) underwater visibility, grottos, and coral gardens teeming with sea life. It has the United States' only underwater national monument. The US Forest Service protects St John, the least developed and most tranquil of the islands. The US Virgin Islands National Park covers more than two-thirds of St John, including Trunk Bay— a long, wide beach considered one of the most beautiful beaches in the West Indies. One third of the park is underwater. Other attrac-

tions in St John are Cruz Bay, the capital; a re-creation of a West Indian village; and Annaberg Ruins, the site of a 1700s Danish sugar mill and plantation.

Puerto Rico is 30 minutes by plane, and many eastern US cities are a three- or four-hour flight. Travel between islands is by ferry.
Map ref: page 797 F9

WAKE ISLAND

Formerly known as Halcyon Island, Wake Island is 3 square miles (7.8 sq km) and in the central Pacific Islands. It is located roughly midway between Guam and the Hawaiian Islands—2,300 miles (3,701 km) west of Honolulu. The territory is actually made up of three coral islets—Wake, Peale, and Wilkes—connected by a roadway. Formerly known as Enenkio, it was named for British sea captain William Wake who landed here in 1796. Spanish explorers reported seeing the islands in 1568 and in 1796 British explorers visited. In 1898 the United States formally occupied Wake Island, and in 1934 it was placed under the jurisdiction of the US Navy. In 1935 a commercial air base was established to serve transpacific flights, and in 1939 construction began on a naval air base and a submarine base. Japanese air and naval forces attacked and captured the island in World War II. They surrendered to the United States in 1945. It is now under the authority of the US Army Space and Strategic Defense Command and is an unincorporated territory. Population is 140.
Map ref: page 798 D4

US Territories and Dependencies in the Caribbean

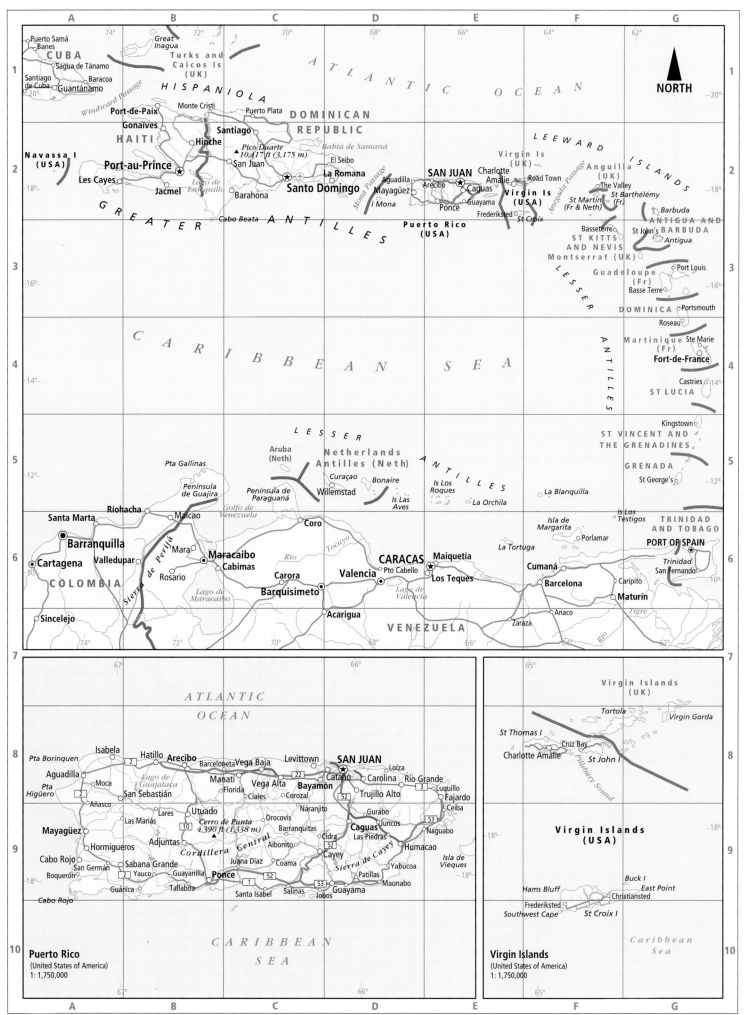

US Territories and Dependencies in the Pacific

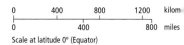

Scale at latitude 0° (Equator)

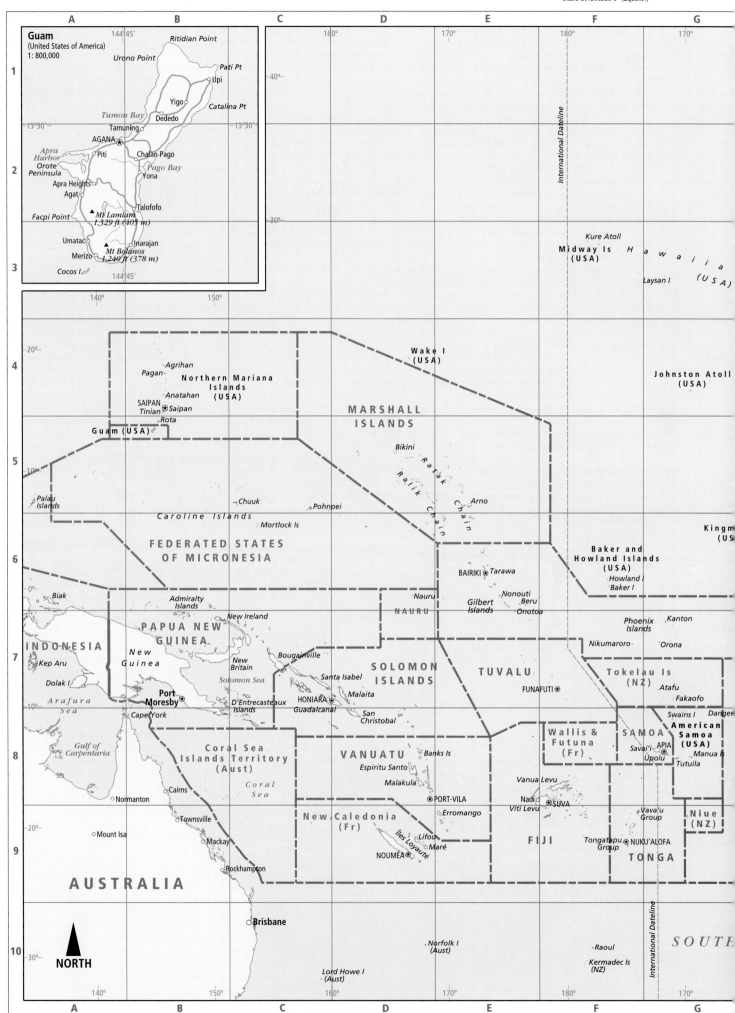

Guam
(United States of America)
1: 800,000

Ritidian Point

Urono Point

Pati Pt

Upi

Yigo

Catalina Pt

Tumon Bay

Dededo

Tamuning

AGANA

Apra Harbor

Piti

Chalan Pago

Orote Peninsula

Pago Bay

Yona

Apra Heights

Agat

Talofofo

Facpi Point

▲ *Mt Lamlam 1,329 ft (405 m)*

Umatac

Inarajan

Merizo

▲ *Mt Bolanos 1,240 ft (378 m)*

Cocos I

International Dateline

Kure Atoll

Midway Is H a w a i i a n

(USA)

Laysan I (U S A)

Wake I
(USA)

Johnston Atoll
(USA)

Agrihan

Pagan

Northern Mariana Islands
(USA)

Anatahan

SAIPAN

Tinian Saipan

Rota

MARSHALL ISLANDS

Guam (USA)

Bikini

Ratak Chain

Chuuk

Pohnpei

Arno

Ralik Chain

Palau Islands

Caroline Islands

Mortlock Is

Kingm
(US

FEDERATED STATES OF MICRONESIA

Baker and
Howland Islands
(USA)

Howland I

Baker I

Biak

BAIRIKI Tarawa

Admiralty Islands

Nauru

Nonouti

Beru

Phoenix
Islands

Kanton

PAPUA NEW GUINEA

New Ireland

NAURU

Gilbert
Islands

Onotoa

Nikumaroro

Orona

INDONESIA

New Guinea

New Britain

Bougainville

SOLOMON ISLANDS

TUVALU

Tokelau Is
(NZ)

Kep Aru

Santa Isabel

Atafu

Dolak I

Solomon Sea

Malaita

FUNAFUTI

Fakaofo

Arafura Sea

Port Moresby

D'Entrecasteaux Islands

HONIARA

Guadalcanal

San Christobal

Swains I

Danger

Cape York

Wallis & Futuna
(Fr)

SAMOA

American Samoa
(USA)

Gulf of Carpentaria

Coral Sea Islands Territory
(Aust)

VANUATU

Banks Is

Savai'i

APIA

Manua Is

Upolu

Tutuila

Normanton

Cairns

Coral Sea

Espiritu Santo

Vanua Levu

Malakula

PORT-VILA

Nadi

SUVA

Vava'u Group

Niue
(NZ)

Townsville

New Caledonia
(Fr)

Erromango

Viti Levu

Mount Isa

Lifou

Vava'u Group

FIJI

Tongatapu Group

NUKU'ALOFA

Mackay

Îles Loyauté

Maré

NOUMÉA

TONGA

Rockhampton

AUSTRALIA

▲ **NORTH**

Brisbane

Norfolk I
(Aust)

Raoul

S O U T H

Lord Howe I
(Aust)

Kermadec Is
(NZ)

International Dateline

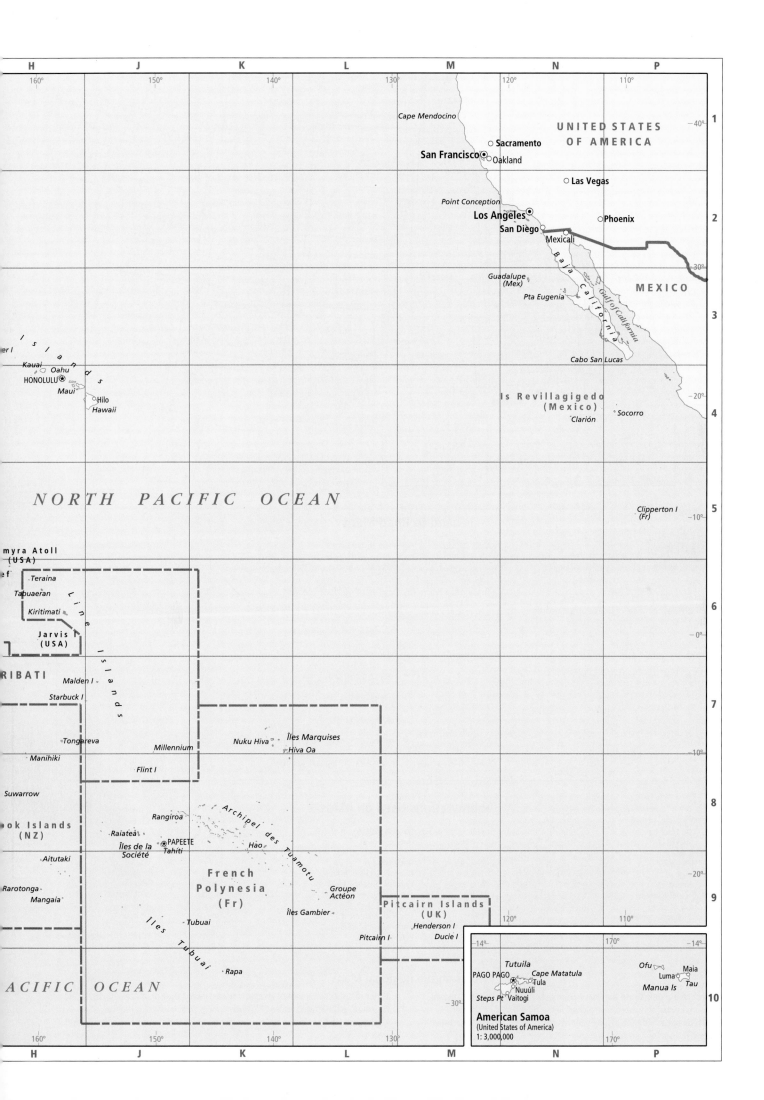

H   J   K   L   M   N   P

160°   150°   140°   130°   120°   110°

Cape Mendocino

UNITED STATES OF AMERICA

○ Sacramento
San Francisco ◉
○ Oakland

○ **Las Vegas**

Point Conception

Los Angeles ◉
San Diego ◉
○ Mexicali

○ **Phoenix**

Baja California

MEXICO

Guadalupe (Mex)

Pta Eugenia

Gulf of California

Cabo San Lucas

Is Revillagigedo (Mexico)

Clarión ·

· Socorro

er I
Kauai ○ Oahu
HONOLULU ⊛
Maui ○
○ Hilo
Hawaii

Islands

NORTH PACIFIC OCEAN

Clipperton I (Fr)

−40°
−30°
−20°
−10°

myra Atoll
(USA)
ef

· Teraina
Tabuaeran ·
Kiritimati ·

Line Islands

Jarvis I
(USA)

RIBATI

Malden I ·
Starbuck I ·

· Tongareva
· Manihiki

Millennium ·
Flint I ·

Îles Marquises
Nuku Hiva ·
Hiva Oa ·

−10°
−0°

Suwarrow ·

ok Islands
(NZ)

· Aitutaki

Rarotonga ·
Mangaia ·

Rangiroa ·
Raiatea ·
Îles de la
Société
⊛ PAPEETE
Tahiti
Hao ·

Archipel des Tuamotu

Groupe
Actéon ·

Îles Gambier ·

**Pitcairn Islands
(UK)**

Henderson I ·

· Tubuai

**French
Polynesia
(Fr)**

Îles Tubuai

· Rapa

Pitcairn I ·

Ducie I ·

120°   110°

ACIFIC OCEAN

160°   150°   140°   130°

−14°
Tutuila
PAGO PAGO Cape Matatula
Tula
Nuuúli
Steps Pt Vaitogi

170°

Ofu
Luma ○
Manua Is

Maia
Tau

−14°
−30°

American Samoa
(United States of America)
1: 3,000,000

170°

H   J   K   L   M   N   P

1
2
3
4
5
6
7
8
9
10

Key to Road Maps

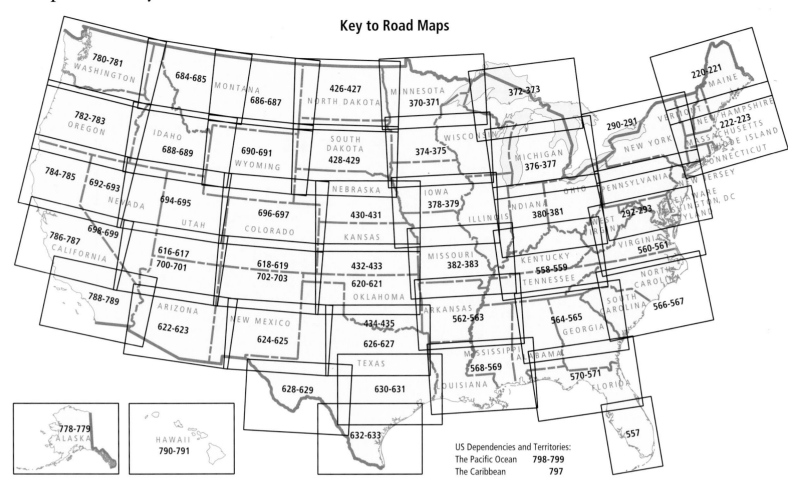

US Dependencies and Territories:
The Pacific Ocean 798-799
The Caribbean 797

Legend to Road Maps

Toll limited-access highway		International border
Free limited-access highway with interstate route marker		Major built-up area with state capital city (small and large)
Principal highway with US route marker		Major city or town, other towns
Other through highway with state or provincial route marker		Major airport; landmark or point of interest; mountain peak; volcano
Other highway		Major river; other watercourse
Mexican federal route, Trans-Canadian route marker		Perennial lake; dry or intermittent lake
Road distances in miles, major and intermediate		Swamp; glacier or ice field
Railroad		Military camp or reservation
Ferry route		Native American land
Continental divide		National park, monument, reserve, wildlife refuge, recreation area
State border		National forest; national grassland

Abbreviations Used on Maps

AFB	Air Force Base	NAS	Naval Air Station	Pt	Point
Arch	Archipelago	Nat Forest	National Forest	R	River
Ck	Creek	Nat Mil Park	National Military Park	Ra	Range
Fwy	Freeway	Nat Park	National Park	Res	Reserve
Hwy	Highway	Nat Rec Area	National Recreation Area	Resn	Reservation
I-	Interstate	NHP	National Historic Park	Resr	Reservoir
I, Is	Island, Islands	NHR	National Historic Reserve	St, Ste	Saint, Sainte
L	Lake	NHS	National Historic Site	Thwy	Thruway
Mil Resn	Military Reservation	NM	National Monument	Tpk	Turnpike
Mt	Mount	NWR	National Wildlife Refuge	WA	Wilderness Area
Mtn	Mountain	Pen	Peninsula	WMA	Wildlife Management Area
Mts	Mountains	Pkwy	Parkway	WRC	Wildlife Research Center

Notes on the Regional Maps

- Volcanoes shown are only those that have been active during recorded history.
- Airports shown are major airports with scheduled airline services; smaller airports with commercial airline services for nearby popular tourist attractions are also shown.

- Minor distances are shown for many roads; cumulative distances, however, are shown only for limited-access highways.
- Alaska and Hawaii do not appear on the small location maps for the mainland states.

INDEX TO PART 1: THE STORY OF AMERICA

This is an index to the subjects in this book (places are in a separate index). Page numbers for pictures are *italic*, and page numbers for major discussions of a subject are **bold**.

INDEX TO PART 2: PLACES

Abbreviations used in this index

United States of America

AL	Alabama
AK	Alaska
AR	Arkansas
AZ	Arizona
CA	California
CO	Colorado
CT	Connecticut
DC	District of Columbia
DE	Delaware
FL	Florida
GA	Georgia
HI	Hawaii
IA	Iowa
ID	Idaho
IL	Illinois
IN	Indiana
KS	Kansas
KY	Kentucky
LA	Louisiana
MA	Massachusetts
MD	Maryland
ME	Maine
MI	Michigan
MN	Minnesota
MO	Missouri
MS	Mississippi
MT	Montana
NC	North Carolina
ND	North Dakota
NE	Nebraska
NH	New Hampshire
NJ	New Jersey
NM	New Mexico
NV	Nevada
NY	New York
OH	Ohio
OK	Oklahoma
OR	Oregon
PA	Pennsylvania
RI	Rhode Island
SC	South Carolina
SD	South Dakota
TN	Tennessee
TX	Texas
UT	Utah
VA	Virginia
VT	Vermont
WA	Washington
WV	West Virginia
WI	Wisconsin
WY	Wyoming

- This index contains the names of settlements, national parks, national forests and other national reserves shown on the detailed regional maps at the end of each section, and the names of the US dependencies and territories and the settlements on them.
- Numbers in **bold** indicate an entry in the text pages.
- Names with a symbol (settlements) on the maps are indexed according to the location of the symbol. Names without a symbol are referenced according to the start or center of the name.
- Words abbreviated on the map, for example NWR (for National Wildlife Refuge), are spelt out in this index.
- The country name, the USA, is not given for places within the USA. However, it does appear in paratheses after the names of US territories and dependencies, for example Guam (USA).

A

Abbeville AL 564 E10, 570 E2
Abbeville GA 565 J9, 571 H1
Abbeville LA **493**, 568 D8
Abbeville MS 563 L6
Abbeville SC 565 L4
Abbotsford WI 375 L3
Abbott AR 562 B4
Abbott NM 619 K7
Abbott TX 627 H9, 630 G2
Abbott VA 560 C7
Abbott WV 560 C3
Abbottsburg NC 566 G5
Abercrombie ND 427 N8
Aberdeen ID 689 H7
Aberdeen KY 558 D6
Aberdeen MD 293 J6
Aberdeen MS 563 M8
Aberdeen NC 566 E3
Aberdeen OH 381 J8
Aberdeen SD 427 K10, 429 K1
Aberdeen WA **773**, 780 B6
Aberfoil AL 564 E9, 570 D1
Abernathy TX 625 N4
Abilene KS **389**, 431 J9
Abilene TX **602**, 626 C7
Abingdon IL 379 L5
Abingdon VA 559 N7
Abington MA 222 F6
Abiquiu NM 618 F7
Abita Springs LA 569 J7
Abo NM 624 D2
Aboite IN 380 F2
Abraham UT 695 H8
Abraham Lincoln Birthplace National Historic Site KY **483**
Abrams WI 372 C10, 376 B1
Absaroka Beartooth Wilderness MT 689 M2, 690 B2
Absarokee MT 685 N10, 686 D10, 689 P1, 690 D1
Absecon NJ 293 M7
Academy SD 429 J6
Acadia National Park ME **190–191**, 221 K9, 221 L9, 223 K2, 223 L1
Accident MD 292 C6
Accomac VA 561 L6
Ace TX 631 L5
Ace Basin National Wildlife Refuge SC 565 P7, 566 C9
Acequia ID 688 G8
Achille OK 435 K4
Ackerman MS 563 L9
Ackley IA 374 G9, 378 F1
Acme LA 568 E5
Acme NM 625 H5
Acme TX 626 C3
Acme WA 780 E2
Acme WY 691 H2
Acoma NV 700 E3
Acoma Pueblo NM **590**, 618 D10, 624 B1
Acomita NM 618 D10, 623 P1, 624 B1
Acorn VA 561 K5
Acra NY 291 M8
Acree GA 565 H10, 570 G2
Acton CA 788 F4
Acton MT 686 E9
Acworth GA 564 F4
Acy LA 568 G7
Ada KS 431 H9
Ada LA 568 B2
Ada MN 370 B6
Ada OH 381 J3
Ada OK 433 L10, 435 J2
Ada WI 376 B4
Adair IA 378 D3
Adair IL 379 L6
Adair OK 433 N6
Adairsville GA 564 F3
Adairville KY 558 D7

Adak AK 778 B10
Adams IN 380 F6
Adams KY 559 M4
Adams MA 222 B5
Adams MN 374 G7
Adams ND 427 L3
Adams NE 431 L5
Adams NY 291 J4
Adams OR 781 L9
Adams TN 558 D7
Adams WI 375 M6
Adams Center NY 291 J4
Adamstown PA 293 J5
Adamsville TN 558 A10, 563 N4
Adamsville TX 626 F10, 630 E3
Adamsville UT 700 G2
Addicks TX 631 K7
Addie NC 559 L10, 565 J1
Addieville IL 383 L4
Addington OK 434 G3
Addis LA 568 F7
Addison AL 564 B4
Addison IL 376 B8
Addison NY 290 G8
Addison OH 381 M8
Addy WA 781 M3
Adel GA 571 H3
Adel IA 378 E3
Adel OR 783 J9, 785 J1
Adelanto CA 788 G4
Adena OH 381 P4
Adgateville GA 565 H6
Adin CA 784 G3
Adirondack Park NY **253**
Adjuntas, Puerto Rico (USA) 797 B9
Admiralty Island National Monument AK 779 N8
Adna WA 780 D7
Adolphus KY 558 E7
Adrian GA 565 L8
Adrian MI 377 H9
Adrian MN 374 B7
Adrian MO 382 B4
Adrian OR 783 N5
Adrian TX 619 N9
Advance MO 383 K7
Advance NC 560 C10, 566 C1
Aeneas WA 781 K2
Affton MO 383 J3
Afton CA 787 P10, 789 J2
Afton IA 378 D5
Afton NM 624 C8
Afton NY 291 K8
Afton OK 433 P6
Afton WY 689 M8, 690 A8
Agana, Guam (USA) 798 A2
Agar SD 429 H2
Agassiz National Wildlife Refuge MN 370 C3
Agat, Guam (USA) 798 A2
Agate CO 697 K8
Agate Beach OR 782 B3
Agate Fossil Beds National Monument NE **396**, 428 A8
Agawam MA 222 C6
Agawam MT 685 J4
Agawam OK 433 H10, 434 G1
Agenda KS 431 J7
Agnes TX 626 G6
Agness OR 782 B8
Agnew NE 431 K4
Agnos AR 562 F2
Agoura Hills CA 788 E5
Agra KS 430 F7
Agra OK 433 K8
Agricola KS 431 N10, 433 N1
Agricola MS 569 M6
Agua Dulce TX 633 H5
Agua Fria National Monument AZ **577**, 622 F3
Agua Nueva TX 632 F7
Aguadilla, Puerto Rico (USA) 797 A8
Aguanga CA 789 H6
Aguila AZ 622 D4
Aguilar CO 703 J4
Aguilares TX 632 E6
Ahloso OK 433 L10, 435 J2
Ahoskie NC 561 J9
Ahwahnee CA 787 H4
Aibonito, Puerto Rico (USA) 797 C9
Aid OH 381 L8

Aiea HI 790 G4
Aiken SC 565 M5, 566 A7
Aiken TX 625 N3
Ailey GA 565 L9
Ainsworth IA 379 J4
Ainsworth NE 429 H8
Aitkin MN 370 F8
Ajo AZ 622 D7
Akeley MN 370 E7
Akers MO 382 G6
Akhiok AK 779 H8
Akiak AK 778 G6
Akin IL 383 M5
Akra ND 427 L2
Akron AL 563 P10, 564 A7, 569 N1
Akron CO 697 M6
Akron IA 374 A9
Akron IN 380 E2
Akron KS 433 K4
Akron MI 377 J4
Akron NY 290 E6
Akron OH **354**, 377 N10, 381 N2
Akron PA 293 H5
Akutan AK 778 E9
Alabaster AL 564 B6
Alabaster MI 377 J3
Alachua FL 571 K6
Aladdin WY **679**, 691 M3
Alakanuk AK 778 F5
Alameda CA 786 C3
Alameda NM 618 E9, 624 D1
Alamo CA 786 C3
Alamo GA 565 K9, 571 J1
Alamo ND 426 B2
Alamo NV 700 C4
Alamo TN 563 L3
Alamo Alto TX 624 D10, 628 A1
Alamo Heights TX 630 D8, 632 G1
Alamogordo NM **590–591**, 624 E6
Alamosa CO 702 G4
Alamosa National Wildlife Refuge CO 702 G4
Alamota KS 430 D10, 432 D1
Alanreed TX 620 C9, 626 B2
Alanson MI 373 H8
Alapaha GA 571 J2
Alaska Maritime National Wildlife Refuge AK 778 C9, 778 F2, 778 G1
Alaska Peninsula National Wildlife Refuge AK 778 G8
Alba MI 373 H9, 376 G1
Alba TX 627 L6
Albany CA 786 C3
Albany GA **473**, 564 G10, 570 G2
Albany KY 558 G7
Albany LA 569 H7
Albany MN 370 E10, 374 D2
Albany MO 378 D6
Albany NY **253**, 291 N7
Albany OH 381 M7
Albany OR **755**, 782 C3
Albany TX 626 D7
Albany WI 375 N9
Albany WY 696 F4
Albemarle NC 566 D2
Alberhill CA 788 G6
Albert KS 430 F10, 432 F1
Albert City IA 374 D9
Albert Lea MN 374 F7
Alberta AL 564 A9, 569 P2
Alberta VA 560 G8
Alberton MT 684 E6
Albertville AL 564 D4
Albertville MN 374 F3
Albertville WI 375 J3
Albia IA 378 G5
Albin MS 563 J7
Albin WY 697 K3
Albion CA 784 B8
Albion IA 378 F2
Albion ID 688 G8
Albion IL 380 A9, 383 P4
Albion IN 376 F10, 380 F2
Albion ME 221 H8
Albion MI 376 G8
Albion NE 429 L10, 431 H2
Albion NY 290 E6
Albion OK 435 M2
Albion PA 290 A9

Albion TX 627 M4
Albion WA 781 N7
Alborn MN 371 H7
Albright WV 560 D2
Albuquerque NM **591–592**, 618 E10, 624 C1
Alburg VT 220 B7
Alburnett IA 375 J10, 379 J2
Alcalde NM 618 G7
Alcatraz Island CA **731**
Alcester SD 429 P7
Alco AR 562 E3
Alcolu SC 566 D6
Alcova WY 691 H8
Alda NE 430 G4
Alden IA 374 F10, 378 F1
Alden KS 433 H2
Alden MN 374 F7
Alden Bridge LA 562 C10, 568 A1
Alder MT 685 J10, 689 K1
Alder WA 780 E7
Alder Creek NY 291 K5
Alderdale WA 781 J9
Alderley WI 376 A5
Alderpoint CA 784 B6
Alderson WV 560 B6
Aldine TX 631 K7
Aledo IL 379 K4
Aledo TX 626 G7
Aleknagik AK 778 G7
Alex OK 433 H10, 434 G1
Alexander AK 779 J6
Alexander AR 562 E6
Alexander GA 565 M7
Alexander IA 374 F9
Alexander KS 430 E10, 432 E1
Alexander ME 221 M7
Alexander ND 426 B4
Alexander TX 626 F8, 630 E1
Alexander WV 560 C3
Alexander City AL 564 D7
Alexandria IN 380 F4
Alexandria KY 559 J1
Alexandria LA **493**, 568 D5
Alexandria MN 370 D9, 374 C1
Alexandria MO 379 J6
Alexandria NE 431 J6
Alexandria OH 381 L5
Alexandria PA 292 E4
Alexandria SD 429 M5
Alexandria TN 558 F8
Alexandria VA **542**, 561 J3
Alexandria Bay NY 291 J3
Alfalfa OR 782 G4
Alford FL 570 D4
Alfred ME 222 F3
Alfred NY 290 F8
Alfred TX 633 H5
Algerita TX 626 E10, 630 C3
Algoa TX 631 L8, 633 N1
Algodones NM 618 F9
Algoma ID 684 B3
Algoma MS 563 M7
Algoma WI 372 D10, 376 C2
Algona IA 374 E8
Algona WA 780 E6
Algonac MI 377 L7
Algood TN 558 G8
Alhambra CA 788 F5
Ali Chukson AZ 622 F9
Alibates Flint Quarries National Monument TX 620 A8
Alice ND 427 M7
Alice TX 633 H5
Aliceville AL 563 N9
Aliceville KS 433 N2
Alicia AR 563 H3
Aline OK 432 G6
Aliquippa PA 292 A4
Alkabo ND 426 B2
Allagash Wilderness Waterway ME 221 H4
Allakaket AK 779 J4
Allamoore TX 628 C2
Allandale FL 571 N8
Allardt TN 559 H8
Alleene AR 562 B8
Allegan MI 376 E7
Allegany NY 290 D8
Alleghany CA 784 G8
Alleghany VA 560 C6

Rio Verde AZ 622 G4
Rio Vista CA 786 D2
Rio Vista TX 627 H8, 630 F1
Rion SC 565 N3, 566 B5
Ripley CA 789 M6
Ripley IL 379 L7
Ripley MS 563 M5
Ripley NY 290 B8
Ripley OH 381 J8
Ripley TN 563 K3
Ripley WV 559 N2
Riplinger WI 375 L4
Ripon CA 786 E3
Ripon WI 375 P6
Rippey IA 378 D2
Rippon WV 560 G2
Ririe ID 689 K5
Risco MO 383 L8
Rising City NE 431 J4
Rising Fawn GA 564 E2
Rising Star TX 626 E8, 630 C1
Rising Sun IN 380 G7
Rising Sun MD 293 J6
Rison AR 562 F7
Rita Blanca National Grassland TX
    619 N6
Rittman OH 381 M2
Ritzville WA 781 L6
River Falls WI 375 H4
River Hills WI 376 B5
River Sioux IA 378 A3
Riverbank CA 698 E3, 786 E3
Riverdale CA 786 G6
Riverdale GA 564 G5
Riverdale IL 376 B9, 380 B1
Riverdale KS 433 J4
Riverdale ND 426 F5
Riverdale NE 430 F5
Riverhead NY 222 C9
Riverside CA 788 G5
Riverside IA 379 J3
Riverside OR 783 M5
Riverside TX 631 K4
Riverside WA 781 J2
Riverside WY 696 E3
Riverton IA 378 B5
Riverton IL 379 N4
Riverton KS 433 P5
Riverton LA 568 E2
Riverton NE 430 G6
Riverton OR 782 A6
Riverton UT 695 K5
Riverton VA 560 G3
Riverton WV 560 E3
Riverton WY 682, 690 E7
Rivervale AR 563 J3
Riverview FL 557 B2
Riverview FL 569 P6, 570 A4
Riverview MI 377 K8
Riverview WY 691 N6
Rives TN 563 L1
Rives Junction MI 377 H7
Rivesville WV 560 C1
Riviera AZ 616 D9, 622 A1
Riviera TX 633 H6
Riviera Beach FL 557 G5
Rixon Lake ND 427 J9
Roach NV 700 B8, 789 L1
Roachdale IN 380 D5
Roads OH 381 L7
Roads End CA 787 K7
Roan Mountain TN 559 N8
Roann IN 380 E3
Roanoke AL 564 E6
Roanoke IL 379 N5
Roanoke IN 380 F3
Roanoke TX 627 H6
Roanoke VA 543, 560 D7
Roanoke Rapids NC 561 H9
Roanoke River National Wildlife
    Refuge NC 561 H9, 567 K1
Roaring Gap NC 560 B9
Roaring Spring PA 292 E4
Roaring Springs TX 625 P4, 626 A4
Robards KY 558 C5
Robbin MN 370 A3
Robbins CA 784 F9
Robbins NC 566 E2
Robbins TN 559 H8
Robbinsville NC 559 K10, 565 H1
Robbs IL 383 N6

Robe WA 780 F3
Robeline LA 568 B4
Robersonville NC 567 J1
Robert LA 569 H7
Robert Lee TX 626 B9
Roberta GA 565 H7
Roberts ID 689 K5
Roberts IL 380 A3
Roberts MD 293 J7
Roberts MS 569 K2
Roberts MT 685 P10, 686 D10,
    689 P1, 690 D1
Roberts WI 375 H3
Robertsburg WV 559 N2
Robertsdale AL 569 N6
Robertson WY 695 M3
Robesonia PA 293 J4
Robin ID 689 J8
Robinson IL 380 B7, 383 P2
Robinson KS 431 N7
Robinson KY 559 J3
Robinson ND 427 H6
Robinson TX 627 H10, 630 G3
Robinsonville MS 563 J5
Robstown TX 633 H5
Roby MO 382 F6
Roby TX 626 B7, 434 B7
Roca NE 431 K5
Rochelle FL 571 L7
Rochelle GA 565 J9, 571 H1
Rochelle IL 379 N2
Rochelle TX 626 D10, 630 C3
Rocheport MO 378 G10, 382 E2
Rochert MN 370 C7
Rochester IL 379 N8
Rochester IN 380 E2
Rochester KY 558 D6
Rochester MI 377 K7
Rochester MN 342, 375 H6
Rochester NH 222 F3
Rochester NY 260, 290 F6
Rochester OH 377 L10, 381 L2
Rochester PA 292 A3
Rochester TX 626 C5
Rochester WA 780 D7
Rochford SD 428 B4
Rock KS 433 K4
Rock MI 372 D7
Rock Cave WV 560 C3
Rock Creek KS 431 M8
Rock Creek MN 370 G10, 374 G2
Rock Creek OH 377 P9, 381 P1
Rock Creek OR 781 H10, 783 H1
Rock Falls IA 374 G8
Rock Falls IL 379 M3
Rock Hall MD 293 H7
Rock Hill SC 565 N2, 566 B3
Rock Island IL 379 L3
Rock Island TX 631 H8, 633 L1
Rock Island WA 781 H5
Rock Rapids IA 374 B7
Rock River WY 691 K10, 696 G2
Rock Spring GA 564 E2
Rock Springs AZ 622 F3
Rock Springs MT 687 J7
Rock Springs WY 682, 690 D10,
    695 P2, 696 A2
Rock Valley IA 374 A8
Rockaway Beach OR 780 B10
Rockbridge IL 379 L9, 383 K2
Rockbridge OH 381 L6
Rockbridge WI 375 L7
Rockdale IL 376 A9, 380 A1
Rockdale TX 630 G5
Rockerville SD 428 B5
Rockfield IN 380 D3
Rockfield WI 376 B5
Rockford AL 564 D7
Rockford IA 374 G8
Rockford ID 689 J6
Rockford IL 375 P10, 379 N1
Rockford MI 376 F6
Rockford MN 374 F3
Rockford NC 560 B9
Rockford NE 431 L6
Rockford OH 380 G3
Rockford WA 781 N5
Rockham SD 429 K2
Rockholds KY 559 J7
Rockingham NC 566 E3
Rocklake ND 427 J2

Rockland ID 689 H8
Rockland ME 221 J9, 223 J1
Rockland MI 371 N7, 372 A5
Rockland TX 631 M4
Rockland WI 375 K6
Rockledge AL 564 D4
Rockledge FL 557 E1, 571 P10
Rocklin CA 784 F9, 786 E1
Rockmart GA 564 F4
Rockport CA 784 B7
Rockport IL 379 K8, 383 H1
Rockport IN 380 C10
Rockport KY 558 D5
Rockport MA 222 G5
Rockport MO 378 B6
Rockport MS 569 H3
Rockport TX 633 K4
Rockport WA 780 F3
Rockport WV 559 P1, 560 A3
Rocksprings TX 629 N5, 630 A6
Rockton IL 375 P10, 379 N1
Rockville CT 222 C7
Rockville IN 380 C5
Rockville MD 292 G7
Rockville MO 382 C4
Rockville NE 430 G4
Rockville SC 566 D9
Rockville UT 700 G4
Rockwall TX 627 K6
Rockwell IA 374 G8
Rockwell NC 566 C2
Rockwell City IA 374 D10, 378 D1
Rockwood ME 221 H5
Rockwood MI 377 K8
Rockwood PA 292 C5
Rockwood TN 559 H9
Rockwood TX 626 D10, 629 P1,
    630 B3
Rocky OK 432 F9, 434 E1
Rocky Boy MT 685 N3, 686 C3
Rocky Comfort MO 382 C8
Rocky Ford CO 703 L2
Rocky Ford GA 565 M7
Rocky Fork TN 559 M9
Rocky Gap VA 560 A7
Rocky Hill CT 222 C7
Rocky Hill NJ 293 L4
Rocky Hill OH 381 L7
Rocky Mount NC 560 G10, 567 H1
Rocky Mount VA 560 D8
Rocky Mountain National Park CO
    646, 696 G6
Rocky River OH 377 M10, 381 M1
Rodanthe NC 567 N2
Rodarte NM 618 G7
Rodeo CA 786 C2
Rodeo NM 623 M9
Rodessa LA 562 B10
Rodman IA 374 D8
Rodman SC 565 N2, 566 B4
Rodney IA 374 B10, 378 A2
Roe AR 562 G6
Roebuck SC 565 M2
Roellen TN 563 L2
Roff OK 435 J2
Roganville TX 631 N4
Rogers AR 457, 562 B1
Rogers ND 427 L6
Rogers NE 431 K3
Rogers TX 630 G4
Rogers City MI 373 K8
Rogerson ID 688 E9, 694 E1
Rogersville AL 564 B2
Rogersville MO 382 E7
Rogersville TN 559 L8
Roggen CO 697 J6
Rogue River OR 782 C8
Rogue River National Forest OR 782
    C9, 782 D8, 784 C1
Rogue Umpqua Divide Wilderness
    Area OR 782 D7
Rohnerville CA 784 A5
Rohwer AR 562 G8
Roland AR 562 E5
Roland OK 562 A4
Rolette ND 427 H2
Rolfe IA 374 D9
Rolinda CA 786 G6
Roll AZ 622 B6
Roll IN 380 F4
Roll OK 432 E8

Rolla KS 432 A4
Rolla MO 382 G5
Rolla ND 427 H2
Rolling Fork MS 563 H10, 568 G1
Rolling Prairie IN 376 D9, 380 D1
Rollins MN 371 J6
Rollins MT 684 F4
Rollinsford NH 222 F4
Rollinsville CO 697 H7
Roma-Los Saenz TX 632 F8
Romayor TX 631 L5
Rome GA 564 F4
Rome IL 379 N5
Rome KS 433 J5
Rome KY 558 D4
Rome MO 382 E8
Rome MS 563 J7
Rome NY 260, 291 K6
Rome PA 291 H9, 293 H1
Rome TN 558 F8
Rome City IN 376 F10, 380 F1
Romeo CO 702 G4
Romeo FL 571 K8
Romeo MI 377 K6
Romeoville IL 376 A9, 380 A1
Romero TX 619 M8
Romeroville NM 619 H8
Romney TX 626 E8, 630 C1
Romney WV 560 F2
Romoland CA 789 H6
Romulus MI 377 K8
Ronan MT 684 F5
Ronceverte WV 560 C6
Ronda NC 560 B10
Roodhouse IL 379 L8, 383 J1
Roopville GA 564 F6
Roosevelt AZ 623 H4
Roosevelt MN 370 D2
Roosevelt OK 432 F10, 434 E1
Roosevelt UT 695 N6
Roosevelt Beach NY 290 D5
Roosevelt Campobello International
    Park ME 188
Roper GA 565 K10, 571 K1
Roper KS 433 M3
Roper NC 561 K10, 567 K1
Ropesville TX 625 M5
Rosalia KS 433 L3
Rosalia WA 781 N6
Rosamond CA 787 L10, 788 F3
Rosanky TX 630 F7
Rosario WA 780 D2
Rosati MO 382 G5
Rosboro AR 562 C6
Rosburg WA 780 C8
Roscoe IL 375 P10, 379 N1
Roscoe MT 685 N10, 686 D10,
    689 P1, 690 D1
Roscoe NE 430 B4
Roscoe NY 291 L9
Roscoe SD 427 J10, 429 J1
Roscoe TX 626 B7
Roscommon MI 377 H2
Rose Bud AR 562 F4
Rose City MI 377 H2
Rose Creek MN 374 G7
Rose Hill IA 378 G4
Rose Hill IL 380 A7, 383 N2
Rose Hill KS 433 K4
Rose Hill NC 567 H4
Rose Hill VA 558 F9
Rose Lake National Wildlife Refuge
    ND 427 K4
Roseau MN 370 C2
Roseboro NC 566 G3
Rosebud MO 383 H4
Rosebud MT 687 J8
Rosebud SD 428 F6
Rosebud TX 630 G4
Roseburg OR 767, 782 C6
Rosebush MI 376 G4
Rosedale MD 293 H7
Rosedale MS 563 H8
Rosedale OK 433 K10, 435 H1
Rosedale TN 559 J8
Rosedale WV 560 B3
Roseglen ND 426 E5
Roseland LA 569 H6
Roseland NE 430 G5
Roselle IL 376 B8
Roselle MO 383 J6

Rosemark TN 563 K4
Rosemont NE 430 G6
Rosendale MN 374 D3
Rosendale NY 291 M9, 293 M1
Rosendale WI 375 P6, 376 A4
Rosepine LA 568 B5
Rosetta MS 568 F5
Rosette UT 688 G10, 694 G2
Roseville CA 784 F9, 786 E1
Roseville IL 379 L5
Roseville MN 374 G3
Roseville OH 381 M5
Rosewood MN 370 B4
Rosewood OH 381 J4
Roseworth ID 688 E8, 694 D1
Rosharon TX 631 K8, 633 N1
Rosholt SD 427 N9
Rosholt WI 372 A10, 375 N4
Rosiclare IL 383 N6
Rosier GA 565 L7
Rosita CO 703 H2
Rosita TX 632 F8
Rosita TX 632 G5
Roslyn SD 427 M10, 429 M1
Roslyn WA 780 G6
Rosman NC 565 K1
Ross MN 370 C2
Ross ND 426 D3
Ross OH 380 G7
Ross TX 627 H9, 630 G2
Ross Fork MT 685 N6, 686 C6
Ross Lake National Recreation Area
    WA 780 G1
Rosser TX 627 K7
Rossford OH 377 J9, 381 J1
Rossie IA 374 C8
Rosston AR 562 C8
Rosston OK 432 E5
Rossville GA 564 E2
Rossville IA 375 K8
Rossville IL 380 B4
Rossville IN 380 D4
Rossville KS 431 M9
Roswell GA 564 G4
Roswell NM 597, 624 G5
Rotan TX 626 B6
Rothsay MN 370 B8
Rothschild WI 375 M4
Rotterdam NY 291 M7
Rougemont NC 560 E10
Rough Rock AZ 617 N6
Roulette PA 290 E9, 292 E1
Round Lake FL 570 D4
Round Mountain NV 693 P9,
    699 M1
Round Mountain TX 630 D5
Round Oak GA 565 J6
Round Pond AR 563 H5
Round Prairie MN 370 D9, 374 D1
Round Rock AZ 617 N6
Round Rock TX 630 F5
Round Top TX 631 H6
Roundhead OH 381 J4
Roundup MT 686 E8
Roundup TX 625 M4
Rouses Point NY 291 N1
Rouseville PA 290 B10, 292 B2
Rover AR 562 C5
Rover TN 558 E9
Rowan IA 374 F9
Rowden TX 630 B1
Rowden TX 626 D8
Rowe NM 618 G9
Rowena SD 429 P6
Rowena TX 626 C9, 629 N1, 630 A2
Rowesville SC 565 P6, 566 B7
Rowland NC 566 E4
Rowland NV 688 D9, 694 C2
Rowlesburg WV 560 D2
Rowlett TX 627 J6
Rowley MA 222 F5
Rowley UT 695 H4
Rowsburg OH 381 M3
Rox NV 700 D5
Roxboro NC 560 E9
Roxbury NY 291 L8
Roxbury PA 292 F5
Roxie MS 568 G4
Roxton TX 627 L5
Roy ID 689 H9, 695 H1

ACKNOWLEDGMENTS

The Publisher believes that permission for use of the historical images in this publication, listed below, has been correctly obtained, however if any errors or omissions have occurred, Global Book Publishing would be pleased to hear from copyright owners.

The Art Archive
58 bottom, 64 top, 66 bottom, 72 top, 73 bottom, 75 bottom, 86 bottom, 92 top left, 92 bottom, 95 top right, 95 bottom, 97 bottom, 98 top, 100 bottom, 115 top, 119 top left, 119 top right, 120 top, 138 top, 154 bottom.

Australian Picture Library/Corbis
63 top, 77 top, 82 bottom, 84 top, 87 bottom, 88–89, 90 top, 91 top, 91 bottom, 92 top, right, 93, 94 bottom, 94, 96 middle, 96 bottom, 99 top, 99 bottom, 101 top, 102 top, 102 bottom, 103, 104 bottom, 105 top, 105 bottom, 106 top, 106 bottom, 107 top left, 107 top right, 108 center, 108 bottom, 109, 110 top right, 111 top, 111 bottom, 115 bottom, 147 top left, 150 bottom, 152, 153 top, 154 top, 155 bottom, 156, 157 top left, 157 top right, 162 bottom, 163 top, 164 bottom, 166 top, 166 bottom, 167 bottom, 170 top, 170 bottom, 171 bottom.

The Kobal Collection
151 top, 153 bottom, 160 top, 160 bottom, 161 bottom, 163 center, 165 top.

PHOTOGRAPHERS
Rob Blakers, Claver Carroll, Paul Huntley, Richard I'Anson, Ionas Kaltenbach, Robert M. Knight, Mike Langford, David McGonigal, Tom McKnight, Barry Stone, Oliver Strewe, J.Peter Thoeming, James Young.

CAPTIONS FOR DOUBLE PAGE PICTURES

16–17: left to right, see pages 22, 28, 30, 37, 44, 51, 68, 81, 121, 130, 191, 123, 228, 169.

18–19: Around Logan Pass, Glacier National Park, Montana.

52–53: Etching of Interview of Howe's Messenger with Washington by M. A. Wageman.

88–89: Launch of the space shuttle Discovery, September 29, 1988, Kennedy Space Center, Cape Canaveral, Florida.

112–13: Lincoln Memorial, Washington, DC.

134–35: Trumpet player, Mississippi.

172–73: left to right, see pages 193, 229, 238, 262, 443, 231, 456, 478, 516, 537, 677, 542, 767, 794.

174–175: Fall colors, New Hampshire.

224–25: Pittsburgh, Pennsylvania.

294–95: Bull riding, National High School Finals Rodeo, Springfield, Illinois.

384–85: Roadscape, Montana.

436–37: Jetty, Lake Arthur, Louisiana.

572–73: Monument Valley, Arizona.

634–35: Sneffels Range from the Dallas Divide, Uncompagre, Colorado.

704–05: Mountains in Denali National Park, Alaska.